Accountants' Guide

Accountants' Guide

A Handbook of Standards and Statements for Accountants

The Certified Accountants Educational Trust

The Certified Accountants Educational Trust
29 Lincoln's Inn Fields
London WC2A 3EE

First published 1986
Second edition 1987
Reprinted 1988
Third edition 1989
Fourth edition 1990
Fifth edition 1992
Sixth edition 1993
Seventh edition 1994
Eighth edition 1995
ISBN 1-898291-13-6

Typeset by ACCA, Glasgow and printed in Great Britain by Bell & Bain

Section 1
Introduction

Contents

Accountants' Guide
Contents

Preface

The Accountants' Guide is an up-to-date handbook of Statements of Standard Accounting Practice (SSAPs), Statements of Recommended Practice (SORPs), Financial Reporting Standards (FRSs), Auditing Standards and Guidelines, Statements of Auditing Standards, Rules of Professional Conduct andStatements of Standards for Reporting Accountants which are relevant to The Chartered Association of Certified Accountants' examinations.

The material contained in the Accountants' Guide is drawn from the Members' Handbook of The Chartered Association of Certified Accountants.

This edition of the Accountants' Guide does not contain all of the Rules of Professional Conduct which members of the Association are required to observe. Instead, only those which students will find the most relevant to their studies have been included for publication.

References to the Companies Acts in the Guide

References in the Guide are made to the Companies Acts of 1985 and 1989. In 1985, company legislation was consolidated by assembling in one statute the provisions of the Companies Acts 1948, 1967, 1976, 1980 and 1981. The 1989 Act has introduced new provisions, many of which have been inserted directly into the 1985 Act. References to the Companies Act 1985 will therefore now include those provisions which have been amended or inserted by the Companies Act 1989.

Section 2
Rules of Professional Conduct

Contents

Rules of professional conduct — Introduction

Introduction

1 Members of the Association are required to observe proper standards of professional conduct and specifically to refrain from what is described in the Association's bye-laws as misconduct, which includes, but is not confined to, any act or default likely to bring discredit to themselves, the Association or the accountancy profession. Members who fail to observe such standards may be required to answer a complaint before the Investigations and Disciplinary Committees.

It is not possible to specify all those combinations of circumstances in which a member may be held by the Disciplinary Committee to have committed professional misconduct as defined above, but this section of the Members' Handbook (which may be added to or varied from time to time) sets out the Association's ethical requirements in relation to those professional situations that most commonly arise.

Members who are in doubt as to their correct course of action in particular cases should obtain further advice through the Legal Department of the Association.

Relationship between the Investment Business Rules and the Rules of Professional Conduct

2 Firms that are authorised by the Association to conduct investment business pursuant to the Financial Services Act 1986, are bound by the Association's Investment Business Rules. Where the Rules of Professional Conduct are more stringent than the Investment Business Rules (or vice versa) the more stringent rule applies.

Overseas members

3 Members in practice overseas in a country in which the profession is controlled by a reputable body or by law, may adhere to the local guidance, even though to do so may not be in accordance with the ethical guidance of the Association. Members in practice in a country in which the profession is not so controlled should follow the guidance of the Association unless well established and generally accepted local practice of reputable firms is to the contrary.

Students

4 Students, as affirmed by their signature to the application forms to be enrolled as registered students, are bound by the ethical requirements of the Association. They also remain bound during the period between the successful completion of the examinations and their admission to membership, at which point, of course, they become subject to the same requirements in their new capacity.

Failure to follow the Rules

5 The effect of failure to comply with the Rules is set out in bye-law 27 (c) as follows:

"In deciding whether a member, relevant firm or student has been guilty of misconduct, regard may be had to any code of practice, ethical or technical, adopted by the Council, and to any regulations affecting members, relevant firms or students laid down or approved by the Council."

Enforcement of the Rules

6 The power of the Association to enforce ethical standards is, in accordance with the Charter and bye-laws, entrusted to three Committees appointed by Council, each of which is, in respect of these powers, independent of the Council.

7 The Investigations Committee, operating under bye-law 29, considers complaints against the conduct of members, relevant firms and students, and is empowered to initiate disciplinary action.

8 If having considered the facts before it and any representations made by the member, relevant firm or student, the Investigations Committee is of the opinion that in all the circumstances those facts amount to misconduct and is of the further opinion that disciplinary proceedings should be brought, it will refer a formal complaint to the Disciplinary Committee. Complaints against members or relevant firms which give rise to or include questions of public concern the Investigations Committee may alternatively refer the matter to the Joint Disciplinary Scheme.

It is the Disciplinary Committee operating under bye-law 30 which, alone, can determine, subject to the right of appeal referred to below, whether a complaint of misconduct is proved.

9 From the Disciplinary Committee the member, relevant firm or student has a right of appeal to the Appeal Committee. (Bye-law 31 refers.)

Further advice

10 Members, whether in practice or not, and students who are in doubt as to their ethical position in any matter, and who cannot resolve this doubt by reference to these Rules, should consult the Legal Department.

Professional and technical standards

11 Fundamental Principle 4 calls for a member to carry out his professional work with proper regard for the technical and professional standards expected of him as a member. However, an employed member who, in the performance of his professional work, may be subject to directions from his employers may be faced with a conflict of loyalties in seeking to apply this Fundamental Principle. The difficulty is of particular importance where the outcome of the work is to be published.

12 When a member has sole responsibility for the preparation and approval of information, including management information, which is to be made public or is to become available, on however restricted a basis, outside the organisation to which it refers, he should ensure that such information complies with the standards referred to in Fundamental Principle 4 or, if it does not so comply, that the reasons for non-compliance are stated truthfully, unambiguously and fairly.

13 When his is not the sole responsibility, he should use his best endeavours to achieve compliance or, if the information does not comply with the standards referred to in Fundamental Principle 4, to ensure that the reasons for non-compliance are stated truthfully unambiguously and fairly.

14 The standards referred to in Fundamental Principle 4 include Statements of Standard Accounting Practice, the City Code on Takeovers and Mergers, and the Rules and Regulations of the International Stock Exchange. Firms which are authorised by the Association to carry out investment business are also referred to Rule 11(4) of the Investment Business Rules 1988.

Status

15 While the considerations set out above apply to all employed members, the more senior the position occupied by the member the greater will be his opportunity to influence events, practices and attitudes and thus the more onerous will be his responsibilities.

Fundamental principles

16.1 Members should behave with integrity in all professional, business and personal financial relationships. Integrity implies not merely honesty but fair dealing and truthfulness.

16.2 Members should strive for objectivity in all professional and business judgements. Objectivity is the state of mind which has regard to all considerations relevant to the task in hand but no other. It presupposes intellectual honesty.

16.3 Members should not accept or perform work which they are not competent to undertake unless they obtain such advice and assistance as will enable them competently to carry out the work.

16.4 Members should carry out their professional work with due skill, care, diligence and expedition and with proper regard for the technical and professional standards expected of them as members.

16.5 Members should behave with courtesy and consideration towards all with whom they come into contact during the course of performing their work.

Integrity, objectivity and independence

Introduction

1 The Fundamental Principles require that a member should behave with integrity in all professional, business and financial relationships and that he (or she) should strive for objectivity in all professional and business judgements. Objectivity is a state of mind, but in certain roles the preservation of objectivity needs to be protected and demonstrated by the maintenance of a member's independence from influences which could affect his objectivity.

2 Section A of this Statement deals with the independence required of an auditor.

3 Section B calls for a similar degree of independence to be exercised by a member in financial reporting and similar roles outside the audit.

4 Section C deals with situations outside the areas dealt with in Sections A and B where certain aspects of the independence guidance are relevant, and where a member must remain conscious of the need to preserve his (or her) objectivity and to observe appropriate safeguards so that his judgement is not swayed by considerations of self interest or the interests of connected parties.

5 Whenever a relationship or situation exists, or a business or other interest is held by a member or practice, whereby objectivity may be threatened, or appear to be threatened, the member concerned should consider the need to disclose the relationship, situation or interest to any relevant party in an appropriate manner.

6 Conflicts of interest have an important bearing on independence and hence also on the public perception of a member's objectivity. (Attention is drawn to the guidance in Section 2.25, 'Conflicts of Interest'.)

7 The attention of members in practice overseas is drawn to paragraph 3 of the Introduction to the Rules of Professional Conduct.

Section A — Independence and the audit

8 PRINCIPLE: A member's objectivity must be beyond question if he (or she) is to report as an auditor. That objectivity can only be assured if the member is, and is seen to be, independent.

9 The Certified Accountants' Qualification and Audit Regulations 1991 include requirements as to control of firms designed, in conformity with the Companies Act 1989, to ensure that these are controlled by qualified persons and that their independence from outside influences is assured. The guidance which follows indicates areas of risk arising from various situations and relationships in which a member's independence as auditor, and hence his objectivity, may be threatened.

10 The attention of members is drawn to paragraphs 77 to 83, in which key terms used in the guidance are defined.

11 Though the guidance is framed in terms of audit under the Companies Acts, and an audit client is therefore generally referred to as a 'Company', the spirit of the guidance applies equally to other audit situations, e.g., audit of trusts.

12 The threat to independence may be reduced by the nature and extent of the precautions taken by the practice to guard against loss of objectivity. (See paragraphs 68 to 76 below.)

Area of risk — undue dependence on an audit client

13 Objectivity may be threatened or appear to be threatened by undue dependence on any audit client or group of connected clients.

Discussion

14 It is not possible to specify precisely all the circumstances in which objectivity may be so threatened because these may involve a variety of factors including the size and nature of the practice and the size and nature of the audit client and its relationship with the practice.

15 The weight of some factors, such as the desire of a practice not to lose a prestigious client, may be difficult to assess. Nor is it possible to set rigid limits even to more quantifiable factors such as the proportion of fee income received. Nevertheless and subject to the next paragraph, the public perception of a member's objectivity is likely to be in jeopardy where the fees for audit and other recurring work paid by one client or group of connected clients exceed 15 per cent of the gross practice income or, in the case of a member practising part-time, 15 per cent of his or her gross earned income. Where the public interest is involved it is particularly important that objectivity is seen to be preserved, and in the case of listed and other public interest companies the appropriate figure should be 10 per cent of the gross practice income. (And see paragraph 66 below.)

16 It is recognised that a new practice seeking to establish itself or an established practice reducing its activities may not be able to comply with this criterion. Such practices therefore should take particular care to safeguard their independence.

17 The figures in paragraph 15 indicate only the extremes beyond which the public perception of a member's objectivity is likely to be at risk. It is the duty of the practice regularly to satisfy itself that it is not open to criticism in respect of any audit engagement, having regard to all the circumstances of the case. For this purpose a practice should, before accepting an audit appointment and as part of its annual review (see paragraphs 68 to 76), carefully consider against the criteria set out in this Statement the propriety of accepting or retaining each audit client or group of associated clients the fees from which for audit and other recurring work represent 10 per cent or more of the gross practice income or of the gross earned income of a member practising part-time. In the case of a listed company or other public interest company — see paragraphs 82 and 83 (Definitions) — a figure of not more than 5 per cent is the appropriate point to initiate review.

18 The fees from a number of non-recurring assignments could, if taken together with recurring work, give rise to a problem of undue dependence on an audit client. Any such dependency should be assessed and dealt with as above.

19 If, after such a review, the engagement is accepted or continued it is essential that safeguards should be set up within the practice on the lines indicated in paragraphs 68 to 76. (For the special position of sole practitioners and small firms see paragraphs 72 to 76.)

20 In circumstances where a member is dependent for his or her income on the profits of any one office within a practice and the gross income of that office is regularly dependent on one client or a group of connected clients for more than 15 per cent of its gross fees (in the case of a listed company or other public interest company — see paragraphs 82 and 83 (Definitions) — 10 per cent), a partner from another office of the practice should take final responsibility for any report made by the practice on the affairs of that client. The same considerations apply to every partner whose income from the practice depends significantly on the retention of a specific audit client or group of clients.

Area of risk — overdue fees

21 The existence of significant overdue fees from an audit client or group of associated clients can be a threat or appear to be a threat to objectivity akin to that of a loan (see paragraph 54 et seq.).

Discussion

22 Before an audit is accepted in these circumstances the situation should be reviewed to ascertain whether the overdue fees, taken together with the fees for the current assignment, could be regarded as a significant loan.

Area of risk — actual or threatened litigation

23 A firm's objectivity may be threatened or appear to be threatened when it is involved in, or even threatened with, litigation in relation to a client.

Discussion

24 Litigation between an auditor and his (or her) client is likely to represent a breakdown in the relationship of trust which should exist between them unless the amount of the claim is insignificant to both the client and the auditor. When a client company or its subsidiaries or associates commence, or express an intention to commence, legal action against an audit firm, or vice versa, the firm and the company may be placed in adversarial positions which could call into question the objectivity of the auditor and thus his ability to report fairly and impartially on the company's accounts. At the same time, the existence of such action (or threat of action) could affect the willingness of the management of the company to disclose relevant information to the auditor.

25 The issue by the audit client of a writ for negligence against the auditor or the commencement of litigation by the auditor alleging, for example, fraud or deceit by the officers of the company, would be considered to impair independence. Such impairment may not necessarily result where litigation arises solely out of a fee dispute, or where the firm is obliged to sue for its fees, provided that the amount of the fees in question is not significant.

26 It is not possible to specify precisely the point at which it would become improper for a firm to continue as auditors. However a firm should have regard to circumstances where litigation might reasonably be perceived by the public as in contemplation, e.g. where publicity is given to matters adversely affecting a listed or other public interest company and reference is made to the company's reliance on accounts or other financial statements prepared by the firm.

Area of risk — associated firms; influences outside the practice

27 A firm's objectivity may be threatened or appear to be threatened as a result of pressures arising from associated practices or organisations, or from other external sources, such as bankers, solicitors, government or those introducing business.

Discussion

28 The factors referred to in paragraphs 14 and 15 as potentially threatening objectivity, in particular the desire not to lose a prestigious client, may arise in connection with the activities of an associated practice or organisation, in the same country or overseas, which acts or has been acting for the client or an associate of the client.

29 The possibility of a threat to independence arising from pressures exerted upon the auditing firm by an associate or external source should be borne in mind and provided for in the firm's review machinery (see paragraphs 68 to 76). Factors include the closeness of the association, and the strength of the associate's interest in the firm's retaining the client.

Area of risk — family and other personal relationships

30 A member's objectivity may be threatened or appear to be threatened as a consequence of a family or other close personal or business relationship.

Discussion

31 By way of example, problems may arise where the practice or anyone closely connected with it has a mutual business interest with a client, or with an officer or employee of a client. Such problems can also exist where an officer or employee is closely connected with a partner or staff member. Where an engagement involving such relationships is accepted or continued, safeguards should be set up within the practice on the lines indicated in paragraphs 68 to 71. (For the special position of sole practitioners and small firms see paragraphs 72 to 76.)

32 The Companies Act, 1989, Section 27, prohibits an officer or employee of a company, or a partner or employee of such a person from accepting appointment as auditor of that company.

33 Problems can also arise if an officer or senior employee of an audit client is so closely connected with the partner or senior staff member responsible for the conduct of the audit as to give rise to real fears of a lack of independence. For the purposes of this paragraph only, 'closely connected' persons include additionally adult children and their spouses, brothers and sisters and their spouses, and any relative to whom regular financial assistance is given, or who is otherwise indebted financially to the partner or senior staff member.

34 The threat to independence may be less where a partner or senior staff member is not personally engaged on the audit in question, where his or her office is distant from the reporting office and where appropriate safeguards are in place in the internal procedures of the practice. Similarly, a connection with a junior staff member of the practice is less likely to be a threat than a connection with a senior staff member or partner.

35 A member should not personally take part in the conduct of the audit of a company if he or she has, during the period upon which the report is to be made, or at any time in the two years prior to the first day thereof been an officer (other than auditor) or employee of that company.

36 A practice should not report on a company if a company associated with the practice fills the appointment of secretary to the client. There is no objection to the practice providing assistance to the company secretary.

Area of risk — beneficial interests in shares and other investments

37 A member's objectivity may be threatened or appear to be threatened where he (or she) holds a beneficial interest in the shares or other forms of investment in a company upon which the practice reports.

Discussion

38 A practice should ensure that it does not have as an audit client a company in which a partner or anyone closely connected with a partner is the holder of a beneficial investment, nor should it employ on the audit a member of staff if that member of staff, or a person closely connected with him or her is a beneficial holder of such investments.

39 The above is not intended to preclude a beneficial holding in an authorised unit or investment trust or Lloyd's syndicate which holds shares in a client company.

40 Thus, a member should not have a Personal Equity Plan which has among its investments any audit clients. However he may have a Personal Equity Plan which invests solely in unit trusts or in an investment trust, provided that the member's practice does not report upon the trust.

41 Where a partner inherits shares or marries a shareholder, or a relevant investment occurs as a result of a take-over, the investment should be disposed of at the earliest practicable date, being a date at which the transaction would not amount to insider dealing. Similar action should be taken where a beneficial investment is held in a company becoming an audit client. Where the necessary disposal cannot be achieved within the time scale envisaged the practice should not continue as auditor.

42 Where a provision in the Articles of Association of a company or an Act of Parliament requires the auditor to be a shareholder the auditor should hold no more than the minimum number of shares necessary to comply with that provision in the Articles or with the Act, and the share holding should be disclosed in the accounts, in the Directors' Report or the Audit Report.

43 Para. 38 is not intended to preclude a partner or a person closely connected with a partner from holding or continuing to hold, in the normal course of business and on normal commercial terms, an insurance or pension policy with a client insurance company or society, though an engagement partner should not take out a new policy with such a client.

Area of risk — beneficial interests in trusts

44 The objectivity of a practice may be threatened or appear to be threatened where a partner or a person closely connected with the partner has a beneficial interest in a trust having a share holding in an audit client company.

Discussion

45 Where a trust, in which a partner or a person closely connected with a partner is a beneficiary, holds or acquires shares in a company audited by the practice:

(a) where the partner is and wishes to remain a trustee, the share holding should be regarded as equivalent to a beneficial share holding, and the practice should cease to report;

(b) where the partner is not a trustee, he should cease personally to report as soon as he becomes aware of the share holding.

46 Where an employee has an interest in a trust having a share holding in an audit client, that employee should not be employed on the audit of that client.

Area of risk — trustee investments

47 A member's objectivity may be threatened or appear to be threatened by trustee share holdings and other trustee investments.

Discussion

48 Independence will be in issue whenever a practice carries out the audit of a company, at a time when a partner, a member of staff employed on the audit, or a person closely connected with either is trustee of a trust holding shares in that company. The threat to objectivity is patent where the share holding is in excess of 10 per cent of the issued share capital of the company or of the total assets of the trust.

49 Where the trust holds shares in a listed company or public interest company — see paragraphs 82 and 83 (Definitions) — and the holding is in excess of 10 per cent of the issued share capital of the company or the trust's aggregate investment in the company exceeds 10 per cent of the total assets comprised in the trust, the practice should not accept or continue appointment as auditors. The holdings (in relation to the issued share capital of the company) of trusts of which partners or staff members of the firm are trustees should be regarded as aggregated for the purposes of this paragraph, provided that, in the case of staff member trustees, the trusteeship is client-related and not of a personal or family nature.

50 A practice should adopt measures appropriate to every other case of a trustee investment. These would include:

(a) a trustee, or someone with whom a trustee is closely connected, should not act as the partner or person responsible for the audit of the company in which the trust is a shareholder;

(b) a sole practitioner should not accept or continue appointment as auditor unless the practitioner is able to arrange for the consultation referred to in paragraphs 72 to 75, and the consultation confirms the propriety of accepting or continuing appointment;

(c) in any case of a trustee investment where the practice does report, the investment should be disclosed in the accounts, in the Directors' Report or in the Audit Report, save in the case of trustee share holdings where the aggregate of all relevant share holdings is less than 1 per cent of the issued capital of the company;

(d) where a close personal relationship develops in the course of a trustee share holding, a member should also have regard to the review procedures recommended in paragraphs 68 to 76.

51 Similar considerations apply when a person closely connected with the practice is a director or employee of a trust company which acts as trustee of a trust holding investments in a company on which the practice reports.

52 Similar considerations to those applying to trustee share holdings (see paragraph 47, et seq. above) apply also in the case of nominee share holdings and 'bare trustee' share holdings.

Area of risk — voting on audit appointments

53 Where a partner or staff member holds shares in any capacity in a company which is an audit client of the practice they should not be voted at any general meeting of the company in relation to the appointment, removal or remuneration of auditors.

Area of risk — loans

54 Objectivity may be threatened or appear to be threatened by a loan to or from an audit client.

Discussion

55 A practice or anyone closely connected with it should not, either directly or indirectly, or by way of a trust or other intermediary:

(a) make a loan to or guarantee borrowings by a company or organisation audited by the practice,

(b) accept a loan from such a company or organisation, or

(c) have borrowings guaranteed by such a company or organisation.

56 This advice does not normally apply to any account in credit with a client clearing bank or similar financial institution.

57 Paragraph 55 is not intended to preclude a loan, overdraft or home mortgage being accepted from an audit-client financial institution in the normal course of business and on normal commercial terms by a partner or staff member, provided that:

(i) the loan is not applied so as to subscribe to partnership capital, and

(ii) the partner is not an engagement partner in relation to the client.

Area of risk — goods and services; hospitality

58 Objectivity may be threatened or appear to be threatened by acceptance of goods, services or hospitality from an audit client.

Discussion

59 Goods or services should not be accepted by a practice or anyone closely connected with it unless the value of any benefit is modest.

60 Acceptance of undue hospitality poses a similar threat.

Area of risk — provision of other services to audit clients

61 There are occasions where objectivity may be threatened or appear to be threatened by the provision to an audit client of services other than the audit.

Discussion

62 There is no objection in principle to a practice providing to a client services additional to the audit. However, care must be taken not to perform management functions or to make management decisions.

63 In the case of many audit clients it is common to provide a range of accountancy services, which may include participation in the preparation of accounting records.

64 However in the case of a listed company or public interest company audit client (in relation to which see paragraphs 82 to 83 (Definitions)) a practice should not participate in the preparation of the company's accounting records save:

(a) in relation to assistance of a mechanical nature. Such assistance might include, for example, work on the finalisation of statutory accounts, including consolidations and tax provisions. However, the scale and nature of such work should be regularly reviewed, or

(b) in emergency situations.

65 In all cases in which a practice is concerned in the preparation of accounting records for an audit client the following safeguards should be observed:

(a) the client must accept responsibility for the records as its own.

(b) the practice must not assume the role of management conducting the operations of an enterprise.

(c) the practice should always make appropriate audit tests even where it has processed or maintained certain records.

66 Members are warned in particular of the dangers of being inadvertently drawn into the provision of management functions where a range of services has been provided to an audit client over a period of years. A member must be careful not to go beyond the advisory role and drift into the management sphere. Where consultancy or similar work is carried out on a regular basis it may become 'recurring work' such as to attract the provisions of paragraphs 15 to 20 (above).

67 Recruitment of key financial and administrative staff for an audit client company is an instance where a practice should proceed with care. Whilst it is acceptable for the practice to advertise for and interview prospective staff and produce a 'short list' and recommendations, the final decision in every case as to whom to engage must be left to the client.

(a) A firm should not audit a client's financial statements which include the product of a specialist valuation carried out by it or an associated practice or organisation in the same country or overseas.

Review procedures

68 Because of the need to guard against loss of independence every audit firm should establish adequate review machinery, including an annual review, in order to satisfy itself that each engagement may properly be accepted or be continued having regard to the guidance given in this Statement, and to identify situations where independence may be at risk and where the appropriate safeguards should be applied.

69 Wherever the review procedures indicate that an audit assignment should be accepted or continued only with additional safeguards against loss of independence the engagement partner's decision and the range of safeguards appropriate to the assignment should be subject to independent review by a partner unconnected with the engagement.

Discussion

70 Examples of such safeguards against loss of independence include the following according to the size and circumstances of the practice and the size and circumstances of the clients:

(a) the inclusion of a manager or other qualified staff in the audit team;

(b) rotation of the engagement partner; and

(c) rotation of senior staff.

71 It may be prudent to adopt a procedure under which staff engaged on an audit assignment are able in the last resort to report any area of concern to a partner other than the engagement partner.

Sole practitioners and small firms

72 Since all the safeguards suggested above will not be available to the sole practitioner within his (or her) practice, the practitioner should set up alternative standing arrangements to consult externally with another member. Such arrangements could include provisions as to the maintenance by the latter of client confidentiality and an undertaking not to accept instructions from any client whose work is the subject of review for a period of two years thereafter.

73 To the extent that a small firm may also find difficulty in implementing the safeguards in paragraphs 68 to 71 the partners should set up external consultation arrangements appropriate to their particular circumstances.

Discussion

74 Where the practitioner's own review indicates that an audit engagement should only be accepted or continued with additional safeguards to protect the practitioner's independence, he or she should undertake such consultation before proceeding further. The extent of the consultation will vary according to the nature of the problem; in some cases it may be confined to a discussion of principles; in others it may involve an examination of the file or a discussion of personal relationships.

75 A sole practitioner should not accept or continue appointment as auditor of a company at a time when he or she is trustee of a trust holding shares in that company, unless he or she has made arrangements for such consultation. (See paragraph 50.)

76 Firms are recommended to keep records of all reviews carried out, of the considerations examined, the advice given, the conclusions arrived at and the reasons therefor.

Definitions

'Closely connected'

77 Various paragraphs of this statement refer to persons 'closely connected' with a member, a partner or a practice. This phrase has been chosen because it is not possible in an advisory document such as this to stipulate precisely the relationships beyond which the independence of a practitioner may be put in jeopardy. Persons not related in any way by blood or marriage, for example, may nevertheless enjoy a friendship closer than many blood relationships. Conversely, two spouses may have lived apart from each other for many years without any financial dependency upon or contact with each other.

78 Bearing in mind however the need to maintain, not merely independence, but also the manifest appearance of independence, the following persons will (save for the special case of paragraph 33 (q.v.)) normally be regarded as closely connected with a person, namely:

(a) his (or her) spouse or cohabitee other than a spouse from whom the person is separated, or, in the case of a share holding, a spouse or cohabitee of whose financial affairs the person has been denied knowledge;

(b) his (or her) minor children, including stepchildren;

(c) a company in which he or she has a 20 per cent interest or more.

79 In the event of a complaint a member shall be presumed to have knowledge of the financial affairs of his (or her) spouse or cohabitee unless he demonstrates the contrary.

80 Similarly, the following persons will normally be regarded as being closely connected with a practice:

(a) a partner or, in the case of a corporate practice, a director or shareholder;

(b) a person closely connected with (a);

(c) an employee of the practice.

For the reasons mentioned earlier these categories are not exhaustive of the relationships which might threaten independence.

'Shares and share holdings'

81 Reference to shares and share holdings should be taken to include debenture and other loan stock and the equivalent, and rights to acquire shares, debentures or other loan stock. Share holdings also include options to purchase or sell such securities. A person's holdings include holdings by a nominee on behalf of that person or by a trust created by that person for his or her personal benefit. Share holdings in parent, subsidiary or associated companies of a client company should normally be regarded on the same basis as share holdings in the client company itself. However, if the practice is auditor only of a company or companies which taken together constitute an insignificant part of a group, independence of the parent company, etc., is not required.

'Listed companies'

82 For the purposes of this Statement, reference to listed companies should be taken to include the following:

(a) companies whose shares or securities have been admitted to listing by a recognised stock exchange;

(b) companies whose equity share capital is marketed under the regulations of a recognised stock exchange, e.g. companies whose shares are dealt with on the USM, and the Third Market.

'Public interest companies'

83 There are some unlisted companies and organisations, in both the private and public sectors, which are 'in the public eye' because of their size, or the product or service they provide. Members should regulate themselves in their dealings with such entities as though they were in fact listed companies.

(a) 'Specialist Valuations'

For the purposes of this Statement 'Specialist Valuations' include actuarial valuations, valuations of intellectual property and brands, other than intangible assets, property and unquoted investments but not:

- valuations of shares in accordance with a valuation and report produced in accordance with Section 108 Companies Act 1985, before the allotment of shares of a public company otherwise than for cash.

The term 'specialist valuation' is not intended to cover the giving of normal advice or discussion, or work of a confirmatory nature, on the adequacy of provisions or the valuation of assets or liabilities which are to be determined by the directors or others.

Section B — Independence in financial reporting and similar non-audit roles

Introduction

84 There are roles other than the audit in which a member is required to report with similar authority on financial matters, as follows:

Financial Reporting

85 The considerations which make it essential for a member to be and be seen to be independent when he or she carries out an audit are also relevant to other financial reporting assignments requiring a professional opinion, including reporting assignments where a document has been prepared in contemplation that a third party may rely on it.

Discussion

86 For reports commissioned by management for management's internal use only see Section C, paragraphs 90 to 92.

Litigation support

87 Members called upon to report or undertake work in connection with civil proceedings or with a criminal prosecution should appreciate that such work may be tendered as evidence in a court of law and/or involve the member in giving evidence upon oath. Members should, therefore, be and be seen to be independent when they accept and carry on such an assignment.

Specialist valuation

88 A member should be independent when carrying out a specialist valuation the results of which may be included in financial accounts or public documents.

Arbitration

89 It is a requirement of law that an arbitrator must act independently of the parties and of the issues involved in an arbitration.

Section C — Independence in professional roles other than those covered in Sections A and B

90 This Section deals with work other than the work covered by Sections A and B of this Statement including:

- taxation services;
- preparation of accounts;
- corporate advisory services other than the preparation of documents for public use;
- management consultancy;
- reporting to management/secondment to management.

91 In these circumstances independence in the strict sense applicable to audit assignments (Section A above) is not essential, provided that the practice is not also auditor to the client and that any relevant relationships and conflicts of interest are appropriately disclosed.

92 There are nevertheless certain factors affecting independence which, by their nature are a threat to objectivity in any professional role. Accordingly the following considerations referred to in Section A (above) apply to the professional assignments referred to in para. 90 above:

Area of risk — family and other personal relationships

93 An objective approach to any assignment may be threatened or appear to be threatened as a consequence of a family or other close personal or business relationship.

Discussion

94 In particular, problems may arise where the practice or anyone closely connected with it has a mutual business interest with a client or with an officer or employee of a client. Where an engagement involving such relationships is accepted, or where such an interest arises in the course of an engagement, appropriate safeguards should be set up within the practice. The safeguards should include:

(a) initial consideration by the member/s involved as to whether it is proper to accept appointment in the context of any conflict of interest which may exist;

(b) adequate disclosure of every such conflict to all relevant parties;

(c) continual review of the appropriateness of the practice continuing to act, including, if necessary, e.g. in the case of sole or small practitioners, arrangements to consult with a member outside the practice.

Area of risk — loans

95 Loans to or from a client constitute a threat or an apparent threat to objectivity, and the considerations set out in paragraphs 54 and 57 of Section A apply to the professional assignments referred to in paragraph 90 above.

Discussion

96 The attention of members is also drawn to the warning in paragraph 21 of Section A, that the existence of significant overdue fees from a client can be a threat to objectivity akin to that of a loan.

Area of risk — goods and services; hospitality

97 Objectivity may be threatened or appear to be threatened by acceptance of goods, services or hospitality from a client.

Discussion

98 Goods or services should not be accepted by a practice or anyone closely connected with it unless the value of any benefit is modest.

99 Acceptance of undue hospitality poses a similar threat.

Beneficial interests in shares and other investments

100 A member or practice should avoid any investment in any company with which the practice has a professional relationship where the value of the investment to the investing member or practice is such as to cast doubts on the objectivity of the practice in performing the role or roles which it has contracted to discharge.

101 In this connection the attention of members is drawn to:

(a) the guidance on improper use of confidential information in Section 2.2 Professional duty of confidence in relation to defaults and unlawful acts of clients and others; and

(b) the wide definition in paragraph 81 of Section A of 'Shares and Share holdings', which includes debenture and other loan stock and rights to acquire the same.

Business advisers

102 Where a member or a practice acts as business adviser to a client, he or it may invest in that client, and, if the client is a company, act as sponsor or promoter of its shares, provided that the relationship is clearly declared to relevant parties.

Discussion

103 Members who hold office in a client company, or have a comparable business relationship with a client, should be aware of the dangers inherent in seeking to combine such a role with that of adviser, whereby their necessary objectivity as a professional adviser is imperilled, or perceived to be so by third parties. In such circumstances, members should be aware of the distinctive nature of each of the roles in which they are engaged, and observe the disclosure requirements in paragraph 5 of the Introduction to the Statement.

Second and other opinions

Specific circumstances

104 Where the opinion of a member is sought on the application of accounting standards or principles to specific circumstances or transactions, either completed or contemplated, of an entity with which the member does not have an ongoing professional relationship to provide audit services, he should be alert to the possibility of his opinion creating undue pressure on the judgement and objectivity of the auditor. Accordingly he should seek to minimise the risk of giving inappropriate guidance by ensuring that he has access to all relevant information.

Discussion

105 When the opinion of a member is sought on an accounting treatment by or on behalf of a company or entity which is not an existing audit client, there is a danger that the opinion he expresses may not be based on the same set of facts as is available to the auditor, or may be based on inadequate evidence and that the opinion may be difficult to modify if further facts come to light. It is important, therefore, that the member whose opinion is sought in such cases should ascertain the circumstances of his being consulted and all the other available facts relevant to formulating a professional judgement. For this purpose he should contact the auditor to provide an opportunity for the latter to bring to his attention any relevant facts and should be prepared, given his client's permission, to provide a copy of his opinion to the auditor. If the company or entity seeking the opinion will not permit the member to communicate with the auditor then he should decline to act.

106 Not at issue are opinions provided pursuant to litigation, expert testimony and assistance provided to other firms and their clients jointly.

General circumstances

107A member giving an opinion on the application of accounting standards or principles, relating to a hypothetical situation and not based on the specific facts or circumstances of a particular organisation, should ensure that the nature of the opinion is made clear.

Professional duty of confidence in relation to defaults and unlawful acts of clients and others

Introduction

1 The principal statutory and common law criminal offences which members may encounter in the course of their work are as follows:

(a) theft, obtaining by deception, false accounting, and suppression of documents;

(b) fraud, forgery and offences in relation to companies;

(c) perjury and offences under the Prevention of Corruption Act;

(d) bankruptcy or insolvency offences, frauds on creditors, false trade descriptions, and offences arising out of relations between employers and employees;

(e) conspiracy, soliciting or inciting to commit crime and attempting to commit crime;

(f) offences in relation to direct and indirect taxation (including value added tax and excise duties);

(g) insider dealing.

2 A member who acquires knowledge indicating that a client or an officer or employee of the client may have been guilty of some default or unlawful act should normally raise the matter with the management of the client at an appropriate level. If his concerns are not satisfactorily resolved, he should consider reporting the matter to non-executive directors or to the client's audit committee where these exist. Where this is not possible or fails to resolve the matter a member may wish to consider making a report to a third party. Guidance is provided below on reporting suspected defaults or unlawful acts to third parties.

Relationship between a member and his client

3 It is the duty of a member to make it clear to a client that he may only act for him if the client agrees to disclose in full to the member all information relevant to the engagement. In the absence of this agreement the member should not consent to act. Firms which are authorised to carry on investment business by the Association, and act in connection with a take-over merger or acquisition, must co-operate with the Panel on Take-overs and Mergers (See Rule 11(4) (b) of the Investment Business Rules.)

4 If, during the course of an engagement, a member is unable to obtain from his client information which he considers necessary, he has a duty to indicate this fact in any report that he may make. Furthermore, in the case of an audit report he has a statutory obligation to do so by virtue of Section 237(3) of the Companies Act 1985. In either case, he may consider that he can no longer act.

Note: The word 'client' throughout this Section includes a 'former client'.

It is an offence under the Companies Act 1985 Section 389A(2) for an officer of a company knowingly or recklessly to make a statement to the auditors of the company (whether orally or in writing) which conveys, or purports to convey, any information or explanation which the auditors require, or are entitled to require, in their capacity as auditors of the company and which is misleading, false or deceptive in a material particular.

5 Sometimes in the course of his work a member may obtain information from a client that has a bearing on information supplied to him by another client. In such circumstances it would be a breach of confidence to reveal the information to the second client without the permission of the first client and, in all probability, any attempt to obtain that permission would result in a breach of the duty of confidence owed to the second client. The member should instead, therefore, endeavour to substantiate the information with evidence obtained from the books and records of the second client. If this proves impossible, the member should seek the consent of the second client for him to obtain direct confirmation of the information concerned. If the member is seeking confirmation in connection with his work as auditor of the second client and consent is refused he should consider qualifying his report or resigning and, where relevant, making an appropriate statement under the Companies Act 1985 Section 394, without revealing the name of the first client. In other cases where consent is refused the member should consider ceasing to act.

Disclosure of defaults or unlawful acts

6 Confidentiality is an implied term of member's contract with his client. For this reason a member should not, as a general rule, disclose to other persons, against his client's wishes, information about the client's affairs acquired during and as a result of their professional relationship.

7 It is in the public interest that this confidential relationship be maintained. Without the benefit of confidentiality a client might be reluctant to seek advice from a member. Because clients are able to discuss their plans in confidence, unintended defaults or unlawful acts may be averted as a result of the client acting on a member's advice.

8 A member who becomes aware that a client has committed a default or unlawful act is normally under no legal obligation to disclose what he knows to any persons other than the directors of the client or some person having their authority. There are, however, circumstances in which, in spite of the contractual position, a member may be obliged to disclose or even if not obliged to disclose, he may be free to do so if he concludes that it is right to do so in the public interest or for his own protection.

Obligatory disclosure

9 Where a member believes that his client has committed terrorist offences connected with Northern Ireland affairs, or has reasonable cause to believe that his client has committed treason, he is bound to disclose that knowledge to the proper authorities immediately.

10 A member must disclose information if compelled by process of law, for example under a court order. A member may also, in certain circumstances, be obliged to disclose certain information to the liquidator, administrative receiver or administrator of a client (Section 235, Insolvency Act 1986). Whereas a barrister, solicitor and the clerk or intermediate agent of either, is not required to disclose oral or documentary communication passing between him and his client in professional confidence without the express consent of the client, this privilege does not apply to communications between a member and his client.

Firms which are authorised to carry on investment business by the Association, and act in connection with a take-over, merger or acquisition, must co-operate with the Panel on Take-overs and Mergers (See Rule 11(4)(b) of the Investment Business Rules.)

A member is, however, entitled to the benefit of the ordinary privilege that he need not disclose any information which would incriminate the member himself.

Voluntary disclosure

11 In certain cases members are free to disclose information, whatever its nature:

(a) Disclosure in the public interest

A member may disclose information, which would otherwise be confidential, if disclosure can be justified in the 'public interest'. Whilst it is a concept recognised by the courts, no definition of 'public interest' has ever been given by the courts, which places members in a difficult position as to whether or not disclosure is justified in the 'public interest'. However, it is clear that these exceptions to the duty of confidentiality cover only disclosure to 'one who has a proper interest to receive the information' (Per Denning LJ in *Initial Services* v. *Putterill,* 1968). The proper authorities may, for example, be the Police, the Department of Trade and Industry or the Stock Exchange, and will depend upon the particular circumstances.

When considering whether or not disclosure is justified, the member should take the following into account:

(i) the relative size of the amounts involved and the extent of the likely financial damage;

(ii) whether members of the public are likely to be affected;

(iii) the possibility or likelihood of repetition;

(iv) the reasons for the client's unwillingness to disclose the matters to the proper authority himself;

(v) the gravity of the matter; and

(vi) any legal advice obtained.

Determination of where the balance of public interest lies will require very careful consideration and it will often be appropriate to take legal advice before making a decision. The reasons underlying any decision whether or not to disclose should be fully documented.

(b) Disclosure to protect the member's interests

A member may disclose to the proper authorities information concerning his client where the member's own interests require disclosure of that information:

(i) to enable the member to defend himself against a criminal charge or to clear himself of suspicion; or

(ii) to resist proceedings for a penalty in respect of a taxation offence, for example in a case where it is suggested that he assisted or induced his client to make or deliver incorrect returns or accounts; or

(iii) to resist a legal action brought against him by his client or some third person; or

(iv) to enable the member to defend himself against disciplinary proceedings or criticism of him which is the subject of enquiry under the joint disciplinary scheme; or

(v) to enable the member to sue for his fees.

(c) Disclosure authorised by statute

There are cases of express statutory provision where disclosure of information to a proper authority overrides the duty of confidentiality for example, in the Drug Trafficking Offences Act 1986. Each such statute should be considered carefully as the protection offered to the person making the disclosure varies from statute to statute.

(d) Disclosure by non-governmental bodies
Members may be approached by recognised but non-governmental bodies seeking information concerning suspected acts of misconduct not amounting to a crime or civil wrong. Some of these bodies have statutory powers to require persons to supply information, in which case members should comply. Where there is no such statutory power, the member should not supply information without the client's consent.

Prosecution of a client or former client

12 Where a member is approached by the police, the Inland Revenue, the Customs and Excise authorities or other public authority making enquiries which may lead to the prosecution of a client or former client for an offence (other than treason or certain terrorist offences), the member should act with caution. He should ascertain whether or not the person requesting information has a statutory right to demand it, seek legal advice before giving information; and consider the nature of the alleged offence and whether if he were to give the information he would be justified because of an overriding public interest in disclosure or would be acting contrary to professional ethics.

13 Unless ordered by the court or acting under a statutory authority the member should decline to give the information until he has obtained his client's authority or received independent legal or other professional advice that he should or may give the information whether or not his client consents. He should state that in the meantime he is not in a position to discuss his client's affairs. He should, however, keep in close touch with his legal or other professional advisor on the legal aspects of his position.

Appearance as a witness

14 If a member is invited to appear in court as a witness against a client or former client, he should normally refuse until served with a subpoena or other form of witness summons.

15 He must answer any questions that are put to him, even though he may thus disclose information obtained in a confidential capacity but he may appeal to the Court for guidance on whether he is obliged to answer particular questions.

16 If the Court directs a member to produce any documents in his ownership or possession, then he must do so. He will generally be warned in advance of the intention to call for such documents.

Members' relations with the authorities on clients' behalf

17 A practising member acting in any professional capacity, has access to much information of a private nature. It is essential that he should normally treat such information as available to him for the purpose only of carrying out the professional duties for which he has been engaged. To divulge information about a client's affairs would normally be a breach of professional confidence, which might have the most serious legal and professional consequences.

Members' own relations with authorities

Criminal offences

18 A member himself commits a criminal offence:

(a) if he incites a client to commit a criminal offence, whether or not the client accepts his advice; or

(b) if he helps or encourages a client in the planning or execution of a criminal offence which is committed; or

(c) if he agrees with a client or anyone else to pervert or obstruct the course of justice by concealing, destroying or fabricating evidence or by misleading the police by statements which he knows to be untrue.

19 Where a member knows or believes that the client has committed an arrestable offence the member would himself commit a criminal offence if he were with knowledge or belief that the client had committed an arrestable offence to do any act with the intention of impeding the arrest or prosecution of client unless the member has lawful authority of reasonable excuse. The mere fact that he was the client's accountant would not be a reasonable excuse. (Criminal Law Act 1967 Section 4(1)). An arrestable offence is one — for which the sentence is fixed by the law or for which a person not previously convicted may under or by virtue of any enactment be sentenced to imprisonment for a term of five years'. (Criminal Law Act 1967 Section 2(1)).

20 A member would have to do some positive act to assist the client to escape arrest or prosecution for an arrestable offence in order to be convicted of the offence of impeding the arrest of prosecution of the client. If a member refuses to answer questions by the police about the client's affairs or refuses to produce documents relating to the client's affairs without the client's consent, the refusal would not be an act to impede the arrest or prosecution of the client.

21 Where a member knows or believes the client has committed an arrestable offence and the member has information which might be of material assistance in the prosecution of the client for the offence, the member would be committing a criminal offence if he were to accept or agree to accept any consideration in return for not disclosing that information.

22 In these circumstances, the acceptance of a reasonable fee for professional services rendered would not be an offence. However, if the fee were wholly or partly paid in consideration for the member not disclosing information, the member would be committing an offence. The acceptance of an unusually large fee might be used as evidence against a member.

23 If a member knows that client has committed treason or certain terrorist offences and the member fails to disclose what he knows to the proper authority, the member commits a criminal offence.

Company investigation

24 Where a member is acting as auditor of a company governed by the Companies Act 1985, his client is the company and not the director.

25 If it is necessary for the auditor to qualify his report on the accounts, the qualifications should indicate clearly the circumstances which give rise to the shareholders and others who may see the accounts, the fact that offences have been committed. The auditor will not be able to avoid bringing to the attention of shareholders circumstances which may indicate that offences have been committed by resigning his office without reporting. Section 394 of the Companies Act 1985 requires him to include in his notice of resignation a statement of any circumstances connected with his resignation which he believes should be brought to the notice of the members or creditors or the company or else a statement to the effect that there are no such circumstances. His resignation will be treated as ineffective unless he complies with this obligation. In many cases, the interests of the members and creditors will best be served if the auditor completes his audit and reports to shareholders on the accounts in accordance with Section 235 of the Companies Act 1985; he may then indicate his unwillingness to accept re appointment at the next Annual General Meeting. Where the auditor believes that he may need to refer to the commission of offences, either in his report on the accounts or in his notice of resignation, he should be aware of the danger of an action for defamation. He should therefore seek legal advice as to the terms in which he should either report or make a statement in his notice of resignation (see paragraph below).

Transmission of report to shareholders

26 In normal circumstances an auditor's duty is fulfilled when he sends his report to the secretary or directors of the company for onward transmission to the shareholders of the company. But if he knows or had good reason to believe that, for example:

(i) his report has not been sent to shareholders; or

(ii) his report has been sent to shareholders in an altered form; or

(iii) his report has been sent to shareholders unaltered in a misleading context;

it will be necessary for him to consider the steps that he should take to rectify the situation. These steps may include communicating directly with the shareholders. Often the mere threat of taking such steps will result in the desired action, but if a direct communication has to be made the auditor must guard against the danger of an action for defamation being brought against him and must take special care in the exceptional cases where the difficulty of communication or the urgency of the situation necessitate some public announcement. As soon as the possibility of making such a communication arises, therefore, he should seek legal advice about his duty to the shareholders in the particular circumstances of the case, as to the method of any communication his duty requires and as to the terms in which the communication should be made. If the auditor is aware of third parties who may be affected by the situation he should also consider taking the steps outlined in paragraphs 28 or 30 below as appropriate.

Urgent cases

27 An auditor may sometimes learn facts which suggest that offences or other unlawful acts or defaults have been committed by a director(s) or an employee(s) of the company. The facts may be of such a nature that, even though they may ultimately give rise to a qualification of the auditor's report, it would be contrary to the interests of the company for their disclosure to await the transmission of his report. On the occasions when this arises, it is likely to be because the conduct is both serious and liable to be repeated. In such a case it will be necessary for an auditor to report at once to the directors. There may also be cases in which the involvement of the directors themselves will make it necessary for the auditor to consider taking further steps to ensure that the matter is brought promptly to the attention of shareholders. These steps may include resignation by a notice stating the circumstances or even direct communication with shareholders. Occasions which call for such steps will be rare, and an auditor who is considering taking them should seek legal advice.

Past accounts and reports

28 Where the auditor discovers that past accounts on which he has reported are defective, he must consider the position in relation to the shareholders, regulatory bodies and the Inland Revenue and third parties.

(a) Shareholders
The action which the auditor should take to bring to the attention of shareholders defects in accounts on which he has reported is described in paragraphs 7-10 of the Auditing Guideline 'Events after the balance sheet date'.

(b) Inland Revenue
The auditor should follow the same procedure as in the case of an individual client.

(c) Other third parties
An auditor may be civilly liable if he has prepared a report which he subsequently discovers to be false in some material respect, and fails to take appropriate action to correct it. In such circumstances, therefore, the auditor should ordinarily take legal advice as to the steps which are appropriate. These might include the following:

(i) Where the report was prepared for the company alone or for statutory purposes, the auditor's appropriate course will generally be to disclose the relevant facts to the directors and ascertain what steps they intend to take to bring it to the attention of third parties who are affected.

(ii) If the directors fail to take such steps, the proper course for the auditor to adopt will depend on the gravity of the error and the nature of the reliance which has been or is likely to be placed upon it by the third party.

Resignation of the auditor

(iii) The courses open to the auditors include resignation by a notice which contains a statement of the relevant facts and of the directors' failure to bring those facts to the attention of those affected. If a notice containing such a statement is deposited at the company's registered office, the company is required by Section 394 of the Companies Act 1985 to send a copy within 14 days to the Registrar of Companies and to every person having a statutory right to receive the accounts. The auditor may also require the directors of the company to convene (at the company's expense) an extraordinary general meeting of the company to receive, and consider such explanation of the circumstances connected with his resignation as he may wish to place before the meeting. Where the auditor has resigned and deposited a statement of the relevant facts, it will often be unnecessary to take any further steps to bring the facts to the attention of the third parties.

(iv) There may, however, be cases in which reliance has been placed or may be placed upon the auditor's report by a third party who is not likely to receive a copy of the auditor's notice of resignation and statement of reasons, either because he is not one of those entitled to receive copies of the accounts or because the company does not propose to send the notice and statement to such persons or does not intend to do so sufficiently quickly. In these cases it may be appropriate for the auditor to communicate directly with a third party known to be affected, stating that he has resigned, that a statement of his reasons for resigning has been deposited with the company to be forwarded to, inter alia, the Registrar of Companies, and that those reasons may affect the interests of persons who have read the company's accounts and his report upon them.

(v) An auditor who believes that a company may fail to forward a copy of his notice of resignation and statement of reasons to the Registrar of Companies may, and in some cases should, notify the Registrar of Companies that he has deposited such a notice and statement with the company and enquire whether it has been received. He should also inform the company that he has notified the Registrar.

Save in exceptionally urgent cases it will usually be appropriate to notify the company in advance of what the auditor intends to do, so that the company may have an opportunity themselves to bring the relevant facts to the attention of those affected.

29 An auditor may sometimes be instructed to prepare a report (other than a statutory report) for the purpose of being submitted to a third party. Such a report will usually amount in law to a representation made by the auditor himself to that third party. Where this is the case and the auditor subsequently discovers that it is false in a material respect, he is entitled to communicate a correction directly to the third party, and should normally do so.

Removal of the auditor

30 The distinction between the directors and the shareholders will sometimes have little or no relevance, either because the directors hold a controlling interest or because all the shareholders are directors. When in these circumstances the directors fail to comply with the auditor's advice they may wish to prevent the auditor from completing his audit and making a report containing qualifications. They could achieve this by calling a general meeting at which the sole business would be the removal of the auditor. If this procedure is followed the auditor may wish to take one of two courses. He may wish to make to the company the written representations which he is authorised to make under Section 391A of the Companies Act 1985 or to exercise his right under Section 391 of the Companies Act 1985 to attend the meeting and be heard. Alternatively, he may resign before the meeting, including a statement of the circumstances in his notice of resignation as he is bound to by Section 394 of the Companies Act 1985. Where there are persons who would be affected by a qualification to the report and who would not be entitled to receive representations under Section 391A or to attend the meeting, resignation with a statement of the circumstances will often be the more appropriate course.

Providing information to a liquidator, receiver, administrative receiver or administrator of a client company

31 Liquidators, administrators and administrative receivers have a statutory right under Section 235 of the Insolvency Act 1986 to call for 'such information concerning the company and its promotion, formation, business, dealings, affairs or property as the (liquidator, administrator or administrative receiver) may . . . reasonably require', from any person who is or was at any time an officer of the company. The courts have held that an auditor is an 'officer' of a company.

32 A member who is required by a liquidator, administrative receiver or administrator to supply information in these classes should normally do so unless the liquidator, administrator or administrative receiver is acting beyond his powers, or for a purpose unrelated to his official functions or in breach of his duties. A liquidator, administrative receiver or administrator will ordinarily have vested in him the sole right to manage the company's assets and affairs. A member dealing with him in good faith is accordingly entitled to assume that he is acting within his powers.

33 A receiver, as opposed to an administrative receiver or an administrator, has no general statutory power to obtain information. Moreover, although the extent of his powers will depend on the terms of the deed or court order pursuant to which he was appointed, it is unlikely that his powers will extend to requiring information from a member without the specific consent of the company or an order of the Court.

Auditors of companies in liquidation

34 Although the appointment of an auditor of a company is made by the shareholders in general meeting (or in the case of a newly formed company by the directors) his appointment is by the company as a legal entity and his duty of confidence is to the company as distinct from the individual shareholders. If the company goes into liquidation the company's rights remain vested in the company as an entity and it is therefore still the company to which the auditor has a duty of confidence. The liquidator will, however, normally be the proper agent of the company for the purpose of enforcing any rights which the company could have enforced, including the company's right to permit its auditors to provide information to others. Moreover a liquidator is entitled to exercise the statutory power conferred upon him by Section 235 of the Insolvency Act 1986, referred to at paragraph 31 above.

35 The auditor of a company which is in liquidation may be approached by the police for assistance in enquiries which may lead to a director or other individual being prosecuted. The auditor is under no legal obligation to give to the police any information obtained in the course of his professional duties and normally he should not do so unless he has the permission of the liquidator (the liquidator being the person who could exercise the right of the company to release the auditor from his duty of confidence). If such permission is not forthcoming unless the considerations of public interest in paragraph 11(a) above applies the auditor should explain to the police that the information is confidential and may not be disclosed without permission.

36 The liquidator may consider it his duty to make a report to the Director of Public Prosecutions under Section 218 of the Insolvency Act 1986 to the effect that a past or present officer or member of the company may have been guilty of a criminal offence in relation to the company. If the Director of Public Prosecutions institutes proceedings following such a report the auditor is one of the persons having a statutory duty to give assistance to the Director of Public Prosecutions so that in these circumstances his duty of confidence is over-ridden.

Companies under investigation

37 Under Section 434 of the Companies Act 1985 the auditor is one of the persons who has a statutory duty to produce documents, to attend before Inspectors when required to do so and to give assistance to Inspectors. This Section gives powers to Inspectors to require such information or assistance from any person, other than an officer or agent of the company, or other body corporate, whom they consider is, or may be, in possession of any information concerning its affairs. A member having a professional relationship with a company other than that of auditor may therefore be required by law to provide information to, or otherwise assist Inspectors. It seems that these powers may include the power to require production of an accountant's working papers. By Section 436 of the Companies Act 1985, refusal to comply with a request made under Section 434 of the Act is punishable as a contempt of court.

38 Section 447 of the Companies Act 1985 gives wide powers to the Department of Trade and its officers. They may at any time, if they think there is good reason so to do, require any books or papers to be produced by a company or by any person who appears to the Department or officer to be in possession of them. If the books or papers are produced, they may take copies of or extracts from them, or have them explained. If the books or papers are not produced, they may require the person who was required to produce them to state, to the best of his knowledge and belief, where they are. Where the person who is ordered to produce books or papers claims a lien on them the production is without prejudice to the lien. It is an offence, punishable by fine, not to comply with a requirement imposed by virtue of Section 447 to produce books or papers or provide an explanation or make a statement; but where a person is charged with an offence in respect of a requirement to produce any books or papers, it is a defence to prove that they were not in his possession or under his control and that it was not reasonably practicable for him to comply with the requirement.

39 Also, the Companies Act 1985 contains provisions relating to entry and search of premises (Section 448), the security of information obtained under Section 447 (Section 449), the penalisation of destroying, mutilating or falsifying company documents (Section 450) and the penalisation of furnishing false information in purported compliance with a requirement imposed under Section 447 (Section 451). Where any of the provisions referred to in this paragraph apply, the auditor's duty of confidence is over-ridden by his statutory duty.

Investigations by the Commission of the European Economic Community

40 Article 65 of the EEC Treaty prohibits agreements in widely defined categories having the object or effect of preventing, restricting or distorting competition within the Common Market. Article 86 of the Treaty prohibits abuses by undertakings of a dominant position which they may hold within the Common Market, by engaging in specified kinds of restrictive practices or agreements. The Commission has a duty under other Articles of the Treaty to enforce these provisions, and for this purpose extensive powers of investigation are conferred upon it by Council Regulation 17. Both the Treaty and the Regulation have the force of law in England.

Article 1 of Regulation 17 empowers the Commission, through its authorised officers, to require any undertakings (including an accountant) to supply information provided that the request is made in writing specifying its legal basis and purpose. An accountant must supply the information requested, and to that extent his duty of confidence is over-ridden. Further, if an accountant fails to supply it the Commission may, by decision, require him to do so within a specified time limit, failing which he is liable to be fined.

Foreign law

41 This section refers to the application of foreign law to members in practice in the United Kingdom providing professional services in the United Kingdom. It is assumed that the professional relationship pursuant to which the member provides his services is one governed by English law. There may, however, be cases in which either by express agreement or by implication from the circumstances, a foreign law will apply. In these circumstances a member should consider taking legal advice from a lawyer qualified to practice in the jurisdiction in question.

42 As outlined in paragraph 6 above it is an implied term of a member's contract with his client that he will not, as a general rule, disclose to other persons information about his client's affairs, acquired during and as a result of their professional relationship, against his client's wishes. Therefore if the member becomes aware, in the course of his professional relationship with either a foreign client or a United Kingdom client with overseas branches, of contraventions by his client of foreign law he is under no duty in English law to disclose that matter to the relevant foreign authority. He may, however, be under such a duty in foreign law. Furthermore, if a member is specifically requested by the foreign authority to provide information relating to possible contraventions of foreign law he should only make disclosure:

(a) if he is compelled to do so by the process of law; or

(b) where the member's own interest requires such disclosure (see paragraph 11(b); or

(c) by way of qualification (in appropriate cases) of his audit report (see paragraph 25).

In any event a member should seek legal advice before making any disclosure.

Defamation

43 If an auditor forms the view that unlawful acts or defaults have occurred and communicates the relevant facts to persons who have a legitimate interest in receiving them, he will enjoy qualified privilege from liability for defamation. Unless malice is proved against him, that privilege will amount to a complete defence, even if the facts should prove to be wrong. While this statement gives general guidance on the circumstances in which an auditor may have a duty to communicate such facts, each case must be considered in the light of its own particular circumstances and an auditor who is in any doubt as to the courses which are properly open to him should take legal advice about his rights and duties.

In particular an auditor who is contemplating making a public announcement or communicating directly with shareholders should bear in mind that such an announcement, even if justified by the particular circumstances of the case, may cause serious damage to the company or to individuals, and such a step should not normally be taken without taking legal advice.

Member's working papers

44 A member's working papers are his own property and any request for their production should normally be refused.

However, if an Inspector of Taxes or one of the special investigative offices of the Inland Revenue requests the production of the working papers relating to a particular client whose affairs are under investigation, the member should bear in mind that it is his duty to act in the best possible interests of his client. If, in his opinion, his client would best be served by producing the documents, then provided that the client does not object, he may do so. In some instances schedules, notes, etc., may well be helpful in supporting the member's report and contentions. Correspondence and notes of interviews with the client and/or his legal advisers will frequently be of an extremely confidential nature and should only be produced in exceptional circumstances — and even then only with the authority of the client. In all such cases the need to take legal advice should be considered and, where appropriate, recommended to the client.

45 The decision whether or not to produce working papers is entirely one for the member, even if the client concerned has no objection to the disclosure of information contained therein. References should also be made to Section 2.6 'Ownership of books and papers.'

46 Occasionally a member is approached by one of the special investigative offices of the Inland Revenue and asked to supply a sample of his working papers. Such a request may arise as the result of an investigation into the affairs of a particular client or from a more general scrutiny of cases handled in an inspector's office. In either case it may be presumed that the Inland Revenue has serious doubts as to the member's standards and therefore wishes to seek further evidence to either confirm or dispel its suspicions. It is understandable that a member who believes his standards to be satisfactory should resent the request, but, nevertheless, he should be aware of the consequences that could ensue from a refusal to co-operate, viz. (i) the investigative office could inform tax inspectors that the member's work is suspect — this could have a damaging effect not only on the member but also on his clients; (ii) the Inland Revenue might institute proceedings against the member for the levy of penalties under Section 99 of the Taxes Management Act 1970 (assisting in the delivery or making of incorrect returns or accounts). Once a penalty has been exacted under this section the Inland Revenue is empowered under Section 20A of the Taxes Management Act 1970 to obtain documents relating to any of the member's clients (but see paragraph 17(c)).

The Association therefore advises members to take a positive attitude and to suggest to the investigative office that an independent accountant be appointed to examine a sample of working papers and to report his findings to the Revenue. In the event that the findings of the independent accountant confirm that there are irregularities in the member's work the Association suggests that the member should consider placing the entire matter in the hands of the independent accountant who may be able to negotiate a settlement with the Inland Revenue on the member's behalf. However, it is for the individual member to decide what is the best course of action for him to take in the particular circumstances.

Taxation offences

47 Among the wrongful acts of clients discovered by members, taxation offences of various kinds are likely to be among the more frequent.

48 Any act or omission directed to or resulting in the evasion or attempted evasion of tax may be the subject of charges under statute or at common law. The taxing statutes prescribe a number of offences for which monetary penalties are recoverable. The recovery of a penalty against a taxpayer does not rule out the possibility of criminal proceedings against him. But this would be unusual. The Commissioners of Inland Revenue have statutory authority to compound any proceeding for the recovery of fines or penalties and in back duty and accounts investigations it is customary for the Inland Revenue to draw the taxpayer's attention to its power to accept a settlement as an alternative to proceedings.

49 When a member finds that a client has misinformed or misled him as to his affairs for the purpose of obtaining some tax advantage, the member must consider carefully, not only the client's but also his own position vis-a-vis the Revenue, particularly in relation to the following:

(a) Past accounts

The member may discover that accounts already prepared and/or reported on by him and/or computations and returns based thereon are no longer accurate.

If these have already been submitted to the Inland Revenue, the member cannot allow the Revenue to continue to rely on them. He should advise the client to make full disclosure or to authorise him to do so without delay.

If the client refuses to make or authorise disclosure, the member should inform him that he can no longer act for him and that it will be necessary to inform the Inland Revenue that since the accounts or statements concerned were submitted, he has obtained information which shows that the accounts or other documents are such that he would no longer be prepared to report on them in the same terms as previously and that he has ceased to act for the client. In so informing the Revenue the member is under no duty to indicate in what way the accounts are defective and should not normally do so unless the client has consented to such disclosure.

(b) Current accounts

Where the information obtained affects accounts or statements that the member is currently preparing or auditing, the member is in a position to deal with the matter himself. That is to say if the client fails to provide such information as the member may require or objects to the manner in which the member considers that the accounts should be presented, it is the member's professional duty to qualify his report on the accounts in such a way as will make clear the respects in which they are defective.

(c) New clients

A member preparing or auditing accounts for a new client may become aware that accounts previously submitted to the Revenue are defective. If so, the member should advise the client to make full and prompt disclosure. The member has no responsibility for past accounts except in so far as they affect the accuracy of accounts that he is preparing or auditing. If they do, then he must inform the client that an appropriate adjustment must be made in the current accounts. If the client is unwilling to agree to such an adjustment, the member should qualify his report on the accounts accordingly.

(d) Business accounts and private returns

A member who is acting for a client in relation to his business affairs may sometimes discover that the client has been guilty of concealment of information from the Revenue in relation to his private income. In that event, the member should advise the client to make full disclosure. If he refuses to do so, the member is under no obligation to take any further steps. In particular, it would be improper for him to make any disclosure to the Revenue without the client's consent, but he may continue to act for the client in business matters. Often he will prefer to terminate the engagement.

The above is based on the premise that the member has acted for the client only in relation to the taxation of his business profits and has been in no way concerned with his private returns. Where, however this is not the case the member should, on refusal of the client to make disclosure, inform the client that he can no longer act for him and that it will be necessary to inform the Inland Revenue accordingly and to dissociate himself from any returns or accounts that may be affected by the client's concealment. The member is under no duty to give the Revenue any further details and it would be improper for him to do so without the client's permission.

(e) Professional responsibility towards clients

Whatever line of conduct may be appropriate for the member to protect his own position, he is still under a professional duty to ensure so far as he can that the client understands the seriousness of offences against the Revenue and the probable consequences of a notification from the member to the Revenue that he is no longer acting for the client. In other words, the member should always urge on the client the desirability of authorising him to make full disclosure. The taxing statutes provide that any accounts submitted on behalf of a taxpayer are deemed to be submitted by him and/or with his consent unless he proves otherwise.

This emphasises the need for the member to obtain appropriate instructions from the client and to ensure that he has signed or otherwise approved the accounts.

Where a member has not been instructed to deal with taxation work for a client, he has no authority to deal with the Inland Revenue. If therefore he should receive any enquiry from the Inland Revenue, he need say no more than that he is not dealing with tax matters and that all enquiries should be made of the client.

(f) Disclosure should be prompt
The provisions of Section 7 of the Taxes Management Act 1970 should always be borne in mind. It provides that where incorrect returns or accounts are submitted by a person neither fraudulently nor negligently and he learns that they are incorrect, he must remedy the error without unreasonable delay, failing which the returns or accounts will be treated as having been submitted negligently. This involves liability to money penalties.

50 The Inland Revenue has been granted wide powers to seek disclosure of information as follows:

(a) Summons to appear
General or special commissioners may in any appeal against an assessment or similar proceeding

(i) require a party to the proceedings to produce such books, accounts or other documents as may be specified — but this power is not exercisable against a member in respect of a client's affairs — Section 51 Taxes Management Act 1970;

(ii) summon any other person (including a member) to appear for examination; a member so summoned is bound to appear (or incur a penalty), but he may (and generally should) decline to be sworn or to answer questions and by so doing will incur no penalty — Section 52 Taxes Management Act 1970.

(b) Notice to provide information
The Revenue may by notice require certain persons to provide such information as may be specified. Generally this power is exercisable against the taxpayer, but in some cases it may be directed towards other persons, e.g.,

(i) a person who, as agent, receives or has received rents or other payments arising from land may be required to furnish particulars — Section 19, Taxes Management Act 1970;

(ii) a person who receives or has received income from securities other than beneficially, may be required to furnish particulars — Section 24 Taxes Management Act 1970;

(iii) a person who is acting or has acted on behalf of others in any transaction reasonably thought to involve the transfer of assets abroad may be required to furnish particulars — Section 745 Income and Corporation Taxes Act 1988.

(c) Notice to produce documents
Under Section 20 Taxes Management Act 1970 (as amended) an inspector may by notice call on any third party to produce documents in his possession containing or reasonably thought to contain information about a taxpayer's liability.

The persons who may be treated as 'the taxpayer' include a company which has ceased to exist and an individual who has died.

Third parties covered by the notice will include accountants. Notice cannot be given unless authorised by the Board of Inland Revenue and a general or special commissioner. The notice must specify the documents required and the time within which they must be produced but need not identify the taxpayer or taxpayers concerned, provided the commissioner has been satisfied that certain other conditions have been fulfilled. But by Section 20B(9) such notice does not apply to audit papers, defined as:

"... papers which are the property of the person appointed as an auditor under [any statutory provision] and which have been prepared by, or for, that person in order to carry out the statutory duties of an auditor ..."

In practice the Revenue will allow equivalent protection where an accountant is appointed to carry out a non-statutory, independent audit to standards similar to those required for a Companies Act audit or to standards laid down by the client's professional body, provided the work on the audit is kept separate from any work on the preparation of the accounts.

Under Section 20A Taxes Management Act 1970 a tax accountant who after 30 July 1976, has been convicted in any UK court of a tax offence or has incurred a penalty for assisting in the preparation of a return or account (other than for VAT) knowing it to be incorrect may be required by notice to produce documents in his possession or power relating to the tax liability of any of his clients. No such notice may be issued:

(i) more than twelve months after the date of conviction of the tax accountant or award of the penalty against him; or

(ii) in respect of documents relating to the conduct of a pending appeal by the client; or

(iii) without the consent of a circuit judge in England and Wales, a sheriff in Scotland or a county court judge in Northern Ireland.

The exemption from producing working papers conferred on a tax accountant by Section 20B(9) does not apply to a notice issued under Section 20A.

(d) Power of entry and seizure

Where there is a reasonable ground for suspecting that evidence of a tax fraud may be found, a Revenue officer may enter premises, by force if necessary, and seize and remove any material which it is reasonably thought may be required in subsequent proceedings.

The Revenue officer must provide a list of the material seized on request by the occupier of the premises or any person having custody of the material seized. Any such entry and seizure, however, requires the warrant of a circuit judge in England and Wales, a sheriff in Scotland or a county court judge in Northern Ireland, and application for such a warrant by a Revenue officer requires the specific authority of the Board of Inland Revenue itself (as distinct from that of a superior officer acting under the Board's authority). The warrant lapses 14 days after issue. General reference — Section 20C Taxes Management Act 1970.

51 In spite of the Revenue's statutory powers an inspector may sometimes ask for the same information to be provided voluntarily. Though the client is not obliged to comply the member may in some cases think it advisable for him to do so. In others the member may feel that he should decline and await the exercise of statutory powers by the Revenue.

Errors in the taxpayer's favour

52 The Inland Revenue may mistakenly make an excessive repayment of tax to the taxpayer, even though full disclosure of the facts has been made to it. Where an excessive repayment is paid directly to the client, the member, as soon as he becomes aware of the error, should urge his client to refund the excess sum to the Revenue. Once the client has knowledge of the error and fails to correct it, he could be committing an offence under the Theft Act 1968. Should the client refuse to refund the payment to the Revenue, the member should consider whether in all the circumstances he should continue to act for the client.

Where the excessive repayment is made to the member on the client's behalf, the member should correct the error. Failure to do so could involve both the member and the client in an offence under the Theft Act 1968.

Value added tax

53 VAT, which has been charged since 1st April 1973, was first regulated by the Finance Act 1972. The 1972 Act and subsequent Finance Acts were consolidated in the Value Added Tax Act 1983, itself supplemented by subsequent Finance Acts by the Customs & Excise Management Act 1979 and regulations made under these Acts. In addition, every person registered for VAT is supplied with the VAT General Guide (Notice No. 700) and other VAT Notices and Leaflets, listed in the General Guide, can be obtained from H.M. Customs & Excise.

VAT offences and related offences

54 The Value Added Tax Act 1983 Section 39 (as amended) creates a number of specific criminal offences relating to VAT e.g.

(a) The fraudulent evasion of VAT or taking steps with a view to such evasion is an indictable offence under the Value Added Tax Act 1983 Section 39(1) when committed not only by the taxpayer, but also by any other person knowingly concerned with the evasion. The penalty on summary conviction is £2,000 or three times the amount of the tax, whichever is the greater, or up to 6 months' imprisonment, or both. The penalty on conviction following indictment is an unlimited monetary amount or imprisonment for no more than 7 years, or both.

(b) Under Section 39(2) of the 1983 Act (as amended), it is an indictable offence to produce, furnish, send or make use of, a document which is false in a material particular with intent to deceive; or when furnishing information, to make a statement knowing it to be false in a material particular; or recklessly to make a statement which is false in a material particular. The penalty on conviction following indictment is an unlimited monetary amount or imprisonment for no more than 7 years, or both. The penalty on summary conviction depends partly on the nature of the document concerned. Where the document is a return or the information furnished relates to a return, the penalty is the greater of £2,000 and three times the amount falsely claimed as credit for input tax and the amount by which the output tax was falsely understated, or no more than 6 months' imprisonment, or both. If the document is a claim for a refund or repayment or the information furnished relates to such a claim, the penalty is the greater of three times the amount falsely claimed and £2,000, or no more than 6 months' imprisonment, or both. Otherwise it is either £2,000 or no more than 6 months' imprisonment, or both.

A member may be alleged to have 'furnished or sent information' within the meaning of Section 39(2) if he has assisted his client with the completion of his VAT return, or filed it with the Custom & Excise Authorities on the client's behalf.

55 Under the Customs & Excise Management Act 1979 Section 171(4), if a member is a director, secretary or similar officer of a company, he could be guilty of an offence, in respect of VAT, if the company with the member's consent or connivance, or due to his neglect, commits an offence.

Under Section 152 of the Customs & Excise Management Act 1979, the Commissioners of Customs & Excise have power to compound proceedings relating to VAT offences. The Commissioners may decide to accept an offer made by an offender, or they may themselves offer to compound on the payment of a stated sum, or they may decide to prosecute, even though an offender has offered to compound.

If the Commissioners have offered to compound, and their offer is refused, this will not in any way prejudice the institution of criminal proceedings. The Commissioners are free to decide on the course of action they wish to pursue. The Commissioners reach their decision after due consideration of the seriousness of the case, and any mitigating or aggravating facts or circumstances.

Where VAT offences are criminal offences, they are not arrestable offences.

Knowledge of VAT offences

56 If a member suspects that a client has committed VAT offences, he must ensure that he in no way assists the client to commit any criminal offence. If criminal charges are likely to be made against the client, the member should advise the client to seek legal advice. Where it seems likely that the Commissioners will settle without proceedings, the member should advise his client to make a full disclosure to the Customs & Excise Authorities and provide full facilities for investigations, so that a private settlement can be obtained, rather than having proceedings brought against him with the accompanying publicity.

57 Civil penalties

In addition to the criminal offences described in paragraphs 21 and 22, there are several acts of commission or omission that give rise to civil penalties. These acts include:

(a) acts and omissions involving dishonesty (Section 13 Finance Act 1985);

(b) serious misdeclaration or neglect* (Section 14 Finance Act 1985);

(c) persistent misdeclaration (Section 14A Finance Act 1985);

(d) failure to notify liability for registration (Section 15 Finance Act 1985);

(e) failure by exempted person to notify a material change in the nature of his taxable supplies (Section 15 Finance Act 1985);

(f) unauthorised issue of tax invoices (Section 15 Finance Act 1985);

(g) breach of walking possession agreements (Section 16 Finance Act 1985);

(h) failure to notify end of liability or entitlement to be registered (Section 17 Finance Act 1985);

(i) failure to keep records, furnish information or produce documents (Section 17 Finance Act 1985);

(j) failure to comply with orders, regulations or rules (Section 17 Finance Act 1985);

(k) failure to furnish returns or pay tax (Section 17 Finance Act 1985);

(l) failure to preserve records (Section 17 Finance Act 1985).

VAT errors

58 Under Section 39(2)(b) of the Value Added Tax Act 1983, any person who makes a statement which he knows to be false in a material particular commits an offence. All errors in VAT returns should therefore be put right in the next return submitted after discovery

*The serious misdeclaration or neglect penalty under Section 14 Finance Act 1985 is yet to come into effect.

of the error. Failure to do so may not only give rise to an offence under Section 39(2)(b) but also to liability to civil penalties under sections 13 or 14 of the Finance Act 1985. The Customs & Excise Authorities have indicated that, if as a result of an error there is an under declaration of VAT of more than £1,000, the taxpayer should nevertheless not wait until the next return is due to be made but would be well advised to inform his local VAT office immediately he discovers the error in order to avoid suspicion that the error was deliberate. It follows that a member who discovers such an error should advise his client accordingly. The same principle applies where there is an over declaration of tax repayable of more than £1,000. For his own protection, in the event that the matter comes to the notice of the Customs & Excise Authorities before the client has disclosed it, the member should ensure that his records of his advice to his client are such as to rebut any allegation that the member himself was knowingly concerned in the commission of any offence.

VAT and accounts

59 If a member acquires information indicating that accounts he has prepared or audited, which have been submitted to the Customs & Excise Authorities, are defective, the member should proceed in accordance with the guidance contained in paragraph 49 above.

VAT assessments

60 Schedule 7 paragraph 4 to the Value Added Tax Act 1983 empowers the Customs & Excise Authorities to raise VAT assessments in the following circumstances:

(a) where a taxable person has failed to make any returns required under the Act;

(b) where a taxable person has failed to keep any documents and afford the facilities necessary to verify any returns; or

(c) where it appears to the Customs & Excise Authorities that the returns are incomplete or incorrect.

Assessments may therefore be raised where there are accounting errors; insufficient records; taxable trading prior to registration; lack of evidence of input tax borne, incorrect rate of VAT applied, an incorrect date has been adopted on a change of VAT rate; incorrect proportions taken in connection with retail schemes or where part of the business is subject to VAT and part is not.

These assessments may be subject to appeal.

61 When a member becomes aware that the Customs & Excise Authorities have raised an assessment on a client he should consider whether the basis of the assessment is likely to have a material effect on any accounts with which he has been associated. If so, he should adopt the procedures set out in paragraphs 16(a) and 30 as appropriate. The member should also consider his position with regard to paragraph 2.

Appendix 1

Examples of offences

1 This appendix gives examples of the principal offences (both arrestable and otherwise) of which a member may become aware in the course of his professional duties. The summaries which follow are necessarily incomplete. An auditor who is contemplating taking steps on the basis that criminal offences have been committed, should take legal advice as to the application of the precise words of the statute to the particular facts which are relevant.

Theft

2 The basic definition of theft is to be found in the Theft Act 1968.

Section 1 of the Act provides:

"(1) A person is guilty of theft if he dishonestly appropriates property belonging to another with the intention of permanently depriving the other of it; and 'thief' and 'steal' shall be construed accordingly.

(2) It is immaterial whether the appropriation is made with a view to gain, or is made for the thief's own benefit."

Theft is an arrestable offence, and punishable on conviction on indictment by imprisonment for a term not exceeding ten years.

3 Sections 2 to 6 of the Theft Act 1968 further define the expressions 'appropriates', 'property', 'belonging to another', and 'with the intention of permanently depriving the other of it'. The Act does not define dishonesty, that being a question of fact to be decided on the circumstances of each case. The Act does, however, provide for certain circumstances in which the appropriation of property belonging to another is not to be treated as dishonest. These include cases in which a person appropriating property does so in the belief that he has in law the right to deprive the other of it, or in the belief that he would have had the other's consent if the other had known of the appropriation and the circumstances of it.

Reference to certain sections of the Act shows that:

(a) any assumption of the rights of an owner is an appropriation;

(b) property which can be stolen includes money and all other property, real or personal, including things in action and other intangible property, but does not include land or things forming part of land and severed from it by the person appropriating it or by his directions, except in three cases:

   (i) when he is a trustee or personal representative, or is authorised by power of attorney, or as liquidator of a company, or otherwise, to sell or dispose of land belonging to another, and he appropriates the land or anything forming part of it by dealing with it in breach of the confidence reposed in him; or

   (ii) when he is not in possession of the land and appropriates anything forming part of the land by severing it or causing it to be severed, or after it has been severed; or

   (iii) when, being in possession of the land under a tenancy, he appropriates the whole or part of any fixture or structure let to be used with the land;

(c) property is regarded as belonging to any person having possession or control of it or any proprietary right or interest in it (not being an equitable interest arising only from an agreement to transfer or grant an interest); if property is subject to a trust, a person who has a right to enforce the trust is an owner of it as against a person who receives property from or on account of another and is under an obligation to him to retain or deal with the property or its proceeds in a particular way, that other is the owner;

(d) the intention of permanently depriving a person of a thing includes a case in which, without meaning the other permanently to lose the thing itself, the person appropriating it has the intention to treat the thing as his own to dispose of regardless of the other's rights.

Obtaining property, or pecuniary advantage, by deception

4 (a) Under Section 15 of the Theft Act 1968, a person who by any deception dishonestly obtains property belonging to another with the intention of permanently depriving the other of it commits an arrestable offence. Obtaining property covers obtaining ownership, possession or control of it. 'Obtain' includes obtaining for another, or enabling another to obtain or retain. 'Deception' means any deception, deliberate or reckless, by words or conduct as to fact or law, including a deception as to the present intentions of the person using the deception or any other person.

(b) Under Section 16 of the Theft Act 1968, a person who by any deception (defined as above) dishonestly obtains for himself or another any pecuniary advantage commits an arrestable offence. A pecuniary advantage within the meaning of Section 16 is obtained for a person where:

(i) he is allowed to borrow by way of overdraft, or to take out any policy of insurance or annuity contract, or obtains an improvement of the terms on which he is allowed to do so; or

(ii) he is given the opportunity to earn remuneration or greater remuneration in an office or employment, or to win money by betting.

(c) The Theft Act 1978 creates a range of offences and replaces Section 16(2)(a) of the Theft Act 1968. The offences created are:

(i) dishonestly obtaining services from another by deception;

(ii) evading liability by deception. The offence is committed where a person by deception dishonestly secures the remission of a liability to make payment, or, with intent to make permanent default, dishonestly induces a creditor or person claiming payment on his behalf to wait for or forgo payment, or dishonestly obtains exemption from or abatement of liability to make payment.

(iii) dishonestly making off without payment, where it is known that payment on the spot is required or expected, and with intent to avoid payment.

False accounting

5 Under section 17 of the Theft Act 1968, it is an arrestable offence:

(a) dishonestly to destroy, deface, conceal or falsify any account or record or document made or required for any accounting purpose; or

(b) in furnishing information for any purpose dishonestly to produce or make use of any account or any record or document as aforesaid which, to the knowledge of the person producing or making use of it, is or may be misleading, false or deceptive in a material particular, with a view to gain for oneself or another or with intent to cause loss to another.

For this purpose, a person who makes or concurs in making an entry which is or may be misleading, false or deceptive in a material particular, or who omits or concurs in omitting a material particular, is treated as falsifying the account or document.

Under Section 34(2) 'gain' and 'loss' are to be construed for the purposes of the Theft Act as extending only to gain or loss in money or other property, but as extending to any such gain or loss whether temporary or permanent; and 'gain' includes a gain by keeping what one has, as well as a gain by getting what one has not, and 'loss' includes a loss by not getting what one might get, as well as a loss by parting with what one has.

Liability of company officers for certain offences by company

6 Under Section 18 of the Theft Act 1968, where the offences of obtaining property by deception, obtaining pecuniary advantage by deception or false accounting are committed by a body corporate and are proved to have been committed with the consent or connivance of any director, manager, secretary or other similar officer of the body corporate, or any person who was purporting to act in any such capacity, he as well as the body corporate is guilty of the offence and is liable to be proceeded against and punished accordingly.

False statements by directors, etc.

7 Under Section 19 of the Theft Act 1968, where an officer of a body corporate or an unincorporated association (or person purporting to act as such), with intent to deceive members or creditors about its affairs, publishes or concurs in publishing a written statement or account which to his knowledge is or may be misleading, false or deceptive in a material particular, he commits an arrestable offence.

Failure to keep proper books of account

8 Failure to keep proper accounting records can, in the case of an individual, form the basis of a criminal charge under the Insolvency Act 1986, Section 361. In the case of a company, a corresponding offence exists under Section 221(5) of the Companies Act 1985 (which reproduces the effect of previous legislation).

Forgery

9 The Forgery and Counterfeiting Act 1981 creates a number of arrestable offences. In particular:

(a) It is an offence to make a false instrument with the intention of inducing somebody to treat it as a genuine instrument and act upon it to his prejudice.

(b) It is an offence for a person to copy what he knows to be a false instrument with the intention of inducing somebody to treat it as a copy of a genuine instrument and to act on it to his prejudice.

(c) It is an offence to use what is known to be a false document or a copy of a false document for these purposes.

(d) An 'instrument' for the purpose of these offences includes any document whether of a formal or informal or of an official or unofficial nature, and any disc, tape, soundtrack or electronic record.

Payment and receipt of bribes

10 Under Section 1 of the Prevention of Corruption Act 1906 it is an offence for an agent (including an employee) corruptly to receive or agree to receive a bribe or an inducement or reward for doing or forbearing to do or for having done or forborne to do any act in relation to the business or affairs of his principal (or employer) or for showing or forbearing to show favour or disfavour to any person in relation to the business or affairs of his principal (or employer). It is also an offence to give or agree to give a bribe for any such purpose. These are not arrestable offences.

11 Corresponding offences relating to public bodies or officials are created by the Public Bodies Corrupt Practices Act 1889 and the Prevention of Corruption Act 1916. Under Section 1 of the latter Act, if the matter or a transaction in relation to which the offence is committed is a contract or a proposal for a contract with Her Majesty or any government department or any public body, or is a subcontract subordinate to such a contract, the offence is punishable by imprisonment for up to 7 years and is therefore an arrestable offence.

Insider dealing

12 The Company Securities (Insider Dealing) Act 1985 (the Act), as amended by the Financial Services Act 1986 makes it a criminal offence to engage in certain forms of insider dealing. The provisions of the Act are complex, and legal advice should be taken on their precise effect. Its essential features can be summarised as follows:

(a) An 'insider' includes a person who within six months preceding the dealing in question has been knowingly 'connected' with a company. Relevant connections include the fact that he has been a director of the company or a related company, or has some other relationship with that company or a related company of a kind which could reasonably be expected to give him access to confidential unpublished price-sensitive information about the securities of either company.

(b) An 'insider' is prohibited by Section 1 of the Act from dealing in the securities of a company with which he is connected (in the above sense) if by virtue of his connection he holds relevant confidential information which he knows to be unpublished and price-sensitive.

(c) A person 'deals in securities' if he (whether as agent or principal) buys or sells or agrees to buy or sell investments within paragraph 9 of Schedule 1 to the Financial Services Act 1986. That is, where the purpose or pretended purpose of the contract is to secure a profit or avoid a loss wholly or partly by reference to fluctuations in the value or price of securities.

(d) There are provisions of the Act extending criminal liability to other cases in which the use of information is less direct. These include:

(i) Cases in which the 'insider' deals in the securities of another company, with which he is not connected, having acquired information about some transaction between or involving that company and a company with which he is connected;

(ii) Cases in which a person, although not himself an insider, deals in securities having knowingly obtained confidential unpublished price-sensitive information from an 'insider'. In this case both the recipient of the information and the insider who communicated it may be liable;

(iii) Cases in which an 'insider' who could not himself lawfully deal in securities advises another person to do so (without necessarily communicating the confidential information to him).

(e) There are special provisions dealing with the case where the information in question is information about a take-over bid which is or has been contemplated.

(f) The Act provides protection for jobbers or market makers on The Stock Exchange or a recognised investment exchange acting in the ordinary course of their business, for persons dealing in international bonds, and for a number of other special cases.

(g) These are not arrestable offences.

13 Under Section 177 Financial Services Act 1986, the Secretary of State may appoint inspectors to carry out investigations to determine whether or not there have been contraventions of Sections 1, 2, 4, or 5 of the Company Securities (Insider Dealing) Act 1985. It is the duty of any person whom the inspectors consider able to give information concerning a contravention to produce documents, attend before the inspectors and give all assistance in connection with the investigation which he is reasonably able to give (s.177(3)).

Conspiracy to defraud

14 It is an offence at common law for two or more persons to agree by dishonesty to deprive a person of something which is his or to which he would or might be entitled, or to induce a person to act in some way in which he would not otherwise have acted. The offence will often involve deception, but need not necessarily do so. The offence consists in every case in the making of the agreement, and it is not essential to the offence that it should actually have been carried out.

Miscellaneous other offences

15 Other offences of which members may become aware in the course of carrying out their professional duties include fraudulent trading by a company (Companies Act 1985, section 458), offences against the Estate Agents Act 1974, the Banking Act 1987 and similar legislation.

Appendix 2

Administrative receiver

A receiver or manager of the whole or substantially the whole of a company's property appointed by (or on behalf of) the holders of any debenture of the company secured by a floating charge or by such a charge and one or more other securities.

Administrator

The person appointed under an administration order to manage a company to achieve the purpose set out in the order.

Liquidator

The name given to a person, other than the official receiver, who is responsible for dealing with the winding up of a company; where the official receiver acts, he is known as 'the official receiver and liquidator'.

Receiver

The general term applied to the person administering any type of receivership; the powers of a receiver vary and if they include powers to manage a business, the receiver is called a receiver and manager.

Advertising, publicity and obtaining professional work

Introduction

1 Subject to the rules which follow, a member may seek publicity for his services and achievements and may advertise his services and products in any way he thinks fit.

Section 56 of the Financial Services Act 1986 provides that investment agreements entered into as a result of certain unsolicited calls will be unenforceable. The relevant provisions governing firms authorised by the Association to conduct investment business are set out in rule 18(1) of the Investment Business Rules 1988.

2 A member may inform the public of the services he is capable of providing by means of advertising or other forms of promotion subject to the general requirement that the medium should not, in the opinion of Council, reflect adversely on the member, the Association or the accountancy profession, nor should the advertisement or promotional material, in the opinion of Council:

(a) as to content or presentation, bring the Association into disrepute or bring discredit to the member, firm or the accountancy profession;

(b) discredit the services offered by others whether by claiming superiority for the member's or firm's own services or otherwise;

(c) be misleading, either directly or by implication;

(d) fall short of the requirements of the British Code of Advertising Practice and the IBA Code of Advertising Standards and Practices, notably as to legality, decency, clarity, honesty, and truthfulness.

Firms which are authorised by the Association to carry on investment business are referred also to rule 18(2) and Appendix 5 of the Investment Business Rules 1988.

3 An advertisement should be clearly distinguishable as such.

Fees

4 If reference is made in promotional material to fees, the basis on which fees are calculated, or to hourly or other charging rates, the greatest care should be taken to ensure that such reference does not mislead as to the precise range of services and time commitment that the reference is intended to cover. Members should not make comparisons in such material between their fees and the fees of other accounting practices, whether members or not.

5 The danger of giving a misleading impression is particularly pronounced when constraints of space limit the amount of information which can be given. For this reason it will seldom be appropriate to include information about fees in short advertisements.

6 A member may offer a free consultation at which levels of fees will be discussed.

Promotional material

7 Promotional material may contain any factual statement the truth of which a member is able to justify but should not make unflattering references to or unflattering comparisons with the services of others.

Introductions

8 A member should not give or offer any commission, fee or reward to a third party, not being either his employee or another public accountant or in the context of investment business another authorised firm, in return for the introduction of a client. In relation to investment business, see also rule 12 of the Investment Business Rules 1988. (For the special situation of introducing insolvency business, see Rules of Professional Conduct, 20, Insolvency Practice, paragraphs 5 and 6.) The purpose of this paragraph is to ensure that introductions made by third parties should only be made by persons governed by ethical standards comparable to those observed by members.

Responsibility for promotional activities

9 For the purpose of this Section, promotional activities carried out in the name of a firm should be construed as promotional activities carried out by the individual members of that practice, whether carried out personally or through agents.

Descriptions

(Effective October 1992)

Members' descriptions

1 (a) Members of the Association may be either Associates or Fellows and both are entitled to use the professional designation "Certified Accountant".

(b) Members may use the designatory letters "ACCA" (for associates) or "FCCA" (for fellows).

(c) A member who is a sole practitioner may describe himself as a "Member of the Chartered Association of Certified Accountants".

(d) A member who holds a current insolvency licence may describe himself as a "Licensed Insolvency Practitioner". A member who holds a practising certificate may describe himself as a Registered Auditor.

(e) Where members belong to two or more accountancy bodies they should either use all their designatory letters on their professional stationery or none at all.

(f) No member is permitted to add Honours or Hons. after his designation or designatory letters even though he may have earned a place of merit in the final examination and have been so shown in the pass list. No honours are awarded in the Association's examinations.

(g) Members may use on their professional stationery words showing membership of other accountancy bodies or of organisations in any field related to accountancy.

Practice descriptions

2 (a) A firm/practice may use the description "Certified Accountants" only where members of the Association constitute at least half of the partners and control at least 51% of the votes under the firm's partnership agreement.

(b) A firm/practice in which all the partners are Certified Accountants may use the description "Members of the Chartered Association of Certified Accountants".

(c) Firms and practices which are authorised by the Association to carry on investment business are referred also to rule 11(1) of the Investment Business Rules 1988. The wording which has been approved by Council for the purpose of the rule 11(1) is as follows:

"Authorised to conduct investment business by the Chartered Association of Certified Accountants".

(d) Firms authorised to conduct investment business may, without undue prominence, use the logo of IFA Promotion Ltd on their professional stationery.

(e) A mixed firm/practice of Chartered or Certified accountants is not permitted to use the description Chartered and Certified Accountants.

(f) A firm/practice may use a description indicating a specialism in any area of work e.g. "Tax advisers", "Accountants and auditors" provided that:

(i) it is competent to provide the specialisms shown;

(ii) the content and presentation of the descriptions does not bring the Association into disrepute or bring discredit to the firm/practice or the accountancy profession.

(g) A firm/practice may include on its professional stationery a list of services it provides.

(h) UK/Irish firms/practices where partners holding practising certificates issued by the Association constitute at least half of the partners and control at least 51% of the votes under the firm's partnership agreement may describe themselves as Registered Auditors. UK/Irish firms/practices holding auditing certificates issued by the Association may describe themselves as "Registered Auditors" and may also add the following statement to their business stationery: "Registered as auditors by the Chartered Association of Certified Accountants".

Where appropriate, the above statement may be combined with the investment business statement detailed in 2(c) above as follows: "Registered as auditors and authorised to conduct investment business by the Chartered Association of Certified Accountants".

The holder of a UK/Irish practising certificate may use the term "Registered Auditor" as a personal description on business stationery, even where the firm/practice in which he is a partner is not authorised as a firm of Registered Auditors. Members are reminded that, under the terms of the Association's recognition under the UK Companies Act 1989, the term "Registered Auditor(s)" must be used when signing any company audit report. This includes limited company audits, audits of other bodies specified under the Companies Act 1989 or other entities required by their constitutions to be audited by a Registered Auditor.

(N.B. the term "firm" includes a sole practitioner's firm.)

Other descriptions

3 The name of any person, who is other than a principal of the practice, may be shown on the professional stationery of a practice, together with a description e.g. 'Manager', 'Tax Consultant', etc. provided that:

(a) the person named is competent to provide any specialism shown;

(b) the name and description are clearly separated from the name(s) of the principal(s), so that they could not be mistaken for principals; and

(c) the description does not bring the Association into disrepute or bring discredit to the practice or the accountancy profession.

Other designatory letters

4 (a) A member who holds a civil or service honour (such as CBE, DSO, DFC etc.) or a civil office (such as MP, etc.) is entitled to use the appropriate designatory letters on his professional stationery if he so wishes. The letters JP may not be shown on professional stationery.

(b) Nevertheless, before doing so he should consider carefully how far (if at all) a statement of such honours or offices is relevant to the professional services he offers.

(c) In the opinion of the Council any reference to such honours or appointments would be entirely inappropriate in signing any audit report or other expression of professional opinion.

Changes in professional appointments

General

1 An accountant who is asked to accept appointment for any recurring professional work must, save where the client has not previously had an accountant acting for him in respect of such work, request the prospective client's permission to communicate with the existing accountant. If such permission is refused he should decline the appointment.

2 If the prospective accountant receives permission from the client, he should write to the existing accountant requesting all the information which ought to be made available to him to enable him to decide whether or not he is prepared to accept the appointment. Communication with the existing accountant is not just a matter of professional courtesy. Its main purpose is to enable the prospective accountant to ensure that there has been no action by the client which would, on ethical grounds, preclude him from accepting the appointment, and that after considering all the facts, the client is someone for whom he would wish to act.

3 Before replying to the prospective accountant, the existing accountant should obtain the client's permission to discuss his affairs fully with the prospective accountant.

4 If the existing accountant is duly authorised by the client to discuss the client's affairs with the prospective accountant, then he may communicate to the latter any relevant information he believes to be true, including the reasons for the proposed change and any other matter of which he considers that the prospective accountant should be made aware. He may prefer to communicate with the prospective accountant orally and the latter must be prepared to facilitate this. The prospective accountant must treat any information given by the existing accountant in the strictest confidence and should weigh this carefully in reaching a decision whether or not to accept the appointment.

5 If the client refuses the existing accountant authority to discuss his affairs with the prospective accountant, the existing accountant should inform the prospective accountant accordingly and the latter should at once intimate to the client that he is not prepared to accept nomination. If the client has neglected to authorise the existing accountant to discuss its affairs with the prospective accountant, then it is for the existing accountant to decide on his course of action. If, for instance, the client has failed or refused to supply him with information properly required by him for the performance of his duties, then he should so inform the prospective accountant. If, on the other hand he suspects that the client has been guilty of some unlawful act, e.g. defrauding the Inland Revenue, but has no proof, it must be left to him to determine whether and to what extent his suspicions should be conveyed to the prospective accountant.

6 If the existing accountant considers that there are reasons of a professional nature to prevent the prospective accountant accepting nomination it is not enough that he should merely say so — he must be prepared to specify what they are. The prospective accountant should also endeavour to ascertain the reasons for the change of accountant. If, having done so, he is of the opinion that the existing accountant is being treated unfairly, he may well decide to refuse nomination. He would, for instance, be justified in forming such an opinion if it appeared that the existing auditor in the conscientious exercise of his duty as an independent professional man had encountered the client's opposition and had declined to give way to the latter in relation to what he considered an important matter of principle or practice.

7 If the prospective accountant receives no reply to his letter of enquiry to the existing accountant, he should make every endeavour to contact him by other means. If he fails to do so or to obtain a satisfactory reply, before accepting appointment, he should send a further letter, by registered or recorded delivery, saying that unless he receives a reply within a stated period, say seven days, he will assume that there are no professional or other reasons to prevent him accepting instructions and will proceed to do so.

Unpaid fees of previous accountant

8 Where there are fees owing to the existing accountant, the prospective accountant is not on that account expected to refuse to act. Whether he does so or not is entirely a matter for his own judgement and so, too, is the related question how far he may properly go in assisting the existing accountant to recover those fees. Normally he would be expected to draw the attention of the client to the fact that the fees are due and unpaid and to suggest that they should be met.

Transfer of books and papers

9 Once a new accountant has been appointed, the former accountant should ensure that all books and papers belonging to the client which are in his possession are promptly transferred, except where he claims to exercise a lien on them in respect of unpaid fees.

Transfer information

10 (a) In the same way, the former accountant should promptly provide the new accountant with all reasonable carry-over information for which the new accountant may ask, in order to ensure continuity of the treatment of the client's affairs, notwithstanding that there may be unpaid fees.

(b) 'Reasonable carry-over information' in (a) above is defined as:

(i) a copy of the last set of accounts formally approved by the client; and

(ii) a detailed trial balance that is in agreement with the accounts referred to in (i) above.

(c) Any further information is provided purely at the discretion of the former accountant who may render a charge to the person requesting the information.

Company auditor

11 The auditor of a company holds office from the conclusion of the general meeting, at which he is appointed or reappointed, to the conclusion of the next general meeting at which accounts are submitted.

12 If the shareholders wish to replace the existing auditors they are free to do so provided that the prescribed statutory procedure is observed (see in particular Section 391A, Companies Act 1985).

13 The provisions set out in paragraph 1-10 above apply equally to a change in the appointment of a company auditor.

Casual vacancy in the auditorship

14 Where there is a casual vacancy in the auditorship of the company, that vacancy will normally be filled by the directors. Any member invited to fill a casual vacancy should follow a course of action similar to that already outlined. If the casual vacancy is due to the death or incapacity of the previous auditor, then the necessary contacts will have to be made with his partners, if any, or with the person who is temporarily responsible for maintaining his practice.

Removal of the auditor

15 The auditor of a company may be removed by ordinary resolution of the members in general meeting, even though his term of office has not expired and despite any agreement between the company and him. This is, however, without prejudice to any right to compensation or damages to which the auditor may be entitled as a result of such removal.

16 Special notice must be given of any resolution for the removal of an auditor. On receipt of that notice the company must send a copy to the auditor, who may then make representations to the company in writing and also request that copies be sent to members, in default of which the auditor may require his representations to be read out at the meeting.

17 But such representations need not be circulated or read out if the court, on the application of the company or other aggrieved person, is satisfied that the rights conferred are being abused to secure needless publicity for defamatory matter; and the court may further direct that the cost of such application shall be paid by the auditor.

18 A removed auditor is entitled to attend the general meeting of the company at which his term of office would normally have expired and any general meeting at which the vacancy caused by his removal is to be filled. On ceasing to hold office, the auditor must deposit at the company's registered office a statement of any circumstances connected with his ceasing to hold office which he feels ought to be brought to the attention of members, or, alternatively, a statement that there are no such circumstances (Section 394 Companies Act 1985).

In connection with the removal of auditors, members should refer to Sections 391 and 391A of the Companies Act 1985.

Resignation of the auditor

19 The auditor of a company may resign by giving notice in writing to the company and his resignation will become effective as from the date of notice or any later date specified therein. In addition the notice must contain:

(a) a statement that there are no circumstances connected with the resignation which the auditor thinks should be brought to the notice of the members or creditors of the company; or

(b) a statement of any such circumstances.

20 On receipt of a statement under paragraph 19(b) above, the company must within 14 days send a copy to all shareholders, debenture holders and other persons entitled under Section 394 of the Companies Act 1985, unless the court on the application of the company or other person aggrieved directs otherwise on the ground that the rights conferred are being used to secure needless publicity for defamatory matter. It may further direct that the costs of such an application shall be paid by the auditor.

21 A resigning auditor submitting such a statement may at the same time require the directors to convene an extraordinary general meeting to consider his explanation of the circumstances leading to his resignation and to circulate a written statement of these circumstances with the notice of meeting. In default thereof the statement must be read out at the meeting.

22 Compliance with the foregoing requirements as to publication of the auditor's statement may be waived by the court, at the instance of the company or other person aggrieved, if the court is satisfied that the auditor is using the Statement to secure needless publicity for defamatory matter; and the court may direct that the costs of such an application shall be paid by the auditor.

23 A resigning auditor is entitled to attend any meeting of the company convened in connection with his resignation or replacement and to receive all relevant notices and to be heard.

24 In connection with the resignation of auditors, members should refer to Sections 392 and 392A of the Companies Act 1985.

Additional professional work

25 A member may be asked to undertake professional work additional to work already being carried out by the client's existing accountant who is not being replaced or superseded. Before accepting such work the member shall communicate as a matter of professional courtesy with the accountant employed by the client and shall inform the accountant as to the general nature of the work being done.

In very exceptional circumstances, the member may not be required to communicate with the accountant. Members are responsible for checking with the Legal Department whether in their particular circumstances they can dispense with the usual practice of communicating with the accountant.

Ownership of books and papers

Determination of ownership

1 Where particular documents and records are not owned by the member they generally belong to the client. In order to determine whether documents and records belong to the member it may be necessary to consider:

(a) the contract between the member and his client usually as evidenced in an engagement letter;

(b) the capacity in which the member acts in relation to his client; and

(c) the purpose for which the documents and records exist or are brought into being.

The contract

2 In *Leicestershire County Council* v. *Michael Faraday & Partners Limited* (1941) 2 K.B. 205, the Court of Appeal stated that if an agent brings into existence certain documents whilst in the employment of his principal, they are the principal's documents and the principal can claim that the agent should hand them over. Some areas of a member's practice involve his acting as agent for his client. Examples of this relationship are where the member is instructed to negotiate the client's tax liabilities with the Inland Revenue or to file accounts with the Registrar of Companies. In such cases the contract is between a principal (the client) and his agent (the member) and the statement of the Court of Appeal applies.

3 Whilst documents belong to the client where they are brought into being by the member acting as agent, this is not usually so where the member acts as principal, for example, where the member is acting as auditor. In such cases the member's working papers belong to the member unless the contract between the client and the member requires otherwise. The contract between the member and his client may set out expressly the agreed position regarding the ownership of documents and records on which the member will work or which are created in the course of that work. Alternatively, the contract may determine the ownership by implication. The ownership of documents and records will therefore vary according to the terms, express or implied, of the contract. Where those terms are such that one party owns the documents and records, the nature of the documents and records is irrelevant and it is not necessary to look further. In the following paragraphs it is assumed that the terms of the contract are silent on the question of ownership.

4 As a general rule where the relationship between the member and his client is that of principal, documents brought into being by the member on the instruction of the client belong to the client. On the other hand, documents prepared, acquired or brought into being by the member solely for his own purpose as principal belong to the member.

Auditing

5 In acting as an auditor, the member is acting as a principal. The end product of his work is to give an auditor's report. Documents prepared by the member solely for the purpose of carrying out his duties as auditor belong to the member. The ownership of documents or records is decided without reference to whether the audit is carried out under statutory provisions or not. If the work involved includes both auditing and accountancy, it may be necessary to consider the purpose for which the documents were prepared in order to determine their ownership.

Accountancy

6 Where the work of the member is solely accountancy the question of ownership will depend on the nature of the work to be done. For example, if the work is to prepare accounting records for the client, the records belong to the client. If the work is to prepare for the client financial statements from the client's records, the financial statements belong to the client, while the member's draft and office copy of those financial statements belong to the member. If, however, the client has specifically asked for drafts to be prepared for him, they will belong to the client as the drafts are the 'product' which is required by the client.

7 Similar considerations apply in connection with the preparation of other documents such as reports, memoranda and notes. If the final documents are specifically prepared for the client at his request, they belong to the client and the member's drafts and office copy will belong to the member. If, however, the client has specifically asked for drafts to be prepared for him the drafts will belong to the client, as they are the 'product' which is required by the client. In *Chantrey Martin & Co* v. *Martin* (1953) 2 Q.B. 286, the draft items referred to above were held to be the property of the member as they were not documents which the client had required the member to produce for him. On the above principles, analyses of banking accounts prepared by the member and correspondence with third parties for the purpose of producing financial statements would normally belong to the member.

8 If the member's work is to produce financial statements from incomplete records, and he is not instructed by the client to work on the records themselves, schedules which he prepares for the purpose of producing the financial statements would normally belong to the members. However, in the case of a body incorporated under statutory provisions, the position is different. For example, Section 221 of the Companies Act 1985 sets out the accounting records which a company must keep. Where such records have not been kept, and a court took the view that such schedules were prepared for the client company in order that it should comply with Section 221 they would belong to the company. In other situations also, records which are required by law to be kept, but which are prepared by the member, would normally belong to the client.

Taxation including VAT

9 Where the member's work relates to taxation, the question of ownership will depend on the nature of the work to be done. If the work is of a tax compliance nature, the accounts, schedules and computations belong to the client. The preparation and submission of accounts, returns and computations to the Inland Revenue or VAT returns to Customs and Excise and the agreement of the client's tax liabilities including those following 'in depth' investigations are examples of work of a tax compliance nature. In *Chantrey Martin & Co* v. *Martin* the Court of Appeal followed its own earlier statement (see paragraph 4) and held that calculations and correspondence between a firm of accountants and the Inland Revenue in regard to a client's accounts and tax computations (both the copies of letters sent and the original letters received) were the property of the client on the basis that the accountants had been acting as agents for the client for the purpose of negotiating with the Inland Revenue the client's tax liability. Where a report is made to a client for submission to the authorities in connection with an accounts investigation the member will be acting as a principal. The report and supporting schedules accordingly belong to the client while the papers used in preparing the report belong to the member.

Advice

10 If the work to be done is to give tax, investment or other advice, the member is acting as principal and drafts, internal memoranda and similar documents in connection with that work belong to the member. However, letters or documents giving the advice belong to the client. Difficult questions may arise in cases where in the course of dealing with these matters a member communicates with third parties. These questions are considered in paragraph 12.

Communications between a member and his client

11 Letters received by a member from his client belong to the member. A member's copy of any letter written to his client is made solely for his own purposes and also belongs to the member. (Re Wheatcroft (1877) 6 Ch. D. 97). A member's notes of questions and answers between the client and the member belong to the member.

Communications with third parties

12 Ownership of copies of communications between a member and third parties depends on the relationship between a member and his client. Where the member is an agent, the copies belong to his client. An example is tax correspondence on behalf of the client (see paragraph 9). Similarly, where a member seeks specialist advice (as opposed to information) from a third party such as a valuer or a solicitor, he will normally be doing so on his client's behalf and the communications which result will normally belong to the client. On the other hand, where the member is acting as principal, it is probable that the courts would hold that the copies belong to the member. This would include documents which are not the end product of the member's work, for example:

(a) documents confirming or otherwise the balance of an account between a third party and the client, such as those in respect of bank balances or custody of securities; and

(b) other documents which the member has obtained solely for his own use in carrying out his duties as principal. These will normally include correspondence between the member and the client's solicitors in which the member is giving or receiving information (as opposed to advice).

General and particular liens

13 A lien is a right of a person to retain possession of the owner's property until the owner pays what he owes to the person in possession. A general lien is a lien over property which can be retained until payment of the whole of the indebtedness of the owner to the person in possession on any account whatsoever. However, such liens can rarely be established. A particular lien is a lien over property which can be retained only until payment of a particular debt due in respect of it is paid. The courts favour particular liens as being equitable between debtor and creditor.

14 An accountant has a particular lien over documents belonging to his client in respect of which the accountant has performed work for which he has not been paid the fee due. In the Court of Appeal in *Woodworth* v. *Conroy* (1976) Q.B. 884, Lord Justice Lawton (with whom the rest of the court agreed) said: "I would adjudge that accountants in the course of doing their ordinary professional work of producing and auditing accounts, advising on financial problems, and carrying on negotiations with the Inland Revenue in relation to both taxation and rating have at least a particular lien over any books of account, files and papers which their clients delivered to them and also over any documents which have come into their possession in the course of acting as their client's agents in the course of their ordinary professional work". He added that accountants may enjoy a wider lien than this but that it was unnecessary for the purpose of the case to deal with that question. Despite the fact that the point was kept open, counsel advises that in the absence of a special contractual provision accountants do not have a right of general lien in law and members are advised that it would not be worthwhile to assert such a right against a client unless they are expressly given that right by their contract with the client.

Conditions for the exercise of a particular lien

15 A right of particular lien will only exist where all four of the following circumstances apply:

(a) the documents retained must be the property of the client who owes the money and not of a third party, no matter how closely connected with the client;

(b) the documents must have come into the possession of the member by proper means;

(c) work must have been done by the member upon the documents and a fee note rendered; and

(d) the fees for which the lien is exercised must be outstanding in respect of such work and not in respect of other unrelated work.

Special cases

16 There are various special cases where the normal position regarding the existence and enforcement of liens does not apply. Special cases may arise as a result of the provisions of a particular statute, or from considerations of general public policy and include the following.

Statutory books of companies

17 An established line of authority exists in which the courts have held that no lien can exist over books or documents of a registered company which, either by statute or by the articles of association of the company, have to be available for public inspection or to be kept at the registered office or some other specified place or be dealt with in any special way. The main cases are Re Capital Fire Insurance Association (1883), 24 Ch. D. 408 and Re The Anglo-Maltese Hydraulic Dock Co Limited (1885), 54 L.J. Ch. 730. Although those cases concerned solicitors' liens, the same principles apply in the case of accountants. Examples of documents which those cases held could not become the subject of a lien are the register of members and directors' minute books which the articles of association would almost certainly, expressly or impliedly, require to be kept available at all material times for the use of directors.

Accounting records of companies

18 Counsel advises that a lien would probably not be upheld in relation to the accounting records which a company must keep in order to comply with Section 221 of the Companies Act 1985. Such records are documents which must by reason of that Section be kept by the company, and which under Section 222 must be kept at the registered office of the company or at such other place as the directors of the company think fit and must at all times be open to inspection by the officers of the company. It should be appreciated that 'accounting records' within the meaning of Section 221 covers a wide range of documents.

19 One of the plaintiffs in *Woodworth* v. *Conroy* was a limited company and Lord Justice Lawton referred to the fact that the plaintiffs had a statutory obligation to produce and file accounts and wanted their papers from the accountants for this purpose. In making the general statement as to the accountants' right to a lien which is quoted in paragraph 15, the judge added no qualification as to the position of companies. However, during the case, the court was not referred to the authorities cited in paragraph 18 concerning lien in relation to companies. Those authorities were accordingly not considered by the court. Counsel advises that in a future case involving a company, *Woodworth* v. *Conroy* would not be regarded as overriding those earlier authorities when read in conjunction with Section 221 of the Companies Act 1985 (see paragraph 18).

Administrative receiverships and receiverships

20 Where a member has a lien over the books of account or other documents of a company, counsel considers that the appointment of a receiver does not affect the lien as a lien is a charge given by the general law and arises from the company's carrying on its business in the ordinary course.

21 Although a debenture may prevent a company from creating any mortgage or charge in priority to the debenture, a member's lien is not a mortgage or charge 'created by the company'. Debenture holders cannot therefore prevent a member from acquiring a lien which the general law allows. A member's lien would be untouched by debenture holders taking possession and by their appointing a receiver, (*Brunton* v. *Electrical Engineering Corporation,* (1892) I Ch. 434). Even where a receiver is appointed by the court, the lien will be unaffected unless the court orders otherwise.

Administration and liquidations

22 Where a company is the subject of an administration order, or is in liquidation or has a provisional liquidator appointed to it, then a member cannot exercise a lien or other right to retain possession of any of the books, papers or other records of the company to the extent that the enforcement of the lien would deny possession of those items to the administrator or liquidator. This is the result of Section 246 of the Insolvency Act 1986. Therefore, if a member is requested by either an administrator or liquidator to hand over such records as he may hold, he is obliged to do so. The only exception is where the lien is on documents which give title to property (for example, title deeds, share certificates or bills of lading pledges or held as security for some liability of the company), and the documents in question are held on that basis. This exception is likely to be of practical importance to members only in cases where in the course of dealing with the affairs of a client they have obtained from a third party (such as a bank) documents which have been pledged or mortgaged to that third party. In such cases the member will normally have been required to undertake to hold them to the order of the third party and he will accordingly hold them as the third party's agent. Where an arrangement of this kind exists the exception to Section 246 applies, and the documents should not without the express consent of the third party be delivered to the administrator or liquidator. This, however, is a difficult area and members may wish to take legal advice on the operation of the exception in any particular case.

Bankruptcy

23 As in liquidations, a lien or other right to retain possession of any books, papers or other records of the bankrupt is unenforceable against the Official Receiver or the Trustee in Bankruptcy, unless that lien is on documents which give a title to property and are held on that basis. This is the result of Section 349 of the Insolvency Act 1986. The principles which apply are similar to those governing Section 246 of the Insolvency Act 1986. As with the situation dealt with in paragraph 22, this is also a difficult area in which members may wish to take legal action.

Fee disputes

24 When a member is about to render a bill which is substantially different from bills rendered to the same client on earlier occasions for which the work is, or may appear to the client to be, comparable, it is good practice to explain to the client the reason for the variation. Where the increase is caused by extra work being necessary, the reason for the extra work can be explained. Where the increase is caused by increased costs, this also can be explained. In many cases both factors will affect the total fee and any explanation will be mutually helpful.

25 Cases do, however, arise where a member presents a bill to a client which the client considers to be excessive. In such cases the client may be prepared to pay a smaller sum and may tender that amount. There is no legal disadvantage in accepting the amount offered provided it is made clear by the member, preferably in writing, at the time of acceptance, that the sum is accepted as a part payment only and not in full discharge of the debt.

26 When a client behaves in this manner it is possible that he has genuine doubts as to the propriety of the fee, and is not actuated by malice or lack of means. In this connection, members are reminded that the President is prepared, on the written application of both parties to the dispute, to appoint an arbitrator.

27 Where arbitration is resorted to or where a writ has been served for the fees, it is clear that in due course the matter of the fees will be settled. In either case, the client may apply to the court for an order requiring the member to surrender the papers notwithstanding his lien, and the court will ordinarily make such an order on condition that the client pays the sum in dispute into court to abide by the result of the arbitration or action. For this reason it will often be appropriate for a member to abandon his lien upon the client agreeing to place the sum in dispute in the hands of a third party with instructions not to release it until the dispute has been resolved.

28 The exercise of a lien in fee disputes is perfectly legal, but members should remember that its nuisance value is likely to promote ill-will not only between the parties, but also towards the profession as a whole.

29 Where a legal right of lien exists, the Council supports the exercise of that lien in appropriate circumstances.

30 Members should, however, consult their solicitors before seeking to exercise a lien in any but the most straightforward of cases. Similarly a client disputing the right of lien of a member should be advised to consult his own solicitors. Where the member's right is well founded the advice the client receives may change his attitude both to the lien and the bill.

Retention of books, files, working papers and other documents

Introduction

1 In determining the period for which audit, tax and other working papers should be retained consideration needs to be given to the following:

(a) legal requirements which specify the period of retention;

(b) the period of time during which actions may be brought in the Courts for which the working papers may need to be available as evidence;

(c) the period of time for which information in the working papers may be required for use in compiling tax returns;

(d) the possibility that a company may seek a quotation on the Stock Exchange or the Unlisted Securities Market.

Firms which are authorised by the Association to conduct investment business are referred also to rules 13(5); 14(4);17(2)(d); 18(2)(e); 18(3)(d); and 21(5) of the Investment Business Rules 1988.

Companies Acts

2 Section 221 of the Companies Act 1985 requires that every company should keep accounting records sufficient to show and explain the company's transactions. The accounting records must contain details of sums of money received and paid, a record of the assets and liabilities of the company, statements of stock held at the end of each financial year, statements of stocktakings and statements of goods sold and purchased.

3 A private company is required to maintain the accounting records for a period of three years from the date on which they were made and all other companies must maintain them for six years.

General position in law

4 There is a general principle in English law that after the passing of a given period of time an action may not be brought before the courts. This general principle arises from two main considerations. Firstly, actions which have lain dormant for a long period of time may be pursued for reasons of personal animosity rather than for justice. Secondly, after the elapse of a long period of time a defendant may have lost or destroyed evidence which is relevant to the case. For these reasons the law requires that persons with a legitimate cause should make their claim within a reasonable period of time.

5 Many statutes lay down specific periods of time within which an action must be commenced. For example the Truck Act 1896 requires that claims for the recovery of improper deductions from wages must be commenced within six months, the Employment Act 1980 requires claims for unfair dismissal to be commenced within three months whereas the Nuclear Installations Act 1965 allows claims for injury to be commenced up to thirty years after the event.

6 In the absence of specific time limits in legislation, the Limitation Act of 1980 sets out the general position concerning time limits as follows:

(a) twelve years for actions upon a specialty or a judgment given by the Courts (a specialty is a contract under seal or an obligation under a seal securing a debt);

(b) six years for actions based upon a simple contract or tort, or three years from the earliest date on which the plaintiff or any person in whom the cause of action was vested before him first had both the knowledge required for bringing an action for damages in respect of the relevant damage and a right to bring such an action subject to a maximum period of fifteen years.

(c) three years for actions based upon personal injuries.

Taxation

7 Section 34 of the Taxes Management Act 1970 provides that subject to any other provisions of the Taxes Acts allowing a longer period in any particular case, an assessment to tax may be made at any time not later than six years after the end of the chargeable period to which the assessment relates. Where any form of fraud or wilful default has been committed by or on behalf of any person in connection with or in relation to tax, assessments on that person to tax may, for the purpose of making good to the Crown any loss of tax attributable to the fraud or wilful default, be made at any time.

8 The Inland Revenue adopts a selective approach to the examination of accounts and taxation computations submitted to them. Normally the accounts and taxation computations are accepted as the basis for settling a taxpayer's liability. Queries are not normally raised where they involve only minor computational or related matters. Where it appears to a District Inspector, in the light of his judgement, experience and knowledge of local conditions, that there might be something wrong with the basic records from which the taxpayer's accounts are made up an in-depth enquiry into the records and underlying information may be made.

9 The selection of an account for a more detailed examination will not, in itself, imply a lengthy examination. As soon as the inspector is satisfied that the accounts are sound, or have been correctly adjusted his enquiry will end. Some cases will turn out to require more exhaustive treatment and the inspector will have to satisfy himself fully that the basic records are correct and complete. Where an account has been selected for detailed examination the initial approach will always be made to the client's accountant, where he has one. The inspector will seek to establish the extent and value of the records available and what the accountant has done to convert these records into balanced accounts.

10 Paragraph 7 of Schedule 7 of the Value Added Tax Act 1983 requires value added tax records to be preserved for a period of six years. The Customs and Excise make routine inspections of VAT records approximately once in every three years. However assessments for VAT may be raised for periods up to six years after the end of the quarter for which a VAT return was rendered.

11 Capital transfer tax payments are calculated with reference to total chargeable transfers within the previous ten years. Agricultural property relief may be available in respect of land which has been owned for seven years. Settlements without interests in possession are subject to a ten year anniversary tax on relevant property. UK residents may acquire a domicile in the UK when they have resided in the UK for seventeen out of the last twenty years. Interests in some accumulation and maintenance settlements are required to vest within twenty-five years.

12 All the limitation periods may be extended where there has been fraud or mistake and in some cases of disability or where there has been acknowledgement or part payment.

Prospectus requirements

13 When a company seeks a quotation on the Stock Exchange or the Unlisted Securities Market the reporting accountants are required to provide a long form report covering the previous six years. The reporting accountants will need to be satisfied that proper audits have been carried out during this period, that financial statements have been prepared on a consistent basis, that the results of discontinued operations are presented separately and that the business has been conducted in accordance with acceptable standards.

Trusteeships

14 Where a member acts as a trustee he has a continuing responsibility to the beneficiaries and all records should be retained, at least until all transactions have been independently audited and a discharge received from all interested persons.

Insolvency — Companies Winding-up by the Court and Bankruptcy

15 Under Statutory Instrument Number 1994 of 1986 a liquidator, on the authorisation of the official receiver, during his tenure of office or on vacating office, or the official receiver while acting as liquidator or trustee, at any time may sell, destroy or otherwise dispose of the books, papers and other records of the insolvent.

Insolvency — Companies Voluntary Winding-up

16 The person who was the last liquidator of a company which has been dissolved may, at any time after the expiration of a period of one year from the date of dissolution, destroy or otherwise dispose of the books, papers and other records of the company.

General considerations

17 The retention of working papers involves expenditure on storage space and staff costs. Members may therefore consider that they have a greater responsibility to retain working papers for clients for whom they continue to act than for those for whom they no longer act.

Minimum periods for retention

18 Members should use their own judgement in determining the period for which working papers should be retained. The minimum period for which working papers should be retained are as follows:

Audit working papers	7 years;
Files on clients' or former clients' chargeable assets and gifts	11 years (then return them to the client or former client or obtain authority from the client or former client for their destruction);
Files of member as trustee	For the period of trusteeship and 7 years thereafter;
Liquidator's working papers in a voluntary liquidation	5 years or a lesser period if approved by the creditors or members.

19 In the case of tax files and other papers which are legally the property of the client or former client, they should be returned to the client or former client after seven years or his specific authority obtained for their destruction.

20 Where it is possible that a defect in advice rendered to a client or former client may not become apparent until up to fifteen years after the advice was given, members may consider it prudent to retain working papers in such instances for at least this period of time.

Historical records

21 When working papers are no longer required members should consider the possibility of making certain records available (with the client's consent) to the County Archivist, the Business Archives Council or the Accounting History Committee of the CCAB. No enterprise is too small for this purpose. Indeed, from the point of view of social history it is the smaller business whose records most require preservation.

Activities through corporate or non-corporate organisations

Provision of accountancy services through companies

1 (a) A Certified Accountant may participate, whether as director and/or member and/or employee, in a limited or unlimited company, which offers auditing and/or accountancy services to the public, provided that in doing so he does not contravene the law of the country in which he practises

(b) Under English law, the following appointments must be held by individuals:

(i) An auditor appointed under the provisions of the Companies Acts;

(ii) A receiver, liquidator and trustee in bankruptcy and under deeds of arrangement.

(c) Where a Certified Accountant becomes a director of a limited or unlimited company which offers auditing services to the public, he shall hold a practising certificate from the Association.

For the purpose of this sub-paragraph 'auditing services' shall include the provision of reports and/or certificates pertaining to financial statements.

(d) Limited or unlimited companies referred to in (a) above are permitted to advertise in accordance with the rules contained in Section 2.3.

Non-accountancy services

2 (a) A Certified Accountant may participate in any capacity, in organisations, whether corporate or non-corporate, which offer services other than accountancy services to the public ('non-accountancy organisations').

(b) Where a Certified Accountant participates in a non-accountancy organisation, and in addition, participates in an organisation offering accountancy services to the public:

(i) both organisations may operate from the same address;

(ii) the non-accountancy organisation may, if linked with the other organisation, indicate the connection in its name, but the name must differ distinctively from that of the other organisation, and the non-accountancy organisation must not, in any other way, be used to attract audit or accountancy work to the other organisation.

(c) A non-accountancy organisation may:

(i) advertise its services in accordance with Section 2.3;

(ii) use any appropriate description, but may not describe itself as 'Certified Accountants'.

Organisations offering accountancy and non-accountancy services

3 There is nothing to prevent a Certified Accountant from participating in any capacity, in a corporate or non-corporate organisation which offers both accountancy and non-accountancy services to the public, but in such a case the member must comply with the rules contained in Section 2 which relate to accountancy organisations.

Appointed representatives under the Financial Services Act 1986

4 (a) In order that a firm at all times be, and be seen to be, free in the actions it undertakes of any interest which might detract from its objectivity it should not enter in any association or arrangement with any person other than the client which may result in the practice being constrained or induced to recommend to a client transactions in some investments but not others, with some persons but not others, or through the agency of some persons but not of others, unless so constrained by law.

(b) Firms which are authorised by the Association to carry on investment business are referred to rule 12 of the Investment Business Rules 1988. This provides that (subject to rule 19) neither the partners nor the employees of such firms may accept an appointment as a person's representative in accordance with Section 44 of the Financial Services Act 1986.

(c) Practising members who are not authorised to conduct investment business, whilst not covered by the Investment Business Rules should nevertheless safeguard their independence by regarding the injunction in sub-paragraph (a) (above) as applying to them.

General

5 (a) A member who engages in activities pursuant to this subsection is, save as otherwise provided in this subsection, subject to the same ethical requirements as any other member.

(b) Any member in doubt about the application of these provisions to his own circumstances should consult the Legal Department and, if necessary, obtain the approval of the Membership Committee before undertaking any activities hereunder.

Fees

Basis of fee

1 A member is entitled to charge for his services such fee as he may consider appropriate for the work undertaken.

2 Members are recommended to mention fees and the general basis on which fees are normally computed in a letter of engagement to the client or potential client. Often, the basis of the fee will be agreed with the client beforehand (whether explicitly or by virtue of custom in certain specialised areas). Where this is not the case a member should charge a fee which is fair and reasonable having regard to:

(a) the seniority and professional expertise of the persons necessarily engaged on the work;

(b) the time expended by each;

(c) the degree of responsibility which the work entails;

(d) the urgency of the work to the client;

(e) the overhead expenses of the firm; and

(f) the importance of the work to the client together with any expenses properly incurred.

Percentage and contingency fees

3 In order to preserve members' independence, fees should not normally be charged on a percentage, contingency or similar basis, save where that course is generally accepted practice for certain specialist work or as provided for in the succeeding paragraphs.

Insolvency work

4 In bankruptcies, liquidations, receiverships, administrations, voluntary arrangements and similar work, the remuneration is dependent upon the manner of appointment and the relevant statutes. The remuneration is often calculated by a percentage of realisations and a percentage of distributions, but this basis should be avoided where possible and practicable. There is no reason why a member should not have regard to the considerations listed in paragraph 2 in determining what he regards as suitable percentages which when applied to the realisations and distributions will produce adequate remuneration for this highly technical and responsible work.

The matter rests however with those who have the power to fix the remuneration and it is unlikely that they will approve percentages which appear to be excessive even though lower percentages will produce an inadequate reward.

For example, where a great amount of difficult and responsible work has been involved but the value of the assets is small. It must therefore be recognised by members who undertake insolvency work that some of it may prove particularly remunerative and some of it may be highly unprofitable.

Work of this kind is subject to a certain amount of jurisdiction by or appeal to the courts and it must be accepted that by long-standing custom and sometimes by statutory requirement, a percentage basis is often used. Members who act as insolvency practitioners should have regard to the provisions of Rules of Professional Conduct, 20 'Insolvency

Practice' and should not make any arrangements whereby their remuneration is shared with representatives or creditors or with any persons other than their partners. This does not preclude payment for professional services rendered to insolvency practitioners; such payment should, however, in cases of liquidation and bankruptcy be previously approved by the liquidator or creditors' Committee, or by the creditors as appropriate, and shown separately in the accounts, including those submitted to the Department of Trade and Industry.

Management buy-out and raising venture capital

5 There are circumstances, such as advising on a management buy-out or the raising of venture capital, where fees cannot realistically be charged save on a contingency basis: to require otherwise would be to deprive potential clients of professional assistance. For example, where the capacity of the client to pay is dependent upon the success or failure of the venture.

6 Where work is subject to a contingency or percentage fee, the capacity in which a member has worked and the basis of his remuneration should be made clear in any document upon which a third party may rely.

Fee quotations

7 The fact that a member secures work by quoting a fee lower than another is not improper provided care is taken to ensure that the client is not misled:

(a) as to the precise range of services that a quoted fee is intended to cover; and

(b) as to the likely level of fees for any work undertaken for the client.

8 If, in the course of an investigation into allegations of unsatisfactory work, there is evidence of the work having been obtained or retained through quoting a fee that is not economic in terms of the factors mentioned in paragraph 2 above, that fact may be taken into account in considering the member's conduct having regard to Fundamental Principle 3.

Bills

9 The firm should be prepared to furnish, on request and without further charge, further details of the work done to enable the client to understand the work that has been prepared on their behalf.

Investment business

10 Firms which are authorised by the Association to carry on investment business are referred to Rule 12(4) of the Investment Business 1988.

Advertisements

11 The attention of members is drawn to the guidance contained in Rules of Professional Conduct, 3, 'Advertising, publicity and obtaining professional work', relative to the mention of fees in advertisements.

Commission on indemnity terms

12 Members may receive commission in respect of transactions effected from clients on the basis that this must be repaid in certain circumstances. For example, the rules of the Life Assurance and Unit Trusts Regulatory Organisation (LAUTRO) provide that in any case where commission is paid before all the premiums are received, there must be an agreement in place which requires repayment of commission in the event that the premium is not paid. In these circumstances the member may agree with the client any one of the following options:

(i) to delay refunding the client's commission until the expiry of the term; or

(ii) to place the commission into a delegated deposit account until the expiry of the term and then to refund the commission to the client with interest; or

(iii) to rebate the client's commission annually over the term; or

(iv) to request the person paying commission to pay only the commission due each year, retaining the balance; or

(v) to forgo all commission; or

(vi) to instruct the person offering commission to retain the commission for the benefit of the client's pension or other policy.

It would remain open to the member to refund the commission to the client either with or without the client's confirmation that he would reimburse the member in the event that commission became repayable.

Professional liability of accountants and auditors

Members' attention is drawn to the principal areas in which actions for negligence may be brought against them by clients or third parties and suggests steps which they may properly be able to take to reduce the risk of such claims. The expressions of law included in this statement have the approval of Counsel. This statement does not deal with the position under the law of the Republic of Ireland.

Introduction

1 This statement is concerned only with the liability for professional negligence which a member may incur because of an act or default by him or by one of his employees or associates which results in financial loss to a person to whom a duty of care is owed. It does not deal with liability arising from other causes (for example criminal acts, breaches of trust, or breaches of contract other than the negligent performance of its terms, and certain heads of liability arising by statute independently of contract).

2 Negligence in this statement therefore means some act or omission which occurs because the person concerned has failed to exercise that degree of professional care and skill, appropriate to the circumstances of the case, which is expected of accountants and auditors. It would be a defence to an action for negligence to show:

(i) that there has been no negligence, or

(ii) that no duty of care was owed to the plaintiff in the circumstances, or

(iii) in the case of actions in tort that no financial loss has been suffered by the plaintiff.

The third defence would not be available to a claim in contract, but only nominal damages would be recoverable and in those circumstances it is unlikely that such an action would be brought.

3 In recent years there have been a number of cases where substantial sums have been claimed as damages for negligence against accountants and auditors. In a number of cases it appears that the claims may have arisen as a result of some misunderstanding as to the degree of responsibility which the accountant was expected to assume in giving advice or expressing an opinion. It is therefore important to distinguish between:

(i) disputes arising from misunderstandings regarding the duties assumed and

(ii) negligence in carrying out agreed terms.

The use of engagement letters

4 There is a contractual relationship between an accountant and his client. Unless an express agreement is made between them to the contrary, the standard of work required of an accountant is defined by Section 13 of the Supply of Goods and Services Act 1982: in a contract for the supply of a service where the supplier is acting in the course of a business, there is an implied term that the supplier will carry out the service with reasonable skill and care. The degree of skill and care required will depend principally on the nature of the work undertaken. An accountant who undertakes work of an unusually specialised nature, or work of a kind whose negligent performance is particularly liable to cause substantial loss, will usually be taken to have assumed a duty to exercise a higher degree of skill and care than would be appropriate to less demanding work. This will, especially, be the case if he holds himself out as being experienced in the kind of work in question. In no case, however, is the duty likely to be absolute. Opinions expressed or advice given will not give rise to claims merely because in the light of later events they prove to have been wrong.

5 The accountant should ensure that at the time he agrees to perform certain work for the client the scope of his responsibilities is made clear, preferably in writing, and the terms of his contract with his client are properly defined. Wherever possible, a letter of engagement should be prepared setting out in detail the actual services to be performed and the terms of the engagement should be accepted by the client so as to minimise the risk of disputes regarding the duties assumed (see Engagement Letters). It may also be helpful for the avoidance of misunderstandings to indicate any significant matters which are not included in the scope of responsibilities undertaken, although it will rarely be possible to provide a comprehensive list of matters excluded. Firms which are authorised by the Association to the conduct investment business are referred to the requirement for a client agreement set out in Rule 14 of the Investment Business Rules 1988.

Excluding or restricting liability to a client

6 It should be borne in mind that an agreement with a client designed to exclude or restrict a member's liability will not always be effective in law. The following are the main relevant considerations.

Auditors under the Companies Acts

7 Section 310 of the Companies Act 1985 makes void any provision in a company's articles or any contractual arrangement purporting to exempt the auditor from or to indemnify him against any liability for negligence, default, breach of duty or breach of trust. Although Section 727 of the Companies Act 1985 empowers the court in certain circumstances to grant relief either wholly or in part from any of such liabilities, it appears that these powers have seldom been exercised and it would be prudent to assume that an auditor might not be relieved of liability.

Other cases

8 Appropriate reference should be made in the letter of engagement to any exclusion or restriction of liability (other than as auditor of a limited company) because if an attempt is made to introduce such a provision into an existing relationship or in relation to a transaction for which instructions have already been accepted, difficulty may be experienced in showing that there is any legal consideration for the client's agreement to submit to the exemption provisions.

The Unfair Contract Terms Act 1977

9 This Act introduces extensive restrictions upon the enforceability of exclusions of liability for negligence and breaches of contract. Section 2 of the Act, which applies in England, Wales and Northern Ireland, makes void any contractual exclusion or restriction of liability for negligence, even in a case where the client has agreed to it and where legal consideration exists, unless the person seeking to rely on that exclusion or restriction can show that it was reasonable. Part II of the Act contains somewhat similar provisions applying as part of the law of Scotland. There is, at present, little case law which affords guidance as to what exclusions or restrictions of liability for negligence will be regarded as reasonable. However, unless the work undertaken presents unusual difficulties or is required to be carried out in unusually difficult circumstances, it would be prudent to assume that an exclusion of liability for negligence may be treated by the courts as unreasonable. A limitation of liability for negligence to a particular sum, will more readily be treated by the courts as reasonable, particularly if the accountant relying upon it can show that he would have difficulty in obtaining professional indemnity insurance for any greater sum.

10 An exclusion or restriction of an accountant's liability will not generally avail him against a third party. Third party liability is dealt with separately in paragraphs 14-28 below.

Advice on limited information

11 Besides reporting under the Companies Act 1985 accountants are called upon to give opinions and advice, including financial advice, in connection with many other matters, for example, investigation or management consultancy assignments, the preparation or audit of the accounts of sole traders, partnerships and charities, and in the field of taxation. A member undertaking to carry out work of this nature should make clear to his client the extent of the responsibility he agrees to undertake, making particular reference to the information supplied to him as a basis for his work and to those areas (if any) to be excluded from his examination. In particular, if the client requires a 'snap' answer to a complicated problem, a member would be well advised to record in writing (or alternatively to state orally and forthwith confirm in writing) that the problem is a complicated one, that he has been given a very limited time in which to study it, that further time is required in order to consider it in depth and that the opinion or advice tendered might well be revised if further time were available to him. He should also state that the client is responsible for the accuracy of the information supplied to the accountant. Except in the case of a genuine emergency the client should be warned against acting on the 'snap' advice tendered before further investigation has been carried out.

12 Statements and warnings of the kind considered in the preceding paragraph are not exclusions or restrictions of liability, but definitions of the work undertaken, and will protect an accountant from a claim for negligence based on the contention that his enquiries should have been more extensive than those so defined. (Sole traders and partnerships are dealt with in Section 8.1 paragraphs 36-43).

13 There is an increasing tendency for accountants to be required to express an opinion on financial statements relating not to past (and therefore ascertainable) results but to the expected results of future periods. The specific considerations which arise in such circumstances are set out in the Audit Brief and Statement, 5, 'Accountants' reports on profit forecasts' to which reference should be made.

Liability to third parties

14 An accountant may be liable for negligence not only in contract, but in tort if a person to whom he owed a duty of care has suffered loss as a result of the accountant's negligence. An accountant will almost always owe a duty of care to his own client, but that duty is likely to be coextensive with his contractual duty. In practice, the possibility of liability in tort will be important mainly in the context of claims by third parties.

15 Recent decisions of the courts, including three important decisions of the House of Lords, have expanded the classes of case in which a person professing some special skill (as an accountant does) could be liable for negligence to someone other than his own client: *Hedley Byrne and Co Ltd* v. *Heller and Partners* (1964) A.C. 465, *Anns* v. *Merton*

London Borough Council (1978) A.C. 728, and *Junior Books Ltd* v. *Veitschi Co Ltd* (1982) 3 W.L.R. 477. Such liability may arise whenever a professional person does work for his client in circumstances where he knows or ought to know;

(i) that his work is liable to be relied upon by a third party and

(ii) that the third party may suffer financial loss if the work in question has been done negligently.

Liability will arise when the work in question is of a kind which it was reasonable for the third party to rely on for his particular purpose. If these conditions are satisfied, the third party is a person whom in the eyes of the law the professional man ought to have in mind in applying his skills to the work in question.

16 (a) The decision of the House of Lords in the case of *Caparo Industries plc* v. *Dickman and others* (1990) I All E.R. 568 has clarified the extent of auditors' liability by defining three criteria for the imposition of a duty of care as follows:

(i) It must be reasonably foreseeable by the defendant that the statements will be relied on by the plaintiff.

(ii) There has to be a 'relevant degree of proximity' between the parties.

(iii) It must be just and reasonable to impose a duty of care on the part of the defendant to the plaintiff.

(b) While it followed from this ruling that the auditors in question did not owe a duty of care either to individual shareholders or to potential investors, auditors will continue to have a duty to shareholders as a group, presumably as represented by the company. Nor will the decision reduce the exposure of accountants who produce or report upon financial statements of various kinds (whether for a fee or not) which are liable to be relied upon by persons other than those for whom they were originally prepared.

17 An accountant may sometimes be informed, before he carries out certain work, that a third party will rely upon the results. An example likely to be encountered in practice is a report upon the business of a client which the accountant has been instructed to prepare for the purpose of being shown to a potential purchaser or potential creditor of that business. In such a case it would be prudent for an accountant to assume that he will be held to owe the same duty to the third party as to his client.

18 Even where the accountant is not specifically informed that a third party will rely upon the results of his work, he would be wise to consider whether this is likely to be the case. Where the accountant knows the purpose of the work and identity of the third party, to whom the information prepared or reported on will be shown, he may be held to owe a duty of care to that third party. An example of such circumstances would be involvement in the production of management accounts or projection for presentation to a bank in support of a loan application.

Avoiding liability to third parties

19 In many cases there are no steps which an accountant can reasonably take to limit the circulation of his work or the use which is made of it. Some documents, such as the reports of auditors of public companies are by their nature incapable of being restricted in this way. In other cases, however, there may be steps which an accountant can take to reduce his exposure to the claims of third parties. These cases cannot be exhaustively defined but the following are some of the more important examples of them.

Documents published generally

20 An accountant may publish a document which is prepared neither in response to the instructions of a particular client nor for any statutory or public purpose: e.g. a text book or a newsletter. In such cases there will often be no circumstances which would enable a third party to assume that it had necessarily been prepared with all due skill and care, and substantial reliance upon it would not be reasonable. An accountant can reinforce his legal position in relation to documents of this kind by including a disclaimer of liability in the document itself. The form of the disclaimer will depend upon the nature of the document. In many cases a disclaimer along the following lines will be found appropriate:

> "While every care has been taken in the preparation of this document, it may contain errors for which we cannot be responsible."

Work done for special purposes

21 An accountant may be instructed to prepare or report upon financial material for some particular purpose. He will not usually be liable to a third party who relies on it for any other purpose for which it is or may be unsuitable. In such a case the accountant would usually have no reason to suppose that such reliance would be placed upon it. Moreover, it would be unreasonable for a third party to rely on it for such a purpose. Members would, however, be well advised to make the position clear by including in the document itself a short statement of the purpose for which it was prepared, if that is not apparent.

Confidential reports

22 Certain reports or statements may appropriately include a rubric specifically restricting its circulation. For example:

> "CONFIDENTIAL.
>
> This report (statement) has been prepared for the private use of X (the client) only and on condition that it must not be disclosed to any other person without the written consent of Y (the accountant)."

Current practice is that clients will respect a rubric of this kind. Accordingly, when a document is so marked but is nevertheless relied upon by a third party without the accountant's consent, the accountant will as a general rule be able to resist liability on the basis that the third party was not a person whom he should have had in mind as being likely to suffer loss by his negligence. Such a rubric should be introduced only where the circumstances warrant it, as it would tend to be devalued by indiscriminate use in connection with documents which by their nature must receive a wide distribution. Where a document is prepared in the first instance for discussion with or approval by the client or others, and is liable to be altered before it appears in its final form, this fact should be made clear so as to prevent persons from placing undue reliance upon it. This may be done by overstamping the document on each page: 'Unrevised draft'.

Documents intended to be checked; accounts prepared for tax purposes

23 An accountant may prepare a report or statement to be issued by his client in circumstances where he can reasonably expect his client to check it for fairness or accuracy before any use is made of it involving third parties. Accounts prepared for the purpose of being submitted to the Inland Revenue for the assessment of taxation will frequently, although not invariably, fall within this category. In such cases, the effective cause of any loss suffered by a third party will ordinarily be the negligence of the person in whose name it was issued and who ought to have checked the document, and not that of the accountant.

Disclaimers of liability to third parties

24 A disclaimer of liability to third parties may sometimes be made in circumstances where liability would or might otherwise arise. Such a disclaimer might for example, be introduced along the following lines:

> "This report is prepared for the use of X (the client) only. No responsibility is assumed to any other person."

Members should, however, be aware that such a disclaimer will often be inappropriate or ineffective. Disclaimers will be inappropriate in circumstances where their use will tend to impair the status of practising accountants by indicating a lack of confidence in their professional work. It would not, for example, be proper to endorse copies of accounts filed in accordance with Sections 226 and 241 of the Companies Act 1985 with a disclaimer by the auditor of liability to persons other than shareholders.

25 The following paragraphs deal with those cases in which there are no professional objections to the use of disclaimers, but in which reservations must be made as to their effectiveness.

Information prepared for the client and passed to third parties

26 Where a statement or report is prepared by an accountant for his client, which is not confidential and can be expected in the ordinary course to be relied upon by third parties, a disclaimer which purports to apply only as against the third parties presents particular difficulties as a matter of law. By it, the accountant seeks in effect to assume a dual standard of care, the one applicable in so far as his work is read by the client and the other in so far as it is read by the third party. Since the third party will normally rely on the report because he expects the accountant to have performed his duty to the client, and since that expectation will normally be reasonable, the attempt to assume such a dual standard is unlikely to succeed.

Information passed directly to third parties

27 Where an accountant (necessarily with the authority of his client) passes information directly to a third party there is no question of a dual standard of liability because the third party is generally the only person who is intended to rely on the accountant's work. In such a case the effectiveness of a disclaimer will depend upon the nature of the information. For example, when giving references or assurances regarding creditworthiness or similar matters, the normal commercial practice is to state that although the reference or assurance is given in good faith the accountant accepts no financial responsibility for the opinion he expresses. Such disclaimers will generally be effective because such references or assurances are not information of the kind which is expected to be the result of extensive research by the accountant. Sometimes, however, an accountant may supply directly to a third party information of a kind which the third party (unless he is told otherwise) can reasonably expect to be the result of research of a more or less extensive kind. As applied to such information, a disclaimer will generally be ineffective in England (although not in Scotland) because of Section 2 of the Unfair Contract Terms Act 1977 (see the following paragraph).

Unfair Contract Terms Act 1977, Section 2

28 The effect of this provision is that where a person is in principle liable for negligence, he cannot exclude that liability by a reference to a notice, except where the notice is reasonable. If an accountant prepares a report or statement in circumstances where it can reasonably be expected that a third party may rely on it, a notice excluding liability to him would only exceptionally be regarded as reasonable. The law on this point is different in Scotland, because the equivalent section of the Act which applies as part of Scots law, Section 16, does not refer to notices but only to terms of contract. Accordingly, in Scotland an appropriately worded disclaimer may be effective to exclude liability to third parties whether or not it is reasonable.

Inclusion of the accountant's name on a document issued by a client

29 Members should endeavour to ensure that no statement or document issued by their client (other than unabridged accounts which have been reported on by them as auditors) will bear their name unless their prior consent has been obtained. It is often desirable for a suitable paragraph to be included in the engagement letter.

30 There have been occasions when the use of a member's name in a document (other than accounts reported on him as auditor) has been interpreted by third parties as implying that the company is financially sound and well conducted, whether or not this is in fact the case. If a member learns that a client proposes to cite his name he should inform the client that his permission must first be obtained and in appropriate cases he should withhold his permission.

Specialist advice

31 In expressing an opinion or giving advice on difficult and complicated matters (for example in the field of taxation) members should bear in mind the magnitude of the financial consequences for their client should the advice tendered be incorrect or misconceived and the implications for them of a possible result in financial loss. An accountant in general practice is deemed by the law only to undertake to bring a fair and reasonable degree of skill and competence to the problem on which he is required to advise, and in appropriate circumstances he may wish to obtain the approval of his client for consulting another person with specialist experience of the matter in question. Occasions may also arise when a member may wish to consider declining a particular assignment because, for example, he is of the opinion that the matter on which his advice is sought does not fall within the normal scope of a professional accountancy practice and the client would therefore receive better assistance from a member of another profession.

Receiverships, trust and secretarial work

32 A member acting as a receiver incurs personal liability for his acts and may, in particular, incur liability under commercial contracts irrespective of negligence on his part. Accordingly if a member appointed by a debenture holder to act in this capacity has to manage a business he should endeavour to ensure that he is fully indemnified by the person who appoints him against all loss and damage arising out of his management. If such an indemnity cannot be obtained, he should endeavour to ensure that contracts into which he enters on behalf of that business include a clause to the effect that he assumes no personal liability thereunder.

33 It is often prudent for a member who is appointed to act as a trustee or asked to carry out certain secretarial work such as cheque signing to obtain an appropriate indemnity. In the former case an instrument creating a trust can give a wide form of indemnity if the settlor is willing to approve its inclusion in the deed; in the latter, the member should arrange for an indemnity to be obtained from his client.

Conclusions

34 Although it is not possible to guard against every circumstance in which an accountant or auditor may run the danger of incurring liability for professional negligence, the following matters should be borne in mind:

(a) before carrying out any work for a client a member should ensure that the exact duties to be performed and in particular any significant matters to be excluded have been agreed with the client in writing by a letter of engagement or otherwise. If the accountant is asked to perform any additional duties at a later date, these should also be defined in writing (paragraph 5);

(b) in giving 'snap' advice at the request of a client or advice which must necessarily be based on incomplete information, a member should make it clear that such advice is subject to limitations and that consideration in depth may lead him to revise the advice given (paragraph 11);

(c) when publishing documents generally a member may find it advantageous to include in the document a clause disclaiming liability (paragraph 20);

(d) when submitting unaudited accounts or other unaudited financial statements or reports to the client, a member should ensure that any special purpose for which the statements or reports have been prepared is recorded on their face, and in appropriate cases should introduce a clause recording that the report or statement is confidential and has been prepared solely for the private use of the client (paragraphs 21 and 22);

(e) it should be recognised that there are areas of professional work (for example when acting as an auditor under the Companies Acts) where it is not possible for liability to be limited or excluded, and that there are other areas of professional work (for example when preparing reports on a business for the purpose of being submitted to a potential purchaser) where although such a limitation or exclusion may be included, its effectiveness will depend on the view which a court may subsequently form of its reasonableness (paragraphs 24 and 25);

(f) when giving references to a third party with regard to future transactions (e.g. payment of rent) a member should state that his opinion is given without financial responsibility on his part (paragraph 27);

(g) where the circumstances appear to warrant it because of the complexity of an assignment or otherwise a member should advise his client that he considers it desirable to take specialist advice. In certain circumstances it may be appropriate for a member either to consult another accountant or to suggest to his client that the advice of a member of another profession should be sought (paragraph 31);

(h) where a member acts as receiver he should endeavour to ensure that the person appointing him executes an appropriate letter of indemnity in his favour or should include appropriate exclusions of his personal liability in contracts with third parties. A member should also arrange for additional professional indemnity insurance cover of a realistic amount and should ascertain from his brokers whether or not cover is provided for the special risks involved (paragraph 32).

Note: Responsibility for obtaining adequate cover lies with individual members. In the UK a scheme has been negotiated by the Association on behalf of members. Insurance proposal forms for several brokers, who will be able to provide quotations, are available for the Membership Department of the Association.

The incapacity or death of a sole practitioner

General

1 The grant of a practising certificate is conditional on provision being made for continuity in the management of a practice, in the event of death or incapacity.

2 A sole practitioner in practice must enter into an arrangement to enable his practice to continue with minimum disruption in the event of his death or incapacity. Provision for continuity in the proper management of a practice may be made in either of the following ways:

(a) by entering into an agreement with another sole practitioner or with a firm of practising accountants;

(b) by satisfying the Association that other adequate provision has been made.

3 Members must ensure that their executors and family will be aware, in the event of death or incapacity, of the arrangements made for the management of the practice.

Continuity agreement

4 Where an agreement is made with another sole practitioner or practising firm, it may take the form of an agreement to manage the practice or may be an agreement to sell the practice on a predetermined basis. When choosing a sole practitioner or firm with which to enter into such an arrangement, a member should try to find a compatible practice where audit procedures, fee structure and the work in general are of a similar kind.

Management agreement

Terms of the management agreement

5 The arrangement made with the sole practitioner or firm should be in the form of a written agreement and include the following matters:

(a) The precise nature of the legal relationship between the principal and the assisting member.

(b) The circumstances which bring the arrangement into operation. Also the maximum duration of the arrangement and provision for a review of the arrangement should the circumstances warrant an extension of time.

(c) The assisting member's obligations.

(d) The assisting member's powers relating to such matters as engaging and dismissing staff, and operating the bank accounts.

(e) The basis on which the assisting member will be remunerated.

(f) The form of a letter, to be sent to clients in the event of the principal's death or incapacity.

Ethical considerations

6 (a) The assisting member, who acts as manager of a practice of a deceased or incapacitated sole practitioner, must not seek any personal gain from the arrangement apart from reasonable remuneration for the work he undertakes. He should not accept clients from the practice he is assisting without the express agreement of the principal or his personal representatives during the period from the commencement of his appointment as manager, to 2 years after the arrangement is terminated, except where he acquires the practice as in (b) below. Failure to observe this rule could result in disciplinary action being taken against the assisting member.

In order to protect the continuity of the practice, the assisting member should, whenever possible, interview clients and staff at the principal's office.

(b) The assisting member may wish to acquire the practice from the incapacitated member or his personal representatives and this is in no way unethical, and may be a very satisfactory solution. The assisting member should negotiate with the personal representatives of a deceased member (who should normally be independently advised), or in the case of incapacity with the member himself or his representatives. Different considerations arise an the incapacity of a sole practitioner from those which arise on death and, therefore, each is dealt with separately below.

Incapacity of a sole practitioner

7 The principal, in spite of his incapacity, will continue as owner of the practice and will be responsible for the actions of the member appointed to manage the practice in his absence. It is of the utmost importance that professional indemnity and other insurances are renewed by reference to the new circumstances. Also, if the incapacity is likely to be of some duration, steps should be taken to inform clients of the arrangements for the continuance of the service to them.

Death of a sole practitioner

8 The advantage of appointing executors is particularly evident in cases of this kind, for if the late practitioner has done so, his executors can act at once to protect the practice. It would obviously be an advantage if one of the executors was professionally qualified. If, on the other hand, he dies intestate, his administrators have no authority to act until they have obtained a grant of administration. Matters acquiring particular attention in both cases are as follows:

(a) the fact that the personal representatives of the deceased have taken over conduct of the practice means that it cannot strictly be described as Certified Accountant(s); nevertheless, for a temporary period the old name and description of the practice may normally be retained for the purpose of realisation, provided that the fact that the practice is under management is indicated;

(b) insurers should be advised of the changed circumstances, especially those concerned with professional indemnity insurance;

(c) as in the case of incapacity, steps should be taken to record in an agreement the scope of the assisting member's authority for administration of the practice including control of staff, operation of banking accounts, etc.

Statutory audits

9 The incapacitated member will retain his appointment as a statutory auditor and can only be removed in accordance with the appropriate statutory procedures (except in the case of Friendly/Industrial and Provident Societies where a member who has ceased to act as auditor because of incapacity is not eligible for automatic re appointment). Some kinds of incapacity are more permanent than others and obviously considerations of practical common sense will indicate the course to be followed, possibly resignation.

The director or other persons responsible for the appointment of the auditor should, if the incapacity is likely to be of considerable duration or affect the normal audit procedures, be fully informed of the circumstances and the arrangements made for the continuation of the practice. If the directors wish to appoint the assisting member, he may quite properly accept, emphasising that he does so on a temporary basis.

Sometimes, however, he may subsequently find himself in a somewhat embarrassing situation if the clients then wish to invite him to accept the appointment permanently. He is free to accept if he wishes, but in that event the Council would expect him to be ready to negotiate with an incapacitated member or his agent as to the financial terms on which he does so. Otherwise the value of the practice would be diminished.

Articled clerks

10 Contracts of articles terminate on the death of a sole practitioner and each articled clerk will need to enter into fresh articles. It is the obligation of the personal representatives to ensure that the necessary arrangements are made. Articled clerks of the assisting member may serve their articles with the managed practice which for this purpose is regarded as a client of the principal. In order to avoid any prejudice to the position of the articled clerk, Council has power to determine that an articled clerk will not count in the complement of clerks allowed to a new principal. Also, Council may allow any break of service to be treated as service under articles.

Descriptions

11 The name of an assisting member who is managing the practice should be disclosed on the letter heading as soon as possible, e.g.

David J. Smith

Certified Accountant

Manager Henry R. Jones, FCCA

or

Managers: Davies and Jones,

Certified Accountants

Clients' monies

General

1 A member in practice is strictly accountable for all clients' monies which he receives. In this Section, the term "clients' monies" includes all monies received by a practice to be held or disbursed by it on the instructions of the person from whom or on whose behalf they are received.

Firms which are authorised by the Association to carry on investment business are referred to Rule 20 of the Investment Business Rules 1988, which governs the treatment of investment business client money. The remaining paragraphs of this Section are concerned only with clients' monies which are not governed by Rule 20.

Clients' accounts

2 Clients' monies should be paid without delay into a bank account, separate from other accounts of the firm, which may be either a general account or an account in the name of the specific client but which should in all cases include in its title the word "client". Any such bank account is referred to herein as "a client account". Where it is anticipated that the monies of an individual client in excess of £10,000 will be held by the firm for more than 30 days, the money should be paid into a separate bank account designated by the name of the client or number allocated to the client account. The term "bank" is defined in paragraph 16 below.

3 Whenever a firm opens a client account it should give written notice in clear terms to the bank at which the account is to be opened of the nature of the account, requiring the bank to acknowledge in writing that it accepts the terms of the notice. Legal advice has been received to the effect that if this is done no question will arise, in the event of the member's bankruptcy, or set-off by the bank against the practice's other accounts or of sequestration by a Trustee in Bankruptcy of a member of the amounts held in the client account for the benefit of the general creditors.

4 Where a firm receives a cheque or draft which includes both client's monies and other monies it should cause the same to be credited to a client account. Once the monies have been received into such client account a firm should withdraw from that account such part of the sum received as can properly be transferred to an office account in accordance with the guidance set out in paragraphs 6 and 7 below.

5 Save as referred to in paragraph 4 above, no monies other than clients' monies should be paid into a client account.

6 The following may be withdrawn from a client bank account, provided that the sums withdrawn do not exceed the total of the monies held for the time being in the account of the client concerned:

(a) monies properly required for a payment to or on behalf of a client,

(b) monies properly required for or towards payment of a debt due to the practice from the client, otherwise than in respect of fees or commissions earned by the firm,

(c) monies properly required for or towards payment of fees or commissions payable to the practice by the client,

(d) monies drawn on a client's authority or in conformity with any contract between the firm and the client.

7 Monies should not be withdrawn from a client bank account for or towards payment of fees or commissions payable under paragraph 6(c) above unless:

(a) the client has been notified in writing that monies held or received on the client's behalf will be applied against those fees or commissions, and has not disagreed,

(b) a principal of the firm has expressly authorised the withdrawal, and

(c) 30 days have elapsed since the date of delivery to the client of the notification, or

(d) the precise amount to be withdrawn has been agreed with the client or has been finally determined by a Court or Arbitrator.

8 A firm should be careful to differentiate, both in its records and, where appropriate, in its use of client accounts, between monies held on behalf of a client in that client's personal capacity and those, within the knowledge of the firm, held on behalf of the same client as trustee for others. A separate client account should be opened to receive the trust monies of each separate trust.

Interest payable on client account monies

9 A firm should pay each client interest of not less than the amount which would have been earned by way of gross interest, if all clients' monies held by the firm for the client had been kept in a separate interest-bearing account, at the small deposit rate, with the bank concerned.

10 The above guidance may be over-ridden by express written agreement between the firm and the client. For instance a client could agree to forego sums of interest of less than £10, or in respect of bank credits until they have been cleared.

Monies held by the firm as stakeholder

11 Monies held by a member as stakeholder should be regarded as clients' monies and should be paid into a separate bank account maintained for the purpose or into a client bank account. The position in law is that such money does not belong to any specific client until the happening of the deciding event and there is therefore no legal requirement to account for any interest earned thereon up to the date of that event.

Maintaining records

12 Every firm should at all times maintain records so as to show clearly the monies it has received, held or paid on account of its clients, and the details of any other monies dealt with by it through a client account, clearly distinguishing the monies of each client from the monies of other clients and from firm monies.

Fees and fee disputes

13 The attention of members is drawn to the guidance on fees contained in Section "Fees". A member has no right to withhold due payment out of monies to clients for the sole reason that a dispute exists in relation to fees billed by the firm, and in the interests of good practice, should not do so.

Bank

14 The term 'bank' comprises an institution authorised within the meaning of the Banking Act 1987, the Bank of England, the Central bank of another member state of the European Community, and a building society within the meaning of the Building Societies Act 1986 (which has adopted the power to provide unrestricted money transaction services).

The Financial Services Act 1986

(Issued April 1989)

1 Section 3 of the Financial Services Act 1986 prohibits any person from carrying on, or purporting to carry on, investment business in the United Kingdom without proper authorisation or exemption.

Breach of this provision is a criminal offence, and a person convicted of contravening Section 3 is liable on conviction on indictment to imprisonment for up to two years, or to a fine of any amount, or both. On summary conviction, the penalties are imprisonment for a term not exceeding six months or a fine not exceeding the statutory maximum, or both.

In addition, contracts made in contravention of Section 3, or as a result of anything done by a person acting in breach of Section 3, are unenforceable against the other party without a court order which will only be granted in limited circumstances. The other party to the contract is entitled to recover any money paid or property transferred by him under the agreement, and to compensation for any loss sustained as a result of parting with it.

The Act also provides that injunctions can be obtained to restrain breaches of Section 3, and for restitution orders to restore the parties to a transaction made in breach of Section 3 to the position they were in before the transaction was entered into.

Investment business

2 The definition of 'investment business', which is very widely drawn and sometimes difficult to interpret, is contained in Section 1 and Schedule 1 of the Act, as amended by subsequent statutory investments. The definition covers not only investment advice, but also dealing and arranging deals in investments; managing investments; and establishing, operating and winding up a collective investment scheme. It is the firm (the company, partnership, or sole practitioner) which carries on investment business which must obtain authorisation or exemption under the Act, and not its individual employees. In view of the width of the Act and the severity of the sanctions, the Association recommends its members in public practice to apply for authorisation for their firms.

A fuller explanation of investment business and the need for authorisation is contained in the Association's Members' Guide to the Financial Services Act 1986. This is available on request from the Practice Regulation Department of the Association.

Restrictions on advertising

3 Section 57 of the Act provides that no person other than an authorised person shall issue, or cause to be issued, an investment advertisement in the United Kingdom, unless its contents have been approved by an authorised person. Contravention of this Section is a criminal offence punishable by up to two years imprisonment, an unlimited fine, or both.

Disciplinary action in respect of convictions before the Courts

1 Council believes it is necessary to issue guidance to members and students on the disciplinary action which is likely to ensue should members or students be convicted of offences before the Courts.

Under the provisions of bye-law 27 disciplinary action can arise in the case of members or students whether or not they were such when the offence occurred. It would, of course, be necessary for the member or student to come into membership or studentship before the disciplinary machinery could be activated.

2 Liability to action arises whenever a member or student is guilty of misconduct, and the circumstances in which such liability may arise are defined in bye-law 27. Under these provisions of the bye-law misconduct includes, but is not confined to acts or defaults likely to bring discredit upon:

(a) the member himself, or

(b) the Association, or

(c) the accountancy profession

The fact that a member or student has pleaded guilty to, or been found guilty of such an offence before a Court of superior jurisdiction in the United Kingdom, or in a superior Court of any country whose judgements are registerable in the United Kingdom, will be treated as conclusive proof of misconduct.

In addition, a finding in civil proceedings that a member acted fraudulently or dishonestly will be treated as conclusive proof of misconduct. Accordingly, where such facts are established before a disciplinary tribunal of the Association, that tribunal will concern itself only with mitigating circumstances which should be taken into account in reaching its decision as to how it should deal with the member or student concerned. It should be borne in mind that liability to disciplinary action may arise from any act of misconduct or default whether in the course of professional work or otherwise.

3 Thus, it is clear that members and students are subject to disciplinary action even when the convictions are wholly unrelated to their professional duties. The question then arises as to what offences are "discreditable or derogatory" within the meaning of the bye-law.

Convictions relating to a member's or student's personal life, such as obtaining money or goods by false pretences, forgery, theft and other offences involving dishonesty amount to prima facie cases of misconduct "discreditable to a member or derogatory to the Association or the accountancy profession". It is essential that members of the accountancy profession, because of the nature of their work and the trust their clients place in them, are honest both in their professional and personal activities. A very serious view must be taken of any lack of honesty in a member's or student's behaviour outside his professional work. But, cases can be envisaged where an Investigations Committee might take a lenient view; e.g. if a student is convicted of a petty theft which the Committee considers to be merely a student prank, the Committee might decide that the conviction should merely remain on the student's file to be taken into consideration with any future instances of misconduct. Similarly, an isolated incident of disorderly behaviour by a member due to intoxication might be considered by the Investigations Committee, after having taken into account all the circumstances, to be a case which should not be referred to the Disciplinary Committee.

4 The criminal law embraces a vast range of offences and Council has examined some of the different categories of offence in an endeavour to identify which should be accepted as "discreditable or derogatory" conduct within the meaning of bye-law 27(a). After careful consideration it has concluded that it is dangerous to lay down rigid rules and that justice is more likely to be done if the Disciplinary Committee is left free to decide each case on its merits.

5 Once the Disciplinary Committee has found a charge of misconduct proved, it then has to determine what penalty, if any, should be imposed on the member or student concerned.

6 In the case of Re. H (a barrister) (1981) 3 All E.R., a case concerning disciplinary proceedings in the Inns of Court, Mr Justice Latey laid down three general principles with regard to sentencing:

(a) A distinction should be drawn between professional misconduct and misconduct outside the profession.

(b) An unsuccessful plea of not guilty is a factor which it is proper for the disciplinary tribunal to weigh with all others, but it should not be the predominant factor.

(c) The disciplinary tribunal should have regard to sentences imposed in comparable cases. The judgement stated:

"For this purpose, we think that the record of the decisions ought to state matters such as the penalty imposed by the criminal court, the approximate length of the barrister's standing at the Bar, whether or not he is a practising barrister, and other matters material to the sentence which can be readily stated."

It seems clear that these three general guidelines should equally be applied to the determining of penalties by the Association's Disciplinary and Appeal Committees, and a record of precedents in relation to the Association's disciplinary decisions is maintained, which is available to the committees at each meeting.

7 In conclusion, the Disciplinary and Appeal Committees will reach their own conclusions as to whether a particular conviction amounts to misconduct within the meaning of bye-law 27(a) ascertaining into account the facts of the particular case, society's current attitude to that offence, the country in which the offence has been committed together with local attitudes, and earlier decisions of the committees. Penalties imposed will be related to the view which the committees take in respect of the individual offences with which they have to deal and the degree of gravity of the matter under consideration.

Corporate finance advice including take-overs

(Issued September 1989)

Introduction

1 Corporate finance activities are wide-ranging in their nature. In many cases an auditor will give corporate finance advice incidental to the audit relationship. The role and nature of advice expected of a member may change in character when the client becomes involved in or anticipates a particular transaction, such as a take-over bid or issue of securities. It is at that point that problems of independence and conflict of interest can arise. The guidance which follows is designed to assist members who find themselves advising in these and related circumstances.

The take-over panel

2 Attention is drawn to the need to comply with the City Code on Take-Overs and Mergers and the Rules Governing Substantial Acquisitions of Shares, which are expressly applied to professional advisers as well as to those engaged in the securities markets.

Objectivity and integrity

3 Provided that a member maintains objectivity and integrity throughout, both in regard to the client and to other interested parties there can be no objection to his or her accepting an engagement which is designed primarily with a view to advancing the client's case. The concept of impartiality has no application in these circumstances.

Conflicts of interest

4 (a) It may be in the best interests of a client company for financial advice to be provided by its auditor and there is nothing improper in the auditor supporting a client in this way. There are however a variety of situations in which conflict can arise.

(b) It is not on the face of it improper for the firm to continue to act as auditors to both parties in a take-over situation, even if the take-over is contested.

(c) A firm may find itself acting as auditors or advisers for two or more parties involved in a take-over subject to the City Code. For the firm to cease to act for a client within the limited period of the take-over, on the basis that conflict might arise, could damage the client's interests.

Accordingly in such circumstances a firm may continue to act for more than one party as auditors, as reporting accountants on any profit forecast, and in the provision of incidental advice consistent with these roles. However the firm should not act as a lead adviser for any party involved, or issue a critique of a client's accounts, and should implement proper safeguards (see below).

The attention of firms is also directed to those sections of the City Code dealing with conflict of interest, including the possession of 'material confidential information'. Members in doubt as to their position under the Code should consult the Take-over Panel.

(d) Where a take-over is not subject to the City Code, and there is no substantial public interest involved, a firm may, subject to the implementation of appropriate safeguards (see paragraph 7 below), continue to advise both sides. However the firm should ensure that the interests of minority shareholders are protected, and should consider the desirability of one company having a wholly independent adviser.

(e) A firm should not underwrite or sponsor an issue to the public of the shares or securities of a client which it audits or on which it has reported or will report, or undertake to accept nomination as auditor of the company being sponsored. Financial involvement of this kind would endanger the independence of the firm in the audit and/or reporting function. An auditor may however assist a client in raising capital by approaching institutional investors.

(f) It is not inappropriate for a member to conduct an acquisition search, which could identify another client as a target, provided the search is based solely on information which is not confidential to that client.

Avoiding conflicts of interest

5 (a) All reasonable steps should be taken to ascertain whether a conflict of interest exists or is likely to arise in the future between a firm and its clients, both in regard to new engagements and to the changing circumstances of existing clients, and including any implications arising from the possession of confidential information. Relationships with clients and former clients need to be reviewed before accepting a new appointment and regularly thereafter. A relationship which ended over two years before is unlikely to constitute conflict. Where it is clear that a material conflict of interest exists a firm should decline to act as financial adviser.

(b) It would be neither reasonable nor necessary to discontinue acting in any capacity in anticipation of every potential conflict. It could in some instances give rise to harmful rumour or speculation for a firm to disengage from a situation before a bid had become public knowledge.

(c) Where there appears to be a conflict of interest between clients but after careful consideration the firm considers that the conflict is not material and unlikely seriously to prejudice the interests of any of those clients, the firm may accept or continue the engagement, but not without first informing the clients concerned.

(d) A firm should not act or continue to act for two or more clients if the disclosure called for in the previous sub-paragraph could seriously prejudice the interests of a client.

(e) Where a conflict of interests is likely seriously to prejudice the interests of a client an engagement should not be accepted or continued even at the informed request of the clients concerned.

6 Where a firm is required for any reason to disengage from an existing client it should do so as speedily as practicable having regard to the interests of the client.

Safeguards

7 Where a firm acts or continues to act for two or more clients following disclosures in accordance with the previous paragraphs, all reasonable steps should be taken to manage the conflict which arises and thereby avoid any adverse consequences. These steps will include some or all of the following safeguards:

(a) the use of different partners and teams for different engagements;

(b) all necessary steps to prevent the leakage of confidential information between different teams and sections within the firm;

(c) regular review of the situation by a senior partner or compliance officer not personally involved with either client; and

(d) advising the clients to seek additional independent advice.

8 Any decision on the part of a sole practitioner must take account of the fact that the safeguards at (a) to (c) of the previous paragraph will not be available to him or her. Similar considerations apply to a small practice.

Documents for public use

9 (a) Where in the course of corporate finance advice a firm prepares information for a client — for example a critique of the accounts of another company — it may be called upon to do so:

(i) in a document which is for the consumption of the client only;

(ii) in order to assist the client to produce a document which will go out solely under the client's name and authority, whether including quotations from the original document or not; or

(iii) as part of a document which is to be published over the name of the member firm.

(b) Any statements or observations in a document prepared for a client must be such as, taken individually and as a whole, are justifiable on an objective examination of the available facts.

(c) A firm is, in the absence of any indication to the contrary, entitled to assume that the published accounts of the company on which it is commenting have been prepared properly and in accordance with all relevant SSAPs. Where scope for alternative accounting treatment exists, and the accuracy of the comment or observation is dependent on an assumption as to the actual accounting treatment chosen, that assumption must be stated, together with any other assumptions material to the commentary. Where the firm is not in possession of sufficient information to warrant a clear opinion this should be declared in the document.

(d) In the case of a document prepared solely for the client and his professional advisers, it should be a condition of the engagement that the document should not be disclosed to any third party without the firm's express permission.

(e) A firm must take responsibility for anything published under its name, and the published document should make clear the client for whom the firm is acting. To prevent misleading or out-of-context quotations, it should be a condition of the engagement that, if anything less than the full document is to be published, the form of the text and its context would have to be agreed with the firm.

(f) Any document whether for private or public use should be prepared in accordance with normal professional standards of integrity and objectivity and with a proper degree of care.

Fees

10 Where a member undertakes an engagement for a fee which is contingent upon the successful outcome of a transaction such as a bid, offer, purchase, sale or raising finance, the member should take particular care to ensure that the arrangements do not prejudice his or her independence and objectivity with regard to any other role which he or she may have, such as auditor or reporting accountant of either the bidder or the target.

Overseas transactions

11 This Statement has been drafted with regard to the situation in the United Kingdom and the Republic of Ireland. Members should apply the spirit of the guidance, subject to local legislation and regulation, to overseas transactions of a similar nature.

Confidentiality

Improper disclosure

1 Information acquired in the course of professional work should not be disclosed except where consent has been obtained from the client, employer or other proper source, or where there is a legal right or duty to disclose.

General

2 Where there is a right (as opposed to a duty) to disclose information a member should only make disclosure in pursuit of a public duty or professional obligation.

3 Questions which may arise as to the propriety of disclosing clients' affairs are dealt with at length in Rules of Professional Conduct 'Professional duty of confidence in relation to defaults and unlawful acts of clients and others'. Paragraphs 6 to 23 in particular set out the general legal position in relation to disclosure of information acquired in the course of a professional assignment.

4 A member faced with a problem in this area is strongly recommended to take legal advice as to the correct course of action.

5 Where a member in business is in doubt as to whether he has a right or duty to disclose he should, if appropriate, initially discuss the matter fully within the organisation in which he works. If that is not appropriate, or if it fails to resolve the problem, he should take legal advice and/or consult the Legal Department.

Improper use of information

6 A member acquiring information in the course of professional work should neither use nor appear to use that information for his personal advantage or for the advantage of a third party.

Examples

7 When a member changes his firm or employment he should distinguish between experience gained in the previous firm or employment and confiential information acquired there.

8 A member should not deal in the shares of a company with which he has a professional association at such a time or times as might make it seem that he was turning to his own advantage information obtained by him in his professional capacity. Firms which are authorised by the Association to carry on investment business are also referred to Rule 11(5) of the Investment Business Rules 1988.

The names of practising firms

General

1 For the purpose of this Section a practising firm is a firm the main business of which is the provision of services customarily provided by Certified Accountants. The term 'firm' includes partnerships, corporations and sole practitioners. Subject to the bye-laws and the following rules, a member may practise under whatever name or title he sees fit.

2 A practice name should be consistent with the dignity of the professional in the sense that it should not project an image inconsistent with that of a professional practice bound by high ethical and technical standards.

3 A practice name should not be misleading.

4 A practice name would be objectionable if in all the circumstances there was a real risk that it could be confused with the name of another firm, even if the member(s) of the practice could lay justifiable claim to the name.

5 There is no objection to a practice name indicating the range or type of services offered by the firm.

6 It has been the custom of the profession for members to practise under a firm's name based on the names of past or present members of the firm itself or of a firm with which it has merged or amalgamated. A practice name so derived will usually be in conformity with this guidance.

Examples

7 It would be misleading for a firm with a limited number of offices to describe itself as 'international' even if one of them was overseas.

8 There is no objection to a practice trading under different names from different offices provided that this does not mislead.

9 There is no objection to membership of a trading association being indicated on the firm's note paper or elsewhere in proximity to the practice name. However, the practice name of such a firm should be clearly distinguishable from the name of the associated firm or group. Thus, it would be misleading for a member of a trading group to bear the same name as the group, but there could be no objection to a firm practising under its own name "as a member of (a named) accountancy group".

10 It would be misleading for a sole practitioner to add the suffix 'and Associates' to the name of his practice unless formal arrangements were agreed with two or more consultants or firms.

11 The same objection does not apply to the suffix '& Co' because it merely indicates the trading, as opposed to the personal, status of the name. (NOTE: Both suffixes will attract the provisions of the Business Names Act 1985).

Authorised firms

12 Investment Business Certificates issued by the Association authorise the firm named on the certificate to carry on investment business in that name only. Accordingly, if a firm wishes to conduct investment business under another practice name, it must apply for a separate Investment Business Certificate.

Legal requirements

13 A practice name must comply with partnership and company law as appropriate, and with the Business Names Act 1985.

Overseas firms

14 Overseas firms are required to comply with any local laws as to practice names so far as overseas offices are concerned. Subject thereto, they may describe themselves in any manner conformable to the practice of the profession locally provided that the principles set out in paragraphs 2 and 3 above are observed.

New and changed names

15 Save where the name of a firm is based on the name of past or present members of the firm itself or of a firm with which it has merged or amalgamated, when a new firm is to be set up and when it is desired to change the name of an existing firm members are recommended, as a means of ensuring compliance with this guidance, to consult the Legal Department, as to the propriety of the proposed name. Firms which are authorised to conduct investment business by the Association should note that a new Investment Business Certificate is required in the event that there is a change of the firm's name.

Conflicts of interest

Conflict between member's and client's interest

1 A firm should always place its client's interests before its own. For this reason a firm should not accept or continue an engagement in which there is or is likely to be a significant conflict of interests between the firm and the client.

2 Any form of financial gain which accrues or is likely to accrue to the firm as a result of the engagement otherwise than in the form of fees or other reward from the client for its services, or commission, etc. properly earned and declared under the provisions of paragraph 3, will always amount to a significant conflict of interests for the purpose of paragraph 1 above. Whether any other form of interest is such as to amount to significant conflict will depend on all the circumstances of the case. The test is whether a reasonable observer, seized with all the facts, would consider the interest as likely to affect the judgement of the firm.

Commission

3 Where any commission, fee or reward is earned by the practice or anyone in it in return for the introduction of a client, or as a result of advice given to a client, the client should be informed, in writing, both of the fact that such commission, fee or reward will be received and, as soon as practicable, of its amount and terms. Where the commission, fee or reward results from advice given to the client, special care should be taken that the advice is in fact in the best interests of the client.

Conflict between interests of different clients

4 There is, on the face of it, nothing improper in a firm having two or more clients whose interests may be in conflict. In such a case however, the work of the firm should be so managed as to avoid the interests of one client adversely affecting those of another. Where the acceptance or continuance of an engagement would, even with safeguards, materially prejudice the interests of any client the appointment should not be accepted or continued.

5 Such prejudice might arise in a variety of ways, including the leakage of information from one client to another and the firm being forced into a position where it has to choose between the interests of different clients.

Managing conflict between clients' interests

6 All reasonable steps should be taken to ascertain whether any conflict of interests exists or is likely to arise in the future, both in regard to new engagements and to the changing circumstances of existing clients, and including any implications arising from the possession of confidential information. Relationships with clients and former clients need to be reviewed before accepting a new appointment and regularly thereafter. A relationship whieh ended over two years before is unlikely to constitute conflict. The nature of the engagement is relevant in this connection. (Members are referred to Rules of Professional Conduct no. 22 'Corporate finance advice including take-overs'.)

Disclosure

7 Wherever there is identified a material conflict of interests between clients or potential clients sufficient disclosure should be made to the clients concerned so that they may make an informed decision as to whether to engage the firm or continue their relationship with the firm.

Safeguards

8 Where a firm becomes aware of a possible conflict between the interests of two or more clients all reasonable steps should be taken to manage it and thereby avoid any adverse consequences. These steps may include some or all of the following safeguards:

(a) the use of different partners and teams for different engagements;

(b) standing instructions and all other steps necessary to prevent the leakage of confidential information between different teams and sections within the firm;

(c) regular review of the situation by a senior partner or compliance officer not personally involved with either client; and

(d) advising one or both clients to seek additional independent advice.

Sole practitioners and small firms

9 Any decision on the part of a sole practitioner should take account of the fact that the safeguards at (a) to (c) of the previous paragraph will not be available to him. Similar considerations apply to a small firm.

Disengagement

10 Wherever a firm is required by paragraph 1 or 3 above to disengage from an existing engagement it should do so as speedily as is compatible with the interests of the clients concerned.

The ethical responsibilities of members in business

Introduction

1 While the first duty of an employed member is towards his employer, such a member is also bound by the same Fundamental Principles and the same standards of behaviour and competence as apply to all other members of the Association. Indeed, it may be that this was one of the reasons why the member was employed.

2 The Introduction to the Rules of Professional Conduct and Section 'Confidentiality', are also of application to the member in business and should be read in conjunction with this Section.

3 All members, whether in business or not, are liable to disciplinary action under the bye-laws.

NOTE: References in this Section to an employed member include members, whether employed or not, who are engaged in work relevant to their qualification as a member other wise than in a practising office.

For observations on the legal position of the employed accountant see the remarks of Lord Denning MR in *Alfred Crompton Amusements* v. *Commissioners of Customs & Excise* (No. 2) (1972) 2 All ER. 353.

Independence

4 The concept of independence, which is central to the role of the practising accountant, has no direct relevance to the employed member, whose first duty is towards his employer. Even for the practising accountant independence is not an end in itself: it is merely a means of securing a more important end, namely an objective approach to work. The requirement for objectivity is of equal application to all members. Without the capacity of being fully independent of his employer it is all the more important that the employed member should strive constantly to maintain objectivity in every aspect of his work.

Objectivity

5 Objectivity is described in Fundamental Principle 2 as the state of mind which has regard to all considerations relevant to the task in hand but no other. It presupposes intellectual honesty. It follows that the interests of a member's employer should no more affect the objectivity of a member's judgement in a professional matter than his own interests.

Example

6 A crucial example concerns the preparation of financial statements and reports, whether designed for external exposure or not. Any report for which an employed member is responsible (whether it bears his signature or not) should be prepared with integrity and objectivity.

This means for example that while a report prepared by an employed member may properly present only one side of the case (for example his employer's) and may present that case to its best advantage, the report should be accurate, truthful and, within its scope, balanced.

It should not rely on ambiguities or half truths, but should, be objectively justifiable and should not be based on unreasonable assumptions. (See also Section 2.22, 'Corporate finance advice including take-overs.)

7 While an employed member must observe the terms of his employment, these cannot require him to be implicated in any dishonest transaction. If he is instructed or encouraged to engage in any enterprise which is unlawful he is entitled and required to decline. In practice, there may be many grey areas, for example as to whether an activity is indeed unlawful and how best to deal with the situation. (Advice on these matters is to be found in Section 2.2, 'Professional duty of confidence in relation to defaults or unlawful acts'. Though written for practising members, much of this guidance may be applied by analogy to the situation of the employed member.)

Financial and other involvement

8 An employed member should recognise the problems which may be created by financial involvements or personal relationships which, whether sanctioned by his contract of employment or not, could nevertheless by reason of their nature or degree threaten his objectivity.

Share dealings

9 In owning and dealing in shares in any organisation in which he is employed or holds office an employed member should take care to observe:

(a) relevant legislation,

(b) the requirements of the Stock Exchange, the Takeover Panel and similarly regulatory bodies as appropriate. Firms which are authorised by the Association to conduct investment business are also referred to Rule 11(4) of the Investment Business Rules 1988; and

(c) his own terms of service.

He should also be aware of the risks attendant on financial involvement referred to in the previous paragraph.

Receiving gifts

10 An employed member should be aware of the difficulties which may arise from the offer or the acceptance of any gift, favour or hospitality which may be intended to influence the recipient or which could be interpreted by a reasonable person in possession of the facts as likely to have that effect. Subject to this, gifts, favours and hospitality of modest value may be accepted to the extent that they may be permitted by the member's employer.

Professional and technical standards

11 Fundamental Principle 4 calls for a member to carry out his professional work with proper regard for the technical and professional standards expected of him as a member. However, an employed member who, in the performance of his professional work, may be subject to directions from his employers may be faced with a conflict of loyalties in seeking to apply this Fundamental Principle. The difficulty is of particular importance where the outcome of the work is to be published.

12 When a member has sole responsibility for the preparation and approval of information, including management information, which is to be made public or is to become available, on however restricted a basis, outside the organisation to which it refers he should ensure that such information complies with the standards referred to in Fundamental Principle 4 or, if it does not so comply, that the reasons for non-compliance are stated truthfully, unambiguously and fairly.

13 When his is not the sole responsibility, he should use his best endeavours to achieve compliance or, if the information does not comply with the standards referred to in Fundamental Principle 4, to ensure that the reasons for non-compliance are stated truthfully, unambiguously and fairly.

14 The standards referred to in Fundamental Principle 4 include Statements of Standard Accounting Practice, the City Code on Take-overs and Mergers, and the Rules and Regulations of the International Stock Exchange.

Status

15 While the considerations set out above apply to all employed members, the more senior the position occupied by the member the greater will be his opportunity to influence events, practices and attitudes and thus the more onerous will be his responsibilities.

Members' Advisory Service

16 An employed member faced with any ethical problem may call upon the Members' Advisory Service for confidential advice.

Section 3
Statements of Standard Accounting Practice (UK and Ireland)

Contents

Foreword to Accounting Standards

(Issued June 1993)

Introduction

1 This foreword explains the authority, scope and application of accounting standards issued or adopted by the Accounting Standards Board (the Board)*. The foreword also considers the procedure by which the Board issues accounting standards and their relationship to International Accounting Standards, issued by the International Accounting Standards Committee.

2 The Board at its meeting on 24 August 1990 agreed to adopt the 22 extant Statements of Standard Accounting Practice (SSAPs) issued by the Councils of the six major accountancy bodies following proposals developed by the Accounting Standards Committee (ASC)†. Adoption by the Board gave these SSAPs the status of accounting standards within Part VII of the Companies Act 1985,‡ (the Act) and within Part VIII of the Companies (Northern Ireland) Order 1986** (the Order). This status will apply until each SSAP is amended, rescinded or replaced by new accounting standards.

3 Accounting standards developed by the Board are designated Financial Reporting Standards (FRSs). Accounting standards developed by the ASC and adopted by the Board continue to be known as SSAPs.

4 FRSs are based on the Statement of Principles for Financial Reporting currently in issue, which addresses the concepts underlying the information presented in financial statements. The objective of this Statement of Principles is to provide a framework for the consistent and logical formulation of individual accounting standards. The framework also provides a basis on which others can exercise judgement in resolving accounting issues.

* The Accounting Standards Board is a Committee of The Accounting Standards Board Limited. The Accounting Standards Board Limited is prescribed as a standard setting body for the purposes of Section 256(1) of the Companies Act 1985 with effect from 20 August 1990 by the Accounting Standards (Prescribed Body) Regulations 1990 (S.I. 1990 No. 1667). The Accounting Standards Board Limited is prescribed as a standard setting body for Northern Ireland for the purposes of Article 264(1) of the Companies (Northern Ireland) Order 1986 with effect from 15 October 1990 by the Accounting Standards (Prescribed Body) Regulations (Northern Ireland) 1990 (S.R. 1990 No. 338).

† Prior to 1 August 1990 accounting standards in the United Kingdom and Republic of Ireland were issued by the Councils of the six major accountancy bodies following proposals developed by the ASC. Since 1 August 1990 the Board has taken over the role of issuing accounting standards applicable in the United Kingdom. The Institute of Chartered Accountants in Ireland issues accounting standards applicable in the Republic of Ireland.

‡ References to the Companies Act 1985 are to that Act as amended by, *inter alia*, the Companies Act 1989 and the Companies Act 1985 (Bank Accounts) Regulations 1991 (S.I. 1991 No. 2705).

** References to the Companies (Northern Ireland) Order 1986 (S.I. 1986 No. 1032 (N.I. 6)) are to that Order as amended by, *inter alia*, the Companies (Northern Ireland) Order 1990 (S.I. 1990 No. 593 (N.I. 5)) the Companies (No. 2) (Northern Ireland) Order 1990 (S.I. 1990 No. 1504 (N.I. 10)) and the Companies (1986 Order) (Bank Accounts) Regulations (Northern Ireland) Order (S.R. 1992 No. 258).

5 The Board may issue pronouncements other than FRSs, including the Urgent Issues Task Force 'Abstracts'. The Board will indicate the authority, scope and application of pronouncements other than FRSs as they are issued. UITF Abstracts are the subject of a separate foreword.

Aims of the Accounting Standards Board

6 The aims of the Board are set out in the document 'The Accounting Standards Board — Statement of Aims'.

Authority of accounting standards

7 FRSs issued and SSAPs adopted by the Board are 'accounting standards' for the purposes of the Act, which requires accounts, other than those prepared by small or medium-sized companies (as defined by the Act), to state whether they have been prepared in accordance with applicable accounting standards and to give particulars of any material departure from those standards and the reasons for it. References to accounting standards in the Act are contained in paragraph 36A of Schedule 4, paragraph 49 of Part I of Schedule 9 and paragraph 18B of Part I of Schedule 9A. The equivalent references in the Order are in paragraph 36A of Schedule 4, paragraph 49 of Part I of Schedule 9 and paragraph 18B of Part I of Schedule 9A.

8 Directors of companies incorporated under the Companies Acts are required by the Act to prepare accounts that give a true and fair view of the state of affairs of the company, and where applicable the group, at the end of the financial year and of the profit or loss of the company or the group for the financial year.

9 The Consultative Committee of Accountancy Bodies (CCAB) is committed to promoting and supporting compliance with accounting standards by its member bodies and by their members, whether as preparers or auditors of financial information.

10 The Councils of the CCAB bodies therefore expect their members who assume responsibilities in respect of financial statements to observe accounting standards. The Councils have agreed that:

(a) where this responsibility is evidenced by the association of members' names with such financial statements in the capacity of directors or other officers, other than auditors, the onus will be on them to ensure that the existence and purpose of accounting standards are fully understood by fellow directors and other officers. Members should also use their best endeavours to ensure that accounting standards are observed and that significant departures found to be necessary are adequately disclosed and explained in the financial statements.

(b) where members act as auditors or reporting accountants, they should be in a position to justify significant departures to the extent that their concurrence with the departures is stated or implied. They are not, however, required to refer in their report to departures with which they concur, provided that adequate disclosure has been made in the notes to the financial statements.

11 The CCAB bodies, through appropriate committees, may enquire into apparent failures by their members to observe accounting standards or to ensure adequate disclosure of significant departures.

12 The Board notes the continuing application of previously adopted SSAPs in the Republic of Ireland through their on-going promulgation by the Institute of Chartered

Accountants in Ireland (ICAI). It further notes ICAI's intention of maintaining close liaison with the Board on promulgating, with appropriate modifications for legal differences, FRSs for application in the Republic of Ireland. The objective of the Board and ICAI is a regime of accounting standards common to both the United Kingdom and the Republic of Ireland.

Scope and application of accounting standards

13 Accounting standards are applicable to financial statements of a reporting entity that are intended to give a true and fair view of its state of affairs at the balance sheet date and of its profit or loss (or income and expenditure) for the financial period ending on that date. Accounting standards need not be applied to immaterial items.

14 Accounting standards should be applied to United Kingdom and Republic of Ireland group financial statements (including any amounts relating to overseas entities that are included in those financial statements). Accounting standards are not intended to apply to financial statements of overseas entities prepared for local purposes.

15 Where accounting standards prescribe information to be contained in financial statements, such requirements do not override exemptions from disclosure given by law to, and utilised by, certain types of entity.

Compliance with accounting standards

16 Accounting standards are authoritative statements of how particular types of transaction and other events should be reflected in financial statements and accordingly compliance with accounting standards will normally be necessary for financial statements to give a true and fair view.

17 In applying accounting standards it is important to be guided by the spirit and reasoning behind them. The spirit and reasoning are set out in the individual FRSs and are based on the Board's Statement of Principles for Financial Reporting.

18 The requirement to give a true and fair view may in special circumstances require a departure from accounting standards. However, because accounting standards are formulated with the objective of ensuring that the information resulting from their application faithfully represents the underlying commercial activity, the Board envisages that only in exceptional circumstances will departure from the requirements of an accounting standard be necessary in order for financial statements to give a true and fair view.

19 If in exceptional circumstances compliance with the requirements of an accounting standard is inconsistent with the requirement to give a true and fair view, the requirements of the accounting standard should be departed from to the extent necessary to give a true and fair view. In such cases informed and unbiased judgement should be used to devise an appropriate alternative treatment, which should be consistent with the economic and commercial characteristics of the circumstances concerned. Particulars of any material departure from an accounting standard, the reasons for it and its financial effects should be disclosed in the financial statements. The disclosure made should be equivalent to that given in respect of departures from specific accounting provisions of companies legislation.

20 The Financial Reporting Review Panel (the Review Panel) and the Department of Trade and Industry have procedures for receiving and investigating complaints regarding the annual accounts of companies in respect of apparent departures from the accounting requirements of the Act, including the requirement to give a true and fair view.* The Review Panel will be concerned with material departures from accounting standards, where as a result the accounts in question do not give a true and fair view, but it will also cover other departures from the accounting provisions of the Act. The Review Panel is empowered by regulations made under the Act to apply to the court for a declaration or declarator that the annual accounts of a company do not comply with the requirements of the Act and an order requiring the directors of the company to prepare revised accounts.† The Department of Trade and Industry has similar powers.

The public sector

21 The prescription of accounting requirements for the public sector in the United Kingdom is a matter for the Government. Where public sector bodies prepare annual reports and accounts on commercial lines, the Government's requirements may or may not refer specifically either to accounting standards or to the need for the financial statements concerned to give a true and fair view. However, it can be expected that the Government's requirements in such cases will normally accord with the principles underlying the Board's pronouncements, except where in the particular circumstances of the public sector bodies concerned the Government considers these principles to be inappropriate or considers others to be more appropriate.

22 In the Republic of Ireland accounting standards will normally be applicable to reporting entities in the public sector as such entities are either established under companies legislation or are established under special legislation which requires them to produce financial statements which give a true and fair view.

The issue of a Financial Reporting Standard

23 Topics that become the subject of FRSs are identified by the Board either from its own research or from external sources, including submissions from interested parties.

24 When a topic is identified by the Board as requiring the issue of an FRS the Board commissions its staff to undertake a programme of research and consultation. This programme involves consideration of and consultation on the relevant conceptual issues, existing pronouncements and practice in the United Kingdom, the Republic of Ireland and overseas and the economic, legal and practical implications of the introduction of particular accounting requirements.

25 When the issues have been identified and debated by the Board a discussion draft is normally produced and circulated to parties who have registered their interest with the Board. When the issues require a more discursive treatment a discussion paper may be published instead. The purpose of either of these documents is to form a basis for discussion with parties particularly affected by, or having knowledge of, the issues raised in the proposals. An exposure draft of an accounting standard (a Financial Reporting Exposure Draft or FRED) is then published to allow an opportunity for all interested parties to comment on the proposals and for the Board to gauge the appropriateness and level of acceptance of those proposals.

* Similar provisions exist for receiving and investigating complaints regarding the annual accounts of companies in respect of apparent departure from the accounting requirements of the Order.

† The Review Panel does not operate in the Republic of Ireland.

26 The exposure draft is refined in the light of feedback resulting from the period of public exposure. There may follow another period of public or selective exposure prior to the issue of an FRS. Although the Board weighs carefully the views of interested parties, the ultimate content of an FRS must be determined by the Board's own judgement based on research, public consultation and careful deliberation about the benefits and costs of providing the resulting information.

Applicability of an accounting standard to transactions entered into before the standard was issued

27 When a new accounting standard is issued the question arises whether its provisions should be applied to transactions which took place prior to the promulgation of the standard. The general policy of the Board is that the provisions of accounting standards should be applied to all material transactions irrespective of the date at which they are entered into. This is because exemption of certain transactions leads to similar transactions being accounted for differently in the same set of accounts, and can also hinder the comparison of the accounts of one entity with another.

28 In a few instances, application of the provisions of accounting standards to past transactions will entail a considerable amount of work and may result in information which is difficult for the user of accounts to interpret. In such a case, in drafting the standard, the Board will consider incorporating an exclusion for transactions which took place prior to the promulgation of the standard.

29 In some instances, a new standard may have unforeseen consequences where financial statements are used to monitor compliance with contracts and agreements. The most widespread example is the covenants contained in banking and loan agreements, which may impose limits on measures such as net worth or gearing as shown in the borrower's financial statements.

30 The Board considers that the developing nature of accounting requirements is a long-established fact that would be known to the parties when they entered into the agreement. It is up to the parties to determine whether the agreement should be insulated from the effects of a future accounting standard or, if not, the manner in which it might be renegotiated to reflect changes in reporting rather than changes in the underlying financial position.* The Board, therefore, has no general policy of exempting transactions occurring before a specific date from the requirements of new accounting standards.

Early adoption of Financial Reporting Exposure Drafts †

31 An exposure draft is issued for comment and is subject to revision. Until it is converted into an accounting standard the requirements of any existing accounting standards that would be affected by proposals in the exposure draft remain in force.

32 Some companies or other reporting entities may wish to provide additional information reflecting proposals in an exposure draft. In the Board's view there are two ways that this can be achieved:

(a) insofar as the information does not conflict with existing accounting standards, it could be incorporated in the financial statements. It should be remembered,

* The British Bankers' Association has indicated that it does not believe that problems arising from breaches in covenants consequent upon changes in accounting policies will occur frequently in practice.

† Similar considerations apply to discussion documents issued by the Board.

however, that the proposals may change before forming part of an accounting standard and the consequences of a change to the proposals should be considered.

(b) the information could be provided in supplementary form.

Reviews of accounting standards

33 Accounting standards are issued against the background of a business environment that evolves over time. The Board is, therefore, receptive to comments on accounting standards, recognising that, for some, a substantial period may be needed before their effectiveness can be judged, while in other cases there may be special reasons why an earlier review is necessary. However, the Board believes that it will normally be appropriate to allow new accounting standards a period in which to become established before commencing a process of formal post-issue review.

Accounting standards and the legal framework

34 In its debates on any accounting topic the Board initially develops its views by considering how its principles of accounting apply to the possible accounting options available for that topic. However, in deciding what is the most appropriate treatment the Board must also consider the environment in which its standards are to be applied. The legislation with which reporting entities must comply forms an important part of that environment. Accordingly, FRSs are drafted in the context of current United Kingdom and Republic of Ireland legislation and European Community Directives with the aim of ensuring consistency between accounting standards and the law.

35 The status of accounting standards under United Kingdom legislation is addressed in the Opinion by Miss Mary Arden QC* 'The true and fair requirement', which is published as an appendix to this Foreword.

International Accounting Standards

36 FRSs are formulated with due regard to international developments. The Board supports the International Accounting Standards Committee in its aim to harmonise international financial reporting. As part of this support an FRS contains a section explaining how it relates to the International Accounting Standard (IAS) dealing with the same topic. In most cases, compliance with an FRS automatically ensures compliance with the relevant IAS. Where the requirements of an accounting standard and an IAS differ, the accounting standard should be followed by entities reporting within the area of application of the Board's accounting standards.

Withdrawal of Explanatory Foreword to Statements of Standard Accounting Practice

37 The 'Explanatory Foreword' to SSAPs, issued by the ASC in May 1975 and revised in May 1986, is superseded by this Foreword and is accordingly withdrawn.

* Now The Honourable Mrs Justice Arden.

Appendix

Opinion

1 This Opinion is concerned with the effect of recent changes in the law on the relationship between accounting standards and the requirement in Sections 226 and 227 of the Companies Act 1985 (as amended) that accounts drawn up in accordance with the Companies Act 1985 give a true and fair view of the state of affairs of the company, and where applicable the group, at the end of the financial year in question and of the profit or loss of the company or group for that financial year. (I shall call this requirement "the true and fair requirement"). As is well known, the true and fair requirement is overriding. Thus both sections provide that where in special circumstances compliance with the requirements of the Act as to the matters to be included in the accounts would be inconsistent with the true and fair requirement there must be a departure from those requirements to the extent necessary to give a true and fair view (Sections 226(5) and 227(6)). The meaning of the true and fair requirement, as it appeared in earlier legislation, was discussed in detail in the Joint opinions which I wrote in 1983 and 1984 with Leonard Hoffmann Q.C. (now the Right Hon. Lord Justice Hoffmann).

2 As stated in those Opinions, the question whether accounts satisfy the true and fair requirement is a question of law for the Court. However, while the true and fair view which the law requires to be given is not qualified in any way, the task of interpreting the true and fair requirement cannot be performed by the Court without evidence as to the practices and views of accountants. The more authoritative those practices and views, the more ready the Court will be to follow them. Those practices and views do not of course stand still. They respond to such matters as advances in accounting and changes in the economic climate and business practice. The law will not prevent the proper development of the practices and views of accountants but rather, through the process of interpretation, will reflect such development.

3 Up to August 1990 the responsibility for developing accounting standards was discharged by the Accounting Standards Committee ("the ASC"). Since August 1990 that responsibility has been discharged by the Accounting Standards Board ("the Board"). The Foreword to Accounting Standards approved by the Board describes in particular the circumstances in which accounts are expected to comply with accounting standards. For this purpose the key paragraph is paragraph 16, which provides

> "Accounting standards are authoritative statements of how particular types of transaction and other events should be reflected in financial statements and accordingly compliance with accounting standards will normally be necessary for financial statements to give a true and fair view."

The Foreword also describes the extensive process of investigation and consultation which precedes the issue of a standard and explains that the major accountancy bodies expect their members to observe accounting standards and may enquire into apparent failures by their members to observe standards or ensure adequate disclosure of departures from them.

4 What is the role of an accounting standard? The initial purpose is to identify proper accounting practice for the benefit of preparers and auditors of accounts. However, because accounts commonly comply with accounting standards, the effect of the issue of standards has also been to create a common understanding between users and preparers of accounts as to how particular items should be treated in accounts and accordingly an expectation that save where good reason exists accounts will comply with applicable accounting standards.

5 The Companies Act 1989 now gives statutory recognition to the existence of accounting standards and by implication to their beneficial role in financial reporting. This recognition is achieved principally through the insertion of a new section (Section 256) into the Companies Act 1985 and of a new disclosure requirement into Schedule 4 to that Act. Section 256 provides:

> "256. (I) In this Part "accounting standards" means statements of standard accounting practice issued by such body or bodies as may be prescribed by regulations.
>
> (2) References in this Part to accounting standards applicable to a company's annual accounts are to such standards as are, in accordance with their terms, relevant to the company's circumstances and to the accounts.
>
> (3) The Secretary of State may make grants to or for the purposes of bodies concerned with —
>
> (a) issuing accounting standards,
>
> (b) overseeing and directing the issuing of such standards, or
>
> (c) investigating departures from such standards or from the accounting requirements of this Act and taking steps to secure compliance with them.
>
> (4) Regulations under this section may contain such transitional and other supplementary and incidental provisions as appear to the Secretary of State to be appropriate."

In addition the notes to financial statements prepared under Schedule 4 must now comply with the following new requirement*:

> "36A. It shall be stated whether the accounts have been prepared in accordance with applicable accounting standards and particulars of any material departure from those standards and the reasons for it shall be given."

6 Another significant change brought about by the 1989 Act is the introduction of a procedure whereby the Secretary of State or a person authorised by him may ask the Court to determine whether annual accounts comply with *inter alia* the true and fair requirement (Section 245B of the Companies Act 1985). The Financial Reporting Review Panel ("the Review Panel") has been authorised by the Secretary of State for this purpose. By agreement with the Department of Trade and Industry the ambit of the Review Panel is normally public and large private companies, with the Department exercising its powers in other cases.

7 The changes brought about by the Companies Act 1989 will in my view affect the way in which the Court approaches the question whether compliance with an accounting standard is necessary to satisfy the true and fair view requirement. The Court will infer from Section 256 that statutory policy favours both the issue of accounting standards (by

* This requirement also applies to group accounts drawn up under Schedule 4A. In addition the accounts of banking and insurance companies and groups drawn up under Schedules 9 and 9A must make the same disclosure. There is an exemption for small and medium-sized companies and for certain small and medium-sized groups.

a body prescribed by regulation) and compliance with them: indeed Section 256(3)(C) additionally contemplates the investigation of departures from them and confers power to provide public funding for such purpose. The Court will also in my view infer from paragraph 36A of Schedule 4 that (since the requirement is to disclose particulars of non-compliance rather than of compliance) accounts which meet the true and fair requirement will in general follow rather than depart from standards and that departure is sufficiently abnormal to require to be justified. These factors increase the likelihood, to which the earlier Joint Opinions referred, that the Courts will hold that in general compliance with accounting standards is necessary to meet the true and fair requirement.

8 The status of accounting standards in legal proceedings has also in my view been enhanced by the changes in the standard-setting process since 1989. Prior to the Companies Act 1989 accounting standards were developed by the ASC, which was a committee established by the six professional accountancy bodies who form the Consultative Committee of Accountancy Bodies ("the CCAB") and funded by them. The standard-setting process was reviewed by a committee established by the CCAB under the chairmanship of Sir Ron Dearing CB. The report of that Committee (the Dearing Report), which was published in 1988 and is entitled The Making of Accounting Standards, contained a number of recommendations, including recommendations leading to what are now paragraph 36A and Section 245B and the further recommendation that the standard-setting body should be funded on a wider basis. As a result of the implementation of these recommendations the standard-setting body no longer represents simply the views of the accountancy profession. Its members are appointed by a committee drawn from the Council of the Financial Reporting Council Limited ("the FRC"). The Council includes representatives of the Government, representatives of the business and financial community and members of the accountancy profession. Moreover, the Board is now funded, via the FRC, jointly by the Government, the financial community and the accountancy profession.

9 The statements referred to in Section 256 are of *standard* accounting practice. Parliament has thus recognised the desirability of standardisation in the accountancy field. The discretion to determine the measure of standardisation is one of the matters left to the Board. By definition, standardisation may restrict the availability of particular accounting treatments. Moreover the Act does not require that the practices required by a standard should necessarily be those prevailing or generally accepted at the time.

10 As explained in the earlier Joint Opinions in relation to statements of standard accounting practice, the immediate effect of the issue of an accounting standard is to create a likelihood that the court will hold that compliance with that standard is necessary to meet the true and fair requirement. That likelihood is strengthened by the degree to which a standard is subsequently accepted in practice. Thus if a particular standard is generally followed, the court is very likely to find that accounts must comply with it in order to show a true and fair view. The converse of that proposition, that non-acceptance of a standard in practice would almost inevitably lead a court to the conclusion that compliance with it was not necessary to meet the true and fair requirement, is not however the case. Whenever a standard is issued by the Board, then, irrespective of the lack in some quarters of support for it, the court would be bound to give special weight to the opinion of the Board in view of its status as the standard-setting body, the process of investigation, discussion and consultation that it will have undertaken before adopting the standard and the evolving nature of accounting standards.

11 The fact that paragraph 36A envisages the possibility of a departure from an "applicable accounting standard" (in essence, any relevant standard: see Section 256(2), above) does not mean that the Companies Act permits a departure in any case where the disclosure is given. The departure must have been appropriate in the particular case. If the Court is satisfied that compliance with a standard is necessary to show a true and fair view in that case, a departure will result in a breach of the true and fair requirement even if the paragraph 36A disclosure is given.

12 Experience shows that from time to time and for varying reasons deficiencies in accounting standards appear. Following a recommendation in the Dearing Report, the Board has established a sub-committee called the Urgent Issues Task Force ("the UITF") to resolve such issues on an urgent basis in appropriate cases. The members of the UITF include leading members of the accountancy profession and of the business community. The agenda of the UITF is published in advance to allow for public debate. The UITF's consensus pronouncements (contained in abstracts) represent the considered views of a large majority of its members. When the UITF reaches its view, it is considered by the Board for compliance with the law and accounting standards and with the Board's future plans. If an abstract meets these criteria the Board expects to adopt it without further consideration. It will then be published by the Board. The expectation of the CCAB, the Board and the profession is that abstracts of the UITF will be observed. This expectation has been borne out in practice. Accordingly in my view, the Court is likely to treat UITF abstracts as of considerable standing even though they are not envisaged by the Companies Acts. This will lead to a readiness on the part of the Court to accept that compliance with abstracts of the UITF is also necessary to meet the true and fair requirement.

13 The Joint Opinions were particularly concerned with the effect of standards on the concept of true and fair. The approach to standards taken in the Joint Opinions is consistent with the approach of the Court in *Lloyd Cheyham* v. *Littlejohn* [1987] BCLC 303 at 313. In that case Woolf J. (as he then was) held that standards of the ASC were "very strong evidence as to what is the proper standard which should be adopted".

14 As regards the concept of true and fair, I would emphasise the point made in the Joint Opinions that the true and fair view is a dynamic concept. Thus what is required to show a true and fair view is subject to continuous rebirth and in determining whether the true and fair requirement is satisfied the Court will not in my view seek to find synonyms for the words "true" and "fair" but will seek to apply the concepts which those words imply.

15 It is nearly a decade since the Joint Opinions were written. Experience and legislative history since then have both illustrated the subtlety and evolving nature of the relationship between law and accounting practice. Accounting standards are now assured as an authoritative source of the latter. In consequence it is now the norm for accounts to comply with accounting standards. I would add this. Just as a custom which is upheld by the courts may properly be regarded as a source of law, so too, in my view, does an accounting standard which the court holds must be complied with to meet the true and fair requirement become, in cases where it is applicable, a source of law in itself in the widest sense of that term.

Mary Arden
Erskine Chambers, Lincoln's Inn, 21st April 1993

Operating and Financial Review

(Issued July 1993)

Introduction

Many listed companies' annual reports already include detailed and penetrating reviews of operations and financing. This Statement developed from the ASB's earlier Discussion Paper of April 1992, is voluntary and not an accounting standard but aims to build on the foundations of existing best practice by providing a framework within which directors can discuss the main factors underlying the company's financial performance and position.

An Operating and Financial Review (OFR) would include a discussion and interpretation of the business, the main factors, features as well as uncertainties, that underlie it and the structure of its financing. Although it is a report on the year under review, not a forecast of future results, it should nevertheless draw out those aspects of the year under review that are relevant to an assessment of future prospects. It would therefore give users of the annual report a more consistent foundation on which to make investment decisions regarding the company.

Confidentiality

Directors will naturally be concerned to ensure that the benefits to the users of the annual report of particular disclosures, and, in competitive capital markets, the consequent benefit to the company, outweigh the potential commercial damage to the business from the disclosure of sensitive information to competitors. Accordingly, the emphasis in this Statement is on discussion of matters of significance to the business as a whole, and it is expected that in most cases directors will be able to provide a reasonably comprehensive and informative OFR whilst avoiding disclosures of a confidential or sensitive nature.

Scope

This Statement has been drafted with listed companies in mind, but it is also applicable to other large corporations where there is a legitimate public interest in their financial statements. The detailed guidance is particularly relevant to major corporations who are better placed to lead the way in developing this form of communication with shareholders. Other listed companies, especially smaller ones or those operating in specialised or highly competitive industries, are urged to follow the spirit of the Statement and use their best endeavours to adapt the detailed guidance to their own circumstances.

The Operating and Financial Review

1 The Operating and Financial Review (OFR) is a framework for the directors to discuss and analyse the business's performance and the factors underlying its results and financial position in order to assist users to assess for themselves the future potential of the business.

2 Directors are encouraged to develop the presentation of their OFR in a way that best complements the format of their annual report as a whole. The proposals are not intended to result in the duplication of information already provided in the annual report. It is for each company's directors to decide whether to deal with the matters addressed in this Statement in a separate, stand-alone section, or by incorporating them within the structure of one or more other sections such as a chief executive's report. If the latter course is adopted, care should be taken to ensure that the combination of OFR information with other material does not obscure its impact or impair the balance and objectivity envisaged by this Statement.

Essential features of an OFR

3 The essential features of an OFR are as follows:

- It should be written in a clear style and as succinctly as possible, to be readily understandable by the general reader of annual reports, and should include only matters that are likely to be significant to investors;
- It should be balanced and objective, dealing even-handedly with both good and bad aspects;
- It should refer to comments made in previous statements where these have not been borne out by events;
- It should contain analytical discussion rather than merely numerical analysis;
- It should follow a 'top-down' structure discussing individual aspects of the business in the context of a discussion of the business as a whole;
- It should explain the reason for, and effect of, any changes in accounting policies;
- It should make it clear how any ratios or other numerical information given relate to the financial statements;
- It should include discussion of:
  - — trends and factors underlying the business that have affected the results but are not expected to continue in the future; and
  - — known events, trends and uncertainties that are expected to have an impact on the business in the future.

4 In discussing trends and uncertainties, the OFR should explain their significance to the business; but it is not intended that the OFR should necessarily include a forecast of the outcome of such uncertainties; nor is it suggested that the OFR should contain anything of the nature of a profit forecast.

5 In some cases, the directors may conclude that a proper discussion of some aspect of the business would require disclosure of confidential or commercially sensitive information, where they consider the potential damage to the company to be greater than the benefits of disclosure. Where the directors decide not to disclose such information, the OFR should ensure that the user is not misled by a discussion that is no longer complete and balanced.

Detailed guidance

6 The following sections indicate how the general principles set out above can be developed, covering two main areas, the operating review and the financial review. In applying this guidance, directors should consider what matters are of significance in the circumstances of their business.

7 The detailed guidance should not be regarded as a comprehensive list of all matters that might be relevant, nor are all items listed relevant to all businesses. The OFR should focus on those matters that are of greatest significance to that business.

Operating review

8 The principal aim of the operating review is to enable the user to understand the dynamics of the various lines of business undertaken — that is, the main influences on the overall results, and how these interrelate. Thus the OFR needs to identify and explain the main factors that underlie the business, and in particular those which either have varied in the past or are expected to change in the future.

Operating results for the period

9 The OFR should discuss the significant features of operating performance for the period covered by the financial statements, covering all aspects of the profit and loss account to the level of profit on ordinary activities before taxation, and focusing on the overall business and on those segments or other divisions that are relevant to an understanding of the performance as a whole. This should cover changes in the industry or the environment in which the business operates, developments within the business, and their effect on the results. Examples are:

- Changes in market conditions;
- New products and services introduced or announced;
- Changes in market share or position;
- Changes in turnover and margins;
- Changes in exchange rates and inflation rates;
- New activities, discontinued activities and other acquisitions and disposals.

10 In the case of material acquisitions, the discussion should comment on the extent to which the expectations at the time of acquisition have been realised. Where a seasonal business has been acquired in the period under review, and the results of the acquisition consolidated are not indicative of those for a full year, this should be indicated.

11 The discussion should cover any other special factors that have affected the results for the period under review; this includes influences whose effect cannot be quantified, as well as specific 'exceptional items'.

Dynamics of the business

12 The OFR should also discuss the main factors and influences that may have a major effect on future results, whether or not they were significant in the period under review. This would include a discussion identifying the principal risks and uncertainties in the main lines of business, together with a commentary on the approach to managing these risks and, in qualitative terms, the nature of the potential impact on results. Examples of matters that may be relevant, depending on the nature of the business, are:

- Scarcity of raw materials;
- Skill shortages and expertise of uncertain supply;
- Patents, licences and franchises;
- Dependence on major suppliers or customers;
- Product liability;
- Health and safety;
- Environmental protection costs and potential environmental liabilities;
- Self insurance;

- Exchange rate fluctuations;
- Rates of inflation differing between costs and revenues, or between different markets.

Although some items of this nature will be referred to in the contingent liabilities note within the financial statements, to which reference may be made in the OFR, the discussion should cover a wider range of risks and uncertainties relating to the business.

Investment for the future

13 Users of annual reports are interested in the extent to which the directors have sought to maintain and enhance future income or profits. The OFR should therefore discuss the business's main activities in this area. This would include activities and expenditure of the period under review which are intended wholly or partly to enhance future profitability and which can be varied, at the discretion of management, over a relatively wide range without significantly affecting current trading.

14 Capital expenditure is a particularly important element, because of both the amounts involved and the long lead time in implementing projects. The OFR should discuss the current level of capital expenditure together with planned future expenditure (both committed, and authorised but not committed). This discussion should indicate the overall level of expenditure, the major business segments and geographical areas accounting for material elements of the total, and the major projects involved.

15 Information should also be given on the likely benefits expected from capital expenditure. This should cover both those benefits arising in the period under review as a result of previous expenditure, and the future benefits expected.

16 In addition to capital expenditure, many other activities and expenditure can be regarded, to a greater or lesser extent, as a form of investing in the future. By their very nature, the definition of such items will vary from one business to another, and particularly from one industry to another. Furthermore, it is often difficult to split such expenditure between that benefiting the current accounting period and that benefiting future periods; nor is the level of activity always measured meaningfully by the expenditure involved. Thus the absolute level of expenditure is less relevant to the user than the impact on current reported profitability of changes in the levels of such activities and expenditure, the potential effect on future earnings of these changes, and management policies in these areas.

17 Examples of such activities and expenditure for the enhancement of future profits include:

- Marketing and advertising campaigns;
- Training programmes;
- Refurbishment and maintenance programmes;
- Pure and applied research which may lead to potential new products and services;
- Development of new products and services;
- Technical support to customers.

18 The OFR should discuss the nature of the business's activities in these areas, with particular emphasis on changes in the level of activity and management policy, and should also refer to the benefits expected from such activities.

Profit for the financial year, total recognised gains and losses and shareholders' perspective

19 The OFR should discuss the overall return attributable to shareholders, in terms of dividends and increases in shareholders' funds, commenting on the contributions from the operating performance of the various business units and on other items reported as part of total recognised gains and losses.

20 This discussion should comment on the significant gains and losses that were previously simply accounted for as reserve movements and are now given prominence in the statement of total recognised gains and losses. For many businesses, especially those that are wholly or partly investment businesses, unrealised gains and losses that are recognised in the statement of total gains and losses form an essential component of the overall performance for the year, and should be discussed as such.

Profit for the financial year, dividends and earnings per share

21 The OFR should include a commentary on the comparison between profit for the financial year and dividends, both in total and in per share terms, indicating the directors' overall dividend policy. Other measures of earnings per share which, as permitted by FRS 3, the directors have shown in the profit and loss account — for example, as providing a more useful indication of future trends — should also be discussed.

Accounting policies

22 In applying accounting policies, it is sometimes necessary for directors to make subjective judgements and relatively arbitrary allocations which may have very significant effects in the reported results. Many of these are a consequence of the need to report within the arbitrary timescale of a financial year the results of transactions whose life extends for a considerable period beyond the financial year. Whilst to refer to all subjective areas would be confusing, the OFR should indicate and explain any subjective judgements to which the financial statements are particularly sensitive.

Financial review

23 The principal aim of this section of the OFR is to explain to the user of the annual report the capital structure of the business, its treasury policy and the dynamics of its financial position — its sources of liquidity and their application, including the implications of the financing requirements arising from its capital expenditure plans.

24 The discussion should concentrate on matters of significance to the position of the business as a whole. It should be a narrative commentary, supported by figures where these assist understanding of the policies and their effect in practice. The following paragraphs indicate specific matters that should be addressed where these are important to an understanding of the business.

Capital structure and treasury policy

25 The OFR should contain a discussion of the capital structure of the business, in terms of maturity profile of debt, type of capital instruments used, currency, and interest rate structure. This should include comments on relevant ratios such as interest cover and debt/equity ratios.

26 The discussion should state the capital funding and treasury policies and objectives. These will cover the management of interest rate risk, the maturity profile of borrowings, and the management of exchange rate risk. The OFR should also discuss the implementation of these policies in the period under review in terms of:

- The manner in which treasury activities are controlled;
- The currencies in which borrowings are made and in which cash and cash equivalents are held;
- The extent to which borrowings are at fixed interest rates;
- The use of financial instruments for hedging purposes;
- The extent to which foreign currency net investments are hedged by currency borrowings and other hedging instruments.

27 The purpose and effect of major financing transactions undertaken up to the date of approval of the financial statements should be explained.

28 The effect of interest costs on profits and the potential impact of interest rate changes should be discussed.

Taxation

29 Where the overall tax charge is significantly different from a 'standard' tax charge (i.e. the normal UK tax rate applied to the profit before taxation), the main components of the reconciliation between the actual and 'standard' tax charges should be discussed.

Funds from operating activities and other sources of cash

30 The cash generated from operations and other cash inflows during the period under review should be discussed, commenting on any special factors that influenced these.

31 Although segmental analysis of profit may be indicative of the cash flow generated by each segment, this will not always be so — for example, because of fluctuations in capital expenditure. Where segmental cashflows are significantly out of line with segmental profits, this should be indicated and explained.

Current liquidity

32 The business's liquidity at the end of the period under review should be discussed. This should include comment on the level of borrowings at the end of the period under review, the seasonality of borrowing requirements, indicated by the peak level of borrowings during that period, and the maturity profile of both borrowings and committed borrowing facilities.

33 Reference should be made to the funding requirements for capital expenditure commitments and authorisations.

34 The discussion should refer to any restrictions on the ability to transfer funds from one part of the group to meet the obligations of another part of the group where these represent, or might foreseeably come to represent, a significant restraint on the group. Such constraints would include exchange controls and taxation consequences of transfers.

35 Where the business has entered into covenants with lenders which could have the effect of restricting the use of credit facilities, and negotiations with the lenders on the operation of these covenants are taking place or are expected to take place, this fact should be indicated in the OFR. Where a breach of a covenant has occurred or is expected to occur, the OFR should give details of the measures taken or proposed to remedy the situation.

Going concern

36 The Cadbury Report* Code of Best Practice proposed that directors of listed companies should state in the annual report their opinion that the company is a going concern, and the Report recommended that the accountancy bodies, together with representatives of listed companies, should develop guidance on the form such confirmation should take. Subject to what such guidance says when available, the going concern confirmation may appropriately be made as part of the OFR discussion of financial position.

Balance sheet value

37 The OFR could also give a commentary on strengths and resources of the business whose value is not reflected in the balance sheet (or only partially shown in the balance sheet). Such items could include brands and similar intangible items. Where considered appropriate, the value of such items, and increases or decreases in their value, could be discussed. It is not intended that an overall valuation of the business be given, nor, in the case of listed companies, for net asset value to be reconciled to market capitalisation.

Statement of compliance

38 As this is a statement of voluntary best practice, directors are not expected to include in the annual report any formal confirmation that they have complied with the principles set out in this Statement, although the inclusion of some comment on the extent to which the Statement has been followed may be helpful to the user. Where it is implied, through the use of the words 'operating and financial review' or otherwise, that the directors have endeavoured to follow these principles, they should signal any fundamental departure from them.

*Report of the Committee on the Financial Aspects of Corporate Governance, December 1992.

Accounting for associated companies

(Issued January 1971; amended August 1974; revised April 1982)

The provisions of this statement of standard accounting practice should be read in conjunction with the explanatory foreword to accounting standards *and need not be applied to immaterial items. The provisions apply to financial statements prepared under the historical cost convention and to financial statements prepared under the current cost convention.*

Part 1 — Explanatory note

1 Statement of Standard Accounting Practice 1 'Accounting for the results of associated companies' (SSAP 1) was issued in January 1971 to introduce a standard accounting treatment for investments in companies, the policies of which, although they are not subsidiaries of the investing company, are subject to significant influence by the investing company.

2 It is generally accepted accounting practice for a company not to take credit in its own (i.e., non-consolidated) profit and loss account and balance sheet for its share of the profits of other companies which have not been declared as dividends. The view is taken that the inclusion of undistributed profits would ignore the separate legal status of the entities concerned and, as regards the investing company, be contrary to the practice of not taking credit for investment income until it is received or receivable.

3 However, where a company conducts an important part of its business through the medium of other companies, the mere disclosure of dividend income (or mere inclusion of dividend income alone) from these companies is unlikely to be sufficient to give adequate information regarding the sources of their income and the manner in which their funds are being employed.

4 At one time such operations were usually carried out through the medium of subsidiary companies. It was for this reason that companies legislation required the preparation of group accounts, normally in the form of consolidated accounts. At the time of the original SSAP there had been two important developments. One was the growing practice of companies to conduct parts of their business through other companies (frequently consortium or joint venture companies) in which they had a substantial but not a controlling interest. The other was the importance which investors had come to attach to earnings per share and the price/earnings ratio. To ensure that the investing company's financial statements as a whole gave adequate information and provided a total of earnings from which the most useful ratios could be calculated, it was considered necessary that the coverage of consolidated financial statements should be extended to include (within the framework of the existing law) the share of earnings or losses of companies which were defined as associated companies.

5 This approach recognised a difference in principle between the nature of investments in associated companies (as defined in SSAP 1) and other forms of trade investment. The essence of the distinction was that an investing company actively participates in the commercial and policy decisions of its associated companies; it thus has a measure of direct responsibility for the return on its investment, and should account for its stewardship accordingly. However, it will not normally seek to exert direct management influence over the operating policy of other companies in which it invests and should continue to deal with them in accordance with traditional accounting methods.

6 The broad concept underlying the accounting treatment of the results of associated companies was the adoption in modified form of the consolidation procedures used for subsidiary companies. It followed from this that the investing company's share of associated companies' profits and losses would be reflected in its consolidated profit and loss account, and its share of their post-acquisition retained profits or accumulated deficits would be reflected in its consolidated balance sheet, though not in its own balance sheet as a legal entity. This is generally referred to as the equity method of accounting.

7 As part of its normal programme of reviewing standards the Accounting Standards Committee (ASC) has reconsidered the principles contained in the first edition of SSAP 1.

8 This SSAP continues the basic principles and requirements of the original SSAP. However, as part of the review ASC has incorporated some changes both in the definition of an associated company and in the presentation of the information involved. The presentation requires separate disclosure of the goodwill component.

9 This SSAP is intended to apply to companies incorporated under the Companies Acts. The principles laid down in it are, nevertheless, applicable to financial statements of any entity, whether incorporated or not, which invests in another entity or entities.

10 In some cases, partnerships or non-corporate joint ventures can have features which justify accounting for a proportionate share of individual assets and liabilities as well as profits or losses.

Part 2 — Definition of terms

11 A *company* includes any enterprise which comes within the scope of statements of standard accounting practice. In particular, references to investments in companies include not only investments in corporate enterprises but can include investments in non-corporate joint ventures and consortia.

12 A *group* comprises a holding company and its subsidiaries.

13 An *associated company* is a company not being a subsidiary of the investing group or company in which:

(a) the interest of the investing group or company is effectively that of a partner in a joint venture or consortium and the investing group or company is in a position to exercise a significant influence over the company in which the investment is made; or

(b) the interest of the investing group or company is for the long term and is substantial and, having regard to the disposition of the other shareholdings, the investing group or company is in a position to exercise a significant influence over the company in which the investment is made.

Significant influence over a company essentially involves participation in the financial and operating policy decisions of that company (including dividend policy) but not necessarily control of those policies. Representation on the board of directors is indicative of such participation, but will neither necessarily give conclusive evidence of it nor be the only method by which the investing company may participate in policy decisions.

14 Where the interest of the investing group or company is not effectively that of a partner in a joint venture or consortium but amounts to 20 per cent or more of the equity voting rights of a company, it should be presumed that the investing group or company has the ability to exercise significant influence over that company unless it can clearly be demonstrated otherwise. For example, there may exist one or more other large shareholdings which prevent the exercise of such influence.

15 Where the interest of the investing group or companyis not effectively that of a partner in a joint venture or consortium and amounts to less than 20 per cent of the equity voting rights of a company it should be presumed that the investing group or company does not have the ability to exercise significant influence unless it can clearly demonstrate otherwise. Unless there are exceptional circumstances, this demonstration should include a statement from the company in which the investment is made that it accepts that the investing group or company is in a position to exercise significant influence over it.

16 Where different companies in a group hold shares in a company, the investment in that company should be taken as the aggregate of the holdings of the investing company together with the whole of those of its subsidiaries but excluding those of its associates in determining whether or not significant influence is presumed to exist.

17 The term 'associated company' should be restricted to the definition given in this SSAP.

Part 3 — Standard accounting practice

Bases of accounting for associated companies

18 Income from investments of a company or its subsidiaries in associated companies (as defined in Part 2 above) should be brought into account on the following bases:

(a) *In the investing company's own financial statements:* dividends received and receivable.

(b) *In the investing group's consolidated financial statements (or the equivalent prepared in accordance with paragraphs 24 and 35 below):* the investing group's share of profits less losses of associated companies.

These bases need not be applied to interests in partnerships or non-corporate joint ventures where such arrangements have features which justify accounting for a proportionate share of individual assets and liabilities as well as profits or losses.

Profit and loss account items

19 *Profit before tax.* The investing group should include in its consolidated financial statements the aggregate of its share of before-tax profits less losses of associated companies. This item should be shown separately and suitably described, for example as 'share of profits less losses of associated companies'.

20 *Taxation.* The tax attributed to the share of profits of associated companies should be disclosed separately within the group tax charge in the consolidated financial statements.

21 *Extraordinary items.* The investing group's share of aggregate extraordinary items dealt with in the associated companies' financial statements should be included with the group's extraordinary items to the extent that the group's share of the items involved would be classified, on the basis of the criteria set out in SSAP 6, as extraordinary in the context of the financial statements of the investing group. Where that share is material in the context of the group's results it should be disclosed separately from extraordinary items arising from companies belonging to the group.

22 *Net profit retained by associated companies.* The investing group's share of aggregate net profits less losses retained by associated companies should be shown separately in the financial statements of the investing group.

23 *Other items.* The investing group should not include its share of associated companies' items such as turnover and depreciation in the aggregate amounts of these items disclosed in its consolidated financial statements. If the results of one or more associated companies are so material in the context of the financial statements of the investing group that more detailed information about them would assist in giving a true and fair view, this information should be given by separate disclosure of the total turnover of the associated companies concerned, their total depreciation charges, their total profits less losses before taxation and the amount of such profits less losses attributable to the investing group. In judging materiality regard should be had not merely to the group's share of the net profit of an associated company but also to the scale of its operations in relation to those of the group.

24 Except where it is a wholly owned subsidiary, an investing company which does not prepare consolidated financial statements should show the information required by paragraphs 19 to 23 of this SSAP by preparing a separate profit and loss account or by adding the information in supplementary form to its own profit and loss account in such a way that its share of the profits of the associated companies is not treated as realised for the purposes of the Companies Acts 1948 to 1981. (References in this SSAP to investing groups and consolidated financial statements are to be taken as embracing this information in the case of investing companies which do not have subsidiaries or which do not otherwise prepare consolidated financial statements.)

Balance sheet items

25 *Investing company's interests in associated companies.* Unless shown at a valuation, the amount at which the investing company's interests in associated companies should be shown in the investing company's own financial statements is the cost of the investment less any amounts written off.

26 *Investing group's interests in associated companies.* The amount at which the investing group's interests in associated companies should be shown in the consolidated balance sheet is the total of:

(a) the investing group's share of the net assets other than goodwill of the associated companies stated, where possible, after attributing fair values to the net assets at the time of acquisition of the interest in the associated companies, and

(b) the investing group's share of any goodwill in the associated companies' own financial statements, together with

(c) the premium paid (or discount) on the acquisition of the interests in the associated companies in so far as it has not already been written off or amortised.

Item (a) should be disclosed separately but items (b) and (c) may be shown as one aggregate amount.

27 *Loans to associated companies.* The total of loans to associated companies from the group should be separately disclosed in the consolidated financial statements.

28 *Loans from associated companies.* The total of loans from associated companies to the group should be separately disclosed in the consolidated financial statements.

29 *Trading balances.* Balances arising from unsettled normal trading transactions between the associated companies and the investing group should be included under current assets or liabilities as appropriate, with separate disclosure if material in the context of the financial statements of the investing group.

30 *Other items.* More detailed information about the associated companies' tangible and intangible assets and liabilities should be given if the interests in the associated companies are so material in the context of the financial statements of the investing group that more detailed information about them would assist in giving a true and fair view. In judging materiality, regard should be had not merely to the net carrying amount of the investment in an associated company, but also to the scale of its operations in relation to those of the group.

31 *Accumulated reserves.* The investing group's share of the post-acquisition accumulated reserves of associated companies and any movements therein should be disclosed in the consolidated financial statements. In arriving at the amount to be disclosed, it will also be necessary to take account of and disclose movements on associated companies' reserves which have not arisen from amounts passing through the profit and loss account, for example surpluses on revaluation of fixed assets. If the accumulated reserves of associated companies overseas would be subject to further tax on distribution, this should be made clear.

32 *Permanent impairment in value.* Where there has been permanent impairment in the value of any goodwill (including any premium paid) attributable to an investment in an associated company, it should be written down, and the amount written off in the accounting period separately disclosed. Because an impairment in the value of the underlying net assets would normally be reflected in the books of the associated company, further provision against the investing group's share of these net assets should not usually be necessary.

33 *Deficiency of net assets.* Where an associated company has a deficiency of net assets but is still regarded as a long-term investment it will usually be supported by its shareholders (either by way of loans or by way of an agreement, either formal or informal, to support it). In these circumstances, the investing group should reflect its share of the deficiency of net assets in its consolidated financial statements.

34 *Investment in an unincorporated entity.* Where an investment is made in an unincorporated entity, a liability could arise which would be in excess of that resulting from taking account only of the investing group's share of net assets of the associated company (e.g., as a result of joint and several liability in a partnership). In such circumstances it may be necessary to consider whether it would be prudent either to include an additional provision, or to recognise a contingent liability for this excess.

35 Except where it is a wholly owned subsidiary, an investing company which does not prepare consolidated financial statements should show the information required by paragraphs 25 to 34 of this SSAP by preparing a separate balance sheet or by adding the information in supplementary form to its own balance sheet.

Inclusion of the results of associated companies in the consolidated financial statements of the investing group.

36 The financial statements used for the purpose of including the results of associated companies should be either coterminous with those of the investing group or made up to date which is either not more than six months before, or shortly after, the date of the financial statements of the investing group. In relation to associated companies which are listed on a recognised stock exchange, only published financial information should be disclosed in the financial statements of the investing group.

37 Before incorporating the results of an associated company based on financial statements issued before completion of those of the investing group, care should be taken to ensure that later information has not materially affected the view shown by the financial statements of the associated company. If financial statements not coterminous with those of the investing group are used and the effect is material the facts and the dates of year-ends should be disclosed.

38 Where the interest of the investing group or company in any company other than a subsidiary is not effectively that of a partner in a joint venture or consortium and the investing group or company holds 20 per cent or more of the equity voting rights of that company but does not account for that company as an associated company, details of the accounting treatment adopted, and the reason for doing so, should be stated by way of note to the financial statements. In those cases where disclosure of the reason would be harmful to the business, the directors may omit the information, after consultation with their auditors (in a comparable manner to that permitted by the Companies Acts for subsidiaries where the disclosure would be harmful to the business, except that Department of Trade approval would not be required in this case). Conversely, where the investing group or company holds less than 20 per cent of the equity voting rights of a company but accounts for that company as an associate, the basis on which significant influence is exercised should be stated.

Accounting adjustments

39 Wherever the effect is material, adjustments similar to those adopted for the purpose of presenting consolidated financial statements should be made to exclude from the investing group's consolidated financial statements such items as unrealised profits on stocks transferred to or from associated companies and to achieve reasonable consistency with the accounting policies adopted by the investing group.

Restrictions on distribution

40 If there are significant restrictions on the ability of an associated company to distribute its retained profits (other than those shown as non-distributable) because of statutory, contractual or exchange control restrictions, the extent of the restrictions should be indicated.

Minority interests

41 Where the investment in an associated company is held by a subsidiary in which there are minority interests, the minority interests shown in the consolidated financial statements of the group should include the minority share of the subsidiary's interest in the results and net assets of the associated company.

Investments by associated companies

42 Where an associated company itself has subsidiary or associated companies, the results and net assets to be dealt with in the investing group's consolidated financial statements are its attributable proportion of the results and net assets of the group (including the appropriate proportion of the results and net assets of its associated companies) of which the associated company is the holding company.

Loss of status as associated company

43 When an investment in a company ceases to fall within the definition of an associated company, it should be stated in the consolidated balance sheet of the investing group at the carrying amount under the equity method at that date. However, the carrying value should be adjusted if dividends are subsequently paid out of profits earned prior to the change of status. Provision should be made against the investment if there has been any impairment in value.

Effective date of acquisition or disposal

44 The effective date for both acquisition and disposal of an interest, or any portion of an interest, in an associated company should be the earlier of:

(a) the date on which consideration passes: or

(b) the date on which an offer becomes unconditional.

This applies even if the acquiring company has the right under the agreement to share in the profits of the acquired business from an earlier date.

Treatment of associated companies in current cost accounts

45 Investments in associated companies should be shown in the investing group's current cost consolidated balance sheet as in paragraph 26 of this SSAP, except that the figure for net assets, other than goodwill, should be based on current costs, or the directors' best estimate thereof. The figures for goodwill, being the investing group's share of goodwill in the associated companies' own financial statements and any premium arising on the acquisition of interests in the associated companies, should be the same as in the historical cost balance sheet, provided that fair values were attributed to the other assets at the dates of each acquisition.

46 The investing group's current cost consolidated profit and loss account should include either the investing group's share of the current cost profits less losses of the associated companies, stated before tax but after interest and the associated companies' separate gearing adjustments, or the directors' best estimate thereof.

47 The investing group's gearing adjustment should be calculated by applying the gearing ratio, calculated from the investing group's current cost consolidated balance sheet, to the total of the investing group's current cost adjustments including an adjustment for the associated companies. The adjustment for the associated companies should be the investing group's share of the current cost adjustments, including gearing, of the associated companies.

48 Where the associated companies do not themselves prepare current cost accounts and as a result the investing group includes information based on directors' best estimates, this fact should be disclosed.

Disclosure of particulars of associated companies

49 Subject to Parts 4 and 5, the names of the principal associated companies should be disclosed in the financial statements of the investing group showing for each of these associated companies:

(a) the proportion of the number of the issued shares of each class held by the investing group; and

(b) an indication of the nature of its business.

Corresponding amounts

50 On first introducing the amended standard method of accounting set out in this SSAP the corresponding amounts for the preceding period should be appropriately stated on a comparable basis.

Date from which effective

51 The amended method of accounting for associated companies set out in this SSAP should be adopted as soon as possible and regarded as standard in respect of financial statements relating to accounting periods starting on or after 1 January 1982.

Part 4 — Note on legal requirements in Great Britain

Relative to group accounts prepared in compliance with the requirements of Section 152 of the Companies Act 1948

52 Section 1(2) of the Companies Act 1981 inserts a new Schedule 8 to the Companies Act 1948. All paragraph references below are to the new Schedule 8 ('the Schedule').

53 The term 'related company' is defined in paragraph 91 of the Schedule as "any body corporate (other than one which is a group company in relation to that company) in which that company holds on a long-term basis a qualifying capital interest for the purpose of securing a contribution to that company's own activities by the exercise of any control or influence arising from that interest". The definition of related company is wider than that of associated company.

54 The profit and loss account formats in the Schedule require separate disclosure of income from shares in related companies.

55 The balance sheet formats in the Schedule require separate disclosure of:

(a) shares in related companies;

(b) loans to related companies;

(c) amounts owed by related companies (showing separately amounts falling due after more than one year);

(d) amounts owed to related companies (showing separately amounts falling due after more than one year).

If all investments falling within the scope of related companies are dealt with as associated companies, the term 'related companies' does not have to be used in the balance sheet or profit and loss account. However the notes should make it clear that there are no other related companies besides those shown as associated companies.

56 The equity method of accounting as required by this statement of standard accounting practice is now specifically permitted in consolidated financial statements by paragraph 65 of the Schedule where it appears to the directors of a holding company that a body corporate is so closely associated with a member of the group as to justify the use of that method in dealing with investments by that or any other member of the group in the shares of that body corporate.

57 Further disclosure requirements relative to investments (including related companies) are contained in paragraphs 31(3), 31(4), 42, 45 and 53(4) of the Schedule and Sections 3 and 4 of the Companies Act 1981.

58 It should be noted that Section 4(5) of the Companies Act 1981 states that where investments are included in the accounts or notes thereto by way of the equity method of valuation then information otherwise required by Section 4(3) need not be given, namely:

(a) the aggregate capital and reserves of each investee company as at the end of the most recent financial year; and

(b) the profit or loss of each investee for that year.

Relative to group accounts prepared in compliance with the requirements of Section 152A of the Companies Act 1948*

59 Schedule 8A to the Companies Act 1948, ('Schedule 8A') requires certain information to be given about unlisted equity investments in the absence of a directors' valuation. The information required to be given by this SSAP may not fully satisfy the requirements of the Act and so it may be necessary either to re-arrange the information appropriately or, if this is impracticable, to provide it by way of a separate note.

60 Schedule 8A also requires the amount respectively of income from listed investments and income from unlisted investments to be shown in the profit and loss account.

61 In the case of an associated company which is either incorporated outside the United Kingdom or carries on business outside the United Kingdom, Section 4(3) of the Companies Act 1967 provides that disclosures of a company's name and other particulars need not be made if in the opinion of the directors and with the concurrence of the Department of Trade such disclosures would be harmful.

62 The valuation basis for investments permitted in paragraph 5A of Schedule 8A is not appropriate for the valuation of associated companies in consolidated financial statements.

Part 5 — Note on legal requirements in Ireland

Northern Ireland

63 Schedule 6 to the Companies Act (Northern Ireland) 1960 permits a valuation basis for investments which may not conform with the requirements of this SSAP. Furthermore paragraph 12(1)(g) of Schedule 6 requires that the amount of income from investments, distinguishing between trade investments and other investments, shall be shown in the profit and loss account.

64 Schedule 2 and Article 15(3) of the Companies (Northern Ireland) Order 1978 will, when brought into operation, make legal requirements in Northern Ireland similar to those outlined at paragraphs 59-62 above.

Republic of Ireland

65 Schedule 6 to the Companies Act 1963 permits a valuation basis for investments which may not be in accordance with the SSAP. Furthermore paragraph 12(g) of Schedule 6 requires that the amount of income from investments should be shown in the profit and loss account.

66 The obligation to prepare group accounts is set out in Section 150(1) of the Companies Act 1963, which refers only to public companies. It should be noted that SSAP 14 'Group accounts' goes beyond this minimum legal requirement and applies also to private companies. Reference should be made to paragraphs 15 and 56 of SSAP 14.

* Applicable to (a) banking, insurance and certain shipping companies and (b) other companies for accounting periods beginning before the appointed day.

67 Paragraph 23 of this SSAP requires that additional information, including total turnover, should be given about associated companies in certain circumstances. Disclosure of total turnover, which is not mandatory under the Companies Act 1963, is required in the interests of informative reporting.

Part 6 — Compliance with International Accounting Standard No. 3

'Consolidated financial statement'

68 The requirements of International Accounting Standard No. 3 'Consolidated financial statements' covering the basis of accounting for associated companies accord very closely with the content of the United Kingdom and Irish SSAP 'Accounting for associated companies' and accordingly compliance with SSAP 1 (revised) will ensure compliance with the requirements of IAS 3 on associated companies in all material respects.

The Accounting Standards Board has issued an interim statement which amends SSAP 1. You should refer to the 'Interim Statement — Consolidated Accounts' (which can be found at the end of Section 3 pages 323-342) for guidance.

Disclosure of accounting policies

(Issued November 1971)

It is fundamental to the understanding and interpretation of financial accounts that those who use them should be aware of the main assumptions on which they are based. The purpose of the statement which follows is to assist such understanding by promoting improvement in the quality of information disclosed. It seeks to achieve this by establishing as standard accounting practice the disclosure in financial accounts of clear explanations of the accounting policies followed in so far as these are significant for the purpose of giving a true and fair view. The statement does not seek to establish accounting standards for individual items; these will be dealt with in separate statements of standard accounting practice issued from time to time.

Part 1 — Explanatory note

Fundamental accounting concepts, accounting bases and accounting policies

1 In accounting usage terms such as 'accounting principles', 'practices', 'rules', 'conventions', 'methods', or 'procedures' have often been treated as interchangeable.* For the purpose of this statement it is convenient to distinguish between fundamental accounting concepts, accounting bases and accounting policies.

2 Fundamental accounting concepts are here defined as broad basic assumptions which underlie the periodic financial accounts of business enterprises. It is expedient to single out for special mention four in particular: (a) the 'going concern' concept (b) the 'accruals' concept (c) the 'consistency' concept and (d) the 'prudence' concept.** The use of these concepts is not necessarily self-evident from an examination of accounts, but they have such general acceptance that they call for no explanation in published accounts and their observance is presumed unless stated otherwise. They are practical rules rather than theoretical ideals and are capable of variation and evolution as accounting thought and practice develop, but their present generally accepted meanings are restated in paragraph 14 below.

3 Accounting bases are the methods which have been developed for expressing or applying fundamental accounting concepts to financial transactions and items. By their nature accounting bases are more diverse and numerous than fundamental concepts, since they have evolved in response to the variety and complexity of types of business and business transactions, and for this reason there may justifiably exist more than one recognised accounting basis for dealing with particular items.

4 Accounting policies are the specific accounting bases judged by business enterprises to be most appropriate to their circumstances and adopted by them for the purpose of preparing their financial accounts.

* In this series 'accounting practices' has been adopted as a generic term to encompass all aspects of financial accounting methods and presentation.

** It is emphasised that it is not the purpose of this statement to develop as basic theory of accounting. An exhaustive theoretical approach would take an entirely different form and would include for instance many more propositions than the four fundamental concepts referred to here. It is, however, expedient to recognise them as working assumptions having general acceptance at the present time.

Particular problems in application of the fundamental concepts

5 The main difficulty in applying the fundamental accounting concepts arises from the fact that many business transactions have financial effects spreading over a number of years. Decisions have to be made on the extent to which expenditure incurred in one year can reasonably be expected to produce benefits in the form of revenue in other years and should therefore be carried forward, in whole or in part; that is, should be dealt with in the closing balance sheet, as distinct from being dealt with as an expense of the current year in the profit and loss account because the benefit has been exhausted in that year.

6 In some cases revenue is received for goods or services the production or supply of which will involve some later expenditure. In this case a decision must be made regarding how much of the revenue should be carried forward, to be dealt with in subsequent profit and loss accounts when the relevant costs are incurred.

7 All such decisions require consideration of future events of uncertain financial effect, and to this extent an element of commercial judgement is unavoidable in the assessment.

8 Examples of matters which give rise to particular difficulty are: the future benefits to be derived from stocks and all types of work in progress at the end of the year; the future benefits to be derived from fixed assets, and the period of years over which these will be fruitful; the extent to which expenditure on research and development can be expected to produce future benefits.

Purpose and limitations of accounting bases

9 In the course of practice there have developed a variety of accounting bases designed to provide consistent, fair and as nearly as possible objective solutions to these problems in particular circumstances; for instance, bases for calculating such items as depreciation, the amounts at which stocks and work in progress are to be stated, and deferred taxation.

10 Accounting bases provide an orderly and consistent framework for periodic reporting of a concern's results and financial position, but they do not, and are not intended to, substitute for the exercise of commercial judgement in the preparation of financial reports. Where a choice of acceptable accounting bases is available judgement must be exercised in choosing those which are appropriate to the circumstances and are best suited to present fairly the concern's results and financial position; the bases thus adopted then become the concern's accounting policies. The significance of accounting bases is that they provide limits to the area subject to the exercise of judgement, and a check against arbitrary, excessive or unjustifiable adjustments where no other objective yardstick is available. By definition it is not possible to develop generalised rules of the exercise of judgement, though practical working rules may be evolved on a pragmatic basis for limited use in particular circumstances. Broadly, the longer a concern's normal business cycle — the period between initiation of business transactions and their completion — the greater the area subject to judgement and its effect on periodic financial accounts, and the less its susceptibility to close regulation by accounting bases. These limitations to the regulating powers of accounting bases must be recognised.

Significance of disclosure of accounting policies

11 In circumstances where more than one accounting basis is acceptable in principle, the accounting policy followed can significantly affect a concern's reported results and financial position and the view presented can be properly appreciated only if the policies followed in dealing with material items are also explained. For this reason adequate disclosure of the accounting policies is essential to the fair presentation of financial accounts. As accounting standards become established through publication of statements of standard accounting practice, the choice of accounting bases regarded as generally available will diminish, but it has to be recognised that the complexity and diversity of business renders total and rigid uniformity of bases impracticable.

12 The items with which this statement is mainly concerned are those which are subject to the exercise of judgement as to how far they should be dealt with in the profit and loss account for the period under review or how far all or part should be carried forward in the balance sheet as attributable to the operations of future periods. The determination of the annual profit and loss of nearly every business substantially depends on a systematic approach to a few material items of this type. For the better appreciation of the view they give, annual accounts should include a clear explanation of the accounting policies followed for dealing with these few key items (some examples of which are given in paragraph 13 below). The intention and spirit of this statement are that management should identify those items of thc type described which are judged material or critical for the purpose of determining and fully appreciating the company's profit or loss and its financial position, and should make clear the accounting policies followed for dealing with them.

Examples of matters for which different accounting bases are recognised

13 Significant matters for which different accounting bases are recognised and which may have a material effect on reported results and financial position include:

depreciation of fixed assets
treatment and amortisation of intangibles such as research and development expenditure, patents and trademarks
stocks and work in progress
long-term contracts
deferred taxation
hire purchase or instalment transactions
leasing and rental transactions
conversion of foreign currencies
repairs and renewals
consolidation policies
property development transactions
warranties for products or services.

This list is not exhaustive, and may vary according to the nature of the operations conducted.

Part 2 — Definition of terms

14 Fundamental accounting concepts are the broad basic assumptions which underlie the periodic financial accounts of business enterprises. At the present time the four following fundamental concepts (the relative importance of which will vary according to the circumstances of the particular case) are regarded as having general acceptability:

(a) the 'going concern' concept: the enterprise will continue in operational existence for the foreseeable future. This means in particular that the profit and loss account and balance sheet assume no intention or necessity to liquidate or curtail significantly the scale of operation;

(b) the 'accruals' concept: revenue and costs are accrued (that is, recognised as they are earned or incurred, not as money is received or paid), matched with one another so far as their relationship can be established or justifiably assumed, and dealt with in the profit and loss account of the period to which they relate; provided that where the accruals concept is inconsistent with the 'prudence' concept (paragraph (d) below), the latter prevails. The accruals concept implies that the profit and loss account reflects changes in the amount of net assets that arise out of the transactions of the relevant period (other than distributions or subscriptions of capital and unrealised surpluses arising on revaluation of fixed assets). Revenue and profits dealt with in the profit and loss account are matched with associated costs and expenses by including in the same account the costs incurred in earning them (so far as these are material and identifiable);

(c) the 'consistency' concept: there is consistency of accounting treatment of like items within each accounting period and from one period to the next;

(d) the concept of 'prudence': revenue and profits are not anticipated, but are recognised by inclusion in the profit and loss account only when realised in the form either of cash or of other assets the ultimate cash realisation of which can be assessed with reasonable certainty; provision is made for all known liabilities (expenses and losses) whether the amount of these is known with certainty or is a best estimate in the light of the information available.

15 Accounting bases are the methods developed for applying fundamental accounting concepts to financial transactions and items for the purpose of financial accounts, and in particular: (a) for determining the accounting periods in which revenue and costs should be recognised in the profit and loss account; and (b) for determining the amounts at which material items should be stated in the balance sheet.

16 Accounting policies are the specific accounting bases selected and consistently followed by a business enterprise as being, in the opinion of the management, appropriate to its circumstances and best suited to present fairly its results and financial position.

Part 3 — Standard accounting practice

Disclosure of adoption of concepts which differ from those generally accepted

17 If accounts are prepared on the basis of assumptions which differ in material respects from any of the generally accepted fundamental concepts defined in paragraph 14 above, the facts should be explained. In the absence of a clear statement to the contrary, there is a presumption that the four fundamental concepts have been observed.

Disclosure of accounting policies

18 The accounting policies (as defined in paragraph 16 above) followed for dealing with items which are judged material or critical in determining profit or loss for the year and in stating the financial position should be disclosed by way of note to the accounts. The explanations should be clear, fair and as brief as possible.

Date from which effective

19 The accounting practices set out in this statement should be adopted as soon as possible and regarded as standard in respect of reports relating to accounting periods starting on or after 1 January, 1972.

Earnings per share

(Issued February 1972; revised August 1974)

The original statement of standard accounting practice on earnings per share (SSAP 3) was issued in February 1972.

Although little change is needed in the basic definition of earnings per share or in the standard accounting practice, other parts of the statement have been brought up to date to take account of:

(a) the change in the basis of taxation in the United Kingdom from the former system of corporation tax to the imputation system;

(b) the issue by the councils of the bodies participating in the Accounting Standards Steering Committee of a number of statements of accounting practice; in particular SSAP 8 'The treatment of taxation under the imputation system in the accounts of companies'.

The Council of the Stock Exchange stated in note 28 of the listing agreement that it will "expect the accounts of listed companies to be drawn up in accordance with the standards approved by these accountancy bodies". This requirement to apply the accounting standard on earnings per share is extended by note 6 of the listing agreement to the computation of the figure of earnings per share to be shown in preliminary profits announcements for the year or other full accounting period.

This statement is intended to apply to the audited accounts of listed companies. The circumstances of smaller unlisted companies and the problems of computation (particularly when a company is financed by interest-free loans from directors) are often such that an earnings per share figure would not be meaningful.

Part 1 — Explanatory note

1 The original call for a standard accounting practice for the disclosure of earnings per share was based on the increasing use of the price-earnings ratio as a standard stock market indicator. Despite the complication introduced by the imputation system of corporation tax and the limitation of dividends by Government regulation in the United Kingdom price-earnings ratios remain one of the most commonly used stock market indicators. Although they are not strictly comparable because of differences between one country's tax system and another's, they are, nevertheless, used on a world-wide basis.

2 The continued use of price-earnings ratios requires that the earnings per share, on which that ratio is based, should be calculated and disclosed on a comparable basis as between one company and another and as between one financial period and another, so far as this is possible.

3 As between one company and another, the main problem arising from the imputation system of corporation tax is the treatment of irrecoverable advance corporation tax (ACT)*. After the transitional period, only a small proportion of listed companies is likely to have irrecoverable ACT (or unrelieved overseas tax arising from a dividend) included in their tax charge for the year. These companies will mainly be those whose earnings arise overseas or who have large capital allowances for corporation tax, such as the oil, mining,

*Recoverable and irrecoverable ACT are defined in SSAP 8 'The treatment of taxation under the imputation system in the accounts of companies'.

plantation and shipping companies. The calculation of earnings per share when there is irrecoverable ACT is considered in paragraphs 7-9.

4 One of the features of the change from the former system to the imputation system of corporation tax is that, whereas before April 1973 earnings after corporation tax were available to cover gross dividends before deduction of income tax, the earnings after corporation tax under the new system are available to cover the actual cash dividends payable to the shareholders. The transitional arrangements also give rise to problems of comparison.

5 In calculating the earnings for the equity shareholders it is not the former gross dividend but the amount of the dividend declared and payable to the preference shareholders, which falls to be deducted from the profit after tax, since, under the imputation system, post-tax profits are available to cover cash dividends.

6 Before calculating earnings per share under the new system, it is necessary to examine carefully the charge for taxation to be deducted in arriving at the earnings figure. The tax charge will always include some elements which are constant, in that they will not vary with the proportion of the profit distributed by way of dividend; the charge may however include other elements which do vary according to the amount of profit distributed and which would be absent if no distributions were made. These components may be classified as follows:

Constant

Corporation tax on income.
Tax attributable to dividends received.
Overseas tax unrelieved because the rate of overseas tax exceeds the rate of UK corporation tax.

Variable

Irrecoverable ACT.
Overseas tax unrelieved because dividend payments restrict the double tax credit available.

7 Two alternative methods of computing earnings per share under the imputation system have been propounded. One would take account of all the elements of the taxation charge listed above, both constant and variable; this is called the net basis. The other would recognise only the constant elements, and because it seeks to arrive at what the earnings would be if the distributions were nil, it is called the nil basis. It can be expected that most companies, in normal circumstances, will not incur either of the variable elements of taxation, so that for them calculations on the net basis and the nil basis will produce the same result. The companies where the two methods are most likely to produce divergent figures are those which have income taxed overseas a significant proportion of which is distributed.

8 The advantage of the nil basis is that it produces a figure of earnings which is not dependent on the level of distribution, and so provides an indicator of one company's performance more closely comparable with that of another. The argument which is preferred is that the net basis takes account of all the relevant facts, including the additional tax liabilities inherent in the dividend policy pursued by the company, for which the directors should no less be accountable to shareholders. It is considered therefore that quoted companies should report in their accounts earnings per share primarily on the net basis.

9 Where, however, there is a material difference between earnings per share calculated on the net basis and on the nil distribution basis, it is most desirable that the latter also be shown although the disclosure requirements in respect of the treatment of taxation in accounts* will enable this earnings per share on a nil basis to be calculated by the user.

Part 2 — Definitions

Earnings per share

10 The profit in pence attributable to each equity share, based on the consolidated profit of the period after tax and after deducting minority interests and preference dividends, but before taking into account extraordinary items, divided by the number of equity shares in issue and ranking for dividend in respect of the period.

Net basis of calculating earnings per share

11 In determining earnings per share on the net basis, the charge for taxation used in determining earnings includes:

(a) any irrecoverable advance corporation tax (ACT);

(b) any unrelieved overseas tax arising from the payment or proposed payment of dividends.

Nil distribution basis of calculating earnings per share

12 In determining earnings per share on the nil basis, the charge for taxation used in determining earnings generally excludes (a) and (b) above (except in so far as these arise in respect of preference dividends).

Part 3 — Standard accounting practice

Applicable to listed companies

13 This accounting standard shall apply to companies having a listing on a recognised stock exchange for any class of equity, other than companies claiming exemption from the disclosure requirements under Part III of Schedule 2 of the Companies Act 1967.

14 In the audited accounts of such listed companies, the earnings per share should be shown on the face of the profit and loss account on the net basis both for the period under review and for the corresponding previous period. (The desirability of showing also the earnings per share on the nil distribution basis where materially different from those on the net basis is emphasised in paragraph 9.)

15 The basis of calculating earnings per share should be disclosed, either in the profit and loss account or in a note thereto. In particular, the amount of the earnings and the number of equity shares used in the calculation should be shown.

16 Where a company has at the balance sheet date contracted to issue further shares after the end of the period, or where it has already issued shares which will rank for dividend later, the effect may be to dilute future earnings per share. In addition, therefore, to the basic earnings per share, as set out above, the fully diluted earnings per share should be shown on the face of the profit and loss account of quoted companies in the following circumstances:

*See SSAP 8 'The treatment of taxation under the imputation system in the accounts of companies'.

(a) where the company has issued a separate class of equity shares which do not rank for any dividend in the period under review, but which will do so in the future;

(b) where the company has issued debentures or loan stock (or preference shares) convertible into equity shares of the company;

(c) where the company has granted options or issued warrants to subscribe for equity shares of the company.

In each case:

(i) the basis of calculation of fully diluted earnings per share should be disclosed;

(ii) the fully diluted earnings per share need not be given unless the dilution is material. Dilution amounting to 5 per cent or more of the basic earnings per share is regarded as material for this purpose;

(iii) fully diluted earnings per share for the corresponding previous period should not be shown unless the assumptions on which it was based still apply;

(iv) equal prominence should be given to basic and fully diluted earnings per share wherever both are disclosed.

Date from which effective

17 The disclosure of earnings per share became an accounting standard in respect of accounts relating to periods starting on or after 1 January 1972. This standard has been revised to take into account the imputation system of corporation tax which was introduced with effect from 6 April, 1973.

Application in Republic of Ireland

18 The calculation of earnings per share should be based on the consolidated profits for the period after corporation profits tax and income tax and after deducting minority interests and preference dividends, but before taking into account extraordinary items.

19 Earnings per share should be described as follows: "Earnings per share after deducting corporation profits tax and income tax".

Appendix 1

20 This appendix is for general guidance and does not form part of the statement of standard accounting practice.

Guidelines for the determination of earnings per share

Primary considerations

Preliminary

21 In simple terms, the earnings per share figure is calculated by apportioning the total amount earned for the equity share capital in a financial period over the number of shares in issue and ranking for dividend in respect of that period.

Earnings for equity

22 The amount earned for equity should normally be the consolidated profit of the year after tax, minority interests and preference dividends, but before extraordinary items*, net

* Extraordinary items are defined in SSAP 6 'Extraordinary items and prior year adjustments'.

of taxation and minority interests. It would include the earnings of associated companies — see SSAP 1 'Accounting for the results of associated companies'.

Preference dividends

23 Under the imputation system, the preference dividend has ceased to be the gross dividend but is now the cash amount declared and payable to the shareholder. This is the amount to be deducted from the profit after tax in calculating earnings per share.

24 Where the preference shares are cumulative, the dividend for the period should be taken into account, whether or not it has been earned or declared. Subject to this, arrears of preference dividend paid during the year should be ignored. In the case of a non-cumulative dividend the deduction should be the amount of the preferential dividend paid or proposed.

25 The fixed part of the dividend on participating preference shares should be treated in the same way as a preference dividend. If the participating element is limited (e.g. maximum 10 per cent) the whole dividend for the period may be deducted. If it is unlimited, then the appropriate proportion of the earnings for the period to allow for the participating element should be deducted before arriving at the earnings for the ordinary shares.

Losses

26 Where a loss is incurred the amount earned for equity is a negative figure, the earnings per share should be determined in the normal manner and the result shown as a loss per share.

27 Where the tax charge is reduced by losses brought forward, the tax charge for the year shown in the profit and loss account (rather than a notional tax charge) should be used in the calculation of earnings per share accompanied by an adequate explanation of the effects of the incidence of tax relief on earnings per share for the year under review and for the preceding year.

Sinking fund

28 Transfers to a loan redemption reserve or to a sinking fund (even though supported by a corresponding transfer of cash) merely divide the profits between those available for immediate distribution and those distributable later; they do not reduce the earnings, of the period, and should not be deducted in calculating the earnings of the period.

Corresponding amounts for the previous period

29 Earnings per share for the corresponding previous period should be shown.

Equity share capital

30 Where there is only one class of equity share capital ranking for dividend, the calculation of earnings per share should be based on the number of such shares in issue during the period. Where there is more than one class of equity shares or where some of the shares are not fully paid, the earning should be apportioned over the different classes of shares in accordance with their dividend rights or other right to participate in profits.

Subsequent changes in capital

31 Where there has been a change in the capital structure after the accounting date but before the preliminary announcement of the results of the period, the earnings per share shown in the profit and loss account should not take this into account; however, it is desirable that the effect on the basic earnings per share of any capitalisation issue, share split, or bonus element inherent in a rights issue should be disclosed.

Summary

32 Earnings per share should be calculated by apportioning the earnings (that is, normally, the consolidated profit of the period after taxation, minority interests and preference dividends but before extraordinary items — see paragraph 2 above) over the number of equity shares in issue and ranking for dividend during the period. A simple example is given below.

33 EXAMPLE

A CAPITAL STRUCTURE

Issued share capital

£500,000 in 10% (now 7% + tax credit)*
cumulative preference share of £1
(issued before 6 April 1973)

£1,000,000 ordinary shares of 25p
= 4,000,000 shares

B TRADING RESULTS

	Year ended 31 December	
	Year 2	*Year 1*
Profit after tax	£535,000	£435,000

Assumptions:
No change in the issued share capital during the two years

C CALCULATION OF EARNINGS PER SHARE

	Year 2	*Year 1*
	£	£
Profit after tax	535,000	435,000
Less Preference dividend	35,000	35,000
Earnings	500,000	400,000
Number of ordinary shares	4,000,000	4,000,000

D ILLUSTRATION OF PRESENTATION IN THE PROFIT AND LOSS ACCOUNT

	Year ended 31 December	
	Year 2	*Year 1*
Earnings per ordinary share of 25p	$12\frac{1}{2}$p	10p

Note. The calculation of earnings per share is based on earnings of £500,000 (Year 1 £400,000) and four million ordinary shares in issue throughout the two years ended 31 December, Year 2.

*See paragraph 18 of SSAP 8 'The treatment of taxation under the imputation scheme in the accounts of companies'.

Treatment of changes in equity share capital

34 Where further equity shares have been issued during the financial year, they will probably have been issued by one of the following methods:

Issue at full market price
Capitalisation issue
Share exchange
Rights issue at less than full market price

Each of these circumstances is likely to affect the method of determining the earnings per share and the effect is summarised below.

Issue at full market price

35 Most issues for cash in this country are in the form of rights issues rather than at full market price. If, however, new equity shares have been issued either for cash at full market price or as consideration for the acquisition of an asset the earnings should be apportioned over the average number of shares ranking for dividend during the period weighted on a time basis.

Capitalisation issue

36 Where new equity shares have been issued by way of capitalisation during the period, the earnings should be apportioned over the number of shares ranking for dividend after the capitalisation. The corresponding figures for all earlier periods should be adjusted accordingly. Similar considerations apply where equity shares are split into shares of smaller nominal value.

Share exchange

37 Where shares (ranking for dividend) or loan stock have been issued during the period as consideration for shares in a new subsidiary, it should be assumed that, for the purpose of calculating the earnings per share, these securities were issued on the first day of the period for which the profits of the new subsidiary are included in the earnings of the group.

Rights issue at less than full market price

38 Earnings per share for prior years — where equity shares are issued by way of rights during the period it is recommended that the factor for adjustment of past earnings per share after a rights issue be based on the closing price* on the last day of quotation of the shares cum rights. The factor is therefore:

$$\frac{\text{Theoretical } \textbf{ex rights} \text{ price}}{\text{Actual } \textbf{cum rights} \text{ price on the last day of quotation cum rights}}$$

Where a rights issue is made during the year under review, the earnings per share for the previous year, and for all earlier years, will need to be adjusted by the factor, calculated as above, to correct for the bonus element in the rights issue.

39 Earnings per share for the year in which a rights issue is made. For the current year in which a rights issue is made it would be undesirable to split the earnings into two periods, one before the rights issue and one after this event. It is necessary to adjust the weighted average share capital by taking the proportion of the capital in issue before the rights issue, applying to this figure the reciprocal of the factor set out above, i.e.

*i.e. the official middle market quotations published on the following day.

$$\frac{\text{Actual \textbf{cum rights} price}}{\text{Theoretical \textbf{ex rights} price}}$$

adding the proportion in issue after the rights issue.

Fully diluted earnings per share

Introduction

40 The earnings per share calculations considered up to this point have been based on either the weighted average share capital ranking for dividend in the period or, in the case of a capitalisation issue, the equity share capital ranking for dividend at the financial year-end.

41 Where a listed company has outstanding:

- a separate class of equity shares which do not rank for dividend in the period but will do so in the future (see paragraph 50 below); or
- debentures or loan stock (or preference shares) convertible into equity shares of the company (see paragraph 51 below); or
- options or warrants to subscribe for equity shares of the company (see paragraph 52 below);

the company has entered into obligations which may dilute the earnings per share in the future. In these circumstances, in addition to the basic earnings per share, the fully diluted earnings per share should be calculated and shown on the face of the profit and loss account in accordance with paragraph 37 and paragraphs 43-49 below.

42 In each of these cases, full information as to the rights of the holders (existing shareholders, convertible stockholders, preference shareholders or holders of options or warrants) should be set out in the accounts.

43 Depending on the terms of the conversion rights or the options to subscribe, it is possible that the calculation of an earnings per share figure, based on the assumption that these rights or options had been exercised at the beginning of the period, would result in increasing the earnings per share above the basic figure. In these circumstances, it is likely that the conversion rights or options would not be exercised. The resultant figure (i.e. increased earnings per share rather than diluted earnings per share) should not be shown if it is in excess of the basic earnings per share.

44 The fully diluted earnings per share need not be given if the dilution is not material, in which event that fact should be stated. Dilution amounting to 5 per cent or more of the basic earnings per share is regarded as material for this purpose.

45 The fully diluted earnings per share should not be shown when the basic earnings per share is a negative figure (i.e. a loss).

46 Since the fully diluted earnings per share is concerned with future dilution, a corresponding amount for the previous period may not be meaningful; it should not be shown unless the assumptions on which it was based are still applicable.

47 Where the dilution is material and the fully diluted earnings per share is shown, the basis of calculation should be disclosed.

48 A listed company may, in any period, have more than one type of convertible debenture or loan stock (or preference shares) in issue with differing conversion rights or may also have issued shares to rank in a future period or have granted options or warrants to subscribe. In this event, the fully diluted earnings per share should take into account only those convertibles or shares or options or warrants which would have a diluting effect on the earnings per share and should disregard those which have no such diluting effect.

49 Wherever fully diluted earnings per share are disclosed in addition to the basic earnings per share, they should both be given equal prominence.

Another class of equity share ranking for dividend in the future

50 Where a listed company has in issue a class of equity shares* not yet ranking for dividend but which will do so in the future (by conversion or otherwise), in addition to the basic earnings per share (calculated on the equity shares ranking for all or any dividends in respect of the period), the fully diluted earnings per share should be calculated on the assumption that this class of shares ranked for dividend from the beginning of the period (or such later date as they were issued).

Convertible securities

51 Where a company has convertible loan stock in issue at any time during the period, in addition to the basic earnings per share, the fully diluted earnings per share should be calculated on the assumption that the maximum number of new equity shares had been issued on conversion and that this conversion had taken place on the first day of the period (or on the date of issue of the convertible loan stock if later). The earnings for the period should be adjusted by adding back the assumed saving of interest on the stock so converted, net of corporation tax.

Options or warrants to subscribe

52 Where a listed company has granted options or issued warrants to subscribe for equity shares of the company, in addition to the basic earnings per share, the fully diluted earnings per share should be calculated on the assumption that the maximum number of new shares had been issued under the terms of the options or warrants and that these had been exercised on the first day of the period (or the date of issue if later.) The earnings for the period should be adjusted on the basis that the proceeds of subscription had been invested in 2½ per cent Consolidated Stock on the first day of the period at the closing price of the previous day.

Exceptions

53 In the circumstances dealt with in paragraphs 50-52 fully diluted earnings per share should be shown on the face of the profit and loss account subject to the exceptions stated in paragraphs 43-46.

Final conversion or subscription during the year

54 Where the convertible loan stock has been finally converted during the year (unless it was converted on the first day of the year and the shares issued have, therefore, ranked for dividend for the full year), it will still be necessary to show the fully diluted earnings per share in the accounts for the year in which that final conversion took place.

55 Similar considerations apply on final subscriptions in the case of options or warrants to subscribe.

*'New' shares of the same class as existing equity shares, which are separately quoted for a time, only because they are transferable in a different form or because they rank for a later (e.g. final) but not for an earlier (e.g. interim) dividend in respect of the period under review, should not be treated as a separate class of shares.

Appendix 2

56 This appendix is for general guidance and does not form part of the statement of standard accounting practice.

Financial statistics in the historical summary

57 In order to present a fair comparison over the period of the historical summary the basic earnings per share figures will need to be adjusted for subsequent changes in capital on the basis set out in the three following paragraphs. The resultant figures should be described as the adjusted earnings per share and should be set out separately from the other financial data which is not so adjusted, e.g. in a separate box.

Adjustments for capitalisation issues

58 Where new equity shares have been issued by way of capitalisation of reserves during any financial year, or where shares have been split into shares of lower nominal value, the earnings per share for all earlier years will need to be adjusted by the appropriate factor, i.e. the number of equity shares before the capitalisation divided by the number of such shares after the capitalisation.

Adjustments for rights issues

59 Where equity shares have been issued by way of rights in any financial year, the earnings per share for all earlier years should be adjusted by the factor set out in paragraph 38 of Appendix 1 of this statement.

Cumulative adjustment

60 Where there is more than one capitalisation or rights issue, both these factors will operate cumulatively.

Dividends per share

61 Where there have been capitalisation or rights issues in the period covered by the summary a straight record of the equity dividends actually paid would not, however be comparable with the adjusted earnings per share. It is therefore suggested that a record of the equity dividends should be set out in the form of pence per share, the dividends being adjusted by the same factors for capitalisation and rights issues (set out above) as the earnings per share. This record should cover the same period, being described as the adjusted equity dividends, and should be set alongside the adjusted basic earnings per share (e.g. in the box referred to in paragraph 57).

Equity dividend cover

62 Dividend cover will normally be found by dividing earnings by dividends under the imputation system of taxation but this simple relationship will not always apply, since the payment of additional dividends may involve the company in the payment of further taxation either in the United Kingdom or overseas. It is the theoretical maximum dividend, after allowing for such additional taxation, which should then be divided by the actual dividend to give the cover.

The Accounting Standards Board has issued Financial Reporting Standard 3: Reporting Financial Performance which amends SSAP 3. You should refer to FRS 3 (which can be found on pages 419-452 for guidance.)

Accounting for government grants

(Issued April 1974, revised July 1990)

The provisions of this statement of standard accounting practice should be read in conjunction with the explanatory foreword to accounting standards *and need not be applied to immaterial items.*

Part 1 — Explanatory note

Introduction

1 Government assistance takes many forms, including grants, equity finance, subsidised loans and advisory assistance. This statement deals with the accounting treatment and disclosure of government grants and other forms of government assistance. It is also indicative of best practice for accounting for grants and assistance from other sources.

2 Government grants are made in order to persuade or assist enterprises to pursue courses of action which are deemed to be socially or economically desirable. The range of grants available is very wide and changes regularly, reflecting changes in government policy. More significantly, different grants tend to be given on different terms as to eligibility, manner of determination, manner of payment and conditions to be fulfilled. While this statement has been written in the context of the grants available at the time of its preparation, it is intended that it will be equally applicable to other grants that may be created in the future.

3 For the purposes of this statement, the term 'government' is defined widely. Thus, it includes not only the national government and all of the various tiers of local and regional government of any country, but also government agencies and 'non-departmental public bodies' (or quangos). It also includes the Commission of the European Communities and other EC bodies, together with other international bodies and agencies.

Basic concepts

4 The 'accruals' concept requires that revenue and costs are accrued, matched with one another so far as their relationship can be established or justifiably assumed, and dealt with in the profit and loss account of the period to which they relate. Government grants should therefore be recognised in the profit and loss account so as to match them with the expenditure towards which they are intended to contribute.

5 The 'prudence' concept requires that revenue and profits are not anticipated, but are recognised by inclusion in the profit and loss account only when realised in the form either of cash or of other assets the ultimate cash realisation of which can be established with reasonable certainty. Accordingly, government grants should not be recognised in the profit and loss account until the conditions for their receipt have been complied with and there is reasonable assurance that the grant will be received.

6 In many cases, the grant-making body has the right to recover all or part of a grant paid if the enterprise has not complied with the conditions under which the grant was made. On the assumption that the enterprise is a going concern, the application of the prudence concept does not normally require postponement of the recognition of the grant in the profit and loss account solely because there is a possibility that it might have to be repaid in the future. The enterprise should consider regularly whether there is a likelihood of a breach of the conditions on which the grant was made. If such a breach has occurred, or appears likely to occur, and it is probable that some grant will have to be repaid, provision should be made for the liability.

7 The treatment for taxation purposes of government grants varies according to the terms of the grant and the particular statute or regulation under which it is made. At one extreme, some grants are free of all tax; at the other, some are taxed as income on receipt. It is sometimes suggested that because grants are taxed as income on receipt they are intended to be regarded as income and should be credited to the profit and loss account as they are received. However, the treatment of an item for tax purposes does not necessarily determine its treatment for accounting purposes, and immediate recognition in the profit and loss account may result in an unacceptable departure from the principle that government grants should be matched with the expenditure towards which they are intended to contribute. Any timing differences that may arise between a tax charge and the recognition of the corresponding credit in the profit and loss account should be dealt with in accordance with SSAP 15 'Accounting for deferred tax'.

Establishing the relationship between grants received and expenditure

8 The matching of grants received and expenditure is straightforward if the grant is made as a contribution towards specified items of expenditure (whether capital, revenue or a particular combination) and is described as such.

9 Difficulties arise where the terms of the grant do not specify precisely the expenditure it is intended to meet, but use such phrases as 'to assist with a project' or 'to encourage job creation', or where the basis of calculation is related to two or more criteria (for example the capital expenditure incurred and the number of jobs created). In these circumstances, it is usually appropriate to consider the circumstances which give rise to the payment of instalments of the grant. If the grant is paid when evidence is produced that certain expenditure has been incurred, the grant should be matched with that expenditure. If the grant is paid on a different basis, it will usually be paid on the achievement of a non-financial objective, such as the creation of a specified number of new jobs; in these circumstances, the grant should be matched with the identifiable costs of achieving that objective, for example the cost of creating and, if applicable, maintaining for the required period the specified new jobs.

10 In some cases, there may be persuasive evidence that the actual expenditure towards which the grant is intended to contribute differs from the expenditure that forms the basis of payment. Such evidence may be contained in the formal application for the grant and subsequent correspondence and negotiation with the grant-making body. Where such evidence exists and is sufficiently persuasive, it is appropriate to match the grant received with the identified expenditure and this approach should be preferred to that outlined in the previous paragraph. For example, a discretionary grant might be given 'to assist with a project', with instalments of the grant being payable on the production of evidence that specific capital expenditure had been incurred; but it might be clear from correspondence that the grant had been made as a contribution to other costs as well, such as the provision of working capital or the meeting of initial training costs.

11 Where a grant is paid on the achievement of a non-financial objective, the costs of achieving that objective must be identified or estimated on a reasonable basis. For example, if a grant is given on condition that jobs are created and maintained for a minimum period, the grant should be matched with the cost of providing jobs for that period, taking due account of the incidence of the costs incurred. As the costs of job creation will often be higher in the early stages of a project, because of start-up costs and the fact that a significant element of wage costs will initially be non-productive, the matching principle may require that an equivalent, higher proportion of the grant should be recognised in the earlier periods.

Recognition of grants in the profit and loss account

12 Once the relationship between the grant and the related expenditure has been established, the recognition of the grant in the profit and loss account will follow. The grant should be recognised in the same period as the related expenditure.

13 In certain circumstances, government grants may be given for the immediate financial support or assistance of an enterprise or for the reimbursement of costs previously incurred, without conditions regarding the enterprise's future actions or a requirement to incur further costs. Government grants may also be given to finance the general activities of an enterprise over a specified period or to compensate for a loss of income; in some instances, the extent of these grants may be such as to constitute a major source of income for the enterprise. Grants that are payable on this basis should be recognised in the profit and loss account of the period in respect of which they are paid or, if they are not stated to be paid in respect of a specified period, in the profit and loss account of the period in which they become receivable.

14 Where an enterprise is required to repay a government grant, either in whole or in part, the full amount to be repaid, after taking into account any unamortised deferred income relating to the grant, should be charged to the profit and loss account immediately it becomes repayable. Where appropriate, the repayment should be dealt with in accordance with SSAP 6 'Extraordinary items and prior year adjustments'.

Balance sheet treatment of grants

15 The application of this statement may result in part or all of a grant that has been received not being recognised immediately in the profit and loss account. Any unrecognised amounts should normally be included in the balance sheet as deferred income. Where a grant is made as a contribution towards expenditure on fixed assets, there are two possible balance sheet treatments, both of which result in the grant being matched with the related expenditure in the profit and loss account. These are:

(a) to treat the amount of the grant as deferred income which is credited to the profit and loss account by instalments over the expected useful economic life of the related asset on a basis consistent with the depreciation policy; or

(b) to deduct the amount of the grant from the purchase price or production cost of the related asset, with a consequent reduction in the annual charge for depreciation.

It is considered that both treatments are acceptable and are capable of giving a true and fair view. However, the CCAB has received Counsel's opinion that paragraphs 17 and 26 of Schedule 4 to the Companies Act 1985 have the effect of prohibiting enterprises to which the legislation applies from accounting for grants made as a contribution towards expenditure on fixed assets by deducting the amount of the grant from the purchase price or production cost of the related asset.

16 Where a government grant takes the form of a transfer of non-monetary assets, the amount of the grant is the fair value of the assets transferred.

Disclosure

17 The financial statements should disclose the accounting policy adopted in respect of government grants in terms which make clear the method or methods adopted. The period or periods over which grants are credited to the profit and loss account should be disclosed in so far as this is practicable given the number and variety of grants that are being received.

Normally, it will be sufficient to give a broad indication of the future periods in which grants already received will be recognised in the profit and loss account.

18 Where the results for the period have been affected materially by amounts credited in respect of government grants, and/or where the results of future periods are expected to be affected materially by the recognition in the profit and loss account of grants already received, it is important for an understanding of the financial statements that the effects on the results or the financial position of the enterprise should be disclosed.

19 Government assistance to an enterprise may also be given in a form other than grants, for example consultancy and advisory services, subsidised loans and credit guarantees. Where such assistance has had a material effect on the results for the period, the nature and, where measurable, the effects of the assistance should be disclosed.

20 Under SSAP 18 'Accounting for contingencies' potential liabilities to repay grants should only be provided for to the extent that repayment is probable. A material contingent loss not so provided for should be disclosed, except where the possibility of repayment is remote.

Part 2 — Definition of terms

21 *Government* includes government and inter-governmental agencies and similar bodies whether local, national or international.

22 *Government grants* are assistance by government in the form of cash or transfers of assets to an enterprise in return for past or future compliance with certain conditions relating to the operating activities of the enterprise.

Part 3 — Standard accounting practice

23 Subject to paragraph 24 of this statement, government grants should be recognised in the profit and loss account so as to match them with the expenditure towards which they are intended to contribute. In the absence of persuasive evidence to the contrary, government grants should be assumed to contribute towards the expenditure that is the basis for their payment. To the extent that grants are made as a contribution towards specific expenditure on fixed assets, they should be recognised over the expected useful economic lives of the related assets. Grants made to give immediate financial support or assistance to an enterprise or to reimburse costs previously incurred should be recognised in the profit and loss account of the period in which they become receivable. Grants made to finance the general activities of an enterprise over a specific period or to compensate for a loss of current or future income should be recognised in the profit and loss account of the period in respect of which they are paid.

24 The foregoing requirements are subject to the proviso that a government grant should not be recognised in the profit and loss account until the conditions for its receipt have been complied with and there is reasonable assurance that the grant will be received.

25 Where the recognition in the profit and loss account of part or all of a grant that has been received is deferred, the amount so deferred should be treated as deferred income. To the extent that the grant is made as a contribution towards expenditure on a fixed asset, in principle it may be deducted from the purchase price or production cost of that asset. The CCAB has received Counsel's opinion, however, that the option to deduct government grants from the purchase price or production cost of fixed assets is not available to companies governed by the accounting and reporting requirements of the Companies Act 1985, as outlined in paragraph 34.

26 Grants relating to leased assets in the accounts of lessors should be accounted for in accordance with the requirements of SSAP 21 'Accounting for leases and hire purchase contracts'.

27 Potential liabilities to repay grants either in whole or in part in specified circumstances should only be provided for to the extent that repayment is probable. The repayment of a government grant should be accounted for by setting off the repayment against any unamortised deferred income relating to the grant. Any excess should be charged immediately to the profit and loss account.

Disclosure

28 The following information should be disclosed in the financial statements:

(a) the accounting policy adopted for government grants;

(b) the effects of government grants on the results for the period and/or the financial position of the enterprise;

(c) where the results of the period are affected materially by the receipt of forms of government assistance other than grants, the nature of that assistance and, to the extent that the effects on the financial statements can be measured, an estimate of those effects.

29 Potential liabilities to repay grants in specified circumstances should, if necessary, be disclosed in accordance with paragraph 16 of SSAP 18 'Accounting for contingencies'.

Transitional provisions

30 Any adjustments arising as a result of a change in accounting policy to comply with the requirements of this statement should be accounted for in accordance with paragraph 18 of SSAP 6 'Extraordinary items and prior year adjustments'.

Date from which effective

31 The accounting practices set out in this statement should be adopted as soon as possible. They should be regarded as standard accounting practice in respect of financial statements relating to accounting periods beginning on or after 1 July 1990.

Part 4 — Legal requirements in Great Britain and Northern Ireland

References are to the Companies Act 1985 and the Companies (Northern Ireland) Order 1986.

32 The balance sheet formats in Schedule 4 require that accruals and deferred income should be shown either under the heading 'Creditors' or separately as 'Accruals and deferred income'. This is relevant to the disclosure of deferred income in relation to government grants. (Standard paragraph 25.)

33 Paragraph 12 of Schedule 4 requires that the amount of any item shall be determined on a prudent basis and, in particular, that only profits realised at the balance sheet date shall be included in the profit and loss account. (Paragraph 91 of the Schedule defines realised profits in relation to a company's accounts as "such profits of the company as fall to be treated as realised profits for the purposes of those accounts in accordance with principles generally accepted with respect to the determination for accounting purposes of realised profits at the time when those accounts are prepared".) (Standard paragraph 24.)

34 Paragraph 17 of Schedule 4 requires that, subject to any provision for depreciation or diminution in value, the amount to be included in the balance sheet in respect of any fixed asset shall be its purchase price or production cost. Paragraph 26(1) states that the purchase price of an asset shall be determined by adding to the actual price paid any expenses incidental to its acquisition. The CCAB has received Counsel's opinion that these paragraphs have the effect of prohibiting enterprises to which the legislation applies from accounting for grants made as a contribution towards expenditure on fixed assets by deducting the amount of the grant from the purchase price or production cost of the related asset. (Standard paragraph 25.)

35 Paragraph 50 (2) of Schedule 4 provides that "The following information shall be given with respect to any other contingent liability not provided for:

(a) the amount or estimated amount of that liability;

(b) its legal nature; and

(c) whether any valuable security has been provided by the company in connection with that liability and if so, what". (Standard paragraph 29.)

Part 5 — Legal requirements in the Republic of Ireland

References are to the Companies (Amendment) Act 1986 and the Schedule to that Act unless otherwise stated.

36 Note 8 to the balance sheet formats in the Schedule provides that government grants included in the item 'Accruals and deferred income' must be shown separately in a note to the accounts if not shown separately in the balance sheet. However, Note 8 does not impose an obligation to include government grants under 'Accruals and deferred income' and such grants may, therefore, be placed under a separate heading. This separate heading is often placed between liabilities and share capital/reserves. If a new heading is adopted (using Section 4(12)), the requirement under Note 8 to have a separate mention of the amount is not applicable. (Standard paragraph 25.)

37 Section 5(c) of the Act requires that the amount of any item shall be determined on a prudent basis and, in particular, that only profits realised at the balance sheet date shall be included in the profit and loss account. (Paragraph 72 of the Schedule defines realised profits in relation to a company's accounts as "such profits of the company as fall to be treated as realised profits for the purposes of those accounts in accordance with principles generally accepted with respect to the determination for accounting purposes of realised profits at the time when those accounts are prepared".) (Standard paragraph 24.)

38 Paragraph 5 of the Schedule requires that, subject to any provision for depreciation or diminution in value, the amount to be included in respect of any fixed asset shall be its purchase price or production cost. Paragraph 14(1) states that the purchase price of an asset shall be determined by adding to the actual price paid any expenses incidental to its acquisition. The CCAB has received legal opinion that the equivalent paragraphs in UK legislation have the effect of prohibiting enterprises to which the legislation applies from accounting for grants made as a contribution towards expenditure on fixed assets by deducting the amount of the grant from the purchase price or production cost of the related asset. (Standard paragraph 25.)

39 Paragraph 36(2) of the Schedule provides that "The following information shall be given with respect to any other contingent liability not provided for:

(a) the amount or estimated amount of that liability;

(b) its legal nature; and

(c) whether any valuable security has been provided by the company in connection with that liability and if so, what". (Standard paragraph 29.)

40 The Companies (Amendment) Act 1983, Section 40 requires the convening of an extraordinary general meeting not later than 28 days from the earliest day on which it is known to a director of the company that its net assets have fallen to half or less of the company's called-up share capital (that a 'financial situation' exists). The 1983 Act also extends the reporting duties of auditors by requiring auditors to state whether in their opinion there existed at the balance sheet date a 'financial situation' in the context of Section 40 which would require the convening of an extraordinary general meeting. For the purpose of calculating the net assets of the company, the term 'liability' should be taken to include not only creditors, but also provisions for liabilities and charges, accruals and deferred income. Government grants treated as deferred income should, therefore, be regarded as a liability for the purposes of calculating net assets under Section 40.

Part 6 — Compliance with International Accounting Standard No.20 'Accounting for Government Grants and Disclosure of Government Assistance'

41 The requirements of International Accounting Standard No. 20 'Accounting for Government Grants and Disclosure of Government Assistance' accord very closely with the content of the United Kingdom and Irish Accounting Standard No. 4 (Revised) 'Accounting for government grants' and accordingly compliance with SSAP 4 (Revised) will ensure compliance with IAS 20 in all material respects.

Accounting for value added tax

(Issued April 1974)

This statement seeks by presenting a standard accounting practice, to achieve uniformity of accounting treatment of VAT in financial statements.

Part 1 — Explanatory note

1 VAT is a tax on the supply of goods and services which is eventually borne by the final consumer but collected at each stage of the production and distribution chain. As a general principle, therefore, the treatment of VAT in the accounts of a trader should reflect his role as a collector of the tax and VAT should not be included in income or in expenditure whether of a capital or of a revenue nature. There will, however, be circumstances, as noted below, in which a trader will himself bear VAT and in such circumstances the accounting treatment should reflect that fact.

Persons not accountable for VAT

2 Persons not accountable for VAT will suffer VAT on inputs. For them VAT will increase the cost of all goods and services to which it applies and should be included in such costs. In particular, the VAT on fixed assets should be added to the cost of the fixed assets concerned.

Accountable persons who also carry on exempted activities

3 In the case of persons who also carry on exempted activities there will be a residue of VAT, which will fall directly on the trader and which will normally be arrived at by division of his activities as between taxable outputs (including zero-rated) and those which are exempt. In such cases, the principle that such VAT will increase the costs to which it applies and should be included in such costs will be equally applicable. Hence the appropriate portion of the VAT allocable to fixed assets should, if irrecoverable, be added to the cost of the fixed assets concerned and the proportion allocable to other items should, if practicable and material, be included in such other items. In some cases, e.g. where financial and VAT accounting periods do not coincide, an estimate may be necessary.

Non-deductible inputs

4 All traders will bear tax in so far as it relates to non-deductible inputs (e.g. motor cars other than for resale and certain business entertaining expenses). Such tax should therefore be included as part of the cost of those items. A similar situation exists in the Republic of Ireland where traders dealing in products such as motor cars, radios and television sets, will bear some non-deductible VAT on the input cost of these items.

Amounts due to or from the Revenue authorities

5 The net amount due to or from the Revenue authorities in respect of VAT should be included of as part of debtors or creditors and will not normally require separate disclosure.

Capital commitments

6 The estimated amount of capital commitments should include the appropriate amount, if any, of irrecoverable VAT.

Comparisons

7 Where it has been customary for purchase tax (or sales taxes in the Republic of Ireland) to be included in turnover, it may be desirable in the initial years of VAT to disclose the turnover periods in which such tax applied both gross and net of tax so as to assist in comparisons. In some cases, for example retailers, it may not be possible to ascertain the amount of purchase tax (or sales tax) included in turnover; in those cases an explanatory note will be desirable. Where customs or excise duties are included in turnover and such duties are reduced to take account of VAT, an explanatory note may be necessary.

Part 2 — Standard accounting practice

Turnover

8 Turnover shown in the profit and loss account should exclude VAT on taxable outputs. If it is desired to show also the gross turnover, the VAT relevant to that turnover should be shown as a deduction in arriving at the turnover exclusive of VAT.

Irrecoverable VAT

9 Irrecoverable VAT allocable to fixed assets and to other items disclosed separately in published accounts should be included in their cost where practicable and material.

Date from which effective

10 The accounting practices set out in this statement should be adopted as soon as possible and regarded as standard in respect of accounting periods starting on or after 1 January 1974.

The treatment of taxation under the imputation system in the accounts of companies

(Issued August 1974: Appendix 3 added December 1977)

The imputation system of company taxation started in the UK in April 1973 and in the Republic of Ireland in 1976. The purpose of this statement is to establish a standard treatment of taxation in company accounts, with particular reference to advance corporation tax and 'mainstream' corporation tax. This statement has been prepared for use when the imputation system of corporation tax is fully implemented. It does not deal in detail with the problems arising in the transitional periods, which should be resolved in the light of the principles herein.

In order to obviate the need to amend the statement whenever there are changes in the rates of taxation the following have been assumed:

(a) corporation tax 50%

(b) advance corporation tax - three sevenths of the amount of qualifying distributions.

The small companies rate should be substituted where warranted by the circumstances.

The application of this statement to companies subject to taxation in the Republic of Ireland is dealt with in Appendix 3.

Part 1 — Explanatory note

Introduction

1 The principal features of the imputation system of corporation tax are broadly as follows. Corporation tax is charged at a single rate on a company's income whether distributed or undistributed; in the absence of a dividend the whole of the tax is payable on a date which may be a year or more after the end of the relevant accounting period. When in an accounting period a company makes a distribution to shareholders, it does not withhold income tax from the payment, but is required to make an advance payment of corporation tax ('ACT'). This ACT will normally be set off against the company's total liability for corporation tax on its income (but not on its chargeable gains) of the same accounting period. The resultant net liability is known as the mainstream corporation tax. The charge for corporation tax therefore comprises the mainstream corporation tax and the ACT. From the paying company's point of view the concept of 'gross' dividends and the deduction of income tax at source therefrom has disappeared. However, an individual shareholder receiving the dividend is chargeable to tax on an amount of income equivalent to the dividend plus the imputed tax credit. This tax credit (generally equivalent to the ACT paid by the company) will discharge the basic rate liability to income tax of a United Kingdom resident or would in certain circumstances be recoverable. For corporate shareholders the concept of franked investment income continues.

2 The ACT set off against the final corporation tax bill is effectively restricted to 30% (assuming a 50% tax rate) of the company's taxable income. Any ACT thereby unrelieved (i.e. ACT on a distribution which together with the related ACT is in excess of taxable income) can be carried back for two years or forward without time limit (but cannot be set against corporation tax on income arising before 1 April 1973).

3 The main accounting problems arising from the imputation system are:

(a) the treatment in the profit and loss account of outgoing dividends and the related ACT;

(b) determining the recoverability of ACT;

(c) the treatment of irrecoverable ACT and of unrelieved overseas tax arising from the payment or proposed payment of dividends.;

(d) the treatment in the balance sheet of taxation liabilities, recoverable ACT and dividends;

(e) the treatment of franked investment income.

Dividends and the related ACT

4 The treatment in the profit and loss account of outgoing dividends and the related ACT is concerned with whether ACT should be treated as part of the cost of the dividend or whether it should be treated as part of tax on the company's profits. The right of a company to deduct income tax from dividends no longer applies. Whatever percentage or per-share dividend is declared, that is the amount which the company will pay to its members. The fact that the dividend will carry a tax credit is a matter affecting the recipient rather than the company's method of accounting for the dividend. Accordingly it is considered appropriate that dividends should be shown in the profit and loss account at the amount paid or payable to the shareholders and that neither the related ACT nor the imputed tax credit should be treated as part of the cost of the dividend. It follows that the charge for taxation in the profit and loss account should embrace the full amount of corporation tax, and not merely the mainstream liability.

Recoverability of ACT

5 ACT is primarily recovered by being set off against the corporation tax on the income of the year in which the related distribution is made. In the case of dividends paid during the year under review, the taxable income of that year and of the two previous years will normally be available to absorb the relief. Where a proposed dividend is to be paid in the following year, then the related ACT falls to be set off against the corporation tax on the taxable income of the year of payment of the proposed dividend and in default of that, against the taxable income of the year under review or of the year previous to that. In both cases ACT can be carried forward indefinitely if necessary. In each year there is an overriding restriction on the use of ACT for set off, by reference to the taxable income of that year.

6 For accounting purposes it is necessary to decide whether recovery of the ACT is reasonably certain and foreseeable or whether it should be written off in the profit and loss account. If the taxable income of the year under review and the amounts available from the preceding year or years are insufficient to cover the ACT, then recoverability of ACT will depend on the extent to which income is earned in future periods in excess of dividends paid or on the existence of a deferred taxation account of adequate size (see paragraph 7). Although the relief remains available indefinitely it will be prudent to have regard only to the immediate and foreseeable future; how long this future period should be will depend upon the circumstances of each case, but it is suggested that where there is no deferred taxation account it should normally not extend beyond the next accounting period.

7 Where a deferred taxation account is maintained, the attitude to recoverability may be different. The balance on the deferred taxation account usually represents an amount which will be released to profit and loss account over the life of related fixed assets. Unrelieved ACT is available to offset against future taxable profits for an indefinite period. There is thus a similarity between unrelieved ACT and the balance on the deferred taxation account and it is therefore reasonable to regard unrelieved ACT as being available for deduction from the amount at which the deferred taxation account is stated in the accounts. Only a proportion of the balance on the account (at the rates assumed 30% of the amount on which the credit balance of the account has been calculated) can be used for this purpose: this is the extent to which ACT can be set off against the corporation tax liability. It should be noted however that to the extent to which the deferred taxation account represents deferred chargeable gains, it is not available for this purpose.

Irrecoverable ACT

8 Any irrecoverable ACT (i.e. ACT the recoverability of which is not reasonably certain and foreseeable) should be written off in the profit and loss account in which the related dividend is shown.

9 There are two differing views on the presentation in the profit and loss account of irrecoverable ACT written off. One view is that irrecoverable ACT should be treated as part of the tax charge upon the company to be deducted in arriving at profits after tax: the other that the irrecoverable ACT, being a cost stemming from the payment of a dividend, should be treated as an appropriation like the dividend itself. Of the two methods the first is supported as the appropriate accounting treatment because unrelieved ACT constitutes tax upon the company or group, as opposed to tax on the shareholders, and is not an appropriation of profits. It is appreciated however that some readers or analysts of accounts may wish for their purposes to regard irrecoverable ACT in some other manner. The amount of irrecoverable ACT should therefore be separately disclosed if material.

10 The question remains whether irrecoverable ACT could appropriately be treated as an 'extraordinary item' as defined in SSAP 6*. The test laid down in that document needs to be applied to each individual case, but it is unlikely that a cost arising from the payment of a normal dividend would be derived from 'transactions outside the ordinary activities of the business', and accordingly irrecoverable ACT will normally constitute part of the ordinary tax charge.

Unrelieved overseas tax

11 Although for tax purposes unrelieved overseas tax cannot be carried forward, the accounting treatment of unrelieved overseas tax arising from the payment of a dividend is similar to that of irrecoverable ACT. This matter is dealt with more fully in Appendix 2.

Franked investment income

12 The concept of franked investment income established under earlier tax systems is continued under the imputation system. Franked investment income comprises the amount of a qualifying distribution received from another UK resident company with the addition of the related tax credit. The net amount can be redistributed to shareholders of the recipient company without payment of ACT and the related tax credit remains attached from the viewpoint of the shareholder.

*SSAP 6 'Extraordinary items and prior year adjustments'.

13 There are several possible methods of dealing with franked investment income in accounts. The two main possibilities are:

(a) to bring into the profit and loss account the cash amount received or receivable (i.e. excluding the tax credit) or

(b) to bring in the amount of the franked investment income (i.e. including the tax credit, an equivalent amount then being treated as part of the charge for taxation).

The first method would involve treating the income either as an item of profit before taxation, or as an addition to the profit after taxation — both alternatives are open to objection. The second method would allow recognition of the income both at the pre-tax and at the after-tax stage in a way which is consistent with other elements of profit, and is therefore adopted as the standard accounting practice.

Mainstream corporation tax

14 Apart from ACT the dates of payments of corporation tax under the new system remain as before. Depending on the date to which a company makes up its accounts, the balance sheet should contain either (a) one liability for mainstream corporation tax, being that on the profit of the year, or (b) two liabilities. In the latter case they will be the mainstream corporation tax on the profits of the previous year payable within nine months of the balance sheet date, and mainstream corporation tax for the year under review payable twelve months later than the above liability. These liabilities should be separately disclosed, under current liabilities or otherwise as appropriate. If they are not shown under current liabilities, the due date of payment should be stated.

ACT

15 ACT on dividends paid will either have been paid by the balance sheet date or will be due for payment shortly afterwards. Where the ACT is regarded as recoverable then it will normally be deducted from the full corporation tax charge based on the profit of the period in arriving at the mainstream corporation tax liability shown in the balance sheet.

16 In the case of dividends proposed but not paid at the balance sheet date, the related ACT will become due for payment within about three months of the dividend itself, and should be shown as a current liability. The right of set-off, however, (assuming the ACT is regarded as recoverable) will not arise for at least 21 months from the balance sheet date. The right is, therefore, in the nature of a deferred asset, and should be shown as such on the balance sheet unless there is a deferred tax account from the balance of which the amount may be deducted.

17 If ACT on dividends paid or proposed is treated as irrecoverable (see paragraphs 8-10) there is no corresponding asset to be dealt with in the balance sheet.

Preference shares

18 Any dividend right established before 6 April 1973 at a gross rate or a gross amount was reduced by the Finance Act 1972, Schedule 23 para. 18* to seven-tenths of its former rate or amount. Steps should therefore be taken to distinguish, for example, a 10% preference share issued before 6 April 1973 on which the dividend is now 7%, from such a preference share issued after that date. A change in the basic rate of income tax and a corresponding change in the rate of ACT would not affect this once-for-all 'netting down'. Thus a former 10% preference share may in the future yield, with related tax credit, either

* Subsequent changes in the rate of ACT have varied the rate of tax credit but not the amount of the cash dividend payable to shareholders.

more or less than 10% on nominal value. The new rate of dividend on preference shares* should therefore be incorporated in the description of the shares in the balance sheet, e.g.

		Authorised	*Issued*
100,000	10% (now 7% + Tax Credit) Preference Shares of £1.	£100,000	£100,000

Appendices

19 Certain accounting considerations arising from the imputation system of corporation tax are considered to be supplementary to the main purpose of this statement. These considerations have been dealt with as follows:

Appendix 1 Examples of the taxation items to be disclosed.
Appendix 2 Further practical points:

(a) unrelieved overseas tax

(b) earnings and dividends in the historical summary.

Appendix 3 Application to companies subject to taxation in the Republic of Ireland.

Part 2 — Definition of terms

Recoverable ACT

20 That amount of the ACT paid or payable on outgoing dividends paid and proposed which can be:

(a) set off against a corporation tax liability on the profits of the period under review or of previous periods; or

(b) properly set off against a credit balance on deferred tax account; or

(c) expected to be recoverable taking into account expected profits and dividends — normally those of the next accounting period only.

Irrecoverable ACT

21 ACT paid or payable on outgoing dividends paid and proposed other than recoverable ACT.

Part 3 — Standard accounting practice

Profit and loss account

22 The following items should be included in the taxation charge in the profit and loss account and, where material, should be separately disclosed:

(a) the amount of the United Kingdom corporation tax specifying:

(i) the charge for corporation tax on the income of the year (where such corporation tax includes transfers between the deferred taxation account and the profit and loss account these also should be separately disclosed where material);

(ii) tax attributable to franked investment income;

(iii) irrecoverable ACT;

* Including participating preference and preferred ordinary shares where the former rate of dividend forms part of the title.

(iv) the relief for overseas taxation;

(b) the total overseas taxation relieved and unrelieved, specifying that part of the unrelieved overseas taxation which arises from the payment or proposed payment of dividends.

23 If the rate of corporation tax is not known for the whole or part of the period covered by the accounts, the latest known rate should be used and disclosed.

24 Outgoing dividends should not include either the related ACT or the attributable tax credit.

25 Incoming dividends from United Kingdom resident companies should be included at the amount of cash received or receivable plus the tax credit.

Balance sheet

26 Dividends proposed (or declared and not yet payable) should be included in current liabilities without the addition of the related ACT. The ACT on proposed dividends (whether recoverable or irrecoverable) should be included as a current tax liability.

27 If the ACT on proposed dividends is regarded as recoverable, it should be deducted from the deferred tax account if such an account is available for this purpose. In the absence of a deferred taxation account ACT recoverable should be shown as a deferred asset.

28 Where the title of a class of preference shares (or participating or preferred ordinary shares) issued before 6 April 1973, includes a fixed rate of dividend, the new rate of dividend should be incorporated in the description of the shares in the balance sheet.

Date from which effective for companies subject to taxation in the UK

29 The accounting practices set out in this statement should be adopted as soon as possible and regarded as standard in respect of financial statements relating to accounting periods beginning on or after 1 January 1975.

Date from which effective for companies subject to taxation in the Republic of Ireland

30 The accounting practices set out in Appendix 3 relating to companies subject to taxation in the Republic of Ireland should be regarded as standard in respect of financial statements relating to accounting periods beginning on or after 1 January 1988.

Appendices

The appendices are for general guidance and do not form part of the statement of standard accounting practice.

Appendix 1

31 This example indicates one method of showing (by way of note) the taxation items required to be disclosed under the Companies Act 1967 and Part 3 of this standard. In simple cases taxation may be dealt with entirely within the profit and loss account.

	£000
Corporation tax on income at x% (including £*b* transferred to/from deferred taxation account)	*a*
Less relief for overseas taxation	*c*
	d
Overseas taxation*	*e*
Tax credit on UK dividends received	*f*
Irrecoverable advance corporation tax	*g*
	H

* Including £J arising from the payment of dividends (see paragraphs 1 and 2 of Appendix 2).

Appendix 2 — Further practical points

Unrelieved overseas tax

32 If the rate of overseas tax on the overseas income of a UK company exceeds the rate of UK mainstream corporation tax thereon, then part of the overseas tax will be unrelieved. If the company pays all or part of a dividend out of its overseas income (i.e. if it pays a dividend which, together with the related ACT is substantially in excess of its, or its group's taxable UK income) then the ACT on the dividend paid out of overseas income will not be available for the purpose of calculating overseas tax credit. Thus, the payment of a dividend in these circumstances may give rise to unrelieved tax (depending on the rate of overseas tax) but this unrelieved tax, unlike the irrecoverable ACT, is not available for carry forward.

33 Following the same reasoning as applied to the accounting treatment of irrecoverable ACT, unrelieved overseas tax which arises from an outgoing dividend should be treated as part of the tax charge to be deducted in arriving at profits after tax. The amount should be separately disclosed, if material.

Earnings and dividends in the historical summary

34 The change to the imputation system destroyed the comparability, as between one period and another, of many of the figures in the historical records. For example, earnings were formerly available to cover gross dividends before deduction of income tax, but under the imputation system they are now available to cover the actual cash dividends payable to the preference or equity shareholders. Hence, in calculating earnings for equity under the imputation system, preference dividends should be deducted at the amount declared and payable to the shareholders — not at the former gross amount.

35 In general, it is likely to be either impracticable or unsatisfactory to attempt to adjust profits earned under one system of taxation to another tax system. Furthermore, if a company had been taxed differently, it might have taken different financial decisions. Most of the items in the historical summary should therefore be left as originally published.

36 Figures such as earnings and dividends based on the old system of taxation should, however, be carefully distinguished from those based on the new system. It may be helpful to describe dividends paid under the old system of taxation as 'gross dividends' to distinguish them from dividends paid under the new system.

37 The transitional period, which may cover more than one accounting year, presents particular problems. It would usually be preferable (where practicable) to show an overlap with the figures calculated both ways for the straddling period, or alternatively to indicate in some other manner the points where comparability has been destroyed by a change in the system to taxation (i.e. 1965 and 1973). Figures relating to earlier periods can then be shown entirely on the old basis with subsequent figures being entirely on the new basis.

38 To calculate the gross dividends for the straddling year (for the purpose of historical summaries only) any dividends relating to that year paid on or after 6 April 1973 may be increased by the amount of the appropriate tax credits and added to any dividends paid before 6 April 1973. To calculate the equivalent 'new' dividends from gross dividends, the gross dividends may be reduced by 30%.

Appendix 3

(This appendix was added in December 1977 and revised in 1988)

Appendix 3 contains the statement of standard accounting practice for application to companies subject to taxation in the Republic of Ireland.

Preface

This revision of the appendix is issued following the introduction of advance corporation tax (ACT) in the Republic of Ireland.

This statement is based on taxation legislation in force up to and including the Finance Act 1987.

In order to obviate the need to amend this statement whenever there are changes in the rates of taxation the following have been assumed:

(a) corporation tax 50%

(b) advance corporation tax 35/65ths of the amount of qualifying distributions.

The computation of earnings per share on a net basis is now relevant in the Republic of Ireland. For this purpose the principle enunciated in SSAP 3 should be applied (except paragraphs 18 and 19 which no longer have effect).

Part 1 — Explanatory note

Introduction

39 The principal features of the imputation system of corporation tax are broadly as follows. Corporation tax is charged at a single rate on a company's profits whether distributed or undistributed; the whole of the tax is generally payable six months after the end of the relevant accounting period. Where a company makes a distribution it is required to make an advance payment of corporation tax. This ACT paid and not repaid will normally be set off against the company's liability for corporation tax on its income (but not on its chargeable gains) of the accounting period in which the distribution is made. An individual shareholder receiving a dividend is chargeable to income tax on an amount of income equivalent to the dividend plus the imputed tax credit. This tax credit will discharge the equivalent amount of income tax of a Republic of Ireland resident or is, in certain circumstances, recoverable. For corporate shareholders, the concept of franked investment income continues.

40 Any unrelieved ACT (known in the legislation as surplus ACT) can be carried back against any corporation tax payable in respect of accounting periods ending within the 12 months prior to the period in which the ACT liability arises or forward without time-limit for set off against the company's corporation tax liability on income. A carry-back claim must be made within two years of the end of the accounting period in which the distribution is made.

41 The main accounting problems arising from the imputation system are:

(a) the treatment in the profit and loss account of outgoing dividends and related ACT;

(b) determining the recoverability of ACT;

(c) the treatment of irrecoverable ACT arising from the payment or proposed payment of dividends;

(d) the treatment of any unrelieved overseas tax;

(e) the treatment of franked investment income;

(f) the balance sheet treatment of taxation liabilities, recoverable ACT and dividends;

(g) the title of preference shares.

Each of these matters is dealt with below.

Dividends and the related ACT

42 The treatment in the profit and loss account of outgoing dividends and related ACT, is concerned with whether ACT should be treated as part of the cost of the dividend or whether it should be treated as part of tax on the company's profits. Whatever percentage or per-share dividend is declared, that is the amount which the company will pay to its members. The fact that the dividend will carry a tax credit is a matter affecting the recipient rather than the company's method of accounting for the dividend. Accordingly, it is considered appropriate that dividends should be shown in the profit and loss account at the amount paid or payable to the shareholders and that neither the related ACT nor the imputed tax credit should be treated as part of the dividend. It follows that the charge for taxation in the profit and loss account should embrace the full amount of corporation tax and not merely the reduced liability after ACT set off.

Recoverability of ACT

43 ACT is primarily recovered by being set off against the corporation tax on the income of the year in which the distribution is made. In the case of dividends paid during the year under review, the corporation tax on the income of that year and of accounting periods ended in the previous year may be available to absorb the ACT. Where a proposed dividend is to be paid in the following year, then the related ACT falls to be set off against the corporation tax on the taxable income of the year of payment of the proposed dividend, and failing that against the corporation tax on the income of the year under review. Any surplus can be carried forward as outlined in paragraph 2 above.

44 For accounting purposes it is necessary to decide whether recovery of the ACT is reasonably certain and foreseeable, or whether it should be written off in the profit and loss account. If the corporation tax on the income of the year under review and the amounts available from the preceding year are insufficient to cover the ACT, then recoverability of ACT will depend on the extent to which corporation tax payable in future periods is in excess of ACT on dividends paid and proposed or on the existence of a deferred taxation account of adequate size. Although the relief remains available indefinitely, it will be prudent to have regard only to the immediate and foreseeable future; how long this future period should be will depend upon the circumstances of each case, but where there is no deferred taxation account it should not normally extend beyond the next accounting period.

45 The approach to be adopted to recoverable ACT should be consistent with SSAP 15 (revised) paragraphs 31 and 32 which read as follows:

31 Debit balances arising in respect of advance corporation tax on dividends payable or proposed at the balance sheet date should be carried forward to the extent that it is foreseen that sufficient corporation tax will be assessed on the profits or income of the succeeding accounting period, against which the advance corporation tax is available for offset.

32 Debit balances arising in respect of advance corporation tax other than on dividends payable or proposed at the balance sheet date should be written off unless their recovery is assured beyond reasonable doubt. Such recovery will normally only be assured where the debit balances are recoverable out of corporation tax arising on profits or income of the succeeding accounting period, without replacement by equivalent debit balances.

It should be noted that paragraph 31 dealing with payable or proposed dividends permits ACT carry forward with replacement by an equivalent debit whereas paragraph 32 dealing with paid dividends does not.

46 The more stringent standard applying to paid dividends is justified since one would normally expect the ACT on dividends paid to be set off against the current year's corporation tax liability. Carrying forward the ACT for set off against the following year's tax liability amounts to a second opportunity for set-off which could create a revolving backlog of unrecovered ACT. The carry forward is allowed where the backlog can be cleared in the following year — otherwise it is not permitted.

47 On the other hand for dividends proposed the first possible set-off is against the following year's tax liability. In the event of inadequacy of the following year's liability the more stringent condition will be applied in the year subsequent to the following year when ACT carry forward is then being considered.

48 Where there is a provision for deferred taxation on income, the attitude to recoverability will be different. The balance on the deferred taxation account represents an amount of corporation tax which is expected to be payable in the future. Unrelieved ACT is available to off set against future corporation tax on income for an indefinite period. It is therefore reasonable to regard unrelieved ACT as being available for deduction from the amount at which the deferred taxation account is stated in the accounts. It should be noted, however, that to the extent to which the deferred taxation account represents deferred chargeable gains, it is not available for this purpose.

Irrecoverable ACT

49 Any irrecoverable ACT (i.e. ACT the recoverability of which is not reasonably certain and foreseeable) should be written off in the profit and loss account in which the related dividend is shown, or in the first subsequent period in which ACT, which was previously regarded as recoverable, is considered to have become irrecoverable.

50 There are two differing views on the presentation in the profit and loss account of irrecoverable ACT written off. One view is that irrecoverable ACT should be treated as part of the tax charge upon the company to be deducted in arriving at profits after tax; the other that the irrecoverable ACT being a cost stemming from the payment of a dividend should be treated as an appropriation like the dividend itself. Of the two methods the first is supported as the appropriate accounting treatment because unrelieved ACT constitutes tax upon the company or group, as opposed to tax on the shareholders and is not an appropriation of profits. It is appreciated, however, that some readers or analysts of accounts may wish for their purposes to regard irrecoverable ACT in some other manner.

The amount of irrecoverable ACT should therefore be separately disclosed if material.

51 The question remains whether irrecoverable ACT should be treated as an extraordinary item as defined in SSAP 6. The test laid down in that document needs to be applied to each individual case, but it is unlikely that a cost arising from the payment of a normal dividend would be derived from transactions outside the ordinary activities of the business, and accordingly irrecoverable ACT will normally constitute part of the ordinary tax charge.

Unrelieved overseas tax

52 Unrelieved overseas tax cannot be carried forward for tax purposes. The accounting treatment of unrelieved overseas tax is similar to that of irrecoverable ACT.

Franked investment income

53 Franked investment income comprises the amount of a distribution received from another Irish resident company with the addition of the related tax credit. The net amount can usually be redistributed to shareholders of the recipient company without payment of ACT, and the related tax credit remains attached from the viewpoint of the shareholder.

54 There are several possible methods of dealing with franked investment income in accounts. The two main possibilities are:

(a) to bring into the profit and loss account the cash amount received or receivable (i.e. excluding the tax credit) or

(b) to bring in the amount of the franked investment income i.e. including the tax credit, an equivalent amount then being treated as part of the charge for taxation.

The first method would involve treating the income either as an item of profit before taxation, or as an addition to the profit after taxation — both alternatives are open to objection. The second method would allow recognition of the income both at the pre-tax and after tax stages in a way which is consistent with other elements of profit, and is therefore adopted as the standard accounting practice.

55 Where franked investment income includes a tax credit at less than the normal amount, due to export sales relief, manufacturing relief or Shannon exemption, the income should be grossed up at the rate of the imputed tax credit which would itself be shown as a component of the tax charge in the accounts. If the amount of franked investment income from manufacturing, exports sales, or Shannon exempt sources is material, it is recommended that the amount of relief should be disclosed in the financial statements.

Balance sheet treatment of taxation liabilities and ACT

56 In most cases the balance sheet will contain one liability for corporation tax, being that on the profit of the year which is generally payable within six months of the end of the accounting period and thus shown as a current liability. In some cases Corporation Tax may be payable more than 12 months after the balance sheet date. Liabilities should be shown as current or non-current as appropriate. If shown as non-current the due date(s) of payment or periods over which payment is due should be stated.

57 ACT on dividends paid will be due for payment six months after the end of the accounting period in which the distribution is made. Where this ACT can be set off against corporation tax on the income of the year under review and the income of the preceding year, no separate liability for ACT should be shown (ACT being covered by the corporation tax liability); if this is not possible, the ACT should be shown as a separate current liability.

58 In the case of dividends proposed but not paid at the balance sheet date, the related ACT will become due for payment eighteen months after the end of the accounting period and should be shown as a separate non-current liability. Where the provision for corporation tax on the income of the period under review, as reduced by ACT on dividends paid, exceeds the liability for ACT on dividends proposed, no separate liability need be recorded for ACT on dividends proposed.

59 Where ACT is regarded as recoverable (see paragraphs 5-10) the amount should be shown as a non-current asset where it is not expected to be recovered within a year, or, where there is a deferred tax account, the amount should be debited to that account to the extent that the balance on that account represents tax on income.

60 Where ACT is regarded as irrecoverable (see paragraphs 11-13) the amount should be charged to profit and loss account. Where there is a substantial contingent asset in the form of irrecoverable ACT written off, the disclosure of the existence of this asset should be considered in the light of SSAP 18.

Preference shares

61 Any dividend right established before April 6,1976 at a gross rate or a gross amount is reduced (by Section 178 of Corporation Tax Act 1976 as amended by Section 28 of Finance Act 1978) to such an amount as would, with the tax credit, amount to the original gross rate. Steps should therefore be taken to distinguish, for example a 10% preference share issued before April 6, 1976 on which the dividend is now at a rate which, together with the tax credit, would amount to 10%. A change from year to year in the rate of tax credit used in the formula will affect this 'netting down' but not the gross rate. For example, a change in the rate of tax credit from 30% to 35% means the gross rate of 10% remains unchanged but its composition changes from net 7% plus tax credit 3% to net 6.5% plus tax credit 3.5%. The description of these shares in the balance sheet should show that the gross rate includes a tax credit. The 'netted down' rate of dividend applicable in the year in question on pre-1976 preference shares should therefore be incorporated in the description of the shares in the balance sheet e.g.

		Authorised	*Issued*
100,000	10% (including tax credit) preference share of IR£1	IR£100,000	IR£100,000

NOTE: At the balance sheet date the composition of the gross dividend was 3.5% tax credit and 6.5% net dividend.

'Preference' shares include participating preference shares and preferred ordinary shares issued prior to April 6, 1976 where the rate of dividend forms part of the title by which the share is described.

62 Where companies have claimed manufacturing relief, the Finance Act 1980, Sections 45-46, contains special provision relating to the tax credit attaching to distributions. Broadly speaking distributions must first be made from the pool of profits, called the 'primary fund', that have benefited from manufacturing relief. Such distributions have reduced tax credit attached to them of 1/18 of the distribution. In the interests of informative reporting, disclosure of the amount of the 'primary fund' is recommended.

Legal requirements

63 Attention is drawn to the requirements of Companies (Amendment) Act 1986 and, in particular, to paragraphs 32(1) (b) and (c), 33 and 40 of the Schedule.

Part 2 — Definition of terms

Recoverable ACT

64 The amount of the ACT paid or payable on outgoing dividends paid and proposed:

(a) which can be properly set off against a credit balance on deferred tax account, or

(b) which can be recovered against the corporation tax liability on the income of any accounting period up to and including the period under review, or

(c) which cannot be set off or recovered under (a) or (b) above but

(i) where relating to a dividend paid in the period under review or in a previous period, can be set off against the expected corporation tax liability on the income of the subsequent period without replacement by an equivalent debit balance;

(ii) where relating to a dividend payable in the subsequent period, can be set off against the expected corporation tax liability on the income of that period.

Recoverable ACT includes any ACT meeting this definition notwithstanding it has been written off previously as irrecoverable.

Irrecoverable ACT

65 ACT paid or payable on outgoing dividends paid and proposed other than recoverable ACT.

Part 3 — Standard accounting practice

Profit and loss account

66 The following items should be included in the taxation charge or credit in the profit and loss account and, where material, should be separately disclosed:

(a) the amount of corporation tax specifying:

(i) the charge or credit for corporation tax on the income of the year;

(ii) transfers between the deferred taxation account and the profit and loss account;

(iii) the relief for overseas taxation;

(b) the total overseas taxation relieved and unrelieved;

(c) tax attributable to franked investment income;

(d) irrecoverable ACT (specifying the basis of the charge);

(e) ACT previously written off as irrecoverable now recovered or regarded as recoverable (specifying the basis of the credit).

Material adjustments in respect of previous periods should be disclosed. Where a company benefits from export sales relief, manufacturing relief or Shannon exemption this should be disclosed together with the dates of expiry of the relief. Where the tax charge is materially affected by timing differences not provided for, this should be disclosed.

67 The rate of corporation tax used should be disclosed. If the rate of corporation tax is not known for the whole or part of the period covered by the accounts the latest known rate should be used.

68 Outgoing dividends should not include either the related ACT or the attributable tax credit. However, the tax credit attaching to dividends paid or proposed should be disclosed in the notes to the accounts.

69 Incoming dividends from Republic of Ireland resident companies should be included in profit before taxation at the amount of cash received or receivable plus the tax credit.

Balance sheet

70 Dividends proposed (or declared and not yet payable) should be included in current liabilities, without the addition of the related ACT.

71 Where ACT on dividends paid in the accounting period under review is exceeded by provisions for corporation tax on the income of the accounting period under review and/or the preceding accounting period(s) (against which that ACT can be set), no separate liability for this ACT should be recorded as ACT would not result in any increase in the overall tax liability. To the extent that this ACT exceeds such provisions it should be provided for as a separate current liability.

72 Where ACT on both dividends paid and dividends proposed in the accounting period under review is exceeded by the provision for corporation tax on the income of that period no separate liability needs to be recorded for ACT on the proposed dividends because the fact that the current period's corporation tax is available to discharge the subsequent period's ACT ensures that the ACT on the proposed dividends will not result in any increase in the overall tax liability. To the extent that ACT on dividends proposed exceeds the corporation tax provision, as reduced by ACT on dividends paid, it should be provided for as a separate non-current liability.

73 If a separate liability for ACT has to be provided for under paragraphs 33 and/or 34 above, the corresponding asset which arises if this ACT is regarded as recoverable should be deducted from any provision for deferred taxation on income in the balance sheet and, to the extent that such provision is inadequate to cover it, the recoverable ACT should be shown as a current or non-current asset as appropriate. At each subsequent balance sheet date, the recoverability of this asset should be re-assessed. If the ACT for which a separate liability has to be provided for under paragraph 32 and/or 33 above is not regarded as recoverable, the provision for the liability should be created by a charge to profit and loss account for irrecoverable ACT (see paragraph 28(d) above).

74 Where the title of a class of preference shares (or participating preference or preferred ordinary shares) issued before April 6, 1976 includes a fixed rate of dividend, the fact that the rate in the title now includes a tax credit should be indicated in the description of the shares in the balance sheet or notes to the balance sheet. The composition of the gross rate at the balance sheet date between net dividend and the tax credit should also be disclosed.

Date from which effective for companies subject to taxation in the Republic of Ireland

75 The accounting practices set out in this Statement should be regarded as standard in respect of financial statements relating to accounting periods beginning on or after January 1, 1988 and earlier adoption is encouraged.

Appendix

This appendix is for general guidance and does not form part of the Statement of Standard Accounting Practice.

1 Profit and loss account

This example indicates one method of showing (by way of note to the profit and loss account) the taxation items required to be disclosed under the Companies (Amendment)

Act 1986 and Part 3 of this standard. In simple cases, taxation may be dealt with entirely within the profit and loss account.

	IR£
Corporation tax on income at 50% (including £b transferred to/from deferred taxation account)	*a*
Less relief for overseas taxation	*c*
	d
Overseas taxation	*e*
Tax credit on Republic of Ireland dividends received	*f*
Irrecoverable advance corporation tax (explain basis)	*g*
	h

NOTE: The taxation charge has been reduced by IR£x in respect of export sales relief/manufacturing relief/Shannon exemption. Export sales relief expires on April 5, 1990; no relief may be claimed for any accounting period or part of a period commencing after that date.

2 Balance sheet

(a) Paragraph 33 refers to the treatment of ACT on dividends paid as a current liability. Under the formats in the Schedule (the Schedule) to the Companies (Amendment) Act 1986 such ACT may be classified as follows:

Format 1 C8

Format 2 C8

(b) Paragraph 34 refers to the treatment of ACT on proposed dividends as a non-current tax liability. Such ACT may be classified in the Schedule formats as follows:

Format 1 F8

Format 2 C8 but including the ACT in the amounts falling due after more than one year.

(c) Paragraph 35 refers to the treatment of recoverable ACT as a current or non-current asset as appropriate. Such ACT may be classified in the Schedule formats as follows:

Format 1 BII

Format 2 BII

with non-current ACT recoverable being included in the amount falling due after more than one year.

Stocks and long-term contracts

(Issued May 1975. Part 6 added August 1980; revised September 1988)

The provisions of this statement of standard accounting practice should be read in conjunction with the explanatory foreword to accounting standards *and need not be applied to immaterial items.*

Part 1 — Explanatory note

Stocks

1 The determination of profit for an accounting year requires the matching of costs with related revenues. The cost of unsold or unconsumed stocks will have been incurred in the expectation of future revenue, and when this will not arise until a later year it is appropriate to carry forward this cost to be matched with the revenue when it arises; the applicable concept is the matching of cost and revenue in the year in which the revenue arises rather than in the year in which the cost is incurred. If there is no reasonable expectation of sufficient future revenue to cover cost incurred (e.g. as a result of deterioration, obsolescence or a change in demand) the irrecoverable cost should be charged to revenue in the year under review. Thus, stocks normally need to be stated at cost, or, if lower, at net realisable value.

2 The comparison of cost and net realisable value needs to be made in respect of each item of stock separately. Where this is impracticable, groups or categories of stock items which are similar will need to be taken together. To compare the total realisable value of stocks with the total cost could result in an unacceptable setting off of foreseeable losses against unrealised profits.

3 In order to match costs and revenue, 'costs' of stocks should comprise that expenditure which has been incurred in the normal course of business in bringing the product or service to its present location and condition. Such costs will include all related production overheads, even though these may accrue on a time basis.

4 The methods used in allocating costs to stocks need to be selected with a view to providing the fairest possible approximation to the expenditure actually incurred in bringing the product to its present location and condition. For example, in the case of retail stores holding a large number of rapidly changing individual items, stock on the shelves has often been stated at current selling prices less the normal gross profit margin. In these particular circumstances this may be acceptable as being the only practical method of arriving at a figure which approximates to cost.

Net realisable value

5 Net realisable value is the estimated proceeds from the sale of items of stock less all further costs to completion and less all costs to be incurred in marketing, selling and distributing directly related to the items in question.

Replacement cost

6 Items of stock have sometimes been stated in financial statements at estimated replacement cost where this is lower than net realisable value. Where the effect is to take account of a loss greater than that which is expected to be incurred, the use of replacement cost is not regarded as acceptable. However, in some circumstances (e.g. in the case of materials, the price of which has fluctuated considerably and which have not become the subject of firm sales contracts by the time the financial statements are prepared) replacement cost may be the best measure of net realisable value. Also, where a company adopts the alternative accounting rules of the Companies Act 1985, items of stock may be stated at the lower of current replacement cost and net realisable value.

Long-term contracts

7 Separate consideration needs to be given to long-term contracts. Owing to the length of time taken to complete such contracts, to defer recording turnover and taking profit into account until completion may result in the profit and loss account reflecting not so much a fair view of the result of the activity of the company during the year but rather the results relating to contracts that have been completed in the year. It is therefore appropriate to take credit for ascertainable turnover and profit while contracts are in progress in accordance with paragraphs 8 to 11 below.

8 Companies should ascertain turnover in a manner appropriate to the stage of completion of the contracts, the businesses and the industries in which they operate.

9 Where the business carries out long-term contracts and it is considered that their outcome can be assessed with reasonable certainty before their conclusion, the attributable profit should be calculated on a prudent basis and included in the accounts for the period under review. The profit taken up needs to reflect the proportion of the work carried out at the accounting date and to take into account any known inequalities of profitability in the various stages of a contract. The procedure to recognise profit is to include an appropriate proportion of total contract value as turnover in the profit and loss account as the contract activity progresses. The costs incurred in reaching that stage of completion are matched with this turnover, resulting in the reporting of results that can be attributed to the proportion of work completed.

10 Where the outcome of long-term contracts cannot be assessed with reasonable certainty before the conclusion of the contract, no profit should be reflected in the profit and loss account in respect of those contracts, although, in such circumstances, if no loss is expected it may be appropriate to show as turnover a proportion of the total contract value using a zero estimate of profit.

11 If it is expected that there will be a loss on a contract as a whole, all of the loss should be recognised as soon as it is foreseen (in accordance with the prudence concept). Examples of how this can be achieved are given in Appendix 3. Initially, the foreseeable loss will be deducted from the work in progress figure of the particular contract, thus reducing it to net realisable value. Any loss in excess of the work in progress figure should be classified as an accrual within 'Creditors' or under 'Provisions for liabilities and charges' depending upon the circumstances. Where unprofitable contracts are of such magnitude that they can be expected to utilise a considerable part of the company's capacity for a substantial period, related administration overheads to be incurred during the period to the completion of those contracts should also be included in the calculation of the provisions for losses.

Disclosure in financial statements

12 A suitable description of the amount at which stocks (excluding long-term contract balances) are stated in financial statements would be 'at the lower of cost and net realisable value'.

13 In the case of long-term contracts:

(a) long-term contract balances classified under the balance sheet heading of 'Stocks' are stated at total costs incurred, net of amounts transferred to the profit and loss account in respect of work carried out to date, less foreseeable losses and applicable payments on account. A suitable description in the financial statements would be 'at net cost, less foreseeable losses and payments on account'.

(b) cumulative turnover (i.e. the total turnover recorded in respect of the contract in the profit and loss accounts of all accounting periods since inception of the contract) is compared with total payments on account. If turnover exceeds payments on account an 'amount recoverable on contracts' is established and separately disclosed within debtors. If payments on account are greater than turnover to date, the excess is classified as a deduction from any balance on that contract in stocks, with any residual balance in excess of cost being classified with creditors.

14 In order to give an adequate explanation of the affairs of the company, the accounting policies followed in arriving at the amount at which stocks and long-term contracts are stated in the financial statements should be set out in a note. Where differing bases have been adopted for different types of stocks and long-term contracts, the amount included in the financial statements in respect of each type will need to be stated.

Further practical considerations

15 The basic considerations which must be taken into account in determining cost and net realisable value in relation to stocks and long-term contracts are set out in Parts 2 and 3 of this statement. The majority of problems which arise in practice in determining these amounts result from considerations which are relevant to particular businesses and are not of such universal application that they can be the subject of a statement of standard accounting practice. Accordingly, Appendix 1 sets out in more detail some general guidelines which may be of assistance in determining cost and net realisable value and in identifying those situations in which net realisable value is likely to be less than cost. Appendix 1 also sets out considerations which need to be borne in mind in calculating the amount of profit to be taken into account in respect of long-term contracts.

Part 2 — Definition of terms

16 Stocks comprise the following categories:

(a) goods or other assets purchased for resale;

(b) consumable stores;

(c) raw materials and components purchased for incorporation into products for sale;

(d) products and services in intermediate stages of completion;

(e) long-term contract balances; and

(f) finished goods.

17 Cost is defined in relation to the different categories of stocks as being that expenditure which has been incurred in the normal course of business in bringing the product or service to its present location and condition. This expenditure should include, in addition to cost of purchase (as defined in paragraph 18), such costs of conversion (as defined in paragraph 19) as are appropriate to the location and condition.

18 Cost of purchase comprises purchase price including import duties, transport and handling costs and any other directly attributable costs, less trade discounts, rebates and subsidies.

19 Cost of conversion comprises:

(a) costs which are specifically attributable to units of production, e.g. direct labour, direct expenses and sub-contracted work;

(b) production overheads (as defined in paragraph 20);

(c) other overheads, if any, attributable in the particular circumstances of the business to bringing the product or service to its present location and condition.

20 Production overheads: overheads incurred in respect of materials, labour or services for production, based on the normal level of activity, taking one year with another. For this purpose each overhead should be classified according to function (e.g. production, selling or administration) so as to ensure the inclusion, in cost of conversion, of those overheads (including depreciation) which relate to production, notwithstanding that these may accrue wholly or partly on a time basis

21 Net realisable value: the actual or estimated selling price (net of trade but before settlement discounts) less:

(a) all further costs to completion; and

(b) all costs to be incurred in marketing, selling and distributing.

22 Long-term contract: a contract entered into for the design, manufacture or construction of a single substantial asset or the provision of a service (or of a combination of assets or services which together constitute a single project) where the time taken substantially to complete the contract is such that the contract activity falls into different accounting periods. A contract that is required to be accounted for as long-term by this accounting standard will usually extend for a period exceeding one year. However, a duration exceeding one year is not an essential feature of a long-term contract. Some contracts with a shorter duration than one year should be accounted for as long-term contracts if they are sufficiently material to the activity of the period that not to record turnover and attributable profit would lead to a distortion of the period's turnover and results such that the financial statements would not give a true and fair view, provided that the policy is applied consistently within the reporting entity and from year to year.

23 Attributable profit: that part of the total profit currently estimated to arise over the duration of the contract, after allowing for estimated remedial and maintenance costs and increases in costs so far as not recoverable under the terms of the contract, that fairly reflects the profit attributable to that part of the work performed at the accounting date. (There can be no attributable profit until the profitable outcome of the contract can be assessed with reasonable certainty.)

24 Foreseeable losses: which are currently estimated to arise over the duration of the contract (after allowing for estimated remedial and maintenance costs and increases in costs so far as not recoverable under the terms of the contract). This estimate is required irrespective of:

(a) whether or not work has yet commenced on such contracts;

(b) the proportion of work carried out at the accounting date;

(c) the amount of profits expected to arise on other contracts.

25 Payments on account: all amounts received and receivable at the accounting date in respect of contracts in progress.

Part 3 — Standard accounting practice

Stocks

26 The amount at which stocks are stated in periodic financial statements should be the total of the lower of cost and net realisable value of the separate items of stock or of groups of similar items.

27 Stocks should be sub-classified in the balance sheet or in the notes to the financial statements so as to indicate the amounts held in each of the main categories in the standard balance sheet formats (as adapted where appropriate) of Schedule 4 to the Companies Act 1985, Schedule 4 to the Companies (Northern Ireland) Order 1986 and, in the Republic of Ireland, the Schedule to the Companies (Amendment) Act 1986.

Long-term contracts

28 Long-term contracts should be assessed on a contract by contract basis and reflected in the profit and loss account by recording turnover and related costs as contract activity progresses. Turnover is ascertained in a manner appropriate to the stage of completion of the contract, the business and the industry in which it operates.

29 Where it is considered that the outcome of a long-term contract can be assessed with reasonable certainty before its conclusion, the prudently calculated attributable profit should be recognised in the profit and loss account as the difference between the reported turnover and related costs for that contract.

30 Long-term contracts should be disclosed in the balance sheet as follows:

(a) the amount by which recorded turnover is in excess of payments on account should be classified as 'amounts recoverable on contracts' and separately disclosed within debtors;

(b) the balance of payments on account (in excess of amounts (i) matched with turnover; and (ii) offset against long-term contract balances) should be classified as payments on account and separately disclosed within creditors;

(c) the amount of long-term contracts, at costs incurred, net of amounts transferred to cost of sales, after deducting foreseeable losses and payments on account not matched with turnover, should be classified as 'long-term contract balances' and separately disclosed within the balance sheet heading 'Stocks'. The balance sheet note should disclose separately the balance of:

   (i) net cost less foreseeable losses; and

   (ii) applicable payments on account;

(d) the amount by which the provision or accrual for foreseeable losses exceeds the costs incurred (after transfers to cost of sales) should be included within either provisions for liabilities and charges or creditors as appropriate.

31 Consequent upon the application of this revised standard, the corresponding amounts in the financial statements will need to be restated on a comparable basis.

Statement of accounting policies

32 The accounting policies that have been applied to stocks and long-term contracts, in particular the method of ascertaining turnover and attributable profit, should be stated and applied consistently within the business and from year to year.

Date from which effective

33 The accounting practices set out in this statement should be adopted as soon as possible and regarded as standard in respect of financial statements relating to accounting periods beginning on or after 1 July 1988.

Part 4 — Note on legal requirements in Great Britain and Northern Ireland

All paragraph references unless otherwise indicated are to Schedule 4 to the Companies Act 1985 and Schedule 4 to the Companies (Northern Ireland) Order 1986.

34 Paragraph 22 requires that, under the historical cost accounting rules, 'the amount to be included in respect of any current asset shall be its purchase price or production cost'. Paragraph 23(1) provides for the inclusion of the asset at net realisable value if lower than purchase price or production cost.

35 Paragraph 90 (paragraph 89 of Schedule 4 to the Companies (Northern Ireland) Order 1986) provides that "the purchase price of any asset . . . includes any consideration (whether in cash or otherwise) given by the company in respect of that asset". Counsel's opinion, obtained by the ASC, has indicated that one purpose of this paragraph is to enable debtors to be stated at face value, that is, at amounts which include a profit element and that this does not conflict with paragraph 22.

36 Paragraph 26 requires expenses incidental to the acquisition of an asset to be included in the purchase price. It also requires the inclusion of directly attributable production overheads in the production cost of an asset and permits the inclusion of overheads which are only indirectly attributable to the production of an asset and interest on borrowed capital. In cases where interest is included the fact must be stated and the amount of interest included must be disclosed in a note to the financial statements. Paragraph 26 also prohibits the inclusion of distribution costs.

37 Paragraph 27 allows the following methods for valuation of stocks (but requires that the method chosen must be one which appears to the directors to be appropriate in the circumstances of the company):

(a) the method known as 'first in, first out' (FIFO);

(b) the method known as 'last in, first out' (LIFO);

(c) a weighted average price; and

(d) any other method similar to any of the methods mentioned above.

38 This standard requires the use of a method which provides a fair approximation to the expenditure actually incurred. The use of some of the methods allowed by paragraph 27 of the Schedule will not necessarily meet this requirement.

39 In particular, the use of the LIFO method can result in the reporting of current assets at amounts that bear little relationship to recent costs. This may result in not only a significant misstatement of balance sheet amounts but also a potential distortion of current and future results. This places a special responsibility on the directors to be assured that the circumstances of the company require the adoption of such a valuation method in order for the accounts to give a true and fair view.

40 Paragraph 27(3) requires a company to state in a note to the accounts the difference between the replacement cost of stocks and their book amount — as determined by 37(a) to (d) above — where this difference is material.

41 It is further provided in paragraph 27(5) that if the most recent actual purchase price or production cost before the balance sheet date appears to the directors of the company to constitute a more appropriate standard of comparison, then that amount may be used as a surrogate for replacement cost.

42 Paragraph 31(5) provides that, where a company adopts the alternative accounting rules, 'stocks may be included at their current cost'.

43 Paragraph 89 (paragraph 88 of Schedule 4 to the Companies (Northern Ireland) Order 1986) provides that provisions are amounts "retained as reasonably necessary for the purpose of providing for any liability or loss which is either likely to be incurred, or certain to be incurred but uncertain as to amount or as to the date on which it will arise".

44 Paragraph 91 [paragraph 90 of Schedule 4 to the Companies (Northern Ireland) Order 1986] declares that realised profits are "such profits of a company as fall to be treated as realised profits for the purposes of those accounts in accordance with principles generally accepted with respect to the determination for accounting purposes of realised profits". It is a 'generally accepted principle' that it is appropriate to recognise profit on long-term contracts when the outcome can be assessed with 'reasonable certainty'. The principle of recognising profit on long-term contracts under this standard, therefore, does not contravene this paragraph.

Part 5 — Note on legal requirements in the Republic of Ireland

45 The legal requirements in Great Britain and Northern Ireland are mirrored, in respect of the Republic of Ireland, in the Schedule to the Companies (Amendment) Act 1986. The following table indicates the corresponding paragraphs in respect of all of the references contained in Part 4 of this statement.

Schedule 4 to the Companies Act 1985	*Schedule 4 to the Companies (Northern Ireland) Order 1986*	*The Schedule to the Companies (Amendment) Act 1986*
Paragraph 22	Paragraph 22	Paragraph 10
Paragraph 23(1)	Paragraph 23(1)	Paragraph 11(1)
Paragraph 26	Paragraph 26	Paragraph 14
Paragraph 27	Paragraph 27	Paragraph 15*
Paragraph 27(4)	Paragraph 27(4)	Paragraph 15(4)*
Paragraph 27(5)	Paragraph 27(5)	Paragraph 15(5)
Paragraph 31(5)	Paragraph 31(5)	Paragraph 19(5)
Paragraph 89	Paragraph 88	Paragraph 70
Paragraph 90	Paragraph 89	Paragraph 71
Paragraph 91	Paragraph 90	Paragraph 72

*There is no provision for the LIFO method of stock valuation in paragraph 15 of the Schedule to the Companies (Amendment) Act 1986.

Part 6 — Compliance with International Accounting Standard No.2 'Valuation and presentation of inventories in the context of the historical cost system' and No 11 'Accounting for construction contracts'

46 The requirements of International Accounting Standard No 2 'Valuation and presentation of inventories in the context of the historical cost system' and International Accounting Standard No 11 'Accounting for construction contracts' accord very closely with the content of the United Kingdom and Irish Accounting Standard No 9 (Revised) 'Stocks and long-term contracts' and accordingly compliance with SSAP 9 will ensure compliance with both IAS 2 and IAS 11 in all material respects.

Appendix 1

This appendix is for general guidance and does not form part of the statement of standard accounting practice.

Further practical considerations

Many of the problems involved in arriving at the amount at which stocks and long-term contracts are stated in financial statements are of a practical nature rather than resulting from matters of principle. This appendix discusses some particular areas in which difficulty may be encountered.

The allocation of overheads

47 Production overheads are included in cost of conversion (as defined in Part 2) together with direct labour, direct expenses and sub-contracted work. This inclusion is a necessary corollary of the principle that expenditure should be included to the extent to which it has been incurred in bringing the product 'to its present location and condition' (paragraph 17 of Part 2). However, all abnormal conversion costs (such as exceptional spoilage, idle capacity and other losses) which are avoidable under normal operating conditions need, for the same reason, to be excluded.

48 Where firm sales contracts have been entered into for the provision of goods or services to customer's specification, overheads relating to design, and marketing and selling costs incurred before manufacture may be included in arriving at cost.

49 The costing methods adopted by a business are usually designed to ensure that all direct material, direct labour, direct expenses and sub-contracted work are identified and charged on a reasonable and consistent basis, but problems arise on the allocation of overheads which must usually involve the exercise of personal judgement in the selection of an appropriate convention.

50 The classification of overheads necessary to achieve this allocation takes the function of the overhead as its distinguishing characteristic (e.g. whether it is a function of production, marketing, selling or administration), rather than whether the overhead tends to vary with time or with volume.

51 The costs of general management, as distinct from functional management, are not directly related to current production and are, therefore, excluded from cost of conversion and, hence, from the cost of stocks and long-term contracts.

52 In the case of smaller organisations whose management may be involved in the daily administration of each of the various functions, particular problems may arise in practice in distinguishing these general management overheads. In such organisations the cost of management may fairly be allocated on suitable bases to the functions of production, marketing, selling and administration.

53 Problems may also arise in allocating the costs of central service departments, the allocation of which should depend on the function or functions that the department is serving. For example, the accounts department will normally support the following functions:

(a) production — by paying direct and indirect production wages and salaries, by controlling purchases and by preparing periodic financial statements for the production units;

(b) marketing and distribution — by analysing sales and by controlling the sales ledger;

(c) general administration — by preparing management accounts and annual financial statements and budgets, by controlling cash resources and by planning investments.

Only those costs of the accounts department that can reasonably be allocated to the production function fall to be included in the cost of conversion.

54 The allocation of overheads included in the valuation of stocks and long-term contracts needs to be based on the company's normal level of activity, taking one year with another. The governing factor is that the cost of unused capacity should be written off in the current year. In determining what constitutes 'normal' the following factors need to be considered:

(a) the volume of production which the production facilities are intended by their designers and by management to produce under the working conditions (e.g. single or double shift) prevailing during the year;

(b) the budgeted level of activity for the year under review and for the ensuing year;

(c) the level of activity achieved both in the year under review and in previous years.

Although temporary changes in the load of activity may be ignored, persistent variation should lead to a revision of the previous norm.

55 Where management accounts are prepared on a marginal cost basis, it will be necessary to add to the figure of stocks so arrived at, the appropriate proportion of those production overheads not already included in the marginal cost.

56 The adoption of a conservative approach to the valuation of stocks and long-term contracts has sometimes been used as one of the reasons for omitting selected production overheads. In so far as the circumstances of the business require an element of prudence in determining the amount at which stocks and long-term contracts are stated, this needs to be taken into account in the determination of net realisable value and not by the exclusion from cost of selected overheads.

Methods of costing

57 It is frequently not practicable to relate expenditure to specific units of stocks and long-term contracts. The ascertainment of the nearest approximation to cost gives rise to two problems:

(a) the selection of an appropriate method for relating costs to stocks and long-term contracts (e.g. job costing, batch costing, process costing, standard costing);

(b) the selection of an appropriate method for calculating the related costs where a number of identical items have been purchased or made at different times (e.g. unit cost, average cost or FIFO).

58 In selecting the methods referred to in paragraphs 11 (a) and (b) above, management must exercise judgement to ensure that the methods chosen provide the fairest practicable approximation to cost. Furthermore, where standard costs are used they need to be reviewed frequently to ensure that they bear a reasonable relationship to actual costs obtaining during the period. Methods such as base stock and LIFO are not usually appropriate methods of stock valuation because they often result in stocks being stated in the balance sheet at amounts that bear little relationship to recent cost levels. When this happens, not only is the presentation of current assets misleading, but there is potential distortion of subsequent results if stock levels reduce and out of date costs are drawn into the profit and loss account.

59 The method of arriving at cost by applying the latest purchase price to the total number of units in stock is unacceptable in principle because it is not necessarily the same as actual cost and, in times of rising prices, will result in the taking of a profit which has not been realised.

60 One method of arriving at cost, in the absence of a satisfactory costing system, is the use of selling price less an estimated profit margin. This is acceptable only if it can be demonstrated that the method gives a reasonable approximation of the actual cost.

61 In industries where the cost of minor by-products is not separable from the cost of the principal products, stocks of such by-products may be stated in accounts at their net realisable value. In this case the costs of the main products are calculated after deducting the net realisable value of the by-products.

The determination of net realisable value

62 The initial calculation of provisions to reduce stocks from cost to net realisable value may often be made by the use of formulae based on predetermined criteria. The formulae normally take account of the age, movements in the past, expected future movements and estimated scrap values of the stock, as appropriate. Whilst the use of such formulae establishes a basis for making a provision which can be consistently applied, it is still necessary for the results to be reviewed in the light of any special circumstances which cannot be anticipated in the formulae, such as changes in the state of the order book.

63 Where a provision is required to reduce the value of finished goods below cost, the stocks of the parts and sub-assemblies held for the purpose of the manufacture of such products, together with stocks on order, need to be reviewed to determine if provision is also required against such items.

64 Where stocks of spares are held for sale special consideration of the factors in paragraph 16 of this appendix will be required in the context of:

(a) the number of units sold to which they are applicable;

(b) the estimated frequency with which a replacement spare is required;

(c) the expected useful life of the unit to which they are applicable.

65 Events occurring between the balance sheet date and the date of completion of the financial statements need to be considered in arriving at the net realisable value at the balance sheet date (e.g. a subsequent reduction in selling prices). However, no reduction falls to be made when the realisable value of material stocks is less than the purchase price, provided that the goods into which the materials are to be incorporated can still be sold at a profit after incorporating the materials at cost price.

The application of net realisable value

66 The principal situations in which net realisable value is likely to be less than cost are where there has been:

(a) an increase in costs or a fall in selling price;

(b) physical deterioration of stocks;

(c) obsolescence of products;

(d) a decision as part of a company's marketing strategy to manufacture and sell products at a loss;

(e) errors in production or purchasing.

Furthermore, when stocks are held which are unlikely to be sold within the turnover period normal in that company (i.e. excess stocks), the impending delay in realisation increases the risk that the situations outlined in (a) to (c) above may occur before the stocks are sold and needs to be taken into account in assessing net realisable value.

Long-term contracts

67 In ascertaining costs of long-term contracts it is not normally appropriate to include interest payable on borrowed money. However, in circumstances where sums borrowed can be identified as financing specific long-term contracts, it may be appropriate to include such related interest in cost, in which circumstances the inclusion of interest and the amount of interest so included should be disclosed in a note to the financial statements.

68 In some businesses, long-term contracts for the supply of services or manufacture and supply of goods exist where the prices are determined and invoiced according to separate parts of the contract. In these businesses the most appropriate method of reflecting profits on each contract is usually to match costs against performance of the separable parts of the contract, treating each such separable part as a separate contract. In such instances, however, future revenues from the contract need to be compared with future estimated costs and provision made for any foreseen loss.

69 Turnover (ascertained in a manner appropriate to the industry, the nature of the contracts concerned and the contractual relationship with the customer) and related costs should be recorded in the profit and loss account as contract activity progresses. Turnover may sometimes be ascertained by reference to valuation of the work carried out to date. In other cases, there may be specific points during a contract at which individual elements of work done with separately ascertainable sales values and costs can be identified and appropriately recorded as turnover (e.g., because delivery or customer acceptance has taken place). This accounting standard does not provide a definition of turnover in view of the different methods of ascertaining it as outlined above. However, it does require disclosure of the means by which turnover is ascertained.

70 In determining whether the stage has been reached at which it is appropriate to recognise profit, account should be taken of the nature of the business concerned. It is necessary to define the earliest point for each particular contract before which no profit is taken up, the overriding principle being that there can be no attributable profit until the outcome of a contract can reasonably be foreseen. Of the profit which in the light of all the circumstances can be foreseen with a reasonable degree of certainty to arise on completion of the contract, there should be regarded as earned to date only that part which prudently reflects the amount of work performed to date. The method used for taking up such profits needs to be consistently applied.

71 In calculating the total estimated profit on the contract, it is necessary to take into account not only the total costs to date and the total estimated further costs to completion (calculated by reference to the same principles as were applied to cost to date) but also the estimated future costs of rectification and guarantee work, and any other future work to be undertaken under the terms of the contract. These are then compared with the total sales value of the contract. In considering future costs it is necessary to have regard to likely increases in wages and salaries, to likely increases in the price of raw materials and to rises in general overheads so far as these items are not recoverable from the customer under the terms of contract.

72 Where approved variations have been made to a contract in the course of it and the amount to be received in respect of these variations has not yet been settled and is likely to be a material factor in the outcome, it is necessary to make a conservative estimate of the amount likely to be received and this is then treated as part of the total sales value. On the other hand, allowance needs to be made for foreseen claims or penalties payable arising out of delays in completion or from other causes.

73 The settlement of claims arising from circumstances not envisaged in the contract or arising as an indirect consequence of approved variations is subject to a high level of uncertainty relating to the outcome of future negotiations. In view of this, it is generally prudent to recognise receipts in respect of such claims only when negotiations have reached an advanced stage and there is sufficient evidence of the acceptability of the claim in principle to the purchaser, with an indication of the amount involved also being available.

74 The amounts to be included in the year's profit and loss account will be both the appropriate amount of turnover and the associated costs of achieving that turnover, to the extent that these amounts exceed corresponding amounts recognised in previous years. The estimated outcome of a contract which extends over several accounting years will nearly always vary in the light of changes in circumstances and for this reason the result of the year will not necessarily represent the proportion of the total profit on the contract which is appropriate to the amount of work carried out in the period: it may also reflect the effect of changes in circumstances during the year which affect the total profit estimated to accrue on completion.

Appendix 2

This appendix is for general guidance and does not form part of the statement of standard accounting practice.

Glossary of terms

The use of the following terms in describing the accounting policies adopted in arriving at the amount at which stocks and long-term contracts are stated in financial statements should be restricted in conformity with the definitions given to each. Where these definitions are inapplicable, alternative expressions should be used and explained.

Average cost

75 The calculation of the cost of stocks on the basis of the application to the unit of stocks on hand of an average price computed by dividing the total cost of units by the total number of such units. This average price may be arrived at by means of a continuous calculation, a periodic calculation or a moving periodic calculation.

Base stock

76 The calculation of the cost of stocks on the basis that a fixed unit value is ascribed to a predetermined number of units of stock, any excess over this number being valued on the basis of some other method. If the number of units in stock is less than the predetermined minimum, the fixed unit value is applied to the number in stock.

Completed long-term contract

77 A long-term contract on which no further work, apart from maintenance work, is expected to take place.

Current cost

78 Of stock is the lower of:

(a) its net current replacement cost; and
(b) its net realisable value.

FIFO (first in, first out)

79 The calculation of the cost of stocks on the basis that the quantities in hand represent the latest purchases or production.

LIFO (last in, first out)

80 The calculation of the cost of stocks on the basis that the quantities in hand represent the earliest purchases or production.

Replacement cost

81 The cost at which an identical asset could be purchased or manufactured.

Standard cost

82 The calculation of the cost of stocks on the basis of periodically predetermined costs calculated from management's estimates of expected levels of cost and of operations and operational efficiency and the related expenditure.

Unit cost

83 The cost of purchasing or manufacturing identifiable units of stocks.

Appendix 3

This appendix is for general guidance and does not form part of the statement of standard accounting practice.

Long-term contracts: further consideration of financial statement presentation

84 The classification of an 'amount recoverable on contracts' within debtors is a somewhat unfamiliar concept which needs careful consideration.

85 The determination of the point at which ownership of completed work passes from the contractor to the customer is a complex matter of legal form and industry practice.

86 An 'amount recoverable on contracts' may not have the contractual status of a debtor in strict legal form. However, it is well established under the accruals concept of revenue and cost recognition that this should not preclude debtors and creditors from being recorded, where this is necessary to reflect the substance of a transaction.

87 An essential test for an 'amount recoverable on contracts' to be recorded as an asset is that it should be realisable. This applies equally whether the balance is classified as a debtor or as an element of work in progress.

88 An 'amount recoverable on contracts' represents an excess of the value of work carried out to date (which has been recorded as turnover) over cumulative payments on account. The amount and realisability of the balance therefore depend on the value of work carried out being ascertained appropriately. The balance arises as a derivative of this process of contract revenue recognition and is directly linked to turnover. In substance, it represents accrued revenue receivable and has the attributes of a debtor.

89 Accordingly, the standard concludes that 'amounts recoverable on contracts' should be classified as debtors, although separate disclosure is prescribed. Counsel's opinion obtained by the ASC confirms that 'amounts recoverable on contracts' should be classified under 'Debtors' and cannot be classified under 'Stocks'.

90 In determining the amounts at which long-term contracts should be included in the financial statements, contracting activity should be reviewed on an individual contract by contract basis. The following example (Example 1) illustrates the process of applying the principles set out in the standard to long-term contracts.

PROJECT 1

Profit and Loss Account — cumulative

Included in turnover		145
Included in cost of sales		(110)
Gross profit		35

Balance Sheet

The amount to be included in debtors under 'amounts recoverable on contracts' is calculated as follows:

Cumulative turnover		145
less: Cumulative payments on account	(100)	
Included in debtors		45

In this case, all the costs incurred to date relate to the contract activity recorded as turnover and are transferred to cost of sales, leaving a zero balance in stocks.

NB If the outcome of the contract could not be assessed with reasonable certainty, no profit would be recognised. If no loss is expected, it may be appropriate to show as turnover a proportion of the total contract value using a zero estimate of profit.

PROJECT 2

Profit and Loss Account — cumulative

Included in turnover		520
Included in cost of sales		(450)
Gross profit		70

Balance Sheet

As cumulative payments on account are greater than turnover there is a credit balance, calculated as follows:

Cumulative turnover		520
less: Cumulative payments on account	(600)	
Excess payments on account		(80)

Example 1

Project Number

	1	2	3	4	5	Balance Sheet Total	Profit & Loss Account
Recorded as turnover — being value of work done	145	520	380	200	55		1,300
Cumulative payments on account	(100)	(600)	(400)	(150)	(80)		
Classified as amounts recoverable on contracts	45			50		95DR	
Balance (excess) of payments on account		(80)	(20)		(25)		
Applied as an offset against long-term contract balances see below		60	20		15		
Residue classified as payments on account		(20)	—		(10)	(30)CR	
Total costs incurred	110	510	450	250	100		
Transferred to cost of sales	(110)	(450)	(350)	(250)	(55)		(1,215)
	—	60	100	—	45		
Provision/accrual for foreseeable losses charged to cost of sales				(40)	(30)		(70)
		60	100		15		
Classified as provision/accrual for losses				(40)		(40)CR	
Balance (excess) of payments on account applied as offset against long-term contract balances		(60)	(20)		(15)		
Classified as long-term contract balances		—	80		—	80DR	
Gross profit or loss on long-term contracts	35	70	30	(90)	(30)		15

This credit balance should firstly be offset against any debit balance on this contract included in stocks and then any residual amount should be classified under creditors as a payment received on account as follows:

Total cost incurred to date		510
less: Cumulative amounts recorded as cost of sales		(450)
		60
less: Excess payments on account (above)		(80)
Included in creditors		(20)

The amount to be included in stocks is zero and the credit balance of 20 is classified as a payment received on account and included in creditors.

The balance sheet note on stocks should disclose separately the net cost of 60 and the applicable payments on account of 60.

PROJECT 3

Profit and Loss Account — cumulative

Included in turnover	380
Included in cost of sales	(350)
Gross profit	30

Balance Sheet

As with Project 2, cumulative payments on account are greater than turnover and there is a credit balance calculated as follows:

Cumulative turnover		380
less: Cumulative payments on account	(400)	
Excess payments on account		(20)

This credit balance should firstly be offset against any debit balance on this contract included in stocks and the residual amount, if any, should be classified under creditors as a payment received on account.

The amount to be included in stocks under long-term contract balances is calculated as follows:

Total costs incurred to date	450
less: Cumulative amounts recorded as cost of sales	(350)
	100
less: Excess payments on account (above)	(20)
Included in long-term contract balances	80

The balance sheet note on stocks should disclose separately the net cost of 100 and the applicable payments on account of 20.

PROJECT 4

Profit and Loss Account — cumulative

Included in turnover		200
Included in cost of sales		(290)
Gross loss		(90)

Balance Sheet

The amount to be included in debtors under 'amounts recoverable on contracts' is calculated as follows:

Cumulative turnover		200
less: Cumulative payments on account	(150)	
Included in debtors		50

The amount to be included as a provision/accrual for foreseeable losses is calculated as follows:

Total costs incurred to date		250
less: Transferred to cost of sales	(250)	
Foreseeable losses on contract as a whole	(40)	
		(290)
Classified as provision/accrual for foreseeable losses		(40)

Note that the credit balance of 40 is not offset against the debit balance of 50 included in debtors.

PROJECT 5

Profit and Loss Account — cumulative

Included in turnover		55
Included in cost of sales		(85)
Gross loss		(30)

Balance Sheet

As cumulative payments on account are greater than turnover there is a credit balance, calculated as follows:

Cumulative turnover		55
less: Cumulative payments on account	(80)	
Excess payments on account		(25)

The credit balance should firstly be deducted from long-term contract balances (after having deducted foreseeable losses) and the residual balance included in creditors under payments received on account as follows:

Total costs incurred to date		100
less: Transferred to cost of sales	(55)	
Foreseeable losses on contract as a whole	(30)	
		(85)
		15
less: Excess payments on account (above)		(25)
Included in creditors		(10)

The balance sheet note on stocks should disclose separately the net cost of 15 and the applicable payments on account of 15.

Accounting for depreciation

(Issued December 1977; amended November 1981; revised January 1987)

The provisions of this statement of standard accounting practice should be read in conjunction with the explanatory foreword to accounting standards *and need not be applied to immaterial items.*

Part 1 — Explanatory note

1 Fixed assets are those assets which are intended for use on a continuing basis in the enterprise's activities. This statement deals with the depreciation of fixed assets (other than investment properties, goodwill, development costs and investments), including the depreciation of amounts capitalised in respect of finance leases.

2 Virtually all fixed assets have finite useful economic lives. In order for the financial statements to reflect properly all the costs of the enterprise it is necessary for there to be a charge against income in respect of the use of such assets. This charge is referred to as depreciation (or amortisation in the case of leasehold property).

3 Depreciation is the measure of the wearing out, consumption or other reduction in the useful economic life of a fixed asset, whether arising from use, effluxion of time or obsolescence through technological or market changes. Depreciation should be allocated so as to charge a fair proportion of cost or valuation of the asset to each accounting period expected to benefit from its use.

4 The assessment of depreciation, and its allocation to accounting periods, involves the consideration of three factors:

(a) the carrying amount of the asset (whether cost or valuation);

(b) the length of the asset's expected useful economic life to the business of the enterprise, having due regard to the incidence of obsolescence; and

(c) the estimated residual value of the asset at the end of its useful economic life in the business of the enterprise.

5 Where an asset is carried at historical cost, the carrying amount is either the cost of acquisition or, in the case of a self-constructed asset, the cost of its production. It has, however, become increasingly common for enterprises to revalue their fixed assets, in particular freehold and leasehold property, and to incorporate these revalued amounts in their financial statements. This gives useful and relevant information to users of accounts. This statement does not prescribe how frequently assets should be revalued but, where a policy of revaluing assets is adopted, the valuations should be kept up to date.

6 An asset's useful economic life may be:

(a) pre-determined, as in the case of a lease;

(b) directly governed by extraction or consumption, as in the case of a mine;

(c) dependent on its physical deterioration through use or effluxion of time;

(d) reduced by economic or technological obsolescence.

7 The useful economic lives of assets should be reviewed regularly and, when necessary, revised. Such a review would normally be undertaken at least every five years, and more frequently where circumstances warrant it. Realistic estimation and regular review of asset lives should result in there being few fully depreciated assets still in economic use. The omission of depreciation on such assets should not be sufficiently material to impair the true and fair view.

8 There is a range of acceptable depreciation methods. Management should select the method regarded as most appropriate to the type of asset and its use in the business so as to allocate depreciation as fairly as possible to the periods expected to benefit from the asset's use. Although the straight line method is the simplest to apply, it may not always be the most appropriate.

9 It is not appropriate to omit charging for the depreciation of an asset on the grounds that its current market value is greater than its net book amount. If account is taken of such increased value by writing up the net book amount of a fixed asset, then an increased charge for depreciation will become necessary.

Part 2 — Definition of terms

10 *Depreciation* is the measure of the wearing out, consumption or other reduction in the useful economic life of a fixed asset whether arising from use, effluxion of time or obsolescence through technological or market changes.

11 *The useful economic life* of an asset is the period over which the present owner will derive economic benefits from its use.

12 *Residual value* is the realisable value of the asset at the end of its useful economic life, based on prices prevailing at the date of acquisition or revaluation, where this has taken place. Realisation costs should be deducted in arriving at the residual value.

13 *Recoverable amount* is the greater of the net realisable value of an asset and, where appropriate, the amount recoverable from its further use.

Part 3 — Standard accounting practice

Scope

14 This statement applies to all fixed assets other than:

(a) investment properties, which are dealt with in SSAP 19 'Accounting for investment properties';

(b) goodwill, which is dealt with in SSAP 22 'Accounting for goodwill';

(c) development costs, which are dealt with in SSAP 13 'Accounting for research and development'; and

(d) investments.

Accounting treatment

15 Provision for depreciation of fixed assets having a finite useful economic life should be made by allocating the cost (or revalued amount) less estimated residual value of the assets as fairly as possible to the periods expected to benefit from their use. The depreciation methods used should be the ones which are the most appropriate having regard to the types of asset and their use in the business.

16 The accounting treatment in the profit and loss account should be consistent with that used in the balance sheet. Hence, the depreciation charge in the profit and loss account for the period should be based on the carrying amount of the asset in the balance sheet, whether historical cost or revalued amount. The whole of the depreciation charge should be reflected in the profit and loss account. No part of the depreciation charge should be set directly against reserves. Supplementary depreciation, namely that in excess of the depreciation based on the carrying amount of the assets, should not be charged in the profit and loss account. This does not, however, preclude the appropriation of retained profits to, for example, a reserve specially designated for replacement of fixed assets.

17 It is essential that asset lives are estimated on a realistic basis. Identical asset lives should be used for the calculation of depreciation both on an historical cost basis and on any bases that reflect the effects of changing prices.

18 The useful economic lives of assets should be reviewed regularly and, when necessary, revised. The allocation of depreciation to accounting periods involves the exercise of judgement by management in the light of technical, commercial and accounting considerations and, accordingly, requires regular review. When, as a result of experience or of changed circumstances, it is considered that the original estimate of the useful economic life of an asset requires revision, the effect of the change in estimate on the results and financial position needs to be considered. Usually, when asset lives are reviewed regularly, there will be no material distortion of future results or financial position if the net book amount is written off over the revised remaining useful economic life. Where, however, future results would be materially distorted, the adjustment to accumulated depreciation should be recognised in the accounts in accordance with SSAP 6 'Extraordinary items and prior year adjustments'. This means that such an adjustment will usually be dealt with in arriving at the profit on ordinary activities. It will only be treated as an extraordinary item if it is derived from an extraordinary event such as the discontinuance of a business segment. The nature and amount of the adjustment should be disclosed.

19 If at any time there is a permanent diminution in the value of an asset and the net book amount is considered not to be recoverable in full (perhaps as a result of obsolescence or a fall in demand for a product), the net book amount should be written down immediately to the estimated recoverable amount, which should then be written off over the remaining useful economic life of the asset. If at any time the reasons for making such a provision cease to apply, the provision should be written back to the extent that it is no longer necessary.

20 In the case of an asset that has not been revalued, provisions for permanent diminution in value of an asset (and any reversals) should be charged (credited) in the profit and loss account for the period. (This paragraph does not discuss the treatment of provisions for permanent diminution in value in the case of previously revalued assets.)

21 A change from one method of providing depreciation to another is permissible only on the grounds that the new method will give a fairer presentation of the results and of the financial position. Such a change does not, however, constitute a change of accounting policy; the net book amount should be written off over the remaining useful economic life, commencing with the period in which the change is made.

22 Where it is an enterprise's policy to include some or all of its fixed assets in the financial statements at revalued amounts, the charge for depreciation of such assets should be based on the revalued amounts and the remaining useful economic lives. Depreciation charged prior to the revaluation should not be written back to the profit and loss account, except to the extent that it relates to a provision for permanent diminution in value which is subsequently found to be unnecessary.

23 Freehold land does not normally require a provision for depreciation, unless it is subject to depletion by, for example, the extraction of minerals. However, the value of freehold land may be adversely affected by considerations such as changes in the desirability of its location and in these circumstances it should be written down.

24 Buildings are no different from other fixed assets in that they have a limited useful economic life, albeit usually significantly longer than that of other types of assets. They should, therefore, be depreciated having regard to the same criteria.

Disclosure

25 The following should be disclosed in the financial statements for each major class of depreciable asset:

(a) the depreciation methods used;

(b) the useful economic lives or the depreciation rates used;

(c) total depreciation charged for the period; and

(d) the gross amount of depreciable assets and the related accumulated depreciation.

26 Where there has been a change in the depreciation method used, the effect, if material, should be disclosed in the year of change. The reason for the change should also be disclosed.

27 Where assets have been revalued, the effect of the revaluation on the depreciation charge should, if material, be disclosed in the year of revaluation.

Date from which effective

28 The accounting and disclosure requirements set out in this statement should be adopted as soon as possible and regarded as standard in respect of financial statements relating to accounting periods beginning on or after 1 January 1987.

Part 4 — Note on legal requirements in the United Kingdom and the Republic of Ireland

United Kingdom

29 Paragraphs 30-33 relate to companies which, in Great Britain, prepare their accounts in accordance with Sections 228 and 230 of the Companies Act 1985 or, in Northern Ireland, prepare them in accordance with Articles 236 and 238 of the Companies (Northern Ireland) Order 1986. References to 'the Schedule' are to Schedule 4 to the Companies Act 1985 and Schedule 4 to the Companies (Northern Ireland) Order 1986.

30 Paragraph 1(1) of the Schedule requires that fixed assets be shown in the balance sheet under the headings of intangible assets, tangible assets and investments. Further specified subdivisions within those headings are also required.

31 Under paragraph 17 of the Schedule the initial carrying amount of any fixed asset must be its purchase price or production cost. A company may, however, avail itself of the alternative accounting rules in Part II Section C of the Schedule under which intangible fixed assets, other than goodwill, may be included at their current cost and tangible fixed assets may be included at market value (as at the date of the last valuation) or at their current cost.

32 Where a fixed asset has a limited useful economic life, paragraph 18 of the Schedule requires that its cost less estimated residual value be reduced by provisions for depreciation so as to write it off systematically over its useful economic life. If the alternative accounting rules are followed, under paragraph 32(1) of the Schedule, the starting point for calculating depreciation is the current cost or market value. Provision must also be made for any permanent diminution in the value of a fixed asset (paragraph 19(2) of the Schedule) but where such a provision is no longer considered to be necessary, paragraph 19(3) of the Schedule requires that it be written back. Disclosure must be made, either on the face of the profit and loss account or in the notes (paragraphs 1(1) and 3(4) of the Schedule), of the depreciation charge and any charge or credit in respect of provisions for diminution in value.

33 The following additional information must also be disclosed (paragraph 42 of the Schedule).

(a) For each fixed asset balance sheet heading:
   (i) the cost or revalued amount at the beginning and end of the year;
   (ii) movements in respect of revaluations, acquisitions, disposals and transfers;
   (iii) the accumulated depreciation at the beginning and end of the period and movements in respect of the depreciation charge for the year, disposals of fixed assets and any other adjustments.

(b) Where fixed assets are accounted for using the alternative accounting rules paragraph 33 of the Schedule requires disclosure of the comparable amounts determined under the historical cost accounting rules or the difference between these amounts and those shown in the balance sheet.

(c) Where fixed assets are carried at revalued amounts paragraph 43 of the Schedule requires disclosure of the years of the valuations, the values given in those years and, for assets valued during the financial year, the names or qualifications of the valuers and the valuation bases used.

Republic of Ireland

Accounts prepared under the Companies Act 1963

34 Paragraphs 35-39 below relate to companies which prepare their accounts in compliance with Sections 149 and 152 of the Companies Act 1963. References to 'the Schedule' are to the Sixth Schedule to that Act.

35 Paragraph 4 of the Schedule requires that reserves, provisions, liabilities and fixed and current assets be classified under headings appropriate to the company's business, fixed assets being distinguished from current assets. In addition the method of arriving at the amount of fixed assets must be disclosed.

36 Under paragraph 5(1) of the Schedule the amount of the fixed assets must be the difference between the cost (or valuation) and the accumulated provisions in respect of depreciation and diminution in value. This does not apply to goodwill, patents or trademarks.

37 Disclosure is required, under paragraph 5(3) of the Schedule, of the total cost (or valuation) of fixed assets and the total depreciation or amounts written off.

38 Paragraph 12(a) of the Schedule requires disclosure of the profit and loss account charge in respect of depreciation, renewals or diminution in value of fixed assets.

39 If depreciation or replacement of fixed assets is provided for by some method other than a depreciation charge or provision for renewals or is not provided for at all, paragraph 14(2) of the Schedule requires disclosure of the method or the fact that no provision has been made.

Accounts prepared under the Companies (Amendment) Act 1986

40 Paragraphs 41-44 relate to companies which prepare their accounts in compliance with section 3 of the Companies (Amendment) Act 1986 ('the 1986 Act'). References to 'the Schedule' are to the Schedule to that Act.

41 Section 4 of the Act and Part I of the Schedule require that fixed assets be shown in the balance sheet under the headings of intangible assets, tangible assets and financial assets. Further specified sub-divisions within these headings are also required.

42 Under paragraph 5 of the Schedule the initial carrying amount of any fixed asset must be its purchase price or production cost. A company may, however, avail itself of the alternative accounting rules in Part III of the Schedule under which intangible fixed assets, other than goodwill, may be included at their current cost and tangible fixed assets may be included at market value (as at the date of the last valuation) or at their current cost.

43 Where a fixed asset has a limited useful economic life, paragraph 6 of the Schedule requires that its cost less estimated residual value be reduced by provisions for depreciation so as to write it off systematically over its useful economic life. If the alternative accounting rules are followed, under paragraph 20(1) of the Schedule, the starting point for calculating depreciation is the current cost or market value. Provision must also be made for any permanent diminution in the value of a fixed asset (paragraph 7(2) of the Schedule) but where such a provision is no longer considered to be necessary, paragraph 7(3) of the Schedule requires that it be written back. Disclosure must be made, either on the face of the profit and loss account or in the notes (Section 4(1) and (6) of the 1986 Act), of the depreciation charge and any charge or credit in respect of provisions for permanent diminution in value.

44 The following additional information must also be disclosed (paragraph 29 of the Schedule).

(a) For each fixed asset balance sheet heading:

(i) the cost or revalued amount at the beginning and end of the year;

(ii) movements in respect of revaluations, acquisitions, disposals and transfers;

(iii) the accumulated depreciation at the beginning and end of the period and movements in respect of the depreciation charge for the year, disposals of fixed assets and any other adjustments.

(b) Where fixed assets are accounted for using the alternative accounting rules, paragraph 21 of the Schedule requires disclosure of the comparable amounts determined under the historical cost accounting rules or the difference between these amounts and those shown in the balance sheet.

(c) Where fixed assets are carried at revalued amounts, paragraph 30 of the Schedule requires disclosure of the years of the valuations, the values given in those years and, for assets valued during the financial year, the names or qualifications of the valuers and the valuation bases used.

Part 5 — Compliance with International Accounting Standard No 4 'Depreciation Accounting'

45 Compliance with the requirements of this statement will automatically ensure compliance with International Accounting Standard No 4 'Depreciation Accounting' so far as assets within the scope of this statement are concerned.

Accounting for research and development

(Issued December 1977, revised January 1989)

The provisions of this statement of standard accounting practice should be read in conjunction with the explanatory foreword to accounting standards *and need not be applied to immaterial items.*

Part 1 — Explanatory note

Basic concepts

1 The accounting policies to be followed in respect of research and development expenditure must have regard to the fundamental accounting concepts including the 'accruals' concept by which revenue and costs are accrued, matched and dealt with in the period to which they relate and the 'prudence' concept by which revenue and profits are not anticipated but are recognised only when realised in the form either of cash or of other assets the ultimate cash realisation of which can be established with reasonable certainty. It is a corollary of the prudence concept that expenditure should be written off in the period in which it arises unless its relationship to the revenue of a future period can be established with reasonable certainty.

The different types of research and development expenditure

2 The term 'research and development' is currently used to cover a wide range of activities, including those in the services sector. The definitions of the different types of research and development used in this statement are based on those used by the Organisation for Economic Co-operation and Development for the purposes of collecting data world-wide.

3 Classification of expenditure is often dependent on the type of business and its organisation. However, it is generally possible to recognise three broad categories of activity, namely pure research, applied research and development. The definitions of the individual categories are set out in Part 2.

4 The dividing line between these categories of expenditure is often indistinct and particular expenditure may have characteristics of more than one category. This is especially so when new products or services are developed through research and development to production, when the activities may have characteristics of both development and production.

5 Research and development activity is distinguished from non-research based activity by the presence or absence of an appreciable element of innovation. If the activity departs from routine and breaks new ground it should normally be included — if it follows an established pattern it should normally be excluded.

6 Examples of activities that would normally be included in research and development are:

(a) experimental, theoretical or other work aimed at the discovery of new knowledge, or the advancement of existing knowledge;

(b) searching for applications of that knowledge;

(c) formulation and design of possible applications for such work;

(d) testing in search for, or evaluation of, product, service or process alternatives;

(e) design, construction and testing of pre-production prototypes and models and development batches;
(f) design of products, services, processes or systems involving new technology or substantially improving those already produced or installed;
(g) construction and operation of pilot plants.

7 Examples of activities that would normally be excluded from research and development include:

(a) testing and analysis either of equipment or product for purposes of quality or quantity control;
(b) periodic alterations to existing products, services or processes even though these may represent some improvemnt;
(c) operational research not tied to a specific research and development activity;
(d) cost of corrective action in connection with break-downs during commercial production;
(e) legal and administrative work in connection with patent applications, records and litigation and the sale or licensing of patents;
(f) activity, including design and construction engineering, relating to the construction, relocation, rearrangement or start-up of facilities or equipment other than facilities or equipment whose sole use is for a particular research and development project;
(g) market research.

The accounting treatment of research and development

8 Expenditure incurred on pure and applied research can be regarded as part of a continuing operation required to maintain a company's business and its competitive position. In general, no one particular period rather than any other will be expected to benefit and therefore it is appropriate that these costs should be written off as they are incurred. Expenditure on pure or applied research may not be treated as an asset (Companies Act 1985, Schedule 4, paragraph 3(2)(c)).

9 The development of new products or services is, however, distinguishable from pure and applied research. Expenditure on such development is normally undertaken with a reasonable expectation of specific commercial success and of future benefits arising from the work, either from increased revenue and related profits or from reduced costs. On these grounds it may be argued that such expenditure, to the extent that it is recoverable, should be deferred to be matched against the future revenue.

10 It will only be practicable to evaluate the potential future benefits of development expenditure if:

(a) there is a clearly defined project; and
(b) the related expenditure is separately identifiable.

11 The outcome of such a project would then need to be examined for:

(a) its technical feasibility; and
(b) its ultimate commercial viability considered in the light of factors such as:
    (i) likely market conditions (including competing products or services);
    (ii) public opinion;

(iii) consumer and environmental legislation.

12 Furthermore a project will only be of value:

(a) only if further development costs to be incurred on the same project together with related production, selling and administration costs will be more than covered by related future revenues; and

(b) adequate resources exist, or are reasonably expected to be available, to enable the project to be completed and to provide any consequential increases in working capital.

13 The elements of uncertainty inherent in the considerations set out in paragraphs 11 and 12 are considerable. There will be a need for different persons with different types of judgement to be involved in assessing the technical, commercial and financial viability of the project. Combinations of the possible differing assessments which they might validly make can produce different assessments of the existence and amounts of future benefits.

14 If these uncertainties are viewed in the context of the concept of prudence, the future benefits of most development projects would be too uncertain to justify carrying the expenditure forward. Nevertheless, in certain industries it is considered that there are a number of major development projects that satisfy the stringent criteria set out in paragraphs 10 to 12. Accordingly, when the expenditure on development projects is judged on a prudent view of available evidence to satisfy these criteria, it may be carried forward and amortised over the period expected to benefit.

15 At each accounting date the unamortised balance of development expenditure should be examined project by project to ensure that it still fulfills the criteria in paragraphs 10 to 12. Where any doubt exists as to the continuation of those circumstances the balance should be written off.

16 Fixed assets may be acquired or constructed in order to provide facilities for research and/or development activities. The use of such fixed assets usually extends over a number of accounting periods and accordingly they should be capitalised and written off over their useful life. The depreciation so written off should be included as part of the expenditure on research and development and disclosed in accordance with SSAP 12.

Exceptions

17 Where companies enter into a firm contract:

(a) to carry out development work on behalf of third parties on such terms that the related expenditure is to be fully reimbursed, or

(b) to develop and manufacture at an agreed price calculated to reimburse expenditure on development as well as on manufacture,

any such expenditure which has not been reimbursed at the balance sheet date should be dealt with as contract work-in-progress.

18 Expenditure incurred in locating and exploiting oil, gas and mineral deposits in the extractive industries does not fall within the definition of research and development used in this accounting standard. Development of new surveying methods and techniques as an integral part of research on geological phenomena should, however, be included in research and development.

Disclosure

19 While there are uncertainties inherent in research and development projects, such activities are important in forming a view of a company's future prospects. Detailed disclosure raises considerable problems of definition and the disclosure requirements of this standard are therefore limited to:

(a) accounting policy as required by SSAP 2;

(b) disclosure of the total amount of research and development expenditure charged in the profit and loss account, distinguished between the current year's expenditure and amounts amortised from deferred expenditure;

(c) the movements on deferred development expenditure during the year.

20 Having regard to the problems of definition and disclosure referred to above, the scope of disclosure required under paragraph 19(b) is (except in the case of Republic of Ireland companies) restricted in effect to companies which are public limited companies, or special category companies, or subsidiaries of such companies, or which exceed by a multiple of 10 the criteria for defining a medium-sized company under the Companies Act 1985.

Part 2 — Definition of Terms

21 The following definition is used for the purpose of this statement:

Research and development expenditure means expenditure falling into one or more of the following broad categories (except to the extent that it relates to locating or exploiting oil, gas or mineral deposits or is reimbursable by third parties either directly or under the terms of a firm contract to develop and manufacture at an agreed price calculated to reimburse both elements of expenditure):

(a) pure (or basic) research: experimental or theoretical work undertaken primarily to acquire new scientific or technical knowledge for its own sake rather than directed towards any specific aim or application;

(b) applied research: original or critical investigation undertaken in order to gain new scientific or technical knowledge and directed towards a specific practical aim or objective;

(c) development: use of scientific or technical knowledge in order to produce new or substantially improved materials, devices, products or services, to install new processes or systems prior to the commencement of commercial production or commercial applications, or to improving substantially those already produced or installed.

Part 3 — Standard Accounting Practice

Scope

22 This standard applies to all financial statements intended to give a true and fair view of the financial position and profit or loss, but, except in the case of Republic of Ireland companies (see paragraphs 45 and 46), the provisions set out in paragraph 31 regarding the disclosure of the total amounts of research and development charged in the profit and loss account need not be applied by an entity that:

(a) is not a public limited company or a special category company (as defined by Section 257 of the Companies Act 1985)* or a holding company that has a public limited company or a special category company as a subsidiary; and

* There is no exact equivalent of 'special category companies' in the Republic of Ireland. The Sixth Schedule to the 1963 Act refers to 'special classes of company' which include banking, discount and assurance companies but not shipping companies.

(b) satisfies the criteria, multiplied in each case by 10, for defining a medium-sized company under Section 248 of the Companies Act 1985, as amended from time to time by statutory instrument and applied in accordance with the provisions of Section 249 of the Act.*

Accounting treatment

23 The cost of fixed assets acquired or constructed in order to provide facilities for research and development activities over a number of accounting periods should be capitalised and written off over their useful lives through the profit and loss account.

24 Expenditure on pure and applied research (other than that referred to in paragraph 23) should be written off in the year of expenditure through the profit and loss account.

25 Development expenditure should be written off in the year of expenditure except in the following circumstances when it may be deferred to future periods:

(a) there is a clearly defined project, and

(b) the related expenditure is separately identifiable, and

(c) the outcome of such a project has been assessed with reasonable certainty as to:

  (i) its technical feasibility, and

  (ii) its ultimate commercial viability considered in the light of factors such as likely market conditions (including competing products), public opinion, consumer and environmental legislation, and

(d) the aggregate of the deferred development costs, any further development costs, and related production, selling and administration costs is reasonably expected to be exceeded by related future sales or other revenues, and

(e) adequate resources exist, or are reasonably expected to be available, to enable the project to be completed and to provide any consequential increases in working capital.

26 In the foregoing circumstances development expenditure may be deferred to the extent that its recovery can reasonably be regarded as assured.

27 If an accounting policy of deferral of development expenditure is adopted, it should be applied to all development projects that meet the criteria in paragraph 25.

28 If development costs are deferred to future periods, they should be amortised. The amortisation should commence with the commercial production or application of the product, service, process or system and should be allocated on a systematic basis to each accounting period, by reference to either the sale or use of the product, service, process or system or the period over which these are expected to be sold or used.

* Equivalent legal references

Great Britain	Northern Ireland	Republic of Ireland
Companies Act 1985	*Companies (Northern Ireland) Order 1986*	*Companies (Amendment) Act 1986*
Section 248	Article 256 (as amended)	Section 8
Section 249	Article 257	Section 9
		Companies Act 1963
Section 257	Article 265	Sixth Schedule paragraph 23

29 Deferred development expenditure for each project should be reviewed at the end of each accounting period and where the circumstances which have justified the deferral of the expenditure (paragraph 25) no longer apply, or are considered doubtful, the expenditure, to the extent to which it is considered to be irrecoverable, should be written off immediately project by project.

Disclosure

30 The accounting policy on research and development expenditure should be stated and explained.

31 The total amount of research and development expenditure charged in the profit and loss account should be disclosed, analysed between the current year's expenditure and amounts amortised from deferred expenditure.

32 Movements on deferred expenditure and the amount carried forward at the beginning and the end of the period should be disclosed. Deferred development expenditure should be disclosed under intangible fixed assets in the balance sheet.

Date from which effective

33 The accounting and disclosure requirements set out in this statement should be adopted as soon as possible and regarded as standard in respect of financial statements relating to accounting periods beginning on or after 1 January 1989.

Part 4 — Note on legal requirements in Great Britain and Northern Ireland

All paragraphs references unless otherwise indicated are to the Companies (Northern Ireland) Order 1986.

34 Paragraph 3(1) of Schedule 4 enables any items required to be shown in a company's balance sheet or profit and loss account to be shown in greater detail than required by the format adopted.

35 Paragraph 3(2)(c) of Schedule 4 provides that a company's balance sheet or profit and loss account may include an item representing or covering the amount of any asset or liability, income or expenditure not otherwise covered by any of the items listed in the accounts format adopted. Cost of research shall not be treated as an asset in any company's balance sheet.

36 Paragraph 19(1) of Schedule 4 does not allow provision to be made for a temporary diminution in value other than for a fixed asset investment.

37 Paragraph 19(2) of Schedule 4 requires provision for diminution in value to be made in respect of any fixed asset which has diminished in value if the reduction is expected to be permanent (whether its useful economic life is limited or not) and the amount to be included in respect of it to be reduced accordingly. Any such provisions not shown in the profit and loss account shall be disclosed (either separately or in aggregate) in a note to the accounts.

38 Paragraph 19(3) requires that where the reasons for which any provision was made have ceased to apply to any extent, then the provision shall be written back to the extent that it is no longer necessary. Any amounts written back in accordance with this sub-paragraph which are not shown in the profit and loss account shall be disclosed (either separately or in aggregate) in a note to the accounts.

39 Paragraph 20(1) of Schedule 4 requires that notwithstanding that an item in respect of development costs is included under fixed assets in the balance sheet formats set out in Part

1 of Schedule 4, an amount may only be included in a company's balance sheet in respect of development costs in special circumstances.

40 Paragraph 20(2) of Schedule 4 requires that if any amount is included in a company's balance sheet in respect of development costs the following information shall be given in a note to the accounts:

(a) the period over which the amount of those costs originally capitalised is being or is to be written off; and

(b) the reasons for capitalising the development costs in question.

41 Paragraph 6(c) of Schedule 7 requires the Directors' Report to contain an indication of the activities (if any) of the company and its subsidiares in the field of research and development.

42 Section 269(2)(b) of the Companies Act 1985 on the treatment of development costs requires that where the unamortised development expenditure carried forward is not treated as a realised loss when determining distributable reserves, the notes to the financial statements shall disclose:

(a) the fact that the amount of the unamortised development expenditure is not to be treated as a realised loss for the purposes of calculating profits; and

(b) the circumstances that the directors relied upon to justify their decision not to treat the unamortised development expenditure as a realised loss.

Part 5 — Note on legal requirements in Republic of Ireland

References are to the Companies (Amendment) Act 1986 and to the Schedule to that Act unless otherwise stated.

43 Section 4(5) of the Act enables any items required to be shown in a company's balance sheet or profit and loss account to be shown in greater detail than required by the format adopted.

44 Section 4(12) of the Act provides that the balance sheet, or profit and loss account, of a company may include an item representing or covering the amount of any asset or liability or income or expenditure not otherwise covered by any of the items listed in the format adopted but that costs of research shall not be treated as assets in the balance sheet of a company.

45 Paragraph 43(4) of the Schedule requires the amount expended on research and development in the financial year, and any amount committed in respect and development in subsequent years, to be stated.

46 Paragrah 43(5) of the Schedule provides that where, in the opinion of the directors, the disclosure of any information required by Paragraph 43(4) would be prejudicial to the interests of the company, that information need not be disclosed, but the fact that any such information has not been disclosed shall be stated.

47 Paragraph 7(1) of the Schedule does not allow provision to be made for a temporary diminution in value other than for a fixed asset investment.

48 Paragraph 7(2) of the Schedule requires provision for diminution in value to be made in respect of any fixed asset which has diminsihed in value if the reduction is expected to be permanent (whether its useful economic life is limited or not) and the amount to be included in respect of it shall be reduced accordingly. Any such provisions which are not shown in the profit and loss account shall be disclosed (either separately or in aggregate) in a note to the accounts.

49 Paragraph 7(3) of the Schedule requires that where the reasons for which any provision was made have ceased to apply to any extent, then the provision should be written back to the extent that it is no longer necessary. Any amounts written back in accordance with this sub-paragraph which are not shown in the profit and loss account shall be disclosed (either separately or in aggregate) in a note to the accounts.

50 Paragraph 8(1) of the Schedule requires that notwithstanding that an item in respect of development costs is included under fixed assets in the balance sheet formats set out in Part 1 of the Schedule, an amount may only be included in a company's balance sheet in respect of development costs in special circumstances.

51 Paragraph 8(2) of the Schedule requires that if any amount is included in a company's balance sheet in respect of development costs, the following information shall be given in a note to the accounts:

(a) the period over which the amount of those costs originally capitalised is being or is to be written off, and

(b) the reasons for capitalising the development costs in question.

52 Section 13(c) of the Act requires the Directors' Report to contain an indication of the activity, if any, of the company and its subsidiaries, if any, in the field of research and development.

53 Section 45A of the Companies (Amendment) Act 1983 on the treatment of develop ment costs, provides that where the development costs are shown in a company's accounts any amount shown as an asset in respect of those costs shall be treated as a realised loss for the purpose of determining profits available for distribution. This provision does not apply to any part of that amount representing an unrealised profit made on revaluation of these costs; nor does it apply if:

(a) there are special circumstances justifying the directors of the company concerned in deciding that the amount mentioned in respect thereof in the company's accounts shall not be treated as a realised loss, and

(b) the note to the accounts required by paragraph 8(2) of the Schedule states that the amount is not to be so treated and explains the circumstances relied upon to justify the decision of the directors to that effect.

Part 6 — Compliance with International Accounting Standard No. 9 'Accounting for research and development activites'

54 The requirements of International Accounting Standard No. 9 'Accounting for research and development activities' accord very closely with the content of the United Kingdom and Irish Accounting Standard No. 13 (Revised) 'Accounting for research and development' and accordingly compliance with SSAP 13 (Revised) will ensure compliance with IAS 9 in all material respects.

Accounting for deferred tax

(Issued October 1978; revised May 1985)

The provisions of this statement of standard accounting practice should be read in conjunction with the explanatory foreword to accounting standards *and need not be applied to immaterial items.*

Part 1 — Explanatory note

Scope

1 This statement is concerned with accounting for tax on profits and surpluses which are recognised in the financial statements in one period but assessed in another. It thus relates primarily to deferred corporation tax and income tax in the United Kingdom and in the Republic of Ireland and, in so far as the principles are similar, to overseas taxes on profits payable by UK and Irish enterprises or their subsidiaries.

2 A number of other taxes, including value added tax, petroleum revenue tax and some overseas taxes, are not assessed directly on profits for an accounting period and are therefore not addressed specifically in this statement. For such taxes, enterprises should generally follow the principle underlying this statement, that deferred tax should be provided to the extent that it is probable that a liability or asset will crystallise but not to the extent that it is probable that a liability or asset will not crystallise.

Background

3 The amount of tax payable on the profits of a particular period often bears little relationship to the amount of income and expenditure appearing in the financial statements. This results from the different basis on which profits are arrived at for the purpose of tax computations as opposed to the basis on which profits are stated in financial statements.

4 The different basis of arriving at profits for tax purposes derives from two main sources. Firstly, certain types of income are tax-free and certain types of expenditure are disallowable, giving rise to 'permanent differences' between taxable and accounting profits. Permanent differences also arise where there are tax allowances or charges with no corresponding amount in the financial statements. Secondly, there are items which are included in the financial statements of a period different from that in which they are dealt with for tax purposes, giving rise to 'timing differences'; thus revenue, gains, expenditure and losses may be included in financial statements either earlier or later than they enter into the computation of profit for tax purposes.

5 Extraordinary items, prior year adjustments and movements on reserves are not included in profit or loss on ordinary activities but may also have an impact on the total tax payable.

Basis of provision

6 There are three principal bases for computing deferred tax.

7 The first is called 'nil provision' or 'flow through' and is based on the principle that only the tax payable in respect of a period should be charged in that period. No provision for deferred tax would therefore be made. Those who hold this view argue that any tax liability arises on taxable profits, not accounting profits, and therefore consider that it is necessary to provide tax only on taxable profits. Further, any tax liability arising on timing differences will depend on the incidence of future taxable profits and may therefore be difficult to quantify.

8 A basis radically different from nil provision is 'full provision', sometimes called 'comprehensive allocation'. This is based on the principle that financial statements for a period should recognise the tax effects, whether current or deferred, of all transactions occurring in that period.

9 An advantage of either of these bases is that the amounts involved can be precisely quantified. However, a crucial disadvantage is that they can lead to a purely arithmetical approach, in which certainty of calculation is given precedence over a reasoned assessment of what the tax effects of transactions will actually be.

10 The effect of timing and other differences on tax charges in relation to reported profits would be of little significance if taxation were not regarded as relevant to the performance of the enterprise for the period, and hence the only accepted indicator of performance were to be the result before tax. However, the result after tax is also widely regarded as an important indicator of performance and this will be distorted by accounting for deferred tax where it is probable that a liability or asset will not crystallise, or by failing to account for deferred tax where it is probable that a liability or asset will crystallise.

11 So far as the balance sheet is concerned, the amount of shareholders' funds and its relationship with the amount of funds from other sources may similarly be distorted by accounting for deferred tax where it is probable that a liability or asset will not crystallise, or by failing to account for deferred tax where it is probable that a liability or asset will crystallise.

12 A third basis is 'partial provision', which requires that deferred tax should be accounted for in respect of the net amount by which it is probable that any payment of tax will be temporarily deferred or accelerated by the operation of timing differences which will reverse in the foreseeable future without being replaced. Partial provision recognises that, if an enterprise is not expected to reduce the scale of its operations significantly, it will often have what amounts to a hard core of timing differences so that the payment of some tax will be permanently deferred. On this basis, deferred tax has to be provided only where it is probable that tax will become payable as a result of the reversal of timing differences. Because it is based on an assessment of what will actually be the position, partial provision is preferable to the other bases described above.

Method of computation

13 There are two principal methods of computation. The first is the deferral method, under which the tax effects of timing differences are calculated using the tax rates current when the differences arise. No adjustments are made subsequently if tax rates change. Reversals are accounted for using the tax rates in force when the timing differences originated, although in practice the effects of reversals and new timing differences are sometimes accounted for as one item. Those who support this method recognise that, when tax rates change, this method will not give an indication of the amount of tax payable or recoverable. Any deferred tax balance will therefore be a deferred tax credit or charge rather than a liability or asset. When tax rates change there is no need to revise the deferred tax already provided. Thus the tax charge or credit for the period relates solely to that period and is not distorted by any adjustments relating to prior periods.

14 The other method is the liability method, under which deferred tax provisions are calculated at the rate at which it is estimated that tax will be paid (or recovered) when the timing differences reverse. Usually the current tax rate is used as the best estimate, unless changes in tax rates are known in advance. As a result, deferred tax provisions are revised to reflect changes in tax rates. Thus the tax charge or credit for the period may include adjustments of accounting estimates relating to prior periods. The deferred tax provision represents the best estimate of the amount which would be payable or recoverable if the relevant timing differences reversed.

15 The liability method is the method consistent with the aim of partial provision, which is to provide the deferred tax which it is probable will be payable or recoverable.

Method of presentation

16 It is generally accepted that, however they have been calculated, tax effects should be shown in financial statements separately from the items or transactions to which they relate. An alternative would be to treat the tax effects of timing differences as integral parts of the revenue or expenditure, assets, provisions or liabilities to which they relate, rather than showing them separately. This 'net of tax' method recognises that the value of assets and liabilities is affected by tax considerations, in particular tax deductibility. On the other hand, it fails to distinguish between a transaction and its tax consequences and therefore should not be used in financial statements.

Part 2 — Definition of terms

17 *Deferred tax* is the tax attributable to timing differences.

18 *Timing differences* are differences between profits or losses as computed for tax purposes and results as stated in financial statements, which arise from the inclusion of items of income and expenditure in tax computations in periods different from those in which they are included in financial statements. Timing differences originate in one period and are capable of reversal in one or more subsequent periods.

19 A loss for tax purposes which is available to relieve future profits from tax constitutes a timing difference.

20 The revaluation of an asset (including an investment in an associated or subsidiary company) will create a timing difference when it is incorporated in the balance sheet, in so far as the profit or loss that would result from realisation at the revalued amount is taxable, unless disposal of the revalued asset and of any subsequent replacement assets would not result in a tax liability, after taking account of any expected rollover relief.

21 The retention of earnings overseas will create a timing difference only if:

(a) there is an intention or obligation to remit them; and

(b) remittance would result in a tax liability after taking account of any related double tax relief.

22 *Financial statements* are balance sheets, profit and loss accounts, statements of source and application of funds, notes and other statements, which collectively are intended to give a true and fair view of financial position and profit or loss.

23 The *liability method* is a method of computing deferred tax whereby it is calculated at the rate of tax that it is estimated will be applicable when the timing differences reverse. Under the liability method deferred tax not provided is calculated at the expected long-term tax rate.

Part 3 — Standard accounting practice

General

24 Deferred tax should be computed under the liability method.

25 Tax deferred or accelerated by the effect of timing differences should be accounted for to the extent that it is probable that a liability or asset will crystallise.

26 Tax deferred or accelerated by the effect of timing differences should not be accounted for to the extent that it is probable that a liability or asset will not crystallise.

27 The assessment of whether deferred tax liabilities or assets will or will not crystallise should be based upon reasonable assumptions.

28 The assumptions should take into account all relevant information available up to the date on which the financial statements are approved by the board of directors, and also the intentions of management. Ideally this information will include financial plans or projections covering a period of years sufficient to enable an assessment to be made of the likely pattern of future tax liabilities. A prudent view should be taken in the assessment of whether a tax liability will crystallise, particularly where the financial plans or projections are susceptible to a high degree of uncertainty or are not fully developed for the appropriate period (see paragraph 52).

29 The provision for deferred tax liabilities should be reduced by any deferred tax debit balances arising from separate categories of timing differences and any advance corporation tax which is available for offset against those liabilities (see Appendix paragraphs 16 and 17).

30 Deferred tax net debit balances should not be carried forward as assets, except to the extent that they are expected to be recoverable without replacement by equivalent debit balances (see Appendix paragraphs 74-90).

31 Debit balances arising in respect of advance corporation tax on dividends payable or proposed at the balance sheet date should be carried forward to the extent that it is foreseen that sufficient corporation tax will be assessed on the profits or income of the succeeding accounting period, against which the advance corporation tax is available for offset.

32 Debit balances arising in respect of advance corporation tax other than on dividends payable or proposed at the balance sheet date should be written off unless their recovery is assured beyond reasonable doubt. Such recovery will normally be assured only where the debit balances are recoverable out of corporation tax arising on profits or income of the succeeding accounting period, without replacement by equivalent debit balances.

Profit and loss account

33 Deferred tax relating to the ordinary activities of the enterprise should be shown separately as a part of the tax on profit or loss on ordinary activities, either on the face of the profit and loss account or in a note.

34 Deferred tax relating to any extraordinary items should be shown separately as part of the tax on extraordinary items, either on the face of the profit and loss account or in a note.

35 The amount of any unprovided deferred tax in respect of the period should be disclosed in a note, analysed into its major components.

36 Adjustments to deferred tax arising from changes in tax rates and tax allowances should normally be disclosed separately as part of the tax charge for the period. However, the effect of a change in the basis of taxation, or of a significant change in government fiscal

policy, should be treated as an extraordinary item where material.

Balance sheet

37 The deferred tax balance, and its major components, should be disclosed in the balance sheet or notes.

38 Transfers to and from deferred tax should be disclosed in a note.

39 Where amounts of deferred tax arise which relate to movements on reserves (e.g. resulting from the expected disposal of revalued assets) the amounts transferred to or from deferred tax should be shown separately as part of such movements.

40 The total amount of any unprovided deferred tax should be disclosed in a note analysed into its major components.

41 Where the potential amount of deferred tax on a revalued asset is not shown because the revaluation does not constitute a timing difference under paragraph 20, the fact that it does not constitute a timing difference and that tax has therefore not been quantified should be stated.

42 Where the value of an asset is shown in a note because it differs materially from its book amount, the note should also show the tax effects, if any, that would arise if the asset were realised at the balance sheet date at the noted value.

Groups

43 Where a company is a member of a group, it should, in accounting for deferred tax, take account of any group relief which, on reasonable evidence, is expected to be available and any charge which will be made for such relief. Assumptions made as to the availability of group relief and payment therefore should be stated.

44 Deferred tax in respect of the remittance of overseas earnings should be accounted for in accordance with the provisions of this statement. Where deferred tax is not provided on earnings retained overseas, this should be stated.

Date from which effective

45 The accounting practices set out in this statement should be adopted as soon as possible and regarded as standard in respect of financial statements relating to accounting periods beginning on or after 1 April 1985.

Part 4 — Note on legal requirements in Great Britain

Relative to financial statements prepared in compliance with the requirements of Sections 228 and 230 of the Companies Act 1985

46 The references to 'the Schedule' below are to Schedule 4 to the Companies Act 1985. Format references are to the formats in paragraph 8 of the Schedule.

47 Deferred tax provisions should be included in the balance sheet under the heading 'Provisions for liabilities and charges' as part of the provision for 'Taxation, including deferred taxation' (balance sheet format 1-I, 2, format 2 - liabilities B, 2). Paragraph 89 of the Schedule describes provisions for liabilities or charges as "any amount retained as reasonably necessary for the purpose of providing for any liability or loss which is either likely to be incurred, or certain to be incurred but uncertain as to the amount or as to the date on which it will arise".

48 The amount of any provisions for taxation other than deferred taxation has to be stated (paragraph 47 of the Schedule). Taking this requirement together with that referred to in paragraph 47 above, the balance of deferred tax will be ascertainable as the remaining figure. Tax provisions are distinguished from tax liabilities falling due within, or after more than, one year, which are shown separately under creditors in the balance sheet (balance sheet format l-E, 8 and H, 8, format 2 — liabilities C, 8 and note 9 on the balance sheet format).

49 Paragraph 46(1) of the Schedule requires the information set out in paragraph 46(2) of the Schedule to be given where any amount is transferred to any provisions for liabilities and charges or from any provision for liabilities and charges, except where the transfer is for the purpose for which the provision was established. The information required in paragraph 46(2) of the Schedule is:

"(a) the amount of the reserves or provisions as at the date of the beginning of the financial year and as at the balance sheet date respectively;

(b) any amounts transferred to or from the reserves or provisions during that year; and

(c) the source and application respectively of any amounts so transferred."

50 Any deferred tax carried forward as an asset should be included under the heading of 'Prepayments and accrued income' either within 'Current Assets/Debtors', if it is current, or separately under main heading D. In the former case, any amount falling due after more than one year should be shown separately (note 5 on the balance sheet formats).

51 In determining the aggregate amount of deferred tax, this statement requires deferred tax debit balances to be matched with deferred tax liabilities against which they will be able to be offset. This is in accordance with paragraph 14 of the Schedule as individual deferred tax debit balances and liabilities which can be offset for tax purposes are not separate items, which under paragraph 5 of the Schedule cannot be offset but are elements of an aggregate deferred tax asset or liability.

52 The amount of any item has to be determined on a prudent basis. In particular, all liabilities and losses which have arisen or are likely to arise in respect of the financial year to which the accounts relate or a previous financial year have to be taken into account (paragraph 12 of the Schedule).

53 Paragraph 50(2) of the Schedule requires information to be given with respect to the amount or estimated amount of any contingent liability not provided for, its legal nature and any valuable security provided. The ASC has obtained legal advice to the effect that unprovided deferred tax is a contingent liability, except where the prospect of it becoming payable is so remote that it does not amount to a contingent liability at all.

54 Where a company is a member of a group, any contingent deferred tax liability on behalf of other members of the group has to be shown separately in the financial statements of any company which has undertaken the commitment, analysed between amounts in respect of any subsidiary and amounts in respect of any holding company or fellow subsidiary (paragraph 50(6) of the Schedule).

55 The tax treatment of amounts credited or debited to the revaluation reserve has to be disclosed (paragraph 34(4) of the Schedule).

56 The basis on which the charge for United Kingdom tax is computed has to be stated (paragraph 54(1) of the Schedule). Particulars are required of any special circumstances affecting the tax liability for the financial year or succeeding financial years (paragraph 54(2) of the Schedule).

57 Paragraph 54(3) of the Schedule requires the amounts shown under the items 'tax on profit or loss on ordinary activities' and 'tax on extraordinary profit or loss', to be analysed between:

(a) United Kingdom corporation tax, before and after any double tax relief;

(b) United Kingdom income tax; and

(c) overseas tax.

Deferred tax is not specifically referred to in the profit and loss account formats. However, this statement requires any deferred tax to be separately shown as part of the tax on profit or loss on ordinary activities or of the tax on extraordinary profit or loss, as appropriate, either on the face of the profit and loss account or in a note.

Relative to financial statements prepared in compliance with the requirements of Sections 258 and 259 of the Companies Act 1985

58 Sections 258 and 259 of the Companies Act 1985 are applicable to some banking, insurance and shipping companies and their holding companies, as laid down in section 257 of the Act. The references to 'the Schedule' below are to Schedule 9 to the Companies Act 1985.

59 Paragraph 9 of the Schedule requires that any amount set aside to prevent undue fluctuation in charges for taxation should be disclosed. If any of that sum is used for another purpose, that fact has to be disclosed together with the amount (paragraph 13(14) of the Schedule).

60 Paragraph 13(7) of the Schedule requires the general nature of all contingent liabilities not provided for to be stated and, where practicable, the aggregate amount or estimated amount of those liabilities, if it is material. The ASC has obtained legal advice to the effect that unprovided deferred tax is a contingent liability, except where the prospect of it becoming payable is so remote that it does not amount to a contingent liability at all.

61 Paragraph 14(1)(c) of the Schedule requires the tax charge to be analysed between:

(a) United Kingdom corporation tax, before and after any double tax relief;

(b) United Kingdom income tax; and

(c) overseas tax.

There is no requirement in the Schedule for deferred tax to be disclosed separately in the profit and loss account or the notes thereto. However, this statement requires any deferred tax to be shown separately, distinguishing between deferred tax on profit or loss on ordinary activities and deferred tax on extraordinary profit or loss, either on the face of the profit and loss account or in a note.

62 The basis on which the charge for United Kingdom taxation is computed has to be stated (paragraph 18(3) of the Schedule). Particulars are required of any special circumstances affecting the liability for the financial year or succeeding financial years (paragraph 18(4) of the Schedule).

Part 5 — Note on legal requirements and other matters in Ireland
Northern Ireland

63 The legal requirements described in Part 4, paragraphs 47 to 57, apply equally to Northern Ireland by virtue of Schedule 6 to the Companies Act (Northern Ireland), 1960, as inserted by Article 3 of The Companies (Northern Ireland) Order 1982. The Schedule references are the same except for paragraph 89 (paragraph 47 above) and paragraph 34(4) (paragraph 55 above), for which the equivalent references in Northern Ireland are paragraphs 88 and 34(5) respectively.

64 The legal requirements described in Part 4, paragraphs 59 to 62, apply equally to Northern Ireland by virtue of Schedule 6A to the Companies Act (Northern Ireland), 1960 as renumbered by Article 3 of The Companies (Northern Ireland) Order 1982. Schedule 6A is applicable to some banking, insurance and shipping companies and their holding companies as laid down in Schedule 2 to The Companies (Northern Ireland) Order 1982. The equivalent references in Northern Ireland are set out below:

SSAP	GB	NI
59	9	7A
59	13(14)	11(8A)
60	13(7)	11(5)
61	14(1)(c)	12(1)(c)
62	18(3)	14(3)
62	18(4)	14(3A)

Republic of Ireland

65 The references to 'the Schedule' below are to the Sixth Schedule to the Companies Act, 1963, which sets out general provisions as to the balance sheet and profit and loss account of companies registered in the Republic of Ireland.

66 Paragraph 4 of the Schedule requires that liabilities shall be classified under headings appropriate to the company's business. Amounts set aside to meet future tax liabilities or for tax equalisation (deferred tax) purposes shall be treated as provisions but separately indicated.

67 Paragraph 11(4) of the Schedule requires the general nature of contingent liabilities not provided for and, where practicable, the aggregate amount or estimated amount of those liabilities to be shown. Paragraph 11(9) of the Schedule requires to be shown the basis on which the amount, if any, set aside for taxation on profits is computed.

68 Paragraph 12(c) of the Schedule requires to be shown the amount of the charge for income tax and other taxation on profits including income tax and other taxation payable outside the State on profits and distinguishing where practicable between income tax and other taxation.

69 Paragraph 14(3) of the Schedule requires to be shown the basis on which the charge for income tax and other taxation on profits, whether payable in or outside the State, is computed.

70 Differences exist between United Kingdom law and Republic of Ireland law on advance corporation tax. Deferred tax is affected by advance corporation tax in the following respects: (a) the offset of advance corporation tax against a deferred tax liability; and (b) the carry forward of a net debit balance on the deferred tax account represented by advance corporation tax. The general provisions of the statement in regard to these two matters will be applicable to Republic of Ireland companies with one exception. Because advance corporation tax is payable six months from the end of the accounting period in which the dividend is paid, it will be necessary to consider the possibility of offsetting an advance corporation tax liability against the asset representing advance corporation tax recoverable. If such an offset were probable the advance corporation tax recoverable would not be deducted from a deferred tax credit balance under paragraph 29 or recognised as a deferred tax debit balance under paragraphs 31 and 32.

71 Certain Irish companies and branches of foreign companies are totally relieved of corporation tax or are subject to tax at reduced rates on profits arising from the export of manufactured goods and services (export sales relief and 'Shannon' relief). Where such companies have timing differences originating during the period of total relief or of reduced relief and it is probable that these differences will reverse after expiry of the relief period — or when the reduced rates no longer apply — and that a tax liability will crystallise, then provision should be made for taxation deferred. The amount of tax to be deferred in respect of such timing differences should be calculated by reference to the effective rate estimated to be applicable in the years of reversal.

72 A reduced rate of corporation tax applies to companies in regard to income arising from the sale of goods manufactured in the Republic of Ireland. Under present legislation the relief is for sales made in periods up to 31 December, 2000. In calculating deferred tax provisions where a reduced rate applies, similar considerations to those given in the preceding paragraphs should be taken into account.

Part 6 — Compliance with International Accounting Standard No. 12 'Accounting for taxes on income"

73 Compliance with the requirements of Statement of Standard Accounting Practice No. 15 (revised) 'Accounting for deferred tax' will automatically ensure compliance with International Accounting Standard No. 12 'Accounting for taxes on income' so far as deferred tax is concerned.

Appendix

Note. This appendix is for guidance only and does not form part of the statement of standard accounting practice.

Deferred tax effects of current tax legislation in the United Kingdom and Republic of Ireland

Introduction

74 This appendix gives guidance on the accounting treatment of the tax effects of permanent and timing differences between taxable and accounting income resulting from current tax legislation in the United Kingdom and Republic of Ireland. It reflects legislation current as at May 1985 and will need to be amended when necessary to reflect changes in legislation.

75 The principal areas of difference are:

(a) permanent differences;

(b) timing differences;

(c) losses;

(d) items not included in profit or loss on ordinary activities; and

(e) advance corporation tax.

Items not included in profit or loss on ordinary activities are dealt with in paragraphs 34 and 39 of this statement and accordingly are not considered in this appendix.

Permanent differences

76 Examples of permanent differences are UK entertaining and fines (disallowable) and regional development grants and interest on tax repayments (tax free). Stock relief in the Republic of Ireland is effectively a permanent difference. These differences will not reverse in future periods and thus give rise to no tax effects in other periods.

Timing differences

77 The combined effect of timing differences should be considered when attempting to assess whether a tax liability will crystallise, rather than looking at each timing difference separately. Paragraphs 27 and 28 of the standard indicate that reasonable assumptions, by reference to suitable financial plans or projections covering a period of years, are required when making this assessment. The period may be relatively short — say three to five years — where the pattern of timing differences is expected to be regular. However, it may need to be longer for an enterprise with an irregular pattern of timing differences. The length of the lives of the relevant assets and the enterprise's assumptions on growth in capital expenditure also affect the length of the period which needs to be considered.

78 A number of timing differences arise from the use of the receipts and payments basis for tax purposes and the accruals basis in financial statements. Examples of these and other timing differences are:

(a) interest receivable accrued in the accounting period, but taxed when received;

(b) dividends from foreign subsidiaries accrued in a period prior to that in which they arise for tax purposes;

(c) intra-group profits in stock deferred upon consolidation until realisation to third parties;

(d) interest or royalties payable accrued in the accounting period, but allowed when paid;

(e) pension costs accrued in the financial statements but allowed for tax purposes when paid or contributed at some later date;

(f) provisions for repairs and maintenance made in the financial statements but not allowed for tax purposes until the expenditure is incurred;

(g) bad debt provisions not allowed for tax purposes unless and until they become 'specific';

(h) provisions for revenue losses on closing down plants or for costs of re-organisation upon which tax relief is not obtained until the costs or losses are incurred; and

(i) revenue expenditure deferred in the financial statements, such as development or advertising, if it is allowed for tax purposes as it is incurred.

79 A number of these differences are 'short term' timing differences in that they can be identified with specific transactions and normally reverse in the accounting period following that in which they originated. Short term and other timing differences need to be considered together when attempting to assess whether a tax liability will crystallise.

Accelerated capital allowances

80 Accelerated capital allowances are timing differences which arise from the availability of capital allowances in tax computations which are in excess of the related depreciation charges in financial statements. The reverse may also occur, whereby the depreciation charges in financial statements exceed the capital allowances available in tax computations.

81 In many businesses, timing differences arising from accelerated capital allowances are of a recurring nature and reversing differences are themselves offset, wholly or partially, or are exceeded, by new originating differences, thereby giving rise to continuing tax reductions or the indefinite postponement of any liability attributable to the tax benefits received. Thus an enterprise having a relatively stable or growing investment in depreciable assets can take tax relief year by year on capital expenditure. This tax relief may equal or exceed the additional tax which would otherwise have been payable in consequence of the reversal of the original timing differences through depreciation. Where for economic or other reasons a spasmodic or highly irregular pattern of capital allowances is forecast, a substantial period of time will need to be considered in attempting to assess whether a tax liability will crystallise. Where there is a declining availability of capital allowances, any originating timing differences will usually reverse, and deferred tax should be provided unless it is probable for other reasons that no tax liability will crystallise.

Revaluations of fixed assets

82 When a fixed asset is revalued above cost a timing difference potentially arises in that, in the absence of rollover relief, tax on a chargeable gain may be payable if and when the asset is disposed of at its revalued amount. Where it is probable that a liability will crystallise, provision for the tax payable on disposal is required to be made out of the revaluation surplus, based on the value at which the fixed asset is carried in the balance sheet. Whether or not a liability will crystallise can usually be determined, in the absence of rollover relief, at the time the enterprise decides to dispose of the asset.

Revaluations not incorporated in the accounts

83 Paragraph 42 of the standard requires that, where the value of an asset is not incorporated in the balance sheet but is given elsewhere such as in a note, the tax effects, if any, which would arise if the asset were realised at the noted value should also be shown. This also applies where the value is given in the directors' report instead of in the notes.

Rollover relief

84 Rollover relief has the effect of deferring the reversal of the timing difference arising on the revaluation of an asset beyond the date of sale, or of creating a timing difference on the sale of an asset that has not been revalued, or a combination of the two. Where rollover relief has been obtained on the sale of an asset, with the 'base cost' of the replacement asset for tax purposes thereby being reduced, and the potential deferred tax has not been disclosed, the standard requires disclosure of the fact that the revaluation does not constitute a timing difference and that tax has therefore not been quantified, as it will not otherwise be evident from the accounts.

Overseas assets

85 Translation of the financial statements of overseas subsidiaries or associated companies is not regarded as creating a timing difference. Gains and losses arising on translation of an enterprise's own overseas assets (including investments in subsidiaries and associated companies) and liabilities may give rise to timing differences depending on whether or not the gains or losses have a tax effect.

Losses

86 Paragraph 30 of the standard requires that deferred tax assets, including those arising from losses, should be recognised only when they are expected to be recoverable without replacement by equivalent debit balances. Recovery may be affected, among other things, by the period of time for which losses are available to be carried forward for tax purposes.

87 Deferred tax relating to current trading losses may be treated as recoverable when:

(a) the loss results from an identifiable and non-recurring cause; and

(b) the enterprise, or predecessor enterprise, has been consistently profitable over a considerable period, with any past losses being more than offset by income in subsequent periods; and

(c) it is assured beyond reasonable doubt that future taxable profits will be sufficient to offset the current loss during the carry-forward period prescribed by tax legislation.

88 Deferred tax relating to capital losses may be treated as recoverable when:

(a) a potential chargeable gain not expected to be covered by rollover relief is present in assets which have not been revalued in the financial statements to reflect that gain and which are not essential to the future operations of the enterprise; and

(b) the enterprise has decided to dispose of these assets and thus realise the potential chargeable gain; and

(c) the unrealised chargeable gain (after allowing for any possible loss in value before disposal) is sufficient to offset the loss in question, such that it is assured beyond reasonable doubt that a tax liability on the relevant portion of the chargeable gain will not crystallise.

Advance corporation taxation (ACT)

89 The minimum tax charge in the profit and loss account in any accounting period will normally be the amount payable as ACT (net of any recovery) plus any amounts charged in respect of overseas tax. As noted in paragraph 7 of SSAP 8 'The treatment of tax under the imputation system in the accounts of companies', ACT which cannot be recovered out of the corporation tax liability on the income of the year but which is carried forward to be recovered out of the corporation tax liability on the income of future periods may, subject to certain limitations, be deducted from the deferred tax account. Where there is no balance on the deferred tax account or to the extent that the balance is insufficient for this purpose, consideration will need to be given as to whether the ACT is recoverable out of the corporation tax liability on the income of future periods.

90 It may be incorrect to carry forward an amount of ACT to offset an equal credit amount of deferred tax. This is because ACT may only be carried forward at the basic rate of income tax on the gross amount of any distribution, to be set off against corporation tax at the full or small companies rates on the same gross amount of taxable income, excluding chargeable gains.

Amendment to SSAP 15 'Accounting for deferred tax' — December 1992

Preface

This amendment to Statement of Standard Accounting Practice No. 15 'Accounting for deferred tax' (SSAP 15) arises from the interaction between, on the one hand, SSAP 15 and, on the other hand, SSAP 24 'Accounting for pension costs', together with UITF Abstract No. 6 'Accounting for post-retirement benefits other than pensions' (UITF 6).

When SSAP 15 was originally issued in 1978 (and indeed when it was revised in 1985) the normal practice in accounting for pensions and other post-retirement benefits was to adopt a cash basis, and consequently there were few significant deferred tax implications. Subsequently, SSAP 24 (issued in 1988) introduced, and UITF 6 is in the process of introducing, major changes in the way these long-term and somewhat uncertain obligations are treated in financial statements, with very significant deferred tax implications. Under SSAP 24 and UITF 6 these long-term obligations are accounted for on a full provision basis, even though in many cases it is likely that they will continually roll over (i.e. as one obligation is settled another will arise) and it has been argued that it is difficult to justify a prohibition, as SSAP 15 would otherwise require, on the related deferred tax being treated on a similar basis if it, too, continually rolls over.

This amendment permits preparers of financial statements, where they consider it appropriate in their particular circumstances, to use the same recognition criteria for the tax implications of pensions and other post-retirement benefits as in accounting for the obligations to provide those benefits. This option would not have been available previously under SSAP 15. The inconsistencies in the approaches adopted by SSAPs 15 and 24 have been pointed out in papers published by the Pensions Research Accountants Group in 1989 and the Institute of Chartered Accountants in England and Wales (TR794) in 1990. Attention is drawn to the statement in TR794 that "the tax consequences of pensions cannot be accounted for in isolation from potential deferred tax effects from other sources", as, for example, "deferred tax arising from sources other than pensions may enhance the prospective recoverability of tax arising in respect of pension payments".

The Urgent Issues Task Force recommended that an amendment be made to SSAP 15. The Accounting Standards Board (the Board) accepted the recommendation and on 9 November 1992 issued Financial Reporting Exposure Draft No. 2 'Amendment to SSAP 15 "Accounting for deferred tax"' (FRED 2) as part of the normal process of consultation. The consultations that the Board has conducted over the last year have indicated that both SSAP 15 and SSAP 24 are high on the list of standards that should be subject to a comprehensive review in the medium term and at that time the inconsistencies in the approaches adopted, as noted above, can be considered more fully. The Board considers that until resources and the allocation of priorities permit these reviews of existing standards to be undertaken, this amendment will remove an inconsistency between two standards that could inhibit proper accounting for long-term post-retirement obligations and allow preparers of financialstatements to adopt the most appropriate accounting treatment in their particular circumstances or the often complex matters dealt with by these standards.

Statement of Standard Accounting Practice

1 SSAP 15 is amended by the insertion of an additional paragraph after paragraph 32 and before paragraph 33 as follows:

> "**32A** Notwithstanding the other requirements of this Statement of Standard Accounting Practice, either the full provision basis or the partial provision basis may be used in accounting for the deferred tax implications of pensions and other post-retirement benefits accounted for in accordance with SSAP 24 'Accounting for pension costs' and UITF 6 'Accounting for post-retirement benefits other than pensions'. The policy adopted should be disclosed."

2 SSAP 15 is also amended by the insertion of an additional heading and paragraphs after paragraph 12 and before paragraph 13 as follows:

"Pensions and other post-retirement benefits

> **12A** Paragraph 32A permits preparers of financial statements, where they consider it appropriate in their particular circumstances, to use the same recognition criteria for the deferred tax implications of pensions and other post-retirement benefits as in accounting for the obligations to provide those benefits.
>
> **12B** Where an enterprise is contemplating the recognition of a deferred tax asset that is permitted by paragraph 32A in respect of a provision for pensions or other post-retirement obligations it should be noted that the normal rules regarding the recoverability of assets are applicable."

3 If an enterprise changes its accounting policy in respect of certain deferred tax items, the normal rules regarding such changes, set out in FRS 3 'Reporting financial performance', are applicable.

4 As this amendment is a relaxation of the existing requirements of SSAP 15 it is effective immediately.

'Amendment to SSAP 15 "Accounting for deferred tax" — December 1992' was adopted by the unanimous vote of the eight members of the Accounting Standards Board.

Members of the Accounting Standards Board

David Tweedie (Chairman)

Allan Cook (Technical Director)

Robert Bradfield

Sir Bryan Carsberg

Michael Garner

Donald Main

Roger Munson

Graham Stacy

Accounting for post balance sheet events

(Issued August 1980)

The provisions of this statement of standard accounting practice should be read in conjunction with the explanatory foreword to accounting standards *and need not be applied to immaterial items. The provisions apply equally to financial statements prepared under the historical cost convention and to financial statements prepared under the current cost convention.*

Part 1 — Explanatory note

1 Events arising after the balance sheet date need to be reflected in financial statements if they provide additional evidence of conditions that existed at the balance sheet date and materially affect the amounts to be included.

2 To prevent financial statements from being misleading, disclosure needs to be made by way of notes of other material events arising after the balance sheet date which provide evidence of conditions not existing at the balance sheet date. Disclosure is required where this information is necessary for a proper understanding of the financial position.

3 A post balance sheet event for the purpose of this standard is an event which occurs between the balance sheet date and the date on which the financial statements are approved by the board of directors. It is not intended that the preliminary consideration of a matter which may lead to a decision by the board of directors in the future should fall within the scope of this standard.

4 Events which occur after the date on which the financial statements are approved by the board of directors do not come within the scope of this standard. If such events are material the directors should consider publishing the relevant information so that users of financial statements are not misled.

5 The process involved in the approval of financial statements by the directors will vary depending on the management structure and procedures followed in preparing and finalising financial statements. However, the date of approval will normally be the date of the board meeting at which the financial statements are formally approved, or in respect of unincorporated enterprises the corresponding date. In respect of group accounts, the date of approval is the date the group accounts are formally approved by the board of directors of the holding company.

Classification of post balance sheet events

6 Events occurring after the balance sheet date may be classified into two categories: 'adjusting events' and 'non-adjusting events'.

7 Adjusting events are events which provide additional evidence relating to conditions existing at the balance sheet date. They require changes in amounts to be included in financial statements. Examples of adjusting events are given in the appendix.

8 Some events occurring after the balance sheet date, such as a deterioration in the operating results and in the financial position may indicate a need to consider whether it is appropriate to use the going concern concept in the preparation of financial statements. Consequently these may fall to be treated as adjusting events.

9 Non-adjusting events are events which arise after the balance sheet date and concern conditions which did not exist at that time. Consequently they do not result in changes in amounts in financial statements. They may, however, be of such materiality that their disclosure is required by way of notes to ensure that financial statements are not misleading. Examples of non-adjusting events which may require disclosure are given in the appendix.

10 Disclosure would be required of the reversal or maturity after the year end of transactions entered into before the year end, the substance of which was primarily to alter the appearance of the company's balance sheet. Such alterations include those commonly known as 'window dressing'.

11 There are certain post balance sheet events which, because of statutory requirements or customary accounting practice, are reflected in financial statements and so fall to be treated as adjusting events. These include proposed dividends, amounts appropriated to reserves, the effects of changes in taxation and dividends receivable from subsidiary and associated companies.

Disclosure in financial statements

12 Separate disclosure of adjusting events is not normally required as they do no more than provide additional evidence in support of items in financial statements.

13 In determining which non-adjusting events are of sufficient materiality to require disclosure, regard should be had to all matters which are necessary to enable users of financial statements to assess the financial position.

Part 2 — Definition of terms

14 *Financial statements* are balance sheets, profit and loss accounts, statements of source and application of funds, notes and other statements, which collectively are intended to give a true and fair view of financial position and profit or loss.

15 *Company* includes any enterprise which comes within the scope of statements of standard accounting practice.

16 *Directors* include the corresponding officers of organisations which do not have directors.

17 *The date on which the financial statements are approved by the board of directors* is the date the board of directors formally approves a set of documents as the financial statements. In respect of unincorporated enterprises, the date of approval is the corresponding date. In respect of group accounts, the date of approval is the date when the group accounts are formally approved by the board of directors of the holding company.

18 *Post balance sheet events* are those events, both favourable and unfavourable, which occur between the balance sheet date and the date on which the financial statements are approved by the board of directors.

19 *Adjusting events* are post balance sheet events which provide additional evidence of conditions existing at the balance sheet date. They include events which because of statutory or conventional requirements are reflected in financial statements.

20 *Non-adjusting events* are post balance sheet events which concern conditions which did not exist at the balance sheet date.

Part 3 — Standard accounting practice

21 Financial statements should be prepared on the basis of conditions existing at the balance sheet date.

22 A material post balance sheet event requires changes in the amounts to be included in financial statements where:

(a) It is an adjusting event; or

(b) It indicates that application of the going concern concept to the whole or a material part of the company is not appropriate.

23 A material post balance sheet event should be disclosed where:

(a) it is a non-adjusting event of such materiality that its non-disclosure would affect the ability of the users of financial statements to reach a proper understanding of the financial position; or

(b) it is the reversal or maturity after the year end of a transaction entered into before the year end, the substance of which was primarily to alter the appearance of the company's balance sheet.

24 In respect of each post balance sheet event which is required to be disclosed under paragraph 23 above, the following information should be stated by way of notes in financial statements:

(a) the nature of the event; and

(b) an estimate of the financial effect, or a statement that it is not practicable to make such an estimate.

25 The estimate of the financial effect should be disclosed before taking account of taxation, and the taxation implications should be explained where necessary for a proper understanding of the financial position.

26 The date on which the financial statements are approved by the board of directors should be disclosed in the financial statements.

Date from which effective

27 The accounting practices set out in this statement should be adopted as soon as possible and regarded as standard in respect of financial statements relating to accounting periods beginning on or after 1 September 1980.

Part 4 — Compliance with International Accounting Standard No. 10 'Contingencies and events occurring after the balance sheet date'

28 The requirements of International Accounting Standard No. 10 'Contingencies and events occurring after the balance sheet date' concerning post balance sheet events accord very closely with the content of the United Kingdom and Irish accounting standard No. 17 'Accounting for post balance sheet events' and accordingly compliance with SSAP 17 will ensure compliance with IAS 10 in all material respects so far as post balance sheet events are concerned.

Appendix

29 This appendix is for general guidance and does not form part of the statement of standard accounting practice. The examples are merely illustrative and the lists are not exhaustive.

The examples listed distinguish between those normally classified as adjusting events and as non-adjusting events. However, in exceptional circumstances, to accord with the prudence concept, an adverse event which would normally be classified as non-adjusting may need to be reclassified as adjusting. In such circumstances, full disclosure of the adjustment would be required.

Adjusting events

30 The following are examples of post balance sheet events which normally should be classified as adjusting events:

(a) *Fixed assets.* The subsequent determination of the purchase price or of the proceeds of sale of assets purchased or sold before the year end.

(b) *Property.* A valuation which provides evidence of a permanent diminution in value.

(c) *Investments.* The receipt of a copy of the financial statements or other information in respect of an unlisted company which provides evidence of a permanent diminution in the value of a long-term investment.

(d) *Stocks and work in progress.*

(i) The receipt of proceeds of sales after the balance sheet date or other evidence concerning the net realisable value of stocks.

(ii) The receipt of evidence that the previous estimate of accrued profit on a long-term contract was materially inaccurate.

(e) *Debtors.* The renegotiation of amounts owing by debtors, or the insolvency of a debtor.

(f) *Dividends receivable.* The declaration of dividends by subsidiaries and associated companies relating to periods prior to the balance sheet date of the holding company.

(g) *Taxation.* The receipt of information regarding rates of taxation.

(h) *Claims.* Amounts received or receivable in respect of insurance claims which were in the course of negotiation at the balance sheet date.

(i) *Discoveries.* The discovery of errors or frauds which show that the financial statements were incorrect.

Non-adjusting events

31 The following are examples of post balance sheet events which normally should be classified as non-adjusting events:

(a) Mergers and acquisitions.

(b) Reconstructions and proposed reconstructions.

(c) Issues of shares and debentures.

(d) Purchases and sales of fixed assets and investments.

(e) Losses of fixed assets or stocks as a result of a catastrophe such as fire or flood.

(f) Opening new trading activities or extending existing trading activities.

(g) Closing a significant part of the trading activities if this was not anticipated at the year end.

(h) Decline in the value of property and investments held as fixed assets, if it can be demonstrated that the decline occurred after the year end.

(i) Changes in rates of foreign exchange.

(j) Government action, such as nationalisation.

(k) Strikes and other labour disputes.

(l) Augmentation of pension benefits.

Accounting for contingencies

(Issued August 1980)

The provisions of this statement of standard accounting practice should be read in conjunction with the explanatory foreword to accounting standards *and need not be applied to immaterial items. The provisions apply equally to financial statements prepared under the historical cost convention and to financial statements prepared under the current cost convention.*

Part 1 — Explanatory note

1 The term contingency used in this statement is applied to a condition which exists at the balance sheet date, where the outcome will be confirmed only on the occurrence or non-occurrence of one or more uncertain future events. It is not intended that uncertainties connected with accounting estimates should fall within the scope of this statement, for example the lives of fixed assets, the amount of bad debts, the net realisable value of inventories, the expected outcome of long-term contracts or the valuation of properties and foreign currency balances.

2 Contingencies existing at the balance sheet date should be taken into consideration when preparing financial statements. Estimates of the outcome and of the financial effect of contingencies should be made by the board of directors of the company. These estimates will be based on consideration of information available up to the date on which the financial statements are approved by the board of directors and will include a review of events occurring after the balance sheet date. As an example, in the case of a substantial legal claim against a company, the factors to be considered would include the progress of the claim at the date on which the financial statements are approved, the opinion of legal experts or other advisers and the experience of the company in similar cases.

3 The treatment of a contingency existing at the balance sheet date is determined by its expected outcome. In addition to accruals under the fundamental concept of prudence in SSAP 2 'Disclosure of accounting policies', contingent losses will be accrued in financial statements where it is probable that a future event will confirm a loss which can be estimated with reasonable accuracy at the date on which the financial statements are approved by the board of directors.

4 Existing conventions preclude contingent gains from being accrued in financial statements. The existence of a contingent gain should be disclosed only if it is probable that the gain will be realised. When the realisation of the gain becomes reasonably certain, then such a gain is not a contingency and accrual is appropriate.

5 Subject to paragraphs 3 and 4 above, a material contingency which is not accounted for under existing requirements should be disclosed by way of notes in order to ensure that financial statements do not present a misleading position. Such disclosure should indicate the nature of the contingency, the uncertainties which are expected to affect the ultimate outcome and either a prudent estimate of the financial effect or a statement that it is not practicable to make such an estimate.

6 A contingency may be reduced or avoided because it is matched by a related counter-claim or claim by or against a third party. In such cases any accrual, or the amount to be disclosed in financial statements by way of notes, should be reduced by taking into account the probable outcome of the claim. However, the likelihood of success, and the probable amounts of the claim and the counter-claim, should be separately assessed, and separately disclosed where appropriate.

7 In disclosing the financial effect of a contingency, the amount should be stated before taking account of taxation, and the taxation implications of a contingency crystallising should be explained where necessary for a proper understanding of the financial position.

8 There are some contingencies where the possibility of the ultimate outcome having a material effect on the financial statements is so remote that disclosure could be misleading. This statement does not require disclosure of remote contingencies.

9 This statement should be read in conjunction with Part 4 — Note of legal requirements.

Part 2 — Definition of terms

10 *Financial statements* are balance sheets, profit and loss accounts, statements of source and application of funds, notes and other statements, which collectively are intended to give a true and fair view of financial position and profit or loss.

11 *Company* includes any enterprise which comes within the scope of statements of standard accounting practice.

12 *Directors* include the corresponding officers of organisations which do not have directors.

13 *The date on which the financial statements are approved by the board of directors* is the date the board of directors formally approves a set of documents as the financial statements. In respect of unincorporated enterprises the date of approval is the corresponding date. In respect of group accounts the date of approval is the date when the group accounts are formally approved by the board of directors of the holding company.

14 *Contingency* is a condition which exists at the balance sheet date, where the outcome will be confirmed only on the occurrence or non-occurrence of one or more uncertain future events. A contingent gain or loss is a gain or loss dependent on a contingency.

Part 3 — Standard accounting practice

15 In addition to amounts accrued under the fundamental concept of prudence in SSAP 2 'Disclosure of accounting policies', a material contingent loss should be accrued in financial statements where it is probable that a future event will confirm a loss which can be estimated with reasonable accuracy at the date on which the financial statements are approved by the board of directors.

16 A material contingent loss not accrued under paragraph 15 above should be disclosed except where the possibility of loss is remote.

17 Contingent gains should not be accrued in financial statements. A material contingent gain should be disclosed in financial statements only if it is probable that the gain will be realised.

18 In respect of each contingency which is required to be disclosed under paragraphs 16 and 17 above, the following information should be stated by way of notes in financial statements:

(a) the nature of the contingency; and

(b) the uncertainties which are expected to affect the ultimate outcome; and

(c) a prudent estimate of the financial effect, made at the date on which the financial statements are approved by the board of directors; or a statement that it is not practicable to make such an estimate.

19 Where there is disclosure of an estimate of the financial effect of a contingency, the amount disclosed should be the potential financial effect. In the case of a contingent loss, this should be reduced by:

(a) any amounts accrued; and

(b) the amounts of any components where the possibility of loss is remote. The net amount only need be disclosed.

20 The estimate of the financial effect should be disclosed before taking account of taxation, and the taxation implications of a contingency crystallising should be explained where necessary for a proper understanding of the financial position.

21 Where both the nature of, and the uncertainties which affect a contingency in respect of an individual transaction are common to a large number of similar transactions, the financial effect of the contingency need not be individually estimated but may be based on the group of similar transactions. In these circumstances the separate contingencies need not be individually disclosed.

Date from which effective

22 The accounting practices set out in this statement should be adopted as soon as possible and regarded as standard in respect of financial statements relating to accounting periods beginning on or after 1 September 1980.

Part 4 — Note of legal requirements

23 Paragraph 11 (5) of Schedule 2 to the Companies Act 1967, paragraph 11 (4) of Schedule 6 to the Companies Act 1963 (Republic of Ireland) and paragraph 11 (5) of Schedule 6 to the Companies (Northern Ireland) Act 1960 or when implemented, paragraph 11 (5) of Schedule 2 to the Companies (Northern Ireland) Order 1978 require the following to be stated by way of note on, or in a statement or report annexed to, the balance sheet:

"The general nature of any other contingent liabilities not provided for and, where practicable, the aggregate amount or estimated amount of those liabilities, if it is material".

Part 5 — Compliance with International Accounting Standard No. 10 'Contingencies and events occurring after the balance sheet date'

24 The requirements of International Accounting Standard No. 10 'Contingencies and events occurring after the balance sheet date' concerning contingencies accord very closely with the content of the United Kingdom and Irish accounting standard No. 18 'Accounting for contingencies' and accordingly compliance with SSAP 18 will ensure compliance with IAS 10 in all material respects so far as contingencies are concerned.

Accounting for Investment Properties

(Issued November 1981; Amended July 1994)

Preface

The provisions of this statement of standard accounting practice should be read in conjunction with the Explanatory Foreword to accounting standards. The provisions apply equally to financial statements prepared under the historical cost convention and to financial statements prepared under the current cost convention. They need not be applied to immaterial items.

Part 1—Explanatory note

1 Under the accounting requirements of SSAP 12 'Accounting for depreciation', fixed assets are generally subject to annual depreciation charges to reflect on a systematic basis the wearing out, consumption or other loss of value whether arising from use, effluxion of time or obsolescence through technology and market changes. Under those requirements it is also accepted that an increase in the value of such a fixed asset does not generally remove the necessity to charge depreciation to reflect on a systematic basis the consumption of the asset.

2 A different treatment is, however, required where a significant proportion of the fixed assets of an enterprise is held not for consumption in the business operations but as investments, the disposal of which would not materially affect any manufacturing or trading operations of the enterprise. In such a case the current value of these investments, and changes in that current value, are of prime importance rather than a calculation of systematic annual depreciation. Consequently, for the proper appreciation of the financial position, a different accounting treatment is considered appropriate for fixed assets held as investments (called in this standard 'investment properties').

3 Investment properties may be held by a company which holds investments as part of its business such as an investment trust or a property investment company.

4 Investment properties may also be held by a company whose main business is not the holding of investments.

5 Where an investment property is held on a lease with a relatively short unexpired term, it is necessary to recognise the annual depreciation in the financial statements to avoid the situation whereby a short lease is amortised against the investment revaluation reserve whilst the rentals are taken to the profit and loss account.

6 This statement requires investment properties to be included in the balance sheet at open market value. The statement does not require the valuation to be made by qualified or independent valuers; but (in paragraph 12) calls for disclosure of the names or qualifications of the valuers, the bases used by them and whether the person making the valuation is an employee or officer of the company. However, where investment properties represent a substantial proportion of the total assets of a major enterprise (e.g. a listed company) the valuation thereof would normally be carried out :

(a) annually by persons holding a recognised professional qualification and having recent post qualification experience in the location and category of the properties concerned; and

(b) at least every five years by an external valuer.

Part 2 — Definition of terms

7 For the purposes of this statement, but subject to the exceptions in paragraph 8 below an investment property is an interest in land and/or buildings:

(a) in respect of which construction work and development have been completed; and

(b) which is held for its investment potential, any rental income being negotiated at arm's length.

8 The following are exceptions from the definition:

(a) A property which is owned and occupied by a company for its own purposes is not an investment property.

(b) A property let to and occupied by another group company is not an investment property for the purposes of its own accounts or the group accounts.

Part 3 — Standard accounting practice

9 This statement does not apply to investment properties owned by charities.

10 Investment properties should not be subject to periodic charges for depreciation on the basis set out in SSAP 12, except for properties held on lease which should be depreciated on the basis set out in SSAP 12 at least over the period when the unexpired term is 20 years or less.

11 Investment properties should be included in the balance sheet at their open market value.

12 The names of the persons making the valuation, or particulars of their qualifications, should be disclosed together with the bases of valuation used by them. If a person making a valuation is an employee or officer of the company or group which owns the property this fact should be disclosed.

13 Subject to paragraph 14 below, changes in the value of investment properties should not be taken to the profit and loss account but should be taken to the statement of total recognised gains and losses (being a movement on an investment revaluation reserve), unless a deficit (or its reversal) on an individual investment property is expected to be permanent, in which case it should be charged (or credited) in the profit and loss account of the period. In the special circumstances of investment companies as defined in companies legislation (as mentioned in paragraphs 31 and 66 of FRS 3 'Reporting Financial Preformance') and of property unit trusts it may not be appropriate to deal with such deficits in the profit and loss account. In such cases they should be shown only in the statement of total gains and losses.

14 Paragraph 13 does not apply to the financial statements of:

(a) insurance companies and groups (and consolidated financial statements incorporating such entities) where changes in market value of investment properties (including those comprising assets of the long-term business) are included in the profit and loss account.

(b) pension funds where changes in market value of investment properties are dealt with in the relevant fund account.

15 The carrying value of investment properties and the investment revaluation reserve should be displayed prominently in the financial statements.

Date from which effective

16 The accounting and disclosure requirements in this statement should be adopted as

soon as possible and regarded as standard in respect of financial statements relating to accounting periods starting on or after 1 July 1981.

Part 4 — Legal requirement in UK and Ireland

17 The application of this standard will usually be a departure, for the overriding purpose of giving a true and fair view, from the otherwise specific requirement of the law to provide depreciation on any fixed asset which has a limited useful economic life. In this circumstance there will need to be given in the notes to the accounts 'particulars of that departure, the reasons for it, and its effect'. UITF Abstract 7 'True and fair view override disclosures' gives guidance on the interpretation of this statutory requirement.

18 In Great Britain paragraphs 19 and 32 of Schedule 4 (for banking companies and groups paragraphs 26 and 42 of Schedule 9) to the Companies Act 1985 set out the legal requirements relating to provisions for diminution in value that are expected to be permanent. In the case of insurance companies and groups reporting under the amended Schedule 9A to the Companies Act 1985 (introduced by SI 1993/3246) note 9 on the profit and loss account format on paragraph 29(7) of the Schedule set out the relevant statutory requirements.

19 There are legal requirements similar to Schedule 4 in Northern Ireland (the Companies (Northern Ireland) Order 1986 Schedule 4 paragraphs 19 and 32 and Schedule 9 paragraphs 26 and 42) and in the Republic of Ireland (the Companies (Amendment(Act 1986 (the Schedule paragraphs 7 and 20) and the European Communities (Credit Institutions: Accounts) Regulations 1992 (the Schedule paragraphs 26 and 42)). Requirements similar to the amended Schedule 9A are expected to be enacted in Northern Ireland and the Republic of Ireland.

Amendment to SSAP 19 Accounting for Investment Properties

— July 1994

Preface

This limited amendment to Statement of Standard Accounting Practice 19 'Accounting for investment properties' (SSAP 19) changes the requirements concerning the treatment of certain deficits that are inconsistent with the spirit of Financial Reporting Standard 3 'Reporting Financial Performance' (FRS 3).

FRS 3 introduced a new performance statement — the statement of total recognised gains and losses — which is intended to deal with all recognised gains and losses in a period, including valuation surpluses and deficits on investment property assets. SSAP 19 previously required the amount by which an aggregate deficit exceeds the amount in the investment revaluation reserve to be charged in the profit and loss account only in respect of write-downs of fixed assets expected to be permanent.

The amendment changes the part of paragraph 13 of SSAP 19 that deals with the situation where a charge should be made in the profit and loss account. It recognises that deficits on individual investment properties that are expected to be permanent should be charged to the profit and loss account, as required by companies legislation, and requires all other valuation movements in investment properties to be shown in the statement of total recognised gains and losses (as movements on the investment revaluation reserve) even if this results in a temporary revaluation deficit. Consequential elaboration has been made to the legal requirements section of the standard, which is also updated for changes in the law since SSAP 19 was promulgated in 1981.

The Urgent Issues Task Force recommended that such an amendment should be implemented and the Accounting Standards Board has accepted that it is appropriate to make this amendment at this time.

A number of commentators on the exposure draft (FRED 9) asked for guidance on certain related questions, such as the distinction between temporary and permanent diminutions in value and whether the measurement of a deficit should be in relation to cost or the revalued carrying amount. However, these questions apply more widely than to investment properties and will be considered by the Board in due course as part of its valuations project.

Statement of Standard Accounting Practice

1 Paragraph 13 of SSAP 19 is amended to read as follows:-

"Subject to pragraph 14 below, changes in the market value of investment properties should not be taken to the profit and loss account but should be taken to the statement of total recognised gains and losses (being a movement on an investment revaluation reserve), unless a deficit (or its reversal) on an individual investment property is expected to be permanent, in which case it should be charged (or credited) in the profit and loss account of the period. In the special circumstances of investment companies as defined in companies legislation (as mentioned in paragraphs 31 and 66 of FRS3 'Reporting Financial Performance') and of property unit trusts it may not be appropriate to deal with such deficits in the profit and loss account. In such cases they should be shown only in the statement of total recognised gains and losses.

2 Paragraph 14 of SSAP 19 is amended to read as follows:

"Paragraph 13 does not apply to the financial statements of:

(a) insurance companies and groups (and consolidated financial statements incorporating such entities) where changes in the market value of investment properties (including those comprising assets of the long-term business) are included in the profit and loss account.

(b) pension funds where changes in the market value of investment properties are dealt with in the relevant fund account."

3 Paragraph 17 of SSAP 19 is amended by the deletion of the first sentence and the addition at the end of the paragraph of the following sentence:

"UITF Abstract 7 'True and fair view override disclosures' gives guidance on the interpretation of this statutory requirement."

4 SSAP 19 is also amended by the insertion of an additional paragraph after paragraph 17 as follows:

"18. in Great Britain paragraphs 19 and 32 of Schedule 4 (for banking companies and groups paragraphs 26 and 42 of Schedule 9) to the Companies Act 1985 set out the legal requirements relating to provisions for diminution in value that are expected to be permanent. In the case of insurance companies and groups reporting under the amended Schedule 9A to the Companies Act 1985 (introduced by SI 1993/3246) note 9 on the profit and loss account format on paragraph 29(7) of the Schedule set out the relevant statutory requirements."

5 The previous paragraph 18 of SSAP 19 is deleted and replaced by a new paragraph 19 to read as follows:

"There are legal requirements similar to Schedule 4 in Northern Ireland (the Companies (Northern Ireland) Order 1986 Schedule 4 paragraphs 19 and 32 and Schedule 9 paragraphs 26 and 42) and in the Republic of Ireland (the Companies (Amendment(Act 1986 (the Schedule paragraphs 7 and 20) and the European Communities (Credit Institutions: Accounts) Regulations 1992 (the Schedule paragraphs 26 and 42)). Requirements similar to the amended Schedule 9A are expected to be enacted in Northern Ireland and the Republic of Ireland."

6 If an enterprise changes its presentation of revaluation deficits as a result of this amendment, the classification of reserves and comparative figures should be restated in accordance with FRS 3 'Reporting Financial Performance'.

7 The accounting practices set out in this amendment to SSAP 19 should be regarded as standard in respect of financial statements relating to accounting periods ending on or after 22 September 1994. Earlier adoption is encouraged but not required.

Foreign currency translation

(Issued April, 1983)

The provisions of this statement of standard accounting practice should be read in conjunction with the explanatory foreword to accounting standards *and need not be applied to immaterial items. The provisions apply to financial statements prepared under either the historical cost convention or the current cost convention.*

This statement sets out the standard accounting practice for foreign currency translation but does not deal with the method of calculating profits or losses arising from a company's normal currency dealing operations; neither does it deal specifically with the determination of distributable profits.

Part 1 — Explanatory note

Background

1 A company may engage in foreign currency operations in two main ways:

(a) Firstly, it may enter directly into business transactions which are denominated in foreign currencies; the results of these transactions will need to be translated into the currency in which the company reports.

(b) Secondly, foreign operations may be conducted through a foreign enterprise which maintains its accounting records in a currency other than that of the investing company; in order to prepare consolidated financial statements it will be necessary to translate the complete financial statements of the foreign enterprise into the currency used for reporting purposes by the investing company.

Objectives of translation

2 The translation of foreign currency transactions and financial statements should produce results which are generally compatible with the effects of rate changes on a company's cash flows and its equity and should ensure that the financial statements present a true and fair view of the results of management actions. Consolidated statements should reflect the financial results and relationships as measured in the foreign currency financial statements prior to translation.

Procedures

3 In this statement the procedures which should be adopted when accounting for foreign operations are considered in two stages, namely:

(a) the preparation of the financial statements of an individual company; and

(b) the preparation of consolidated financial statements.

The individual company stage

4 During an accounting period a company may enter into transactions which are denominated in a foreign currency. The result of each transaction should normally be translated into the company's local currency using the exchange rate in operation on the date on which the transaction occurred; however, if the rates do not fluctuate significantly, an average rate for a period may be used as an approximation. Where the transaction is to be settled at a contracted rate, that rate should be used; where a trading transaction is covered by a related or matching forward contract, the rate of exchange specified in that contract may be used.

5 Once non-monetary assets, e.g. plant, machinery and equity investments, have been translated and recorded they should be carried in the company's local currency. Subject to the provisions of paragraph 30 concerning the treatment of foreign equity investments financed by foreign currency borrowings, no subsequent translations of these assets will normally need to be made.

6 At the balance sheet date monetary assets and liabilities denominated in a foreign currency, e.g. cash and bank balances, loans and amounts receivable and payable, should be translated by using the rate of exchange ruling at that date, or, where appropriate, the rates of exchange fixed under the terms of the relevant transactions. Where there are related or matching forward contracts in respect of trading transactions, the rates of exchange specified in those contracts may be used.

7 An exchange gain or loss will result during an accounting period if a business transaction is settled at an exchange rate which differs from that used when the transaction was initially recorded, or, where appropriate, that used at the last balance sheet date. An exchange gain or loss will also arise on unsettled transactions if the rate of exchange used at the balance sheet date differs from that used previously.

8 Exchange gains or losses arising on settled transactions in the context of an individual company's operations have already been reflected in cash flows, since a change in the exchange rate increases or decreases the local currency equivalent of amounts paid or received in cash settlement. Similarly, it is reasonably certain that exchange gains or losses on unsettled short-term monetary items will soon be reflected in cash flows. Therefore, it is normally appropriate, because of the cash flow effects, to recognise such gains and losses as part of the profit or loss for the year; they should be included in profit or loss from ordinary activities unless they arise from events which themselves would fall to be treated as extraordinary items, in which case they should be included as part of such items.

9 When dealing with long-term monetary items, additional considerations apply. Although it is not easy to predict what the exchange rate will be when a long-term liability or asset matures, it is necessary, when stating the liability or the asset in terms of the reporting currency, to make the best estimate possible in the light of the information available at the time; generally speaking translation at the year-end rate will provide the best estimate, particularly when the currency concerned is freely dealt in on the spot and forward exchange markets.

10 In order to give a true and fair view of results, exchange gains and losses on long-term monetary items should normally be reported as part of the profit or loss for the period in accordance with the accruals concept of accounting; treatment of these items on a simple cash movements basis would be inconsistent with that concept. Exchange gains on unsettled transactions can be determined at the balance sheet date no less objectively than exchange losses; deferring the gains whilst recognising the losses would not only be illogical by denying in effect that any favourable movement in exchange rates had occurred but would also inhibit fair measurement of the performance of the enterprise in the year. In particular, this symmetry of treatment recognises that there will probably be some interaction between currency movements and interest rates and reflects more accurately in the profit and loss account the true results of currency involvement.

11 For the special reasons outlined above, both exchange gains and losses on long-term monetary items should be recognised in the profit and loss account. However, it is necessary to consider on the grounds of prudence whether the amount of the gain or the amount by which exchange gains exceed past exchange losses on the same items, to be recognised in the profit and loss account should be restricted in the exceptional cases where there are doubts as to the convertibility or marketability of the currency in question.

12 Gains or losses on exchange arising from transactions between a holding company and its subsidiaries, or from transactions between fellow subsidiaries, should normally be reported in the individual company's financial statements as part of the profit or loss for the year in the same way as gains or losses arising from transactions with third parties.

The consolidated financial statements stage

13 The method used to translate financial statements for consolidation purposes should reflect the financial and other operational relationships which exist between an investing company and its foreign enterprises.

14 In most circumstances the closing rate/net investment method, described in paragraphs 15-20, should be used and exchange differences accounted for on a net investment basis. However, in certain specified circumstances (see paragraphs 21-24) the temporal method should be used.

The closing rate/net investment method

15 This method recognises that the investment of a company is in the net worth of its foreign enterprise rather than a direct investment in the individual assets and liabilities of that enterprise. The foreign enterprise will normally have net current assets and fixed assets which may be financed partly by local currency borrowings. In its day-to-day operations the foreign enterprise is not normally dependent on the reporting currency of the investing company. The investing company may look forward to a stream of dividends but the net investment will remain until the business is liquidated or the investment disposed of.

16 Under this method the amounts in the balance sheet of a foreign enterprise should be translated into the reporting currency of the investing company using the rate of exchange ruling at the balance sheet date. Exchange differences will arise if this rate differs from that ruling at the previous balance sheet date or at the date of any subsequent capital injection (or reduction).

17 Amounts in the profit and loss account of a foreign enterprise should be translated at the closing rate or at an average rate for the accounting period. The use of the closing rate is more likely to achieve the objective of translation, stated in paragraph 2, of reflecting the financial results and relationships as measured in the foreign currency financial statements prior to translation. However, it can be argued that an average rate reflects more fairly the profits or losses and cash flows as they arise to the group throughout an accounting period. The use of either method is therefore permitted, provided that the one selected is applied consistently from period to period.

18 No definitive method of calculating the average rate has been prescribed, since the appropriate method may justifiably vary as between individual companies. Factors that will need to be considered include the company's internal accounting procedures and the extent of seasonable trade variations; the use of a weighting procedure will in most cases be desirable. Where the average rate used differs from the closing rate, a difference will arise which should be dealt with in reserves.

19 The results of the operations of a foreign enterprise are best reflected in the group profit and loss account by consolidating the net profit or loss shown in its local currency financial statements without adjustment (other than for normal consolidation adjustments). If exchange differences arising from the retranslation of a company's net investment in its foreign enterprise were introduced into the profit and loss account, the results from trading operations, as shown in the local currency financial statements, would be distorted. Such differences may result from many factors unrelated to the trading performance of financing operations of the foreign enterprise; in particular, they do not represent or measure changes in actual or prospective cash flows. It is therefore inappropriate to regard them as profits or losses and they should be dealt with as adjustments to reserves.

20 Although equity investments in foreign enterprises will normally be made by the purchase of shares, investments may also be made by means of long-term loans and inter-company deferred trading balances. Where financing by such means is intended to be, for all practical purposes, as permanent as equity, such loans and inter-company balances should be treated as part of the investing company's net investment in the foreign enterprise; hence exchange differences arising on such loans and inter-company balances should be dealt with as adjustments to reserves.

The temporal method

21 For most investing companies in the UK and Ireland foreign operations are normally carried out through foreign enterprises which operate as separate or quasi-independent entities rather than as direct extensions of the trade of the investing company.

22 However, there are some cases in which the affairs of a foreign enterprise are so closely interlinked with those of the investing company that its results may be regarded as being more dependent on the economic environment of the investing company's currency than on that of its own reporting currency. In such a case the financial statements of the foreign enterprise should be included in the consolidated financial statements as if all its transactions had been entered into by the investing company itself in its own currency. For this purpose the temporal method of translation should be used; the mechanics of this method are identical with those used in preparing the accounts of an individual company, as stated in paragraphs 4-12.

23 It is not possible to select one factor which of itself will lead a company to conclude that the temporal method should be adopted. All the available evidence should be considered in determining whether the currency of the investing company is the dominant currency in the economic environment in which the foreign enterprise operates. Amongst the factors to be taken into account will be:

(a) the extent to which the cash flows of the enterprise have a direct impact upon those of the investing company;

(b) the extent to which the functioning of the enterprise is dependent directly upon the investing company;

(c) the currency in which the majority of the trading transactions are denominated;

(d) the major currency to which the operation is exposed in its financing structure.

24 Examples of situations where the temporal method may be appropriate are where the foreign enterprise:

(a) acts as a selling agency receiving stocks of goods from the investing company and remitting the proceeds back to the company;

(b) produces a raw material or manufactures parts or sub-assemblies which are then shipped to the investing company for inclusion in its own products;

(c) is located overseas for tax, exchange control or similar reasons to act as a means of raising finance for other companies in the group.

The treatment of foreign branches

25 For the purpose of this statement, foreign operations which are conducted through a foreign branch should be accounted for in accordance with the nature of the business operations concerned. Where such a branch operates as a separate business with local finance, it should be accounted for using the closing rate/net investment method. Where the foreign branch operates as an extension of the company's trade and its cash flows have a direct impact upon those of the company, the temporal method should be used.

Areas of hyper-inflation

26 Where a foreign enterprise operates in a country in which a very high rate of inflation exists it may not be possible to present fairly in historical cost accounts the financial position of a foreign enterprise simply by a translation process. In such circumstances the local currency financial statement should be adjusted where possible to reflect current price levels before the translation process is undertaken.

The special case of equity investment financed by foreign borrowings

27 Under the procedures set out in this statement, exchange gains or losses on foreign currency borrowings taken up by an investing company or foreign enterprise would normally be reported as part of that company's profit or loss from ordinary activities and would flow through into the consolidated profit and loss account.

28 Where an individual company has used borrowings in currencies other than its own to finance foreign equity investments or where the purpose of such borrowings is to provide a hedge against the exchange risk associated with existing equity investments, the company may be covered in economic terms against any movement in exchange rates. It would be inappropriate in such cases to record an accounting profit or loss when exchange rates change.

29 Therefore, provided the conditions set out in this paragraph apply, the company may denominate its foreign equity investments in the appropriate foreign currencies and translate the carrying amounts at the end of each accounting period at the closing rates of exchange. Where investments are treated in this way, any resulting exchange differences should be taken direct to reserves and the exchange gains or losses on the borrowings should then be offset, as a reserve movement, against these exchange differences. The conditions which must apply are as follows:

(a) in any accounting period, exchange gains or losses arising on the borrowings may be offset only to the extent of exchange differences arising on the equity investments;

(b) the foreign currency borrowings, whose exchange gains or losses are used in the offset process, should not exceed, in the aggregate, the total amount of cash that the investments are expected to be able to generate, whether from profits or otherwise; and

(c) the accounting treatment adopted should be applied consistently from period to period.

30 Similarly, within a group, foreign borrowings may have been used to finance group investment in foreign enterprises or to provide a hedge against the exchange risk associated with similar existing investments. Any increase or decrease in the amount outstanding on the borrowings arising from exchange movements will probably be covered by corresponding changes in the carrying amount of the net assets underlying the net investment (which would be reflected in reserves). Since in this case the group will be covered in economic terms against any movement in exchange rates, it would be inappropriate to record an accounting profit or loss when exchange rates change.

31 In the consolidated financial statements, therefore, subject to certain conditions, the exchange gains or losses on such foreign currency borrowings, which would otherwise have been taken to the group profit and loss account, may be offset as reserve movements against exchange differences on the retranslation of the net investments. The conditions which must apply are as follows:

(a) the relationship between the investing company and the foreign enterprises concerned should be such as to justify the use of the closing rate method for consolidation purposes;

(b) in any accounting period, exchange gains or losses arising on foreign currency borrowings may be offset only to the extent of the exchange differences arising on the net investments in foreign enterprises;

(c) the foreign currency borrowings, whose exchange gains or losses are used in the offset process, should not exceed, in the aggregate, the total amount of cash that the net investments are expected to be able to generate, whether from profits or otherwise; and

(d) the accounting treatment adopted should be applied consistently from period to period.

32 Where the provisions of paragraph 29 have been applied in the investing company's financial statements to a foreign equity investment which is neither a subsidiary nor an associated company, the same offset procedure may be applied in the consolidated financial statements.

Part 2 — Definition of terms

33 *Financial statements* are balance sheets, profit and loss accounts, statements of source and application of funds, notes and other statements, which collectively are intended to give a true and fair view of the financial position and profit or loss.

34 *Company* includes any enterprise which comes within the scope of statements of standard accounting practice.

35 An *exempt company* is one which:

(a) is registered in Great Britain and does not prepare its accounts in accordance with either Sections 149 and 152 of the Companies Act 1948; or

(b) is registered in Northern Ireland and is exempted from full disclosure by Part 3 of Schedule 6A to the Companies Act (Northern Ireland) 1960 as amended by the Companies (Northern Ireland) Order 1982; or

(c) is registered in the Republic of Ireland and is exempted from full disclosure by Part 3 of Schedule 6 to the Companies Act 1963.

36 A *foreign enterprise* is a subsidiary, associated company or branch whose operations are based in a country other than that of the investing company or whose assets and liabilities are denominated mainly in a foreign currency.

37 A *foreign branch* is either a legally constituted enterprise located overseas or a group of assets and liabilities which are accounted for in foreign currencies.

38 *Translation* is the process whereby financial data denominated in one currency are expressed in terms of another currency. It includes both the expression of individual transactions in terms of another currency and the expression of a complete set of financial statements prepared in one currency in terms of another currency.

39 A company's *local currency* is the currency of the primary economic environment in which it operates and generates net cash flows.

40 An *exchange rate* is a rate at which two currencies may be exchanged for each other at a particular point in time; different rates apply for spot and forward transactions.

41 The *closing rate* is the exchange rate for spot transactions ruling at the balance sheet date and is the mean of the buying and selling rates at the close of business on the day for which the rate is to be ascertained.

42 A *forward contract* is an agreement to exchange different currencies at a specified future date and at a specified rate. The difference between the specified rate and the spot rate ruling on the date the contract was entered into is the discount or premium on the forward contract.

43 The *net investment* which a company has in a foreign enterprise is its effective equity state and comprises its proportion of such foreign enterprise's net assets; in appropriate circumstances, intra-group loans and other deferred balances may be regarded as part of the effective equity stake.

44 *Monetary items* are money held and amounts to be received or paid in money and, where a company is not an exempt company, should be categorised as either short-term or long-term. Short-term monetary items are those which fall due within one year of the balance sheet date.

Part 3 — Standard accounting practice

45 When preparing the financial statements of an individual company the procedures set out in paragraphs 46-51 should be followed. When preparing consolidated financial statements, the procedures set out in paragraphs 52-58 should be followed.

Individual companies

46 Subject to the provisions of paragraphs 48 and 51 each asset, liability, revenue or cost arising from a transaction denominated in a foreign currency should be translated into the local currency at the exchange rate in operation on the date on which the transaction occurred; if the rates do not fluctuate significantly, an average rate for a period may be used as an approximation. Where the transaction is to be settled at a contracted rate, that rate should be used. Where a trading transaction is covered by a related or matching forward contract, the rate of exchange specified in that contract may be used.

47 Subject to the special provisions of paragraph 51, which relate to the treatment of foreign equity investments financed by foreign currency borrowings, no subsequent translations should normally be made once non-monetary assets have been translated and recorded.

48 At each balance sheet date, monetary assets and liabilities denominated in a foreign currency should be translated by using the closing rate or, where appropriate, the rates of exchange fixed under the terms of the relevant transactions. Where there are related or matching forward contracts in respect of trading transactions, the rates of exchange specified in those contracts may be used.

49 All exchange gains or losses on settled transactions and unsettled short-term monetary items should be reported as part of the profit or loss for the year from ordinary activities (unless they result from transactions which themselves would fall to be treated as extraordinary items, in which case the exchange gains or losses should be included as part of such items).

50 Exchange gains and losses on long-term monetary items should also be recognised in the profit and loss account; however, it is necessary to consider on the grounds of prudence whether, in the exceptional cases outlined in paragraph 11, the amount of the gain, or the amount by which exchange gains exceed past exchange losses on the same items to be recognised in the profit and loss account, should be restricted.

51 Where a company has used foreign currency borrowings to finance, or provide a hedge against, its foreign equity investments and conditions set out in this paragraph apply, the equity investments may be denominated in the appropriate foreign currencies and the carrying amounts translated at the end of each accounting period at closing rates for inclusion in the investing company's financial statements. Where investments are treated in this way, any exchange differences arising should be taken to reserves and the exchange gains or losses on the foreign currency borrowings should then be offset, as a reserve movement, against these exchange differences. The conditions which must apply are as follows:

(a) in any accounting period, exchange gains or losses arising on the borrowings may be offset only to the extent of exchange differences arising on the equity investments;

(b) the foreign currency borrowings, whose exchange gains or losses are used in the offset process, should not exceed, in the aggregate, the total amount of cash that the investments are expected to be able to generate, whether from profits or otherwise; and

(c) the accounting treatment adopted should be applied consistently from period to period.

Consolidated financial statements

52 When preparing group accounts for a company and its foreign enterprises, which includes the incorporation of the results of associated companies or foreign branches into those of an investing company, the closing rate/net investment method of translating the local currency financial statements should normally be used.

53 Exchange differences arising from the translation of the opening net investment in a foreign enterprise at the closing rate should be recorded as a movement on reserves.

54 The profit and loss account of a foreign enterprise accounted for under the closing rate/ net investment method should be translated at the closing rate or at an average rate for the period. Where an average rate is used, the difference between the profit and loss account translated at an average rate and at the closing rate should be recorded as a movement on reserves. The average rate used should be calculated by the method considered most appropriate for the circumstances of the foreign enterprise.

55 In those circumstances where the trade of the foreign enterprise is more dependent on the economic environment of the investing company's currency than that of its own reporting currency, the temporal method should be used.

56 The method used for translating the financial statements of each foreign enterprise should be applied consistently from period to period unless its financial and other operational relationships with the investing company change.

57 Where foreign currency borrowings have been used to finance, or provide a hedge against, group equity investments in foreign enterprises, exchange gains or losses on the borrowings, which would otherwise have been taken to the profit and loss account, may be offset as reserve movements against exchange differences arising on the retranslation of the net investments provided that:

(a) the relationships between the investing company and the foreign enterprises concerned justify the use of the closing rate method for consolidation purposes;

(b) in any accounting period, the exchange gains and losses arising on foreign currency borrowings are offset only to the extent of the exchange differences arising on the net investments in foreign enterprises;

(c) the foreign currency borrowings, whose exchange gains or losses are used in the offset process, should not exceed, in the aggregate the total amount of cash that the net investments are expected to be able to generate, whether from profits or otherwise; and

(d) the accounting treatment is applied consistently from period to period.

58 Where the provisions of paragraph 51 have been applied in the investing company's financial statements to a foreign equity investment which is neither a subsidiary nor an associated company, the same offset procedure may be applied in the consolidated financial statements.

Disclosure

59 The methods used in the translation of the financial statements for foreign enterprises and the treatment accorded to exchange differences should be disclosed in the financial statements.

60 The following information should also be disclosed in the financial statements:

(a) for all companies, or groups of companies, which are not exempt companies, the net amount of exchange gains and losses on foreign currency borrowings less deposits, identifying separately:

  (i) the amount offset in reserves under the provisions of paragraphs 51, 57 and 58; and

  (ii) the net amount charged/credited to the profit and loss account;

(b) for all companies, or groups of companies, the net movement on reserves arising from exchange differences.

Dates from which effective

61 The accounting and disclosure requirements set out in this statement should be adopted as soon as possible. They should be regarded as standard in respect of financial statements relating to accounting periods beginning on or after 1 April 1983.

Part 4 — Legal requirements in UK and Ireland

62 Paragraphs 63 to 69 below apply to companies preparing accounts in compliance with Sections 149 and 152 of the Companies Act 1948 or with Sections 143 and 146 of the Companies Act (Northern Ireland) 1960. The references to the Schedule which follow are to Schedule 8 to the Companies Act 1948 (as inserted by Section 1 of the Companies Act 1981). References to the Schedule will also be to Schedule 6 to the Companies Act (Northern Ireland), 1960, as inserted by Article 3 of the Companies (Northern Ireland) Order 1982, when this is brought into operation on 1 July 1983.

63 Paragraph 12 of the Schedule required that the amount of any item shall be determined on a prudent basis and, in particular, that only profits realised at the balance sheet date shall be included in the profit and loss account. (Paragraph 90 of the Schedule defines realised profits in relation to a company's accounts as "such profits of the company as fall to be treated as realised profits for the purposes of those accounts in accordance with principles generally accepted with respect to the determination for accounting purposes of realised profits at the time when those accounts are prepared.")

64 Paragraph 15 of the Schedule permits a departure from paragraph 12 of the Schedule if it appears to the directors that there are special reasons for such a departure. Particulars of any departure, the reasons for it and its effect must be given in a note to the accounts.

65 For companies other than exempt companies, all exchange gains taken through the profit and loss account, other than those arising on unsettled long-term monetary items, are realised. For such companies the application of paragraph 50 of this statement may result in unrealised exchange gains on unsettled long-term monetary items being taken to the profit and loss account. In this statement the need to show a true and fair view of results, referred to in paragraph 10 above, is considered to constitute a special reason for departure from the principle under paragraph 15 of the Schedule.

66 This statement is based on the assumption that the process of translation at closing rates for the purposes of this statement does not constitute a departure from the historical cost rules under Section C of the Schedule nor does it give rise to a diminution in value of an asset under Section B of the Schedule.

67 Paragraph 58(1) of the Schedule requires that, where sums originally denominated in foreign currencies are brought into balance sheet or profit and loss account, the basis on which those sums have been translated into sterling shall be stated.

68 Part 1 of the Schedule lays down the choice of formats permitted for the presentation of accounts. Distinction is drawn between operating and other income and expense. For this reason it is necessary to consider the nature of each foreign exchange gain or loss and to allocate each accordingly. Gains or losses arising from trading transactions should normally be included under "Other operating income or expense" while those arising from arrangements which may be considered as financing should be disclosed separately as part of "Other interest receivable/payable and similar income/expense". Exchange gains or losses which arise from events which themselves fall to be treated as extraordinary items should be included as part of such items.

69 Paragraph 46 of the Schedule required the following information to be disclosed about movements on any reserve:

(a) the amount of the reserve at the date of the beginning of the financial year and as at the balance sheet date respectively;

(b) any amounts transferred to or from the reserve during that year; and

(c) the source and application respectively of any amounts so transferred.

70 Paragraph 1 and 2 of Schedule 2 to the Companies Act 1981 permit certain companies to prepare accounts in compliance with Section 149A and 152A of and Schedule 8A to the Companies Act 1948 instead of Sections 149 and 152 and Schedule 8. Paragraph 11(9) of Schedule 8A requires disclosure of the basis on which foreign currencies have been converted into sterling. Schedule 2 to the Companies (Northern Ireland) Order 1982 will permit similar companies registered in Northern Ireland to prepare accounts in accordance with Sections 143A and 146A of and Schedule 6A to the Companies Act (Northern Ireland) 1960 which require the same disclosure.

71 Similar legal requirements are expected to be enacted in the Republic of Ireland.

Part 5 — Compliance with International Accounting Standard No. 21 'Accounting for the effects of changes in foreign exchange rates'

72 Compliance with the requirements of Statement of Standard Accounting Practice No. 20 'Foreign currency translation' will automatically ensure compliance with International Accounting Standard No. 21 'Accounting for the effects of changes in foreign exchange rates'.

Accounting for leases and hire purchase contracts

(Issued August 1984)

The provisions of this statement of standard accounting practice should be read in conjunction with the explanatory foreword to accounting standards *and* **need not be applied to immaterial items.** *The provisions apply equally to financial statements prepared under the historical cost convention and to financial statements prepared under the current cost convention.*

This statement does not apply to lease contracts concerning the rights to explore for or to exploit natural resources such as oil, gas, timber, metals and other minerals. Nor does it apply to licensing agreements for items such as motion picture films, video recordings, plays, manuscripts, patents and copyrights.

Part 1 — Explanatory note

Background

1 Leases and hire purchase contracts are means by which companies obtain the right to use or purchase assets. In the UK there is normally no provision in a lease contract for legal title to the leased asset to pass to the lessee.

2 A hire purchase contract has similar features to a lease except that under a hire purchase contract the hirer may acquire legal title by exercising an option to purchase the asset upon fulfilment of certain conditions (normally the payment of an agreed number of instalments).

3 Current tax legislation provides that in the normal situation capital allowances can be claimed by the lessor under a lease contract but not by the hirer under a hire purchase contract.

4 Lessors fall into three broad categories. They may be companies, including banks and finance houses, which provide finance under lease contracts to enable a single customer to acquire the use of an asset for the greater part of its useful life; they may operate a business which involves the renting out of assets for varying periods of time probably to more than one customer; or they may be manufacturer or dealer lessors who use leasing as a means of marketing their products, which may involve leasing a product to one customer or to several customers.

5 As a lessor and lessee are both parties to the same transaction it is appropriate that the same definitions should be used and the accounting treatment recommended should ideally be complementary. However, this will not mean that the recorded balances in both financial statements will be the same because the taxation consequences and hence the pattern of cash flows will be different.

Forms of lease

6 Leases can appropriately be classified into finance leases and operating leases. The distinction between a finance lease and an operating lease will usually be evident from the terms of the contract between the lessor and the lessee.

7 An operating lease involves the lessee paying a rental for the hire of an asset for a period of time which is normally substantially less than its useful economic life. The lessor retains most of the risks and rewards of ownership of an asset in the case of an operating lease.

8 A finance lease usually involves payment by a lessee to a lessor of the full cost of the asset together with a return on the finance provided by the lessor. The lessee has substantially all the risks and rewards associated with the ownership of an asset, other than the legal title. In practice all leases transfer some of the risks and rewards of ownership to the lessee, and the distinction between a finance lease and an operating lease is essentially one of degree.

9 Sometimes, the lessor may receive part of his return in the form of a guarantee from an independent third party, in which case the lease may be a finance lease as far as the lessor is concerned, but not from the lessee's point of view.

10 Briefly, this standard requires that a finance lease should be capitalised by the lessee, that is, accounted for as the purchase of rights to the use and enjoyment of the asset with simultaneous recognition of the obligation to make future payments. A hire purchase is normally accounted for in a similar way. Under an operating lease, only the rental will be taken into account by a lessee.

11 The effect of a lease is to create a set of rights and obligations related to the use and enjoyment by the lessee of a leased asset for the term of the lease. Such rights constitute the rewards of ownership transferred under the lease to the lessee whilst the obligations, including in particular the obligation to continue paying rent for the period specified in the lease, constitute the risks of ownership so transferred. Where the rights and obligations of the lessee are such that his corresponding rewards and risks are, despite the absence of the ability to obtain legal title, substantially similar to those of an outright purchaser of the asset in question, the lease will be a finance lease.

12 Conceptually, what is capitalised in the lessee's accounts is not the asset itself but his rights in the asset (together with his obligation to pay rentals). However, the definition of a finance lease is such that a lessee's rights are for practical purposes little different from those of an outright purchaser. Hence, it is appropriate that lessees should include these assets in their financial statements, but they should describe them as "leased assets" to distinguish them from owned assets.

Part 2 — Definition of terms

13 *Company* includes any enterprise which comes within the scope of statements of standard accounting practice.

14 A *lease* is a contract between a lessor and a lessee for the hire of a specific asset. The lessor retains ownership of the asset but conveys the right to use of the asset to the lessee for an agreed period of time in return for the payment of specified rentals. The term 'lease' as used in this statement also applies to other arrangements in which one party retains ownership of an asset but conveys the right to the use of the asset to another party for an agreed period of time in return for specified payments.

15 A *finance lease* is a lease that transfers substantially all the risks and rewards of ownership of an asset to the lessee. It should be presumed that such a transfer of risks and rewards occurs if at the inception of a lease the present value of the minimum lease payments, including any initial payment, amounts to substantially all (normally 90 per cent or more) of the fair value of the leased asset. The present value should be calculated by using the interest rate implicit in the lease (as defined in paragraph 24). If the fair value of the asset is not determinable, an estimate thereof should be used.

16 Notwithstanding the fact that a lease meets the conditions in paragraph 15, the presumption that it should be classified as a finance lease may in exceptional circumstances be rebutted if it can be clearly demonstrated that the lease in question does not transfer substantially all the risks and rewards of ownership (other than legal title) to the lessee. Correspondingly, the presumption that a lease which fails to meet the conditions in paragraph 15 is not a finance lease may in exceptional circumstances be rebutted.

17 An *operating lease* is a lease other than a finance lease.

18 A *hire purchase contract* is a contract for the hire of an asset which contains a provision giving the hirer an option to acquire legal title to the asset upon the fulfilment of certain conditions stated in the contract.

19 The *lease term* is the period for which the lessee has contracted to lease the asset and any further terms for which the lessee has the option to continue to lease the asset, with or without further payment, which option it is reasonably certain at the inception of the lease that the lessee will exercise.

20 The *minimum lease payments* are the minimum payments over the remaining part of the lease term (excluding charges for services and taxes to be paid by the lessor) and:

(a) in the case of the lessee, any residual amounts guaranteed by him or by a party related to him; or

(b) in the case of the lessor, any residual amounts guaranteed by the lessee or by an independent third party.

21 The *gross investment* in a lease at a point in time is the total of the minimum lease payments and any unguaranteed residual value accruing to the lessor.

22 The *net investment* in a lease at a point in time comprises:

(a) the gross investment in a lease (as defined in paragraph 21): less

(b) gross earnings allocated to future periods.

23 The *net cash investment* in a lease at a point in time is the amount of funds invested in a lease by a lessor, and comprises the cost of the asset plus or minus the following related payments or receipts:

(a) government or other grants receivable towards the purchase or use of the asset;

(b) rentals received;

(c) taxation payments and receipts, including the effect of capital allowances;

(d) residual values, if any, at the end of the lease term;

(e) interest payments (where applicable);

(f) interest received on cash surplus;

(g) profit taken out of the lease.

24 The *interest rate implicit in a lease* is the discount rate that at the inception of a lease, when applied to the amounts which the lessor expects to receive and retain produces an amount (the present value) equal to the fair value of the leased asset. The amounts which the lessor expects to receive and retain comprise (a) the minimum lease payments to the lessor (as defined in paragraph 20), plus (b) any unguaranteed residual value, less (c) any part of (a) and (b) for which the lessor will be accountable to the lessee. If the interest rate implicit in the lease is not determinable, it should be estimated by reference to the rate which a lessee would be expected to pay on a similar lease.

25 *Fair value* is the price at which an asset could be exchanged in an arm's length transaction less, where applicable, any grants receivable towards the purchase or use of the asset.

26 *Unguaranteed residual value* is that portion of the residual value of the leased asset (estimated at the inception of the lease), the realisation of which by the lessor is not assured or is guaranteed solely by a party related to the lessor.

27 *Finance charge* is the amount borne by the lessee over the lease term, representing the difference between the total of the minimum lease payments (including any residual amounts guaranteed by him) and the amount at which he records the leased asset at the inception of the lease.

28 *Gross earnings* comprise the lessor's gross finance income over the lease term, representing the difference between his gross investment in the lease (as defined in paragraph 21) and the cost of the leased asset less any grants receivable towards the purchase or use of the asset. Where a lessor selects option (b) of paragraph 41 the grants to be deducted should be the grossed-up amount.

29 The *inception of a lease* is the earlier of the time the asset is brought into use and the date from which rentals first accrue.

30 *Initial direct costs* are those costs incurred by the lessor that are directly associated with negotiating and consummating leasing transactions, such as commissions, legal fees, costs of credit investigations and costs of preparing and processing documents for new leases acquired.

Part 3 — Standard accounting practice

Hire purchase and leasing

31 Those hire purchase contracts which are of a financing nature should be accounted for on a basis similar to that set out below for finance leases. Conversely, other hire purchase contracts should be accounted for on a basis similar to that set out below for operating leases.

Accounting by lessees

32 A finance lease should be recorded in the balance sheet of a lessee as an asset and as an obligation to pay future rentals. At the inception of the lease the sum to be recorded both as an asset and as a liability should be the present value of the minimum lease payments, derived by discounting them at the interest rate implicit in the lease.

33 In practice in the case of a finance lease the fair value of the asset will often be a sufficiently close approximation to the present value of the minimum lease payments and may in these circumstances be substituted for it.

34 The combined benefit to a lessor of regional development and other grants together with capital allowances, which reduce tax liabilities, may enable the minimum lease payments under a finance lease to be reduced to a total which is less than the fair value of the asset. In these circumstances, the amount to be capitalised and depreciated should be restricted to the minimum lease payments. A negative finance charge should not be shown.

35 Rentals payable should be apportioned between the finance charge and a reduction of the outstanding obligation for future amounts payable. The total finance charge under a finance lease should be allocated to accounting periods during the lease term so as to produce a constant periodic rate of charge on the remaining balance of the obligation for each accounting period, or a reasonable approximation thereto.

36 An asset leased under a finance lease should be depreciated over the shorter of the lease term (as defined in paragraph 19) and its useful life. However, in the case of a hire purchase contract which has the characteristics of a finance lease, the asset should be depreciated over its useful life.

37 The rental under an operating lease should be charged on a straight-line basis over the lease term, even if the payments are not made on such a basis, unless another systematic and rational basis is more appropriate.

Accounting by lessors

38 The amount due from the lessee under a finance lease should be recorded in the balance sheet of a lessor as a debtor at the amount of the net investment in the lease after making provisions for items such as bad and doubtful rentals receivable.

39 The total gross earnings under a finance lease should normally be allocated to accounting periods to give a constant periodic rate of return on the lessor's **net cash investment** in the lease in each period. In the case of a hire purchase contract which has characteristics similar to a finance lease, allocation of gross earnings so as to give a constant periodic rate of return on the finance company's **net investment** will in most cases be a suitable approximation to allocation based on the net cash investment. In arriving at the constant periodic rate of return, a reasonable approximation may be made.

40 As an alternative to paragraph 39, an allocation may first be made out of gross earnings of an amount equal to the lessor's estimated cost of finance included in the net cash investment calculation, with the balance being recognised on a systematic basis.

41 Tax free grants which are available to the lessor against the purchase price of assets acquired for leasing should be spread over the period of the lease and may be dealt with either:

(a) by treating the grant as non-taxable income; or

(b) by grossing up the grant and including the grossed-up amount in arriving at profit before tax.

Where treatment (b) is adopted, the lessor should disclose the amount by which the profit before tax and the tax charge have been increased as a result of grossing up such grants.

42 An asset held for use in operating leases by a lessor should be recorded as a fixed asset and depreciated over its useful life.

43 Rental income from an operating lease, excluding charges for services such as insurance and maintenance, should be recognised on a straight-line basis over the period of the lease, even if the payments are not made on such a basis, unless another systematic and rational basis is more representative of the time pattern in which the benefit from the leased asset is receivable.

44 Initial direct costs incurred by a lessor in arranging a lease may be apportioned over the period of the lease on a systematic and rational basis.

Manufacturer/dealer lessor

45 A manufacturer or dealer lessor should not recognise a selling profit under an operating lease. The selling profit under a finance lease should be restricted to the excess of the fair value of the asset over the manufacturer's or dealer's cost less any grants receivable by the manufacturer or dealer towards the purchase, construction or use of the asset.

Sale and leaseback transactions

Accounting by the seller/lessee

46 In a sale and leaseback transaction which results in a finance lease any apparent profit or loss (that is, the difference between the sale price and the previous carrying value) should be deferred and amortised in the financial statements of the seller/lessee over the shorter of the lease term and the useful life of the asset.

47 If the leaseback is an operating lease:

(a) any profit or loss should be recognised immediately, provided it is clear that the transaction is established at fair value;

(b) if the sale price is below fair value, any profit or loss should be recognised immediately except that if the apparent loss is compensated by future rentals at below market price it should to that extent be deferred and amortised over the remainder of the lease term (or, if shorter, the period during which the reduced rentals are chargeable);

(c) if the sale price is above fair value, the excess fair value should be deferred and amortised over the shorter of the remainder of the lease term and the period to the next rent review (if any).

Accounting by the buyer/lessor

48 A buyer/lessor should account for a sale and leaseback in the same way as he accounts for other leases, that is, using the methods set out in paragraphs 38-45 above.

Disclosure by lessees

49 The gross amounts of assets which are held under finance leases* together with the related accumulated depreciation should be disclosed by each major class of asset. The total depreciation allocated for the period in respect of assets held under finance leases* should be disclosed by each major class of asset.

50 The information required by paragraph 49 may, as an alternative to being shown separately from that in respect of owned fixed assets, be integrated with it such that the totals of gross amount, accumulated depreciation, net amount and depreciation allocated for the period for each major class of asset are included with similar amounts in respect of owned fixed assets. Where this alternative treatment is adopted, the net amount of assets held under finance leases* included in the overall total should be disclosed. The amount of depreciation allocated for the period in respect of assets held under finance leases* included in the overall total should also be disclosed.

51 The amounts of obligations related to finance leases* (net of finance charges allocated to future periods) should be disclosed separately from other obligations and liabilities, either on the face of the balance sheet or in the notes to the accounts.

52 These net obligations under finance leases* should be analysed between amounts payable in the next year, amounts payable in the second to fifth years inclusive from the balance sheet date, and the aggregate amounts payable thereafter. This analysis may be presented either (a) separately for obligations under finance leases* or (b) where the total

* Including the equivalent information in respect of hire purchase contracts which have characteristics similar to that type of lease (see paragraph 31).

of these items is combined on the balance sheet with other obligations and liabilities, by giving the equivalent analysis of the total in which it is included. If the analysis is presented according to (a) above, a lessee may, as an alternative to analysing the net obligations, analyse the gross obligations, with future finance charges being separately deducted from the total.

53 The aggregate finance charges allocated for the period in respect of finance leases* should be disclosed.

54 Disclosure should be made of the amount of any commitments existing at the balance sheet date in respect of finance leases* which have been entered into but whose inception occurs after the year end.

55 The total of operating lease rentals* charged as an expense in the profit and loss account should be disclosed, analysed between amounts payable in respect of hire of plant and machinery and in respect of other operating leases*.

56 In respect of operating leases*, the lessee should disclose the payments which he is committed to make during the next year, analysed between those in which the commitment expires within that year, in the second to fifth years inclusive and over five years from the balance sheet date, showing separately the commitments in respect of leases of land and buildings and other operating leases*.

57 Disclosure should be made of the policies adopted for accounting for operating leases* and finance leases*.

Disclosure by lessors

58 The net investment in (i) finance leases and (ii) hire purchase contracts at each balance sheet date should be disclosed.

59 The gross amounts of assets held for use in operating leases*, and the related accumulated depreciation charges, should be disclosed.

60 Disclosure should be made of:

(a) the policy adopted for accounting for operating leases* and finance leases* and, in detail, the policy for accounting for finance lease income*;

(b) the aggregate rentals receivable in respect of an accounting period in relation to (i) finance leases* and (ii) operating leases*; and

(c) the cost of assets acquired, whether by purchase or finance lease*, for the purpose of letting under finance leases*.

Date from which effective for lessors and finance companies

61 The accounting practices set out in this statement should be adopted as soon as possible and regarded as standard for financial statements relating to accounting periods beginning on or after 1 July 1984 in respect of leases and hire purchase contracts (a) entered into on or after 1 July 1984 or (b) which have five years or more to run on 1 July 1984. If the provisions of this statement are not applied retroactively to all leases and hire purchase contracts existing at 1 July 1984, lessors and finance companies should disclose the amounts of gross earnings from finance leases and hire purchase contracts for the current year and the comparative period which have arisen under each of the principal bases used.

***Including the equivalent information in respect of hire purchase contracts which have characteristics similar to that type of lease (see paragraph 31).**

Date from which effective for lessees and hirers

62 The accounting practices set out in this statement should be adopted by lessees and hirers as soon as possible and regarded as standard in respect of financial statements relating to accounting periods beginning on or after 1 July 1987. However, the disclosure requirements in paragraphs 52 and 54-57 should be regarded as standard in respect of financial statements relating to accounting periods beginning on or after 1 July 1984.

Part 4 — Legal requirements in Great Britain

63 Paragraph 50(5) of Schedule 8* provides that "Particulars shall also be given of any other financial commitments which:

(a) have not been provided for; and

(b) are relevant to assessing the company's state of affairs."

In so far as finance leases are capitalised by lessees, the obligations under finance leases *are* provided for in the accounts. This will not be the case to the extent that lessees take advantage of the delayed implementations of capitalisation as set out in paragraph 62.

64 Paragraph 53(6) of Schedule 8 requires disclosure of the "amount charged to revenue in respect of sums payable in respect of the hire of plant and machinery" (standard, paragraphs 49, 50, 53 and 55 and guidance notes).

65 The balance sheet formats in Schedule 8 require that creditors falling due within one year should be shown separately from creditors falling due after more than one year (standard, paragraph 52 and guidance notes).

66 The balance sheet formats in Schedule 8 provide that the "amount falling due after more than one year shall be shown separately for each item included under debtors". This is relevant to the disclosure of amounts receivable by a lessor (standard, paragraph 58 and guidance notes).

Part 5 — Legal requirements in Ireland

Northern Ireland

67 The Schedule references in Part 4 (paragraphs 63-66) apply equally to Schedule 6 of the Companies Act (Northern Ireland) 1960, as inserted by Article 3 of the Companies (Northern Ireland) Order 1982.

Republic of Ireland

68 General provisions as to accounts are set out in the Sixth Schedule to the Companies Act 1963. There are no legal requirements in the Republic of Ireland similar to those outlined in Part 4.

Part 6 — Compliance with International Accounting Standard No. 17 'Accounting for leases'

69 The requirements of International Accounting Standard No. 17 'Accounting for leases' accord very closely with the content of the United Kingdom and Irish Account ing Standard No. 21 'Accounting for leases and hire purchase contracts' and accordingly compliance with SSAP 21 will ensure compliance with IAS 17 in all material respects.

*All references to Schedule 8 refer to the new Schedule 8 to the Companies Act 1948, as inserted by Section 1 of the Companies Act 1981.

Accounting for goodwill

(Issued December 1984; revised July 1989)

FRS 7 *Fair values in acquisition accounting,* published September 1994, supersedes paragraphs 14, 23, 27, 30 and 33 of this standard. Following publication of FRS 7, SSAP 22 is to be interpreted in the light of FRS 7; references to 'separable net assets' should be interpreted as 'identifiable assets and liabilities'.

FRS 6 *Acquisitions and mergers,* published September 1994, supersedes disclosure paragraphs 48–51; amended disclosure requirements are included in FRS 6.

The provisions of this statement of standard accounting practice should be read in conjunction with the explanatory foreword to accounting standards. *The standard need not be applied to immaterial items. The provisions apply to financial statements prepared under either the historical cost convention or the current cost convention.*

Part 1 — Explanatory note

Nature and meaning of goodwill

1 It is usual for the value of a business as a whole to differ from the value of its separable net assets. The difference, which may be positive or negative, is described as goodwill.

2 Goodwill is therefore by definition incapable of realisation separately from the business as a whole; this characteristic of goodwill distinguishes it from all other items in the accounts. Its other characteristics are that:

(a) the value of goodwill has no reliable or predictable relationship to any costs which may have been incurred;

(b) individual intangible factors which may contribute to goodwill cannot be valued;

(c) the value of goodwill may fluctuate widely according to internal and external circumstances over relatively short periods of time; and

(d) the assessment of the value of goodwill is highly subjective.

Thus, any amount attributed to goodwill is unique to the valuer and to the specific point in time at which it is measured, and is valid only at that time, and in the circumstances then prevailing.

3 'Purchased goodwill' (positive or negative) is established when a business combination is accounted for as an acquisition; it includes goodwill arising on consolidation, and on the acquisition of an interest in an associated company* or of an unincorporated business. On the purchase of a company, the shares acquired are recorded at cost, being the fair value of the consideration given. For the purposes of consolidated accounts, the cost of the shares is allocated amongst the separable net assets acquired, with purchased goodwill emerging as the difference. Similar principles apply on the acquisition of an unincorporated business.

4 Goodwill can also be attributed to businesses which are not the subject of an acquisition (non-purchased goodwill, as defined in paragraph 24), in that as going concerns they are worth more (positive goodwill), or less (negative goodwill), than the sum of the fair values of their separable net assets . However, except when goodwill is evidenced by a purchase transaction, it is not an accepted practice to recognise it in financial statements.

*See paragraph 26(c) of SSAP 1 'Accounting for associated companies'.

5 There is no difference in character between purchased goodwill and non-purchased goodwill. However, the value of purchased goodwill, although arising from a subjective valuation of the business, is established as a fact at a particular point in time by a market transaction; this is not true of non-purchased goodwill.

The accounting treatment of purchased goodwill

6 The standard requires that purchased goodwill should normally be eliminated from accounts by immediate write-off. (In this context, the term 'write-off' does not imply an equivalent actual loss of value — see paragraph 7 below.) The principal reason for this is that immediate write-off of purchased goodwill is consistent with the accepted practice of not including non-purchased goodwill in accounts. Thus, if purchased goodwill is treated as an asset whilst non-purchased goodwill is not, a balance sheet does not present the total goodwill of a company (or group); it reflects only the purchased goodwill of the acquired business(es) at the date of acquisition, to the extent that it has not been written off.

7 The standard requires that the immediate write-off of purchased goodwill should be made against reserves, not as a charge in the profit and loss account. This is because (a) purchased goodwill is written off as a matter of accounting policy, that is, in order to achieve consistency of treatment with non-purchased goodwill, rather than because it has suffered a permanent diminution in value and (b) the write-off is not related to the results of the year in which the acquisition was made.

8 There will be cases where the fair value of the separable net assets exceeds the value of the business as a whole. This difference is termed 'negative goodwill'. Negative goodwill, which is the mirror image of positive goodwill, should be credited to reserves. Where negative goodwill arises, the amounts allocated to the relevant separable net assets will need to be reviewed particularly carefully to ensure that the fair values ascribed to them are not overstated.

9 It is recognised that there is an alternative way of looking at positive goodwill. This is that, although goodwill is intangible, it is a reality, it exists and when a business is purchased the price paid includes an amount attributable to purchased goodwill; thus capital has been expended in exchange for an asset — goodwill — which should be recognised and treated in the same way as any other capital asset.

10 Whilst providing that companies should normally follow the preferred treatment of writing off goodwill immediately against reserves, the standard also allows a company to carry positive goodwill as an asset and to amortise it through the profit and loss account over its useful economic life.

11 Guidance on factors to be considered in determining the useful economic life of purchased goodwill is contained in Appendix 1. As the factors which affect the estimates of the useful economic life of purchased goodwill are likely to vary according to the different circumstances of different acquisitions, there is no requirement in the standard to select the same useful economic life for the goodwill arising on different acquisitions.

12 It is envisaged that most companies will select the policy of elimination of goodwill immediately on acquisition and that only a limited number will select the policy of amortisation. There may, however, be cases where an individual company's circumstances require that it adopt different policies in relation to the goodwill which arises on different acquisitions; for example, a company may in general follow the preferred policy of immediate write-off but it may need to adopt the policy of amortising the goodwill on an unusually large acquisition because of the effect which immediate write-off would have on its reserves.

Goodwill and separable net assets

13 In deciding whether a particular asset falls into the category of separable net assets, the test is whether that asset could be identified and sold separately without disposing of the business as a whole. For example, an asset may be an essential part of a company's manufacturing operations, and it may be that the asset would be of very little value other than in its present use; but it could be sold separately or bought from its manufacturers, whereas goodwill could not be — it could only be either acquired or sold as part of the process of acquiring or selling the business as a whole. Separable net assets may include identifiable intangibles such as those specifically mentioned in the balance sheet formats in the Companies Act 1981, i.e. "concessions, patents, licences, trade marks and similar rights and assets"; other examples include publishing titles, franchise rights and customer lists. (This list of examples is not intended to be comprehensive.) Identifiable intangibles such as these form part of the separable net assets which are recorded in an acquiring company's accounts at fair value, even if they were not recorded in the acquired company's accounts.

14 When ascribing fair values to separable net assets at the time of an acquisition, a provision may be needed in respect of items which were taken into account in arriving at the purchase price, that is, anticipated future losses or costs of re-organisation. Where such provision is needed, it forms part of the liabilities which are set up at the time of the acquisition and is therefore not considered to be part of the goodwill arising on the acquisition. Such a provision may be needed whether goodwill is positive or negative.

Special types of asset

15 Some property assets are valued on a basis which has regard to the trading potential which attaches to the property*. This trading potential is sometimes thought of as goodwill, but such a basis of valuation would normally exclude any goodwill which is personal to the present owner or management and which would not pass with the property on a sale with vacant possession. This practice is acceptable in certain limited categories of business. Where it is followed, the assets concerned should be disclosed separately and the notes to the accounts should make clear that this practice has been followed and that the amount at which the assets concerned are stated does not exceed their open market value**, having regard to the trading potential of the business. This treatment is not dealt with in Part 3 of the standard as it concerns the treatment of other assets, not of goodwill.

Goodwill in the accounts of individual entities and holding companies and in consolidated accounts

16 The standard requires that the amount to be attributed to purchased goodwill should be the difference between the fair value of the consideration given and the aggregate of the fair values of the separable net assets acquired. This applies equally to the accounts of an individual entity, to the accounts of a holding company and to consolidated accounts. However, the circumstances of each require separate consideration.

*See the Royal Institution of Chartered Surveyors' Guidance Notes on the Valuation of Assets (2nd edition), Background Paper No. 7, 'Open market valuations having regard to trading potential'. Paragraph 2 of the Paper notes that "there are certain types of property designed or adapted for particular uses, which invariably change hands in the open market at prices based directly on trading potential for a strictly limited use. Examples of such properties which normally are sold as fully operational business units include hotels, public houses, cinemas, theatres, bingo clubs, gaming clubs, petrol filling stations, betting shops, specialised leisure and sporting facilities."

**In the context of land and buildings the term 'open market value' is commonly used for what is described elsewhere in this standard as 'fair value'.

17 Where an individual entity acquires an unincorporated business, it will account for the cost of the business acquired by attributing fair values to the separable net assets it has acquired. If the fair value of the consideration given differs from the aggregate of the fair values of the separable net assets acquired, the difference will be purchased goodwill and it will be identified separately in the entity's accounting records. This purchased goodwill should then be eliminated from the accounts as set out in the standard.

18 Where a holding company acquires another company and merger accounting is not used, it will include in its own balance sheet the shares in the acquired company at cost, based on the fair value of the consideration given. From the point of view of the holding company, the separable net assets will be the shares in the acquired company, not the individual assets and liabilities of the acquired company. Since the fair value of the shares acquired will normally be equal to the fair value of the consideration given, no purchased goodwill will arise in the accounting records of the holding company. The standard does not require an adjustment to be made in the holding company's accounts to the carrying value of the shares in the acquired company in respect of any consolidation goodwill written off either in the group accounts or in the accounts of the subsidiary or associate, except to the extent that the carrying value of the investment in shares should be written down to reflect any permanent diminution in value.

19 On consolidation, the cost of the investment is attributed to the separable net assets of the acquired company - that is, the fixed and net current assets less long-term liabilities — by stating them at their fair values. Any difference between that total and the carrying value of the investment (i.e. the fair value of the purchase consideration) represents purchased goodwill arising on consolidation. This goodwill should then be eliminated from the accounts as set out in the standard.

Explanatory note on additional disclosure

20 Paragraphs 47-53 of SSAP 22 require certain additional disclosures to be made when recording acquisitions and disposals. These are intended to improve the financial reporting of business combinations within the scope of this standard by enabling users of financial statements to gain a better appreciation of the business acquired and of the extent to which the results of the combined entity after an acquisition are attributable to trading performance as opposed to other factors, such as the disposal of part of the business or the release of unutilized provisions established when the business combination occurred. These additional disclosures will complement appropriate accounting treatments and not be a substitute for them.

21 The requirements include the disclosure of the fair value of the consideration. While this is a figure which could be calculated from the other disclosures already made in relation to acquisitions, it will be helpful to have it separately disclosed, particularly if the basis of calculation is given in those cases where the fair value could differ considerably according to the valuation method chosen.

22 The amount of purchased goodwill shown in the accounts may be different from that arising from an acquisition where, for example, the statutory provisions of the UK Companies Act 1985 relating to merger relief are applied and only the residual figure after application of merger relief is disclosed. This effective netting of goodwill against merger reserve without explicit mention in the financial statements can convey the misleading impression that the consideration for the purchase was less than was actually the case. To avoid this result, the amount of purchased goodwill arising on an acquisition should be shown in the year of acquisition in all cases.

23 When ascribing fair values to separable net assets at the time of an acquisition, adjustments may have to be made on consolidation to the book amount of assets and liabilities of the acquired company. Such adjustments may include revaluations; applying the acquiring group's accounting policies to the acquiree; making provisions; and recognising previously unrecorded assets such as intangible assets. Disclosure of details of the consolidation adjustments made and of movements on provisions related to acquisitions, analysed under the headings of paragraph 48, will provide valuable information to the user of financial statements on the acquisition itself and enables post-acquisition trading performance to be distinguished from the effects of, for example, the release of unutilized provisions. Appropriate disclosure will also help allay the concern expressed by some commentators that, in certain instances, profits may have benefited from provisions made at acquisition but which subsequently did not prove necessary.

24 The disclosure of the profit or loss on disposals of businesses, or business segments, previously acquired also enables post-combination trading performance to be separated from the effect of other factors. Some commentators have suggested that the disclosure of the profit or loss on disposal may not, on its own, provide sufficient information about the disposal in the absence of details of the extent to which attributable goodwill arising on the earlier acquisition has previously been written off to reserves. It is accepted that, where a reorganisation has taken place since an acquisition, an element of estimation may be required in determining the goodwill attributable to the disposal. However, it is not considered that the calculation problems are insurmountable, particularly where the goodwill is allocated on or soon after acquisition, in the knowledge that this information may be required later. For disposals of businesses, or business segments, acquired before the effective date of this standard, goodwill need not be attributed and disclosed where it would be impractical to do so but, in these circumstances, this fact should be disclosed. Although goodwill is defined in paragraph 26 by reference to the business as a whole, goodwill can be allocated over different business segments.

25 Enterprises that amortise goodwill are encouraged but not required to disclose earnings per share before goodwill amortisation in addition to following the present requirements of SSAP 3 (Revised) — Earnings per share. This will help the comparison of their results with those of enterprises which charge no amortisation for purchased goodwill on acquisition as they have written it off immediately against reserves. The basis on which the additional earnings per share figure has been calculated should be disclosed. It should be clearly stated that the additional calculation differs from that required by SSAP 3. Earnings per share on the SSAP 3 basis is required by SSAP 3 to be shown on the face of the profit and loss account.

Part 2 — Definition of terms

26 *Goodwill* is the difference between the value of a business as a whole and the aggregate of the fair values of its separable net assets.

27 *Separable net assets* are those assets (and liabilities) which can be identified and sold (or discharged) separately without necessarily disposing of the business as a whole. They include identifiable intangibles.

28 *Purchased goodwill* is goodwill which is established as a result of the purchase of a business accounted for as an acquisition. Goodwill arising on consolidation is one form of purchased goodwill.

29 *Non-purchased goodwill* is any goodwill other than purchased goodwill.

30 *Fair value* is the amount for which an asset (or liability) could be exchanged in an arm's length transaction.

31 *Useful economic life* of purchased goodwill is the best estimate of the life of such goodwill at the date of purchase.

32 *Company,* for the purpose of this standard, includes any enterprise or group which comes within the scope of statements of standard accounting practice.

33 *Acquisition adjustments* are those accounting adjustments to the assets or liabilities of an acquired business made for any matters arising in consequence of or in anticipation of an acquisition.

34 A *business segment* is a material and separately identifiable component of the business operations of a company or group whose activities, assets and results can be clearly distinguished from the remainder of the company's activities. A business segment will normally have its own separate product lines or markets.

Part 3 — Standard accounting practice

General

35 No amount should be attributed to non-purchased goodwill in the balance sheets of companies or groups.

36 The amount to be attributed to purchased goodwill should be the difference between the fair value of the consideration given and the aggregate of the fair values of the separable net assets acquired.

37 The amount attributed to purchased goodwill should not include any value for separable intangibles. The amount of these, if material, should be included under the appropriate heading within intangible fixed assets in the balance sheet.

38 Purchased goodwill should not be carried in the balance sheet of a company or group as a permanent item.

39 Purchased goodwill (other than negative goodwill) should normally be eliminated from the accounts immediately on acquisition against reserves ('immediate write off').

40 Any excess of the aggregate of the fair values of the separable net assets acquired over the fair value of the consideration given (negative goodwill) should be credited directly to reserves.

41 Purchased goodwill (other than negative goodwill) may be eliminated from the accounts by amortisation through the profit and loss account in arriving at profit or loss on ordinary activities on a systematic basis over its useful economic life ('amortisation'). When this treatment is selected, the following points apply:

(a) Purchased goodwill should not be revalued. If there is a permanent diminution in value of purchased goodwill, it should be written down immediately through the profit and loss account to its estimated recoverable amount.

(b) The useful economic life should be estimated at the time of acquisition. It should not include any allowance for the effects of subsequent expenditure or other circumstances subsequently affecting the company since these would have the effect of creating non-purchased goodwill.

(c) The estimated useful economic life over which purchased goodwill is being amortised may be shortened but may not be increased.

42 Nothing in this standard precludes a company from using both the immediate write-off treatment and the amortisation treatment in respect of the goodwill which relates to different acquisitions, so long as the accounting policies provide for the elimination of goodwill on a basis consistent with the standard.

Disclosure

43 The accounting policy followed in respect of goodwill should be explained in the notes to the accounts.

44 The amount of goodwill recognised as a result of any acquisitions during the year should be shown separately for each acquisition where material.

45 Where the amortisation treatment is selected, purchased goodwill should be shown as a separate item under intangible fixed assets in the balance sheet until fully written off. In addition, the following should be disclosed:

(a) the movement on the goodwill account during the year, showing the cost, accumulated amortisation and net book value of goodwill at the beginning and end of the year, and the amount of goodwill amortised through the profit and loss account during the year; and

(b) the period selected for amortising the goodwill relating to each major acquisition.

46 If the accounting treatment of goodwill existing at the date of introduction of the standard is different from the policy followed in respect of all other goodwill, that treatment and the amounts involved should be disclosed.

47 The fair value of the consideration and the amount of purchased goodwill arising on each acquisition during the period should be separately disclosed. Disclosure should identify the method of dealing with goodwill arising and whether it has been set off against merger reserve or other reserves or has been carried forward as an intangible asset (for the use of 'merger reserve' in relation to Republic of Ireland companies, see paragraph 65).

48 A table should be provided showing the book values, as recorded in the acquired company's books at the date of acquisition but before any acquisition adjustments, and the fair values of each major category of assets and liabilities acquired. An explanation of the reasons for differences between values should be given for each major category of assets and liabilities and these adjustments should be analysed between:

(i) revaluations;

(ii) provisions for future trading losses;

(iii) other provisions;

Any amounts that cannot be classified within (i)-(iii) above should be analysed between:

(iv) bringing accounting policies into line with those of the acquiring group;

(v) any other major item.

49 Movements on provisions related to acquisitions should be disclosed and analysed between the amounts used and the amounts released unused or applied for another purpose. Sufficient details should be given to identify the extent to which the provisions have proved unnecessary.

50 Where the fair value of the assets and liabilities, or the consideration, can only be determined on a provisional basis at the end of the accounting period in which the acquisition took place, this should be stated and the reasons given. Where there are subsequent material adjustments to such provisional fair values, with a consequent adjustment to goodwill, those adjustments should be disclosed and explained.

51 The disclosures required by paragraph 47-50 should be made separately for each material acquisition and in aggregate for other acquisitions where these are material in total although not so individually.

52 The following should be disclosed in respect of each material disposal of a previously acquired business or business segment:

(a) the profit or loss on the disposal;

(b) the amount of purchased goodwill attributable to the business or business segment disposed of and how it has been treated in determining the profit or loss on disposal;

(c) the accounting treatment adopted and the amount of the proceeds in situations where no profit or loss is recorded on a disposal because the proceeds have been accounted for as a reduction in the cost of the acquisition.

53 The provisions in paragraph 52 relating to goodwill on disposals should apply to all disposals where the relevant information is obtainable and in all cases where disposals relate to acquisitions made after the effective date for this section. Where, in relation to acquisitions prior to the effective date, it is impossible or impractical to ascertain the attributable goodwill on a disposal this should be stated and the reasons given.

Date from which effective

54 The accounting practices set out in this statement should be adopted as soon as possible. Except as stated in paragraph 55 below they should be regarded as standard accounting practice in respect of financial statements relating to accounting periods beginning on or after 1 January 1985.

55 The accounting practices set out in paragraphs 47-53 of this statement should be adopted as soon as possible and regarded as standard in respect of accounting periods beginning on or after 1 January 1989.

Part 4 — Legal requirements in Great Britain and Northern Ireland

References are to the Companies Act 1985 and the Companies (Northern Ireland) Order 1986.

General

56 Set out below is a summary of the main legal requirements which are directly relevant to goodwill in Great Britain. In each case a brief description of the point is given, together with the relevant Companies Act reference and a note of the paragraph(s) in the standard where the point is covered. It should be noted that in general these legal provisions apply to the accounts of both individual companies and groups. However, paragraphs 59 and 61 apply only to individual companies.

57 The accounting policy adopted by the company in respect of goodwill should be disclosed (4 Sch. 36; standard, paragraph 43).

58 The balance sheet formats in Schedule 4 require that purchased goodwill, to the extent that it has not been written off, should be shown under the heading of intangible fixed assets. Goodwill should be shown separately from other intangible assets such as patents, licences and trade marks (CA 1985 4 Sch. formats and note 3 to the balance sheet formats; standard, paragraphs 37 and 45).

59 If goodwill is treated as an asset (i.e. where it is not written off immediately), it should be amortised systematically over a period chosen by the directors (4 Sch. 21(2); standard, paragraph 41). The period chosen should not exceed the useful economic life of the goodwill in question (4 Sch. 21(3); standard, paragraph 41). The period chosen and the reasons for choosing that period should be disclosed in a note (4 Sch. 21(4); standard, paragraph 45(b) and paragraph 4 of Appendix 1).

60 Goodwill may not be revalued (4 Sch. 31(1); standard, paragraph 41 (a)).

61 In the case of a permanent diminution in value of goodwill which is carried as an asset, a provision should be made and the carrying amount of goodwill should be reduced accordingly. The provision should either be shown in the profit and loss account or disclosed in a note (4 Sch. 19(2); standard, paragraph 41 (a)).

62 The movements on the goodwill account should be disclosed. The same level of disclosure is required as for other fixed assets (CA 1985 4 Sch. 42; standard, paragraph 45 (a)).

Note on realised profits

63 Realised profits are defined by paragraph 91 of Schedule 4 Companies Act 1985 (paragraph 90 of Schedule 4 to the Companies (Northern Ireland) Order 1986) as being those which "fall to be treated as realised profits ... in accordance with principles generally accepted with respect to the determination for accounting purposes of realised profits at the time when those accounts are prepared". Appendix 2 gives guidance on the effect of accounting for goodwill on realised profits.

Part 5 — Legal requirements in the Republic of Ireland

64 The legal requirements in Great Britain and Northern Ireland are mirrored, in respect of the Republic of Ireland, in the Schedule to the Companies (Amendment) Act 1986. The following table indicates the corresponding paragraphs in respect of all the references contained in Part 4 of this statement.

Schedule 4 to the Companies Act 1985	*Schedule 4 to the Companies (Northern Ireland) Order 1986*	*The Schedule to the Companies (Amendment) Act 1986*
Formats and note 3 to the balance sheet formats	Formats and note 3 to the balance sheet formats	Formats and note 2 to the balance sheet formats
Paragraph 19	Paragraph 19	Paragraph 7
Paragraph 21	Paragraph 21	Paragraph 9
Paragraph 31	Paragraph 31	Paragraph 19
Paragraph 36	Paragraph 36	Paragraph 24
Paragraph 42	Paragraph 42	Paragraph 31
Paragraph 91	Paragraph 90	Paragraph 72

65 No legislation equivalent to the merger relief in the Companies Act 1985 currently exists in the Republic of Ireland. Until such a time as equivalent legislation is enacted no explicit relief from the requirement to establish a share premium account (Section 62(1), Companies Act 1963) is available.

Part 6 — Compliance with International Accounting Standard No 22 'Accounting for business combinations'

66 The requirements of International Accounting Standard No 22 'Accounting for business combinations' which related to accounting for goodwill accord very closely with the content of the United Kingdom and Irish Accounting Standard No 22 'Accounting for goodwill' and accordingly compliance with SSAP 22 will ensure compliance in all material respects with the requirements of IAS 22 which relate to accounting for goodwill.

Appendix 1

This appendix is for guidance only and does not form part of the statement of standard accounting practice.

Factors to be considered in determining the useful economic life of purchased goodwill

67 Where a company employs the amortisation treatment, it will need to determine the useful economic life of the goodwill in respect of each acquisition. The useful economic life of goodwill is also relevant to the transfer from unrealised to realised reserves as referred to in paragraph 2 of Appendix 2. The useful economic life of purchased goodwill is the period over which benefits may reasonably be expected to accrue from that goodwill in the acquired company which existed and was identified at the time of acquisition. In the period following the acquisition, the value of the purchased goodwill is considered to diminish although it may be replaced by non-purchased goodwill. The total goodwill (purchased and non-purchased) may remain constant or may increase or decrease. However, in determining the useful economic life of purchased goodwill, the effects of subsequent expenditure or other circumstances affecting the company after the date of the acquisition should not be taken into account, since these would have the effect of creating non-purchased goodwill. The purchased goodwill whose useful life is being determined is only that which existed and was recognised at the time of the acquisition.

68 There are a number of factors which may be relevant to a determination of the useful economic life of purchased goodwill. These factors should be assessed at the time the acquisition was made, and include: expected changes in products, markets or technology; the expected period of future service of certain employees; and expected future demand, competition or other economic factors which may affect current advantages.

69 It is sometimes argued that the value of an investment at a given point in time can be regarded as the present value of the future net cash flows from the investment. Consequently, the period of time during which returns can reasonably be anticipated from the investment would set an upper limit on the amortisation period. This factor may suggest a relatively short amortisation period such as the five years envisaged by the general rule of the EC 4th Directive. However, in implementing the 4th Directive, the UK took advantage of the Member State option to permit amortisation over a period exceeding five years, but not exceeding the useful economic life. The standard also provides for amortisation of goodwill over its useful economic life and, accordingly, it is inappropriate to indicate any maximum period in numerical terms.

70 It is not possible to specify general rules regarding the useful economic life over which purchased goodwill should be amortised in any particular case, and it is likely that different useful economic lives will be selected for the goodwill arising on different acquisitions. Paragraph 45 of the standard requires, *inter alia,* disclosure of the amortisation period(s) selected in relation to major acquisitions. Further, as noted in paragraph 59, there is a legal requirement for disclosure of the reasons for choosing the amortisation period. The amortisation period will generally have been selected because it represents the useful economic life of the goodwill and a statement to that effect would appear to satisfy the requirement.

Appendix 2

This appendix is for guidance only and does not form part of the statement of standard accounting practice.

Effect of elimination of goodwill on realised profits

71 Paragraph 63 of the standard sets out the legal definition of realised profits. This is relevant only in the case of an individual company. In the case of goodwill arising on consolidation, the distinction between realised and unrealised reserves is not relevant. Distributions are made from the profits of individual companies, not by groups, and hence the elimination of consolidation goodwill has no effect on the distributable profits of any company.

72 Where it is the policy of an individual company to eliminate goodwill against reserves immediately on acquisition, the question arises whether such elimination constitutes a reduction of realised reserves. To the extent that the goodwill is considered to have suffered an actual diminution in value, the write-off should be charged against realised reserves. In other cases, where goodwill is written off on acquisition as a matter of accounting policy, rather than because of an actual diminution in value realised reserves should not be reduced immediately. However, the standard is based on the concept in the UK Companies Acts that purchased goodwill has a limited useful life so that ultimately its elimination must constitute a realised loss. It may in some circumstances (e.g. where a company lacks sufficient distributable reserves to cover the purchase cost of the goodwill) be appropriate to charge the elimination of goodwill initially to a suitable unrealised reserve, thereby spreading the effect of the elimination of goodwill on realised reserves over its useful life rather than impairing realised reserves immediately. The Accounting Standards Committee is advised by the Department of Trade and Industry that the restriction regarding the use of the revaluation reserve set out in paragraph 34(3) of Schedule 4 has the effect that this reserve should not be charged with the write-off of goodwill. A suitable unrealised reserve may exist as a result of the crediting to reserves of negative goodwill — see paragraph 3 below. To maintain parity of effect as regards distributable reserves with the amortisation method permitted by paragraph 41 of the standard, the amount written off should then be transferred from unrealised reserves to realised reserves so as to reduce realised reserves on a systematic basis in the same way as if the goodwill had been amortised. In case of doubt on the points in this paragraph, legal advice should be sought.

73 Where negative goodwill arises in the accounts of an individual company it should be credited initially to an unrealised reserve, from which it may be transferred to realised reserves in line with the depreciation or realisation of the assets acquired in the business combination which gave rise to the goodwill in question. On the introduction of this standard, amounts representing negative goodwill which arose on prior acquisitions may already have been credited to reserves. To the extent that the assets acquired have, on the introduction of this standard, been depreciated or realised, the relevant amount of reserves may be regarded as realised.

Appendix 3

This appendix is for guidance only and does not form part of the statement of standard accounting practice.

Fair value table

74 The following example is given to indicate a format for the fair value table and adjustments required by paragraph 48. This example is neither exhaustive nor prescriptive but is for general guidance. In practice only material adjustments need be separately disclosed.

Fair value table

Acquisition — XYZ LTD *Date* — 19.2.89

Consideration — 100,000 £1 ordinary shares were issued to acquire the following assets. The fair value of the consideration, using the mid-market price on 19.2.89 of £3.06, was £306,000 giving rise to goodwill of £100,000.

	Book value	Revaluation	Provisions for trading losses	Other provisions	Accounting policy alignment	Other major items	Fair value to the group
	£000	£000	£000	£000	£ 000	£000	£000
Fixed assets							
Intangible						80 [f]	80
Tangible	160	20 [a]					180
Investments	20	5 [b]					25
Current assets							
Stock	40		(4) [c]	(5) [d]	(2) [e]		29
Debtors	35						35
Investments	10						10
Cash at bank	12						12
Total assets	277	25	(4)	(5)	(2)	80	371
Liabilities							
Provisions:							
Pensions	30						30
Taxation	45					10 [g]	55
Other	10		8 [c]				18
Creditors:							
Debenture	2						2
Bank loans	15						15
Trade creditors	30						30
Other creditors	10						10
Accruals	5						5
Total liabilities	147		8			10	165
Net assets	130	25	(12)	(5)	(2)	70	206

	Adjustments	Explanations
(i)	**Revaluations**	
	Note a	Increases in value of freehold properties since last revaluation in 1981.
	Note b	Increase in value of shares of USM investment since purchase in 1983.
(ii)	**Provisions for Trading losses**	
	Note c	Losses expected to be incurred prior to closing down small tools division.
(iii)	**Other provisions**	
	Note d	Write-down following reassessment of realisable value of stock which is more than one year old.
(iv)	**Accounting policy alignments**	
	Note e	Change of stock valuation from weighted average cost to FIFO which is used by the group.
(v)	**Other major Items**	
	Note f	Recognition of intangibles — relating to publishing titles and brands acquired.
	Note g	Adjustment to deferred tax arising from the incorporation of fair values.

Accounting for pension costs

(Issued May 1988)

The provisions of this statement of standard accounting practice should be read in conjunction with the explanatory foreword to accounting standards *and need not be applied to immaterial items.*

Part 1 — Explanatory note

Importance of pension costs

1 The provision of a pension is part of the remuneration package of many employees. Pension costs form a significant proportion of total payroll costs and they give rise to special problems of estimation and of allocation between accounting periods. Accordingly, it is important that standard accounting practice exists concerning the recognition of such costs in the employers' financial statements. This statement deals with the accounting for, and the disclosure of, pension costs and commitments in the financial statements of enterprises that have pension arrangements for the provision of retirement benefits for their employees.

Types of pension schemes

2 Pension arrangements can take different forms. The employer may have a commitment arising from the contract of employment, the provision of pensions may have arisen from custom and practice or *ex gratia* arrangements may be made on a case by case basis. This Statement covers a scheme where an enterprise has entered into a commitment, whether legal, contractual or implicit in the employer's actions, to provide pensions for its employees. It also addresses situations where *ex gratia* or discretionary payments are made in the absence of such a commitment.

3 Pension schemes to which this Statement applies may basically be divided into defined contribution schemes and defined benefit schemes. In a defined contribution scheme, the employer will normally discharge his obligation by making agreed contributions to a pension scheme and benefits paid will depend upon the funds available from these contributions and investment earnings thereon. The cost to the employer can, therefore, be measured with reasonable certainty. A number of pension schemes in the United Kingdom and Ireland, including many smaller ones, are defined contribution schemes.

4 In a defined benefit scheme, however, the benefits to be paid will usually depend upon either the average pay of the employee during his or her career or, more typically, the final pay of the employee. In these circumstances, it is impossible to be certain in advance that the contributions to the pension scheme, together with the investment return thereon, will equal the benefits to be paid. The employer may have a legal obligation to provide any unforeseen shortfall in funds or, if not, may find it necessary to meet the shortfall in the interest of maintaining good employee relations. Conversely, if a surplus arises the employer may be entitled to a refund of, or reduction in, contributions paid into the pension scheme. Thus, in this type of scheme the employer's commitment is generally more open than with defined contribution schemes and the final cost is subject to considerable uncertainty. The larger UK and Irish schemes are generally of the defined benefit kind and these cover the great majority of members of schemes.

5 Pension schemes may also be classified by the way in which they are financed, namely funded schemes or schemes where the benefits are paid directly by the employer. The same accounting principles apply to both types of scheme.

6 The trustees of a funded scheme may make use of the services of an insurance company — an approach that is particularly common amongst the smaller schemes. Insurance companies offer a wide variety of contracts, but, in the case of defined benefit schemes, these contracts are normally no more than investment management and administrative arrangements, possibly with life cover included, and do not relieve the employer of the responsibility to ensure that the scheme is adequately financed.

Actuarial considerations

7 In view of the very long-term nature of the pensions commitment, it is necessary to make use of actuarial calculations in determining the pension cost charge in respect of defined benefit schemes. In the case of defined contribution schemes there is no need for actuarial advice in order to establish the pension cost although such advice may be required for other purposes in connection with the operation of the scheme.

8 In defined benefit schemes, the choice of assumptions and the choice of valuation method can each have a major effect on the contribution rate calculated at each valuation. The choice of assumptions can be as significant as the choice of method.

9 The assumptions which the actuary must make in carrying out his valuation will be about matters such as future rates of inflation and pay increases, increases to pensions in payment, earnings on investments, the number of employees joining the scheme, the age profile of employees and the probability that employees will die or leave the company's employment before they reach retiring age. The actuary will view the assumptions as a whole; he will make assumptions which are mutually compatible, in the knowledge that, if experience departs from the assumptions made, the effects of such departures may well be offsetting, notably in the case of investment yields and increases in prices and earnings.

10 Most pension schemes undergo a formal actuarial valuation on a triennial basis. In such cases it is not intended that any special valuation exercise should be carried out by enterprises for the purpose of implementing this Statement for the first time.

11 The Councils of the Institute and Faculty of Actuaries published a paper in May 1986 entitled 'Pension Fund Terminology: specimen descriptions of commonly used valuation methods'. In addition the Auditing Practices Committee has published an Audit Brief entitled 'The work of a pension scheme actuary'. This covers matters such as the valuation of defined benefit and defined contribution schemes, valuation assumptions and interprofessional co-operation. A glossary of pensions terminology for pension schemes has been published by The Pensions Management Institute and The Pensions Research Accountants Group.

The funding plan

12 The funding methods developed by actuaries are designed to build up assets in a prudent and controlled manner in advance of the retirement of the members of the scheme, in order that the obligations of the scheme may be met without undue distortion of the employer's cash flow. The actuary's main concern is that the present and estimated future contribution levels should be at least sufficient to provide security for the payment of the promised benefits.

13 A range of actuarial methods is available for determining the level of contributions needed to meet the liabilities of the pension scheme. Some methods will tend to lead to higher levels of funding in the scheme than others.

14 In practice, it is common for actuaries to aim at a level contribution rate, as a proportion of pensionable pay in respect of current service. The contribution rate thus determined depends on the particular actuarial method used and the assumptions made regarding new entrants to the scheme. In broad terms, in projecting a stable contribution rate, accrued benefits methods rely on the assumption that the flow of new entrants will be such as to preserve the existing average age of the work-force; prospective benefits methods, on the other hand, normally look only to the existing work-force and seek a contribution rate that will remain stable for that group despite its increasing age profile until the last member retires or leaves. In a mature scheme both types of method may in practice achieve stable contribution rates but the size of the fund under a prospective benefits method will tend to be larger than under an accrued benefits method because it is intended to cover the ageing of the existing work-force.

15 From time to time it may be necessary to improve the level of funding because of deficiencies (where these are not expected to be offset by future surpluses). This may be done by an increase in the ordinary annual rate of contribution or by additional special payments over a limited period. On occasion the employer may make additional lump sum contributions which have the effect of reducing his future liabilities, if to do so is convenient in the context of the financial policy of the employer's business. Conversely, a previously high level of funding may be lowered by reducing or interrupting the contributions if there is a surplus in the fund or in times of financial stringency for the company. However, whilst the financial position of the sponsoring employer may influence the pattern of funding it will not provide a satisfactory basis for determining the pension charge for the period.

The accounting objective

16 From the point of view of the employee a pension may be regarded as deferred remuneration; from the point of view of the employer it is part of the cost incurred in obtaining the employee's services. The accounting objective therefore requires the employer to recognise the cost of providing pensions on a systematic and rational basis over the period during which he benefits from the employees' services. Many companies have, until now, simply charged the contributions payable to the pension scheme as the pension cost in each accounting period. In future, in order to comply with this Statement, it will be necessary to consider whether the funding plan provides a satisfactory basis for allocating the pension cost to a particular accounting period.

Defined contribution schemes

17 In the case of a defined contribution scheme the employer's obligation at any point in time is restricted to the amount of the contributions payable to date. The pension cost is, therefore, the amount of the contributions payable in respect of the particular accounting period.

Defined benefit schemes

18 The selection of the actuarial method and assumptions to be used in assessing the pension cost of a defined benefit scheme is a matter of judgement for the actuary in consultation with his client, taking account of the circumstances of the specific company and its workforce. This Statement requires that the actuarial valuation method and assumptions used for accounting purposes should satisfy the accounting objective. In order that full provision may be made over the employees' service lives for the expected costs of their pensions, the effect of expected future increases in earnings, include merit increases, up to the assumed retirement date or earlier date of withdrawal or death in service, should be recognised. Account will also need to be taken of expected future increases in deferred pensions and pensions in payment where the employer has an express or implied commitment to grant such increases. The calculation of benefit levels should be based on the situation most likely to be experienced and not on a contingent event not likely to occur. The actuarial method selected should be used consistently and should be disclosed. If there is a change of method this fact should be disclosed and the effect quantified. The actuarial assumptions and the actuarial method taken as a whole should be compatible and should lead to the actuary's best estimate of the cost of providing the pension benefits promised.

19 If the funding plan does not provide a satisfactory basis for determining the pension cost charge, separate actuarial calculations will be required.

Regular pension costs and variations in cost

20 The total cost of pensions in a year can notionally be divided into the regular cost, which is the consistent ongoing cost recognised under the actuarial method used, and variations from the regular cost. Where a stable contribution rate for regular contributions, expressed as a percentage of pensionable earnings, has been determined, that rate will provide an acceptable basis for calculating the regular cost under the stated accounting objective so long as it makes full provision for the expected benefits over the anticipated service lives of employees.

21 Variations from the regular cost may arise from:

(a) experience surpluses or deficiencies:

(b) the effects on the actuarial value of accrued benefits of changes in assumptions or method;

(c) retroactive changes in benefits or in conditions for membership;

(d) increases to pensions in payment or to deferred pensions for which provision has not previously been made.

Spreading variations from regular cost

22 Experience deficiencies or surpluses are part of the ongoing process of revising the estimate of the ultimate liabilities which will fall on the employer. Any effect on the cost should normally be taken into account by adjusting the current and future costs charged in the accounts and should not be treated as a prior year adjustment.

23 In accordance with the accounting objective, the normal period over which the effect of material deficiencies or surpluses should be spread for accounting purposes is the expected remaining service lives of the current employees in the scheme after making suitable allowances for future withdrawals. A period representing the average remaining service lives of the current membership may be used if desired. This period, which will vary from scheme to scheme and from time to time, should be determined by the actuary. It would not be appropriate to credit or charge the entire surplus or deficiency against profits in one accounting period, except as provided in paragraphs 81 to 83.

24 The only circumstances in which there may be a departure from the normal principle of spreading material surpluses or deficiencies as set out in paragraph 23 are summarised in this paragraph and in paragraph 29 below. The full conditions which must be satisfied before there may be a departure from the normal spreading requirements are set out in paragraphs 81 to 83. The circumstances referred to below represent situations that properly lie outside the actuarial assumptions and normal running of the scheme and, accordingly, are expected to arise infrequently. They are:

(a) where there is a significant reduction in the number of employees covered by the company's and/or group's pension scheme arrangements;

(b) where, in the circumstances set out in paragraph 82, prudence requires a material deficiency to be recognised over a shorter period.

25 In many companies, there have been reorganisation programmes in recent years that have involved significant redundancies. These have often led to large non-reversing surpluses building up in related pension schemes. This Statement recognises that in such instances it would not be appropriate to spread the effect of the refund of such surpluses over the remaining service lives of the current employees in the scheme.

26 In the circumstances set out in paragraph 24(a) a refund of a surplus, contributions holiday or reduction in contributions should be accounted for as it becomes receivable and should not be anticipated, that is, if it is agreed that contributions will be reduced for a period of years the reduction should be recognised on a year by year basis and not accumulated and reflected in the financial statements in the period the first reduction becomes effective. Where a reduction in the number of employees is related to an extraordinary event, such as the closure of a business segment, it is accepted that it may not be possible to apply the rule set out in this paragraph. This is because SSAP 6 (Revised) 'Extraordinary items and prior year adjustments' requires the individual elements of income and expenditure which derive from a single extraordinary event to be aggregated and so it may not be appropriate to defer recognition of an associated pension cost or credit.

27 The exemption from the normal spreading principle relating to significant reductions in the total number of employees covered by a group's or company's pension arrangements does not cover situations where employees are transferred from one group to another one.

28 As stated in paragraph 24(b), in strictly limited circumstances prudence may require that a material deficiency should be recognised over a period shorter than the expected remaining service lives of current employees in the scheme. A precondition of invoking this section is that significant additional contributions have had to be paid into the pension scheme. Furthermore the additional payments should have been made as stated in paragraph 24 in respect of a major transaction or event outside the actuarial assumptions and normal running of the scheme. A possible example of such a situation would be where there had been a major mismanagement of a pension scheme's assets. However, it is emphasised that each situation must be judged on its particular merits.

29 Where a refund that is subject to deduction of tax in accordance with the provisions of the UK Finance Act 1986, or equivalent legislation, is made to the employer, the enterprise may depart from the normal spreading principle and instead recognise the refund in the period in which it occurs. The accounting treatment adopted in respect of such refunds should be disclosed.

Changes in assumptions, valuation method and benefits

30 The effect of changes in the assumptions or valuation method on the cost of providing for past service is analogous to an experience deficiency or surplus and should be accounted for in a similar way.

31 Retroactive changes in benefits and membership are decided upon currently and it is thus not appropriate to charge any part of the costs arising from these decisions as a prior year adjustment. Past service costs should normally be written off over the remaining service lives of the current employees.

32 Where a surplus in a pension fund is utilised to provide benefits for which the company had previously established a provision in its financial statements, the provision, to the extent that it is no longer required, should be released over the estimated remaining service lives of the current employees.

Increases to pensions in payment and deferred pensions

33 Increases to pensions in payment up to a certain level may be specified in the rules of the pension scheme. Other increases may be granted in response to pensioners' needs and in the interests of continuing good industrial relations. In the United Kingdom, increases to deferred pensions, that is the prospective pensions of early leavers, are required by law to be made up to a special level.

34 Increases specified in the pension scheme rules or required by law will be taken into account in the actuarial assumptions. The cost will, therefore, be charged over the service lives of the employees. Any divergence between the assumptions and experience will be accounted for as an element of any overall experience deficiency or surplus.

35 Other increases are, at least in form, discretionary at the time they are awarded, whether they are paid through the scheme or directly by the employer. Discretionary increases may be granted on the basis that the rules require there to be an annual review or because the employer has announced an intention to grant increases but no previous commitment has been made. The preferred treatment is for such increases, where they are likely to be granted on a regular basis, to be allowed for in the actuarial assumptions. They will then be recognised as part of the pension cost over the working lives of the beneficiaries.

36 Once an increase has been awarded it is very unlikely that it will be withdrawn and so it should be regarded thereafter as part of the employer's commitments. Accordingly, this Statement provides that, if provision has not been made for the increase in the actuarial assumptions, the capitalised amount of the increase should be provided for in the period in which it is granted to the extent that it is not covered by a surplus.

37 Where a non-recurring ('one-off') increase is granted which applies to the current period but will not affect pensions paid in future periods, it should be treated as purely *ex gratia* and its cost should be charged in the period in which it is granted to the extent that it is not covered by a surplus.

38 Employers may occasionally grant *ex gratia* pensions to employees at the time of their retirement. An example would be a pension granted to a long-serving employee who for some reason had not been a member of the company's scheme and for whom the company decided to make provision. As with discretionary pension increases, the capital cost of any such *ex gratia* pensions should be charged in the period in which they are granted to the extent that they are not covered by a surplus.

Hybrid schemes

39 A few schemes are hybrid in nature combining features of defined contribution and defined benefit schemes. In such instances the rules or trust deed should be carefully studied and the operation of the scheme in practice, or its proposed method of operation, taken into account when determining the appropriate accounting treatment. The accounting treatment adopted should be in accordance with the underlying substance of the scheme.

Discounting

40 By their nature actuarial valuations make allowance for interest so that future cash flows are discounted to their present value. Financial statements, however, normally include items at their face value without discounting them. The question of whether items should be discounted in financial statements is a general one and this Statement does not attempt to establish standard practice. Interest effects arising from short-term timing differences between the payment of contributions and the recognition of cost are not likely to be material and can be ignored. If the difference is long-term, the situation becomes akin to that arising in respect of an unfunded scheme. If a scheme is unfunded the provision for pension costs is assessed and reviewed on a discounted basis and adjusted each year by an amount comprising two elements: a charge for the year (equivalent to a contribution in a funded scheme) and interest on the unfunded liability.

Foreign schemes

41 In principle, the pension costs charged in respect of all pension schemes included in group accounts should conform to the accounting objective and a consolidation adjustment should be made where the cost charged in the individual accounts of a group company does not do so.

42 No adjustment would normally be necessary in respect of UK and Irish schemes as the pension cost in the individual company accounts should already conform to the requirements of this Statement. On the other hand, in the case of foreign schemes, the commitment of the employer regarding the provision of pensions may be very different from that which is customary in the United Kingdom and Ireland so that it would be inappropriate to adjust the pension cost charged. In some cases, for example, the employer's obligation may be discharged by prescribed payments under a nationwide or industry-wide scheme with characteristics similar to those of the State scheme in the United Kingdom. In such cases charging the contributions payable will satisfy the requirements of this Statement.

43 In other instances the nature of the employer's commitment may be similar to that in the UK and Ireland and the different determination of the pension cost charge may be caused solely by different accounting policies. An adjustment to the charge would then be appropriate although it is recognised that it may sometimes be impractical to make such an adjustment because of the difficulties and cost of obtaining compatible actuarial valuations in order to be able to recalculate the pension charge in accordance with the full provisions of this Statement. In such circumstances while an adjustment to the charge is not mandatory it is encouraged and suitable disclosure should be made.

Deferred taxation

44 For many enterprises the pension cost charge for the period has in the past been equal to the contributions payable. Under the requirements of this Statement the charge in the financial statements could be different from the contributions payable if, for example, a deficiency on valuation is being spread forward in the financial statements over the estimated remaining service lives of current employees although an additional lump-sum payment has been paid into the pension fund. Since taxation relief is generally granted in respect of payments made to the pension fund, accounting for pension costs in the manner prescribed by this Statement may have deferred tax implications. Where these occur they should be accounted for in accordance with SSAP 15 (Revised) 'Accounting for Deferred Tax'.

Disclosures

45 Sufficient information should be disclosed to give the user of the financial statements a proper understanding of the impact of the pension arrangements on the group's and/or the company's financial statements.

46 For a defined contribution scheme it will usually suffice to indicate the nature of the scheme and the amounts included in the profit and loss account and balance sheet.

47 For a defined benefit scheme more extensive disclosures are needed because of the greater and more uncertain obligations of the employer. Disclosures required include the accounting policy, the actuarial valuation method and major actuarial assumptions adopted, the cost charged, with explanations of it, and certain actuarial valuation information. In view of the significant long-term variable commitment of the employer, the disclosures should not only relate to the amounts in the financial statements for the periods presented but should also give an indication of significant changes in future costs that are expected under the actuarial assumptions and method used. Examples of how a small company and a large group may satisfy the disclosure requirements are given in Appendix 1.

48 As explained in paragraph 14, the effect of aiming for a level contribution rate varies according to the actuarial method used and the assumption made regarding new entrants. It is therefore necessary to disclose what assumption has been made in this regard unless it is immediately apparent from the disclosure of the actuarial method used.

49 This Statement requires the disclosure of an outline of the results of the most recent formal actuarial valuation or later review of the pension scheme on an ongoing basis. Specific disclosures to be made include the market value of scheme assets at the date of their valuation or review and the level of funding expressed in percentage terms. In certain instances it may be necessary to provide further information in order that details on the level of funding may be seen in their proper context. The level of funding and/or market values of scheme assets at the date of valuation or review may, for example, have subsequently changed markedly as a result of changes in general stock market values or in the level of contributions paid into the pension scheme. In particular, it should be considered whether the figures disclosed relating to the last valuation or review need to be amplified by a discussion of changes that have occurred since that date.

50 Disclosure is also required of changes in the group and/or company's pension scheme arrangements where these have had, or will have, a material effect on the future cost of providing pensions.

51 Where a company or group has more than one scheme it will often be necessary to give information on a combined basis in order to keep the volume of disclosures within reasonable limits. However, it is important that the combined figures should provide a proper understanding of the impact of the pension arrangements on the group's and/or company's financial position.

Group schemes

52 It is quite common for a number of companies within the same group to contribute to a single group scheme. With such schemes it is normally accepted that the same contribution rate, expressed as a percentage of payroll, should apply to the different member companies even though, if calculated on an individual company basis, the rate payable may vary between the employers within a group. This statement permits the use of a common group rate for contributions payable by sponsoring employers. If a group scheme is in operation it may not be possible to estimate the pension obligations for which a particular group company is responsible and it would not be meaningful to provide information relating to the group as a whole in the subsidiary's financial statements. Provision is therefore made for reduced disclosure in the financial statements of subsidiary companies that are members of group schemes. The full details relating to the pension scheme should be disclosed in the financial statements of the holding company.

Transitional provisions

53 When, on implementing this Statement for the first time, a cumulative adjustment arises in respect of prior years, this may either be dealt with in accordance with the other provisions of this Statement or accounted for in accordance with the provisions of SSAP 6 (Revised) 'Extraordinary items and prior year adjustments'. That is, the cumulative adjustment may, except as discussed below, be spread over the expected remaining service lives of current employees in the scheme or accounted for as a prior year adjustment. To the extent that the adjustment relates to a variation from regular cost that, in accordance with the provisions of paragraphs 81 and 82, would not be eligible to be spread over the remaining service lives it should be accounted for as a prior year item. (An example of such an adjustment would be one arising from a significant reduction in the number of employees covered by a company's pension scheme arrangements.) Similar considerations may also arise in respect of paragraphs 84 and 85 which deal with discretionary and *ex gratia* pension increases and *ex gratia* pensions. The cumulative adjustment should be calculated, as at the beginning of the accounting period in which this Statement is first applied, as the actuarial value of the surplus or deficiency on an ongoing basis as adjusted by any existing provision for unfunded pension costs or any existing pensions prepayment. In order that enterprises do not have to undertake a special valuation exercise for the purposes of implementing this Statement, they may base the calculation of the cumulative adjustment on the results of the last actuarial valuation so long as it was carried out on a basis broadly consistent with the requirements of this Statement. In arriving at the adjustment any surplus or deficiency at the last valuation date should be adjusted to take account of any additional payments or reduced contributions made since that date as a consequence of it. It may also be necessary to make allowance for major changes affecting the pension scheme since the last valuation.

The Republic of Ireland

54 The Republic of Ireland, unlike the United Kingdom, currently does not have any legislative requirement for defined benefit pension schemes to be actuarially assessed and the actuarial profession's involvement with pension schemes has tended to be less than in the United Kingdom. Legislation is to be introduced based on the recommendations contained in the First Report of the National Pensions Board but the first actuarial valuation for a number of schemes will not take place until the beginning of the next decade. Accordingly, the provisions of paragraphs 77, 79 to 85 and 88(g) and 88(h) will not be mandatory for non-quoted companies registered in the Republic of Ireland in respect of the financial statements of periods commencing before 1 January 1993. Such companies are, however, encouraged to comply with the full requirements of this Statement as soon as possible.

55 The full requirements of this Statement will apply to companies registered in the Republic of Ireland and quoted on the International Stock Exchange of the United Kingdom and the Republic of Ireland Limited from the same date as it applies to companies registered in the United Kingdom.

Part 2 — Definition of terms

56 Accrued benefits are the benefits for service up to a given point in time, whether the rights to the benefits are vested or not. They may be calculated in relation to current earnings or protected final earnings.

57 An **accrued benefits method** of actuarial valuation is a valuation method in which the actuarial value of liabilities relates at a given date to:

(a) the benefits including future increases promised by the rules, for the current and deferred pensioners and their dependants; and

(b) the benefits which the members assumed to be in service on the given date will receive for service up to that date only.

Allowance may be made for expected increases in earnings after the given date, and/or for additional pension increases not promised by the rules. The given date may be a current or future date. The further into the future the adopted date lies, the closer the results will be to those of a prospective benefits valuation method.

58 The **average remaining service life** is a weighted average of the expected future service of the current members of the scheme up to their normal retirement dates or expected dates of earlier withdrawal or death in service. The weightings can have regard to periods of service, salary levels of scheme members and future anticipated salary growth in a manner which the actuary considers appropriate having regard to the actuarial method and assumptions used.

59 A **current funding level valuation** considers whether the assets would have been sufficient at the valuation date to cover liabilities arising in respect of pensions in payment, preserved benefits for members whose pensionable service has ceased and accrued benefits for members in pensionable service, based on pensionable service to and pensionable earnings at, the date of valuation including revaluation on the statutory basis or such higher basis as has been promised.

60 An ***ex gratia*** **pension** or **discretionary** or ***ex gratia*** **increase** in a pension is one which the employer has no legal, contractual or implied commitment to provide.

61 A **defined benefit scheme** is a pension scheme in which the rules specify the benefits to be paid and the scheme is financed accordingly.

62 A **defined contribution scheme** is a pension scheme in which the benefits are directly determined by the value of contributions paid in respect of each member. Normally the rate of contribution is specified in the rules of the scheme.

63 An **experience surplus or deficiency** is that part of the excess or deficiency of the actuarial value of assets over the actuarial value of liabilities, on the basis of the valuation method used, which arises because events have not coincided with the actuarial assumptions made for the last valuation.

64 A **funding plan** is the timing of payments in an orderly fashion to meet the future cost of a given set of benefits.

65 A **funded scheme** is a pension scheme where the future liabilities for benefits are provided for by the accumulation of assets held externally to the employing company's business.

66 The **level of funding** is the proportion at a given date of the actuarial value of liabilities for pensioners' and deferred pensioners' benefits and for members' accrued benefits that is covered by the actuarial value of assets. For this purpose the actuarial value of future contributions is excluded from the value of assets.

67 An **ongoing actuarial valuation** is a valuation in which it is assumed that the pension scheme will continue in existence and (where appropriate) that new members will be admitted. The liabilities allow for expected increases in earnings.

68 **Past service** is used in this Statement to denote service before a given date. It is often used, however, to denote service before entry into the pension scheme.

69 **Pensionable payroll/earnings** are the earnings on which benefits and/or contributions are calculated. One or more elements of earnings (e.g. overtime) may be excluded, and/or there may be a reduction to take account of all or part of the state scheme benefits which the member is deemed to receive.

70 A **pension scheme** is an arrangement (other than accident insurance) to provide pension and/or other benefits for members on leaving service or retiring and, after a member's death, for his/her dependants.

71 A **prospective benefits method** of valuation is a valuation method in which the actuarial value of liabilities relates to:

(a) the benefits for current and deferred pensioners and their dependants, allowing where appropriate for future pension increases; and

(b) the benefits that active members will receive in respect of both past and future service, allowing for future increases in earnings up to their assumed exit dates, and where appropriate for pension increases thereafter.

72 **Regular cost** is the consistent ongoing cost recognised under the actuarial method used.

Part 3 — Standard accounting practice

Scope

73 This Statement applies where the employer has a legal or contractual commitment under a pension scheme or one implicit in the employer's actions, to provide, or contribute to, pensions for his employees. It also addresses discretionary and *ex gratia* increases in pensions and *ex gratia* pensions. The same principles apply irrespective of whether the scheme is funded or unfunded.

74 This Statement applies to defined contribution schemes and defined benefit schemes.

75 Although this Statement primarily addresses pensions, its principles may be equally applicable to the cost of providing other post-retirement benefits.

76 This Statement does not apply to either state social security contributions or redundancy payments.

Pension cost

77 The accounting objective is that the employer should recognise the expected cost of providing pensions on a systematic and rational basis over the period during which he derives benefit from the employees' services. The ways in which this is to be achieved are detailed in paragraphs 78 to 92.

Defined contribution schemes

78 For defined contribution schemes the charge against profits should be the amount of contributions payable to the pension scheme in respect of the accounting period.

Defined benefit schemes

79 For defined benefit schemes the pension cost should be calculated using actuarial valuation methods which are consistent with the requirements of this Statement. The actuarial assumptions and method, taken as a whole, should be compatible and should lead to the actuary's best estimate of the cost of providing the pension benefits promised. The method of providing for expected pension costs over the service lives of employees in the scheme should be such that the regular pension cost is a substantially level percentage of the current and expected future pensionable payroll in the light of the current actuarial assumptions.

80 Subject to the provisions of paragraphs 81 to 83, variations from the regular cost should be allocated over the expected remaining service lives of current employees in the scheme. A period representing the average remaining service lives may be used if desired.

81 The provisions of paragraph 80 should not be applied where, and to the extent that, a significant change in the normal level of contributions occurs because contributions are adjusted to eliminate a surplus or deficiency resulting from a significant reduction in the number of employees covered by the enterprise's pension arrangements. Except where such treatment would be inconsistent with SSAP 6 in relation to an extraordinary item, any reduction in contributions arising in these circumstances should be recognised as it occurs. Amounts receivable may not be anticipated; for example, the full effect of a contribution holiday should not be recognised at the outset of the holiday, but rather spread over its duration.

82 In strictly limited circumstances prudence may require that a material deficit be recognised over a period shorter than the expected remaining service lives of current employees in the scheme. Such circumstances are limited to those where a major event or transaction has occurred which has not been allowed for in the actuarial assumptions, is outside the normal scope of those assumptions and has necessitated the payment of significant additional contributions to the pension scheme.

83 Where a refund that is subject to deduction of tax in accordance with the provisions of the UK Finance Act 1986, or equivalent legislation, is made to the employer, the enterprise may depart from the requirements of paragraph 80 and account for the surplus or deficiency in the period in which the refund occurs.

Ex gratia pensions and discretionary and ex gratia pension increases

84 Where *ex gratia* pensions are granted the capital cost, to the extent not covered by a surplus, should be recognised in the profit and loss account in the accounting period in which they are granted.

85 Where allowance for discretionary or *ex gratia* increases in pensions is not made in the actuarial assumptions, the capital cost of such increases should, to the extent not covered by a surplus, be recognised in the profit and loss account in the accounting period in which they are initially granted.

Balance sheet

86 If the cumulative pension cost recognised in the profit and loss account has not been completely discharged by payment of contributions or directly paid pensions, the excess should be shown as a net pension provision. Similarly, any excess of contributions paid or directly paid pensions over the cumulative pension cost should be shown as a prepayment.

Disclosures

87 The following disclosures should be made in respect of a defined contribution scheme:

(a) the nature of the scheme (i.e. defined contribution);

(b) the accounting policy;

(c) the pension cost charge for the period;

(d) any outstanding or prepaid contributions at the balance sheet date.

88 The following disclosures should be made in respect of a defined benefit scheme:

(a) the nature of the scheme (i.e. defined benefit);

(b) whether it is funded or unfunded;

(c) the accounting policy and, if different, the funding policy;

(d) whether the pension cost and provision (or asset) are assessed in accordance with the advice of a professionally qualified actuary and, if so, the date of the most recent formal actuarial valuation or later formal review used for this purpose. If the actuary is an employee or officer of the reporting company, or of the group of which it is a member, this fact should be disclosed;

(e) the pension cost charge for the period together with explanations of significant changes in the charge compared to that in the previous accounting period;

(f) any provisions or prepayments in the balance sheet resulting from a difference between the amounts recognised as cost and the amounts funded or paid directly;

(g) the amount of any deficiency on a current funding level basis, indicating the action, if any, being taken to deal with it in the current and future accounting periods;

(h) an outline of the results of the most recent formal actuarial valuation or later formal review of the scheme on an ongoing basis.

This should include disclosure of:

(i) the actuarial method used and a brief description of the main actuarial assumptions;

(ii) the market value of scheme assets at the date of their valuation or review;

(iii) the level of funding expressed in percentage terms;

(iv) comments on any material actuarial surplus or deficiency indicated by (iii) above;

(i) any commitment to make additional payments over a limited number of years;

(j) the accounting treatment adopted in respect of a refund made in accordance with the provisions of paragraph 83 where a credit appears in the financial statements in relation to it;

(k) details of the expected effects on future costs of any material changes in the group's and/or company's pension arrangements.

89 Where a company or group has more than one pension scheme disclosure should be made on a combined basis, unless disclosure of information about individual schemes is necessary for a proper understanding of the accounts. For the purposes of paragraph 88(g) above, however, a current funding level basis deficiency in one scheme should not be set off against a surplus in another.

Group schemes

90 A subsidiary company which is a member of a group scheme should disclose this fact in its financial statements and disclose the nature of the group scheme indicating, where appropriate, that the contributions are based on pension costs across the group as a whole. Such a company is exempt from the disclosure requirements of paragraph 88(g) and (h) and should instead state the name of the holding company in whose financial statements particulars of the actuarial valuation of the group scheme are contained. This exemption only applies if the holding company is registered in the United Kingdom or the Republic of Ireland.

Foreign schemes

91 Where, in respect of foreign operations, the employer has an obligation to provide pensions, the pension charge should reflect that obligation and, therefore, be dealt with in accordance with the requirements of this Statement. An adjustment on consolidation will be necessary where the charge is not already calculated in accordance with the basis set out in this Statement, unless the nature of the employer's commitment is very different from that which is customary in the United Kingdom and Ireland. It is recognised, however, that in some cases it may be impractical to make the adjustment because of the difficulties and cost of obtaining the necessary actuarial information. In such cases, the amount charged to the profit and loss account and the basis of the charge should, as a minimum, be disclosed in the consolidated financial statements.

Transitional provisions

92 When, on implementing this Statement for the first time, a cumulative adjustment arises in respect of prior years this may either be dealt with in accordance with the other provisions of this Statement or accounted for in accordance with the provisions of SSAP 6 (Revised) 'Extraordinary items and prior year adjustments'. The way in which the transitional provisions have been applied should be disclosed in the financial statements for the period in which this Statement is first implemented.

Date from which effective

93 The accounting and disclosure requirements set out in this Statement should be adopted as soon as possible and, except in the case of certain companies registered in the Republic of Ireland as provided in paragraph 94, regarded as standard in respect of financial statements relating to accounting periods beginning on or after 1 July 1988.

94 In the case of companies that are registered in the Republic of Ireland and not quoted on the International Stock Exchange of the United Kingdom and Ireland paragraphs 77, 79 to 85 and 88(g) and 88(h) should be adopted as soon as possible and regarded as standard in respect of financial statements relating to accounting periods beginning on or after 1 January 1993. The remainder of the required accounting practices and disclosures should be regarded as standard in respect of financial statements relating to accounting periods beginning on or after 1 July 1988. A cumulative adjustment that arises in respect of paragraph 84 on *ex gratia* pensions may either be dealt with in accordance with SSAP 6 (Revised) or allocated over the expected remaining service lives of current employees in the scheme.

Part 4 — Legal requirements in Great Britain and Northern Ireland

References are to the Companies Act 1985 and the Companies (Northern Ireland) Order 1986.

95 Paragraph 50(4) of Schedule 4 requires a company to give details of any pension commitments provided for in the company's balance sheet and also of any such commitments for which no provision has been made. Particulars of pension commitments to past directors of the company must be disclosed separately.

96 Paragraph 50(6) of Schedule 4 requires that disclosure under paragraph 50(4) should separately include details of commitments undertaken on behalf of, or for the benefit of, any holding company or fellow subsidiary of the company and any subsidiary of the company.

97 Paragraph 56(4) of Schedule 4 requires companies to disclose the total pension costs incurred in the year on behalf of all employees of the company, together with separate disclosure of social security costs incurred on their behalf.

98 By virtue of paragraphs 61 and 68 of Schedule 4, the above requirements also apply to group accounts.

99 Banking, insurance and shipping companies are exempt from the above requirements of Schedule 4.

100 Paragraph 28 of Schedule 5 requires companies to disclose the total amount of pension paid to directors or past directors, other than pensions funded substantially through a pension scheme. If they are so funded, the amount disclosed as emoluments has to include contributions to the scheme (paragraph 22).

Part 5 — Legal requirements in the Republic of Ireland

101 In this part references to companies legislation have been abbreviated as follows:

Companies Act 1963 — The 1963 Act

The Schedule to the Companies (Amendment) Act 1963 — The Schedule

102 Section 191 of the 1963 Act requires disclosure of the aggregate amount of directors' and past-directors' pensions, other than pensions under a scheme where contributions are substantially adequate for the maintenance of the scheme. The Section also requires disclosure of the aggregate amount of directors' emoluments; for the purpose of the Section emoluments include contributions paid in respect of directors to any pension scheme.

103 Paragraph 36(4) of the Schedule requires disclosure of any pension commitments included in the company's balance sheet and any such commitments for which no provision has been made. Where any such commitment relates wholly or partly to pensions payable to past directors of the company, separate particulars shall be given of that commitment so far as it relates to such pensions.

104 Information required to be disclosed under paragraph 36(5) of the Schedule is as follows:

(a) the nature of every pension scheme operated by or on behalf of the company including information as to whether or not each scheme is a defined benefit scheme or a defined contribution scheme;

(b) whether each such scheme is externally funded or internally financed;

(c) whether any pension costs and liabilities are assessed in accordance with the advice of a professionally qualified actuary and, if so, the date of the most recent relevant actuarial valuation;

(d) whether, and if so where, any such actuarial valuation is available for public inspection.

Part 6 — Compliance with International Accounting Standard No19 'Accounting for Retirement Benefits in the Financial Statements of Employers'

105 Compliance with the requirements of this Statement will automatically ensure compliance with International Accounting Standard No 19 'Accounting for Retirement Benefits in the Financial Statements of Employers'.

Appendix 1

This appendix is for general guidance and does not form part of the statement of standard accounting practice.

Examples of disclosures

106 *(a) Defined contribution scheme*

The company operates a defined contribution pension scheme. The assets of the scheme are held separately from those of the company in an independently administered fund. The pension cost charge represents contributions payable by the company to the fund and amounted to £500,000 (1986 £450,000). Contributions totalling £25,000 (1986 £15,000) were payable to the fund at the year-end and are included in creditors.

107 *(b) Defined benefit scheme*

(i) Small company

The company operates a pension scheme providing benefits based on final pensionable pay. The assets of the scheme are held separately from those of the company, being invested with insurance companies. Contributions to the scheme are charged to the profit and loss account so as to spread the cost of pensions over employees' working lives with the company. The contributions are determined by a qualified actuary on the basis of triennial valuations using the projected unit method*. The most recent valuation was as at 31 December 1987. The assumptions which have the most significant effect on the results of the valuation are those relating to the rate of return on investments and the rates of increase in salaries and pensions. It was assumed that the investment returns would be 9% per annum, that salary increases would average 7% per annum and that present and future pensions would increase at the rate of 4% per annum.

The pension charge for the period was £50,000 (1986 £48,000). This included £5,200 (1986 £5,000) in respect of the amortisation of experience surpluses that are being recognised over 10 years, the average remaining service lives of employees.

*These and other actuarial funding methods are described in 'Pension Fund Terminology: specimen descriptions of commonly used valuation methods' issued by the Institute and Faculty of Actuaries.

The most recent actuarial valuation showed that the market value of the scheme's assets was £1,200,000 and that the actuarial value of those assets represented 104% of the benefits that had accrued to members, after allowing for expected future increases in earnings. The contributions of the company and employees will remain at 11% and 5% of earnings respectively.

(ii) Large group

The group operates a number of pension schemes throughout the world. The major schemes, which cover 85% of scheme members, are of the defined benefit type. With the exception of the main scheme in Germany, the assets of the schemes are held in separate trustee administered funds.

The total pension cost for the group was £2,050,000 (1986 £1,585,000) of which £300,000 (1986 £285,000) relates to the overseas schemes. The pension cost relating to the UK schemes is assessed in accordance with the advice of a qualified actuary using the attained age method*. The latest actuarial assessment of those schemes was at 31 December 1985. The assumptions which have the most significant effect on the results of the valuation are those relating to the rate of return on investments and the rates of increase in salaries and pensions. It was assumed that the investment return would be 9% per annum, that salary increases would average 7% per annum and that present and future pensions would increase at the rate of 4% per annum. The cost has risen significantly as a result of the acquisition of ABC Limited at the beginning of the period and the resultant increase in group scheme members. Of the total cost, £350,000 (1986 £300,000) is attributable to amortisation of past service liabilities that are being written off over a ten-year period ending in 1988.

At the date of the latest actuarial valuation, the market value of the assets of the UK scheme was £32.1m and the actuarial value of the assets was sufficient to cover 85% of the benefits that had accrued to members, after allowing for expected future increases in earnings. This deficiency should be eliminated by 1991 at the current employer's contribution rate of 12% of pensionable earnings.

The element of the total pension cost relating to foreign schemes includes £280,000 (1986 £250,000) where the charge has been determined in accordance with local best practice and regulations in the Federal Republic of Germany.

A provision of £5,500,000 (1984 £5,000,000) is included in creditors, this being the excess of the accumulated pension cost over the amount funded. The major part of this provision relates to the unfunded German scheme.

*These and other actuarial funding methods are described in 'Pension Fund Terminology: specimen descriptions of commonly used valuation methods' issued by the Institute and Faculty of Actuaries.

Segmental reporting

(Issued June 1990)

The provisions of this statement of standard accounting practice should be read in conjunction with the explanatory foreword to accounting standards *and need not be applied to immaterial items.*

Part 1 — Explanatory note

Purpose of segmental information

1 Many entities carry on several classes of business or operate in several geographical areas, with different rates of profitability, different opportunities for growth and different degrees of risk. It is not usually possible for the user of the financial statements of such an entity to make judgements about either the nature of the entity's different activities or their contribution to the entity's overall financial results unless the financial statements provide some segmental analysis of the information they contain. The purpose of segmental information is, therefore, to provide information to assist the users of financial statements:

(a) to appreciate more thoroughly the results and financial position of the entity by permitting a better understanding of the entity's past performance and thus a better assessment of its future prospects; and

(b) to be aware of the impact that changes in significant components of a business may have on the business as a whole.

2 This accounting standard should ensure as far as possible that the segmental information reported by an entity is disclosed on a consistent basis, year by year. However, caution should be exercised if comparing similar segments in different entities, because, in addition to any differences in accounting policies adopted, the basis of accounting for intersegment sales or the treatment of common costs may not be consistent between entities.

Scope and applicability

3 This accounting standard contains provisions relating to the statutory segmental disclosure requirements contained in companies legislation in the United Kingdom and the Republic of Ireland. All companies are required to comply with these provisions.

4 This accounting standard also contains provisions relating to the disclosure of intersegment turnover, geographical segment result, segment net assets, origin of turnover, and segmental information about associated undertakings, which are not required by companies legislation. These provisions apply to any entity that:

(a) is a public limited company or has a public limited company as a subsidiary; or

(b) is a banking or insurance company or group (as defined for the purposes of Part VII of the Companies Act 1985); or

(c) exceeds the criteria, multiplied in each case by 10, for defining a medium-sized company under Section 248 of the Companies Act 1985, as amended from time to time by statutory instrument.

However, a subsidiary that is not a public limited company or a banking or insurance company need not comply with these provisions if its parent provides segmental information in compliance with this accounting standard.

5 All entities are encouraged to apply the provisions of this accounting standard in all financial statements intended to give a true and fair view of the financial position and profit or loss.

6 Where, in the opinion of the directors, the disclosure of any information required by this accounting standard would be seriously prejudicial to the interests of the reporting entity, that information need not be disclosed; but the fact that any such information has not been disclosed must be stated. This repeats the exemption contained in paragraph 55(5) of Schedule 4 to the Companies Act 1985* in the wider context of this accounting standard.

Determining reportable segments

7 Information contained in financial statements can be segmented in two principal ways — by class of business and geographically. The Companies Act 1985 recognises both of these bases in paragraph 55 of Schedule 4, referring to the geographical areas as 'markets'. Paragraph 55 states that in analysing the source (in terms of either business or market) of turnover or profit or loss the directors should have regard to the manner in which the company's activities are organised. Paragraph 55 also states that it is for the directors to determine whether the company has carried on business of two or more classes or has supplied markets that differ substantially from each other and that where, in the opinion of the directors, the classes of business or the markets do not differ substantially from each other they may be treated as one.

8 In identifying separate reportable segments, the directors should have regard to the overall purpose of presenting segmental information (as set out in paragraph 1) and the need of the user of the financial statements to be informed where an entity carries on operations in different classes of business or in different geographical areas that:

(a) earn a return on investment that is out of line with the remainder of the business; or

(b) are subject to different degrees of risk; or

(c) have experienced different rates of growth; or

(d) have different potentials for future development.

9 Each class of business or geographical segment that is significant to an entity as a whole should be identified as a reportable segment. For the purposes of this accounting standard a segment should normally be regarded as significant if:

(a) its third party turnover is ten per cent or more of the total third party turnover of the entity; or

(b) its segment result, whether profit or loss, is ten per cent or more of the combined result of all segments in profit or of all segments in loss, whichever combined result is the greater; or

(c) its net assets are ten per cent or more of the total net assets of the entity.

10 The directors should review the definitions of the segments annually and re-define them when appropriate. In doing so the directors should have regard to the fundamental objective of this accounting standard, which is to achieve, as far as possible, consistency and comparability between years.

*Throughout this statement of standard accounting practice, references to paragraph 55 of Schedule 4 to the Companies Act 1985 should be read in the Republic of Ireland as references to paragraph 41 of the Schedule to the Companies (Amendment) Act 1986.

Classes of business

11 A separate class of business is a distinguishable component of an entity that provides a separate product or service or a separate group of related products or services.

12 When deciding whether or not an entity operates in different classes of business, the directors should take into account the following factors:

(a) the nature of the products or services;

(b) the nature of the production processes;

(c) the markets in which the products or services are sold;

(d) the distribution channels for the products;

(e) the manner in which the entity's activities are organised;

(f) any separate legislative framework relating to part of the business, for example, a bank or an insurance company.

13 Although it is possible to identify certain characteristics that differentiate between classes of business, no single set of characteristics is universally applicable nor is any single characteristic determinative in all cases. Consequently, determination of an entity's classes of business must depend on the judgement of the directors.

Geographical segments

14 A geographical segment is a geographical area comprising an individual country or a group of countries in which an entity operates, or to which it supplies products or services.

15 A geographical analysis should help the user of the financial statements to assess the extent to which an entity's operations are subject to factors such as the following:

(a) expansionist or restrictive economic climates;

(b) stable or unstable political regimes;

(c) exchange control regulations;

(d) exchange rate fluctuations.

16 It is not practicable to define a method of grouping that will reflect all the differences between international business environments and that would apply to all entities. The selected grouping should reflect the purpose of presenting segmental information (as set out in paragraph 1) and the factors noted in paragraphs 8 and 15. Although geographical proximity may indicate similar economic trends and risks, this will not necessarily be the case.

Information to be disclosed

General

17 The entity should define in its financial statements each reported class of business and geographical segment.

Turnover

18 The factors listed in paragraph 15 apply both to the geographical locations of the entity's operations and to the geographical locations of its markets. The user of the financial statements gains a fuller understanding of the entity's exposure to these factors, if turnover is disclosed according to both location of operations and location of markets. For the purposes of this accounting standard, origin of turnover is the geographical area *from* which products or services are supplied to a third party or another segment. Destination of turnover is the geographical area *to* which goods or services are supplied. Because disclosure relating to segment results and net assets will generally be based on location of operations, an analysis of turnover on the same basis will enable the user to match turnover, result and net assets on a consistent basis, and to relate all three to the perceived risks and opportunities of the segments. For these reasons this accounting standard requires the disclosure of sales by origin, but reporting entities should also disclose turnover by destination unless there is no material difference between the two. If there is no material difference, a statement to that effect is required.

19 Inter-segment sales and transfers are often a material part of the total turnover of the reportable segments and in such cases they should be analysed segmentally and shown separately. The geographical analysis of inter-segment turnover should be disclosed by origin. Analysis by destination usually has little or no value and would not normally be provided.

20 The Companies Act 1985 and the Companies (Northern Ireland) Order 1986 contain provisions exempting banking and insurance companies and groups from the requirement to disclose turnover in certain circumstances. In the Republic of Ireland, similar exemptions are extended to special classes of companies (banking, discount and insurance companies) under the Companies Act 1963. Certain other entities — for example, building societies — are subject to different statutory rules from those applied to companies. Where turnover is not required by statute to be disclosed, it is not required by this accounting standard to be disclosed segmentally. The fact that such turnover has not been disclosed segmentally should be stated.

Segment result

21 The entity should disclose the result of each reportable segment before accounting for taxation, minority interests and extraordinary items. The geographical analysis of segment result should normally be based on the areas from which products or services are supplied.

22 In the majority of entities, different classes of business or geographical segments are financed by different proportions of interest-bearing debt and equity. The interest earned or incurred by individual segments is therefore a result of the entity's overall financial policy rather than a proper reflection of the results of the various segments. Consequently, comparisons of profit between segments or between different years for the same segment are likely to be meaningless if interest is included in arriving at the result. For these reasons, it will normally be appropriate for segment results to be disclosed before taking account of interest. However, where all or part of the entity's business is to earn and/or incur interest (as in the financial sector, for example), or where interest income or expense is central to the business (as in the contracting or travel businesses, for example), interest should normally be included in arriving at the segment result.

Common costs

23 Common costs are costs relating to more than one segment. They should be treated in the way that the directors deem most appropriate in pursuance of the objectives of segmental reporting. Entities may apportion some common costs for the purposes of internal reporting and, in such cases, it may be reasonable for such costs to be similarly apportioned for external reporting purposes. If the apportionment would be misleading, common costs should not be apportioned in the segmental disclosures but should be deducted from the total of the segment results. Costs that are directly attributable to individual reportable segments are not common costs for the purposes of this accounting standard and therefore should be allocated to those segments, irrespective of the fact that they may have been borne by a different segment or by the Head Office.

Segment net assets

24 The net assets of each reportable segment should be disclosed. In most cases these will be the non-interest bearing operating assets less the non-interest bearing operating liabilities. However, to the extent that the segment result is disclosed after accounting for interest as described in paragraph 22, the corresponding interest-bearing operating assets and liabilities should also be included.

25 Segment operating assets and liabilities may include assets and liabilities relating exclusively to one segment and also an allocated portion of assets and liabilities that relate jointly to more than one segment. Assets and liabilities used jointly by more than one segment should be allocated to the segments on a reasonable basis. Assets and liabilities that are not used in the operations of any segment should not be allocated to segments. Operating assets of a segment should not normally include loans or advances to, or investments in, another segment unless interest therefrom has been included in arriving at the segment result on the basis set out in paragraph 22.

Associated undertakings

26 Sometimes associated undertakings form a significant part of a reporting entity's results or assets. In such circumstances the following information should be analysed segmentally and shown separately in the segmental report:

(a) the reporting entity's share of the profits or losses of associated undertakings before accounting for taxation, minority interests and extraordinary items; and

(b) the reporting entity's share of the net assets of associated undertakings (including goodwill to the extent that it has not been written off) stated, where possible, after attributing fair values to the net assets at the date of acquisition of the interest in each associated undertaking.

However, it is recognised that this information might be unobtainable or publication might be prejudicial to the business of the associate. In such circumstances the disclosure is not required but the reason for non-disclosure should be stated by way of note, together with a brief description of the omitted business or businesses.

27 For the purposes of this accounting standard, associated companies form a significant part of the reporting entity's results or assets if, in total, they account for at least 20% of the total result or 20% of the total net assets of the reporting entity.

General

28 The total of the amounts disclosed by segment should agree with the related total in the financial statements. If it does not, the reporting entity should provide a reconciliation between the two figures. Reconciling items should be properly identified and explained.

29 Comparative figures for the previous accounting period should be provided. If a change is made to the definitions of the segments or to the accounting policies that are adopted for reporting segmental information, the nature of the change should be disclosed. The reason for the change and the effect of the change should be stated. The previous year's figures should be restated to reflect the change.

Part 2 — Definition of terms

30 A *class of business* is a distinguishable component of an entity that provides a separate product or service or a separate group of related products or services.

31 A *geographical segment* is a geographical area comprising an individual country or group of countries in which an entity operates, or to which it supplies products or services.

32 *Origin* of turnover is the geographical segment from which products or service are supplied to a third party or to another segment.

33 *Destination* of turnover is the geographical segment to which products or services are supplied.

Part 3 — Standard accounting practice

34 If an entity has two or more classes of business, or operates in two or more geographical segments which differ substantially from each other, it should define its classes of business and geographical segments in its financial statements, and it should report with respect to each class of business and geographical segment the following financial information:

(a) turnover, distinguishing between (i) turnover derived from external customers and (ii) turnover derived from other segments;

(b) result, before accounting for taxation, minority interests and extraordinary items; and

(c) net assets.

The reporting entity should disclose the geographical segmentation of turnover by origin. It should also disclose turnover to third parties by destination or state where appropriate that this amount is not materially different from turnover to third parties by origin. Segment result will normally be disclosed before taking account of interest. However, where all or part of the entity's business is to earn and/or incur interest, or where interest income or expense is central to the business, interest should normally be included in arriving at the segment result. Net assets will normally be non-interest bearing operating assets less the non-interest bearing operating liabilities, but to the extent that the segment result is disclosed after accounting for interest the corresponding interest-bearing assets or liabilities should also be included.

35 When both parent and consolidated financial statements are presented, segmental information should be presented on the basis of the consolidated financial statements.

36 The reporting entity should disclose the following information segmentally in relation to its associated undertakings if these account for at least 20% of its total result or 20% of its total net assets:

(a) the entity's share of the results of associated undertakings before accounting for taxation, minority interests and extraordinary items; and

(b) the entity's share of the net assets of associated undertakings (including goodwill to the extent it has not been written off) stated, where possible, after attributing fair values to the net assets at the date of acquisition of the interest in each associated undertaking.

The segmental disclosure should be of the aggregate amounts for all associated undertakings for which the information is available and should be shown separately in the segmental report. However, this information need not be disclosed if it is unobtainable or publication would be prejudicial to the business of the associate. In such circumstances, the reason for non-disclosure should be stated by way of note, together with a brief description of the omitted business or businesses.

37 The total of the amounts disclosed by segment should agree with the related total in the financial statements. If it does not, the reporting entity should provide a reconciliation between the two amounts. Reconciling items should be properly identified and explained.

38 Comparative figures for the previous accounting period should be provided. If, however, on the first occasion on which an entity provides a segmental report the necessary information is not readily available, comparative figures need not be provided.

39 The directors should re-define the segments when appropriate. If a change is made to the definitions of the segments or to the accounting policies that are adopted for reporting segmental information, the nature of the change should be disclosed. The reason for the change and its effect should be stated. The previous year's figures should be re-stated to reflect the change.

40 This accounting standard contains provisions relating to the statutory segmental disclosure requirements contained in companies legislation in the United Kingdom and the Republic of Ireland. All companies are required to comply with these provisions.

41 This accounting standard also contains provisions relating to segmental disclosures which are not required by companies legislation.* These provisions apply to any entity that:

(a) is a public limited company or that has a public limited company as a subsidiary; or

(b) is a banking or insurance company or group (as defined for the purposes of Part VII of the Companies Act 1985); or

(c) exceeds the criteria, multiplied in each case by 10, for defining a medium-sized company under Section 247** of the Companies Act 1985, as amended from time to time by statutory instrument.

However, a subsidiary that is not a public limited company or a banking or insurance company need not comply with these provisions if its parent provides segmental disclosures in compliance with this accounting standard.

42 All other entities are encouraged to apply the provisions of this accounting standard in all financial statements intended to give a true and fair view of the financial position and profit or loss.

43 Where, in the opinion of the directors, the disclosure of any information required by this accounting standard would be seriously prejudicial to the interests of the reporting entity, that information need not be disclosed. The fact that any such information has not been disclosed must be stated.

44 Entities that are not required by statute to disclose turnover in their financial statements are not required by this accounting standard to disclose turnover segmentally. The fact that turnover has not been disclosed segmentally should be stated in the financial statements.

*Disclosures not required by the Companies Act 1985 are those set out in paragraphs 34(a)ii, 34(b) in so far as it relates to geographical segment result, 34(c), 34 in so far as it relates to origin of turnover, and 36.

****Equivalent legal references**

Great Britain	Northern Ireland	Republic of Ireland
Companies Act 1985	*Companies (Northern Ireland) Order 1986*	*Companies (Amendment) Act 1986*
Section 247	Article 256 (as amended)	Section 8

Date from which effective

45 The provisions of this statement of standard accounting practice should be adopted as soon as possible and regarded as standard in respect of financial statements relating to accounting periods beginning on or after 1 July 1990.

Part 4 — Legal and International Stock Exchange requirements in Great Britain and Northern Ireland

Company law

All paragraph references, unless otherwise indicated, are to the Schedules to the Companies Act 1985 and the Companies (Northern Ireland) Order 1986.

46 Paragraph 55(1) of Schedule 4 requires all companies that, in the course of the financial year, have carried on business of two or more classes that (in the opinion of the directors) differ substantially from each other to state:

(a) a description of each class of business;

(b) the amount of turnover attributable to each class of business; and

(c) the amount of the profit or loss of the company before taxation that is, in the opinion of the directors, attributable to each class of business.

47 Paragraph 55(2) of Schedule 4 requires all companies that, in the course of the financial year, have supplied geographical markets that (in the opinion of the directors) differ substantially from each other to state the amount of the turnover attributable to each market.

48 Paragraph 55(3) of Schedule 4 provides that, in analysing the source (in terms of either classes of business or markets) of turnover or profit or loss for the purposes of paragraph 55, the directors of the company shall have regard to the manner in which the company's activities are organised.

49 Paragraph 55(4) of Schedule 4 provides that, for the purposes of paragraph 55:

(a) classes of business which, in the opinion of the directors, do not differ substantially from each other shall be treated as one class;

(b) markets which, in the opinion of the directors, do not differ substantially from each other shall be treated as one market; and

(c) any amounts properly attributable to one class of business or to one market which are not material may be included in the amount stated in respect of another.

50 Paragraph 55(5) of Schedule 4 states that where, in the opinion of the directors, the disclosure of any information required by paragraph 55 would be seriously prejudicial to the interests of the company, that information need not be disclosed but the fact that any such information has not been disclosed must be stated.

51 Schedule 9 deals with the special provisions for banking and insurance companies and groups. Paragraph 17 of Schedule 9 requires the following matters to be stated by way of note, if not otherwise shown:

(a) the turnover for the financial year, except in so far as it is attributable to the business of banking or discounting;

(b) if some or all of the turnover is omitted by reason of its being attributable to the business of banking or discounting, the fact that it is so omitted; and

(c) the method by which turnover stated is arrived at.

52 Paragraph 17(5) of Schedule 9 provides that a company should not be subject to the requirements of paragraph 17 if it is neither a parent company nor a subsidiary undertaking and the turnover which, apart from sub-paragraph 17(5), would be required to be stated does not exceed £1 million.

53 Schedule 10 deals with the directors' report where accounts are prepared in accordance with the special provisions for banking or insurance companies or groups. Paragraph 2 provides that where a company prepares group accounts in accordance with the special provisions and, in the course of the financial year to which the accounts relate, the group has carried on business of two or more classes (other than banking or discounting of a class prescribed for the purpose of paragraph 17(2) of that Schedule) that in the opinion of the directors differ substantially from each other, there shall be contained in the directors' report a statement of:

(a) the proportions in which the turnover for the financial year (so far as stated in the consolidated accounts) is divided amongst those classes (describing them); and

(b) as regards business of each class, the extent or approximate extent (expressed in money terms) to which, in the opinion of the directors, the carrying on of business of that class contributed to, or restricted, the profit or loss of the company for that year (before taxation).

Classes of business which, in the opinion of the directors, do not differ substantially from each other, are to be treated as one class.

International Stock Exchange

54 The International Stock Exchange of the United Kingdom and the Republic of Ireland Ltd sets out its requirements for segmental information in the 'Admission of Securities to Listing'. Section 5, Chapter 2, paragraph 21 (c) of that publication requires:

> "a geographical analysis of both net turnover and contribution to trading results of those trading operations carried on by the company (or group) outside the United Kingdom and the Republic of Ireland".

55 No analysis of the contribution to trading results is required unless the contribution to profit or loss from a specific area is 'abnormal' in nature. 'Abnormal' is defined as substantially out of line with the normal ratio of profit to turnover.

Part 5 — Legal and International Stock Exchange requirements in the Republic of Ireland

Company law

All paragraph references, unless otherwise indicated, are to the Schedule to the Companies (Amendment) Act 1986.

56 Paragraph 41(1) requires all companies that, in the course of the financial year, have carried on business of two or more classes that (in the opinion of the directors) differ substantially from each other to state:

(a) a description of each class of business; and

(b) the amount of turnover attributable to each class of business.

57 Paragraph 41(2) requires all companies that, in the course of the financial year, have supplied geographical markets that (in the opinion of the directors) differ substantially from each other, to state the amount of the turnover attributable to each market.

58 Paragraph 41(3) provides that, in analysing the source (in terms of either classes of business or markets) of turnover, the directors of the company shall have regard to the manner in which the company's activities are organised.

59 Paragraph 41(4) provides that, for the purposes of paragraph 41:

(a) classes of business which, in the opinion of the directors, do not differ substantially from each other shall be treated as one class;

(b) markets which, in the opinion of the directors, do not differ substantially from each other shall be treated as one market; and

(c) any amounts properly attributable to one class of business or to one market which are not material may be included in the amount stated in respect of another.

60 Paragraph 41(5) states that where, in the opinion of the directors; the disclosure of any information required by paragraph 41 would be seriously prejudicial to the interests of the company, that information need not be disclosed but the fact that any such information has not been disclosed must be stated.

61 Banking, discount and insurance companies are regarded as special classes of companies and as such come within Part III of the Sixth Schedule to the Companies Act 1963 which exempts them from the disclosure requirements of the Schedule to the Companies (Amendment) Act 1986.

62 The International Stock Exchange of the United Kingdom and the Republic of Ireland Ltd sets out its requirements for segmental information in the 'Admission of Securities to Listing'. Section 5, Chapter 2, paragraph 21 (c) of that publication requires:

> "a geographical analysis of both net turnover and contribution to trading results of those trading operations carried on by the company (or group) outside the United Kingdom and the Republic of Ireland".

63 No analysis of the contribution to trading results is required unless the contribution to profit or loss from a specific area is 'abnormal' in nature. 'Abnormal' is defined as substantially out of line with the normal ratio of profit to turnover.

Part 6 — Compliance with International Accounting Standard No. 14 'Reporting Financial Information by Segment'

64 Compliance with the requirements of this accounting standard will ensure compliance with IAS 14 in all material respects, except in the following circumstances:

(a) This accounting standard does not require the basis of inter-segment pricing to be disclosed. This information must be disclosed in order to comply with IAS 14.

(b) This accounting standard requires the disclosure of segment 'net assets', whereas IAS 14 refers to 'assets employed'. However, as stated in paragraph 34, net assets will normally be the non-interest bearing operating assets less the non-interest bearing operating liabilities, and in those cases net assets will not be materially different from assets employed.

(c) This accounting standard gives the following exemptions which do not appear in IAS 14.

   (i) An entity need not disclose segmental information if disclosure would be seriously prejudicial to its interests.

   (ii) An entity that is not required by statute to disclose turnover is not required to disclose turnover segmentally.

   (iii) A subsidiary that is not a public limited company or a banking or insurance company need not make the segmental disclosures required by this accounting standard if its parent does so.

Appendix: Illustrative segmental report

This Appendix is for general guidance only and does not form part of the Statement of Standard Accounting Practice

CLASSES OF BUSINESS	Industry A		Industry B		Other industries		Group	
	1990 £000	1989 £000	1990 £000	1989 £000	1990 £000	1989 £000	1990 £000	1989 £000
TURNOVER								
Total sales	33,000	30,000	42,000	38,000	26,000	23,000	101,000	91,000
Intersegment sales	(4,000)	—	—	—	(12,000)	(14,000)	(16,000)	(14,000)
Sales to third parties	29,000	30,000	42,000	38,000	14,000	9,000	85,000	77,000
PROFIT BEFORE TAXATION								
Segment profit	3,000	2,500	4,500	4,000	1,800	1,500	9,300	8,000
Common costs							300	300
Operating profit							9,000	7,700
Net interest							(400)	(500)
							8,600	7,200
Group share of the profits before taxation of associated undertakings	1,000	1,000	1,400	1,200	—	—	2,400	2,200
Group profit before taxation							11,000	9,400
NET ASSETS								
Segment net assets	17,600	15,000	24,000	25,000	19,400	19,000	61,000	59,000
Unallocated assets							3,000	3,000
							64,000	62,000
Group share of the net assets of associated undertakings	10,200	8,000	8,800	9,000	—	—	19,000	17,000
Total net assets							83,000	79,000

GEOGRAPHICAL SEGMENTS	United Kingdom		North America		Far East		Other		Group	
	1990	1989	1990	1989	1990	1989	1990	1989	1990	1989
TURNOVER	£000	£000	£000	£000	£000	£000	£000	£000	£000	£000
Turnover by destination										
Sales to third parties	34,000	31,000	16,000	14,500	25,000	23,000	10,000	8,500	85,000	77,000
Turnover by origin										
Total sales	38,000	34,000	29,000	27,500	23,000	23,000	12,000	10,500	102,000	95,000
Intersegment sales	—	—	(8,000)	(9,000)	(9,000)	(9,000)	—	—	(17,000)	(18,000)
Sales to third parties	38,000	34,000	21,000	18,500	14,000	14,000	12,000	10,500	85,000	77,000
PROFIT BEFORE TAXATION										
Segment profit	4,000	2,900	2,500	2,300	1,800	1,900	1,000	900	9,300	8,000
Common costs									300	300
Operating profit									9,000	7,700
Net interest									(400)	(500)
									8,600	7,200
Group share of the profits before taxation of associated undertakings	950	1,000	1,450	1,200	—	—	—	—	2,400	2,200
Group profit before taxation									11,000	9,400
NET ASSETS										
Segment net assets	16,000	15,000	25,000	26,000	16,000	15,000	4,000	3,000	61,000	59,000
Unallocated assets									3,000	3,000
									64,000	62,000
Group share of the net assets of associated undertakings	8,500	7,000	10,500	10,000	—	—	—	—	19,000	17,000
Total net assets									83,000	79,000

Unallocated assets consist of the Group's head office in London amounting to £2.4million (1989 £2.5 million) and at the Group's regional office in Hong Kong amounting to £0.6 million (1989 £0.5 million)

Consolidated accounts — Interim Statement

Reproduced with the permission of the Accounting Standards Board

Statement on the interpretation of the Companies Act for the preparation of consolidated accounts and changes to SSAP 1 'Accounting for associated companies' and SSAP 14 'Group accounts' to remove inconsistencies with the 1985 Act as amended .

Preface

This statement is in two parts. Part 1 gives guidance on how the provisions of the 1985 Companies Act, as amended in 1989, are to be interpreted in the preparation of consolidated accounts. Part 2 amends SSAP 1 'Accounting for associated companies' and SSAP 14 'Group accounts' refer to this guidance and to eliminate inconsistencies with the law that have arisen since the publication or revision of those standards. Some sections of these standards are being withdrawn and certain minor wording changes are being made. Reference to this statement is now made in SSAP 1 and SSAP 14 which has the effect of giving this statement the force of an accounting standard. These amendments do not apply to companies registered in the Republic of Ireland.

Introduction

1 The Accounting Standards Board has issued this interim statement to give timely guidance on the interpretation of certain of the recent legislative changes in Great Britain and Northern Ireland for the preparation of consolidated accounts and to make the changes in SSAP 1 'Accounting for associated companies' and SSAP 14 'Group accounts' that are required as a consequence of the legal changes and the Board's statement. Changes in the law relating to the preparation of group accounts were introduced into the Companies Act 1985 by the Companies Act 1989. The 1985 Act as amended is referred to in this statement as 'the Act'. In due course the Board expects to conduct a full review of the issues raised in the preparation of consolidated accounts, including the treatment of associated undertakings and joint ventures, and to issue accounting standards as appropriate.

2 The Board adopted SSAP 1 and SSAP 14 together with other accounting standards of its predecessor body, the Accounting Standards Committee, at its first meeting on 24 August 1990. Incorporating references to this guidance in SSAP 1 and SSAP 14 has the effect of giving this guidance itself the force of an accounting standard. Where the accounting procedures set out in SSAP 1 and SSAP 14 are unchanged they should still be followed if they are relevant.

3 Part 1 of this statement gives guidance on how the provisions of the 1985 Companies Act, as amended in 1989, are to be interpreted in the preparation of consolidated accounts. The Board's guidance is given directly by reference to the relevant sections of the Act. The guidance given in this statement can serve to explain or clarify the effect of the legal provisions. In the interests of good accounting the Board may also set limits to the use of treatments allowed but not required by the Act. However it should be noted that the Board's guidance is given in addition to the Act in order to aid its application and should be read in conjunction with the provisions of the Act. These remain paramount for companies reporting under it.

4 Part 2 of this statement amends certain paragraphs of SSAP 1 'Accounting for associated companies' and SSAP 14 'Group accounts'. These amendments are required either as a result of the changes in the law or to make the accounting standards consistent with this statement.

5 A commentary on this statement is provided in the Appendix. The commentary on Part 1 discusses the statement in the context of the comments received on ED 50 'Consolidated Accounts'. The commentary on Part 2 gives the reasons for the amendments to SSAP 1 and SSAP 14.

Application of the statement in Ireland

Republic of Ireland

6 This statement amends SSAP 1 and SSAP 14 in order to make them consistent with the Companies Act 1985, as amended. Accordingly, the amendments do not apply to the operation of SSAP 1 and SSAP 14 in the Republic of Ireland. The Board notes the continuing application of these accounting standards in their unamended form to companies registered in the Republic of Ireland through their continuing promulgation by the Council of the Institute of Chartered Accountants in Ireland.

Northern Ireland

7 This statement applies in Northern Ireland as in Great Britain except that the changes in the law relating to the preparation of consolidated accounts were introduced into the Companies (Northern Ireland) Order 1986 by the Companies (Northern Ireland) Order 1990. Reference to 'the Act' in this statement should be read as referring to the relevant Articles, when commended, in the amended 1986 Order.

Date from which the statement is effective

8 This statement is effective for financial years commencing on or after 23 December 1989.

Part 1 — Guidance on interpretation of the Act

Identifying a parent undertaking and its subsidiary undertaking

9 The 1989 amendments to the 1985 Act change the circumstances in which an undertaking is to be treated as a parent undertaking in relation to another undertaking, its subsidiary undertaking. The main provisions of the Act dealing with this question are in Section 258, where the Act provides how 'parent undertaking' and 'subsidiary undertaking' are to be construed, and Schedule 10A, which explains certain expressions used in Section 258. The Board considers that, in the main, these provisions by themselves provide a sufficient framework for the effective application of the Act. However the Act introduces several new expressions on which there is a need for additional guidance to clarify how such expressions should be applied in the preparation of consolidated accounts. Indeed there was an expectation in drafting the Act that accounting standards should provide such additional guidance.

10 Section 258(4) gives one of the new conditions by which the Act requires one undertaking to treat another as its subsidiary undertaking.

"An undertaking is also a parent undertaking in relation to another undertaking, a subsidiary undertaking, if it has a participating interest in the undertaking and:

(a) it actually exercises a dominant influence over it, or

(b) it and the subsidiary undertaking are managed on a unified basis."

'Dominant influence', 'actually exercises' and 'managed on a unified basis' are expressions used for the first time in the Act, which it would be helpful for an accounting standard to interpret. Similarly, some further guidance is useful on the circumstances under which an interest may be said to be 'held on a long-term basis'.

11 'Participating interest' is defined in the Act (s.260) essentially as "an interest held by an undertaking in the shares of another undertaking which it holds on a long-term basis for the purpose of securing a contribution to its activities by the exercise of control or influence arising from or related to that interest". A holding of 20 per cent or more of the shares of an undertaking is presumed to be a participating interest unless the contrary is shown. An interest in shares for the purpose of this definition includes an interest which is convertible into an interest in shares as well as an option to acquire shares or any such interest.

Dominant influence

12 'Dominant influence' is used in two distinct ways in the Act. It is first used in a very restricted sense in Section 258(2)(c) in relation to provisions in the undertaking's memorandum or articles or a control contract. This meaning is discussed in paragraphs 16-18 below. The more general meaning of 'dominant influence' relates to the case where the actual exercise of dominant influence over an undertaking, combined with a participating interest in that undertaking, leads to that undertaking being a subsidiary undertaking for the purpose of the Act. 'Dominant influence' as used in this context is discussed in paragraph 13 below.

'Dominant influence' and 'actually exercises' — for Section 258(4)

13 Dominant influence is effective control with or without the legal rights that normally signify control. Control over an undertaking is the ability to direct that undertaking. In the context of consolidated accounts, control means the ability of an undertaking to direct the financial and operating policies of another undertaking with a view to gaining benefits from its activities.

14 Actual exercise of dominant influence is not defined in the Act but the result of the actual exercise of dominant influence is that major decisions will be taken in accordance with the wishes of the dominant party whether these are expressed or perceived. The actual exercise could be either active involvement of the dominant party in directing the operating and financial policies of another undertaking or a more passive approach. In the latter case, a dominant undertaking might have put itself in a position to be able to provide general guidance on the financial and operating policies of another undertaking without regular or day to day involvement but with a veto on any policies of which the dominant undertaking disapproved; the result being that the directors of the undertaking which is dominated in practice follow what are perceived to be the wishes of the dominant undertaking. A power of veto over the financial and operating policies of another undertaking can indicate that the undertaking holding the veto has a dominant influence over that other undertaking if the veto is held only by the dominant undertaking, or undertakings connected with it, and no similar veto is held by any other undertaking. It would generally be appropriate to presume that a dominant influence is actually being exercised when one undertaking holds reserve powers which could be exerted to ensure that another undertaking aligned its financial and operating policies in accordance with the wishes of the undertaking holding the reserve powers.

15 In making a judgement on whether one undertaking actually exercises a dominant influence over another it is important to consider in full the relationship between the two undertakings and the effect of any agreements, formal and informal, between them. Commercial relationships such as that of a supplier, customer or lender do not of themselves constitute dominant influence.

'Dominant influence' — for Section 258(2)(c)

16 Section 258(2)(c) states that an undertaking is a parent undertaking in relation to another undertaking, a subsidiary undertaking, if — "it has the right to exercise a dominant influence over the undertaking—

(i) by virtue of provisions contained in the undertaking's memorandum or articles, or

(ii) by virtue of a control contract."

17 Schedule 10A.4(1) of the Act states that "for the purposes of Section 258(2)(c) an undertaking shall not be regarded as having the right to exercise a dominant influence over another undertaking unless it has a right to give directions with respect to the operating and financial policies of that other undertaking which its directors are obliged to comply with whether or not they are for the benefit of that other undertaking". This is a much more restrictive definition than the interpretation of 'actually exercises dominant influence' given above in paragraphs 13-15. However, the Act specifically provides that this paragraph (Sch 10A.4(3)) shall not be read as affecting the construction of the expression 'actually exercises a dominant influence'.

18 There exists a common law duty for the directors of any company to act in the best interests of that company. For this reason there is some doubt whether a right to exercise a dominant influence, as defined in Sch I10A.4(1), would be legal for companies established under the laws of the United Kingdom under the standard long form of objects clause in general use. It would seem that, as a minimum, a control contract giving such influence could only be legal where the subsidiary undertaking's objects clause properly authorised the entry into such a contract.

'Managed on a unified basis'

19 Two or more undertakings are managed on a unified basis if the whole of the operations of the undertakings are integrated and they are managed as a single unit. Unified management does not arise solely by virtue of an undertaking's managing another.

'Held on a long-term basis'

20 An interest should be considered as held on a long-term basis where it is held other than 'exclusively with a view to subsequent resale'.

Exclusion of a subsidiary undertaking from consolidation

21 The Act requires that all subsidiary undertakings of the parent company should be consolidated except where the exclusion of a subsidiary undertaking is permitted or required in the Act. Section 229 sets out the grounds on which a subsidiary need not be or should not be consolidated by its parent undertaking.

Exclusions permitted by the Act

22 A subsidiary undertaking may be excluded from consolidation:

(a) "if its inclusion is not material for the purpose of giving a true and fair view; but two or more undertakings may be excluded only if they are not material taken together";

(b) "where severe long-term restrictions substantially hinder the exercise of the rights of the parent company over the assets or management of that undertaking";

(c) "the information necessary for the preparation of group accounts cannot be obtained without disproportionate expense or undue delay";

(d) "the interest of the parent company is held exclusively with a view to subsequent resale and the undertaking has not previously been included in consolidated group accounts prepared by the parent company".

23 The value of the information provided about a group by its consolidated accounts depends on the extent to which the information about the group is complete. The information is complete if all the undertakings that are part of the group, i.e., that are subsidiary undertakings, are included in the consolidation. Thus a subsidiary undertaking should be excluded from consolidation only in exceptional circumstances. Most special circumstances relating to a subsidiary undertaking are best dealt with by disclosure, for example by giving segmental information where its activities or risks differ from those of other members of the group or by giving details of any relevant restrictions on the movement or use of its assets, rather than by not consolidating it.

24 Exceptionally, circumstances may exist that make it inappropriate to consolidate a subsidiary undertaking. In these circumstances that undertaking should be required, and not merely allowed, to be excluded from consolidation with the rest of its group. In order to help preparers identify the exceptional cases where it is inappropriate to consolidate a subsidiary undertaking, the circumstances under which the Act allows or requires a subsidiary undertaking not to be included in the consolidation of its group are discussed below.

Subsidiary undertaking(s) not material — s.229(2)

25 The Board does not intend its accounting standards to apply to immaterial items as, by definition, choices on how they should be treated do not affect the view given by the accounts.

Severe long-term restrictions — s.229(3)(a)

26 Where severe long-term restrictions substantially hinder the exercise of the rights of the parent undertaking over the assets and management of its subsidiary undertaking, the Board considers that such a subsidiary undertaking should not be consolidated. However, the restrictions must indeed be severe. A subsidiary undertaking should not be excluded merely because restrictions are threatened or another party has the power to impose them; restrictions must actually be in place on a day-to-day basis. Generally, restrictions are dealt with better by disclosure than by non-consolidation. For example, difficulties in making remittances do not of themselves necessarily amount to severe long-term restrictions that justify non-consolidation. However, severe difficulties in making remittances may indicate that severe long-term restrictions over the assets and management of the subsidiary undertaking are in force.

Disproportionate expense and undue delay in obtaining the necessary information — s.229(3)(b)

27 The Board considers that the information given about a group in its consolidated accounts must be complete in order to be of value and in order to be capable of giving a true and fair view of the group. Thus 'disproportionate expense' and 'undue delay' can only be relevant when considered in the context of a non-material subsidiary. Neither expense nor delay can justify excluding from the consolidated accounts of the group a subsidiary undertaking that is material in the context of the group.

Interest is held exclusively with a view to subsequent resale — s.229(3)(c)

28 An interest in another undertaking is held exclusively with a view to subsequent resale if a purchaser has been identified or is being sought and the interest is reasonably expected to be disposed of within one year of the date of acquisition of that interest. An interest which is acquired involuntarily, for example on the crystallising of a security held for a loan, should also be treated as held exclusively with a view to a subsequent resale, unless the interest has become part of the continuing activities of the group of the holder acts as if it intends the interest to form part of such activities of the group.

Exclusion required by the Act

Different activities

29 Section 229(4) of the Act requires that subsidiary undertakings be excluded from consolidation "where the activities of one or more subsidiary undertakings are so different from those of other undertakings to be included in the consolidation that their inclusion would be incompatible with the obligation to give a true and fair view". This does not apply "merely because some of the undertakings are industrial, some commercial and some provide services, or because they carry on industrial or commercial activities involving different products or provide different services". Because consolidated information can be analysed further in the notes, or on the face of the primary statements, it is exceptional that the activities of a subsidiary undertaking should so differ from those of other undertakings included in the consolidation that including that subsidiary in the consolidation would be incompatible with the obligation to give a true and fair view.

30 The circumstances under which a subsidiary undertaking's activities are so different that its inclusion in the consolidated accounts would be incompatible with the obligation to show a true and fair view are so exceptional that the Board considers it misleading to link them to any particular contrast of activities. Unless, exceptionally, there are conclusive grounds for believing that the inclusion of a subsidiary undertaking in the consolidated accounts is incompatible with showing a true and fair view of the group, all subsidiary undertakings, whatever their activities, should be consolidated with the group. The grounds for considering that the inclusion of such a subsidiary undertaking would not be compatible with the true and fair view should be explained in a note to the accounts.

Elimination of group transactions

31 The Act allows the elimination of the profits and losses resulting from transactions between undertakings included in the consolidation to be made in proportion to the group's interest in the shares of the undertakings (Schedule 4A.6). In line with a clear majority of the opinions expressed on ED 50, the Board requires that transactions of any sort between group undertakings should be eliminated in full. Profit or loss adjustments in relation to such eliminated transactions should be set against both the controlling interest and the minority in proportion to their interests in the undertaking whose individual accounts recorded such profits or losses.

Joint ventures

32 The Act introduces the term 'joint venture' for the first time into company law. Schedule 4A. 19 describes a joint venture and permits a joint venture that is neither a body corporate nor a subsidiary to be dealt with in the consolidated accounts by the method of proportional consolidation. In the Act, a joint venture is essentially an undertaking jointly managed by one undertaking included in the consolidation with one or more undertakings not included in the consolidation. The Act uses 'joint management' to describe something which could in fact more aptly be described as joint control. The Act's provisions do not require the involvement of the joint venturers in the day-to-day operation of the venture's business nor do they exclude from the definition of a joint venture an undertaking which is managed on a day-to-day basis by a single operator. The Board considers that the general description of a joint venture in the Act can usefully be supplemented by a definition which identifies those key characteristics of a joint venture that distinguish it from other kinds of undertaking.

Definition of a joint venture

33 A joint venture is an undertaking by which its participants expect to achieve some common purpose or benefit. It is controlled jointly by two or more venturers. Joint control is the contractually agreed sharing of control.

Quasi subsidiaries

34 The Board has now received the comments on ED 49 'Reflecting the substance of transactions in assets and liabilities'. When the Board has completed its review of the comments, it intends to issue an accounting standard which will identify certain undertakings as quasi subsidiaries and which will set out how such quasi subsidiaries are to be treated.

Reference to Appendix

35 Paragraphs A I A 12 of the Appendix to this statement expand, where appropriate, the Board's reasons for adopting certain interpretations and, in particular, explain how the comments received on ED 50 'Consolidated accounts' have influenced the guidance given.

Part 2 — Changes to SSAP 1 and SSAP 14

Introduction

36 This part of the statement sets out the changes made to SSAP 1 'Accounting for associated companies' and SSAP 14 'Group accounts' for Great Britain and Northern Ireland to add references to this guidance and to remove inconsistencies with the Companies Act 1985 as amended by the Companies Act 1989 (the Act). These changes consist mainly of the withdrawal of sections that are inconsistent, although some minor wording changes are also necessary. The most important additions are those in paragraph

18 of SSAP 1 and in paragraph 15 of SSAP 14 which add references to this statement to SSAP 1 and SSAP 14. Elsewhere, the Board has sought only the minimum adjustments necessary to bring SSAPs 1 and 14 in line with the Act and avoid inconsistency in applying SSAP 1 and SSAP 14 as accounting standards within the meaning of Section 256 of the Act. As noted in paragraph 6 of this statement, the amendments made do not apply to companies registered in the Republic of Ireland.

37 The changes do not amount to a full review of SSAP 1 and SSAP 14 by the Accounting Standards Board. The Board is conducting a full review of these Standards in the light of the comments received on the Accounting Standards Committee's (ASC's) exposure draft ED 50 'Consolidated accounts'. In due course, the Board will publish its requirements on the appropriate treatments of matters now covered by SSAPs 1 and 14 and the old accounting standards will be withdrawn.

Change to SSAP 1 'Accounting for Associated Companies'.

38

Changes made (SSAP 1 references)	***Amended paragraphs***
Paragraph 10 — insert "other" between "partnerships or" and "non-corporate"	**10** In some cases, partnerships or other non-corporate joint ventures can have features which justify accounting for a proportionate share of individual assets and liabilities as well as profits or losses.
Paragraph 13 (a) — withdrawn (b) — "and is substantial" withdrawn	**13** (b) the interest of the investing group or company is for the long term and, having regard to the disposition of the other share- holdings, the investing group or company is in a position to exercise a significant influence over the company in which the investment is made.
Paragraph 14 — "is not effectively that of a partner in a joint venture or consortium and" withdrawn	**14** Where the interest of the investing group or company amounts to 20 per cent or more of the equity voting rights of a company, it should be presumed that the investing group or company has the ability to exercise significant influence over that company unless it can clearly demonstrate otherwise. For example, there may exist one or more other large shareholdings which prevent the exercise of such influence.

Changes made (SSAP 1 references)	Amended paragraphs
Paragraph 15 — "is not effectively that of a partner in a joint venture or consortium and" withdrawn	**15** Where the interest of the investing group or company amounts to less than 20 per cent of equity voting rights of a company it should be presumed that the investing group or company does not have the ability to exercise significant influence unless it can clearly demonstrate otherwise. Unless there are exceptional circumstances, this demonstration should include a statement from the company in which the investment is made that it accepts that the investing group or company is in a position to exercise significant influence over it.
Paragraph 17 —withdrawn	
Paragraph 18 — "(as defined in Part 2 above)" withdrawn — insert "other" between "partnerships or" and "non-corporate" — at last line, add "Associated companies should be accounted for in accordance with the Companies Act 1985 as amended in 1989 (the Act). The Act should be applied by referring to the Interim Statement — Consolidated Accounts issued by the Accounting Standards Board and dated December 1990."	**18** Income from investments of a company or its subsidiaries in associated companies should be brought into account on the following bases: (a) *In the investing company's own financial statements:* dividends received and receivable. (b) *In the investing group's consolidated financial statements (or the equivalent prepared in accordance with paragraphs 24 and 35 below):* the investing group's share of profits less losses of associated companies. These bases need not be applied to interests in partnerships or other non-corporate joint ventures where such arrangements have features which justify accounting for a proportionate share of individual assets and liabilities as well as profits or losses. Associated companies should be accounted for in accordance with the Companies Act 1985 as amended in 1989 (the Act). The Act should be applied by referring to the Interim Statement — Consolidated Accounts issued by the Accounting Standards Board and dated December 1990.

Changes made (SSAP 1 references)	***Amended paragraphs***
Paragraph 19 — "for example . . . associated companies" withdrawn.	**19** *Profit before tax.* The investing group should include in its consolidated financial statements the aggregate of its share of before tax profits less losses of associated companies. This item should be shown separately and suitably described.
Paragraph 24 —"Except where it is a wholly owned subsidiary" withdrawn; "unless the investing company is exempt from preparing consolidated financial statements, or would be exempt, if it had subsidiaries. Information about the associated companies should be reported" inserted between "its own profit and loss account" and "in such a way". —the next "its" after the insertion to be replaced by "the investing company's " and the following "the" to becomes "its". — reference to "the Companies Acts 1948 to 1981" to be replaced by "the Companies Act 1985". — in the last bracketed sentence "which do not have subsidiaries or which do not otherwise prepare consolidated financial statements" replaced by "showing the results of their associated companies in this way".	**24** An investing company which does not prepare consolidated financial statements should show the information required by paragraphs 19 to 23 of this SSAP by preparing a separate profit and loss account or by adding the information in supplementary form to its own profit and loss account unless the investing company is exempt from preparing consolidated financial statements, or would be exempt, if it had subsidiaries. Information about the associated companies should be reported in such a way that the investing company's share of the profits of its associated companies is not treated as realised for the purposes of the Companies Act 1985. (References in this SSAP to investing groups and consolidated financial statements are to be taken as embracing this information in the case of investing companies showing results of their associated companies in this way.)
Paragraph 35 —"a wholly owned subsidiary" withdrawn and replaced by "exempt from preparing consolidated accounts".	**35** Except where it is exempt from preparing consolidated accounts, an investing company which does not prepare consolidated financial statements should show the information required by paragraphs 25 to 34 of this SSAP by preparing a separate balance sheet or by adding the information in the supplementary form to its own balance sheet.

Changes made (SSAP 1 references)	***Amended paragraphs***
Paragraph 38 — "is" added in first line between "or company" and "in any company". — "is not effectively that of a partner in a joint venture or consortium" withdrawn and replaced by "or a proportionately consolidated joint venture". — "Department of Trade" changed to "the Secretary of State's".	**38** Where the interest of the investing group or company is in any company other than a subsidiary or a proportionately consolidated joint venture and the investing group or company holds 20 per cent or more of the equity voting rights of that company but does not account for that company as an associated company, details of the accounting treatment adopted, and the reason for doing so, should be stated by way of note to the financial statements. In those cases where disclosure of the reason would be harmful to the business, the directors may omit the information, after consultation with their auditors, (in a comparable manner to that permitted by the Companies Acts for subsidiaries where the disclosure would be harmful to the business except that the Secretary of State's approval would not be required in this case). Conversely, where the investing group or company holds less than 20 per cent of the equity voting rights of a company but accounts for that company as an associate, the basis on which significant influence is exercised should be stated.
Paragraph 49 — "Subject to Parts 4 and 5" withdrawn.	**49** The names of the principal associated companies should be disclosed in the financial statements of the investing group showing for each of these associated companies: (a) The proportion of the number of the issued shares of each class held by the investing group; and (b) an indication of the nature of its business.
Part 4 — note on legal requirements in Great Britain withdrawn.	
Part 5 — paragraphs 63-64 — Note on legal requirements in Northern Ireland withdrawn.	
Part 6 — compliance with International Accounting Standard No. 3 "Consolidated Financial Statements" withdrawn.	

Changes to SSAP 14 "Group Accounts"

39

Changes made (SSAP 14 references)	***Amended paragraphs***
Introductory section — 2nd paragraph withdrawn *"Compliance with this standard ... associated companies"* withdrawn.	
Paragraph 1 — last sentence "Alternative . . . conditions" withdrawn.	**1** Group accounts showing the state of affairs and profit or loss of a holding company and its subsidiaries have been required by law in most instances in the United Kingdom and Ireland for many years. In practice the group accounts usually take the form of consolidated financial statements which present the information contained in the separate financial statements of the holding company and its subsidiaries as if they were the financial statements of a single entity.
Paragraph 2 — withdrawn.	
Paragraph 7 — withdrawn.	
Paragraph 8 — "as defined above" withdrawn .	**8** *Holding company.* A company is a holding company of another if but only if that other is its subsidiary.
Paragraph 12 — "One form of group" withdrawn and replaced by "are". — "s" dropped from "presents".	**12** *Consolidated financial statements* are accounts which present the information contained in the separate financial statements of a holding company and its subsidiaries as if they were the financial statements of a single entity.

Changes made (SSAP 14 references)	***Amended paragraphs***
Paragraph 15 — 2nd sentence "The only . . . below." withdrawn and replaced by "Consolidated accounts should be prepared in accordance with the Companies Act 1985 as amended in 1989 (the Act). The Act should be applied by referring to the Interim Statement — Consolidated Accounts issued by the Accounting Standards Board and dated December 1990."	**15** A holding company should prepare group accounts in the form of a single set of consolidated financial statements covering the holding company and its subsidiary companies, at home and overseas. Consolidated accounts should be prepared in accordance with the Companies Act 1985 as amended in 1989 (the Act). The Act should be applied by referring to the Interim Statement — Consolidated Accounts issued by the Accounting Standards Board and dated December 1990. A description of the bases on which subsidiary companies have been dealt with in the group accounts should be given.
Paragraph 18 — "and if it is not practicable . . . as necessary)" withdrawn.	**18** If a subsidiary does not prepare its formal financial statements to the same date as the holding company appropriate adjustments should be made to the consolidated financial statements for any abnormal transactions in the intervening period. The following additional information should be given for each principal subsidiary with a different accounting date: (a) its name; and (b) its accounting date; and (c) the reason for using a different accounting date. Where the accounting period of a principal subsidiary was of a different length from that of the holding company the accounting period involved should be stated.
Paragraph 20 — "a wholly owned subsidiary" withdrawn and replaced by "exempt from the requirements to prepare consolidated accounts".	**20** When a company is not exempt from the requirements to prepare consolidated accounts and it does not prepare group accounts dealing with all its subsidiaries for one of the other reasons permitted under the Companies Acts, the reasons for the exclusion of any subsidiary must be stated. Consideration will need to be given to whether the resulting financial statements give a true and fair view of the position of the group as a whole.

Changes made (SSAP 14 references)	Amended paragraphs
Paragraph 21 — withdrawn.	
Paragraph 22 — withdrawn.	
Paragraph 23 — "on the grounds set out in paragraph 21(a)" withdrawn.	**23** Where a subsidiary is excluded from consolidation because of dissimilar activities, the group accounts should include separate financial statements for that subsidiary. They may be combined with the financial statements of other subsidiaries with similar operations, if appropriate. The separate financial statements should include the following information: (a) a note of the holding company's interest; (b) particulars of intra-group balances; (c) the nature of transactions with the rest of the group; and (d) a reconciliation with the amount included in the consolidated financial statements for the group's investment in the subsidiary which should be stated under the equity method of accounting.
Paragraph 24 —withdrawn.	
Paragraph 25 — "on the grounds set out in paragraph 21 (c)" withdrawn.	**25** Where a subsidiary is excluded from consolidation because of severe restrictions, the amount of the group's investment in the subsidiary should be stated in the consolidated balance sheet at the amount at which it would have been included under the equity method of accounting at the date the restrictions came into force. No further accruals should be made for its profits or losses. However, if the amount at which the investment is stated in the consolidated financial statements on this basis has been impaired by a decline in value of the investment (other than temporarily) provision for the loss should be made through the consolidated profit and loss account. For this purpose, investments should be considered individually and not in the aggregate.

Changes made (SSAP 14 references	***Amended paragraphs***
Paragraph 26 — "on the grounds set out in paragraph 21 (c)" withdrawn and replaced by "because of severe restrictions".	**26** Where a subsidiary is excluded from consolidation because of severe restrictions the following information should be disclosed in the group accounts: (a) its net assets; (b) its profits or losses for the period; (c) any amounts included in the consolidated profit and loss account in respect of: (i) dividends received; (ii) writing down of the investment.
Paragraph 27 — "set out in paragraph 21(d) that control is intended to be temporary" withdrawn and replaced by "that it is held exclusively for subsequent resale". — "temporary" in the next phrase withdrawn.	**27** Where a subsidiary is excluded from consolidation on the grounds that it is held exclusively for subsequent resale, the investment in the subsidiary should be stated in the consolidated balance sheet as a current asset at the lower of cost and net realisable value.
Part 4 — Note of legal requirements in Great Britain withdrawn.	
Part 5 — Section A, Note of legal requirements in Northern Ireland withdrawn.	
Part 6 — compliance with International Accounting Standard No 3 "Consolidated Financial Statements" withdrawn.	

40 SSAP 1 and SSAP 14 do not use the same terminology as the Act. However, this statement does not attempt to correct this as that would require reference to all the points where different usage arises. The main differences in terminology are:

Terminology

SSAPs 1 and 14	*The Act*
"company"	"undertaking"
"associated company"	"associated undertaking"
"subsidiary"	"subsidiary undertaking"
"holding company"	"parent undertaking"
"parent"	"parent undertaking"
"consolidated financial statements"	"consolidated accounts"

Reference to Appendix

41 The Appendix to this statement (paragraphs A13-A23) explains the changes made to SSAP 1 and SSAP 14.

APPENDIX

In developing its interim guidance, the Board has considered the comments that it has received to date on ED 50 'Consolidated accounts'. A request was made for comment by 15 October 1990 on the sections of ED 50 that relate directly to the application in the preparation of consolidated accounts of the amendments to the 1985 Act. Thirty-five letters of comment were received in time to be considered by the Board in drafting this statement. Of those, thirteen comments were from companies, seventeen from accounting firms and accountants' representative bodies and five from others.

Commentary on Part 1— Guidance on interpretation of the Act

Identifying a parent undertaking and its subsidiary undertaking

42 If an undertaking has a participating interest in another undertaking and actually exercises a dominant influence over it, the Act identifies these as a parent undertaking and its subsidiary undertaking. These terms are new to the law and the Board gives guidance on the meaning of 'dominant influence' and 'actually exercises'. The comments received in general supported the ED 50 definition (paragraph 78 of ED 50) but several commentators expressed unease with a definition of "actually exercises dominant influence" which included "the passive influence that can derive from the holding of a legal or effective power of veto". It was pointed out that joint venturers may have an effective power of veto arising from their joint venture agreements and the ability to block a special resolution could also be regarded as an effective veto. In neither of these cases would such a veto of itself make consolidation appropriate. The Board has drafted its guidance to preserve the thrust of ED 50 while clarifying what was meant by passive influence and power of veto in a way which avoids the problems identified by the commentators.

43 Dominant influence is defined as effective control; thus the meaning of control affects the application of this part of the Act. Commentators pointed out that the ED 50 definition of control could be read as excluding loss making subsidiaries because it was phrased so that the achievement of benefits was key rather than the ability to achieve benefits. The

Board's guidance on 'control' is based on the ED 50 definition but small changes have been made to stress that it is the ability to benefit and not the actual receipt of benefit that is relevant for this purpose.

44 'Managed on a unified basis' is the second condition where a participating interest will lead to an undertaking becoming a subsidiary undertaking of the holder of the interest. The first condition is 'actually exercises dominant influence' and both of these conditions were adopted as part of one option in the Seventh Directive. The Board considers that it will be unusual for two undertakings to be managed on a unified basis where one does not also have dominant influence over the other. However, to make the meaning given in ED 50 for 'managed on a unified basis' of practical use where such cases exist, the Board's guidance states that the undertakings should be 'integrated' rather than requiring complete integration as in ED 50.

Exclusion of a subsidiary undertaking from consolidation

45 The comments received on ED 50 were in the main supportive of the ASC's attempts to limit very severely the circumstances where subsidiary undertakings might be excluded from consolidation. The Board supports the limiting of the grounds on which subsidiary undertakings should be excluded from consolidation. It believes that the information given by group accounts is more useful in general where all of the subsidiary undertakings of a group have been consolidated. The Board is also aware of the possibility of abuse if the grounds on which subsidiary undertakings should be excluded are left too general.

46 The two grounds for exclusion on which there was most comment were the exclusion permitted in the Act where the subsidiary undertaking is held exclusively for resale and the exclusion required in the Act where the consolidation of the subsidiary undertaking is incompatible with the obligation to give a true and fair view because of the undertaking's different activities. Even on these two grounds there was wide support for the ED 50 proposals which interpreted these conditions strictly. However, in developing its own guidance on these points, the Board has borne in mind the points raised in the comments and has made certain changes to meet these.

47 Where the parent undertaking has voluntarily acquired a subsidiary undertaking, the grounds on which that subsidiary undertaking should be excluded from consolidation because it is held exclusively for resale have not changed from the ED 50 proposals except that the expectation of a disposal within one year now has to be 'reasonable'. However, the Board has taken note of the comments which pointed out the special difficulties that could be experienced by parent undertakings which acquired their subsidiary undertakings involuntarily, such as in the case of distress. In these cases, the subsidiary undertaking should be treated as held exclusively for resale, unless the interest has become part of the continuing activities of the group or the parent undertaking acts as if it intends that interest to form part of the continuing activities of the group.

48 Although the comments in general supported ED 50 in its treatment of exclusion for incompatibility arising from different activities, some of the comment criticised ED 50 on the grounds that it was misleading that the crucial incompatibility for exclusion was restricted to Schedule 9 banking and insurance companies. Some commentators considered that the necessary incompatibility may arise for some banking and insurance companies but there are many cases where consolidation of such businesses would be compatible with the obligation to give a true and fair view. Equally commentators considered that incompatibility might arise in some cases where parent or subsidiary undertakings were not-for-profit organisations. From the comments received it seemed that some had taken ED 50 to mean that banking and insurance companies should in general be excluded from consolidation in mixed groups. If a subsidiary undertaking is a Schedule 9 company and its parent undertaking is not, or vice versa, this does not necessarily mean that such a subsidiary undertaking should be excluded from consolidation; only if, exceptionally, it is incompatible with the obligation to give a true and fair view to consolidate that subsidiary undertaking should it not be consolidated.

49 The guidance drafted by the Board is intended to be more strict than the ED 50 proposals because it stresses that the key criterion for excluding a subsidiary undertaking is that there are conclusive grounds for believing that its consolidation is incompatible with the obligation to give a true and fair view. The guidance explains that such incompatibility is so exceptional that it would be misleading to link it to any particular activities. Where a subsidiary undertaking is excluded because its inclusion would be incompatible with the obligation to give a true and fair view, the consolidated accounts should explain in a note why it is believed that that subsidiary undertaking should be excluded.

Joint ventures

50 The comments received supported the need for an accounting standard to define a joint venture. The Board has drafted its guidance on the meaning of 'joint venture' in the light of comment received. In particular, the ED 50 definition was criticised for implying that the existence of a joint venture agreement was a necessary condition for an undertaking to be a joint venture. It also seemed to suggest that participants had to have been involved in the set up of the undertaking if that undertaking was to be taken as their joint venture. Thus, the definition might not have covered the interests of those who did not participate in the venture until it was established. The definition of a joint venture offered in this guidance is closer to that of the IASC proposals than the ED 50 definition.

51 The Board has not issued interim guidance on the accounting treatment of joint ventures under the Act. The comments revealed no consensus on how joint ventures should be treated. This is also an area where the Act conflicts with the preferred treatments proposed by several commentators. The International Accounting Standards Committee is soon to publish its standard on the treatment of joint ventures. The Board reserves its opinion on how joint ventures should be treated until it has the time to consider this as part of its full review of consolidated accounts.

Disproportionate expense and undue delay

52 The Act allows a subsidiary undertaking to be excluded from consolidation if information necessary for the preparation of group accounts cannot be obtained without disproportionate expense or undue delay. The Board considers that this can only be relevant for a subsidiary which is not material in the context of the group. In all cases the statutory time limit for delivery of accounts must be observed.

Venture capital companies

53 The Board has considered representations from venture capitalists that their interest in their investments is so different from that of other investors in companies that their investments should be treated differently from those of other companies. This applies particularly where a venture capitalist holds an interest in another undertaking that qualifies as its associated or subsidiary undertaking. The Board considers that the treatment for associated or subsidiary undertakings that is appropriate for other companies is also appropriate for venture capitalists. The venture capitalists may, however, wish to disclose further information about their investments which will be of use to their investors.

Commentary on Part 2 — Changes to SSAP 1 and SSAP 14

54 Where SSAP 1 uses the terms 'joint ventures', 'partnerships' and 'consortia' these references are dropped as the Act now refers only to associated undertakings or joint ventures. The Act requires undertakings which are associated undertakings to be equity accounted. 'Associated undertaking' is defined in the Act not to include non-corporate joint ventures where the option to use proportional consolidation has been taken (paragraphs 10, 14, 15, 18 and 38 of SSAP 1).

55 The changes made to paragraph 13 of SSAP 1 arise mainly as a result of the way 'associated undertaking' is defined in the Act. The definition is set out in Schedule 4A.20 and broadly provides that an associated undertaking is one where the investing undertaking has a participating interest and exercises a significant influence.

56 Paragraph 17 of SSAP 1 is withdrawn. The term 'associated company' is now out of date so that restrictions on its use are meaningless.

57 Paragraph 19 of SSAP 1 gives an example of the heading under which the results of associated undertakings should be recorded. This does not comply with the Act so the reference is withdrawn.

58 When SSAPs 1 and 14 were revised or published wholly owned subsidiaries were the only companies which were not required to prepare group accounts. The Act has now extended the exemptions from preparing group accounts so that a different phrase is now required to denote exempt companies (paragraphs 24, 35 of SSAP 1 and paragraph 20 of SSAP 14)

59 In paragraph 38 of SSAP 1 the reference to the Department of Trade has been updated to the Secretary of State.

60 SSAP 14 was drawn up to accord with the legal definitions of subsidiary and parent at that time. These have been changed by the 1989 amendments to the 1985 Companies Act which set out the new circumstances under which one undertaking is a subsidiary undertaking and another is its parent undertaking. This has led to the withdrawal of paragraph 7 of SSAP 14 and changes to paragraph 8 of SSAP 14.

61 The Act no longer allows the presentation of group accounts other than by consolidation. This necessitates the changes to paragraphs 1, 2 and 22 of SSAP 14.

62 The Act has changed the circumstances under which a subsidiary undertaking is allowed or required to be excluded from consolidation. Paragraphs 15, 21, 22, 23, 24, 25, 26 and 27 of SSAP 14 are affected by this change.

63 The law has been changed in relation to those cases where the financial year of a subsidiary undertaking does not coincide with its parent undertaking (Schedule 4A.2(2)). The phrase withdrawn from paragraph 18 is thus no longer necessary.

64 Part 4 and Part 5 (paragraphs 6364) of SSAP 1 and Part 4 and Section A of Part 5 of SSAP 14 give the legal requirements in Great Britain and Northern Ireland. These have been withdrawn in full as they are now out of date and bringing them up to date would require extensive changes. This affects the drafting of paragraph 49 of SSAP 1. Part 6 of SSAP 1 and SSAP 14 deals with compliance with international statements and has also been withdrawn as the International Accounting Standard referred to, IAS 3 'Consolidated Financial Statements', has now been superseded. In SSAP 14 this necessitates withdrawing the paragraph referring to IAS 3 from the introductory passage.

Section 4
Financial Reporting Standards

Contents

Cash flow statements

Reproduced with the permission of the Accounting Standards Board

Summary

a Financial Reporting Standard No. 1 'Cash Flow Statements' (the FRS) establishes standards for cash flow reporting. It supersedes Statement of Standard Accounting Practice No. 10 'Statements of Source and Application of Funds' (SSAP 10) and requires reporting entities which fall within its scope to prepare a cash flow statement as part of their financial statements setting out on a standard basis their cash generation and absorption for a period. The FRS sets out the required structure of the cash flow statement and minimum level of disclosure.

b The Statement of Principles for Financial Reporting being developed by the Accounting Standards Board (the Board) recognises that users of financial statements need information on the liquidity, viability and financial adaptability of the entity concerned. Deriving this information involves the user in making assessments of the future cash flows of the entity. Accruals accounting, used in producing profit and loss (or income and expenditure) accounts and balance sheets, adjusts cash flows to measure results for a period and this is the primary basis for projections. Nevertheless, long-term provisions and other allocations associated with accruals accounting need to be eliminated in order to reveal the leads and lags in historical cash flows, thereby improving understanding of a reporting entity's cash generating or cash absorption mechanisms and providing a basis for the assessment of future cash flows.

c In order to promote understanding and to help to achieve the objectives of cash flow reporting by securing the useful presentation of information, the FRS requires that individual cash flows should be classified under certain standard headings according to the activity that gave rise to them. The standard headings required in a cash flow statement are:

- operating activities;
- returns on investments and servicing of finance;
- taxation;
- investing activities; and
- financing.

In addition, the FRS requires that the cash flow statement should show a total giving the net cash inflow or outflow before financing. The FRS specifies particular cash flows to be separately reported under each of the standard headings apart from operating activities. Analysis of net cash flow from operating activities on the so-called 'direct method' is encouraged but not required.

d In order to ensure that it reflects clearly the substance of a reporting entity's cash management, the cash flow statement deals with flows of cash equivalents as well as with cash flows.

e A reconciliation between the operating profit reported in the profit and loss (or income and expenditure) account and the net cash flow from operating activities should be given as a note to the cash flow statement. This reconciliation should disclose separately the movements in stocks, debtors and creditors related to operating activities and other differences between cash flows and profits. A reconciliation of the amounts shown in the balance sheet of the reporting entity in respect of items reported within the financing section of the cash flow statement with the equivalent figures in the previous year's balance sheet, disclosing separately the movements resulting from cash flows, differences arising from changes in foreign currency exchange rates and other movements, should also be given as a note to the cash flow statement.

Small reporting entities

f The FRS exempts most small reporting entities from the requirement to include a cash flow statement as part of their financial statements. The exemption does not extend to public companies, banking companies, insurance companies, authorised persons under the Financial Services Act 1986, or members of a group containing one or more of the above mentioned entities.

Wholly owned subsidiary undertakings

g A wholly owned subsidiary undertaking of a parent undertaking established under the law of a member State of the European Community is exempt from the requirements of the FRS if:

(i) the parent undertaking publishes, in English, consolidated financial statements which include the subsidiary undertaking concerned, drawn up in accordance with United Kingdom or Republic of Ireland companies legislation or the EC Seventh Company Law Directive; and

(ii) those consolidated financial statements include a consolidated cash flow statement dealing with the cash flows of the group; and

(iii) that cash flow statement gives sufficient information to enable a user of the financial statements to derive the totals of the amounts required to be shown under each of the standard headings set out in the FRS.

Objective

1 The objective of the FRS is to require reporting entities falling within its scope to report on a standard basis their cash generation and cash absorption for a period. To this end reporting entities are required to provide a primary financial statement analysing cash flows under the standard headings of 'operating activities', 'returns on investments and servicing of finance', 'taxation', 'investing activities' and 'financing', disclosed in that sequence, in order to assist users of the financial statements in their assessment of the reporting entity's liquidity, viability and financial adaptability. The objective of the standard headings is to ensure that cash flows are reported in a form that highlights the significant components of cash flow and facilitates comparison of the cash flow performance of different businesses.

Definitions

The following definitions shall apply for the purposes of this FRS and in particular the statement of standard accounting practice set out in paragraphs 7 to 46.

2 *Cash.* Cash in hand and deposits repayable on demand with any bank or other financial institution. Cash includes cash in hand and deposits denominated in foreign currencies.

3 *Cash equivalents.* Short-term, highly liquid investments which are readily convertible into known amounts of cash without notice and which were within three months of maturity when acquired; less advances from banks repayable within three months from the date of the advance. Cash equivalents include investments and advances denominated in foreign currencies provided that they fulfil the above criteria.

4 *Cash flow.* An increase or decrease in an amount of cash or cash equivalent resulting from a transaction.

5 *Companies Act 1985.* Companies Act 1985 as amended by the Companies Act 1989.

6 *Companies (Northern Ireland) Order 1986.* Companies (Northern Ireland) Order 1986 as amended by the Companies (Northern Ireland) Order 1990 and the Companies (No. 2) (Northern Ireland) Order 1990.

Statement of Standard Accounting Practice

The statement of standard accounting practice set out in paragraphs 7 to 46 of the FRS should be read together with the Objective of the FRS as stated in paragraph 1, the definitions set out in paragraphs 2 to 6 and also the Foreword to Accounting Standards and the Statement of Principles for Financial Reporting issued from time to time by the Board.

The Explanation section of the FRS, set out in paragraphs 48 to 84, shall be regarded as part of the statement of standard accounting practice in so far as it assists in interpreting that statement.

7 Reporting entities falling within the scope of paragraph 8 of the FRS are required to provide as a primary statement within the reporting entity's financial statements a cash flow statement drawn up in accordance with the standard accounting principles set out in paragraphs 9 to 46 of the FRS.

Scope

8 This FRS applies to all financial statements intended to give a true and fair view of the financial position and profit or loss (or income and expenditure) except those of entities that are:

(a) companies incorporated under the Companies Acts and entitled to the exemptions available in Sections 246 to 249 of the Companies Act 1985* for small companies when filing accounts with the Registrar of Companies; or

(b) entities which would have come under category (a) above had they been companies incorporated under companies legislation; or

(c) wholly owned subsidiary undertakings of a parent undertaking which is established under the law of a member State of the European Community where:

(i) the parent undertaking publishes, in English, consolidated financial statements which include the subsidiary undertaking concerned, drawn up in accordance with United Kingdom or Republic of Ireland companies legislation or the EC Seventh Company Law Directive; and

(ii) those consolidated financial statements include a consolidated cash flow statement dealing with the cash flows of the group; and

(iii)that cash flow statement gives sufficient information to enable a user of the financial statements to derive the totals of the amounts required to be shown under each of the standard headings set out in this FRS; or

(d) Building Societies, as defined by the Building Societies Act 1986 in the United Kingdom and by the Building Societies Act 1989 in the Republic of Ireland, but only so long as they are required by law to prepare as part of their financial statements a statement of source and application of funds in a prescribed format; or

(e) mutual life assurance companies.

* The equivalent references in Northern Ireland legislation are Sections 254 to 257 of the Companies (Northern Ireland) Order 1986.

The equivalent references in Republic of Ireland legislation are Sections 8, 9, 10 and 12 of the Companies (Amendment) Act 1986.

9 The cash flow statement provided with group financial statements should reflect the cash flows of the group.

10 Insurance companies, other than mutual life assurance companies to which the FRS does not apply, should include the cash flows of their long-term life, pensions and annuity businesses only to the extent that the cash flows are those of the insurance company itself rather than cash flows of the long-term funds.

Preparation of cash flow statements

11 The cash flow statement should include all the reporting entity's inflows and outflows of cash and cash equivalents except those movements within cash and cash equivalents that result from the purchases and sales for cash or cash equivalents of holdings which form part of that entity's cash equivalents. Transactions which do not result in cash flows of the reporting entity should not be reported in the cash flow statement.

Format for cash flow statements

12 The cash flow statement should list the inflows and outflows of cash and cash equivalents for the period classified under the following standard headings:

- operating activities;
- returns on investments and servicing of finance;
- taxation;
- investing activities; and
- financing

in that order and showing a total for each standard heading and a total of the net cash inflow or outflow before financing. Examples of formats for cash flow statements are provided in the illustrative examples annexed to the FRS.

Classification of cash flows

13 The cash flow statement should disclose separately, where material, the individual categories of cash flows under the standard headings set out in paragraphs 15 to 30 except in the extremely rare circumstances where this presentation would not be a fair representation of the activities of the reporting entity. In such cases informed judgement should be used to devise an appropriate alternative treatment. The cash flow classifications may be subdivided further to give a fuller description of the activities of the reporting entity or to provide segmental information.

14 Where a cash flow is not specified in the categories set out in paragraphs 15 to 30 below then it should be shown under the most appropriate standard heading.

Classification of cash flows by standard heading

Operating activities

15 Cash flows from operating activities are in general the cash effects of transactions and other events relating to operating or trading activities. Net cash flow from operating activities represents the net increase or decrease in cash and cash equivalents resulting from the operations shown in the profit and loss account in arriving at operating profit.

16 Operating cash flows may be reported in the cash flow statement on a net or gross basis.

17 A reconciliation between the operating profit (for non-financial companies normally profit before interest) reported in the profit and loss account and the net cash flow from operating activities should be given as a note to the cash flow statement. This reconciliation should disclose separately the movements in stocks, debtors and creditors related to operating activities and other differences between cash flows and profits.

Returns on investments and servicing of finance

18 'Returns on investments and servicing of finance' are receipts resulting from the ownership of an investment and payments to providers of finance excluding those items required by paragraphs 15 and 24 to 30 to be classified under operating, investing or financing activities.

19 Cash inflows from returns on investments and servicing of finance include:

(a) interest received, including any related tax recovered;

(b) dividends received (disclosing separately dividends received from equity accounted entities), net of any tax credits.

20 Cash outflows from returns on investments and servicing of finance include:

(a) interest paid (whether or not the charge is capitalised), including any tax deducted and paid to the relevant tax authority;

(b) dividends paid, excluding any advance corporation tax;

(c) the interest element of finance lease rental payments.

Taxation

21 The cash flows included under the heading taxation are cash flows to or from taxation authorities in respect of the reporting entity's revenue and capital profits. Cash flows in respect of other taxation, including payments and receipts in respect of Value Added Tax, other sales taxes, property taxes and other taxes not assessed on the profits of the reporting entity should be dealt with as set out in paragraphs 34 and 35 of this FRS.

22 Taxation cash inflows include cash receipts from the relevant tax authority of tax rebates, claims or returns of overpayments.

23 Taxation cash outflows include cash payments to the relevant tax authority of tax, including payments of advance corporation tax and purchases of certificates of tax deposit.

Investing activities

24 The cash flows included in investing activities are those related to the acquisition or disposal of any asset held as a fixed asset or as a current asset investment (other than assets included within cash equivalents).

25 Cash inflows from investing activities include:

(a) receipts from sales or disposals of fixed assets;

(b) receipts from sales of investments in subsidiary undertakings net of any balances of cash and cash equivalents transferred as part of the sale;

(c) receipts from sales of investments in other entities with separate disclosure of divestments of equity accounted entities;

(d) receipts from repayment or sales of loans made to other entities by the reporting entity or of other entities' debt (other than cash equivalents) which were purchased by the reporting entity.

26 Cash outflows from investing activities include:

(a) payments to acquire fixed assets;

(b) payments to acquire investments in subsidiary undertakings net of balances of cash and cash equivalents acquired;

(c) payments to acquire investments in other entities with separate disclosure of investments in equity accounted entities;

(d) loans made by the reporting entity and payments to acquire debt of other entities (other than cash equivalents).

Financing

27 Financing cash flows comprise receipts from or repayments to external providers of finance of amounts in respect of principal amounts of finance.

28 Financing cash inflows include:

(a) receipts from issuing shares or other equity instruments;

(b) receipts from issuing debentures, loans, notes, and bonds and from other long and short-term borrowings (other than those included within cash equivalents).

29 Financing cash outflows include:

(a) repayments of amounts borrowed (other than those included within cash equivalents);

(b) the capital element of finance lease rental payments;

(c) payments to re-acquire or redeem the entity's shares;

(d) payments of expenses or commissions on any issue of shares, debentures, loans, notes, bonds or other financing.

30 The amounts of any finance cash flows received from or paid to equity accounted entities should be disclosed separately.

Exceptional and extraordinary items

31 Where cash flows relate to items that are classed as exceptional items in the profit and loss account these exceptional cash flows should be shown under the appropriate standard headings, according to the nature of each item. Sufficient disclosure of the nature of cash flows relating to exceptional items should be given in a note to the cash flow statement to allow a user of the financial statements to gain an understanding of the effect on the reporting entity's cash flows of the underlying transactions.

32 Where cash flows relate to items that are classed as extraordinary items in the profit and loss account these extraordinary cash flows should be shown separately under the appropriate standard headings, according to the nature of each item. In the extremely rare circumstances where it is inappropriate to include a cash flow relating to an extraordinary item under one or more of the standard headings within the cash flow statement the cash flows should be shown within a separate section in the cash flow statement.

33 Sufficient disclosure of the nature of cash flows relating to extraordinary items should be given in a note to the cash flow statement to allow a user of the financial statements to gain an understanding of the effect on the reporting entity's cash flows of the underlying transactions.

Value Added Tax and other taxes

34 Cash flows should be shown net of any attributable Value Added Tax or other sales tax unless the tax is irrecoverable by the reporting entity. The net movement on the amount payable to, or receivable from, the taxing authority should be allocated to cash flows from operating activities unless a different treatment is more appropriate in the particular circumstances concerned. In circumstances where sales taxes paid by the reporting entity are irrecoverable cash flows should be shown gross by including the associated sales tax unless this is impracticable, in which case the irrecoverable tax should be included under the most appropriate standard heading.

35 Taxation cash flows excluding those in respect of the reporting entity's revenue and capital profits and Value Added Tax, or other sales tax, should be included within the cash flow statement under the same standard heading as the cash flow which gave rise to the taxation cash flow, unless a different treatment is more appropriate in the particular circumstances concerned.

Foreign currencies

36 Where a portion of a reporting entity's business is undertaken by a foreign entity, the cash flows of that entity are to be included in the cash flow statement on the basis used for translating the results of those activities in the profit and loss account of the reporting entity.

Hedging transactions

37 Cash flows that result from transactions undertaken to hedge another transaction should be reported under the same standard heading as the transaction that is the subject of the hedge.

Groups

38 A group cash flow statement should only deal with flows of cash and cash equivalents external to the group. Accordingly, cash flows that are internal to the group should be eliminated in the preparation of the group cash flow statement. Dividends paid to any minority interests should be reported under the heading returns on investments and servicing of finance, and disclosed separately.

39 The cash flows of any entity which is equity accounted in consolidated financial statements should only be included in the group cash flow statement to the extent of the actual cash flows between the group and the entity concerned.

Acquisitions and disposals

40 Where a group acquires or disposes of a subsidiary undertaking, the amounts of cash and cash equivalents paid or received in respect of the consideration should be shown net of any cash and cash equivalent balances transferred as part of the purchase or sale of the subsidiary undertaking. In addition, a note to the cash flow statement should show a summary of the effects of acquisitions and disposals indicating how much of the consideration comprised cash and cash equivalents and the amounts of cash and cash equivalents transferred as a result of the acquisitions and disposals.

41 Where a subsidiary undertaking joins or leaves a group during a financial year the cash flows of the group should include the cash flows of the subsidiary undertaking concerned for the same period as that for which the group's profit and loss account includes the results of the subsidiary undertaking.

42 Material effects on amounts reported under each of the standard headings reflecting the cash flows of a subsidiary undertaking acquired or disposed of in the period should be disclosed, as far as practicable, as a note to the cash flow statement. This information need only be given in the financial statements for the period in which the acquisition or disposal occurs.

Major non-cash transactions

43 Material transactions not resulting in movements of cash or cash equivalents of the reporting entity should be disclosed in the notes to the cash flow statement if disclosure is necessary for an understanding of the underlying transactions.

Reconciliation with balance sheet figures

44 The movements in cash and cash equivalents and the items shown within the financing section of the cash flow statement should be reconciled to the related items in the opening and closing balance sheets for the period. The reconciliations should disclose separately for cash and cash equivalents and for financing items the movements resulting from cash flows, differences arising from changes in foreign currency exchange rates (those relating to the retranslation of any opening balances of cash and cash equivalents and financing items and those resulting from the translation of the cash flows of foreign entities at exchange rates other than the year end rate) and other movements. Where several balance sheet amounts or parts thereof have to be combined to permit a reconciliation, sufficient detail should be shown to enable the movements to be understood. Possible formats for such reconciliations are provided in the illustrative examples annexed to the FRS.

Comparative figures

45 Comparative figures should be given for all items in the cash flow statement and such notes thereto as are required by the FRS.

Date from which effective

46 The accounting practices set out in this FRS should be adopted as soon as possible and regarded as standard in respect of financial statements relating to accounting periods ending on or after 23 March 1992.

Financial Reporting Standard No. 1 'Cash Flow Statements' was adopted by the unanimous vote of the nine members of the Accounting Standards Board.

Members of the Accounting Standards Board

David Tweedie (Chairman)

Sir Bryan Carsberg (Vice Chairman)

Allan Cook (Technical Director)

Robert Bradfield

Elwyn Eilledge

Michael Garner

Donald Main

Roger Munson

Graham Stacy

Compliance with International Accounting Standards

47 Compliance with the FRS ensures compliance with International Accounting Standard No. 7 'Statement of Changes in Financial Position'. The FRS is also broadly in line with the exposure draft of a proposed International Accounting Standard 'Cash Flow Statements' issued by the International Accounting Standards Committee in July 1991.

Explanation

The need for cash flow information

48 Historical cash flow information may assist users of financial statements in making judgements on the amount, timing and degree of certainty of future cash flows; it gives an indication of the relationship between profitability and cash generating ability, and thus of the quality of the profit earned. In addition, analysts and other users of financial information often, formally or informally, develop models to assess and compare the present value of the future cash flows of entities. Historical cash flow information could be useful to check the accuracy of past assessments and indicate the relationship between the entity's activities and its receipts and payments.

49 A cash flow statement in conjunction with a balance sheet provides information on liquidity, viability and financial adaptability. The balance sheet provides information about an entity's financial position at a particular point in time including assets, liabilities and equity and their relationship with each other at the balance sheet date. The balance sheet is often used to obtain information on liquidity, but the information is incomplete for this purpose as the balance sheet is drawn up at a particular point in time.

50 A cash flow statement shows information about the reporting entity's cash flows in the reporting period, but this provides incomplete information for assessing future cash flows. Some cash flows result from transactions that took place in an earlier period and some cash flows are expected to result in further cash flows in a future period. Accordingly, cash flow statements should normally be used in conjunction with profit and loss accounts and balance sheets when making an assessment of future cash flows.

Cash instead of working capital

51 The Board believes that the information provided by a cash flow statement has the following advantages over that provided by a working capital based funds flow statement:

(a) Funds flow data based on movements in working capital can obscure movements relevant to the liquidity and viability of an entity. For example, a significant decrease in cash available may be masked by an increase in stock or debtors. Entities may, therefore, run out of cash while reporting increases in working capital. Similarly, a decrease in working capital does not necessarily indicate a cash shortage and a danger of failure;

(b) As cash flow monitoring is a normal feature of business life and not a specialised accounting technique, cash flow is a concept which is more widely understood than are changes in working capital;

(c) Cash flows can be a direct input into a business valuation model and, therefore, historical cash flows may be relevant in a way not possible for funds flow data;

(d) A funds flow statement is based largely on the difference between two balance sheets. It reorganises such data, but does not provide new data. The cash flow statement and associated notes required by the FRS may include data not disclosed in a funds flow statement.

Cash and cash equivalents

52 Entities often invest cash in excess of immediate needs in short-term highly liquid investments or borrow on a short-term basis to cover a peak in working capital requirements. Whether an entity's liquid resources comprise cash or a financial instrument that is readily convertible to a known amount of cash is largely irrelevant to users' assessments of liquidity and future cash flows. It is also irrelevant whether a cash flow results in a decrease in a cash balance or results in an increase in an overdraft or short-term bank loan. The Board, therefore, decided that a statement of cash flows should focus on the aggregate of cash and cash equivalents and that cash equivalents should be calculated net of short-term bank advances.

53 Entities' cash management programmes vary in the range of short to medium term deposits and instruments which they manage as a cash or near cash portfolio. In adopting the definition of cash equivalents for the purposes of the FRS the Board distinguished between those deposits and instruments that are effectively available immediately at face value and those that are placed for a longer term and would consequently incur some price risk if they were to be utilised at an earlier date. Thus cash equivalents, apart from any offset of overdrafts and other short term bank borrowings, must be highly liquid, convertible into known amounts of cash without notice and not have any significant risk of changes in value owing to changes in interest rates.

54 The Board believes that a reasonable cut-off for cash equivalents is represented by a three month maturity threshold on the grounds that instruments within three months of maturity do not have any significant risk of changes in value due to changes in interest rates. The Board believes that the same cut-off point of three months should be used for bank borrowings. An investment purchased with more than three months to maturity does not become a cash equivalent when its remaining maturity is three months. Similarly, bank borrowings with a maturity of more than three months when drawn down do not become cash equivalents when their remaining maturity becomes three months because in these circumstances no transaction has taken place and it would be misleading to represent the approach of maturity as a cash flow.

55 Some entities, particularly banks and other financial institutions, hold highly liquid financial instruments for investment or trading purposes and not as part of their cash management programme. The Board's definition of cash equivalents includes highly liquid instruments only if they had less than three months remaining to maturity when purchased. The Board believes that consistency between the cash flow statements of different reporting entities is desirable, as far as possible, and accordingly highly liquid instruments held by financial institutions for trading purposes should be included as part of their cash equivalents only if they fall within the definition of cash equivalents set out in paragraph 3.

Cash or net debt

56 The Board believes that the focus of the cash flow statement should be not only cash flows but also the movements in a reporting entity's net cash or debt position. By separating the servicing of finance from the movements in principal amounts of finance, by requiring a total giving the net cash inflow or outflow before financing and by requiring disclosure of movements in the reporting entity's financing, the Board believes that information on the movements in the net cash or debt position is given an appropriate degree of prominence. The Board has not specified the form of presentation of the change in cash and cash equivalents because the significance of this item may be expected to differ for individual reporting entities. The illustrative examples show two out of a number of possible forms of presentation.

Scope

57 The Board has examined the circumstances of small reporting entities and has exempted most of them from the requirement to include a cash flow statement as part of their financial statements. This exemption does not extend to public companies that have the powers under their constitutions to offer their shares or debentures to the public and may lawfully exercise that power, or to banking companies, insurance companies, authorised persons under the Financial Services Act 1986, or members of a group containing one or more of the above mentioned entities. The scope of the exemption may be restricted at a later date as part of a wider examination of the reporting requirements of small entities.

58 The Board believes that the small entities exemption is justified because the costs for small entities, which are often owner managed, of producing historical cash flow information in a highly standardised form are likely to be disproportionate to the benefits. The Board has restricted the definition so that entities that are authorised to hold public money or offer securities to the public are required to produce a cash flow statement. However, the Board encourages small reporting entities to include a cash flow statement as part of their financial statements if it would provide useful information to users of those financial statements and the benefits of doing so outweigh the costs of providing the information.

59 The Board recognises that trade and other creditors may be users of financial statements, but has taken into account the fact that small companies or groups of companies as defined by the Companies Act 1985 are able to take advantage of provisions in that Act allowing them to file abbreviated accounts with the Registrar of Companies. These abbreviated accounts need not include a cash flow statement or an equivalent, and thus the information would not necessarily be within the public domain.

60 The Board has examined and rejected the proposition that wholly owned subsidiary undertakings should have to include a cash flow statement as part of their financial statements. Wholly owned subsidiary undertakings are legal entities in their own right and thus have legal obligations to creditors. They are, however, often controlled and managed on a day to day basis by their parent and the group may have a centralised treasury or other cash/debt management operation which results in a wholly owned subsidiary undertaking's cash flow being wholly or partly dependent on the group's overall cash or funding position. In view of the fact that cash balances can be moved around a group rapidly, historical cash flow information of individual group companies is limited in the information that it can contribute to an assessment of future cash flows. Accordingly, the Board believes that a cash flow statement is not meaningful in relation to wholly owned subsidiary undertakings.

61 The Board has examined the proposition that a cash flow statement would not be particularly useful in respect of financial institutions, particularly banks, insurance companies and building societies.

62 The main reasons advanced for these views in respect of banks are that a bank's cash is its stock in trade and that more useful information would be given by a statement dealing with the capital resources available to the bank. The Board agrees that capital resources are an important indicator of the viability and financial adaptability of financial institutions, but also believes that a cash flow statement provides users of financial statements published by banks with useful information on the sources of cash and how it has been utilised and thus no exemption from the requirements of the FRS is given to banks.

63 The Board does, however, believe that the reporting of gross operating cash flows for a bank would not provide a user of the bank's financial statements with useful information, because many of the gross operating cash flows are essentially cash flows originated as a result of a decision by third parties who hold deposits or have loans with the bank to move funds to or from their accounts with the bank and thus these cash flows are beyond the day-to-day control of the bank's management. However, the FRS allows reporting entities to report cash flows from operations on a net basis (i.e. gross cash flows after deduction of other cash flows) and the Board believes that the reporting of net operating cash flows, together with cash flow information on a bank's investing and financing activities, provides useful information to users of the bank's financial statements. The illustrative examples annexed to the FRS include an example of a cash flow statement for a bank.

64 The main reason advanced for an exemption from the requirement to publish a cash flow statement as part of financial statements of an insurance company is that the cash inflows for an insurance company, unlike those of a manufacturing company, relate to premiums which by their nature precede the cash outflows in respect of claims, sometimes by a long period of time, and thus a cash flow statement gives little information on the liquidity, viability and financial adaptability of an insurance company. However, the Board believes that cash flow statements are useful to users of insurance company financial statements because, if used in conjunction with profit and loss accounts and balance sheets, they can assist the user of the financial statements to obtain a rounded picture of financial performance, position and adaptability. Accordingly, no general exemption from the requirements of the FRS is given to insurance companies.

65 However, the Board believes that cash flows arising from 'long-term assurance' business (life, annuity and pensions) of an insurance company should not be dealt with in the cash flow statement except to the extent that the cash flows are those of the insurance company itself (e.g. cash withdrawn from the long-term funds by the insurance company) rather than cash flows of the long-term funds. The Board believes that this presentation is appropriate, as the shareholders of an insurance company generally have restricted rights to any profits, and associated cash surpluses, made by the long-term funds. In addition, the Board believes that this presentation is consistent with the manner in which many insurance companies currently draw up their profit and loss accounts, balance sheets and statements of source and application of funds. The illustrative examples annexed to the FRS include an example of a cash flow statement for an insurance company. The same considerations apply to mutual life assurance companies that are owned by the policy holders and, accordingly, these companies are exempt from the requirements of the FRS.

66 Users of the financial statements of financial institutions, including insurance companies, may find it useful to have information on total liquid assets when making assessments of liquidity, viability and financial flexibility. In these circumstances the financial institutions concerned may wish to provide additional information on the amounts and flows of those liquid assets not dealt with in the cash flow statement. A possible way of presenting such information is set out in the notes to illustrative example 6 — 'XYZ Insurance Company Limited'.

67 Building Societies in the United Kingdom are required by Section 72(1)(C) of the Building Societies Act 1986 to prepare a statement of source and application of funds as part of their annual financial statements. The format of this statement, which is prescribed, is set out in Schedule 3 of the Building Societies (Accounts and Related Provisions)

Regulations 1987. The equivalent requirement to prepare a statement of source and application of funds in Republic of Ireland legislation is set out in Section 77 of the Building Societies Act 1989. The Board believes that the cost to Building Societies of including a cash flow statement in addition to the statement of source and application of funds would outweigh the benefits to users of Building Society financial statements. Accordingly, Building Societies are exempt from the provisions of the FRS during the period that they are required by law to include a statement of source and application of funds in their financial statements in a separately prescribed format.

Classification of cash flows

68 The Board believes that, in order to promote understanding and to help achieve the objectives of cash flow reporting by presenting the information in a useful way, individual cash flows should be classified according to the activity which gave rise to them. In order to promote comparability amongst different entities the FRS prescribes certain standard headings. The standard headings to be identified in a cash flow statement are 'operating activities', 'returns on investments and servicing of finance', 'taxation', 'investing activities' and 'financing'. The Board believes that the totals of the amounts within each standard heading provide useful information for general comparison purposes. However, the significance of the components within each standard heading may vary from reporting entity to reporting entity and accordingly the FRS requires subdivision of the amounts shown under each standard heading. In order to provide users of cash flow statements with a standard set of information that they can use in their analyses the FRS specifies certain standard subdivisions which should be separately disclosed, if material, but reporting entities are encouraged to disclose additional information relevant to their particular circumstances.

Reporting net cash flow from operating activities

69 The Board considered the respective merits of the so-called 'direct' and 'indirect' methods for reporting net cash flow from operating activities. The direct method shows operating cash receipts and payments (including, in particular, cash receipts from customers, cash payments to suppliers and cash payments to and on behalf of employees), aggregating to the net cash flow from operating activities. The indirect method starts with operating profit and adjusts it for non-cash charges and credits to reconcile it to the net cash flow from operating activities.

70 The principal advantage of the direct method is that it shows operating cash receipts and payments. Knowledge of the specific sources of cash receipts and the purposes for which cash payments were made in past periods may be useful in assessing future cash flows. However, the Board does not believe at present that in all cases the benefits to users of this information outweigh the costs to the reporting entity of providing it and, therefore, has not required the information to be given. Nevertheless, in those circumstances where the benefits to users of the information given by the direct method outweigh the costs of providing it the Board encourages reporting entities to provide the relevant information.

71 The principal advantage of the indirect method is that it highlights the differences between operating profit and net cash flow from operating activities. Many users of financial statements believe that such a reconciliation is essential to give an indication of the quality of the reporting entity's earnings. Some investors and creditors assess future cash flows by estimating future income and then allowing for accruals adjustments; thus information about past accruals adjustments may be useful to help estimate future adjustments.

72 The Board believes that it is important that cash flow statements produced by different reporting entities are comparable as far as possible in the circumstances and thus believes that it should prescribe the outline format of the statement. Accordingly, the FRS requires the cash flow statement to show the net cash flow from operating activities, supplemented by a note reconciling this to the reporting entity's operating profit for the period. This reconciliation should not be given in the primary cash flow statement, in order to avoid confusing operating profit and the reconciling items with cash flows. The result is that reporting entities must give the information required by the indirect method, but may also give the information required by the direct method.

Interest and dividend payments and receipts

73 The Board believes that the presentation of net cash flow from operating activities should not be affected by the capital structure of the reporting entity, that payments resulting from the servicing of finance should be shown together and that the cash flow statement format should be consistent with the other primary statements including the profit and loss account wherever possible. Accordingly, interest and dividends paid are normally required to be classified under a separate heading entitled 'returns on investments and servicing of finance'. Cash flows in relation to interest rate hedging instruments such as interest rate swaps (other than those purchased or sold by a financial institution as part of its operating activities) should also be included under returns on investments and servicing of finance because these cash flows are equivalent to interest or are hedges of interest receipts or payments.

74 Interest and dividends received may result from investment activities, investment of cash and cash equivalents, or in some cases operating activities. The Board believes that, in general, interest received and paid should be shown in the same category within the cash flow statements, that dividends received should be shown under the same heading as interest and that the most appropriate category is returns on investments and servicing of finance. However, investment companies that show interest and dividends received in their profit and loss accounts prior to arriving at their operating profit should include interest and dividends received as part of their operating cash flows. Similarly banks that show interest received and paid in their profit and loss account prior to arriving at their operating profit should include interest received and paid as part of their operating cash flows and insurance companies that include interest and dividends received and certain interest paid in their profit and loss account prior to arriving at their operating profit should include the cash flows relating to those amounts as part of their operating cash flows.

Taxation

75 The taxation cash flows of a reporting entity in relation to revenue and capital profits may result from complex computations that are affected by the operating, investing and financing activities of an entity The Board believes that it is not useful to divide taxation cash flows into constituent parts relating to the activities that gave rise to them because the apportionment will, in many cases, have to be made on an arbitrary basis. As taxation cash flows generally arise from activities in an earlier period, apportioning the taxation cash flows would not necessarily report the taxation cash flows along with the transactions that gave rise to them. In addition, the Board notes that a taxation cash flow is not normally a collection of individual cash inflows and outflows and thus analysing it in this manner would require preparers of financial statements to allocate individual cash flows over the standard headings and would not necessarily give information on the entity's underlying cash flows.

76 Accordingly, the Board believes that taxation cash flows in relation to revenue and capital profits should be disclosed in a separate section within the cash flow statement entitled taxation.

77 The existence of Value Added Tax (VAT), and other sales taxes, raises the question of whether the relevant cash flows should be reported gross or net of the tax element and how the balance of tax paid to, or repaid by, the taxing authorities should be reported.

78 Generally sales taxes, including VAT, are payable by the ultimate consumer of the goods or services concerned. A business providing goods or services on which VAT is payable (even if at a zero rate) is generally able to reclaim the VAT incurred by it in providing those goods or services. However, businesses that make exempt supplies are unable to reclaim VAT. Between these two categories are partially exempt businesses that can reclaim part of the VAT incurred by them.

79 The cash flows of an entity include VAT where appropriate and thus strictly the various elements of the cash flow statement should include VAT. However, this treatment does not take into account the fact that normally VAT is a short-term timing difference as far as the entity's overall cash flows are concerned and the inclusion of VAT in the cash flows may distort the allocation of cash flows to standard headings. In order to avoid this distortion and to show cash flows attributable to the reporting entity's activities, the Board believes that cash flows should be shown net of sales taxes and the net movement on the amount payable to, or receivable from, the taxing authority should be allocated to cash flows from operating activities unless a different treatment is more appropriate in the particular circumstances concerned.

80 Taxation cash flows excluding those in respect of the reporting entity's revenue and capital profits and Value Added Tax, or other sales tax, should be included within the cash flow statement under the same standard heading as the cash flow that gave rise to the taxation cash flow unless a different treatment is more appropriate in the particular circumstances concerned. This presentation is consistent with the manner in which transactions are presented in profit and loss accounts and balance sheets.

Investing activities

81 Investing activities are sometimes undertaken to maintain an entity's current level of operations and sometimes to expand or contract the level of operations. In addition investing activities may have consequential effects on operating activities, for example by creating a need for further working capital. The Board decided that criteria for distinguishing expenditure to expand the level of operations from expenditure to maintain the level of operations would vary from reporting entity to reporting entity and would distort the comparability provided by the standard headings. Similar problems arise in analysing changes in working capital. Reporting entities that find it useful to make such distinctions are encouraged to do so within the standard headings or by way of note.

Hedging transactions

82 Entities may undertake hedging transactions that result in cash flows. Often the hedging transactions are carried out with investment instruments that would normally be reported as cash flows under investing activities or returns on investments and servicing of finance. However, reporting hedging cash flows separately from the transactions being hedged would not result in the cash flow statement accurately reflecting the commercial effect of the linked transactions. Accordingly, the Board believes that cash flows which result from transactions undertaken to hedge another transaction should be reported under the same standard heading as the transaction that is the subject of the hedge.

Major non-cash transactions

83 Consideration for transactions may be in a form other than cash. The purpose of a cash flow statement is to report cash flows and non-cash transactions should, therefore, not be reported in a cash flow statement. However, to obtain a full picture of the alterations in financial position caused by the transactions for the period, separate disclosure of material non-cash transactions (such as a vendor placing, the exchange of major assets or the inception of a finance lease contract) is also necessary.

Identification with balance sheet figures

84 The amounts of cash and cash equivalents and amounts shown in the financing section of the cash flow statement should be reconciled to the related items in the opening and closing balance sheets for the period in order to facilitate the use of both cash flow and balance sheet information in assessing the liquidity viability and financial adaptability of the reporting entity.

Illustrative examples

These illustrative examples are for general guidance and do not form part of the Financial Reporting Standard. In particular, the analyses of net cash flows from operating activities under the direct method, the sub-totalling in the reconciliation of operating profit to net cash flow from operating activity for a bank, and the disclosure of total liquid assets for an insurance company, shown in the examples in italics, are optional disclosures.

This section sets out examples of cash flow statements for six types of reporting entity. The examples, which are for illustrative purposes only, do not include comparative figures, except where they are required for a better understanding of the example.

1. Single company.
2. Group, including equity accounted entities, with acquisitions and a disposal during the year.
3. Property investment company.
4. Investment company.
5. Bank.
6. Insurance company.

Illustrative example 1 — Single company

XYZ LIMITED

Cash flow statement for the year ended 31 March 1992

	£000	£000
Net cash inflow from operating activities		6,889
Returns on investments and servicing of finance		
Interest received	3,011	
Interest paid	(12)	
Dividends paid	(2,417)	
Net cash inflow from returns on investments and servicing of finance		582
Taxation		
Corporation tax paid (including advance corporation tax)	(2,922)	
Tax paid		(2,922)
Investing activities		
Payments to acquire intangible fixed assets	(71)	
Payments to acquire tangible fixed assets	(1,496)	
Receipts from sales of tangible fixed assets	42	
Net cash outflow from investing activities		(1,525)
Net cash inflow before financing		3,024
Financing		
Issue of ordinary share capital	211	
Repurchase of debenture loan	(149)	
Expenses paid in connection with share issues	(5)	
Net cash inflow from financing		57
Increase in cash and cash equivalents		3,081

Notes to the cash flow statement

1. Reconciliation of operating profit to net cash inflow from operating activities.

	£000
Operating profit	6,022
Depreciation charges	893
Loss on sale of tangible fixed assets	6
Increase in stocks	(194)
Increase in debtors	(72)
Increase in creditors	234
Net cash inflow from operating activities	6,889

2. Analysis of changes in cash and cash equivalents during the year.

	£000
Balance at 1 April 1991	21,373
Net cash inflow	3,081
Balance at 31 March 1992	24,454

3. Analysis of changes in cash and cash equivalents during the year.

	1992	1991	Change in year
	£000	£000	£000
Cash at bank and in hand	529	681	(152)
Short-term investments	23,936	20,700	3,236
Bank overdrafts	(11)	(8)	(3)
	24,454	21,373	3,081

4. Analysis of changes in financing during the year.

	Share capital	Debenture loan
	£000	£000
Balance at 1 April 1991	27,411	156
Cash inflow/(outflow) from financing	211	(149)
Profit on repurchase of debenture loan for less than its book value		(7)
Balance at 31 March 1992	27,622	—

Illustrative example 2 — Group

XYZ GROUP PLC

Cash flow statement for the year ended 31 March 1992

	£000	£000
Operating activities		
Cash received from customers	*195,016*	
Cash payments to suppliers	*(109,225)*	
Cash paid to and on behalf of employees	*(56,434)*	
Other cash payments	*(12,345)*	
Net cash inflow from continuing operating activities	*17,012*	
Net cash outflow in respect of discontinued activities and reorganisation costs	*(990)*	
Net cash inflow from operating activities		16,022
Returns on investments and servicing of finance		
Interest received	508	
Interest paid	(2,389)	
Interest element of finance lease rentals payments	(373)	
Dividend received from associated undertaking	15	
Dividends paid	(2,606)	
Net cash outflow from returns on investments and servicing of finance		(4,845)
Taxation		
UK corporation tax paid	(2,880)	
Overseas tax paid	(7)	
Tax paid		(2,887)
Investing activities		
Purchase of tangible fixed assets	(3,512)	
Purchase of subsidiary undertakings (net of cash and cash equivalents acquired) (See note 7)	(18,221)	
Sale of plant and machinery	1,052	
Sale of business (See note 8)	4,208	
Sale of trade investment	1,595	
Net cash outflows in respect of unsuccessful takeover bid	(3,811)	
Net cash outflow from investing activities		(18,689)
Net cash outflow before financing		(10,399)
Financing		
Issue of ordinary share capital	(49)	
New secured loan repayable in 1995	(1,091)	
New unsecured loan repayable in 1993	(1,442)	
New short-term loans	(2,006)	
Repayment of amounts borrowed	847	
Capital element of finance lease rental payments	1,342	
Net cash inflow from financing		(2,399)
Decrease in cash and cash equivalents		(8,000)
		(10,399)

Notes to the cash flow statement

1. Reconciliation of operating profit to net cash inflow from operating activities.

	£000
Operating profit	20,249
Depreciation charges	3,158
Profit on sale of tangible fixed assets	(50)
Increase in stocks	(12,263)
Increase in debtors	(3,754)
Increase in creditors	9,672
Net cash inflow from continuing operating activities	17,012
Net cash outflow in respect of discontinued activities and reorganisation costs	(990)
Net cash inflow from operating activities	16,022

2. Analysis of changes in cash and cash equivalents during the year.

	£000
Balance at 1 April 1991	78
Net cash outflow before adjustments for the effect of foreign exchange rate changes	(8,000)
Effect of foreign exchange rate changes	(102)
Balance at 31 March 1992	(8,024)

3. Analysis of the balances of cash and cash equivalents as shown in the balance sheet.

	1992 £000	1991 £000	Change in year £000
Cash at bank and in hand	1,041	1,279	(238)
Bank overdrafts	(9,065)	(1,201)	(7,864)
	(8,024)	78	(8,102)

4. Analysis of changes in financing during the year.

	Share capital (including premium)	Loans and finance lease obligations
	£000	£000
Balance at 1 April 1991	10,334	7,589
Cash inflows from financing	49	2,350
Shares issued for non-cash consideration	9,519	
Loans and finance lease obligations of subsidiary undertakings acquired during the year		3,817
Inception of finance lease contracts		2,845
Balance at 31 March 1992	19,902	16,601

[Note to preparers of financial statements

The disclosures set out below in respect of non-cash transactions may be combined with information disclosed elsewhere in the financial statements, e.g., the disclosure in respect of subsidiary undertakings acquired during the year could be combined with the disclosures required by paragraph 13(5) of Schedule 4A to the Companies Act 1985.]

5. Major non-cash transactions.

(a) During the year the group entered into finance lease arrangements in respect of assets with a total capital value at the inception of the leases of £2,845,000.

(b) Part of the consideration for the purchases of subsidiary undertakings and the sale of a business that occurred during the year comprised shares and loan notes respectively. Further details of the acquisitions and the disposal are set out below.

6. Purchase of subsidiary undertakings.

	£000
Net assets acquired	
Tangible fixed assets	12,194
Investments	1
Stocks	9,384
Debtors	13,856
Taxation recoverable	1,309
Cash at bank and in hand	1,439
Creditors	(21,715)
Bank overdrafts	(6,955)
Loans and finance leases	(3,817)
Deferred taxation	(165)
Minority shareholders' interests	(9)
	5,522
Goodwill	16,702
	22,224
Satisfied by	
Shares allotted	9,519
Cash	12,705
	22,224

The subsidiary undertakings acquired during the year contributed £1,502,000 to the group's net operating cash flows, paid £1,308,000 in respect of net returns on investments and servicing of finance, paid £522,000 in respect of taxation and utilised £2,208,000 for investing activities.

7. Analysis of the net outflow of cash and cash equivalents in respect of the purchase of subsidiary undertakings.

	£000
Cash consideration	12,705
Cash at bank and in hand acquired	(1,439)
Bank overdrafts of acquired subsidiary undertakings	6,955
Net outflow of cash and cash equivalents in respect of the purchase of subsidiaries	18,221

8. Sale of business.

	£000
Net assets disposed of	
Fixed assets	775
Stocks	5,386
Debtors	474
	6,635
Loss on disposal	(1,227)
	5,408
Satisfied by	
Loan notes	1,200
Cash	4,208
	5,408

The business sold during the year contributed £200,000 to the group's net operating cash flows, paid £252,000 in respect of net returns on investments and servicing of finance, paid £145,000 in respect of taxation and utilised £209,000 for investing activities.

Illustrative example 3 — Property investment company

XYZ PROPERTY INVESTMENTS LIMITED

Cash flow statement for the year ended 31 March 1992

	£m	£m
Operating activities		
Cash received from tenants	*263.8*	
Cash payments in respect of direct property costs	*(14.4)*	
Cash paid to and on behalf of employees	*(9.0)*	
Other cash payments	*(8.9)*	
Net cash inflow from operating activities		231.5
Returns on investments and servicing of finance		
Interest received	145.1	
Interest paid	(111.1)	
Dividends paid	(75.7)	
Net cash outflow from returns on investments and servicing of finance		(141.7)
Taxation		
Corporation tax paid	(55.3)	
Tax paid		(55.3)
Investing activities		
Purchase of property	(361.6)	
Sales of property	80.6	
Purchase of plant and machinery and fixtures & fittings	(1.2)	
Sale of plant and machinery and fixtures & fittings	0.1	
Other cash outflows from investing activities	(0.3)	
Net cash outflow from investing activities		(282.4)
Net cash outflow before financing		(247.9)
Financing		
Issue of ordinary share capital	(0.9)	
Issue of Convertible Bonds	(175.0)	
Issue of Unsecured Loan Notes	(3.9)	
Repayments of debenture stocks	11.9	
Amounts paid in respect of the expenses of the issues of Convertible Bonds and Unsecured Loan Notes	3.3	
Net cash inflow from financing		(164.6)
Decrease in cash and cash equivalents		(83.3)
		(247.9)

Notes to the cash flow statement

1. Reconciliation of operating profit to net cash inflow from operating activities.

	£m
Operating profit	241.1
Depreciation charges	1.5
Increase in debtors	(32.5)
Increase in creditors	21.0
Effect of other deferrals and accruals of operating activity cash flow	0.4
Net cash inflow from operating activities	231.5

2. Analysis of changes in cash and cash equivalents during the year.

	£m
Balance at 1 April 1991	350.5
Net cash outflow	(83.3)
Balance at 31 March 1992	267.2

3. Analysis of the balances of cash and cash equivalents as shown in the balance sheet.

	1992	1991	Change in year
	£m	£m	£m
Cash at bank and in hand	0.4	3.4	(3.0)
Short-term deposits	266.8	347.1	(80.3)
	267.2	350.5	(83.3)

4. Analysis of changes in financing during the year.

	Share capital (including premium)	Loans including convertible bonds
	£m	£m
Financing at 1 April 1991	503.7	1,113.5
Cash inflows from financing	0.9	167.0
Financing at 3 1 March 1992	504.6	1280.5

Illustrative example 4 — Investment company

XYZ INVESTMENT COMPANY PLC

Cash flow statement for the year ended 31 March 1992

	£000	£000
Operating activities		
Cash received from investments	*9,491*	
Interest received	*2,870*	
Investment management fees paid	*(1,057)*	
Cash paid to and on behalf of directors	*(35)*	
Other cash payments	*(720)*	
Net cash inflow from operating activities		*10,549*
Returns on investments and servicing of finance		
Interest paid	(114)	
Dividends paid	(6,642)	
Net cash outflow from returns on investments and servicing of finance		(6,756)
Taxation		
UK corporation tax paid	(1,286)	
Overseas tax paid	(362)	
Total tax paid		(1,648)
Investing activities		
Purchase of investments	(149,770)	
Sales of investments	114,097	
Net cash outflow from investing activities		(35,673)
Net cash outflow before financing		(33,528)
Financing		
Issue of Equity Index Unsecured Loan Stock 2004	(60,000)	
Expenses paid in respect of the loan stock issue	1,162	
Net cash inflow from financing		(58,838)
Increase in cash and cash equivalents		25,310
		(33 ,528)

Notes to the cash flow statement

1. Reconciliation of operating profit to net cash inflow from operating activities.

	£000
Income before interest payable and taxation	12,475
Increase in accrued income	(46)
Decrease in other debtors	243
Decrease in creditors	(23)
Tax on franked investment income included within income from UK companies	(2,100)
Net cash inflow from operating activities	10,549

2. Analysis of changes in cash and cash equivalents during the year.

	£000
Balance at 1 April 1991	10,359
Net cash inflow	25,310
Balance at 31 March 1992	35,669

3. Cash and cash equivalents.
The balance for cash and cash equivalents is shown in the balance sheet as 'Cash at bank and in hand' £35,669,000 (1991 — £10,359,000).

4. Analysis of changes in financing during the year.

	Share capital £000	Loans including equity index loan stock £000
Balance at 1 April 1991	55,902	476
Cash inflow from financing		60,000
Change in value of Equity Index Loan Stock		(253)
Balance at 31 March 1992	55,902	60,223

Illustrative example 5 — Bank

XYZ INTERNATIONAL BANK LIMITED
Cash flow statement for the year ended 31 March 1992

	£m	£m
Net cash inflow from operating activities		1,106.9
Returns on investments and servicing of finance		
Dividends received from associated undertakings	9.9	
Ordinary dividends paid	(57.2)	
Preference dividends paid	(10.4)	
Dividends paid to minority shareholders in subsidiary undertaking	(0.2)	
Net cash outflows from returns on investments and servicing of finance		(57.9)
Taxation		
Corporation tax paid	(73.8)	
Overseas tax paid	(14.2)	
Total tax paid		(88.0)
Investing activities		
Purchase of trade investments	(14.7)	
Sale of trade investments	5.7	
Investment in associated undertaking	(56.1)	
Sale of investment in associated undertaking	71.2	
Purchase of tangible fixed assets	(121 .4)	
Sales of tangible fixed assets	40.1	
Net cash outflow from investing activities		(75.2)
Net cash inflow before financing		885.8
Financing		
Issue of ordinary share capital	(6.3)	
Repayments of loan capital	12.3	
Net cash outflow from financing		6.0
Increase in cash and cash equivalents		879.8
		885.8

Notes to the cash flow statement

1. Reconciliation of operating profit to net cash inflow from operating activities.

	£m
Operating profit	241.4
Increase in interest receivable and prepaid expenses	(161.2)
Increase in interest payable and accrued expenses	118.1
Provision for loan losses	20.8
Release of provisions against rescheduled country debt	(50.7)
Depreciation	53.2
Profit on sale of tangible fixed assets	(0.9)
Effect of other deferrals and accruals of operating activity cash flow	1.1
Net cash flow from trading activities	*221.8*
Net increase in deposits and commercial paper	2,542.8
Net increase in loans to customers	(1,419.1)
Net change in finance lease balances receivable	(241.2)
Decrease in securities held (other than those treated as investment activities)	39.9
Increase in collections on other banks	(18.7)
Net increase in placings with banks (repayable beyond 3 months)	(18.6)
Net cash inflow from operating activities	1,106.9

2. Analysis of changes in cash and cash equivalents during the year.

	£m
Balance at 1 April 1991	6,322.9
Net cash inflow before adjustments for the effect of foreign exchange rate changes	879.8
Effect of foreign exchange rate changes	(142.3)
Balance at 31 March 1992	7,060.4

3. Analysis of the balances of cash and cash equivalents as shown in the balance sheet.

	1992	1991	Change in year
	£m	£m	£m
Coin, bank notes and balances with central banks	912.5	736.9	175.6
Money at call and short notice	5,322.4	4,781.6	540.8
Marketable bills of exchange	562.5	584.8	(22.3)
Certificates of deposit	263.0	219.6	43.4
	7,060.4	6,322.9	737.5

The group is required to maintain balances with the Bank of England which, at 31 March 1992, amounted to £54.0 million (1991 — £43.3 million).

Certain subsidiary undertakings of the group are required by law to maintain average reserve balances with the Federal Reserve Bank in the United States of America. Such reserve balances amounted to $30.4 million at 31 March 1992 (1991 — $28.6 million).

4. Analysis of changes in financing during the year.

	Share capital (including premium) *£000*	Loan capital *£000*
Balance at 1 April 1991	435.3	1,248.1
Effect of foreign exchange differences		(115.7)
Cash inflow/(outflow) from financing	6.3	(12.3)
Other movements	(0.1)	
Balance at 31 March 1992	441.5	1,120.1

Illustrative example 6 — Insurance company

XYZ INSURANCE COMPANY LIMITED

Cash flow statement for the year ended 31 March 1992

	£m	£m
Operating activities		
Premiums received from customers	*2,410.8*	
Reinsurance premiums paid	*(400.3)*	
Claims paid	*(1,634.2)*	
Reinsurance receipts in respect of claims	*350.3*	
Cash received from long-term funds	*85.3*	
Cash paid to and on behalf of employees	*(127.5)*	
Interest received	*152.5*	
Dividends received	*166.3*	
Interest paid	*(22.0)*	
Other operating cash payments	*(656.8)*	
Net cash inflow from operating activities		324.4
Returns on investments and servicing of finance		
Interest paid	(20.0)	
Dividends paid	(79.2)	
Net cash outflow from returns on investments and servicing of finance		(99.2)
Taxation		
Corporation tax paid (including advance corporation tax)	(132.5)	
Tax paid		(132.5)
Investing activities		
Purchase of liquid investments (other than cash equivalents)	(382.1)	
Purchase of other investments (other than cash equivalents)	(50.0)	
Sale of liquid investments (other than cash equivalents)	363.8	
Sale of other investments (other than cash equivalents)	48.0	
Purchase of tangible fixed assets	(16.7)	
Net cash outflow from investing activities		(37.0)
Net cash inflow before financing		55.7
Financing		
Issue of ordinary share capital	6.1	
Repayment of long-term loan	(60.1)	
Net cash outflow from financing		(54.0)
Increase in cash and cash equivalents		1.7

Notes to the cash flow statement

1. Reconciliation of operating profit to net cash inflow from operating activities.

	£m
Operating profit	181.8
Depreciation charges	12.0
Increase in debtors	(90.4)
Increase in amount owed by long-term funds	(16.7)
Increase in unearned premiums	47.2
Increase in claims provisions	206.3
Increase in creditors	12.2
Tax on franked investment income included within operating income	(28.0)
Net cash inflow from operating activities	324.4

2. Analysis of changes in cash and cash equivalents and other liquid investments during the year.

	Cash and cash equivalents	Other liquid investments	Total
	£m	*£m*	*£m*
Balance at 1 April 1991	23.7	3,720.4	3,744.1
Net cash inflow	1.7		1.7
Purchase of investments		382.1	382.1
Sale of investments		(363.8)	(363.8)
Change in market value		331.3	331.3
Balance at 31 March 1992	25.4	4,070.0	4,095.4

3. Analysis of the balances of cash and cash equivalents and other liquid investments as shown in the balance sheet.

	1992	1991	Change in year
	£m	*£m*	*£m*
Cash at bank and in hand	59.9	34.6	25.3
Bank overdrafts	(34.5)	(10.9)	(23.6)
Total cash and cash equivalents	25.4	23.7	1.7
Other liquid investments	*4,070.0*	*3,720.4*	*349.6*
	4,095.4	*3,744.1*	*351.3*

4. Analysis of changes in financing during the year.

	Share capital (including premium)	Long term loan
	£m	*£m*
Financing at 1 April 1991	296.5	346.2
Cash inflow/(outflow) from financing	6.1	(60.1)
Financing at 31 March 1992	302.6	286.1

The development of the standard

This section does not form part of the Financial Reporting Standard.

Summary of the principal changes from Statement of Standard Accounting Practice No. 10 'Statements of source and application of funds'

1 Statement of Standard Accounting Practice No. 10 (SSAP 10), issued July 1975, sought to establish the practice of providing statements of source and application of funds as a part of audited financial statements and to lay down a minimum standard of disclosure in such statements.

2 The objective of the statement of source and application of funds required by SSAP 10 was to show the manner in which the operations of a reporting entity had been financed and in which its financial resources had been used. The information disclosed in the statement is essentially a rearrangement of the information given in the profit and loss (or income and expenditure) account and balance sheet.

3 SSAP 10 was drafted to allow preparers of accounts flexibility in the preparation of funds flow statements. It did not provide a definition of funds or set out a basic structure for a statement. It did, however, specify certain key information which was required to be given in the statement and also provided two examples for general guidance in an appendix, which did not form part of the statement of standard accounting practice.

4 The FRS requires reporting entities to report cash flows rather than accrual based funds flows and the basic structure of the cash flow statement is prescribed.

5 SSAP 10 applied to all financial statements intended to give a true and fair view of the financial position and profit or loss (or income and expenditure) other than those entities with turnover or gross income of less than £25,000 per annum although consideration was to be given to providing the statement for small entities whenever it was desirable. The FRS allows exemptions to a much larger number of reporting entities including most small reporting entities and wholly owned subsidiary undertakings.

6 SSAP 10 allowed the purchase or disposal of subsidiary undertakings to be dealt with either by showing the consideration paid or received as a separate item within the statement of source and application of funds or by reflecting the effects of the acquisition or disposal on the separate assets and liabilities dealt with in the statement. The FRS requires purchase or sales consideration (unless merger accounting is used) to be shown under investing activities and the method reflecting the effects on the separate assets and liabilities, the so-called 'line by line' method, is not permitted.

Summary of the principal changes from Exposure Draft No. 54 'Cash flow statements'

1 The proposed Statement of Standard Accounting Practice set out in Exposure Draft No. 54 (ED 54), issued in July 1990 by the ASC, sought to replace the statement of source and application of funds required by SSAP 10 with a cash flow statement and to set out a general format for such a statement.

2 The requirements of the FRS have been based upon ED 54 and the comments received on it together with the Board's own research, consultation and careful deliberation about the benefits and costs of providing the information. The vast majority of commentators on ED 54 were supportive of the overall approach adopted. The principal differences in the requirements of the FRS and ED 54 are set out below.

Scope

3 ED 54 proposed that the standard should apply to all financial statements intended to give a true and fair view of the financial position and profit or loss (or income and expenditure) other than those entities that do not report under the Companies Act and which have turnover or revenue of less than £25,000 per annum. This scope, which allowed fewer exemptions than those allowed by SSAP 10, was criticised by some commentators, who believed that small companies and wholly owned subsidiary undertakings subsidiaries should be exempted in certain circumstances. The FRS allows exemptions from its requirements to a much larger number of reporting entities including most small reporting entities and wholly owned subsidiary undertakings.

Classification of cash flows

4 ED 54 identified the same major classes of activity (i.e.. operating, investing and financing) as the FRS, but the FRS requires certain cash flows to be reported differently from the proposals contained in ED 54 as explained in paragraphs 5 to 8 below. In addition the FRS requires cash flows arising from financing activities to be divided into two separate categories; cash flows resulting from movements of principal amounts of finance, and returns on investments and servicing of finance.

Reporting net cash flow from operating activities

5 ED 54 considered two methods, direct and indirect, for reporting net cash flow from operating activities and allowed either method to be used. The Board notes that many users of financial statements require the reconciliation between operating profit and net cash flow from operating activities. Some respondents to ED 54 stated that they believed that it would be costly to implement the direct method as they did not currently collect information in such a form directly from their accounting systems. Particular problems would be encountered by multinational groups implementing the direct method. Accordingly, the FRS allows the net cash flow from operating activities to be reported on a net or gross basis, but, in addition, a note to the cash flow statement should give a reconciliation between the reporting entity's operating profit and the net cash flow from operating activities. Thus reporting entities must give the information required by the indirect method, but may also give the information required by the direct method and the Board encourages reporting entities to give a breakdown of their cash flows under the direct method in those circumstances where the benefits to users of the information outweigh the costs of providing it.

Interest and dividend receipts and payments

6 ED 54 required interest received and paid to be included under operating activities. However, there was no consensus in the comments on ED 54 concerning the treatment of interest received and paid in a cash flow statement and in order to present the cash flow information in a useful way the FRS requires that interest received and paid should normally be shown under returns on investments and servicing of finance.

7 ED 54 drew a distinction between interest paid, which is contractual, and dividends paid, which are discretionary, although both are paid to providers of capital. It proposed that dividends paid be included under the reporting entity's financing activities and dividends received under operating activities. However, there was no consensus in the comments on ED 54 concerning the treatment of dividends received and paid in a cash flow statement and in order to present cash flow information in a useful way that is consistent with the presentation of receipts and payments of interest the FRS does not make such a distinction and requires both dividends received and dividends paid to be shown under returns on investments and servicing of finance.

Taxation

8 ED 54 required taxation cash flows in relation to income and capital gains to be shown as operating activities unless material elements of the cash flows related to another activity, when an apportionment could be made. Many commentators on ED 54 did not agree with this presentation, but preferred that taxation be disclosed separately within its own section in order to present the information in a more useful way or to avoid arbitrary apportionments. The Board agrees with these views and accordingly the FRS requires such cash flows to be shown in a separate section of the statement entitled 'taxation'.

9 ED 54 required cash flows to be disclosed inclusive of any attributable Value Added Tax, or other sales taxes, but the FRS requires cash flows to be reported net of any such taxes unless the tax is not recoverable by the reporting entity, when cash flows should normally include the irrecoverable tax. There was no consensus in the comments on ED 54 on the treatment of Value Added Tax, although some commentators believed that problems would be encountered in the production and interpretation of tax inclusive cash flows.

Cash or net debt

10 Many commentators on the exposure draft stated that they believed that a statement that analysed the movement in a reporting entity's net cash or debt position would be more useful than one which reported the movement in cash and cash equivalents alone. These commentators noted that the cash position of an entity must be considered along with obligations that the entity may have. The Board agrees with these comments, but believes that the main focus of the cash flow statement should still be cash flows. However, by splitting the servicing of finance from the movements in principal amounts of finance, requiring a total giving the net cash flow before financing and by requiring a reconciliation of the items within the financing section of the statement to the opening and closing balance sheets the Board believes that the information required by these commentators is given.

Accounting for subsidiary undertakings

Reproduced with the permission of the Accounting Standards Board

Summary

a Financial Reporting Standard No 2 'Accounting for Subsidiary Undertakings' (the FRS) sets out the conditions under which an undertaking that is the parent undertaking of other undertakings (its subsidiary undertakings) should prepare consolidated financial statements. The FRS also sets out the manner in which consolidated financial statements are to be prepared. The purpose of consolidated financial statements is to provide financial information about the economic activities of a group. The Companies Act 1985, as amended by the Companies Act 1989, (the amended Act is referred to as 'the Act') defines a parent undertaking and its subsidiary undertakings that together make up a group. The FRS adopts these definitions.

b The FRS supersedes Statement of Standard Accounting Practice No 14 — 'Group Accounts' and the Board's 'Interim Statement: Consolidated Accounts' except for the following paragraphs of the Interim Statement: paragraphs 32 and 33, 50 and 51 on joint ventures and paragraphs 38, 54 - 59 and 64 dealing with the amendments to SSAP 1 'Accounting for Associated Companies'.

c The FRS applies to all parent undertakings. A parent undertaking that does not report under the Act should comply with the requirements of the FRS except to the extent that these are not permitted by any statutory framework under which the undertaking reports.

d A parent undertaking should prepare consolidated financial statements for its group in accordance with the standard accounting practice set out in the FRS unless it uses one of the exemptions permitted by the Act and set out in paragraph 21 of the FRS.

e The Act and the FRS exempt a parent undertaking from preparing consolidated financial statements if:

(i) its group is small or medium-sized and not an ineligible group as defined in Section 248; or

(ii) it is a wholly-owned or majority-owned subsidiary undertaking and its immediate parent undertaking is established under the law of a member state of the European Community. Exemption is conditional on compliance with certain further conditions in Section 228; or

(iii) all of its subsidiary undertakings are permitted or required to be excluded from consolidation by Section 229.

f The consolidated financial statements should be prepared by consolidating financial information for the parent undertaking and all its subsidiary undertakings, except for any subsidiary undertakings that are to be excluded from consolidation by virtue of the requirements of the Act and the FRS.

g A subsidiary undertaking is to be excluded from consolidation if:

(i) severe long-term restrictions substantially hinder the exercise of the parent undertaking's rights over the subsidiary undertaking's assets or management; or

(ii) the group's interest in the subsidiary undertaking is held exclusively with a view to subsequent resale and the subsidiary undertaking has not previously been consolidated; or

(iii) the subsidiary undertaking's activities are so different from those of other undertakings to be included in the consolidation that its inclusion would be incompatible with the obligation to give a true and fair view.

The Act permits rather than requires exclusion in cases (i) and (ii) above. The FRS requires exclusion in these circumstances because the same conditions that justify permitting exclusion also make consolidation inappropriate. In addition, the FRS requires the circumstances in which subsidiary undertakings are to be excluded from consolidation to be interpreted strictly. It is important that only those subsidiary undertakings whose consolidation would be inappropriate are excluded from consolidation so that consolidated financial statements reflect in full the resources, obligations and results of the group.

h The FRS requires additional disclosures for subsidiary undertakings excluded from consolidation and requires them to be accounted for as follows.

(i) Subsidiary undertakings excluded from consolidation because of severe long-term restrictions are to be treated as fixed asset investments. They are to be included at their carrying amount when the restrictions came into force, subject to any write down for permanent diminution in value, and no further accruals are to be made for profits or losses of those subsidiary undertakings, unless the parent undertaking still exercises significant influence. In the latter case they are to be treated as associated undertakings.

(ii) Subsidiary undertakings excluded from consolidation because they are held exclusively for resale and have not previously been consolidated are to be included as current assets at the lower of cost and net realisable value.

(iii) Subsidiary undertakings excluded from consolidation because of their different activities are to be accounted for using the equity method as required by the Act.

i Minority interests in total should be reported separately in the consolidated balance sheet and profit and loss account. When an entity becomes a subsidiary undertaking the assets and liabilities attributable to its minority interest should be included on the same basis as those attributable to the interest held by the parent and other subsidiary undertakings. The effect of this for an acquisition is that all the subsidiary undertaking's identifiable assets and liabilities are included at fair value as required by the Act. No goodwill should be attributed to the minority interest.

j Intra-group transactions may result in profits or losses being included in the book value of assets to be included in the consolidation; the FRS requires the elimination in full of any such profits or losses because, for the group as a whole, no profits or losses have arisen.

k Uniform group accounting policies should generally be used in preparing the consolidated financial statements; in exceptional cases different policies may be used with disclosure.

l The financial statements of all subsidiary undertakings to be used in preparing consolidated financial statements should have the same financial year end and be for the same accounting period as those of the parent undertaking of the group. Where the financial year of a subsidiary undertaking differs from that of the parent undertaking of the group, interim financial statements for that subsidiary undertaking prepared to the parent undertaking's accounting date should be used. If this is impracticable, earlier financial statements of the subsidiary undertaking may be used, provided they are prepared for a financial year that ended not more than three months earlier.

m Changes in membership of a group occur on the date control passes, whether by a transaction or other event. Changes in the membership of the group during the period should be disclosed.

n When a subsidiary undertaking is acquired the FRS requires its identifiable assets and liabilities to be brought into the consolidation at their fair values at the date that undertaking becomes a subsidiary undertaking, even if the acquisition has been made in stages. When a group increases its interest in an undertaking that is already its subsidiary undertaking, the identifiable assets and liabilities of that subsidiary undertaking should be revalued to fair value and goodwill arising on the increase in interest should be calculated by reference to that fair value. This revaluation is not required if the difference between fair values and carrying amounts of the identifiable assets and liabilities attributable to the increase in stake is not material.

o The effect of consolidating the parent and its subsidiary undertakings may be that aggregation obscures useful information about the different undertakings and activities included in the consolidated financial statements. Parent undertakings are encouraged to give segmental analysis to provide readers of consolidated financial statements with useful information on the different risks and rewards, growth and prospects of the different parts of the group. The specification of such analysis, however, falls outside the scope of the FRS.

p The accounting practices set out in the FRS should be adopted as soon as possible and regarded as standard for periods ending on or after 23 December 1992, except for Republic of Ireland companies, who should regard it as standard after the date of application of the Irish legislation implementing the European Community Seventh Directive. Such Irish companies should adopt the accounting practices in the FRS as soon as possible after the enactment of the implementing legislation.

Objective

1 The objective of this FRS is to require parent undertakings to provide financial information about the economic activities of their groups by preparing consolidated financial statements.* These statements are intended to present financial information about a parent undertaking and its subsidiary undertakings as a single economic entity to show the economic resources controlled by the group, the obligations of the group and the results the group achieves with its resources.**

* 'Financial statements' is the term used in the FRS to mean the same as the term 'accounts' used in the Companies Acts.

** The Companies Act 1985, as amended by the 1989 Act, contains detailed provisions relating to consolidated financial statements. The FRS considers the application of the Act and adds to its provisions where necessary.

Definitions

The following definitions apply for the purposes of the FRS and in particular the statement of standard accounting practice set out in paragraphs 18 to 56.

The terms defined below which are also defined in the Act have the same meaning in the FRS as in the Act, notwithstanding that in some cases the FRS definition is a summary or explanation rather than a repetition of the definition in the Act. The definitions should therefore be interpreted by reference to the full provisions of the Act. The marginal notes give the main references in the Act. References to sections and schedules are to those of the Act unless otherwise stated.

2 *The Act*
Companies Act 1985 as amended by the Companies Act 1989.

3 *Companies (Northern Ireland) Order 1986*
Companies (Northern Ireland) Order 1986 as amended by the Companies (Northern Ireland) Order 1990 and the Companies (No 2) (Northern Ireland) Order 1990.

4 *Consolidated financial statements*
The financial statements of a group prepared by consolidation.

5 *Consolidation*
The process of adjusting and combining financial information from the individual financial statements of a parent undertaking and its subsidiary undertakings to prepare consolidated financial statements that present financial information for the group as a single economic entity.

6 *Control*
The ability of an undertaking to direct the financial and operating policies of another undertaking with a view to gaining ecomomic benefits from its activities.

7 *Dominant influence*
Influence that can be exercised to achieve the operating and financial policies desired by the holder of the influence, notwithstanding the rights or influence of any other party.

- **a** In the context of paragraph 14(C) and Section 258(2)(C) *the right to exercise a dominant influence* means that the holder has a right to give directions with respect to the operating and financial policies of another undertaking with which its directors are obliged to comply, whether or not they are for the benefit of that undertaking. [From 10A Sch4(1)]
- **b** *The actual exercise of dominant influence* is the exercise of an influence that achieves the result that the operating and financial policies of the undertaking influenced are set in accordance with the wishes of the holder of the influence and for the holder's benefit whether or not those wishes are explicit. The actual exercise of dominant influence is identified by its effect in practice rather than by the way in which it is exercised. [FRS defining phrase used in s.258(4)(a)]

8 *Equity method*
A method of accounting for an investment that brings into the consolidated profit and loss account the investor's share of the investment undertaking's results and that records the investment in the consolidated balance sheet at the investor's share of the investment undertaking's net assets including any goodwill arising to the extent that it has not previously been written off.

9 *Group*
A parent undertaking and its subsidiary undertakings. [From s. 262]

10 *Interest held on a long-term basis*
An interest which is held other than *exclusively with a view to subsequent resale.* [FRS defining phrase used in s. 260]

11 *Interest held exclusively with a view to subsequent resale* [FRS defining phrase used in s. 229 (3) (c)]

a An interest for which a purchaser has been identified or is being sought, and which is reasonably expected to be disposed of within approximately one year of its date of acquisition; or

b an interest that was acquired as a result of the enforcement of a security, unless the interest has become part of the continuing activities of the group or the holder acts as if it intends the interest to become so.

12 *Managed on a unified basis* [FRS defining phrase used in s. 258 (4) (b)]
Two or more undertakings are managed on a unified basis if the whole of the operations of the undertakings are integrated and they are managed as a single unit. Unified management does not arise solely because one undertaking manages another.

13 *Minority interest in a subsidiary undertaking* [From 4A Sch 17]
The interest in a subsidiary undertaking included in the consolidation that is attributable to the shares held by or on behalf of persons other than the parent undertaking and its subsidiary undertakings.

14 *Parent undertaking and subsidiary undertaking* [From s. 258 and 10A Sch]
An undertaking is the parent undertaking of another undertaking (a subsidiary undertaking) if any of the following apply.

a It holds a majority of the voting rights in the undertaking. [From s. 258 (2) (a)]

b It is a member of the undertaking and has the right to appoint or remove directors holding a majority of the voting rights at meetings of the board on all, or substantially all, matters. [From s. 258 (2) (b) and 10A Sch 3]

c It has the right to exercise a dominant influence over the undertaking [From s. 258 (2) (c) and 10A Sch 4]

(i) by virtue of provisions contained in the undertaking's memorandum or articles; or

(ii) by virtue of a control contract. The control contract must be in writing and be of a kind authorised by the memorandum or articles of the controlled undertaking. It must also be permitted by the law under which that undertaking is established. [From 10A Sch 4 (2)]

d It is a member of the undertaking and controls alone, pursuant to an agreement with other shareholders or members, a majority of the voting rights in the undertaking. [From s. 259 (2) (d)]

e It has a participating interest in the undertaking and: [From s. 258 (4)]

(i) it actually exercises a dominant influence over the undertaking; or

(ii) it and the undertaking are managed on a unified basis.

f A parent undertaking is also treated as the parent undertaking of the subsidiary undertakings of its subsidiary undertakings. [From s. 258 (5)]

For the purpose of Section 258 [parent and subsidiary undertakings] an undertaking shall be treated as a member of another undertaking: [From s. 258 (3)]

(i) if any of its subsidiary undertakings is a member of that undertaking; or

(ii) if any shares in that other undertaking are held by a person acting on behalf of the parent undertaking or any of its subsidiary undertakings.

Any shares held, or powers exercisable, by a subsidiary undertaking should be treated as held or exercisable by its parent undertaking. [From 10A Sch 9]

15 *Partitipating interest* [From s. 260]

An interest held by an undertaking in the shares of another undertaking which it holds on a long-term basis for the purpose of securing a contribution to its activities by the exercise of control or influence arising from or related to that interest.

a A holding of 20% or more of the shares of an undertaking shall be presumed to be a participating interest unless the contrary is shown.

b An interest in shares includes an interest which is convertible into an interest in shares, and includes an option to acquire shares or any interest which is convertible into shares.

c An interest held on behalf of an undertaking shall be treated as held by that undertaking.

16 *Undertaking* [From s. 259]

A body corporate, a partnership or an unincorporated association carrying on a trade or business with or without a view to profit.

17 *Voting rights in an undertaking* [From 10A Sch 2 (1)]

Rights conferred on shareholders in respect of their shares or, in the case of an undertaking not having a share capital, on members, to vote at general meetings of the undertaking on all, or substantially all, matters. Schedule 10A deals with the attribution of voting rights in certain circumstances.

Statement of Standard Accounting Practice

The statement of standard accounting practice set out in paragraphs 18 to 56 of the FRS should be read in the context of the Objective of the FRS as stated in paragraph 1, the definitions set out in paragraphs 2 to 17 and also of the Foreword to Accounting Standards and the Statement of Principles for Financial Reporting currently in issue.

In the statement of standard accounting practice marginal notes give the main references to the Act. If no marginal reference is given the requirement is that of the FRS alone. The statement of standard accounting practice should be interpreted by reference to the full provisions of the Act notwithstanding that the statement summarises certain provisions of the Act. References to sections and schedules are to those of the Act unless otherwise stated.

The Explanation section of the FRS, set out in paragraphs 59 to 94, shall be regarded as part of the statement of standard accounting practice insofar as it assists in interpreting that statement.

Scope

18 This standard applies to all parent undertakings that prepare the financial statements described below whether or not they report under the Act. Parent undertakings that prepare consolidated financial statements intended to give a true and fair view of the financial position and profit or loss (or income and expenditure) of their group should prepare such statements in accordance with the requirements of the FRS. A parent undertaking that uses one of the exemptions from preparing consolidated financial statements (described in paragraph 21) but prepares individual financial statements intended to give a true and fair view of its own financial position and profit or loss (or income and expenditure) should include the statement required by paragraph 22. The FRS does not otherwise deal with the individual financial statements of a parent undertaking.

19 Parent undertakings that do not report under the Act should comply with the requirements of the FRS, and of the Act where referred to in the FRS, except to the extent that these requirements are not permitted by any statutory framework under which such undertakings report.

Consolidated financial statements

Preparation of consolidated financial statements

20 A parent undertaking should prepare consolidated financial statements for its group unless it uses one of the exemptions set out in paragraph 21 . [s. 227, s. 228 and s. 248]

Exempt parent undertakings

21 A parent undertaking is exempt from preparing consolidated financial statements for its group on any one of the following grounds.

- **a** The group is small or medium-sized and is not an ineligible group as defined in Section 248. A group is ineligible if any of its members is a public company, a banking institution, an insurance company or an authorised person under the Financial Services Act 1986. [s.248]
- **b** The parent undertaking is a wholly-owned subsidiary undertaking and its immediate parent undertaking is established under the law of a member state of the European Community. Exemption is conditional on compliance with certain further conditions set out in Section 228(2). A parent undertaking is not exempt

if any of its securities is listed on a stock exchange in any European Community country. [s.228]

c The parent undertaking is a majority-owned subsidiary undertaking and meets all the conditions for exemption as a wholly-owned subsidiary undertaking set out in Section 228(2) as well as the additional conditions set out in Section 228(1)(b). [s. 228]

d All of the parent undertaking's subsidiary undertakings are permitted or required to be excluded from consolidation by Section 229. (The conditions for exclusion of Section 229 are more fully described in paragraph 25 and are elaborated on in paragraphs 76 to 78.) [s.229(5)]

22 The Act sets out disclosure requirements for parent companies not required to prepare consolidated financial statements. In addition to providing this information, a parent undertaking making use of an exemption from preparing consolidated financial statements should state that its financial statements present information about it as an individual undertaking and not about its group. This statement should include or refer to a note giving the grounds on which the parent undertaking is exempt from preparing consolidated financial statements, as required by Schedule 5 paragraph 1(4). [s. 231 and 5 Sch Part 1]

Undertakings to be included in the consolidation

23 As required by the Act, the consolidated financial statements should include the parent undertaking and all its subsidiary undertakings, except those that are required to be excluded under the conditions set out in paragraph 25 below. [s.229(1)]

Disproportionate expense and undue delay

24 Neither disproportionate expense nor undue delay in obtaining the information necessary for the preparation of consolidated financial statements can justify excluding from consolidation subsidiary undertakings that are individually or collectively material in the context of the group. [FRS allows s.229 (3) (b) exclusion only where the undertaking is not material]

Subsidiary undertakings to be excluded from consolidation

25 The exclusions required by this paragraph are based on the exclusions permitted or required by Section 229 (3) and (4). A subsidiary undertaking should be excluded from consolidation where [s.229 (3) and (4)]:

a severe long-term restrictions substantially hinder the exercise of the rights of the parent undertaking over the assets or management of the subsidiary undertaking. The rights referred to are those by reason of which the parent undertaking is defined as such under Section 258 and in the absence of which it would not be the parent undertaking; [FRS requires exclusion permitted by s. 229 (3) (a)] or

b the interest in the subsidiary undertaking is held exclusively with a view to subsequent resale (as defined in paragraph 11) and the subsidiary undertaking has not previously been consolidated in group accounts prepared by the parent undertaking; [FRS requires exclusion permitted by s. 229 (3) (c)] or

c the subsidiary undertaking's activities are so different from those of other undertakings to be included in the consolidation that its inclusion would be incompatible with the obligation to give a true and fair view. It is exceptional for such circumstances to arise and it is not possible to identify any particular contrast of activities where the necessary incompatibility with the true and fair view generally occurs. The Act provides that exclusion on the grounds of different activities does not apply 'merely because some of the undertakings are industrial, some commercial and some provide services, or because they carry on industrial or commercial activities involving different products or provide different services'. [s. 229 (4)]

26 As required by the Act, subject to the conditions and exemptions of Section 231, the names of any subsidiary undertaking excluded from the consolidation and the reasons why they have been excluded should be given. [s. 231 and 5 Sch 15 (4)]

Accounting for excluded subsidiary undertakings

Severe long-term restrictions

27 A subsidiary undertaking excluded on the grounds set out in paragraph 25(a) [severe long-term restrictions] should be treated as a fixed asset investment. If restrictions were in force at its acquisition date, the subsidiary undertaking should be carried initially at cost; if restrictions came into force at a later date, the subsidiary undertaking should be carried at a fixed amount calculated using the equity method at that date. While the restrictions are in force, no further accruals should be made for the profits or losses of that subsidiary undertaking, unless the parent undertaking still exercises a significant influence over it. If this is the case, it should treat the subsidiary undertaking as an associated undertaking using the equity method. The carrying amount of subsidiary undertakings subject to severe long-term restrictions should be reviewed and written down for any permanent diminution in value. In assessing diminution in value, each subsidiary undertaking should be considered individually. Any intragroup amounts due from subsidiary undertakings excluded on the grounds of severe long-term restrictions should also be reviewed and written down, if necessary.

28 When the severe restrictions cease and the parent undertaking's rights are restored, the amount of the unrecognised profit or loss that accrued during the period of restriction for that subsidiary undertaking should be separately disclosed in the consolidated profit and loss account of the period in which control is resumed. Similarly, any amount previously charged for permanent diminution that needs to be written back as a result of restrictions ceasing should be separately disclosed.

Held exclusively with a view to subsequent resale

29 A subsidiary undertaking that is excluded from consolidation on the grounds set out in paragraph 25(b) [held exclusively with a view to subsequent resale] should be recorded in the consolidated financial statements as a current asset at the lower of cost and net realisable value.

Different activities [4A Sch 18]

30 A subsidiary undertaking excluded on the grounds set out in paragraph 25(c) [different activities] should be recorded in the consolidated financial statements using the equity method, as required by the Act.

Disclosures for subsidiary undertakings excluded from consolidation [s. 231 and 5 Sch 15-20]

31 In addition to the disclosures required by Schedule 5, subject to Section 231, the following information should be given in the consolidated financial statements for subsidiary undertakings not included in the consolidation:

a particulars of the balances between the excluded subsidiary undertakings and the rest of the group;

b the nature and extent of transactions of the excluded subsidiary undertakings with the rest of the group;

c for an excluded subsidiary undertaking carried other than by the equity method, any amounts included in the consolidated financial statements in respect of:

(i) dividends received and receivable from that undertaking; and

(ii) any write-down in the period in respect of the investment in that undertaking or amounts due from that undertaking;

d for subsidiary undertakings excluded because of different activities, the separate financial statements of those undertakings. Summarised information may be provided for undertakings that individually, or in combination with those with similar operations, do not account for more than 20% of any one or more of operating profits, turnover or net assets of the group. The group amounts should be measured by including all excluded subsidiary undertakings.

32 Disclosures for excluded subsidiary undertakings in general apply to individual excluded subsidiary undertakings. However, if the information about excluded subsidiary undertakings is more appropriately presented for a sub-unit of the group comprising more than one excluded subsidiary undertaking, the disclosures may be made on an aggregate basis. Any individual sub-unit for these disclosures is to include only subsidiary undertakings excluded under the same subsection of Section 229. Individual disclosures should be made for any excluded subsidiary undertaking, including its sub-group where relevant, that alone accounts for more than 20% of any one or more of operating profits, turnover or net assets of the group. The group amounts should be measured by including all excluded subsidiary undertakings.

Disclosures for principal subsidiary undertakings

33 In addition to the disclosures required by Schedule 5. and, like those, subject to the exemptions and conditions of Section 231, the following should be shown for each subsidiary undertaking whose results or financial position principally affects the figures in the consolidated financial statements. [s. 231 and 5 Sch Part II]

a the proportion of voting rights held by the parent and its subsidiary undertakings; and

b an indication of the nature of its business.

Disclosure of the basis of dominant influence

34 Where an undertaking is a subsidiary undertaking only because its parent undertaking has a participating interest in it and actually exercises a dominant influence over it, the consolidated financial statements should disclose the basis of the parent undertaking's dominant influence in addition to the disclosures required, subject to Section 231, by Schedule 5 paragraph 15(5). [s. 231 and 5 Sch 15 (5)]

Minority interests

35 The consolidated balance sheet should show separately the aggregate of the capital and reserves attributable to minority interests at the end of the period under 'Minority interests' in accordance with Schedule 4A paragraph 17(2). This amount represents the aggregate share of net assets or liabilities of subsidiary undertakings included in the consolidation that are attributable to the minority interests. [4A Sch 17 (2)]

36 The consolidated profit and loss account should show separately the aggregate of profit or loss on ordinary activities for the period attributable to the minority interests under 'Minority interests' in accordance with Schedule 4A paragraph 17(3). Any extraordinary profit or loss attributable to minority interests should be shown separately in accordance with Schedule 4A paragraph 17(4). [4A Sch 17(3) and (4)]

37 Profits or losses arising in a subsidiary undertaking should be apportioned between the controlling and minority interests in proportion to their respective interests held over the period in which the profits or losses arose. Where the losses in a subsidiary undertaking attributable to the minority interest result in its interest being one in net liabilities rather than net assets, the group should make provision to the extent that it has any commercial or legal obligation (whether formal or implied) to provide finance that may not be recoverable in respect of the accumulated losses attributable to the minority interest.

38 Whether the assets and liabilities of a subsidiary undertaking are included at fair values or adjusted carrying amounts*, those attributable to the minority interest should be included on the same basis as those attributable to the interests held by the parent and its other subsidiary undertakings. However, goodwill arising on acquisition should only be recognised with respect to the part of the subsidiary undertaking that is attributable to the interest held by the parent and its other subsidiary undertakings. No goodwill should be attributed to the minority interest.

Where the merger method of accounting is to be used, Schedule 4A paragraph 11 requires the assets and liabilities of the subsidiary undertaking to be consolidated at the amounts at which they stand in that undertaking's financial statements, subject to any adjusments authorised or required by the Act.

Consolidation adjustments

Intragroup transactions

39 To the extent that they are reflected in the book value of assets to be included in the consolidation, profits or losses on any intra-group transactions should be eliminated in full. Amounts in relation to debts and claims between undertakings included in the consolidation should also be eliminated. The elimination of profits or losses relating to intra-group transactions should be set against the interests held by the group and the minority interest in respective proportion to their holdings in the undertaking whose individual financial statements recorded the eliminated profits or losses. All profits or losses on transactions that would be eliminated if they were between undertakings included in the consolidation should also be eliminated if one party is a subsidiary undertaking excluded because of its different activities (paragraph 25(c)). [FRS requirement in relation to 4a Sch 6. The Act allows partial elimination but the FRS requires elimination in full.]

* Where the acquisition method of accounting is to be used in consolidating a subsidiary undertaking. Schedule 4A paragraph 9 requires the identifiable assets and liabilities of the undertaking acquired to be included in the consolidation at their fair values as at the date of acquisition.

Accounting policies

40 Subject to paragraph 41 below, uniform group accounting policies should be used for determining the amounts to be included in the consolidated financial statements, if necessary by adjusting for consolidation the amounts which have been reported by subsidiary undertakings in their individual financial statements. [4A Sch 3(1)]

41 In exceptional cases, different accounting policies may be used. Where the directors of the parent undertaking depart from the Act's general requirement to use the same group accounting rules to value or otherwise determine the assets and liabilities to be included in the consolidated financial statements, Schedule 4A paragraph 3(2) requires disclosure of the particulars, which should include the different accounting policies used. [4A Sch 3(2)]

Accounting periods and dates

42 The financial statements of all subsidiary undertakings to be used in preparing the consolidated financial statements should, wherever practicable, be prepared to the same financial year end and for the same accounting period as those of the parent undertaking of the group.

43 Where the financial year of a subsidiary undertaking differs from that of the parent undertaking of the group, interim financial statements should be prepared to the same date as those of the parent undertaking of the group for use in the preparation of the consolidated financial statements. If it is not practicable to use such interim financial statements, the financial statements of the subsidiary undertaking for its last financial year should be used, providing that year ended not more than three months before the relevant year end of the parent undertaking of the group. In this case any changes that have taken place in the intervening period that materially affect the view given by the group's financial statements should be taken into account by adjustments in the preparation of the consolidated financial statements. [FRS preference of alternatives permitted by 4A Sch 2(2)]

44 The following information should be given for each subsidiary undertaking which is included in the consolidated financial statements on the basis of information prepared to a different date or for a different accounting period from that of the parent undertaking of the group: [Subject to s.231, 5 Sch 19 requires disclosures for different financial year ends]

- **a** the name of the subsidiary undertaking;
- **b** the accounting date or period of the subsidiary undertaking; and
- **c** the reason for using a different accounting date or period for the subsidiary undertaking.

Changes in composition of a group

Date of changes in group membership

45 The date for accounting for an undertaking becoming a subsidiary undertaking is the date on which control of that undertaking passes to its new parent undertaking. This date is the date of acquisition for Schedule 4A paragraph 9 or the date of merger. The date for accounting for an undertaking ceasing to be a subsidiary undertaking is the date on which its former parent undertaking relinquishes its control over that undertaking.

Ceasing to be a subsidiary undertaking

46 When an undertaking ceases to be a subsidiary undertaking during a period, the consolidated financial statements for that period should include the results of that subsidiary undertaking up to the date that it ceases to be a subsidiary undertaking and any gain or loss arising on that cessation, to the extent that these have not been already provided for in the consolidated financial statements.

47 The gain or loss directly arising for the group on an undertaking ceasing to be its subsidiary undertaking is calculated by comparing the carrying amount of the net assets of that subsidiary undertaking attributable to the group's interest before the cessation with any remaining carrying amount attributable to the group's interest after the cessation together with any proceeds received. The net assets compared should include any related goodwill not previously written off through the profit and loss account. This calculation of gain or loss applies whether the cause of the undertaking ceasing to be a subsidiary undertaking is a direct disposal, a deemed disposal or other event.

48 In addition to the disclosures required by Schedule 4A paragraph 15, the consolidated financial statements should give the name of any material undertaking that has ceased to be a subsidiary undertaking in the period, showing any ownership interest retained. Where any material undertaking has ceased to be a subsidiary undertaking other than by the disposal of at least part of the interest held by the group, the circumstances should be explained. [4A Sch 15]

Becoming or ceasing to be a subsidiary undertaking other than by a purchase or exchange of shares

49 Where an undertaking has become or ceased to be a subsidiary undertaking other than as a result of a purchase or exchange of shares, the circumstances should be explained in a note to the consolidated financial statements.

Changes in stake

Acquiring a subsidiary undertaking in stages

50 Schedule 4A paragraph 9 requires that the identifiable assets and liabilities of a subsidiary undertaking be included in the consolidation at fair value at the date of its acquisition, that is, the date it becomes a subsidiary undertaking. This requirement is also applicable where the group's interest in the undertaking that becomes a subsidiary undertaking is acquired in stages. [4A Sch 9]

Increasing an interest held in a subsidiary undertaking

51 When a group increases its interest in an undertaking that is already its subsidiary undertaking, the identifiable assets and liabilities of that subsidiary undertaking should be revalued to fair value and goodwill arising on the increase in interest should be calculated by those fair values. This revaluation is not required if the difference between net fair values and carrying amounts of the assets and liabilities attributable to the increase in stake is not material.

Reducing an interest held in a subsidiary undertaking

52 Where a group reduces its interest in a subsidiary undertaking, it should record any profit or loss arising calculated as the difference between the carrying amount of the net assets of that subsidiary undertaking attributable to the group's interest before the reduction and the carrying amount attributable to the group's interest after the reduction together with any proceeds received. The net assets compared should include any related goodwill not previously written off through the profit and loss account. Where the undertaking remains a subsidiary undertaking after the disposal, the minority interest in that subsidiary undertaking should be increased by the carrying amount of the net identifiable assets that are now attributable to the minority interest because of the decrease in the group's interest. No amount for goodwill that arose on acquisition of the group's interest in that subsidiary undertaking should be attributed to the minority interest.

Distributions

Restrictions on distribution

53 Where significant statutory, contractual or exchange control restrictions on distributions by subsidiary undertakings materially limit the parent undertaking's access to distributable profits, the nature and extent of the restrictions should be disclosed.

Tax on the accumulated reserves of overseas subsidiary undertakings

54 The extent to which deferred tax has been accounted for in respect of future remittances of the accumulated reserves of overseas subsidiary undertakings should be disclosed. Where deferred tax has not been provided in respect of all the accumulated reserves of overseas subsidiary undertakings the reasons for not fully providing should be given.

Date from which effective

55 The accounting practices set out in this statement should be adopted as soon as possible and regarded as standard in respect of consolidated financial statements relating to periods ending on or after 23 December 1992 except for those companies considered below. The accounting practices in this statement should be adopted by Republic of Ireland companies as soon as possible after the enactment of the Irish legislation implementing the European Community Seventh Directive and regarded as standard in respect of consolidated financial statements for periods specified in the date of application of that legislation.

Withdrawal of SSAP 14 'Group accounts' and 'Interim Statement: Consolidated Accounts'

56 The FRS supersedes SSAP 14 'Group accounts' and the references to SSAP 14 in other accounting standards should be treated as follows:

- **a** SSAP 1: paragraph 66 — last two sentences referring to SSAP 14 are deleted;
- **b** SSAP 6: paragraph 5 — "as required by SSAP 14 'Group accounts'" deleted;
- **c** SSAP 23: paragraph 1 — line 5 "SSAP 14 'Group accounts'" replaced by "FRS 2 'Accounting for subsidiary undertakings'" and last two sentences deleted;

  paragraph 16 — "in accordance with the requirements of SSAP 14" deleted;
  paragraph 22 — "as required by SSAP 14" deleted.

The FRS also supersedes the 'Interim Statement: Consolidated Accounts' except for paragraphs 32 and 33, A9 and A10 on joint ventures and the amendments to SSAP 1 'Accounting for Associated Companies' contained in paragraph 38 of the Interim Statement and the related commentary A13 - A18 and A23. The paragraphs not superseded remain in force.

Financial Reporting Standard No 2 'Accounting for Subsidiary Undertakings' was adopted by the unanimous vote of the nine members of the Accounting Standards Board.

Members of the Accounting Standards Board

David Tweedie (Chairman)

Allan Cook (Technical Director)

Robert Bradfield

Sir Bryan Carsberg

Elwyn Eilledge

Michael Garner

Donald Main

Roger Munson

Graham Stacy

Compliance with International Accounting Standards

57 Compliance with the FRS ensures compliance with International Accounting Standard No 27 'Consolidated Financial Statements' (IAS 27) except that IAS 27 does not have an exclusion from consolidation for a subsidiary undertaking based on the grounds that its activities are dissimilar from those of other undertakings to be included in the consolidation. The exclusion for different activities is an exclusion required by statute. As explained in the FRS, this is expected to apply only exceptionally when the inclusion of a subsidiary undertaking would not be compatible with the obligation to give a true and fair view.

58 The IASC has issued E45 'Proposed Statement — Business Combinations' which includes proposals to implement its harmonisation programme. E45 proposes as the benchmark treatment that, when an entity becomes a subsidiary undertaking and is not wholly-owned, minority interests should be measured at the pre-acquisition carrying amounts of their attributable identifiable assets and liabilities. The FRS requires the minority interests to be measured at their proportion of the amount at which the identifiable assets and liabilities are included in the consolidation; for an acquisition this is fair value at that date. This treatment is proposed by the IASC as an allowed alternative.

Explanation

The purpose of consolidated financial statements

59 For a variety of legal, tax and other reasons undertakings generally choose to conduct their activities not through a single legal entity but through several undertakings under the ultimate control of the parent undertaking of that group. For this reason the financial statements of a parent undertaking by itself do not present a full picture of its economic activities or financial position. Consolidated financial statements are required in order to reflect the extended business unit that conducts activities under the control of the parent undertaking.

The legal background to the FRS

60 In the United Kingdom the preparation of consolidated financial statements for companies is governed by the Act and the Companies (Northern Ireland) Order 1986. These implement in their respective jurisdictions the provisions of the European Community Seventh Directive. The FRS is drafted to be consistent with the Act, supplementing it with guidance on its application and additional requirements where necessary. The definitions and statement of standard accounting practice contain marginal notes that give references to the Act where these are relevant. Any differences in the application of the FRS in Northern Ireland are explained in the sections setting out the legal provisions in that jurisdiction (paragraph 97). The application of the FRS in the Republic of Ireland is explained in the section on the legal requirements in the Republic of Ireland (paragraph 98).

Parent undertakings not subject to the Act

61 The FRS is drafted in terms derived from the Act but applies to all parent undertakings that prepare financial statements intended to give a true and fair view. A parent undertaking not subject to the Act should comply with the requirements of the FRS, and of the Act where referred to in the FRS, except to the extent that these requirements are not permitted by any statutory framework under which the undertaking reports. By reference to the Act, which in most cases accords with requirements the FRS might otherwise introduce itself in respect of such undertakings, the FRS achieves a single set of requirements relating to the preparation of consolidated financial statements both for companies that report under the Act and for other undertakings.

The relationship between the legal background and accounting principles

62 The accounting concept that underlies the presentation of consolidated financial statements for a group as a single economic entity is summarised in the definition of control in paragraph 6. Although the definitions of parent and subsidiary undertakings in the Act are founded mainly on the accounting concept of control, Section 258 uses a list of tests rather than relying on control directly to determine which undertakings are parent and subsidiary undertakings. In the main the effect of applying the tests in the Act is the same as using a criterion based directly on the accounting concept of control. However, in some cases the tests of the Act may either fail to identify as a subsidiary undertaking one that is controlled by another undertaking or identify as a subsidiary undertaking one that is not controlled by its parent undertaking. In other cases Section 258 may identify more than one undertaking as the parent undertaking of the same subsidiary undertaking. Where more than one undertaking is thereby identified as a parent of one subsidiary undertaking, not more than one of those parents can have control as defined in paragraph 6.

63 In practice such apparent differences between the effects of applying the Act and the standard can generally be resolved by taking into account the following factors:

- **a** the existence of a quasi subsidiary (paragraph 64); or
- **b** the existence of severe long-term restrictions on the rights of the parent undertaking (paragraph 65); or
- **c** the existence of a joint venture agreement, whether formal or informal (paragraphs 66 and 67).

64 Undertakings that are directly or indirectly controlled by another undertaking and are sources of benefit to that other, but do not qualify according to the tests in the Act as subsidiary undertakings, are described as 'quasi subsidiaries'. The definition and treatment of quasi subsidiaries are not dealt with in this standard*.

65 The Act allows a subsidiary undertaking to be excluded from consolidation if the parent undertaking suffers severe long-term restrictions that substantially hinder the exercise of its rights over the assets or management of the subsidiary undertaking. Paragraph 78(c) discusses severe long-term restrictions further.

66 The control that identifies undertakings as parent and subsidiary undertakings should be distinguished from shared control for example as in a joint venture. It is the parent undertaking's sole control of its subsidiary undertakings that gives it access to its subsidiary undertakings' resources. The parent undertaking extends its economic activities through its subsidiary undertakings using their assets and liabilities in a similar way to its own. The ability of an undertaking that shares control to direct the operating and financial policies of the undertaking in which control is shared is circumscribed by the need to take account of the wishes of the other parties that share control. An

* At the time of issue of the FRS, the Board is in the course of developing a separate standard dealing *inter alia* with quasi subsidiaries.

undertaking identified as a parent by Section 258 that shares control over its subsidiary undertaking may be suffering from severe long-term restrictions as discussed in paragraph 78(c) in relation to the undertaking in which it shares control.

67 Where the tests of the Act identify more than one undertaking as the parent of one subsidiary undertaking it is likely that they have shared control and therefore their interests in the subsidiary undertaking are in effect interests in a joint venture and should be treated accordingly. Alternatively one or more of the undertakings identified under the Act as a parent undertaking may exercise a non-controlling but significant influence over its subsidiary undertaking in which case it would be more appropriate to treat that subsidiary undertaking in the same way as an associated undertaking rather than to include it in the consolidation.

Identifying parent and subsidiary undertakings

68 Parent and subsidiary undertakings are defined in the FRS by applying the provisions of Section 258, which are repeated in an abbreviated form in paragraph 14 of the FRS. In addition, the FRS defines some of the phrases that are used in the Act to define undertakings that are parent or subsidiary undertakings. Paragraphs 69-74 below consider some of the terms used.

Dominant influence

69 The Act uses 'dominant influence' as a key phrase in two of the conditions of section 258 that identify parent and subsidiary undertakings.

70 Section 258(2)(c) identifies an undertaking as a parent undertaking if it has the right to exercise a dominant influence over another undertaking:

- **a** by virtue of provisions contained in the undertaking's memorandum or articles; or
- **b** by virtue of a control contract.

Schedule 10A paragraph 4(1) states that for the purposes of Sub-section 258(2)(c) 'an undertaking shall not be regarded as having the right to exercise a dominant influence over another undertaking unless it has a right to give directions with respect to the operating and financial policies of that other undertaking which its directors are obliged to comply with whether or not they are for the benefit of that other undertaking'. This forms the basis of the definition set out in paragraph 7(a) of the FRS. In the United Kingdom directors are bound by a common law duty to act in the best interests of their company. For this reason there may, in some cases, be a risk that accepting a right to exercise dominant influence, as here defined, would be in breach of the above duty.

71 In a second reference to dominant influence, Section 258(4)(a) identifies an undertaking as the subsidiary undertaking of another (its parent undertaking) if that other has a participating interest in it and actually exercises a dominant influence over it. Schedule 10A paragraph 4(3) provides that the definition of the 'right to exercice a dominant influence' for the purposes of Section 258(2)(c) shall not affect the construction of 'actually exercises a dominant influence' in Section 258(4)(a). The FRS defines 'actual exercise of dominant influence', as the exercise of an influence that achieves the result that the operating and financial policies of the undertaking influenced are set in accordance with the wishes of the holder of the influence and for its benefit (whether or not those wishes are explicit).

72 As indicated in paragraph 7(b) of the FRS, the actual exercise of dominant influence is identified by its effect in practice rather than the means by which it is exercised. The effect of the exercise of dominant influence is that the undertaking under influence implements the operating and financial policies that the holder of the influence desires. Thus a power of veto or any other reserve power that has the necessary effect in practice can form the basis whereby one undertaking actually exercises a dominant influence over another. However, such powers are likely to lead to the holder actually exercising a dominant influence over an undertaking only if they are held in conjunction with other rights or powers or if they relate to the day-to-day activities of that undertaking and no similar veto is held by other parties unconnected to the holder. The full circumstances of each case should be considered, including the effect of any formal or informal agreements between the undertakings, to decide whether or not one undertaking actually exercises a dominant influence over another. Commercial relationships such as that of supplier, customer or lender do not of themselves constitute dominant influence.

73 A parent undertaking may actually exercise its dominant influence in an interventionist or non-interventionist way. For example, a parent undertaking may set directly and in detail the operating and financial policies of its subsidiary undertaking or it may prefer to influence these by setting out in outline the kind of results it wants achieved without being involved regularly or on a day-to-day basis. Because of the variety of ways that dominant influence may be exercised evidence of continuous intervention is not necessary to support the view that dominant influence is actually exercised. Sufficient evidence might be provided by a rare intervention on a critical matter. Once there has been evidence that one undertaking has exercised a dominant influence over another, then the dominant undertaking should be assumed to continue to exercise its influence until there is evidence to the contrary. However, it is still necessary for the preparation of the consolidated financial statements to examine the relationship between the undertakings each year to assess any evidence of change in status that may have arisen.

Managed on a unified basis

74 Section 258(4)(b) identifies an undertaking as a parent undertaking of another undertaking (its subsidiary undertaking) if it has a participating interest in that other undertaking and they are managed on a unified basis. Undertakings are managed on a unified basis if the whole of the operations of the undertakings are integrated and they are managed as a single unit. Unified management does not arise solely because one undertaking manages another because this may not fulfil the condition that the operations of the undertakings are integrated.

Preparation of consolidated financial statements

75 The requirements of the FRS apply to all parent undertakings that prepare consolidated financial statements intended to give a true and fair view of the financial position and profit or loss of the group. In giving such a view the same accounting principles apply in general to consolidated financial statements as would apply to the financial statements of a single entity. Parent undertakings should comply with the requirements of the FRS in preparing consolidated financial statements giving a true and fair view, even if the parent undertaking is not specifically required to prepare consolidated financial statements.

Exclusion of subsidiary undertakings from consolidation

76 The Act requires that all the subsidiary undertakings of a parent undertaking are to be included in the consolidated financial statements for that group subject to the exceptions permitted or required by Section 229(2)-(4). The circumstances in which the Act permits or requires a subsidiary undertaking to be excluded from consolidation are the following:

Permissive exclusions

a 'if its inclusion is not material for the purpose of giving a true and fair view; but two or more undertakings may be excluded only if they are not material taken together'; or

b 'where the information necessary for the preparation of group accounts cannot be obtained without disproportionate expense or undue delay'; or

c 'where severe long-term restrictions substantially hinder the exercise of the rights of the parent company over the assets or management of that undertaking'; or

d 'where the interest of the parent company is held exclusively with a view to subsequent resale and the undertaking has not previously been included in consolidated group accounts prepared by the parent company'.

Required exclusion

e 'where the activities of one or more subsidiary undertakings are so different from those of other undertakings to be included in the consolidation that their inclusion would be incompatible with the obligation to give a true and fair view'.

77 Within this statutory framework the FRS elaborates on the conditions for exclusion set out in the Act so that these identify as far as possible only those undertakings defined as subsidiary undertakings by Section 258 that are not controlled by their parent undertaking in a way that would in principle justify consolidation. This gives effect to the Board's view that a parent undertaking should consolidate all those undertakings that are its subsidiary undertakings unless there are circumstances that make consolidation inappropriate. Under the circumstances set out in paragraph 78(c) and (d) below the FRS requires the parent undertaking to exclude a subsidiary undertaking because the same conditions that justify permitting exclusion of a subsidiary undertaking also make consolidation of that undertaking inappropriate. Exclusion from consolidation is not the only way of clarifying the effect on the group of the circumstances affecting some of its subsidiary undertakings; exclusion should only be used exceptionally. In many cases circumstances such as restrictions or activities with special risks are better dealt with by disclosure for example by giving additional segmental information rather than by exclusion from consolidation of the subsidiary undertakings concerned.

78 In order to help preparers identify the exceptional cases where it is inappropriate to consolidate a subsidiary undertaking the exclusions allowed or required by Section 229(2)-(4) are discussed below.

Materiality

a The FRS deals only with material items. Thus this ground for exclusion requires no special mention in the FRS. The Act only allows exclusion for two or more subsidiary undertakings if they are not material taken together.

Disproportionate expense and undue delay

b In principle neither expense nor delay can justify excluding from consolidation subsidiary undertakings that are individually or collectively material in the context of the group.

Severe long-term restrictions

c Restrictions are only relevant to justify the exclusion of a subsidiary undertaking from consolidation if the restrictions substantially hinder the exercise of the rights of the parent undertaking over the assets or management of the subsidiary undertaking. The rights affected must be those by reason of which the undertaking holding them is the parent undertaking and without which it would not be the parent undertaking. Severe long-term restrictions justify excluding a subsidiary undertaking from consolidation only where the effect of those restrictions is that the parent undertaking does not control its subsidiary undertaking. Severe long-term restrictions are identified by their effect in practice rather than by the way in which the restrictions are imposed For example a subsidiary undertaking should not be excluded because restrictions are threatened or because another party has the power to impose them unless such threats or the existence of such a power has a severe and restricting effect in practice in the long-term on the rights of the parent undertaking. Generally restrictions are dealt with better by disclosure than by non-consolidation. However the loss of the parent undertaking's control over its subsidiary undertaking resulting from severe long-term restrictions would make it misleading to include that subsidiary undertaking in the consolidation. Where a subsidiary undertaking is subject to an insolvency procedure in the United Kingdom control over that undertaking may have passed to a designated official (for example an administrator, administrative receiver or liquidator) with the effect that severe long-term restrictions are in force. A company voluntary arrangement does not necessarily lead to loss of control. In some overseas jurisdictions even formal insolvency procedures may not amount to loss of control.

Interest held exclusively with a view to subsequent resale

d This exclusion applies only to those undertakings that have never formed a continuing part of group activities and have not previously been included in consolidated financial statements prepared by the parent undertaking. Paragraph 11 defines the two sets of circumstances in which an interest in a subsidiary undertaking is considered to be held exclusively with a view to subsequent resale .The first set of circumstances (paragraph 11(a)) depends on an immediate intention to sell and the expectation of a sale within approximately one year. An interest for which a sale is not completed within a year of its acquisition may still fulfil the conditions of paragraph 11(a) if, at the date the accounts are signed, the terms of the sale have been agreed and the process of disposing of that interest is substantially complete. The second set of circumstances (paragraph 11(b)) depends on the way in which the interest was acquired, that is whether it was acquired as a result of the enforcement of a security. The provisions of Schedule 10A paragraph 8(b) may be relevant in determining whether such an interest has been acquired. This paragraph provides that rights attached to shares held as a security are to be treated as held by the person providing the security where the shares are held in connection with the granting of loans as part of normal business activities and apart from the right to exercise them to preserve the value of the security or to realise it the rights are exercisable only in the interests of the provider of the security.

Different activities

e The key feature of this exclusion is that it refers only to a subsidiary undertaking whose activities are so different from those of other undertakings included in the consolidation that to include that subsidiary undertaking in the consolidation would be incompatible with the obligation to give a true and fair view. Cases of this sort are so exceptional that it would be misleading to link them in general to any particular contrast of activities. For example the contrast between Schedule 9 and 9A companies (banking and insurance companies and groups) and other companies or between profit and not-for-profit undertakings is not sufficient of itself to justify non-consolidation. The different activities of undertakings included in the consolidation can better be shown by presenting segmental information rather than by excluding from consolidation the subsidiary undertakings with different activities.

79 Treatment of excluded subsidiary undertakings.

Severe long-term restrictions

a Where severe long-term restrictions are in force so that a subsidiary undertaking is no longer under the control of its parent undertaking that subsidiary undertaking should not be consolidated. From the date severe long-term restrictions come into force and until they are lifted the subsidiary undertaking subject to the restrictions should be excluded from consolidation and treated instead as a fixed asset investment. If restrictions are in force when the subsidiary undertaking is acquired it should be carried initially at cost; if restrictions came into force at a later date the subsidiary undertaking should be carried at a fixed amount calculated using the equity method as at the date the restrictions came into force. If in spite of severe long-term restrictions the parent undertaking retains significant influence over a subsidiary undertaking the investment should be treated as an associated undertaking using the equity method. Because severe long-term restrictions may give rise to diminutions in value the FRS requires the value of the excluded subsidiary undertaking to be reviewed to assess whether any permanent diminution in value has occurred. Any intra-group amounts due from such excluded subsidiary undertakings may also be affected by severe long-term restrictions, particularly if the restrictions extend to remittances. These balances should also be reviewed and provision made as necessary.

Held exclusively for resale

b A subsidiary undertaking held exclusively for resale and not previously included in the consolidated financial statements of the parent undertaking does not form part of the continuing activities of the group. Although the parent undertaking (as identified by Section 258 and paragraph 14 of the FRS) may control such a subsidiary undertaking, its control is temporary and is not used to deploy the underlying assets and liabilities of that subsidiary undertaking as part of the continuing group's activities for the benefit of the parent undertaking of the group. The subsidiary undertaking is therefore excluded from consolidation and the temporary nature of the parent undertaking's interest is recognised by carrying it as a current asset at the lower of cost and net realisable value.

Different activities make consolidation incompatible with giving a true and fair view

c Even where a subsidiary undertaking's activities are, exceptionally, so different from those of other undertakings included in the consolidation that its consolidation is not compatible with the obligation to give a true and fair view, that subsidiary undertaking contributes to the wealth and performance of the group. The net assets and results of such a subsidiary undertaking should, therefore, be reflected in the consolidated financial statements and, because it is inappropriate to do this by consolidation, the equity method should be used instead. The use of the equity method is required by Schedule 4A paragraph 18. The FRS also requires separate financial statements for such excluded subsidiary undertakings to accompany the consolidated financial statements so that the information given is complete and fully reflects the different type of assets and liabilities used in the activities of the group as a whole.

Intra-group guarantees re excluded subsidiary undertakings

d Liabilities to third parties of one group member guaranteed by another are themselves included in the consolidated financial statements so that intra-group guarantees do not normally require disclosure. Guarantees in respect of subsidiary undertakings excluded from consolidation have to be treated in the same way as guarantees given by members of the group to third parties because, in these cases, the intragroup guarantees relate to liabilities that are not included gross in the consolidated financial statements.

Minority interests

80 Despite the title 'Minority interests', there is in principle no upper limit to the proportion of shares in a subsidiary undertaking which may be held as a minority interest while the parent undertaking still qualifies as such under Section 258 of the Act (describcd in paragraph 14 of the FRS). The amounts reported in the consolidated balance sheet and profit and loss account for the minority interests indicate the extent to which the assets and liabilities and profits and losses of subsidiary undertakings included in the consolidation are attributable to shareholders other than the parent or its other subsidiary undertakings. The effect of the existence of minority interests on the returns to investors in the parent undertaking is best reflected by presenting the net identifiable assets attributable to minority interests on the same basis as those attributable to group interests. Using the same basis for including group assets and liabilities, irrespective of the extent to which they are attributable to the minority interest, presents the assets and liabilities on a consistent basis for the group as a whole.

81 The FRS requires that losses be attributed to the minority interest in a loss making subsidiary undertaking, regardless of whether or not this leads to a debit balance for the minority interest; to do otherwise would obscure the comparison between the assets and liabilities and results attributable to the minority interest and those attributable to the group interests both during the periods when the accumulated losses accrue and afterwards, if these are then made good by later profits. Accumulated losses of subsidiary undertakings do not of themselves necessarily require funding by the parent undertaking and a debit balance for minority interests represents net liabilities attributable to the shares held by the minorities in that subsidiary undertaking rather than a debt due from them. The group should provide for any commercial or legal obligation (whether formal or implied) to provide finance that may not be recoverable in respect of the accumulated losses attributable to the minority interests. Provisions of this sort would include the minorities' share of any liability guaranteed by the group, or any liability that the group itself would be likely to settle for commercial or other reasons, if the subsidiary undertaking could not do so itself. Any provision made with respect to minority debit balances should be set directly against the minority interest amount in the profit and loss account and the balance sheet.

82 The FRS requires that the goodwill arising on acquisition of a subsidiary undertaking that is not wholly owned should be recognised only in relation to the group's interest and that none should be attributed to the minority interest. Although it might be possible to estimate by extrapolation or valuation an amount of goodwill attributable to the minority when a subsidiary undertaking is acquired, this would in effect recognise an amount for goodwill that is hypothetical because the minority is not a party to the transaction by which the subsidiary undertaking is acquired.

Consolidation adjustments and intra-group transactions

83 Presenting information about the economic activities of the group as a single economic entity in consolidated financial statements requires adjustment for intra-group transactions of the amounts reported in the individual financial statements of the parent and its subsidiary undertakings. Intra-group transactions may result in a profit or loss that is included at least temporarily in the book value of group assets. To the extent that such assets are still held in the undertakings included in the consolidation at the balance sheet date, the related profits or losses recorded in the individual financial statements have not arisen for the group as a whole and must therefore be eliminated from group results and asset values. The elimination should be in full, even where the transactions involve subsidiary undertakings with minority interests. Transactions between undertakings included in the consolidation deal with the assets and liabilities that are wholly within the group's control, even if they are not wholly owned. From the perspective of the group as a single entity no profit or loss arises on intra-group transactions because no increase or decrease in the group's net assets has occurred. Where there are subsidiary undertakings excluded from consolidation because of their different activities, transactions with those subsidiary undertakings, which would be eliminated if they related wholly to subsidiary undertakings included in the consolidation, should also be eliminated. Profits or losses arising on transactions with undertakings excluded from consolidation because they are held exclusively with a view to subsequent resale or because of severe long-term restrictions need not be eliminated, except to the extent appropriate where significant influence is retained and the subsidiary undertaking is treated as an associated undertaking. However, it is important to consider whether it is prudent to record any profit arising from transactions with subsidiary undertakings excluded on these grounds.

Changes in composition of a group

84 The date on which an undertaking becomes or ceases to be another undertaking's subsidiary undertaking marks the point at which a new accounting treatment for that undertaking is applied. The relevant date is the date on which control passes and paragraph 45 of the FRS is framed in these terms. This date should also be the one on which an undertaking begins or ceases to qualify as a parent or subsidiary undertaking under Section 258. The date on which control passes is a matter of fact and cannot be backdated or otherwise altered.

85 Where control is transferred by a public offer, the date control is transferred is the date the offer becomes unconditional, usually as a result of a sufficient number of acceptances being received. For private treaties, the date control is transferred is generally the date an unconditional offer is accepted. Where an undertaking becomes or ceases to be a subsidiary undertaking as a result of the issue or cancellation of shares, the date control is transferred is the date of issue or cancellation. The date that control passes may be indicated by the acquiring party commencing its direction of the operating and financial policies of the acquired undertaking or by changes in the flow of economic benefits. The date on which the consideration for the transfer of control is paid is often an important indication of the date on which a subsidiary undertaking is acquired or disposed of. However, the date the consideration passes is not conclusive evidence of the date of the transfer of control because this date can be set to fall on a date other than that on which control is transferred with compensation for any lead or lag included in the consideration. Consideration may also be paid in instalments.

86 An undertaking may cease to be a subsidiary undertaking as a result of the parent undertaking losing control over it because of changes in the rights it holds or in those held by another party in that subsidiary undertaking. A parent undertaking may also lose control of its subsidiary undertaking because of changes in some other arrangement that gave it control without there being any change in the former parent undertaking's holding in its former subsidiary undertaking. For example, control may pass if there is a change in voting rights or in how these are allocated. In these circumstances neither a gain nor a loss accrues in the consolidated financial statements, unless there is a payment for the transfer of control, because there is no change in the net assets attributable to the group's holding in the former subsidiary undertaking. The assets and liabilities of the former subsidiary undertaking should cease to be consolidated but should be shown instead as an associated undertaking or investment as appropriate.

87 An undertaking usually ceases to be a subsidiary undertaking because the group reduces its proportional interest in that undertaking. The reduction of the group's interest may result from its directly disposing of part of the interest it holds or from a deemed disposal. Any reduction in the group's proportional interest other than by a direct disposal is a deemed disposal. Disposals and deemed disposals may give rise to profits or losses for the group, which should be calculated as set out in paragraph 47. There may be other losses or gains that arise for the group as a result of an undertaking ceasing to be a subsidiary undertaking. These are not part of the direct gain or loss described here but may need to be provided for, if they are quantifiable, or otherwise disclosed to show the full effect of the cessation. Deemed disposals may arise where the group's interest in a subsidiary undertaking is reduced, *inter alia:*

- **a** because the parent undertaking and its group do not take up their full allocation of rights in a rights issue; or
- **b** because the parent undertaking and its group do not take up their full share of scrip dividends while other equity holders in that subsidiary undertaking take up some, at least, of their share; or
- **c** because another party has exercised its options or warrants; or
- **d** because the subsidiary undertaking has issued shares to parties other than the parent undertaking and its group.

Changes in stake

88 When an undertaking is first consolidated, its identifiable assets and liabilities are initially brought into the consolidation at their fair values at the date of its acquisition as a subsidiary undertaking (the acquisition method of accounting as provided by Schedule 4A paragraph 9). Where a subsidiary undertaking is acquired in stages, its net identifiable assets and liabilities are to be included in the consolidation at their fair values on the date it becomes a subsidiary undertaking, rather than at the date of the earlier purchases. Using other methods to compute the amounts to be included in the consolidation would fail to give a full picture of the assets and liabilities acquired that now comprise part of the group's resources.

89 The effect of the Schedule 4A paragraph 9 method of acquisition accounting is to treat as goodwill, or negative goodwill, the whole of the difference between, on the one hand, the fair value, at the date an undertaking becomes a subsidiary undertaking, of the group's share of its identifiable assets and liabilities and, on the other hand, the total acquisition cost of the interests held by the group in that subsidiary undertaking. This applies even where part of the acquisition cost arises from purchases of interests at earlier dates. In the generality of cases this method provides a practical means of applying acquisition accounting because it does not require retrospective assessments of the fair values of the identifiable assets and liabilities of the acquired undertaking. In special circumstances, however, not using fair values at the dates of earlier purchases, while using an acquisition cost part of which relates to earlier purchases, may result in accounting that is inconsistent with the way the investment has been treated previously and, for that reason, may fail to give a true and fair view. For example, an undertaking that has been treated as an associated undertaking by a group may then be acquired by that group as a subsidiary undertaking. Using the method required by Schedule 4A paragraph 9 to calculate goodwill on such an acquisition has the effect that the group's share of profits or losses and reserve movements of its associated undertaking becomes reclassified as goodwill (usually negative goodwill). A similar problem may arise where the group has substantially restated its investment in an undertaking that subsequently becomes its subsidiary undertaking. For example where a provision has been made against such an investment for permanent diminution in value the effect of applying the Schedule 4A paragraph 9 method of acquisition accounting would be to increase reserves and create an asset (goodwill). In the rare cases where the Schedule 4A paragraph 9 calculation of goodwill would be misleading goodwill should be calculated as the sum of goodwill arising from each purchase of an interest in the relevant undertaking adjusted as necessary for any subsequent diminution in value. Goodwill arising on each purchase should be calculated as the difference between the cost of that purchase and the fair value at the date of that purchase of the identifiable assets and liabilities attributable to the interest purchased. The difference between the goodwill calculated on this method and that calculated on the method provided by the Act is shown in reserves. Section 227(6) sets out the disclosures required in cases where the statutory requirement is not applied.

90 Where a group increases its stake in an undertaking that is already its subsidiary undertaking the consideration paid may not be equal to the fair value of the identifiable assets and liabilities previously attributed to the minority and now acquired from the minority. If the assets and liabilities were not revalued to fair values before calculating the goodwill arising on the change in stake then the difference between the consideration paid and the relevant proportion of the carrying value of net assets acquired would be made up in part of goodwill and in part of changes in value. The FRS requires that the assets and liabilities of the subsidiary undertaking be revalued to fair value at the date of the increase in stake unless the difference between the fair values and the carrying amounts of the share of net assets acquired is not material.

91 Where the group decreases its stake in an undertaking whether or not it continues to be a subsidiary undertaking, a profit or loss generally arises. Consolidated financial statements are prepared from the perspective of investors in the parent undertaking of the group. Where the group disposes of part of its interest in a subsidiary undertaking it transacts directly with third parties and a profit or loss for the group arises and is reported in the consolidated financial statements. This can be contrasted with the treatment of intra-group transactions where no profit or loss arises for the group as a whole because the transaction involves only undertakings included in the consolidation and under common control and does not directly involve any third party.

Distributions

92 SSAP 15 'Accounting for deferred tax' states that the retention of earnings overseas will create a timing difference only if:

- **a** there is an intention or obligation to remit them; and
- **b** remittance would result in a tax liability after taking account of any related double tax relief.

It also requires that, where deferred tax is not provided on earnings retained overseas, this should be stated. In addition this FRS requires disclosure of the extent to which deferred tax has been accounted for in respect of future remittances of the accumulated reserves of overseas subsidiary undertakings. Where deferred tax has not been provided for in full, the reason for not providing fully should be given, for example, that the amounts are considered to be permanently reinvested overseas and are not intended to be remitted.

Disclosures

93 The FRS refers to the disclosure requirements of the Act and, where appropriate, adds further disclosure requirements of its own. By referring to certain of the disclosure requirements in the Act in the text of the statement of standard accounting practice the FRS extends these disclosure requirements to parent undertakings not subject to the Act. Requirements of the Act are identified by section or schedule numbers; reference to the Act itself is necessary to ascertain the full disclosures required.

Segmental information

94 Segmental information has a particular importance in group financial reporting. The aggregation and adjustments required to consolidate financial information for the parent undertaking and its subsidiary undertakings may obscure information about the different undertakings and activities included in the consolidated financial statements. The information about the separate group activities that may be obscured by consolidation can be restored by giving information about the group on a segmental basis. Parent undertakings should consider how to provide segmental information for their group, indicating the different risks and rewards, growth and prospects of the different parts of the group and treating the requirements of SSAP 25 'Segmental reporting' as a minimum rather than a limit to disclosure. Two examples of how segmental information could supplement consolidated financial statements are given below.

Segmentation rather than exclusion for certain subsidiary undertakings

a Where the FRS discusses excluding subsidiary undertakings from consolidation, it stresses the importance of the completeness of the information presented in the consolidated financial statements. Thus, where subsidiary undertakings engage in different activities or are subject to certain restrictions that are not such as to require exclusion from consolidation under the FRS, the most complete picture is presented by consolidating the subsidiary undertakings concerned and giving additional information or by identifying the assets, liabilities and results attributable to undertakings engaging in those activities or subject to those restrictions .

Minority interests

b Users of consolidated financial statements who are interested in assessing the effect of the existence of minority interests in certain parts of the group on the expected returns to investors in the rare undertaking may find it helpful to have information showing the amounts attributable to the minority interest in different group segments .

Note of legal requirements

Legal requirements in Great Britain

References are to the Companies Act 1985 as amended by the Companies Act 1989.

Readers should refer to the Act itself for an understanding of the relevant points of law. This section lists only the main sections in the Act containing provisions in relation to subsidiary undertakings. The provisions of the Act are not considered further here because they are dealt with in the many references to the Act in the other sections of the FRS.

Main sections of the Companies Act

95 The main sections of the Companies Act containing provisions relating to the preparation of consolidated financial statements are the following.

Section 227	'Duty to prepare group accounts'
Section 228	'Exemption for parent companies included in accounts of larger group'
Section 229	'Subsidiary undertakings included in the consolidation'
Section 230	'Treatment of individual profit and loss account where group accounts prepared'
Section 231	'Disclosure required in notes to accounts: related undertakings'
Section 248	'Exemption for small and medium-sized groups'
Section 249	'Qualification of group as small or medium-sized'
Section 258	'Parent and subsidiary undertakings'
Section 259	'Meaning of "undertaking" and related expressions'
Section 260	'Participating interests'
Section 262	'Minor definitions'
Section 262A	'Index of defined expressions'
Schedule 4A (All paragraphs)	'Form and Content of Group Accounts'
Schedule 5 (All paragraphs)	'Disclosure of Information: Related Undertakings'
Schedule 10A (All paragraphs)	'Parent and Subsidiary Undertakings: Supplementary Provision'

Disclosure requirements

96 The following sections and paragraphs give the main disclosure requirements of the Act with respect to consolidated financial statements.

Section 227(4) - (6)

Section 228(2)

Section 231

Schedule 4A — Paragraphs 3, 4, 13, 14, 15, 17

Schedule 5 'Disclosure of Information: Related Undertakings'

Part I 'Companies not Required to Prepare Group Accounts'

Part II 'Companies Required to Prepare Group Accounts'

Legal requirements in Northern Ireland

97 The legal requirements in Northern Ireland are very similar to those in Great Britain. The following table shows the Articles and Schedules in the Companies (Northern Ireland) Order 1986 which correspond to the legal references in paragraphs 95-96 above.

Companies Act 1985 (as amended)	The Companies (Northern Ireland) Order 1986 (as amended)
Section 227	Article 235
Section 228	Article 236
Section 229	Article 237
Section 230	Article 238
Section 231	Article 239
Section 248	Article 256
Section 249	Article 257
Section 258	Article 266
Section 259	Article 267
Section 260	Article 268
Section 262	Article 270
Section 262A	Article 270A
Schedules	
Schedule 4A (all paragraphs)	Schedule 4A (all paragraphs)
Schedule 5 (Parts I & II) (all paragraphs)	Schedule 5 (Parts I & II) (all paragraphs)
Schedule 10A (all paragraphs)	Schedule 10A (all paragraphs)

Legal requirements in the Republic of Ireland

98 Implementation of the European Community Seventh Directive in the Republic of Ireland is still awaited at the date of printing. Following implementation of the Directive, Republic of Ireland companies will come within the scope of FRS 2. When the legal references for the Republic of Ireland are available, the Accounting Standards Board will publish them, together with the effective date for adoption by Irish companies, on a separate sheet. Copies of that sheet, when available, can be obtained free of charge on request to:

The Accounting Standards Board
Holborn Hall
100 Gray's Inn Road
London
WC1X 8AL

Any further printing of the FRS will contain the Republic of Ireland references and effective date for adoption for Irish companies.

The development of the standard

This section does not form part of the Financial Reporting Standard.

History of the FRS

1 Statement of Standard Accounting Practice No 14 (SSAP 14) — 'Group Accounts', issued September 1978, dealt with the presentation of group accounts for a group of companies. The practice of preparing group accounts for companies and their subsidiaries had been well established in the United Kingdom and Ireland since 1947. However, the issue of International Accounting Standard No 3 — 'Consolidated Financial Statements' made it desirable for there to be a domestic standard on the subject.

2 SSAP 14 was drafted to accord with relevant provisions of the Companies Acts then in force. At that time the Companies Acts did not include detailed rules regarding the preparation of group accounts.

3 SSAP 14 defined a holding company and a subsidiary company by reference to the legal definitions current at that time. The terms now used are 'parent undertaking' and 'subsidiary undertaking' which are defined in the Companies Act 1985, as amended by the Companies Act 1989 (the Act). The Act now contains new provisions on group accounts to implement the European Community Seventh Company Law Directive with the result that the requirements of SSAP 14 are no longer entirely consistent with current legislation.

4 The need to revise SSAP 14 for changes in the law has provided an opportunity to conduct a thorough review of the standard. This was undertaken initially by the Accounting Standards Committee whose proposals were issued as ED 50 — 'Consolidated Accounts' in June 1990. The Accounting Standards Board issued the 'Interim Statement: Consolidated accounts' in December 1990, to give timely guidance on how certain provisions of the Act were to be interpreted in the preparation of consolidated accounts. The Interim Statement also made the changes to SSAP 14 — 'Group Accounts' that were required as a consequence of the statutory changes. The issue of the FRS by the Accounting Standards Board completes the review process.

Summary of the principal changes from Statement of Standard Accounting Practice No 14 — 'Group Accounts'

5 SSAP 14 defined a company as a subsidiary of another 'if but only if

(a) that other either:

(i) is a member of it and controls the composition of its board of directors; or

(ii) holds more than half in nominal value of its equity share capital; or

(b) the first mentioned company is a subsidiary of any company which is that other's subsidiary and it otherwise comes within the terms of Section 154 of the Companies Act 1948' (now repealed).

The FRS defines a parent undertaking and a subsidiary undertaking in the same way as the Act using a set of conditions that are based on whether one undertaking controls another. These are set out in paragraph 14 of the FRS.

6 The FRS requires a parent undertaking not making use of an exemption to prepare consolidated financial statements for its group. SSAP 14 exceptionally allowed alternative forms of group reporting if the resulting group accounts were considered to give a fairer view of the financial position of the group as a whole than would consolidated financial statements.

7 SSAP 14 exempted from the obligation to prepare group accounts only holding companies that were wholly owned subsidiaries not otherwise required by law to prepare group accounts. The FRS follows the Act in allowing other exemptions from preparing consolidated financial statements. A parent undertaking is in general exempt from the requirement to prepare consolidated financial statements if its group is a small or medium-sized one; or if it is wholly or majority-owned by an undertaking established under the law of a member state of the European Community; or if all its subsidiary undertakings fall within the exclusions from consolidation.

8 The circumstances in which subsidiary undertakings are to be excluded from the consolidation have changed in certain respects from those in SSAP 14.

(a) SSAP 14 required a subsidiary to be excluded from consolidation if its activities were so dissimilar from those of other companies within the group that its consolidation would be misleading and information would be better provided by presenting financial statements for the excluded subsidiary separate from the financial statements for the rest of the group. The FRS requires a subsidiary undertaking to be excluded from consolidation if exceptionally its activities are so different from other subsidiary undertakings included in the consolidation that its inclusion in the consolidation would be incompatible with the obligation to give a true and fair view.

(b) SSAP 14 required a subsidiary to be excluded from consolidation if the holding company held more than half of the subsidiary's equity share capital but either (a) it did not own share capital carrying more than half the votes; or (b) contractual or other restrictions were imposed on its ability to appoint the majority of the board of directors. Although the FRS does not have the same exclusion the FRS will in most cases have the same practical effect because (a) an undertaking is a subsidiary undertaking if another undertaking holds a majority of its voting rights and (b) exclusion is required where severe long-term restrictions substantially hinder the rights of the parent undertaking over the assets or management of its subsidiary undertaking.

(c) SSAP 14 required exclusion from consolidation of a subsidiary where control was intended to be temporary. The FRS requires consolidation where one undertaking controls another and therefore has not based exclusion on control being temporary. However it does require exclusion from consolidation of a subsidiary undertaking held exclusively with a view to resale which has not previously been consolidated. This condition for exclusion is more restrictive than the temporary control test.

9 SSAP 14 required that the consolidated financial statements should contain sufficient information about material subsidiaries acquired or sold to enable shareholders to appreciate the effect on the consolidated results. There are now specific disclosure requirements in the law, as well as in accounting standards in respect of acquisitions, and the general SSAP 14 requirement is not repeated in the FRS. In addition FRS 1 — 'Cash flow Statements' contains a requirement to show the cash flow effects of acquisitions and disposals.

10 SSAP 14 sets out the effective date of acquisition or disposal as the earlier of the date on which consideration passes or the date on which an offer becomes or is declared unconditional. This is replaced in the FRS by a single triggering date which is the date control of the undertaking passes. This date is a matter of fact and cannot be backdated or otherwise altered.

11 SSAP 14 required that debit balances for the minority interests should only be recognised in the balance sheet if there was a binding obligation on minority shareholders to make good losses incurred which they were able to meet. The FRS requires minority interests to be debited in full with their share of any loss whether or not this results in a debit balance, subject to the need for a provision discussed below. A debit for minority interests does not represent a liability of the minority shareholders and it may be misleading to refer to their being obliged to make good losses. The group should make provision to the extent that it has any commercial or legal obligation (whether formal or implied) to provide finance that may not be recoverable in respect of the accumulated losses attributable to minority interests.

Summary of the principal changes from the Board's 'Interim Statement: Consolidated Accounts'

12 In December 1990 the Board issued the 'Interim Statement: Consolidated Accounts' to give timely guidance on the application of certain provisions of the new Act to the preparation of consolidated financial statements. The Interim Statement dealt mainly with the interpretation of the new phrases used in the conditions that identified parent and subsidiary undertakings and with the exclusions from consolidation permitted or required by the Act for certain subsidiary undertakings. Although the drafting has changed to fit the format of an accounting standard, the FRS incorporates the guidance given by the Interim Statement except in the following areas.

(a) Dominant influence is now defined without explicit reference to control although the effect of dominant influence is the same as control.

(b) The explanation dealing with subsidiary undertakings whose activities are so different that consolidation is incompatible with the obligation to give a true and fair view now states explicitly that the contrast between Schedule 9 and 9A companies and other companies or between profit and not-for-profit undertakings is not sufficient of itself to justify non consolidation.

(c) The Interim Statement defined a joint venture. The FRS deals only with accounting for subsidiary undertakings leaving joint ventures as a separate project.

Summary of the principal changes from Exposure Draft No 50 — 'Consolidated Accounts'

13 Exposure Draft No 50 (ED 50) — 'Consolidated Accounts' was issued in June 1990 by the Accounting Standards Committee. It proposed standard accounting practice for the preparation of consolidated accounts covering both accounting for subsidiary undertakings and accounting for associated undertakings and joint ventures. The FRS deals only with accounting for subsidiary undertakings in consolidated financial statements. The Board is engaged in another project considering accounting for associated undertakings and joint ventures.

14 The Explanatory Note in ED 50 considered the purpose of consolidated accounts, the basis of consolidation and the meaning of control. The FRS deals only briefly in its explanation section with the conceptual background to financial reporting for groups. The conceptual basis of consolidated financial statements and consideration of the group as a reporting entity are to be considered by the Board in the chapter of its Statement of Principles dealing with the boundaries of the reporting entity.

15 ED 50 used the terms 'subsidiary', 'parent' and 'enterprise' in line with earlier accounting standards. Commentators on its proposals considered that it would be more appropriate to use the terminology of the Act on which the FRS is based. The FRS now refers to 'subsidiary undertaking', 'parent undertaking' and 'undertaking'. However in line with the Board's other published work, the FRS uses 'financial statements' instead of 'accounts' as used in the Act.

16 ED 50 proposed definitions for the phrases used in the Act in the criteria for identifying parent and subsidiary undertakings. The FRS elaborates on these definitions in the light of the comments received on the ED. The general thrust of the definitions remains the same but the following changes are worth noting:

(a) 'Dominant influence' is no longer defined in terms of control but by its ability to achieve the operating and financial policies desired by the holder of the influence notwithstanding the rights or influence of any other party. The actual exercise of dominant influence is identified by its effect in practice rather than the way in which it is exercised. The effect of dominant influence is the same as the effect of control.

(b) The role of reserve powers and powers of veto in the actual exercise of dominant influence has been clarified.

17 ED 50 proposed that a parent undertaking using an exemption from preparing consolidated accounts should make additional disclosures if its individual financial statements alone were not sufficient to give a true and fair view of its financial position. ED 50 noted that in some cases such additional information might better be presented by providing consolidated financial statements for the whole group. This proposal attracted adverse comment because in certain circumstances, its effect would be to take away all exemption given by the Act. The FRS requires a parent undertaking using an exemption to state that its financial statements present information about it as an individual undertaking and not about its group. Parent undertakings using any of the exemptions should also make the disclosures set out in Schedule 5 Part 1 of the Companies Act.

18 ED 50 proposed definitions for the phrases used in the Act to set the conditions under which a subsidiary undertaking was permitted or required to be excluded from consolidation. As a result of the comments received the guidance of the FRS on how these conditions are to be interpreted has changed slightly from that given in ED 50 although the emphasis remains on interpreting these conditions restrictively. The main changes are set out below.

(a) *Interests held exclusively with a view to subsequent resale.* A second part has been added bringing acquisitions as a result of the enforcement of a security within the definition of interests held exclusively with a view to subsequent resale unless the subsidiary undertaking has become part of the continuing activities of the group or the holder acts as if it intends the interest to become so.

(b) *Activities so different that consolidation would be incompatible with the obligation to give a true and fair view.* ED 50 proposed that such an incompatibility could arise only from consolidating a Schedule 9 or 9A company with non Schedule 9 or 9A companies. Several commentators considered that a requirement not to consolidate Schedule 9 and 9A companies with others might result in a loss of useful and comparable information on group activities as a whole. Linking incompatibility with the true and fair view to issues relating to the format in which financial statements were presented was considered unsatisfactory. The FRS, therefore stresses that the key feature of this exclusion is that including a given subsidiary undertaking in the consolidation is incompatible with the obligation to give a true and fair view. The FRS notes that this incompatibility will be so exceptional in practice that it would be misleading to associate it with any particular contrast of activities. For example the contrasts between Schedule 9 or 9A companies and other companies or between profit and not-for-profit undertakings would not of themselves be sufficient to justify non-consolidation.

19 ED 50 followed SSAP 14 and proposed that losses should only be debited to minority interests where they resulted in a debit balance if there was a binding and reliable obligation on the minority to make good any such losses. The FRS's treatment for the minority's share of losses is explained in paragraph 11 above.

20 ED 50 proposed dropping the requirement of SSAP 14 (paragraph 18) that appropriate adjustments should be made to the consolidated financial statements for any abnormal transactions in the intervening period between the end of the period of a subsidiary and the later one of the group. Commentators considered that some disclosure of this sort would be useful. The FRS requires that where a subsidiary undertaking's financial year end differs from that of the parent undertaking the consolidated financial statements should be prepared using interim financial statements or only if this is impracticable its financial statements for its last financial year ending not more than three months before that of the group's parent undertaking. In this latter case adjustment is required for changes in the intervening period that materially affect the view given by the consolidated financial statements.

21 ED 50 proposed that the effective date of acquisition or disposal be the earlier of:

(a) the date on which the consideration passes; or

(b) the date at which an offer becomes or is declared unconditional; or

(c) the date of such other event at which control is gained or ceases to exist.

The FRS now sets the date of changes in membership of the group as the date that control passes. The Explanation (paragraphs 84 and 85) considers the transactions and events that indicate when control passes.

22 ED 50 proposed that its requirement to include the appropriate proportion of the results of a subsidiary undertaking that has been disposed of should be subject to the requirements of SSAP 6 — 'Extraordinary items and prior year adjustments' (paragraphs 11-14) dealing with the disposal of a segment. The FRS does not refer to SSAP 6 and requires that the consolidated profit and loss account should include the results of a subsidiary undertaking up to the date of its disposal. The Board is proposing to supersede SSAP 6 with an FRS developed from FRED 1 — 'The Structure of Financial Statements — Reporting of Financial Performance'.

23 The FRS has dropped the proposed requirement of ED 50 in respect of disposals to disclose the amount of purchased goodwill attributable to business or business segments disposed of and how that goodwill has been treated in determining the profit or loss on disposal. These disclosures are still required by paragraph 52(b) of SSAP 22 — 'Accounting for Goodwill'. The treatment of goodwill on disposal is set out in paragraph 47, which requires that the net assets disposed of include any related goodwill not previously written off through the profit and loss account.

24 In response to criticism of the ED 50 proposals, the FRS changes the treatment for increases in stake in a subsidiary undertaking. ED 50 did not propose to require a revaluation to fair value on an increase in stake, and, consequently, the goodwill balance arising could have consisted of an amount relating to revaluation of net identifiable assets as well as goodwill. The FRS requires that the goodwill should be calculated by revaluing the subsidiary undertaking's assets and liabilities to fair value at the date of the change in stake, unless the difference between fair values and carrying amounts is not material.

Reporting financial performance

Reproduced with the permission of the Accounting Standards Board.

Summary

a Financial Reporting Standard No. 3 'Reporting Financial Performance' (the FRS) introduces: changes to the format of the profit and loss account; a note of historical cost profits and losses; a statement of total recognised gains and losses; and a reconciliation of movement in shareholders' funds. The FRS supersedes Statement of Standard Accounting Practice No. 6 (Revised) 'Extraordinary items and prior year adjustments' (SSAP 6), amends SSAP 3 'Earnings per share' and makes consequential changes to a number of other accounting standards.

b A layered format is to be used for the profit and loss account to highlight a number of important components of financial performance:

(i) results of continuing operations (including the results of acquisitions);

(ii) results of discontinued operations;

(iii) profits or losses on the sale or termination of an operation, costs of fundamental reorganisation or restructuring and profits or losses on the disposal of fixed assets; and

(iv) extraordinary items.

The thrust of this approach can be illustrated diagrammatically as follows:

Continuing	*Discontinued*
Normal operations	Normal operations
The items listed in b (iii) above	The items listed in b (iii) above
Extraordinary items — being unusual items outside ordinary activities	

c In presenting the profit and loss account the following requirements should be observed:

(i) The analysis between continuing operations, acquisitions (as a component of continuing operations) and discontinued operations should be disclosed to the level of operating profit (which for non-financial reporting entities is normally profit before income from shares in group undertakings). The analysis of turnover and operating profit is the minimum disclosure required in this respect on the face of the profit and loss account.

(ii) All exceptional items, other than those in (iii) below, should be included under the statutory format headings to which they relate. They should be separately disclosed by way of note or, where it is necessary in order that the financial statements give a true and fair view, on the face of the profit and loss account.

(iii) The following items, including provisions in respect of such items, should be shown separately on the face of the profit and loss account after operating profit and before interest:

— profits or losses on the sale or termination of an operation;
— costs of a fundamental reorganisation or restructuring; and
— profits or losses on the disposal of fixed assets.

(iv) Extraordinary items should be disclosed.

d Earnings per share should be calculated on the profit attributable to equity shareholders of the reporting entity, after accounting for minority interests, extraordinary items, preference dividends and other appropriations in respect of preference shares. Where a reporting entity wishes to present an additional earnings per share calculated on another level of earnings the additional indicator should be presented on a consistent basis over time and, wherever disclosed, reconciled to the amount required by the FRS. Such a reconciliation should list the items for which an adjustment is being made and disclose their individual effect on the calculation. The earnings per share required by the FRS should be at least as prominent as any additional version presented and the reason for calculating the additional version should be explained.

e The note of historical cost profits and losses is a memorandum item, the primary purpose of which is to present the profits or losses of reporting entities that have revalued assets on a more comparable basis with those of entities that have not. It is an abbreviated restatement of the profit and loss account which adjusts the reported profit or loss, if necessary, so as to show it as if no asset revaluations had been made. Unless the historical cost information is unavailable, the note is required whenever there is a material difference between the result as disclosed in the profit and loss account and the result on an unmodified historical cost basis; it should be presented immediately following the profit and loss account or the statement of total recognised gains and losses.

f The statement of total recognised gains and losses is a primary financial statement that enables users to consider all recognised gains and losses of a reporting entity in assessing its overall performance. It, therefore, includes the profit or loss for the period together with all other movements on reserves reflecting recognised gains and losses attributable to shareholders. The statement is not intended to reflect the realisation of gains recognised in previous periods nor does it deal with transfers between reserves, which should continue to be shown in the notes to the financial statements.

g The reconciliation of movements in shareholders' funds brings together the performance of the period, as shown in the statement of total recognised gains and losses, with all the other changes in shareholders' funds in the period, including capital contributed by or repaid to shareholders.

h Prior period adjustments should be accounted for by restating the comparative figures for the preceding period in the primary statements and notes and adjusting the opening balance of reserves for the cumulative effect. The cumulative effect of the adjustments should also be noted at the foot of the statement of total recognised gains and losses of the current period. The effect of prior period adjustments on the results for the preceding period should be disclosed where practicable.

i The accounting practices set out in the FRS should be adopted as soon as possible and regarded as standard in respect of financial statements relating to accounting periods ending on or after 22 June 1993.

Objective

1 The objective of the FRS is to require reporting entities falling within its scope to highlight a range of important components of financial performance to aid users in understanding the performance achieved by a reporting entity in a period and to assist them in forming a basis for their assessment of future results and cash flows.

Definitions

The following definitions apply for the purposes of the FRS and in particular the statement of standard accounting practice set out in paragraphs 12 to 33.

2 *Ordinary activities.* Any activities which are undertaken by a reporting entity as part of its business and such related activities in which the reporting entity engages in furtherance of, incidental to, or arising from, these activities. Ordinary activities include the effects on the reporting entity of any event in the various environments in which it operates, including the political, regulatory, economic and geographical environments, irrespective of the frequency or unusual nature of the events.

3 *Acquisitions.* Operations of the reporting entity that are acquired in the period.

4 *Discontinued operations.* Operations of the reporting entity that are sold or terminated and that satisfy all of the following conditions.

(a) The sale or termination is completed either in the period or before the earlier of three months after the commencement of the subsequent period and the date on which the financial statements are approved.

(b) If a termination, the former activities have ceased permanently.

(c) The sale or termination has a material effect on the nature and focus of the reporting entity's operations and represents a material reduction in its operating facilities resulting either from its withdrawal from a particular market (whether class of business or geographical) or from a material reduction in turnover in the reporting entity's continuing markets.

(d) The assets, liabilities, results of operations and activities are clearly distinguishable, physically, operationally and for financial reporting purposes.

Operations not satisfying all these conditions are classified as continuing.

5 *Exceptional items.* Material items which derive from events or transactions that fall within the ordinary activities of the reporting entity and which individually or, if of a similar type, in aggregate, need to be disclosed by virtue of their size or incidence if the financial statements are to give a true and fair view.

6 *Extraordinary items.* Material items possessing a high degree of abnormality which arise from events or transactions that fall outside the ordinary activities of the reporting entity and which are not expected to recur. They do not include exceptional items nor do they include prior period items merely because they relate to a prior period.

7 *Prior period adjustments.* Material adjustments applicable to prior periods arising from changes in accounting policies or from the correction of fundamental errors. They do not include normal recurring adjustments or corrections ofaccounting estimates made in prior periods.

8 *Total recognised gains and losses.* The total of all gains and losses of the reporting entity that are recognised in a period and are attributable to shareholders.

9 *Companies Act 1985.* The Companies Act 1985 as amended by the Companies Act 1989.

10 *Companies (Northern Ireland) Order 1986.* The Companies (Northern Ireland) Order 1986 as amended by the Companies (Northern Ireland) Order 1990 and the Companies (No.2) (Northern Ireland) Order 1990.

11 *Companies (Amendment) Act 1986.* The Republic of Ireland Companies (Amendment) Act 1986 as amended by the Companies Act 1990 and by the European Communities (Companies: Group Accounts) Regulations 1992 *(the 1992 Regulations).*

Statement of Standard Accounting Practice

The statement of standard accounting practice set out in paragraphs 12 to 33 of the FRS should be read in the context of the Objective of the FRS as stated in paragraph 1, the definitions set out in paragraphs 2 to 11 and also of the Foreword to Accounting Standards and the Statement of Principles for Financial Reporting currently in issue.

The Explanation section of the FRS, set out in paragraphs 35 to 66, shall be regarded as part of the statement of standard accounting practice insofar as it assists in interpreting that statement.

Scope

12 The FRS applies to all financial statements intended to give a true and fair view of a reporting entity's financial position and profit or loss (or income and expenditure). Every such reporting entity should apply the requirements of the FRS except to the extent that these requirements are not permitted by the statutory framework (if any) under which the entity reports.

Profit and loss account

13 All gains and losses recognised in the financial statements for the period should be included in the profit and loss account or the statement of total recognised gains and losses. Gains and losses may be excluded from the profit and loss account only if they are specifically permitted or required to be taken directly to reserves by this or other accounting standards or, in the absence of a relevant accounting standard, by law.

Continuing and discontinued operations

14 The aggregate results of each of continuing operations, acquisitions (as a component of continuing operations) and discontinued operations should be disclosed separately. The results of acquisitions included in continuing operations should not include those that are also discontinued in the same period. The minimum disclosure required down to the operating profit level on the face of the profit and loss account in respect of continuing operations, acquisitions and discontinued operations is the analysis of turnover and operating profit (which for non-financial reporting entities is normally profit before income from shares in group undertakings). The analysis between continuing operations, acquisitions (as a component of continuing operations) and discontinued operations of each of the other statutory profit and loss account format items between turnover and operating profit should be given by way of note where not shown on the face of the profit and loss account. In those circumstances where a reporting entity presents allocations of interest or tax between continuing and discontinued operations, the method and underlying assumptions used in making the allocations should be disclosed.

15 Where an acquisition, or a sale or a termination, has a material impact on a major business segment this should be disclosed and explained.

Acquisitions

16 Where it is not practicable to determine the post-acquisition results of an operation to the end of the current period, an indication should be given of the contribution of the acquisition to the turnover and operating profit of the continuing operations in addition to the information required by the Companies Act 1985*. If an indication of the contribution of an acquisition to the results of the period cannot be given this fact and the reason should be explained.

Discontinued operations

17 Only income and costs directly related to discontinued operations should appear under the heading of discontinued operations. Reorganisation or restructuring of continuing operations resulting from a sale or termination should be treated as a part of continuing operations.

The consequences of a decision to sell or terminate an operation

18 If a decision has been made to sell or terminate an operation, any consequential provisions should reflect the extent to which obligations have been incurred that are not expected to be covered by the future profits of the operation or the disposal of its assets. This principle requires that the reporting entity should be demonstrably committed to the sale or termination. This should be evidenced, in the former case, by a binding sale agreement and, in the latter, by a detailed formal plan for termination from which the reporting entity cannot realistically withdraw. The provision should cover only (a) the direct costs of the sale or termination and (b) any operating losses of the operation up to the date of sale or termination, in both cases, after taking into account the aggregate profit, if any, to be recognised in the profit and loss account from the future profits of the operation

* Companies Act 1985 Schedule 4A paragraph 13.

The equivalent reference in Northern Ireland legislation is the Companies (Northern Ireland) Order 1986 Schedule 4A paragraph 13.

The nearest equivalent reference in the Republic of Ireland is the 1992 Regulations Section 27 which sets out a general requirement for disclosure in the case of changes in the composition of a group.

or disposal of its assets. Unless the operation qualifies as a discontinued operation in the period under review, the write down of assets and any provisions should appear in the continuing operations category. In the subsequent period when the operation does qualify as discontinued, the provisions should be used to offset the results of the operation in the discontinued category. The related disclosure in that subsequent period, however, should be to show the results of the discontinued operation under each of the statutory format headings with the utilisation of the provision analysed as necessary between the operating loss and the loss on sale or termination of the discontinued operation and disclosed on the face of the profit and loss account immediately below the relevant items.

Exceptional items

19 All exceptional items, other than those included in the items listed in paragraph 20, should be credited or charged in arriving at the profit or loss on ordinary activities by inclusion under the statutory format headings to which they relate. They should be attributed to continuing or discontinued operations as appropriate. The amount of each exceptional item, either individually or as an aggregate of items of a similar type, should be disclosed separately by way of note, or on the face of the profit and loss account if that degree of prominence is necessary in order to give a true and fair view. An adequate description of each exceptional item should be given to enable its nature to be understood.

20 The following items, including provisions in respect of such items should be shown separately on the face of the profit and loss account after operating profit and before interest, and included under the appropriate heading of continuing or discontinued operations:

(a) profits or losses on the sale or termination of an operation;

(b) costs of a fundamental reorganisation or restructuring having a material effect on the nature and focus of the reporting entity's operations; and

(c) profits or losses on the disposal of fixed assets.

In calculating the profit or loss in respect of the above items consideration should only be given to revenue and costs directly related to the items in question.

When the net amount of (a) or (c) above is not material, but the gross profits or losses are material, the relevant heading should still appear on the face of the profit and loss account with a reference to a related note analysing the profits and losses. Relevant information regarding the effect of these items on the taxation charge and, in the case of consolidated financial statements, any minority interests should both be shown in a note to the profit and loss account. As a minimum the related tax and the minority interest should both be shown in aggregate, but if the effect of the tax and minority interests differs for the various categories of items further information should be given where practicable, to assist users in assessing the impact of the different items on the net profit or loss attributable to shareholders. The taxation effects of these items are also referred to in paragraphs 23 and 24.

Profit or loss on the disposal of an asset

21 The profit or loss on the disposal of an asset should be accounted for in the profit and loss account of the period in which the disposal occurs as the difference between the net sale proceeds and the net carrying amount, whether carried at historical cost (less any provisions made) or at a valuation.

Extraordinary items

22 Any extraordinary profit or loss should be shown separately on the face of the profit and loss account, after the profit or loss on ordinary activities after taxation but before deducting any appropriations such as dividends paid or payable and, in the case of consolidated financial statements, after the figure for minority interests. The amount of each extraordinary item should be shown individually either on the face of the profit and loss account or in a note and an adequate description of each extraordinary item should be given to enable its nature to be understood. The tax on extraordinary profit or loss and, in the case of consolidated financial statements, the extraordinary profit or loss attributable to minority shareholders should be shown separately as a part of the extraordinary item either on the face of the profit and loss account or in a note. Any subsequent adjustments to the tax on extraordinary profit or loss in future periods should be shown as an extraordinary item.

Taxation

23 Any special circumstances that affect the overall tax charge or credit for the period, or that may affect those of future periods, should be disclosed by way of note to the profit and loss account and their individual effects quantified. Such disclosures should include any special circumstances affecting the tax attributable to the items specified in paragraph 20. The effects of a fundamental change in the basis of taxation should be included in the tax charge or credit for the period and separately disclosed on the face of the profit and loss account.

24 The tax on items of the type listed in paragraph 20 or on an extraordinary profit or loss should be determined by computing the tax on the profit or loss on ordinary activities as if the items did not exist, and comparing this notional tax charge with the tax charge on the profit or loss for the period (after extraordinary items). Any additional tax charge or credit (including deferred tax) arising should be attributed to the items. If there are items in both groups in the same period, the tax on the items combined should be calculated then apportioned between the two groups in relation to their respective amounts, unless a more appropriate basis of apportionment is available. If a more appropriate basis is adopted the method of apportionment should be disclosed.

Earnings per share

25 Paragraph 10 of SSAP 3 concerning the definition of earnings per share is withdrawn and replaced by the following paragraph:

> '10 The profit in pence attributable to each equity share, based on the profit (or in the case of a group the consolidated profit) of the period after tax, minority interests and extraordinary items and after deducting preference dividends and other appropriations in respect of preference shares, divided by the number of equity shares in issue and ranking for dividend in respect of the period.'

If an additional earnings per share calculated at any other level of profit is presented it should be presented on a consistent basis over time and, wherever disclosed, reconciled to the amount required by the FRS. Such a reconciliation should list the items for which an adjustment is being made and disclose their individual effect on the calculation. The earnings per share required by the FRS should be at least as prominent as any additional version presented and the reason for calculating the additional version should be explained. The reconciliation and explanation should appear adjacent to the earnings per share disclosure, or a reference should be given to where they can be found.

Note of historical cost profits and losses

26 Where there is a material difference between the result as disclosed in the profit and loss account and the result on an unmodified historical cost basis, a note of the historical cost profit or loss for the period should be presented. Where full historical cost information is unavailable or cannot be obtained without unreasonable expense or delay, the earliest available values should be used. The note of the historical cost profit or loss should include a reconciliation of the reported profit on ordinary activities before taxation to the equivalent historical cost amount and should also show the retained profit for the financial year reported on the historical cost basis. The note should be presented immediately following the profit and loss account or the statement of total recognised gains and losses.

Statement of total recognised gains and losses

27 A primary statement should be presented, with the same prominence as the other primary statements, showing the total of recognised gains and losses and its components. The components should be the gains and losses that are recognised in the period insofar as they are attributable to shareholders*.

Reconciliation of movements in shareholders' funds

28 A note should be presented reconciling the opening and closing totals of shareholders' funds of the period.

Prior period adjustments

29 Prior period adjustments should be accounted for by restating the comparative figures for the preceding period in the primary statements and notes and adjusting the opening balance of reserves for the cumulative effect. The cumulative effect of the adjustments should also be noted at the foot of the statement of total recognised gains and losses of the current period. The effect of prior period adjustments on the results for the preceding period should be disclosed where practicable.

Comparative figures

30 Comparative figures should be given for all items in the primary statements and such notes thereto as are required by the FRS. The comparative figures in respect of the profit and loss account should include in the continuing category only the results of those operations included in the current period's continuing operations.

Investment companies

31 Investment companies as defined in companies legislation should include in the profit and loss account only profits available for distribution.

Date from which effective

32 The accounting practices set out in the FRS should be adopted as soon as possible and regarded as standard in respect of financial statements relating to accounting periods ending on or after 22 June 1993.

* As explained in UITF Abstract 3 and paragraphs 6 and 7 of SSAP 22 — 'Accounting for Goodwill', the immediate write-off to reserves of purchased goodwill is not a recognised loss.

Withdrawal of SSAP 6 and amendment of other statements

33 The FRS supersedes SSAP 6 and amends SSAP 3 in accordance with paragraph 25 of the FRS. Related changes to SSAP 3 and other accounting standards follow:

(a) *SSAP 1:* paragraph 21, line 4 "SSAP 6" is replaced by "FRS 3 'Reporting Financial Performance'";

(b) *SSAP 3:* paragraphs 18 and 19 are deleted;

(c) *SSAP 3:* Appendix 1 paragraph 2 — the first sentence is replaced by "The amount earned for equity should be the profit (or, in the case of a group, the consolidated profit) of the period after tax, minority interests and extraordinary items and after deducting preference dividends and other appropriations in respect of preference shares." The footnote to this paragraph is deleted;

(d) *SSAP 3:* Appendix 1 paragraph 12 —line 2 "normally, the consolidated profit of the period after taxation, minority interests and preference dividends but before extraordinary items" is replaced by "the profit (or, in the case of a group, the consolidated profit) of the period after tax, minority interests and extraordinary items and after deducting preference dividends and other appropriations in respect of preference shares";

(e) *SSAP 4:* paragraph 14 — line 5 "SSAP 6 'Extraordinary Items and Prior Year Adjustments'" is replaced by "FRS 3 'Reporting Financial Performance' as an exceptional item";

(f) *SSAP 4:* paragraph 30 is replaced by "Any adjustments arising as a result of a change in accounting policy to comply with the requirements of this statement should be accounted for as a prior year adjustment in accordance with FRS 3 'Reporting Financial Performance'".

(g) *SSAP 8:* paragraph 10 and Appendix 3 paragraph 13 are each replaced by "Irrecoverable ACT should be treated as part of the tax on ordinary activities." The footnote to paragraph 10 is deleted;

(h) *SSAP 12:* paragraph 18 — line 12 "SSAP 6 'Extraordinary Items and Prior Year Adjustments'" is replaced by "FRS 3 'Reporting Financial Performance' as an exceptional item included under the same statutory format heading as the ongoing depreciation charge." The penultimate and prepenultimate sentences of paragraph 18 are deleted;

(i) *SSAP 15:* paragraph 36 — the last sentence is deleted;

(j) *SSAP 19:* paragraph 13 — line 6 "investment trust companies (as mentioned in paragraph 10 of SSAP 6)" is replaced by "Companies Act investment companies (as mentioned in paragraph 66 of FRS 3 'Reporting Financial Performance')";

(k) *SSAP 24:* paragraph 26 — the last two sentences are replaced by "Where a reduction in the number of employees is related to an event such as the sale or termination of an operation, it is accepted that it may not be possible to apply the rule set out in this paragraph. This is because FRS 'Reporting Financial Performance' requires provisions consequent on the sale or termination of an operation to be made after taking account of future profits of the operation or the disposal of its assets. It may therefore not be appropriate to defer recognition of an associated pension cost or credit.";

(l) *SSAP 24:* paragraph 53 line 3 "SSAP 6 (Revised) 'Extraordinary Items and Prior Year Adjustments'" is replaced by "FRS 3 'Reporting Financial Performance'";

(m) *SSAP 24:* paragraph 81 — the second sentence is replaced by "Where the significant reduction in the number of employees is related to the sale or termination of an operation, the associated pension cost a credit should be recognised immediately to the extent necessary to comply with the requirements of paragraph 18 of FRS 3 'Reporting Financial Performance'. In all other cases where there is a reduction in contributions arising from a significant reduction in employees the reduction of contributions should be recognised as it occurs.";

(n) *SSAP 24:* paragraph 92 — line 3 "SSAP 6 (Revised) 'Extraordinary items and prior year adjustments'" is replaced by "FRS 3 'Reporting Financial Performance'";

(o) *SSAP 24:* paragraph 94 — line 8 "SSAP 6 (Revised)" is replaced by "FRS 3 'Reporting Financial Performance'";

(p) *UITF Abstract 1:* Paragraph 6 — line 2 "SSAP 6" is replaced by "FRS 3". In the references section "Statement of Standard Accounting Practice 6 — Extraordinary Items and Prior Year Adjustments'' is replaced by "FRS 3 'Reporting Financial Performance'";

(q) *UITF Abstract 2:* is withdrawn;

(r) *UITF Abstract 5:* references section "Statement of Standard Accounting Practice 6 — Extraordinary Items and Prior Year Adjustments — paragraph 33" is replaced by 'FRS 3 Reporting Financial Performance' — paragraph 13".

Financial Reporting Standard No. 3 'Reporting Financial Performance' was adopted by a vote of eight of the nine members of the Accounting Standards Board. Mr Bradfield dissented. His dissenting view is set out on pages 48 to 50.

Members of the Accounting Standards Board

David Tweedie (Chairman)

Allan Cook (Technical Director)

Robert Bradfield

Sir Bryan Carsberg

Elwyn Eilledge

Michael Garner

Donald Main

Roger Munson

Graham Stacy

Compliance with International Accounting Standards

34 The requirements of the FRS are consistent with International Accounting Standard 5 'Information to be Disclosed in Financial Statements' and International Accounting Standard 8 'Unusual and Prior Period Items and Changes in Accounting Policies'. The FRS is also consistent with the exposure draft of a proposed revised International Accounting Standard 'Extraordinary Items Fundamental Errors and Changes in Accounting Policies' issued by the International Accounting Standards Committee in July 1992.

Explanation

Components of financial performance

35 The many parts of a reporting entity's activities exhibit features which differ in stability, risk and predictability, indicating a need for the separate disclosure of components of financial performance in the profit and loss account and in the statement of total recognised gains and losses. The disclosure of these components is designed to facilitate understanding of the performance achieved in a period and to assist users in deciding on the extent to which past results are useful in helping to assess potential future results. A component, of whatever nature, should be shown separately if it has a special significance for the assessment of some aspect of performance.

36 The total of all recognised gains and losses attributable to shareholders of a reporting entity includes the following components:

(a) profit or loss before the deduction of dividends;

(b) adjustments to the valuation of assets; and

(c) differences in the net investment in foreign enterprises arising from changes in foreign currency exchange rates.

37 The profit and loss account and statement of total recognised gains and losses are intended to present all the entity's gains and losses recognised in a particular period. Profit or loss of a period focuses on what a reporting entity earns for its output (revenue) and what it sacrifices to obtain that output (expenses). Gains and losses may be excluded from the profit and loss account only if they are specifically permitted or required to be taken directly to reserves by this or other accounting standards or, in the absence of a relevant accounting standard, by law. For example, a gain on the revaluation of a fixed asset should be reflected directly in the statement of total recognised gains and losses of the period in which the revaluation takes place. The realisation, or part realisation, of such a gain on the sale of the asset in a subsequent period is not itself a gain of that later period but, rather, confirmation of a gain that had already occurred by the time of the revaluation. Consequently, the gain or loss on the disposal of the asset is to be calculated as the difference between the net sale proceeds and the net carrying amount.

Profit and loss account

Continuing and discontinued operations

38 The objective of reporting separately the results of continuing operations, acquisitions (as a component of continuing operations) and discontinued operations is to assist users, first, in assessing the financial performance of these aspects of a reporting entity's operations and, secondly, in forming a basis for the assessment of future income. Separate presentation assists analysis of the significance of the part of a reporting entity's operations that has ceased and of new operations that have been acquired. The various aspects of the definition and requirements regarding discontinued operations are explained in paragraphs 41 to 44. In respect of acquisitions, the requirement is to disclose their post-acquisition results for the period in which the acquisition occurs. In some circumstances it may also be useful to users for the results of acquisitions for the first full financial year for which they are a part of the reporting entity to be disclosed in the notes.

39 The FRS requires each of the statutory profit and loss account headings between turnover and operating profit to be analysed between continuing operations, acquisitions (as a component of continuing operations) and discontinued operations. For non-financial reporting entities operating profit is normally profit before income from shares in group undertakings, although in certain cases income from associated undertakings or from other participating interests may be considered to be part of operating profit. In order to avoid too much data on the face of the profit and loss account, the minimum disclosure required there in respect of continuing operations, acquisitions and discontinued operations is the analysis of turnover and operating profit. A similar analysis is required between continuing and discontinued operations for the items specifically required to be disclosed by paragraph 20; where practicable this analysis should identify, either on the face of the profit and loss account or in the notes, the amounts arising in respect of acquisitions.

40 The analysis in respect of continuing operations, acquisitions and discontinued operations is required only to the profit before interest level because interest payable is often a reflection of a reporting entity's overall financing policy, involving both equity and debt funding considerations on a group wide basis, rather than an aggregation of the particular types of finance allocated to individual segments of the reporting entity's operations. Any allocation of interest would involve a considerable degree of subjectivity, that could leave the user uncertain as to the relevance and reliability of the information. If a reporting entity wishes to provide such an allocation, the FRS requires that the method and underlying assumptions used in making the allocation be disclosed.

Discontinued operations

41 The FRS requires operations to be classified as discontinued when the sale or termination is completed either in the period or before the earlier of three months after the commencement of the subsequent period and the date on which the financial statements are approved. Only the results of operations up to the balance sheet date should be included; operations in the subsequent period should be included in the results of that period, separately classified as discontinued if material. Any income and costs associated with a sale or termination that has not been completed are to be included in the continuing category. In some cases it may be appropriate to disclose separately in a note to the profit and loss account the results of operations which although not discontinued are in the process of discontinuing, but they should not be classified as discontinued.

42 To be included in the category of discontinued operations, a sale or termination must have a material effect on the nature and focus of the reporting entity's operations and represent a material reduction in its operating facilities resulting either from its withdrawal from a particular market (whether class of business or geographical) or from a material reduction in turnover in its continuing markets. The nature and focus of a reporting entity's operations refers to the positioning of its products or services in their markets including the aspects of both quality and location. For example, if a hotel company which had traditionally served the lower end of the hotel market sold its existing chain and bought luxury hotels then, while remaining in the business of managing hotels, the group would be changing the nature and focus of its operations. A similar situation would arise if the same company were to sell its hotels in, say, the United States of America and buy hotels in Europe. The regular sales and replacements of material assets which are undertaken by a reporting entity as part of the routine maintenance of its portfolio of assets should not be classified as discontinuances and acquisitions. In the example, the sale of hotels and the purchase of others within the same market sector and similar locations would be treated as wholly within continuing operations.

43 To be classified as discontinued a sale or termination should have resulted from a strategic decision by the reporting entity either to withdraw from a particular market (whether class of business or geographical) or to curtail materially its presence in a continuing market (i.e. 'downsizing'). The sale or termination of a component of a reporting entity's operations which is undertaken primarily in order to achieve productivity improvements or other cost savings is a part of that entity's continuing operations and the effects of the sale or termination should be included under that heading.

44 To be classified as discontinued, the assets, liabilities, results of operations and activities of an operation must be clearly distinguishable, physically, operationally and for financial reporting purposes. If the financial results of a sold or terminated operation are not identifiable separately from the accounting records or to a material extent can only be derived through making allocations of income or expenses, then the operation cannot be classified as a discontinued operation. For example, a manufacturing facility that is closed down but which lacks an external market price for its output cannot be classified as a discontinued operation.

The consequences of a decision to sell or terminate an operation

45 Paragraph 18 sets out the principle underlying the establishment of provisions as a consequence of a decision to sell or terminate an operation. This principle focuses on the fact that an obligation arises at the point when the reporting entity becomes demonstrably committed to the sale or termination. Evidence of the commitment might be the public announcement of specific plans, the commencement of implementation, or other circumstances effectively obliging the reporting entity to complete the sale or termination. A binding contract entered into after the balance sheet date may provide additional evidence of asset values and commitments at the balance sheet date. In the case of an intended sale for which no legally binding sale agreement exists, no obligation has been entered into by the reporting entity; accordingly, provisions for the direct costs of the decision to sell and for future operating losses should not be made. In accordance with normal practice, however, any permanent diminutions in asset values should be recorded.

Exceptional items

46 Exceptional items are defined in paragraph 5. They are an inherent part of the normal activities of a reporting entity and are included in the computation of profit or loss on ordinary activities but, because of their exceptional size or incidence, require separate disclosure to explain the performance of a period. Exceptional items may arise from a variety of sources and for larger or more complex businesses they are likely to occur in one form or another in most periods They should not be aggregated on the face of the profit and loss account under one heading of exceptional items but, rather, each should be included within its natural statutory format heading or paragraph 20 category and separately disclosed in accordance with the requirements of paragraphs 19 and 20 The nature of exceptional items makes it necessary to distinguish exceptional profits from exceptional losses, in the notes if not on the face of the profit and loss account. The profits or losses on the disposal of fixed assets in paragraph 20 (c) are not intended to include profits and losses that are in effect no more than marginal adjustments to depreciation previously charged. In any references to profit or loss as including or excluding exceptional items, an explanation should be given of the relevance of their inclusion or exclusion (as the case may be) in the context of considering the results of the period or assessing maintainable earnings.

47 Exceptional items may occur in either continuing or discontinued operations and need to be identified individually as belonging to one or other category. In showing the amount of each exceptional item, individual items or groups of a similar type of item should not be combined if separately they relate to continuing and to discontinued operations.

Extraordinary items

48 Extraordinary items are defined in paragraph 6. Extraordinary items should be shown on the face of the profit and loss account before deducting any appropriations such as dividends paid or payable and, in the case of consolidated financial statements, after the figure for minority interests. Extraordinary items are extremely rare as they relate to highly abnormal events or transactions that fall outside the ordinary activities of a reporting entity and which are not expected to recur. In view of the extreme rarity of such items no examples are provided. Items falling into the category of exceptional in accordance with the terms of the FRS cannot, by definition, be extraordinary.

49 The FRS follows companies legislation in requiring the tax on extraordinary profit or loss and, in the case of consolidated financial statements, the minority shareholders' interest in an extraordinary profit or loss, to be shown separately.

Taxation

50 Companies legislation requires disclosure in the notes of the details of any special circumstances that affect any liability to taxation, whether for the financial year in question or for future years, and whether in respect of profits, income or capital gains. Such special circumstances could include, for example, the effect on the tax charge of losses whether utilised or carried forward. This disclosure can be useful in understanding the period's charge or credit in respect of taxation, particularly when there are items of the type specified in paragraph 20. It is recognised that analysing an entity's total taxation charge between component parts of its result for a period can involve arbitrary allocations that tend to become less meaningful the more components there are. However, in respect of items such as disposal profits or losses the tax can often be identified with the exceptional item concerned and the relationship between the profit or loss and the attributable tax may be significantly different from that in respect of operating profits or losses. In such circumstances it is relevant to identify the tax charge or credit more specifically. Disclosure of special circumstances can also be useful in assessing likely future amounts of taxation. Therefore, the FRS requires that the notes should not only disclose the existence of any special circumstances but should also quantify their individual effects.

51 The application of the fundamental accounting concept of consistency requires that the tax effects of an extraordinary item should themselves be treated as extraordinary. This principle would apply even where an extraordinary item and its tax effects are recognised in different periods, such as where the tax relief in respect of an extraordinary loss is not recognised until it is utilised in a subsequent period.

Earnings per share

52 It is not possible to distil the performance of a complex organisation into a single measure. Undue significance, therefore, should not be placed on any one such measure which may purport to achieve this aim. To assess the performance of a reporting entity during a period all components of its activities must be considered. For this reason and to provide a starting point for analysis, the FRS requires earnings per share to be calculated on profit attributable to equity shareholders of the reporting entity. If preparers wish to highlight any other version of earnings per share, they are required to provide an explanation of the particular significance they are attaching to that version and to itemise and quantify the adjustments they are making to the earnings per share required by the FRS.

Segmental reporting

53 It is important for a thorough understanding of the results and financial position of a reporting entity that the impact of changes on material components of the business should be highlighted. To assist in this objective, if an acquisition, a sale or a termination has a material impact on a major business segment the FRS requires that this impact should be disclosed and explained.

Note of historical cost profits and losses

54 The note of historical cost profits and losses is a memorandum item that is an abbreviated restatement of the profit and loss account adjusting the reported profit or loss, if necessary, so as to show it as if no asset revaluations had been made. Adjustments are made for such items as:

(a) gains recognised in prior periods in the statement of total recognise gains and losses and realised in the current period; for example, the difference between the profit on the disposal of an asset calculated on depreciated historical cost and that calculated on a revalued amount; and

(b) the difference between an historical cost depreciation charge and the depreciation charge calculated on the revalued amount included in the profit and loss account of the period.

55 Two reasons for disclosing the profit or loss for a period on the unmodified historical cost basis of accounting are commonly cited. The first is, that for as long as discretion exists on the timing or scale of revaluations included in financial statements, the unmodified historical cost basis will give the reported profits or losses of different reporting entities on a more comparable basis. The second is the wish of certain users to assess the profit or loss on sale of assets based on their historical cost, rather than, as the FRS requires, on their revalued carrying amount. In acknowledgement of these concerns, the Board has made the provision of a note of historical cost profits and losses a requirement of the FRS in those circumstances where there is a material difference between the result as disclosed in the profit and loss account and the result on an unmodified historical cost basis. Where full historical cost information is unavailable or cannot be obtained without unreasonable expense or delay, the earliest available values should be used. The note of historical cost profits and losses should be presented immediately following the profit and loss account or the statement of total recognised gains and losses. In consolidated financial statements, the profit and loss account figure for minority interests should be amended for the purposes of this note to reflect the adjustments made where they affect subsidiary companies with a minority interest. For the purpose of paragraph 26 the following are not deemed to be departures from the historical cost convention: (a) adjustments necessarily made to cope with the impact of hyperinflation on foreign operations and (b) the practice of market makers and other dealers in investments of marking to market where this is an established industry practice.

Statement of total recognised gains and losses

56 The range of important components of financial performance which the FRS requires reporting entities to highlight would often be incomplete if it stopped short at the profit and loss account, since certain gains and losses are specifically permitted or required by law or an accounting standard to be taken directly to reserves. An example is an unrealised gain, such as a revaluation surplus on fixed assets. It is necessary to consider all gains and losses recognised in a period when assessing the financial performance of a reporting entity during that period. Accordingly, the FRS requires, as a primary statement, a statement of total recognised gains and losses to show the extent to which shareholders' funds have increased or decreased from all the various gains and losses recognised in the period. It follows from this perspective that the same gains and losses should not be recognised twice (for example, a holding gain recognised when a fixed asset is revalued should not be recognised a second time when the revalued asset is sold).

57 Statements of total recognised gains and losses contribute further to the purposes of financial reporting by:

(a) combining information about operating and related performance with other aspects of a reporting entity's financial performance; and

(b) providing information (jointly with the other primary statements) that is useful for assessing the return on investment in a reporting entity.

If a reporting entity has no recognised gains or losses other than the profit or loss for the period a statement to this effect immediately below the profit and loss account will satisfy the requirement of paragraph 27.

58 Where there is a material recognised movement between the amount attributable to different classes of shareholders which does not affect total shareholders' funds an explanatory footnote to the statement may be appropriate. An example might be an appropriation of profit to accrue a premium on redemption of preference shares.

Reconciliation of movements in shareholders' funds

59 The profit and loss account and the statement of total recognised gains and losses reflect the performance of a reporting entity in a period. There are, however, other changes in shareholders' funds that can also be important in understanding the change in the financial position of the entity. The purpose of the reconciliation of movements in shareholders' funds is to highlight those other changes. If included as a primary statement, the reconciliation should be shown separately from the statement of total recognised gains and losses.

Prior period adjustments

60 The majority of items relating to prior periods arise mainly from the corrections and adjustments which are the natural result of estimates inherent in accounting and more particularly in the periodic preparation of financial statements. They are dealt with in the profit and loss account of the period in which they are identified and their effect is stated where material. They are not exceptional or extraordinary merely because they relate to a prior period; their nature will determine their classification. Prior period adjustments, that is prior period items which should be adjusted against the opening balance of retained profits or reserves, are rare and limited to items arising from changes in accounting policies or from the correction of fundamental errors.

61 Estimating future events and their effects requires the exercise of judgement and will require reappraisal as new events occur, as more experience is acquired or as additional information is obtained. Because a change in estimate arises from new information or developments, it should not be given retrospective effect by a restatement of prior periods. Sometimes a change in estimate may have the appearance of a change of accounting policy and care is necessary to avoid confusing the two.

62 It is a fundamental accounting concept that there is consistency of accounting treatment within each accounting period and from one period to the next. A change in accounting policy may therefore be made only if it can be justified on the grounds that the new policy is preferable to the one it replaces because it will give a fairer presentation of the result and of the financial position of a reporting entity. It is a characteristic of a change in accounting policy that it is the result of a choice between two or more accounting methods. Therefore it does not arise from the adoption or modification of an accounting method necessitated by transactions or events that are clearly different in substance from those previously occurring. Following a change in accounting policy, the amounts for the current and corresponding periods should be restated on the basis of the new policies. The cumulative adjustments should also be noted at the foot of the statement of total recognised gains and losses of the current period and included in the reconciliation of movements in shareholders' funds of the corresponding period in order to highlight for users the effect of the adjustments.

63 In exceptional circumstances it may be found that financial statements of prior periods have been issued containing errors which are of such significance as to destroy the true and fair view and hence the validity of those financial statements. The corrections of such fundamental errors and the cumulative adjustments applicable to prior periods have no bearing on the results of the current period and they are therefore not included in arriving at the profit or loss for the current period. They are accounted for by restating prior periods, with the result that the opening balance of retained profits will be adjusted accordingly and highlighted in the reconciliation of movements in shareholders funds. As the cumulative adjustments are recognised in the current period, they should also be noted at the foot of the statement of total recognised gains and losses of the current period.

Comparative figures

64 Comparative figures should be given for all items in the primary statements and such notes thereto as are required by the FRS. To aid comparison, the comparative figures in respect of the profit and loss account should be based on the status of an operation in the financial statements of the period under review and should, therefore, include in the continuing category only the results of those operations included in the current period's continuing operations. The comparative figures appearing under the heading 'continuing operations' may include figures which were shown under the heading of acquisitions in that previous period; no reference need be made to the results of those acquisitions, since they are not required to be presented separately in the current year. Where, however, information on acquisitions is provided voluntarily in respect of the first full year, it may be helpful to provide comparative figures for those acquisitions. Similarly, the comparative figures for discontinued operations will include both amounts relating to operations discontinued in the previous period and amounts relating to operations discontinued in the period under review, which in the previous period would have been included as part of continuing operations. The analysis of comparative figures between continuing and discontinued operations is not required on the face of the profit and loss account.

Investment companies

65 The FRS is based on the view that the profit and loss account for the period should include and show separately all gains and losses which are recognised in that period, except for those which are specifically permitted or required by this or other accounting standards to be taken directly to reserves or, in the absence of a relevant accounting standard, specifically permitted or required by law to be taken directly to reserves. This is a concept which applies to all types of reporting entity, although the precise form of presentation of the results of financial performance will vary between types of reporting entity.

66 Investment companies as defined in Section 266 of the Companies Act 1985* (Companies Act investment companies) have special legal provisions regarding the recording of unrealised capital losses, with the result that their profit and loss accounts are not comparable with those of other reporting entities. In the case of such investment companies all recognised gains and losses of a capital nature should be shown only in the statement of total recognised gains and losses leaving the profit and loss account to be confined to profits available for distribution.

Note on legal requirements

Great Britain

General

67 The requirements of Schedules 4 and 4A to the Companies Act 1985* relating to the form and content of company and group financial statements set out formats for the profit and loss account allowing some flexibility in certain circumstances in the manner in which the information is presented. The provisions of the FRS supplement those legal requirements, while remaining within their bounds.

Disclosure

68 Companies Act 1985 Schedule 4 paragraph 54

'(1) The basis on which the charge for United Kingdom corporation tax and United Kingdom income tax is computed shall be stated.

* The equivalent legislation in Northern Ireland is Article 274 of the Companies (Northern Ireland) Order 1986.

The equivalent legislation in the Republic of Ireland is Section 47 of the Companies (Amendment) Act 1983.

(2) Particulars shall be given of any special circumstances which affect liability in respect of taxation of profits, income or capital gains for the financial year or liability in respect of taxation of profits, income or capital gains for succeeding financial years.'

69 Companies Act 1985 Schedule 4A paragraph 13

'(1) The following information with respect to acquisitions taking place in the financial year shall be given in a note to the accounts.'

'(4) The profit or loss of the undertaking or group acquired shall be stated:

(a) for the period from the beginning of the financial year of the undertaking or, as the case may be, of the parent undertaking of the group, up to the date of the acquisition; and

(b) for the previous financial year of that undertaking or parent undertaking;

and there shall also be stated the date on which the financial year referred to in paragraph (a) began.'

70 Companies Act 1985 Schedule 4A paragraphs 15 and 16

'15 Where during the financial year there has been a disposal of an undertaking or group which significantly affects the figures shown in the group accounts, there shall be stated in a note to the accounts:

(a) the name of that undertaking or, as the case may be, of the parent undertaking of that group; and

(b) the extent to which the profit or loss shown in the group accounts is attributable to profit or loss of that undertaking or group;

16 The information required by paragraph 13, or . . . 15 above need not be disclosed with respect to an undertaking which:

(a) is established under the law of a country outside the United Kingdom; or

(b) carries on business outside the United Kingdom;

if in the opinion of the directors of the parent company the disclosure would be seriously prejudicial to the business of that undertaking or to the business of the parent company or any of its subsidiary undertakings and the Secretary of State agrees that the information should not be disclosed.'

Definition

71 Companies Act 1985 Section 266

'(1) In Section 265 "investment company" means a public company which has given notice in the prescribed form (which has not been revoked) to the registrar of companies of its intention to carry on business as an investment company, and has since the date of that notice complied with the requirements specified below.

(2) Those requirements are:

(a) that the business of the company consists of investing its funds mainly in securities, with the aim of spreading investment risk and giving members of the company the benefit of the results of the management of its funds;

(b) that none of the company's holdings in companies (other than those which are for the time being in investment companies) represents more than 15 per cent by value of the investing company's investments;

(c) that distribution of the company's capital profits is prohibited by its memorandum or articles of association;

(d) that the company has not retained, otherwise than in compliance with this Part, in respect of any accounting reference period more than 15 per cent of the income it derives from securities.'

Northern Ireland

72 Schedules 4 and 4A of the Companies (Northern Ireland) Order 1986 are similar to Schedules 4 and 4A of the Companies Act 1985 as referred to in paragraph 67.

73 Paragraph 54 of Schedule 4 of the Companies (Northern Ireland) Order 1986 is similar to paragraph 54 of Schedule 4 of the Companies Act 1985 as set out in paragraph 68.

74 Paragraphs 13, 15 and 16 of Schedule 4A of the Companies (Northern Ireland) Order 1986 are similar to paragraphs 13, 15 and 16 of Schedule 4A of the Companies Act 1985 as set out in paragraphs 69 and 70.

75 Article 274 of the Companies (Northern Ireland) Order 1986 is similar to Section 266 of the Companies Act 1985 as set out in paragraph 71.

Republic of Ireland

76 The Schedule of the Companies (Amendment) Act 1986 is similar to Schedule 4 of the Companies Act 1985 as referred to in paragraph 67.

77 Paragraph 40 of the Schedule of the Companies (Amendment) Act 1986 is similar to paragraph 54 of Schedule 4 of the Companies Act 1985 as set out in paragraph 68.

78 Section 27 of the 1992 Regulations sets out a general requirement for disclosure in the case of changes in the composition of a group. There are no specific equivalents to paragraphs 13(4), 15 and 16 of Schedule 4A of the Companies Act 1985 as set out in paragraphs 69 and 70.

79 Section 47 of the Companies (Amendment) Act 1983 is similar to Section 266 of the Companies Act 1985 as set out in paragraph 71.

Illustrative examples

These illustrative examples are for general guidance and do not form part of the Financial Reporting Standard. The best form of the disclosure will depend on individual circumstances.

The example on pages 434 to 439 includes two profit and loss accounts along with a statement of total recognised gains and losses, a note of historical cost profits and losses, a reconciliation of movements in shareholders' funds and certain related notes. The following matters should also be noted:

The entity is a group of companies.

The group has made acquisitions and disposals of operations during the year under review.

In this example there is no extraordinary item. However the positioning of such an item on the face of the profit and loss account is shown although in practice the caption would not appear if no extraordinary items existed.

The profit and loss account examples include the disclosure of earnings per share numbers and a pro forma reconciliation statement for adjusted earnings per share numbers is also shown.

The profit and loss account examples have been prepared using Format 1* as contained in Schedule 4 of the Companies Act 1985. Equivalent information should be shown if any of the other statutory formats are used.

The example on page 439 is one of a Companies Act investment company.

* The requirements relating to banking and insurance companies and groups are set out in Schedule 9 to the Companies Act 1985.

Profit and loss account example 1

	1993	1993	1992 as restated
	£m	£m	£m
Turnover			
Continuing operations	550		550
Acquisitions	50		
	600		
Discontinued operations	175		190
		775	690
Cost of sales		(620)	(555)
Gross profit		155	135
Net operating expenses		(104)	(83)
Operating profit			
Continuing operations	50		40
Acquisitions	6		
	56		
Discontinued operations	(15)		12
Less 1992 provision	10		
		51	52
Profit on sale of properties in continuing operations		9	6
Provision for loss on operations to be discontinued			(30)
Loss on disposal of discontinued operations	(17)		
Less 1992 provision	20		
		3	
Profit on ordinary activities before interest		63	28
Interest payable		(18)	(15)
Profit on ordinary activities before taxation		45	13
Tax on profit on ordinary activities		(14)	(4)
Profit on ordinary activities after taxation		31	9
Minority interests		(2)	(2)
[Profit before extraordinary items]		29	7
[Extraordinary items] (included only to show positioning)		—	—
Profit for the financial year		29	7
Dividends		(8)	(1)
Retained profit for the financial year		21	6
Earnings per share		**39p**	**10p**
Adjustments		Xp	Xp
[to be itemised and an adequate description to be given]			
Adjusted earnings per share		Yp	Yp
[Reason for calculating the adjusted earnings per share to be given]			

Profit and loss account example 2

	Continuing operations		Discontinued operations	Total	Total
		Acquisitions			
	1993	**1993**	**1993**	**1993**	**1992** as restated
	£m	*£m*	*£m*	*£m*	*£m*
Turnover	550	50	175	775	690
Cost of sales	(415)	(40)	(165)	(620)	(555)
Gross profit	135	10	10	155	135
Net operating expenses	(85)	(4)	(25)	(114)	(83)
Less 1992 provision			10	10	
Operating profit	50	6	(5)	51	52
Profit on sale of properties	9			9	6
Provision for loss on operations to be discontinued					(30)
Loss on disposal of discontinued operations			(17)	(17)	
Less 1992 provision			20	20	
Profit on ordinary activities before interest	59	6	(2)	63	28
Interest payable				(18)	(15)
Profit on ordinary activities before taxation				45	13
Tax on profit on ordinary activities				(14)	(4)
Profit on ordinary activities after taxation				31	9
Minority interests				(2)	(2)
[Profit before extraordinary items]				29	7
[Extraordinary items] (included only to show positioning)				—	—
Profit for the financial year				29	7
Dividends				(8)	(1)
Retained profit for the financial year				21	6
Earnings per share				**39p**	**10p**
Adjustments				Xp	Xp
[to be itemised and an adequate description to be given]					
Adjusted earnings per share				Yp	Yp

[Reason for calculating the adjusted earnings per share to be given]

Statement of total recognised gains and losses

	1993	1992 as restated
	£m	£m
Profit for the financial year	29	7
Unrealised surplus on revaluation of properties	4	6
Unrealised (loss)/gain on trade investment	(3)	7
	30	20
Currency translation differences on foreign currency net investments	(2)	5
Total recognised gains and losses relating to the year	28	25
Prior year adjustment (as explained in note x)	(10)	
Total gains and losses recognised since last annual report	18	

Note of historical cost profits and losses

	1993	1992 as restated
	£m	£m
Reported profit on ordinary activities before taxation	45	13
Realisation of property revaluation gains of previous years	9	10
Difference between a historical cost depreciation charge and the actual depreciation charge of the year calculated on the revalued amount	5	4
Historical cost profit on ordinary activities before taxation	59	27
Historical cost profit for the year retained after taxation, minority interests, extraordinary items and dividends	35	20

Notes to the financial statements

Note required in respect of profit and loss account example 1

	1993			1992 (as restated)		
	Continuing	Discontinued	Total	Continuing	Discontinued	Total
	£m	£m	£m	£m	£m	£m
Cost of sales	455	165	620	385	170	555
Net operating expenses						
Distribution costs	56	13	69	46	5	51
Administrative expenses	41	12	53	34	3	37
Other operating income	(8)	0	(8)	(5)	0	(5)
	89	25	114	75	8	83
Less 1992 provision	0	(10)	(10)			
	89	15	104			

The total figures for continuing operations in 1993 include the following amounts relating to acquisitions: cost of sales £40 million and net operating expenses £4 million (namely distribution costs, £3 million, administrative expenses £3 million and other operating income £2 million).

Note required in respect of profit and loss account example 2

	1993			1992 (as restated)		
	Continuing	Discontinued	Total	Continuing	Discontinued	Total
	£m	£m	£m	£m	£m	£m
Turnover				500	190	690
Cost of sales				385	170	555
Net operating expenses						
Distribution costs	56	13	69	46	5	51
Administrative expenses	41	12	53	34	3	37
Other operating income	(8)	0	(8)	(5)	0	(5)
	89	25	114	75	8	83
Operating profit				40	12	52

The total figure of net operating expenses for continuing operations in 1993 includes £4 million in respect of acquisitions (namely distribution costs £3 million, administrative expenses £3 million and other operating income £2 million).

Reconciliation of movements in shareholders' funds

	1993	1992 as restated
	£m	£m
Profit for the financial year	29	7
Dividends	(8)	(1)
	21	6
Other recognised gains and losses relating to the year (net)	(1)	18
New share capital subscribed	20	1
Goodwill written off	(25)	
Net addition to shareholders' funds	15	25
Opening shareholders' funds (originally £375 million before deducting prior year adjustment of £10 million)	365	340
Closing shareholders' funds	380	365

Reserves

	Share premium account	Revaluation reserve	Profit and loss account	Total
	£m	£m	£m	£m
At beginning of year as previously stated	44	200	120	364
Prior year adjustment			(10)	(10)
At beginning of year as restated	44	200	110	354
Premium on issue of shares (nominal value £7 million)	13			13
Goodwill written off			(25)	(25)
Transfer from profit and loss account of the year			21	21
Transfer of realised profits		(14)	14	0
Decrease in value of trade investment		(3)		(3)
Currency translation differences on foreign currency net investments			(2)	(2)
Surplus on property revaluations		4		4
At end of year	57	187	118	362

Note: Nominal share capital at end of year £18 million (1992 £11 million).

Companies Act investment company

Profit and loss account

	1993	1992
	£m	£m
Revenue	35	30
Expenses	(11)	(10)
	24	20
Interest payable	(5)	(7)
Profit on ordinary activities before taxation	19	13
Tax on profit on ordinary activities	(4)	(3)
Profit on ordinary activities after taxation	15	10
Minority interests	(1)	(1)
Profit available for distribution	14	9
Dividends	(13)	(8)
Transfer to revenue reserves	1	1

Statement of total recognised gains and losses

	1993	1992
	£m	£m
Capital profit on investments		
Realised gains and losses	52	70
Unrealised gains and losses	138	75
	190	145
Tax	(16)	(22)
Minority interest	(1)	(4)
	173	119
Unrealised surplus on revaluation of tangible fixed assets	4	2
Capital surplus for the year	177	121
Revenue profit available for distribution	14	9
Total recognised gains and losses for the year	191	130
Distributable profits		
Revenue profit available for distribution	14	9
Dividends	(13)	(8)
Transfer to distributable reserves	1	1
Non-distributable profits		
Transfer to non-distributable reserves	177	121
	178	122

Dissenting view

Mr Bradfield dissents from the FRS because he fears that it could frequently produce misleading measures of performance. He notes that it emphasises the components of pre-tax profit, which are now to include the results of business disposals. Shareholders will attach a different level of significance to each of these components — profits from trading being the most important in assessing the underlying performance. However, the FRS ignores, so far as the face of the profit and loss account is concerned, the often material impact in the eyes of shareholders of tax, minority interests and the issue of further shares on each of these components. Here, he believes, the FRS meets neither its own objective nor the intent of many passages in the Board's Statement of Principles.

Under the FRS, the results from trading and business disposals are shown as separate components of profit before tax but are combined thereafter. Information on the tax and minority interests relating to disposals is required, where practicable, to be given in the notes. However, there is no requirement to identify the disposals component of 'profit before tax', 'profit after tax and minorities' or 'earnings per share'. Under SSAP 6, which the FRS replaces, business disposal profits were excluded from all these measures.

Business disposal profits reflect internally generated goodwill often accrued over many years, together with an element of inflation; they are different in kind from the trading results of the year. Pending realisation, they constitute a hidden reserve. They may attract little tax and rarely contain a minority interest. By contrast, Mr Bradfield notes, it is the magnitude and quality of the earnings from trading, after tax and minority interests, that are the focus of attention for the shareholder as he uses the financial statements to assess the continuity of the source of dividends.

Mr Bradfield believes it imperative that users should clearly see the effects of tax and minorities on trading results attributable to shareholders. If, in an international group of companies, the pre-tax trading profits in a low tax regime were to fall and those in a high tax regime were to rise by an identical amount, the shareholder would be materially worse off. SSAP 6 clearly displayed this decline; the FRS serves only to mask it.

Mr Bradfield notes that increasing tax and minority interests can convert an improvement in trading profit, from one year to the next, into a decline in profit attributable to shareholders. Also, where both disposal profits and losses arise, a modest pre-tax result from disposals can be transformed into a substantial after-tax result. Superimposing these elements of profit, as opposed to displaying them separately, may create a reassuring facade which will hide the underlying trend from many users of accounts. If, in addition, there has been a rights issue or an acquisition for shares, users will be left without a single indicator of whether the entity has done well or badly. SSAP 6, when faithfully applied, coped with all these situations.

In Mr Bradfield's view, such outcomes conflict with many of the qualities of financial statements referred to in chapter 2 of the draft Statement of Principles ('The Objective of Financial Statements and Qualitative Characteristics of Financial Information'). These qualities include:

'comparability', whereby 'users must be able to compare the financial statements of an enterprise over time to identify trends in its financial ... performance' (paragraph 34); and

'understandability', whereby information should be 'readily understandable by users' (paragraph 38).

Furthermore, Mr Bradfield believes that the main subtotals from 'profit before taxation on ordinary activities' downwards impart no useful information to the user. They therefore conflict with the twin primary characteristics of 'relevance' (paragraph 23) and 'reliability' (paragraph 26); in the latter case because of failure to 'represent faithfully the effect of the transactions and other events' (paragraph 28). Mr Bradfield therefore believes that the FRS will fail to meet the reasonable expectations of users of financial statements.

Mr Bradfield has suggested some alternative routes for the FRS. One would require each of the headings 'profit before tax', 'profit after tax and minorities' and 'earnings per share' to be analysed into two parts: one from trading and one from disposals. This remains an option open to preparers. He believes that it would enable individual profit and loss accounts, five year summaries and summary financial statements to present helpful and realistic pictures that accord with users' expectations of financial reporting.

The development of the standard

General

i SSAP 6, which is superseded by FRS 3, was originally issued in 1974 and was based on the 'all-inclusive' concept of profit. It was revised as recently as 1986, but, in spite of a number of improvements that were included, there remained significant problems with its interpretation in practice, particularly in respect of the variety of treatments of apparently similar events as either ordinary or extraordinary items in the profit and loss account. The 1986 revision had not achieved the objective of narrowing the differences and variety of accounting practice in this area and calls for change had been heard from users of financial statements as well as from many preparers and auditors involved with the problem.

ii The Board responded by proposing a major change to the presentation of financial performance both in the profit and loss account itself and for items passing through reserves. Its initial proposals were issued in a discussion draft in April 1991 and these were developed in Financial Reporting Exposure Draft 1 'The Structure of Financial Statements — Reporting of Financial Performance' (FRED 1) published in December 1991.

iii The FRS has retained the essential features of FRED 1, in particular the shift of emphasis from a single performance indicator. The Board believes that the performance of complex organisations cannot be summarised in a single number and has therefore adopted an 'information set' approach that highlights a range of important components of performance. This approach inevitably means that financial statements will sometimes appear more complex than under the former standard. However, it is widely accepted that certain totals in the profit and loss account, such as profit before tax and earnings per share, have been used too simplistically and have obscured the significance of relevant underlying components of financial performance. The presentation and disclosure requirements of the FRS should provide a framework which will facilitate the analysis and interpretation of the various aspects of performance.

iv Under the previous SSAP 6 approach, the inconsistencies underlying earnings per share (calculated before extraordinary items) were not clearly evident to users of financial statements and automatic reliance was often placed on the resultant numbers without there being sufficient awareness of the subjective judgements of the preparers in what was included or excluded. In future earnings per share will be all-inclusive with the result that significant variations from one period to another or the absence of expected variations, whatever the cause, will demand some explanation. Earnings per share will tend to be more volatile than under SSAP 6, because, for example, they will include all business disposal profits and losses, but, as indicated above, there was, in any event, significant inconsistency in how SSAP 6 was applied in practice. Moreover, the FRS permits preparers of financial statements to present additional versions of earnings per share provided that (a) the assumptions on which they are based are explicitly disclosed, (b) the reasons for presenting the additional versions are explained and (c) there is consistency in the approach adopted. It is recognised that users may develop methods to calculate and publish an adjusted earnings per share of individual reporting entities on the basis of an independent assessment of financial statements. The FRS should facilitate such assessments by requiring the provision of a range of relevant information.

v It will be for users to identify particular components that they consider of significance in varying circumstances. This is a feature of the information set approach. For the reasons stated above, it will not be appropriate under FRS 3 (any more than it was in practice under SSAP 6) for users to pay particular attention to any 'headline' number on the face of the profit and loss account or statement of total recognised gains and losses without considering the number's composition. Using the information required by the FRS either on the face of the financial statements or in the notes, users should adapt any headline number to give the performance measure required. The Board considers that the FRS is an important step forward in providing the requisite information to users in a form designed to assist a more mature understanding and analysis of financial performance. Where summarised or highlighted information is presented, (such as a preliminary announcement) it will be the responsibility of the presenters of such information to emphasise the particular components of performance which are of significance in their specific circumstances.

Principal changes from FRED 1

The consequences of a decision to sell or terminate an operation

vi FRED 1 did not address the making of provisions in respect of operations that are to be discontinued in future periods. In response to comments received, this issue has been addressed in the FRS.

Exceptional items

vii In the light of the proposed severe restrictions on what should be categorised as extraordinary, FRED 1 proposed that a material profit or loss on the sale or termination of an operation should always be shown on the face of the profit and loss account. The FRS has extended this disclosure to two other items — costs of a fundamental reorganisation or restructuring having a material effect on the nature and focus of the reporting entity's operations and profits or losses on the disposal of fixed assets. FRED 1 also proposed that the tax and minority interest attributable to a profit or loss on sale or termination should be shown in a note. In view of the additional items required to be shown on the face of the profit and loss account by the FRS, the Board has given further thought to the question of attributable tax and minority interests and has added paragraphs requiring as a minimum that the aggregate tax and minority interest related to these three items should be disclosed. Preparers should provide further information, where practicable and relevant, identifying the tax and minority interest related to individual categories of these items, in order to assist users in assessing the impact of individual items on the net profit or loss attributable to shareholders.

viii A concern was expressed by respondents to FRED 1 about exceptional items and the prominence they were to be given. In summary, the view was that exceptional items should not be transferred to a single heading of 'exceptional', because profit before exceptional items could then become the focus of financial statement presentations, with the implication that no exceptional items are expected in the future. To meet this concern the FRS requires all exceptional items (other than three specific types of item) to be included in the income or expense heading to which they relate.

Revenue investment (discretionary expenditure)

ix The discussion draft introduced the concept of discretionary expenditure. Users of financial statements had encouraged the Board to require disclosure of expenses that are incurred largely for the benefit of future periods and that can therefore be varied by material amounts without affecting current revenues. The draft sought to do this by including a definition along these lines and amplifying it by reference to common examples of such expenses, viz., research and development expense, training, advertising and major maintenance.

x In FRED 1 the concept of discretionary expenditure was developed and in the process the name 'discretionary expenditure' was changed to 'revenue investment'. More detailed guidance was given as to what should be included under this heading and a minimum disclosure requirement was proposed. This was for the disclosure, where material, of the charges to the profit and loss account of the period in respect of research and development, training, advertising and major maintenance and refurbishment. A requirement for an explanation of all material changes between the current and prior period in the level of revenue investment was also proposed.

xi These revenue investment proposals failed to attract support in the context of the proposed accounting standard, and the Board therefore concluded that they should not be pursued by that means. The Board remains of the view that appropriate disclosures of this kind can be of assistance to users of financial statements but in the light of the responses to FRED 1 concluded that the concept can best be developed within the Board's proposals for an Operating and Financial Review to support a company's annual report — i.e. as part of a wider discussion of a company's performance. The Board's decision on the FRED 1 proposal on revenue investment does not in any way affect the existing requirements of SSAP 13 — 'Accounting for research and development' and the Companies Act 1985 regarding the disclosure of research and development activities.

Reconciliation of movements in shareholders' funds

xii Several respondents to FRED 1, in commenting on the statement of total recognised gains and losses, suggested it should be extended to provide a complete reconciliation of the movements in shareholders' funds. The Board agreed that changes in shareholders' funds other than those included in the statement of total recognised gains and losses can also be important in understanding the change in the financial position of a reporting entity and concluded that this additional information should be required in a reconciliation of movements in shareholders' funds. In order not to divert attention from the components of performance of the total of recognised gains and losses for the period, it specified that if included as a primary statement, the reconciliation should be shown separately from the statement of total recognised gains and losses.

Amendment to FRS 3 'Reporting Financial Performance': Insurance Companies — June 1993

Reproduced with the permission of the Accounting Standards Board.

Preface

This limited amendment to Financial Reporting Standard No. 3 'Reporting Financial Performance' (FRS 3), exempts insurance companies from certain requirements to the extent that they relate to investments. These requirements are contained in paragraphs 13 and 21 of FRS 3 which are as follows:

> "**13** All gains and losses recognised in the financial statements for the period should be included in the profit and loss account or the statement of total recognised gains and losses. Gains and losses may be excluded from the profit and loss account only if they are specifically permitted or required to be taken directly to reserves by this or other accounting standards or, in the absence of a relevant accounting standard, by law."

> "**21** The profit or loss on the disposal of an asset should be accounted for in the profit and loss account of the period in which the disposal occurs as the difference between the net sale proceeds and the net carrying amount, whether carried at historical cost (less any provisions made) or at a valuation."

New legislative requirements in respect of the accounts of insurance companies are expected to take effect from 1 January 1995 to implement the EC Council Directive on the annual accounts and consolidated accounts of insurance undertakings (91/674/EEC). If insurance companies were to be required to comply with these requirements of FRS 3 prior to the requirements of the new legislation being known, it would be possible that they would have to make significant changes to their accounting twice within a three year period.

In the circumstances the Board concluded that at this time the cost to insurance companies of compliance with the specific requirements of FRS 3 would probably be greater than the benefit to users. The Board will reconsider the accounting by insurance companies for their investments once the requirements of the new legislation are known and will decide at that time whether the requirements of FRS 3 should apply or whether there should be alternative requirements.

Statement of Standard Accounting Practice

1 FRS 3 is amended by the insertion of an additional heading and paragraph after paragraph 31 and before paragraph 32 as follows:

"Insurance businesses

31A The requirements of paragraphs 13 and 21 do not apply to the financial statements of insurance companies or insurance groups as defined in companies legislation* for the gains or losses arising on the holding or disposal of investments. Additionally, the requirements of paragraphs 13 and 21 do not apply to consolidated financial statements to the extent they include insurance companies or insurance groups."

2 As this amendment is a relaxation of the existing requirements of FRS 3 it is effective immediately.

'Amendment to FRS 3 "Reporting Financial Performance": Insurance Companies June 1993' was adopted by the unanimous vote of the eight members of Accounting Standards Board.

Members of the Accounting Standards Board

David Tweedie (Chairman)

Allan Cook (Technical Director)

Robert Bradfield

Ian Brindle

Sir Bryan Carsberg

Michael Garner

Donald Main

Graham Stacy

*Companies Act 1985 Section 744 and Section 255A(5).

The equivalent legislation in Northern Ireland is the Companies (Northern Ireland) Order 1986 Article 2 and Article 263A(5).

The equivalent legislation in the Republic of Ireland is the Companies (Amendment) Act 1986 Section 2(3) and the European Communities (Companies: Group Accounts) Regulations 1992 regulation 6(2)(g).

Capital instruments

Reproduced with the permission of the Accounting Standards Board

Summary

a Financial Reporting Standard 4 'Capital Instruments' requires capital instruments to be presented in financial statements in a way that reflects the obligations of the issuer. The FRS prescribes methods to be used to determine the amounts to be ascribed to capital instruments and their associated costs and specifies relevant disclosures.

b The amount of shareholders' funds attributable to equity and non-equity interests is to be disclosed. In consolidated financial statements a similar analysis of minority interests is to be disclosed. If any capital instrument other than shares contains an obligation to transfer economic benefits it is to be classified as a liability. Convertible debt is to be displayed separately from other liabilities. The key distinctions may be summarised as follows:

Item	Analysed between	
Shareholders' funds	Equity interests	Non-equity interests
Minority interests in subsidiaries	Equity interests in subsidiaries	Non-equity interests in subsidiaries
Liabilities	Convertible liabilities	Non-convertible liabilities

c The direct costs incurred in connection with the issue of capital instruments should be deducted from the proceeds of the issue. This treatment applies only to those costs that can be demonstrated to relate directly to the instrument in question. Other costs are to be charged as expenses when incurred.

d The finance costs associated with liabilities and non-equity shares are to be allocated to periods at a constant rate based on the carrying amount. The amount to be attributed to these instruments initially is the net amount of the issue proceeds. The finance cost for a period is added to the carrying amount and payments deducted from it. In the case of a redeemable instrument this will result in the carrying amount at the time it is redeemed being equal to the amount payable at that time.

e The FRS applies to all reporting entities whose financial statements are intended to give a true and fair view, irrespective of size or ownership.

f The requirements of the FRS apply to all transactions and to all instruments irrespective of the date at which they are issued.

Objective

1 The objective of this FRS is to ensure that financial statements provide a clear coherent and consistent treatment of capital instruments in particular as regards the classification of instruments as debt, non-equity shares or equity shares; that costs associated with capital instruments are dealt with in a manner consistent with their classification and for redeemable instruments allocated to accounting periods on a fair basis over the period the instrument is in issue; and that financial statements provide relevant information concerning the nature and amount of the entity's sources of finance and the associated costs commitments and potential commitments.

Definitions

The following definitions shall apply in this FRS and in particular in the Statement of Standard Accounting Practice set out in paragraphs 18-67.

2 *Capital instruments:* All instruments that are issued by reporting entities as a means of raising finance including shares, debentures loans and debt instruments options and warrants that give the holder the right to subscribe for or obtain capital instruments. In the case of consolidated financial statements the term includes capital instruments issued by subsidiaries except those that are held by another member of the group included in the consolidation.

3 *Companies Act 1985:* The Companies Act 1985 as amended by the Companies Act 1989.

4 *Companies (Northern Ireland) Order 1986:* The Companies (Northern Ireland) Order 1986 as amended by the Companies (Northern Ireland) Order 1990 and the Companies (No 2) (Northern Ireland) Order 1990.

5 *Companies (Amendment) Act 1986:* The Republic of Ireland Companies Acts 1963-1990 and the European Communities (Companies: Group Accounts) Regulations 1992.

6 *Debt:* Capital instruments that are classified as liabilities.

7 *Equity shares*: Shares other than non-equity shares.

8 *Finance costs:* The difference between the net proceeds of an instrument and the total amount of the payments (or other transfers of economic benefits) that the issuer may be required to make in respect of the instrument.

9 *Investment companies:* Investment companies as defined in Section 266 of the Companies Act 1985 or in Section 274 of the Companies (Northern Ireland) Order 1986 or in Section 47(3) of the Companies (Amendment) Act 1983.

10 *Issue costs:* The costs that are incurred directly in connection with the issue of a capital instrument that is those costs that would not have been incurred had the specific instrument in question not been issued.

11 *Net proceeds:* The fair value of the consideration received on the issue of a capital instrument after deduction of issue costs.

12 *Non-equity shares: Shares* possessing any of the following characteristics:

(a) any of the rights of the shares to receive payments (whether in respect of dividends in respect of redemption or otherwise) are for a limited amount that is not calculated by reference to the company's assets or profits or the dividends on any class of equity share.

(b) any of their rights to participate in a surplus in a winding up are limited to a specific amount that is not calculated by reference to the company's assets or profits and such limitation had a commercial effect in practice at the time the shares were issued or if later at the time the limitation was introduced.

(c) the shares are redeemable either according to their terms or because the holder or any party other than the issuer can require their redemption.

13 *Participating dividend:* A dividend (or part of a dividend) on a non-equity share that, in accordance with a company's memorandum and articles of association is always equivalent to a fixed multiple of the dividend payable on an equity share.

14 *Share:* Share in the share capital of the reporting company (or, in the context of consolidated financial statements, the holding company of a group) including stock.

15 *Shareholders' funds:* The aggregate of called up share capital and all reserves, excluding minority interests.

16 *Term (of a capital instrument):* The period from the date of issue of the capital instrument to the date at which it will expire, be redeemed or be cancelled.

If either party has the option to require the instrument to be redeemed or cancelled and under the terms of the instrument it is uncertain whether such an option will be exercised, the term should be taken to end on the earliest date at which the instrument would be redeemed or cancelled on exercise of such an option.

If either party has the right to extend the period of an instrument, the term should not include the period of the extension if there is a genuine commercial possibility that the period will not be extended.

17 *Warrant:* An instrument that requires the issuer to issue shares (whether contingently or not) and contains no obligation for the issuer to transfer economic benefits.

Statement of Standard Accounting Practice

Scope

18 Financial Reporting Standard 4 applies to all financial statements intended to give a true and fair view of a reporting entity's financial position and profit or loss (or income and expenditure) for a period. The terminology used in this statement will be appropriate for those reporting entities that are companies. Entities other than companies should adapt the terminology as appropriate.

19 The FRS applies to accounting for capital instruments by entities that issue them. It does not address accounting for investments in capital instruments issued by other entities.

20 The scope of the FRS includes capital instruments denominated in a foreign currency. However the FRS does not address the translation of foreign currency amounts relating to such instruments into the reporting currency or the accounting for foreign exchange differences arising from such translations.

21 The requirements of the FRS apply to all capital instruments with the following exceptions:

(a) warrants issued to employees under employee share schemes;

(b) leases which should be accounted for in accordance with SSAP 21;

(c) equity shares issued as part of a business combination that is accounted for as a merger.

22 In applying the requirements of the FRS, capital instruments that are issued at the same time in a composite transaction should be considered together. They should be accounted for as a single instrument unless they are capable of being transferred, cancelled or redeemed independently of each other.

Classification of capital instruments

23 All capital instruments should be accounted for in the balance sheet within one of the following categories:

— liabilities

— shareholders' funds

— in the case of consolidated financial statements, minority interests.

24 Capital instruments (other than shares which are addressed at paragraphs 37-45 below) should be classified as liabilities if they contain an obligation to transfer economic benefits (including a contingent obligation to transfer economic benefits). Capital instruments that do not contain an obligation to transfer economic benefits should be reported within shareholders' funds.

Debt

Convertible debt

25 Conversion of debt should not be anticipated. Convertible debt should be reported within liabilities and the finance cost should be calculated on the assumption that the debt will never be converted. The amount attributable to convertible debt should be stated separately from that of other liabilities.

26 When convertible debt is converted the amount recognised in shareholders' funds in respect of the shares issued should be the amount at which the liability for the debt is stated as at the date of conversion. No gain or loss should be recognised on conversion.

Carrying amount and allocation of finance costs

27 Immediately after issue debt should be stated at the amount of the net proceeds.

28 The finance costs of debt should be allocated to periods over the term of the debt at a constant rate on the carrying amount. All finance costs should be charged in the profit and loss account except in the case of investment companies which are addressed in paragraph 52.

29 The carrying amount of debt should be increased by the finance cost in respect of the reporting period and reduced by payments made in respect of the debt in that period.

30 Accrued finance costs may be included in accruals rather than in the carrying amount of debt to the extent that the finance costs have accrued in one accounting period and will be paid in cash in the next. Any such accrual should be included in the carrying amount of the debt for the purposes of calculating finance costs and gains and losses arising on repurchase or early settlement.

31 Where the amount of payments required by a debt instrument is contingent on uncertain future events such as changes in an index, those events should be taken into account in the calculation of the finance costs and the carrying amount once they have occurred.

Repurchase of debt

32 Gains and losses arising on the repurchase or early settlement of debt should be recognised in the profit and loss account in the period during which the repurchase or early settlement is made.

The maturity of debt

33 An analysis of the maturity of debt should be presented showing amounts falling due:

(a) in one year or less or on demand;

(b) between one and two years;

(c) between two and five years; and

(d) in five years or more.

34 The maturity of debt should be determined by reference to the earliest date on which the lender can require repayment.

35 Where committed facilities are in existence at the balance sheet date that permit the refinancing of debt for a period beyond its maturity the earliest date at which the lender can require repayment should be taken to be the maturity date of the longest refinancing permitted by a facility in respect of which all the following conditions are met:

(a) The debt and the facility are under a single agreement or course of dealing with the same lender or group of lenders;

(b) The finance costs for the new debt are on a basis that is not significantly higher than that of the existing debt;

(c) The obligations of the lender (or group of lenders) are firm: the lender is not able legally to refrain from providing funds except in circumstances the possibility of which can be demonstrated to be remote;

(d) The lender (or group of lenders) is expected to be able to fulfil its obligations under the facility.

36 Where the maturity of debt is assessed by reference to that of refinancing permitted by facilities in accordance with paragraph 35, the amounts of the debt so treated analysed by the earliest date on which the lender could demand repayment in the absence of the facilities should be disclosed.

Shares and warrants

37 Shares and warrants should be reported as part of shareholders' funds. In the period in which shares or warrants are issued the net proceeds should be reported in the reconciliation of movements in shareholders' funds.

38 The balance sheet should show the total amount of shareholders' funds.

39 Where shares are repurchased or redeemed shareholders' funds should be reduced by the value of the consideration given.

The analysis of shareholders' funds

40 Shareholders' funds should be analysed between the amount attributable to equity interests and the amount attributable to non-equity interests. The amount of shareholders' funds attributable to equity interests is the difference between total shareholders' funds and the total amount attributable to non-equity interests. The amount attributable to non-equity interests is the aggregate of amounts relating to all classes of equity shares and warrants for non-equity shares.

The amount attributable to non-equity shares within the analysis of shareholders' funds and the allocation of finance costs

41 Immediately after the issue of a non-equity instrument the amount of non-equity shareholders' funds attributable to it should be the net proceeds of the issue. This amount should be increased by the finance costs in respect of the period and reduced by dividends or other payments made in respect of the instrument in that period.

42 The finance costs for non-equity shares should be calculated on the same basis as the finance costs for debt set out in paragraphs 27-31 above.

43 Where the entitlement to dividends in respect of non-equity shares is calculated by reference to time, the dividends should be accounted for on an accruals basis except in those circumstances (for example where profits are insufficient to justify a dividend and dividend rights are non-cumulative) where ultimate payment is remote. All dividends should be reported as appropriations of profit.

44 Where the finance costs for non-equity shares are not equal to the dividends the difference should be accounted for in the profit and loss account as an appropriation of profits.

Equity shares and warrants

45 The net proceeds from the issue of equity shares and warrants for equity shares should be credited direct to shareholders' funds. The amount attributed to equity shares or warrants should not be subsequently adjusted to reflect changes in the value of the shares or warrants.

46 When a warrant is exercised the amount previously recognised in respect of the warrant should be included in the net proceeds of the shares issued.

47 When a warrant lapses unexercised the amount previously recognised in respect of the warrant should be reported in the statement of total recognised gains and losses.

Scrip dividends

48 Where shares are issued (or proposed to be issued) as an alternative to cash dividends, the value of such shares should be deemed to be the amount receivable if the alternative of cash had been chosen. Where the number of shareholders who will elect to receive the shares is uncertain the whole amount should be treated as a liability to pay cash dividends.

Shares issued by subsidiaries

49 Shares issued by subsidiaries (other than shares held by companies within the group) should be accounted for in consolidated financial statements as liabilities if the group taken as a whole has an obligation to transfer economic benefits in connection with the shares for example where another member of the group has given a guarantee of payments to be made in respect of the shares. In all other cases they should be reported as minority interests.

50 The amount of minority interests shown in the balance sheet should be analysed between the aggregate amount attributable to equity interests and amounts attributable to non-equity interests.

51 The amounts attributed to non-equity minority interests and their associated finance costs should be calculated in the same manner as those for non-equity shares. The finance costs associated with such interests should be included in minority interests in the profit and loss account.

Investment companies

52 Investment companies may include the finance costs in respect of capital instruments and any gains or losses recognised in accordance with paragraph 32 in the statement of total recognised gains and losses to the extent that these items relate to capital. The amount so treated should be disclosed within the statement, and the accounting policy for determining the allocation of finance costs between revenue and capital should be stated.

Disclosures

53 The disclosures required by the following paragraphs should be made in addition to those required by paragraphs 25, 33, 36, 38, 40, 50 and 52 above.

54 Where the disclosures required by paragraphs 25, 40 and 50 of convertible debt non-equity interests in shareholders' funds and non-equity interests in minority interests are given in the notes to the financial statements rather than on the face of the balance sheet the relevant caption on the face of the balance sheet should state that convertible debt or non-equity interests (as the case may be) are included.

Disclosures relating to shares

55 An analysis should be given of the total amount of non-equity interests in shareholders funds relating to each class of non-equity shares and series of warrants for non-equity shares.

56 A brief summary of the rights of each class of shares should be given. This should include the following:

(a) the rights to dividends;

(b) the dates at which the shares are redeemable and the amounts payable in respect of redemption;

(c) their priority and the amounts receivable on a winding up;

(d) their voting rights.

This information will usually make clear why a class of share has been classified as equity or non-equity but if necessary additional information should be given to explain the classification. Where rights vary according to circumstances these circumstances and the variation should be described.

57 The disclosure required by paragraph 56 need not be given for equity shares that have all the following features:

(a) no right to dividends other than those that may be recommended by the directors;

(b) no redemption rights;

(c) unlimited right to share in the surplus remaining on a winding up after all liabilities and participation rights of other classes of shares have been satisfied;

(d) one vote per share.

58 Where warrants or convertible debt are in issue that may require the company to issue shares of a class that is not currently in issue the information set out in paragraph 56 should be given in respect of that class.

59 The aggregate dividends for each class of share should be disclosed including the total amount in respect of each of: dividends on equity shares; participating dividends; and other dividends on non-equity shares. Any other appropriation of profit in respect of non-equity shares should also be disclosed. Where there are amounts relating to non-equity shares and the above information is not given on the face of the profit and loss account the relevant caption should make clear that such amounts are included.

Disclosures relating to minority interests

60 The minority interests charge in the profit and loss account should be analysed between equity and non-equity minority interests.

61 Where there are non-equity minority interests a description should be given of any rights of holders of the shares against other group companies.

Disclosures relating to debt

62 In respect of convertible debt, details of the dates of redemption and the amount payable on redemption should be disclosed. The number and class of shares into which the debt may be converted and the dates at or periods within which the conversion may take place should be stated. It should also be stated whether conversion is at the option of the issuer or at that of the holder.

63 A brief description should be given of the legal nature of any instrument included in debt where it is different from that normally associated with debt, for example where the debt is subordinated or where the obligation to repay is conditional. Where amounts are included in debt that represent instruments in respect of which the amount payable, or the claim that would arise on a winding up, is significantly different from that at which the instrument is stated in the financial statements, that amount should be stated. This information may be summarised and need not be given for each individual instrument.

64 Gains and losses arising on the repurchase or early settlement of debt should be disclosed in the profit and loss account as separate items within or adjacent to 'interest payable and similar charges'.

General

65 Where the brief summaries required by paragraphs 56, 58, 61, 62 or 63 cannot adequately provide the information necessary to understand the commercial effect of instruments that fact should be stated in the accounts together with particulars of where the relevant information may be obtained. The principal features of the instruments should in any event be stated.

Date from which effective

66 The accounting practices set out in the FRS should be regarded as standard in respect of financial statements relating to accounting periods ending on or after 22 June 1994. Earlier adoption is encouraged but not required.

Withdrawal of UITF Abstract 1 and Abstract 8

67 The FRS supersedes UITF Abstract 1 and Abstract 8.

Explanation

Capital instruments

68 The definition of capital instruments, given in paragraph 2 includes all kinds of shares and debt instruments as well as options and warrants to obtain such instruments. It characterises capital instruments as a means of raising finance: an instrument may be within the definition whether or not the consideration given for its issue takes the form of cash. Capital instruments may take the form of contracts between two parties (for example a borrower and its bank) as well as an issue of transferable securities.

Identification of distinct capital instruments

69 In order to apply the requirements of the FRS it is necessary to determine whether instruments issued at the same time should be accounted for individually or not. Accounting for the individual instruments is required by paragraph 22 if (and only if) the instruments are capable of being transferred, cancelled or redeemed independently of each other. For example, if debt and warrants are issued simultaneously and the warrants can be transferred, cancelled or redeemed independently of the debt, the two components should be accounted for separately. It would be necessary in such a case to apportion the proceeds of the issue to each component.

The classification of capital instruments

70 The FRS contains requirements for determining whether capital instruments should be accounted for as liabilities. Special considerations, discussed at paragraphs 82-87 below, arise in connection with shares of the entity and these requirements accordingly do not apply to them.

71 The FRS requires capital instruments to be accounted for as liabilities if they contain an obligation to transfer economic benefits (paragraph 24). The most common example of such an obligation is the requirement to make cash payments to the holder of the instrument, but an obligation to transfer other kinds of property would also cause the instrument to be classified as a liability. The payments may be described in various ways, for example as interest, or as an amount payable on redemption; how the obligation is described is not relevant to the classification of the instrument.

72 If a capital instrument contains an obligation for the issuer to transfer economic benefits to another party it should be classified as debt even if the obligation is contingent. For example an instrument that gives the holder the right to require either the transfer of cash or the issue of an equity share imposes an obligation on the issuer and should therefore be classified as a liability. The only obligations to transfer economic benefits that should not be taken into account are those that would not be considered in accordance with the going concern concept, that is, those that would arise only on the insolvency of the issuer and, where the issuer is expected to be able to comply with covenants on loan and similar agreements, those that would follow a breach of those covenants.

The term of debt

73 The FRS requires debt and non-equity interests to be accounted for by allocating finance costs over the term of the instrument at a constant rate. The term of the instrument is usually self-evident but where either party has the option to extend the term, or to require the instrument to be redeemed early, such options should be carefully evaluated. If there is an option for early redemption, the term should be taken to end on the earliest date the option could be exercised, unless there is no genuine commercial possibility that the option will be exercised. The term should not include any period for which the instrument might be extended unless such an extension is virtually certain at the time the instrument is issued: that is, there is no genuine commercial possibility that the period will not be extended.

74 In evaluating the commercial possibilities of options, it should be assumed that the parties will act in accordance with their economic interests. A severe deterioration in the creditworthiness of the issuer should not be anticipated, but should be taken into account when it occurs. For example, in the case of a zero coupon bond, the return to the lender consists entirely of the amount received at maturity. If the lender under such an instrument had the right to require early redemption, but on exercise of that right he would receive only the original issue price, it would be unrealistic to assume that he would exercise it unless the issuer's creditworthiness deteriorated to a significant extent. The term of such a bond would therefore normally be taken to extend to its final maturity.

Finance costs

75 The FRS requires finance costs to be recognised at a constant rate on the carrying amount of debt. In some instances the nominal yield on the debt will not be materially different from the amount required by the FRS to be recognised and in these circumstances calculations will not be necessary in order to derive the information required by the FRS.

76 The FRS also requires all finance costs to be charged in the profit and loss account. However, the FRS does not prohibit the capitalisation of finance costs as part of the cost of an asset by way of a simultaneous transfer from the profit and loss account that is separately disclosed.

The maturity of debt

77 The FRS requires the maturity of debt to be assessed according to the earliest date on which the lender could demand repayment, taking account of facilities granted by the same lender before the balance sheet date that may permit the refinancing of the debt. For example, a bank loan may fall due three months after the balance sheet date but the borrower may have obtained a commitment from the bank before the balance sheet date to provide a further loan for the same amount for a further three years. In such a case, providing the conditions required by the FRS are met, the debt would be included in the analysis of the maturity of debt as falling due between two and five years from the balance sheet date.

78 The restriction to facilities provided by the same lender or group of lenders ensures that the facility and the borrowings in question are related. It is also consistent with the requirements of companies legislation.* For this purpose lenders should be regarded as part of the same group if they are parties to the same agreement or course of dealing, even if it is not always the same members of the group who participate in individual financings entered into under that agreement or in the course of dealing. This may be the case for some multi-option facilities. However, under commercial paper arrangements funds are raised from lenders who are not parties to an agreement that provides for finance beyond the maturity of existing indebtedness. The maturity of such arrangements should therefore be taken to be that of the existing debt, even if there is an agreement with other lenders to refinance the debt if fresh commercial paper cannot be issued.

79 An increase in the price of debt is as significant as its refinancing: for this reason the FRS requires the maturity of borrowings to be assessed by reference to borrowings under related facilities only where the finance costs for the new debt are not on a basis that is significantly higher than that of the existing debt. Where the cost of finance under a facility is determined by reference to a base rate (such as LIBOR) a change in that base rate should not be regarded as an increase in the level of finance costs for this purpose.

80 It would be right to have regard to facilities only if there are objective grounds for believing that the lender will fulfil its commitment. The FRS therefore requires that the facilities must be committed and that there must be no circumstances expected or likely that would either permit the lender to refrain from providing new borrowings or prevent it from providing them. The expectation that the new borrowings will be available, if required, must have existed at the balance sheet date and be reviewed in the light of any post balance sheet events to ensure that it remains reasonable on the date the financial statements are approved by the directors.

81 Particular care should be taken in considering the circumstances in which the lender may refrain from providing new borrowings. If these circumstances are described in a way

*Companies Act 1985, Schedule 4 paragraph 85. The equivalent legislation in Northern Ireland is the Companies (Northern Ireland) Order 1986, Schedule 4 paragraph 84, and in the Republic of Ireland is the Companies (Amendment) Act 1986, the Schedule paragraph 67.

that may be interpreted subjectively — for example if further finance may be withheld if the borrower's financial condition suffers an 'adverse change' and that term is not further defined — it will be unsafe to rely on borrowings under the facility being available. For that reason, the FRS requires that it can be demonstrated that any circumstances that would enable the lender to withhold finance are remote.

Shares and warrants

82 The FRS requires all shares to be reported within shareholders' funds. Warrants are also required to be reported within shareholders' funds since, by definition, they do not contain an obligation to transfer economic benefits.

83 Certain kinds of shares have features that make them economically similar to debt. Nonetheless, the requirement to classify capital instruments as debt if they contain an obligation to transfer economic benefits does not apply to shares. The legal status of shares is well established and understood and there are specific conditions in UK and Irish legislation that have to be satisfied if any payment is made in respect of them. In addition, the balance sheet formats prescribed by companies legislation require called up share capital to be stated separately from liabilities.

84 The FRS requires shareholders' funds to be analysed to show the amount relating to equity and non-equity interests. The definition of non-equity shares is widely drawn, so that any right to a dividend or to a redemption payment that is for a limited amount will have the effect that the shares will be considered non-equity shares, irrespective of the other rights they may enjoy.

85 It is possible that in rare circumstances shares will be classified as non-equity shares in accordance with the requirements of the FRS even though they fall within the definition of equity share capital contained in companies legislation. If this situation arises further explanation would be required to clarify the position.

86 As financial statements are usually prepared on a going concern basis, rights of shares to participate on a winding up do not usually affect the accounting for the shares. But if winding up is foreseeable when shares are issued, the limitation of rights has a commercial effect. Such a circumstance could arise, for example, where a group raises finance by way of an issue of shares of a special purpose subsidiary with a predetermined life. For this reason the definition requires that a limitation on the rights to participate on a winding up is taken into account only where, at the date it was introduced, it was likely that it would have a commercial effect in practice.

87 Shares that the issuer may or will be required to redeem are classed as non-equity shares, since they do not form part of the residual interest in the company. Furthermore, since the amount payable in respect of redemption must be fixed prior to redemption, the rights of the shares in respect of redemption will be restricted.

Shares issued by subsidiaries

88 Usually, where subsidiaries have shares in issue that are not held by another company in the group they are reported in the consolidated financial statements within minority interests but in some cases they are required by the FRS to be reported within liabilities, that is, as debt.

89 Consolidated financial statements are prepared on the basis that the undertakings included in the consolidation form a single entity ('the group'). Therefore, where a subsidiary has shares in issue it is necessary to look at the effect on the group as a whole when the consolidated financial statements are being prepared and to consider the rights attaching to the shares in conjunction with any agreements to which other group companies are a party. For example, if another company in the group has provided guarantees in respect of dividends or redemption, or has undertaken to purchase the shares in the event of the subsidiary failing to make the expected payments, the group as a whole will be unable to avoid the transfer of economic benefits irrespective of the financial condition of the subsidiary: accordingly the issue will constitute a liability of the group and should be reported as such. This will also be the case where the shares are issued by a subsidiary incorporated in a jurisdiction where it cannot avoid paying dividends or amounts in respect of redemption even if there are insufficient profits, in which case funds would have to be provided by other group companies.

90 Particular care is necessary in assessing the effect of subordinated guarantees given by group companies in respect of shares issued by subsidiaries, as the degree of subordination varies widely. The intent of some such guarantees is that the rights of the holder of the shares against the group are the same as those of the holder of preference shares of the parent. All the rights and remedies of the holders of the subsidiary undertaking's shares against group companies should be considered and the shares should be reported as liabilities unless it is clear that the intended equivalence of the rights to those attaching to preference shares of the parent is actually attained. If it is, the shares should be reported as non-equity minority interests.*

91 Where it is determined that it is appropriate to report shares issued by subsidiaries in consolidated financial statements within minority interests rather than as a liability, it is necessary to determine whether they represent an equity interest or a non-equity interest. Companies legislation** requires the balance sheet to show as minority interests the amount of capital and reserves attributable to shares in subsidiary undertakings included in the consolidation held by or on behalf of persons other than the parent company and its subsidiary undertakings. Where the shares are equity shares the relevant amount of minority interests will be the proportionate share of net identifiable assets. If the shares are non-equity shares the amount of capital and reserves attributable to the shares will correspond to the amount determined by the requirements of the FRS: that is the net proceeds plus recognised finance costs less payments made.

Issue costs

92 The FRS requires issue costs, as defined, to be accounted for as a reduction in the proceeds of a capital instrument. Such costs are not assets as defined in the Board's draft Statement of Principles because they do not provide access to any future economic benefits.

93 In the case of shares, issue costs are integral to a transaction with owners and for this reason the FRS requires them to be taken into account in determining the net proceeds that are reported in the reconciliation of movements in shareholders' funds. They should not be disclosed in the statement of total recognised gains and losses.

* Even if the rights of the holders of shares in a subsidiary against all companies in a group are equivalent to those of holders of a class of shares in the parent, the precise means by which those rights will be enforced, if the need arises, will differ. There will also inevitably be a risk that future events will show that the presumed equivalence does not exist. For these reasons, it would never be right to show shares issued by a subsidiary within the shareholders' funds of the group.

** Companies Act 1985, Schedule 4A paragraph 17. The equivalent legislation in Northern Ireland is the Companies (Northern Ireland) Order 1986, Schedule 4A paragraph 17, and in the Republic of Ireland is the European Communities (Companies Group Accounts) Regulations 1992, the Schedule, paragraph 8.

94 In the case of most debt instruments, the issuer has the use of funds during the life of the instrument, and in return pays interest. The benefit obtained from the issue costs is reflected in the interest expense: indeed, issue costs are in some cases economically indistinguishable from a discount on issue. Issue costs are therefore appropriately accounted for as an adjustment to the amount of the liability, which effectively results in their being charged over the life of the instrument. If it became clear that the instrument would be redeemed early, then the amortisation of the issue costs and any discount on issue would have to be accelerated.

95 Where the life of an instrument is indeterminate the benefit of the issue costs is reflected in terms of the financing indefinitely. In such a case, the issue costs are therefore not taken to the profit and loss account until such time as the instrument is redeemed or cancelled.

96 Care should be taken in the determination of the amount that falls to be treated as issue costs to avoid the danger of overstating finance costs over the life of the instrument in question. For this reason the definition of issue costs is deliberately restrictive. The definition does not admit costs of researching and negotiating sources of finance or of ascertaining the suitability or feasibility of particular instruments, nor allocations of internal costs that would have been incurred had the instrument not been issued: for example management remuneration. The costs incurred in connection with a financial restructuring or renegotiation also do not qualify as issue costs; such costs relate to previous sources of finance and not to any instrument that may be issued following the restructuring or renegotiation. Costs that do not qualify as issue costs should be written off to the profit and loss account as incurred.

97 The requirement of the FRS that issue costs are reflected in the amounts charged to the profit and loss account over the term of a capital instrument is not intended to prohibit the subsequent charging of issue costs to the share premium account by means of a transfer between reserves. The amounts that may be charged to the share premium account are determined by the requirements of companies legislation.

Investment companies

98 Paragraph 52 of the FRS permits investment companies (provided certain conditions are met) to deal with some gains and costs relating to capital instruments in the statement of total recognised gains and losses rather than in the profit and loss account. This exemption has been included in view of the requirements of companies legislation that such companies distinguish revenue and capital and distribute as dividends a large proportion of their revenue and none of their capital. If special provisions were not included in respect of investment companies, the introduction of the FRS might result in inequitable consequences: for example, in the case of split capital investment trusts the distribution of returns as between one class of shareholder and another might be changed in a way that was contrary to the previous expectations of the shareholders and the company. The Board is considering whether guidance on accounting by investment companies, including the distinction between revenue and capital, is required.

Scrip dividends

99 The FRS requires that where scrip dividends are issued or proposed the value of shares issued or to be issued should be taken to be the amount of the cash dividend. Where, as is often the case, a scrip dividend takes the legal form of a bonus issue of shares, the appropriation should be written back as a reserve movement, and appropriate amounts transferred between reserves and share capital to reflect the capitalisation of reserves.

Disclosure requirements

100 The FRS requires non-equity interests in shareholders' funds, non-equity interests in minority interests, and convertible debt to be disclosed separately from amounts relating to equity interests and non-convertible debt respectively. Because these distinctions have fundamental implications for the forecasting of future cash flows, they are extremely important and in many cases where such instruments are in issue it will be necessary for this information to be given on the face of the balance sheet. In the assessment of materiality in connection with convertible securities, consideration should be given not only to their carrying amount but also to the implications of conversion. In some cases, however, on grounds of materiality, this information may be disclosed in the notes to the financial statements rather than on the face of the balance sheet. Where this is the case, paragraph 54 requires that the caption on the face of the balance sheet should indicate that the balance sheet total includes non-equity interests or convertible debt. Similarly, paragraph 59 requires the captions used in the profit and loss account to indicate the existence of non-equity interests the details of which are disclosed only in the notes.

101 There is a presumption that amounts included in debt relate to conventional borrowing agreements. As this may not always be the case, paragraph 63 requires a brief description of the obligations and legal arrangements relating to any debt that are different from those usually associated with debt. This would apply, for example, to subordinated debt, to non-recourse debt and to those shares issued by subsidiary undertakings that are classified as debt in accordance with the FRS.

102 Although the FRS does not require the disclosure of the market values of capital instruments, such information may be useful to users of financial statements as it provides an insight into the economic burden represented by the debt. Where information on market values would assist users, its disclosure should be considered.

Application Notes

These Application Notes specify how some of the requirements of FRS 4 are to be applied to transactions that have certain features. However, the Notes are not an exhaustive guide to all the requirements that may be relevant and should therefore be read in conjunction with the FRS itself.

Capital instruments may have a combination of features and accordingly more than one Note may be relevant to a single capital instrument.

The illustrations shown in the shaded areas are provided as an aid to understanding and shall not be regarded as part of the Statement of Standard Accounting Practice.

CONTENTS

Convertible debt with enhanced interest

Debt issued with warrants

Deep discount bonds

Income bonds

Index linked loans

Limited recourse debt

Participating preference shares

Perpetual debt

Repackaged perpetual debt

Stepped interest bonds

Subordinated debt

Auction Market Preferred Shares ('AMPS')

Features

AMPS are preference shares that are entitled to dividends determined in accordance with an auction process in which a panel of investors participates, the shares being transferred at a fixed price to the investor who will accept the lowest dividend. If the auction process fails — for example because no bids are received — the shares remain in the ownership of the former holder and the dividend is increased to a rate, known as the default rate, that is calculated in accordance with a prescribed formula. (This default rate may change if there is any change in the credit rating of the issuer.) In some cases dividends may be passed at the option of the issuer and in any event will not be paid by a UK company if there are insufficient distributable profits. If the dividend is not paid the holders of the AMPS do not obtain any additional rights, for example to demand redemption. AMPS are redeemable at the option of the issuer, usually at the issue price.

Analysis and required accounting

As AMPS are shares, dividends cannot be paid in respect of them except out of distributable profits, nor can they be redeemed unless the redemption is financed out of distributable profits or by a fresh issue of shares. Because they are redeemable at a fixed amount, and because the dividend rights are limited, AMPS constitute non-equity shares.

In accordance with the requirements of the FRS, AMPS should be reported within shareholders' funds as non-equity shares and included in the amount attributable to non-equity shares (paragraph 40). The finance cost for each period should be the dividend rights accruing in respect of the period.

Capital contributions

Features

Capital contributions are sometimes made by a holding company to its wholly-owned subsidiary in order to provide the finance necessary for the subsidiary where it is not desired that this should be by way of debt and there would be adverse consequences (for example, tax consequences) arising from a subscription for new shares. Whilst a capital contribution enhances the value of the holding company's investment in its subsidiary, there is no requirement for the subsidiary to bear any servicing cost, nor can it be required to repay the contribution.

Analysis and required accounting

From the standpoint of the subsidiary, a capital contribution does not contain an obligation to transfer economic benefits. In accordance with paragraph 24 of the FRS it should be reported within shareholders' funds. In the year in which the capital contribution is made, it should be reported in the reconciliation of movements in shareholders' funds.

Convertible capital bonds

Features

The detailed provisions of convertible capital bonds vary but the following are typical. Convertible capital bonds are debt instruments on which interest is paid periodically, issued by a special purpose subsidiary incorporated outside the UK. Prior to maturity they may be exchanged for shares of the subsidiary which, at the option of the bondholder, are either immediately redeemed or immediately exchanged for ordinary shares of the parent. The bonds and payments in respect of the shares of the subsidiary are guaranteed by the parent. The parent has the right to issue convertible redeemable preference shares of its own in substitution for the bonds should it wish to do so.

Analysis and required accounting

From the standpoint of the subsidiary, convertible capital bonds are clearly debt since the obligation to pay interest is an obligation to transfer economic benefits. In addition, paragraph 25 of the FRS requires that conversion of debt should not be anticipated. In the subsidiary's financial statements the bonds should therefore be accounted for as debt.

From the standpoint of the group they are also liabilities. Even though the parent has the option to issue convertible preference shares in substitution for the bonds, the requirements of paragraph 25 of the FRS again entail that such conversion should not be anticipated. Whilst non-equity shares have a particular legal status that justifies their inclusion in shareholders' funds, this does not justify reporting within shareholders' funds an instrument that does not have that status and may never be converted into one that does.

Since the liabilities are convertible, the amount attributable to convertible capital bonds should be included in the amount of convertible debt, which should be stated separately from other liabilities.

Convertible debt with a premium put option

Features

Convertible debt with a premium put option contains an option for the holder to demand redemption (either at the maturity of the debt or at some earlier date) for an amount that is in excess of the amount originally received for the debt. At the time the debt is issued, it is uncertain whether the debt will be converted before the redemption option may be exercised, and hence whether the premium on redemption will be paid.

Analysis and required accounting

The premium put option provides a higher guaranteed return to the holder of the debt than would be received on identical debt without such a put option. Often this higher return corresponds to that which the holder would have expected to receive on non-convertible debt. The holder's decision as to whether to exercise the option will depend on the relative values of the shares to which he would be entitled on conversion and the cash receivable, including the premium, on exercise of the option.

In accordance with the definition of the term of an instrument contained in paragraph 16 of the FRS, the term of convertible debt with a premium put option should be considered to end on the earliest date at which the holder has the option to require redemption. The premium payable on exercise of the premium put option falls to be included in the calculation of the finance costs for the debt.

On conversion, in accordance with paragraph 26 of the FRS, the proceeds of the shares issued should be deemed to be the carrying amount of the debt, including accrued premium, immediately prior to conversion.

Convertible debt with enhanced interest

Features

As an alternative to the premium put structure discussed above, convertible debt may contain an undertaking that the interest will be increased at a date in the future. At the time the debt is issued, it is uncertain whether the debt will be converted before the enhanced interest is payable.

Analysis and required accounting

The enhanced rate of interest increases the guaranteed return to the holder. Often this higher return corresponds to that which the holder would have expected to receive on non-convertible debt. The holder's decision as to whether to convert the debt will take into account the interest forgone by such a decision.

In accordance with the definitions set out in paragraphs 8 and 16 of the FRS, the interest for the full term of the convertible debt should be taken into account in the allocation of finance costs, which should be allocated at a constant rate in accordance with paragraph 28.

Illustration

Convertible debt is issued on 1 January 2000 for £1,000 and is redeemable at the same amount on 31 December 2014. It carries interest of £59 a year (a nominal rate of 5.9 per cent) for the first five years, after which the rate rises to £141 a year (a nominal rate of 14.1 per cent).

In order to comply with paragraph 28 of the FRS the finance costs should be allocated to accounting periods at the rate of 10 per cent a year. The movements on the carrying amount over the term of the debt would be as follows:

Year ending	*Balance at beginning of year*	*Finance costs for year (10%)*	*Cash paid during year*	*Balance at end of year*
	£	*£*	*£*	*£*
31.12.2000	1,000	100	(59)	1,041
31.12.2001	1,041	104	(59)	1,086
31.12.2002	1,086	109	(59)	1,136
31.12.2003	1,136	113	(59)	1,190
31.12.2004	1,190	119	(59)	1,250
31.12.2005	1,250	125	(141)	1,234
31.12.2006	1,234	124	(141)	1,217
31.12.2007	1,217	122	(141)	1,198
31.12.2008	1,198	120	(141)	1,177
31.12.2009	1,177	118	(141)	1,154
31.12.2010	1,154	116	(141)	1,129
31.12.2011	1,129	113	(141)	1,101
31.12.2012	1,101	110	(141)	1,070
31.12.2013	1,070	107	(141)	1,036
31.12.2014	1,036	105*	(141 + 1,000)	—

*Increased by £1 rounding difference.

Debt issued with warrants

Features

Debt is sometimes issued with warrants. The issue is often made for the par value of the debt and the debt will be redeemed at the same amount. The warrants and the debt are capable of being transferred separately.

Analysis and required accounting

In accordance with paragraph 22 of the FRS, the proceeds of the issue should be allocated between the debt and the warrants. As a result, the amount of the proceeds deemed to relate to the debt will be less than par value. The discount on issue should be treated as finance costs and apportioned to accounting periods so that the total finance costs on the debt will have a constant relationship to the outstanding obligation. Accounting for warrants is specified at paragraphs 45-47 of the FRS.

Illustration

Debt and warrants are issued together for £1,250. The debt is redeemable at the same amount. The term of the debt is five years from 1 January 2000 and it carries interest at 4.7 per cent (£59 a year). It is determined (for example by reference to the market values for the debt and the warrants immediately after issue) that the fair value of the debt and the warrants are respectively £1,000 and £250.

The debt would initially be recognised at £1,000. The finance cost of the debt is the difference between the payments required by the debt which total £1,545 ((5 x £59) + £1,250) and the deemed proceeds of £1,000 that is, £545. In order to allocate these costs over the term of the debt at a constant rate on the carrying amount (as required by paragraph 28 of the FRS) they must be allocated at the rate of 10 per cent. The movements on the carrying amount of the debt over its term would be as follows:

Year ending	*Balance at beginning of year*	*Finance costs for year (10%)*	*Cash paid during year*	*Balance at end of year*
	£	£	£	£
31.12.2000	1,000	100	(59)	1,041
31.12.2001	1,041	104	(59)	1,086
31.12.2002	1,086	109	(59)	1,136
31.12.2003	1,136	113	(59)	1,190
31.12.2004	1,190	119	(1,250 + 59)	—

Deep discount bonds

Features

Deep discount bonds are bonds that carry a low nominal rate of interest and accordingly are issued at a discount to the value at which they will be redeemed. In the extreme case where no interest at all is payable they are sometimes referred to as zero coupon bonds.

Analysis and required accounting

The cost to the borrower of issuing a deep discount bond comprises the discount on issue as well as any interest payments. It is clear that deep discount bonds represent liabilities of the issuer since they contain an obligation to make cash payments. In accordance with the definition of 'finance costs' in paragraph 8 of the FRS the finance costs will constitute the difference between the net proceeds and the total payments that the issuer may be required to make in respect of the instrument. In accordance with paragraph 28 of the FRS the finance costs will be allocated to periods at a constant rate on the carrying amount, with the result that the carrying amount of the bond immediately prior to redemption will equate to the amount at which it is to be redeemed. The discount should not be treated as an asset.

Accounting for a deep discount bond is illustrated above in connection with debt issued with warrants.

Income bonds

Features

The distinctive feature of income bonds is that interest is payable only in the event that the issuer has sufficient reported profits (after allowing for interest on other kinds of debt) to make the payment. If profits are insufficient the issuer is not in default and no additional rights accrue to the holder of the bond, although interest payments may be cumulative. Income bonds must be redeemed by the issuer at a fixed amount on a specific date.

Analysis and required accounting

The requirement to redeem the bonds is an obligation to transfer economic benefits. The bonds must therefore be accounted for as a liability as required by paragraph 24 of the FRS. Even if the issuer were not required to redeem the bonds, they would still be classed as a liability, because of the obligation to pay interest. The fact that the obligation to pay is dependent on the existence of profits makes the obligation contingent, but it does not remove the obligation.

Index linked loans

Features

Sometimes loan agreements do not state a specific amount for the payments: instead they include a formula to be used for their calculation. For example, in the case of floating rate loans, the amount of periodic payments of interest will be calculated by reference to a base rate e.g. LIBOR + 2 per cent. Another example is that of index linked loans which may be redeemable at the principal amount multiplied by an index.

Analysis and required accounting

Paragraph 31 requires that finance costs contingent on uncertain events such as changes in an index should be adjusted to reflect those events only once they have occurred. The effect is that the initial carrying amount will take no account of those events but the carrying amount at each subsequent balance sheet date will be recalculated to take account of the changes occurring in that reporting period. The resulting change in carrying amount is accounted for as an increase or decrease in finance costs for the period.

Illustration

A loan of £1,250 is issued on 1 January 2000 on which interest of 4 per cent (£50) is paid annually and the principal amount is repayable based on an index. The balance at the end of each year is found by multiplying the original principal amount by the index at the end of the year: the change in the amount is treated as additional finance costs.

Year ending	*Balance at beginning of year* £	*Finance costs for year (10%)* £	*Cash paid during year* £	*Balance at end of year* £	*Index at end of year* £
31.12.2000	1,250	125	(50)	1,325	106
31.12.2001	1,325	100	(50)	1,375	110
31.12.2002	1,375	75	(50)	1,400	112
31.12.2003	1,400	150	(50)	1,500	120
31.12.2004	1,500	175	(1,625 + 50)	—	130

Limited recourse debt

Features

Sometimes debt is raised on terms that the lender's recourse is limited. Although the borrower is expected to meet the obligations of the debt out of his general resources, in the event of default the lender can obtain repayment only by enforcing his rights against the particular security that is identified in the loan agreement. If the proceeds of the security are insufficient to repay the loan, the lender must bear the loss and has no further rights against the borrower.

Analysis and required accounting

Limited recourse debt constitutes an obligation on the part of the borrower to repay, and hence should be accounted for as a liability*. The borrower will normally have all the

*The Board's project on reporting the substance of transactions addresses the limited circumstances in which non-recourse finance should be accounted for using a linked presentation.

benefits of the security (including the right to receive the sale proceeds) and will have to meet the obligation to repay the debt in order to preserve these rights. Although if the security declines in value the borrower may possibly be able to elect to hand it over to the lender and thus avoid any further liability in respect of the debt, such an eventuality would be unusual, and therefore should not be reflected in the accounting until such time as the asset is transferred.

Limited recourse debt is one of the kinds of debt envisaged in paragraph 63 of the FRS in that its legal nature differs from that usually associated with debt. A brief description of its nature should be given. An illustration of such disclosure is set out below.

Illustration of disclosures

'The limited recourse debt of £xxx is secured on the company's investment in an industrial warehouse at Allington Industrial Estate, Barsetshire, which has a market and book value of £YYY. In the event of non-payment of the interest or principal on this debt, the lenders have the right to require the sale of the property and will be paid all the sale proceeds up to the amount of the debt but have no other rights against the company.'

Participating preference shares

Features

Participating preference shares are similar to other familiar kinds of preference shares except that they are entitled, in addition to a fixed dividend for each accounting period, to a proportion of the dividends paid on equity shares.

Analysis and required accounting

Because participating preference shares contain an entitlement to share in profits that is of a restricted amount and has priority over the other classes of shares, they are non-equity shares in accordance with the definition in paragraph 12 of the FRS and their interest in shareholders' funds should be presented in the balance sheet within the aggregate amount attributable to non-equity shares as required by paragraph 40. The fixed and participating elements of the dividend will be disclosed separately as required by paragraph 59.

Perpetual debt

Features

Perpetual debt is debt in respect of which the issuer has neither the right nor the obligation to repay the principal amount of the debt. Usually, interest is paid at a constant rate, or at a fixed margin over a benchmark rate such as LIBOR.

Analysis and required accounting

Sometimes it is suggested that as the principal amount will never be repaid there is no need for the balance sheet to reflect a liability in respect of the debt. However, the obligation to pay interest is an obligation to transfer economic benefits and hence the instrument is a liability. As there are no repayments of principal the burden of this liability never diminishes. The FRS is based on the principle that debt should be accounted for having regard to all the payments required by the debt, irrespective of their legal description, in the determination of the appropriate finance charge and capital repayment for each accounting period. In the case of perpetual debt where interest is paid at a constant rate, or at a fixed margin over a benchmark, the correct finance charge will be equal to the coupon payable for each period. Hence no part of the repayments will reduce the carrying amount and the debt will always be shown at the amount of net proceeds. If the amount of the claim that would arise on a winding up is different from the carrying amount of the debt, it should be stated in accordance with paragraph 63.

Repackaged perpetual debt

Features

Sometimes perpetual debt is issued that carries interest at a relatively high rate for a number of years ('the primary period'), and then bears no further interest, or only a nominal amount. As the debt cannot be required to be redeemed, its value after the primary period has expired is negligible and, in practice, there will usually be arrangements to transfer it to a party friendly to the issuer or to enable the issuer to elect, in effect, to redeem the debt for a token amount.

Analysis and required accounting

The substance of such an arrangement is that the debt is repaid over the primary period. The payments required by the debt should be apportioned between a finance charge for each accounting period and the effective reduction of the principal amount. It would be necessary to make full disclosure of the arrangement in the financial statements.

The finance costs of the debt (as defined in paragraph 8 of the FRS) will be the difference between the net proceeds and the payments which the issuer is required to make. This will be allocated to periods over the primary period at a constant rate on the carrying amount, as required by paragraph 28 of the FRS.

Illustration

On 1 January 2000 a company borrows £1,250 which is stated to be irredeemable and to carry interest of 16.275 per cent for the first ten years after which no further payments are required. The annual payments would be £203. The substance of the arrangement is that the ten payments of £203 would repay the amount borrowed and the finance charge would be allocated using a rate of 10 per cent. The accounting would be as follows:

Year ending	*Balance at beginning of year*	*Finance costs for year (10%)*	*Cash paid during year*	*Balance at end of year*
	£	*£*	*£*	*£*
31.12.2000	1,250	125	(203)	1,172
31.12.2001	1,172	117	(203)	1,086
31.12.2002	1,086	108	(203)	991
31.12.2003	991	99	(203)	887
31.12.2004	887	88	(203)	772
31.12.2005	772	77	(203)	646
31.12.2006	646	64	(203)	507
31.12.2007	507	50	(203)	354
31.12.2008	354	35	(203)	186
31.12.2009	186	17*	(203)	—

*Reduced by £1 rounding difference

Stepped interest bonds

Features

The stated rate of interest payable in respect of stepped interest bonds increases progressively over the period of issue.

Analysis and required accounting

In the case of stepped interest bonds, the stated rate of interest for each accounting period does not reflect the true economic cost of borrowing in any period during the time the bond is outstanding, since low rates of interest in one period are compensated for by higher rates in another.

Under the requirements of paragraph 28 of the FRS the pattern of the interest payments does not affect the allocation of finance costs. The payments required by the debt should be apportioned between a finance charge for each accounting period at a constant rate on the outstanding obligation and a reduction of the carrying amount. The effect of this accounting on a stepped interest bond is that the overall effective interest cost will be charged in each accounting period: an accrual will be made in addition to the cash payments in earlier periods and will reverse, partially offsetting the higher cash payments, in later periods. It would be necessary to make full disclosure of the arrangement in the financial statements.

Illustration

A loan of £1,250 is entered into on 1 January 2000 under which interest is payable according to the following schedule:

Year ending	*Rate of interest (as a percentage of nominal amount)*	*Amount of interest* £
31.12.2000	6.0	75
31.12.2001	8.0	100
31.12.2002	10.0	125
31.12.2003	12.0	150
31.12.2004	16.4	205

The overall effective rate can be found to be 10 per cent. The movement on the loan over its period in issue would be as follows:

Year ending	*Balance at beginning of year* £	*Finance costs for year (10%)* £	*Cash paid during year* £	*Balance at end of year* £
31.12.2000	1,250	125	(75)	1,300
31.12.2001	1,300	130	(100)	1,330
31.12.2002	1,330	133	(125)	1,338
31.12.2003	1,338	134	(150)	1,322
31.12.2004	1,322	133	(1,250 + 205)	—

Subordinated debt

Features

Subordinated debt is debt under which the rights of the lender are not as great as those of other creditors of the issuer. The methods of subordination vary widely. For example, one method is for subordinated debt to be repaid only when certain conditions are met, which are intended to ensure that the interests of other creditors are not impaired by the repayment. Another method of subordination is a prohibition on repayment of the debt whilst other creditors remain unpaid.

Analysis and required accounting

Irrespective of the means of subordination that is used, the lender on subordinated terms does not forgo the right to be repaid: he simply accepts that under certain conditions repayment will be postponed. It follows that, despite the subordination, the company has an obligation to repay (that is, an obligation to transfer economic benefits) and therefore subordinated debt should be accounted for as a liability.

Subordinated debt is one of the kinds of debt envisaged in paragraph 63 of the FRS in that its legal nature differs from that usually associated with debt. A brief description of its nature should be given. An illustration of such disclosure is set out below.

Illustration of disclosures

'The only event of default in relation to the subordinated debt is non-payment of principal or interest. The only remedy available to the holders of the subordinated debt in the event of default is to petition for the winding up of the company. In a winding up no amount will be paid in respect of the subordinated debt until all other creditors have been paid in full.'

ADOPTION OF FRS 4 BY THE BOARD

Financial Reporting Standard 4 'Capital Instruments' was approved for issue by the eight members of the Accounting Standards Board.

David Tweedie (Chairman)

Allan Cook (Technical Director)

Robert Bradfield

Ian Brindle

Sir Bryan Carsberg

Michael Garner

Donald Main

Graham Stacy

APPENDIX I

NOTE ON LEGAL REQUIREMENTS

1 The following note sets out certain of the requirements of the law relating to accounting for capital instruments and, where necessary, explains the relationship between the requirements of the FRS and the legal requirements.

Great Britain

Presentation of shareholders' funds

2 Paragraph 40 of the FRS requires the aggregate amount of shareholders' funds to be analysed between the amount attributable to equity interests and the amount attributable to non-equity interests. It is envisaged that this analysis will be presented as supplementary to the information required by the Companies Act 1985 (the amounts of called up share capital, share premium account, revaluation reserve, other reserves (with a sub-analysis of this amount) and profit and loss account). The FRS does not require any of the individual components of shareholders' funds to be analysed between equity and non-equity interests.

3 Sections 130-133 of the Companies Act 1985 contain requirements for amounts to be taken to the share premium account and for the application of that account. The FRS does not contain any requirements concerning the amounts to be taken to the share premium account or called up share capital and therefore does not conflict with these requirements of the law. For example, nothing in the FRS affects the availability of merger relief under section 131 of the Act.

Minority interests

4 Paragraph 1 of Schedule 4A to the Companies Act 1985 requires group accounts to be prepared as if the group were a single company. Paragraph 17 of that Schedule requires the amount of capital and reserves attributable to shares in consolidated subsidiary undertakings held by persons other than the parent company or other group companies to be shown under minority interests. Paragraph 49 of the FRS addresses the interaction of those requirements where the shareholder of a subsidiary has other rights against group companies, for example under a guarantee given by a parent. It requires the accounting to reflect such an obligation, by recognising a liability in respect of it. Where this accounts entirely for the arrangement there will be no amount remaining that represents an interest in the capital and reserves of the subsidiary.

Discount on issue and premium on redemption

5 Paragraph 24 of Schedule 4 to the Companies Act 1985 permits the excess of the amount repayable on a debt over the consideration received to be treated as an asset. As this treatment is not, however, mandatory, the FRS, which, in accordance with its principles, requires a different treatment, is not in conflict with the Act.

6 Paragraph 3(2) of Schedule 4 to the Companies Act 1985 prohibits treating the expenses of and commission on any issue of shares or debentures as an asset.

Maturity of debt

7 Paragraph 85 of Schedule 4 to the Companies Act 1985 requires a loan to be treated as falling due for repayment on the earliest date on which the lender could require repayment if he exercised all options and rights available to him. The requirements of the FRS are consistent with this requirement.

Other requirements

8 Schedule 4 to the Companies Act 1985 also requires the following information to be disclosed:

(a) In respect of shares (paragraph 38(1)):

(i) the authorised share capital; and

(ii) where there are shares of more than one class, the number and aggregate nominal value of shares of each class allotted.

(b) In the case of allotted redeemable shares (paragraph 38(2)):

(i) the earliest and latest dates on which the company may redeem them;

(ii) whether redemption is mandatory, or is at the option of either the company or the shareholder; and

(iii) whether any (and, if so, what) premium is payable on redemption.

(c) Where the company has allotted any shares during the year (paragraph 39):

(i) the reason for the allotment;

(ii) the classes of shares allotted; and

(iii) in respect of each class of shares, the number allotted, their aggregate nominal value and the consideration received by the company.

(d) In respect of contingent rights to the allotment of further shares (such as options to subscribe or rights relating to the conversion of shares or securities) the following information (paragraph 40):

(i) the number, description and amount of the shares involved;

(ii) the period during which the right is exercisable; and

(iii) the price to be paid for the shares allotted.

(e) Where the company has issued any debentures during the year (paragraph 41(1)):

(i) the reason for making the issue;

(ii) the classes of debentures issued; and

(iii) in respect of each class of debentures, the amount issued, and the consideration received by the company.

(f) Particulars of any redeemed debentures which the company has power to reissue (paragraph 41(2)).

(g) Where debentures are held by a nominee or trustee for the company, the nominal amount and the amount at which the debentures are stated in the accounting records (paragraph 41(3)).

(h) In respect of each item under creditors (paragraph 48):

(i) the total amount that is not repayable by instalments and is not due for repayment within five years of the balance sheet date;

(ii) the total amount that is repayable by instalments, some of which fall due beyond five years from the balance sheet date, disclosing separately the amount that falls due beyond five years. (This is not required for amounts that are included in a category of creditors falling due within one year);

(iii) the terms of repayment and interest on each debt details of which are given under (i) or (ii) above; or, if this would result in a statement of excessive length, a general indication of the terms of payment or repayment and the rates of interest; and

(iv) the total amount in respect of which any security has been given, and an indication of the nature of the security.

(i) In respect of dividends and reserve transfers:

(i) the profit and loss account must show the amounts set aside to or withdrawn from reserves and the aggregate amount of any dividends paid and proposed (paragraph 3(7));

(ii) the aggregate amount which is recommended for distribution by way of dividend (paragraph 51(3)); and

(iii) the amount of any arrears of fixed cumulative dividends on any class of the company's shares, and the period for which they are in arrears (paragraph 49).

(j) The amount of interest on or similar charges in respect of each of (paragraph 53(2)):

(i) bank loans and overdrafts, and other loans which are not repayable by instalments and fall due within five years of the balance sheet date;

(ii) bank loans and overdrafts, and other loans which are repayable by instalments the last of which falls due for payment within five years of the balance sheet date;

(iii) other loans.

(k) The amount of convertible loans shall be shown separately from other debenture loans (note (7) on the balance sheet formats).

Banking and insurance companies and groups

9 Schedule 4 to the Companies Act 1985 does not apply to banking and insurance companies and groups. Requirements equivalent to those of Schedule 4 for banking companies and groups are contained in Schedule 9 (as amended by the Companies Act 1985 (Bank Accounts) Regulations 1991); those for insurance companies and groups are contained in Schedule 9A to the Companies Act 1985, which is expected to be amended shortly by the Companies Act 1985 (Insurance Companies Accounts) Regulations.

Northern Ireland

10 The Companies (Northern Ireland) Order 1986 requires similar information in respect of share capital and reserves to that required by the Companies Act 1985, as referred to in paragraph 2 above.

11 Articles 140-143 of the Companies (Northern Ireland) Order 1986 are similar to sections 130-133 of the Companies Act 1985, referred to in paragraph 3 above.

12 Schedules 4 and 4A to the Companies (Northern Ireland) Order 1986 are similar to Schedules 4 and 4A to the Companies Act 1985.

13 Schedule 9 to the Companies (Northern Ireland) Order 1986, as amended by the Companies (1986 Order) (Bank Accounts) Regulations (Northern Ireland) 1992 is similar to Schedule 9 to the Companies Act 1985 (as amended by the Companies Act 1985 (Bank Accounts) Regulations 1991) Schedule 9A to the Companies (Northern Ireland) Order 1986, which is expected to be amended shortly, is similar to Schedule 9A to the Companies Act 1985.

Republic of Ireland

14 The Companies (Amendment) Act 1986 requires similar information in respect of share capital and reserves to that required by the Companies Act 1985, as referred to in paragraph 2.

15 Section 62 of the Companies Act 1963 is similar to Section 130 of the Companies Act 1985. There are no requirements in the legislation of the Republic of Ireland equivalent to Sections 131-133 of the Companies Act 1985.

16 The following table shows the references to the requirements of legislation of the Republic of Ireland which correspond to the provisions of Schedule 4A to the Companies Act 1985 mentioned above.

Companies Act 1985 Schedule 4A paragraph 1

European Communities (Companies: Group Accounts) Regulations paragraph 15

Companies Act 1985 Schedule 4A paragraph 17

European Communities (Companies: Group Accounts) Regulations, the Schedule paragraphs 8-9

17 The following table shows the references to the requirements of legislation of the Republic of Ireland which correspond to the provisions of Schedule 4 to the Companies Act 1985 mentioned above.

Great Britain: Companies Act 1985 Schedule 4	*Republic of Ireland: Companies (Amendment) Act 1986 Schedule (unless otherwise stated)*
Paragraph 3(2)	Section 4(12)
3(7)	Section 4(15)
24	Paragraph 12
38(1)	26(1)
38(2)	26(2)
39	27
40	No equivalent
41(1)	28(1)
41(2)	28(2)
41(3)	28(3)
48	34
49	35
51(3)	37(3)
53(2)	39(2)
85	67
Note (7) on the balance sheet formats	Note (5) on the balance sheet formats

18 Schedule 6 to the Companies Act 1963, as amended by the European Communities (Credit Institutions: Accounts) Regulations 1992 is similar to Schedule 9 to the Companies Act 1985 (as amended by the Companies Act 1985 (Bank Accounts) Regulations 1991). Schedule 6 to the Companies Act 1963, insofar as it relates to insurance companies, is expected to be amended shortly to implement the EC Insurance Accounts Directive.

APPENDIX II

Compliance with International Accounting Standards

The requirements of the FRS are consistent with existing International Accounting Standards. However, the International Accounting Standards Committee (IASC) has issued an exposure draft (E40) that is a draft of a proposed standard on Financial Instruments.

The principal areas where the proposals of the IASC exposure draft and the FRS are at variance are:

a The IASC exposure draft proposes that certain preferred shares, for example those where the holder has the right to require redemption, should be accounted for as liabilities. For the reasons given in paragraphs 5-6 of Appendix III, the FRS requires all shares to be reported within shareholders' funds.

b The IASC exposure draft proposes that the proceeds of instruments that have both liability and equity rights should be allocated between the component parts. For the reasons given in paragraphs 14-18 of Appendix III, the FRS requires such instruments to be accounted for wholly as a liability.

The IASC has announced that a revised exposure draft, E48, Financial Instruments will be published on 1 January 1994. It is not expected that the proposals of E48 will differ from those of E40 in respect of the above matters.

APPENDIX III

The development of the FRS

1 The Board undertook the development of an FRS on accounting for capital instruments in view of the increasing number and variety of capital instruments that have been introduced in recent years. Accounting for some of the new instruments has not always been uniform, and a variety of arguments have been advanced to justify differing treatments. Some of these arguments have called into question methods of accounting for capital instruments that have been used for many years and had previously appeared uncontroversial. The central issues that required resolution were the criteria to be used to determine whether a capital instrument represents debt or equity and the treatment of instruments such as convertible debt that will or may be exchanged for other instruments.

2 The contents of the FRS are closely based on the proposals contained in FRED 3 'Accounting for Capital Instruments' which was issued in December 1992. In turn, the proposals in that FRED were based on those set out in the Board's Discussion Paper 'Accounting for Capital Instruments' which was published in December 1991. The considerations that the Board found persuasive in framing the principal proposals in the FRS are summarised in paragraphs 3-23 below. Paragraphs 24-44 summarise the principal comments made by respondents to the FRED and discuss consequent modifications to the proposals of the FRED that have been made in response to those comments.

The rationale of the FRS

The distinction between debt and equity

3 The Board's draft Statement of Principles defines a liability as follows:

> "Liabilities are an entity's obligations to transfer economic benefits as a result of past transactions or events."

4 Thus the criterion used in the FRS to determine whether a capital instrument represents a liability is whether it contains an obligation to transfer economic benefits.

5 This criterion is not, however, used to determine the accounting for a company's shares. Shares have a distinct legal status reflected *(inter alia)* in the limitations imposed by companies legislation on the circumstances in which payments may be made in respect of them. It is also impossible to classify shares as liabilities within the constraints of the statutory formats for the balance sheet.

6 Although there are practical and legal difficulties in classifying shares as liabilities, another distinction — that between equity and non-equity shares — is practicable and is of great significance in assessing the financial position of the company. Equity shares represent the residual interest in a company. They have no claim on the company's assets that ranks prior to any other claim, but obtain the exclusive right to any increase in the net assets. Therefore the FRS requires the interests of equity shareholders in the company to be stated prominently, clearly distinguished from those of shares that have any element of priority. Priority requires some limitation in the amount to which priority attaches, and so the definition of 'non-equity shares' focuses on limitation of rights.

7 As explained in paragraphs 88-91 of the Explanation, it is sometimes the case that shares issued by subsidiaries, when considered in the context of the group, are liabilities of the group. Where this is the case, the FRS requires them to be accounted for as liabilities. In other cases, the FRS proposes that an analysis be presented of minority interests between the amount attributable to equity and non-equity interests. This analysis is similar to that of shareholders' funds and is required for the same reasons.

Warrants

8 When a company issues warrants its only obligation is to issue shares at a fixed price, if so required by the holder.

9 The price paid for a warrant can be thought of as part of the subscription price for a share that may (or may not) be issued at a future date. For this reason, the FRS requires warrants to be reported within shareholders' funds.

10 Once the warrant expires unexercised the amount paid for the warrant accrues to the benefit of the shareholders. For this reason, the FRS requires that on the expiry of a warrant the amount previously recognised in shareholders' funds be recognised in the statement of total recognised gains and losses. Showing the gain in that statement rather than in the profit and loss account is consistent with the role of the statement of total recognised gains and losses as providing a summary of changes in total reserves.

11 The Board acknowledges that the subject of warrants raises wider issues than are dealt with in the FRS. In particular, it is sometimes argued that, when the amount paid on exercise of warrants is lower than the fair value of the shares issued, there is an additional, implicit consideration that needs to be reflected in the financial statements. If this view is accepted, the question arises whether the estimate of fair value for this purpose should be made as at the issue date of the warrants or as at the exercise date.

12 Another view of warrants, which is that of a minority of the Board, is that, in substance, they are transactions with owners. Those who subscribe to this view would disagree with the proposal of the FRS that where a warrant lapses unexercised the amount previously recognised should be reported in the statement of total recognised gains and losses as they consider that that statement should not be affected by capital transactions between owners and the company. The Board rejected this view as it considers that the warrant holders are not owners of the company; the issue of warrants that are not subsequently exercised therefore represents a gain that should be reflected in the statement of total recognised gains and losses.

13 The problem involves conceptual and practical issues requiring research and consultation that the Board believes would be better conducted as a separate project. The FRS, therefore, excludes from its scope warrants and share options issued under employee share schemes, which are the most common example of warrants giving rise to these wider issues. If and when the Board addresses these issues it will also review the definition and treatment of warrants specified in this FRS.

Convertible instruments

14 There are a number of possible approaches to accounting for convertible debt, but the most usual is to report it as a liability. Although this is uncontroversial where conversion is uncertain or unlikely, it is sometimes argued that where conversion is probable convertible debt should be reported outside liabilities.

15 The FRS, however, requires convertible debt to be reported within liabilities irrespective of the probability of future conversion. This is because the balance sheet is a record of the financial position of the company at a point in time, rather than a forecast of future events. (This is not, of course, to deny that financial statements may be useful in forming an assessment of future events.) There are difficulties with the idea that convertible debt should be classified according to the probability of conversion, notably in specifying how the probability of conversion should be judged, whether convertible debt should be reclassified if the probability of conversion changes, and whether the interest on convertible debt that is not reported as a liability should be deducted in arriving at profit before taxation.

16 One of the criticisms of reporting convertible debt as a liability is that it ignores the equity rights that are inherent in an issue of convertible debt. Two methods of accounting that attempt to address this are 'split accounting' and 'the imputed interest method'.

17 The IASC's exposure draft E40 proposes that split accounting should be required for convertible debt. Under this method the proceeds of an issue of convertible debt are allocated between two components: the equity rights, and the liability. Because the amount at which the liability is initially recognised is reduced, compared with more conventional accounting, the reported finance charges over the term of the debt are increased, and would normally be similar to those that would arise on an issue of non-convertible debt. The overall accounting effect is similar to that of an issue of debt issued with warrants as illustrated in the Application Notes.

18 The Discussion Paper illustrated 'split accounting' and 'the imputed interest method' and sought respondents' views on them, although it did not propose that these methods should be required. The FRED also sought respondents' views on methods of accounting for convertible debt. The majority of the respondents who addressed the issue agreed that these methods should not be required, giving as their reasons complexity and subjectivity.

Accounting for debt and non-equity interests

19 The FRS requires finance costs to be allocated to periods at a constant rate of interest on the outstanding amount. This method reflects the fact that finance costs are a function of the amount outstanding and the passage of time. It is also a familiar method because it is already required by SSAP 21 to be used by lessees to account for their obligations under finance leases.

20 A minority of the Board believes that the method by which the FRS requires finance costs to be allocated can result in significant distortions, for example where long-term debt is issued at a time when interest rates are expected to change significantly. For this reason, the minority takes the view that the FRS should at least have permitted finance costs to be spread by reference to the term structure of interest rates implicit in the terms of the financing. The Discussion Paper discussed this method and also methods based on the market values of liabilities. They were rejected mainly on grounds of subjectivity and complexity. The Discussion Paper also rejected the allocation of finance costs on a straight line basis because it does not reflect the relationship between finance costs and the amount outstanding.

Scope of the FRS

21 Although the FRS applies to the majority of capital instruments, certain exclusions have been made.

22 The FRS does not deal with accounting for warrants and options issued to employees under employee share schemes, for the reasons explained at paragraphs 8-13 above.

23 Equity shares issued as part of a business combination that is accounted for as a merger, and leases have been excluded from the scope of the FRS as the Board did not wish to reconsider accounting for business combinations or for leases as part of the development of this FRS. The Board issued FRED 6 'Acquisitions and Mergers' in May 1993 and expects to issue an FRS on that subject in due course. The Board has not yet determined whether it will reconsider accounting for leases.

Matters considered in the light of responses to the FRED

24 Most of the respondents to the FRED agreed with its principal proposals. The following paragraphs describe those points on which respondents expressed concern and, where appropriate, explain the Board's reasons for the changes from the proposals of the FRED.

Consistency between FRS 4 and 'Reporting the Substance of Transactions'

25 Several respondents expressed concern that the proposals in FRED 3 seemed to be inconsistent with those contained in FRED 4 'Reporting the Substance of Transactions'. They contrasted the objective of FRED 4 that transactions should be accounted for in accordance with their substance, with the proposals of FRED 3 which, in their view, suggested that the legal form of capital instruments rather than their substance should determine how they were accounted for. Examples that were cited included the proposal that convertible debt should be reported as a liability until such time as it is actually converted, irrespective of the probability of conversion. Some respondents suggested that if conversion was probable, the substance of the instrument was that of equity.

26 The Board noted that convertible debt typically contains an obligation to make payments in respect of interest up to the time of conversion and that this alone would be sufficient to justify reporting it as a liability. More fundamentally, however, it concluded that, even where conversion is probable, this does not affect the substance of the relationship prevailing between the issuer and the holder of convertible debt prior to conversion which is that of debtor and creditor. Although FRED 4 states that exercise of an option should be assumed where there is no genuine commercial possibility that the option will not be exercised, it will not typically be the case that the option to convert debt is of this kind, given the volatile changes that affect companies and hence the value of their equity. Although conversion of convertible debt is sometimes probable, it is not usually certain. Furthermore, the legal nature of the relationship between the issuer and the holder of the debt has important economic consequences: for example in the case of a deterioration in the financial condition of the issuer, the holder of convertible debt has a much more valuable set of legal rights to secure recovery of his investment than a shareholder. Indeed in some cases this may be why the investor has chosen to make his investment in the form of convertible debt. The Board therefore concluded that requiring convertible debt to be accounted for as a liability was faithful both to its economic substance and to its legal form.

27 Another proposal that respondents considered to require accounting that was inconsistent with the substance of an instrument was that non-equity shares should be reported within shareholders' funds rather than as a liability. The Board's reasons for not requiring non-equity shares to be reported as liabilities are explained at paragraphs 5 and 6 above. The Board takes the view that whilst some non-equity shares may have characteristics of liabilities, the clear distinction of the amount attributable to such shares from equity shareholders' funds ensures that the amount of equity shareholders' funds is clearly stated and alerts the user to the existence of non-equity shares, the characteristics of which may need to be analysed carefully.

Disclosure requirements

28 Most respondents agreed with the items for which FRED 3 proposed disclosure, and accordingly they have largely been retained in the FRS. Several respondents, however, disagreed with the proposals of the FRED that certain distinctions should be drawn on the face of the primary financial statements, which they considered excessive; in their view making this disclosure in this way could make the accounts more difficult to understand.

29 As stated in paragraph 100 of the Explanation, the Board believes that the items for which separate disclosure on the face of the balance sheet was proposed are important, and that such disclosure will be necessary in many cases. Although the Board does not agree with respondents that disclosure on the face of the primary financial statements will often result in excessive detail, it decided that it would be adequate for the FRS to leave it to the discretion of preparers as to where this information was best given in their particular circumstances, provided that in making a decision they bear in mind the fundamental requirement for the accounts to give a true and fair view and that, if the information is given in the notes, that fact is indicated on the face of the primary financial statements.

30 The FRS does not retain the requirement proposed in the FRED to disclose the accounting policy used for capital instruments. The Board agreed with, respondents that disclosure of this was already required by SSAP 2 and, in the case of companies that prepare their accounts in accordance with Schedule 4, by paragraph 36 of that Schedule.

31 Another disclosure requirement that was proposed in the FRED but has not been retained in the FRS is that of the market value of debt and non-equity shares, where such a value could be readily ascertained. Such a disclosure is useful to users of financial statements as it provides an insight into the economic burden represented by the debt. However, respondents, and some Board members, objected to this requirement on the grounds that the disclosure might be misleading; for example, it might imply that a company would be able to take advantage of short-term changes in the value of its debt when it was not, in fact, able to do so. The information might also be considered to be of limited usefulness as the market value disclosure would often be given for only part of a company's total exposure. In particular it is beyond the scope of the FRS to develop similar disclosure requirements for off balance sheet instruments. The Board concluded that it would not be appropriate to require disclosure of market values at this time, but that it should be encouraged, and that the desirability of such disclosure would be considered in the Board's future work in conjunction with that of other standard-setting bodies.

32 The requirement to disclose participating dividends separately from other dividends on non-equity shares has been introduced to meet the concern that a division of dividends simply into equity and non-equity failed properly to reflect the fact that participating dividends are directly linked to the dividend on equity shares.

Maturity of liabilities

33 The FRS retains the proposal of the FRED that in general the maturity of debt should be assessed by reference to its contractual maturity and that a departure from this should be made only where the same lender (or group of lenders) has agreed to provide a further loan on substantially the same terms as the existing debt.

34 The Board carefully considered the views expressed by respondents who pointed out that commercial paper (which is a form of short-term debt) is frequently reported as long-term because the issuer holds back-up facilities that would permit its refinancing. Under the proposals of the FRED commercial paper would be reported as short-term notwithstanding the back-up facilities because the facility is not granted by the lender but by another party and because the rate of interest on the debt permitted by the facility is greater than that payable on the commercial paper. The considerations that influenced the Board in reaching its decision are summarised below.

35 The Board noted that issuers who regard commercial paper as a long-term source of funds normally expect to be able to refinance commercial paper by further issues of commercial paper. The purpose of the back-up facility is to provide funds in the event that further commercial paper cannot be issued, a circumstance that may arise either for reasons specific to the issuer or because of events of a more general nature. Although the possibility of an issuer's not being able to issue commercial paper may be remote in the larger markets for such paper, this is not necessarily the case where commercial paper is issued in smaller markets. As noted above, the borrowings that the issuer may make under a back-up facility are not similar to borrowings under commercial paper. The Board does not therefore consider that such facilities could reasonably be regarded as an extension of the indebtedness created by the commercial paper; rather they are arrangements entered into to safeguard the issuer from the remote possibility that it may be unable to finance the redemption of commercial paper from a fresh issue or from other sources. The Board was also aware that it was sometimes suggested that back-up facilities might not be available in the circumstances where fresh commercial paper cannot be issued.

36 The analysis of maturity that is secured by the requirements of the FRS indicates the time at which new borrowings may have to be entered into. This is important information for users of accounts because entering into new borrowings causes the price and other terms of the borrowings to change. The Board noted that, given the range of financial instruments that are now available, no single analysis will provide all the information that a user of financial statements may require. It considers, however, that the most objective and relevant basis for financial reporting is that which is founded on the actual instruments in issue, rather than one which reports the combined effect of various arrangements that may not always be intrinsically linked, which consequently may obscure the underlying financial flexibility. The Board noted that its statement on the Operating and Financial Review encourages companies to give a narrative discussion of their capital structure and liquidity. The Review provides an opportunity to explain the company's overall financial structure and how the instruments reflected in the accounts integrate with other instruments and facilities for the execution of its financial policy.

37 The Board also noted that the Companies Act requires that "*A loan is treated as falling due for repayment ... on the earliest date on which the lender could require repayment ...*

if he exercised all options and rights available to him." (Companies Act 1985, Schedule 4 paragraph 85). The Board takes the view that the requirements of the FRS are consistent with that requirement, but that alternatives favoured by respondents might not be.

Repurchase of debt

38 The FRS includes requirements in respect of repurchase of debt, which was not specifically addressed in the FRED. The subject was addressed in Abstract 8 of the Board's Urgent Issues Task Force, issued in March 1993. The requirements of the FRS are substantially the same as those of the Abstract.

39 The FRS requires gains and losses arising on the repurchase or other settlement of debt to be recognised at that time and not deferred, for example over the period of the original borrowing. This requirement is based on the view that the finance cost reported by an entity should normally reflect only its current borrowing arrangements, and not be influenced by any previous borrowings that have now been terminated.

40 UITF 8 included two exceptions to the requirement for immediate recognition of a gain or loss arising on the repurchase of debt. The first prohibited a gain or loss being recognised where the agreement to repurchase the debt was coupled with its refinancing on substantially the same terms; the second prohibited a gain or loss being recognised where the repurchase was not at fair value and the shortfall or excess was compensated for by other terms of the transactions. As explained in FRED 4 'Reporting the Substance of Transactions', the substance of such a series of transactions should be determined by viewing the series as a whole. Accordingly, gains and losses on such linked transactions should be recognised only where justified by a change in the substance of the entity's assets and liabilities.

Renegotiation of debt

41 In response to comments made on the FRED, the Board considered whether the FRS should address the accounting for the renegotiation of debt, that is the agreement by a creditor to a reduction or a deferral of payments due under the debt with the effect that the borrower's obligations are significantly reduced.

42 The question arises in such circumstances whether the concession should be recognised as a gain at the time it is granted or whether its effect should be spread over the remaining period of the debt as a reduction in finance charges. Deferral of the recognition of the effect of a renegotiation can have the result that an agreement that has significant economic consequences is not reported in the period in which those consequences arise and that liabilities and finance costs for subsequent periods are shown at amounts that do not properly represent the agreement then in force. The Board therefore concluded that in principle the gain should be recognised in the period in which renegotiation is concluded. Proposals to that effect were published in July 1993.

43 A further question is whether, in recognising the gain and determining the subsequent finance costs, the accounting should be based on the market values prevailing at the time of renegotiation or whether the revised payments should be discounted at the rate inherent in the original debt. The Board's proposals were that the market values prevailing at the time of the renegotiation should be used, as this would result in the carrying amount of the debt following the renegotiation and finance costs for subsequent periods that reflected the economic circumstances that prevailed at the time of renegotiation. Several respondents objected to this aspect of the proposals, pointing out that if (as would often be the case in practice) fair values had to be estimated by a process of discounting, it seemed wrong to use a relatively high rate reflecting the distressed circumstances of the borrower, since this would increase the recorded gain. The Board also noted that the IASC was preparing a revised exposure draft on Financial Instruments that differed from its original exposure draft on this point in that it proposed the use of the original inherent rate.

44 In the light of these concerns, the Board concluded that the FRS should not address accounting for renegotiation of debt. The Board will continue to monitor the developments of the IASC project and may readdress the issue at a later date.

Reporting the substance of transactions

Summary

General

a Financial Reporting Standard 5 'Reporting the Substance of Transactions' requires an entity's financial statements to report the substance of the transactions into which it has entered. The FRS sets out how to determine the substance of a transaction (including how to identify its effect on the assets and liabilities of the entity), whether any resulting assets and liabilities should be included in the balance sheet, and what disclosures are appropriate. The FRS also contains some provisions in respect of how transactions should be reported in the profit and loss account and the cash flow statement.

b The FRS will not change the accounting treatment and disclosure of the vast majority of transactions. It will mainly affect those more complex transactions whose substance may not be readily apparent. The true commercial effect of such transactions may not be adequately expressed by their legal form and, where this is the case, it will not be sufficient to account for them merely by recording that form.

c Transactions requiring particularly careful analysis will often include features such as:

(i) the party that gains the principal benefits generated by an item is not the legal owner of the item;

(ii) a transaction is linked with others in such a way that the commercial effect can be understood only by considering the series as a whole; or

(iii) an option is included on terms that make its exercise highly likely.

d The FRS sets out principles that willl apply to all transactions. In addition, there are five Application Notes that describe the application of the FRS to transactions with certain features: consignment stock; sale and repurchase agreements; factoring; securitised assets; and loan transfers. The Application Notes need not be referred to in all cases. At the start of each Note there is a 'Features' section that may serve as a quick reference point to determine whether further study is required. In addition, each Note concludes with a table summarising its main provisions.

Identification and recognition of the substance of transactions

e A key step in determining the substance of any transaction is to identify whether it has given rise to new assets or liabilities for the entity and whether it has increased or decreased the entity's existing assets or liabilities. Assets are, broadly, rights or other access to future economic benefits controlled by an entity; liabilities are, broadly, an entity's obligations to transfer economic benefits.

f The future economic benefits inherent in an asset are never completely certain in amount; there is always some risk that the benefits will turn out to be greater or less than expected. Whether the entity gains or suffers from such variations in benefits is evidence of whether it has an asset.

g The definition of a liability requires an obligation to transfer benefits. Evidence that an entity has such an obligation is given if there is some circumstance in which the entity is unable to avoid an outflow of benefits.

h Once identified, an asset or liability should be recognised (i.e. included) in the balance sheet, provided that there is sufficient evidence that an asset or liability exists, and the asset or liability can be measured at a monetary amount with sufficient reliability.

i Following its recognition, an asset may be affected by a subsequent transaction. Where the transaction does not significantly alter the entity's rights to benefits or its exposure to risks, the entire asset should continue to be recognised. Conversely, where the transaction transfers to others all significant rights to benefits and all significant exposure to risks, the entity should cease to recognise the asset in its entirety. Finally, in other cases where not all significant benefits and risks have been transferred, it may be appropriate to amend the description or monetary amount of an asset and, where necessary, recognise a liability for any obligations it has assumed.

Linked presentation for certain non-recourse finance arrangements

j A special form of presentation, termed a 'linked presentation', should be used for certain non-recourse finance arrangements. This presentation shows, on the face of the balance sheet, the finance deducted from the gross amount of the item it finances. It should be used where, although the entity has significant rights to benefits and exposure to risks relating to a specific item, the item is financed in such a way that the maximum loss the entity can suffer is limited to a fixed monetary amount. For use of a linked presentation it is necessary that both:

(i) the finance will be repaid only from proceeds generated by the specific item it finances (or by transfer of the item itself) and there is no possibility whatsoever of a claim on the entity being established other than against funds generated by that item (or the item itself), and

(ii) there is no provision whatsoever whereby the entity may either keep the item on repayment of the finance or re-acquire it at any time.

Disclosure of the substance of transactions

k Adequate disclosure of a transaction is important to an understanding of its commercial effect. For most transactions, the disclosures currently required will be sufficient for this purpose. However, where the nature of any recognised asset or liability differs from that of items usually found under the relevant balance sheet heading, the differences should be explained. Furthermore, to the extent that a transaction has not resulted in the recognition of assets or liabilities, disclosure may nevertheless be required in order to give an understanding of its commercial effect.

Quasi-subsidiaries

l Sometimes assets and liabilities are placed in an entity (a 'vehicle') that is in effect controlled by the reporting entity but does not meet the legal definition of a subsidiary. Where the commercial effect for the reporting entity is no different from that which would result were the vehicle a subsidiary, the vehicle will be a 'quasi-subsidiary'.

m The FRS requires the assets, liabilities, profits, losses and cash flows of any quasi-subsidiary to be included in the consolidated financial statements of the group that controls it in the same way as if they were those of a subsidiary. However, where a quasi-subsidiary is used to finance a specific item in such a way that the provisions of paragraph j above are met from the point of view of the group, the assets and liabilities of the quasi-subsidiary should be included in consolidated financial statements using the linked presentation described in paragraph j.

n Disclosure is required, in summary form, of the financial statements of quasi-subsidiaries.

Financial Reporting Standard 5

Objective

1 The objective of this FRS is to ensure that the substance of an entity's transactions is reported in its financial statements. The commercial effect of the entity's transactions, and any resulting assets, liabilities, gains or losses, should be faithfully represented in its financial statements.

Definitions

The following definitions shall apply in this FRS and in particular in the Statement of Standard Accounting Practice set out in paragraphs 11-39.

2 *Assets:* Rights or other access to future economic benefits controlled by an entity as a result of past transactions or events.

3 *Contol in the context of an asset:* The ability to obtain the future economic benefits relating to an asset and to restrict the access of others to those benefits.

4 *Liabilities:* An entity's obligations to transfer economic benefits as a result of past transactions or events.

5 *Risk:* Uncertainty as to the amount of benefits. The term includes both potential for gain and exposure to loss.

6 *Recognition:* The process of incorporating an item into the primary financial statements under the appropriate heading. It involves depiction of the item in words and by a monetary amount and inclusion of that amount in the statement totals.

7 *Quasi-subsidiary:* A quasi-subsidiary of a reporting entity is a company, trust, partnership or other vehicle that, though not fulfilling the definition of a subsidiary, is directly or indirectly controlled by the reporting entity and gives rise to benefits for that entity that are in substance no different from those that would arise were the vehicle a subsidiary.

8 *Control of another entity:* The ability to direct the financial and operating policies of that entity with a view to gaining economic benefit from its activities.

9 *Subsidiary:* A subsidiary undertaking as defined by companies legislation.

10 *Companies legislation:*

(a) In Great Britain, the Companies Act 1985;

(b) In Northern Ireland, the Companies (Northern Ireland) Order 1986; and

(c) In the Republic of Ireland, the Republic of Ireland Companies Acts 1963-1990 and the European Communities (Companies: Group Accounts) Regulations 1992.

Statement of Standard Accounting Practice

Scope

11 Subject to paragraph 12, Financial Reporting Standard 5 applies to all transactions of a reporting entity whose financial statements are intended to give a true and fair view of its financial position and profit or loss (or income and expenditure) for a period. In the FRS, the term 'transaction' includes both a single transaction or arrangement and also a group or series of transactions that achieves or is designed to achieve an overall commercial effect.

12 The following are excluded from the scope of the FRS, unless they are a part of a transaction that falls within the scope of the FRS:

(a) Forward contracts and futures (such as those for foreign currencies or commodities);

(b) Foreign exchange and interest rate swaps;

(c) Contracts where a net amount will be paid or received based on the movement in a price or an index (sometimes referred to as 'contracts for differences');

(d) Expenditure commitments (such as purchase commitments) and orders placed, until the earlier of delivery or payment;

(e) Employment contracts.

13 Where the substance of a transaction or the treatment of any resulting asset or liability falls not only within the scope of this FRS but also directly within the scope of another FRS, a Statement of Standard Accounting Practice ('SSAP'), or a specific statutory requirement governing the recognition of assets or liabilities, the standard or statute that contains the more specific provision(s) should be applied.

General

The substance of transactions

14 A reporting entity's financial statements should report the substance of the transactions into which it has entered. In determining the substance of a transaction, all its aspects and implications should be identified and greater weight given to those more likely to have a commercial effect in practice. A group or series of transactions that achieves or is designed to achieve an overall commercial effect should be viewed as a whole.

Quasi-subsidiaries

15 Where the entity has a quasi-subsidiary, the substance of the transactions entered into by the quasi-subsidiary should be reported in consolidated financial statetments.

The substance of transactions

Identifying assets and liabilities

16 To determine the substance of a transaction it is necessary to identify whether the transaction has given rise to new assets or liabilities for the reporting entity and whether it has changed the entity's existing assets or liabilities.

17 Evidence that an entity has rights or other access to benefits (and hence has an asset) is given if the entity is exposed to the risks inhernt in the benefits, taking into account the likelihood of those risks having a commercial effect in practice.

18 Evidence that an entity has an obligation to transfer benefits (and hence has a liability) is given if there is some circumstance in which the entity is unable to avoid, legally or cornmercially, an outflow of benefits.

19 Where a transaction incorporates one or more options, guarantees or conditional provisions, their commercial effect should be assessed in the context of all the aspects and implications of the transaction in order to determine what assets and liabilities exist.

Recognition of assets and liabilities

20 Where a transaction results in an item that meets the definition of an asset or liabiiity, that item should be recognised in the balance sheet if:

(a) There is sufficient evidence of the existence of the item (including, where appropriate, evidence that a future inflow or outflow of benefit will occur); and

(b) The item can be measured at a monetary amount with sufficient reliability.

Transactions in previously recognised assets

Continued recognition of an asset in its entirety

21 Where a transaction involving a previously recognised asset results in no significant change in:

(a) The entity's rights or other access to benefits relating to that asset; or

(b) Its exposure to the risks inherent in those benefits,

the entire asset should continue to be recognised. In particular this will be the case for any transaction that is in substance a financing of a previously recognised asset, unless the conditions for a linked presentation given in paragraphs 26 and 27 are met, in which case such a presentation should be used.

Ceasing to recognise an asset in its entirety

22 Where a transaction involving a previously recognised asset transfers to others:

(a) All significant rights or other access to benefits relating to that asset; and

(b) All significant exposure to the risks inherent in those benefits,

the entire asset should cease to be recognised.

Special cases

23 Paragraph 21 and 22 deal with most transactions affecting items previously recognised as assets. In other cases where there is a significant change in the entity's rights to benefits and exposure to risks but the provisions of paragraph 22 are not met, the description or monetary amount relating to an asset should, where necessary, be changed and a liability recognised for any obligations to transfer benefits that are assumed. These cases arise where the transaction takes one or more of the following forms:

(a) A transfer of only part of the item in question;

(b) A transfer of all of the item for only part of its life; and

(c) A transfer of all of the item for all of its life but where the entity retains some significant right to benefits or exposure to risk.

24 In the special cases referred to in paragraph 23, where the amount of any resulting gain or loss is uncertain, full provision should be made for any probable loss but recognition of any gain, to the extent it is in doubt, should be deferred. In addition, where the uncertainty could have a material effect on the financial statements, this fact should be disclosed in the notes to the financial statements.

The meaning of 'significant'

25 In applying paragraphs 21-23 above and paragraph 26 below, 'significant' should be judged in relation to those benefits and risks that are likely to occur in practice, and not in relation to the total possible benefits and risks.

Linked presentation for certain non-recourse finance arrangements

26 Where a transaction involving an item previously recognised as an asset is in substance a financing — and therefore meets the condition of paragraph 21 regarding no significant change in the entity's access to benefits or exposure to risks — but the financing 'ring-fences' the item such that:

(a) The finance will be repaid only from proceeds generated by the specific item it finances (or by transfer of the item itself) and there is no possibility whatsoever of a claim on the entity being established other than against funds generated by that item (or the item itself);

(b) There is no provision whatsoever whereby the entity may either keep the item on repayment of the finance or re-acquire it at any time;

(c) All of the conditions given in paragraph 27 are met;

the finance should be shown deducted from the gross amount of the item it finances on the face of the balance sheet within a single asset caption (a 'linked presentation'). The gross amounts of the item and the finance should be shown on the face of the balance sheet and not merely disclosed in the notes to the financial statements. A linked presentation should also be used where an item that is financed in such a way that all of the above three conditions are met has not been recognised previously as an asset.

27 A linked presentation should be used only where all of the following are met:

(a) The finance relates to a specific item (or portfolio of similar items) and, in the case of a loan, is secured on that item but not on any other asset of the entity;

(b) The provider of the finance has no recourse whatsoever, either explicit or implicit, to the other assets of the entity for losses and the entity has no obligation whatsoever to repay the provider of finance;

(c) The directors of the entity state explictly in each set of financial statements where a linked presentation is used that the entity is not obliged to support any losses, nor does it intend to do so;

(d) The provider of the finance has agreed in writing (in the finance documentation or otherwise) that it will seek repayment of the finance, as to both principal and interest, only to the extent that sufficient funds are generated by the specific item it has financed and that it will not seek recourse in any other form, and such agreement is noted in each set of financial statements where a linked presentation is used;

(e) If the funds generated by the item are insufficient to pay off the provider of the finance, this does not constitute an event of default for the entity; and

(f) There is no provision whatsoever, either in the financing arrangement or otherwise, whereby the entity has a right or an obligation either to keep the item upon repayment of the finance or (where title to the item has been transferred) to re-acquire it at any time. Accordingly:

  (i) where the item is one (such as a monetary receivable) that directly generates cash, the provider of the finance will be repaid out of the resulting cash receipts (to the extent these are sufficient); or

  (ii) where the item is one (such as a physical asset) that does not directly generate cash, there is a definite point at which either the item will be sold to a third party and the provider of the finance repaid from the proceeds (to the extent these are sufficient) or the item will be transferred to the provider of the finance in full and final settlement.

Where all of these conditions hold for only part of the finance, a linked presentation should be used for only that part. In such cases, the maximum future payment that the reporting entity could make (other than from funds generated by the specific item being financed) should be excluded from the amount deducted on the face of the balance sheet.

28 In respect of an arrangement for which a linked presentation is used, profit should be recognised on entering into the arrangement only to the extent that the non-returnable proceeds received exceed the previous carrying value of the item. Thereafter, any profit or loss deriving from the item should be recognised in the period in which it arises. The net profit or loss recognised in each period should be included in the profit and loss account and separate disclosure of its gross components should be given in the notes to the financial statements.

Offset

29 Assets and liabilities should not be offset. Debit and credit balances should be aggregated into a single net item where, and only where, they do not constitute separate assets and liabilities, i.e. where, and only where, all of the following conditions are met:

(a) The reporting entity and another party owe each other determinable monetary amounts, denominated either in the same currency, or in different but freely convertible currencies. For this purpose a freely convertible currency is one for which quoted exchange rates are available in an active market that can rapidly absorb the amount to be offset without significantly affecting the exchange rate;

(b) The reporting entity has the ability to insist on a net settlement. In determining this, any right to insist on a net settlement that is contingent should be taken into account only if the reporting entity is able to enforce net settlement in all situations of default by the other party; and

(c) The reporting entity's ability to insist on a net settlement is assured beyond doubt. It is essential that there is no possibility that the entity could be required to transfer economic benefits to another party whilst being unable to enforce its own access to economic benefits. For this to be the case it is necessary that the debit balance matures no later than the credit balance. It is also necessary that the reporting entity's ability to insist on a net settlement would survive the insolvency of the other party.

Disclosure of the substance of transactions

30 Disclosure of a transaction in the financial statements, whether or not it has resulted in assets or liabilities being recognised or ceasing to be recognised, should be sufficient to enable the user of the financial statements to understand its commercial effect.

31 Where a transaction has resulted in the recognition of assets or liabilities whose nature differs from that of items usually included under the relevant balance sheet heading, the differences should be explained.

Quasi-subsidiaries

Identification of quasi-subsidiaries

32 In determining whether another entity (a 'vehicle') gives rise to benefits for the reporting entity that are in substance no different from those that would arise were the vehicle a subsidiary, regard should be had to the benefits arising from the net assets of the vehicle. Evidence of which party gains these benefits is given by which party is exposed to the risks inherent in them.

33 In determining whether the reporting entity controls a vehicle regard should be had to who, in practice, directs the financial and operating policies of the vehicle. The ability to prevent others from directing those policies is evidence of control, as is the ability to prevent others from enjoying the benefits arising from the vehicle's net assets.

34 Where the financial and operating policies of a vehicle are in substance predetermined, contractually or otherwise, the party possessing control will be the one that gains the benefits arising from the net assets of the vehicle. Evidence of which party gains these benefits is given by which party is exposed to the risks inherent in them.

Accounting for quasi-subsidiaries

35 Subject to paragraph 37, the assets, liabilities, profits, losses and cash flows of a quasi-subsidiary should be included in the group financial statements of the group that controls it in the same way as if they were those of a subsidiary. Where an entity has a quasi-subsidiary but no subsidiaries and therefore does not prepare group financial statements, it should provide in its financial statements consolidated financial statements of itself and the quasi-subsidiary, presented with equal prominence to the reporting entity's individual financial statements.

36 Paragraph 35 should be applied by following the requirements regarding the preparation of consolidated financial statements set out in companies legislation and in FRS 2 'Accounting for Subsidiary Undertakings'. However, quasi-subsidiaries should be excluded from consolidation only where the interest in the quasi-subsidiary is held exclusively with a view to subsequent resale* and the quasi-subsidiary has not previously been included in the reporting entity's consolidated financial statements.

37 Where a quasi-subsidiary holds a single item or a single portfolio of similar items and the effect of the arrangement is to finance the item in such a way that the provisions of paragraphs 26 and 27 are met from the point of view of the group, the quasi-subsidiary should be included in consolidated financial statements using a linked presentation.

Disclosure of quasi-subsidiaries

38 Where one or more quasi-subsidiaries are included in consolidated financial state-

*As defined in FRS 2, paragraph 11.

ments, this fact should be disclosed. A summary of the financial statements of each quasi-subsidiary should be provided in the notes to the financial statements, unless the reporting entity has more than one quasi-subsidiary of a similar nature, in which case the summary may be given on a combined basis. These summarised financial statements should show separately each main heading in the balance sheet, profit and loss account, statement of total recognised gains and losses and cash flow statement for which there is a material item, together with comparative figures.

Date from which effective

39 The accounting practices set out in the FRS should be regarded as standard in respect of financial statements relating to accounting periods ending on or after 22 September 1994. Earlier adoption is encouraged but not required.

Explanation

Scope

40 The scope of the FRS, as set out in paragraph 11, extends to all kinds of transactions, subject only to the exclusions given in paragraph 12. Most transactions are straighfforward, giving rise to a number d standard rights and obligations with the result that their substance and commercial effect are readily apparent. Applying established accounting practices will be sufficient to ensure that the substance of such transactions is properly reported in the financial statements, without the need to refer to the FRS.

41 Conversely, applying established accounting practices may not be sufficient to portray the substance of more complex transactions whose commercial effect may not be readily apparent. For such transactions it will be necessary to refer to the FRS in order to ensure that their substance is correctly identified and properly reported.

Exclusions from the FRS

42 Paragraph 12 excludes from the FRS certain contracts for future performance except where they are merely a part of a transaction (or of a group or series of transactions) that falls within the FRS. For example, an interest rate swap forming part of a securitisation would fall to be considered under the FRS in relation to its role in the securitisation. Conversely, an interest rate swap that was no more than a part of an entity's overall treasury management activities would fall outside the scope of the FRS.

Other standards

43 The FRS sets out general principles relevant to reporting the substance of all transactions. Other accounting standards, the Application Notes of the FRS and companies legislation apply general principles to particular transactions or events. It follows that where a transaction falls within the scope of both the FRS and another accounting standard or statute, whichever contains the more specific provisions should be applied. Nevertheless, the specific provisions of any standard or statute should be applied to the substance of the transaction and not merely to its legal form and, for this purpose, the general principles set out in FRS 5 will be relevant.

44 Pension obligations are an example of an item falling within the scope of both FRS 5 and another standard, the latter being SSAP 24 'Accounting for pension costs'. As SSAP 24 contains the more specific provisions on accounting for pension obligations and does not require consolidation of pension funds, such funds should not be consolidated as quasi-subsidiaries. FRS 5, however, contains the more specific provisions in respect of certain other transactions that may take place between an entity and its pension fund, for example a sale and repurchase agreement relating to one of the entity's properties.

45 The relationship between SSAP 21 'Accounting for lease and hire purchase contracts' and FRS 5 is particularly close. In general, SSAP 21 contains the more specific provisions governing accounting for stand-alone leases that fall wholly within its parameters, although the general principles of the FRS will also be relevant in ensuring that leases are classified as finance or operating leases in accordance with their substance. However, for some lease arrangements, and particularly for those that are merely one element of a larger arrangement, the FRS will contain the more specific provisions. An example is a sale and leaseback arrangement where there is also an option for the seller/lessee to repurchase the asset; in this case the provisions of Application Note B are more specific than those of SSAP 21.

The substance of transactions

General principles

46 Paragraph 14 of the FRS sets out general principles for reporting the substance of a transaction. Particularly for more complex transactions, it will not be sufficient merely to record the transaction's legal form, as to do so may not adequately express the commercial effect of the arrangements. Notwithstanding this caveat, the FRS is not intended to affect the legal characterisation of a transaction, or to change the situation at law achieved by the parties to it.

Features of more complex transactions

47 Transactions requiring particularly careful analysis will often include features such as:

(a) The separation of legal title to an item from rights or other access to the principal future economic benefits associated with it and exposure to the principal risks inherent in those benefits*;

(b) The linking of a transaction with others in such a way that the commercial effect can be understood only by considering the series as a whole; or

(c) The inclusion of options or conditions on terms that make it highly likely that the option will be exercised or the condition fulfilled.

(a) Separation of legal title from benefits and risks

48 A familiar example of the separation of legal title from benefits and risks is a finance lease. Another is goods sold under reservation of title. In both cases, the location of legal title will not normally be expected to have a commercial effect in practice. Thus the party having the benefits and risks relating to the underlying property should recognise an asset in its balance sheet even though it does not have legal title. Arrangements involving the separtion of legal title from benefits and risks are dealt with in detail in Application Note B.

(b) Linking of transactions

49 The linking of two or more transactions extends the possibilities for separating legal

*For ease of reading, 'rights or other access to future economic benefits' are frequently referred to hereafter as 'rights to benefits' or 'benefits', and 'exposure to the risks inherent in those benefits' is frequently referred to hereafter as 'exposure to risks' or 'risks'.

title from benefits and risks, a sale of goods linked with a commitment to repurchase may leave the original owner with the principal benefits and risks relating to the goods if the re-purchase price is set at the costs, including interest, incurred by the other party in holding the goods. In such a case, application of the FRS will result in the transaction being accounted for as a financing rather than a sale, showing the asset and a corresponding liability on the balance sheet of the original owner.

(c) Inclusion of options

50 Some sale transactions are accompanied by an option, rather than a commitment, for either the original owner to repurchase or the buyer to resell. Often the commercial effect of such an arrangement is that an economic penality (such as the foregoing of a profit) would be suffered by the party having the option if it failed to exercise it. Some transactions incorporate both a put option for the buyer and a call option for the original owner, in such a way that it will almost certainly be in the commercial interests of one of the parties to exercise its option (as for example where both options have the same exercise price and are exercisable on the same date). In such cases, there will be no genuine commercial possibility that the original owner will fail to repurchase the item and application of the FRS will again result in the transaction being accounted for as a financing rather than a sale.

Assessing commercial effect by considering the position of other parties

51 Whatever the substance of a transaction, it will normally have commercial logic for each of the parties to it. If a transaction appears to lack such logic from the point of view of one or more parties, this may indicate that not all related parts of the transaction have been identified or that the commercial effect of some element of the transaction has been incorrectly assessed.

52 It follows that in assessing the commercial effect of a transaction, it will be important to consider the position of all of the parties to it, including their apparent expectations and motives for agreeing to its various terms. In particular, where one party to the transaction receives a lender's return but no more (comprising interest on its investment perhaps together with a relatively small fee), this indicates that the substance of the transaction is that of a financing. This is because the party that receives a lender's return is not compensated for assuming any significant exposure to loss other than that associated with the creditworthiness of the other party, nor is the other party compensated for giving up any significant potential for gain.

Identifying assets and liabilities

53 In accounting terms, the substance of a transaction is portrayed through the assets and liabilities, including contingent assets and liabilities, resulting from or altered by the transaction. A key step in reporting the substance of any transaction is therefore to identify its effect on the assets and liabilities of the entity.

Assets — control of access to benefits

54 The definition of an asset requires that access to future economic benefits is controlled by the entity. Access to future economic benefits will normally rest on a foundation of legal rights, although legally enforceable rights are not essential to secure access. Control is the means by which the entity ensures that the benefits accrue to itself and not to others. Control can be distinguished from management (i.e. the ability to direct the use of an item that generates the benefits) and, although the two often go together, this need not be so. For example, the manager of a portfolio of securities does not have control of the securities, as he does not have the ability to obtain the economic benefits associated with them. Such control rests with his appointer who has delegated to the manager the right to take day-to-day decisions about the composition of the portfolio.

Assets — risk

55 The future economic benefits inherent in an asset are never completely certain in amount; there is always the possibility that the actual benefits will be greater or less than those expected, or will arise sooner or later than expected. For instance, the value of stocks may rise or fall as market conditions change; foreign currency balances may become worth more or less because of exchange rate movements; debtors may default or be slow in paying. This uncertainty regarding the eventual benefit is referred to as 'risk', with the term encompassing both an upside element of potential for gain and a downside element of exposure to loss.

56 The entity that has access to the benefits will usually also be the one to suffer or gain if these benefits turn out to be different from those expected. Hence, evidence of whether an entity has access to benefits (and hence has an asset) is given by whether it has the risks inherent in those benefits.

Liabilities — obligations to transfer benefits

57 The definition of liabilities requires an obligation to transfer economic benefits. Whilst most obligations are legally enforceable, a legal obligation is not a necessary condition for a liability. An entity may be commercially obliged to adopt a certain course of action that is in its long-term best interests in the widest sense, even if no third party can legally enforce that course. As illustrated in paragraph 50 above, the prospect of a commercial or economic penalty if a certain action is not taken may negate a legal right to refrain from taking that action.

58 The notion of obligation implies that the entity is not free to avoid an outflow of resources. Where there is some circumstance in which the entity is unable to avoid such an outflow whether for legal or commercial reasons, it will have a liability. However, in accordance with SSAP 18 'Accounting for contingencies' if the entity's obligation is contingent on the occurrence of one or more uncertain future events (as under a stand-alone guarantee given by the entity) its liability may not be recognised.

Options

59 On its own, an option to acquire an item of property in the future represents a different asset from ownership of the property itself. For example, when an option to purchase shares at a future date is acquired, the only asset is the option itself; the asset 'shares' will be acquired only on exercise of the option. Similarly, an unconditional obligation is not the same as a contingent commitment to assume such an obligation at another party's option. Although both are liabilities, they are different liabilities and if recognised in the balance sheet their descriptions will be different.

60 Where an option is part of a more complex transaction, it may not necessarily represent a separate asset or liability of the type discussed in paragraph 59. For example, an option may serve, in conjunction with the other aspects of the transaction, to give one party access to the future benefits arising from an item of property without legal ownership. Alternatively the terms of an option, together with other aspects of the overall transaction, may in effect create an unconditional obligation even though the legal obligation is expressed as being conditional on the exercise of the option. Options of this kind should be accounted for by considering the substance of the transaction as a whole.

61 In determining the substance of a transaction incorporating options, in accordance with paragraph 14, greater weight must be given to those aspects and implications more likely to have a commercial effect in practice. This will involve considering the extent to which there is a genuine commercial possibility that the option will be exercised or, alternatively, that it will not be exercised. In extreme cases, there will be no genuine commercial possibility that the option will be exercised, in which case the existence of that option should be ignored; alternatively, there will be no genuine commercial possibility that an option will fail to be exercised, in which case its future exercise should be assumed. For example, a transaction may be structured in such a way that the cost of exercising an option will almost inevitably be lower (or, alternatively, higher) than the benefits obtained from its exercise. As another example, there may be a combination of put and call options such that it will almost certainly be in the commercial interests of one or other party to exercise its option. In both these cases, the substance of the overall transaction is that the parties have outright, and not optional or conditional, obligations and access to benefits. In less extreme cases, further analysis will be required. It may be necessary to consider the true commercial objectives of the parties and the commercial rationale for the inclusion of such options in the transaction. This may reveal either that the parties in substance have outright obligations and access to benefits, or, alternatively, that the parties' obligations and access to benefits are genuinely optional or conditional.

62 In assessing the commercial effect of an option, all the terms of the transaction and the circumstances of the parties that are likely to be relevant during the exercise period of the option should be taken into account. It should be assumed that each of the parties will act in accordance with its economic interests. Any actions that the parties would take only in the event of a severe deterioration in liquidity or creditworthiness should not be anticipated but should be taken into account only when such a deterioration occurs (for example, when creditworthiness has declined because of the prospect of imminent cash flow difficulties).

Guarantees and conditional provisions

63 Paragraphs 59-62 should also be applied to guarantees and other conditional provisions. The commercial effect of such provisions should in all cases be determined in the context of the overall transaction.

Recognition of assets and liabilities

64 Once it appears from analysis of a transaction that an asset or liability has been acquired or assumed by an entity, it is necessary to apply various recognition tests to determine whether the asset or liability should be included in the balance sheet.

65 The general criteria set out in paragraph 20* require that an asset or liability should be recognised only where it can be measured with 'sufficient' reliability. The effect of prudence is that less reliability of measurement is acceptable when recognising items that involve decreases in equity (e.g. increases in liabilities) than when recognising items that do not (e.g. increases in assets). It follows that, particularly for liabilities, where a reasonable estimate of the amount of an item is available, the item should be recognised.

*These criteria are drawn from Chapter 4 of the Board's draft Statement of Principles

Transactions in previously recognised assets

66 Following its recognition, an asset may be affected by a subsequent transaction and it will be necessary to consider whether, as a result of the transaction, the description or monetary amount of the asset needs to be changed. In this regard paragraphs 21-28 and 67-88 will apply.

Continued recognition of an asset in its entirety

67 Paragraph 21 requires that where there is no significant change in the entity's rights to benefits, its previously recognised asset should continue to be recognised. In the same way, the entity will continue to have an asset where its exposure to the risks inherent in the benefits of the asset is not significantly altered. Even if the proceeds generated by the asset are directed in the first instance to another party, provided the entity gains or suffers from all significant changes in those proceeds it should be regarded as having the benefits of the asset and should continue to recognise it. For example, a 'sale' of debts with recourse to the seller for all bad debts and provision for the seller to pay a finance charge that reflects the speed of payment by debtors leaves the seller with all significant risks relating to the debts (the risks being the speed of payment and the degree of non-payment). This is so even if actual cash receipts are collected directly by the buyer and only a net surplus or deficit settled with the seller. In such cases the seller would continue to recognise an asset equal in amount to the debts, although the transfer of legal title would be disclosed.

68 Thus, under paragraph 21, it will not be appropriate to cease to recognise any part of an asset where the transaction entered into is in substance a financing of that asset, even if the financing is without recourse. Such financing transactions leave the entity with those rights to benefits and exposures to risks (including potential for gain) that are likely to have a commercial effect in practice, as well as creating a liability to repay the finance. The only exception to this is non-recourse finance arrangements that meet the conditions for a linked presentation given in paragraphs 26-27. Although such arrangemennts are in substance financings, their particular features are such that a linked presentation is required to portray all the effects of the arrangement. This is explained further in paragraphs 76-80 below.

Ceasing to recognise an asset in its entirety

69 Conversely, paragraph 22 requires that where a transaction transfers to others all significant rights to benefits and all significant exposure to risks that relate to a previously recognised asset, the entire asset should cease to be recognised. An example would be a sale of debts for a single non-returnable cash payment.

Special cases

70 Paragraphs 21 and 22 deal with the great majority of transactions affecting previously recognised assets. However, in other cases there may be a significant change in the entity's rights to benefits and exposure to risks but not a complete transfer of all significant benefits and risks. In such cases, it will be necessary to consider whether the description or monetary amount of the asset needs to be changed and also whether a liability needs to be recognised for any obligations assumed or risks retained. These special cases arise where the transaction takes one or more of the following forms:

(a) A transfer of only part of the item in question;

(b) A transfer of all of the item for only part of its life; and

(c) A transfer of all of the item for all of its life but where the entity retains some significant right to benefits or exposure to risk.

(a) Transfer of only part of an item

71 Transfer of part of an item that generates benefits may occur in one of two ways. The most straightforward is where a proportionate share of the item is transferred. For example, a loan transfer might transfer a proportionate share of a loan (including rights to receive both interest and principal), such that all future cash flows, profits and losses arising on the loan are shared by the transferee and transferor in fixed proportions. A second, less straightforward way of transferring a part of an item arises where the item comprises rights to two or more separate benefit streams, each with its own risks. A part of the item will be transferred where all significant rights to one or more of those benefit streams and associated exposure to risks are transferred whilst all significant rights to the other(s) are retained. An example would be a 'strip' of an interest-bearing loan into rights to two or more different cash flow streams that are payable on different dates (for instance 'interest' and 'principal'), with the entity retaining rights to only one of those streams (for instance 'principal'). In both these cases, the entity would cease to recognise the part of the original asset that has been transferred by the transaction, but would continue to recognise the remainder. A change in the description of the asset might also be required.

(b) Transfer of an item for only part of its life

72 Paragraph 23 also applies to a transaction that transfers all of an item that generates benefits for only part of its life. Provided that the entity's access to benefits and exposure to risks following the transaction are both significantly different from those it had before the transaction, the description or monetary amount of the asset previously recognised would need to be changed. For example, an entity may sell an item of property but agree to repurchase it in a substantially depreciated form (as for example where the item will be used for most of its life by the buyer). In this case the entity's original asset has changed from being the original item of property to a residual interest in that item and, in addition, the entity has assumed a liability of its obligation to pay the repurchase price. Sale and repurchase agreements are dealt with further in Application Note B.

(c) Transfer of an item for all of its life with some benefit or risk retained

73 Finally, paragraph 23 applies to a transaction that transfers an item that generates benefits for all of its life, but leaves the entity with significant rights to benefits or exposure to risks relating to that item. Whilst control has passed to the transferee, the retention of significant rights to benefits or exposure to risks has the result that the transaction fails to meet the conditions in paragraph 22 for ceasing to recognise an asset in its entirety. For example, an entity may sell an investment in a subsidiary with the consideration including an element of deferred performance-related consideration. Provided that significant rights to benefits and exposure to risks associated with the subsidiary have passed to the buyer (as will be the case where the deferred consideration is only a portion of the subsidiary's profits arising in only a limited period), both the description and the monetary amount of the asset will need to be changed. This reflects the fact that the asset is no longer an investment in a subsidiary but rather is a debtor for the performance-related consideration (although, under the provisions of SSAP 18, the debtor may be measured at nil and therefore not recognised but merely disclosed). As another example, an entity may sell equipment subject to a warranty in respect of the condition of the equipment at the time of sale, or subject to a guarantee of its residual value. This would normally transfer all significant rights to benefits and some significant exposure to risks to the buyer (these being those arising from the equipment's future use and resale), but leave the seller with some significant risk in the form of obligations relating to the equipment's future performance or residual value. The seller would therefore cease to recognise the equipment as an asset, but would recognise a liability for its warranty obligation or guarantee (with the liability being accounted for in accordance with the provisions of SSAP 18).

Measurement and profit recognition

74 In any of the above three classes of transaction, there arises the issue of how to measure the change in the entity's assets or liabilities and any resulting profit or loss. This measurement process requires that the previous carrying value of the asset is apportioned into an amount relating to those benefits and risks disposed of and an amount relating to those retained. In some cases, measurement will be relatively easy; for instance this might be the case where a proportionate share of the original asset is retained as described in paragraph 71 above or where there are similar and frequent transactions in liquid and freely accessible markets. In other cases, measurement may be more difficult with the result that the amount of any gain or loss is uncertain. In such cases, in accordance with the provisions of SSAP 18, paragraph 24 requires a prudent approach to be adopted, with full provision being made for any probable loss but recognition of any gain, to the extent it is in doubt, being deferred.

The meaning of 'significant'

75 In applying paragraphs 21-23 and 26 it may be necessary to determine whether certain rights to benefits or exposure to risks are 'significant'. When this is done, greater weight should be given to what is likely to have a commercial effect in practice. In particular. whether any retained risk is 'significant' should be judged not against the total possible variation in benefits, but against that variation which is likely to occur in practice. For instance, if for a portfolio of debts of 100, bad debts are expected to be 2 and the debts are sold with recourse to the entity for bad debts of up to 5, the seller will have retained all significant risk of non-payment. Thus the debts would continue to be recognised in their entirety (unless the conditions for a linked presentation are met).

Linked presentation for certain non-recourse finance arrangements

General principles

76 Sometimes an entity finances an item on terms that the provider of the finance has recourse to only the item it has financed and not to the entity's other assets. It is sometimes argued that the effect of such arrangements is that the entity no longer has an asset in respect of the item, nor does it have a liability for the finance. For the purpose of determining the appropriate accounting treatment, non-recourse finance arrangements can be classified into two types.

Separate presentation of an asset and liability

77 The first type of arrangement is where, although in the event of default the provider of the finance can obtain repayment only by enforcing its rights against the specified item, the entity retains rights to all the benefits generated by the item and can repay the finance from its general resources in order to preserve those rights. In such a case the entity has both an asset (its access to all the benefits generated by the item) and a liability (its obligation to repay the finance) and they should be included in the balance sheet in the normal way.

Linked presentation

78 The second type of non-recourse finance arrangement is where the finance will be repaid only from benefits generated by the specified item. Although the entity has rights to any surplus benefits remaining after repayment of the finance, it has no right or obligation to keep the item or to repay the finance from its general resources. In these cases the entity does not have an asset equal to the gross amount of the item (as it does not have access to all the future benefits generated by it), nor a liability for the full amount of the finance (as the financier will be repaid only from benefits generated by the specific item and not from benefits generated by any other assets of the entity). However, the entity does retain rights to those benefits and exposure to those risks that are likely to have a commercial effect in practice — i.e. the significant benefits and risks. It is retention of the significant benefits and risks that distinguishes this type of non-recourse financing from the transactions described in paragraph 23 that transfer a part of an asset. Where there is no transfer of significant benefits and risks the transaction is in substance a financing arrangement and the other party would usually receive a lender's return and no more. Conversely, the transactions described in paragraph 23 involve a transfer of significant benefits and risks. Indications of such transactions are where the other party has rights to benefits greater than those associated with a lender's return and has corresponding exposure to some significant risk.

79 For example, assume an entity transfers title to a portfolio of high quality debts of 100 in exchange for non-returnable proceeds of 90. The entity cannot be required to repay these non-returnable proceeds in any circumstance or in any form, nor can it be required to make any other payment in respect of the debts. In addition, the entity retains rights to a further sum (calculated as 10 less any bad debts and a finance charge) whose amount depends on whether and when the debtors pay. In this situation the entity does not have a liability for the non-returnable proceeds of 90 (as it can never be required to repay them except out of cash generated by the debts portfolio), nor an asset of 100 (as the first 90 of benefits generated by the debts must be passed to the transferee). However, the entity does have a new asset in its rights to future benefits of up to 10, which depends principally on the performance of the entire portfolio of 100. If any one debt proves to be completely bad or if all debts prove to be partly bad, the entity bears the entire loss (subject to the ceiling of 10) as its future cash receipts are reduced accordingly. Although it has transferred catastrophe risk (of benefits being less than 90), the entity has retained all the variation in benefits likely to occur in practice — i.e. the significant benefits and risks. The catastrophe risk that is transferred is not significant since, although the potential losses involved are large in absolute terms, it is extremely unlikely that such losses will occur in practice.

80 For this type of arrangement, a special presentation (a 'linked presentation') is required to give a true and fair view of the entity's position. This presentation involves giving additional information on the face of the balance sheet about the entity's new net asset (of 10 in the above example). In the above example, the linked presentation would be as follows:

Debts subject to financing arrangements:

Debts (after providing for expected bad debts of 1)	99
Less: non-returnable amounts received	(90)
	9

This linked presentation shows both that the entity retains significant benefits and risks relating to all the debts, and that the claim of the provider of the finance is limited strictly to the funds generated by them.

Detailed conditions for use of a linked presentation

81 A linked presentation is appropriate only where the commercial effect for the entity is that the item is being sold but the sale process is not yet complete. Thus there must be no doubt whatsoever that the claim of the provider of the finance is limited strictly to funds generated by the specific item it finances. It must be clear that there is no legal, commercial or other obligation under which the entity may fund any losses (from whatever cause) on the items being financed or transfer any economic benefits (apart from those generated by the item). In addition, the entity must have no right or obligation to repay the finance from its general resources, to keep the item on repayment of the finance or to re-acquire it in the future. These principles are reflected in the detailed conditions for use of a linked presentation set out in paragraph 27.

82 Condition 27(a) requires that the finance relates to a specific item or group of similar items. A linked presentation should not be used where the finance relates to two or more items that are not part of a portfolio, or to a portfolio containing items that would otherwise be shown under different balance sheet captions. Similarly, a linked presentation should not be used where the finance relates to any kind of business unit, or for items that generate the funds required to repay the finance only by being used in conjunction with other assets of the entity. The item must generate the funds required to repay the finance either by unwinding directly into cash (as in the case of a debt), or by its sale to a third party.

83 Conditions 27(b)-(e) require that there is no recourse and no other condition (legal, commercial or other) that could result in the entity supporting losses, from whatever cause, on the items being financed (or, as discussed in the next paragraph, supporting such losses beyond a fixed monetary ceiling). Recourse could take a number of forms, for instance: an agreement to repurchase non-performing items or to substitute good items for bad ones; a guarantee given to the provider of the finance or any other party (of performance, proceeds or other support); a put option under which items can be transferred back to the entity; a swap of some or all of the amounts generated by the item for a separately determined payment; or a penalty on cancelling an on-going arrangement such that the entity bears the cost of any items that turn out to be bad. Normal warranties given in respect of the condition of the item at the time the non-recourse finance arrangement is entered into would not breach this condition; however, warranties relating to the condition of the item in the future or to its future performance would do so.

84 If there is partial recourse for losses up to a fixed monetary ceiling, a linked presentation may still be appropriate in respect of that part of the finance for which there is no recourse. However, where the entity provides any kind of open-ended guarantee (i.e. one that does not have a fixed monetary ceiling) a linked presentation should not be used.

An example of such an open-ended guarantee would be a guarantee of completion provided by a property developer.

85 The following example illustrates the effect of partial recourse. An entity transfers title to a portfolio of debts of 100 (for which expected bad debts are 4) in return for proceeds of 95 plus rights to a future sum whose amount depends on whether and when debtors pay. In addition, there is recourse to the entity for the first 10 of any losses. Assuming the conditions set out in paragraphs 26-27 are met, the arrangement would be presented as follows:

Debts subject to financing arrangements:

Gross debts (after providing for bad debts)	96
Less: non-returnable proceeds	(85)
	11

The remaining 10 of the finance would be included within liabilities.

86 Condition 27(f) requires there to be no provision for the entity to repurchase the item being financed. For instance, where legal title to the item has been transferred, a linked presentation should not be used to the extent that one party has a put or a call option to effect repurchase, or where there is an understanding between the parties that the item will be re-acquired in the future.

Profit or loss recognition and presentation

87 Where a linked presentation is used, profits or losses should be recognised in the period in which they arise so as to reflect the fact that the entity continues to gain or suffer from the performance of the underlying gross item. For example, on entering into the arrangement, a gain will arise only to the extent that the non-returnable proceeds received exceed the previous carrying value of the item. In subsequent periods, a gain (or loss) will arise to the extent that the income from the item exceeds (or falls short of) the amounts due to the provider of finance in respect of that period. Finally, any gain resulting from an onward sale of the item to a third party will arise only in the period in which the onward sale occurs.

88 Where a linked presentation is adopted in the balance sheet, normally it will be sufficient for only the net amount of any income or expense recognised in each period to be included in the profit and loss account, with the gross components being disclosed by way of note. However, the gross components should be shown on the face of the profit and loss account by using a linked presentation where the effect of the arrangement on the performance of the entity is so significant that to include merely the net amount of income or expense within the captions shown on the face of the profit and loss account would not be sufficient to give a true and fair view.

Offset

89 Offsetting is the process of aggregating debit and credit balances and including only the net amount in the balance sheet. In order to present the commercial effect of transactions, it is necessary that any separate assets and liabilities that result are not offset.

90 Offset is permissible, and indeed necessary, between related debit and credit balances that are not separate assets and liabilities as defined in the FRS. For this to be the case, it is necessary that all of the conditions given in paragraph 29 are met, such that there is no possibility that the entity could be required to pay another party and later find it was unable to obtain payment itself. In this respect, the requirement in condition (c) in paragraph 29 that the debit balance matures no later than the credit balance will be met if, at its own discretion, the reporting entity can ensure that result by accelerating the maturity of the debit balance or deferring the maturity of the credit balance. Where the reporting entity or the other party is a group, particular care must be taken to ensure that the reporting entity, through its constituent legal entities, can insist on a net settlement of the amounts to be offset in all situations of default and that this ability would survive the insolvency of any of the separate legal entities that constitute the other party.

91 Where the conditions for a linked presention given in paragraphs 26-27 are met, the entity's asset is the net amount. Such a presentation does not constitute offset of an asset and a liability; rather it is the provision of additional information about an asset (which is the net amount), necessary in order to give a true and fair view.

Disclosure of the substance of transactions

92 Paragraph 30 requires that disclosure of a transaction should be sufficient to enable the user of the financial statements to understand its commercial effect. For the vast majority of transactions this involves no more than those disclosures currently required. However, this may not be sufficient to portray fully the commercial effect of more complex transactions, in which case further information will need to be disclosed.

93 Assets and liabilities resulting from more complex transactions will not necessarily be exactly the same as those resulting from more straightforward transactions. The greater the differences the greater the need for disclosure. For example, certain assets may not be available for use as security for liabilities of the entity; or certain liabilities, whilst not qualifyng for the linked presentation set out in pararaphs 26-27 may, in the event of default, be payable only to the extent that the assets which they are secured yield sufficient benefits.

94 Even where a transaction does not result in any items being recognised in the balance sheet, the need for disclosure should still be considered. The transaction may give rise to guarantees, commitments or other rights and obligations which, although not sufficient to require recognition of an asset or liability, require disclosure in order that the financial statements give a true and fair view.

Quasi-susidiaries

Identification of quasi-subsidiaries

95 An entity may directly control access to future economic benefits or may control such access through the medium of another entity, normally a subsidiary. Control through the medium of another entity is of such widespread significance that it underlies the statutory definition of a subsidiary undertaking and is reflected in the requirement for the preparation of consolidated accounts. However, such control is not confined to cases where another entity is a subsidiary as defined in statute. 'Quasi-subsidiaries' are sometimes established by arrangements that give as much effective control over another entity as if that entity were a subsidiary.

Benefits

96 In deciding whether or not an entity is a quasi-subsidiary, access to the whole of the benefit inflows arising from its gross assets and responsibility for the whole of the benefit outflows associated with its liabilities are not the key considerations. In practice, many subsidiaries do not give rise to a possible benefit outflow for their parent of an amount equal to their gross liabilities — indeed, the limiting of benefit outflows in the event of losses occurring may have been a factor for the parent in establishing a subsidiary. In addition, as the liabilities of a subsidiary have a prior claim on its assets, the parent will not have access to benefit inflows of an amount equal to those gross assets. For this reason, it is necessary to focus on the benefit flows associated with the net assets of the entity. Often evidence of where these benefits lie is given by which party stands to suffer or gain from the financial performance of the entity — i.e. which party has the risks inherent in the benefits.

Control

97 Control is the means by which one entity determines how the assets of another entity are employed and by which the controlling entity ensures that the resulting benefits accrue to itself and not to others. Control may be evidenced in a variety of ways depending on its basis (e.g. ownership or other rights) and the way in which it is exercised (interventionist or not). Control includes the ability to restrict others from directing major policies, but a power of veto will not of itself constitute control unless its effect is that major policy decisions are taken in accordance with the wishes of the party holding that power. One entity will not control another where there is a third party that has the ability to determine all major issues of policy.

98 In some cases, arrangements are made for allocating the benetits arising from the activities of an entity such that active exercise of control is not necessary. The party or parties who will gain the benefits (and bear their inherent risks) are irreversibly specified in advance. No party has direct control in the sense of day-to-day direction of the entity's financial and operating policies, since all such matters are predetermined. In such cases, control will be exercised indirectly via the arrangements for allocating the benefits and it will be necessary to look at the effects of those arrangements to establish which party has control. It follows that, for the reasons set out in paragraph 96 above, the party possessing control will be the one that gains the benefits arising from the net assets of the entity.

Accounting for quasi-subsidiaries

99 In essence, consolidation is founded on the principle that all the entities under the control of the reporting entity should be incorporated into a single set of financial statements. Applying this principle has the result that the assets, liabilities, profits, losses and cash flows of any entity that is a quasi-subsidiary should be included in group financial statements in the same way as if they were those of a member of the statutory group (this is referred to below as 'inclusion of a quasi-subsidiary in group financial statements').

100 The entities that constitute a group are determined by companies legislation. Companies legislation also requires that where compliance with its provisions would not be sufficient to give a true and fair view, the necessary additional information shall be given in the accounts or in a note to them*. Inclusion of a quasi-subsidiary in group financial statements is necessary in order to give a true and fair view of the group as legally defined and thus constitutes provision of such additional information.

*In Great Britain section 227(5) of the Companies Act 1985. Equivalent references for Northern Ireland and the Republic of Ireland are given in paragraphs 5 and 6 respectively of Appendix 1 'Note on legal requirements'.

101 Companies legislation and FRS2 'Accounting for subsidiary undertakings' permit or require subsidiaries to be excluded from consolidation in certain circumstances. However, as inclusion of a quasi-subsidiary in group financial statements is required in order that those financial statements give a true and fair view of the group, these exclusions are generally not appropriate for a quasi-subsidiary. The following considerations are relevant:

(a) An immaterial quasi-subsidiary is outside the scope of this FRS, which need not be applied to immaterial items.

(b) Where severe long-term restrictions substantially hinder the exercise of the rights of the reporting entity over the assets or management of another entity, the reporting entity will not have the control necessary for the definition of a quasi-subsidiary to be met. Where the financial and operating policies of another entity are predetermined, this affects the manner in which control, of that entity is exercised, but does not preclude the entity from being a quasi-subsidiary.

(c) Disproportionate expense or undue delay in obtaining information justifies excluding a quasi-subsidiary only if it is immaterial.

(d) Where there are significant differences between the activities of a quasi-subsidiary and those of the group that controls it, these should be disclosed. However, the quasi-subsidiary should nevertheless be included in the consolidation in order that the group financial statements present a true picture ot the extent of the group's activities.

It is appropriate to exclude a quasi-subsidiary from consolidation only where the interest in the quasi-subsidiary is held exclusively with a view to subsequent resale and the quasi-subsidiary has not previously been included in the reporting entity's consolidated financial statements. In determining if this exclusion is appropriate in a particular instance, reference should be made to FRS2.

102 Some arrangements for financing an item on a non-recourse basis involve placing the item and its finance in a quasi-subsidiary as a means of 'ring-fencing' them. Where, as a result, the conditions of paragraphs 26 and 27 are met from the point of view of the group as legally defined, the item and its finance should be included in the group financial statements by using a linked presentation. As noted above, the inclusion of a quasi-subsidiary in group financial statements forms additional information, necessary in order to give a true and fair view of the group as legally defined — the quasi-subsidiary is not part of that group. Where an item and its finance are effectively ring-fenced in a quasi-subsidiary, a true and fair view of the position of the group is given by presenting them under a linked presentation. In this situation, the group does not have an asset equal to the gross amount of the item, nor a liability for the full amount of the finance. However, where the item and its finance are similarly ring-fenced in a subsidiary, a linked presentation may not be used. This is because the subsidiary is part ot the group as legally defined — hence the item and its finance, being an asset and a liability of the subsidiary, are respectively an asset and liability of the group. The subsidiary would be consolidated in the normal way in accordance with companies legislation and a linked presentation would not be used (unless a linked presentation were appropriate in the subsidiary's individual financial statements).

Disclosure of quasi-subsidiaries

103 When one or more quasi-subsidiaries are included in the consolidated financial statements of a statutory group, companies legislation requires the fact that such additional information has been included, and the effect of its inclusion, to be clearly disclosed*.

APPLICATION NOTES

These Applicatian Notes specify how the requirements of FRS5 are to be applied to transactions that have certain features. For such transactions, observance of the Notes will normally be sufficient to ensure compliance with the requirements of FRS5.

The tables and illustrations shown in the shaded areas are provided as an aid to understanding and shall not be regarded as part of the Statement of Standard Accounting Practice.

It is not intended that the accounting treatment determined by FRS5 or the terminology used in the Application Notes should change the situation at law achieved by the parties. Accordingly, it is not intended that the legal effectiveness of any transfer should be affected.

CONTENTS

Application Note A — Consignment Stock

NB Although this Application Note is drafted in terms of the motor trade it applies equally to similar arrangements in other industries.

Features

A1 Consignment stock is stock held by one party (the 'dealer') but legally owned by another (the 'manufacturer'), on terms that give the dealer the right to sell the stock in the normal course of its business or, at its option, to return it unsold to the legal owner. The stock may be physically located on the premises of the dealer, or held at a car compound or other site nearby. The arrangement has a number of commercial advantages for both parties: the dealer is able to hold or have faster access to a wider range of stock than might otherwise be practicable; the manufacturer can avoid a build-up of stock on its premises by moving it closer to the point of sale; and both benefit from the greater sales potential of the arrangement.

*In Great Britain Section 227 of the Companies Act 1985. Equivalent references for Northern Ireland and the Republic of Ireland are given in paragraphs 5 and 6 respectively of Appendix I 'Note on legal requirements'.

A2 The main features of a consignment stock arrangement are as follows:

(a) The manufacturer delivers goods to the dealer, but legal title does not pass until one of a number of events takes place, e.g. the dealer has held the goods for a specified period, adopts them by using them as demonstration models, or sells them to a third party. Until such a crystallising event, the dealer is entitled to return the goods to the manufacturer or the manufacturer is able to require their return or insist that they are passed to another dealer.

(b) Once legal title passes, the transfer price becomes payable by the dealer. This price may be fixed at the date goods are delivered to the dealer, it may vary with the period between delivery and transfer of title, or : may be the manufacturer's list price at the date of transfer of title.

(c) The dealer may also be required to pay a deposit to the manufacturer, or to pay the latter a display or financing charge. This deposit or charge may be fixed for a period (e.g. one year) or may fluctuate. Its amount is usually set with reference to the dealer's past sales of the manufacturer's goods or to average or actual holdings of consignment stock. It may (or may not) bear interest. In some cases, a finance company will pay the deposit or charge to the manufacturer and will charge interest thereon to the dealer.

(d) Other terms of the arrangement will usually cover items such as inspection and access rights of the manufacturer, and responsibility for damage, loss or theft and related insurance. These are usually of minor importance in determining the accounting treatment.

Analysis

A3 The purpose of the analysis below is to determine whether, at any particular time, the dealer has an asset in the stock and a corresponding liability to pay the manufacturer for it. To this end, it is necessary to identify whether the dealer has access to the benefits of the stock and exposure to the risks inherent in those benefits. From the dealer's perspective, the principal benefits and risks of consignment stock are as follows:

Benefits:

(i) The future cash flows from sale to a third party and the right to retain items of stock in order to achieve such a sale;

(ii) Insulation from changes to the transfer price charged by the manufacturer for its stock (e.g. because the manufacturer has increased its list price); and

(iii) The right to use the stock (e.g. as a demonstration model) by adopting it.

Risks:

(i) The risk of being compelled to retain stock that is not readily saleable or is obsolete, resulting in no sale or a sale at a reduced price; and

(ii) The risk of slow movement, resulting in increased costs of financing and holding the stock and an increased risk of obsolescence.

Paragraphs A5-A10 show how the various features of a consignment stock agreement will determine where the above benefits and risks lie. The stock should be included on the dealer's balance sheet where the dealer has access to its principal benefits and bears the principal risks inherent in those benefits.

A4 In determining the substance of an agreement, it will be necessary to look at all its features and give greater weight to those that are more likely to have a commercial effect in practice. In addition, it will be necessary to consider the interaction between the features and to evaluate the arrangement as a whole.

Manufacturer's right of return (benefit (i))

A5 The dealer's access to the benefits of the stock will be constrained by any right of the manufacturer to require goods to be returned or transferred to another dealer. The likely commercial effect of this constraint should be assessed. For instance, if a high proportion of the consignment stock is returned or transferred without compensation, this indicates that the stock is not an asset of the dealer. Conversely, if the dealer is able to resist requests made by the manufacturer for transfers and in practice actually does so, or in practice the manufacturer compensates the dealer for agreeing to transfer stock in accordance with the manufacturer's wishes, this indicates that the stock is an asset of the dealer.

Dealer's right of return (risk (i))

A6 If the dealer has a right to return stock without payment of a penalty, it will not bear obsolescence risk. This indicates that the dealer has neither the asset 'stock', nor a liability to pay the manufacturer for it. Again, the likely commercial effect of any such right of return and the significance of obsolescence risk should be considered. If the right of return is exercised frequently or the manufacturer regularly provides a significant incentive (such as a price discount or a free extension to the consignment period) to persuade the dealer not to return stock where it would otherwise do so, this indicates that the stock is not an asset of the dealer. Conversely, if the dealer either has no right to return stock, or in practice does not exercise its right or is charged a significant penalty for doing so, this indicates that the dealer bears the principal risks relating to the stock and the stock is an asset for it. In such cases the dealer will also have a corresponding liability (legal or commercial) to pay for the stock.

Stock transfer price and deposit (benefit (ii), risk (ii))

A7 Whether the dealer is insulated from changes in the prices charged by the manufacturer for its stock depends on how the stock transfer price is determined. Where the price is based on the manufacturer's list price at delivery, then the manufacturer is unable to pass on any subsequent price changes, which indicates that the stock became an asset of the dealer at the date of delivery. Conversely, if the price charged to the dealer is the manufacturer's list price at the date of the transfer of legal title, this indicates that the stock remains an asset of the manufacturer until legal title is transferred.

A8 The stock transfer price will also affect the incidence of slow movement risk and who bears the variable cost of financing the stock until sold. In a simple arrangement where there is no deposit and stock is supplied for a fixed price that is payable by the dealer only when legal title is transferred it will be clear that the manufacturer bears the slow movement risk. The manufacturer will bear the slow movement risk wherever the transfer price is not determined by reference to the length of time for which stock is held (such as where the transfer price is the manufacturer's list price at either delivery or transfer of legal title). Conversely, if in the same basic arrangement, the price to be paid by the dealer increases by a factor that varies with the time the stock is held and approximates to commercial interest rates, then it will be equally clear that the dealer bears the slow movement risk. This may be so even where the financing element of the price charged to the dealer is based on average past movements of stocks held by that dealer (e.g. for administrative convenience), or is levied in another form (e.g. a display charge).

A9 The existence of a deposit complicates the analysis. The main question to be answered is whether the effect of the deposit is that the dealer, rather than the manufacturer, bears variations in the stock financing costs that are due to slow movement. For example, this could be achieved by a substantial, interest-free deposit whose amount is related to levels of stock held by the dealer. Alternatively, a finance company might advance the deposit to the manufacturer and charge interest thereon (in whatever form) to the dealer.

Dealer's right to use the stock (benefit (iii))

A10 Whilst a right for the dealer to use the stock in its business will not, of itself, be sufficient to make the stock an asset of the dealer, the exercise of the right will usually have this effect. Such exercise will usually cause the transfer of legal title to the dealer and give rise to an unconditional obligation for it to pay the manufacturer.

Required accounting

Substance of the transaction is that the stock is an asset of the dealer

A11 Where it is concluded that the stock is in substance an asset of the dealer, the stock should be recognised as such on the dealer's balance sheet together with a corresponding liability to the manufacturer. Any deposit should be deducted from the liability and the excess classified as a trade creditor. The notes to the financial statements should explain the nature of the arrangement, the amount of consignment stock included in the balance sheet and the main terms under which it is held, including the terms of any deposit.

Substance of the transaction is that the stock is not an asset of the dealer

A12 Where it is concluded that the stock is not in substance an asset of the dealer, the stock should not be included on the dealer's balance sheet until the transfer of title has crystallised. Any deposit should be included under 'other debtrors'. The notes to the financial statements should explain the nature of the arrangement, the amount of consignment stock held at the year-end, and the main terms under which it is held, including the terms of any deposit.

Table

Indications that the stock is not an asset of the dealer at delivery	Indications that the stock is an asset of the dealer at delivery
Manufacturer can require the dealer to return stock (or transfer stock to another dealer) without compensation; or Penalty paid by the dealer to prevent returns/transfers of stock at the manufacturer's request.	Manufacturer cannot require dealer to return stock or transfer stock; or Financial incentives given to persuade dealer to transfer stock at manufacturer's request.
Dealer has unfettered right to return stock to the manufacturer without penalty and actually exercises the right in practice.	Dealer has no right to return stock or is commercially compelled not to exercise its right of return.
Manufacturer bears obsolescence risk. e.g. — obsolete stock is returned to the manufacturer without penalty; or — financial incentives given by manufacturer to prevent stock being returned to it (e.g. on a model change or if it becomes obsolete).	Dealer bears obsolescence risk, e.g. — penalty charged if dealer returns stock to manufacturer; or — obsolete stock cannot be returned to the manufacturer and no compensation is paid by manufacturer for losses due to obsolescence.
Stock transfer price charged by manufacturer is based on manufacturer's list price at date of transfer of legal title. Manufacturer bears slow movement risk, e.g. — transfer price set independently of time for which dealer holds stock and there is no deposit.	Stock transfer price charged by manufacturer is based on manufacturer's list price at date of delivery. Dealer bears slow movement risk. e.g. — dealer is effectively charged interest as transfer price or other payments to manufacturer vary with time for which dealer holds stock; or — dealer makes a substantial interest-free deposit that varies with the levels of stock held.

Application Note B — Sale and repurchase agreements

NB For ease of reading the parties to a sale and repurchase agreement are referred to below as 'seller' and 'buyer', notwithstanding that analysis of the transaction in accordance with this Application Note may result in the seller continuing to show an asset on its balance sheet.

Features

B1 Sale and repurchase agreements are arrangements under which assets are sold by one party to another on terms that provide for the seller to repurchase the asset in certain circumstances. A similar commercial effect may be achieved by arrangements under which one party holds an asset on behalf of another: although such arrangements are not sale and repurchase agreements, a similar analysis is appropriate and these are therefore covered by this Application Note.

B2 The main features of a sale and repurchase agreement will usually be:

(a) The sale price — this may be market value or another agreed price (analysed in paragraph B9)

(b) The nature of the repurchase provision — this may be: an unconditional commitment for both parties; an option for the seller to repurchase (a call option); an option for the buyer to resell to the seller (a put option); or a combination of put and call options; (analysed in paragraphs B10-B12)

(c) The repurchase price — this may: be fixed at the outset; vary with the period for which the asset is held by the buyer; or be the market price at the time of repurchase. It may also be designed to permit the buyer to recover incidental holding costs (e.g. insurance) if these do not in fact continue to be met by the seller; (analysed in paragraphs B13-B14); and

(d) Other provisions, including where appropriate: for the seller to use the asset whilst it is owned by the buyer; for determining the time of repurchase; or for remarketing the asset if it is to be sold to a third party; (analysed in paragraphs B15-B18).

Analysis

Overview of basic principles

B3 The purpose of the analysis is to determine both whether the seller has an asset (and what is the nature of that asset), and whether the seller has a liability to repay the buyer some or all of the amounts received from the latter.

B4 In a straightforward case, the substance of a sale and repurchase agreement will be that of a secured loan — i.e. the seller will retain all significant rights to benefits relating to the original asset and all significant exposure to the risks inherent in those benefits and will have a liability to the buyer for the whole of the proceeds received. For example, this would be the case where the seller has in effect an unconditional commitment to repurchase the original asset from the buyer at the sale price plus interest. The seller should account for this type of arrangement by showing the original asset on its balance sheet together with a liability for the amounts received from the buyer.

B5 In certain more complex cases, it may be determined that a sale and repurchase agreement is not in substance a financing transaction and that the seller retains access to only some of the benefits of the original asset and retains only some of their inherent risks. Where this is so, in accordance with paragraph 23, the description or monetary amount of the original asset should be changed and a liability recognised for any obligation to transfer benefits that is assumed. It will also be necessary to give full disclosure of these more complex arrangements in the notes to the financial statements.

B6 The substance of the arrangement may be more readily apparent if the position of both buyer and seller are considered, together with their apparent expectations and motives for agreeing to its various terms. In particular, where the substance is that of a secured loan, the buyer will require that it is assured of a lender's return on its investment and the seller will require that the buyer earns no more than this return. Thus whether or not the buyer earns such a return is an important indicator of the substance of the transaction.

Benefits and risks

B7 The analysis that follows shows how the features set out in paragraph B2 may result in the seller having a liability to the buyer or in the seller retaining rights to some or all of the benefits of the original asset and exposure to some or all of the risks inherent in those benefits. These benefits and risks will usually include some or all of the following:

Benefits

(i) The benefit of any expected increase in the value of the asset; and

(ii) Benefits arising from use or development of the asset.

Risks:

(i) The risk of an unexpected variation (adverse or favourable) in the value of the asset;

(ii) The risk of obsolescence; and

(iii) Where repurchase is not at a set date, the risk of a variation in the cost of financing the asset because of the variable period between sale and repurchase.

B8 In analysing any specific agreement in practice, it will be necessary to look at all the features of the agreement and give greater weight to those that are more likely to have a commercial effect in practice. In addition, it will be necessary to consider the interaction between the features in order to determine the substance of the arrangement as a whole.

Feature (a) — Sale price

B9 A sale price of other than the market value of the asset at the time of sale indicates that some benefit and risk have been retained by the seller, such that the seller has an asset (either the original asset or a new one) or a liability to the buyer. Even where the sale price is the asset's market value, the seller may nevertheless have an asset or a liability since the other terms of the arrangement may result in the seller retaining significant benefits and risks.

Feature (b) — Nature of repurchase provision

1. Commitment

B10 Any type of unconditional commitment for the seller to repurchase will give rise to both a liability and an asset for the seller: the liability being the seller's commitment to pay the repurchase price; and the asset being continued access to some or all of the benefits of the original asset that forms the subject of the sale and repurchase agreement. The price at which repurchase will occur and the other provisions of the arrangement will determine the exact nature of the seller's asset; these are dealt with in paragraphs B13-B18 below.

B11 There may in effect be a commitment to repurchase even without a strict legal obligation. In particular, this will be the case where there is an option (or a combination of options) on terms that leave no genuine commercial possibility that the option will fail to be exercised. For example, the exercise price of a call option may be set at a significant discount to expected market value, the seller may need the asset to use on an ongoing basis in its business, or the asset may provide in effect the only source of the seller's future sales. Unwritten understandings between the parties may also result in a commercial commitment for the seller to repurchase even in the absence of a strict legal obligation. Such a commitment is more likely to exist where the buyer's business does not usually involve it in taking on risks of a kind associated with the asset.

2. Put and call options

B12 In some cases the seller may have a call option to repurchase the asset but have no commitment to do so, or the buyer may have a put option to transfer the asset back to the seller without the seller having an equivalent right to insist on repurchase. It will be important to determine why the parties have agreed to such a one-sided option and to assess the commercial effect of the option with regard to all aspects of the arrangement, including whether the seller has a commercial need to repurchase the asset. This analysis may reveal that, in substance, there is a commitment to repurchase as discussed above. Conversely, such an analysis may reveal that the buyer assumes significant benefits and risks relating to the original asset, indicating that the seller has neither the original asset, nor a liability for the option's exercise price. In such a case, where the seller holds a call option it will have a new asset in the form of the option itself; where the buyer has a put option, the seller will have a contingent liability to the buyer for the exercise price of the option (contingent on the buyer exercising its option). In both cases, the seller's new asset or liability should be recognised or disclosed, on a prudent basis, following the principles set out in SSAP 18 'Accounting for contingencies'.

Feature (c) — Repurchase price and provision for a lender's return

B13 In the most straightforward case, the repurchase price will be the sum of the original sale price, plus any major costs incurred by the buyer and a lender's return (comprising interest on the sale price and costs incurred by the buyer, perhaps with a relatively small fee), but no more. In this case, even if the repurchase provision takes the form of an option, the repurchase price indicates that the substance of the transaction is that of a secured loan, with the benefits and risks of the asset remaining with the seller. This is because the buyer is not compensated for assuming any significant exposure to loss, nor is the seller compensated for giving up any significant potential for gain, thus indicating that the transaction is, in substance, a financing. It will be necessary to look at the arrangement as a whole to establish whether the buyer receives a lender's return since the means of providing it will vary. For example, it may be achieved by lease or other regular payments, licence fees, adjustment to the original sales price or the calculation of the repurchase price.

B14 Conversely, if the buyer is not assured of a lender's return, this indicates that some benefit and risk have been passed to the buyer such that the seller has not retained the original asset. The seller may, nevertheless, have a different asset (and a corresponding liability). For example, if a manufacturer sells equipment but agrees to repurchase it in a substantially different form towards the end of its economic life, the manufacturer has both a liability (to pay the repurchase price) and an asset (the equipment as at the repurchase date).

Feature (d) — Other provisions

1. Ability to use the asset

B15 Whilst the ability of the seller to determine the use of the original asset does not, of itself, result in the substance of the transaction being that of a secured loan, it will usually indicate this is so. Continued use of the asset by the seller may indicate that it has a commercial obligation to repurchase even if it has no legal obligation to do so, for instance if there is a commercial need for the seller to repurchase or an expectation that it will do so.

B16 Where the seller continues to use the asset in its business by entering into a sale and leaseback transaction, the provisions of both SSAP 2 I 'Accounting for leases and hire purchase contracts' and this Application Note will be relevant. Where, in the terms of this Application Note, the substance of the transaction is that of a secured loan, it will be structured so that no significant benefits or risks are passed to the buyer, with the rentals and other lease payments providing the buyer with a lender's return. Thus, in the terms of SSAP 2I, 'substantially all the risks and rewards of ownership' of the asset will remain with the seller, the leaseback will be classified as a finance lease, and the transaction will be accounted for as the raising of finance secured on the asset. If, on the other hand, the leaseback is in substance an operating lease, the transaction will be accounted for as a sale of the original asset.

2. Profits or losses on a sale of the asset to a third party

B17 In some cases, the seller may retain access to any increase in the value of the asset via provisions that pass to it substantially all of any profit arising on a sale by the first buyer to a third party (subject to the buyer receiving a lender's return). In addition the buyer may be protected from risk of loss, for instance by the seller being obliged to reimburse the whole or part of any loss on a sale to a third party, or the original sale price being such that losses are unlikely to occur in practice. The substance of such an arrangement is that of a secured loan.

3. Use of special entities ('vehicles')

B18 Some cases may involve a sale to a special entity (a 'vehicle') that is partly or wholly financed by a party other than the seller (e.g. a financial institution). In such a case, the seller will usually retain access to any increase in the value of the asset and, where relevant, the benefits from its use, via a right either to repurchase the asset or, in the event that the seller does not repurchase, to receive the majority of any profits from a future sale to a third party. In addition, the seller may provide protection against loss to the other investors in the vehicle, e.g. by providing a subordinated loan to the vehicle that acts as a cushion to absorb any losses or by guaranteeing the value of the asset in the event that it is sold on to a third party. Such provisions are clear indications that the substance of the transaction is that of a secured loan. Where the terms of the arrangement taken as a whole mean that the investors in the vehicle are reasonably assured of recovering their original investment and earning a lender's return (but no more) thereon, the substance of the transaction will be that of a secured loan.

Required accounting

Substance of the transaction is that of a secured loan

B19 Where the substance of the transaction is that of a secured loan, the seller should continue to recognise the original asset and record the proceeds received from the buyer as a liability. Interest — however designated — should be accrued. The carrying amount of the asset should be reviewed and provided against if necessary. The notes to the financial statements should describe the principal features of the arrangement, including the status of the asset and the relationship between the asset and liability.

B20 Where the transaction is a sale and leaseback, no profit should be recognised on entering into the arrangement and no adjustment made to the carrying value of the asset. As stated in the guidance notes to SSAP 2 I, this represents the substance of the transaction, "namely the raising of finance secured on an asset that continues to be held and that is not disposed of".

Substance of the transaction is that the seller has a different asset

B21 Where the seller has a new asset or liability (for example, merely a call option to repurchase the original asset), it should recognise or disclose that new asset or liability on a prudent basis in accordance with the provisions of SSAP 18. In particular, the seller should recognise (and not merely disclose) a liability for any kind of unconditional obligation it has entered into. Where doubts exist regarding the amount of any gain or loss arising, full provision should be made for any expected loss but recognition of any gain, to the extent that it is in doubt, should be deferred until it is realised. The notes to the financial statements should describe the main features of the arrangement, including: the status of the asset; the relationship between the asset and the liability; and the terms of any provision for repurchase (including any options) and of any guarantees.

Table

Indications of sale of original asset to buyer (nevertheless, the seller may retain a different asset)	Indications of no sale of original asset to buyer (secured loan)
	Sale price does not equal market value at date of sale.
No commitment for seller to repurchase asset. e.g. — Call option where there is a real possbility the option will fail to be exercised.	Commitment for seller to repurchase asset, e.g. — Put and call option with the same exercise price; — Either a put or a call option wlth no genuine commercial possiblilty that the option will fail to be exercised; or — Seller requires asset back to use in its business or asset is in effect the only source of seller's future sales.
Risk of changes in asset value borne by buyer such that buyer does not receive solely a lender's return e.g. — Both sale and repuchase price equal market value at date of sale/repurchase.	Risk of changes in asset value borne by seller such that buyer receives solely a lender's return. e.g. — Repurchase price equals sale price plus costs plus interest — Original purchase price adjusted retrospectively to pass variations in the value of the asset to the seller: — Seller provides residual value guarantee to buyer or subordinated debt to protect buyer from falls in the value of the asset.
Nature of the asset is such that it will be used over the life of the agreement, and seller has no rights to determine its use. Seller has no rights to determine asset's development or future sale.	Seller retains right to determine asset's use, development or sale, or rights to profits therefrom.

Illustrations

Illustration 1

A, a house-builder, agrees with B, a bank, to sell to B some of the land within its land bank. The arrangements surrounding the sale are as follows:

(a) the sales price will be open market value as determined by an independent surveyor;

(b) B grants A the right to develop the land at any time during B's ownership, subject to its approval of the development plans, which approval shall not be unreasonably withheld; for this right, A pays all the outgoings on the land plus an annual fee of 5 per cent of the purchase price;

(c) B will maintain a memorandum account in respect of the land for the purpose of determining the price to be paid by A should A ever re-acquire the land or any adjustments necessary to the original purchase price. In this account will be entered the purchase price, any expenses incurred by B in relation to the transaction, a sum added quarterly (or on the sale by B of the land) calculated by referencc to B's base lending rate plus 2 per cent applied to the daily balance on the account; and from the account will be deducted any annual fees paid by A to B;

(d) B grants A an option to acquire thc land at any time within the next five years; the acquisition price is to be the balance on the memorandurn account at the time of exercising the option;

(e) A grants B an option to require it to repurchase the land at any time within the next five years, the price to be the balance on the memorandum account at that time;

(f) on the expiry of five years from the date of acquiring the land, B will offer it for sale generally; and at any time prior to that it may with the consent of A offer the land for sale; and

(g) in the event of B selling the land to a third party, the proceeds of sale shall be deducted from the memorandum account maintained by B and the balance on the account shall be settled between A and B in cash, as a retrospective adjustment of the price at which B originally purchased the land from A.

The commercial effect of the above arrangement is that of a secured loan. A continues to bear all significant benefits and risks relating to the land, retains control of its development, and bears all resulting gains and losses (via either exercise of its call option, or adjustment to the purchase price on sale of the land to a third party). This latter feature also gives rise to a liability for A to repay the whole of the sale proceeds received from B. In addition, B is assured of a lender's return (and no more): whilst the regular payments by A to B to secure the right to develop the land are not sufficient to provide this, B's return is guaranteed through the operation of the memorandum account and its role in determming the option price on a resale.

Illustration 2

This illustration is similar to the first but makes use of V, a vehicle company, and a subordinated loan to effect the purchase. A agrees wiith B (the bank) and V to sell land within its land bank to V. Relevant terms are as follows:

(a) the sale price is open market value;

(b) B grants V a loan of 60 per cent of the market value to effect the purchase, with A providing V with a subordinated loan of the balance of the consideration. B's loan bears interest at the bank's base rate plus 2 per cent: A's loan bears interest at 10 per cent. All payments of interest and capital; on A's loan are subordinated to all sums due to B in any period;

c) V grants A the right to develop the land at any time during V's ownership, subject to its approval. For this right, A pays V a market rental on the land. If this is less than the interest payable on V's loan from B, then A will advance the amount of the shortfall as an addition to its subordinated loan;

(d) V grants A an option to acquire the land at any time within the next five years, at a price equal to the original sales price plus any incidental costs incurred by V;

(e) on the expiry of five years from the date of acquiring the land, V will offer it for sale generally, and at any time before then may with the consent of A offer the land for sale; and

(f) in the event of V selling the land, to the extent that the proceeds of sale and any other cash accumulated in V exceed any sums due to B and A under the terms of their respective loans, an immediate payment shall be made to A as a retrospective adjustment of the price at which V originally purchased the land from A.

In this illustration, the substance of the transaction is that of a secured loan. A continues to bear all significant benefits and risks relating to the land, it continues to have the ability to develop it and access to the whole of any profits from its future sale. In addition, the subordinated loan from A provides a cushion to absorb losses on the disposal of the land by the vehicle; this ensures that all foreseeable losses accrue to A and thus protects the position of the bank. In practice, such subordinated loans are often sufficiently large to make any loss by the bank through a loss in value of the land extremely remote. Where this is not the case or there is no subordinated loan, the necessary protection may be provided through put options — such as are incorporated within Illustration I — which enable the buyer to require the seller to repurchase the asset. Where the substance of the transaction is that of a secured loan, the buyer will require that the terms of the arrangement taken as a whole mean it is reasonably assured of receiving return of the purchase price and any costs it incurs plus a lender's return (but no more) on its investment.

Application Note C — Factoring of debts

NB For ease of reading the parties to a factoring agreement are referred to in this Application Note as 'seller' and 'factor', notwithstanding that analysis of the transaction in accordance with this Application Note may result in the seller continuing to show the factored debts as an asset on its balance sheet.

Features

C1 Factoring of debts is a well established method of obtaining finance, sales ledger administration services, or protection from bad debts. The principal features of a factoring arrangement are as follows:

(a) Specified debts are transferred to the factor (usually by assignment). The transfer may be of complete debtor balances or of all invoices relating to named debtors (perhaps subject to restrictions on the amount that will be accepted from any one debtor).

(b) The factor offers a credit facility that permits the seller to draw up to a fixed percentage of the face value of the debts transferred. Normally these advances are repaid as and when the underlying debts are collected, often by paying the money that is collected into a specially nominated bank account for the benefit of the factor.

(c) The factor may also offer a credit protection facility (or insurance cover). This will limit or eliminate the extent to which the factor has recourse to the seller for debts that are in default.

(d) The factor may administer the sales ledger of the seller. Where such a service is provided, the factor becomes responsible for collecting money from debtors and pursuing those that are slow in paying. In such cases the fact that debts have been factored is likely to be disclosed to the seller's customers; this may not be necessary in other circumstances.

C2 On the transfer of debts, the factoring charges levied on the seller will be set by the factor with reference to expected collections from the debtors and any credit protection services provided (sales ledger administration services are usually invoiced separately). These charges may be fixed at the outset or subject to adjustment at a later date to reflect actual collections; they may be payable immediately or on some future date.

Analysis

Overview of basic principles

C3 The purpose of the analysis below is to determine the appropriate accounting treatment in the seller's financial statements. There are three possible treatments:

(a) to remove the factored debts from the balance sheet and show no liability in respect of any proceeds received from the factor ('derecognition');

(b) to show the proceeds received from the factor deducted from the factored debts on the face of the balance sheet within a single asset caption (a 'linked presentation'); or

(c) to continue to show the factored debts as an asset, and show a corresponding liability within creditors in respect of the proceeds received from the factor (a 'separate presentation').

C4 In order to determine the appropriate accounting treatment, it is necessary to answer two questions:

(a) whether the seller has access to the benefits of the factored debts and exposure to the risks inherent in those benefits (referred to below as 'benefits and risks'); and

(b) whether the seller has a liability to repay amounts received from the factor.

Where the seller has transferred all significant benefits and all significant risks relating to the debts, and has no obligation to repay the factor, derecognition is appropriate; where the seller has retained significant benefits and risks relating to the debts but there is absolutely no doubt that its downside exposure to loss is limited, a linked presentation should be used; and in all other cases a separate presentation should be adopted.

Benefits and risks

C5 The main benefits and risks relating to debts are as follows:

Benefits:

(i) the future cash flows from payment by the debtors.

Risks:

(i) slow payment risk; and

(ii) credit risk (the risk of bad debts).

Analysis of benefits

C6 At first glance it may appear that the factor has access to the cash flows from payments by debtors. This may be particularly so if the money that is collected is to be paid direct to the factor (or into a specially nominated bank account for its benefit). However, it may actually be the seller that benefits from payments by debtors, these payments merely representing the primary source from which the factor will be repaid. In particular, where the seller has an obligation to repay any sums received from the factor on or before a set date regardless of the level of collections from the underlying debts, it is clear that the seller has the benefit of payments by debtors, exposure to their inherent risks and a liability to the factor. Such an arrangement should be accounted for by using a separate presentation. Conversely, where the seller receives a single non-returnable cash payment from the factor and the only future payments to be made are by the seller passing to the factor all and any payments from debtors as and when paid, the seller will both have transferred the benefits and risks of the factored debts and have no obligation to repay amounts received from the factor. This latter arrangement would qualify for derecognition.

C7 Considering the benefits in isolation will not normally enable a clear decision to be made on the appropriate accounting treatment for a factoring. The cash flows may appear similar in both of the above arrangements — an initial cash inflow for the seller followed by a later cash outflow (or a sacrifice of a cash inflow that would otherwise occur). For this reason, the risks (both upside potential for gain and downside exposure to loss) are more significant than the benefits.

Slow payment risk: credit facility

C8 The first main risk associated with non-interest bearing debts is slow payment risk (including the upside potential from prompt payment by debtors). Where the finance cost charged by the factor is essentially a fixed sum determined at the time the transfer is made, the factor will bear the risk of slow payment; where it varies to reflect the speed of collection of the debts subsequently, the seller will bear that risk. Close attention to the arrangements and to their commercial effect in practice may be necessary to determine whether a variable finance cost falls upon the seller since it may take various forms, including a bonus for early settlement, or a retrospective adjustment to the purchase price.

Credit risk: credit protection facility

C9 Credit risk is the other main risk associated with trade debts. If there is no recourse to the seller for bad debts, the factor will bear this risk; if there is full recourse, the seller will bear it. Furthermore, as non-payment is merely the ultimate form of slow payment, where credit risk is retained by the seller, the latter will normally also bear at least some risk of slow payment. For example, where the arrangement takes the form of the seller repurchasing debts that remain outstanding after a given time, the seller bears the slow payment risk beyond this time as well as bearing the credit risk.

Administration arrangments and service-only factoring

C10 For the purpose of deciding upon the appropriate accounting treatment, the administration arrangements will not be directly significant (provided they are on an arm's length basis, and for a fee that is commensurate with the service provided). In a service-only factoring arrangement, where the factor administers the sales ledger but cash is received no earlier than if the debts had not been factored, the seller retains access to the benefits of the debts and exposure to their inherent risks. Thus such an arrangement should be accounted for by using a separate presentation.

Derecognition

C11 Derecognition (i.e. ceasing to recognise the factored debts in their entirety) is appropriate only where the seller retains no significant benefits and no significant risks relating to the factored debts.

C12 Whilst the commercial effect of any particular transaction should be assessed taking into account all its aspects and implications, the presence of all of the following indicates that the seller has not retained significant benefits and risks, and derecognition is appropriate:

(a) the transaction takes place at an arm's length price for an outright sale;

(b) the transaction is for a fixed amount of consideration and there is no recourse whatsoever, either implicit or explicit, to the seller for losses from either slow payment or non-payment. Normal warranties given in respect of the condition of the debts at the time of the transfer (e.g. a warranty that goods have been delivered or that the borrower's credit limit had not been breached at the time of granting him credit) would not breach this condition. However, warranties relating to the condition of the debts in the future or to their future performance (e.g. that debtors will not move into arrears in the future) would breach the condition. Other possible forms of recourse are set out in paragraph 83; and

(c) the seller will not benefit or suffer in any way if the debts perform better or worse than expected. This will not be the case where the seller has a right to further sums from the factor which vary according to the future performance of the debts (i.e. according to whether or when the debtors pay). Such sums might take the form of deferred consideration, a retrospective adjustment to the purchase price, or rebates of certain charges; they include all forms of variable finance cost.

C13 Where any of the above three features is not present this indicates that the seller has retained benefits and risks relating to the factored debts and, unless these are insignificant, either a separate presentation or a linked presentation should be adopted.

C14 Whether any benefit and risk retained are 'significant' should be judged in relation to those benefits and risks that are likely to occur in practice, and not in relation to the total possible benefits and risks. For example, if for a portfolio of factored debts of 100, expected bad debts are 5 and there is recourse to the seller for credit losses of up to 10, significant risk will have been retained (as the seller would bear losses of up to twice those expected to occur). Accordingly, in this example, derecognition would not be appropriate and either a linked presentation or a separate presentation should be used. The terms of any roll-over provisions and their effect in practice require careful consideration since these may result in the seller continuing to bear significant risk where, at first sight, it appears that the arrangements do not have this effect. For example, the pricing of future transfers may be adjusted to reflect recent slow payment or bad debt experience and there may be a significant disincentive (e.g. a penalty) for the seller to cancel the arrangement. This may result in the seller continuing to bear significant risk, albeit disguised as revised charges for debts factored subsequently.

Linked presentation

C15 A linked presentation will be appropriate where, although the seller has retained significant benefits and risks relating to the factored debts, there is absolutely no doubt that its downside exposure to loss is limited to a fixed monetary amount. A linked presentation should be used only to the extent that there is both absolutely no doubt that the factor's claim extends solely to collections from the factored debts, and no provision for the seller to re-acquire the debts in the future. The conditions that need to be met in order for this to be the case are set out in paragraph 27 and explained in paragraphs 81-86. When interpreting these conditions in the context of a factoring arrangement the following points apply:

condition (a) (specified assets) —

> a linked presentation should not be used where the debts that have been factored cannot be separately identified.

condition (d) (that the factor agrees in writing there is no recourse, and such agreement is noted in the financial statements) —

> the inclusion of an appropriate statement in the factoring agreement will meet the first part of this condition.

C16 Where debts are factored on an ongoing basis, the arrangements for terminating the agreement must be carefully analysed in order to ensure that the conditions for a linked presentation are met. It will be necessary that, although the factor does not take on any new debts, it continues to bear losses on debts already factored and is not able to transfer them back to the seller. Where this is not the case, there remains the possibility that the factor will return debts that it suspects to be bad by terminating the arrangement. In such a case the seller's exposure to loss is not limited, and a separate presentation should be adopted.

Separate presentation

C17 Where the seller has retained significant benefits and risks relating to the debts and the conditions for a linked presentation are not met, a separate presentation should be adopted.

Required accounting

Derecognition

C18 Where the seller has retained no significant benefits and risks relating to the debts and has no obligation to repay amounts received from the factor, the debts should be removed from its balance sheet and no liability shown in respect of the proceeds received from the factor. A profit or loss should be recognised, calculated as the difference between the carrying amount of the debts and the proceeds received.

Linked presentation

C19 Where the conditions for a linked presentation are met, the proceeds received, to the extent they are non-returnable, should be shown deducted from the gross amount of the factored debts (after providing for bad debts, credit protection charges and any accrued interest) on the face of the balance sheet. An example is given in illustration 2 below. The interest element of the factor's charges should be recognised as it accrues and included in the profit and loss account with other interest charges. The notes to the financial statements should disclose: the main terms of the arrangement; the gross amount of factored debts outstanding at the balance sheet date; the factoring charges recognised in the period, analysed as appropriate (eg between interest and other charges); and the disclosures required by conditions (c) and (d) in paragraph 27.

Separate presentation

C20 Where neither derecognition nor a linked presentation is appropriate, a separate presentation should be adopted, i.e. a gross asset (equivalent in amount to the gross amount of the debts) should be shown on the balance sheet of the seller within assets, and a corresponding liability in respect of the proceeds received from the factor should be shown within liabilities. The interest element of the factor's charges should be recognised as it accrues and included in the profit and loss account with other interest charges. Other factoring costs should be similarly accrued and included in the profit and loss account within the appropriate caption. The notes to the financial statements should disclose the amount of factored debts outstanding at the balance sheet date.

Table

Indication that derecognition is appropriate (debts are not an asset of the seller)	Indications that a linked presentation is appropriate	Indications that a separate presentation is appropriate (debts are an asset of the seller)
Transfer is for a single, non-returnable fixed sum.	Some non-returnable proceeds received, but seller has rights to further sums from the factor (or vice versa) whose amount depends on whether or when debtors pay.	Finance cost varies with speed of collection of debts, e.g. — by adjustment to consideration for original transfer; or — subsequent transfers priced to recover costs of earlier transfers.
There is no recourse to the seller for losses.	There is either no recourse for losses, or such recourse has a fixed monetary ceiling.	There is full recourse to the seller for losses.
Factor is paid all amounts received from the factored debts (and no more). Seller has no rights to further sums from the factor.	Factor is paid only out of amounts collected from the factored debts, and seller has no right or obligation to repurchase debts.	Seller is required to repay amounts received from the factor on or before a set date, regardless of timing or amounts of collections from debtors.

Illustration 1 — Factoring with recourse (separate presentation)

Company S enters into a factoring arrangement with F, with the following principal terms:

(a) S will transfer (by assignment) all its trade debts to F, subject only to credit approval by F and a limit placed on the proportion of the total that may be due from any one debtor;

(b) F administers S's sales ledger and handles all aspects of collection of the debts in return for an administration charge at an annual rate of 1 per cent, payable monthly, based upon the total debts factored at each month-end;

(c) S may draw up to 70 per cent of the gross amount of debts factored and outstanding at any time, such drawings being debited in the books of F to a factoring account operated by F for S;

(d) weekly, S assigns and sends copy invoices to F as they are raised. F sends statements to debtors, following up all overdue invoices by telephone or letter;

(e) F credits collections from debtors to the factoring account, and debits the account monthly with interest calculated on the basis of the daily balances on the account using a rate of base rate plus 2 per cent. Thus this interest charge varies with the amount of finance drawn by S under the finance facility from F, the speed of payment of the debtors and base rate;

(f) any debts not recovered after 90 days are reassigned to S for an immediate cash payment, which is credited to the factoring account;

(g) F pays for all other debts, less any advances and interest charges made, 90 days after the date of their assignment to F, and debits the payment to the factoring account; and

(h) on termination of the agreement the balance on the factoring account is settled in cash.

The commercial effect of the above arrangements is that, although the debts have been legally transferred to F, the benefits and risks are retained by S. S continues to bear the slow payment risk as the interest charged by F varies with the speed of payment by the debtors; S continues to bear all of the credit risk as it must pay for any debts not recovered after 90 days, and it therefore has unlimited exposure to loss. In addition, S in effect has an obligation to repay amounts received from F on or before a set date regardless of the levels of collections from the factored debts — either out of collections from debtors on the day they pay, or from its general resources after 90 days, whichever is the earlier. Thus a separate presentation should be adopted.

Illustration 2 — Factoring without recourse (linked presentation)

S enters into an agreement with F with the following principal terms:

(a) S will transfer (by assignment) to F such trade debts as S shall determine, subject only to credit approval by F and a limit placed on the proportion of the total that may be due from any one debtor. F levies a charge of 0.15 per cent of turnover, payable monthly, for this facility;

(b) S continues to administer the sales ledger and handle all aspects of collection of the debts;

(c) S may draw up to 80 per cent of the gross amount of debts assigned at any time, such drawings being debited in the books of F to a factoring account operated by F for S;

(d) weekly, S assigns and sends copy invoices to F as they are raised;

(e) S is required to bank the gross amounts of all payments received from debts assigned to F direct into an account in the name of F. Credit transfers made by debtors direct into S's own bank account must immediately be paid to F;

(f) F credits such collections from debtors to the factoring account, and debits the account monthly with interest calculated on the basis of the daily balances on the account using a rate of base rate plus 2.5 per cent. Thus this interest charge varies with the amount of finance drawn by S under the finance facility from F, the speed of payment of the debtors and base rate;

(g) F provides protection from bad debts. Any debts not recovered after 90 days are credited to the factoring account, and responsibility for their collection is passed to F. A charge of 1 per cent of the gross value of all debts factored is levied by F for this service and debited to the factoring account;

(h) F pays for the debts, less any advances, interest charges and credit protection charges, 90 days after the date of purchase, and debits the payment to the factoring account; and

(i) on either party giving 90 days' notice to the other, the arrangement will be terminated. In such an event, S will transfer no further debts to F, and the balance remaining on the factoring account at the end of the notice period will be settled in cash in the normal way.

The commercial effect of this arrangement is that, although the debts have been legally transferred to F, S continues to bear significant benefits and risks relating to them. S continues to bear slow payment risk as the interest charged by F varies with the speed of collections of the debts. Hence, the gross amount of the debts should continue to be shown on its balance sheet until the earlier of collection and transfer of all risks to F (i.e. 90 days). However, S's maximum downside loss is limited since any debts not recovered after 90 days are in effect paid for by F, which then assumes all slow payment and credit risk beyond this time. Thus, even for debts that prove to be bad, S receives some proceeds.* Hence, assuming the conditions given in paragraphs 26 and 27 are met, a linked presentation should be adopted. The amount deducted on the face of the balance sheet should be the lower of the proceeds received and the gross amount of the debts less all charges to the factor in respect of them. In the above example, for a debt of 100 this latter amount would be calculated as 100 less the credit protection fee of 1 and the maximum finance charge (calculated for 90 days at base rate plus 2.5 per cent). Assuming the proceeds received of 80 are lower than this, and accrued interest charges at the year-end are 2, the arrangement would be shown as follows:

*For a debt of 100 that subsequently proves to be bad, the proceeds received would be 100, less the credit protection fee of 1, less an interest charge calculated for 90 days at base rate plus 2.5%.

Current Assets		
Stock		x
Debts factored without recourse:		
Gross debts (after providing for credit protection fee and accrued interest)	97	
less: non-returnable proceeds	(80)	
		17
Other debtors		x

In addition, the non-returnable proceeds of 80 would be included within cash and the profit and loss account would include both the credit protection expense of 1 and the accrued interest charges of 2.

Application Note D — Securitsed assets

Features

D1 Securitisation is a means by which providers of finance fund a specific block of assets rather than the general business of a company. The assets that have been most commonly securitised in the UK are household mortgages. Other receivables such as credit card balances, hire purchase loans and trade debts are sometimes securitised, as are non-monetary assets such as property and stocks. This Application Note applies to all kinds of assets.

D2 The main features are generally as follows:

(a) The assets to be securitised are transferred by a company (the 'originator') to a special purpose vehicle (the 'issuer') in return for an immediate cash payment. Additional deferred consideration may also be payable.

(b) The issuer finances the transfer by the issue of debt, usually tradeable loan notes or commercial paper (referred to below as 'loan notes'). The issuer is usually thinly capitalised and its shares placed with a party other than the originator charitable trusts have often been used for this purpose — with the result that the issuer is not classified as a subsidiary of the originator under companies legislation. In addition, the major financial and operating policies of the issuer are usually predetermined by the agreements that constitute the securitisation, such that neither the owner of its share capital nor the originator has any significant continuing discretion over how it is run.

(c) Arrangements are made to protect the loan noteholders from losses occurring on the assets by a process termed 'credit enhancement'. This may take the form of third party insurance, a third party guarantee of the issuer's obligations or an issue of subordinated debt (perhaps to the originator); all provide a cushion against losses up to a fixed amount.

(d) The originator is granted rights to surplus income (and, where relevant, capital profits) from the assets — i.e. to cash remaining after payment of amounts due on the loan notes and other expenses of the issuer. The mechanisms used to achieve this include: servicing or other fees; deferred sale consideration; 'super interest' on amounts owed to the originator (e.g. subordinated debt); dividend payments; and swap payments.

(e) In the case of securitised debts; the originator may continue to service the debts (i.e. to collect amounts due from borrowers, set interest rates etc.). In this capacity it is referred to as the 'servicer' and receives a servicing fee.

(f) Cash accumulations from the assets (e.g. from mortgage redemptions) are reinvested by the issuer until loan notes are repaid. Any difference between the interest rate obtained on reinvestments and that payable on the loan notes will normally affect the originator's surplus under (d) above. The terms of the loan notes may provide for them to be redeemed as assets are realised, thus minimising this reinvestment period. Alternatively, cash accumulations may be invested in a 'guaranteed investment contract' that pays a guaranteed rate of interest (which may be determined by reference to a variable benchmark rate such as LIBOR) sufficient to meet interest payments on the loan notes. Another alternative, used particularly for short-term debts arising under a facility (e.g. credit card balances), is a provision for cash receipts (here from card repayments) to be reinvested in similar assets (e.g. new balances on the same credit card accounts). This reinvestment in similar assets will occur for a specified period only, after which time cash accumulations will either be used to redeem loan notes or be reinvested in other more liquid assets until loan notes are repaid.

(g) In certain circumstances, for example if tax changes affect the payment of interest to the noteholders or if the principal amount of loan notes outstanding declines to a specified level, the issuer may have an option to buy back the notes. Such repurchase may be funded by the originator, in which case the originator will re-acquire the securitised assets.

D3 From the originator's standpoint, the effect of the arrangement is usually that it continues-to obtain the benefit of surplus income (and, where relevant, capital profits) from the securitised assets and bears losses up to a set amount. Usually, however, the originator is protected from losses beyond a limited amount and has transferred catastrophe risk to the issuer.

Analysis

D4 The purpose of the analysis is to determine the following:

(a) the appropriate accounting treatment in the originator's individual company financial statements. There are three possible treatments:

(i) to remove the securitised assets from the balance sheet and show no liability in respect of the note issue, merely retaining the net amount (if any) of the securitised assets less the loan notes as a single item ('derecognition');

(ii) to show the proceeds of the note issue deducted from the securitised assets on the face of the balance sheet within a single asset caption (a 'linked presentation'); or

(iii)to show an asset equivalent in amount to the gross securitised assets within assets, and a corresponding liability in respect of the proceeds of the note issue within creditors (a 'separate presentation');

(b) the appropriate accounting treatment in the issuer's financial statements. Again there are three possible treatments: derecognition, a linked presentation or a separate presentation; and

(c) the appropriate accounting treatment in the originator's group accounts. This involves issues of:

(i) whether the issuer is a subsidiary or (more usually) a quasi-subsidiary of the originator such that it should be included in the originator's group accounts; and

(ii) where the issuer is a quasi-subsidiary, whether a linked presentation should be adopted in the originator's consolidated accounts.

Each of these is considered in more detail below.

(a) Originator's individual accounts

Overview of basic principles

D5 The principles for determining the appropriate accounting treatment in the originator's individual company financial statements are similar to those applied in both Application Note C — 'Factoring of debts' and in Application Note E — 'Loan transfers'. It is necessary to establish what asset and liability (if any) the originator now has, by answering two questions:

(a) whether the originator has access to the benefits of the securitised assets and exposure to the risks inherent in those benefits (referred to below as 'benefits and risks'); and

(b) whether the originator has a liability to repay the proceeds of the note issue.

Where the originator has transferred all significant benefits and risks relating to the securitised assets and has no obligation to repay the proceeds of the note issue, derecognition is appropriate; where the originator has retained significant benefits and risks relating to the securitised assets but there is absolutely no doubt that its downside exposure to loss is limited, a linked presentation should be used; and in all other cases a separate presentation should be adopted.

D6 The benefits and risks relating to securitised assets will depend on the nature of the particular assets involved. In the case of interest bearing loans, the benefits and risks are described in paragraph E6 of Application Note E — 'Loan transfers'.

Derecognition

D7 Derecognition (i.e. ceasing to recognise the securitised assets in their entirety) is appropriate only where the originator retains no significant benefits and no significant risks relating to the securitised assets.

D8 Whilst the commercial effect of any particular transaction should be assessed taking into account all its aspects and implications, the presence of all of the following indicates that the originator has not retained significant benefits and risks, and derecognition is appropriate:

(a) the transaction takes place at an arm's length price for an outright sale;

(b) the transaction is for a fixed amount of consideration and there is no recourse whatsoever, either implicit or explicit, to the originator for losses from whatever cause. Normal warranties given in respect of the condition of the assets at the time of the transfer (e.g. in a mortgage securitisation, a warranty that no mortgages are in arrears at the time of transfer, or that the income of the borrower at the time of granting the mortgage was above a specified amount) would not breach this condition. However, warranties relating to the condition of the assets in the future or to their future performance (e.g. that mortgages will not move into arrears in the future) would breach the condition. Other possible forms of recourse are set out in paragraph 83; and

(c) the originator will not benefit or suffer if the securitised assets perform better or worse than expected. This will not be the case where the originator has a right to further sums from the vehicle that vary according to the eventual value realised for the securitised assets. Such sums could take a number of forms, for instance deferred consideration, a performance-related servicing fee, payments under a swap, dividends from the vehicle, or payments from a reserve fund.

Where any of these three features is not present, this indicates that the originator has retained benefits and risks relating to the securitised assets and, unless these are insignificant, either a separate presentation or a linked presentation should be adopted.

D9 Whether any benefit and risk retained are 'significant' should be judged in relation to those benefits and risks that are likely to occur in practice, and not in relation to the total possible benefits and risks. Where the profits or losses accruing to the originator are material in relation to those likely to occur in practice, significant benefit and risk will be retained. For example, if for a portfolio of securitised assets of 100, expected losses are 0.5 and there is recourse to the originator for losses of up to 5, the originator will have retained all but an insignificant part of the downside risk relating to the assets (as the originator bears losses of up to ten times those expected to occur). Accordingly, in this example, derecognition will not be appropriate and either a linked presentation or a separate presentation should be used.

Linked presentation

D10 A linked presentation will be appropriate where, although the originator has retained significant benefits and risks relating to the securitised assets, there is absolutely no doubt that its downside exposure to loss is limited to a fixed monetary amount. A linked presentation should be used only to the extent that there is both absolutely no doubt that the noteholders' claim extends solely to the proceeds generated by the securitised assets, and there is no provision for the originator to re-acquire the securitised assets, in the future. The conditions that need to be met in order for this to be the case are set out in paragraph 27 and explained in paragraphs 81-86. When interpreting these conditions in the context of a securitisation the following points apply:

condition (a) (specified assets)

— a linked presentation should not be used where the assets that have been securitised cannot be separately identified. Nor should a linked presentation be used for assets that generate the funds required to repay the finance only by being used in conjunction with other assets of the originator;

condition (d) (agreement in writing that there is no recourse; such agreement noted in the financial statements)

— where the noteholders have subscribed to a prospectus or offering circular that clearly states that the originator will not support any losses of either the issuer or the noteholders, the first part of this condition will be met. Provisions that give the noteholders recourse to funds generated by both the securitised assets themselves and third party credit enhancement of those assets would also not breach this condition;

condition (f) (no provision for the originator to repurchase assets)

— where there is provision for the originator to repurchase only part of the securitised assets (or otherwise to fund the redemption of loan notes by the issuer), the maximum payment that could result should be excluded from the amount deducted on the face of the balance sheet. Where there is provision for the issuer (but not the originator) to redeem loan notes before an equivalent amount has been realised in cash from the securitised assets, a linked presentation may still be appropriate provided there is no obligation (legal, commercial or other) for the originator to fund the redemption (e.g. by repurchasing the securitised assets).

D11 These conditions should be regarded as met notwithstanding the existence of an interest rate swap agreement between the originator and the issuer, provided all the following conditions are met:

(a) the swap is on arm's length market-related terms and the obligations of the issuer under the swap are not subordinated to any of its obligations under the loan notes;

(b) the variable interest rate(s) that are swapped are determined by reference to publicly quoted rates that are not under the control of the originator;

(c) at the time of transfer of the assets to the issuer, the originator had hedged exposures relating to these assets (either individually or as part of a larger portfolio) and entering into the swap effectively restores the hedge position left open by their transfer. Thereafter, where the hedging of the originator's exposure under the swap requires continuing management, any necessary adjustments to the hedging position are made on an ongoing basis. This latter requirement will be particularly relevant where any prepayment risk involved cannot be hedged exactly.

The conditions for a linked presentation should also be regarded as met notwithstanding the existence of an interest rate cap agreement between the originator and the issuer provided that, in addition to all the above conditions being met, the securitisation was entered into before 22 September 1994.

D12 In the case of securitisations of revolving assets that arise under a facility (e.g. credit card balances), a careful analysis of the mechanism for repaying the loan notes is required in order to establish whether or not conditions (b) and (f) in paragraph 27 are met. For such assets, the loan notes are usually repaid from proceeds received during a period of time (referred to as the 'repayment period'). The proceeds received in the repayment period will typically comprise both repayments of securitised balances existing at the start of the repayment period and repayments of balances arising subsequently (for example arising from new borrowings in the repayment period on the credit card accounts securitised). In order that the conditions for a linked presentation are met, it is necessary that loan notes are repaid only to the extent that there have been, in total, cash collections from securitised balances existing at the start of the repayment period equal to the amount repaid on the loan notes. This is necessary in order to ensure that the issuer is allocated its proper share of any losses.

D13 It will also be necessary to analyse carefully any provisions that enable the originator to transfer additional assets to the issuer in order to establish whether or not conditions (b) and (f) in paragraph 27 are met. To the extent that the originator is obliged to replace poorly performing assets with good ones, there is recourse to the originator and a linked presentation should not be used. However, where there is merely provision for the originator to add new assets to replace those that have been repaid earlier than expected (and thus to 'top up' the pool in order to extend the life of the securitisation), the conditions for a linked presentation may still be met. For a linked presentation to be used, it is necessary that the addition of new assets does not result in either the originator being exposed to losses on the new or the old assets, or in the originator re-acquiring assets. Provided these features are present, the effect is the same as if the noteholders were repaid in cash and they immediately reinvested that cash in new assets, and a linked presentation may be appropriate.

Separate presentation

D14 Where the originator has retained significant benefits and risks relating to the securitised assets and the conditions for a linked presentation are not met, the originator should adopt a separate presentation.

Multi-originator programmes

D15 There are some arrangements where one issuer serves several originators. The arrangement may be structured such that each originator receives future benefits based on the performance of a defined portfolio of assets (typically those it has transferred to the issuer and continues to service or use). For instance, in a mortgage securitisation, the benefits accruing to any particular originator may be calculated as the interest payments received from a defined portfolio of mortgages, less costs specific to that portfolio (e.g. insurance premiums, payments for credit facilities), less an appropriate share of the funding costs of the issuer. The effect is that each originator bears significant benefits and risks of a defined pool of mortgages, whilst being insulated from the benefits and risks of other mortgages held by the issuer. Thus each originator should show that pool of mortgages for which it has significant benefits and risks on the face of its balance sheet, using either a linked presentation (if the conditions for its use are met) or a separate presentation.

(b) Issuer's accounts

D16 The principles set out in paragraphs D5-D15 for the originator's individual financial statements also apply to the issuer's financial statements. In a securitisation, the issuer usually has access to all future benefits from the securitised assets (in the case of mortgages, to all cash collected from mortgagors) and is exposed to all their inherent risks. Hence, derecognition will not be appropriate. In addition, the noteholders usually have recourse to all the assets of the issuer (these may include the securitised assets themselves, the benefit of any related insurance policies or credit enhancement, and a small amount of cash). In this situation, the issuer's exposure to loss is not limited, and use of a linked presentation will not be appropriate. Thus the issuer should usually adopt a separate presentation.

(c) Originator's group financial statements

D17 Assuming a separate presentation is used in the issuer's financial statements but not in those of the originator, the question arises whether the relationship between the issuer and the originator is such that the issuer should be included in the originator's group financial statements. The following considerations are relevant:

(a) Where the issuer meets the definition of a subsidiary, it should be consolidated in the normal way by applying the relevant provisions of companies legislation and

FRS 2. Where the issuer is not a subsidiary, the provisions of this FRS regarding quasi-subsidiaries are relevant.

(b) In order to meet the definition of a quasi-subsidiary, the issuer must give rise to benefits for the originator that are in substance no different from those that would arise were the entity a subsidiary. This will be the case where the originator receives the future benefits arising from the net assets of the issuer (principally the securitised assets less the loan notes). It is not necessary that the originator could face a possible benefit outflow equal in amount to the issuer's gross liabilities. Strong evidence of whether this part of the definition is met is whether the originator stands to suffer or gain from the financial performance of the issuer.

(c) The definition of a quasi-subsidiary also requires that the issuer is directly or indirectly controlled by the originator. Usually securitisations exemplify the situation described in paragraphs 34 and 98, in that the issuer's financial and operating policies are in substance predetermined (in this case under the various agreements that constitute the securitisation). Where this is so, the party possessing control will be the one that has the future benefits arising from the issuer's net assets.

D18 It follows that it should be presumed that the issuer is a quasi-subsidiary where either of the following is present:

(a) the originator has rights to the benefits arising from the issuer's net assets, i.e. to those benefits generated by the securitised assets that remain after meeting the claims of noteholders and other expenses of the issuer. These benefits may be transferred to the originator in a number of forms as described in paragraph D2(d); or

(b) the originator has the risks inherent in these benefits. This will be the case where, if the benefits are greater or less than expected (e.g. because of the securitised assets realising more or less than expected), the originator gains or suffers.

D19 In general, where an issuer's activities comprise holding securitised assets and the benefits of its net assets accrue to the originator, the issuer will be a quasi-subsidiary of the originator. Conversely, the issuer will not be a quasi-subsidiary of the originator where the owner of the issuer is an independent third party that has made a substantial capital investment in the issuer, has control of the issuer, and has the benefits and risks of its net assets.

D20 Where the issuer is a quasi-subsidiary of the originator, the question arises whether a linked presentation should be adopted in the originator's group financial statements. It follows from paragraph 37 that where the issuer holds a single portfolio of similar assets, and the effect of the arrangement is to ring-fence the assets and their related finance in such a way that the provisions of paragraphs 26 and 27 are met from the point of view of the group, a linked presentation should be used.

Required accounting

Originator's individual financial statements

Derecognition

D21 Where the originator has retained no significant benefits and risks relating to the securitised assets and has no obligation to repay the proceeds of the note issue, the assets should be removed from its balance sheet, and no liability shown in respect of the proceeds of the note issue. A profit or loss should be recognised, calculated as the difference between the carrying amount of the assets and the proceeds received.

Linked presentation

D22 Where the conditions for a linked presentation are met, the proceeds of the note issue (to the extent they are non-returnable) should be shown deducted from the securitised assets on the face of the balance sheet within a single asset caption. Profit should be recognised and presented in the manner set out in paragraphs 28 and 87-88. The following disclosures should be given:

(a) a description of the assets securitised;

(b) the amount of any income or expense recognised in the period, analysed as appropriate;

(c) the terms of any options for the originator to repurchase assets or to transfer additional assets to the issuer;

(d) the terms of any interest rate swap or interest rate cap agreements between the issuer and the originator that meet the conditions set out in paragraph D11;

(e) a description of the priority and amount of claims on the proceeds generated by the assets, including any rights of the originator to proceeds from the assets in addition to the non-recourse amounts already received;

(f) the ownership of the issuer; and

(g) the disclosures required by conditions (c) and (d) in paragraph 27.

D23 Where an originator uses a linked presentation for several different securitisations that all relate to a single type of asset (i.e. all the assets, if not securitised, would be shown within the same balance sheet caption), these may be aggregated on the face of the balance sheet. However, securitisations of different types of asset should be shown separately. In addition, details of each material arrangement should be provided in the notes to the financial statements, unless they are on similar terms and relate to a single type of asset, in which case they may be disclosed in aggregate.

Separate presentation

D24 Where neither derecognition nor a linked presentation is appropriate, a separate presentation should be adopted, i.e. a gross asset (equal in amount to the gross amount of the securitised assets) should be shown on the balance sheet of the originator within assets, and a corresponding liability in respect of the proceeds of the note issue shown within liabilities. No gain or loss should be recognised at the time the securitisation is entered into (unless adjustment to the carrying value of the assets independent of the securitisation is required). Disclosure should be given in the notes to the financial statements of the gross amount of assets securitised at the balance sheet date.

Issuer's financial statements

D25 The requirements set out in paragraphs D21-D24 for the originator's individual financial statements also apply to the issuer's financial statements. For the reasons set out in paragraph D16, in most cases the issuer will be required to adopt a separate presentation, in which case the provisions of paragraph D24 will apply.

Originator's consolidated financial statements

D26 Where the issuer is a quasi-subsidiary of the originator, its assets, liabilities, profits, losses and cash flows should be included in the originating group's consolidated financial statements. Where the provisions of paragraph D20 are met, a linked presentation should be applied in the consolidated financial statements and the disclosures required by paragraphs D22 and D23 should be given; in all other cases a separate presentation should be used and the disclosure required by paragraph D24 should be given.

Table

Indications that de-recognition is appropriate (securitised assets are not assets of the originator)	Indications that a linked presentation is appropriate	Indications that a separate presentation is appropriate (securitised assets are assets of the originator)
Originator's individual financial statements		
Transaction price is arm's length price for an outright sale.	Transaction price is not arm's length price for an outright sale.	Transaction price is not arm's length price for an outright sale.
Transfer is for a single, non-returnable fixed sum.	Some non-returnable proceeds received, but originator has rights to further sums from the issuer, the amount of which depends on the performance of the securitised assets.	Proceeds received are returnable, or there is a provision whereby the originator may keep the securitised assets on repayment of the loan notes or re-acquire them.
There is no recourse to the originator for losses.	There is either no recourse for losses, or such recourse has a fixed monetary ceiling.	There is or may be full recourse to the originator for losses, e.g. —originator's directors are unable or unwilling to state that it is not obliged to fund any losses; —noteholders have not agreed in writing that they will seek repayment only from funds generated by the securitised assets.
Originator's consolidated financial statements		
Issuer is owned by an independent third party that made a substantial capital investment, has control of the issuer, and has the benefits and risks of its net assets.	Issuer is a quasi-subsidiary of the originator, but the conditions for a linked presentation are met from the point of view of the group.	Issuer is a subsidiary of the originator.

Application Note E — Loan transfers

NB In this Application Note, the following terminology is used:

(a) the 'lender' is the party that has rights to principal and interest under the original loan agreement, and is purporting to transfer them;

(b) the 'transferee' is the party purporting to acquire the loan, and includes a new lender (in a novation), an assignee and a sub-participant;

(c) the 'borrower' is the party that has obligations to make payments of principal and interest under the original loan agreement; and

(d) references to the transfer of a 'loan' or 'loans' apply equally to the transfer of both a single loan and a portfolio of loans.

Features

E1 This Application Note deals with the transfer of interest-bearing loans to an entity other than a special purpose vehicle. The main features of a loan transfer are as follows:

(a) Specified loans are transferred from a lender to a transferee by one of the methods set out in paragraph E2 below, in return for an immediate cash payment. The transfer may be of the whole of a single loan, part of a loan, or of all or part of a portfolio of similar loans.

(b) Payments of principal and interest collected from borrowers are passed to the transferee (either direct or via the lender). In some cases, there may be a difference between amounts received from borrowers and those passed to the transferee (the lender retaining or making up the difference), or if a borrower fails to make payments when due, the lender may nevertheless make payments to the transferee.

E2 Loans cannot be 'sold' in the same way as tangible assets. However, there are three methods by which the benefits and risks of a loan can be transferred:

Novation: The rights and obligations under the loan agreement are cancelled and replaced by new ones whose main effect is to change the identity of the lender. Although rights can be transferred by other means, novation is the only method of transferring obligations (e.g. to supply funds under an undrawn loan facility) with the consequent release of the lender.

Assignment: Rights (to principal and interest), but not obligations, are transferred to a third party (the 'assignee'). There are two types of assignment: statutory assignment, which must relate to the whole of the loan and where notice in writing must be given to the borrower and other obligors (e.g. a guarantor); and equitable assignment, which may relate to only part of a loan and which does not require notice to the borrower. Both types are subject to equitable rights arising before notice is received. For example, a right of set-off held by the borrower against the lender will be good against the assignee for any transactions undertaken before the borrower receives notice of the assignment.

Sub-participation: Rights and obligations are not formally transferred but the lender enters into a non-recourse back-to-back agreement with a third party, the 'sub participant', under which the latter deposits with the lender an amount equal to the whole or part of the loan and in return receives from the lender a share of the cash flows arising on the loan.

E3 The terms of a loan transfer will usually not be identical to those of the original loan, and a gain or loss will arise for the lender. This gain or loss may occur in one of two ways:

first, if all future payments made by the borrower (and only such payments) are to be passed to the transferee, the consideration for the transfer will differ from the carrying amount of the loan and the lender's gain or loss will be realised in cash immediately. Alternatively, the consideration for the transfer may be set equal to the carrying amount of the loan, and the amounts to be paid by the borrower and those to be passed on to the transferee will differ. In this case, the lender's gain or loss will be the net present value of this difference and will be realised in cash over the term of the loan.

Analysis

Overview of basic principles

E4 The purpose of the analysis is to determine the appropriate accounting treatment in the financial statements of the lender. There are three possible treatments:

(a) to remove the loan (or a part of it) from the balance sheet and show no liability in respect of the amounts received from the transferee ('derecognition');

(b) to show the amounts received from the transferee deducted from the loan on the face of the balance sheet within a single asset caption (a 'linked presentation'); or

(c) to continue to show the loan as an asset, and show a corresponding liability within creditors in respect of the amounts received from the transferee (a 'separate presentation').

E5 The principles to be applied to determine the appropriate accounting treatment are similar to those applied in both Application Note D — 'Securitised assets' relating to individual (rather than consolidated) financial statements and in Application Note C — 'Factoring of debts'. It is necessary to answer two questions:

(a) whether the lender has access to the benefits of the loans and exposure to the risks inherent in those benefits (referred to below as 'benefits and risks'); and

(b) whether the lender has a liability to repay the transferee.

Where the lender has transferred all significant benefits and risks relating to the loans and has no obligation to repay the transferee, derecognition is appropriate (this would be the case where all future cash flows from borrowers — but only those cash flows — are passed to the transferee as and when received). Where the lender has retained significant benefits and risks relating to the loans but there is absolutely no doubt that its downside exposure to loss is limited, a linked presentation should be used (this is likely to be rare for a loan transfer). In all other cases a separate presentation should be adopted.

Benefits and risks

E6 The main benefits and risks relating to loans are as follows:

Benefits:

(i) the future cash flows from payments of principal and interest.

Risks:

(i) credit risk (the risk of bad debts);

(ii) slow payment risk;

(iii) interest rate risk (the risk of a change in the interest rate paid by the borrower. Included in this risk is a form of basis risk, i.e. the risk of a change in the interest rate paid by the borrower not being matched by a change in the interest rate paid to the transferee);

(iv) reinvestment/early redemption risk (the risk that, where payments from the loans are reinvested by the lender before being paid to the transferee, the rate of interest obtained on the reinvested amounts is above or below that payable to the transferee); and

(v) moral risk (the risk that the lender will feel obliged, because of its continued association with the loans, to fund any losses arising on them).

Analysis of benefits

E7 At first sight it may appear that the transferee has access to the cash collected from borrowers. However, as set out in more detail in paragraphs C6 and C7, the cash flows may appear similar even where different accounting treatments are appropriate and considering the benefits in isolation will not normally enable a clear decision to be made. Rather, it is necessary to determine which party is exposed to the risks relating to the loans (both upside potential for gain and downside exposure to loss).

Analysis of risks

E8 The benefit of cash payments of principal and interest are subject to the five risks outlined in paragraph E6. The first of these, credit risk, will be borne by the lender to the extent there is recourse to it for bad debts; if there is no such recourse, the transferee will bear the credit risk.

E9 The second risk, slow payment, will be borne by the party that suffers (or benefits) if borrowers pay later (or earlier) than expected. If amounts are passed to the transferee only when received from the borrower, the transferee will bear this risk; if the lender pays amounts to the transferee regardless of whether it has received an equivalent payment from the borrower, the lender will bear it.

E10 Interest rate risk will be borne by the lender where the interest it receives from the borrower and payments it makes to the transferee are not directly related*. Where any changes in the interest rate charged to the borrower are passed on to the transferee after a short administrative delay, the lender may not bear significant interest rate risk; however, where any delays are significant the lender will bear significant risk.

E11 The lender will bear reinvestment risk where payments received from the borrower are not immediately passed on to the transferee but are reinvested by the lender for a period. An exception would be where the transferee is entitled to all of any interest actually earned (but no more) on the amounts reinvested by the lender.

E12 The final risk is moral risk. For either derecognition or a linked presentation to be appropriate, the lender must have taken all reasonable precautions to eliminate this risk such that it will not feel obliged to fund any losses. This will include ensuring that the arrangements for servicing the loans reflect the standards of commercial behaviour expected of the lender.

*'Directly related' in this context means that either the interest rates paid and received are both fixed, or the two rates are tied to the same external rate e.g. LIBOR.

Derecognition

E13 Derecognition (i.e. ceasing to recognise the loans in their entirety) is appropriate only where the lender retains no significant benefits and no significant risks relating to the loans. In determining whether any benefit and risk retained are 'significant', greater weight should be given to what is more likely to have a commercial effect in practice.

E14 The three possible methods of transferring the benefits and risks relating to a loan are described in paragraph E2; each may result in derecognition in appropriate cases:

(a) A novation (i.e. the replacement of the original loan by a new one with the consequent release of the lender) will usually transfer all significant benefits and risks, provided that there are no side agreements that leave benefits and risks with the lender.

(b) An assignment (i.e. the transfer of the rights to principal and interest that constitute the original loan, whilst not transferring any obligations) may also transfer all significant benefits and risks, provided that, in addition to there being no side agreements that leave benefits and risks with the lender, there are no unfulfilled obligations (e.g. to supply additional funds in the event of a restructuring of the loan) and any doubts regarding intervening equitable rights are satisfied.

(c) A sub-participation (i.e. the entering into an additional non-recourse back-to-back agreement with the sub-participant rather than the transfer of any of the rights or obligations that constitute the original loan itself) may also transfer all significant benefits and risks, provided that the lender's obligation to pay amounts to the transferee eliminates its access to benefits from the loans but extends only to those benefits. Thus the sub-participant must have a claim on all specified payments from the loans but on only those payments, and there must be no possibility that the lender could be required to pay amounts to the sub-participant where it has not received equivalent payments from the borrower.* Where this is the case, the loans no longer constitute an asset of the lender, nor does the deposit placed by the sub-participant represent a liability—it will therefore be appropriate to derecognise the loans. Particular attention should be paid to the effect of the borrower asking for a rescheduling. The lender may, for commercial reasons, wish to agree to a rescheduling plan, whereas the sub-participant may simply look to the lender for compensation if it is not repaid. Where the lender has an obligation (legal, commercial or other) to provide such compensation, derecognition will not be appropriate.

E15 Whilst the commercial effect of any particular transaction should be assessed taking into account all its aspects and implications, the presence of all of the following indicates that the lender has not retained significant benefits and risks, and derecognition is appropriate:

*Where only part of the payments due under the original loan are eliminated in this way it may be appropriate to derecognise only part of the original loan. This is addressed in paragraphs E19 and E20 below.

(a) the transaction takes place at an arm's length price for an outright sale;

(b) the transaction is for a fixed amount of consideration and there is no recourse whatsoever either implicit or explicit, to the lender for losses from whatever cause. Normal warranties given in respect of the condition of the loans at the time of the transfer (e.g. a warranty that no loan was in arrears at the time of transfer) would not breach this condition. However, warranties relating to the condition of the loans in the future or to their future performance (e.g. that loans will not move into arrears in the future) would breach the condition. Other possible forms of recourse are set out in paragraph 83; and

(c) the lender will not benefit or suffer in any way if the loans perform better or worse than expected. This will not be the case where the lender has a right to further sums that vary according to the future performance of the loans (i.e. according to whether or when borrowers pay, or according to the amounts borrowers pay). Such sums might take the form of an interest differential, deferred consideration, a performance-related servicing fee or payments under a swap.

Where any of these three features is not present, this indicates that the lender has retained benefits and risks relating to the loan and, unless these are insignificant, either a separate presentation or a linked presentation should be adopted.

E16 Whether any benefit and risk retained are 'significant' should be judged in relation to those benefits and risks that are likely to occur in practice, and not in relation to the total possible benefits and risks. Where the profits or losses accruing to the lender are material in relation to those likely to occur in practice, significant benefit and risk will be retained, such that derecognition will not be appropriate and either a linked presentation or a separate presentation should be used.

Linked presentation

E17 A linked presentation will be appropriate where, although the lender has retained significant benefits and risks relating to the loans, there is absolutely no doubt that its downside exposure to loss is limited to a fixed monetary amount. A linked presentation should be used only to the extent that there is both absolutely no doubt that the transferee's claim extends solely to cash collected from the loans, and no provision for the lender to keep or re-acquire the loans by repaying the transferee. The conditions that need to be met in order for this to be the case are set out in paragraph 27 and explained in paragraphs 81-86.

Separate presentation

E18 Where the lender retains significant benefits and risks relating to the loans and the conditions for a linked presentation are not met, a separate presentation should be adopted.

Transfers of part of a loan

E19 In some cases the amount received by the lender from the transferee represents only part of the original loan. As explained in paragraph 71, where the effect of the arrangement is that a part of the loan is transferred, derecognition of that part will be appropriate. This will be the case where each party has a proportionate share of all future cash collected from the loan (and of related profits and losses). For example, were the transferee to be entitled to 40 per cent of any cash flows from payments of both principal and interest as and when paid by the borrower (i.e. it does not receive cash if such payments are not made), the lender should cease to recognise 40 per cent of the loan. Conversely, if the lender bears losses in preference to the transferee and thus retains significant risk relating to the loans, derecognition of any part of them is not appropriate. For example, were the transferee to have first claim on any cash flows arising from a portfolio of loans with the lender's share acting as a cushion to absorb any losses, the lender should continue to show the gross amount of the whole portfolio on the face of its balance sheet (although if the conditions for a linked presentation are met, it should be used).

E20 In other cases, the entire principal amount of a loan may be funded by the transferee, but there may be a difference between the interest payments due from the borrower and those the lender has agreed to pass on to the transferee. In such cases derecognition of a part of the original loan may still be appropriate provided that the lender's interest differential does not result in it bearing significant risks relating to the loan. For instance, if the lender's interest differential is fixed and is in substance no more than a fee for originating or administering the loan, derecognition will be appropriate. Conversely, if the lender's interest differential varies depending on the performance of the loan (as where it acts as a cushion to absorb losses or the lender bears interest rate risk), either a separate presentation or a linked presentation should be used. A linked presentation should be used only where the lender's maximum loss is capped, as might be the case where a variable rate loan is funded by a fixed rate one (if the lender's maximum loss is capped at the fixed interest payments due to the transferee). However, a linked presentation should not be used where the lender's maximum loss is not capped, as will be the case where a fixed rate loan is funded by a variable rate one, or where a loan in one currency is funded by a loan in another. The principles in this paragraph apply equally where the transferee funds only part of the principal amount of the original loan.

Administration arrangements

E21 Whether or not the lender continues to administer the loans is not, of itself, relevant to deciding upon the appropriate accounting treatment. However, the administration arrangements may affect where certain benefits and risks lie. For instance, where the lender's servicing fee is not an arm's length fee for the services provided, this indicates it has retained significant benefits and risks relating to the loans.

Required accounting

Derecognition

E22 Where the lender has retained no significant benefits and risks relating to the loans and has no obligation to repay the transferee, the loans should be removed from its balance sheet and no liability shown in respect of the amounts received from the transferee. A profit or loss may arise for the lender in the two ways set out in paragraph E3. Where the profit or loss is realised in cash it should be recognised, calculated as the difference between the carrying amount of the loans and the cash proceeds received. Where, however, the lender's profit or loss is not realised in cash and there are doubts as to its amount, full provision should be made for any expected loss but recognition of any gain, to the extent it is in doubt, should be deferred until cash has been received.

Linked presentation

E23 Where the conditions for a linked presentation are met, the proceeds received, to the extent they are non-returnable, should be shown deducted from the gross amount of the loans on the face of the balance sheet. Profit should be recognised and presented as set out in paragraphs 28 and 87-88. The notes to the financial statements should disclose: the main terms of the arrangement; the gross amount of loans transferred and outstanding at the balance sheet date; the profit or loss recognised in the period, analysed as appropriate; and the disclosures required by conditions (c) and (d) in paragraph 27.

Separate presentation

E24 Where neither derecognition nor a linked presentation is appropriate, a separate presentation should be adopted, i.e. a gross asset (equivalent in amount to the gross amount of the loans) should be shown on the balance sheet of the lender within assets, and a corresponding liability in respect of the amounts received from the transferee should be shown within creditors. No gain or loss should be recognised at the time of the transfer (unless adjustment to the carrying value of the loan independent of the transfer is required). The notes to the financial statements should disclose the amount of loans subject to loan transfer arrangements that are outstanding at the balance sheet date.

Table

Indications that de-recognition is appropriate (off lender's balance sheet)	Indications that a linked presentation is appropriate	Indications that a separate presentation is appropriate (on lender's balance sheet)
Transfer is for a single, non-returnable fixed sum.	Some non-returnable proceeds received, but lender has rights to further sums whose amount depends on whether or when the borrowers pay.	The proceeds received are returnable in the event of losses occurring on the loans.
There is no recourse to the lender for losses from any cause.	There is either no recourse for losses, or such recourse has a fixed monetary ceiling.	There is full recourse to the lender for losses.
Transferee is paid all amounts received from the loans (and no more), as and when received. Lender has no rights to further sums from the loans or the transferee.	Transferee is paid only out of amounts received from the loans, and lender has no right or obligation to repurchase them.	Lender is required to repay amounts received from the transferee on or before a set date, regardless of the timing or amount of payments by the borrowers.

Adoption of FRS 5 by the Board

Financial Reporting Standard 5 — 'Reporting Substance of Transactions' was approved for issue by the nine members of the Accounting Standards Board

David Tweedie	(Chairman)
Allan Cook	(Technical Director)
Robert Bradfield	
Ian Brindle	
Sir Bryan Carsberg	
Michael Garner	
Raymond Hinton	
Donald Main	
Graham Stacy	

Appendix 1

Note on legal requirements

Great Britain

References are to the Companies Act 1985

Group accounts

1 Definitions of 'parent undertaking' and 'subsidiary undertaking' are set out and explained in Section 258 and Schedule 10A.

2 Other provisions of the Companies Act relevant to the preparation of consolidated accounts are given in paragraphs 95 and 96 of FRS 2 'Accounting for Subsidiary Undertakings'.

3 *The requirement to show a true and fair view*

Section 227 provides the following:

"(1) If at the end of a financial year a company is a parent company the directors shall, as well as preparing individual accounts for the year, prepare group accounts.

(2) Group accounts shall be consolidated accounts comprising—

(a) a consolidated balance sheet dealing with the state of affairs of the parent company and its subsidiary undertakings, and

(b) a consolidated profit and loss account dealing with the profit or loss of the parent undertaking and its subsidiary undertakings.

(3) The accounts shall give a true and fair view of the state of affairs as at the end of the financial year, and the profit or loss for the financial year, of the undertakings included in the consolidation as a whole, so far as concerns members of the company.

(4) A company's group accounts shall comply with the provisions of Schedule 4A as to the form and content of the consolidated balance sheet and consolidated profit and loss account and additional information to be provided by way of notes to the accounts.

(5) Where compliance with the provisions of that Schedule, and the other provisions of this Act, as to the matters to be included in a company's group accounts or in the notes to those accounts, would not be sufficient to give a true and fair view, the necessary additional information shall be given in the accounts or in a note to them.

(6) If in special circumstances compliance with any of those provisions is inconsistent with the requirement to give a true and fair view, the directors shall depart from that provision to the extent necessary to give a true and fair view.

Particulars of any such departure, the reasons for it and its effect shall be given in a note to the accounts."

Section 255A(5) states that, in the case of a banking or insurance company, the references to the provisions of Schedule 4A in Section 227(5) and (6) shall be read as references to those provisions as modified by Part II of Schedule 9.

Offset

4 The Companies Act contains the following provisions relating to offset:

Schedule 4 paragraph 5 (an identical requirement for banking companies and groups is contained in Schedule 9 paragraph 5)

> "Amounts in respect of items representing assets or income may not be offset against amounts in respect of items representing liabilities or expenditure (as the case may be), or vice versa."

Schedule 4 paragraph 14 (an identical requirement for banking companies and groups is contained in Schedule 9 paragraph 21)

> "In determining the aggregate amount of any item the amount of each individual asset or liability that falls to be taken into account shall be determined separately."

Northern Ireland

5 The legal requirements in Northern Ireland are identical to those in Great Britain. In particular:

Article 266 of and Schedule 10A to the Companies (Northern Ireland) Order 1986 are identical to Section 258 of and Schedule 10A to the Companies Act 1985 as referred to in paragraph 1 above.

Other provisions of companies legislation relevant to the preparation of consolidated accounts, as referred to in paragraph 2 above, are given in paragraph 97 of FRS 2 'Accounting for subsidiary undertakings'.

Articles 235 and 263A(5) of the Companies (Northern Ireland) Order 1986 are identical to Sections 227 and 255A(5) respectively of the Companies Act 1985 as referred to in paragraph 3 above.

Paragraphs 5 and 14 of Schedule 4 to the Companies (Northern Ireland) Order 1986 are identical to paragraphs 5 and 14 of Schedule 4 to the Companies Act 1985 as referred to in paragraph 4 above.

Republic of Ireland

6 The legal requirements in the Republic of Ireland are similar to those in Great Britain. In particular:

Regulation 4 of the European Communities (Companies: Group Accounts) Regulations 1992 is similar to Section 258 of and Schedule 10A to the Companies Act 1985 as referred to in paragraph 1 above.

Other provisions of companies legislation relevant to the preparation of consolidated accounts, as referred to in paragraph 2 above, are given in the insert replacing paragraph 98 of FRS 2 'Accounting for subsidiary undertakings'.

Regulations 5, 13 and 14 of the European Communities (Companies: Group Accounts) Regulations 1992 are similar to Section 227 of the Companies Act 1985 as referred to in paragraph 3 above. As regards banks, Section 5(1) of the European Communities (Credit Institutions: Accounts) Regulations 1992 is similar to Section 255A(5) of the Companies Act 1985 as referred to in paragraph 3 above. Pending implementation of the EC Insurance Accounts Directive (91/674 EC) there is no legislation similar to

Section 255A(5) for insurance companies.

Sections 4(11) and 5(e) of the Companies (Amendment) Act 1986 are similar to paragraphs 5 and 14 of Schedule 4 to the Companies Act 1985 as referred to in paragraph 4 above.

Appendix II

Compliance with International Accounting Standards

There is no International Accounting Standard on this subject. The International Accounting Standards Committee (IASC) has issued a 'Framework for the Preparation and Presentation of Financial Statements'. The definitions of assets and liabilities set out in the FRS and the principles underlying it are similar in all material respects to those set out in the IASC's Framework. However, neither International Accounting Standards nor the Framework currently envisage use of a linked presentation for certain non-recourse finance as required by paragraphs 26-28 of the FRS.

Appendix III

The development of the FRS

General

1 The problems of what is commonly referred to as 'off balance sheet financing' became evident during the 1980s. In that period, a number of complex arrangements were developed that, if accounted for in accordance with their legal form, resulted in accounts that did not report the commercial effect of the arrangement. In particular, concern grew over arrangements for financing a company's operations in such a way that, if the arrangement were accounted for merely by recording its legal form, the finance would not be shown as a liability on the balance sheet.

2 At the same time, there was rapid innovation in financial markets. New arrangements for financing assets were developed, the accounting for which was not immediately obvious. An example of one such arrangement is securitisation, whereby an asset and its non-recourse finance are tightly ring-fenced using a separate vehicle company.

3 These developments raised fundamental questions about the nature of assets and liabilities and when they should be included in the balance sheet. Questions were also raised about the accounting for some transactions that had been used by businesses for many years. For example, some queried whether factoring should be accounted for as a secured loan rather than as a sale of debts.

4 The FRS has been developed to address these issues and to deal with the problems caused by the misleading effects that 'off balance sheet financing' can have on the accounts. As that term indicates, the most widely recognised effect is the omission of liabilities from the balance sheet. However, the assets being financed, as well as the finance itself, are excluded, with the result that both the resources of the entity and its financing are understated. There may also be important effects on the profit and loss account. For instance, a profit may be reported on a 'sale' that is, in substance, a secured loan. As another example, what is in substance a finance charge may be either omitted from the profit and loss account altogether or described as some other kind of expense. All of these effects make it harder for the reader of the accounts to assess the true economic position of the reporting entity because they obscure the true extent and nature of its borrowings, its assets and the results of its activities.

5 The Board believes that financial statements should represent faithfully the commercial effects of the transactions and other events they purport to represent. This requires transactions to be accounted for in accordance with their substance and not merely their legal form, since the latter may not fully indicate the commercial effect of the arrangements entered into.

History of documents issued

TR 603

6 The first authoritative document to address this issue was Technical Release 603 (TR 603) — 'Off Balance Sheet Financing and Window Dressing', issued in December 1985 by the Institute of Chartered Accountants in England and Wales. The main provision of this short, preliminary document was that, in determining the accounting treatment of transactions, their economic substance rather than their mere legal form should be considered.

ED 42

7 TR 603 was followed by ED 42 'Accounting for special purpose transactions', which was issued in March 1988 by the Accounting Standards Committee (ASC). ED 42 took a general approach, providing guidance that could be applied to a variety of situations, rather than specifying detailed rules for specific transactions. It proposed that assets and liabilities arising from off balance sheet transactions be included in the balance sheet rather than merely disclosed in the notes. For this purpose, ED 42 described the essential characteristics of assets and liabilities. It also proposed that 'controlled non-subsidiaries' should be consolidated as if they were subsidiaries as legally defined. The definition of a controlled non-subsidiary was substantially the same as that of a quasi-subsidiary given in FRS 5.

ED 49

8 ED 49 'Reflecting the substance of transactions in assets and liabilities' was issued by the ASC in May 1990. ED 49 responded to the comments received on ED 42 as well as certain changes in the law. The ED continued to take a general approach, proposing analysis of the substance of transactions by reference to the essential characteristics of assets and liabilities. It also continued to propose that controlled non-subsidiaries should be consolidated in group accounts, although these vehicle entities were renamed 'quasi-subsidiaries'. The main changes from ED 42 were: the inclusion, for the first time, of general recognition tests; the inclusion of Application Notes specifying how the draft standard was to be applied to five specific transaction types (including securitisation and factoring) — these were included at the specific request of commentators to ED 42 and their inclusion was later supported by the majority of commentators to ED 49; and the addition of guidance on identifying control.

Bulletin 15

9 Respondents to ED 49 raised, *inter alia*, the concern that the treatment it proposed for factoring was inconsistent with that proposed for securitisation. This led the Accounting Standards Board to review the accounting for securitisation and, in October 1991, to issue proposals (in Bulletin 15) under which most securitised assets would be shown on the balance sheet, the arrangement being accounted for as a secured loan. This was on the grounds that, in most securitisations, the originating entity retains significantly all of the profits from the securitised assets. Although the entity has strictly limited its exposure to losses on those assets, the same is true for other non-recourse finance arrangements and for limited liability subsidiaries, where it is accepted that assets and liabilities should be reported gross.

10 The respondents to Bulletin 15 were divided on whether securitisations should be accounted for on balance sheet as a secured loan, or off balance sheet as a sale. Views on both sides of the argument were strongly held, reflecting different beliefs about the primary purpose of the balance sheet. Those who favoured securitisations being accounted for on balance sheet believed that the primary use of the balance sheet is in assessing the amounts, timing and certainty of future cash flows. In their view, the total resources that underlie these future cash flows (and on which income will be earned in the future) should be shown on one side of the balance sheet, and the means by which they are financed should be shown on the other. They also pointed out that typically, the originating entity continues to gain significantly all the profits from the securitised assets and to be exposed to all those losses likely to occur in practice.

11 Those respondents who favoured securitisations being accounted for as a sale and therefore off balance sheet believed that the primary use of the balance sheet is in assessing the maximum possible loss to which the entity is exposed. They thought that the accounting treatment of securitisations (and perhaps other forms of non-recourse finance) should concentrate on showing that the originating entity has a limited downside exposure to loss, and that only a net asset of the amount to which the entity is exposed should be presented.

12 The Board debated in detail the issues raised by the respondents and also consulted numerous interested parties. It concluded that users of accounts need to know *both* the entity's gross resources and finance (as these determine the size of its future income) and the net amount of these (as this is the maximum loss the entity can suffer). Hence the Board developed a new kind of presentation — a 'linked presentation' — under which the finance is deducted from the gross securitised assets on the face of the balance sheet. This presentation shows the gross resources that underlie the business (and on which income will be earned in the future), yet highlights that the entity has a strictly limited exposure to loss.

FRED 4

13 Finally, in February 1993, the Board issued FRED 4 'Reporting the substance of transactions'. This carried through the general principles set out in ED 49 with only two major changes. The first was the introduction of proposals for a linked presentation for certain forms of non-recourse finance (including securitisations), as described above. These proposals attracted general support and are retained in the FRS with only one minor change which is described in paragraphs 29-32 below.

14 The only other major change from ED 49 was the inclusion of detailed criteria for when items may be offset in accounts. These prohibited offset of amounts denominated in different currencies or bearing interest on different bases, on the grounds that, for two items to be offset, they must exactly eliminate one another. Such elimination would not be present where the items were in different currencies or bore interest on different bases, because of the currency or interest rate risk that was present. It was therefore proposed that the two items should not be offset but should be reported as separate assets and liabilities. This proposal has been modified in the FRS, in the light of comments received, as described below.

15 Other, less significant changes from ED 49 were: the inclusion of definitions of assets and liabilities as opposed to a description of their 'essential characteristics' (these definitions are drawn from the Board's draft Statement of Principles); the provision of more guidance on accounting for transactions with options; the inclusion, for the first time, of criteria for when assets should cease to be recognised; the introduction of a distinction between control of an asset and control of another entity, and changes to some of ED 49's recognition tests, including removing the proposal that recognition be based on a 'reasonable accounting analogy'.

Matters considered in the light of responses to FRED 4

16 Most of the respondents to FRED 4 agreed with its principal proposals and these have been largely retained in the FRS. The following paragraphs describe those points on which respondents expressed concern and, where appropriate, explain with reasons, the changes the Board has made to the proposals of FRED 4 or the Board's reasons for not adopting a change.

Complexity of the FRS

17 Several respondents expressed concern that FRED 4 was complex and difficult to understand. In part, this complexity stemmed from the inclusion of proposals for a linked presentation as set out above. Another reason for the FRED being difficult to understand was its general approach of specifying principles applicable to all transactions rather than detailed rules for specific situations. Whilst this general approach was supported, there was concern that the resulting principles appeared somewhat abstract and difficult to comprehend on a first reading.

18 To meet these concerns, the structure and drafting of the FRED have been reviewed and, where possible, simplified. In addition, the Explanation section to the FRS gives examples where appropriate. However, the Board believes this is a complex area that cannot be reduced to a few simple rules without the danger of over-simplification. Indeed, simple rules, mechanically applied, would result in accounts that do not report substance.

Offset

19 As noted above, FRED 4 proposed prohibiting offset of amounts denominated in different currencies or bearing interest on different bases but asked for comments on this prohibition. The majority of those who commented favoured either allowing or requiring offset of such items. Their reasons included: that the balance sheet does not, in general, show currency or interest rate exposures, hence grossing up the items does not necessarily allow a better assessment of these risks, that the currency or interest rate risk may be hedged such that the risk portrayed by grossing up may, in fact, no longer exist; that given freely accessible and liquid foreign exchange markets, monetary items in different currencies can be regarded as being freely convertible, and essentially a single item; and that the balance sheet should focus on portraying credit risk since users expect to get information about credit risk from the balance sheet, but not about currency or interest rate risks. A majority of the Board is persuaded by these arguments and, accordingly, the FRS requires offset of amounts denominated in different currencies or bearing interest on different bases provided that certain criteria are met.

20 The Board also considered whether it should require disclosure of amounts in different currencies or bearing interest on different bases that have been offset. Such disclosure would allow the user to draw up a balance sheet incorporating all items that do not exactly eliminate one another. However, such a balance sheet would give only part of the information needed to assess the entity's exposure to currency and interest rate risk. For a full assessment, it would be necessary to disclose the currency and interest rate profile of all recognised assets and liabilities as well as the effects of 'off balance sheet' instruments such as swaps and options. The Board decided that it was not yet in a position to specify comprehensive disclosure of such risks and that to require disclosures that gave only partial information on currency and interest rate risk would be potentially misleading. Accordingly, the FRS does not require disclosure of amounts that have been offset.

21 FRED 4 also proposed prohibiting offset where the right to settle net was contingent (for example on the counterparty going into liquidation). This was on the basis that as such contingent rights could not have been exercised at the balance sheet date, they should not be reflected in the assets and liabilities reported at that date. After reviewing the comments on this issue, the Board decided that provided: (a) the right to settle net can be invoked in all situations of default; and (b) the entity's debit balance matures no later than its credit balance, the amounts should be offset. This is because in such a situation there is no possibility that the entity could be required to pay out its credit balance without first having recovered its debit balance.

22 Finally, FRED 4 did not propose the approach taken in US and certain other overseas accounting standards that require for offset that the reporting entity intends to settle net; FRED 4 required merely that the reporting entity has the ability to do so. The reason FRED 4 did not propose this approach is that the intended manner of settlement is essentially a matter of administrative convenience and does not affect the economic position of the parties. This reasoning was supported by commentators and, accordingly, the conditions given in the FRS for offset are not based on the intent of the reporting entity.

Ceasing to recognise assets

23 FRED 4 contained criteria for when assets should cease to be recognised. These required both that no significant access to benefits was retained and that any risk retained was immaterial. Commentators were particularly concerned over the second of these conditions: for instance that it might require continued recognition of an asset sold with a residual value guarantee or of a subsidiary sold with deferred performance-related consideration.

24 As a result, the FRS distinguishes three types of transactions. The first is transactions that transfer all significant rights to benefits relating to an asset and all significant exposures to the risks inherent in those benefits. For such transactions, the asset should cease to be recognised in its entirety. Conversely, where a transaction transfers no significant rights to benefits relating to an asset or no significant exposures to their inherent risks, the asset should continue to be recognised in its entirety. The third type of transaction comprises those special cases where not all significant benefits and risks have been transferred, but it is necessary to amend the description or monetary amount of the original asset or to recognise a new liability for any obligations assumed. Examples of this third type of transaction are given in paragraphs 71-73.

Contracts for future performance

25 For the avoidance of doubt, the Board decided that contracts for future performance, such as swaps, forward contracts and purchase commitments, should be removed from the scope of the FRS, except where they are merely a part of a transaction (or of a connected series of transactions) that falls within the FRS. The accounting for such contracts is a complex area that requires further research and consultation before an FRS dealing with their accounting could be issued.

Options

26 FRED 4's approach to options and the new guidance it contained were generally supported. However, the comments revealed some uncertainty over the approach to be taken to options for which there is a genuine commercial possibility both that the option will be exercised and that it will not be exercised, but the transaction is structured such that one or other outcome is significantly more likely. The FRS provides that the commercial effect of an option should be assessed in the context of all the aspects and implications of the transaction. It also explains that it may be necessary to consider the true commercial objectives of the parties and the commercial rationale for the inclusion of the option in the transaction in order to establish whether the parties' rights and obligations are, in substance, optional or conditional or, alternatively, outright.

27 Finally, for the avoidance of doubt, the FRS emphasises that, in assessing the commercial effect of an option, all the terms of the transaction and the circumstances of the parties that are likely to be relevant during the exercise period of the option should be taken into account — and not just conditions existing at the balance sheet date.

Linked presentation for subsidiaries

28 The FRS carries through the proposal in FRED 4 that where an item and its non-recourse finance are 'ring-fenced' in a quasi-subsidiary in such a way that the conditions for a linked presentation are met from the point of view of the group, the quasi-subsidiary should be included in consolidated financial statements using a linked presentation. However, if in a similar arrangement the item and its finance are held by a subsidiary, a linked presentation may not be used. In this case, the subsidiary is part of the group as legally defined: hence the item and its finance, being an asset and liability of the subsidiary, are respectively an asset and a liability of the group and companies legislation requires them to be shown in consolidated accounts in the normal way. Some respondents argued that the commercial effect is the same regardless of whether the vehicle is a subsidiary or a quasi-subsidiary, and hence the same accounting treatment should be adopted. However, companies legislation does not permit this. In legal terms, the inclusion of a quasi-subsidiary constitutes the provision of *additional* information about the group as legally defined and thus a quasi-subsidiary may be included in any way necessary to give a true and fair view of that group. However, a subsidiary is *part of* the group as legally defined and companies legislation requires the subsidiary to be consolidated in the normal way.

The use of swaps in securitisations

29 The Board was asked to clarify whether, in a securitisation, an interest rate swap or an interest rate cap between an originator and an issuer would restrict use of a linked presentation. FRED 4 required, as does the FRS, that, for a linked presentation, there must be 'no recourse whatsoever' to the originator and 'no possibility whatsoever of a claim being established on the entity [i.e. the originator] other than against funds generated by that item [i.e. the securitised assets]'. These provisions would prohibit use of a linked presentation where there is an interest rate swap or an interest rate cap between the originator and the issuer.

30 However, the argument was put to the Board that an exception to this principle was appropriate because the risks are often hedged by the originator as part of its normal hedging activities and thus payments to the issuer under the swap or cap would not represent a net loss to the originator. In many cases, the originator will have hedged any interest rate (and related) risks relating to the securitised assets prior to the securitisation, with the result that the securitisation opens up a gap in the originator's hedging portfolio by removing a hedged asset without removing its hedge. The most natural way to close this gap is for the issuer and the originator to enter into an interest rate swap or cap. Such a swap or cap will also be advantageous to the issuer by providing it with a hedge of the difference in the interest rate received on its newly acquired assets and that paid on its loan notes. It was also stated that, in the case of an interest rate swap (although not in the case of an interest rate cap), the issuer is currently unable to enter into a suitable swap with a third party as there is currently no market for such swaps in the UK (principally because the swap would require an amortising amount of principal to reflect actual repayments of the securitised assets).

31 The Board believes, as a matter of principle, that a linked presentation should be permitted only where there is no recourse whatsoever to the originator and accordingly should not be permitted where there is an interest rate swap or cap between the originator and the issuer. However, it decided with reluctance and as a pragmatic and provisional response to the issue, to permit use of a linked presentation in the originator's accounts notwithstanding the presence of an interest rate swap between the originator and the issuer in a securitisation provided certain strict criteria are met. (These are set out in paragraph D11.) In reaching this decision, the Board took into account the interaction of its decision with the present framework for regulating banks. The Board was also swayed by the fact that there is currently no market for such swaps in the UK and hence the issuer is unable to enter into a suitable swap with anyone other than the originator. For interest rate caps, the Board decided to give a similar concession but to restrict it to those securitisations in existence prior to 22 September 1994 since the availability of a suitable market for interest rate caps means there is no need for future transactions of this kind to be undertaken with the originator. The FRS also requires disclosure of interest rate swaps and caps between the originator and the issuer where a linked presentation is used.

32 The Board's decision with respect to interest rate swaps represents an interim measure and will be reviewed in the light of developments in securitisations and of progress made in the Board's forthcoming project on derivatives.

Disclosures of derecognised assets

33 Three of the Application Notes to FRED 4 contained specific disclosure requirements in respect of derecognised assets. Commentators generally thought these requirements were excessive, and they have not heen retained in the FRS.

Acquisitions and Mergers

Reproduced with the kind permission of the Accounting Standards Board

Financial Reporting Standard 6 is set out in paragraphs 1–39.

The Statement of Standard Accounting Practice set out in paragraphs 4–39 should be read in the context of the Objective as stated in paragraph 1 and the definitions set out in paragraphs 2–3 and also of the Foreword to Accounting Standards and the Statement of Principles for Financial Reporting currently in issue.

The Explanation set out in paragraphs 40–89 shall be regarded as part of the Statement of Standard Accounting Practice insofar as it assists in interpreting that statement.

Appendix III 'The development of the FRS' reviews considerations and arguments that were thought significant by members of the Board in reaching the conclusions on FRS 6.

Summary

a Financial Reporting Standard 6 'Acquisitions and Mergers' sets out the circumstances in which the two methods of accounting for a business combination — acquisition accounting and merger accounting — are to be used.

b Acquisition accounting regards the business combination as the acquisition of one company by another; the identifiable assets and liabilities of the company acquired are included in the consolidated balance sheet at their fair value at the date of acquisition, and its results included in the profit and loss account from the date of acquisition. The difference between the fair value of the consideration given and the fair values of the net assets of the entity acquired is accounted for as goodwill.

c Merger accounting, on the other hand, treats two or more parties as combining on an equal footing. It is normally applied without any restatement of net assets to fair value, and includes the results of each for the whole of the accounting period. Correspondingly, it does not reflect the issue of shares as an application of resources at fair value. The difference that arises on consolidation does not respresent goodwill but is deducted from, or added to, reserves.

d The FRS requires acquisition accounting to be used for any business combination where a party can be identified as having the role of an acquirer, since this method of accounting reflects the application of resources by the acquirer and the net assets acquired.

e Merger accounting is restricted to, and required for, those business combinations where the use of acquisition accounting would not properly reflect the true nature of the combination. A merger is a business combination in which, rather than one party acquiring control of another, the parties come together to share in the future risks and benefits of the combined entity. It is not the augmentation of one entity by the addition of another, but the creation of what is effectively a new reporting entity from the parties to the combination.

f A combination meets the definition of a merger only if it satisfies the five criteria set out in paragraphs 6–11 of the FRS. These criteria relate to:

1. the way the roles of each party to the combination are portrayed;
2. the involvement of each party to the combination in the selection of the management of the combined entity;

3 the relative sizes of the parties to the combination;

4 whether shareholders of the combining entities receive any consideration other than equity shares in the combined entity;

5 whether shareholders of the combining entities retain an interest in the performance of only part of the combined entity.

g Where a combination meets these criteria, acquisition accounting is not permitted as this method would not fairly present the effect of the combination.

h The FRS also contains provisions for applying merger accounting to mergers effected by the creation of a new holding company, and also to certain group reconstructions where acquisition accounting may not be appropriate.

i The FRS contains disclosure requirements applying to business combinations accounted for by using merger accounting so that the transition from separate entities to the merged entity can be understood; and further disclosure requirements, replacing those in SSAP 22 'Accounting for goodwill', for business combinations accounted for by using acquisition accounting, so that the effect of the acquisition can be understood.

Objective

1 The objective of this FRS is: to ensure that merger accounting is used only for those business combinations that are not, in substance, the acquisition of one entity by another but the formation of a new reporting entity as a substantially equal partnership where no party is dominant; to ensure the use of acquisition accounting for all other business combinations; and to ensure that in either case the financial statements provide relevant information concerning the effect of the combination.

Definitions

2 The following definitions shall apply in this FRS and in particular in the Statement of Standard Accounting Practice set out in paragraphs 4–39.

Acquisition: A business combination that is not a merger.

Business combination: The bringing together of separate entities into one economic entity as a result of one entity uniting with, or obtaining control over the net assets and operations of, another.

Equity shares: Shares other than non-equity shares.

Group reconstruction: Any of the following arrangements:

(a) the transfer of a shareholding in a subsidiary undertaking from one group company to another;

(b) the addition of a new parent company to a group;

(c) the transfer of shares in one or more subsidiary undertakings of a group to a new company that is not a group company but whose shareholders are the same as those of the group's parent;

(d) the combination into a group of two or more companies that before the combination had the same shareholders.

Merger: A business combination that results in the creation of a new reporting entity formed from the combining parties, in which the shareholders of the combining entities come together in a partnership for the mutual sharing of the risks and benefits of the combined entity, and in which no party to the combination in substance obtains control over any other, or is otherwise seen to be dominant, whether by virtue of the proportion of its shareholders' rights in the combined entity, the influence of its directors or otherwise.

Non-equity shares: Shares possessing any of the following characteristics:

(a) any of the rights of the shares to receive payments (whether in respect of dividends, in respect of redemption or otherwise) are for a limited amount that is not calculated by reference to the company's assets or profits or the dividends on any class of equity share;

(b) any of their rights to participate in a surplus in a winding up are limited to a specific amount that is not calculated by reference to the company's assets or profits and such limitation had a commercial effect in practice at the time the shares were issued or, if later, at the time the limitation was introduced;

(c) the shares are redeemable, either according to their terms or because the holder, or any party other than the issuer, can require their redemption.

3 References to companies legislation mean:

(a) in Great Britain, the Companies Act 1985;

(b) in Northern Ireland, the Companies (Northern Ireland) Order 1986; and

(c) in the Republic of Ireland, the Companies Acts 1963-90 and the European Communities (Companies: Group Accounts) Regulations 1992 .

Statement of Standard Accounting Practice

The marginal notes give the main references to the Companies Act 1985 in Great Britain. For the equivalent references in companies legislation in Northern Ireland and the Republic of Ireland see Appendix I.

Scope

4 Financial Reporting Standard 6 applies to all financial statements that are intended to give a true and fair view of a reporting entity's financial position and profit or loss (or income and expenditure) for a period. Although the FRS is framed in terms of an entity becoming a subsidiary undertaking of a parent company that prepares consolidated financial statements, it also applies where an individual company or other reporting entity combines with a business other than a subsidiary undertaking.

Use of merger accounting

5 A business combination should be accounted for by using merger accounting if:

(a) the use of merger accounting for the combination is not prohibited by companies legislation (4A Sch 10); and

(b) the combination meets all the specific criteria set out in paragraphs 6–11 below and thus falls within the definition of a merger.

Acquisition accounting should be used for all other business combinations, except as provided in paragraphs 13 and 14.

Criteria for determining whether the definition of a merger is met

6 Criterion 1 — No party to the combination is portrayed as either acquirer or acquired, either by its own board or management or by that of another party to the combination.

7 Criterion 2 — All parties to the combination, as represented by the boards of directors or their appointees, participate in establishing the management structure for the combined entity and in selecting the management personnel, and such decisions are made on the basis of a consensus between the parties to the combination rather than purely by exercise of voting rights.

8 Criterion 3 — The relative sizes of the combining entities are not so disparate that one party dominates the combined entity by virtue of its relative size.

9 Criterion 4 — Under the terms of the combination or related arrangements, the consideration received by equity shareholders of each party to the combination, in relation to their equity shareholding, comprises primarily equity shares in the combined entity; and any non-equity consideration, or equity shares carrying substantially reduced voting or distribution rights, represents an immaterial proportion of the fair value of the consideration received by the equity shareholders of that party. Where one of the combining entities has, within the period of two years before the combination, acquired equity shares in another of the combining entities, the consideration for this acquisition should be taken into account in determining whether this criterion has been met.

10 For the purpose of paragraph 9, the consideration should not be taken to include the distribution to shareholders of:

(a) an interest in a peripheral part of the business of the entity in which they were shareholders and which does not form part of the combined entity; or

(b) the proceeds of the sale of such a business, or loan stock representing such proceeds.

A peripheral part of the business is one that can be disposed of without having a material effect on the nature and focus of the entity's operations.

11 Criterion 5 — No equity shareholders of any of the combining entities retain any material interest in the future performance of only part of the combined entity.

12 For the purposes of paragraphs 6–11 above any convertible share or loan stock should be regarded as equity to the extent that it is converted into equity as a result of the business combination.

Group reconstructions

13 A group reconstruction may be accounted for by using merger accounting, even though there is no business combination meeting the definition of a merger, provided:

(a) the use of merger accounting is not prohibited by companies legislation (4A Sch 10);

(b) the ultimate shareholders remain the same, and the rights of each such shareholder, relative to the others, are unchanged; and

(c) no minority's interest in the net assets of the group is altered by the transfer.

Combination effected by using a new parent company

14 Where a combination is effected by using a newly formed parent company to hold the shares of each of the other parties to a combination, the accounting treatment depends on the substance of the business combination being effected: that is, whether a combination of the entities other than the new parent company would have been an acquisition or a merger. If the combination would have been an acquisition, one entity can be identified as having the role of an acquirer. This acquirer and the new parent company should first be combined by using merger accounting; then the other parties to the business combination should be treated as acquired by this combined company by using the acquisition method of accounting. On the other hand, where the substance of the business combination effected by a new parent company is a merger, the new parent company and the other parties should all be combined by using merger accounting.

Applicability to various structures of business combination

15 The provisions of the FRS, which are explained by reference to an acquirer or issuing entity that issues shares as consideration for the transfer to it of shares in the other parties to the combination, should also be read so as to apply to other arrangements that achieve similar results.

Merger accounting

16 With merger accounting the carrying values of the assets and liabilities of the parties to the combination are not required to be adjusted to fair value on consolidation, although appropriate adjustments should be made to achieve uniformity of accounting policies in the combining entities (4A Sch 11).

17 The results and cash flows of all the combining entities should be brought into the financial statements of the combined entity from the beginning of the financial year in which the combination occurred, adjusted so as to achieve uniformity of accounting policies. The corresponding figures should be restated by including the results for all the combining entities for the previous period and their balance sheets for the previous balance sheet date, adjusted as necessary to achieve uniformity of accounting policies.

18 The difference, if any, between the nominal value of the shares issued plus the fair value of any other consideration given, and the nominal value of the shares received in exchange should be shown as a movement on other reserves in the consolidated financial statements. Any existing balance on the share premium account or capital redemption reserve of the new subsidiary undertaking should be brought in by being shown as a movement on other reserves. These movements should be shown in the reconciliation of movements in shareholders' funds.

19 Merger expenses are not to be included as part of this adjustment, but should be charged to the profit and loss account of the combined entity at the effective date of the merger, as reorganisation or restructuring expenses, in accordance with paragraph 20 of FRS 3 'Reporting Financial Performance'.

Acquisition accounting

20 Business combinations not accounted for by merger accounting should be accounted for by acquisition accounting. Under acquisition accounting, the identifiable assets and liabilities of the companies acquired should be included in the acquirer's consolidated balance sheet at their fair value at the date of acquisition. The results and cash flows of the acquired companies should be brought into the group accounts only from the date of acquisition. The figures for the previous period for the reporting entity should not be adjusted. The difference between the fair value of the net identifiable assets acquired and the fair value of the purchase consideration is goodwill, positive or negative (4A Sch 9).*

Disclosure

Acquisitions and mergers

21 The following information in respect of all business combinations occurring in the financial year, whether accounted for as acquisitions or mergers, should be disclosed in the

*The date of acquisition and the acquisition of a subsidiary undertaking in stages are dealt with in FRS 2, paragraphs 45, 50, 84-85 and 88-89.

financial statements of the acquiring entity or, in the case of a merger, the entity issuing shares (4A Sch 13(2)):

(a) the names of the combining entities (other than the reporting entity);

(b) whether the combination has been accounted for as an acquisition or a merger;

(c) the date of the combination.

Mergers

22 In respect of each business combination accounted for as a merger, other than group reconstructions falling within paragraph 13, the following information should be disclosed in the financial statements of the combined entity for the period in which the merger took place:

(a) an analysis of the principal components of the current year's profit and loss account and statement of total recognised gains and losses into (Extension of 4A Sch 13(4));

(i) amounts relating to the merged entity for the period after the date of the merger, and

(ii) for each party to the merger, amounts relating to that party for the period up to the date of the merger;

(b) an analysis between the parties to the merger of the principal components of the profit and loss account and statement of total recognised gains and losses for the previous financial year (Extension of 4A Sch 13(4));

(c) the composition and fair value of the consideration given by the issuing company and its subsidiary undertakings (4A Sch 13(3));

(d) the aggregate book value of the net assets of each party to the merger at the date of the merger;

(e) the nature and amount of significant accounting adjustments made to the net assets of any party to the merger to achieve consistency of accounting policies, and an explanation of any other significant adjustments made to the net assets of any party to the merger as a consequence of the merger(4A Sch 13(6)); and

(f) a statement of the adjustments to consolidated reserves resulting from the merger (4A Sch 13(6)).

The analysis of the profit and loss account in (a) and (b) above should show as a minimum the turnover, operating profit and exceptional items, split between continuing operations, discontinued operations and acquisitions; profit before taxation; taxation and minority interests; and extraordinary items.

Acquisitions

23 The disclosure requirements for business combinations accounted for as acquisitions apply as follows:

(a) those in paragraphs 24–35 are required for each material acquisition; and, with the exception of those in paragraph 35, should also be given for other acquisitions in aggregate;

(b) the additional disclosure requirements in paragraph 36 apply to substantial acquisitions as defined in paragraph 37.

24 The composition and fair value of the consideration given by the acquiring company and its subsidiary undertakings should be disclosed. The nature of any deferred or contingent purchase consideration should be stated, including, for contingent consideration, the range of possible outcomes and the principal factors that affect the outcome (4A Sch 13(3)).

25 A table should be provided showing, for each class of assets and liabilities of the acquired entity (4A Sch 13(5)):

(a) the book values, as recorded in the acquired entity's books immediately before the acquisition and before any fair value adjustments:

(b) the fair value adjustments, analysed into:

(i) revaluations,

(ii) adjustments to achieve consistency of accounting policies, and

(iii) any other significant adjustments, giving the reasons for the adjustments; and

(c) the fair values at the date of acquisition.

The table should include a statement of the amount of purchased goodwill or negative goodwill arising on the acquisition.

26 In the table required by paragraph 25, provisions for reorganisation and restructuring costs that are included in the liabilities of the acquired entity, and related asset write-downs, made in the twelve months up to the date of acquisition should be identified separately.

27 Where the fair values of the identifiable assets or liabilities, or the purchase consideration, can be determined only on a provisional basis at the end of the accounting period in which the acquisition took place, this should be stated and the reasons given. Any subsequent material adjustments to such provisional fair values, with corresponding adjustments to goodwill, should be disclosed and explained.

28 As required by FRS 3, in the period of acquisition the post-acquisition results of the acquired entity should be shown as a component of continuing operations in the profit and loss account, other than those that are also discontinued in the same period; and where an acquisition has a material impact on a major business segment this should be disclosed and explained.

29 Where it is not practicable to determine the post-acquisition results of an operation to the end of the period of acquisition, an indication should be given of the contribution of the acquired entity to the turnover and operating profit of the continuing operations. If an indication of the contribution of an acquired entity to the results of the period cannot be given, this fact and the reason should be explained.

30 Any exceptional profit or loss in periods following the acquisition that is determined using the fair values recognised on acquisition should be disclosed in accordance with the requirements of FRS 3, and identified as relating to the acquisition.

31 The profit and loss account or notes to the financial statements of periods following the acquisition should show the costs incurred in those periods in reorganising, restructuring and integrating the acquisition. Such costs are those that:

(a) would not have been incurred had the acquisition not taken place; and

(b) relate to a project identified and controlled by management as part of a reorganisation or integration programme set up at the time of acquisition or as a direct consequence of an immediate post-acquisition review.

32 Movements on provisions or accruals for costs related to an acquisition should be disclosed and analysed between the amounts used for the specific purpose for which they were created and the amounts released unused.

33 In accordance with FRS 1, the cash flow statement should show the amounts of cash and cash equivalents paid in respect of the consideration, net of any cash and cash equivalents balances transferred as part of the acquisition. In addition, a note to the cash flow statement should show a summary of the effects of acquisitions indicating how much of the consideration comprised cash and cash equivalents and the amounts of cash and cash equivalents transferred as a result of the acquisition.

34 In accordance with FRS 1, material effects on amounts reported under each of the standard headings reflecting the cash flows of the acquired entity in the period should be disclosed, as far as is practicable, as a note to the cash flow statement. This information need be given only in the financial statements for the period in which the acquisition occurs.

35 For a material acquisition, the profit after taxation and minority interests of the acquired entity should be given for (4A Sch 13(4)):

(a) the period from the beginning of the acquired entity's financial year to the date of acquisition giving the date on which this period began; and

(b) its previous financial year.

Substantial acquisitions

36 For acquisitions meeting the conditions set ut in the next paragraph, the following information should be disclosed in the financial statements of the combined entity for the period in which the acquisition took place (Extension of 4A Sch 13 (4)):

(a) the summarised profit and loss account and statement of total recognised gains and losses of the acquired entity for the period from the beginning of its financial year to the effective date of acquisition, giving the date on which this period began; this summarised profit and loss account should show as a minimum the turnover, operating profit and those exceptional items falling within paragraph 20 of FRS 3; profit before taxation; taxation and minority interests; and extraordinary items;

(b) the profit after tax and minority interests for the acquired entity's previous financial year.

This information should be shown on the basis of the acquired entity's accounting policies prior to the acquisition.

37 The disclosures in paragraph 36 should be given for each business combination accounted for by using acquisition accounting where:

(a) for listed companies, the combination is a Class I or Super Class I transaction under the Stock Exchange Listing Rules;

(b) for other entities, either

(i) the net assets or operating profits of the acquired entity exceed 15 per cent of those of the acquiring entity, or

(ii) the fair value of the consideration given exceeds 15 per cent of the net assets of the acquiring entity;

and should also be made in other exceptional cases where an acquisition is of such significance that the disclosure is necessary in order to give a true and fair view. For the purposes of (b) above, net assets and profits should be those shown in the financial statements for the last financial year before the date of the acquisition; and the net assets should be augmented by any purchased goodwill eliminated against reserves as a matter of accounting policy and not charged to the profit and loss account.

Date from which effective

38 The accounting practices set out in the FRS should be regarded as standard in respect of business combinations first accounted for in financial statements relating to accounting periods commencing on or after 23 December 1994. Earlier adoption is encouraged but not required.

Withdrawal of SSAP 23 and amendment of SSAP 22

39 The FRS supersedes SSAP 23 'Accounting for acquisitions and mergers' and paragraphs 48–51 of SSAP 22 'Accounting for goodwill'.

Explanation

Introduction

40 Two different methods have been used to account for business combinations: merger accounting and acquisition accounting.

41 In merger accounting the financial statements of the parties to the combination are aggregated, and presented as though the combining entities had always been part of the same reporting entity. Accordingly, although the merger may have taken place part of the way through the financial year, the results of the combining entities for the full financial year are reflected in the group accounts for the period and corresponding amounts are presented on the same basis. The accounting policies of the combining entities are adjusted to achieve uniformity, but the assets and liabilities need not be adjusted to reflect fair values at the date of the combination. Under merger accounting, a difference may arise on consolidation between the nominal value of the shares issued, taken together with the fair value of any other consideration, and the aggregate of the nominal values the shares received in exchange. Such difference is not goodwill, as it does not result from the difference between the fair value of the consideration and the fair value of the identifiable net assets. It should be shown as a movement on consolidated reserves. Any share premium accounts and capital redemption reserves of the new subsidiary undertaking are not preserved as such in the consolidated accounts, since they do not relate to the share capital of the reporting entity, but are brought in by being shown as a movement on other reserves.

42 In acquisition accounting the results of the acquired company are brought into the group accounts only from the date of acquisition. The identifiable assets and liabilities acquired are included at fair value in the consolidated accounts and are therefore stated at their cost to the acquiring group. The fair value of the consideration given is set against the aggregate fair value of the net identifiable assets acquired and any resulting balance is goodwill, if positive, or else a negative consolidation difference called negative goodwill.*

43 The fact that a particular business combination does not meet the criteria for merger accounting, and is thus accounted for by using acquisition accounting, does not preclude the acquirer from obtaining merger relief in its individual accounts under the provisions of section 131 of the Companies Act 1985 if the requirements of that section are met. In

*The treatment of such balances is dealt with in SSAP 22 'Accounting for goodwill' and is the subject of a current ASB project.

such cases, in the consolidated accounts, acquisition accounting is applied in the normal way: goodwill is still calculated by comparing the fair value of the shares issued, rather than their nominal or recorded value, with the fair value of the net assets acquired; and any resulting excess over the nominal value of the shares issued, taken together with the fair value of any other consideration, is shown, not as share premium, but as a separate reserve.

Definition of a merger and an acquisition

44 A merger is a rare type of business combination in which two or more parties come together for the mutual sharing of benefits and risks arising from the combined businesses, in what is in substance an equal partnership, each sharing influence in the new entity. No party can be regarded as acquiring control over another, or becoming controlled by another; and the reporting entity formed by the combination must be regarded as a new entity rather than the continuation of one of the combining entities, enlarged by its having obtained control over the others.

45 An acquisition is defined as any business combination that is not a merger. In many acquisitions, the shareholders of the acquired party do not have a continuing interest in the combined entity, but instead sell their shareholdings for cash or other non-equity consideration. Even where all parties in an acquisition retain an interest in the combined entity, the parties do not come together on equal terms; one party has a greater degree of influence than the others, and is seen as acquiring the other entities in exchange for a share in the combined entity. An acquisition is therefore a transaction that is, in substance, the application of resources by the acquiring entity to obtain control of one or more other entities, by the payment of cash, transfer of other assets, the incurring of a liability or the issue of shares.

46 The legal form of a business combination will normally be for one company to acquire shares in one or more others. This fact does not make that company an acquirer in the sense discussed above. Similarly, the question of whether the combined entity should be regarded as a new reporting entity is not affected by whether or not a new legal entity has been formed to acquire shares in others.

Rationale for merger accounting

47 In a merger, no party to the combination can be properly regarded as obtaining control over the other; rather, the parties to the combination join together on an equal footing to form a combined enterprise for their mutual benefit.

48 For such mergers it is misleading to account for the combination as the application of resources by one party to obtain control over the other, since this assumes a distinction in the roles of the parties that does not reflect reality. Furthermore, it is only the legal structure of the combination that would determine which party would be treated under acquisition accounting as the acquirer, and thus determine the party whose net assets would be treated as being acquired and whose goodwill would be recognised.

49 A merger is a true mutual sharing of the benefits and risks of the combined entity. Therefore the joint history of the entities that have combined will be relevant to the combined group's shareholders. This record will be provided by merger accounting because it treats the separate businesses as though they were continuing as before, only now jointly owned and managed. If acquisition accounting were to be used, it would focus artificially on only one of the parties to the combination, which would lead to a discontinuity in information reported on the combined entity.

50 Thus the concept of a merger is of a partnership or pooling of interests, where all the parties to the combination participate in the combined businesses of the merged entity on substantially equal terms; and where the substance of the arrangement is such that the reporting entity cannot be regarded as merely being enlarged by the acquisition of the other entities, but must be considered as effectively a new reporting entity.

51 In a business combination that qualifies as a merger, expenses of the combination are similar in nature to expenses of a fundamental reorganisation or restructuring, and should be charged to the profit and loss account for the period in which the merger occurred, shown as an exceptional item in accordance with paragraph 20 of FRS 3. This is not intended to prohibit the subsequent charging of issue costs to the share premium account by means of a transfer between reserves.

Rationale for acquisition accounting

52 The acquisition of another entity is a transaction by which an entity seeks to increase the assets under its control. Acquisition accounting is appropriate for most business combinations since it reflects in the financial statements the application of resources by one party to the combination in order to obtain control of the other, represented by the fair value of the net assets over which control is obtained together with goodwill.

53 The profits of the acquired company are brought into account only from the date of the combination and the history of the group is seen as the history of the acquirer with occasional additions when it acquires other entities.

Deciding whether a business combination is a merger or an acquisition

54 The FRS requires that to determine whether a business combination meets the definition of a merger, it should be assessed against certain specified criteria; failure to meet any of these criteria indicates that the definition was not met and thus that merger accounting is not to be used for the combination.

55 Individually these tests are insufficient to define the intangible quality of a true merger, and may appear arbitrary. Nevertheless, taken as a whole, they provide a reasonable basis for determining whether a particular business combination meets the definition of a merger and thus should be accounted for by using merger accounting.

56 In applying the criteria, it is necessary to consider the substance and not just the form of the arrangements and to take account of all relevant information related to the combination. It is important to have regard to the transaction as a whole, including any related arrangements that are connected with the business combination either because they are entered into in contemplation of that combination or because they are part of the process by which that combination is effected. The vast majority of business combinations will be acquisitions and only in rare circumstances will a combination fulfil all the detailed conditions for it to be treated as a merger.

Parties to the combination

57 For the purposes of assessing whether a combination is a merger meeting the criteria, the parties to the combination are considered as comprising not solely the business of each entity that is combining but also the management of the entity and the body of its shareholders.

58 Merger accounting is not appropriate for a combination where one of the parties results from a recent divestment by a larger entity, because the divested business will not have been independent for a sufficient period to establish itself as being a party separate from its previous owner. Only once the divested business has established a track record of its own can it be considered as a party to a merger. However, a party to a combination may divest itself of a peripheral part of its business before the combination (or as part of the arrangements for the combination) and still meet the criteria for merger accounting.

59 Where a party to the combination is not a company with share capital, the conditions applying to equity shares should be interpreted as applying to those elements of its capital structure that allocate rights to profits and control.

Criterion 1 — role of the parties

60 An essential feature of a merger is that it represents a genuine combining of the interests of the parties; such a genuine combination of interests cannot exist if one party portrays itself, or another party, as having a dominant role as an acquirer or the subservient role of being acquired.

61 Where the terms of a share-for-share exchange indicate that one party has paid a premium over the market value of the shares acquired, this is evidence that that party has taken the role of an acquirer unless there is a clear explanation for this apparent premium other than its being a premium paid to acquire control.

62 The circumstances surrounding the transaction may provide evidence to indicate the nature of a business combination. The following, while not individually conclusive, would need to be considered: the form by which the combination was achieved, the plans for the combined entity's future operations (for example, whether any closures or disposals related more to one party than another), and the proposed corporate image (such as the name, logo and the location of the headquarters and principal operations). Where a publicly quoted company is a party to a business combination, the content of communications with its shareholders is likely also to be relevant in determining the substance of the transaction.

Criterion 2 — dominance of management

63 An essential feature of the genuine combination of interests underlying the definition of a merger is that all parties to the combination are involved in determining the management of the combined entity and reach a consensus on the appropriate structure and personnel; if decisions can be reached only by the exercise of majority voting rights against the wishes of one of the parties to the merger, or if one party clearly dominates this process, this indicates that the combination is not a genuine pooling of interests. However, this does not preclude the possibility of all, or most, of the management team of the combined entity coming from only one of the parties, provided that this clearly reflects the wishes of the others.

64 In applying this test, it is necessary to consider not only the formal management structure of the combined entity, but also the identity of all persons involved in the main financial and operating decisions and the way in which the decision-making process operates in practice within the combined entity.

65 Normally the management of the combined entity would contain representatives of each of the combining parties. Where the senior management structure and personnel of the combined entity are essentially those of one of the combining parties, this criterion will not have been met unless it is clear that all the parties to the merger genuinely participated in the decision.

66 In applying this test it is necessary to consider only the decisions made in the period of initial integration and restructuring at the time of the combination; but both the short-term effects and expected long-term consequences of decisions made in this period need to be considered.

Criterion 3 — relative size of the parties

67 Where one party is substantially larger than the other parties it would be presumed that the larger party can or will dominate the combined undertaking. This will not be consistent with treating such a business combination as a merger as the combined entity will not be a substantially equal partnership.

68 A party would be presumed to dominate if it is more than 50 per cent larger than each of the other parties to the combination, judged by reference to the ownership interests; that is, by considering the proportion of the equity of the combined entity attributable to the shareholders of each of the combining parties. However, this presumption may be rebutted if it can be clearly shown that there is no such dominance; other factors, such as voting or share agreements, blocking powers or other arrangements, can mean that a party to the combination has more influence, or conversely less influence, than is indicated by its relative size. Circumstances that rebut the presumption of dominant influence based on relative sizes would need to be disclosed and explained.

Criterion 4 — non-equity consideration

69 Criterion 4 is concerned with the extent to which equity shareholders of the combining entities receive any consideration other than equity shares (as defined in paragraph 2 above) in the combined entity. Cash, other assets, loan stock and preference shares are all examples of non-equity consideration.

70 As stated in the note on legal requirements (Appendix I), companies legislation provides that one of the conditions for merger accounting is that the fair value of any consideration other than the issue of equity shares (as defined in companies legislation) did not exceed 10 per cent of the nominal value of the equity shares issued. Criterion 4 requires a further condition to be met, that all but an immaterial proportion of the fair value of the consideration received must be in the form of equity shares (as defined in paragraph 2); this definition of equity, which is that adopted in FRS 4 'Capital instruments', is narrower than that of companies legislation, and is used to avoid the possibility of Criterion 4 being met by the use of shares that, although within the statutory definition of equity, have characteristics that are closer to non-equity.

71 The FRS requires that all arrangements made in conjunction with the combination must be taken into account. Equity shareholders will be considered to have disposed of their shareholding for cash where any arrangement is made in connection with the combination that enabled them to exchange or redeem the shares they received in the combination for cash (or other non-equity consideration); for example, a vendor placing or similar arrangement should be treated as giving rise to non-equity consideration. However, a normal market selling transaction, or privately arranged sale, entered into by a shareholder is not made in conjunction with the combination and does not prevent the criterion being met.

72 A business combination may not be accounted for as a merger if a material part of the consideration that the issuing entity offers the equity shareholders in the other parties is in the form of shares with substantially reduced rights. Such an offer would be contrary to the concept that a merger is the mutual sharing in risks and rewards of the combined entity. Some adjustment to the rights attaching to the shares held by the non-issuing entities' shareholders may be compatible with the combination being a merger, as business combinations result from a negotiating process where different pre-existing rights have to be reconciled. Whether any change in the rights of one group of shareholders is sufficient to prevent that business combination being treated as a merger will depend on the facts in any individual case, taking into account such matters as what rights shareholders originally had, the total arrangement negotiated, time limits and whether any new restrictions apply equally to all sets of shareholders. In determining whether equity shares with reduced rights have been issued, both rights to vote and rights to distributions attaching to the shares would need to be taken into account. If any of these individual rights were significantly reduced or circumscribed the combination would fail to fulfil this condition.

73 If one entity has acquired an interest in another in exchange for non-equity consideration, or equity shares with significantly reduced rights, within the two years before those entities combined, such consideration should be regarded as part of the consideration for the combination for the purpose of determining whether this criterion is met.

74 Sometimes a peripheral part of the business of one of the combining parties will be excluded from the combined entity. The FRS states that shares in the peripheral business, or the proceeds of sale of the business, that are distributed to the shareholders of that party to the combination as part of the arrangements for the combination are not to be counted as part of the consideration for the purposes of this criterion.

Criterion 5 — minorities etc.

75 Criterion 5 is concerned with a party retaining an interest in only part of the combined entity. The concept of a merger is that the participants enter into a mutual sharing of the risks and rewards of the whole of the new entity, including the pooled future results of the combined entity. This concept is incompatible with certain participants having a preferential interest in one part of the combined entity. This criterion would not, therefore, be met if the share of the equity in the combined entity allocated to the shareholders of one of the parties to the combination depended to any material extent on the post-combination performance of the business, or any part of it, formerly controlled by that party.

76 This criterion would similarly not be met where earn-outs or similar performance-related schemes are included in the arrangements to effect a merger. The test is also failed if there is any material minority (defined by companies legislation as 10 per cent) of shareholders left in one of the combining parties that have not accepted the terms of the combination offer.

77 However, the criterion would not necessarily be invalidated by an arrangement whereby the allocation of consideration between the shareholders of the combining parties depended on the determination of the eventual value of a specific liability or asset contributed by one of the parties—such as the eventual outcome of a claim against one of the parties, or the eventual sales value of a specific asset owned by one of the parties — as opposed to the future operating performance of that party.

Group reconstructions

78 In addition to mergers as defined above, merger accounting may also be appropriate for a group reconstruction, provided that the relative rights of the ultimate shareholders are not altered. Such reconstructions include not only the transfer of shares in a subsidiary undertaking within a group, but also arrangements such as the introduction of a new holding company, the splitting off of one or more subsidiary undertakings, as in some demergers, where a separate group is formed, and the bringing together into a new group of two or more companies that were previously under common ownership. Acquisition accounting would require the restatement at fair value of the assets and liabilities of the company transferred, and the recognising of goodwill, which is likely to be inappropriate in the case of a transaction that does not alter the relative rights of the ultimate shareholders.

79 Where a minority interest exists, merger accounting is permitted only for those group reconstructions that do not change the interest of the minority in the net assets of the group. Thus the transfer of a subsidiary undertaking within a sub-group that has a minority shareholder may qualify for merger accounting; but acquisition accounting must be used for the transfer of a subsidiary undertaking out of, or into, such a sub-group. If a minority has effectively acquired, or disposed of, rights to part of the net assets of the group, the FRS requires the transfer to be accounted for by using acquisition accounting rather than merger accounting.

Disclosure

80 The disclosure requirements in the FRS cover and supplement those in companies legislation.

Mergers

81 With merger accounting the financial statements of the combined entity are drawn up by combining the results of the combining entities for the whole of the financial year in which the merger occurred. Users, particularly those who have been assessing the parties to the combination as separate businesses, may require information on the financial performance of the individual parties. The FRS therefore requires an analysis of the profit and loss account and statement of total recognised gains and losses into pre- and post-merger amounts; and a further analysis of the pre-merger amounts between each of the parties to the merger. An analysis between the parties of the preceding financial year is also required. However, it is not necessary, where revaluation gains or losses have been recognised as a result of a valuation at the year-end, to obtain further valuations at the date of the merger in order to apportion the gains or losses between pre- and post-merger periods.

82 Group reconstructions that are accounted for by using merger accounting are exempted from the disclosure requirements in the FRS, but must still give the information required by companies legislation.

Acquisitions

83 The disclosure requirements of the FRS provide information about the resources applied in acquisitions, the net assets acquired and the effects on the consolidated financial statements of the acquiring group. Separate presentation of the results of acquisitions assists analysis of the significance of new operations that have been acquired. In some circumstances it may also be useful to users for the results of acquisitions for the first full financial year for which they are a part of the reporting entity to be disclosed in the notes.

84 Paragraph 23 of the FRS requires the disclosures in paragraphs 24-35 to be given for each material acquisition, and those in paragraphs 24-34 to be given for other acquisitions in aggregate. Materiality must be judged by whether the information relating to the acquisition might reasonably be expected to influence decisions made by the users of general purpose financial statements. Paragraph 36 applies further disclosure requirements to certain substantial acquisitions.

85 In order to give a true and fair view of post-acquisition financial performance, paragraph 30 of the FRS requires disclosure of exceptional profits or losses determined using fair values recognised on an acquisition. Examples include profits or losses on the disposal of acquired stocks where the fair values of stocks sold lead to abnormal trading margins after the acquisition; the release of provisions in respect of an acquired loss-making long-term contract that the acquirer makes profitable; and the realisation of contingent assets or liabilities at amounts materially different from their attributed fair values. In accordance with the requirements of FRS 3, exceptional items would be included in the profit and loss account format headings to which they relate, and would be disclosed by way of note, or on the face of the profit and loss account if necessary to give a true and fair view.

86 FRS 3 requires the profits or losses on the post-acquisition sale or termination of an operation, or on the disposal of fixed assets, to be shown in the profit and loss account below operating profit. Post-acquisition integration, reorganisation and restructuring costs, including provisions in respect of them, would, if material, be reported as exceptional items; but only if the restructuring is fundamental, having a material effect on the nature and focus of the enlarged group's operations, would the costs be shown below operating profit as an item falling under paragraph 20 of FRS 3. Paragraph 31 of FRS 6 requires that costs of reorganising, restructuring and integration that relate to an acquisition, whether relating to a fundamental restructuring or not, should be shown separately from other exceptional items.

87 The costs of reorganising, restructuring and integrating an acquired entity may extend over more than one period. For major acquisitions, therefore, management may wish to state in the notes to the financial statements the nature and amount of such costs expected to be incurred in relation to the acquisition (including asset write-downs), indicating the extent to which they have been charged to the profit and loss account. If part of these costs relate to asset write-downs (beyond any impairments recognised in adjusting to fair values on the acquisition) it may be useful to distinguish these from cash expenditure. An illustrative example of how such information might be shown is included as Appendix IV to the FRS.

Substantial acquisitions

88 Where an acquisition has been made that has a substantial effect on the consolidated results of the acquiring entity, additional disclosures are required to enable the user to assess the effect of the acquisition on the consolidated results. Although control over the acquired entity is obtained only at the date of acquisition, in most cases it is a continuing business that is acquired, and information on the results for the period up to the date of acquisition is relevant to the user. For acquisitions that meet the size tests in paragraph 37, the FRS therefore requires the disclosure of the results of the acquired entity for the part of its financial year up to the date of the acquisition, and for its previous financial year. Since neither of these periods will necessarily be twelve months, their commencing dates should also be indicated.

89 Several components of the pre-acquisition results are required to be shown for the part of the acquired entity's financial year up to the date of acquisition, since this period may be particularly relevant to an understanding of the post-acquisition results and may not otherwise be publicly reported. Equivalent information for the preceding financial year is likely to be of less relevance, and the disclosure requirement is limited to profit after tax and minority interests. The FRS requires this information to be given on the basis of the acquired entity's accounting policies before the acquisition; in some cases, the management of the acquiring entity may consider it helpful in explaining the impact of the acquisition to give, in addition, the same information restated onto the basis of the acquiring entity's accounting policies.

Adoption of FRS 6 by the Board

Financial Reporting Standard 6 — 'Acquisitions and Mergers' was approved for issue by the eight members of the Accounting Standards Board.

Sir David Tweedie (Chairman)

Allan Cook (Technical Director)

Robert Bradfield

Ian Brindle

Michael Garner

Raymond Hinton

Donald Main

Graham Stacy

Appendix 1

Note on legal requirements

Great Britain

References are to the Companies Act 1985

Merger accounting

1 The Companies Act describes the acquisition method of accounting (Schedule 4A paragraph 9) and the merger method of accounting (Schedule 4A paragraph 11). Schedule 4A paragraph 10 lays down the conditions that must be met if a business combination is to be accounted for as a merger. The conditions are:

(a) that at least 10 per cent of the nominal value of the relevant shares (those with unrestricted rights to participate both in distributions and in the assets on liquidation) in the undertaking acquired is held by or on behalf of the parent company and its subsidiary undertakings;

(b) that the proportion referred to in (a) was attained pursuant to an arrangement providing for the issue of equity shares by the parent company or one or more of its subsidiary undertakings;

(c) that the fair value of any consideration other than the issue of equity shares given pursuant to the arrangement by the parent company and its subsidiary undertakings did not exceed 10 per cent of the nominal value of the equity shares issued; and

(d) that adoption of the merger method of accounting accords with generally accepted accounting principles or practice.

2 Where a group is acquired, the Companies Act requirements described in the previous paragraph also apply. References to shares of the undertaking acquired are to be construed as references to the shares of the acquired group's parent and references to the assets and liabilities, income and expenditure, and capital and reserves of the undertaking acquired are to be construed as references to the same elements of the group acquired, after making the necessary set-off and adjustments required for the consolidated accounts (Schedule 4A paragraph 12).

Disclosures

3 The following information shall be given in a note to the accounts for all business combinations taking place in the financial year:

(a) the names of the entities involved;

(b) whether the combination has been accounted for by the acquisition or merger method of accounting (Schedule 4A paragraph 13 (2)).

4 In addition, for any business combination that significantly affects the figures shown in the group accounts, the following further information shall be given:

(a) the composition and fair value of the consideration for the acquisition given by the parent and its subsidiary undertakings (Schedule 4Aparagraph I3(3));

(b) the profit or loss of the undertaking or group acquired for the period up to the date of the acquisition from the beginning of the financial year of that undertaking or group, and for the previous financial year of that undertaking or group. The date on which this financial year began should also be stated (Schedule 4A paragraph 13 (4)) .

5 Where the acquisition method of accounting has been adopted, the book values immediately prior to acquisition and fair values at the date of acquisition of each class of assets and liabilities of the acquired entity shall be stated in tabular form, including a statement of the amount of any goodwill or negative consolidation difference arising on the acquisition, together with an explanation of any significant adjustments made (Schedule 4A paragraph 13(5)).

6 Where the merger method of accounting has been adopted, an explanation shall be given of any significant adjustments made in relation to the amounts of the assets and liabilities of the undertaking or group acquired, together with a statement of any resulting adjustment to the consolidated reserves (including the restatement of opening consolidated reserves) (Schedule 4A paragraph 13 (6)).

7 None of the information required by paragraph 13 of Schedule 4A to the Act need be disclosed for an undertaking which:

(a) is established under the law of a country outside the United Kingdom; or

(b) carries on business outside the United Kingdom.

if, in the opinion of the directors of the parent company, the disclosure would be seriously prejudicial to the business of that undertaking or to the business of the parent company or any of its subsidiary undertakings and the Secretary of State agrees that the information should not be disclosed (Schedule 4A paragraph 16).

Share premium and merger relief

8 Section 130(1) of the Companies Act provides that if a company issues shares at a premium, whether for cash or otherwise, a sum equal to the aggregate amount or value of the premiums on those shares should be transferred to an account called the share premium account. The provisions of the Companies Act relating to the reduction of a company's share capital apply, with exceptions, as if the share premium account were part of its paid-up share capital.

9 Limited relief from the above ('merger relief') is given by sections 131-134.

10 Section 131 of the Companies Act provides, *inter alia,* that, subject to specified conditions, where an issuing company has secured at least a 90 per cent equity holding in another company, section 130 does not apply to the premium on shares issued in the transaction which takes the holding in that other company to at least 90 per cent.

11 Section 133(1) provides that the premium on any shares to which the relief in sections 131 and 132 of the Companies Act applies may also be disregarded in determining the amount at which any shares, or other consideration provided for the shares issued, are to be included in the offeror company's balance sheet.

12 The Companies Act requires the disclosure of additional information where merger relief is taken. Schedule 5 paragraphs 10 and 29 refer respectively to companies that are not obliged to prepare group accounts and those that are. They apply to arrangements attracting merger relief, that is, where a company allots shares in consideration for the issue, transfer or cancellation of shares in another body corporate ('the other company') in circumstances such that section 131(2) (merger relief) applies to the premiums on the shares.

13 If the company makes such an arrangement during the financial year, the following information shall be given:

(a) the name of the other company;

(b) the number, nominal value and class of shares allotted;

(c) the number, nominal value and class of shares in the other company issued, transferred or cancelled; and

(d) particulars of the accounting treatment adopted in the consolidated accounts in respect of the issue, transfer or cancellation.

14 In addition, for companies that are required to prepare group accounts Schedule 5 paragraph 29(2) requires the disclosure of particulars of the extent to which and manner in which the profit or loss for the financial year shown in the consolidated accounts is affected by any profit or loss of the other company, or any of its subsidiary undertakings, that arose before the time of the arrangement.

Accounts of the parent company

15 The FRS deals only with the method of accounting to be used in group accounts; it does not deal with the form of accounting to be used in the acquiring or issuing company's own accounts and in particular does not restrict the reliefs available under sections 131–133 of the Companies Act.

16 Where a dividend is paid to the acquiring or issuing company out of pre-combination profits, it would appear that it need not necessarily be applied as a reduction in the carrying value of the investment in the subsidiary undertaking. Such a dividend received should be applied to reduce the carrying value of the investment to the extent necessary to provide for a diminution in value of the investment in the subsidiary undertaking as stated in the accounts of the parent company. To the extent that this is not necessary, it appears that the amount received will be a realised profit in the hands of the parent company.

Northern Ireland

17 The legal requirements in Northern Ireland are similar to those in Great Britain. The following table shows the references to the Companies (Northern Ireland) Order 1986 that correspond to the marginal references in the FRS and the legal references in paragraphs 1–16 above.

Great Britain: the Companies Act 1985	*Northern Ireland:* the 1986 Order
Merger accounting	
Schedule 4A paragraphs 9–12	Schedule 4A paragraphs 9–12
Disclosures	
Schedule 4A paragraph 13	Schedule 4A paragraph 13
Schedule 4A paragraph 16	Schedule 4A paragraph 16
Share premium and merger relief	
Sections 130–134	Articles 140–144
Schedule 5 paragraph 10	Schedule 5 paragraph 10
Schedule 5 paragraph 29	Schedule 5 paragraph 29

Republic of Ireland

18 The following table shows the references to the European Communities (Companies: Group Accounts) Regulations 1992 and the Companies Act 1963 that correspond to the marginal references in the FRS and the legal references in paragraphs 1–16 above.

Great Britain: the Companies Act 1985	*Republic of Ireland:* the 1992 Regulations
Merger accounting	
Schedule 4A paragraph 9	Paragraph 19
Schedule 4A paragraph 10	Paragraph 21
Schedule 4A paragraph 11	Paragraph 22
Schedule 4A paragraph 12	Paragraph 23
Disclosures	
Schedule 4A paragraph 13(2)	The Schedule paragraph 12(2)
Schedule 4A paragraph 13(3)–13(6)	No exact equivalent; paragraph 27 of the l992 Regulations states that if the composition of the undertakings dealt with in the group accounts has changed significantly in the course of a financial year, the group accounts must include information that makes the comparison of successive setsof group accounts meaningful.
Schedule 4A paragraph 16	No equivalent

Share premium and merger relief

Section 130	Companies Act 1963 section 62
Sections 131–134	No equivalent
Schedule 5 paragraph 10	No equivalent
Schedule 5 paragraph 29	No equivalent

Merger relief in the Republic of Ireland

19 As there is currently no legislation equivalent to merger relief in the Republic of Ireland, no explicit relief from the requirement of section 62(1) of the Companies Act 1963 to establish a share premium account is available.

20 However, section 149(5) of the Companies Act I963 provides that, whilst, in general, pre-acquisition profits of acquired subsidiaries may not be treated in the holding company's accounts as revenue profit, an exemption from that provision is available in that, where the directors and auditors are satisfied and so certify that it would be fair and reasonable and would not prejudice the rights and interests of any person, the profits or losses attributable to any shares in a subsidiary may be treated in a manner otherwise than in accordance with that sub-section.

21 The possible need for legal advice in relation to the application of section 149(5) to merger accounting should be considered before merger accounting is applied to Republic of Ireland companies.

Appendix II

Compliance with International Accounting Standards

The requirements of the FRS are consistent with International Accounting Standard 22 'Business Combinations' (revised 1993), except for the provision in paragraph 13 of that standard relating to reverse acquisitions, which is incompatible with companies legislation in the UK and the Republic of Ireland.

Appendix III

The development of the FRS

History

Before the Companies Act 1981

1 Although some use was made of merger accounting in the UK before the Companies Act 1981, and indeed an exposure draft of an accounting standard, ED 3, was published (in 1971), there was concern that the share premium provisions of the Companies Act 1948 might be interpreted so as to prohibit the use of merger accounting. This view was confirmed by the decision in *Shearer* v. *Bercain* in 1980.

The Companies Act 1981 and SSAP 23

2 The Companies Act 1981 introduced the concept of merger relief, removing the legal obstacle to merger accounting. Following this, the Accounting Standards Committee

(ASC) issued an exposure draft, ED 31, converted into an accounting standard, SSAP 23 'Accounting for acquisitions and mergers', in 1985.

3 SSAP 23 based its concept of a merger on whether or not the arrangements for the combination resulted in material resources leaving the group. This concept was supported by four criteria defining the circumstances in which merger accounting was permitted:

(a) the business combination results from an offer to the holders of all equity shares and the holders of all voting shares that are not already held by the offeror; and

(b) the offeror has secured, as a result of the offer, a holding of (i) at least 90 per cent of all equity shares (taking each class of equity separately), and (ii) the shares carrying at least 90 per cent of the votes of the offeree; and

(c) immediately prior to the offer, the offeror does not hold (i) 20 per cent or more of all equity shares of the offeree (taking each class of equity separately), or (ii) shares carrying 20 per cent or more of the votes of the offeree; and

(d) not less than 90 per cent of the fair value of the total consideration given for the equity share capital (including that given for shares already held) is in the form of equity share capital; not less than 90 per cent of the fair value of the total consideration given for voting non-equity share capital (including that given for shares already held) is in the form of equity and/or voting non-equity share capital.

4 Note, however, that merger accounting remained optional even if these criteria were met.

The EC Seventh Directive and the Companies Act 1989

5 The EC Seventh Company Law Directive introduced more stringent requirements to be met before merger accounting was permitted. The conditions of the Directive were implemented in Great Britain, with some additional provisions, by the Companies Act 1989, as amendments to the Companies Act 1985. These conditions are:

(a) that at least 90 per cent of the nominal value of the relevant shares (those with unrestricted rights to participate both in distributions and in the assets on liquidation) in the undertaking acquired is held by or on behalf of the parent company and its subsidiary undertakings;

(b) that the proportion referred to in (a) was attained pursuant to an arrangement providing for the issue of equity shares by the parent company or one or more of its subsidiary undertakings;

(c) that the fair value of any consideration other than the issue of equity shares given pursuant to the arrangement by the parent company and its subsidiary undertakings did not exceed 10 per cent of the nominal value of the equity shares issued; and

(d) that adoption of the merger method of accounting accords with generally accepted accounting principles or practice.

6 In requiring compliance with generally accepted accounting principles, the Companies Act clearly acknowledged that merger accounting would not be appropriate for all business combinations that met the first three conditions.

7 The comparison, in condition (c), with the nominal value of shares issued is also noteworthy. The nominal value is of no economic significance. In contrast, the corresponding condition (d) of SSAP 23 refers to the fair value of the equity shares issued.

Limiting the use of merger accounting — the ED 48 proposals

8 ED 48 was issued by the ASC in February 1990 in response to widespread concern that the SSAP 23 conditions were too readily circumvented. It proposed to limit the use of merger accounting to a very restricted class of combinations that could be regarded as 'true' mergers. These were to be defined as a combination that was effectively an equal partnership between the combining parties, where no party saw itself as either an acquirer or an acquiree. In addition, there had to be continuing involvement from the management of each of the parties in the combined entity; and the parties were to be of broadly equal size. Any minority not accepting the merger offer was not to exceed 10 per cent, and no material consideration other than equity shares was permitted.

9 ED 48 then proposed that merger accounting would be required, and not merely permitted, for all combinations meeting these conditions (although, as a practical matter, it has been suggested that it would be relatively easy for merging parties to ensure that one of the conditions was not met, without fundamentally altering the commercial substance of the transaction, if they did not wish to use merger accounting — and thus for practical purposes the option to use acquisition accounting might be seen to remain).

10 Although respondents to ED 48 were generally in agreement with its proposals, there was criticism of the conditions for merger accounting, in particular of their subjective nature, which, it was expected, would give rise to difficulties in applying them consistently.

International Accounting Standards

11 The merger concept underlying ED 48 is similar to that proposed for a 'uniting of interests' in the International Accounting Standard 22, revised in 1993, although that standard does not develop tests for identifying when a combination is a merger. IAS 22 defines a uniting of interests as:

> "a business combination in which the shareholders of the combining enterprises combine control over the whole, or effectively the whole, of their net assets and operations to achieve a continuing mutual sharing in the risks and benefits attaching to the combined entity such that neither party can be identified as the acquirer."

FRED 6

12 In considering the application of merger accounting, the Board was concerned by the apparent choice available in many cases between acquisition and merger accounting, and that two business combinations with very similar economic substance could be accounted for in different ways, with substantial differences in reported results and balance sheets not only for the financial year in which the combination occurred but for several years thereafter. The Board also found it difficult to identify any theoretical basis to justify the use of merger accounting for the wide range of business combinations for which it was then permissible.

13 In issuing FRED 6, the Board therefore adopted the intention of ED 48, of narrowing the use of merger accounting.

14 No major changes were proposed, but the Board sought to remove subjectivity where possible. The approach of the FRED was based on the belief that merger accounting should be applied to only a few rare instances of business combinations that were properly regarded as mergers, and that the vast majority of business combinations were more appropriately accounted for as acquisitions.

15 The definition of a merger was redrafted, but its intent was unchanged. The definition of an acquisition was amended to make it clear that all combinations were either mergers or acquisitions.

16 The six conditions under which merger accounting would have been permitted by ED 48 were redrafted as five criteria, as follows:

Criterion 1 — redrafted form of ED 48 condition (a).

Criterion 2 — amended form of ED 48 condition (b), acknowledging that to require the board of a merged entity to have equal participation from each of the parties to the merger might prevent the parties to the merger from choosing the management they considered most appropriate; and might lead to too much focus on the numerical representation of each party on the new board at the expense of considering where the real decision taking influence lay.

Criterion 3 — redrafted form of ED 48 condition (e).

Criterion 4 — redrafted form of ED 48 condition (c).

Criterion 5 — redrafted form of ED 48 conditions (d) and (f), reducing these to a more general principle.

Disclosure

17 The disclosure requirements proposed by ED 48 were extended to require analysis into pre-combination and post-combination periods of several items in the profit and loss account, and the statement of total recognised gains and losses, rather than focusing solely on profit after tax and extraordinary items.

Matters considered in the light of responses to FRED 6

18 A large majority of the respondents to FRED 6 agreed with the proposals it contained, and these are accordingly unchanged. The following paragraphs describe those points on which respondents expressed concern and explain whether or not a change was made and the Board's reasoning for its decision.

Disclosure requirements on an acquisition

19 The full disclosure requirements proposed in the FRED relating to the pre-combination results of the parties to a merger, and the acquired entity in an acquisition, were supported by a majority of respondents, and particularly by users of accounts. Concern was expressed, however, at the practical difficulties in obtaining this information relating to acquisitions, and many preparers of financial statements questioned whether such disclosures were, in practice, of value to users.

20 The Board has therefore reconsidered the extent of the disclosures required in respect of the acquired company, and has made three main relaxations in the requirements:

(a) less detailed analysis of the results of the acquired company up to the date of acquisition is now required;

(b) only the profit after tax and minority interests for its previous financial year is now required to be shown; and

(c) fuller disclosure is now required only for substantial acquisitions, defined as being 'Class I' or 'Super Class I' where the acquirer is a listed company, or in excess of 15 per cent of net assets or profits for others.

The FRS now states that this information is to be given using the accounting policies of the acquired company, instead of being restated using the acquirer's accounting policies.

21 Some respondents suggested that it would be more helpful for all disclosure requirements relating to acquisitions to be consolidated into one standard. The Board has accordingly included in this FRS the proposed disclosure requirements set out in FRED 7 (which were based on those in SSAP 22), amended to take account of responses made to that FRED. It has also incorporated references to the disclosure requirements relating to acquisitions in FRS 1 and FRS 3, unchanged other than to make it clear that the disclosures should be made separately for each material acquisition, and for other acquisitions in aggregate.

Disclosure requirements on a merger

22 The Board concluded that, in the case of a merger, no relaxation of the proposed disclosures was appropriate. Because of the continuing involvement of management of both parties to the merger, the practical difficulties would be less, and the likely significance of the merger to the shareholders would make it desirable to provide fuller information. Although it was argued that analysing pre-merger results among the parties was in some sense contrary to the concept of merger accounting, in that the financial statements were drawn up on the basis that the parties had always been merged, the Board took the view that full information on the combining parties separately was important to an understanding of the combined entity.

Definitions and criteria for merger accounting

23 The definitions of mergers and acquisitions, and the criteria for merger accounting, were generally agreed as appropriate by respondents, and only minor drafting changes have been made. Criterion 4 has been amended to make clear the effect of an entity disposing of part of its business prior to the combination.

Group reconstructions

24 There was general agreement with the proposed use of merger accounting in group reconstructions, but some respondents requested that this should be more widely available. The Board has therefore agreed to widen the definition of group reconstructions, provided minority rights are unaffected, to include situations where a new holding company is created; where a 'horizontal group' of companies under common ownership become a group under the companies legislation definition; and where a part of a group is transferred to a new company, not part of the group but owned by the same shareholders as the group.

Merger expenses

25 The FRED proposed that merger expenses should be charged to the profit and loss account. Although a majority of respondents supported this proposal, there was significant support for deducting such costs from reserves, in a way similar to the costs of issuing an equity instrument under FRS 4. The Board believes, however, that there is a fundamental difference between the costs of issue of an equity instrument, which raises new capital, from which the costs may sensibly be deducted, and the costs of a merger, which does not raise new capital, but which requires an expenditure of resources that should therefore be charged to the profit and loss account. The Board has clarified that these costs should be shown as an exceptional item in accordance with paragraph 20 of FRS 3.

Demergers

26 Several respondents suggested that the FRS should deal with the accounting issues arising on demergers as well. However, the Board took the view that such issues as arise on a demerger are unrelated to those of business combinations, and should not be dealt with in the same FRS (although the restructuring that takes place on a demerger may fall within the group restructuring provisions of this FRS).

Alternative views — prohibiting the use of merger accounting

27 The Preface to the FRED set out an alternative view, that the use of merger accounting should be prohibited (other than for certain group reconstructions). This alternative view attracted little support; most commentators thought that mergers, although rare, were a separate class of business combination for which merger accounting should be available. The Board has, accordingly, not proceeded with that proposal.

Appendix IV

Illustrative Example of Disclosure of Reorganisation and Integration Costs

This example is provided as an aid to understanding and does not form part of the Financial Reporting Standard.

Paragraph 87 of the Explanation suggests that, for major acquisitions, management may wish to include in the notes to the financial statements the amount of reorganisation and other costs to be incurred in relation to the acquisition. The following example indicates one way in which this optional information might be presented. The best form of the disclosure will depend on individual circumstances.

Costs of Reorganising and Integrating Acquisitions

	Acquisition of European business (note (a))	**Other acquisitions**	**TOTAL**
	£ million	*£ million*	*£ million*
Announced but not charged as at the previous year-end	—	25	25
Announced in relation to acquisitions during the year	170	—	170
Adjustments to previous years' estimates	—	(5)	(5)
	170	20	190
Charged in the year			
— operating profit	55	12	67
— elsewhere	65	—	65
	120	12	132
Announced but still to be charged at 31 December 1995	50	8	58

Note (a): Acquisition of European business

		£million
Cost of acquisition		400
Reorganisation and integration expenditure announced		
Fundamental restructuring:		
— withdrawal from existing US business and related redundancies	65	
Other items (to be charged to operating profit):		
— other redundancy costs	75	
— re-branding and redesign costs	30	
Announced reorganisation and integration costs as shown in above table		170
Total investment		570

In addition to the £120 million expenditure shown in the above table, reorganisation and integration costs charged during the year include £30 million in respect of write-downs to fixed assets consequent on the closure of the XYZ plant.

Fair values in acquisition accounting

Financial Reporting Standard 7 is set out in paragraphs 1-31.

The Statement of Standard Accounting Practice set out in paragraphs 4-31 should be read in the context of the Objective as stated in paragraph 1 and the definitions set out in paragraphs 2-3 and also of the Foreword to Accounting Standards and the Statement of Principles for Financial Reporting currently in issue.

The Explanation set out in paragraphs 32-85 shall be regarded as part of the Statement of Standard Accounting Practice insofar as it assists in interpreting that statement.

Appendix III 'The development of the FRS' reviews considerations and arguments that were thought significant by members of the Board in reaching the conclusions on FRS 7. The views of the member who dissented are set out in Appendix IV.

Summary

General

a Financial Reporting Standard 7 'Fair values in acquisition accounting' sets out the principles of accounting for a business combination under the acquisition method of accounting. Companies legislation requires the identifiable assets and liabilities of the acquired entity to be included in the consolidated financial statements of the acquirer at their fair values at the date of acquisition. The difference between these and the cost of acquisition is recognised as goodwill or negative goodwill. The results of the acquired entity are included in the profit and loss account of the acquiring group from the date of acquisition.

Fair values of identifiable assets and liabilities

b The assets and liabilities recognised in the allocation of fair values should be those of the acquired entity that existed at the date of acquisition. They should be measured at fair values that reflect the conditions at the date of the acquisition.

c The liabilities of the acquired entity should not include provisions for future operating losses. Changes in the assets and liabilities resulting from the acquirer's intentions or from events after the acquisition should be dealt with as post-acquisition items. Similarly, costs of reorganisation and integrating the business acquired, whether they relate to the acquired entity or the acquiring group, should be dealt with as post-acquisition costs and do not affect the fair values at the date of acquisition.

d Fair values should be based on the value at which an asset or liability could be exchanged in an arm's length transaction. The fair value of monetary items should take into account the amounts expected to be received or paid and their timing.

e Unless they can be measured at market value, the fair values of non-monetary assets will normally be based on replacement cost, but should not exceed their recoverable amount as at the date of acquisition. The recoverable amount reflects the condition of the assets on acquisition but not any impairments resulting from subsequent events. The FRS specifies the methods for determining fair values of individual categories of assets and liabilities.

Investigation period and goodwill adjustments

f The identification and valuation of assets and liabilities acquired should be completed, if possible, by the date on which the first post-acquisition financial statements of the acquirer are approved by the directors. If it has not been possible to complete the investigation of fair values by that date, provisional valuations should be made; these should be amended if necessary in the next financial statements with a corresponding adjustment to goodwill.

Cost of acquisition

g The cost of acquisition is the amount of cash or cash equivalents paid and the fair value of other purchase consideration given by the acquirer, together with the expenses of the acquisition. The FRS explains the methods used to determine the amounts to be ascribed to constituent parts of the purchase consideration.

h Where the payment of consideration for an acquisition is to be made after the date of acquisition, reasonable estimates of the amounts expected to be paid should be included in the cost of acquisition at their present values.

Objective

1 The objective of this FRS is to ensure that when a business entity is acquired by another, all the assets and liabilities that existed in the acquired entity at the date of acquisition are recorded at fair values reflecting their condition at that date; and that all changes to the acquired assets and liabilities, and the resulting gains and losses, that arise after control of the acquired entity has passed to the acquirer are reported as part of the post-acquisition financial performance of the acquiring group.

Definitions

2 The following definitions shall apply in this FRS and in particular in the Statement of Standard Accounting Practice set out in paragraphs 4–31.

Acquisition: A business combination that is accounted for by using the acquisition method of accounting.

Business combination: The bringing together of separate entities into one economic entity as a result of one entity uniting with, or obtaining control over the net assets and operations of, another.

Date of acquisition: The date on which control of the acquired entity passes to the acquirer. This is the date from which the acquired entity is accounted for by the acquirer as a subsidiary undertaking under FRS 2 'Accounting for subsidiary undertakings'.

Fair value: The amount at which an asset or liability could be exchanged in an arm's length transaction between informed and willing parties, other than in a forced or liquidation sale.

Identifiable assets and liabilities: The assets and liabilities of the acquired entity that are capable of being disposed of or settled separately, without disposing of a business of the entity.

Recoverable amount: The greater of the net realisable value of an asset and, where appropriate, the value in use.

Value in use: The present value of the future cash flows obtainable as a result of an asset's continued use, including those resulting from the ultimate disposal of the asset.

3 References to companies legislation mean:

(a) in Great Britain, the Companies Act 1985;

(b) in Northern Ireland, the Companies (Northern Ireland) Order 1986; and

(c) in the Republic of Ireland, the Companies Acts 1963-90 and the European Communities (Companies: Group Accounts) Regulations 1992.

Statement of Standard Accounting Practice

Scope

4 Financial Reporting Standard 7 applies to all financial statements that are intended to give a true and fair view of a reporting entity's financial position and profit or loss (or income and expenditure) for a period. Although the FRS is framed in terms of the acquisition of a subsidiary undertaking by a parent company that prepares consolidated financial statements, it also applies where an individual company or other reporting entity acquires a business other than a subsidiary undertaking.

Determining the fair values of identifiable assets and liabilities acquired

Principles of recognition and measurement on an acquisition

5 The identifiable assets and liabilities to be recognised should be those of the acquired entity that existed at the date of the acquisition.

6 The recognised assets and liabilities should be measured at fair values that reflect the conditions at the date of the acquisition.

Application of the principles

7 As a consequence of the above principles, the following do not affect fair values at the date of acquisition and therefore fall to be treated as post-acquisition items:

(a) changes resulting from the acquirer's intentions or future actions;

(b) impairments, or other changes, resulting from events subsequent to the acquisition;

(c) provisions or accruals for future operating losses or for reorganisation and integration costs expected to be incurred as a result of the acquisition, whether they relate to the acquired entity or to the acquirer.

8 The application of these principles to specific classes of asset and liability is detailed in paragraphs 9-22 below. Subject to those paragraphs, fair values should be determined in accordance with the acquirer's accounting policies for similar assets and liabilities.

Tangible fixed assets

9 The fair value of a tangible fixed asset should be based on:

(a) market value, if assets similar in type and condition are bought and sold on an open market; or

(b) depreciated replacement cost, reflecting the acquired business's normal buying process and the sources of supply and prices available to it.

The fair value should not exceed the recoverable amount of the asset.

Intangible assets

10 Where an intangible asset is recognised, its fair value should be based on its replacement cost, which is normally its estimated market value.

Stocks and work-in-progress

11 Stocks, including commodity stocks, that the acquired entity trades on a market in which it participates as both a buyer and a seller should be valued at current market prices.

12 Other stocks, and work-in-progress, should be valued at the lower of replacement cost and net realisable value. Replacement cost is for this purpose the cost at which the stocks would have been replaced by the acquired entity, reflecting its normal buying process and the sources of supply and prices available to it — that is, the current cost of bringing the stocks to their present location and condition.

Quoted investments

13 Quoted investments should be valued at market price adjusted if necessary for unusual price fluctuations or for the size of the holding.

Monetary assets and liabilities

14 The fair value of monetary assets and liabilities, including accruals and provisions, should take into account the amounts expected to be received or paid and their timing. Fair value should be determined by reference to market prices, where available, by reference to the current price at which the business could acquire similar assets or enter into similar obligations, or by discounting to present value.

Contingencies

15 Contingent assets and liabilities should be measured at fair values where these can be determined. For this purpose reasonable estimates of the expected outcome may be used.

Business sold or held exclusively with a view to subsequent resale

16 Where an interest in a separate business of the acquired entity is sold as a single unit within approximately one year of the date of acquisition, the investment in that business should be treated as a single asset for the purposes of determining fair values. Its fair value should be based on the net proceeds of the sale, adjusted for the fair value of any assets or liabilities transferred into or out of the business, unless such adjusted net proceeds are demonstrably different from the fair value at the date of acquisition as a result of a post-acquisition event. This treatment should be applied to any business operation, whether a separate subsidiary undertaking or not, provided that its assets, liabilities, results of operations and activities are clearly distinguishable, physically, operationally and for financial reporting purposes, from the other assets, liabilities, results of operations and activities of the acquired entity.

17 Where the business has not been sold by the time of approval of the first financial statements after the date of acquisition, the fair value of the interest in the business should be based on the estimated net proceeds of the sale, provided:

(a) a purchaser has been identified or is being sought; and

(b) the disposal is reasonably expected to occur within approximately one year of the date of the acquisition.

The interest in the business or, if it is not a separate subsidiary undertaking, in the assets of the business, should be shown within current assets. When the sale price is subsequently determined, the original estimate of fair value should be adjusted to reflect the actual sale proceeds.

18 If the subsidiary undertaking or business operation is not, in fact, sold within approximately one year of the acquisition, it should be consolidated normally with fair values attributed to the individual assets and liabilities as at the date of acquisition, and corresponding adjustments to goodwill.

Pensions and other post-retirement benefits

19 The fair value of a deficiency or, to the extent that it is reasonably expected to be realised, a surplus in a funded pension or other post-retirement benefits scheme, or accrued obligations in an unfunded scheme, should be recognised as a liability or an asset of the acquiring group.

20 Changes in pension or other post-retirement arrangements following an acquisition should be accounted for as post-acquisition items and should be dealt with in accordance with the requirements of the standard concerned with pension costs.

Deferred taxation

21 Deferred tax assets and liabilities recognised in the fair value exercise should be determined by considering the enlarged group as a whole.

22 The benefit to the group of any tax losses attributable to an acquired entity at the date of acquisition should be recognised in accordance with the requirements of the standard concerned with deferred tax.

Investigation period and goodwill adjustments

23 The recognition and measurement of assets and liabilities acquired should be completed, if possible, by the date on which the first post-acquisition financial statements of the acquirer are approved by the directors.

24 If it has not been possible to complete the investigation for determining fair values by the date on which the first post-acquisition financial statements are approved, provisional valuations should be made; these should be amended, if necessary, in the next financial statements with a corresponding adjustment to goodwill.

25 Any necessary adjustments to those provisional fair values and the corresponding adjustment to purchased goodwill should be incorporated in the financial statements for the first full financial year following the acquisition. Thereafter, any adjustments, except for the correction of fundamental errors, which should be accounted for as prior period adjustments, should be recognised as profits or losses when they are identified.

Determining the cost of acquisition

26 The cost of acquisition is the amount of cash paid and the fair value of other purchase consideration given by the acquirer, together with the expenses of the acquisition as described in paragraph 28. Where a subsidiary undertaking is acquired in stages, the cost of acquisition is the total of the costs of the interests acquired, determined as at the date of each transaction.

27 Where the amount of purchase consideration is contingent on one or more future events, the cost of acquisition should include a reasonable estimate of the fair value of amounts expected to be payable in the future. The cost of acquisition should be adjusted when revised estimates are made, with consequential corresponding adjustments continuing to be made to goodwill until the ultimate amount is known.

28 Fees and similar incremental costs incurred directly in making an acquisition should, except for the issue costs of shares or other securities that are required by FRS 4 'Capital instruments' to be accounted for as a reduction in the proceeds of a capital instrument, be included in the cost of acquisition. Internal costs, and other expenses that cannot be directly attributed to the acquisition, should be charged to the profit and loss account.

Disclosures

29 The disclosures that should be made relating to an acquisition are set out in paragraphs 21 and 23-37 of FRS 6 'Acquisitions and mergers'.

Date from which effective

30 The accounting practices set out in the FRS should be regarded as standard in respect of business combinations first accounted for in financial statements relating to accounting periods commencing on or after 23 December 1994. Earlier adoption is encouraged but not required.

Amendment of SSAP 22

31 The FRS supersedes paragraphs 14, 23, 27, 30 and 33 of SSAP 22 'Accounting for goodwill'.

The following preamble is inserted in SSAP 22 before the Explanatory note:

> "FRS 7 'Fair values in acquisition accounting', published September 1994, supersedes paragraphs 14, 23, 27, 30 and 33 of this standard. Following publication of FRS 7, SSAP 22 is to be interpreted in the light of FRS 7; references to 'separable net assets' should be interpreted as 'identifiable assets and liabilities'.
>
> FRS 6 'Acquisitions and mergers', published September 1994, supersedes disclosure paragraphs 48-51; amended disclosure requirements are included in FRS 6."

Explanation

Introduction

32 The FRS is consistent with the requirements of companies legislation regarding the acquisition method of accounting. It sets out principles for identifying the assets and liabilities of an acquired entity and determining their fair values, and for determining the cost of acquisition.

33 Under the acquisition method of accounting, the identifiable assets and liabilities acquired are recognised at their fair values as at the date of acquisition, and the difference between these and the cost of acquisition is accounted for as goodwill or negative goodwill.

Determining the fair values of identifiable assets and liabilities acquired

Existing assets and liabilities of the acquired entity

34 The identifiable assets and liabilities over which the acquirer obtains control are those representing rights to future economic benefits and obligations to transfer economic benefits, including contingent rights and obligations, of the acquired entity that were in existence before the date of acquisition.

35 The identifiable assets and liabilities may include items that were not previously recognised in the financial statements of the acquired entity. These include assets and liabilities that are not normally recognised in accounts where no acquisition is involved, because other accounting standards preclude their immediate recognition. Examples are:

(a) pension surpluses or deficiencies identified on an acquisition that are otherwise recognised over several financial years in an entity's financial statements, in accordance with the requirements of SSAP 24 'Accounting for pension costs';

(b) contingent assets that may be assigned a value on acquisition, but cannot otherwise be recognised in financial statements because SSAP 18 'Accounting for contingencies' precludes the recognition of a contingent gain until realisation becomes reasonably certain.

36 The examples given above are included in the identifiable assets and liabilities because when an acquisition is made it is necessary to identify and recognise, so far as possible, all assets and liabilities acquired, provided they can be reliably valued. If this is not done, the reporting of post-acquisition performance is distorted by changes in assets and liabilities not being recognised in the correct period. The usual accounting practice, for example, of deferring recognition of contingent assets, does not apply, because the recognition of an acquired asset represents the expectation that the amounts expended on its acquisition will be recovered; it does not anticipate a future gain. It is, however, necessary to review the recoverable amounts of such assets to ensure that provision is made for any probable losses.

37 Certain contingent assets and liabilities that crystallise as a result of the acquisition would also be recognised provided that the underlying contingency was in existence before the acquisition. An example is where the acquired entity has previously entered into a contract that contains a clause under which obligations are triggered in the event of a change of ownership.

38 Identifiable liabilities include items such as onerous contracts and commitments that existed at the time of acquisition, whether or not the corresponding obligations were recognised as liabilities in the financial statements of the acquired entity. When an acquisition is made, provisions for liabilities would be recognised as identifiable liabilities only if such commitments had been made by the acquired entity before the date of acquisition. In the case of business closure decisions made by the acquired entity before the date of acquisition, the principles for recognising consequential provisions are set out in FRS 3 'Reporting financial performance', which states that obligations are incurred when there is a detailed formal plan for termination from which the entity cannot realistically withdraw*.

Exclusion of post-acquisition costs

39 The FRS does not permit provisions for future losses or for reorganisation costs expected to be incurred as a result of the acquisition to be included as liabilities acquired: they are not liabilities of the acquired entity as at the date of acquisition. As an example, if the acquirer decides to close a factory of the acquired entity as a measure to integrate the combined operations, this is a post-acquisition event. Only if the acquired entity was

*FRS 3, paragraph 18.

already committed to this course of action, and unable realistically to withdraw from it, would it be regarded as pre-acquisition. Similarly, if the acquirer undertakes a reorganisation to integrate the acquired operation or to improve its efficiency, this is also a post-acquisition event.

40 Where provisions for future costs were made by an acquired entity shortly before an acquisition took place, for example during the course of negotiations with the acquirer, it would be necessary to pay particular attention to the circumstances in order to determine whether obligations were incurred by the acquired entity before the acquisition. Only if the acquired entity was demonstrably committed to the expenditure whether or not the acquisition was completed would it have a liability at the date of acquisition. If obligations were incurred by the acquired entity as a result of the influence of the acquirer, it would be necessary to consider whether control of the acquired entity had been transferred at an earlier date and, consequently, whether the date of acquisition under the requirements of FRS 2 'Accounting for subsidiary undertakings' pre-dated such commitments*. Under paragraph 26 of FRS 6 'acquisitions and mergers', disclosure is required of provisions made by the acquired entity within the twelve months preceding the date of acquisition.

Measurement of identifiable assets and liabilities

41 Most acquisitions are not made on the basis of individual transactions in assets and liabilities. The acquisition transaction does not itself determine the values attributed to each asset and liability acquired and for this reason companies legislation and accounting standards require a fair value exercise to determine initial carrying amounts of assets and liabilities on an acquisition.

42 Although the FRS contains specific requirements for determining fair values of different classes of assets and liabilities, the concept of fair value underlying the specific rules is the value at which the asset, or liability, could be exchanged in an arm's length transaction between informed and willing parties.

43 Where similar assets are bought and sold on a readily accessible market, the market price will represent the fair value. Where quoted market prices are not available, market prices can often be estimated, either by independent valuations, or valuation techniques such as discounting estimated future cash flows to their present values. In some cases, where quoted market prices are not available, subsequent sales of acquired assets may provide the most reliable evidence of fair value at the time of the acquisition.

44 Where a fair value is based on a market price, it is important to ensure that such price is appropriate to the circumstances of the acquired business. For example, it may be possible to obtain a price for secondhand plant and machinery of the type used in the business, but the second-hand market may deal in very small volumes; or the items may not be identical in terms of the ability to obtain maintenance or technical support from the manufacturer or for the machinery to be customised to the requirements of the business. In general, unless the acquired business is genuinely able to consider the purchase of second-hand equipment as a viable alternative to purchasing direct from the manufacturer, the fair value of plant and machinery is more appropriately determined from the

* Under paragraph 45 of FRS 2 the date of acquisition may be indicated by the acquiring entity commencing its direction of the operating and financial policies of the acquired undertaking or by changes in the flow of economic benefits.

replacement cost of an equivalent new asset, depreciated where appropriate to reflect its age and condition.

45 The fair value attributed to an asset should not exceed the value the business is able to recover from the asset, either from its disposal or, in the case of a fixed asset, by continuing to use the asset. Where the fair value is based on a market price, the net realisable value will be similar to the fair value, differing only by costs of realisation and the dealer's margin. However, where the fair value is based on depreciated replacement cost or cost of manufacture, the net realisable value and, in the case of a fixed asset, the value in use will also need to be considered.

46 Both net realisable value and value in use at the time of the acquisition are unaffected by the acquirer's intentions for the future use of the asset. Net realisable value represents the amount for which the business would be able to sell the asset, whether or not such sale is intended. Similarly, the value in use of a fixed asset at the time of the acquisition depends, not on the intended use, but on the most profitable possible use of the asset.

Impaired assets

47 Where the replacement cost of an acquired asset is not recoverable in full (owing, for example, to lack of profitability, under-utilisation or obsolescence), the fair value is the estimated recoverable amount. The FRS requires that a valuation at recoverable amount should reflect the condition of the asset on acquisition but not any impairments resulting from subsequent events.

48 Where acquired assets that had not been impaired before acquisition are disposed of after acquisition for a reduced price (for example, as part of a post-acquisition reorganisation of the enlarged group), any losses resulting from their disposal would be treated as post-acquisition losses, i.e. attributed to the reorganisation, and would not reduce the fair values as at the date of acquisition.

49 In some cases recoverable amount can be determined only by considering as a whole a group of assets that are used jointly, rather than by attempting to determine the recoverable amount of each identifiable asset in that group. Aggregation in such cases serves to facilitate the attribution of cash flows to the assets that help to generate them.

Tangible fixed assets

50 Where reliable market values are obtainable—for example, for quoted investments and certain types of property—fair value would be based on current market values of similar assets. As explained in paragraph 44 above, for many types of fixed asset—for example most plant and machinery, and specialised properties specific to the business—fair value is represented by gross replacement cost reduced by depreciation to take account of the age and condition of the asset. Depreciation rates need to reflect estimated asset lives and residual amounts used by the acquirer for similar types of asset; otherwise, without there being any change in the asset's use or intended use, the first post-acquisition profit and loss account would reflect the adjustment from the previous management's depreciation rate to the acquirer's depreciation rate.

51 For certain assets it is not easy to determine current replacement cost; neither is it possible to estimate the value of the future services that an asset can provide through its continued use, because of the inherent subjectivity of such a valuation. In such circumstances the historical cost of the asset updated by the use of price indices may be the most reliable means of estimating replacement cost. Where prices have not changed materially it would be acceptable to use a carrying value based on historical cost as a reasonable proxy for fair value.

Stocks and work-in-progress

52 Where stocks are replaced by purchasing in a ready market — for example, commodities and dealing stocks — to which the acquired entity has access, fair value is represented by market value. Where there is no ready market for a category of stocks — for example, most manufactured stocks — fair value is represented by the current cost to the acquired company of reproducing the stocks.

53 The FRS requires account to be taken of the way the acquired business purchased or manufactured the stocks. For example, for a business purchasing in wholesale markets the replacement cost would be the wholesale price; and the replacement cost of the finished goods of a manufacturer will be the current cost of manufacture, not the cost of buying in finished goods from another manufacturer. Although this replacement cost takes account of the effects of input price changes during the period the stocks are held, no addition would be made for unrealised profit that would not normally be recognised in the acquired entity until the stocks are sold.

54 The current cost of manufacture for finished goods and work-in-progress would be based on current standard costs where these are employed. In practice, where there is a short manufacturing cycle, replacement cost may not be materially different from historical cost.

55 For long-term, maturing stocks, replacement cost would be based on market values if stocks at similar stages of completion are regularly traded in the market. In other cases, where such market transactions do not occur because either there is no market or the market is very thin, and where it is difficult to find replacement cost because replacement would be impossible in the short term, a surrogate for replacement cost may be found in the historical cost of bringing the stocks to their present location and condition, including an amount representing an interest cost in respect of holding the stock.

56 For long-term contracts, SSAP 9 'Stocks and long-term contracts' requires turnover and cost of sales to be recognised as the contract progresses, and attributable profit to be recognised prudently as it is earned. For this reason, no adjustments to book values would be required to such contracts, other than adjustments that would normally result from assessing the outcome of the contract under SSAP 9, or reflecting the change-over to the acquirer's accounting policies.

57 In estimating the net realisable value of stocks, an acquirer may reach a judgement about the value of slow-moving or redundant stocks that differs from that of the management of the acquired entity. However, any material write-down of the carrying value of stocks in the acquired entity's books before or at the time of the acquisition would need to be justified by the circumstances of the acquired entity before acquisition. If exceptional profits appear to have been earned on the realisation of stocks after the date of the acquisition, it will be necessary to re-examine the fair values determined on acquisition as required by paragraphs 23-25 of the FRS and, if necessary, to make an adjustment to these values and a corresponding adjustment to goodwill. If, alternatively, the profit is attributable to post-acquisition events it should be disclosed as an exceptional item as required by paragraph 30 of FRS 6.

Quoted investments

58 The fair value of quoted investments will normally be their market price. However, it may be necessary to adjust the market price to allow for short-term fluctuations or, in the case of large holdings, to reflect either a lower realisable value representing the difficulties of disposal or a higher value for a holding representing a substantial voting block.

Monetary assets and liabilities

59 Most short-term monetary assets and liabilities, including trade debtors and creditors, would be recognised at amounts expected to be received or paid on settlement or redemption.

60 The fair values of certain long-term monetary items may, however, be materially different from their book values. One example is where an acquired entity is carrying material amounts of long-term debt at fixed rates that do not reflect current borrowing rates. The fair value will be greater or lower than book value depending on the direction of changes in interest rates since the debt was issued. Another example is a material long-term debtor where the delay in settlement is not compensated by an interest charge reflecting current market rates.

61 The FRS requires monetary items to be stated at fair values where these are materially different from book values. Where the monetary item is a quoted security, its fair value is normally its market price. The fair values of other monetary items may be determined by considering the current terms on which a similar monetary asset or liability could be acquired or assumed, or by discounting to their present values the total amounts expected to be received or paid. The choice of interest rate to be applied to long-term borrowings would be affected by current lending rates for an equivalent term, the credit standing of the issuer and the nature of any security. For long-term debtors (after any necessary provisions have been made) the interest rate would be based on current lending rates.

62 The differences between fair values arrived at by discounting and the total amounts receivable or payable in respect of the relevant items represent discounts or premiums on acquisition that would be dealt with in the financial statements of the acquiring group as interest income or expense — that is, by allocation to accounting periods over the term of the monetary items at a constant rate based on their carrying amounts.

63 Where debt instruments issued by the acquired company are quoted, market values at the date of acquisition would be used instead of present values. However, in cases where a reduced pre-acquisition market value of an acquired entity's debt reflected the market's perception that it was at risk of being unable to fulfil its repayment obligations, the reduction would not be recognised in the fair value allocation if the debt was expected to be repaid at its full amount.

Contingencies

64 The value attributed to a contingent asset or liability needs to reflect the best estimate of the likely outcome; otherwise the post-acquisition profit and loss account will reflect the change from the previous management's estimate to the acquirer's estimate, without any related event or change in circumstances. In rare cases where a commitment or a contingent asset is of a kind that is normally assumed or acquired in an arm's length transaction (for example, underwriting commitments), its fair value would reflect the market price for such transactions.

Business sold or held exclusively with a view to subsequent resale

65 Where the acquisition of a group of companies includes a subsidiary undertaking or a discrete business operation that has been sold, or is expected to be sold, as a single unit within approximately a year of the acquisition it is appropriate to treat the investment in this business as a single asset, and to assign a single fair value to the whole investment rather than assign individual fair values to the various assets and liabilities that are included in the operation to be sold. The asset the group acquires is regarded as the investment in the subsidiary undertaking or business operation, rather than the individual items; and the actual net realised value will normally provide the most reliable evidence of fair value at the date of acquisition. One effect of this treatment is that goodwill is effectively apportioned between the part of the acquired group that is to be kept and the part sold, with the result that no further adjustment to write off the goodwill relating to the business disposed of, to comply with UITF Abstract 3 'Treatment of goodwill on disposal of a business', would be necessary. Where the effect is material, the net proceeds would be discounted to obtain their present value at the date of acquisition (taking into account any distribution of profits from the business). The principle explained in paragraph 85 below for attributing expenses to the cost of an acquisition would also apply to the costs of disposals.

66 Where the disposal has not been completed at the time of the first financial statements after the acquisition, the fair value is based on the estimated sales proceeds. Any initial estimate of fair value would normally be adjusted to actual net realised value within the period allowed for completing the investigation of fair values, with the change being adjusted against goodwill.

67 Such intended disposals would neither have been previously consolidated by the acquirer, nor have formed a continuing part of the activities of the acquiring group. In these circumstances, for an interest in a subsidiary undertaking, companies legislation* permits, and FRS 2 requires, the interest to be recognised as a current asset in the acquirer's consolidated accounts. The results of its operations during the holding period are excluded from the profit and loss account of the acquiring group.

68 The FRS requires the same principles of valuation to be applied to disposals of other business operations that are not subsidiary undertakings. Therefore, for example, the assets of a division held for resale would be shown as a single separately described current asset.

69 In the following circumstances it would be appropriate to estimate separately fair values at the acquisition date and to record a post-acquisition profit or loss on disposal:

(a) the acquirer has made a material change to the acquired business before disposal;

(b) specific post-acquisition events occur during the holding period that materially change the fair value of the business from the fair value estimated at the date of acquisition; or

(c) the disposal is completed at a reduced price for a quick sale.

Pensions and other post-retirement benefits

70 The FRS requires that where an acquired entity sponsors a defined-benefit pension scheme, or a defined-benefit post-retirement scheme other than a pension scheme, the allocation of fair values should include an asset in respect of a surplus in a funded scheme

* In Great Britain, the Companies Act 1985 , Section 229(3)(c); in Northern Ireland, the Companies (Northern Ireland) Order 1986, Article 237 (3)(c); and in the Republic of Ireland the European Communities (Companies: Group Accounts) Regulations 1992, Regulation 11(c).

and a liability in respect of a deficiency in a funded scheme or accrued obligations relating to an unfunded scheme. These assets or liabilities are in substitution for existing prepayments or provisions that have accumulated in the accounts of the acquired entity under the requirements of SSAP 24.

71 The fair value attributed to a surplus in a funded scheme would be determined by taking into account not only the actuarial surplus of the fund, but also the extent to which the surplus could be realised in cash terms, by way of reduction of future contributions or otherwise, and the timescale of such potential realisations.

72 This treatment differs from the normal requirements of SSAP 24, which in many circumstances do not permit the immediate recognition of assets and liabilities in respect of surpluses or deficiencies, but require them to be recognised systematically over the average remaining service lives of the employees in the scheme. Whilst SSAP 24 is primarily concerned with the allocation of pension costs to a company's profit and loss account on a continuing basis over several financial years, accounting for an acquisition transaction necessitates the recognition in the acquirer's group accounts of all assets and liabilities of the acquired entity identified at the date of acquisition. A pension asset, however, would be recognised only insofar as the acquired entity or the acquirer was able to benefit from the existing surplus.

73 The valuation of the pension fund surplus or deficit depends on several assumptions: interest rates, inflation and investment returns; the likely turnover of staff; and future salary increases; and the acquirer would apply its own judgement in determining these assumptions. However, the FRS requires changes in pension or other post-retirement arrangements following an acquisition to be accounted for as post-acquisition items. An example is the cost of improvements to benefits granted to members of an acquired scheme as part of a policy of harmonising remuneration packages in the enlarged group. This treatment is consistent with accounting for any changes stemming from the acquisition that affect the pension arrangements of the acquirer's own workforce, and has the effect of treating changes in pension arrangements on the same basis as the realignment of any other aspects of remuneration. The cost of post-acquisition changes to pension and other post-retirement arrangements would be dealt with in accordance with the requirements of SSAP 24 relating to variations in pension cost.

Deferred taxation

74 Deferred tax has to be determined on a group basis; at the end of the accounting period in which the acquisition occurred, the enlarged group's deferred tax provision will be calculated as a single amount, on assumptions applicable to the group. To determine the deferred tax of the acquired company at the date of acquisition using different assumptions from those applying to the group as a whole would result in the post-acquisition profit and loss account reflecting the change from one set of assumptions to another, rather than any real change in the circumstances of the group.

75 The benefit to the group of any tax losses in an acquired entity at the date of acquisition would be recognised on acquisition in accordance with the requirements of SSAP 15 'Accounting for deferred tax'. The losses would therefore be treated as timing differences, and would be recognised as reductions in deferred tax liabilities (if any), with any remainder recognised as deferred tax assets provided that the criteria for recognition specified in SSAP 15 are met. Application of these principles may result in deferred tax assets that were previously unrecognised in the acquired entity's financial statements being recognised on acquisition. If the criteria for the recognition of the benefits of tax losses in the group financial statements are not met as at the date of acquisition or within the permitted period for completing the fair value exercise, the benefits (if any) will be recognised in post-acquisition periods when the criteria are met, and any necessary disclosure required by paragraph 23 of FRS 3 will be given.

Determining the cost of acquisition

Fair values of the components of the purchase consideration

76 In order to apply the requirements of the FRS, it is necessary to determine the fair values of the constituent parts of the purchase consideration. The purchase consideration may comprise:

(a) cash or other monetary items, including the assumption of liabilities by the acquirer;

(b) capital instruments issued by the acquirer, including shares, debentures, loans and debt instruments, share warrants and other options relating to the securities of the acquirer; or

(c) non-monetary assets, including securities of another entity.

Cash and other monetary consideration

77 Where the purchase consideration is in the form of cash or other monetary assets given or liabilities assumed, its fair value is normally readily determinable as the amount paid or payable in respect of the item. When settlement of cash consideration is deferred, fair values are obtained by discounting to their present value the amounts expected to be payable in the future. The appropriate discount rate is the rate at which the acquirer could obtain a similar borrowing, taking into account its credit standing and any security given.

Capital instruments

78 Where shares (and other capital instruments) issued by the acquirer are quoted on a ready market, the market price on the date of acquisition would normally provide the most reliable measure of fair value. Where control is transferred by a public offer, the relevant date is the date on which the offer or, where there is a series of revised offers, the successful offer becomes unconditional, usually as a result of a sufficient number of acceptances being received. Where, owing to unusual fluctuations, the market price on one particular date is an unreliable measure of fair value, market prices for a reasonable period before the date of acquisition, during which acceptances could be made, would need to be considered.

79 Where securities issued by the acquirer are not quoted or, if they are quoted, the market price is unreliable owing, for example, to the lack of an active market in the quantities involved, it would be necessary to make a valuation of those securities. The fair value would be estimated by taking into account items such as:

(a) the value of similar securities that are quoted;

(b) the present value of the future cash flows of the instrument issued;

(c) any cash alternative to the issue of securities; and

(d) the value of any underlying security into which there is an option to convert.

Where it is not possible to value the consideration given by any of the above methods, the best estimate of its value may be given by valuing the entity acquired.

Non-monetary consideration

80 Where the purchase consideration takes the form of non-monetary assets, fair values would be determined by reference to market prices, estimated realisable values, independent valuations, or other available evidence.

Contingent consideration

81 The terms of an acquisition may provide that the value of the purchase consideration, which may be payable in cash, shares or other securities at a future date, depends on uncertain future events, such as the future performance of the acquired company. An example is an 'earn-out', where consideration payable to the vendor takes the form of an initial payment, together with further payments based on a multiple of future profits of the acquired company. By its nature, the fair value of such contingent consideration cannot be determined precisely at the date of acquisition. The FRS requires that the cost of acquisition should include a reasonable estimate of its fair value. Where it is not possible to estimate the total amounts payable with any degree of certainty, at least those amounts that are reasonably expected to be payable would be recognised. Initial estimates would be revised as further and more certain information becomes available.

82 Where contingent consideration is to be satisfied by the issue of shares, there is no obligation to transfer economic benefits and, accordingly, amounts recognised would be reported as part of shareholders' funds, for example as a separate caption representing shares to be issued. In the analysis of shareholders' funds, amounts would be attributed to equity and non-equity interests depending on the nature of the shares to be issued, in accordance with FRS 4 'Capital instruments'. When the shares are issued, appropriate transfers would be necessary between any amounts then held in shareholders' funds in respect of their issue and called up share capital and share premium.

83 If the acquirer can satisfy part of the consideration by the issue of shares or the payment of cash at its option, this part of the future consideration is not a liability because there is no obligation to transfer economic benefits. Consequently, the expected future consideration would be accounted for as a credit to shareholders' funds as explained in paragraph 82 above until an irrevocable decision regarding the form of consideration has been taken. If, however, the vendor has the right to demand cash or shares, the expected future consideration represents an obligation to the vendor and would be accounted for as a liability until the shares are issued or the cash is paid.

84 Acquisition agreements may require payments to be made in various forms, for example as non-competition payments or as bonuses to the vendors who continue to work for the acquired company. In such circumstances, it is necessary to determine whether the substance of the agreement is payment for the business acquired, or an expense such as compensation for services or profit sharing. In the first case the expected payments would be accounted for as contingent purchase consideration; in the other case the payments would be treated as expenses of the period to which they relate.

Acquisition expenses

85 Acquisition expenses to be treated as part of the cost of acquisition include incremental costs such as professional fees paid to merchant banks, accountants, legal advisers, valuers and other consultants. Such expenses exclude any allocation of costs that would still have been incurred had the acquisition not been entered into — for example, the costs of maintaining an acquisitions department or management remuneration; such costs would be charged to the profit and loss account as incurred. Expenses of issuing shares and other capital instruments that qualify as issue costs as defined in FRS 4 would be dealt with in accordance with the requirements of that standard. Such expenses are not added to the cost of acquisition.

Adoption of FRS 7 by the Board

Financial Reporting Standard 7 — 'Fair Values in Acquisition Accounting' was approved for issue by a vote of seven of the eight members of the Accounting Standards Board. Mr Main dissented. His dissenting view is set out in Appendix IV.

Members of the Accounting Standards Board

Sir David Tweedie (Chairman)

Allan Cook (Technical Director)

Robert Bradfield

Ian Brindle

Michael Garner

Raymond Hinton

Donald Main

Graham Stacy

Appendix I

Note on legal requirements

Great Britain

References are to the Companies Act 1985

1 The Companies Act describes the acquisition method of accounting in Schedule 4A paragraph 9:

(a) The identifiable assets and liabilities of the undertaking acquired shall be included in the consolidated balance sheet at their fair values as at the date of acquisition. The 'identifiable' assets or liabilities of the undertaking acquired mean the assets or liabilities that are capable of being disposed of or discharged separately, without disposing of a business of the undertaking (Schedule 4A paragraph 9(2)).

(b) The income and expenditure of the undertaking acquired shall be brought into the group accounts only as from the date of the acquisition (Schedule 4A paragraph 9(3)).

(c) There shall be set off against the acquisition cost of the interest in the shares of the undertaking held by the parent company and its subsidiary undertakings the interest of the parent company and its subsidiary undertakings in the adjusted capital and reserves of the undertaking acquired. The resulting amount if positive shall be treated as goodwill, and if negative as a negative consolidation difference (Schedule 4A paragraph 9(4)-(5))

(d) The 'acquisition cost' is defined as the amount of any cash consideration and the fair value of any other consideration, together with such amount (if any) in respect of fees and other expenses of the acquisition as the company may determine; and 'the adjusted capital and reserves' of the undertaking acquired are defined as the capital and reserves at the date of the acquisition after adjusting the identifiable assets and liabilities of the undertaking to fair values as at that date (Schedule 4A paragraph 9(4)).

Share premium and merger relief

2 Section 130(1) of the Act provides that if a company issues shares at a premium, whether for cash or otherwise, a sum equal to the aggregate amount or value of the premiums on those shares should be transferred to an account called the share premium account. The provisions of the Act relating to the reduction of a company's share capital apply, with exceptions, as if the share premium account were part of its paid-up share capital.

3 Limited relief from the above ('merger relief') is given by Sections 131-134.

4 Section 131 provides, *inter alia*, that, subject to specified conditions, where an issuing company has secured at least a 90 per cent equity holding in another company, Section 130 does not apply to the premium on shares issued in the transaction that takes the holding in that other company to at least 90 per cent.

5 Section 133(1) provides that the premium on any shares to which the relief in Sections 131 and 132 applies may also be disregarded in determining the amount at which any shares or other consideration provided for the shares issued is to be included in the offeror company's balance sheet.

Share premium and fair value

6 Shares forming part of the consideration are valued at their fair value for the purposes of computing acquisition cost and goodwill under paragraph 9(4) of Schedule 4A. By contrast, the value of the share premiums arising on the shares issued, for the purposes of section 130, is based on the value to the issuing company of the consideration it has received. Where these values are different, or where (if the merger relief provisions apply) the premiums are disregarded, the cost of investment in the parent company's books will be different from the cost of acquisition for the purposes of paragraph 9(4). In such circumstances the difference should form a separate element of consolidated reserves, and does not form part of goodwill.

Northern Ireland

7 The legal requirements in Northern Ireland are very similar to those in Great Britain. The following table shows the references to the Companies (Northern Ireland) Order 1986 that correspond to the legal references in paragraphs 1-6 above.

Great Britain	*Northern Ireland*
Schedule 4A paragraph 9	Schedule 4A paragraph 9
Sections 130-134	Articles 140-144

Republic of Ireland

8 The following table shows the references to the European Communities (Companies: Group Accounts) Regulations 1992 and the Companies Act 1963 that correspond to the legal references in paragraphs 1-6 above.

Great Britain	*Republic of Ireland*
Schedule 4A paragraph 9	Regulation 19
Section 130	Companies Act 1963 Section 62
Sections 131-134	No equivalent

Appendix II

Compliance with International Accounting Standards

The International Accounting Standards Committee (IASC) has issued a revised standard IAS 22 'Business Combinations'. The principal areas where the revised IAS 22 and the FRS are at variance* are as follows. First, the revised IAS 22 requires that fair values of identifiable assets and liabilities acquired in an acquisition should be determined by reference to their intended use by the acquirer. The FRS requires the identifiable assets and liabilities to be recorded at their fair values as at the date of acquisition. Secondly, certain adjustments that would be treated as fair value adjustments under the revised IAS 22, for example those for additional liabilities recognised to reflect an acquirer's different intentions regarding an acquisition, would be accounted for as post-acquisition items under the FRS.

Appendix III

The development of the FRS

General and history

1 The principle of attributing fair values in consolidated financial statements to the assets and liabilities of newly acquired subsidiaries has been recognised in UK accounting standards for many years and, since 1989, in companies legislation.

SSAP 14

2 SSAP 14 'Group accounts', which was published in 1978, required the purchase consideration for the acquisition of a subsidiary to be allocated between the underlying net tangible and intangible assets other than goodwill on the basis of the fair value to the acquiring company. The standard gave no guidance on how to determine fair values.

SSAP 22

3 SSAP 22 'Accounting for goodwill', issued in 1984, gave limited guidance on how to identify the assets and liabilities of an acquired business that should be regarded as separable from the purchased goodwill arising on the acquisition. It also sanctioned the practice that had evolved of adjusting the fair values ascribed to the separable net assets acquired to include provisions for anticipated future losses or costs of reorganisation. Such provisions were permitted to be recognised in the fair value exercise if the future losses or costs were taken into account in arriving at the purchase price.

* The Board's reasons for adopting proposals that differ from those of the IASC's revised IAS 22 are set out in Appendix III at paragraphs 15–16 and 27–28.

4 Subsequently, however, concern among users began to emerge over the extent to which the use of provisions could potentially be hidden or abused. The Accounting Standards Committee (ASC) took action to address these concerns by amending SSAP 22 to include some specific disclosure requirements relating to the fair value exercise. The revised SSAP 22, published in 1989, required disclosure of adjustments made to the book values of the assets and liabilities of an acquired business, analysed into revaluations and provisions. It also required disclosure of movements on provisions related to acquisitions, analysed into the amounts used and the amounts released unused or applied for another purpose. At the same time as SSAP 22 was being amended, the ASC was developing an accounting standard on fair value accounting (see paragraph 6 below).

Companies Act 1989

5 The Companies Act 1989 introduced a new Schedule 4A to the Companies Act 1985, which set out rules regarding the form and content of consolidated financial statements. The Act requires that, in accounting for the acquisition of a subsidiary, the subsidiary's identifiable assets and liabilities must be included in the consolidated balance sheet at their fair values as at the date of acquisition. There is no guidance in the Act on how to determine the fair values of assets and liabilities acquired.

ED 53

6 The ASC issued a discussion paper in 1988, followed in 1990 by an exposure draft, ED 53 'Fair value in the context of acquisition accounting'. ED 53 contained proposals for determining fair values of assets and liabilities identified in an acquisition, for dealing with anticipated reorganisation costs and for valuing the consideration given for an acquisition.

7 ED 53 proposed that fair values should be determined from the perspective of the acquiring company, based on circumstances at the date of acquisition. Its proposals for dealing with acquisition provisions did not permit provision to be made for future trading losses of acquired businesses but did, however, continue to permit provisions for reorganisation costs to be made as fair value adjustments if there was a clearly defined programme of reorganisation that had been costed in reasonable detail and there was evidence that the acquirer took account of the plans and costs in formulating the offer.

ASB Discussion Paper

8 In April 1993, the Board published a Discussion Paper, 'Fair values in acquisition accounting'. The Board adopted much of the work of the ASC in framing its proposals, but concluded that a different approach to the recognition of liabilities was necessary to address a number of issues, including those raised in responses to ED 53. A theme common to several of the commentators' responses had been that the basic principles underlying ED 53's approach had not been properly developed and in particular that the exposure draft had failed to rationalise its conclusions on key issues such as the recognition of reorganisation and future loss provisions.

9 The Discussion Paper contained proposals that attempted to draw a clear distinction of principle between recording the elements of the purchase transaction, including accounting for the preacquisition assets and liabilities of the acquired business, and the items that should fall into the post-acquisition period. The proposals would have precluded provisions both for future losses in acquired businesses and, as a departure from ED 53, for reorganisation costs following an acquisition from being included as fair value adjustments. The principal reasons for proposing such a radical change to existing practices were threefold:

(a) the proposals for dealing with the recognition of anticipated future losses and reorganisation costs were consistent with the Board's draft Statement of Principles regarding the recognition of liabilities;

(b) the proposals were consistent with the philosophy behind the 'information set' approach in FRS 3 'Reporting financial performance' in respect of presenting the financial effects of post-acquisition activities, including reorganisation of acquired businesses;

(c) to meet users' concerns on perceived scope for abuse; it was doubtful whether an alternative approach of developing a standard founded on enhanced disclosure of acquisition provisions, supplemented by specific and probably arbitrary rules on cut-off between pre- and post-acquisition items would prove as effective in the long term as an approach built on the Board's draft Statement of Principles.

FRED 7

10 FRED 7 was published in December 1993. It retained the essential features of the proposals in the Discussion Paper, while refining and clarifying them to take account of the comments received.

11 Views on the proposal in the Discussion Paper that all costs of reorganising acquired businesses should be treated as charges to post-acquisition profits had been divided, with a small majority in favour of the proposed treatment. Support had been strongest among user groups, who generally welcomed the transparency of the proposals in providing a proper basis for analysing the financial consequences of acquisition activities. Opposition had been voiced by many — although by no means all — preparers, who argued that the proposals belied the reality of the way acquisitions are handled because they failed to reflect the fact that the cost of an acquisition and subsequent, directly related expenditure are the product of a single investment decision. As an example, many commentators had argued that the costs incurred in the immediate post-acquisition period to implement a business plan to reorganise an acquisition were probably discrete and significant and were an integral part of the investment appraisal process; such costs, they contended, should not be reported in the group's trading results. The purchase and integration of a subsidiary, in their eyes, was in substance a single capital transaction, despite the fact that some elements might be revenue in form.

12 The Board set out in FRED 7 the basis for its conclusions on the proposed treatment of post-acquisition reorganisation costs. The main arguments, which are equally applicable to the FRS, are summarised as follows.

(a) The proposals were made in the context of the fundamental changes to the disclosure of financial performance that were introduced by FRS 3. If a company incurs material revenue expenditure to improve future profitability, the costs are normally charged to the profit and loss account. FRS 3 and the Operating and Financial Review both provide the facility for proper disclosure and explanation of the resulting volatility in the reported results. The Board believed that all such expenditure should be treated similarly, whether it related to a reorganisation following an acquisition or to a reorganisation of an ongoing business. It would be left to investment analysis to assess the benefit to an entity of a reorganisation.

(b) The proposals in respect of the recognition of liabilities were consistent with the Board's draft Statement of Principles. The approach rested on whether there was an obligation in the acquired entity at the acquisition date. The Board recognised that, where an acquisition was made, the acquirer might have taken into account additional costs to reorganise the operations of the combining entities and such costs might have been factored into the investment decision and the amount of purchase consideration to be offered. However, it did not follow that these costs should be deemed to increase the liabilities of the acquired entity existing at the acquisition date.

(c) The proposals, which required reorganisations related to acquisitions to be treated on the same footing as any other reorganisations, set out principles that avoided the need to define cut-off points between items to be included in the fair value exercise and items to be recognised in the post-acquisition period, which would have been difficult to achieve. Framing an alternative approach on the basis of the acquirer's intentions at the time of the acquisition would, in the Board's opinion, have led to artificial distinctions being drawn not only between the treatment of reorganisations affecting the acquired business and consequential changes in the existing business of the acquirer, but also between reorganisations that were planned at the time of acquisition and those that occurred later.

13 Many commentators had argued that the 'acquirer's perspective' should be retained as a principle for attributing fair values to the assets and liabilities acquired. They had contended that because the purchase consideration was based on the acquirer's assessment of the fair value of the acquired entity and its underlying assets and liabilities, it followed that the allocation of the purchase consideration should also be based on the acquirer's perspective.

14 The Board is of the view that under its draft Statement of Principles, management intent is not a sufficient basis for recognising changes to an entity's assets and liabilities. It is events, not intentions for future actions, that increase or decrease an entity's assets or liabilities. When intentions are translated into actions that commit the entity to particular courses of action, the accounting should then reflect any obligations or changes in assets that arise from those actions. In relation to acquisition accounting, the Board concluded that events of a post-acquisition period that resulted in the recognition of additional liabilities or the impairment of existing assets of an acquired entity should be reported as events of that period rather than of the pre-acquisition period.

15 Some commentators expressed concern that the proposals for precluding any reorganisation provisions as fair value adjustments were more restrictive than the requirements in the USA or International Accounting Standards. They urged the Board to go no further than to achieve consistency with US GAAP which, although not permitting provisions for future losses of acquired companies to be recognised as fair value adjustments, would allow adjustments to be made to take account of management intentions in the valuation of acquired assets, including, for example, provisions in respect of the intended closure of facilities in the acquired entity that are duplicated in the enlarged group.

16 In developing FRED 7, the Board took into account the fact that US GAAP in this area considerably pre-dates the development of the present framework of general accounting concepts in the USA, as well as the IASC framework and the UK draft Statement of Principles, which are similar. The Board took the view that its proposals were consistent with the conceptual frameworks that had been developed elsewhere and, in particular, noted that the principle of accounting for obligations rather than management intentions was gaining greater acceptance internationally.

Matters considered in the light of responses to FRED 7

17 The following paragraphs refer to comments made by respondents to FRED 7, and explain with reasons the changes the Board has made to proposals of the FRED or the Board's reasons for rejecting arguments for changes. Individual Board members gave greater weight to some factors than to others.

Reorganisation provisions

18 FRED 7 proposed that the identifiable assets and liabilities recognised in the fair value exercise should be those of the acquired entity that existed at the date of acquisition, and should include provisions neither for future operating losses nor for reorganisation and integration costs expected to be incurred as a result of the acquisition.

19 This proposal met with outright support from institutional investors, analysts and users of accounts; substantial support from accountancy firms and accountancy bodies; and strong, though not unanimous, opposition from preparers of accounts.

20 The main arguments raised by the respondents opposed to the proposals in the FRED are summarised below, together with the Board's response to the arguments.

Commercial reality

21 It was argued that the FRED ignored the commercial reality of the transaction, namely that the acquirer's management takes the reorganisation and integration costs into account in its 'project plan' for the acquisition, and regards these costs as part of the 'investment'; they should therefore be treated as akin to additional consideration. Furthermore, it was argued, under the FRED's proposals the acquisition of a poorly organised business that is then reorganised by the acquirer gives a different accounting result from the acquisition of an equivalent but well-organised business that is not in need of reorganisation.

22 Of those who preferred the status quo on reorganisation provisions, most agreed that the existing situation was unsatisfactory and that tighter definitions and controls were needed; in particular, there was little support for continuing to allow provisions to be made for future losses of the acquired business, and most agreed that there should be rules to restrict the use of reorganisation provisions made as fair value adjustments.

23 The Board has carefully reconsidered the arguments against its proposals, which reiterated the arguments raised by a majority of preparers against the proposals in the Discussion Paper. The Board recognises the strength of feeling held in some quarters against this aspect of its proposals, which changes long-standing accounting practice. It has also balanced these views with those of user and other groups who supported the proposals. While not discounting the reasons or rationale underlying the position of those opposed to its proposals, the Board decided that it should develop an FRS on the basis of the proposals in FRED 7. It believes that this FRS will lead to clearer and more consistent reporting than has been the case under existing practices. Furthermore, the Board remains of the view that the approach adopted in the FRS is more soundly based on principle than would be an alternative approach that sought to improve existing standards by addressing disclosure issues and developing detailed rules that had the principal objective of constraining reorganisation provisions solely in order to prevent abuse.

24 Without repeating all the arguments underlying the Board's position as set out in FRED 7, the Board reaffirms that the principles in the FRS for determining the fair values of the assets and liabilities of the acquired entity adhere closely to the Board's draft Statement of Principles in respect of the recognition of assets and liabilities, and to the philosophy behind FRS 3 (complemented by the Operating and Financial Review) for reporting financial performance and other gains and losses.

25 The FRS, therefore, follows the principle (as set out in the draft Statement of Principles) that identifiable liabilities are limited to obligations of the acquired entity that existed at the date of acquisition and, consequently, other changes should fall into the post-acquisition period. The Board recognises that rationalisation expenditures, whether to improve or to integrate part of the business following an acquisition, are undertaken because they are expected to result in lasting and long-term benefits. However, in the Board's view this does not justify the effective capitalisation of that expenditure as goodwill, irrespective of whether it was planned at the time of the acquisition or whether the plans were formulated after the acquisition took place.

26 The Board also takes the view that the acquisition of a well-organised company is a different transaction from the acquisition of a company in need of reorganisation, and there is no reason why the two transactions should result in the same accounting outcome. In one case the acquirer is reporting the acquisition of a business whose previous management ran it efficiently; in the other, the acquirer is reporting the acquisition of a less efficient business and the subsequent expenditure intended to improve it. In the first case, the success of the business was apparent before the acquirer agreed to buy it; in the second, the value of the reorganisation expenditure will be judged subsequently by the increase in profitability of the acquired business that is achieved.

International competitiveness and international GAAP

27 It was suggested by some respondents that the FRED's approach, by being stricter in some respects than the corresponding provisions of accounting standards in other countries (in particular, US GAAP and the International Accounting Standard) would damage the competitiveness of UK companies. Conversely, others have argued that the existing flexible accounting practices in the UK have encouraged UK companies to overpay for acquisitions compared with foreign companies. The Board takes the view that accounting standards should be neutral as to economic effect. Therefore, the FRS seeks to provide greater clarity in the reporting of acquisition activities. The more transparent accounting resulting from the FRS and from other accounting reforms that the Board has undertaken should contribute to sound economic decisions.

28 The Board carefully considered the international harmonisation issue during the development of FRED 7. As noted in paragraph 16 above, the Board believes that the FRS is consistent with the conceptual frameworks that have been adopted by various standard-setting bodies.

'Socio-economic' consequences

29 Some respondents also claimed that acquirers will be less willing to acquire companies in need of reorganisation, thus allowing inefficient management to remain and preventing rationalisation that is beneficial to the economy as a whole. However, the Board notes that the cash flow effect of a transaction is the same whichever accounting treatment is adopted.

Understandability of financial statements

30 Several preparers of accounts suggested that the reporting of acquisitions would be more difficult to understand, because the full cost to the acquirer will not be clear and the post-acquisition results will be distorted by reorganisation and integration costs. However, users who responded were unanimous that the FRED's proposals would provide them with clearer and more informative information on acquisitions.

31 In response to those commentators who argued that the financial statements should be capable of showing the full cost of the investment in an acquisition, including the intended costs of post-acquisition reorganisation, the FRS has introduced a recommendation that the planned reorganisation expenditure relating to the acquisition should be disclosed in the notes to the financial statements (see paragraph 40 below).

Anti-avoidance measures

32 There was concern that the requirements of the FRS could be circumvented by collusion between the vendor and the acquirer, resulting for example in the vendor entering into obligations to restructure the business on the instructions of the acquirer before the formal transfer of control.

33 The Discussion Paper had proposed that any reorganisation provisions made by the vendor in the six months before the acquisition should be treated as post-acquisition; however, this was generally regarded as unnecessarily draconian and was omitted from the FRED.

34 The FRS deals with the issue in three ways. First, it emphasises that provisions should be included in the balance sheet of the acquired company at the date of acquisition only if that entity had a commitment from which it could not realistically withdraw whether or not the acquisition had been completed. Secondly, it draws attention to the possibility that the effective transfer of control took place at an earlier date than the formal transfer of shares. Thirdly, there is an additional disclosure requirement (included in FRS 6) for any provisions for reorganisation made by the acquired company within 12 months before the date of acquisition to be shown separately in the 'fair value table'.

Conclusion

35 The Board gave careful consideration to the arguments of those opposed to the proposals in the FRED, and acknowledged the strength of feeling particularly among many preparers of accounts. However, it concluded that the arguments put forward were essentially those it had already addressed in coming to its initial views expressed in the Discussion Paper and FRED 7. Moreover, where the arguments concern the understandability of financial statements, due regard must be given to the views of the professional users of accounts—in particular, the institutional investors and analysts, who were fully in support of the proposals.

Other issues

'Acquirer's perspective'

36 Several respondents (including both some of those who supported the FRED'S approach to reorganisation provisions as well as some of those who opposed it) argued that the fair values should be determined from the 'acquirer's perspective'. However, the Board took the view that this term had no single clear meaning, and might be interpreted to indicate that fair values should take into account the decisions of the acquirer taken after the acquisition. For this reason, the Board has avoided using the term in the FRS, but has added more specific descriptions of the extent to which the acquirer's estimates and perceptions are taken into account in determining fair values. The concept of fair value underlying these specific rules remains, however, the value at which the asset, or liability, could be exchanged in an arm's length transaction between informed and willing parties. This concept is independent of the particular circumstances of either the acquirer or the acquired business.

Disclosure of provisions for reorganisation costs

37 Several respondents were concerned that, if reorganisation and similar costs relating to an acquisition were reported in the profit and loss account in accordance with the provisions of FRS 3 such costs might be reported as a deduction from the results of acquisitions, or as part of continuing activities; or, if they related to a fundamental reorganisation of the acquiring entity, as an exceptional item outside operating profit. Users might therefore find it difficult to ascertain the total costs relating to acquisitions. Instead, they proposed that a new category of exceptional item should be defined, to include all costs of reorganisation, restructuring and integration relating to an acquisition, that would not form part of operating profit.

38 The Board concluded that this alternative proposal would confuse different kinds of costs relating to acquisitions, some of which might properly be excluded from operating profit but others of which were just as much an operating cost as the costs of routinely reorganising an existing part of the business. Furthermore, the introduction of a new class of exceptional item would lead to considerable difficulties of definition, as in many cases it was difficult to draw a clear distinction between costs relating to the acquisition, and similar costs relating to the acquirer's existing business that might well still have been incurred had the acquisition not taken place.

39 The Board therefore decided against introducing a new class of exceptional item. FRS 6, which now includes all disclosure requirements relating to acquisitions, sets out in paragraph 86 how the requirements of FRS 3 apply to costs relating to acquisitions.

40 In addition, paragraph 87 of FRS 6 suggests that management may wish to show, in a note to the financial statements, the total expenditure announced in relation to reorganisation and integration of acquisitions, together with the expenditures charged in the profit and loss account in the period and the further amount expected to be incurred. This would provide users with a clear statement of the total costs involved with the acquisition, and companies would be able to add what further explanation and discussion of the figures they think appropriate.

Pension surpluses

41 The FRED proposed that an actuarial surplus or deficit on a pension scheme operated by the acquired company should be recognised as an asset or liability on acquisition. Many respondents thought it imprudent to carry such a surplus as an asset, as it was often uncertain whether it could be realised. They therefore proposed that, whilst provision should still be made for a deficit, a surplus should not be recognised as an asset.

42 The Board has reconsidered the issue, and concluded that, although recognition of a surplus is consistent with the principles on which the FRS is based, it is important that the fair value attributed to such a surplus is justified. The FRS therefore requires the fair value of a surplus to be determined taking into account the extent to which, and timescale over which, the surplus is reasonably expected to be realised, normally in the form of reductions in future contributions.

43 The Board is currently reviewing the existing accounting standard on pension costs, SSAP 24. However, the Board decided that to omit reference to pension surpluses and deficits in the FRS, or to require fair values to be based on the assets or liabilities recognised by the acquired company in its own accounts under SSAP 24, might result in the omission of significant assets and liabilities and subsequent misstatement of profits of the enlarged group.

Acquisition expenses

44 The FRED proposed that the amount of incidental expenses that fall to be treated as an addition to the cost of acquisition should be restricted to incremental costs that would not have been incurred had the acquisition not taken place, and did not permit the capitalisation of internal costs even where they might be directly related to the acquisition. This proposal was consistent with the revised IAS 22 and US GAAP, and took a deliberately restrictive view to avoid the danger of overstating the cost of acquisition.

45 An alternative view is that the incremental cost approach is anomalous where the equivalent services, such as legal advice or acquisition search and investigation services, are provided by in-house departments rather than by external advisers or consultants.

46 There was substantial support from respondents for each view. The Board concluded that the difficulty of defining 'incremental' for in-house facilities might lead to excessive costs being capitalised, with the resulting overstatement of profits. This outweighed the possible anomalies that might arise. The proposals in the FRED have accordingly been carried through to the FRS.

Discounting

47 The FRED proposed that monetary assets and liabilities should be discounted to present value where they were materially different from nominal amounts. Although this was supported, a substantial minority of respondents were concerned over the introduction of discounting on a piecemeal basis, applying only to assets and liabilities of an acquisition, rather than as part of a more general application of discounting to all assets and liabilities.

48 The Board has reaffirmed its view that monetary assets and liabilities acquired in an acquisition should be included at their fair value at the time of the acquisition; this fair value will depend on the estimated amounts and timing of payments, and, in the case of long-term items not bearing interest at current market rates, may be materially different from their face value or nominal value. Significant distortions to reported profits may arise if such items are not included at their fair value. Discounting is an established and widely used valuation technique, and is one method of arriving at an estimate of fair valuue. The Board notes that this treatment is also consistent with the revised IAS 22 and with US GAAP.

Appendix IV

Dissenting view

1 Mr Main dissents from the FRS because of its treatment of the costs an acquiring company incurs to convert an acquired entity into the business unit it envisaged when making the acquisition. He was content at the exposure draft stage to let the proposal go forward in order to elicit a public response. However, he has found his concern reinforced by comments received and therefore feels unable to vote for the FRS.

2 Mr Main believes that it is very rare for a company to acquire another without intending to make changes to the acquired business to enable it to operate efficiently. Such changes may include, on the one hand, investment in, and reorganisation of, the assets being acquired to enable products or services to be provided efficiently, and, on the other hand, reductions of excessive manpower, buildings or equipment to enable an adequate profit to be earned.

3 Mr Main believes that the need for such changes and the likely cost of executing them are invariably known to the acquirer at the time the acquisition is made, and that the normal practice of management when considering a proposed acquisition for approval is to aggregate the acquisition price with these costs of bringing the acquired entity into a state acceptable to the buyer, in order to arrive at the investment total against which the expected earnings are judged.

4 The requirements of the FRS will prevent a company from recognising in the financial statements at the time of acquisition the costs of the intended changes. It is only when such costs are committed irrevocably that they are to be included in the financial statements, and even then, to the extent that these costs are not capital expenditure, they cannot be included as part of the investment cost of the acquisition.

5 For these reasons the financial statements will, in his view, be misleading and fail to provide accountability for the transactions that have taken place.

6 Mr Main supports the view expressed by many commentators on the Discussion Paper and Exposure Draft, as set out in paragraphs 11 and 21 of 'The development of the FRS' (Appendix III), that the costs of an acquisition and subsequent directly related expenditure are the product of a single investment decision; and that the purchase and integration of a subsidiary are in substance a single capital transaction. He believes that the opposition to this view by certain commentators reflected less an endorsement of the principles underlying the FRS than a reaction to perceived abuses in previous practice, including the making of excessive acquisition provisions to cover future trading losses and types of expenditure whose relationship to the acquisition was remote. He would summarise the responses to the exposure draft on this point as follows:

(a) from preparers of accounts:	overwhelming opposition
(b) from users:	acceptance, because they want to know the amount of post-acquisition provisions (which he considers to be a valid point), but a view that they would ignore the amounts charged against profits (indicating that they do not regard such charges as a proper reduction of profit);
(c) from auditors:	acceptance, because it can be very difficult at times to pass judgement on directors' decisions as to the proper capital provision for post-acquisition costs.

7 Mr Main believes that the concerns over past abuses could be met, without overturning long-standing practice, by a standard that provided a stricter definition of what costs should be permitted to be included in acquisition provisions, together with more detailed note disclosure of the provisions made. Provisions would be restricted to costs to be incurred within twelve months of the acquisition, and would exclude any costs relating to the acquiring entity's own activities. Provisions for future losses would also be prohibited. Notes to the financial statements would be required to disclose the separate elements of the provisions involved and the actual expenditure subsequently charged against the provisions. Surplus provisions would be required to be adjusted against goodwill rather than be released to the profit and loss account. He believes that the disclosure requirements in the related FRS 6 would provide sufficient information on the effects of an acquisition without the need for the radical change in practice introduced in FRS 7.

8 Mr Main believes that his alternative would ensure that:

(a) the total cost of the acquisition investment decision would be reflected clearly in the financial statements;

(b) accountability could be measured; and

(c) the potential for abuse would be removed and auditors would have a clear standard against which the contents of the provision could be judged.

Section 5
Statements of Recommended Practice

Contents

Explanatory foreword to statements of recommended practice

Introduction

1 Statements of Recommended Practice ('SORPs') have been developed in the public interest and set out current best accounting practice. The primary aims in issuing SORPs are to narrow the areas of difference and variety in the accounting treatment of the matters with which they deal and to enhance the usefulness of published accounting information.

2 SORPs were initially developed and issued by the Accounting Standards Committee ('ASC'). Alternatively, they have been developed and, after approval and franking by the ASC, issued by an 'industry' group which is representative of the industry concerned for the purpose of developing SORPs specific to that industry and recognised as such by the ASC. Such SORPs are referred to as 'franked SORPs'. (The term 'industry' is intended to refer to specific industries or sectors, including parts of the public sector.)

3 Before approving and franking a franked SORP, the ASC will have reviewed the proposed statement and the procedures involved in its development.

4 The ASC or the appropriate industry group may also develop and issue appendices to, and guidance notes on, SORPs.

Authority

5 SORPs have in the past been issued with the authority of the ASC or the industry group concerned after approval and franking by the ASC. A statement at the beginning of each SORP will explain which body has issued the document.

6 As from August 1990, the ASC has been replaced as the accounting standard setting body for the UK and Ireland by a new two-tier structure, the Financial Reporting Council and the Accounting Standards Board (ASB). In reviewing all of ASC's published statements, ASB then decided not to adopt existing SORPs on the basis that, since they do not have the statutory implications of accounting standards they do not require formal adoption by the Board. Therefore, existing and future SORPs will no longer have the authority of the ASB.

Status

7 Unlike accounting standards, SORPs are not and never have been mandatory on members of the Association and other leading professional bodies.

Scope

8 The scope of each SORP is set out in the text of the SORP itself.

Relationship with accounting standards

9 The authority, scope and application of accounting standards and the obligation of members of the governing bodies of the ASC/ASB to observe them or justify departures from them are set out in the Explanatory Foreword to accounting standards.

10 SORPs will always take account of the principles laid down in accounting standards. They can never be taken as authority to depart from the requirements imposed by

accounting standards, nor to extend the scope of accounting standards to include entities or circumstances which are otherwise excluded from specific accounting standards or accounting standards in general.

11 It is recognised in the Explanatory Foreword to accounting standards that it would be impracticable for accounting standards to cater for all situations. In applying a modified or alternative treatment it is important to have regard to the spirit of and reasoning behind any relevant accounting standards. The recommendations contained in SORPs will always have regard to this spirit and reasoning. They may, therefore, be indicative of the treatment which should be adopted in a situation not specifically catered for by accounting standards.

Future developments

12 In accordance with its new policy, the ASB will not in future issue its own SORPs. SORPs will instead be developed by bodies recognised by the Board to provide guidance on the application of accounting standards to specific industries. The Board will be prepared to recognise such bodies if they fall within its acceptance criteria, turning on the size of the industry or sector in question; the Board being satisfied as to the representative nature of the body proposing to produce the SORP; and the body agreeing to follow the ASB's code of practice for the SORP development process. This code of practice will ensure that the subject matter and scope of the SORP have the ASB's prior approval; that there is adequate due process, including widespread public consultation; and that Exposure Drafts are submitted for consideration before publication.

Since ASB intends in future to play a limited role in the production of SORPs, the process of 'franking' statements, as conducted by the ASC, will be discontinued. Instead, the Board will require to be appended to the SORP a 'negative assurance statement'. This will make clear that the Board is not approving the SORP but is rather confirming that it contains no fundamental points of principle which the Board consider unacceptable in the context of current accounting practice that the SORP is not in conflict with any existing or currently contemplated accounting standard, and that the SORP has been prepared in accordance with the Board's code of practice.

Pension scheme accounts

(Issued December 1985)

This Statement of Recommended Practice ('SORP') sets out recommendations, intended to represent current best practice, on the form and contents of the accounts of pension schemes. It also explains the context in which it has been assumed the accounts will be placed.

The provisions of this statement should be read in conjunction with the Explanatory Foreword to SORPs. Although SORPs are not mandatory, entities falling within their scope are encouraged to follow them and to state in their accounts that they have done so. They are also encouraged to disclose any departure from the recommendations and the reason for it. The provisions need not be applied to immaterial items.

Part 1 — Explanatory note

Introduction

1 The objectives of a pension scheme annual report are to inform members and other users as to:

(a) the general activity, history and development of the scheme;

(b) the transactions of the scheme and the size of its fund;

(c) the progress of the scheme towards meeting its potential liabilities and obligations to members; and

(d) the investment policy and performance of the scheme. To be of value to the users, this information should be provided on a timely basis.

2 In order to achieve these objectives and to present a balanced report on the pension scheme as a whole, the annual report should be made available as soon as possible after the accounting date and should comprise:

(a) A trustees' report. This is primarily a review of, or comment on:
  (i) membership statistics and major changes in benefits, constitution or legal requirements;
  (ii) the financial development of the scheme as disclosed in the accounts;
  (iii) the actuarial position of the scheme as disclosed in the actuary's statement; and
  (iv) the investment policy and performance of the scheme, including details of any delegation of investment management responsibilities by the trustees.

(b) Accounts. These are a stewardship report, designed to give a true and fair view of the transactions of the scheme during the accounting period and of the disposition of its net assets at the period end. An auditors' report on the accounts should be attached if the accounts have been audited.

(c) An actuary's statement. This is a statement by an actuary based on his investigation into, and report on, the ability of the current fund of the pension scheme to meet accrued benefits and the adequacy of the fund and future contribution levels to meet promised benefits when due.

(d) An investment report. Investment policy and performance are important aspects of the stewardship function and accordingly the trustees' report in amplification of the accounts should contain or have appended additional information on investments held and investment income earned and comment on investment policy and performance.

3 As explained in paragraph 2, the information required of the investment report may instead be included in the trustees' report. The accounts and the actuary's statement are, however, two separate expert reports, having fundamentally different objectives. The former is a record of the origin and current size and disposition of the fund and the latter is a statement based on an investigation into, and report on, the present and future ability of the scheme to meet the accrued and prospective obligations to its members. These two reports require to be read in conjunction with each other, but neither should form a part of, or be subsumed into, the other.

Form and context in which the accounts appear

4 The form and context in which the accounts appear can have a significant effect on the overall message conveyed to the reader. It is therefore important that the separate components of the annual report are consistent with each other and do not omit any information which could affect the view given by the annual report as a whole. For example, the trustees' report's review of the financial development of the scheme should be both a fair review and consistent with the accounts. Similarly, the accounts should be presented in conjunction with an actuary's statement which comments comprehensively on the adequacy of the current fund and funding policy.

5 It is suggested, therefore, that when preparing pension scheme accounts one must consider the contents of the remainder of the annual report in order to ensure that the accounts are not submitted to members and employers in a misleading form or context.

Fundamental accounting concepts and materiality

6 The recommendations contained in this statement should be considered in conjunction with the fundamental accounting concepts described in SSAP 2 'Disclosure of accounting policies' and should be applied only after taking into account the materiality of the item or matter involved.

Legislation

7 Legislation designed to regulate certain aspects of pension schemes has been enacted in the United Kingdom. This legislation imposes on most schemes constituted in Great Britain a requirement that they prepare annual reports which include a set of accounts. The legislation also sets out in some detail requirements on the form and contents of the accounts and the principles to be applied in preparing them. As a consequence, some of the recommendations contained in this statement are also embodied in the legislation of Great Britain. This is dealt with further in part 5.

Terminology

8 Although this statement adopts the terms 'revenue account', 'net assets statement' and 'movement of funds statement', alternative terminology may be equally acceptable. The word 'company' is used in this statement to represent any incorporated or unincorporated entity. The statement is intended to be applied to schemes in the United Kingdom and the Republic of Ireland. However, for simplicity, it adopts terms such as 'UK investments' and 'sterling' rather than using phrases such as 'investments in assets domiciled at home' and 'local currency'.

Part 2 — Definition of terms

9 The *accruals concept* is a concept of accounting whereby revenues and costs are recognised as they are earned or incurred (not as money is received or paid) and matched with one another so far as their relationship can be established or justifiably assumed.

10 *Added years* is a form of provision of additional benefits whereby a member is promised benefit for a period in excess of that which would otherwise be taken into account in calculating the pension benefit.

11 *Additional voluntary contributions* are the contributions (over and above the regular contributions, if any, required from a member by the scheme rules) which a member elects to pay in order to secure additional benefits.

12 An *associated company* is a company, not being a subsidiary of the investing group or company, in which:

(a) the interest of the investing group or company is effectively that of a partner in a joint venture or consortium and the investing group or company is in a position to exercise a significant influence over the company in which the investment is made; or

(b) the interest of the investing group or company is for the long term and is substantial and, having regard to the disposition of the other shareholdings, the investing group or company is in a position to exercise a significant influence over the company in which the investment is made.

13 The *closing rate of exchange* is the exchange rate for spot transactions ruling at the accounting date and is the mean of the buying and selling rates at the close of business on that day.

14 *Concentration of investment* arises when a significant proportion of the assets of the scheme is invested in one company and any connected companies and persons, or in one property. For the purpose of this definition, investment includes:

(a) an interest in shares and securities of a company;

(b) mortgages on real property owned by a company;

(c) freeholds and leaseholds owned by the scheme's trustees and effectively leased directly to a company; and

(d) loans made to a company.

15 *A pension scheme is a *fully insured scheme* when the trustees have effected an insurance contract in respect of each member which guarantees benefits corresponding at all times to those promised under the rules.

16 A *fund* of a pension scheme is the net assets held on behalf of the scheme by the trustees for the purpose of meeting benefits when they become due.

17 *The *members* of a pension scheme are all employees and former employees entitled to a benefit from the scheme.

18 *A *money purchase scheme* is a pension scheme in which the benefits are directly determined by the value of contributions paid in respect of each member.

19 *Movement of funds statement* is the term used in this statement of recommended practice to describe the reconciliation of the movement in the net assets of the scheme

*Definition taken from 'Pensions Terminology—A Glossary for Pension Schemes' published by PMI/PRAG in 1984.

during the accounting period when it is presented as a separate statement within the accounts.

20 The *net assets* of the scheme are its assets and its liabilities other than those for pension and other benefits falling due after the date of the accounts.

21 *Net assets statement* is the term used in this statement of recommended practice to describe a summary of the net assets of a pension scheme presented as part of the accounts.

22 *A *pension scheme* is an arrangement (other than for accident insurance) to provide pension and/or other benefits for members on leaving service or retiring and, possibly, after a member's death, for his or her dependants.

23 *Quoted securities* are, for the purposes of this statement, securities for which an established market exists and market prices are readily available. Any other security is an unquoted security.

24 *Revenue account* is the term used in this statement of recommended practice to describe a summary of the financial additions to, and withdrawals from, the fund of a pension scheme presented as part of the accounts.

25 *Self investment* is investment of all or part of a scheme's assets in the business of the scheme employer and any connected companies and persons. For the purpose of this definition, investment includes all investment set out in (a) to (d) of paragraph 14 and, in addition, includes money currently due to the scheme but held by the companies such as employer and employee contributions.

26 *A *state scheme premium* is a payment which may be made when either the pension scheme or a member of it ceases to be contracted out, in return for which the state scheme will provide the equivalent of the whole or a part of the guaranteed minimum pension, i.e. the statutory minimum pension which a pension scheme must provide as one of the conditions of contracting out under the Social Security Pensions Act 1975.

27 *Subsidiary company.* A company is a subsidiary of another if, but only if,

(a) that other either:
   (i) is a member of it and controls the composition of its board of directors; or
   (ii) holds more than half in nominal value of its equity share capital; or

(b) the first mentioned company is a subsidiary of any company which is that other's subsidiary.

28 *Term insurance* is a form of life insurance which provides a lump sum on death before a fixed future date.

Part 3 — Recommended practice

Scope

29 The recommendations contained in this statement are intended to be applicable to all pension schemes other than:

(a) those which have only one member at the accounting date;

(b) those which are unfunded, i.e. those under which benefits are paid out of the employer's revenue and no provision is made for future liabilities by setting aside assets under trusts.

*Definition taken from 'Pensions Terminology — A Glossary for Pension Schemes' published by PMI/PRAG in 1984.

30 As such, the scope of this statement is intended to include, *inter alia:*

(a) schemes which are fully insured and which may not, therefore, have any assets to disclose in the net assets statement; and

(b) schemes which are money purchase schemes and which may, therefore, have no need for an actuary's statement.

Primary addressees

31 The primary addressees of the accounts of a pension scheme are the members, the dependants of deceased former members and the participating employers.

Basis of accounting

32 The accounts should normally be prepared on the basis of the accruals concept.

33 All the assets and liabilities of the scheme at the period end should be included in the net assets statement in order to show the current size and disposition of the fund. The only exceptions to this are:

(a) the liabilities to pay pensions and other benefits in the future, which will be reported upon separately in the actuary's statement (see paragraphs 43 to 45);

(b) insurance policies purchased to match the pension obligations of specific individual members (see paragraphs 61 and 62); and

(c) additional voluntary contributions separately invested from the assets of the principal scheme (see paragraphs 63 and 64).

34 The carrying amount of investments should be the market value at the date of the net assets statement, where such a value is available, or else at the trustees' estimate thereof. This is dealt with further in paragraphs 46 to 54.

35 The carrying amount of all other assets and liabilities recognised in the net assets statement should be based on normal accounting conventions.

Content of accounts

36 The accounts and notes thereto should comprise:

(a) a revenue account which discloses the magnitude and character of the financial additions to, and withdrawals from, the fund during the accounting period;

(b) a net assets statement which discloses the size and disposition of the net assets of the scheme at the period end; and

(c) a reconciliation of the movement in the net assets of the scheme to the revenue account. This reconciliation may be shown as a completely separate statement (i.e. a 'movement of funds statement') or alternatively it may be incorporated into the revenue account or the net assets statement.

37 The revenue account, net assets statement, movement of funds statement (if any), and notes to the accounts should contain as a minimum the items set out in part 4 of this statement.

38 Corresponding amounts should be disclosed. The accounting period will usually be one year in duration. If this is not the case for both the current and corresponding periods, this fact should be clearly stated.

39 The accounts should contain such additional information as is necessary to give a true and fair view of the transactions of the scheme for the accounting period and of the disposition of its net assets at the period end. This will include, for example, information about capital commitments, post balance sheet events and contingencies (other than future liabilities to pay pensions and related outgoings).

Accounting policies

40 The accounting policies followed in dealing with items which are judged material or critical in accounting for or reporting on the transactions and net assets of the scheme should be explained in the notes to the accounts. The explanations should be clear, fair, and as brief as possible.

41 The following are examples of some areas where it will be appropriate to disclose the accounting policies adopted:

(a) the policies adopted in applying the accruals concept to significant categories of income and expenditure, such as contributions, investment income, transfer values and benefits;

(b) the bases adopted for the valuation of assets;

(c) the basis of foreign currency translation;

(d) the treatment of interest on property developments; and

(e) the bases adopted for accounting for investments in subsidiary and associated companies and in joint ventures.

42 It is a fundamental accounting concept that there is consistency of accounting treatment within each accounting period and from one period to the next. A change in accounting policy should not be made unless it can be justified on the ground that the new policy is preferable to the one it replaces because it will give a fairer presentation of the transactions and of the disposition of the net assets of the scheme. When changes are made they should be disclosed, along with the reasons for making the change. If the effect is material it should be accounted for as a prior year adjustment by restating the opening balance of the fund and the corresponding amounts.

Actuarial position

43 The responsibility for reviewing the adequacy of the funding arrangements made to meet expected pensions and other benefits from the fund lies with the actuary to the scheme. This responsibility will normally be discharged by the preparation of an actuary's report which, although usually addressed to the trustees, is also made available to the members. A statement by the actuary based on this report forms a separate component of the annual report.

44 An actuary's report will often not be prepared annually, and, when it is prepared, it will not necessarily coincide with the date of the annual report and accounts. Accordingly, the actuary will often provide an interim or supplementary statement explaining whether he is aware of any changes in circumstances or necessary changes in assumptions which would indicate that his previous statement could not, if prepared at the current date, be made.

45 The accounts should refer to the actuary's statement by way of a note. This note might take the following form:

"The accounts summarise the transactions and net assets of the scheme. They do not take account of liabilities to pay pensions and other benefits in the future. The actuarial position of the fund, which does take account of such liabilities, is dealt with in the statement by the actuary on pages 00 to 00 of the annual report and these accounts should be read in conjunction therewith."

If the actuary's report is not recent and the actuary's statement has not been updated by an interim or supplementary statement, the above wording may need to be amended.

Valuation of investments

46 Investments should be included in the net assets statement at their market value at the date of the net assets statement, where such a value is available, or else at the trustees' estimate thereof. The carrying amount of the principal categories of investment should be arrived at by applying the valuation bases set out below in paragraphs 48 to 54. The bases adopted should be disclosed in the notes to the accounts.

47 Any significant restrictions affecting the ability of the scheme to realise its investments at the accounting date at all or at the value at which they are included in the accounts should be disclosed in a note to the accounts. This will include, for example, legal or contractual restrictions on the surrender of units (e.g. managed funds) or material penalties which would have been suffered if they had been surrendered at the accounting date. It will not include the inherent difficulties in disposing of a large investment.

48 Securities quoted in the UK should be valued at the midpoint of the quotations in the Stock Exchange Daily Official List or at similar recognised market values.

49 Other securities quoted overseas should similarly be valued at middle market prices from overseas stock exchanges translated at closing rates of exchange.

50 Unquoted securities (including venture capital funds where appropriate) should be valued by the trustees.

51 Investments which are held in units should be valued at the average of the unit bid and offer prices at the accounting date. For some unitised funds, offer prices are regularly quoted but bid prices are not. In such circumstances, a basis such as reducing the offer price by an amount which takes account of the specific circumstances is likely to give a suitable valuation. Where unit bid and offer prices are both not available or have otherwise not been used, the basis adopted in arriving at an estimate of market value should be disclosed.

52 Financial futures, options, and forward currency positions should be included or provided for at market value, where such market value is available. If it is not available, a trustees' valuation should be used.

53 Property should be included in the net assets statement at open market value. Guidance on this matter is given in appendix 1 to this statement. The name, or employing firm, and qualification of the valuer should be stated. If the valuer is an employee of the scheme or the participating employers this fact should be stated.

54 If practicable, long-term insurance policies should be valued using a premium valuation method. Where there are difficulties in obtaining this value, however, the latest value established by the actuary for the assessment of the discontinuance position, adjusted by subsequent additions to and withdrawals from the policy, will usually be satisfactory. Guidance on this matter is given in appendix 2 to this statement.

Accounting for associated and subsidiary companies

55 Pension schemes may have investments in associated or subsidiary companies. These companies will be either investment-holding companies or trading companies. The associated companies may include joint ventures such as managed funds or pooled investments.

56 In principle, such investments should be accounted for as follows:

(a) the results, assets and liabilities of subsidiary companies should be consolidated with the transactions, assets and liabilities of the scheme. For investment-holding subsidiaries the basis of this consolidation will usually be a proportional consolidation on a line-by-line basis; for other subsidiaries it will be a single-line equity method of accounting;

(b) investments in associated companies which are joint ventures should be treated in the same way as investments in subsidiary companies; and

(c) investments in associated companies which are not joint ventures should be treated in the same way as ordinary investments by including them in the net assets statement at market value and including only dividends received and receivable in the revenue account.

Where consolidated accounts are prepared, they should be the only accounts of the scheme; there is no need to produce separate 'entity' accounts. The consolidation bases to be used are explained more fully in paragraphs 57 to 60 below.

57 It will usually be appropriate to include in the scheme's accounts, on a line-by-line basis, a proportion of the results, assets and liabilities of subsidiary investment-holding companies based on the percentage equity shareholding of the scheme in the companies.

58 However, if the pension scheme in effect has an interest or obligation in respect of the whole of the results, assets or liabilities of a subsidiary company, for example because it has agreed to acquire or indemnify the minority interests, it will be appropriate to consolidate the whole of the company's results, assets and liabilities and include the minority shareholders' interest in the net assets statement.

59 Uniform group accounting policies should be followed by a pension scheme in preparing its consolidated accounts. For example, investments held by investment-holding subsidiary companies should be included in the consolidated accounts at market value. Where such group accounting policies are not adopted by a subsidiary, adjustments should be made in preparing the consolidated accounts.

60 The scheme's investment in trading subsidiary companies should be included in the net assets statement at market value. Although the same principles as in paragraphs 57 and 58 should be applied in determining the proportion of the net result of such companies which should be included in the scheme's revenue account, this proportion should be included on a single line rather than line-by-line as for investment-holding companies. The unrealised gains arising from the revaluation to market value of investments in trading subsidiaries should be treated in exactly the same way as those on other investments.

Accounting for long-term insurance policies

61 If long-term insurance policies are purchased which match, and fully guarantee, the pension obligations of specific individual members of the scheme, the acquisition costs of the policy should be treated as the cost of discharging the benefits at the time of purchase. Such a policy should not be included in the net assets statement of the scheme.

62 All other long-term insurance policies should be included in the net assets statement.

Accounting for additional voluntary contributions (AVCs)

63 Where AVCs are made to purchase added years or additional defined benefits within the provisions for benefits under the principal scheme, they should be included as contributions receivable from members in the scheme's revenue account and the assets acquired with them should be included in the net asset statement.

64 Where AVCs are separately invested in such a way that the proceeds from the investment determine the benefit to the members, they should either be disclosed separately from the transactions and net assets of the fund but accounted for within the accounts of the scheme or the notes thereto, or referred to by way of note and accounted for and reported on separately to those members making AVCs.

Disclosure items

65 If there is any self-investment in excess of 5% of the value of the net assets of the scheme, then this should be disclosed in a note to the accounts, together with details of the nature and value of the investment involved.

66 Where there is a concentration of investment (other than in UK Government securities) which exceeds 5% of the value of the net assets of the scheme, then this should be disclosed in a note to the accounts, together with details of the amount and nature of the investment and the company involved.

67 Where insurance policies form a material part of the net assets of the scheme, the trustees will usually disclose the main characteristics relevant to the overall investment policy, for instance whether the policies are with or without profits.

Investment report

68 This statement assumes that the annual report includes a report which contains a greater analysis of the investment portfolio and income than is disclosed in the accounts. This analysis will often include:

(a) analysis of investments by industrial sector;

(b) analysis of investments by geographical sector;

(c) details of the ten or twenty largest investments;

(d) details of investments which represent 5% or more of any class of shares of any company; and

(e) details of the extent to which properties are subject to rent reviews.

69 The totals shown in any such report should be reconciled to the amounts shown in the accounts.

Part 4 — Format of accounts

70 The accounts of a pension scheme, and the notes thereto, should contain the items listed below where they are material. These lists are not intended to be recommendations on either the layout or the order of these items.

Revenue account

1. Contributions receivable:

    1.1 from employers:

        1.1.1 normal;
        1.1.2 additional;

    1.2 from members:

        1.2.1 normal;
        1.2.2 additional voluntary (see paragraphs 63 and 64);

    1.3 transfers in:

1.3.1 group transfers in from other schemes;
1.3.2 individual transfers in from other schemes.

2. Investment income:
   - 2.1 income from fixed interest securities;
   - 2.2 dividends from equities;
   - 2.3 income from index-linked securities;
   - 2.4 income from managed or unitised funds;
   - 2.5 net rents from properties. Any material netting-off should be separately disclosed;
   - 2.6 interest on cash deposits
   - 2.7 share of profits/losses of trading subsidiary companies and joint ventures.

3. Other income:
   - 3.1 claims on term insurance policies;
   - 3.2 any other category of income which does not naturally fall into the above classification, suitably described and analysed where material.

4. Benefits payable:
   - 4.1 pensions;
   - 4.2 commutation of pensions and lump sum retirement benefits;
   - 4.3 death benefits;
   - 4.4 payments to and on account of leavers:
     - 4.4.1 refunds of contributions;
     - 4.4.2 state scheme premiums;
     - 4.4.3 purchase of annuities to match preserved benefits;
     - 4.4.4 group transfers out to other schemes;
     - 4.4.5 individual transfers out to other schemes.

5. Other payments:
   - 5.1 premiums on term insurance policies;
   - 5.2 any other category of expenditure which does not naturally fall into the above classification, suitably described and analysed where material.

6. Administrative and other expenses borne by the scheme, with suitable analysis where material.

   Where the administrative expenses are borne directly by a participating employer, that fact should be disclosed.

Net assets statement

7. Investment assets:
   - 7.1 fixed interest securities (analysed between public sector and other);
   - 7.2 equities;
   - 7.3 index-linked securities;
   - 7.4 managed funds (analysed between property and other);
   - 7.5 unit trusts (analysed between property and other);
   - 7.6 trading subsidiary companies and joint ventures;
   - 7.7 freehold and leasehold property;
   - 7.8 cash deposits;
   - 7.9 insurance policies;

7.10 other investments, such as works of art;
7.11 debtors and creditors in respect of investment transactions where these form part of the net assets available for investment within the investment portfolio;
7.12 other assets and liabilities directly connected with investment transactions (e.g. financial futures, options and forward dealings in currencies and, where appropriate, tax recoverable).

Investments should be further analysed between 'UK' and 'foreign' and between 'quoted' and 'unquoted', and freehold and leasehold property should be further analysed between 'short leasehold' and 'other'.

8. Fixed assets, held primarily for reasons other than investment potential.

9. Long-term borrowings:
9.1 sterling; and
9.2 foreign currency.

10. Current assets and liabilities:
10.1 contributions due from employer;
10.2 unpaid benefits; and
10.3 other current assets and liabilities (other than liabilities to pay pensions and other benefits in the future).

Reconciliation of the movement in the net assets of the scheme

11. The reconciliation of the movement in the net assets of the scheme may be incorporated into the revenue account or net assets statement, or alternatively be shown as a separate statement. Whichever method of presentation is adopted it should clearly disclose:
11.1 opening net assets of the scheme;
11.2 net new money invested, per revenue account;
11.3 change in market value of investments (realised and unrealised); and
11.4 closing net assets of the scheme.

71 The amount of sales and of purchases of investments should be disclosed either within one of the accounting statements referred to in paragraph 70 or elsewhere in the notes.

Part 5 — Note on legal requirements in Great Britain, Northern Ireland and the Republic of Ireland

Great Britain

72 Legislation designed to regulate certain aspects of pension schemes, including the periodic preparation of annual reports, has been enacted in Great Britain, and is contained within the Social Security Act 1985 and the Regulations made under the Act.

73 As well as imposing on the trustees the requirement to prepare annual reports, the legislation includes detailed requirements on the form and content of the annual report, including the accounts. These requirements provide a framework for the accounting for and reporting on the transactions, assets and liabilities of pension schemes. The legislation sets out the over-riding principle of the accounts of pension schemes which is that they should give a true and fair view of the transactions of the scheme during the period and of the disposition of its net assets at the period end.

74 The legislation also requires the inclusion as a note to the accounts of a statement explaining whether or not the accounts have been prepared in accordance with the professional guidelines currently issued by the Accounting Standards Committee and, if not, giving particulars of material differences.

75 The recommendations contained in this Statement of Recommended Practice, which are consistent with the legislation in all respects, provide guidance on best practice in complying with the legislation. However, the recommendations deal with some aspects of pension scheme accounting not dealt with in the legislation (for example, accounting for associated and subsidiary companies) and they go further than the legislation in some respects. Examples of respects in which they go further include:

(a) the scope of the recommendations. As explained in paragraph 29, the recommendations are intended to be applicable to all pension schemes other than one-member schemes and unfunded schemes. The accounting requirements of the Social Security Act 1985 apply to all occupational pension schemes other than one-member schemes, unfunded schemes, and public service schemes. 'Occupational pension scheme' is more narrowly defined than this statement's 'pension scheme'; and

(b) the definition of self-investment contained in paragraph 25 of this statement is wider than that adopted in the Act in that 'monies currently due to the scheme from the employer' are included in the statement's definition but not in the Act's.

Northern Ireland and the Republic of Ireland

76 Although the legislation referred to in paragraph 72 includes Northern Ireland within its scope, the requirement to prepare annual reports only applies to schemes constituted in Great Britain. There is no equivalent requirement for pension schemes constituted in Northern Ireland. It is understood, however, that legislation is planned which will introduce requirements similar to those now enacted in Great Britain.

77 There is no equivalent legislation enacted in, or planned for, the Republic of Ireland.

78 Nevertheless, as this statement is complete in itself and does not rely on legislation in any way, its provisions are suitable for application to schemes operating in Northern Ireland and the Republic of Ireland.

79 Paragraph 26 of this statement refers to the Social Security Pensions Act 1975 . This is United Kingdom legislation for which there is no equivalent in the Republic of Ireland. Consequently, the term defined ('state scheme premium') is not relevant in the context of schemes constituted in the Republic of Ireland.

80 Paragraph 27 of this statement adopts a definition of subsidiary company based on the statutory definitions given in the Companies Act 1985 and the Companies Act (Northern Ireland), 1960, as inserted by Article 3 of The Companies (Northern Ireland) Order 1984. However, the Companies Act 1963 (Republic of Ireland) gives a slightly different definition, in that a company in which the holding company holds more than half of the shares carrying voting rights, as distinct from more than half of the equity share capital, is also included. Such companies will normally come within the definition of paragraph 27 because holding more than half of the shares with voting rights will be equivalent to controlling the composition of the board of directors.

Appendix 1

This appendix does not form part of the statement of recommended practice.

Valuation of properties held as investments

Paragraph 53 of the statement recommends that property should be valued annually at open market value for inclusion in the accounts. The annual valuation of all properties by external, qualified valuers may be expensive and time-consuming with no commensurate benefit. This appendix is intended to provide guidance on the matter.

81 Although a valuation of properties should be undertaken annually, it need not necessarily be by a qualified or independent valuer. It will usually be acceptable to have a valuation carried out by a qualified valuer at regular intervals, with an appraisal and, if necessary, update of this valuation carried out by the trustees during the intervening years.

82 The regularity with which the valuation should be carried out by a qualified valuer, and the possible involvement of independent valuers, depends, to some extent, on the proportion of the assets held in the form of properties. In the absence of unusual circumstances a valuation by a qualified valuer should be undertaken every five years.

83 In order to ensure that the trend of the movement in market values is not distorted unnecessarily by carrying out such valuations every five years it may be appropriate to undertake them on a rolling basis, with a proportion of the total property portfolio being valued by a qualified valuer each year.

Appendix 2

This appendix does not form part of the statement of recommended practice.

Valuation of long-term insurance policies

The statement recommends that all investments of the pension scheme, including long-term insurance policies (other than policies referred to in paragraph 61), should be included in the net assets statement at market value. The market value of long-term insurance policies is not readily ascertainable, hence a basis of valuation which is consistent with that adopted for other assets (i.e. a middle-market price) and which is practicable should be used.

84 The main methods of valuing long-term insurance policies are as follows:

(i) surrender value;

(ii) assignment value;

(iii) value determined for an insurance company's own actuarial valuation;

(iv) premium value. This is an estimate of a single premium to purchase the payments at present secured under the policies

(v) modified premium value. Although the premium value does not represent a middle-market price, it can be made similar by excluding the loadings made by the insurer in premium rating for initial expenses, such as issue expenses, brokerage and stamp duty. This 'modified premium value' is lower than the premium value;

(vi) valuation for actuarial assessment of the discontinuance position; and

(vii) valuation for actuarial assessment of the future contribution rate.

85 Surrender value is the value at which the insurer is prepared to buy back the policy and is consequently a realisable value. The surrender value quoted by the insurance company will depend on many factors unrelated to the policy's worth in normal circumstances, such as the willingness of the insurance company to buy the policy and the need to realise assets. Surrender value will therefore be the relevant valuation basis only if it is likely that the policy will be surrendered.

86 An assignment value is also a realisable value. Assignment of pension policies is unusual and the assignment value involved will be a matter of negotiation on each occasion. As such, it will be neither appropriate nor practicable to use such values for accounting purposes unless the policy is to be assigned.

87 The value determined by an insurance company for its own internal purposes will have been calculated on different assumptions and for different purposes than a valuation for use in pension scheme accounts. It will not, therefore, reflect the market value of the policy.

88 Premium value and modified premium value are replacement costs. There may be practical problems in trying to determine these values when certain policy benefits could not be purchased in their existing form, for example those under long established with-profits policies. When premiums are continuing under annual premium contracts the estimated single premium should be such as would, together with the contractual future premiums, purchase the same policy benefits.

89 A valuation for the actuarial assessment of the discontinuance position should be directly comparable to the market values attributed to other assets.

90 A valuation for the actuarial assessment of the future contribution rate will, like the value referred to in 87, have been based on different assumptions to those usually adopted in determining market value.

91 All of these methods are likely to produce different values. Surrender value, assignment value and the value determined by an insurance company for its own internal purposes will generally not be consistent with middle-market values. Premium value or modified premium value is most closely akin to middle-market value and should, therefore, be used. Where this is impractical, the carrying amount should be based on the value established by the actuary for the assessment of the discontinuance position.

92 Such actuarial valuations should be undertaken at least every three years. In the interim years the value determined by the latest actuarial valuation should be adjusted to take account of additions to and withdrawals from the policy.

93 These actuarial values are based on different principles to those on which premium values and modified premium values are based. Consequently they will not necessarily give comparable results. Although arguments can be advanced in favour of the use of actuarial values rather than premium values or vice versa, either of these bases will, as long as it is consistently applied, provide a satisfactory valuation for use in the accounts.

Accounting by charities

(Issued by the Accounting Standards Committee in May 1988)

This Statement of Recommended Practice sets out recommendations, on the way in which a charity should report annually on the resources entrusted to it and the activities it undertakes.

Although the recommendations are not mandatory, charities are encouraged to follow them and to state in their accounts that they have done so. They are also encouraged to disclose any departure from the recommendations and the reason for it. The recommendations *need not be applied to immaterial items.*

The recommendations contained in this statement of recommended practice go beyond the requirements of the Charities Act 1960 and the Charities Act 1985 and have been welcomed by the Charity Commission. Accounts prepared in accordance with these recommendations will therefore be acceptable for filing with the Charity Commission and, if necessary, with the appropriate local authority.

Part 1 — Explanatory note

Introduction

1 The purpose of a charity's annual report is to provide timely and regular information on the charity, enabling the user of the report to gain an understanding of the charity's operations and achievements and a full and proper appreciation of the charity's transactions during the period and of its position at the period end. This statement of recommended practice sets out recommendations on the form and content of the annual report and on the way in which the accounts contained in the report should be prepared.

2 The Accounting Standards Committee's purpose in setting out these recommendations is to help improve the quality of financial reporting by charities. It also wishes to provide assistance to those who are responsible for the preparation of charities' annual reports and accounts. The Accounting Standards Committee hopes that the recommendations will assist in reducing the current diversity in accounting practice and presentation although the intention is not to try to standardise them.

3 Universities are not included within the scope of the recommendations. That apart, the statement is intended to be applicable to all charities in the United Kingdom and the Republic of Ireland, regardless of their constitution, size or complexity. However, it is recognised that some of the recommendations may not be applicable to all charities because of the nature of the particular charity or because of the limited classes or size of the transactions or assets involved. Nevertheless, the full recommendations have been given in this statement, leaving discretion to the trustees of each charity to apply the recommendations according to the character of their charity and the significance of the figures involved.

4 The Accounting Standards Committee has issued 'Accounting by charities: A guide for the smaller charity' in order to assist the trustees of small charities in exercising this discretion.

Interpretation of financial information on charities

5 Charities are highly disparate in character, so any comparison of the financial information they produce must be undertaken with care, even if the charities involved seem to be homogeneous. Also it is important to note that, when interpreting the income and expenditure account of a charity, the amount by which income exceeds expenditure, or expenditure exceeds income, in any one year is not usually a measure of performance or efficiency and does not usually provide an indication of the charity's future needs. Similarly, the balance sheet is not necessarily a measure of the wealth of the charity.

6 This statement recommends that a review and explanation of the accounts be provided in the annual report. It is important that reference be made to this review and explanation by those seeking to interpret the accounts correctly.

Simplified reporting

7 It has been assumed in preparing this statement that a full annual report is to be prepared and that it will include a full set of accounts. However, some charities include simplified accounts in their annual report or include extracts from their annual report in other publications. As the form of such documents will vary considerably depending on the purpose for which they have been prepared, it is not practicable to include detailed recommendations on their preparation in this statement. However, some general principles which ought to be followed are set out below.

(a) Regardless of the intended circulation of any simplified report, a full annual report should always be produced. Details of how this full report can be obtained should be given in the simplified report.

(b) Simplified accounts should carry a statement explaining that they are not the full accounts and that they are not audited.

(c) Simplified accounts should be a fair summary of the full accounts. This means that they should contain information on both the income and expenditure account and the balance sheet and that they should be based on the principles set out in this statement.

Part 2 — Definition of terms

8 A **charity** is any institution established for charitable purposes only. Where the institution is involved in more than one activity, operates more than one fund, or is not centralised into one unit of operation, the term is used in this statement to incorporate all those activities and funds which fall within the scope of a single governing instrument (or instruments supplemental to the main instrument) and any further endowments held within the terms of the original instrument.

9 A **fund** is a pool of unexpended resources, held and maintained separately from other pools because of the circumstances in which the resources were originally received or the way in which they have subsequently been treated. A fund will be one of two kinds: a restricted fund or an unrestricted fund. (The terms 'fund' and 'funds' are used in the statement in this specialised way except when used in the phrases 'fund-raising' and 'statement of source and application of funds'.)

10 Restricted funds are funds subject to specific conditions, imposed by the donor* and binding on the trustees. They represent unspent restricted income and/or assets to which restrictions as to their use apply.

* The conditions may alternatively be imposed not by the donor but by the trusts relating to the donation. For example, if a donation is made in response to a special appeal, its use will be restricted to the purpose of the appeal, notwithstanding the fact that the donor did not impose any restriction on its use.

11 A **permanent endowment** is a particular form of restricted fund in that the fund must be held permanently, although its constituent assets may change from time to time.

12 A **designated fund** is a particular form of unrestricted fund, consisting of amounts of unrestricted funds which have been allocated or designated for specific purposes by the charity itself. The use of designated funds for their designated purpose will remain at the discretion of the trustees.

13 Administration expenses comprise the costs which are not incurred directly on any of the charitable activities or projects of the charity and which are not incurred on fund-raising activities or publicity. Administration expenses will include a proper allocation of items of expenditure involving more than one cost category (e.g. administration expenses, fund-raising expenses etc), but should not include any apportionment of costs which belong to other cost categories.

14 Fund-raising expenses comprise the costs incurred by a charity in inducing others to make voluntary contributions to it. They will also include a proper allocation of items of expenditure involving more than one cost category (e.g. administration expenses, fund-raising, expenses etc.,), but should not include any apportionment of costs which belong to other cost categories.

Part 3 — Recommended practice

The scope of the recommendations

15 These recommendations are intended to be applicable to all charities other than universities. Any departure from the recommendations should be disclosed and explained in the annual report.

The annual report

Activities and funds to be reported on

16 The annual report of a charity should contain information on all the activities and funds of the charity and its non-autonomous branches. If a charity has some branches which are autonomous and which are therefore not dealt with in the report, this fact should be explained.

17 In order for the user to gain a full appreciation of the scope of a charity's activities, the annual report should also provide information on charities which are connected with the reporting charity and on its subsidiary and associated companies. Recommendations on the provision of this information are set out in paragraphs 70 to 73.

18 Funds held by a charity as custodian trustee will not usually fall within the scope of the annual report. Nevertheless, an indication of the extent to which the charity acts as a custodian trustee will need to be provided when explaining the charity's unquantifiable charitable work and the level of its administration expenses incurred.

The content of the annual report

19 The annual report should contain:

(a) legal and administrative details. These details will provide background information on the constitution of the charity. Paragraph 21 sets out the information which should usually be disclosed;

(b) a trustees' report or equivalent statement. This report should, as explained in paragraph 22, include a description of the charity and how it operates and a commentary on the figures shown in the accounts; and

(c) the accounts and notes thereto and, if the accounts have been audited, the auditors' report on them. The accounts are a report, expressed in financial terms, on the activities and resources of the charity. Paragraph 24 describes the accounts in detail, and the remainder of this statement sets out recommendations on their preparation.

Although it has been assumed in this statement that the legal and administrative details, the trustees' report, and the accounts will form three separate parts of the annual report, it is recognised that some or all of the legal and administrative details could just as easily be provided in the trustees' report or in the notes to the accounts.

Responsibility for preparing the annual report

20 The trustees are responsible for the preparation of the annual report and therefore for the form and content of the accounts. They should discharge this responsibility by formally approving and adopting the report. The trustees' report and balance sheet should be signed by at least two trustees on behalf of all of them in order to show this approval. The date of approval should also be disclosed.

Legal and administrative details

21 The legal and administrative details provided in the annual report should include the following information:

(a) an indication of the nature of the governing instrument or legal status of the charity. If applicable, the charity registration number and the company registration number should also be provided;

(b) the names of the trustees and their nominating body (or other method of appointment or election), the names of the members of any management committee and the names of the principal officers of the charity;

(c) the principal or registered address of the charity;

(d) the names and addresses of any other relevant organisations or persons. This may include the names and addresses of those acting as bankers, solicitors, auditors, and investment or other advisers;

(e) details of any restrictions in the way in which the charity can operate. This should include details of any limitations in the trustees' powers of investment including, for example, any restrictions imposed by the Trustee Investments Act 1961.

The trustees' report

22 The trustees' report is the main narrative section of the annual report. It should contain:

(a) an explanation of the objectives of the charity and a description of the way in which the charity is organised. The policies that have been adopted in order to try to achieve these objectives should also be explained. If there have been any significant changes in the objectives, organisation or policies since the last report, this should also be made clear. The purpose of this part of the report is to explain what the charity is trying to achieve and how it is going about it;

(b) a review of the development, activities and achievements of the charity during the year. This review should bring the reader up to date on the charity's progress and achievements. It should also explain the important events which have occurred during the year and how the charity has responded to them. It will be in this part of the report that information enabling the reader to judge the effectiveness of the charity will usually be provided;

(c) a review of the transactions and financial position of the charity, and an explanation of the salient features of the accounts. This review should enable the reader to appreciate the significance of any surpluses or deficits disclosed in the accounts and the purposes for which the charity's assets are being held. It will also put the charity's current financial position in the context of its future plans and commitments, particularly with regard to ongoing items of expenditure, projects not yet completed and obligations not yet met. The purpose of this part of the report is to help ensure that the accounts are properly interpreted.

23 Other information which, if not included in the accounts, could usefully be provided in the trustees' report includes details of voluntary help, donations-in-kind and other intangible income received during the accounting period (see paragraph 36), an indication of the extent to which the charity is dependent upon certain donors and, if the charity was set up to undertake a specific project, cumulative figures on progress of the project.

The accounts

24 The accounts are a report in financial terms on the activities and resources of the charity. They should comprise:

(a) an income and expenditure account that shows the resources made available to the charity and the expenditure incurred by the charity during the period;

(b) a balance sheet that shows the assets, liabilities and funds of the charity. The balance sheet (or its notes, see (f) below) should also provide some indication of how the funds may or, because of restrictions imposed by donors, must be utilised;

(c) a statement of source and application of funds that shows the flow of cash through the charity. However, as explained more fully in paragraph 64, there may be circumstances in which such a statement is neither necessary nor helpful. If this is the case, the statement should not be prepared;

(d) an explanation of the accounting policies used to prepare the accounts;

(e) details of the movement on, and position of, the various funds of the charity; and

(f) other notes which explain or expand upon the information contained in the accounting statements referred to above or which provide other useful information. This will include notes which show an analysis of the figures in the accounts and notes which explain the relationship between the figures.

The corresponding amounts for the previous accounting period should be given for figures disclosed in the accounts or in the notes to the accounts. The duration of the current and corresponding accounting periods should also be shown.

Accounting for separate funds

25 Most charities will hold unrestricted funds. Some may also hold one or more restricted funds, some of which may be permanent endowment funds. Appendix 1 explains in detail the legal position as regards transactions involving these various funds. To summarise, the position is as follows.

(a) The assets and liabilities representing the various funds of the charity need to be distinguished in the accounting records so that it is known which assets and liabilities are held in which funds.

(b) Realised and unrealised profits and losses on assets held in a particular fund form part of that fund. Similarly, provisions for depreciation or for a permanent fall in value of an asset form part of the fund in which the asset is held.

(c) Income generated from assets held in a particular fund may be subject to donor-imposed restrictions as to its use or the fund to which it belongs. However, where this is not the case the income will be unrestricted income.

Accounting for permanent endowment funds

26 Permanent endowment funds represent the capital of a charity. A consequence of this is that increases and decreases in the amount of the permanent endowment funds should not be dealt with in the income and expenditure account, but should instead be taken directly to the relevant permanent endowment fund in the balance sheet. A note to the accounts should disclose all movements on permanent endowment funds.

27 Income derived from assets held within a permanent endowment fund may be subject to donor-imposed restrictions as to its use or the fund to which it belongs. However, where this is not the case the income will be unrestricted income: it will not form part of the permanent endowment fund. It should therefore be included in the income and expenditure account in the normal way.

Accounting for other funds

28 The treatment of movements on all other funds should not be affected by the type of fund involved. This means, for example, that restricted income and unrestricted income received at the same time should be included in the income and expenditure account at the same time. Similarly, expenditure out of restricted funds should be included no sooner or later than expenditure made at the same time out of unrestricted funds.

29 The accounts and notes should provide information on the charity's fund structure and on the significance of each of the major fund balances. There are a number of different ways in which this information could be presented. For example, the accounts could consist of a single set of accounting statements with columnar or note analysis. On the other hand, separate sets of statements could be produced for each major fund. The trustees should decide on the presentation to be adopted. In doing so, they should take into account the complexity of the fund structure and the need to avoid confusion between the movements on the various funds.*

30 Whatever the presentation adopted, the accounts or notes should contain a reconciliation of the total opening funds of the charity to the total closing funds, showing the income less expenditure figure from the income and expenditure account and details of all other movements on the funds during the period. This reconciliation should be analysed between the major funds of the charity. The amount of each major fund should be analysed between the amount that is realised and the amount that is unrealised. The nature and purpose of each major fund should also be disclosed.

31 When disclosing details of movements on the major funds, transfers should be shown separately from allocations to designated funds. Furthermore:

* References in the remainder of the statement to 'the income and expenditure account', 'the balance sheet' and 'the statement of source and application of funds' should be taken to be references to all income and expenditure accounts, balance sheets and statements of source and application of funds prepared by the charity.

(a) material transfers and allocations of income received to designated funds should be separately disclosed, without aggregation or netting off, and should be accompanied by a narrative explanation of the nature and objective of the transfer or allocation;

(b) transfers and allocations should, if they are to be included in the income and expenditure account, be shown separately from, and beneath a subtotal of, the income and expenditure for the period.

Accounting policies

32 In order to understand the accounts it is essential that they are accompanied by an explanation of the basis on which they have been prepared. The accounting policies adopted for dealing with material items should therefore be explained in the notes to the accounts. These explanations should be clear, fair, and as brief as possible.

33 Examples of the accounting policies which should be explained include the policies adopted in the following areas:

(a) the capitalisation and depreciation of fixed assets;

(b) commitments not yet met and the use of designated funds;

(c) determining the amounts at which assets are included in the balance sheet;

(d) donations, legacies and other forms of voluntary income;

(e) grants payable and receivable;

(f) identifying the items to be included within administration expenses, fund-raising expenses, and publicity expenses;

(g) investment income;

(h) netting off of expenses and related income;

(i) realised and unrealised gains and losses on investments and fixed assets;

(j) stock;

(k) subscriptions for life membership.

Where a charity is involved in specialised activities, such as research, it is particularly important that the accounting policies adopted to account for these activities are explained.

34 The accounting policies should be consistently applied throughout the period and from one period to the next. A change in accounting policy should not be made unless the new policy will give a fairer presentation of the transactions or financial position of the charity than the one it replaces. Any change in accounting policy should be disclosed. If the effect of such a change is material, it should be accounted for by restating the opening balance of the fund or funds involved. The corresponding amounts for the previous period should also be adjusted. Any such restatements should be disclosed and explained.

Voluntary income

35 Voluntary income consists of all incoming resources (whether in the form of cash or other assets or in kind) other than incoming resources received for permanent endowment, government and similar grants, investment income and gains, and payments received for services or goods.

36 A charity may receive assistance in the form of donated facilities, voluntary help or beneficial loan arrangements. Such assistance is generally referred to as 'intangible income' or 'donations-in-kind'. Although some intangible income could be included in the income and expenditure account, it will usually be more appropriate to deal with it in the notes to the accounts or in the trustees' report — particularly as its value will often be impossible to quantify. The information disclosed in respect of such income should be sufficient to give a reasonable appreciation of the benefit derived from it.

37 The value of all other voluntary income should be included in the income and expenditure account as soon as it is prudent and practicable to do so. This will usually be when the income is received. Paragraphs 38 to 44 expand upon this general principle. This means, for example, that all legacies (other than those received for permanent endowment) should be included in full in the income and expenditure account as soon as they are received.

Restricted income

38 As explained in paragraph 28, the fact that income is restricted should not affect the manner in which it is accounted for in the income and expenditure account or the timing of its recognition as income. The one exception to this rule is when the restrictions imposed are so onerous that it is impossible to use the income in the way intended. In such circumstances the income should be carried forward in the balance sheet under the heading 'deferred restricted income' and the restrictions involved explained.

Donated assets

39 Incoming resources in the form of donated assets should usually be included in the income and expenditure account as soon as they are received. The amount at which they should be included should be a reasonable estimate of their value to the charity. The basis of valuation should be disclosed. This treatment is appropriate regardless of whether the assets were donated for use, sale or distribution.

40 On occasion it may not be practicable to ascertain the value of assets received, in which case their receipt should instead be disclosed in a note to the accounts. If it later becomes practicable to ascertain a value for them, this value should be included in the income and expenditure account as income at the date of valuation. For example, if an asset cannot be valued at the date of receipt but is later sold, the sale proceeds should be included as income at the date of sale. If the amount of assets included in income in a period other than the period of receipt is significant, this fact should be reported and the amounts involved disclosed.

Cash collections

41 When income has been collected for a charity but has not been received by it by the end of the accounting period, an estimate of the amount not received should in theory be included in the income and expenditure account. Similarly, when some of the charity's income is in collection containers at public premises at the period end, an estimate of the amount in the containers should in theory be included as income. However, because of the practical difficulties which will often be involved, it is not necessary to include such estimates in the income and expenditure account. Whatever treatment is adopted to account for such income should be applied consistently and disclosed.

Life subscriptions

42 Life subscriptions purchase for the subscriber facilities or benefits extending over a number of years. In theory a proportion of each subscription received should be allocated to each of the periods for which it is anticipated the subscription will apply. However, rather than undertake lengthy calculations to estimate the appropriate period to use, it is acceptable to use an approximation, perhaps based on the relationship between the amount of the annual subscription and the amount of the life subscription. The period used should be disclosed.

Grants receivable

43 Government and similar grants should be dealt with in accordance with the terms of the grant. Grants made towards the cost of acquiring a fixed asset should be taken to income and expenditure account over the useful life of the asset concerned (see paragraphs 51 to 55, which deal with accounting for fixed assets). The amount of the grant still to be taken to income and expenditure account should be shown on the balance sheet as a deferred credit or, where appropriate, included in the relevant fund balance.

44 If a grant is to be received after the expenditure to which it relates, a best estimate of the amount to be received should be included in the income and expenditure account.

Gains and losses on investments and fixed assets

45 A realised or unrealised gain or loss arising on an asset will form part of the fund in which the asset involved is (or, in the case of an asset disposed of, was) held.

Realised gains and losses

46 Realised gains and losses on the disposal of investments should either be:

(a) included in the income and expenditure account, in which case they should be disclosed separately from other income; or

(b) disclosed in the statement of investment gains (an example of which is shown in Appendix 2) and then added to or deducted from the appropriate fund in the balance sheet. Statements of investment gains should be disclosed on the face of the accounts, not in the notes.

47 Realised gains and losses on the disposal of fixed assets should be included in the income and expenditure account and, if material, disclosed separately from other income.

Unrealised gains and losses

48 As explained in paragraph 68, investments may be carried in the balance sheet at cost or at market value. Where they are carried at cost, there will be no unrealised gains or losses to account for, except in the case of a permanent diminution in value (see paragraph 69). Where they are carried at market value, unrealised gains and losses will arise. Such gains and losses should be accounted for in a manner which is consistent with realised gains and losses on investments; in other words, if realised gains and losses on investments are included in the income and expenditure account, unrealised gains and losses on investments should be as well.

49 Similarly, unrealised gains or losses will arise if fixed assets are included in the balance sheet at revalued amounts (see paragraph 68). Such gains and losses should not be included in the income and expenditure account: they should be added to or deducted from the appropriate fund in the balance sheet.

Other income

50 If a charity carries out trading activities, the income should be accounted for in accordance with the normal accounting rules for profit-oriented entities. If a charity charges for services which it provides, the charges should be recognised as income in the income and expenditure account as they are earned. For example, if a service is provided over a period of time, the income involved should be recognised over the period of service and not over the period in which the payment is received.

Accounting for fixed assets

Capitalisation of fixed assets

51 All expenditure on the acquisition, production or installation of fixed assets and all receipts of fixed assets by way of gift should be capitalised and included in the balance sheet. This general principle is not affected by the source of finance used to pay for the fixed asset, or the source of finance likely to be used to pay for any future replacement of the asset.

(a) Expenditure on the acquisition, production or installation of fixed assets should be capitalised at the amount expended.

(b) Fixed assets received by way of gift should be capitalised at the value at which the gift was included in income (see paragraph 39).

(c) Fixed assets being capitalised some time after being acquired, for example as a result of a change in accounting policy, should similarly be capitalised at original cost or at the value at which the gift was included in income. However, if neither of these amounts are ascertainable, a reasonable estimate of the asset's current value to the charity should be used.

For the remainder of this statement all of these valuation bases will be referred to as 'cost'.

52 The only exception to this general principle is that a charity need not capitalise a fixed asset which is either:

(a) inalienable (in other words a fixed asset which the charity is prohibited from disposing of) historic (such as a monument or statue); or

(b) for which neither a cost nor a market value is available. This should be an extremely rare occurrence: it will be usually be possible to determine a reasonable estimate of its cost or value without incurring significant expenditure.

A summary of the fixed assets not included in the balance sheet but still in use should be given in the notes to the accounts. These summary details should be sufficient to enable the reader to appreciate the age and scale of fixed assets not included on the balance sheet.

Revaluation of fixed assets

53 If a charity revalues some or all of its fixed assets, this fact, together with the date and bases of valuation, should be stated in the notes to the accounts. In the year of valuation, the names and qualifications of the persons responsible for making the valuation should also be disclosed.

Depreciation of fixed assets

54 Most fixed assets depreciate, that is wear out, get consumed or otherwise suffer a reduction in their useful life through use, the passing of time or obsolescence. Fixed assets which have a finite useful life should be depreciated. Fixed assets which have an indefinite useful life, such as freehold land, should not be depreciated. This means that:

(a) fixed assets with finite useful lives should be included in the balance sheet at cost (or, if revalued, at a revalued amount) less an appropriate provision for depreciation, and

(b) fixed assets with an indefinite useful life should be included at cost (or, if revalued, at a revalued amount).

55 If a fixed asset is revalued its depreciation should be based on the revalued amount, the residual value and remaining useful life of the asset at the date of the revaluation.

Other expenditure and costs

56 All expenditure should be included in the income and expenditure account as soon as it is incurred. The only exception to this is expenditure incurred to acquire assets, that is, expenditure on the acquisition, production or installation of fixed assets, expenditure on stock items, expenditure on the acquisition of investments, advance expenditure or prepayments. Expenditure incurred to acquire assets should be carried forward in the balance sheet.

57 Expenditure is not incurred until consideration for the expenditure has passed, in other words until something is received in exchange for the expenditure. However, in the case of expenditure and grants relating directly to charitable activities an exchange is usually not involved. Where there is no exchange, the expenditure or grant should be recognised in the income and expenditure account when its payment becomes due. An implication of this is that commitments which extend beyond the end of the accounting period and grants which fall to be paid in future accounting periods should be charged in future income and expenditure accounts. (See also paragraph 74 and 75.)

The income and expenditure account

Presentation

58 The income and expenditure should be analysed in a manner appropriate to the charity. This analysis should enable the user of the accounts to gain a proper appreciation of the principal elements of the income and expenditure of the charity, but should not be excessively detailed. The following items should be shown separately in the analysis:

(a) realised and unrealised gains and losses on investments (if included in the income and expenditure account) and, if material, realised gains and losses on the disposal of fixed assets;

(b) fund-raising expenses;

(c) publicity expenses;

(d) administration expenses; and

(e) expenditure and grants relating directly to charitable activities.

Administration expenses, fund-raising expenses and publicity expenses

59 It is not practicable to produce precise definitions of 'administration expenses', 'fund-raising expenses' and 'publicity expenses' or to set out detailed guidance, applicable to all charities, on what expenditure should be included within each heading. The following principles should however be applied.

(a) Items of expenditure which involve more than one category, for example some administration expenses and some expenditure relating directly to charitable activities, should be allocated on a rational basis to the cost categories involved.

(b) Expenditure incurred on activities falling directly within one cost category should not be apportioned to any other cost category.

60 The absence of precise definitions or detailed guidance means that each charity should develop principles for cost allocation suitable to its own circumstances. These principles should be applied consistently. A full description of the items included within each category and of the principles adopted should be disclosed.

Netting-off

61 A minimum of 'netting off' of income and expenditure and of assets and liabilities should take place. However, if a charity has received income from, and incurred expenses on, special fund-raising events or activities, it may occasionally be more informative to include only the net figure in the income and expenditure account. Where netting off takes place, the reason for it and, whenever practicable, the 'gross' figures should be disclosed in the notes.

Tax credits on income

62 Income received after deduction of tax at source and income received by deed of covenant should be grossed up for the tax recoverable and this gross figure included in the income and expenditure account. The tax recoverable should be shown as a debtor until the charity recovers the amount involved.

The statement of source and application of funds

63 The purpose of the statement of source and application of funds is to show the movement of cash through the charity. Some charities believe information on their cash transactions to be more meaningful than information on their income and expenditure because, for example, they are funded on the basis of their cash needs or because their investment activity is directed primarily towards making the proceeds of sales available for charitable purposes. Where this is the case the statement of source and application of funds may be given greater prominence than the income and expenditure account.

64 On the other hand, there may be circumstances in which the preparation of a statement of source and application of funds is neither necessary to give full disclosure of information nor helpful in enabling the user to understand the charity's activities. For example, charities that operate on a cash basis and consequently have no significant assets or liabilities will find that the statement will be similar to their income and expenditure account. In such circumstances, the statement need not be included in the accounts.

65 Where a statement of source and application of funds is prepared:

(a) the analysis of the cash movements and the use of figures which have been netted-off should follow the same principles as those adopted for the income and expenditure account (see paragraphs 35 to 41, and 61); and

(b) the statement should be reconcilable to the income and expenditure account and the balance sheet.

The balance sheet

Presentation

66 The assets of a charity should be analysed in the balance sheet between fixed assets, investments (including investment properties), and current assets; and the liabilities should be analysed between current and long-term liabilities. In addition, the assets and liabilities should be analysed in a way that enables the reader to gain a proper appreciation of their spread and character. The example set of accounts in Appendix 2 illustrates what this might entail.

67 The total amount of the assets less liabilities of a charity should be analysed between its major funds.

(a) Wherever possible it should be made clear which assets and liabilities form part of restricted funds, particularly permanent endowment funds. Where this is not practicable, the notes should provide an indication as to whether or not sufficient resources are held in an appropriate form to enable the funds concerned to be applied in accordance with the restrictions imposed. For example, if a charity has a fund which is to be spent in the near future, it should be made clear in the notes whether or not the assets held in the fund are short-term assets.

(b) Where funds have been divided into wider and narrower ranges under the powers given to trustees by the Trustee Investments Act 1961, the accounts or notes should indicate the investments allowed to each range.

The amounts at which assets and liabilities are included in the balance sheet

68 Except as explained in paragraph 69, the assets and liabilities of a charity should be included in the balance sheet at the following amounts:

(a) fixed assets at cost (or valuation) less an appropriate provision for depreciation;

(b) investments at cost or market value. If the investments are included in the balance sheet at cost, the market value should be disclosed in the notes to the accounts;

(c) current assets at the lower cost and net realisable value; and

(d) liabilities at their settlement value.

69 If an asset suffers a permanent loss (or diminution) in value, the amount at which the asset is carried in the balance sheet should be reduced to the asset's current value by a provision. Where this provision should be charged will depend on the circumstances involved.

(a) If the asset involved is an investment, the provision should be charged to the same place as realised and unrealised losses on the investments (see paragraphs 45 to 48).

(b) If the asset is a fixed asset, the provision should be charged to the income and expenditure account to the extent that it is not covered by a previous gain on revaluation of that asset. To the extent that it is covered by a previous gain, the provision should be used to reduce the gain by deducting it from the appropriate fund in the balance sheet.

In determining whether any asset has suffered a permanent loss, gains in the value of other assets should not be taken into account.

Connected charities

70 A charity may be connected with other charities. It will usually be possible to identify whether charities are connected by considering whether they have common trustees, unity of administration, and common, parallel or related objects and activities.

71 If the reporting charity is connected to other charities, information about the other charities' activities and resources should be included in its annual report. This information should include:

(a) particulars of the connected charities, including principal contact addresses and the nature of the relationship between the charities; and

(b) particulars of any material transactions between the charities.

One way in which the relevant information could be given is by aggregating the accounts of the charity with those of its connected charities. If aggregated accounts are prepared, the basis on which they have been prepared should be disclosed. Separate accounts for the reporting charity should still be prepared.

Subsidiary and associated companies

72 A charity may have one or more subsidiary companies.

(a) The activities of a subsidiary may not be fundamentally different from those of the charity. For example, the subsidiary may be an investment-holding company; it might be concerned solely or largely with fund-raising; or it might be the vehicle used to undertake the charitable activities of the charity. If a charity has such a subsidiary or subsidiaries, it should prepare consolidated accounts for itself and its subsidiary or subsidiaries. Separate accounts for the charity itself should still be prepared.

(b) If a subsidiary undertakes activities which are fundamentally different from those of the charity, for example if it is a trading company, it will not be appropriate to consolidate its accounts with those of the charity. Instead, the investment in the subsidiary should be treated in the same way as other investments are treated. A summary of the transactions, assets and liabilities of the subsidiary, together with an explanation of its activities and their relevance to the charity, should be disclosed in the notes to the accounts. As an alternative to providing a summary of its subsidiary's transactions, assets and liabilities, the charity may if it wishes include the accounts of the subsidiary within its annual report.

73 A charity may have one or more associated companies. Investments in associated companies should be treated in the same way as investments in subsidiaries undertaking activities which are fundamentally different from those of the charity (see paragraph 72).

Other disclosure items

Commitments and designated funds

74 Particulars of all material commitments in respect of specific charitable projects, whether they are legally binding or not, should be disclosed in the accounts. These particulars should include the amounts involved, when the commitments are likely to be met, and the movements on commitments previously reported. Particulars of all other material legally binding commitments should also be disclosed.

75 Commitments can be dealt with either by disclosing them in a note to the accounts or by using designated funds to represent committed unrestricted funds. If designated funds are used, they should be disclosed separately from restricted funds and appropriately described.

76 Guarantees given by the charity, and the conditions under which liabilities might arise as a result of guarantees, should be disclosed in a note to the accounts.

Loans and other liabilities

77 If loans or other liabilities are secured on the assets of a charity then this fact, along with details of the security, should be disclosed in the notes to the accounts. The existence of charges against assets should be disclosed in a similar manner.

78 The amount and interest and repayment terms of all inter-fund loans should be disclosed in the notes to the accounts.

Information relating to transactions with trustees and to employees of the charity

79 Particulars, including the amounts involved, of any transaction, contract or other arrangement between a charity and any of its employees or trustees, or persons connected with them, should be disclosed in the notes to the accounts if the transaction, contract or other arrangement is likely to be significant to the user of the accounts. Employees' contracts of employment are an example of contracts which will not usually be significant to the user.

80 Particulars of any relevant connection of the trustees or officers of a charity (for example, as trustees or officers of charities with which the reporting charity works) should also be disclosed.

81 If some or all of the trustees have received remuneration from the charity or have been reimbursed by the charity for expenses which they have incurred, this fact and the amounts involved should be disclosed in the notes to the accounts. An indication of the type of expenses reimbursed should also be provided. If no remuneration was paid or no expenses reimbursed, this should be reported.

82 The total emoluments (i.e. remuneration and benefits-in-kind) paid to employees during the accounting period and the average number of employees during the period should be disclosed in the notes to the accounts.

Part 4 — Notes on legal requirements in the United Kingdom and the Republic of Ireland

83 A charity constituted in the United Kingdom or the Republic of Ireland may, by virtue of its constitution or activities, be subject to a range of statutory reporting requirements. Some of the more commonly encountered requirements are referred to below. Although the recommendations contained in this statement are intended to represent best practice there may be circumstances in which they conflict with some of the statutory requirements imposed on a charity. This statement cannot overrule such requirements.

84 The recommendations do not incorporate every statutory reporting requirement that may be imposed on a particular charity. For example, an incorporated charity would be required to provide certain additional disclosures and analyses in the notes to the accounts and would also be required to prepare a directors' report containing specified information. Compliance with the recommendations contained in this statement will therefore not necessarily mean that all the statutory reporting requirements that may be imposed on a charity have been met.

England and Wales

Charities Act 1960

85 All charities in England and Wales must comply with the financial reporting requirements of the Charities Act 1960 and the Charities (Statement of Account) Regulations, 1960 ('the 1960 legislation'). This legislation requires charities to keep proper accounting records to enable them to prepare consecutive statements of account. These statements of account should consist of an income and expenditure relating to a period of not more than fifteen months and a balance sheet relating to the end of that period. Each statement of account should contain:

(a) particulars of the charity's assets at the balance sheet date, distinguishing between assets forming part of the permanent endowment and other assets. These particulars should include the names of the persons in whom the assets are vested;

(b) the approximate amount of the charity's liabilities at that date;

(c) the amount of the receipts during the period, classified according to the nature of the receipt and distinguishing between receipts forming part of the permanent endowment and other receipts; and

(d) the amount of the payments made during the period, classified according to the nature of the payment and distinguishing between payments made out of the permanent endowment and other payments.

86 All charities having permanent endowments, other than 'excepted charities', must automatically send to the Commissioners each year a statement of account. All charities, other than 'exempt charities', must send statements of account to the Commissioners on request.

87 The format in which the income and expenditure account and balance sheet should be prepared, and the accounting policies which should be adopted in preparing them, are not specified in the legislation. Although the Charity Commission provides charities with standard forms for the preparation of statements of account, alternative formats can be used as long as the information provided meets the requirements of the legislation.

Charities Act 1985

88 All local charities whose sole or primary object is the relief of poverty, other than exempt charities (as defined in the 1960 legislation) and ecclesiastical charities, must send statements of account prepared in accordance with the 1960 legislation to the 'appropriate local authority'.

Companies Act 1985

89 Many charities are incorporated as limited companies and, as a consequence, are required to follow the reporting requirements set out in the Companies Act 1985 ('the 1985 Act'). In essence, this Act requires all incorporated charities to prepare, in respect of each accounting period, and file an income and expenditure account, a balance sheet, various notes, a directors' report and an auditors' report. If, at the end of the accounting period, the charity has one or more subsidiaries, then group accounts should also be prepared and filed. The accounts of the charity and its group are required to show a true and fair view and, except where it is not consistent with the showing of a true and fair view, should comply with the detailed requirements set out in Schedule 4 to the 1985 Act.

90 Schedule 4 sets out the formats in which the income and expenditure account and balance sheet should usually be prepared. These formats, and the income and expenditure account formats in particular, are not wholly appropriate for the income and expenditure accounts of charities. It is therefore normally necessary to take advantage of paragraph 3(3) of Schedule 4, which allows the formats to be adapted in respect of items to which an Arabic number has been assigned to reflect the special nature of a charity's operations.

91 Although Schedule 4 requires the disclosure of certain information not referred to in this statement, the statement's recommendations, with the following exceptions, are consistent with the Schedule's requirements:

(a) In paragraph 61 it is recognised that, although the netting off of income and expenditure will usually be inappropriate, it may occasionally be acceptable. Schedule 4, paragraph 5 states that no material netting off of separate items should take place.

(b) In paragraph 66 it is recommended that the assets of a charity be analysed between fixed assets, investments, and current assets. Schedule 4 requires assets to be analysed between fixed assets and current assets. Fixed assets and current assets are designated by capital letters in the balance sheet formats. They cannot, therefore, be adapted under paragraph 3(3). However, provided that all the investments are fixed assets it should be possible to satisfy both the Companies Act formats and the recommendations of the SORP.

Scotland

92 Although the Companies Act 1985 extends to incorporated charities constituted in Scotland, there is no equivalent legislation to the Charities Act 1960 or the Charities Act 1985 in Scotland. This means that, whilst incorporated charities have to prepare and file an income and expenditure account, balance sheet and various notes in respect of each accounting period, unincorporated charities constituted in Scotland are not required by law to prepare accounts.

Northern Ireland Charities Act 1964

93 In Northern Ireland charities are governed by the Charities Act (Northern Ireland) 1964. However, this Act requires neither registration nor the preparation or filing of accounts.

Companies (Northern Ireland) Order 1986

94 The Companies (Northern Ireland) Order 1986 is the Northern Ireland legislation equivalent to the Companies Act 1985. The references to the Companies Act 1985 in paragraphs 89 to 91 should therefore also be taken to be references to the 1986 Order.

Republic of Ireland Charities Acts 1961 and 1973

95 In the Republic of Ireland charities are governed by the Charities Act 1961 and 1973. Neither of these Acts requires charities to register or to prepare and submit accounts.

Companies (Amendment) Act 1986

96 The Companies (Amendment) Act 1986 ('the 1986 Act') is the Republic of Ireland legislation equivalent to the Companies Act 1985. The 1986 Act references that are equivalent to those given in paragraphs 89 to 91 are as follows:

The 1985 Act	*The 1986 Act*
Schedule 4	The Schedule
Paragraph 3(3) of Sch 4	Section 4 (13)

Appendix 1 — The funds of a charity

The purpose of this appendix is to explain the legal position as regards the various funds of a charity and the implications this has for the way in which the funds are accounted for.

The types of funds a charity might have

97 A charity's funds can be categorised into restricted funds and unrestricted funds. Restricted funds are funds subject to specific conditions, imposed by the donor, or the trusts under which the donation was made, and binding on the trustees. All other funds are unrestricted funds, which means that as long as they are used in pursuance of the charity's objectives and in a way which is consistent with the charity's charitable status, their use is at the complete discretion of the trustees.

The need to distinguish between the assets and liabilities held in different funds

98 If a profit is made on the disposal of an asset, the profit will form part of the fund in which the asset was held. An unrealised profit on an asset will also form part of the fund in which the asset is held. Similarly, realised and unrealised losses and provisions for depreciation and for the permanent diminution in value of an asset reduce the fund in which the asset is (or, in the case of a realised loss, was) held. In order to ensure that profits, losses and provisions are added to or deducted from the correct fund, it is therefore essential to know which assets and liabilities are held in which fund.

99 The trustees of a charity will be in breach of trust if they use restricted income in a way which is not consistent with the restrictions imposed. To this end it is essential that items of income and expenditure are added to, or deducted from, the appropriate fund. It is also important for the trustees to ensure that the assets and liabilities held in a fund are consistent with the fund type: if a fund which, because of donor restrictions, must be used in the short-term is represented by assets which can only be utilised in the long-term, there is a real possibility that the charity will not be able to meet the restrictions.

Income derived from assets held by the charity

100 Although profits arising on the disposal of an asset will form part of the fund in which the asset was held, this will not necessarily be the case with income derived from the asset. Unless the terms on which the asset was donated make it clear than an alternative treatment should be adopted, income derived from an asset already held by the charity will be unrestricted income, even if the asset is held in a permanent endowment fund.

Permanent endowment funds

101 One particular type of restricted fund is known as a permanent endowment fund. Permanent endowment funds must be held indefinitely. This does not however necessarily mean that the assets held in the permanent endowment fund cannot be disposed of although the terms of the endowment might prohibit this. What it does mean is that the permanent endowment fund cannot be used to make payments to others, and the assets making up the permanent endowment fund cannot be given away. Furthermore, if an asset that is held as part of a permanent endowment fund is disposed of, its place in the fund must be taken by the assets received in exchange.

102 As explained above, if a profit is made on the disposal of an asset held in a permanent endowment fund, the profit will become part of the permanent endowment and the amount of the fund will increase. The other means by which permanent endowment funds will be increased will be by receiving incoming resources received for permanent endowment (whether in the form of new permanent endowment funds or additions to existing ones) and by recognising unrealised gains on assets held in permanent endowments. On the other hand, income derived from assets held within a permanent endowment fund does not affect the amount of permanent endowment unless either the terms of the original endowment require it to do so or the Charity Commission so orders.

103 Similarly, a loss made on the disposal of an asset held in a permanent endowment fund will result in the amount of the fund being decreased. Such losses are in fact the only transactions which can reduce the amount of the permanent endowment. Provisions for the depreciation of assets held in permanent endowment funds or for the permanent diminution in value of assets held in permanent endowment funds, and unrealised losses recognised in the accounts in respect of assets held in permanent endowment funds are the only other means by which a permanent endowment fund can be reduced.

104 Permanent endowment funds, because of their permanence, are tantamount to being the capital of the charity. The statement of recommended practice recognises this by recommending that increases and decreases in the amount of permanent endowment funds are not dealt with in the income and expenditure account.

Appendix 2 — Example set of accounts

105 **Income and Expenditure Account**
Year Ended 31 December 1987

		1987		*15 months ended 31.12.86*
Income	£	£	£	£
Donations and gifts		7,920		8,942
Legacies		3,416		19,761
Covenanted income		15,600		15,500
Voluntary income		26,936		44,203
Grants received		2,793		2,749
Investment income		414		481
		30,143		47,433
Indirect expenditure				
Fund-raising expenses	782		656	
Publicity expenses	534		412	
Administration expenses	1,236		1,471	
		2,552		2,539
Income less indirect expenditure		27,591		44,894
Direct charitable expenditure		30,479		41,684
Income less expenditure		(2,888)		3,210

Statement of Investment Gains
Year Ended 31 December 1987

	1987	*15 months ended 31.12.86*
	£	£
Realised gains on disposal of investments	1,463	912
Change in unrealised gains/(losses) on investments	(1,212)	361
Net investment gains	251	1,273

The income and expenditure account and statement of investment gains should be read in conjunction with the reconciliation and analysis of movements on the funds shown on page . . .

Reconciliation and Analysis of Movements on the Funds for the Year Ended 31 December 1987

	Unrestricted funds			Restricted funds (excluding permanent endowment funds)				Total	Permanent endowment funds
	General	Designated	Total	Core	India	Africa	Total		
	£	£	£	£	£	£	£	£	£
Income	22,038	—	22,038	—	7,112	993	8,105	30,143	—
Indirect expenditure	(1,636)	—	(1,636)	—	(822)	(94)	(916)	(2,552)	—
	20,402	—	20,402	—	6,290	899	7,189	27,591	—
Opening value of funds	938	4,100	5,038	1,513	3,631	1,280	6,424	11,462	234
Funds available for use	21,340	4,100	25,440	1,513	9,921	2,179	13,613	39,053	—
New permanent endowment fund	—	—	—	—	—	—	—	—	1,020
Net investment gains	—	—	—	201	50	—	251	251	596
Charitable expenditure	(15,674)	(7,911)	(23,585)	—	(4,753)	(2,141)	(6,894)	(30,479)	—
	5,666	(3,811)	1,855	1,714	5,218	38	6,970	8,825	1,850
Transfers	(1,387)	—	(1,387)	1,387	—	—	1,387	—	—
Designations	(4,235)	4,235	—	—	—	—	—	—	—
	44	424	468	3,101	5,218	38	8,357	8,825	1,850

Analysis of Fund Balances Between the Net Assets

	Unrestricted funds	Restricted funds (excluding permanent endowment funds)				Permanent endowment funds	Total funds
		Core	India	Africa	Total		
	£	£	£	£	£	£	£
Fixed assets	—	—	4,106	—	4,106	1,355	5,461
Investments	—	3,101	279	38	3,418	495	3,913
Net current assets	716	—	833	—	833	—	1,549
Long-term liabilities	(136)	—	—	—	—	—	(136)
Provisions	(112)	—	—	—	—	—	(112)
	468	3,101	5,218	38	8,357	1,850	10,675
Represented by:							
Realised amounts	468	2,435	5,188	38	7,661	1,619	9,748
Unrealised amounts	—	666	30	—	696	231	927
	468	3,101	5,218	38	8,357	1,850	10,675

Balance Sheet as 31 December 1987

	1987		1986	
	£	£	£	£
Fixed assets		5,461		5,698
Investments		3,913		4,561
Current assets				
Stock	671		631	
Debtors	483		886	
Cash at bank and in hand	816		361	
	1,970		1,878	
Current liabilities	421		216	
Net current assets		1,549		1,662
		10,923		11,921
Long-term liabilities		(248)		(225)
		10,675		11,696
Funds				
Permanent endowment funds		1,850		234
Other restricted funds		8,357		5,911
Unrestricted funds		468		5,551
		10,675		11,696

The balance sheet should be read in conjunction with the reconciliation and analysis of movements on the funds shown on page . . .

Extracts from notes

(NB Although the accounts would normally be accompanied by a full set of notes, only extracts from the notes are included here. The extracts shown illustrate some of the more important or more complex of the recommended disclosures. The notes should be cross referenced to the accounts.)

Fixed assets

	Motor vehicles	*Fixtures and fittings*	*Total*
	£	£	£
Cost			
Opening balance at 1 January 1987	7,531	1,100	8,631
Additions	2,980	—	2,980
Disposals	(2,329)	—	(2,329)
Closing balance at 31 December 1987	8,182	1,100	9,282
Accumulated depreciation			
Opening balance at 1 January 1987	2,383	550	2,933
Charge for the year	2,359	275	2,634
Depreciation on disposals	(1,746)	—	(1,746)
Closing balance at 31 December 1987	2,996	825	3,821
Net book value			
At 31 December 1987	5,186	275	5,461
At 1 January 1987	5,148	550	5,698

Commitments

(a) *Charitable commitments*

As explained in accounting policy note . . ., commitments for specific charitable projects are dealt with by making allocations to designated funds. Therefore, as the reconciliation and analysis of movements on the funds shows, the commitments of the charity in respect of such projects are as follows:

	1987	*1986*
	£	£
Commitments at the beginning of the period	4,100	796
Additional commitments entered into	4,235	8,213
Commitments met	(7,911)	(4,909)
Commitments at the end of the period	424	4,100

It is expected that the commitments outstanding at the period-end will all be met in 1988.

(b) *Other commitments*

In addition to the commitments referred to above, the charity has entered into the following legally-binding commitments:

	1987	*1986*
	£	£
For the purchase of motor vehicles	5,921	2,980

Subsidiary companies

The charity has a subsidiary, ShopCo Ltd, which undertakes trading activities. As these activities are fundamentally different from the activities of the charity, consolidated accounts have not been prepared. ShopCo Ltd operates three shops, located in various parts of the country. It purchases ornaments and artefacts from manufacturers and sells them to the public. The profits earned are passed to the charity by means of a deed of covenant; a fact which is referred to in the company's publicity material. Two trustees of the charity sit on the board of ShopCo Ltd but receive no remuneration for doing so. A summary of ShopCo Ltd's transactions and financial position is set out below.

(a) *Profit and loss account*	*1987*	*1986*
	£	£
Turnover	72,149	68,163
Cost of sales	43,637	40,611
Gross profit	28,512	27,552
Selling costs	9,361	8,800
Administration costs	3,461	3,013
Profit before deed of covenant	15,690	15,739
Deed of covenant	15,600	15,500
Profit before taxation	90	239
Taxation	—	—
Retained profit for the financial year	90	239

(b) *Balance sheet*

	1987 £	1986 £
Current assets		
Stock	9,239	12,576
Cash in hand and at bank	1,610	(311)
	10,849	12,265
Creditors: amounts due within one year		
Trade creditors	840	2,346
	10,009	9,919
Represented by:		
Share Capital	10,000	10,000
Profit and loss account	9	(81)
	10,009	9,919

Connected charities

The trustees of the charity are also the trustees of the Pollington Charity, a charity with which the charity shares administration facilities. Whilst the charity provides assistance and comfort to those being treated for cancer, the Pollington Charity makes grants to persons researching into cures for cancer. From time to time, loans on commercial terms may be made by one of the charities to the other, although there were no such loans outstanding at the year-end. There are no other transactions between the charities. A summarised set of accounts, in which the accounts of the charity and the Pollington Charity have been aggregated, are set out below:

(a) *Income and expenditure account*

	1987 £	1986 £
Voluntary income	34,631	57,351
Grants received	33,961	31,621
Investment income	1,321	1,012
	69,913	89,984
Indirect expenditure	7,264	6,982
	62,649	83,002
Direct charitable expenditure	60,192	73,139
Income less expenditure	2,457	9,863

(b) *Statement of investment gains*

Realised gains	2,651	1,101
Change in unrealised gains	381	1,312
Net investment gains	3,032	2,413

	1987	1986
	£	£
(c) *Balance sheet*		
Fixed assets	5,461	5,698
Investments	28,140	24,163
Current assets	4,136	2,011
Current liabilities	(4,596)	(6,035)
Long-term liabilities	(248)	(225)
	32,893	25,612
Permanent endowment funds	6,211	4,419
Other restricted funds	10,487	9,321
Unrestricted funds	16,195	11,872
	32,893	25,612

The Pollington Charity can be contacted at the following address: . . . (Not shown)

Section 6
Statements of Standards for Reporting Accountants

Contents

Audit exemption reports

Effective date

This Statement of Standards for Reporting Accountants is effective for reports signed on or after 21 December 1994, earlier adoption of the requirements is encouraged.

This statement sets out the basic principles and essential procedures, indicated by paragraphs in bold type, to be observed by reporting accountants engaged to prepare a report for the purposes of section 249A(2) of the Companies Act 1985 ('the Act') on the accounts of a small company; it also includes explanatory and other material which, rather than being prescriptive, is designed to assist reporting accountants.

The limited nature of such a report derives from the relevant legislation and this statement has been prepared in consultation with the DTI.

In this statement, the word 'report' is used to refer to the report for the purposes of section 249A(2). A summary of some of the key points of the legislative background to such reports is given in Appendix l. For a proper understanding of the statutory requirements, however, reference should be made to the Act.

Accountancy work performed by reporting accountants

The directors of small companies usually engage an accounting firm to assist them to comply with their statutory responsibility to prepare annual accounts. Often the same accounting firm is engaged both to assist with accounts preparation (and related accountancy work) and to act as reporting accountants.

The procedures performed by the accounting firm in the preparation of the accounts will often be directly relevant to the report, but will not necessarily be sufficient to enable them to express all of the opinions which the Act requires in the report. However, where the accounting firm has prepared the accounts from the accounting records, and is satisfied that its procedures comply with paragraphs 1 to 17 of this statement, no additional work will be required in order to express the opinions which are to be provided in the report.

Objective of the engagement

1 The reporting accountants should perform such procedures as are necessary to provide a reasonable basis on which to express the opinions which are to be provided in the report.

1.1 The report requires opinions to be expressed on three specific matters and provides assurance only on those matters (see Appendix 1). The reporting accountants' work is designed to provide a reasonable basis for these opinions. As the scope of the opinions is narrow, the reporting accountants' procedures are limited and much less extensive than, for example, in an audit.

1.2 In particular, the reporting accountants do not consider the completeness, accuracy and validity of the accounting records; nor do they consider whether the accounts give a true and fair view, the company's compliance with applicable accounting standards, the treatment of events after the balance sheet date, the appropriateness of the going concern basis, or the company's compliance with other laws and regulations.

Agreeing the terms of the engagement

2 The reporting accountants and the directors should set out in writing and agree on the terms of the engagement.

2.1 To qualify for the exemption it is necessary for the directors to cause a report to be prepared. It is therefore in the interests of both the reporting accountants and the company that the reporting accountants send a letter confirming their acceptance of the appointment and documenting the key terms of the engagement.

2.2 If the reporting accountants already have an appointment as auditors of the company, under terms specified in an existing audit engagement letter, a new engagement letter will need to be agreed. There is no requirement to resign from the appointment as auditors. However, if it appears likely that the company will not require an audit of its accounts for the foreseeable future, then, in order to avoid any possible confusion, the accounting firm may wish to resign as auditors (and to make the statement required by section 394). In such circumstances the reporting accountants and the directors may agree terms of engagement on a continuing rather than an annual basis.

2.3 Matters dealt with in the engagement letter will normally include:

(a) the respective responsibilities of the directors and of the reporting accountants;

(b) the scope of the reporting accountants' work;

(c) the circumstances in which, and the form in which, a report can be issued; and

(d) the terms of any non-statutory professional services to be provided by the reporting accountants (for example, to assist the directors in preparing the accounts).

2.4 The reporting accountants can agree with the directors a limit on any liability arising out of the work. Section 310, which would make void any such agreement made by an auditor, does not apply to this or any other non-audit engagement. Legal advice may be required regarding the terms of any such agreement and on the form of words to be included in the engagement letter.

2.5 An illustrative example of an annual engagement letter for this type of engagement is given in Appendix 2.

Ethical considerations

3 In the conduct of the engagement, the reporting accountants should comply with the ethical guidance issued by their relevant professional body.

3.1 The users of the report will reasonably expect the reporting accountants to have had regard to the appropriate ethical considerations; these include, *inter alia,* integrity, objectivity, professional competence and due care, and confidentiality. In addition, the reporting accountants are required by section 249D(4) to be independent of the company.

Planning

4 The reporting accountants should plan their work so that an effective engagement is performed.

4.1 As part of their planning procedures, the reporting accountants will make specific and timely enquiries to obtain the directors' confirmation that, to the best of their knowledge and belief, they expect that:

(a) the company will satisfy the report conditions; and

(b) the company has not fallen, and will not fall, into any of the cases where the exemption is not available;

and whether they require a report to be prepared. In considering whether a report is to be prepared, the directors will have regard to any undertakings given to third parties which may require an audit to be carried out, for example, where an audit is a condition of a loan covenant.

4.2 Obtaining an understanding of the procedures to be adopted for the accounts to be prepared, and of the form of accounting records kept by the company, is an important part of planning: it assists the reporting accountants to tailor the specific procedures to be performed having regard to the circumstances of the particular engagement. The accounting records are those kept by the company under section 221 and do not include, for example, any statutory register or minute book kept by the company.

Documentation

5 Working papers should adequately record the reporting accountants' planning and the procedures performed, and should provide evidence that the work was carried out in accordance with these standards and support the conclusions drawn.

5.1 The extent of working papers is a matter of professional judgement, since it is neither necessary nor practicable to document every matter the reporting accountants consider.

5.2 Working papers normally include:

- the engagement letter;
- a description of the accounting records kept by the company;
- evidence of the planning process;
- a record of the nature, timing and extent of the procedures undertaken and the results of such procedures (including a copy of any Companies Act accounts disclosure checklist which has been used);
- a written record of any information or explanations from the board of directors which the reporting accountants regard as being of importance to their opinion;
- copies of the final trial balance, of the accounts and of the report.

A separately documented work programme is not necessary, provided the work planned and performed is recorded.

Work delegated to assistants

6 Work delegated to assistants should be directed, supervised and reviewed in a manner which provides confidence that such work is done competently and in accordance with these standards.

6.1 Appropriate arrangement's need to be in place to ensure that any assistants to whom work is delegated are adequately briefed on their responsibilities and the objectives of the procedures they are to perform. The progress of the engagement needs to be monitored and the work performed by each assistant needs to be reviewed by personnel of at least equal competence, to ensure that the procedures have been performed as planned and have been adequately documented, and that any significant matters have been properly identified, so that the objectives of the engagement may be met.

Procedures

Accounts in agreement with the accounting records

7 The reporting accountants should perform such procedures as are necessary to provide a reasonable basis on which to express an opinion on whether the accounts are in agreement with the accounting records.

7.1 Procedures relating to this objective will comprise comparison of the accounts with the accounting records. The reporting accountants will need, *inter alia,* to agree all balances in the accounts with the general ledger, via the trial balance. Postings from the books of prime entry (in whatever form these are kept by the company) to the general ledger will need to be agreed on a test basis, checking items in each direction. In deciding the number of items to test, and the basis of their selection, the reporting accountants will have regard to the need to obtain a reasonable basis for the opinion expressed.

7.2 However, the reporting accountants do not carry out procedures to enable them to form an opinion on whether proper accounting records have been kept, or to check the arithmetical accuracy of the accounting records. Entries in the accounting records do not need to be checked to source documents (such as invoices). In those cases where no other accounting records are kept, source documents can be regarded as constituting the accounting records.

7.3 For the purposes of this opinion the reporting accountants will disregard 'de minimis' differences between the accounts and the accounting records.

Accounts drawn up in a manner consistent with the specified accounting requirements

8 The reporting accountants should perform such procedures as are necessary to provide a reasonable basis on which to express an opinion on whether, having regard only to, and on the basis of, the information contained in the accounting records, the accounts have been drawn up in a manner consistent with the accounting requirements specified in section 249C(6).

8.1 The reporting accountants only consider the information contained in the accounting records. Their objective is to be satisfied that, on the basis of whatever accounting records have been kept by the company, the accounts have been prepared from them in the form laid down by the specified requirements.

8.2 For example, in relatlon to an amount included in the accounting records purporting to represent fixed assets (say, plant and machinery), the reporting accountants will need to consider whether:

- it is included in the balance sheet:
  - — in the appropriate caption in one of the formats prescribed by Schedule 4; and
  - — with an appropriate description prescribed by Schedule 4 ('tangible fixed assets');
- it is included in the balance sheet on a basis permitted by Schedule 4: and
- provision is made for depreciation as required by Schedule 4.

The reporting accountants may find it helpful to use a Companies Act accounts disclosure checklist in this part of the engagement.

8.3 The reporting accountants are not required to perform procedures designed to obtain evidence to support the entries in the accounting records, the existence, ownership or value of assets, or the completeness of income, liabilities and disclosures in the accounts. Nor do they make any assessment of the estimates or judgements made by the directors in the preparation of accounts, or of whether the accounts comply with applicable accounting standards.

Entitlement to exemption from an audit

9 The reporting accountants should perform such procedures as are necessary to provide a reasonable basis on which to form an opinion on whether, having regard only to, and on the basis of, the information contained in the accounting records, the company is entitled to exemption from an audit.

9.1 Procedures relating to this objective will comprise:

(a) inspection of the accounting records to establish whether the report conditions appear to have been met; and

(b) consideration of whether, at any time within the year, the company fell into any of the categories not entitled to the exemption from an audit of the accounts.

9.2 For this purpose the reporting accountants accept the information contained in the accounting records kept by the company, without attempting to further verify or substantiate the basis on which entitlement to the exemption is claimed by the directors. Where the reporting accountants are satisfied that the accounts are in agreement with the accounting records, it may be possible to form the required opinion on entitlement to the exemption on the basis of turnover and balance sheet totals shown in the accounts.

9.3 The reporting accountants' knowledge of the company will normally provide a sufficient basis on which to consider whether the company is in any of the categories of company not entitled to the exemption. The reporting accountants will, however, need to remain alert, throughout the engagement, for any information which might come to light indicating that the company may, at some time in the financial year, have fallen into one of the categories of companies not entitled to the exemption.

Discussions with the board of directors

10 If the reporting accountants either:

(a) have doubts whether the results of their procedures provide a reasonable basis on which to express an affirmative opinion on each of the matters specified by the Act; or

(b) have become aware of information which indicates to them that the accounts may be misleading,

the matters giving rise to their concern should be discussed with the directors.

10.1 The reporting accountants' concern may be dispelled by information and explanations supplied by the directors, or by the directors making appropriate amendments to the accounts (or the accounting records). The reporting accountants do not seek independent evidence to corroborate information or explanations provided by the directors.

10.2 The reporting accountants are not required to perform procedures designed to obtain evidence that the accounts are not misleading. Nevertheless, in the normal course of their work they may become aware of information which may indicate to them that the accounts may be misleading. Practising accountants have a professional responsibility not to allow their names to be associated with accounts which they believe may be misleading, and will therefore discuss with the directors any such matters which have come to their attention.

11 If the reporting accountants conclude that the company did not satisfy the

conditions for exemption from an audit of the accounts, or that it did not fall within the categories of companies entitled to the exemption, or if they are unable to reach a conclusion on either of these matters, no report can be issued. The reporting accountants should notify the directors in writing of the reason without undue delay.

11.1 Section 249C(3) specifies that the report shall 'state that in the opinion of the reporting accountant ... the company satisfied the [report conditions]'; the Act does not permit this opinion to be qualified. Therefore, no report is issued if, in the opinion of the reporting accountants, the report conditions are not satisfied, or if they remain uncertain whether those conditions are satisfied. In such circumstances an audit of the accounts is required

Reporting

12 If the reporting accountants are satisfied that the results of their procedures provide a reasonable basis on which to express an affirmative opinion on each of the matters specified by the Act, they should issue a report including such an opinion.

12.1 An illustrative example of such a report is given in Appendix 3.

13 The report should include the following matters:

(a) a title identifying the shareholders of the company as the persons to whom the report is addressed;

(b) an introductory paragraph identifying the accounts reported on;

(c) a statement that the directors are responsible for the preparation of the accounts;

(d) a description of the basis of the reporting accountants' opinion;

(e) the reporting accountants' opinion;

(f) the name and signature of the reporting accountants;

(g) the date of the report.

Addressee

13.1 The report is to be made to the members of the company, who are normally the shareholders (section 249A(2)).

Directors' responsibilities

13.2 A company is not entitled to the exemption unless the balance sheet includes a statement by the directors acknowledging their responsibilities for ensuring that the company keeps accounting records which comply with section 221 and for preparing accounts which give a true and fair view and which otherwise comply with the requirements of the Act (section 249B(4)(c)). It is sufficient for the report to include a reference to that statement, rather than reproducing it in full.

Basis of opinion

13.3 This section of the report describes the scope of the engagement, to enable the reader to understand the nature of the procedures performed and the assurance expressed .

Name and signature of the reporting accountants

13.4 The copy of the report which is delivered to the registrar of companies is required to state the name of, and to be signed by, the reporting accountants. Copies of the report laid before the company in general meeting, or which are otherwise circulated, published or issued, need only state the name of the reporting accountants.

13.5 The report is signed in the name of the accounting firm, indicating their capacity as reporting accountants.

Date of the report

13.6 The date of the report is the date on which the reporting accountants sign the report. The reporting accountants do not date the report earlier than the date on which the accounts are approved by the directors.

Modification of the report

Disagreement

14 If the reporting accountants conclude that in respect of a particular matter either:

(a) the accounts are not in agreement with the accounting records kept by the company under section 221; or

(b) the accounts have not been drawn up in a manner consistent with the accounting requirements specified in section 249C(6),

they should issue a report including a negative opinion in respect of the relevant part of the opinion section.

14.1 The negative opinion indicates that, in the opinion of the reporting accountants, because of the matter in question, the relevant requirement has not been met. An illustrative example of a report containing a negative opinion is given in Appendix 4.

14.2 If the reporting accountants express a negative opinion in respect of one of the matters specified by the Act, they may need to consider the implications for the other opinions. For example, if the reporting accountants conclude that the accounts do not agree with the accounting records, it will be necessary to consider whether that particular matter raises doubts about the company's entitlement to the exemption from an audit of the accounts.

14.3 However, the fact that the reporting accountants identify a matter giving rise to a negative opinion does not of itself give rise to a need to perform additional or more extensive procedures in relation to other aspects of the accounts or of the accounting records.

Limitation on scope

15 If a limitation on the scope of the reporting accountants' procedures prevents them from obtaining a reasonable basis for an opinion as to whether either:

(a) the accounts are in agreement with the accounting records kept by the company under section 221; or

(b) the accounts have been drawn up in a manner consistent with the accounting requirements specified in section 249C(6),

they should issue a report including a qualified opinion in respect of the relevant part of the opinion section.

15.1 A limitation on scope may be:

(a) imposed by the directors (for example, where they refuse to provide information or explanations requested by the reporting accountants); or

(b) imposed by circumstances (for example, where parts of the accounting records have been lost or destroyed).

15.2 If there is a limitation on scope due to the absence of part of the accounting records, the reporting accountants may nevertheless be able, by comparing the accounts with the remaining accounting records (including any source documents which may be available), to conclude that the company satisfied the report conditions and that a report can be issued (see paragraph 11.1). In such circumstances, the opinion as to whether the accounts are in agreement with the accounting records will be qualified; the reporting accountants will need to consider whether the limitation on scope prevents them from forming an opinion as to whether the accounts have been drawn up in a manner consistent with the specified accounting requirements.

15.3 The qualified opinion indicates that it is expressed 'except for' the matter in question. An illustrative example of a report where there has been a limitation on scope is given in Appendix 5.

The use of an explanatory paragraph

16 If the reporting accountants have become aware of information which indicates to them that the accounts may be misleading, and their concern cannot be resolved by procedures which are within the scope of the examination, they should add an explanatory paragraph to the 'basis of opinion' section of the report, referring to the matter. It should be clearly stated that no opinion is expressed on the matter referred to.

16.1 If the reporting accountants' concerns have not been resolved by discussion with the directors, a negative or qualified opinion will be inappropriate if the matter in question is one that is outside the scope of the opinions required by the Act. In such cases the matter is highlighted by means of an additional explanatory paragraph in the 'basis of opinion' section of the report, to provide readers with a proper understanding of the basis of the opinion. An illustrative example of a report including an explanatory paragraph is given in Appendix 6.

16.2 The inclusion of an explanatory paragraph indicates only that the reporting accountants have become aware of that matter in the course of carrying out their procedures. When no explanatory paragraph is included this does not signify that the reporting accountants have satisfied themselves that the accounts are not misleading, but only that no matters have come to their attention to suggest otherwise.

Circumstances which may lead to resignation

17 If the reporting accountants either:

(a) have become aware of information which indicates to them that the accounts may be misleading, and they conclude that the matter cannot be adequately dealt with by means of modification of their report; or

(b) have serious doubts about the integrity of the directors,

the reporting accountants should resign from the engagement, notifying the directors in writing of the reason without undue delay.

17.1 Where the reporting accountants identify several different matters, each giving rise to a separate reason to modify the report, it will be necessary to consider the nature of the matters in question, and whether their combined effect is such as to raise doubts as to whether the reporting accountants can be associated with the accounts.

17.2 The reporting accountants may need to take legal advice on the wording of any letter of resignation relating to the integrity of the directors.

Appendix 1

Legislative Background

This appendix summarises some of the key points of the legislative background. For a proper understanding of the statutory requirements, however, reference should be made to the Act.[1]

Exemptions from audit

1 The Act confers exemptions from audit for certain categories of small company: under section 249A(1) those companies which meet the 'total exemption conditions' (section 249A(3)) in respect of a financial year are exempt from the obligation to have their annual accounts audited, whilst under section 249A(2) those meeting the 'report conditions' (section 249A(4)) are similarly exempt if the directors cause a report to be prepared in accordance with section 249C and made to the company's members by suitably qualified reporting accountants.

2 No statutory report is required in the case of a company which meets the total exemption conditions.

3 The report conditions specified in section 249A(4) are that:

(a) the company qualifies as a small company in relation to that year for the purposes of section 246;

(b) its turnover for that year is more than £90,000 but not more than £350,000; and

(c) its balance sheet total for the year is not more than £1.4 million.

For a company which is a charity, the report conditions are modified by section 249A(5): the reference to turnover is replaced by gross income, on which the limit is £250,000.

The report

4 Section 249C specifies that the report for the purposes of section 249A(2) is required to state whether in the opinion of the reporting accountants making it:

(a) the accounts of the company for the financial year in question are in agreement with the accounting records kept by the company under section 221; and

(b) having regard only to, and on the basis of, the information contained in those accounting records, those accounts have been drawn up in a manner consistent with the provisions of the Act (i.e. accounting requirements) specified in section 249C(6), so far as they are applicable to the company.

[1] Sections 249A to 249E were inserted by the Companies Act 1985 (Audit Exemption) Regulations 1994 (SI 1994/1935).

5 The report also states that in the opinion of the reporting accountants, having regard only to, and on the basis of, the information contained in the accounting records kept by the company under section 221, the company satisfied the requirements of section 249A(4), modified by section 249A(5) where the company is a charity, for the financial year in question, and did not fall within the categories of company not entitled to the exemption specified in section 249B(1)(a) to (f) at any time within that financial year.

6 The provisions specified in section 249C(6) are:

(a) section 226(3) and Schedule 4 ('Form and content of company accounts');

(b) section 231 and paragraphs 7 to 9A and 13(1), (3) and (4) of Schedule 5 ('Disclosure of information: related undertakings');

(c) section 232 and Schedule 6 ('Disclosure of information: emoluments and other benefits of directors and others'),

where appropriate as modified by section 246(1)(a) and (1A) and section A of Part I of Schedule 8.

Cases where exemptions are not available

7 Section 249B(1) specifies that a company is not entitled to exemption in respect of a financial year if at any time within that year it was:

(a) a public company;

(b) a banking or insurance company;

(c) enrolled in a list maintained by the Insurance Brokers Registration Council under section 4 of the Insurance Brokers (Registration) Act 1977;

(d) an authorised person or appointed representative under the Financial Services Act 1986;

(e) a special register body as defined in section 117(1) of the Trade Union and Labour Relations (Consolidation) Act 1992 or an employers' association as defined by section 122 of that Act; or

(f) a parent company or subsidiary undertaking.

8 Section 249B(4) specifies that a company shall not be entitled to exemption unless the balance sheet includes a statement by the directors acknowledging their responsibilities, *inter alia*, for:

(a) ensuring that the company keeps accounting records which comply with section 221; and

(b) preparing accounts which give a true and fair view and which otherwise comply with the requirements of the Act.

Abbreviated accounts

9 If the directors of a company which satisfies the report conditions propose to take advantage of the exemptions conferred by Part III of Schedule 8 (exemptions with respect to delivery of accounts) and to deliver to the registrar of companies 'abbreviated accounts', a copy of the report for the purposes of section 249A(2) is also to be delivered to the registrar of companies.

10 No special report by the reporting accountants on the abbreviated accounts is required.

11 To avoid any possible confusion, however, the directors may choose to append to the copy of the report that is to be delivered some explanatory words, such as follows:

'The following reproduces the text of the report prepared for the purposes of section 249A(2) Companies Act 1985 in respect of the company's annual accounts, from which the abbreviated accounts (set out on pages .... to ....) have been prepared.'

Appendix 2

Illustrative Example of an Engagement Letter

This example is intended to illustrate the principles set out and the guidance given in the statement. In any particular engagement the letter will need to be tailored to the specific circumstances.

The reporting accountants' professional body may specify other matters which are to be included in an engagement letter.

To the directors of ...

The purpose of this letter is to set out the basis on which we are engaged:

(a) to act as reporting accountants to prepare a report for the purposes of section 249A(2) Companies Act 1985 (the Act), in respect of the company's accounts for the year ended ..., in accordance with section 249C of the Act; and

(b) to provide other professional services to the company;

and the respective responsibilities of the directors and of ourselves.

1 Responsibilities of the directors

1.1 As directors of the company, you are responsible for ensuring that the company maintains proper accounting records and for preparing accounts which give a true and fair view and which have been prepared in accordance with the Act.

1.2 You are also responsible for determining whether, in respect of the year, the company meets the conditions for exemption from an audit of the accounts set out in section 249A of the Act, and for determining whether, in respect of the year, the exemption is not available for any of the reasons set out in section 249B.

1.3 If, in respect of the year, the availability of the exemption from an audit of the accounts is conditional upon your causing a report in respect of these accounts to be prepared for the purposes of section 249A(2), you are responsible for deciding whether that report shall be made and for appointing us as reporting accountants to make that report to the shareholders of the company.

2 Responsibilities of the reporting accountants

2.1 We shall plan our work on the basis that a report for the purposes of section 249A(2) is required for the year, unless you inform us in writing that either:

(a) the company requires an audit of the accounts; or

(b) the company requires neither an audit nor such a report.

2.2 Should you instruct us to carry out an audit, then a separate letter of engagement will be required.

2.3 Should you inform us that the company requires neither an audit nor a report, then we shall have no responsibilities to the company, except those specifically agreed upon between us in respect of other professional services.

2.4 As reporting accountants, we have a statutory responsibility to report to the shareholders of the company whether in our opinion:

(a) the accounts are in agreement with the accounting records kept by the company under section 221 of the Act; and

(b) having regard only to, and on the basis of, the information contained in those accounting records, the accounts have been drawn up in a manner consistent with the accounting requirements specified in section 249C(6) of the Act, so far as they are applicable to the company.

2.5 We also have a statutory responsibility to state that, having regard only to, and on the basis of, the information contained in the accounting records kept by the company under section 221, in our opinion the company satisfied the conditions for exemption from an audit of the accounts specified in section 249A(4) of the Act and did not, at any time within the year, fall within any of the categories, specified in section 249B(1), of companies not entitled to the exemption.

2.6 We do not have any responsibility to report whether any shareholder of the company has notified the company that he or she requires an audit, consequently we have no responsibility to carry out any work in respect of this matter.

2.7 Should our work lead us to conclude that the company is not entitled to exemption from an audit of the accounts, or should we be unable to reach a conclusion on this matter, then we will not issue any report and will notify you in writing of the reasons. In these circumstances, if appropriate, we will discuss with you the need to appoint an auditor.

3 Scope of the reporting accountants' work

3.1 Our engagement will be conducted in accordance with the Statement of Standards for Reporting Accountants issued by the Auditing Practices Board. Our procedures will consist of comparing the accounts with the accounting records kept by the company, and making such limited enquiries of the officers of the company as we may consider necessary for the purposes of our report.

3.2 Our work as reporting accountants will not be an audit of the accounts in accordance with Auditing Standards. Accordingly, we will not seek any independent evidence to support the entries in the accounting records, the existence, ownership or value of assets, or the completeness of income, liabilities and disclosures in the accounts. Nor will we make any assessment of the estimates and judgements made by you in your preparation of the accounts. Consequently our work as reporting accountants will not provide any assurance that the accounting records or the accounts are free from material misstatement, whether caused by fraud, other irregularities or error.

3.3 We have a professional responsibility not to allow our name to be associated with accounts which we consider may be misleading. Therefore, although we are not required to search for such matters, should we become aware, for any reason, that the accounts may be misleading, and the matter cannot be adequately dealt with by means of modification of our report, we will not issue any report and will withdraw from the engagement, and will notify you in writing of the reasons.

3.4 As part of our normal procedures, we may request you to provide written confirmation of any information or explanations given by you orally during the course of our work.

3.5 We attach to this letter a specimen of the form of report, setting out, in the manner specified by the professional standards, the opinions required by the Act.

4 Accounting and other services

4.1 You have asked us to assist you in the maintenance of the accounting records and in the preparation of the accounts, as follows:

(describe the work to be performed or refer to a separate letter of engagement)

4.2 You have also asked us to provide other professional services, in respect of ...

(describe the other services)

4.3 Our engagement with the company as reporting accountants for the purpose of preparing the report is a statutory responsibility and is distinct, and entirely separate, from any obligations or responsibilities arising out of the contractual arrangements agreed between us under which we are to provide the professional services described in [4.1] to [4.2] above.

5 Limitation of liability

5.1 *(The reporting accountants can agree with the directors a limit on any liability arising out of the work. In such circumstances, legal advice may be required regarding the form of words to be included in the engagement letter.)*

6 Fees

6.1 Our fees are computed on the basis of time spent on the company's affairs by the partners and our staff, and on the level of skills and responsibility involved. Our fees will be charged separately for each of the main classes of work described above, will be billed at appropriate intervals during the year and will be due on presentation.

6.2 If, in the circumstances described in [2.7], we do not issue any report, or if, in the circumstances described in [3.3], or for any other reason, it becomes necessary for us to withdraw from the engagement, our fees for work performed will be payable by the company.

7 Agreement of terms

7.1 We shall be grateful if you could confirm in writing your agreement to the terms of this letter, or let us know if they are not in accordance with your understanding.

Yours faithfully

. . .

Appendix 3

Illustrative Example of Report

ACCOUNTANTS' REPORT TO THE SHAREHOLDERS ON THE UNAUDITED ACCOUNTS OF XYZ LIMITED

We report on the accounts for the year ended ... set out on pages ... to ....

Respective responsibilities of directors and reporting accountants

As described on page ... the company's directors are responsible for the preparation of the accounts, and they consider that the company is exempt from an audit. It is our responsibility to carry out procedures designed to enable us to report our opinion.

Basis of opinion

Our work was conducted in accordance with the Statement of Standards for Reporting Accountants, and so our procedures consisted of comparing the accounts with the accounting records kept by the company, and making such limited enquiries of the officers of the company as we considered necessary for the purposes of this report. These procedures provide only the assurance expressed in our opinion.

Opinion

In our opinion:

(a) the accounts are in agreement with the accounting records kept by the company under section 221 of the Companies Act 1985;

(b) having regard only to, and on the basis of, the information contained in those accounting records:

(i) the accounts have been drawn up in a manner consistent with the accounting requirements specified in section 249C(6) of the Act; and

(ii) the company satisfied the conditions for exemption from an audit of the accounts for the year specified in section 249A(4) of the Act[2] and did not, at any time within that year, fall within any of the categories of companies not entitled to the exemption specified in section 249B(1).

[Signature]

Reporting accountants

Date *Address*

[2] The words 'as modified by section 249A(5)' should be included here if the company is a charity.

Appendix 4

Illustrative Example of Report: Opinion Including Disagreement

ACCOUNTANTS' REPORT TO THE SHAREHOLDERS ON THE UNAUDITED ACCOUNTS OF XYZ LIMITED

We report on the accounts for the year ended ... set out on pages ... to ....

Respective responsibilities of directors and reporting accountants

. . .

Basis of opinion

. . .

Opinion — including disagreement

As stated in note ..., the directors have made no provision in the accounts for the depreciation of plant and machinery shown in the balance sheet at £... Paragraph 18 of Schedule 4 to the Companies Act 1985 requires that any fixed asset which has a limited useful economic life be depreciated.

In our opinion:

(a) the accounts are in agreement with the accounting records kept by the company under section 221 of the Companies Act 1985;

(b) having regard only to, and on the basis of, the information contained in those accounting records:

(i) because of the absence of the provision for depreciation referred to above, the accounts have not been drawn up in a manner consistent with the accounting requirements specified in section 249C(6) of the Act; and

(ii) the company satisfied the conditions for exemption from an audit of the accounts for the year specified in section 249A(4) of the Act and did not, at any time within that year, fall within any of the categories of companies not entitled to the exemption specified in section 249B(1).

[Signature]

Reporting accountants

Date *Address*

Appendix 5

Illustrative Example of Report: Opinion Including Limitation on Scope

ACCOUNTANTS' REPORT TO THE SHAREHOLDERS ON THE UNAUDITED ACCOUNTS OF XYZ LIMITED

We report on the accounts for the year ended ... set out on pages ... to ....

Respective responsibilities of directors and reporting accountants

. . .

Basis of opinion

Our work was conducted in accordance with the Statement of Standards for Reporting Accountants, and so our procedures consisted of comparing the accounts with the accounting records kept by the company, and making such limited enquiries of the officers of the company as we considered necessary for the purpose of this report, except that the scope of our work was limited as explained below. These procedures provide only the assurance expressed in our opinion.

Owing to flood damage, certain accounting records relating to sales for the first month of the year have been destroyed, and so we have been unable to compare the sales shown in the accounts with those accounting records.

Opinion — including limitation on scope

In our opinion:

(a) except for the uncertainty relating to sales, which arises from the limitation on the scope of our work described above, the accounts are in agreement with the accounting records kept by the company under section 221 of the Companies Act 1985;

(b) having regard only to, and on the basis of, the information contained in those accounting records:

  (i) the accounts have been drawn up in a manner consistent with the accounting requirements specified in section 249C(6) of the Act; and

  (ii) the company satisfied the conditions for exemption from an audit of the accounts for the year specified in section 249A(4) of the Act and did not, at any time within that year, fall within any of the categories of companies not entitled to the exemption specified in section 249B(1).

[Signature]

Reporting accountants

Date *Address*

Note: In this example the reporting accountants have been able to conclude that the company satistied the report conditions and that the limitation of scope did not prevent them from forming an opinion as to whether the accounts have been drawn up in the manner consistent with the specified accounting requirements.

Appendix 6

Illustrative Example of Report: Including Explanatory Paragraph

ACCOUNTANTS' REPORT TO THE SHAREHOLDERS ON THE UNAUDITED ACCOUNTS OF XYZ LIMITED

We report on the accounts for the year ended ... set out on pages ... to ....

Respective responsibilities of directors and reporting accountants

. . .

Basis of opinion

. . .

Trade debtors

In carrying out our procedures it has come to our attention that the balance sheet total of debtors includes a debt of £... which has been outstanding for in excess of one year. XYZ Limited has no security for this debt. The directors have made no provision against the debt being irrecoverable and they have informed us that they are satisfied that it will be recovered in full. We are not required to and have not performed any procedures to corroborate the directors' views, and we therefore express no opinion on this matter.

Opinion

. . .

[Signature]
Reporting accountants
Date *Address*

Section 7
Auditing Standards and Guidelines

Contents

Auditing Standards and Guidelines

Explanatory Foreword

(Issued April 1980; revised January 1989)

Introduction

1 This Explanatory Foreword explains the scope and authority of Auditing Standards and Auditing Guidelines approved by the Councils of The Institute of Chartered Accountants in England and Wales, The Institute of Chartered Accountants of Scotland, The Institute of Chartered Accountants in Ireland, The Chartered Association of Certified Accountants, The Chartered Institute of Public Finance and Accountancy and The Chartered Institute of Management Accountants (collectively referred to in the following paragraphs as 'the Accountancy Bodies'). It should be read in conjunction with the Auditing Standards and Guidelines to which it forms a collective preface.*

Definitions

2 An 'audit' is the independent examination of, and expression of an opinion on, the financial statements of an enterprise. (When reading Auditing Standards and Guidelines, the term 'enterprise' should be read as embracing any form of entity, whether profit oriented or not.)

3 Unless the relevant Auditing Standard or Auditing Guideline indicates to the contrary, the term 'audit' applies:

(a) where there is a statutory requirement for the auditor to express an opinion in terms of whether the financial statements give a true and fair view (for example, audits under the Companies Acts or the Industrial and Provident Societies Acts);

(b) where there is a statutory requirement for the auditor to express an opinion in terms other than whether the financial statements give a true and fair view (for example, audits of government departments or local authorities); and

(c) where the terms and scope of the engagement are agreed between the auditor and his client (for example, the audit of a sole trader or partnership) or where they are specified in a legal document (for example, a trust deed).

4 Where the term 'the auditor' is used, reference is to the individual, the firm or the organisation carrying out the audit of the enterprise. Where appropriate the term includes the auditor's staff acting within delegated authority, and references to the masculine include the feminine.

5 'Financial statements' comprise all those statements and other financial information which are identified as being within the scope of the audit. These will normally include balance sheets, profit and loss accounts (or other forms of income and expenditure statements) and statements of source and application of funds together with relevant notes.

6 The responsibility for the preparation of financial statements and the presentation of the information included therein rests with the management of the enterprise (in the case of a company, the directors). The auditor's responsibility is to report on the financial statements as presented by management.

* The personal standards relevant to the work of an auditor are described in ethical statements published by the Accountancy Bodies.

Scope and authority of Auditing Standards

7 Auditing Standards are those Statements of Auditing Standards which have been approved for issue by the Councils of the Accountancy Bodies.

8 Auditing Standards prescribe the basic principles and practices which members of the Accountancy Bodies are expected to follow in the conduct of an audit. Auditing Standards apply whenever an audit is carried out by them.

9 Members of the Accountancy Bodies who assume responsibility as auditors are expected to observe Auditing Standards. Apparent failures by members to observe Auditing Standards may be enquired into by the appropriate committees established by the Councils of the Accountancy Bodies, and disciplinary action may result.

10 It would be impracticable to establish a code of rules sufficiently elaborate to cater for all situations and circumstances which an auditor might encounter. Such a code could not provide for innovations in business and financial practice and might hinder necessary development and experiment in auditing practice. In the observance of Auditing Standards, therefore, the auditor must exercise his judgement in determining both the auditing procedures necessary in the circumstances to afford a reasonable basis for his opinion and the wording of his report.

11 Explanatory notes may be added to the text of Auditing Standards. These explanatory notes have the same scope and authority as Auditing Guidelines (see paragraphs 13 and 14 below).

Scope and authority of Auditing Guidelines

12 Auditing Guidelines are those guidelines which have been approved for issue by the Councils of the Accountancy Bodies.

13 Auditing Guidelines are intended to assist the auditor by giving guidance on:

(a) procedures by which Auditing Standards may be applied;
(b) the application of Auditing Standards to specific items appearing in the financial statements of an enterprise;
(c) the application of Auditing Standards to particular sectors, industries and service organisations;
(d) specific types of reporting engagement other than audits as defined in paragraph 2; and
(e) other matters relating to the proper performance of audit work.

14 Auditing Guidelines are intended to be persuasive. They are not prescriptive and there may be occasions when the auditor considers it appropriate to depart from the guidance given. However, they should normally be followed, and the auditor should be prepared to explain departures if called upon to do so.

Auditing Standards and Guidelines and the law

15 Members are advised that a court of law may, when considering the adequacy of the work of an auditor, take into account any pronouncements or publications which it thinks may be indicative of good practice. Auditing Standards and Guidelines are likely to be so regarded.

International auditing pronouncements

16 International Auditing Guidelines are issued by the International Federation of Accountants. The Accountancy Bodies have agreed to incorporate the principles on which International Auditing Guidelines are based into their own Auditing Standards and Guidelines when and to the extent practicable. International Auditing Guidelines are authoritative in the UK and Ireland only to the extent that they have been so incorporated.

Application of Auditing Standards overseas

17 Where the financial statements of an overseas enterprise are to be incorporated into UK or Irish financial statements, the audit of the overseas enterprise should conform to Auditing Standards in so far as this is necessary to ensure that the audit of the UK or Irish financial statements as a whole is in accordance with Auditing Standards.

18 Where a member of the Accountancy Bodies is carrying out an audit overseas for purposes other than UK or Irish reporting, Auditing Standards may not be appropriate. The auditor should therefore observe any generally accepted local standards or practice when carrying out the audit.

Audit Briefs

19 Audit Briefs are issued by the Auditing Practices Committee. They are informative publications on subjects of topical interest and are intended to assist auditors in the discharge of their duties or to stimulate debate on important auditing issues. They do not require the approval of the Councils of the Accountancy Bodies for issue, and they do not have the same authority as either Auditing Standards or Auditing Guidelines.

The auditor's operational standard

(Issued April 1980)

This Auditing Standard should be read in conjunction with the Explanatory Foreword to Auditing Standards and Guidelines *including the glossary of terms. General guidance on procedures by which this Auditing Standard may be complied with are given in Auditing Guidelines:*

Planning, controlling and recording
Accounting systems
Audit evidence
Internal control
Review of financial statements

1 This Auditing Standard applies whenever an audit is carried out.

Planning, controlling and recording

2 The auditor should adequately plan, control and record his work.

Accounting systems

3 The auditor should ascertain the enterprise's system of recording and processing transactions and assess its adequacy as a basis for the preparation of financial statements.

Audit evidence

4 The auditor should obtain relevant and reliable audit evidence sufficient to enable him to draw reasonable conclusions therefrom.

Internal controls

5 If the auditor wishes to place reliance on any internal controls, he should ascertain and evaluate those controls and perform compliance tests on their operation.

Review of financial statements

6 The auditor should carry out such a review of the financial statements as is sufficient, in conjunction with the conclusions drawn from the other audit evidence obtained, to give him a reasonable basis for his opinion on the financial statements.

Effective date

7 This Auditing Standard is effective for the audit of financial statements relating to accounting periods starting on or after 1 April 1980.

Charities

(Issued October 1981)

Preface

This guideline gives guidance on the special factors to be considered in the application of auditing standards to charitable organisations. It is supplementary to, and should be read in conjunction with, 'The auditor's operational standard' and the related auditing guidelines.

Where the auditor is to express an opinion on financial statements intended to give a true and fair view, this guideline should also be read in conjunction with the Auditing Standards, 'The audit report' and 'Qualifications in audit reports' and the Auditing Guideline, 'Audit report examples'.

Aspects relating to audit reports, which are expressed other than in true and fair terms, will be covered in guidance from APC to be published in the future.

The guideline is based on the law as at 1 January 1981.

Special circumstances relating to Scotland and Northern Ireland are set out in the appendices to this guideline. Separate guidance will be issued for the Republic of Ireland in due course.

Background

General

Scope

1 This guidance applies to the independent examination of, and expression of an opinion on, the financial statements of charitable organisations by an appointed auditor in pursuance of that appointment and in compliance with any relevant statutory obligation. It is particularly relevant to the audit of charities which would normally expect to receive a substantial proportion of their income from voluntary sources, including those small charities which have a few voluntary workers and relatively small income.

2 The audit of financial statements of charities may be required by statute, by the charity itself (e.g. by the constitution, by specific request of the governing body) or by the Charity Commissioners (see paragraphs 6 and 7). There are many circumstances, particularly in the case of small charities, where an audit is not required. This guideline does not apply in circumstances where the engagement relates to the preparation of financial statements and not to the audit of those financial statements.

Definitions of charitable purposes

3 For the purposes of the Charities Act 1960 a charity is defined as any institution, corporate or not, which is established exclusively for charitable purposes according to the laws of England and Wales and is subject to the control of the High Court in the exercise of the court's jurisdiction with respect to charities.

4 Although there is no more comprehensive statutory definition of 'charitable purposes' than in the 1960 Act, charitable purposes were classified by Lord MacNaghten in Pemsel's Case in 1891 into four principal divisions:

- (a) the relief of poverty;
- (b) the advancement of education;
- (c) the advancement of religion;
- (d) other purposes beneficial to the community not falling under any of the preceding heads.

Picarda, in *Law and Practice relating to Charities,* and the Goodman Report of Charity Law and Voluntary Organisations (1976), have given more detailed classifications.

Legal status and constitution

5 The objects of a charity are set out in its constitution. The activities performed by the charity should therefore be within the categories of charitable purposes (see paragraph 4) and accord with its objects.

6 Charities are established either by trust deed or constitution, constitution and rules; or as corporations. Charities in this last category are usually incorporated either under the Companies Act 1948 as companies limited by guarantee, or under some other general Act of Parliament (e.g. Acts relating to friendly and industrial and provident societies). More exceptionally, they may be incorporated by special Act of Parliament (e.g. the National Trust) or by Royal Charter (e.g. many universities and colleges). Under Section 4 of the Charities Act 1960 all charities established in England and Wales, with certain exceptions under Section 4(4), are required to register with the Charity Commissioners, and an institution is for all purposes conclusively presumed to be a charity at any time when it is on the register of charities.

Regulatory bodies

7 The Charity Commissioners maintain the Central Register of Charities. If they are satisfied that an institution applying for registration is established for exclusively charitable purposes (and if it is not one of a class of charities exempted from the need to register) they will enter it in the register. The Commissioners can request that the accounts of charities so registered be filed. They can also require the accounts to be audited.

8 The Registrar of Companies maintains a register of companies which must file an annual return and audited accounts. This applies to any charity which is incorporated as a company.

9 War charities for the disabled (which may be, but need not necessarily be, charities within the meaning of the Charities Act 1960) are required to register with the appropriate local authorities under the War Charities Act 1940 and the National Assistance Act 1948 (unless specifically exempt under the Acts).

10 Charities organising house to house collections, street collections, or lotteries or prize competitions must obtain a licence or permit or be registered under separate Acts and under certain regulations may also be required to file an audited return.

Fiscal provisions affecting charities

11 There are various forms of relief and tax advantages which may be enjoyed by charities. It is advisable to be aware of all changes in legislation relating to the items mentioned in paragraphs 12-14.

12 General exemption from tax on income and from VAT is not given to charities. There are, however, specific exemptions from taxation of income which will be granted if a claim is made to the Board of the Inland Revenue. These exemptions are set out in the Income and Corporation Taxes Act 1970 and subsequent legislation. Certain extra statutory and other concessions are allowed in practice.

13 If a charity is carrying on a trade, relevant taxation exemptions will be allowed only if the profits from the trade are applied solely to the purposes of the charity and either:

(a) the trade is exercised in the course of the actual carrying out of a primary purpose of the charity; or

(b) the work in connection with the trade is mainly carried out by the beneficiaries of the charity.

14 There are also certain reliefs in respect of:

(a) corporation tax;
(b) capital gains tax;
(c) capital transfer tax;
(d) stamp duty;
(e) development land tax;
(f) national insurance surcharge;
(g) VAT;
(h) rates.

Accounting

Purposes of financial statements — stewardship

15 Charities exist not to generate profits but to meet an identified objective; consequently their performance is often measured in financial terms, not by the surplus of income over expenditure, but rather by the size of the income and the way in which it has been spent. Thus the primary purpose of the annual financial statements of a charity is to account for the stewardship of the funds entrusted to it by the public, the state and others. Financial statements may also be necessary for other reasons. For example, in the case of a corporate charity, financial statements must be prepared in a manner to comply with statutes.

Form of financial statements

16 Under Section 32 of the Charities Act 1960, charities are required to keep proper books of account and to prepare consecutive statements of account. Where a charity is subject to other statutory regulations, there may be a requirement in these for proper accounting records.

The financial statements usually comprise:

(a) a revenue account, which in many cases provides considerable detail; normally this will take the form of an income and expenditure account, but occasionally it is described as a "statement of transactions or operations";
(b) a balance sheet, or more than one if considered appropriate for specific funds;
(c) a statement of source and application of funds;
(d) notes to the accounts.

17 However, the financial statements of small charities are often a simple document such as a receipts and payments account and a concise statement of assets and liabilities.

Accounting policies

18 It is essential that the financial statements of all charities should include a statement of the main accounting policies in accordance with SSAP 2. The disclosure of significant accounting policies assumes a greater importance than for other enterprises in the absence of specific guidance from the accountancy bodies on the application of statements of standard accounting practice to not-for-profit organisations and charities in particular. The most important accounting policies for a charity will probably include:

(a) the basis on which income has been taken to the credit of the revenue account (for example, accruals or cash basis, policy with regard to legacy income, gross or net profit from trading activities);
(b) the basis on which expenditure has been charged to the revenue account (for example, accruals or cash, costs including VAT);
(c) the accounting treatment of fixed assets and investments, including donated assets;

(d) the presentation of the special funds and the movements thereon;
(e) the treatment of branches.

Statements of standard accounting practice

19 Many charities are subject to a statutory or constitutional requirement for their financial statements to give a true and fair view and in many other cases it is clearly desirable that a true and fair view should be given. As indicated in the Explanatory Foreword to Statements of Standard Accounting Practice, SSAPs apply to all financial statements intended to give a true and fair view of financial position and profit or loss.

20 However, the Explanatory Foreword recognises that "there may be situations in which for justifiable reasons accounting standards are not strictly applicable because they are impracticable or exceptionally, having regard to the circumstances, would be inappropriate or give a misleading view". In considering the appropriateness of particular SSAPs to charities, it must be remembered that SSAPs have been prepared primarily with business enterprises in mind, whereas charities are not-for-profit organisations. As a result it is important for the auditor to use his judgement as to the appropriateness or otherwise of a SSAP to the individual circumstances of the charity concerned. If any specific accounting guidance is issued on the application of SSAPs to charities, the effect on this guideline will be considered following publication of that guidance.

Some areas of activity requiring special attention

21 *Included and excluded activities.* It is often difficult to decide where the charity's activities stop and a third party takes over. The criteria are:

(a) does the charity have control?
(b) is the activity undertaken by a body with a separate constitution?

It is sometimes necessary for a charity to take legal advice to determine which activities form part of the stewardship of the main charitable body and should be accounted for in the financial statements.

22 *Cash income.* In practice a charity may find it difficult to institute procedures to ensure that all cash collections, often by volunteers, are properly accounted for in the books of account.

23 The cut-off date for the cash income of some charities is not always the year-end date, a later date sometimes being adopted because of the importance of accounting for income collected but not yet remitted by voluntary supporters.

24 *Donations in kind.* Charities are sometimes reluctant, or find it impracticable, to bring donations in kind into their books at their market value.

25 *Legacies.* Because legacy income fluctuates considerably, charities frequently employ a Legacy Equalisation Account. Some problems of auditing legacy income are dealt with in paragraphs 33 and 35.

26 *Specific funds.* (See also paragraph 60). Charities may produce separate accounts to detail movements in certain funds for which they act as trustees or which represent monies raised for specific projects. Categories of specific funds include designated, restricted and endowment funds.

27 *Central and local government grants and loans.* (See also paragraphs 34 and 57). Charities can be eligible for a number of grants and loans, which can create problems in respect of:

(a) knowing of the existence of the grant or loan scheme and the right to claim;
(b) using the money for the correct purpose.

28 *Other areas.* The following are considered elsewhere in this guidance:
(a) overseas activities (paragraph 36);
(b) branches (paragraphs 35 and 58);
(c) depreciation (paragraph 59).

Auditing

Scope

29 The scope of the audit will depend on the status of the charity and the form of report to be given. The charity may have been constituted:
(a) by trust deed;
(b) as an unincorporated association;
(c) as a company limited by guarantee under the Companies Acts;
(d) under the Acts relating to friendly and industrial and provident societies;
(e) by Royal Charter; or
(f) by special Act of Parliament.

30 Where the charity is a company, a friendly or an industrial and provident society or in many cases where it is incorporated by special Act of Parliament, the minimum audit requirements are laid down by statute. In other cases, the constitutional documents should be examined to determine audit requirements and discussions held with the trustees of the charity. Even in cases where the audit requirements are well defined, the trustees should be consulted, as they may wish to expand the scope of the audit to cover, for example, specific instructions for the auditors to look for frauds. Once the scope of the audit has been established, it should be defined and explained in a suitably worded letter of engagement.

Key audit areas peculiar to charities

31 *Donations and fund-raising.* It may be difficult to ensure the completeness and accuracy of recording of income from donations and fund-raising activities. Donations can also take the form of capital gifts such as shares or property, which require to be valued.

32 Sources which may require the special attention of the auditor include:
(a) postal receipts;
(b) deeds of covenant;
(c) flag days and door-to-door collections;
(d) functions and meetings;
(e) other fund-raising events;
(f) donations in kind.

33 *Legacies.* These may give rise to problems of completeness where, for example, they involve reversionary gifts. The auditor's review procedures should confirm that, where possible, the charity has followed up legacies.

34 *Central and local government grants and loans.* The auditor should be familiar with the workings of the grant or loan system and the accepted ways of treating grants or loans in the financial statements.

35 *Branches.* Some charities regard a voluntary organiser in a particular area as a branch, whilst others only confer branch status on a local office. It can thus be difficult to decide the status of a branch, and whether its transactions and balances should or can be included in the main financial statements. This is a matter which might usefully be dealt with in a letter of engagement. Where a branch has its own separate constitution which is quite different from that of the main charity, its transactions and balances will properly be excluded from the financial statements of the charity. Where the branch is so independent that it cannot be required to submit independent returns it may not be possible to include its transactions and balances. Where branches are excluded, it is essential that adequate disclosure is made in the financial statements, and consideration given as to whether the auditor's report should be suitably amplified or qualified. There may also be a problem for the auditor in forming an opinion on branches which do not have proper accounting disciplines.

36 *Overseas activities.* Where records are maintained overseas and the amounts are material, the auditor should give consideration to a local audit. If remittances to overseas branches are treated as an expense when made, evidence of receipt will be required.

37 *Specific funds.* Tests will need to be designed to confirm that these funds have been correctly accounted for and applied.

38 *Grants to beneficiaries.* The auditor should confirm that the bona fides of the recipient have been established. For example, the auditor will look for evidence of the payment and bona fides of a sample of grants made by the charity, and scrutinise all grants of an unusual size or nature.

Procedures

39 Paragraph 1 of "The auditor's operational standard" states that

"This auditing standard applies whenever an audit is carried out."

The application of auditing standard is no more onerous in the case of charities than in the case of other organisations.

40 The following procedures amplify those given in the operational guidelines which support "The auditor's operational standard". They do not impose on the auditor any additional requirements. For example, the internal controls operated by some charities, particularly small ones, whilst adequate for their own purposes, may not be sufficient for the purposes of reliance by the auditor in arriving at his opinion. In such cases the auditor would choose a substantive route and not rely upon control which may exist.

41 In all audits, the scope will be determined by, and the audit procedures used will vary in accordance with, the terms of the auditor's appointment. The level of audit evidence to be obtained will be a matter of judgement for the auditor in each individual case.

Planning

42 When planning the audit of a charity the auditor should particularly consider the following:

(a) the scope of the audit (see paragraph 29);

(b) recent recommendations of the Charity Commissioners or the other regulatory bodies;

(c) the acceptability of accounting policies adopted;

(d) changes in circumstances in the sector in which the charity operates;

(e) changes in the scale or nature of the charity's operations;

(f) past experience of the effectiveness of the charity's accounting system;

(g) key audit areas (see paragraphs 31-38);

(h) the amount of detail included in the financial statements on which the auditor is required to report.

Accounting systems

43 Some of the areas of activity requiring special attention when reviewing a charity's accounting system are listed in paragraphs 21-28.

Audit evidence

44 When designing substantive tests for charities the auditor should give special attention to the possibility of:

(a) understatement or incompleteness of the recording of all income including gifts in kind, cash donations, and legacies;

(b) overstatement of cash grants of expenses;

(c) mis-analysis or misuse in the application of funds;

(d) misstatement or omission of assets including donated properties and investments;

(e) the existence of restricted or uncontrollable funds in foreign or independent branches.

45 The extent of testing required will depend on the scope of the audit. For example, the auditor may be required to report on financial statements which include considerable detail. Similarly, whilst the level of audit testing would provide reasonable expectation of detecting material misstatements resulting from fraud, the charity may seek further assurances that fraud has not taken place.

46 Normal analytical review procedures as applied to a commercial enterprise, including the comparison of one year's financial statements with another, may need to be modified in the case of a charity. Particular consideration should be given to the relationship between appeals income and related expenses, and investments and the income from such investments. A comparison of the funds raised by particular branches from one period to the next should also be carried out and explanations obtained for significant differences.

Internal controls

47 The auditor will have to consider whether there are any internal controls on which he may wish to rely, or whether he will need to carry out extensive substantive testing. Large charities should have the internal controls appropriate to any large enterprise, and the auditor should look for and encourage the charity to implement normal internal controls and reporting systems in keeping with the scale of operations.

48 Small charities will generally suffer from internal controls weaknesses common to small enterprises, such as lack of segregation of duties and use of unqualified staff. Shortcomings may arise from the staff's lack of training and also, if they are volunteers, from their attitude, in that they may resent formal procedures. The auditor will have to consider particularly carefully whether he will be able to obtain adequate assurance that the accounting records do reflect all the transactions of the enterprise. Adequate control may often be available in a small charity by means of increased review and authorisation procedures by the trustees or other officials of the charity.

49 In considering internal controls the auditor should bear in mind any related reporting requirements. For example the Friendly Societies Act 1974 requires the auditor to state in his report if a satisfactory system of control over transactions has not been maintained.

50 Generally, the auditor will hope to be able to rely on the internal controls of the charity in one or more key areas wherever the volume of transactions make this reliance desirable.

For example, the auditor might wish to rely on the charity's system of authorising and controlling grants payments by the grants committee. His compliance tests might include checking with the minutes concerned and other documentation.

51 Some indication of the internal controls which might be expected to be present in most charities is given in paragraphs 52-62 below. Other areas where the auditor might seek to rely on internal controls are dealt with in the Auditing Guideline, 'Internal controls'.

52 *Donations — collecting boxes and tins*

(a) Numerical control over collecting boxes and tins.
(b) Satisfactory sealing of boxes and tins so that any opening prior to recording is apparent.
(c) Regular collection and recording of proceeds from collecting boxes.
(d) Dual control over counting and recording of proceeds.

53 *Donations — postal and cash*

(a) Dual control over the opening of mail.
(b) Immediate recording of donations on opening mail or receipt of cash.

54 *Deeds of covenant*

(a) Regular checks and follow-up procedures to ensure due amounts are received.
(b) Regular checks to ensure all tax repayments have been obtained.

55 *Legacies*

(a) Comprehensive correspondence files maintained in respect of each legacy, numerically controlled.
(b) Search agency reports of legacies receivable.
(c) Regular reports and follow-up procedures undertaken in respect of outstanding legacies.

56 *Fund-raising activities*

(a) Records maintained for each fund-raising event.
(b) Comparable controls maintained over receipts as for normal donations.
(c) Comparable controls maintained over expenses as for administrative expenses.

57 *Central and local government grants and loans*

(a) Regular checks that all sources of income or funds are fully exploited and appropriate claims made.
(b) Ensuring income or funds are correctly applied in accordance with the terms of the grant or loan.
(c) Comprehensive records of applications made and follow-up procedures for those not discharged.

58 *Branches*

(a) Any branch, office or individual representatives of the charity should make regular reports or returns to the charity, and checks should be made to ensure that all these are received.
(b) Any report of the misuse of the charity's name should be promptly investigated.
(c) Wherever the trustees of the charity have direct control over the branches, internal controls should be of equivalent standard to that of the main charity.
(d) Consideration of an accounts manual and the standardisation of procedures at all branches.
(e) Proper acknowledgements of remittances to and from abroad.

59 *Fixed assets and depreciation*

(a) A register of fixed assets maintained including donated assets.

(b) Assets vested in the official custodian, where appropriate.
(c) Donated assets recorded at approximate market value, where appropriate.
(d) Depreciation calculated and recorded as for commercial enterprises, where the accounting policy requires.

60 *Specific funds*

Records maintained of:

(a) separate revenue and assets of accounts;
(b) terms controlling application of fund monies;
(c) applications of fund monies.

61 *Grants to beneficiaries*

(a) Records maintained of all requests for material grants received and their treatments.
(b) Checks made of the bona fides of applicants for substantial grants, and that amounts paid are intra vires.
(c) Minutes maintained of all Grants Committee meetings with record of decisions made.
(d) Adequate documentation given to committee for them to base their decision on the accurate facts.

62 *Bank records*

In small charities the following controls will have particular significance:

(a) prompt banking or receipts;
(b) independent agreement of banking records to receipts records;
(c) regular bank reconciliations;
(d) scrutiny of returned cheques for unusual or frequent endorsements;
(e) adequate arrangements for bank signatories.

Review of financial statements

63 The auditor must consider carefully whether the accounting policies adopted are appropriate to the activities, constitution and objectives of the charity, and are consistently applied, and whether the financial statements adequately disclose these policies and fairly present the state of affairs and the results for the accounting period.

64 In particular the auditor should consider the basis of:

(a) disclosing income from fund-raising activities (for example, net or gross);
(b) accounting for income and expenses (accruals or cash);
(c) the capitalising of expenditure on fixed assets;
(d) apportioning administrative expenditure;
(e) recognising income from donations and legacies;
(f) treating exceptional and extraordinary items.

65 In determining whether the financial statements comply with all relevant statutory requirements and other regulations, it is necessary to take account of the legal framework within which a particular charity operates.

66 In determining whether proper disclosures have been made, the auditor should consider the presentation of:

(a) special or irregular income or expenditure;
(b) specific funds;
(c) net surplus/deficit for the period;

(d) allocation of funds;
(e) movements on particular funds;
(f) statements of source and application of funds;
(g) realised and unrealised surpluses/deficits on disposal or revaluation of assets;
(h) branch accounts;
(i) detailed analysis of income and expenses.

67 Charities without significant endowments or accumulated funds will often be dependent upon future income from voluntary sources, in order to meet the financial commitments arising from the continuation of their activities. In these circumstances, the review of the financial statements may lead the auditor to question whether a going concern basis of accounting is appropriate. He should therefore, in forming a conclusion on the matter, take account of the amount of, and trends in, income and expenditure since the accounting date, any forecasts and representations by management as to future income and expenditure and (where relevant) the market value of the charity's tangible assets.

Reporting

68 Where the auditor is to express an opinion on financial statements intended to give a true and fair view this guideline should also be read in conjunction with the Auditing Standards 'The audit report' and 'Qualifications in audit report' together with the Auditing Guideline 'Audit report examples'.

69 The form of auditor's report and the persons to whom it will be addressed will depend on the constitution of the particular charity concerned. For example, the auditor's report on the financial statements of a charity registered under the Companies Acts is determined in accordance with the provisions of those Acts and addressed to the members or appropriate governing body. The auditor's report on the financial statements of a charity registered under the Acts relating to friendly and industrial and provident societies will be in another form and addressed to the charity itself. In other cases, where charities are not governed by statute, the auditor's report will be determined in accordance with the terms of the auditor's appointment. For example, it may be appropriate for the auditor to report only that the financial statements have been prepared in compliance with regulations governing the charity's operations.

70 If applicable, the auditor should identify in his report the statutory provisions under which he has carried out his audit. Where appropriate he should state that the accounts comply with the Companies Acts, relevant Acts relating to friendly and industrial and provident societies or the specific applicable Act of Parliament (for example, the National Trust Act). Where a charity is not incorporated under an Act of Parliament, reference should normally be made to the trust deed or other constitutional document of the charity under which the accounts have been produced.

Form of unqualified audit report

71 "AUDITORS' REPORT TO (THE MEMBERS/TRUSTEES) OF..........................
....

We have audited the financial statements on pages ... to ... in accordance with approved auditing standards.

In our opinion the financial statements give a true and fair view of the state of the charity's affairs at 31 December 19.. and if its surplus/deficit and source and application of funds for the year then ended and comply with (insert relevant statutory and/or constitutional provisions)."

Notes

1. Whether the auditor should report on the surplus/deficit or income and expenditure will depend on the statutory or constitutional provisions under which he is reporting. For example, if reporting under the Companies Acts, then Section 56(2)(b) of the 1967 Act applies and the income and expenditure account should disclose a net surplus or deficit, on which the auditor should express an opinion. However, under the Friendly and Industrial and Provident Societies Act 1968 and the Friendly Societies Act 1974, the auditor's opinion would be on the income and expenditure.
2. Some constitutional documents impose on the auditor additional reporting requirements, which must also be incorporated; for example, a positive confirmation that proper books and records have been kept.

Qualifications in audit reports

72 The basic criteria regarding qualifications in audit reports are the same in charities as in other audits and thus the Auditing Standard, 'Qualifications in audit report' will be applicable, together with the related guidance in the Guideline, 'Audit report examples'.

73 A particular and frequent problem for many small charities is the difficulty of applying proper control over voluntary donations until they are entered in the accounting records. This creates a problem for auditors similar to that which exists in relation to many small businesses regarding evidence of completeness of income. Where such a problem does exist, even after the auditor has taken steps to obtain all the evidence which can reasonably be obtained he may conclude that he is unable to give an unqualified opinion on the financial statements in respect of the completeness of income. In such a case, provided that he has satisfied himself that the system of accounting and control is reasonable having regard to the size and nature of the charity's operations, and that he has no reason to believe that income has been omitted, an example of a form of report which might be used is as follows:

"AUDITORS' REPORT TO (THE MEMBERS/TRUSTEES) OF..............................
....

We have audited the financial statements on pages ... to ....

Our audit was conducted in accordance with approved auditing standards having regard to the matters referred to in the following paragraph.

This charity, in common with many others of similar size and organisation, derives a substantial proportion of its income from voluntary donations which cannot be fully controlled until they are entered in the accounting records, and are not therefore susceptible to independent audit verification.

Subject to the foregoing, in our opinion the financial statements give a true and fair view of the state of the charity's affairs at 31 December 19.. and of its surplus/deficit and source and application of funds for the year ended and comply with (insert relevant statutory and/or constitutional provisions)."

74 It is emphasised that the above example is not automatically appropriate for use in the audits of all charities, since in many, and particularly in larger charities, there can, and should be, adequate internal controls covering all significant types of income.

75 Considerations relating to the disclosure of accounting policies by, and the application of SSAPs to charities are dealt with in paragraphs 18-20 above. Where there are departures from SSAPs with which he concurs and these are adequately disclosed and explained in the financial statements, it should not be necessary for the auditor to refer to these in his report.

Appendix 1

Special circumstances relating to Scotland

Definition of a charity (paragraphs 3 and 4):

76 (a) The definition of 'charity' in the Charities Act 1960 does not apply in Scotland. Lord MacNaghten's four-fold classification of 'charitable purposes' in Pemsel's case also does not form part of the law of Scotland except for the purposes of construing United Kingdom taxing statutes. The general law of Scotland makes no precise definition of the terms 'charity' or 'charitable purposes' but, after earlier suggestions that the term 'charitable' only covered the relief of poverty, it is now generally thought that there is little or no difference in scope between the term 'charitable' in the Scottish sense and 'charitable' in the English sense, and, as indicated above, for taxation purposes, the two senses are identical.

Registration (paragraph 6):

(b) The requirement to register with the Charity Commissioners applies only to charities subject to the jurisdiction of the High Court in England. There is no equivalent system of registration of charities in operation in Scotland.

Charity Commissioners (paragraph 7):

(c) The system of registration and supervision operated by the Charity Commissioners under the Charities Act 1960 does not apply in Scotland. There is no regulatory body akin to the Charity Commissioners operating in Scotland.

Charity recognition (paragraph 7):

(d) In Scotland application is made to the Inland Revenue for recognition as a charity for taxation purposes, and, as indicated earlier, the English law meaning of the term 'charitable' is applied.

Appendix 2

Special circumstances relating to Northern Ireland

Companies Acts:

77 (a) For all references to the Companies Act 1948 to 1967, the corresponding legislation is the Companies Act (Northern Ireland) 1960.

Friendly Societies Acts:

(b) For all references to the Friendly and Industrial Provident Societies Act 1968 and the Friendly Societies Act 1974, the corresponding legislation is the Friendly Societies Act (Northern Ireland) 1970.

Charities Acts:

(c) The Charities Act (Northern Ireland) 1964 governs the operation of charities within Northern Ireland in place of the Charities Act 1960. This Act contains no provision equivalent to Section 4 of the 1960 Act requiring registration. The Department of Finance, which is the regulatory body, is empowered to ask for accounts and documents. There is no requirement to file the audited accounts of with the Inland Revenue to obtain the tax reliefs noted.

Registration (paragraphs 9 and 10):

(d) The requirement referred to in paragraph 9 for registration with appropriate local authorities does not apply to Northern Ireland and the regulations referred to in paragraph 10 covering house to house collections, street collections and lottery or prize competitions are contained in separate enactments specifically related to Northern Ireland.

Reporting (paragraphs 68-75):

(e) Where the auditor is reporting under the Companies Act (Northern Ireland) 1960, an additional paragraph would be added to the auditor's report, to state whether proper books of account have been kept and the accounts are in agreement therewith, and whether the auditor has obtained all the information and explanations he considers necessary.

Building societies in the United Kingdom

(Issued January 1982; revised March 1989)

Preface

This guideline gives guidance on the special factors to be considered in the application of auditing standards to building societies. It is supplementary to, and should be read in conjunction with, the auditor's operational and reporting standards and related guidelines.

This guideline does not apply to building societies registered in the Republic of Ireland.

Guidance on the audit of building societies was first issued in 1982. The Building Societies Act 1986 made significant changes to the accounting and audit requirements for building societies. It also opened up new areas of business activity to societies. The original auditing guideline has, therefore, been thoroughly reviewed and revised both to reflect the legal changes and to take advantage of experience gained since 1982.

This guideline is based on the law contained in the Building Societies Act 1986 which came into effect progressively from 1 January 1987 and is fully implemented, in respect of those sections relating to accounting records and systems, for financial years beginning on or after 1 October 1987.

Section 82(8) of the Building Societies Act 1986 permits auditors to provide information direct to the Building Societies Commission without the society's knowledge in certain circumstances. Guidance on that section was issued in December 1986 and is now incorporated with only minor amendments into the revised guideline.

The contents of this guideline have the approval of the Building Societies Commission and the Treasury.

Introduction

1 This guideline is intended to assist the auditors of a building society ('a society'):

(a) to comply with auditing standards and apply relevant auditing guidelines; and

(b) to understand and comply with the relevant requirements of the Building Societies Act 1986 ('the Act').

In addition it will provide guidance on particular aspects of building society accounting and control procedures. It cannot, however, substitute for the proper study of the Act, regulations and Prudential Notes which is an essential part of the planning and execution of a building society audit.

It is also hoped that directors of building societies (particularly those who have specific audit responsibilities, e.g. members of an audit committee) will find the guideline of value in carrying out their responsibilities under the Act.

2 Before accepting appointment, auditors of a building society should take steps to understand the legal framework under which societies operate and the prudential and reporting requirements that flow therefrom. These differ significantly from those which apply to companies generally, viz:

- Societies are regulated by the Building Societies Commission ('the Commission') which is given by the Act the powers to control the way in which societies conduct their affairs. The functions of the Commission are set out in Section 1(4) of the Act and include promoting the financial stability of societies and the protection of the investments of shareholders and depositors.
- Each year two complementary reports have to be submitted to the Commission. The first has to be signed by the chairman and the chief executive (s. 71(11)). The second

comes from the auditors (s. 82). Both reports are required to state whether, throughout the preceding year, the society had complied fully with the requirements of Section 71 of the Act, and whether at all times there had been in place adequate and effective systems for both control of the business of the society, and for inspection and report to the directors that such controls have been in place and have been working.

A number of consequences for auditors flow from these requirements.

- If the auditors are to report that the systems were operative throughout the year, their visits to the society should normally be carried out at periodic intervals during the year.
- Because the auditors are required to report specifically on the system of control, they should carry out compliance tests on the controls. This means that in the majority of cases, where societies have computer-based systems, the auditors should be able to identify and test the effectiveness of the controls inherent in those systems. They cannot audit 'around' the systems.
- The Commission expects societies and their auditors to report to it, on compliance with Section 71, matters that are significant in relation to the prudential assessment of systems. It is expected by the Commission that there will often be such matters to report and that these will be the subject of discussion between Commission and society, and sometimes the auditor.

3 A building society is a society established under the Act. Section 5(1) of the Act requires that:

> ". . . [the society's] purpose or principal purpose is that of raising, primarily by the subscriptions of the members, a stock or fund for making to them advances secured on land for their residential use."

4 Holding the savings of individuals and providing advances upon mortgage security are the businesses traditionally associated with building societies. In addition, the Act permits societies to carry on a range of activities not previously open to building societies, such as unsecured lending, development and holding of residential property and providing certain financial services or services relating to land (ss. 34 and 14 to 19) (paragraphs 27 to 30 below). A power to carry on such an activity is known as an 'adoptable power'. Both the principal purpose of the society and the 'adoptable powers' which it has adopted must be specified in its memorandum of the purpose and the extent of the powers of the society.

5 A building society audit has many special aspects, the most important being that the statutory reporting requirements are more specific than those required by company legislation, in that auditors are required to form opinions on:

(a) the system of control (s. 82(3)(b));

(b) the system of inspection and report (s. 82(3)(c));

(c) the system of safe custody of documents (s. 82(3)(d);

(d) certain parts of the annual business statement (s. 78(7)); and

(e) the summary financial statement (s. 76(5)), as well as on the annual accounts, the directors' report and the accounting records.

6 Having formed their opinions, the auditors are required to express those opinions in the following reports:

(a) to the members on the annual accounts, annual business statement and directors' report (s. 78(1) and (3)) (paragraphs 131 to 134);

(b) to the members on any statement of particulars of transactions and arrangements with directors and connected persons (s. 78(9)) (paragraphs 135 to 140);

(c) on the summary financial statement prepared for members and depositors (s. 76(5)) (paragraphs 141 to 142); and
(d) to the Commission (paragraphs 17 to 21) on the accounting records; on the systems of control of the society's business and records and of inspection and report; and on the system of safe custody of documents (s. 82) (paragraphs 148 to 159).

The report to the Commission is a feature of a building society audit which has no equivalent in the Companies Act audit requirements, although it has a parallel in audits under the Banking Act 1987 or the Financial Services Act 1986.

7 As well as being required to make the annual reports referred to in the preceding paragraph, the auditors are entitled to make reports to the Commission "if they are satisfied that it is expedient to do so in order to protect the investments of shareholders or depositors", or on request by the Commission (s. 82(8)) (paragraphs 166 to 177). Such *ad hoc* reports will, however, be the exception.

8 The business of a society must be conducted in a prudent manner. Section 45 of the Act sets out the "criteria of prudent management" (paragraphs 22 to 26) and the Commission has provided guidance on these matters in a series of 'Prudential Notes' (paragraph 18).

9 One of the criteria of prudent management is the "maintenance of the requisite accounting records and systems of control of business and of inspection and report". This requirement is set out in more detail in Section 71 of the Act.

10 Section 71(4) identifies three functions of a building society's system of control of its business and records:

(a) the control of the conduct of the business in accordance with the Act;
(b) the control of the conduct of the business in accordance with the decisions of the board of directors; and
(c) the control of the accounting and other records.

11 The system of inspection and report is a society's system for monitoring the operation of the system of control; it is not part of the system of control. Inspection must be carried out on behalf of the board of directors and the results of inspection must be reported to the board (s. 71(5)). Inspection will include assessment of the adequacy, effectiveness and operation of the system of control.

12 A detailed statement in writing of the system of control must be kept available to the board. This is essential; a society which fails to maintain such a written record fails to meet the Act's requirements that the systems be "established and maintained" (s. 71(6)).

13 The two systems (i.e. of control and of inspection and report) must combine to enable the directors and the society to discharge their respective duties and functions (s. 71(6)).

14 The importance of management information to the directors and the society in fulfilling their obligations to control the business is recognised in a requirement (s. 71(7)) for such information to be available with sufficient accuracy, promptness and regularity (or at need). Similarly, information provided to the Commission must be both sufficiently accurate and available as agreed with the Commission.

15 Auditors must note that these issues (particularly paragraph 10(b) above) go wider than those normally considered in the course of a company audit. It is particularly important that the auditors of a building society undertake an engagement only after considering their own competence and the adequacy of their resources to carry out their extensive duties under the Act. Auditors continuing in office should review their competence to act each year, since the nature and complexity of the business of a society may change significantly from year to year. In assessing their competence and resources the auditors should bear in mind the type and range of the society's activities and nature of its systems. For example, highly specialised computer systems will require of the auditors skills different from those necessary to evaluate manual systems. Similarly, different skills may be required of the auditors of a large society offering the full range of services permitted by the Act from those required of the auditors of a small society engaged only in the traditional areas (paragraph 4) of building society business.

Legal background

Legislation

16 The 1986 Act has replaced the Building Societies Act 1962 (and, in Northern Ireland, the Building Societies Act (Northern Ireland) 1967), which consolidated Acts passed between 1874 and 1960 as the single Act governing building societies (ss. 15 and 124 of and Sch. 21 to the Act do not, however, apply to Northern Ireland). Under the Act, statutory provisions relating to building societies may include Orders and Regulations made by the Treasury or by the Commission (usually requiring the consent of the Treasury) and contained in Statutory Instruments.

The Commission

17 Section 1 of the Act makes provision for a Building Societies Commission appointed by the Treasury. The Commission has a supervisory and a regulatory role and is empowered to obtain information, documents and explanations from various sources including the auditors (s. 52(6) and (13)).

18 The Commission publishes "Prudential Notes" (PNs). Generally, these notes explain what, in the Commission's opinion, is required for a society to meet the criteria of prudent management set out in Section 45 of the Act. As explained in the 'General Introduction to Prudential Notes' (PN 1986/1, to be found at the back of 1987/1 on 'Capital Adequacy'), the role of the notes is "as much education as prescriptive". Auditors' attention is drawn in particular to paragraph 12 of Prudential Note 1986/1:

"The guidance in a prudential note will, however, in the context of the Commission deciding whether it appears to it that the criteria of prudent management are met by a society, generally create presumptions in two senses:

- (a) on the one hand, the Commission will start with the presumption that compliance with the guidance in a note **in spirit as well as letter** will secure that the relevant prudential criteria are met, **to the extent that they are covered by that note**; if in a particular case the issue of statutory action arose and if the society could show that it was so complying, the onus would then be on the Commission to establish that the society was nevertheless not meeting the relevant criteria in that respect;
- (b) on the other hand, the **onus would be on a society** which did not comply with the guidance to satisfy the Commission that it was nevertheless meeting the relevant criterion, or criteria, of prudent management."

Among other things the notes are intended "to give both board and auditor guidance on what standards the Commission thinks appropriate in areas where the auditor has to report on a society's compliance with the Act" (PN 1986/1 paragraph 11 (e)).

19 Section 82(8) gives auditors a right to furnish information to the Commission if the auditors of the Commission are satisfied "that it is expedient to do so in order to protect the investments of shareholders or depositors". This right exists notwithstanding any obligation of confidence incumbent on the auditors and whether or not the giving of information is contrary to the interests of the society (paragraphs 166 to 177).

20 The Commission is required to make an annual report to Parliament, copies of which may be obtained from HM Stationery Office. Where the Commission has during the year determined the extent of the powers of any society (under s. 38 of the Act) details will be included in the annual report. The report may also include statistical information and copies of any letters from the Commission to building society chairmen or chief executives. It may, therefore, be a useful source of information for auditors and in particular may indicate likely areas of audit risk.

21 The Commission offers a subscription service which covers statutory instruments, Prudential Notes and notes for guidance; auditors will find this service helps them to keep up to date with the Commission's guidance. Other useful sources of information about building societies are The Building Societies Association (paragraph 37) and the public files maintained by the central office (in Scotland the Assistant Registrar of Friendly Societies for Scotland, elsewhere the Central Office of the Registry of Friendly Societies). The public files are available for inspection by members of the public and include such documents as the memorandum and rules of a society, financial statements and particulars of the chief executive and directors.

Prudent management

22 Section 45 of the Act sets out the criteria of prudent management as:

(a) Maintenance of adequate reserves and other designated capital resources (paragraphs 73 to 77).

(b) Maintenance of a structure of commercial assets which satisfies the requirements of Part III of the Act (paragraphs 78 and 79).

(c) Maintenance of adequate assets in liquid form (paragraph 81).

(d) Maintenance of the requisite arrangements for assessing the adequacy of securities for advances secured on land.

(e) Maintenance of the requisite accounting records and systems of control of business and of inspection and report (paragraphs 44 to 69).

(f) Direction and management —

  (i) by a sufficient number of persons who are fit and proper to be directors, as the case may be, officers, in their respective positions,

  (ii) conducted by them with prudence and integrity.

(g) Conduct of the business with adequate professional skills.

A failure to satisfy any of the first five of these criteria is regarded as a failure by the society's directors to conduct the affairs of the society prudently (s. 45(7)).

23 In order to obtain initial authorisation subsequent to 1 January 1987 to raise funds and borrow money, the board of directors, chief executive and secretary of a society must satisfy the Commission that they:

> "have the capacity and intention to direct the affairs of the society in accordance with the criteria of prudent management ..." (s. 9(4)(c)).

Thereafter, if the society fails to satisfy any of the criteria, the Commission is entitled to assume that the investments of shareholders and depositors are at risk and may, accordingly, impose conditions upon (s. 42) or revoke (s. 43) the society's authorisation. This presumption is of particular interest to auditors in the context of reports to the Commission under Section 82(8) of the Act.

24 The Section 45 criteria do not constitute an exhaustive list and the Commission may quite properly take account of other factors in exercising its powers to revoke or impose conditions upon authorisation.

25 To comply with the fifth criterion of prudent management, the accounting records, systems of control and systems of inspection and report of a building society must be such as, among other things, to enable the directors properly to discharge their functions of direction of the affairs of the society (s. 71(2)(c) and (6)(a)). The systems of control and of inspection and report must be such as to secure, among other things, that the society's business is so conducted and its records so kept that the information necessary to enable the directors to discharge their duties and functions is sufficiently accurate, available with sufficient regularity or at need and sufficiently prompt for these purposes (s. 71 (7)(a)). The primary duty, that of compliance with the requirements of prudent management, rests on the directors. The directors and chief executive have to report annually to the Commission on compliance with Section 71 (s. 71(11)).

26 The auditors must report on compliance with the requirements of Section 71 (s. 82); they must, therefore, consider whether the records and systems enable the board to direct the affairs of the society in accordance with the criteria of prudent management. Prudential Note 1987/4 on 'Systems' (see Appendix) sets out what the Commission considers to be the key issues to be addressed by all societies. The Commission will presume that these issues have been considered by the auditors in preparing their report under Section 82.

Powers to provide services

27 Section 34 empowers building societies to provide certain financial services and services relating to land. The services which a society may provide are set out in Schedule 8 to the Act (as subsequently amended) and in Sections 14 to 19.

28 There are various restrictions specific to the provision of each service permitted under Section 34 of the Act. Certain of the services may be provided by subsidiaries of a society, but not by the society itself. Power to provide any of the Schedule 8 services, and some of the Section 14 to 19 services, may only be exercised by a society which has expressly adopted the relevant power in its memorandum of the purpose and extent of its powers.

29 The auditors should be aware of the extent of the powers of the society they are auditing and should understand all aspects of the society's business. The contents of the memorandum and rules of a society are specified in paragraphs 2 and 3 of Schedule 2 to the Act.

30 Generally, the audit implications of a society, or its subsidiary, providing any of the permitted services will be similar to those of other businesses providing the same service and are not, therefore, discussed in detail in this guideline. (The implications for a society's systems of having subsidiaries or other associated bodies which provide such services are considered at paragraphs 97 to 99 below.)

Annual accounts and other reports by the directors to members

31 The annual accounts and reports to be laid before the annual general meeting of a building society pursuant to Section 81(1) are made up of three parts (paragraph 33 regarding group accounts):

(a) *the annual accounts* — consisting of the balance sheet, the income and expenditure account, the statement of the source and application of funds and the notes to them (s. 72(1) and (10)). These last three are required to be annexed to the balance sheet (s. 80(2));

(b) *the directors' report* — containing (among other things) a fair review of the development of the business during the year and the position at the end of it (s. 75(1)(a)). The directors must also state whether any and, if so, what activities carried on during the year are believed to have been carried on outside the powers of the society (s. 75(1)(c)). The directors' report must be attached to the balance sheet (s. 80(4));

(c) *the annual business statement* — containing the information prescribed by the Commission (s. 74(3)). The annual business statement must be annexed to the balance sheet (s. 80(2)).

32 The contents and form of the annual accounts are prescribed by the Building Societies (Accounts and Related Provisions) Regulations 1987 (SI 1987 No 2072) and include a format for the statement of the source and application of societies' funds. Auditors are required to report on whether the annual accounts, business statement and directors' report conform to the requirements of Part VIII of the Act and regulations thereunder (s. 78(4), (7) and s. 76(5)) and must, therefore, be familiar with the requirements of the regulations.

33 The annual accounts will, where appropriate, include group accounts (consolidated in almost all cases) (s. (72(2)). Group accounts for this purpose differ from those required by company law, as they will contain not only two balance sheets but also two income and expenditure accounts (of the society and of the group), although one statement of source and application of funds for the group alone is sufficient (s. 72(4)).

34 The auditors' report to the members of the society will be attached to the balance sheet (s. 80(2)). Copies of the annual accounts, with the attachments thereto, must be sent to the Commission, and to the Central Office for public filing.

35 In addition to the annual accounts and reports referred to above, a society must prepare a summary financial statement. This contains information derived from the annual accounts, annual business statement and directors' report. It gives a summary account of the society's financial development during and financial position at the end of the year (s. 76(1)). The form and contents of the summary financial statement are prescribed by the Building Societies (Accounts and Related Provisions) Regulations 1987. The summary must contain: (i) a statement that it is only a summary; (ii) a statement that, in so far as it summarises the information in the accounts, those accounts have been audited; and (iii) a statement of the auditors' opinion on certain matters (paragraphs 141 and 142 below).

36 The summary financial statement is the only financial statement required to be sent annually to members (and, in some cases, only to members having a 'qualifying shareholding' which, initially, is £100 unless the rules of the society specify a lesser amount) and it must contain a statement that the accounts, business statement and directors' report will be available to members and depositors free of charge on demand at every office of the society after a specified date. (Some societies may wish to send out full accounts to members in addition to the summary and all societies must send the full annual accounts to their members and depositors on demand.)

37 A society's annual accounts and reports should be drawn up in compliance with the Act and with any regulations thereunder. An overriding requirement of the Act (s. 73(9)) is that the annual accounts shall show a true and fair view. Statements of Standard Accounting Practice (SSAPs) apply to all financial accounts intended to give a true and fair view of financial position and profit or loss. Guidance on accounting and disclosure issues may also be provided by the Commission and by The Building Societies Association through numbered circulars and other documents, and the auditors should ensure that those which are relevant to the accounts and the financial operations of the society are available for their inspection during the course of the audit. (The Building Societies Association, which represents virtually all active building societies, offers a subscription service for its relevant circulars and briefs, which is available for use by auditors.)

The auditors' role

38 Sections 77 to 79, and 82 of the Act set out the statutory duties and rights of auditors, and Schedule 11 to the Act deals with their appointment, tenure and qualifications. The duties imposed by the Act are more extensive than those placed on auditors by the Companies Act, and consequently the scope of the audit is more extensive.

39 The duties imposed by the Act include two distinct reporting functions:

(a) various reports to the members of the society (s. 76(5) and 78); and

(b) a report to the Commission (s. 82).

40 The audit report to the members on the annual accounts includes an opinion expressed in true and fair terms (paragraphs 131 to 134) and to that extent is similar to an audit report under the Companies Act 1985. The auditors of a building society must also report to the members in positive terms on consistency between the directors' report on the one hand and the records and the annual accounts on the other and on compliance with the relevant legislation.

41 In addition, the auditors are required to make two further reports to the members:

(a) on a statement of particulars of transactions and arrangements with directors and persons connected with them (s. 78(9)) (paragraphs 135 to 140); and

(b) on the summary financial statement (s. 76(5)) (paragraphs 141 and 142).

42 The report to the Commission must deal with the society's accounting records; its systems of control and of inspection and report; and the system of safe custody of documents (s.82(2)) (paragraph 148). The Act has introduced a duty to report to the Commission on whether or not the requirements of the Act have been met. In the past auditors were required to report only in cases of non-compliance and then only to the members of the society.

43 As well as the annual reports referred to above, auditors may from time to time be called upon, or decide, to make other reports. These include reports to the Commission:

(a) when societies propose to merge (paragraphs 160 to 162 below);

(b) on conversion of a society to a public limited company (paragraph 163); and

(c) under Section 82(8) of the Act when the auditors or the Commission consider the disclosure of information expedient in order to protect the investments of shareholders or depositors (paragraph 166 to 177).

Accounting records, information and documents

Accounting records

44 Section 71(1) imposes on every building society a duty to keep accounting records. Sections 82(2) and (3) impose on the auditors of a building society a duty to report to the Commission whether the accounting records kept by the society comply with Section 71. The auditors are required, by Section 82(3), to specify each requirement of Section 71 not complied with and the respects in which it was not complied with.

45 The functions of accounting records set out in Section 71(2) are drawn wider than in previous legislation:

"(2) The accounting records of a society must be such as to —

(a) explain its transactions;

(b) disclose, with reasonable accuracy and promptness, the state of the business of the society at any time;

(c) enable the directors properly to discharge the duties imposed on them by or under this Act and their functions of direction of the affairs of the society; and

(d) enable the society properly to discharge the duties imposed on it by or under this Act; and must be kept in an orderly manner."

46 In particular the accounting records must contain entries from day to day of: (a) all sums received and paid by the society; and (b) every other transaction which will or, there is reasonable ground for expecting, may give rise to liabilities or assets of the society other than insignificant assets or liabilities in respect of the management of the society (s. 71(3)(a) and (b)). The accounting records are not just double-entry bookkeeping records; for example, transactions which may give rise to liabilities or assets (other than those which are insignificant or relate to the management of the society) will need to be recorded in some form of register of contingent liabilities and contingent assets.

47 Auditors should consider both the materiality and the remoteness of contingencies in forming an opinion as to the adequacy of the accounting records in the context of Section 71(3)(b). The accounting records must also contain a record of the assets and liabilities of any class specifically regulated by or under Parts II and III of the Act (s. 71(3)(c)).

48 Section 71(9) requires accounting records to be preserved for six years. Auditors should, therefore, in discharging their responsibilities under Section 82(3)(a) and (b), assess the system for securing the retention of documents for this period.

Information for the control of business and for the Commission

49 Section 71 gives statutory recognition to the role of accounting records and systems in the management of an enterprise; societies' systems are, among other things, required by the Act to produce information for the Commission which is sufficiently accurate for the Commission's purpose. Auditors are required to report to the Commission on whether or not these requirements have been met (s. 82). Prudential Notes and letters from the Commission should be reviewed for evidence of the Commission's requirements.

50 The auditors' responsibilities relate to the system which produces the management information; auditors are not expected to carry out detailed investigation of assumptions, data, calculations, decisions or omissions. They must, therefore, consider whether the information system has been established and is maintained in the light of the matters set out in paragraphs 4.3 to 4.7 of Prudential Notes 1987/4 (see Appendix).

51 When assessing the adequacy of a society's accounting records and system for the control of the conduct of the business, the auditors must consider the nature and extent of a society's activities (both present and planned), its board procedures, and what is appropriate to the society (PN 1987/4 paragraph 4.8; see Appendix).

52 In forming an opinion on the records and systems the auditors should carry out compliance tests to satisfy themselves that the system of control as recorded in the 'detailed statement in writing' (paragraphs 58 and 59) is not only adequate in theory but is also operating effectively in practice.

Deeds and other mortgage related documents

53 Every building society is required to establish and maintain a system to ensure the safe custody of all documents relating to property mortgaged to the society (s. 12(12)). The auditors have a statutory obligation to report to the Commission on whether the society's system of safe custody of documents complies with the requirement of Section 12(12). If the system does not so comply, the auditors must specify the respects in which Section 12(12) was not complied with. Consequently, the system should be evaluated and compliance tests carried out to enable the auditors to satisfy themselves that an adequate system is in operation. The society's system should include records of deeds held and controls to ensure that the deeds held are valid, for example, detailed examination of a sample of deeds or positive confirmation of their validity from solicitors. Normally, the auditors will only need to be satisfied that deeds are *prima facie* valid, but should they need to establish more positively the legal validity of particular deeds, it would be appropriate to seek legal advice.

Systems of control and of inspection and report

Introduction

54 Every building society is required to establish and maintain:

(a) a system of control of its business and records (s. 71(1)(b)); and
(b) a system of inspection and report (s. 71(1)(b)).

55 The Act and Prudential Note 1987/4 together codify what has for some time been accepted as best practice in the management of any entity. Directors are responsible for setting business objectives, deciding policies and procedures, controlling and maintaining custody of assets and ensuring that the enterprise meets its liabilities. Directors and the chief executives of building societies are now required by Section 71 (11) to send to the Commission each year a statement of their opinion as to whether the requirements of Section 71 have been complied with. By imposing this duty upon the directors and chief executive of a building society, the Act makes it quite clear where the responsibility for the society's system lies.

56 The auditors' responsibilities in relation to a building society's systems of control and of inspection and report are significantly different from those in relation to the internal controls of a limited company. There are three elements of this difference:

(a) The auditor of a limited company is obliged to assess its internal control systems if, but only if, he wishes to place reliance on those systems in arriving at his opinion on the financial statements. The auditors of a building society, by contrast, must always assess the system of control and of inspection and report (s. 79(1)(b)).
(b) The building society auditors' assessment of the systems of control and of inspection and report goes beyond assessing their reliability in producing accounts which show a true and fair view. Auditors are, therefore, concerned with the system's sufficiency in providing the information which directors need in order to direct the affairs of the society: they must make their assessment of the systems in a management rather than purely accounting context.
(c) The auditors of a building society have an express statutory duty to report to the Commission on the systems of control and of inspection and report.

57 Prudential Note 1987/4 sets out the main issues which need to be addressed in forming an opinion on a society's systems. Auditors are expected to relate the guidance in the note to the particular circumstances and strategic direction of the individual society and additional matters may need to be considered in making their report under Section 82.

Documentation

58 The system of control is only to be treated as established and maintained if a detailed written statement of the system (as in operation for the time being) is kept available to the board (s. 71(6)). Prudential Note 1987/4 (at paragraph 5.2, see Appendix) sets out criteria for evaluating documentation.

59 Any significant failure to keep the required systems documentation will be a matter for report by the auditor to the Commission, under Section 82(3)(b), as a failure to comply with the requirements of Section 71. Auditors are referred to Prudential Note 1987/4 paragraphs 8.2 to 8.4 in determining what is significant. The auditors will need to examine the detailed written statement when reviewing the system of control and to carry out tests to satisfy themselves that it is an accurate statement of the system "as in operation for the time being".

System of control

60 Prudential Note 1987/4 (see Appendix) sets out guidance as to how the Commission expects Section 71 of the Act to work in practice. It deals with systems of business control under the following headings:

Organisational control systems
Management information system
Information for the Commission
Planning systems
Information technology
Human resources

Auditors will find that the Commission's guidance, whilst having a greater emphasis on aspects of organisational and management controls, identifies key elements of control consistent with those identified in the Appendix to the Auditing Guideline 'Internal controls'.

61 Prudential Note 1987/4 sets out the main issues which need to be addressed by all societies in forming an opinion on a society's systems of business control. The Commission has stated (PN 1987/4 paragraph 1.d) that in forming their opinions, the board and chief executive of some societies will need to consider these issues having regard to the particular characteristics and circumstances of their society. Although the issues have been established primarily for the benefit of societies' boards, they should also be addressed by auditors in forming their opinion on the adequacy of the systems.

62 By considering these issues and their application to the individual society, the auditors can ensure that they are addressing the relevant matters in forming their opinion and making their report.

63 Auditors will review and evaluate a building society's systems primarily in order to discharge their duties under Section 82 (report to the Commission), but they will also wish to determine the extent to which, by placing reliance on internal controls, they may limit the level of substantive tests required to form an opinion on the annual accounts. For this purpose three essential points must be recognised by the auditors:

(a) in the case of most building societies, the volume of transactions is so great that it would not be practicable to carry out an audit without obtaining considerable assurance from adequate systems of control, and of inspection and report;

(b) in the case of most commercial organisations, most movements of cash are the result of an equivalent movement of goods. Certain audit assurance can therefore be obtained by reference to this relationship. This is not available, however, in the case of building societies and similar financial organisations. Assurance must therefore be provided by adequate systems of control, and of inspection

report, particularly over the handling of cash; and

(c) there are large volumes of similar transactions and accounting systems which frequently involve the use of computers. The auditors will need to have, or be able to call upon, the necessary expertise to satisfy themselves that they fully understand the systems in operation, firstly in order to comply with their Section 82 responsibility to report to the Commission and, secondly, so that they can justify from their working papers any reliance placed on internal controls in forming an opinion on the accounts.

A system of inspection and report which meets the requirements of the Act (considered below) should be a source of considerable assurance to the auditors concerning the adequacy, effectiveness and operation of the system of control of a society's business and records.

Inspection on behalf of the board

64 A system of inspection and report is a system quite distinct from the system of control. The system of control is a system for day to day control; the system of inspection involves examination of and reporting upon the system of control. The purpose of system of inspection is:

"(a) to provide a continuous appraisal for management and the board as to the overall effectiveness of the control systems, including all proposed changes, and to recommend improvements where considered desirable or necessary.

(b) to determine whether the systems and controls established by the management and the board have operated as laid down (in the society's control documentation) and comply with policies, procedures, laws, regulations, etc.

(c) to assess whether financial and operating information supplied to management and the board is accurate, pertinent, timely and complete." (PN 1987/4 paragraph 6.2.)

65 The key elements of a satisfactory system of inspection are set out in paragraph 6.4 of Prudential Note 1987/4.

66 The auditors should consider the adequacy of the inspection procedures on a similar basis to that set out in the paragraphs on internal audit in the Auditing Guideline 'Internal Controls' and ensure that the system deals adequately with the matters set out in paragraphs 6.3 and 6.4 of Prudential Note 1987/4. The auditors must remember that they are required by the Act to report on whether or not the systems are adequate, and must recognise that this is a major difference from a trading company. Key questions that the auditors should consider regarding the systems of inspection include:

(a) Is the system structured so that it can perform an independent appraisal function?

(b) Is the organisation and staffing adequate?

(c) Do staff have the necessary training, experience and seniority?

(d) Is the work adequately planned and controlled?

(e) Does the programme of inspection ensure comprehensive coverage of the whole system within an adequate period of time? Comprehensive coverage includes assessing the adequacy, effectiveness and operation of the system of controls, including new business/systems development.

(f) Are the inspection techniques used satisfactory?

(g) Is the work adequately documented?

(h) Are reporting procedures adequate, clearly documented and independent?

(i) Is there adequate follow-up of inspection reports?

67 Where the society is unable to establish a full-time inspection department in conjunction with its other review procedures, it must set up an adequate alternative comprising one or more of the following:

(a) the use of a competent independent person on a part-time basis;
(b) consortia arrangements with other societies; and
(c) the use of independent accountants or other external suitably qualified persons.

The nature and degree of technical skills required for a person to be 'competent' to carry out inspection or internal audit functions will depend on the nature of the business and the complexity of the systems on which he is required to report. For example, a person engaged by a society to carry out an inspection of the controls built into a society's computer systems will require specialist knowledge of computer security and control. The auditors will need to be satisfied that the society overcomes any disadvantages inherent in the above alternatives to a full-time inspection department.

68 It is important to recognise that the external auditors are giving an independent opinion. Consequently they must consider very carefully their involvement in matters on which they are required to give that independent opinion. Where a society does not have the necessary expertise available amongst its directors, it may call on its external auditors for advice. The giving of advice on the procedures for establishing and maintaining systems or on the design of systems, or on the interpretation of inspection reports does not necessarily conflict with the giving of an independent opinion. If auditors are asked to assist in carrying out the inspection procedures, they must consider whether such assistance could result in a loss of objectivity, and thus independence, in giving their opinion on the maintenance of systems of inspection.

Reporting to the board

69 The system of report enables the board and management to satisfy themselves that the inspection function is being carried out properly. It is for the board to establish a procedure for receiving reports arising from the inspection function. This task might, for example, be delegated to a committee of the board as suggested in Section 7 of Prudential Note 1987/4. In forming a view on the overall effectiveness of the inspection function, the board and management need to consider the following matters:

(a) adequacy and scope of planning including coverage of the whole group;
(b) adequacy and scope of work performed in relation to the plans and programmes;
(c) regularity and level of reporting of matters arising from the inspections;
(d) conclusions drawn and recommendations made on the adequacy, operation and effectiveness of controls;
(e) disposal of points and recommendations raised, and reasons for any rejection of major points; and
(f) review of overall effectiveness of inspection function.

Auditors also will need to take those matters into consideration when reviewing the reporting procedure; they will need to establish their own relationship with the board or committee of the board which receives inspection reports and discuss their own findings with the board or the appropriate committee.

Managing the balance sheet

Introduction

70 The first four of the seven criteria of prudent management deal with aspects of a society's balance sheet — its reserves, commercial and liquid assets and security for advances secured on land. The last three criteria deal with the records and systems and with the direction and conduct of the business.

71 The balance sheet is a good starting point for auditors seeking to gain an understanding of the business of a building society. Auditors must recognise the significant changes that have taken place (since the previous guideline was issued), such as the raising of non-retail funds, new activities, opportunities for securitisation and off balance sheet finance, and the increasing complexity of financial markets. The following paragraphs consider some of the key elements of balance sheet management in a building society.

Treasury management

72 Treasury management is today a highly technical area with commercial risks heightened by the speed, size and volume of transactions and by the novelty of many of the financial instruments traded. It is essential that the sophistication and strength of a society's systems be adequate to cope with its present, and planned, level of involvement in the financial markets. Societies' planning procedures should establish prudent policies for treasury management and should include plans to secure the services of directors and managers with the levels of experience and knowledge necessary to safeguard the interests of shareholders and depositors. A society's auditors must consider whether its treasury systems meet the requirements of Prudential Note 1987/4. They should refer to any papers and Prudential Notes issued by the Commission specifically on Treasury Risk Management and Treasury Systems and Control.

Capital adequacy

73 The importance of capital is set out in Section 45 as the first criterion of prudent management: "maintenance of adequate reserves and other designated capital resources". The Commission has developed this concept in Prudential Note 1987/1 on 'Capital Adequacy — A framework for assessment'.

74 A building society's need for capital goes much further than the need to cover the risk of loss of capital value of particular groups of assets. The prime role of capital in a deposit-taking institution such as a building society is to ensure the continued viability of the institution and to maintain investors' confidence in that viability. The Commission gives the following examples of that role:

" (a) since, over simplifying somewhat, capital represents the difference between the amount of assets on which the society earns income and the liabilities on which it pays interest, it provides a cushion of income to absorb a squeeze on margins due to competition;

(b) capital provides the society with some ability to ride out 'shocks', and to gain time to adjust successfully to sharp changes in circumstances; and

(c) capital provides reassurance to investors, thereby minimising the risks of loss of confidence which may arise, whether about the viability of the society or otherwise.

Thereafter, it has to cover the specific risks such as credit risk, or interest rate mismatch, on different parts of the society's business." (Paragraph 5.9 of the Commission's response to the Consultations on Capital Adequacy.)

75 The framework involves two measures of a society's required capital, the 'desired level' and the 'minimum acceptable level'. Against these is tested the society's 'standard measure of capital' — a measure of the available capital. The standard measure of capital and the minimum acceptable capital are determined by means of calculations set out by the Commission in its Prudential Note 1987/1. The desired capital is determined by a society's board and is the minimum acceptable capital plus a margin of half per cent (plus an additional requirement for smaller societies) or such higher margin as the society may choose. The Commission has provided in Prudential Note 1987/1 a summary, which auditors may find helpful, of the 'calculus' for the assessment of capital adequacy. The summary (in Part III of the blue pages at the front of the Note) sets out the standard value and capital ratios for certain types of asset and asset groups.

76 The accounting records and the systems of control and of inspection and report should enable the board to monitor and control the society's capital requirements in accordance with Section 71 of the Act; the auditors must, therefore, in preparing their report under Section 82, consider whether the records and systems comply with the requirements.

77 Auditors are not required to report on the arithmetical accuracy of the application of the calculus and of the completion of the Annual Capital Monitoring Return. Their responsibilities under Section 82 do, however, extend to consideration of the management information systems used for the completion of the Annual Capital Monitoring Return. Inaccurate returns may indicate failure to comply with Section 71. Auditors should also note that their agreement is required to the methods of valuation used in relation to: (a) the use of statistical sampling techniques in classifying the existing mortgage book prior to a new system being established by 1 January 1988 and the allocation of redemptions thereafter; and (b) price data of securities (paragraphs 5.20(iii)(b) and 4.24(iv), respectively, of the Commission's statement 'Capital Adequacy — Application of the calculus and completion of the Annual Capital Monitoring Return').

Classes of assets and liabilities

78 The accounting records of a society must contain a record of "assets ... of any class specifically regulated ..." (s. 71(3)(c)). The Building Societies (Accounts and Related Provisions) Regulations 1987 require disclosure in the annual business statement of ratios of assets of certain classes in relation to total commercial assets. The recording and disclosure of classes of assets will, therefore, be matters for consideration by the auditors. Materiality in this area must be judged specifically in relation to the limits set by or under the Act and the auditor should appreciate the absolute nature of those limits; any holding in excess of the limits, however small, is in fact a breach of the requirements of the Act.

79 The Act defines certain 'nature limits' for the assets and liabilities of a society, with which the society must comply at all times. These limits are not of themselves prudential. They exist to ensure that a society retains the basic form and structure of a building society. In certain cases, e.g. wholesale funding, the Commission may for prudential reasons not agree to a society taking advantage of the full extent of the nature limit. To understand fully the structure of the balance sheet of a society, the full range of nature limits needs to be understood.

(a) *Liquid assets*
Section 21 provides that no more than 33¹/₃ per cent of the assets of a society shall be held in liquid form. The various liquid assets that may be held are prescribed by Statutory Instrument which specifies the instruments and types of institutions in which societies can invest their assets.

(b) *Commercial assets*
Commercial assets are not formally defined within the Act. These are, however, those assets other than liquid assets which are used by societies to generate income. There are three categories of commercial assets:

— Class 1 assets cover loans to individuals for the residential use of the borrower or a dependent which are fully secured.

— Class 2 assets are other loans which are fully secured.

— Class 3 assets are those other assets, including unsecured loans to individuals, in which societies have power to invest.

Section 20 of the Act places limits on the proportions into which commercial assets are split. The system of control of the business must assume that the society, at all times, operates within the prescribed commercial asset structure. Initially not less than 90 per cent of commercial assets had to be Class 1 assets. However, the Government has announced that the limit will be gradually lowered to 75 per cent.

(c) *Wholesale funding*
Section 7(3) of the Act restricts the amount of 'non-retail' funds that may be raised by the society. Initially the figure prescribed by the Act was 20 per cent, although the proportion has since been raised to 40 per cent. However, the adjustment is not automatic, and societies will need to agree with the Commission on an individual basis the proportion of non-retail funds that they may hold. In agreeing the percentage for each society the Commission will take account of the strength of the society's system of control of its business, with particular emphasis on its ability to manage its treasury function.

(d) *Liabilities in the form of shares*
Section 8 of the Act requires that not less than 50 per cent of the funds deposited with the society must be in the form of shares.

80 Auditors need to know and understand the relevant limits and definitions, and will have to carry out compliance tests on the systems and substantive tests on balance of assets and liabilities reported in the annual accounts and business statement. Materiality will fall to be judged in relation to the relevant limits.

Liquid assets

81 Significant amounts of the society's funds held as liquid assets are often under the control of a small number of individuals. Particular care must, therefore, be taken by the auditors when examining the systems of control and of inspection and report in this area. Auditors should obtain assurance that the systems ensure that:

(a) the liquid assets of a society are held in accordance with current liquid asset regulations;
(b) the limit on liquid assets is not exceeded; and
(c) information is provided to enable both capital and liquidity adequacy to be monitored.

Liabilities of associated bodies

82 A building society has a statutory obligation (s. 22) to discharge the liabilities of a subsidiary or other associated body linked by resolution which is unable to discharge them out of its own assets. For this reason a society must maintain adequate capital and liquidity which takes account of the liabilities of subsidiaries and associated bodies linked by resolution (PN 1987/1). The Commission has stated that although a society is not statutorily obliged to stand behind those of its associated bodies not 'linked by resolution', in practice it could find itself in the position of having to do so in order to protect its good name (PN 1987/1 paragraph 9.3). Auditors should bear in mind these factors when considering a society's systems for monitoring capital adequacy and disclosure of contingent liabilities in the annual accounts.

Audit testing

This section of the guideline comments on matters peculiar to building societies. It does not comment on key areas which, although they may be of particular importance in the context of a building society, are subject to the same considerations as apply to audits of other types of entity, or are covered by other guidelines. The nature of the business of a society will, in many cases, mean that auditors need to refer to other guidelines.

Advances

83 Almost all of the advances made will be secured, but some societies will make unsecured advances within the current limits. The auditors should carry out appropriate audit tests in order to satisfy themselves that the systems provide that, *inter alia*:

(a) all mortgage advances are to bona fide borrowers, have been made in compliance with the system of control and are properly secured on the title of the property;

(b) security continues to be maintained, including guarantees, endowment policies, insurance cover;

(c) unsecured advances are made to bona fide borrowers and have been made in compliance with the system of control including credit rating procedures where unauthorised overdrafts are possible, the system identifies them and appropriate investigation is made;

(d) all arrears in the repayment of advances, loans and overdrafts are monitored to ensure that they represent nothing more significant than delays in repayment by bona fide borrowers, and are not due to misrecording or defalcation by employees or agents of the society;

(e) provisions for losses are regularly assessed and maintained at adequate levels;

(f) all redemption monies and repayments have been properly accounted for in the society's records;

(g) assets are correctly classified;

(h) limits for classes of assets are not exceeded; and

(i) capital adequacy requirements are monitored.

Investors' accounts

84 A society's procedures should control all types of account and prevent unauthorised access to accounting records and passbooks. Some factors relating to individual accounts make them more susceptible to undetected errors or defalcation where there are weaknesses in control and limited opportunity for segregation of duties. For example:

(a) the investor cannot be traced;

(b) passbooks are held by the society;

(c) requests for non-communication have been received;

(d) fixed amounts are held for a long period; or

(e) there are exceptions to the society's usual procedures.

Auditors will therefore need to consider whether additional testing is needed in relation to particular types of account. Further considerations will arise if the society operates banking-type facilities or uses automated teller machines. Auditors of such societies are referred to the Auditing Guideline 'Banks in the United Kingdom'.

Communication between the society and investors/borrowers

85 It is an important feature of a system of control within a building society that the society should communicate with its investors and borrowers in a proper and timely manner, and that all queries from investors and borrowers which relate to the accounting function are properly monitored and resolved. The auditors should, therefore, take steps to satisfy themselves that this aspect of the society's systems is operating adequately. The system of control should ensure that the statements are sent out in accordance with the society's policies. The statements issued by many building societies ask the recipient to send any queries direct to the external or internal auditors. This enables the auditors to judge the nature and significance of any discrepancies and to assess the system in operation for the resolving of such queries. It must, however, be stressed that it is the society's responsibility to issue statements and to process any queries arising therefrom. It must also be stressed that the monitoring by the external auditors of the system of communication is not necessarily a substitute for circularisation of a sample of investors and borrowers, whether by the internal or external auditors.

Treasury management

86 As indicated in paragraph 72, treasury management is an increasingly important aspect of a society's business. Audit tests of treasury management systems should provide assurance that (among other things):

(a) formal trading policies and dealing limits are adhered to;
(b) deals are only made with approved counterparties;
(c) staff independent of dealers check dealing slips to contract notes received from counterparties and overdue contract notes are followed up;
(d) all alterations to deal slips are authorised by dealers;
(e) sequence controls exist over deal slips;
(f) EDP deal listings are checked with deal slips by staff independent of the dealers and unmatched items followed up;
(g) there is independent review and follow-up of outstanding items on reconciliations;
(h) there is an analysis of deals by broker to ensure no undue concentration of business with any one broker;
(i) independent checks of calculations of all fees and commissions are carried out;
(j) adequate controls exist over input of market prices for revaluation purposes;
(k) that there are adequate controls over data processing;
(l) that controls over physical security of documents are adequate; and
(m) bank mandates cover non-written instructions and that these are related only to the specific accounts.

Liquid assets

87 Audit tests in relation to liquid assets should include tests of the following:

(a) whether investment is in accordance with society policy and legal requirements (paragraph 79);
(b) whether investments may only be made with appropriate authority;
(c) arrangements for the custody of title documents;
(d) independent checks of receipts and calculations of income;
(e) procedures for portfolio review.

Non-retail funds

88 The liabilities of a building society in respect of its non-retail funds and deposits may not exceed 40 per cent of the society's total liabilities (s. 7(3) as amended by SIs 1987 Nos. 378 and 2131). Audit tests should, therefore, seek assurance that the society's systems ensure that:

(a) the source and nature of funds is accurately recorded on receipt;

(b) funds are correctly classified in management information and in information provided to the Commission;

(c) management information is adequate for monitoring compliance with the limit on non-retail funds and is available on a timely basis;

(d) aggregation rules for the liabilities of associated bodies are correctly applied; and

(e) non-retail funds do not exceed 40 per cent of total liabilities.

Branches

89 Many building societies operate a network of branches. The auditors' approach to such branches will principally be determined by the degree of head office control over the accounting function and the conduct of business (e.g. decisions on the provision of mortgage finance and maintenance of mortgage records) and by the effectiveness of the society's own inspection visits. Where the branches maintain separate accounting records, the extent of audit visits will be further influenced by the assets and liabilities involved at each branch. Where the accounting records are maintained at head office rather than at the branches, the auditors should make sufficient branch visits to provide themselves with reasonable assurance that the systems of control and of inspection and report are operating satisfactorily. Particular attention should be given to exceptions to the society's normal control procedures caused by the staffing levels at smaller branches (e.g. the greater difficulty of ensuring adequate segregation of duties) and to the consequent need for an increased level of control from outside the branch.

Agencies

90 Most building societies operate a network of agencies, and the auditors will need to establish the powers and responsibilities of each agency. The systems of control and of inspection and report over such agencies must be established and maintained as with other systems, and in particular should ensure prompt returns from the agency of its receipts. It can be more difficult for a society to monitor whether or not the systems are adhered to by an agent than by a branch, as an agent is not an employee of the society operating from the society's premises. Normally auditors would not expect direct contact with an agent unless a material volume of business is carried out through an individual agency. Where the total volume of business carried out through agencies is material to the society's total business, auditors will need to consider whether it is sufficient to rely on the results of inspection of agency controls and their own tests thereon, without visiting any agencies. Where the volume of business is, or may become, material, each agency agreement should permit access by the society and its auditors to the agent's records, so far as they relate to the society's affairs.

Computer systems

91 Building societies have, in recent years, seen a major increase in the use of computers to process accounting and management information and the introduction of electronic funds transfer systems. As a result, most societies have become dependent on their computer systems to process and control data and records accurately and efficiently. Consequently, the systems of control and of inspection and report established by a society over its computer systems, and over the computer installation itself, form an integral part of the society's total systems of control. Stand-by arrangements for maintaining the integrity of the systems and the information held will be an essential part of a society's system of control. The documentation of key computer controls must be integrated within the overall documentation of a society's system of business control (paragraphs 5.3 and 5.4 of PN 1987/4).

92 As part of their assessment of the systems of control and of inspection and report, the auditors will need to consider the key controls established in each of the principal computer systems and in the computer installation or bureau. The auditors will also need to confirm, by performing specific compliance tests, that these controls have been properly maintained. In addition, it is highly desirable for auditors to be involved in reviewing significant new computer systems, or amendments to existing systems, prior to their implementation in order to satisfy themselves that the appropriate controls have been implemented before the system goes live.

93 It is important that the system of inspection and report adequately cover the society's computer systems and installations and that the detailed statement in writing available to the board (s. 71(6)) covers controls established in the computer systems and installations.

Group considerations

94 A building society may have subsidiaries or invest in other associated bodies, with certain restrictions.

95 The auditors of a building society have a right of access to accounting records of a society and a right to require information and explanations from officers of the society. These rights are extended to require subsidiaries or other associated bodies which are UK bodies corporate to give the same access and information (s. 79(4)(a) and (5)). A society having subsidiaries or other associated bodies which are not UK bodies corporate has a duty to take all reasonable steps to ensure that the auditors are afforded similar access and information (s. 79(4)(b)). Insofar as it is generally applicable, building society auditors should follow the guidance given in the Auditing Guideline 'Group financial statements — reliance on the work of other auditors'. In particular, the paragraphs on 'operational procedures' and 'further considerations' will be helpful.

96 The group accounts of a building society with subsidiaries must deal with, among other things, the income and expenditure of the society and its subsidiaries. Where the subsidiaries are limited companies, and therefore, each is required by statute to produce a profit and loss account, the auditors of the group accounts should bear in mind the difference in reporting requirements. The group auditors should obtain assurance that the audit work carried out by the auditors of the subsidiaries is sufficient to enable them to express an opinion on the income and expenditure (rather than profit or loss) of the subsidiaries for the purpose of inclusion in the society's group accounts.

97 A society has the responsibility to ensure that there are accounting records, a system of control and a system of inspection and report, in relation to the business of the society and its subsidiaries or other associated bodies linked by resolution (s. 71(10)). As explained in paragraph 2.4(f) of Prudential Note 1987/4, a society is permitted by Section 71 to view as a whole the records and systems of the group (taking, in this context, 'the group' to mean the society, its subsidiaries and its associated bodies linked by resolution). Although the systems of control have to be extended to the new areas of a society's business (PN 1987/4 paragraph 1.h), this does not mean that subsidiaries and associated bodies linked by resolution need to have the same higher standards (PN 1987/4 paragraph 1.g) of records and systems as they would if they were building societies. Thus, controls operated by the society might compensate for apparent deficiencies in controls operated at associated body level. The auditors must assess the records and systems on this basis, viewing the group as a whole.

98 A society's own systems must also be adequate for the society to monitor the activities carried out on its behalf by associated bodies not linked by resolution.

99 As part of the overall system of control in its group, a society may require some specific controls to be maintained within its subsidiaries or other associated bodies.

Where this is so, the auditors of the group may wish to seek assurance from the auditors of a subsidiary or other associated body that those specific controls are effective and have been maintained. The auditors of the subsidiary or other associated body have a duty under Section 79(4)(a) to supply information and explanations requested by the society's auditors and should ensure that the scope of their audit work enables them to do so.

Operational guidelines and materiality

The following procedures are complementary to those given in the operational guidelines referred to in the preface to this guideline.

Planning, controlling and recording

100 When planning the audit of a building society, the auditors should particularly consider the following:

(a) the requirements of the Act so far as they affect the audit and the accounts;

(b) the requirements of any relevant orders or regulations issued under statutory instrument;

(c) any relevant Building Societies Association circulars or guidance;

(d) any prudential notes or other guidance notes issued by the Commission;

(e) correspondence between the society and the Commission;

(f) the rules and memorandum of the society;

(g) the range of activities undertaken by the society;

(h) matters dealt with in paragraphs 83 to 93 of this guideline;

(i) any request from the society that the scope of the audit be expanded;

(j) the timing and nature of the audit work to be carried out to enable the auditors' report to be signed within the timetable for distribution of the summary financial statement and the report to the Commission; and

(k) the use of staff with adequate training and experience.

101 The Commission in its summary of Prudential Note 1987/1 on 'Capital Adequacy' sets out the main identifiable financial risks facing building societies as follows:

(a) the risk from a squeeze on margins due to either:

(i) competition; or

(ii) other circumstances in which it may not be possible to pass on to borrowers in full an increase in its cost of funds;

(b) the other risks from concentration in one lending market and in one main source of funds;

(c) the credit risks arising from that society's particular lending policies;

(d) the position risk on its liquid assets and fixed assets; and

(e) in the longer term, the risk of an end to the growth, or even a reduction in the size of either, or both, of the main markets for societies.

When planning an audit, auditors need to consider these risks and their significance for the society in question.

102 The board of a society should also have identified specific areas of risk in order to manage the affairs of the society in a prudent manner and establish the systems of control and of inspection and report required of every society. In order to maintain a satisfactory system the board will need to reconsider the areas of risk as circumstances change. It follows that building society auditors need to assess the areas of potential risk in planning their work to enable them to form a judgement on the compliance of the systems with the requirements of Section 71 of the Act.

103 Where a society has adopted and is exercising any of the powers to undertake activities permitted by Sections 14 to 19 of the Act or to provide services permitted by Schedule 8 to the Act, the auditors should consider those aspects of the society's business in planning their audit approach (paragraphs 27 to 30). In particular, they should bear in mind that the risk inherent in a society's wider activities may be greater than the risk associated with the traditional business of a building society. Consequently there may be greater risk of misstatement in the accounts or weaknesses in systems resulting in loss to the society's members.

104 With the statutory requirement for systems of control and of inspection and report, auditors should expect to be able to place some reliance on the work of internal auditors. They should, therefore, seek to co-ordinate their working methods and those of the internal auditors in accordance with the Auditing Guideline 'Reliance on internal audit'; careful planning will enable auditors to avoid unnecessary duplication of work.

105 With regard to recording their work and the evidence obtained, auditors should recognise that they may be contacted by the Commission in response to reports by the directors and chief executive or by the auditors (PN 1987/4 paragraph 8.6), auditors may then, or at the time of reporting, be asked to produce evidence to support their reports to the Commission, including evidence of the reasons for not commenting on any particular matter.

106 Auditors are, therefore, advised to consider carefully what records they need to maintain. They should bear in mind that records of when information was received and of its source may be helpful if the information could at some time lead to a decision to make or not to make a Section 82(8) report to the Commission.

Accounting systems

107 The Auditing Guideline 'Accounting systems' draws the attention of auditors of enterprises such as building societies to the need to consider their specific duties relating to accounting records. These requirements are set out in Sections 71, 79 and 82 of the Act. The auditors should follow the Auditing Guideline 'Accounting systems' in carrying out these specific duties.

Audit evidence

108 The auditor's operational standard states:

> "The auditor should obtain relevant and reliable audit evidence sufficient to enable him to draw reasonable conclusions therefrom"

and this is expanded on in the Auditing Guideline 'Audit evidence'.

109 The relevance of audit evidence should be assessed in relation to the various reports which building society auditors are required to make. Audit evidence should also be relevant to the nature of the business. The auditors of a building society should always remember the value of evidence obtained from independent sources and of consistent evidence obtained from different sources within the society.

110 The auditors' judgement of what is sufficient evidence to enable them to form their opinions on the annual accounts and other reports of a building society will be influenced by, among other things, their knowledge of the business of the society, the environment in which it operates and the risk of misstatement. This judgement will need to be reviewed if the society starts to undertake the new activities or to provide the new services described in paragraphs 27 to 30.

111 The extent to which reliance may be placed upon the work of internal auditors will depend upon the particular circumstances. Auditors should refer to the Auditing Guidelines 'Internal controls' (paragraph 20 in particular) and 'Reliance on internal audit'.

112 The auditors' evaluation of the system of control, assurance obtained from the internal audit function, the results of compliance tests and the auditors' assessment of materiality in particular audit areas will form the basis of their judgement of the level of substantive tests necessary to provide them with relevant and reliable audit evidence sufficient for them to form an opinion on the annual accounts and other reports. The major substantive tests should be designed to provide audit evidence concerning, among other things:

(a) investors' and borrowers' balances;
(b) existence of deeds;
(c) existence, ownership, and value of premises, equipment, vehicles, investments and cash;
(d) interest received and paid; and
(e) management expenses.

113 In some areas, such as interest received on advances to members and interest paid on shares and deposits, analytical review procedures can provide valuable audit evidence and may enable the auditors to reduce the level of other substantive tests. Similarly, the audit of management expenses may include review procedures such as comparison with the previous year's accounts and budgets and management accounts for the year under review in addition to other substantive tests.

114 Regularly published statistics indicating trends amongst building societies in general should also be examined and any variations from the trend should be investigated. These statistics are the product of regular (principally monthly) returns of financial information made by each society. This information is provided to the Commission. The Building Societies Association, the Central Statistical Office and the Department of the Environment. Auditors should be aware of these statistics and refer to the information contained therein where appropriate.

115 It is just as important for auditors to gather sufficient relevant and reliable audit evidence when forming their opinion on a society's systems as when forming an opinion on the annual accounts and other reports. Evidence of the maintenance of systems is much greater if the directors (or a committee of directors reporting to the full board) approve new procedures which materially affect the control systems, and if they minute any regular review of procedures and of the detailed written statement of the system (required by s. 71(6)). Evidence of the maintenance of inspection systems should be provided by proper documentation of inspection programmes, work carried out, conclusions reached and reports made.

Internal controls

116 The requirements of Section 71 of the Act and Prudential Note 1987/4 on 'Systems' are discussed in paragraphs 54 to 69. Together these should result in not only a strong system of internal control, but also effective inspection and often broader based internal audit procedures. Auditors should, therefore, be able to place considerable reliance on internal control in forming their opinion on the accounts, as well as carrying out their other duties and responsibilities under the Act. However, attention is drawn to the comments in the Auditing Guideline 'Internal controls' on limitations on the effectiveness of internal controls and in particular the observation that:

"No internal control system, however elaborate, can by itself guarantee efficient administration and the completeness and accuracy of the records."

117 The chief executive or individual managers of a building society will generally be able to exercise close control through their detailed personal knowledge and contact throughout the organisation. If, however, the chief executive is, or individual managers are, in a position to override controls, the system of control is incomplete. The smaller the society, the more likely that control procedures will rely extensively on the chief executive. The control and inspection activities of the board over the actions of management to whom the board delegates authority and responsibility are, therefore, particularly important and the board must ensure that the systems are such that no individual can override them; the auditors will need to consider carefully how the directors exercise their responsibilities and comply with the legal requirements.

118 Auditors should recognise that most directors are non-executive and the day-to-day management of the society is delegated to one or more full-time executives. The delegation of management functions should form part of the society's systems of control and should be recorded in the detailed systems' statement (paragraphs 58 and 59). The systems of inspection and report should provide additional assurance that delegated functions are properly controlled and carried out. The controls instituted by directors should include consideration of whether the extent of delegation is reasonable having regard to the capability and seniority of the person to whom the powers are given. As part of their examination of a society's systems, the auditors should form a view as to whether there are adequate systems to control and monitor the delegation of management functions.

119 Irrespective of his day-to-day reporting responsibility, in all cases, the head of the inspection function should always have access to the highest level of management and the board. However, particular consideration must be given to inspection and reporting procedures where there is a senior official able to influence the operation of control overall or in particular parts of the society's operations. In such a case, reporting should be direct to the board and not just to that official.

Review of financial statements

120 The auditors should consider whether the financial statements comply with all statutory requirements and other regulations. The majority of the requirements are contained in the Building Societies (Accounts and Related Provisions) Regulations 1987 (SI 1987 No. 2072). The format of the annual accounts set out in that statutory instrument should be adhered to, unless to do so (with any necessary additional information) would not present a true and fair view of the state of the society's affairs, its income and expenditure or the manner in which the business of the society has been financed and in which its financial resources have been used. Any departure from the regulations on these grounds should be recorded in the notes to the accounts together with the reasons for it and its effects (s. 73(9)). The auditors must also consider whether the accounting policies adopted are such as will enable them to express an unqualified opinion on the accounts.

121 SSAP 2 requires accounting policies to be disclosed. The Regulations require this disclosure to be in a statement of accounting policies which must include a description of policies in respect of the following:

" (a) the depreciation and diminution in value of assets;

(b) the translation of amounts denominated in foreign currencies (if applicable);

(c) the accounting for and valuation of UK Government and other securities;

(d) the valuation of investment properties (if applicable); and

(e) the provision for losses on advances and loans."

122 The Regulations do not prescribe detailed accounting policies. Auditors must satisfy themselves that the policies adopted by the society result in a true and fair view being given, are adequately disclosed and are consistently applied, for example:

(a) discounts and premiums on investments may or may not be spread over the period of maturity; investments may or may not be valued at market valuation;

(b) goodwill should be treated in accordance with the alternatives in SSAP 22, but it may arise either in the society or in a subsidiary. Because of the publication of both a society and a group income and expenditure account, any related treatment of writing-off of loans to subsidiaries would strictly be disclosed differently from the goodwill write-off to reserves. Auditors will need to consider how the writing-off of goodwill and loans can best be disclosed through the accounts and notes;

(c) the costs of establishing new branches, particularly related to new activities, can be material and not immediately matched by income. Whilst prudence and SSAP 13 would indicate that such costs would be written off immediately, the matching concept is used as a basis, for example by estate agencies, to defer revenue costs in the first few months for amortisation over a number of years. Auditors will need to consider the appropriateness of such a policy for building societies, consistency within the group but in different businesses, and, if used, the suitability of the time scale;

(d) building societies will be considering how to develop new sources of finance including the refinancing of mortgages. Auditors will need to consider how such schemes should be disclosed on or off the balance sheet, and in the notes and other statements, recognising the major implications for limits and ratios. They should also review any minutes of discussions held by the society with the Commission.

123 In reviewing the financial statements, the auditors should consider, among other things, the following matters:

(a) whether infrequent or unusual receipts or payments (by type, timing or amount) are properly and consistently treated in the financial statements (on which they are reporting) in relation to income and expenditure for the accounting period;

(b) transactions near the balance sheet date: the auditors should have regard to the requirements of SSAP 17, and in particular should examine transactions which have the effect of showing, as on the balance sheet date, a state of affairs (particularly the society's liquidity) which is materially different from that during the year and shortly after. In addition to such matters as tax or interest payments soon after the balance sheet date, items requiring particular attention are:

(i) large deposits received shortly before the year end and repaid shortly after;

(ii) large loan repayments received shortly before the year end and re-advanced on the same property shortly after;

(iii) unusual delay until after the year end in making payments in accordance with applications received before the year end for withdrawals of shares or deposits;

(iv) an abnormal year end accumulation of commitments for advances followed by the making of the advances shortly after the year end;

(v) significant items in bank reconciliation statements; and

(vi) other transactions which have a significant effect on key ratios disclosed in the annual business statement or summary financial statement.

Materiality

124 The annual accounts of a building society are required to show a true and fair view of various aspects of the society's financial position. In forming their opinion on the annual accounts of a society (or a company) auditors have to consider what is material to the true and fair view. In so doing, they must take account of, *inter alia*:

(a) the different matters on which they are reporting (e.g. income and expenditure as opposed to profit or loss);
(b) the characteristics and nature of the business of building societies as financial institutions and mutual organisations;
(c) the importance of liquidity;
(d) the absolute nature of the various limits imposed on aspects of a society's business;
(e) prudential considerations; and
(f) the views of the Commission.

125 An example of the application of the concept of materiality to particular circumstances is found in a decision by the Central Office of the Registry of Friendly Societies in March 1987. The decision relates to an application by the Thrift and Cheshunt Building Societies for confirmation of a proposed transfer of engagements. Auditors may wish to refer to published extracts from the decision by the Central Office — these are to be found at Annex B on page 60 of the 'Annual Report of the Building Societies Commission 1986-87'. The following points emerge from the decision:

(a) where a full assessment of the financial position of a society has to take account of a number of factors, a change in any one of those factors may of itself constitute a material change in the financial position of a society;
(b) a change within a range of variation previously experienced by the society may be material even though such variations have not in the past accompanied a loss of confidence in the society or indicated serious financial difficulties;
(c) the fact that a change has been explained to the board does not make it immaterial for the members;
(d) a change which has caused the board to take corrective action may nevertheless be material to members;
(e) the uncertainties which face a building society in respect of both inflows and outflows mean that it is unwise to regard any fall in liquidity as temporary until it has actually been reversed;
(f) commitments which are not yet legally binding should not be ignored or regarded as entirely in the control of the society but should be considered in the light of the going concern concept and the need for a society to retain the confidence of its investors.

Auditors should bear these additional considerations in mind when forming a view on whether or not a matter is material in the context of a particular building society audit or a particular report such as that required on a merger (paragraphs 160 to 162).

126 Materiality in the context of financial statements can be explained in relation to the amounts involved and what they stand for in explaining the business of a society. Materiality, in the context of systems and the auditors' report on systems, is a more difficult concept. Although auditors are charged with the responsibility of reporting on whether or not the systems comply with the requirements of the Act, they should not lose sight of the real purpose of their report, which is like that of the annual opinion of the directors and chief executive (PN 1987/4, paragraph 8.1):

"(a) to focus the attention of the board on the need to review and develop systems in line with the changing business environment (risk) to afford adequate protection to investors' funds; and

(b) to be the first step in satisfying the Commission that the board has done so."

127 The auditors are not required to express opinions on the commercial management of the affairs of the society or its subsidiaries and associated bodies. Auditors should however, consider whether the system of control of the business is providing directors and senior management with adequate information on a timely basis. The Commission would expect auditors to comment in their report under Section 82 if this is not the case.

Reporting to management

128 The Auditing Guideline 'Internal controls' emphasises the importance of reporting significant weaknesses in internal controls to management. General guidance on reporting such weaknesses is given in the Auditing Guideline 'Reports to management'.

129 Not only the auditors but also the directors and chief executive of a building society have to report to the Commission on compliance with the Act's requirements for systems of control and of inspection and report. The auditors should, therefore arrange for an exchange of views on the systems with the board, or a committee of the board, in advance of making their report to the Commission. Before the meeting of the board, or its committee, the auditors should provide written notification of the matters they wish to draw to the attention of the board including those matters on which they propose to report to the Commission (this need not be a full management letter but just a note of the key issues). At the meeting, the auditors should explain any matters arising from their audit.

130 Auditors should remember that they are required to send their report to the Commission via the society (s. 82(5)) and the Act gives the society's board an opportunity to comment on the auditors' report. Just as financial statements are signed by directors before the auditors' report to the members is issued, it would be desirable for the directors and chief executive to follow a similar procedure (which can be achieved within the statutory framework) by preparing their report to the Commission in advance of the auditors' report. Auditors are, therefore, advised to agree with the board a timetable for preparing, discussing and submitting their reports.

Reporting to members

On the annual accounts, directors' report and business statement

131 The auditors' report must be addressed to the members of the society. The matters on which the auditors must report are set out in Section 78. As is the case with all auditors' reports, it should clearly indicate those areas of the annual accounts and other reports on which the auditors are reporting. It is usual to deal with this by stating the relevant page numbers in the report. The pages indicated should include those parts of the annual business statement on which the auditors are required to report. The auditors are not required to report on the section of the annual business statement giving information relating to directors and other officers.

132 Set out below is a form of unqualified auditors' report:

AUDITORS' REPORT TO THE MEMBERS OF ... BUILDING SOCIETY

We have audited the accounts on pages ... to ... in accordance with approved Auditing Standards. In our opinion the accounts give a true and fair view of the state of affairs of the Society at ..., of the income and expenditure of the Society for the year then ended, and of the manner in which the business of the Society was financed and in which its financial resources were used during the year.

We have examined the annual business statement on pages ... to ... other than the details of directors and officers upon which we are not required to report. In our opinion the information which we have examined gives a true representation of those matters referred to therein.

We have examined the directors' report on pages ... to ... In our opinion the information given therein is consistent with the accounting records and the annual accounts.

In our opinion the accounts, the business statement and the directors' report have each been prepared so as to conform to the requirements of Part VIII of the Building Societies Act 1986 and regulations thereunder.

Auditors

Date

133 Where a society has subsidiaries the auditors will also be required to report to the members on the group accounts. They should bear in mind, in particular, that they are reporting on the income and expenditure of the group which may include limited company subsidiaries which would normally report profit or loss rather than income and expenditure (paragraph 96 above).

134 Set out below is a form of unqualified auditors' report in respect of a building society, its subsidiaries and associated bodies:

AUDITORS' REPORT TO THE MEMBERS OF ... BUILDING SOCIETY

We have audited the accounts on pages ... to ... in accordance with approved Auditing Standards. In our opinion the accounts give a true and fair view of the state of affairs of the Society and of the Group at ..., of the income and expenditure of the Society and of the Group for the year then ended, and of the manner in which the business of the Group was financed and in which the Group's financial resources were used during the year.

We have examined the annual business statement on pages ... to ... other than the details of directors and officers upon which we are not required to report. In our opinion the information which we have examined gives a true representation of those matters referred to therein.

We have examined the directors' report on pages ... to ... In our opinion the information given therein is consistent with the accounting records and the annual accounts.

In our opinion the accounts, the business statement and the directors' report have each been prepared so as to conform to the requirements of Part VIII of the Building Societies Act 1968 and regulations thereunder.

Auditors

Date

On Section 65 transactions

135 Each building society is required to maintain a register containing copies of certain transactions or arrangements made for a director, or person connected with a director, during the current financial year or previous ten financial years (s. 68(1)). The transactions to be recorded in the register are those falling within Section 65(1) and above certain values (s. 68(1), (7), (8)).

136 Building societies are required by Section 68(3) to make available for inspection by members at certain times a statement containing the requisite particulars of transactions recorded in the Section 68 register. The auditors are required to examine the statement and report to the members on this statement (s. 78(9)).

137 The particulars required by Section 68 to be set out in the statement are the requisite particulars of those transactions and arrangements which were included in the register at any time during the last complete financial year. There are thus two stages to auditors' enquiries:

(a) whether the statement covers all transactions included in the register during the year; and

(b) whether the statement gives the requisite particulars of those transactions.

The auditors are not required to undertake work specifically designed to identify transactions between the society and directors not disclosed in the society's register.

138 Where there are no transactions recorded in the register, the Commission will, nevertheless, expect a 'nil' return and auditors should report on that nil return as appropriate.

139 The auditors' report (which should be annexed to the statement) should state whether in their opinion the statement contains the particulars required by Section 68. If the auditors are of the opinion that it does not, they must include in their report a statement giving the requisite particulars, but only in so far as they are reasonably able to do so (s. 78(10)).

140 A form of report on the statement of Section 65 transactions is set out below. It deals with the situation in which the auditors have no information of Section 65 transactions other than those disclosed by the society and they are satisfied that the requisite particulars have been given in respect of those transactions. (The auditors are not, therefore, in the position of having to form an adverse opinion and give the requisite particulars in so far as they are reasonably able to do so.)

AUDITORS' REPORT TO THE MEMBERS OF ... BUILDING SOCIETY ON THE STATEMENT OF PARTICULARS OF TRANSACTIONS AND ARRANGEMENTS INCLUDED IN THE SECTION 68(1) REGISTER AT ANY TIME DURING THE YEAR ENDED ...

We have examined the foregoing statement of particulars of transactions and arrangements with directors and persons connected with them falling within Section 65(1) of the Building Societies Act 1986.

In our opinion the statement contains the requisite particulars, as required by Section 68 of the Building Societies Act 1986, in relation to those transactions recorded by the society in the register of transactions and arrangements maintained under Section 68(1) of that Act.

Auditors

Date

On the summary financial statement

141 The summary financial statement must include a statement of the auditors' opinion on the summary's consistency with the annual accounts, business statement and directors' report and with its conformity with Section 76 and relevant regulations. The auditors do not report on the summary financial statement in true and fair terms.

142 Set out below is a form of unqualified report on the summary financial statement:

AUDITORS' REPORT TO THE MEMBERS AND DEPOSITORS OF ... BUILDING SOCIETY ON THE SUMMARY FINANCIAL STATEMENT FOR THE YEAR ENDED ...

We have examined the summary financial statement [above/overleaf].

In our opinion the summary financial statement is consistent with the accounts, business statement and directors' report for the year ended ... and conforms to the requirements of Section 76 of the Building Societies Act 1986 and regulations thereunder.

Auditors

Date

Qualified opinions

143 Auditors of building societies are under a duty in preparing their report to members under Section 78 to carry out such investigations as will enable them to form an opinion on the accounting records, on the systems of control and of inspection and report and on agreement of the annual accounts with the underlying records (s. 79(1)).

144 If the auditors are of the opinion that the annual accounts are not in agreement with the accounting records, they are to state that fact in their report to the members (s. 79(2)).

145 If the auditors fail to obtain all the information and explanations and the access to documents which they consider necessary for the purposes of their audit, they are required to state that fact in their report to the members (s. 79(6)).

146 There is no express requirement for the auditors to report to the members their findings as regards accounting records and systems, even if their investigations cause them to form an adverse opinion on these matters. If, however, the grounds for a qualification of the auditors' report to the Commission are such that the annual accounts do not give a true and fair view, the auditors should include the matter in their report to the members, in addition to reporting it, in all cases, to the Commission on accounting records and systems (s. 82(2)).

147 Where the auditors are of the view that a qualified report may be necessary (for whatever reason), they should discuss the matter fully with the directors of the society. If the auditors remain of the view that they must qualify their opinion, the auditors should advise the directors to discuss the matter with the Commission. If the directors will not, for whatever reason, raise the matter with the Commission, the auditors should normally inform the directors of the society of their intention and approach the Commission themselves.

Reporting to the Commission

To the Commission — annual report

148 The auditors of a building society are required to report to the Commission on the conduct of specified aspects of the business of the society during the financial year (s. 82(1)). The report must state the auditors' opinion on whether or not the society has complied with each of the requirements of Sections 12 and 71 as respects:

(a) the accounting records;
(b) the system of control of its business and records;
(c) the system of inspection and report; and
(d) the system of safe custody of documents.

149 The Building Societies Commission will presume, unless the auditors' report indicates to the contrary, that the auditors have addressed the issues indicated in Prudential Note 1987/4 (paragraphs 54 to 69 above and Appendix). It is not obligatory for a society to follow the guidance given by the Commission in its note; it is for the directors to decide whether the requirements of Section 71 can be satisfied by other means. However, the Commission has stated (PN 1986/1, paragraph 10) that where a board considers that it can disregard a specific recommendation in a Prudential Note but still protect investors and meet the criteria of prudent management, the Commission would expect the board to consult and satisfy the Commission first. Where this is the case, auditors should obtain evidence that the Commission has been so satisfied.

150 Circumstances which should normally lead to a qualification of a report on systems include:

"(a) the absence of accounting records, or of systems, or of documentation of those systems, necessary to enable directors or the society to discharge their duties;

(b) a significant weakness or failure in any of these which occurred during the year; and

(c) other matters which resulted, individually or collectively, in there not being reasonable assurance that the requirements of Section 71 have been complied with." (PN 1987/4, paragraph 8.3).

151 Auditors will also find it helpful to note that the Commission accepts that qualifications in the auditors' report do not necessarily call into question the adequacy of protection of investors. Of particular interest to the Commission in considering the effect of a systems weakness on investors' security will be timeliness and effectiveness of corrective action. The Commission may wish to have discussions with a society's board and auditors in order to:

"(a) establish whether or not the matter reported is prudentially significant or not;

(b) understand any proposals for corrective action arising from the report; and

(c) where appropriate, agree a basis for monitoring the implementation and effectiveness of the proposals." (PN 1987/4, paragraph 8.6).

152 The Commission does not require auditors to report all omissions, weaknesses and failures, however minor, in the existence, nature, scope and effectiveness of records and systems. Rather, it requires (PN 1987/4, paragraph 8.2) reports to include matters which individually or collectively are, in the opinion of the auditors, significant and result in there not being reasonable assurance that the requirements of Section 71 have been complied with. The Commission does not wish to receive reports of minor deficiencies in the accounting records or systems of control and of inspection and report, providing that the directors and chief executive and the auditors themselves are satisfied that the deficiencies are not symptomatic of more serious problems (PN 1987/4, paragraph 8.2). The Commission does not expect auditors to report on management's business judgements and decisions unless these are relevant to assessment of systems (PN 1987/4, paragraph 8.4). The assessment of whether the society's affairs have been conducted with prudence and integrity and with adequate professional skills is for the board and the Commission. Nevertheless, to the extent that they are aware of circumstances that could lead to a report under Section 82(8), auditors must themselves make an assessment of whether the society's affairs have been conducted with prudence.

153 Set out below are the likely elements of a report to the Building Societies Commission (although not all would necessarily appear in every such report):

AUDITORS' REPORT TO THE BUILDING SOCIETIES COMMISSION ON... BUILDING SOCIETY FOR THE YEAR ENDED...

We have examined the accounting records, the systems of control and of inspection and report and the system of safe custody of documents maintained by the society during the year ended...

Our examination was carried out in accordance with the Auditing Guideline 'Building Societies in the United Kingdom'.[1] The scope of our work was limited to consideration

[1] These words do not mean that this Auditing Guideline has the status of an Auditing Standard or that any of the procedures described are to be regarded as mandatory. Paragraph 14 of the Explanatory Foreword to Auditing Standards and Guidelines (revised version, issued January 1989) states that there may be occasions when the auditor considers it appropriate to depart from the guidance given in an Auditing Guideline. The Building Societies Commission has confirmed that it is aware of this and that a report including these words will not necessarily imply that there have been no departures from this Auditing Guideline.

of whether the foregoing records and systems complied with the requirements of Sections 12 and 71 of the Building Societies Act 1986 (the Act).

In our opinion during the year ended...

either [some or all of (a) to (d)]

(a) [except for the matters set out at paragraph x of the appendix to this report/ subject to the matters set out at paragraph x of the appendix to this report], the accounting records complied with the requirements of Section 71 of the Act;

(b) [except for the matters set out at paragraph x of the appendix to this report/ subject to the matters set out at paragraph x of the appendix to this report], the system of control of the business and records of the society complied with the requirements of Section 71 of the Act;

(c) [except for the matters set out at paragraph x of the appendix to this report/ subject to the matters set out at paragraph x of the appendix to this report], the system of inspection and report complied with the requirements of Section 71 of the Act; and

(d) [except for the matters set out at paragraph x of the appendix to this report/ subject to the matters set out at paragraph x of the appendix to this report], the system of safe custody of documents complied with the requirement of Section 12(12) of the Act.

and/or [some or all of the following or other qualification (paragraphs 154 and 155)] the accounting records/systems of control/systems of inspection and report/system of safe custody of documents were not established and maintained in accordance with the requirements of [specify section and sub-section of the Act] in the respects set out in the appendix attached to this report.

Auditors

Date

154 The question of whether it is appropriate to report "did comply except for" or "did not comply in the respects set out" is a question of degree. Auditors must use their professional judgement to determine which is the more appropriate form of report.

155 The Commission has given guidance on the criteria for determining compliance and non-compliance and on the matters to be reported to it in paragraphs 8.2 and 8.3 of Prudential Note 1987/4 (Appendix).

156 As with audit reports on financial statements (see the Auditing Standard 'Qualifications in audit reports'), qualifications will depend upon the particular circumstances. However, distinctions may be drawn between circumstances of uncertainty and those of disagreement, and between matters which are material but not fundamental and those which are fundamental. Thus, a 'subject to' qualification might be appropriate when the auditors have been unable to test whether part of the system complied with the requirements of the Act, for example because of accidental destruction of some records; an 'except for' qualification might be appropriate when the auditors are of the opinion that controls over some particular aspect of a society's business did not comply with the requirements of the Act but that the systems as a whole complied with each requirement of the Act.

157 Where a society had, at any time during the year to which the report relates, subsidiaries or other associated bodies linked by resolution, the auditors are also required (s. 82(4)) to report on compliance with Section 71 in its application to the society, its subsidiaries and other associated bodies linked by resolution.

158 The directors and chief executive of the society are also required to report to the

Commission their opinion whether the requirements of Section 71 have been complied with (s. 71(11)). The Act gives the directors and chief executive three months after the end of the financial year in which to make their report to the Commission but gives the auditors between 72 and 90 days (depending upon agreement with the society) to send to the society their report to the Commission. Within 90 days of the year end, the society is required to send the report to the Commission, together with any comments which the directors wish to make (s. 82(5)). If the directors make any comments on the auditors' report to the Commission, they must send a copy of their comments to the auditors before they send them to the Commission (s. 82(7)).

159 Auditors should at the outset of their engagement discuss with the society's board the timing of the auditors' Section 82 report and the Section 71(11) report of the directors and chief executive.

On merger or conversion to a public limited company

160 When building societies propose to merge (whether by amalgamation, transfer of engagements or partial transfer of engagements) each society is required to send a statement to members. The contents of the statement are set out in paragraph 1(4) of Schedule 16 to the Act and in a joint Procedural Note issued by the Commission and the Registry of Friendly Societies. The statement must set out, among other things, the financial position of each society and the key features of the merger agreement, it must be prepared to the same standards as apply to financial statements and directors' reports under the Act. The Commission requires 'letters of comfort' (which will not be published) from each society's auditors before it will approve the Schedule 16 statements. The auditors' letters should state ('Merger Procedures' Guidance Note Section 5.3) whether:

(a) unaudited figures in the statement are reasonable and have been correctly abstracted from the society's records;
(b) the financial information is reasonable in the context in which it appears; and
(c) in reviewing the data relating to the statement anything has come to their attention which would cast doubt on the directors' statement about significant changes.

161 Auditors may also be required (Procedural Note, Annex B paragraphs 3 to 5) to state their opinion of:

(a) outline plans and timetables for integration of accounting, control and inspection systems; and
(b) arrangements to ensure continuity over the integration of accounting records, the system of control, the system of inspection and report and management information.

162 The Schedule 16 statement is intended to give a picture of the relative financial positions of the societies proposing to merge. Where different accounting policies could result in some loss of comparability between the societies, adjustments may be necessary. Any differences or adjustments should be explained. The auditors should consider whether the information given is comparable and be satisfied that any adjustments are reasonable (Procedural Note, Annex C paragraph 8).

163 In order to convert to a public limited company (and thus cease to be a building society), a building society is required by Schedule 17 to the Act to make a transfer statement to members. The statement is similar to that required for a merger. Auditors will be required to report upon the current financial position of the society and either the forecasts for a specially formed company or the financial details of an existing transferee company and its position after transfer.

164 In the case of either a merger or a conversion to a public limited company, auditors are advised to discuss with the Commission what assurance it is seeking and the terms of their engagement. When reporting to the Commission, auditors should state clearly the scope of the work they have carried out and any limitations on that work, including any limitations in the terms of their engagement.

Other reports

165 Under Section 82(9) of the Act, the Treasury may make an order which requires building society auditors to provide information to the Commission. Any such order would set out the circumstances in which the information must be provided and the nature of the information. Were such an order to be made, auditors would be under a duty to provide the information and that duty would outweigh any obligation of confidence which the auditors may owe to their building society client.

Protecting the investments of shareholders or depositors

The statutory provision

166 Section 82(8) of the Act gives the auditors of a building society an express statutory right to provide the Building Societies Commission with information when either the auditors or the Commission are satisfied that it is expedient for them to do so in order to protect the investments of shareholders or depositors.

167 In December 1986, the Commission issued Prudential Note 1986/2 on 'Relationships between Auditors and the Commission'. That Note sets out amongst other things the Commission's understanding of the effect of Section 82(8) of the Act and the circumstances in which the Commission would expect building society auditors to take the initiative and approach the Commission with information in order to protect the investments of shareholders or depositors. Auditors should be aware of the Commission's view of Section 82(8), as set out in the Prudential Note.

168 Confidentiality is an implied term of auditors' contracts with their clients but in Section 82(8) circumstances it does not prevail since auditors are entitled to provide information relating to the conduct of the society's business, or the business of any of its subsidiaries or other associated bodies, to the Commission "notwithstanding any obligation of confidence incumbent on them". Furthermore, auditors have this right to provide information to the Commission in order to protect the investments of shareholders or depositors whether or not to do so would be contrary to the interests of the society. The "obligation of confidence" referred to in Section 82(8) is that which is owed by the building society auditors to the building society and its associated bodies. The Commission recognises that it would not be appropriate for the auditors to report to the Commission information which they have obtained through their professional relationship with another client which is not the building society's associated body.

169 Auditors should realise that there are circumstances in which Section 82(8) would not provide protection, for example, where they could be held to have acted maliciously or in bad faith. The Act does not, therefore, provide complete immunity from all types of legal action by parties affected, or subsequently affected, by the auditors' action in reporting to the Commission. Auditors may, therefore, wish to consider taking legal or other professional advice before making the decision whether or in what manner to report, and in order, for example, to ensure that the form and content of their report are such as to secure the protection of Section 82(8) and that it only includes relevant material. However, auditors should recognise that speed of reporting will often be important in order to protect the investments of shareholders or depositors. There is no protection given by the Act if the auditors fail to report to the Commission.

The normal relationship between societies, auditors and the Commission

170 Prudential Note 1986/2 makes it clear, at paragraph 6, that the long-established relationships between the Commission (or its predecessor the Registry of Friendly Societies), auditors and societies are to continue. Section 82(8) does not replace those relationships, nor is it intended to have a role in the normal relationships between auditors and the Commission. The primary responsibility for providing the Commission with information remains with the directors of building societies.

171 Section 82(8) does, however, provide a mechanism for coping with the exceptional circumstance in which it appears to the auditors, or to the Commission, that the investments of shareholders or depositors would be most effectively protected by the auditors providing information directly to the Commission and, if necessary, without the knowledge of the society. (PN 1986/2, paragraphs 12 and 13).

Protection of investments — the auditors' judgement

172 Section 82(8) operates for the protection of the investments of shareholders or depositors. It is only when there is actual or potential risk material to the security of the investments of shareholders or depositors that those investments may require protection by the use of this provision. The source of the risk is not significant in the context of Section 82(8), what is significant is its effect or potential effect.

173 Auditors should satisfy themselves that their decision will stand up to examination at a future date on the basis of the following considerations:

— what the auditors knew at the time;

— what they should have known in the course of their audit work;

— what they should have concluded; and

— what they should have done.

174 Speed of reporting under Section 82(8) will often be important to the protection of the investments of shareholders or depositors. Auditors should report as soon as they reasonably can after forming the view that it is expedient to do so in order to protect the investments of shareholders or depositors. This may well mean reporting under Section 82(8) in advance of making reports under other provisions of the Building Societies Act 1986, principally the Section 78 report to members and the Section 82(1) report to the Commission. For this reason, a firm of auditors should ensure:

(a) that all its staff working on building society audits are aware of the provisions of Section 82(8) and are able to identify situations in which it might operate; and

(b) that satisfactory procedures exist for any information obtained by audit staff in the course of an audit and likely to be relevant in a Section 82(8) context to be passed on to the partner responsible for the audit without unnecessary delay.

175 Auditors cannot, however, be expected to be aware of all circumstances which, had they known of them, would have led them to exercise their right to report under Section 82(8). That section does not require auditors to change the scope of their audit work, nor the frequency or timing of their audit visits; they have no obligation to seek out grounds for making a report under Section 82(8), i.e. the section does not place an obligation on auditors to conduct their work in such a way that there is reasonable certainty that they will discover circumstances of the kind described in paragraph 172. It is only when auditors become aware in the ordinary course of their audit work of circumstances which might indicate an actual or potential risk material to the security of investments of shareholders or depositors that they should then make detailed enquiries with Section 82(8) specifically in mind.

176 Auditors should ensure that they are made aware of any other relationship which may exist between any department of their firm and the building society which could affect their work. As noted in paragraph 169, the Act does not give protection to auditors if a matter is not reported to the Commission. Auditors should, therefore ensure that they are informed of all potentially 'reportable' matters by all other departments within their firm which have a relationship with the building society. It would, therefore, be prudent for such firms to establish adequate systems of inter-departmental communication to ensure any matters which may give rise to a report under Section 82(8) are brought to the attention of the auditors. However, the Commission expects building societies to advise their auditors when they appoint a third party (including another department of the same firm) to review, investigate or report on any aspects of their records and systems and to provide them with copies of reports by such a third party promptly after their receipt.

177 In forming a view as to whether it is expedient to report a matter to the Commission in order to protect the investments of shareholders or depositors, auditors should: (a) take into account the degree of probability that there is an actual or potential risk material to the security of investments of shareholders or depositors; and (b) follow the procedures in making enquiries and obtaining and assessing relevant evidence which are a normal part of forming a professional judgement in relation to an audit.

178 Appendix — Prudential Note 1987/4 — Systems

1 Introduction

1.a The role of this note is twofold:

(a) to explain to societies and their external auditors the purpose underlying Sections 71 and 82 of the Building Societies Act 1986; and

(b) to set out what the Commission considers to be the key issues that a society needs to address if its systems are to satisfy the requirements of Section 71 of the Act, thereby satisfying the fifth criterion of prudent management, and to some degree the seventh, in Section 45(3) of the Act. The Commission will presume that these issues have been considered by a society's board and its external auditors in preparing their respective reports to the Commission under Sections 71 and 82.

The purpose and applications of Sections 71 and 82 of the Act

1.b Experience in building societies and other financial institutions has demonstrated the critical importance for the protection of investors of having adequate systems. That need is enhanced by the increasing complexity of societies' operations, and the increasing pace of change and risks in financial markets. Section 71 accordingly generally strengthened the provisions of previous legislation, requiring societies to maintain adequate accounting records and to establish and maintain systems of control of business and inspection and report, and codified best practice. The Act also introduced a new requirement for explicit reports by the board and by auditors to the Commission on compliance with the strengthened requirements on systems.

1.c The Act specifies the respective roles of the board, external auditors and Commission. As with other prudential provisions, it is for the board to ensure that the requirements of Section 71 are being met and to be ready to demonstrate that to the Commission. The Commission see as the essential elements in giving effect to this:

(a) the board establishing arrangements for the continuous review of systems including systems relative to new business;

(b) confirmation to the society's external auditors that appropriate arrangements have been established and maintained during the reporting period;

(c) the board's assessment of whether the society has complied with the requirements of the Act for the period under review, and where necessary the identification of matters which the board proposes to rectify together with corrective actions proposed;

(d) the preparation and submission of the opinions required by the board and the auditors to the Commission; and

(e) the discussion, on a confidential basis, with the Commission of these opinions and, where appropriate, actions taken or planned.

Satisfying the requirements of the Act

1.d The Note sets out the main issues which, in the opinion of the Commission, need to be addressed by the board and chief executive. The Note provides a framework which the Commission believes can be applied to all societies. However, the Commission recognises that there is considerable diversity in the scale and scope of the societies' operations. Therefore, in forming their opinions, the board and chief executive of a society will need to consider these issues having regard to the particular characteristics, circumstances and business strategy of their society.

1.e The Commission will presume that, in relation to the reports received, the issues set out in this Note, as with other Prudential Notes, will have been addressed. It is not obligatory for a society to follow the guidance and it is for it to decide whether the requirements of Section 71 of the Act can be satisfied by other means. The auditor would also have to be similarly satisfied. Where a society departs from the guidance it must be ready at some stage to satisfy the Commission that it is nevertheless meeting the requirements of Section 71 and so the fifth criterion of prudent management in Section 45(3). This requirement may arise during the course of the Commission's normal prudential contact with a society, an inspection visit or as part of the annual review meeting.

Auditing Practices Committee

1.f The Auditing Practices Committee of the accountancy bodies will shortly be issuing to auditors a revision of the Auditing Guideline for Building Societies. That will set out more fully the professional requirements in respect of the report by the auditors.

Business standards

1.g The 1986 Act recognises that the board and management of a society have a fiduciary duty to the members of the society; the duty is analogous to that of the board and management of a public company to its shareholders. A society's board and management also have an extra duty of care in respect of investors' (shareholders' and depositors') money placed with the society. Hence the requirement to meet the criteria of prudent management. This extra duty of care laid on a society means that it needs to maintain a higher level of business standards than that for the generality of businesses in respect of those activities which relate to, or have a direct consequence for, investors' funds.

1.h Moreover, the fundamental change over the last few years in the markets in which societies are operating, to which the Commission drew attention in the Response to the Consultation on Capital Adequacy (paragraphs R5.2 to 5.6), has increased the requirements for management systems just as it has for capital. Societies need the capacity to assess more quickly the potential consequences of decisions, to carry through decisions taken, and to monitor the outcome. The systems of control also have to be extended into the new areas of a society's business.

2. Statutory background

2.1 Section 76 of the 1962 Act required every building society to:

"(a) cause to be kept proper books of account with respect to its transactions and its assets and its liabilities; and

(b) establish and maintain a system of control and inspection of its books of account and a system for supervising its cash holdings and all receipts and remittances."

Proper books of account were not deemed to have been kept (sub-section 2) unless they were such as to give a true and fair view of the state of affairs of the society and explain its transactions. There was also a specific requirement for every society to establish and maintain a system to ensure the safe custody of all documents of title belonging to the society, and of the deeds relating to property mortgaged to the society.

2.2 Section 71 of the 1986 Act develops in more explicit terms the scope of the requirements for accounts, records and systems and codifies best practice as previously promoted by the Registry of Friendly Societies. In particular it now expressly requires a society to establish and maintain a 'system of control of its business' covering the totality of the business process. Further, Section 45(10) makes it clear that "'business' includes business which the society proposes to carry on" and "the business of the society includes, where other bodies are associated with it, ... the business of those associated bodies".

2.3 Section 71 of the 1986 Act states that every building society shall cause accounting records to be kept in accordance with the section. It includes a list of:

(a) the minimum objectives of the accounting records of a society; and

(b) the minimum contents of such accounting records.

2.4 Section 71 states that every building society shall establish and maintain systems of control of its business and records and of inspection and report, in accordance with the section. It includes:

(a) the definition of the systems of control as a system for the control of the conduct of its business in accordance with the Act and the decisions of the board of directors and for the control of the accounting and other records of the business;

(b) a definition of the system of inspection and report as a system of inspection on behalf of and report to the board of directors on the operation of the system of control of the society's business and records;

(c) a specification of the minimum objectives of the systems of control and of inspection and report;

(d) a provision that no such system of control shall be treated as established or maintained unless there is kept available to the board a detailed statement in writing of the system as in operation for the time being;

(e) a provision that the systems of control and of inspection and report must provide that the information made available to the board, and to the Commission, is sufficiently accurate for its purposes; and

(f) a provision that where a society has subsidiaries or bodies linked by resolution (the group) the society shall secure that the group keeps such accounting records, and establishes and maintains such systems of control and of inspection and report that will enable the society to comply with the requirements of Section 71 in relation to the business of the group taken as a whole.

2.5 There is a further requirement introduced by Section 71(11). A society's directors are required within a period of three months after the end of the society's financial year to make and send to the Commission a statement of their opinion as to whether the requirements of the section have been complied with in respect of that year. The statement is to be signed by the chairman and by the chief executive. In addition to the opinion expressed by the directors and chief executive, a society's auditors are required by Section 82 of the Act to report to the Commission whether in their opinion the society has complied with Section 71.

3. Accounting records and systems

3.1 The principal reasons why a building society needs to maintain adequate accounting and other records include:

(a) to provide the directors and management of the society with adequate financial information to enable them to conduct its business in a prudent manner on a day-to-day basis;

(b) to enable the directors of a society to fulfil their statutory duties as regards preparing annual accounts in accordance with Section 72 and regulations made under Section 73 of the Act;

(c) to safeguard the assets of the society and the interests of investors; and

(d) to provide the directors and management of the society with sufficiently accurate and timely information to enable them to submit the information required or requested by the Commission.

3.2 When forming their opinion on whether the accounting and other records are adequate, the board, chief executive and auditors of a society need to satisfy themselves that they are:

(a) such that they capture and record on a timely basis and in an orderly fashion every transaction and commitment which a society enters into with sufficient information in respect of each to explain (other than insignificant assets or liabilities in respect of the management of the society):

(i) its nature and purpose;

(ii) the asset(s) and/or liability(ies), actual and contingent, which arise or may arise from it; and

(iii) the income and/or expenditure, current and deferred, which arise from it (them).

(b) maintained in an integrated and orderly manner to disclose, with reasonable accuracy and promptness, the state of the business at any time.

4. Systems of business control

Organisational control systems

4.1 Societies, in common with good practice elsewhere, need:

(a) clearly defined organisational arrangements together with a defined structure of authorities and responsibilities distinguishing between decisions to be reserved for the board and those to be delegated to managers and other employees; and

(b) arrangements for reviewing the compliance and effectiveness of organisational controls.

4.2 In forming their opinion on systems of business control, the board, chief executive and auditors of a society need to establish whether:

(a) the society's overall organisational arrangements are adequately defined and documented, for example through an organisation manual;

(b) the society's decision-making processes together with authority limits and responsibilities are properly defined and documented, for example through operating manuals; and

(c) compliance with approved authority limits is effectively monitored and controlled.

Management information system

4.3 Section 71(7) requires the board and management of each society to maintain information systems to:

(a) enable directors to direct and control the society's business (which includes the business it proposes to carry on) — Section 71(7)(a); and

(b) provide the information required by the Commission in its role of prudential supervisor — Section 71 (7)(b).

4.4 In evaluating whether a society has complied with Section 71(7)(a), the board and management of a society need to satisfy themselves that:

(a) the information is sufficient to enable the board to determine whether it is meeting the criteria of prudent management;

(b) the information available for the different areas of a society's business is sufficient for the proper assessment of the potential risks for the society and the proper determination of its need for capital and liquidity;

(c) the information available is sufficiently comprehensive to provide the board with a clear statement of the performance and financial position of the society;

(d) management information reports are prepared at a frequency consistent with the dynamics of the business area reported on;

(e) actual performance is compared with planned or budgeted performance; and

(f) sufficient attention is focused on key factors affecting income and expenditure and that appropriate performance indicators are employed.

4.5 In forming a view on whether the management information system is sufficiently comprehensive, the board and management of a society need to consider whether, where relevant, the substance of reports provides a clear statement of:

(a) the capital position of the society;

(b) its liquidity position;

(c) the positions and exposures arising from treasury management operations;

(d) the balance sheet ratios in relation to the 'nature limits' set out in the 1986 Act, Sections 7(3), 8(1), 20(2) and (3), and 21(3);

(e) profits and losses, assets and liabilities, and funds flows; and

(f) the profitability of products, services and subsidiaries.

Information for the Commission

4.6 Section 71 (7)(b) requires the systems of control and of inspection and report to be maintained so as to ensure that the information reported to the Commission is sufficiently accurate for its purpose and is regularly reported. Because of the fiduciary duty of a society to account properly for investors' and borrowers' balances, it is expected that actual outturn financial information will be available sufficiently promptly and accurately. In the case of items requiring estimates or judgement by management there will inevitably be a degree of approximation involved. In these cases, whether they relate to outturn information or forecasts, the approximations should be capable of being clearly explained, and should be based on stated assumptions.

4.7 The Commission recognises that there will be other circumstances where, to enable a return to be made available to the Commission on time, a certain element of approximation may be acceptable. In these circumstances the amount of approximation should give a fair representation of the matters being reported. In specific cases the Commission may provide further guidance on required accuracy and acceptable degrees of approximation in the guidance notes for particular returns.

Planning systems

4.8 The board and management of a society have to satisfy the criteria of prudent management not only in respect of its present business but also the further business of the society. For this reason, the board and management need to satisfy the Commission that not only are they currently meeting the criteria of prudent management but that they also have the capacity and intention to continue to do so. A satisfactory planning system is essential for this purpose. It will be for each society to decide what is an appropriate planning horizon and to maintain and develop planning systems appropriate to its individual circumstances and the changing business environment.

4.9 It is important to have an integrated system for planning, budgeting, financial accounting, monitoring of actual against budget and feedback of results into management decisions and back into the planning process. The planning-related issues on which the board and management need to satisfy themselves in relation to the particular circumstances and strategic direction of the individual society are:

General

(a) the planning system is clearly defined, appropriately documented and planning related tasks and decision-making are clearly allocated within the organisation;

(b) the conclusions, recommendations, projections and assumptions set out in any plan are adequately supported by analysis, and are based on adequate data obtained from both internal and external sources, and are properly documented for comparison with actuals;

(c) consideration of a range of possible outcomes in relation to varying risks and the need for an appropriate level of capital backing;

Short-term planning

(d) directors and management have available to them adequate short-term financial and operating plans as a basis for measuring performance and taking tactical decisions;

Medium-term planning

(e) the planning system provides for the setting, review and revision of medium-term financial and other objectives, strategies and targets;

(f) new business activities are adequately researched, analysed and appraised in terms of feasibility, financial returns and requirements for capital;

Strategic plans

(g) the planning process is sufficiently developed to enable the directors and management to form a view on the society's position in the market for savings and loans products and provision of services;

(h) the society has a clear perception of its strengths and weaknesses, the opportunities available and potential threats, particularly where strategic change and new products are being considered; and

(i) key resources, such as information technology and human resources, have been appropriately identified and built into the planning process.

Information technology

4.10 The rapid expansion of information technology (IT) brings with it some considerable risks as well as significant benefits. Some of the issues which the board and management of a society need to address are:

(a) the extent to which the society's IT strategy is consistent with its business strategies;

(b) whether the procedures for evaluating significant IT investments are sufficiently comprehensive to ensure that the technical and business cases for the investment are clearly demonstrated;

(c) relative to the society's dependence on IT and the implications for the individual society and societies generally of a major hardware or software failure, or major incident such as a fire, whether the society has adequate standby arrangements; and whether these arrangements are adequately reviewed and tested;

(d) whether systems are properly documented;

(e) whether the physical and other security measures are sufficient to minimise risk of unauthorised access to facilities and systems, to identify such access; and

(f) whether the scope of work of internal audit is sufficiently comprehensive to assure the board and management that system controls are effective.

Human resources

4.11 The increase in the level of competition on both sides of the balance sheet, together with the opportunities afforded by the new legislation, create an environment where each society will need to consider the overall development of the organisation. Such considerations include the planning for, and development of, human resources where societies are proposing to enter fields of business activity with which they might not be familiar. In particular the board and management of a society need to be satisfied that:

(a) the society has identified its present and future manpower and skill requirements relative to its business activities and has defined recruitment, training and development plans to achieve them; and

(b) there are arrangements for securing the supply of appropriately skilled directors, managers and staff.

5. Documentation of systems

5.1 Section 71(6) provides that there must be kept available to the board a detailed statement, in writing, of the systems of control. The need for documentation of systems is primarily twofold:

(a) whilst control systems might be operated satisfactorily for a time without documentation, its absence makes it impossible to ensure that they are maintained over time; and

(b) the board and others (e.g. external auditors and those carrying out the inspection function) have specific statutory responsibilities in respect of the control systems. The absence of documentation makes it impossible for those reviewing the systems to satisfy themselves that the controls being operated are those that have been authorised, that they are complete and that they are adequate for their purpose.

Criteria for evaluating documentation

5.2 The board and management of a society will establish their own criteria for evaluating control system documentation. Such criteria would include, but not necessarily be limited to, the following, that:

(a) *It should be comprehensive.* It should cover all material aspects of the operations and business of the society.

(b) *It should be integrated.* Separate elements of the system should be interrelated and cross-referred in such a way that the whole system can be viewed as an integrated totality.

(c) *It should identify the controls.* The controls need to be identified and their purpose defined so that their effectiveness can be evaluated and so that the relationship and interdependency with other controls can be established.

(d) *It should attribute responsibility for operating the controls.* There need to be named persons or posts for each control operation, alternatives in case of absence and continuity of standards of control during absence.

(e) *It should state how operation of the control is to be evidenced.* Evidencing would normally require signatures or initials; records and registers; retention of control documents; staff attendance records.

(f) *It should establish a control discipline.* The instructions should be clear and precise avoiding expressions in relation to control functions such as 'normally' and 'if possible'.

(g) *It should be capable of practical day-to-day use.* The separate specifications of controls should have a practical role in the review and improvement of systems, for example, through the inspection function.

(h) *It should always be up to date.* There should be an accurate description of the system that has been established and is operating. When changes or modifications are made to the systems the appropriate systems of control need to be both established and documented by the time the changes become operative.

(i) *It should require confirmation of compliance.* Managers in branches and different areas of a society's business are key control points within the overall control system. They should periodically be required to confirm to the board, to the best of their knowledge and belief, compliance of the controls within the system which has been established.

Computer controls

5.3 The documentation of computer controls must be integrated within the overall documentation of a society's system of business control. Operating manuals provided by a computer supplier can often form a useful part of a society's procedures documentation but it is unlikely that such manuals will be in a form which enables them to comprise part of the control documentation. The criteria set out in paragraph 5.2 apply equally to the controls surrounding computer systems.

5.4 There will be a number of key controls performed within the computer programs and a society will need to ensure that it documents all such controls if it is placing reliance on them.

6. Systems of inspection and report

6.1 The requirement to establish and maintain a system of inspection and report to the board of a society is distinct from the requirement to establish and maintain a system of control. In many societies the system of inspection will be undertaken as part of the role of an Internal Audit Department with appropriately wider terms of reference. Such practice is recommended and may be considered essential for larger societies.

Purpose of the system

6.2 The purpose of a system of inspection is:

(a) to provide a continuous appraisal for management and the board as to the overall effectiveness of the control systems, including all proposed changes, and to recommend improvements where considered desirable or necessary;

(b) to determine whether the systems and controls established by the management and the board have operated as laid down (in the society's control documentation) and comply with policies, procedures, laws, regulations, etc.;

(c) to assess whether financial and operating information supplied to management and the board is accurate, pertinent, timely and complete.

6.3 The board and management of a society will need to satisfy themselves that the following considerations have been satisfactorily addressed within the context of the scale, range, complexity and pace of developments of the society's business and accounting systems:

(a) To maintain the objectivity of the inspection function it must be independent of the functions it inspects;

(b) Sufficient manpower resources are available to achieve the agreed objectives of the inspection function;

(c) Qualifications, experience and training of the individuals performing the inspection function are adequate in relation to the objectives;

(d) Status and reporting relationship of the head of the inspection function is sufficient to maintain the independence and objectivity of the function.

It is important to ensure that the head of the inspection function has the right of direct access to the highest level of management and the board.

Key elements of a system

6.4 The key elements of a satisfactory system of inspection include:

(a) *Terms of reference.* These should be specified with precision and should include, amongst other matters, scope and objectives of the inspection function, access to records, powers to obtain information/explanations from staff, and reporting requirements. They should be approved by management and the board.

(b) *Risk analysis.* Risks and/or control objectives should be identified in each area or cycle of the society's business and the adequacy of the specific controls which have been established to address these risks/control objectives should be assessed.

(c) *Inspection plan.* On the basis of the risk analysis an inspection plan should be developed which in the opinion of directors satisfies the requirements of Section 71 of the Act.

(d) *Detailed programmes.* These should be based upon the inspection plan together with the controls and their objectives specified in the control documentation.

Each programme should be comprehensive, specifying the frequency with which the various parts of the programme are to be carried out and how the work is to be performed (sample sizes, methods of selection, etc.).

(e) *Working papers.* Adequate working papers should be maintained to evidence the individual who performed the programmed work, how it was controlled and supervised, and to record the conclusions reached, with cross referencing to the reports made and action taken.

(f) *System of reporting.* Provision should be made for the submission of formal reports at the conclusion of each area of programmed work stating the areas covered together with any recommendations and conclusions reached.

Reporting and review

6.5 The board and management need to satisfy themselves that the inspection function is being properly carried out. To enable it to review the overall effectiveness of the inspection function it needs to consider the following aspects:

(a) adequacy and scope of planning;

(b) adequacy and scope of work performed in relation to the plans and programmes;

(c) regularity and level of reporting on matters arising from the inspections;

(d) disposal of points and recommendations raised, and reasons for any rejection of major points; and

(e) review of overall effectiveness of inspection function.

7. Compliance with the Building Societies Act and other legislation

Board review and oversight

7.1 The Commission considers that, for a board to discharge effectively its responsibilities in relation to the matters covered in this Note, it needs — in all but the most exceptional circumstances — to have the services of a committee (an audit committee or one of its standing committees) consisting either entirely of, or including a substantial majority of, non-executive directors, to advise it. The matters on which such a committee might advise include:

(a) the review of the adequacy of the society's systems of business control, and in particular its arrangements for evaluating risks in relation to its existing and future business and related capital requirements;

(b) the review of the adequacy of reports made available to the board;

(c) the review of the annual accounts prior to their approval by the board;

(d) the preparation and supervision of the society's inspection programme; and

(e) the receiving of reports from the internal auditor and reporting to the board on the inspection programme together with recommendations for improvements.

Compliance with statutory and other requirements

7.2 Societies are now having to meet not only the requirements of the Building Societies Act 1986, but also of an increasing range of other legislation: in particular virtually all will have to meet, directly or indirectly, requirements under the Financial Services Act 1986. The board of a society may wish to consider whether in its case it would be desirable to appoint a compliance officer, at board or senior management level. Such an officer would have the responsibility of reporting to, and advising, the board on the necessity for and effectiveness of arrangements for ensuring compliance by a society, in respect of existing and prospective legislation. These arrangements would have to cover not only the pattern of society's business, but also its practices and methods. It would cover primary legislation and also statutory instruments made under it, and also the rules of self-regulatory organisations. It would have to cover not only the present business of a society, but more particularly an extension of it. Such compliance with statutory requirements is distinct from the requirement for the board to establish and maintain adequate systems of control and inspection and report which is the subject of this Note.

8. Directors' and chief executive's statement of their opinion and auditors' report

Directors' and chief executive's statement of their opinion

8.1 The purpose of the annual opinion of the directors and chief executive are:

(a) to focus the attention of the board on the need to review and develop systems in line with the changing business environment (risk) to afford adequate protection to investors' funds; and

(b) to be the first step in satisfying the Commission that the board has done so.

In forming the opinion, directors and chief executives will need to consider the matters which are set out in Section 71 of the Act and this Note.

Criteria for determining compliance and non-compliance

8.2 The Commission considers that the Act requires matters to be reported which individually or collectively are significant and result in there not being reasonable assurance that the requirements of Section 71 have been complied with in some significant respect at any time during the year. Where minor deficiencies are identified in the accounting records, or systems of control and of inspection and report, provided that directors and the chief executive satisfy themselves that those deficiencies were not symptomatic of more serious problems, the Commission does not consider that they need be reported. Where significant deficiencies are identified and accordingly reported, the Commission would expect the report to state the corrective measures taken, or to be taken.

Matters to be reported to the Commission

8.3 Circumstances which should normally lead to a qualification of the opinion include:

(a) the absence of accounting records, or of systems or of documentation of those systems, necessary to enable directors or the society to discharge their duties;

(b) a significant weakness or failure in any of these which occurred during the year; and

(c) other matters which resulted, individually or collectively, in there not being reasonable assurance that the requirements of Section 71 have been complied with.

Auditors' reports to the Commission

8.4 The report to the Commission is a report on compliance with Sections 12(12) and 71 of the Act. Auditors are not required, in this report under Section 82(1) to 82(4), to express opinions generally on the commercial management of the affairs of the society, its subsidiaries and associated bodies linked by resolution. The exception to that is if a commercial decision, in their opinion, leads to a failure to comply with Section 71.

The Commission's response to reports received

8.5 The reports received from societies and auditors will, together with other information, be used by the Commission as part of its evaluation of the prudential position of each society:

(a) in relation to the requirements of Section 71; and

(b) the criteria of prudent management — Section 45.

8.6 The Commission will need to consider, when it receives a qualified report, whether the corrective action appears sufficient, and whether it calls in question the adequacy of the protection of investors. A qualification of either report may well not do so, provided that it also reports timely and effective corrective action. Before reaching its conclusion the Commission may wish to meet a society's board and auditors, either separately or together, to:

(a) establish whether or not the matter reported is prudentially significant or not;

(b) understand any proposals for corrective action arising from the report; and

(c) where appropriate, agree a basis for monitoring the implementation and effectiveness of the proposals.

8.7 Whether or not the report is qualified, the Commission may wish to explore the basis of the assessment in the report. It may ask the society to satisfy the Commission on how it had dealt with the various issues in this Note. In some such cases it may also wish to review and discuss the report by the auditors with the society.

Trade unions and employers' associations

(Issued August 1984)

Preface

This guideline gives guidance on the special factors to be considered in the application of auditing standards to trade unions and employers' associations. It is supplementary to, and should be read in conjunction with, 'The auditor's operational standard' and the related auditing guidelines.

The auditor's opinion on the accounts contained in the annual return submitted to the Certification Officer under the provisions of the Trade Union and Labour Relations Act 1974 should be expressed in true and fair terms. The terms of the audit report on the annual financial statements, prepared under the rules of the trade unions or employers' association, will depend on the requirements set out in those rules and should be confirmed, preferably in an engagement letter. In most cases, however, the audit report on the annual financial statements will also be required in true and fair terms. Where the auditor expresses an opinion in true and fair terms, this guideline should be read in conjunction with the Auditing Standards 'The audit report' and 'Qualifications in audit reports' and the Auditing Guideline 'Audit report examples'.

This guideline is based on the law at 31 July 1984. Members are advised to keep up to date with changes in the law relating to trade unions and employers' associations. The possible effects on auditors of a Bill on trade unions, which is being considered by Parliament at the date of publication, are described in Appendix 2.

Special circumstances relating to Northern Ireland are set out in Appendix 3 to this guideline. Special factors relating to the Republic of Ireland are currently being considered and separate guidance may be issued; at present there is no legal requirement for the auditor's report on the accounts to be expressed in true and fair terms.

Introduction

1 Section 28(1) of the Trade Union and Labour Relations Act 1974 ('the Act') defines a trade union as:

"An organisation (whether permanent or temporary) which either:

(a) consists wholly or mainly of workers of one or more descriptions and is an organisation whose principal purposes include the regulation of relations between workers of that description or those descriptions and employers or employers' associations; or

(b) consists wholly or mainly of:

(i) constituent or affiliated organisations which fulfil the conditions specified in paragraph (a) above (or themselves consist wholly or mainly of constituent or affiliated organisations); or

(ii) representatives of such constituent or affiliated organisations;

and in either case is an organisation whose principal purposes include the regulation of relations between workers and employers or between workers and employers' associations, or include the regulation of relations between its constituent or affiliated organisations."

2 Section 28(2) of the Act defines an employers' association as:

"An organisation (whether permanent or temporary) which either:

(a) consists wholly or mainly of employers or individual proprietors of one or more descriptions and is an organisation whose principal purposes include the regulation of relations between employers of that description or those descriptions and workers or trade unions; or

(b) consists wholly or mainly of:

(i) constituent or affiliated organisations which fulfil the conditions specified in paragraph (a) above (or themselves consist wholly or mainly of constituent or affiliated organisations which fulfil those conditions); or

(ii) representatives of such constituent or affiliated organisations;

and in either case is an organisation whose principal purposes include the regulation of relations between employers and workers or between employers and trade unions, or include the regulation of relations between its constituent or affiliated organisations."

Throughout this guideline, references to trade unions, should, where appropriate, be interpreted as including both trade unions and employers' associations as defined in Section 28 of the Act.

3 This guideline gives guidance not only on the audit of trade union accounts contained in annual returns but also on the audit of annual financial statements prepared under the rules of the trade union and laid before the members at conference and/or circulated to individual members or branches ('annual financial statements'). In most cases, the same auditor is required to report on both, and as a result much of the work that needs to be carried out in order to form an opinion on one, assists him in forming an opinion on the other.

4 This guideline extends to the audit of branches where for purposes of the Act they are deemed to be separate trade unions or where they submit separate annual returns. The principles contained in this guideline will also give assistance in respect of the audit of branches not required under the Act to submit an annual return but which prepare (annual financial statements).

5 Some trade unions are constituted as companies incorporated under the Companies Acts. In addition, some trade unions may carry out activities, which may or may not be directly connected with the rules or objects of the trade union, by way of separate entities. As a result, auditors may also be required to report under the terms of the Companies Acts, the Friendly and Industrial and Provident Societies Acts, the Insurance Companies Acts etc.. Regard should be paid to any additional accounting and auditing requirements set out in this other legislation.

6 Some audit areas peculiar to trade unions and employers' associations may require the special attention of the auditor. These areas, which are considered elsewhere in this guideline, are: branches and branch auditors who may not necessarily be qualified; separate funds and the allocation of income and expenditure and assets and liabilities to those funds; and maintenance of membership records.

7 For the purposes of this guideline, the term 'branch' includes all types of district and local area organisations such as areas, regions, sections, and chapels. The term 'fund' relates to those separate accounts maintained in respect of specific purposes.

Background

Legal

8 Every trade union has rules which set out its objects and constitution. Such rules normally specify the extent to which the powers of the union can be exercised by or delegated to specific officials, councils, committees or branches. They also normally incorporate provisions relating to the preparation and audit of annual financial statements.

The wording of such provisions varies widely from trade union to trade union and may be phrased in general or specific terms.

9 A copy of every trade union's rules must be sent each year to an official entitled the Certification Officer for Trade Unions and Employers' Associations ('the Certification Officer'). Under the Act, the Employment Protection Act 1975 and the Employment Act 1980, the Certification Officer is responsible for:

(a) maintaining lists of trade unions and employers' associations;
(b) determining the independence of trade unions;
(c) reimbursing certain expenses incurred by independent trade unions in conducting secret postal ballots;
(d) seeing that trade unions and employers' associations keep accounting records, have their accounts properly audited and submit annual returns;
(e) ensuring the periodical examination of members' superannuation schemes;
(f) securing observance of statutory procedures for transfers of engagements, amalgamations and changes of name;
(g) supervising the statutory requirements as to the setting up and operation of political funds and dealing with complaints by members about political fund rules.

10 The Trade Union Act 1913 enables a trade union to include the furtherance of political objects among its objects. Payments in the furtherance of political objects, however, must be made out of a separate political fund. A trade union is also required when completing its annual return to show the income and expenditure for the year and the balance at the end of the year on political fund account.

Taxation

11 Trade unions are liable to corporation tax on income and chargeable gains. For this purpose, funds derived from members (contributions, entrance fees, levies, fines etc.) do not rank as income, but corporation tax is chargeable on trading profits, investment and rental income, and gains arising on the disposal of chargeable assets. Section 338 of the Income and Corporation Taxes Act 1970, however, specifically exempts trade unions from tax on income (except trading income), and chargeable gains which are applicable and applied for the purpose of provident benefits.

12 Under the Finance Act 1972, trade unions having as their main object the negotiation on behalf of members of the terms and conditions of their employment, are exempt from value added tax for membership benefits supplied or available in return for subscriptions. Exemption is not available however, for the supply of goods and services which members pay for separately. Such supplies to members, and in addition supplies to third parties, will normally be taxable supplies and the trade union will be required to register and account for tax accordingly, subject to the minimum turnover limit.

13 Trade unions are not exempted bodies under the provisions of the Development Land Tax Act 1976 and are accordingly liable to such tax in the appropriate circumstances.

Accounting

14 Section 10 of the Act requires every trade union (except one which consists wholly or mainly of representatives of constituents or affiliated organisations) to:

(a) establish and maintain a satisfactory system of control of its accounting records, its cash holdings and its receipts and remittances; and
(b) keep proper accounting records with respect to its transactions, assets and liabilities.

These records must be such as to give a true and fair view of the state of affairs of the trade union and to explain its transactions.

15 Under Section 11(2) of the Act every trade union to which Section 10 applies is also required (unless it has been in existence for less than twelve months) to submit an annual return, relating to its affairs, to the Certification Officer. Schedule 2 of the Act requires the annual return to be for a calendar year and to be filed by 1 June, except where the Certification Officer directs that it should be for a different period and amends the time limit for filing. It also provides that the annual return shall be in such form as the Certification Officer may require. Currently, he requires trade unions to complete Form AR21 and employers' associations to complete Form AR27. Both forms contain sections for the insertion of the accounts. The Certification Officer does allow trade unions or employers' associations incorporated under the Companies Acts, however, to submit with their Forms AR21 or 27 a copy of their accounts prepared under the Companies Acts, and so avoid the duplication of broadly similar accounts. This concession does not enable such trade unions and employers' associations to avoid any of their responsibilities under the Act. Accordingly it is still necessary for the auditor's report on Form AR21 and Form AR27 to be provided as required by paragraphs 70-75 of this guideline.

16 Under the Act, the responsibilities of trade unions and employers' associations include preparing revenue and other accounts and a balance sheet which give a true and fair view of the matters to which they relate (Schedule 2 of the Act). In this context, it is preferable for a trade union working through branches to include the transactions, assets and liabilities of all the branches unless the accounts relating to certain branches are included in, or covered by, separate annual returns. It should also include those transactions, assets and liabilities relating directly to the rules or objects of the trade union, even where they are dealt with by way of a separate entity such as a limited company or a registered friendly society.

17 Schedule 2 of the Act also requires the revenue accounts to be prepared on an income and expenditure basis and not on a receipts and payments basis. The accounting records of the trade union should therefore be maintained in such a manner as to enable the revenue accounts to be produced on the basis laid down in the Act. This would involve the inclusion of members' contributions in arrear except where, after any necessary provisions for contributions which are not considered to be collectable, the amount is immaterial.

18 Failure to comply with Section 10 (maintenance of a system of control and accounting records), Section 11 (annual returns, appointment of auditors etc.) and Schedule 2 (administrative provisions) of the Act, involves the trade union, and the officers responsible, in an offence under Section 12 of the Act. The rules of a trade union are secondary to and not in substitution of the Act.

19 Three main problems arise from the way in which the requirements of the Act cut across the autonomy traditionally enjoyed by the branches of certain trade unions in financial and other matters. Firstly, while in some cases the accounting records of the trade unions may be centralised, in others head office and individual branches will maintain separate accounting records. Under the Act, however, a trade union cannot avoid responsibility for the accounting records solely because they are maintained at branch level. It is important that proper accounting records are maintained in respect of all trade union activities carried out and all funds maintained by the trade union, whether they be at head office or branch level. Head office should therefore exercise control and supervision over the accounting records maintained at branch level unless separate annual returns are filed.

20 Secondly, branch year ends sometimes differ from that of the trade union itself.

Consequently, adjustments may have to be made when the figures are combined.

21 Thirdly, some funds managed by branches have no direct connection with the rules or the objects of the trade union or the branch as such, and should not be included in an annual return. Examples of such funds include monies collected for recreational, charitable or social purposes, contributions to which are totally voluntary and not a condition for trade union membership.

22 If trade union funds are established for specific purposes in accordance with trade union rules or conference decisions and if the specific purpose cannot be changed other than by a decision taken at an appropriate level of the trade union, then such funds should be separately identified in the annual return.

23 In most instances the contents of the annual financial statements are similar to those of the accounts contained in the annual return. Revenue accounts indicating income and expenditure tend to disclose much more information regarding the trade union's activities compared with the statutory profit and loss accounts for companies. In many cases full details of income and expenditure during the year and all branch funds are included in the annual financial statements on the same basis as the accounts contained in the annual return.

24 As indicated in the Explanatory Foreword to Statements of Standard Accounting Practice, SSAPs apply to all financial statements intended to give a true and fair view of the financial position or profit or loss. Trade unions are subject to a statutory requirement for the accounts contained in their annual returns to give a true and fair view. It must be recognised, however, that the trade union rules may not specifically require the annual financial statements to give a true and fair view or may require particular accounting policies to be used for certain transactions. Nevertheless, it is clearly desirable that a true and fair view should be given and that the same accounting policies and bases should be followed in the accounts contained in the annual return and in the annual financial statements.

25 In considering the appropriateness of particular SSAPs to trade unions, it must be remembered that SSAPs have been prepared primarily with business enterprises in mind, whereas most trade union activities are not-for-profit. As a result, it is important for the auditor to use his judgement as to the appropriateness or otherwise of an SSAP to the individual circumstances of the trade union concerned.

26 In the absence of specific guidance from the accountancy bodies on the application of SSAPs to organisations such as trade unions, most of whose activities are not-for-profit, it is essential that accounts contained in annual returns and annual financial statements include a statement of the main accounting policies followed. These will probably include:

(a) the basis for accounting for contribution income;
(b) the basis for inclusion of transactions, assets and liabilities of branches;
(c) the accounting bases adopted in connection with separate funds, including any political funds set up in accordance with the Trade Union Act 1913.

27 As indicated in paragraphs 21 and 22 above, the accounts contained in the annual return and the annual financial statements of many trade unions may include separate fund accounts. Certain items of income or expenditure may be credited or charged direct to such fund accounts rather than passed through income and expenditure accounts. It is important that there is adequate disclosure of all the individual movements comprising any net movement on the fund accounts. Given the tax position of most trade unions, however, it will not usually be appropriate to deal with extraordinary items net of tax or distinguish between figures for income before and after tax.

28 Compliance with SSAP 10 requires that a source and application of funds statement is produced unless the gross income of the trade union is less than £25,000. Since the Forms AR21 and AR27 do not include sections for such a statement, it will need to be attached separately.

Audit

29 Section 11(3) requires every trade union to appoint an auditor to audit the accounts contained in its annual return. Schedule 2 of the Act prescribes who may be appointed and provides that the auditor of a trade union should make a report to the trade union on the accounts audited by him and contained in its annual return. This report should state whether in the opinion of the auditor those accounts give a true and fair view of the matters to which they relate. The auditor also has a duty to carry out such investigations as will enable him to form an opinion on whether proper accounting records have been kept, whether a satisfactory system of control over transactions has been maintained and whether the accounts are in agreement with the accounting records. If these statutory requirements have not in the auditor's opinion been satisfied, or if he fails to obtain the necessary information and explanations, he must state that fact in his report.

30 Schedule 2 of the Act provides the auditor with the following rights:

(a) the right of access at all times to the accounting records of the trade union, including those of branches dealt with in its annual return, and to all other documents relating to its affairs;

(b) the right to require from officers of the trade union, or of any of its branches, such information and explanations as he considers necessary;

(c) the right to attend general meetings of members or of delegates of members and to receive due notices of such meetings;

(d) the right to be heard at such meetings on any part of the business which concerns him as auditor.

31 Schedule 2 of the Act also requires the trade union rules to contain provision for the appointment and removal of auditors and also prescribes both the scope of the audit and the terms of the auditor's report on the accounts included in the annual return. The auditor's responsibilities in connection with the annual financial statements may not be specifically covered in the trade union rules regarding audit ('audit rules') on such matters as:

(a) the scope of his audit;

(b) to whom he is reporting; and

(c) the terms of his report.

Problems can also arise where the audit rules provide that the auditor's responsibilities will be determined by the executive committee or senior officials.

Auditing procedures

32 The following procedures are supplementary to those given in the operational auditing guidelines.

Planning

33 Because of the problems indicated in paragraph 31 above, the auditor should pay particular attention to the wording of the audit rules and to minutes recording decisions regarding audit made by the executive committee. He should send an engagement letter to confirm his understanding of the terms of his appointment. The letter should indicate that the auditor is required to state whether in his opinion the accounts contained in the annual return give a true and fair view. It should also indicate the matters which he is required to state in his report on the annual financial statements. In most cases, these will include his opinion on whether these statements give a true and fair view. The auditor should also use the engagement letter to exclude any requirements which he cannot reasonably fulfil, such as a requirement for the auditor to 'certify' the annual financial statements as being 'correct'. Where the rules provide that the auditor should report in terms such as 'the financial statements are in accordance with the books and records' the auditor should bear in mind his statutory obligation to report in true and fair terms on the accounts contained in the AR21 and AR27.

34 The engagement letter should deal with the treatment of branch funds within the annual return and the annual financial statements and the extent to which such branch funds are included within the scope of the auditor's responsibilities. It should also clarify the scope of the audit in respect of any activities where the connection with the rules or objects of the trade union is in doubt (see paragraphs 5, 16 and 21 above).

35 The auditor will need to consider the extent to which it is necessary to visit and examine the records maintained at branches. He will take into account the manner in which head office exercises its responsibilities for control and supervision over the accounting records maintained at branch level and whether separate branch auditors are appointed.

36 Branch financial statements are frequently audited by individuals or firms other than the auditors of the trade unions themselves. Such branch auditors may be either professionally qualified or unqualified. The trade union auditor, however, is responsible for reporting on the accounts contained in the annual return and/or the annual financial statements prepared by the trade union and, if these incorporate branch transactions, he should take this matter into account when planning his audit. He will need to consider the extent to which he can rely on other auditors.

37 The trade union auditor should consider preparing a standard form of audit programme which could be used by branch auditors and requiring it to be completed, signed and submitted direct to himself, together with any questionnaire which he might think is appropriate. This does not, however, relieve the trade union auditor from the need to consider the adequacy of audit arrangements and to communicate further with branch auditors to the extent he considers necessary.

38 Where a professionally unqualified person audits a branch whose transactions, assets or liabilities represent a significant proportion of those of the trade union, it is unlikely that a standard audit programme on its own will satisfactorily meet the situation. In such circumstances, the auditor may have to carry out further work himself and, if this is the case, he should discuss with the trade union the extra costs arising from the use of unqualified auditors' work. If the auditor is of the view that the use of unqualified auditors may be such as to prejudice the audit being conducted in accordance with approved auditing standards, his discussions with the trade union should also cover the possibility of his needing to qualify his report on the grounds of uncertainty — material amounts not being adequately audited in accordance with approved auditing standards.

39 It is not unusual for the auditor of the trade union to provide advice and significant assistance in respect of the preparation of the annual return and/or the annual financial statements. In these circumstances, it is essential that proper consideration is given to avoiding any impairment of independence.

40 When planning the audit of a trade union the auditor should also consider:

(a) the need, when reporting on the accounts contained in the annual return, to carry out investigations to enable him to form an opinion as to whether the trade union has maintained a satisfactory system of control over its transactions;

(b) the degree of reliance that he may wish to place on internal controls in order to arrive at an opinion on the accounts contained in the annual return and/or the annual financial statements;

(c) the amount of detail included in the financial statements on which he is required to report (see paragraph 23);

(d) decisions of the annual conference or executive committees of the trade union which affect the audit or the matters upon which he is required to report;

(e) any comments made by the Certification Officer following the submission of the previous year's annual return;

(f) the reports issued by the Certification Officer and the guidance notes contained within the form of annual return for the current year;

(g) any changes which might have taken place in the law relating to trade unions and employers' associations.

Accounting systems

41 Paragraph 8 of the Auditing Guideline 'Accounting systems' states that "the auditor will need to obtain an understanding of the enterprise as a whole and how the accounting system reflects assets and liabilities and transactions". In connection with this requirement, a trade union auditor will have to examine the system whereby branches within the scope of his audit account for trade union contributions and other items of income and expenditure administered on behalf of the trade union. This will involve the auditor in assessing the adequacy of periodic returns from branches as a basis for the preparation of accounts. If a branch does not submit periodic returns the auditor should ascertain whether or not the excluded branches are submitting their own annual returns to the Certification Officer. He should also examine the rules and any supplementary decisions made under the rules to ascertain the rights and responsibilities of the branches concerned and the degree of their accountability to head office.

42 Members' contributions represent the largest source of income for most trade unions. It will therefore be necessary for the auditor to obtain an understanding of the accounting system in respect of contributions. In order to make an assessment of its adequacy he will have to consider its completeness. This will involve him examining the methods for updating membership and contribution records, the procedures for ensuring that all contributions due (including those collected by employers) are properly received and the arrangements for ensuring that all contributions are banked promptly and intact. He should also examine the systems dealing with arrears of contributions.

43 In particular, where there are delays between the date of collection and remittance to the trade union, the auditor will need to satisfy himself as to the appropriateness of the method of determining arrears and the reasonableness of the figures produced.

Audit evidence

44 Paragraph 4 of the 'The auditor's operational standard' states that "the auditor should obtain relevant and reliable evidence sufficient to enable him to draw reasonable conclusions therefrom". Particularly important sources of evidence in respect of a trade union are the membership and contribution records mentioned in paragraph 42 above. Normally, an examination of these records, and the figures contained within them, will assist the auditor in obtaining the assurance that he requires in respect of members' contribution income for the trade union as a whole and for the separate funds.

45 There may be circumstances, however, where the trade union auditor is himself unable to examine the membership and contribution records kept at some branches and where communication with branch auditors may not be available. Similarly it may not be possible to obtain adequate evidence as to the completeness of contributions deducted by employers under the check-off scheme. In such circumstances and where alternative auditing procedures are not available, the auditor reporting on accounts contained in an annual return should consider whether he has received all the information and explanations that he requires in order to form an opinion. He may have to conclude that there is uncertainty as to whether:

(a) the accounts show a true and fair view;

(b) the trade union has kept proper accounting records; and

(c) the trade union has maintained a satisfactory system of control over its transactions.

46 Two other important sources of audit evidence are the rules and minuted decisions. The latter represent an important source because many significant decisions affecting financial matters may be taken by conference or delegated down to specific councils, committees or branches. Key areas where the auditor will have to rely on trade union rules and minuted decisions are as follows:

(a) *Contributions (including political fund contributions) and entrance fees*
The auditor will have to consider whether contributions and entrance fees have been collected at the correct rates.

(b) *Fines and special levies receivable*
The auditor will have to consider whether the trade union has power to enforce fines and certain special levies.

(c) *Benefits payable*
Most benefits are recurring expenditure for which the trade union rules lay down the basis of entitlement, the scales of benefit and the terms and conditions of benefit. One of the principal conditions is usually that the applicant is not in arrears with his contributions.

(d) *Travel, subsistence and attendance payments and allowances*
Apart from day-to-day travel and subsistence of officials or employees in the course of trade union business, payments are frequently made in connection with attendance at conferences, negotiating committees and fraternal delegations. The auditor will have to consider whether such payments made are in accordance with agreed scales.

(e) *Dispute payments and receipts*
Industrial disputes sometimes involve payment of dispute benefit (strike pay) and related expenses, and occasionally involve the receipt of donations at local or national level. Although these situations are usually referred to in the trade union rules, they are normally too infrequent and the circumstances too varied to warrant detailed treatment. The conduct of such disputes is accordingly usually determined by decisions of the appropriate executive committee. The auditor should, therefore, take note of the detailed proposals for the conduct of the dispute as expressed in the relevant minutes or satisfy himself that decisions

taken are in accordance with properly delegated authority. He should also devise tests to check whether receipts and payments are in accordance with the system laid down and are properly evidenced.

47 Representations by management are one source of audit evidence. Such representations should be confined to matters which are material to the financial statements and which are mainly considerations affecting judgement and opinion. Matters of fact can also be included, however, where they are material and where knowledge of the fact is confined to management. In the case of a trade union, knowledge of the fact that all trade union funds and transactions for the period have been disclosed to the auditor may be confined to senior officials and therefore may need to be confirmed in writing. A letter addressed to the auditor confirming such representations should be approved by the body responsible for approving the financial statements and should be signed on its behalf by the general secretary or some other designated officer of the trade union.

Internal controls

48 The Auditing Guideline 'Internal controls' has particular relevance to the audit of trade unions. This is because of:

(a) the specific requirement (see paragraph 14) on most trade unions to establish and maintain satisfactory systems of control over their accounting records, their cash holdings, receipts and remittances;

(b) the duties (see paragraph 29) on auditors reporting on accounts contained in annual returns to carry out investigations into and, where necessary, to report on such systems.

49 Large trade unions should have the internal controls appropriate to any large enterprise, and the auditor should look for and encourage such a trade union to implement normal internal controls and reporting systems in keeping with the scale of operation.

50 Small trade unions and branches, even those of large trade unions, will generally suffer from internal control weaknesses common to small enterprises, such as lack of segregation of duties and use of unqualified or part-time staff. Shortcomings may possibly arise in the implementation of formal procedures from the staff's lack of training particularly if they are volunteers. Adequate control may often be available by means of increased review and authorisation procedures by committee members or other officials of the trade union.

51 Some indications of the internal controls which might be present in most trade unions are given in paragraphs 52-61 below. Other types of internal control, on which the auditor might seek to rely, are dealt with in the Auditing Guideline 'Internal controls'.

52 *Financial organisation*

(a) Preparation and appraisal of budgets.

(b) Comparison of actual performance against budgets.

(c) Monitoring in detail by specific committees or officers of expenditure incurred.

53 *Contributions (including political fund contributions) and entrance fees*

(a) Regular checks to ensure that the membership and contribution records are being kept up to date.

(b) Ensuring that contributions and entrance fees are collected at the appropriate rates.

(c) Reconciliations between contributions and entrance fees received and the membership and contribution records.

(d) Investigation of arrears by officials. Where possible, these officials should not be responsible for collecting or handling contributions or entrance fee monies.

(e) Checks to ensure that any amounts accounted for by branch officers or other persons collecting contributions are in accordance with agreed rates and any deductions for collecting commissions or locally incurred expenditure are properly controlled.

54 *Fines and special levies receivable*

Regular checks to ensure that fines and special levies receivable are properly imposed and recorded, and are in accordance with agreed rates.

55 *Benefits payable*

(a) Regular checks to ensure that benefits payable are properly recorded.

(b) Checks to ensure that applicants fulfil all conditions necessary before receiving benefit.

56 *Travel, subsistence and attendance payments and allowances*

(a) Regular checks to ensure that claims are bona fide.

(b) Ensuring that payments are made in accordance with agreed scale rates.

(c) Checks to ensure that claims for loss of earnings are properly supported.

57 *Dispute payments and receipts*

(a) Ensuring that dispute payments and receipts are properly recorded.

(b) Checks to ensure that dispute payments and receipts are dealt with in accordance with the trade union rules, minuted decisions or decisions made by officials with appropriate authority.

58 *Separate funds*

Checks to ensure that income and expenditure, assets and liabilities and numbers of members contributing are properly identified and recorded in respect of each separate fund.

59 *Cash and bank*

(a) Prompt banking of receipts.

(b) Independent agreement of banking records to receipt records.

(c) Regular bank reconciliations.

(d) Adequate arrangements for bank signatories.

(e) Periodic checking of petty cash by an independent official.

60 *Investments*

(a) Ensuring that investments are properly recorded.

(b) Periodic checks to ensure that all investment income due is in fact received.

(c) Proper authorisation of purchases and disposals of investments.

(d) Regular checking of the register of investments with evidence of title.

61 *Properties*

(a) Ensuring that all property transactions are properly authorised.

(b) Ensuring that all properties are properly recorded and that all rental income due is in fact received.

62 Where there are branches not submitting separate annual returns to the Certification Officer, the auditor reporting on the accounts contained in the annual return should satisfy himself that the trade union head office has complied with Section 11(8) of the Act. In other words, that the head office has taken steps to ensure that satisfactory controls have been established for all transactions which are accounted for in the head office annual return. Such steps should include:

(a) making arrangements to receive regular reports and checking to ensure that these are received;

(b) carrying out enquiries promptly where adverse matters come to light;

(c) regular agreement of transactions and balances due between head office and the branches;

(d) regular agreement of amounts to be retained by branches, for example branch retentions of contributions.

63 A problem area is the concentration of control in a particular senior official such as a general or branch secretary. As a result, such an official may be in a position to override certain of the internal controls of the trade union. In such circumstances, the auditor should consider placing less reliance on internal controls and extending the level of his substantive tests.

Review of financial statements

64 In addition to those accounting policies highlighted in paragraph 26, the auditor should review the basis:

(a) for apportioning administrative expenses and taxation between funds (including any political funds set up in accordance with the Trade Union Act 1913); and

(b) of hypothecation. This is a term applied to the irrevocable appropriation of assets and income for the benefit of a specific fund or towards meeting specific expenditure.

65 Many trade unions adopt a system of budgetary control over expenses. During his general review, therefore, the auditor should compare the income and expenditure for the period under review with budgeted figures and consider the explanations for any variances arising.

66 During his general review, the auditor should consider the additional information included in the annual return not included in the accounts, such as the details of membership including numbers of those contributing or not contributing to the political fund. This information may help him in forming an opinion on the accounts contained in the annual return and/or the annual financial statements.

67 In connection with the presentation and disclosure, the auditor should consider whether:

(a) the treatment of transactions, assets and liabilities relating to the rules and objects of the trade union is appropriate;

(b) the treatment of branch funds is appropriate;

(c) there has been proper disclosure of separate funds, including any political funds set up in accordance with the Trade Union Act 1913;

(d) there has been appropriate disclosure of the allocation of the income and expenditure between funds and of any transfers between funds;

(e) a single statement of source and application of funds is appropriate where there are several revenue accounts produced, each covering separate activities of the trade union.

68 Where the annual return is completed some considerable time after the auditor has signed his audit report on the annual financial statements, the auditor should update his review of events after the balance sheet date and consider the effect that this might have on his report on the accounts contained in the annual return.

69 In reviewing the accounts contained in the annual return and/or the annual financial statements to ensure compliance with requirements, the auditor should consider:

(a) the trade union rules and if relevant, delegated decisions; and

(b) the Act and any regulations made thereunder.

Reporting

70 This section sets out the general reporting principles to be followed. For suggested wording of reports to be used in specific circumstances, references should be made to Appendix 1.

The audit report on the accounts contained in the annual return

71 The audit report on the accounts contained in the annual return is required to be expressed in 'true and fair' terms. As a result, this section of the guideline should be read in conjunction with the Auditing Standards 'The audit report' and 'Qualifications in audit reports' and the Auditing Guideline 'Audit report examples'.

72 The audit report should be dated. It should also identify the trade union as the body to whom it is addressed and also identify those pages or paragraphs of the annual return which contain the audited accounts and the year to which the annual return relates. The auditor should also state expressly in his report whether:

(a) the accounts have been audited in accordance with approved auditing standards;

(b) in his opinion, the accounts give a true and fair view of the state of the trade union's financial affairs, transactions, and where applicable, source and application of funds.

73 Under Schedule 2 of the Act the auditor must also state the fact in his report, where in his opinion:

(a) proper accounting records have not been maintained;

(b) a satisfactory system of control over its transactions has not been maintained;

(c) the accounts are not in agreement with the accounting records; or

(d) he has not obtained the necessary information and explanations that he requires.

In these circumstances the auditor should include in his report a separate 'explanatory' paragraph outlining the facts giving rise to qualification. The auditor is not required, however, to state in his report whether the accounts contained in the annual return comply with the Act.

74 Failure to meet reporting deadlines may mean that information concerning the financial affairs of certain branches is not received by head office. As a result the trade union may include estimated figures in its annual return or exclude the financial affairs of the branches concerned from its annual return entirely. In these circumstances, the auditor should consider using the example audit report (a) (iii) or (iv) given in Appendix 1.

75 Where a statement of source and application of funds is required to comply with SSAPs but has not been attached to the annual return form, the auditor will have to consider including in his audit report a separate paragraph using the wording set out in the Auditing Standard 'The audit report'.

The audit report on the annual financial statements

76 The audit report on the annual financial statements should identify the members of the trade union as the persons to whom it is addressed, unless the trade union rules require it to be addressed to other persons such as the 'Executive Committee'. It should also identify the financial statements to which it relates.

77 The terms of the audit report will depend on the requirements set out in the trade union rules as confirmed in the engagement letter (note paragraph 80). In most cases, however, the audit report will be required to be in true and fair terms. Consequently, regard will normally have to be paid to the Auditing Standards 'The audit report' and 'Qualifications in audit reports' and the Auditing Guideline 'Audit report examples'.

78 In some cases the annual financial statements which the auditor is required to audit will be those of head office and will exclude the financial affairs of all the branches. In such cases an emphasis of matter paragraph should be included in the audit report to explain that condition. It is unlikely that the annual financial statements which the auditor is required to audit will include the financial affairs of head office and of only some of many branches.

79 Where the annual financial statements show income and expenditure relating to one fund account on another fund account, the principles outlined in the example report (a) (vii) in Appendix 1 should be followed.

80 Where a trade union is a company incorporated under the Companies Acts, the audit report on the financial statements should additionally be in terms required by Section 14 of the Companies Act 1967, and should state where appropriate, that the financial statements comply with the Companies Acts 1948-1981.

Appendix 1

Audit report examples

81 As with the Auditing Guideline 'Audit report examples', the examples of audit reports set out below are intended merely to illustrate possible forms of wording for use in different circumstances. Since qualifications must be expressed in terms chosen to fit the particular circumstances to which they relate, it is impracticable, and could be misleading to suggest standard forms of wording.

The forms of qualified reports and the manner in which materiality should be judged in deciding to qualify an audit opinion are described in the Auditing Standard 'Qualifications in audit reports'.

The following examples should be addressed to the trade union or the employers' association as applicable.

(a) Example audit reports on the accounts contained in the annual return.

(i) *Unqualified audit report: annual return covering both head office and all branches*

"AUDITORS' REPORT TO THE ... ON THE ACCOUNTS CONTAINED IN ITS ANNUAL RETURN FOR THE YEAR ENDED ....

We have audited the accounts set out on pages ... to ... of this return in accordance with approved Auditing Standards.

In our opinion the accounts give a true and fair view of the state of the financial affairs at 31 December .... and of its transactions and source and application of funds for the year then ended."

(ii) *Unqualified audit report. Emphasis of matter: branches submitting separate annual returns*

"AUDITORS' REPORT TO THE ... ON THE ACCOUNTS CONTAINED IN ITS ANNUAL RETURN FOR THE YEAR ENDED ...

We have audited the accounts set out on pages ... to ... of this return in accordance with approved Auditing Standards.

We draw your attention to note ... which indicates that information concerning the financial affairs of certain branches has been excluded from these accounts but has been included in a separate annual return submitted under the Trade Union and Labour Relations Act 1974 to the Certification Officer for Trade Unions and Employers' Associations.

In our opinion the accounts give a true and fair view of the state of the trade union's financial affairs excluding those branches indicated above at 31 December .... and of its transactions and source and application of funds for the year then ended."

(iii) *Qualified audit report. Uncertainty — subject to: inclusion of estimated branch revenue*

"AUDITORS' REPORT TO THE ... ON THE ACCOUNTS CONTAINED IN ITS ANNUAL RETURN FOR THE YEAR ENDED ....

We have audited the accounts set out on pages ... to ... of this return in accordance with approved Auditing Standards.

As explained in note ... certain financial information relating to the affairs of a number of branches has not been received and accordingly revenue expenditure totalling £... in respect of (type of expenditure) has been estimated.

Subject to any adjustments that may be required when the actual amount of revenue expenditure referred to above is known, in our opinion the accounts give a true and fair view of...."

(iv) *Qualified audit report. Disagreement — except: omission of branch financial affairs*

"AUDITORS' REPORT TO THE ... ON THE ACCOUNTS CONTAINED IN ITS ANNUAL RETURN FOR THE YEAR ENDED ....

We have audited the accounts set out on pages ... to ... of this return. Our audit was conducted in accordance with approved Auditing Standards except that the scope of our work was limited by the matter referred to below.

As explained in note ... certain financial information relating to the affairs of a number of branches has not been received and nothing has been included in the accounts in respect thereof. In these circumstances we were unable to carry out all the auditing procedures, or to obtain all the information and explanations we considered necessary.

Except for the effects of the adjustments which would have been shown to be necessary had the information indicated in the paragraph above been received, in our opinion the accounts give a true and fair view of ...."

(v) *Qualified audit report. Uncertainty — subject to: membership and contribution records at branches cannot be examined*

"AUDITORS' REPORT TO THE ... ON THE ACCOUNTS CONTAINED IN ITS ANNUAL RETURN FOR THE YEAR ENDED ....

We have audited the accounts set out on pages ... to ... of this return. Our audit was conducted in accordance with approved Auditing Standards except that the scope of our work was limited by the matter referred to below.

It was not possible to examine the membership and contribution records kept at a significant number of the branches. Accordingly, we were unable to carry out all the auditing procedures, or to obtain all the information and explanations we considered necessary, or to form an opinion as to whether:

(i) the ... has kept proper accounting records in accordance with Section 10 of the Trade Union and Labour Relations Act 1974;

(ii) the ... has maintained a satisfactory system of control over its transactions in accordance with that section.

Subject to the effects of any adjustments which might have been shown to be necessary had it been practicable for us to examine the membership and contribution records of certain branches, in our opinion the accounts give a true and fair view of the ...."

(vi) *Qualified audit report. Uncertainty — subject to: failure to keep proper accounting records or maintain a satisfactory control over contribution income during part of the year*

"AUDITORS' REPORT TO THE ... ON THE ACCOUNTS CONTAINED IN ITS ANNUAL RETURN FOR THE YEAR ENDED ...

We have audited the accounts set out on pages ... to ... of this return in accordance with approved Auditing Standards.

As stated in note ..., a period occurred during the year when the membership and contribution records became significantly out of date and contribution income was not subject to internal controls in keeping with the scale of operations. Accordingly, in our opinion, the ... has not:

(a) kept proper accounting records in accordance with Section 10 of the Trade Union and Labour Relations Act 1974;

(b) maintained a satisfactory system of control in accordance with that section.

Subject to the effects of any adjustments which might have been shown to be necessary had proper accounting records and a satisfactory system of control been maintained, in our opinion the accounts give a true and fair view of ...."

(vii) *Qualified audit report. Disagreement — except: income or expenditure relating to one fund account shown on another fund account*

"AUDITORS' REPORT TO THE ... ON THE ACCOUNTS CONTAINED IN ITS ANNUAL RETURN FOR THE YEAR ENDED ...

We have audited the accounts set out on pages ... to ... of this return in accordance with approved Auditing Standards.

Payments amounting to ..., in respect of..., have been made out of the A Fund Account as opposed to the B Fund Account.

Except for the matter referred to above, in our opinion the accounts give a true and fair view of ...."

In the event that a payment in furtherance of political objects is made out of a fund other than the political fund, the auditor should also make reference to the fact that this is in contravention of the Trade Unions Act 1913 .

(b) Example audit report on the annual financial statements.

Unqualified audit report: annual financial statements covering both head office and all branches

"AUDITORS' REPORT TO THE MEMBERS OF THE ...

We have audited the financial statements set out on pages ... to ... in accordance with approved Auditing Standards.

In our opinion, the financial statements give a true and fair view of the state of the ... financial affairs at 31 December .... and of its transactions and source and application of funds for the year then ended."

Appendix 2
Trade Union Bill 1983

82 Paragraph 40 of the guideline indicates that when planning the audit of a trade union the auditor should consider any changes in the law relating to trade unions and employers' associations. Currently the Trade Union Bill 1983 is before Parliament, and members are strongly advised to keep up to date with developments relating to this possible legislation. One part of the Bill which, if enacted in its present form will affect the auditor is Part III which lays down more precise requirements as to what constitutes a political fund. Consequently, these detailed provisions would need to be taken into account by the auditor in deciding whether income and expenditure and assets and liabilities have been dealt with through the appropriate fund account.

Appendix 3
Special circumstances relating to Northern Ireland

83 As regards Northern Ireland, the main law relating to trade unions is contained in the Trade Unions Acts 1871-1965. Of these relevant Acts, only three are specific to Northern Ireland, the rest being the equivalent UK Acts of 1871-1913. The three specific to Northern Ireland are the:

Trade Disputes and Trade Unions (Northern Ireland) Act 1927;

Trade Disputes and Trade Unions (Northern Ireland) Act 1958; and

Trade Union (Amalgamations etc.) Act 1965.

The only relevant legislation contained in these Acts for the purposes of the guideline is the requirement of Section 8 of the 1927 Act with respect to the furnishing of annual returns under Section 16 of the 1871 Act by three types of trade unions not registered in Northern Ireland, but carrying on business there. This section is set out below:

Trade Disputes and Trade Unions (Northern Ireland) Act 1927
Section 8

(1) Any trade union carrying on business in Northern Ireland, and being a trade union registered in Great Britain under the Trade Union Acts 1871-1927 (or being unregistered but required by those Acts to furnish returns in Great Britain under Section 16 of Trade Union Act 1871), shall before 1 June in every year transmit to the Registrar of Friendly Societies:

(a) a copy, certified in such a manner as the said Register may decide, of the general statement and other documents transmitted in that year in pursuance of said Section 16, to, and recorded by, the officer acting as Registrar for the purposes of the said section in its application to Great Britain; and

(b) a statement setting forth in relation to business carried on by a trade union in Northern Ireland such particulars of receipts and expenditure of the trade union and other information as the Registrar of Friendly Societies may require.

(2) Section 16 of the 1871 Act applies to every trade union carrying on business in Northern Ireland, but having its principal office outside the United Kingdom.

(3) Every trade union (not registered in Northern Ireland) carrying on business in Northern Ireland shall furnish to the Registrar before 1 June in every year, the names and addresses of one or more persons resident in Northern Ireland authorised to accept on behalf of the trade union, service of process and any notices required to be served on the trade union.

Trade unions registered in Northern Ireland continue to fall within the old definition contained in Section 2 of the 1913 Act.

Trade Union Act 1913

Section 2

(1) Definition of a trade union — any combination whether temporary or permanent, the principal objects of which are under its constitution statutory objects. Provided that any combination which is for the time being registered as a trade union shall be deemed to be a trade union as defined by the Act so long as it continues to be so registered.

The only legislation for such trade unions as regards accounts, annual returns and auditors is contained in Sections 11 and 16 of the 1871 Act. These sections are set out below. This legislation is not as detailed or specific as the requirements of the 1974 Act which represents the basis of the guideline.

Trade Union Act 1871

Section 11

Requires account to be made by the Honorary Treasurer, and audited as laid down under the rules of the union.

Section 16 Annual returns

A general statement of receipts, funds, effects and expenditure of every trade union registered under this Act shall be transmitted to the Registrar before 1 June in every year, and shall show fully the assets and liabilities at the date and the receipts and expenditure during the year preceding the date to which it is made out.

It shall show separately the expenditure in respect of the several objects of the trade union, and shall be prepared and made out up to such date, in such form, and shall comprise such particulars as the Registrar may from time to time require; together with all alterations of rules, new rules and changes of officers.

The audit report required by the Annual Return (Form AR21) currently takes the following form: "In our opinion the foregoing Annual Return for the year ended 31st December .... is properly drawn up, is in agreement with the registered rules, the books of Account and the records of the Union and gives a true and fair view of the matters to which it is addressed (subject to a Special Report dated ... day of...)". If no Special Report is made the words in brackets should be struck out.

Housing associations

(Issued 14 November 1984)

Preface

This guideline gives guidance on the special factors to be considered in the application of auditing standards to housing associations. It is supplementary to, and should be read in conjunction with, the auditor's operational and reporting standards, their related guidelines and, where there are donations or fund raising activities, the Auditing Guideline 'Charities'.

Special considerations relating to Scotland and Northern Ireland are set out in appendices to this guideline.

This guideline is based on the law as at 18 September 1984 and on the third edition of the 'Recommended Form of Published Accounts for Housing Associations'.

Definitions

1 In this guideline:

the 1957 Act means the Housing Act 1957;

the 1964 Act means the Housing Act 1964;

the 1965 Act means the Industrial and Provident Societies Act 1965;

the 1968 Act means the Friendly and Industrial and Provident Societies Act 1968;

the 1972 Act means the Housing Finance Act 1972;

the 1974 Act means the Housing Act 1974;

the 1976 Act means the Rent (Agriculture) Act 1976;

the 1977 Act means the Rent Act 1977;

the 1980 Act means the Housing Act 1980;

the 1984 Act means the Housing and Building Control Act 1984;

the 1982 Order means the Registered Housing Associations (Accounting Requirements) Order 1982 (Statutory Instrument 1982 No. 828);

the Recommended Form means the Housing Corporation booklet 'Recommended Form of Published Accounts for Housing Associations';

housing association means a society, body of trustees or company established for the purpose of, or amongst whose objects are included those of providing constructing, improving, or managing or facilitating or encouraging the construction or improvement of houses or hostels being a society, body of trustees or company who do not trade for profit or whose constitution or rules prohibit the issue of any capital with interest or dividend exceeding the rate for the time being prescribed by the Treasury, whether with or without differentiation as between share or loan capital;

registered housing association means a housing association registered with the Housing Corporation under the 1974 Act;

association (where used without qualification) means a 'registered housing association';

1965 Act Society means an association which is registered with the Registrar of Friendly Societies under the 1965 Act;

charitable housing association means an association (other than a 1965 Act Society) which is a registered charity that is not an exempt charity as defined by the Charities Act 1960;

association with charitable status means an association which is a registered charity or a 1965 Act Society which is an exempt charity (as defined by the Charities Act 1960) through the use of charitable model rules;

co-ownership society means a 1965 Act society in the case of which:

(a) the rules of the society restrict membership to persons who are tenants or prospective tenants of the association and preclude the granting or assignment of tenancies to persons other than members; and

(b) each tenant (or his personal representatives) will under the terms of the tenancy agreement or of the agreement under which he became a member of the society, be entitled, on his ceasing to be a member and subject to any conditions stated in either agreement, to a sum calculated by reference directly or indirectly to the value of his housing accommodation;

almshouse means a corporation or body of persons which is a charity within the meaning of the Charities Act 1960 and which is prevented by its rules or constituent instrument from granting tenancies of dwelling houses occupied for the purposes of the charity;

Hostel Deficit Grant means grant payable under Section 33 of the 1974 Act;

Revenue Deficit Grant means grant payable under Section 32 of the 1974 Act;

Housing Association Grant means grant payable under Section 29 of the 1974 Act, as amended by Section 130 of the 1980 Act;

housing land means land and buildings held by an association for the purpose of providing housing accommodation;

managing body means:

(a) in relation to a 1965 society, the committee of management or other directing body of the society;

(b) in relation to a charitable housing association which is a company incorporated under the Companies Acts, the board of directors of the company;

(c) in relation to a charitable housing association which is a trust, the trustees;

self-build society means a housing association whose object is to provide for sale to, or occupation by, its members, dwellings built or improved principally with the use of its members' own labour.

Introduction

2 Housing associations provide an alternative to local authority and private enterprise housing, either by acquiring and rehabilitating existing dwellings or by undertaking new building with the aim of providing rented accommodation in perpetuity or until purchased by the tenant. In addition, under the 1980 and 1984 Acts, they may sell accommodation to their existing tenants outright or on a shared ownership basis (in certain instances they are obliged to do this); undertake rehabilitation for sale either outright or on a shared ownership basis; build new accommodation for sale on a shared ownership basis.

This guideline applies to the audit of registered housing associations giving guidance on matters prescribed by the Housing Acts or by orders made thereunder. As registered housing associations may be legally constituted in a number of ways, guidance is also given in respect of compliance with other statutes or documents relevant to their constitution. The principles contained in this guideline may also give assistance in respect of the audit of housing associations which are not registered housing associations.

Background

Legal

3 Because registered housing associations can be legally constituted in a number of ways, it is essential for an auditor of such an association to be familiar with the legal framework within which it operates. This guideline is not intended to be a substitute for the proper consideration of the relevant legislation.

4 To receive certain loans, grants and subsidies payable under the Housing Acts, housing associations must register with the Housing Corporation. This corporate body was created by the 1964 Act and was given additional powers by the 1974 and 1980 Acts. In addition to the provision of finance for housing associations, the functions of the Housing Corporation include the promotion and assistance of registered housing associations, and the supervision and control of their activities.

5 The Housing Corporation may only register housing associations which are 1965 Act societies or charitable housing associations. Some 1965 Act societies are in fact charities, either through separate registration with the Charity Commissioners or through the use of charitable model rules. However, such societies are regarded for the purpose of this guideline as 1965 Act societies rather than as charitable housing associations.

6 1965 Act societies are obliged to follow:

(a) their rules, as registered with the Registrar of Friendly Societies;
(b) various Acts applicable to industrial and provident societies, in particular the 1965 and 1968 Acts;
(c) various sections of the 1974 and 1980 Acts.

Charitable housing associations are also obliged to follow certain sections of the 1974 and 1980 Acts. They may either be trusts or companies incorporated under the Companies Acts. Where they are trusts, their operations must be in accordance with their trust deeds, as approved by the Charity Commissioners. Where they are companies, their operations must be in accordance with the Companies Acts and their Memoranda and Articles of Association, as lodged with the Registrar of Companies.

General

7 As mentioned already, the Housing Corporation controls and encourages the housing association movement. In particular, under Section 1 of the 1974 Act, its general functions are to:

(a) promote and assist the development of registered housing associations and of unregistered self-build societies;
(b) facilitate the proper exercise and performance of the functions, and to publicise the aims and principles, of registered housing associations and unregistered self-build societies;
(c) establish and maintain a register of housing associations;
(d) exercise supervision and control over registered housing associations; and
(e) act as agent for the payment of Housing Association Grant to registered housing associations.

The Housing Corporation provides mortgage loan finance, guarantees bank overdrafts and issues circulars of guidance and policy. It also carries out a programme of monitoring associations registered with it and has the power to appoint a nominee to serve on the association's managing body and initiate investigations which may result in the Housing Corporation:

(a) removing any committee member, officer, agent or servant who has been responsible for or privy to misconduct or mismanagement, or has by his conduct contributed to it or facilitated it;
(b) ordering any bank or other person who holds money or securities on behalf of an association not to part with the money or securities without the approval of the

Housing Corporation;

(c) restricting, by order, the transactions which may be entered into, or the nature, or amount of the payments which may be made in the administration of an association without the approval of the Housing Corporation.

8 In addition to the Housing Corporation, the following have a major impact on the housing association movement:

(a) The Department of the Environment and the Welsh Office. These government departments work jointly to determine and control housing policy in England and Wales. The Department of the Environment is also the principal source of revenue and capital grants for housing purposes.

(b) The Scottish Development Department. This is the relevant government department for Scotland.

(c) The Registry of Friendly Societies. This is the body responsible for the administration of the Industrial and Provident Societies Acts, 1965-1978 which are applicable *inter alia* to 1965 Act societies.

(d) The National Federation of Housing Associations ('the NFHA'). This is the central representative body for housing associations, trusts and societies in England and Wales. Although it receives a grant from the Department of the Environment, the NFHA is a wholly independent body whose revenue comes chiefly from its member housing associations. The NFHA provides common services for its members and represents them in discussions with the government, local authorities and other bodies. It arranges training courses and conferences, carries out research and other activities, and produces a monthly magazine 'Voluntary Housing' and other publications as a means of disseminating information.

(e) The Northern Ireland Federation of Housing Associations. This body undertakes in Northern Ireland the functions carried out by NFHA in England and Wales.

(f) Insurance Service for Housing Associations Ltd. This is a company set up by the NFHA (majority shareholder) and the Housing Corporation (minority shareholder) in order to provide insurance services to housing associations.

(g) Housing Association Consultancy and Advisory Service Ltd. This is a company limited by guarantee and jointly owned by the Housing Corporation and the NFHA which provides consultancy services to housing associations.

(h) The Scottish Federation of Housing Associations. This is a voluntary body to which Scottish registered housing associations may belong.

(i) The National Association of Almshouses. This is a voluntary body to which registered housing associations which are almshouses may belong.

(j) Local Authorities. There is usually a close relationship between local authorities and registered housing associations, the former providing finance to enable the latter to provide housing.

9 Appendix 1 sets out the sources of finance and subsidy which are available to registered housing associations. The more common of these are loans from local authorities and the Housing Corporation, and Revenue Deficit Grant, Hostel Deficit Grant and Housing Association Grant from central government.

Taxation

10 Housing associations have no general exemption from taxation, but those with charitable status are entitled to exemptions laid down in Section 360 of the Income and Corporation Taxes Act 1970 and other reliefs available in practice to charities. Housing associations without charitable status may be entitled to certain reliefs under Section 341 of the Income and Corporation Taxes Act 1970, providing they are co-operative housing associations approved by the Inland Revenue, mainly co-ownership societies, or self-build societies. In addition, under Section 93 of the Finance Act 1965, other housing associations may obtain relief from income tax and corporation tax in relation to their housing activities in the form of grants from the Secretary of State for the Environment, for Scotland or for Wales.

Accounting

The Registered Housing Associations (Accounting Requirements) Order 1982 (Statutory Instrument 1982 No. 828)

11 Under Sections 124(1) and 151 of the 1980 Act the Secretary of State for the Environment may, by order, lay down accounting requirements for registered housing associations. The first of these orders, the Registered Housing Associations (Accounting Requirements) Order 1982 lays down requirements, in respect of periods commencing on or after 1 September 1982, with a view to ensuring that accounts disclose certain information, include additional financial statements and give a true and fair view so far as housing activities are concerned.

12 The information that needs to be disclosed is set out in the first Schedule of the Order. It comprises matters to be shown in:

- (a) the balance sheet;
- (b) the balance sheet or in notes to the accounts;
- (c) the summary income and expenditure account, which is defined by the 1982 Order as meaning the revenue account as required by legislation relating to the 1965 Act societies and charitable housing associations;
- (d) the summary income and expenditure account or in notes to the accounts.

Nothing prevents further information from being disclosed.

13 The additional financial statements that need to be prepared are set out in paragraphs 5 and 7 of the 1982 Order. They comprise:

- (a) a source and application of funds statement;
- (b) a general income and expenditure account;
- (c) except in relation to a co-ownership society, a property revenue account and a statement of housing administration costs;
- (d) in relation to a co-ownership society, a housing cost and finance statement.

14 With the exception of the statement of housing administration costs, the accounts (including the additional financial statements) described above need to be accompanied by corresponding amounts for the preceding period. However, as a transitional arrangement, paragraph 9 of the 1982 Order states that corresponding amounts need not be shown where:

- (a) the preceding period began before 1 September 1982; and
- (b) the managing body of the association states that information relating to the preceding period cannot be obtained without unreasonable expense or delay.

15 It is explicitly recognised in the 1982 Order that its requirements should not take precedence over the statutory requirements to give a true and fair view. Where, however, it is necessary to depart from the 1982 Order in order to give a true and fair view, the 1982

Order requires that the fact of the departure, the reasons for it and its effect be recorded in the notes to the accounts. It should be noted that the 1982 Order only deals with matters relating to housing activities whereas Section 3 of the 1968 Act and part 1 of Schedule 16 of the 1980 Act require respectively the accounts of 1965 Act societies and charitable housing associations to give a true and fair view of the society or charity as a whole.

The Registered Housing Associations (Accounting Requirements for Almshouses) Order 1983 (Statutory Instrument 1983 No. 207)

16 This allows almshouse charities to omit the additional financial statements referred to in paragraph 13 above.

The Recommended Form of Published Accounts for Housing Associations and Statements of Standard Accounting Practice

17 The booklet, 'Recommended Form of Published Accounts for Housing Associations', published by the Housing Corporation in association with the NFHA and following consultations with the CCAB and other relevant bodies provides a detailed insight into housing association accounting and the various bases acceptable to the Department of the Environment when it determines eligibility for certain grants. These recommendations do not carry statutory authority, but accounts drawn up in accordance with the Recommended Form should comply with statutory requirements for housing associations. The Recommended Form is therefore essential reading for auditors of housing associations.

18 Because the accounts of 1965 Act societies and charitable housing associations are required to give a true and fair view, registered housing associations fall within the ambit of SSAPs. SSAPs, however, do not specifically deal with housing association accounting and this represents another reason for following the Recommended Form, as it explains how certain SSAPs (notably SSAP 4 'The accounting treatment of government grants' and SSAP 12 'Accounting for depreciation') can be met. It is important that the main accounting policies are set out in the accounts in accordance with SSAP 2.

19 A minority of housing associations are incorporated under the Companies Acts. The financial statements of such associations need additionally to comply with the requirements of the Companies Acts.

Some areas of accounting requiring special attention

20 Cyclical repairs and maintenance. In order to spread the cost of cyclical repairs and maintenance there is need for a provision for future repairs and maintenance, representing amounts set aside by annual charges to the property revenue account. Although provisions are not taken into account for Revenue Deficit Grant purposes, it will be necessary for an association to set aside amounts based on expected future expenditure to enable its accounts to give a true and fair view.

21 Apportionment. This is necessary for three reasons. First, since Revenue Deficit Grant is assessed by reference to the deficit in the property revenue account, certain items (such as management expenses) need to be split between the property revenue account and the general income and expenditure account. Secondly, within the general income and expenditure account, a number of separate apportionments may be necessary in order to comply with the 1982 Order. Thirdly, where an association undertakes any activities which are not housing activities, it is required by the 1982 Order to identify those which relate solely to housing activities and to apportion those items which relate to housing and other activities. In addition, apportionment enables costs to be properly reported and controlled.

22 Housing Association Grant and capital expenditure. Most schemes of acquisition, development and improvement undertaken by registered housing associations are financed by loans (from local authorities or the Housing Corporation) and Housing Association Grant. This is significant as the principles used in determining what are the capital costs of development and improvement and what are major repair schemes for grant purposes may also be relevant in determining what is capital expenditure for the purposes of the accounts. In this connection, guidance given in the Recommended Form should be useful.

23 Property Equity Account. The capital cost of housing accommodation less Housing Association Grant, property equity (or internal funding) account and depreciation, should be capable of being reconciled to outstanding loans, after taking into account loan advances receivable.

24 Grant Redemption Fund. Under Section 131 of the 1980 Act, every registered housing association which has at any time received Housing Association Grant, is required to set up a Grant Redemption Fund and to show separately in its accounts surpluses arising from increased rental income from projects on which grant has been paid. The 1982 Order prescribes how the Grant Redemption Fund is to be constituted and shown in the accounts. In addition, the Department of the Environment has issued The Grant Redemption Fund (Manner of Calculating Surpluses) Determination 1982 (issued on 26 August 1983), which sets out how housing associations should calculate the surpluses which should be transferred to the fund, and The Grand Redemption Fund (Rate of Interest) Determination 1982, which specifies the rate of interest to be charged by the Secretary of State on surpluses recovered. In order to calculate the Grand Redemption Fund, housing associations will need to analyse revenue income and expenditure, and in some cases capital expenditure, between schemes financed by Housing Association Grant, those financed by other means and those with a mixture of funding. The accounting system of an association will need to be in a form that can produce this information.

25 Revenue Deficit Grant and Hostel Deficit Grant. Schedule 1 of the 1982 Order requires the balance sheet to show the amount included in current assets in respect of Revenue Deficit Grant and Hostel Deficit Grant receivable. This may cause problems because associations will be including in their accounts amounts of grant receivable in respect of which claims cannot yet have been made — as they must first be supported by audited accounts and by reports by the auditors on the claims. Although the Secretary of State has discretion over the amounts of grant paid, the Department of the Environment has addressed problems associated with the discretionary nature of the grants by publishing the Principles used by the Department of the Environment and Welsh Office for assessing claims for Revenue Deficit Grant and for Hostel Deficit Grant. It therefore follows that although it is likely that grants receivable will not have been claimed at the date of the audit report, an amount based on a prudent assessment using the above principles should be included in the accounts.

26 Accumulated Surplus and Specific Reserves. All the reserves of an association, other than those which can be shown to have been derived from non-housing sources such as charitable donations and commercial income, will normally be taken into account and offset against deficits in the determination of Revenue Deficit Grant and Hostel Deficit Grant. Accordingly, associations find it convenient to distinguish surpluses arising from non-housing sources in their accounts.

27 Housing land. Schedule 1 of the 1982 Order also lays down rules for calculating the net book value of housing land. These rules differ as between housing land belonging to a co-ownership society and other housing land.

28 Disposals of housing property. Under the 1980 Act, tenants of associations without charitable status were given the right to buy their homes. Associations without charitable status were allowed to undertake rehabilitation schemes for sale and were also allowed to build new homes or rehabilitate existing housing for shared ownership. Accounting for these disposals and properly dealing with the resulting surpluses or deficits including the taxation implications can be complex. In this connection, guidance given in the Recommended Form and circulars issued from time to time by the Housing Corporation should be useful.

Accounting requirements specific to 1965 Act societies or charitable housing associations

29 In addition to the above which apply to registered housing associations in general, there are other matters contained in the Acts which apply specifically to 1965 Act societies or charitable housing associations.

30 1965 Act societies. Under the 1965 and 1968 Acts these societies are required:

(a) to cause to be kept such proper books of account as are necessary to give a true and fair view of their affairs and to explain their transactions;

(b) to establish and maintain satisfactory systems of control of their books of account, their cash holdings and all their receipts and remittances;

(c) to send to the Registrar of Friendly Societies annual returns together with accounts, as defined by Section 3 of the 1968 Act, and the auditor's report thereon;

(d) not to publish any revenue account or balance sheet unless it has been audited and signed by the secretary and two committee members of the society.

31 Charitable housing associations. Part 1 of Schedule 16 of the 1980 Act lays down similar requirements, to those described in paragraph 30(a) and (b) above, in respect of charitable housing associations. However, where such charitable housing associations are trusts, they need only file accounts with the Charity Commissioners if they are specifically requested to do so. Where such charitable housing associations are companies, incorporated under the Companies Acts, it will be necessary for them to maintain accounting records and to file annual returns and audited accounts with the Registrar of Companies in accordance with those Acts. The Companies Registration Office of the Department of Trade has no objection to receiving, for filing, accounts which have been expanded to contain extra information required under another Act.

Auditing

Scope

32 The scope of an audit of a registered housing association depends on the form of audit report required by relevant statutes and any additional requirements laid down by the association's rules, constitutional documents (e.g. trust deeds) or managing body.

33 Statutory provisions relevant for audit reporting purposes include the following:

(a) Section 124(2) of the Housing Act 1980.
This applies to all registered housing associations and requires the auditor's report to state *inter alia* whether in his opinion the financial statements comply with the accounting requirements laid down by order by the Secretary of State i.e. the Registered Housing Associations (Accounting Requirements) Order 1982, and, where relevant, the Registered Housing Associations (Accounting Requirements for Almshouses) Order 1983.

(b) Section 9 of the 1968 Act.

This only applies to those associations which are 1965 Act societies.

(c) Part 1 of Schedule 16 of the 1980 Act.
This only applies to registered charitable housing associations.

(d) Section 14 of the Companies Act 1967.
This only applies to those registered charitable housing associations which are companies. It must be regarded as being additional to part 1 of Schedule 16 of the 1980 Act, and not as being in lieu thereof.

34 The audit reporting requirements of Section 9 of the 1968 Act and part 1 of Schedule 16 of the 1980 Act include the need for the auditor to state whether in his opinion the financial statements give a true and fair view, and are broadly similar in other respects to those of Section 14 of the Companies Act 1967. There are, however, two important differences from the reporting requirements of the Companies Acts.
First, there is no statutory requirement that an auditor should report where information contained outside the audited accounts (i.e. in the directors' report) is not consistent with those accounts. Secondly, the auditor has to state the fact in his report where, in his opinion, a satisfactory system of control over transactions has not been maintained.

35 Given the numerous possible sources of audit reporting requirements, the scope of the audit including statutory requirements should be discussed with the managing body, and then defined and explained in a suitably worded engagement letter.

Key audit areas

36 In addition to the areas of accounting described in paragraphs 20-28 above, key audit areas which may require special consideration include the following.

Rents

37 In respect of the rented accommodation provided by an association, the auditor should be aware that:

(a) except in the case of co-ownership societies and hostels, rents, and increases therein, need to be determined and registered by a rent officer or, on appeal against his registration, with a rent assessment committee;

(b) after November 1983, unless a substantial change has taken place in the accommodation provided or in the terms of the tenancy agreement, an application for a new registered rent cannot be made earlier than three months before the second anniversary of the date of an existing registration;

(c) a rent increase arising on re-registration needs to be phased in respect of any period of delay in accordance with provisions contained in Schedule 6 to the 1976 Act and Schedule 8 of the 1977 Act as amended by Section 60 of the 1980 Act;

(d) For Revenue Deficit Grant purposes, the Department of the Environment will make the assumption that the maximum possible fair rents have been charged. In Grant Redemption Fund calculations, it is also assumed that maximum fair rents under the existing legislation have been charged.

Some associations collect rents in cash, using rent collectors. Such a system of collection can create problems for the auditor because it is sometimes difficult to obtain corroborative evidence such as tenants' rent books.

Service charges and rates

38 Service charges, and in most cases general rates and water rates, are collected with the rents. In this context, the auditor should note that since the 1980 Act rent officers assess fixed service charges on their value to the tenants and variable service charges on the costs to the landlord. However, local variations of practice can occur, and the auditor should be aware of this. The auditor should also note that, where there are intervals or voids between tenancies, the association may be liable for rates. For instance, where a statutory authority has resolved to exercise a power to rate empty properties, an association may after a period of vacancy (normally three months) become liable for void rates. Alternatively, if the association has undertaken a rate collection agreement with the statutory authority in return for a discount or allowance, it will not normally receive the benefit of a free period.

Repairs

39 The volume of repair work carried out by outside contractors is often considerable. In such circumstances, it is important that there are arrangements for ensuring that there are proper ordering procedures such as the obtaining of tenders or quotations, and that the income tax regulations regarding payments to sub-contractors in the construction industry are being properly observed.

Grants

40 As indicated in paragraph 9 and Appendix 1, registered housing associations are eligible for finance from a number of sources. This can create difficulties for associations in respect of:

(a) knowing the existence of a type of grant and the right to claim it;

(b) presenting the claim within the required time limits;

(c) following the correct conditions in order to obtain the grant;

(d) maximising the opportunities for receiving payments on account.

The auditor of a registered housing association should be familiar with the workings of the grants system and the methods of treating grants in financial statements.

Housing land

41 Title deeds for housing land are normally held by lending authorities. Housing land being sold, leased, mortgaged, charged or otherwise disposed of requires the consent of the Housing Corporation, except in the cases of sales to secure tenants exercising their right to buy under the 1980 Act.

Interest on loans incurred

42 Interest accruing on loans during the development period is capitalised and included as part of the cost of a scheme. The total qualifying costs (including interest) will then be financed in part by a repayment mortgage based on the capitalised value of the rental income, net of deductions for management and maintenance, with the balance met by Housing Association Grant. The interest which arises on the repayment mortgage should be charged in full to the property revenue account. Any interest on development costs arising after the repayment account has been set up will be capitalised and met by a final Housing Association Grant payment. Where a grant payment is delayed, interest arising on the outstanding loans to be repaid by grant will be paid by the Department of the Environment directly to the lending authority. This only arises where payment of Housing Association Grant has been delayed and the interest is known as simple interest. If a delay in paying Housing Association Grant is attributable to the association, the simple interest payment by the Department of the Environment will be restricted to 90% and the balance (known as penalty interest) will become due from the association to the lending authority. There are no grants available to fund this liability and it must be met from the association's own resources. If a property is sold, where simple interest has previously been paid by the Department, although the simple interest may not be recorded in the association's books of accounts, the Department will require its repayment out of any proceeds of sales. Such repayment will be abated if the sale is under the right to buy provisions of the 1980 Act.

Prohibited payments

43 Sections 26 and 27 of the 1974 Act (as amended by part 2 of Schedule 16 of the 1980 Act) prohibit registered housing associations in general, and in certain cases (see Section 27) 1965 Act societies only, from making payments or gifts, or from granting benefits, to association officers, committee members and employees, their relatives and various entities with which these persons may be associated. A number of exemptions are given, the most notable being that:

(a) payments can be made, and benefits granted, to an officer or employee under his contract of employment;
(b) payments of expenses can be made to a committee member;
(c) certain charitable housing trusts are empowered under the terms of their trust deed to pay an honorarium to each member of the committee who attends meetings.

The provisions contained in these sections have audit significance as, under the 1982 Order, details of payments, gifts and benefits are required to be shown in the summary income and expenditure account or in the notes to the accounts.

Donations and fund-raising

44 Some registered charitable housing associations can derive a substantial proportion of their income from donations and fund-raising. In such cases the auditor should make use of the guidance given in the Auditing Guideline 'Charities'.

Stocks and work in progress

45 Where associations undertake Improvement for Sale and Shared Ownership Schemes and show development in progress as 'stocks and work in progress' in the balance sheet, it is important that account is taken of any foreseeable losses likely to arise in respect of the ultimate disposal of the units. This is particularly important where an association has completed properties and is unable to sell these within a reasonable time, resulting in an accumulation of interest.

Mortgages receivable

46 At the balance sheet date loan advances may be outstanding from lending authorities in respect of schemes in progress. Such mortgages receivable will be shown as current assets in the associated accounts. It is, however, important that this account does not include items which will not ultimately qualify for loans or grant and therefore represent unfunded capital deficits. Under most circumstances, amounts shown as due at the balance sheet date should have been received before the audit is completed.

Borrowing limits

47 The auditor should carefully consider any constraints on borrowing limits contained within an association's rules. Memorandum and Articles of Association, trust deed, or charity commission scheme. Many associations have a specific borrowing limit which could be exceeded by the gross borrowings for development (including interest awaiting capitalisation), even though residual mortgages after payment of Housing Association Grant would be *intra vires*.

Auditing procedures

Planning

48 Paragraph 2 of the auditor's operational standard states that "the auditor should adequately plan, control and record his work". When planning the audit of a registered housing association, the following should be considered in addition to the matters described in the Auditing Guideline 'Planning, controlling and recording':

(a) the large number of statutes which may affect the association;
(b) the Recommended Form;
(c) new orders made by the Secretary of State under Sections 124(1) and 151 of the 1980 Act;
(d) administrative circulars issued by the Department of the Environment and the Housing Corporation;
(e) changes affecting registered housing associations (these are normally reported in the NFHA's magazine 'Voluntary Housing');
(f) the need to form a separate opinion as to whether a satisfactory system of control has been maintained;
(g) any monitoring report on the association produced by the Housing Corporation.

49 In considering the timing of significant phases in the preparation of the accounts, the auditor should bear in mind time limits for filing accounts. In this respect Section 124(3) of the 1980 Act provides that every registered housing association shall furnish to the Housing Corporation a copy of its accounts and auditor's report within six months of the end of the period to which they relate. In addition Section 39 of the 1965 Act lays down a three month time limit which affects 1965 Act societies.

Accounting systems

50 Paragraph 3 of the Auditing Guideline, 'Accounting systems' states that "the auditor will often have a separate and distinct responsibility to form an opinion as to the adequacy of the accounting records for the purposes of complying with the legislation or regulations to which the enterprise may be subject". Such a responsibility exists in respect of a registered housing association, in whatever manner it may be constituted. The areas of activity requiring special attention, when ascertaining and assessing the accounting system of a housing association, are listed in paragraphs 20-28 and 37-47.

Audit evidence

51 Paragraph 8 of the Auditing Guideline, 'Audit evidence' states that "audit evidence is obtained by carrying out audit tests which may be classified as 'substantive' or 'compliance' according to their primary purpose". The need to review the system of internal control means that the auditor will normally have to carry out compliance tests. When designing substantive tests for registered housing associations, the auditor should give special attention to the possibility of:

(a) understatement or incompleteness of the recording of income including rents, service charges and where appropriate rates receivable from tenants, proceeds from the sale of properties, gifts in kind and cash donations;
(b) grants claimed being disallowed (including capital grants relating to expenditure which may have been the subject of interim mortgage advances);
(c) payments being made for repair work, when no work has in fact been carried out;
(d) prohibited payments made not being disclosed;
(e) housing land being sold, leased, mortgaged, charged or otherwise disposed of without consent being obtained from the Housing Corporation, except in the case of a sale to a sitting tenant exercising his right to buy under the 1980 Act;
(f) housing accommodation being misstated or omitted;
(g) loans incurred not being recorded;
(h) rents in respect of development schemes not being properly accounted for between capital and revenue. Under the Housing Association Grant system, parts

of the rents received during a development period should be capitalised if the scheme exceeds 50 units.

52 Financial statements of housing associations are required to disclose information in greater detail than those of most other enterprises. This will have to be taken into account by the auditor, as the nature and extent of evidence needed to achieve the required level of audit assurance will be influenced by the detail disclosed in the financial statements and the form of report which the auditor is required to give.

53 Analytical review procedures as applied to business enterprises will need to be modified in the case of registered housing associations. In particular, consideration should be given to the relationship between the number of housing units available for occupation, the incidence of empty units and rents receivable. Furthermore, the capital cost of housing accommodation less Housing Association Grant, depreciation and property equity account should be checked to ensure that it equals outstanding loans, after taking into account loan advances receivable.

Internal controls

54 The Auditing Guideline, 'Internal controls' has particular relevance to the audit of registered housing associations. This is because of:

(a) specific requirements (see paragraphs 30 and 31) on 1965 Act societies and charitable housing associations to establish and maintain satisfactory systems of control over their accounting records, their cash holdings, receipts and remittances;

(b) corresponding requirements (see paragraph 34) on the auditors of 1965 Act societies and charitable housing associations to state the fact in their reports when in their opinion a satisfactory system of control over transactions has not been maintained.

55 Large registered housing associations should have the internal controls appropriate to any large enterprise, and the auditor should look for and encourage such an association to implement internal controls and reporting systems in keeping with the scale of operations.

56 Small registered housing associations may often suffer from internal control weaknesses common to small enterprises, such as lack of segregation of duties and use of unqualified or part-time staff. Shortcomings may possibly arise in the implementation of formal procedures from the staff's lack of training, particularly if they are volunteers. Adequate control may often be available in a small association by means of increased review and authorisation procedures by its managing body.

57 Examples of internal controls in areas of particular significance to registered housing associations and which might be expected to be present in most housing associations are set out in paragraphs 58-64 below. Other types of internal control, on which the auditor may seek to rely, are described in the Auditing Guideline, 'Internal controls'.

Rents

58 (a) Periodic checking (by an official other than a rent collector) of notifications of voids, of rent registrations and of changes in the housing stock to the rent ledger and to tenants' rent books.

(b) Reconciliation of rents receivable to the number of units, registered rents and the incidence of voids.

(c) Rotation of collectors and comparisons of their performance.

(d) Arrears procedures by a person who is not responsible for collecting or handling rent monies.

(e) Regular comparisons between the rent ledger and the banking records.

Service charges and, where appropriate, rates

59 (a) Reconciliation of service charges receivable with the number of units, the service charges determined by the rent officer and the incidence of voids.

(b) Arrears procedures by a person who is not responsible for collecting or handling service charge or rate monies.

(c) Procedures to ensure that rate refunds are obtained for void periods and that nil assessments are obtained when the property is uninhabitable.

Property development

60 (a) Proper tendering procedures (e.g. procedures in accordance with "Housing Corporation Schemework Procedure Guide").

(b) Involvement of the managing body in the appointment of consultants.

(c) Authorisation procedures, involving the managing body, before properties are purchased.

(d) Inspection and approval procedures before payment.

Disposal of housing land

61 (a) Authorisation procedures, involving the managing body.

(b) Scrutiny by an independent official to ensure that, where appropriate Housing Corporation consent has been obtained, and that disposal proceeds have been properly received and accounted for.

Grants and loans

62 (a) Regular checks that all sources of income or funds are fully utilised and that appropriate claims have been made.

(b) Procedures to ensure that income or funds are correctly applied in accordance with the grant or loan.

(c) Controls over application for grants and loans.

(d) Reconciliations between property costs and property mortgages.

Housing accommodation

63 Controls to ensure all housing accommodation is recorded and to ensure that all changes are reflected in the records.

Repairs

64 (a) Procedures for obtaining tenders or quotations, particularly in respect of major repair work.

(b) Inspection and approval procedures before payment.

(c) Comparison of repair costs against budgets.

65 Paragraph 21 of the Auditing Guideline, 'Internal controls' states that "it is important that the auditor should report, as soon as practicable, significant weaknesses in internal controls which come to his attention during the course of an audit to an appropriate senior level of management of the enterprise". In the context of a registered housing association, such an appropriately senior level of management will be the managing body, and any letter to it should be sent through its chairman.

66 The auditor of a registered housing association should be aware that:

(a) the Housing Corporation may expect associations to require management letters from auditors;

(b) using its general powers of supervision and control, the Housing Corporation may expect such letters to be made available on request to itself by the association.

Review of financial statements

67 In determining whether the accounts have been prepared on the basis of acceptable accounting policies, consideration should be given to the Recommended Form and SSAPs. Particular attention should be paid to the areas described in paragraphs 20-28, and to:

(a) the basis for valuing schemes still in the course of development;

(b) the matching of development allowances to periods in which administration costs can be expected to arise;

(c) the treatment of interest accruing on loans (see paragraph 42);

(d) the treatment of rents received in respect of development schemes (see paragraph 51 (h));

(e) the basis of providing against rents in arrear;

(f) the possible erroneous inclusion of loan advances receivable relating to non qualifying capital costs under the balance sheet item 'mortgages receivable'.

68 During his review of presentation and disclosure, the auditor of a registered housing association should consider any new factors which affect the presentation or accounting policies adopted. For example, where an association incurs unfunded capital or revenue expenditure by incurring exceptional repairs, or by wrongly anticipating that statutory approval of a purchase of property would be received, or where schemes substantially overrun the original budgets, the auditor should consider whether it is still appropriate for the accounts to be prepared on a going concern basis. Similarly, the auditor will need to consider the adequacy of the financing arrangements disclosed in the note on capital commitments in the accounts.

69 The auditor should also consider whether the main accounting policies are adequately disclosed. Furthermore, where there is a figure for Revenue Deficit Grant or Hostel Deficit Grant, he should expect to see a note to the effect that although the payment of the grant is at the discretion of the Secretary of State, the amount brought into the accounts has been evaluated in accordance with the principles used by the Department of the Environment and Welsh Office for assessing claims for Revenue Deficit Grant and Hostel Deficit Grant published by the Department of the Environment.

70 In determining whether the accounts comply with all statutory requirements and other regulations, account should be taken of the 1982 Order and of the legal framework within which a particular registered housing association operates. Attention should also be paid to the Recommended Form.

Reporting

General

71 Because of the statutory requirements (see paragraph 34) for the auditor's report to include an expression of opinion as to whether the financial statements give a true and fair view, this section of the guideline should be read in conjunction with the Auditing Standards, 'The audit report' and 'Qualifications in audit reports', the Auditing Guideline, 'Audit report examples' and, where there are donations, the Auditing Guideline, 'Charities'.

72 In addition, as stated in paragraph 33, the report should include an expression of opinion as to whether the financial statements comply with the Registered Housing Associations (Accounting Requirements) Order 1982 and, where relevant, the registered Housing Associations (Accounting Requirements for Almshouses) Order 1983 .

73 As explained below, the form of the report and the persons to whom it is addressed will depend on the constitution of the registered housing association.

Audit reports on 1965 Act societies

74 The auditor's report should, in order to comply with Section 9 of the 1968 Act, be addressed to the society. It should include, in addition to the matters dealt with in paragraphs 71 and 72, an expression of opinion as to whether the financial statements comply with the requirements of the Industrial and Provident Societies Acts 1965-1978 .

75 Under Section 9 of the Friendly and Industrial Provident Societies Act 1968, the auditor must also state the fact in his report, where in his opinion:

(a) proper books of account have not been kept in accordance with the requirements of Section 1(1)(a) of that Act;

(b) a satisfactory system of control over transactions has not been maintained in accordance with the requirements of Section 1(1)(b) of that Act;

(c) the revenue account or accounts, the other accounts (if any) to which the report relates, and the balance sheet are not in agreement with the books of account;

(d) he has not obtained all the information and explanations he considers necessary.

76 Set out below is an appropriate form of wording for an unqualified audit report in respect of a 1965 Act society.

"AUDITORS' REPORT TO ... — A HOUSING ASSOCIATION REGISTERED UNDER SECTION 13 OF THE HOUSING ACT 1974

We have audited the financial statements on pages ... to ... in accordance with approved auditing standards.

In our opinion the financial statements, which have been prepared under the historical cost convention, give a true and fair view of the state of the society's affairs at 31 December 19.. and of its income and expenditure and source and application of funds for the year then ended and comply with the requirements of the Industrial and Provident Societies Acts 1965-1978, and the Registered Housing Associations (Accounting Requirements) Order 1982".

Where relevant, reference should also be made to the Registered Housing Associations (Accounting Requirements for Almshouses) Order 1983.

Audit reports on charitable housing associations

77 The auditor's report should, in order to comply with part 1 of Schedule 16 of the 1980 Act, be addressed to the charity. However, it should also be addressed to:

(a) the trustees, where the charity is a trust and there is a specific requirement in the trust deed to report to them;

(b) the members, where the charity is a company incorporated under the Companies Acts.

It should include, in addition to the matters dealt with in paragraphs 71 and 72, an expression of opinion as to whether the financial statements comply:

(a) with part 1 of Schedule 16 of the Housing Act 1980; and

(b) with the trust deed under which the housing association is constituted, or with the

Companies Acts 1948-1981.

78 Under part 1 of Schedule 16 of the Housing Act 1980, the auditor must also state the fact in his report where in his opinion:

(a) proper books of account have not been kept in accordance with that schedule;

(b) a satisfactory system of control has not been maintained in accordance with that schedule;

(c) the accounts are not in agreement with the books;

(d) he has not obtained all the information and explanations he considers necessary.

79 Where a charitable housing association is a trust, there may also be a need to express an opinion on certain additional matters in accordance with the trust deed (e.g. that proper books and records have been kept).

80 Where a charitable housing association is a company, it should be borne in mind that Sections 14 and 23A of the Companies Act 1967 lay down other matters which the auditor may need to state in his report.

81 Set out below is an appropriate form of wording for an unqualified audit report in respect of a charitable housing association:

"AUDITORS' REPORT TO THE (NAME OF THE CHARITY) — A HOUSING ASSOCIATION REGISTERED UNDER SECTION 13 OF THE HOUSING ACT 1974 — AND ITS TRUSTEES/MEMBERS

We have audited the financial statements on pages ... to ... in accordance with approved Auditing Standards.

In our opinion the financial statements, which have been prepared under the historical cost convention, give a true and fair view of the state of the charity's affairs at 31 December 19.. and of its income and expenditure and source and application of funds for the year then ended and comply with the requirements of the trust deed dated ..../Companies Acts 1948-1981, part 1 of Schedule 16 of the Housing Act 1980 and the Registered Housing Associations (Accounting Requirements) Order 1982."

Where relevant, reference should also be made to the Registered Housing Associations (Accounting Requirements for Almshouses) Order 1983.

Qualified audit reports

82 As mentioned in paragraph 56, there is often a need for small registered housing associations to have increased review and authorisation procedures by their managing bodies to overcome internal control weaknesses common to all small businesses. Where, in the auditor's opinion, such review and authorisation procedures have not been carried out, he should consider giving a 'subject to' opinion and including in his report the following explanatory paragraph.

"In common with many registered housing associations of similar size and organisation, there is difficulty in applying certain types of internal control. As a result, there is a need for increased review and authorisation procedures by the committee of management/the trustees/board of directors. In our opinion such review and authorisation procedures have not been carried out and as a result the society/charity has not maintained a satisfactory system of control of transactions in accordance with the requirements of Section 1(1)(b) of the Friendly and Industrial and Provident Societies Act 1968/part 1 of Schedule 16 of the Housing Act 1980."

An auditor qualifying on the grounds indicated above should also consider whether:

(a) proper books of accounts have been kept;

(b) there is a need to qualify his opinion on the financial statements on the grounds of uncertainty.

83 As explained in the Auditing Guideline, 'Charities', a particular and frequent problem for many small charities is the difficulty in applying proper control over voluntary donations until they are entered in the accounting records. Where such a problem exists in relation to a small charitable housing association (or indeed a small 1965 Act society which is a charity), the auditor may conclude that he is unable to give an unqualified opinion on the financial statements in respect of completeness of income. In such a case, the auditor should consider whether the form of audit report discussed and set out in paragraph 73 of the Auditing Guideline 'Charities' is appropriate.

Appendix 1
as at 18 September 1984
Sources of finance and subsidy

84 (a) *Housing Corporation*

Loans under Section 9 of the 1974 Act of up to one hundred per cent of the capital cost of an approved scheme, including legal and professional fees, acquisition and building costs, acquisition and development allowances and capitalised interest. The interest rate is normally fixed over the term of the loan, which is repaid partly through Housing Association Grant and partly by annual repayments on an annuity system.

Guarantees, under Section 10 of the 1974 Act, in respect of the repayment of the principal of and the payment of interest on sums borrowed otherwise than from the Housing Corporation.

The Housing Corporation also has the power to make loans under Section 7 of the Housing Act 1961 and Section 2 of the Housing Act 1964 but these powers are unlikely to be exercised.

85 (b) *Central Government — Department of the Environment*

(i) Housing Association Grant: Section 29 of the 1974 Act and paragraphs 1-7 of Schedule 18 of the 1980 Act

A capital grant on an approved housing project to reduce the loan to an amount, the repayment of which can be supported by the expected rental income net of allowances in respect of the costs of managing and maintaining properties. The circumstances in which this grant may be repayable are set out in the 1974 Act, and in Section 131 of the 1980 Act. Housing Association Grant acquisition and development allowances, initially given by way of loan to finance the administrative costs arising from the acquisition and development of land and buildings, are together with approved capital costs eligible to be met from this grant.

(ii) Revenue Deficit Grant: Section 32 of the 1974 Act and paragraph 9 of Schedule 18 of the 1980 Act

A discretionary grant to cover a deficit on revenue account.

(iii) Hostel Deficit Grant: Section 33 of the 1974 Act and paragraph 10 of Schedule 18 of the 1980 Act

A discretionary grant to cover deficits incurred in the running of hostel accomodation.

(iv) Basic residual subsidy: Section 72 of the 1972 Act

An annual reducing subsidy, introduced originally to compensate for subsidies lost under that Act.

(v) Special residual subsidy: Section 73 of the 1972 Act
An annual reducing subsidy on buildings completed in 1972 and 1973, and in 1974 before the Housing Act 1974 came into operation.

(vi) New building subsidy: Section 75 of the 1972 Act
An annual reducing subsidy on new buildings completed in 1972 and 1973, and in 1974 before the 1974 Act came into operation.

(vii) Hostel subsidy: Section 92 of the 1972 Act
A limited term subsidy for hostels.

(viii) Rent phasing grant:
A grant covering the shortfall between the registered fair rent determined at the completion of a rehabilitation scheme and that paid by each tenant, having regard to pre-modernisation registration and the rent phasing of increases under the 1980 Act.

86 (c) *Local Government*

(i) Loans from Local Authorities: Section 119 of the 1957 Act
Exactly as for (a) above but interest rates not always fixed this will vary from authority to authority.

(ii) Welfare grants: Section 119 of the 1957 Act
Grants for schemes where a welfare element is provided.

(iii) Rate fund contributions
Discretionary support out of general rate fund, paid by a cheque or by deduction from payments due for mortgage interest and repayments.

(iv) Exchequer subsidies
Paid by Central Government to the Local Authority and through it to the housing association, in respect of subsidies provided under the Housing Acts 1967 and 1969 for converted properties.

(v) Housing benefits
Tenants with low incomes or receiving supplementary benefits from the Department of Health and Social Security may be entitled to housing benefits. With the tenant's agreement, these may be paid direct to the housing association landlord.

(vi) Other grants available from Local Authorities include improvement grants, hostel grants, repair grants, smoke control grants, home insulation grants, housing action area, general improvement and conservation area grants. Local authorities may also guarantee bank overdrafts.

87 (d) *Other*

(i) Loans from building societies
These are likely to increase in the future particularly in respect of shared ownership schemes and new initiatives.

(ii) Finance from banks
Banks are usually involved in the provision of temporary or short-term finance such as overdraft facilities.

(iii) Charitable money
Housing associations may receive donations, legacies, covenanted subscriptions or proceeds from fund-raising events. The Housing Associations' Charitable Trust exists to allocate loans and grants to housing associations for purposes in respect of which statutory funds are not available.

(iv) Surpluses arising from in-house architects' and surveyors' departments
Some large housing associations maintain departments which carry out professional services in respect of housing developments. The cost of such services, based on the fees charged by external architects and surveyors, is eligible for mortgage loan finance and is included in Housing Association Grant calculations. Therefore, the difference between the market price of these services which would normally be higher, because of the profit element, and the cost to the housing association of providing them internally represents a source of income for the association.

(v) In addition, finance may also be available from the European Economic Community, and from the Department of Health and Social Security in respect of special care schemes, and from the Department of the Environment and Local Authorities in respect of listed buildings.

Appendix 2
as at 18 September 1984
Bibliography

88 The following is a list of statutes and other documents which may give further assistance to the auditors of housing associations. Relevant documents available may change as developments relating to housing associations take place. In this respect, it will be useful to take account of the NFHA's magazine 'Voluntary Housing' and circulars issued by the Housing Corporation and the Department of the Environment.

Government legislation

Companies Acts 1948-1981
Income and Corporation Taxes Act 1970
Industrial and Provident Societies Act 1965
Finance Act 1965
Friendly and Industrial and Provident Societies Act 1968
Housing Finance Act 1972
Housing Act 1974
Rent (Agriculture) Act 1976
Rent Act 1977
Housing Act 1980
Statutory Instrument No 828: The Registered Housing Associations (Accounting Requirements) Order 1982
Statutory Instrument No 207: The Registered Housing Associations (Accounting Requirements for Almshouses) Order 1983

Department of the Environment

The Grant Redemption Fund (Manner of Calculating Surpluses) Determination 1982
The Grant Redemption Fund (Rate of Interest) Determination 1982
Principles used by the Department of the Environment and the Welsh Office for assessing claims for Revenue Deficit Grant
Principles used by the Department of the Environment and the Welsh Office for assessing claims for Hostel Deficit Grant
HAG manual
Circular 103/77: Calculation and payment of Housing Association Grant
Circular 14/83: Local authorities and housing associations

Housing Corporation

Recommended Form of Published Accounts for Housing Associations
Schemework Procedure Guide and Scottish Guidance Note 8/80 (dealing with tendering procedures)

National Federation of Housing Associations

A Committee Member's Handbook (this contains an extensive appendix which sets out further sources of information)
Various booklets, including in particular a series on the Housing Act 1980
A Manual of Housing Associations Finance (with update service — published jointly with the Chartered Institute of Public Finance and Accountancy)

Appendix 3

Special considerations relating to Scotland

89 The legislation referred to in the text of the guideline is that relating to England and Wales. In Scotland all housing associations are incorporated bodies registered under the Industrial and Provident Societies Acts. All references to other housing associations which are charities registered with the Charity Commission, either incorporated as companies under the Companies Acts or unincorporated bodies governed by their trust deed are therefore irrelevant. This includes all references to Schedule 16 of the Housing Act 1980. Other references in the guideline for which there are different Scottish equivalents, are as follows:

Paragraph	*Reference*	*Scottish equivalent*
1	Providing rented housing accommodation in perpetuity	A long-term basis would be more appropriate as perpetuities as such are not recognised in Scots law.
1, 41, 42 51(e)	Sitting tenants right to buy under the Housing Act 1980	In Scotland tenants have no right to buy but associations are encouraged to develop a voluntary policy of selling to sitting tenants.
11	The Secretary of the Environment may prescribe accounting requirements	In Scotland the authority is the Secretary of State for Scotland acting through the Scottish Development Department. For the first Order the Secretary of State for the Environment, the Secretary of State for Scotland and the Secretary of State for Wales collaborated in promulgating the Accounting Requirements Order (SI 828/1982) operative throughout the United Kingdom.
25 and 69	Principles used by the Department of the Environment and Welsh Office for assessing claims for Revenue Deficit Grant	Principles to be adopted by the Scottish Development Department for assessing claims for Revenue Deficit Grant.
37(b)	Application for registration	In Scotland the relevant date is the

Paragraph	*Reference*	*Scottish equivalent*
	of a new rent three months before the second anniversary of the date of an existing registration	third anniversary of the date of an existing registration. Provisions applicable to registration and valuation of rents are those of Part IV of the Rent (Scotland) Act 1971 as applied by ss.60-68 of the Housing (Financial Provisions) (Scotland) Act 1972 which are amended by the Housing (Financial Provisions) (Scotland) Act 1978 and the Tenants Rights etc. (Scotland) Act 1980.
37(c)	Schedule 8 of the 1977 Rent Act as amended by s.60 of the 1980 Act	Housing (Financial Provisions) (Scotland) Act 1972 s.63 as amended by Housing (Financial Provisions) (Scotland) Act 1978. See also orders under SI 1668/1980 and SI 278/1981.
60(a)	Housing Corporation Schemework Procedure Guide	Scottish Guidance Note 8/80.
Appendix 1		
(a)	s.7 of the Housing Act 1961	s.11 of the Housing (Scotland) Act 1962.
(b)(iv)	s.72 of the Housing Finance Act 1972	s.52 of the Housing (Financial Provisions) (Scotland) Act 1972.
(v)	s.73 of the Housing Finance Act 1972	s.53 of the Housing (Financial Provisions) (Scotland) Act 1972.
(vi)	s.75 of the Housing Finance Act 1972	s.55 of the Housing (Financial Provisions) (Scotland) Act 1972. (each as amended by Housing Act 1974 Sch. 13).
(vii)	s.92 of the Housing Finance Act 1972	s.21 of the Housing (Scotland) Act 1968 as amended by the Housing (Financial Provisions) (Scotland) Act 1972.
(c)(i) and (ii)	s.119 of the Housing Act 1957	cf. s.152 of the Housing (Scotland) Act 1966 as amended by the Housing (Scotland) Act 1974 s.17.
(iv)	Exchequer Subsidies Housing Acts 1967 and 1969	Housing (Scotland) Act 1974.

Appendix 2

Additional government legislation relevant to Scotland comprises:

- Housing (Financial Provisions) (Scotland) Act 1972
- Housing (Financial Provisions) (Scotland) Act 1978
- Housing (Scotland) Act 1974
- Tenants Rights etc. (Scotland) Act 1980

Appendix 4

Special considerations relating to Northern Ireland

90 The legislation referred to in the text of the guideline is that relating to England and Wales. In Northern Ireland all registered housing associations are incorporated bodies registered under the Industrial and Provident Societies Acts (Northern Ireland) 1969 and 1976 and the vast majority of these are charitable bodies. The functions carried out by the Housing Corporation are undertaken in Northern Ireland by the Department of the Environment for Northern Ireland ('DOE NI'). The following legislation is comparable in the context used in the guideline:

Used in guideline	*Equivalent in Northern Ireland*
the 1980 Act	the Housing (Northern Ireland) Orders 1981 and 1983 — the 1981 Order and the 1983 Order
the 1982 Order	the Registered Housing Associations (Accounting Requirements) (Northern Ireland) Order 1983 — the 1983 (AR) Order
the 1965 and 1968 Acts	the Industrial and Provident Societies Acts (Northern Ireland) 1969 and 1976 — the 1969 and 1976 Acts
the Companies Acts	the Companies Acts (Northern Ireland) 1960 to 1983

Other references in the guideline for which there are different equivalents in Northern Ireland are as follows:

Paragraph	*Reference*	*Equivalent in Northern Ireland*
1, 41, 42 5l(c)	Sitting tenant's right to buy under the 1980 Housing Act	In Northern Ireland tenants do not have a right to buy.
7(a)	Housing Corporations act as agent for the payment of Housing Association Grant to registered housing associations	The DOE NI considers applications for and makes payments of grants to registered housing associations.
11	The Secretary of the Environment may prescribe accounting treatments	Under Article 126A of the 1981 Order, the authority is the DOE NI. The first Order (the 1983 (AR) Order) lays down requirements in respect of periods commencing on or after 1 January 1984.
13	The additional financial statements that need to be prepared	Under Articles 5 and 6 of the 1983 (AR) Order the additional financial statements comprise: (a) a source and application of funds statement; (b) a property revenue account; (c) a property development account; (d) if appropriate, a services revenue account; (e) a general income and expenditure account;

Paragraph	*Reference*	*Equivalent in Northern Ireland*
		(f) a statement of housing administration costs.
14(a)	The transitional arrangement date	Under Article 9 of the 1983 (AR) Order, the date is 1 January 1984 not 1 September 1982.
24	Grant Redemption Fund	In Northern Ireland the requirement to set up a grant redemption fund applies to periods commencing on or after 1 January 1984.
	The Grant Redemption Fund (Manner of calculating surpluses) Determination 1982	The Grant Redemption Fund (Manner of calculating surpluses) (Northern Ireland) Determination 1983.
	The Grant Redemption Fund (Rate of Interest) Determination 1982	The Grant Redemption Fund (Rate of Interest) (Northern Ireland) Determination 1983.
25 and 69	Principles used by the Department of the Environment and Welsh Office for assessing claims for Revenue Deficit Grant and for Hostel Deficit Grant	There is no existing equivalent publication in Northern Ireland at present. The DOE NI hope to publish guidance on this topic before the end of 1984.
33 and 34	(a) Section 124(2) of the Housing Act 1980	Article 126A (2)1981 Order.
	(b) Section 9 of the 1968 Act	Section 43 of the 1969 Act.
	(c) Part 1 of Schedule 16 of the 1980 Act	The 1983 (AR) Order.
	(d) Section 14 Companies Act 1967	Article 33 The Companies (Northern Ireland) Order 1978.
37	Rents	The auditor should be aware that the rent to be charged for any housing accommodation provided by a registered housing association shall be such amount as may be determined by the DOE NI.
38	Assessment of fixed and variable service charges	It is the responsibility of the housing association to assess the fixed and variable service charges to ensure that no deficit arises and this is monitored by the DOE NI.
43	Sections 26 and 27 of the 1974 Act	Articles 134 and 135 of the 1981 Order as amended by Schedule 7 of the 1983 Order.
48(c)	New Orders made by the Secretary of State under	New Orders made by the DOE NI under Article 126 (A) (1) of the 1981

Paragraph	*Reference*	*Equivalent in Northern Ireland*
	Sections 124(1) and 151 of the 1980 Act	Order.
49	Section 124(3) of the 1980 Act	Article 126 A (3) of the 1981 Order.
60 (a)	Housing Corporation Scheme Work Procedure Guide	There is no Northern Ireland equivalent but the DOE NI use this document as their guide.
77	Part 1 of Schedule 16 of the Housing Act 1980	The 1983 (AR) Order.
Appendix 1 (b)	Central Government — Department of the Environment	Central Government Department of the Environment for Northern Ireland. (i) Loans from Department of the Environment for Northern Ireland. 100 per cent of capital cost of an approved scheme, including legal and professional fees, acquisition and building costs and capitalised interest. Interest normally fixed over term of loan. Repaid partly through grant (see (ii) below) and the balance on the annuity system. (ii) Housing Association Grant (Article 137 The Housing (Northern Ireland) Order 1981). A capital grant on an approved housing project to reduce the loan to an amount, the repayment of which can be supported by the expected rental income net of costs of managing and maintaining properties. This grant may be repayable if the property is sold or the association is dissolved, or in the event of an abandoned scheme. (iii) Revenue Deficit Grant (Article 139 The Housing (Northern Ireland) Order 1981). A discretionary grant to cover a deficit on revenue account. (iv) Hostel Deficit Grant (Article 140 The Housing (Northern Ireland) Order 1981). A

Paragraph	*Reference*	*Equivalent in Northern Ireland*
		discretionary grant to cover deficits incurred in the running of hostel accommodation.
		(v) Housing benefits from Northern Ireland Housing Executive: Tenants with low incomes or receiving supplementary benefits from the DHSS may be entitled to rent allowances; with the tenants' agreement these may be paid direct to the housing association landlord.
Appendix 1 (d)	Other (iii) Charitable money	Charitable money. Charitable associations may receive donations, proceeds from fund-raising events. With increased government aid, this is less important. The Housing Associations Charitable Trust exists to allocate grants out of funds from donations etc..

The impact of regulations on public sector audits

(Issued March 1988)

Preface

This guideline gives guidance on the consideration to be given to regulatory requirements whether primarily affecting the auditor or the audited body when applying Auditing Standards and Guidelines to a public sector audit assignment. It is supplementary to and should be read in conjunction with the auditor's operational and reporting standards, operational guidelines and, where relevant, other guidelines.

For the purpose of this guideline the public sector includes Government Departments, Non-Departmental Public Bodies, Local Authorities, Health Authorities, Nationalised Industries, Water Authorities and similar bodies some of which may be limited companies. References in this guideline to audits relate specifically to public sector audits. This limited application acknowledges that the public sector is generally subject to a high degree of regulation; it does not imply that the private sector is unregulated.

For most public sector audits, the scope and objective of the audit are affected by the interests and requirements of certain third party organisations such as audit supervisory bodies and government Sponsoring Departments which have specific regulatory responsibilities.

Audit supervisory bodies are charged statutorily with the responsibility for making proper arrangements for one or more of:

(a) the audit of the financial statements of specific classes of organisations;
(b) setting standards (as in codes or manuals) for the conduct of such audits; and
(c) reporting on the activities of such organisations in a manner and to an extent required by legislation or regulation.

Examples of audit supervisory bodies are the Audit Commission for Local Authorities in England and Wales, the Commission for Local Authority Accounts in Scotland, the Department of Health and Social Security, the Department of Trade and Industry and in the Republic of Ireland, the Department of the Environment.

Sponsoring Departments are those Government Departments assigned statutorily or administratively with the responsibility to monitor and advise certain organisations such as Nationalised Industries and Non-Departmental Public Bodies on the discharge of their powers or duties; and who are responsible in conjunction with H.M. Treasury or, in the Republic of Ireland, the Department of Finance for the scope and content of their financial statements. In these cases it is the relevant Secretary of State who is usually responsible for the appointment of auditors and for determining their terms of engagement and to whom in many cases, audit reports are addressed.

Introduction

1 In the public sector most bodies may only carry on those activities for which they have been given general or specific statutory powers, or which are reasonably incidental thereto. The degree of regulation is generally high although it does vary, and there may also be difficulty in ascertaining the extent of regulations and their impact on the conduct of the audit.

2 The auditor of a public sector body is expected to take reasonable steps to consider compliance by the audited body with regulations relevant to its activities and operations.

This guideline provides guidance on the extent to which the particular regulated environment should be identified and taken into account in carrying out an audit.

Background

3 The regulated environment in which an audit takes place is formed by those statutory and other requirements which directly affect the audit, and those which primarily affect the activities of the audited body but may have an indirect effect on the conduct of the audit.

Regulations which directly affect the auditor

4 The manner in which an auditor conducts his work is affected by a combination of approved Auditing Standards and Guidelines, and regulatory influences including:

(a) specific statutory requirements;
(b) requirements of an audit supervisory body or Sponsoring Department;
(c) contractual requirements contained in terms of engagement.

Regulations primarily affecting the activities of the audited body

5 The nature of regulation affecting public sector bodies ranges from statutory to detailed administrative requirements. The regulations may or may not have a fundamental effect on the operations of the organisation; some may even affect its viability.
The regulatory framework normally includes:

(a) statutory or quasi-statutory provisions, such as Royal Charters of Incorporation, the Local Government Finance Act 1982, the Water Act 1973, the National Health Service Act 1977, and Ministerial directions under such provisions;
(b) secondary legislation or Statutory Instruments, such as the Local Authority Accounts and Audit Regulations;
(c) Treasury and Departmental rules or instructions, such as the Government Accounting Manual and Departmental manuals and circulars; and
(d) internal rules and administrative arrangements, such as standing orders, financial regulations and approved procedures, which regulate and influence the activities of the body.

Degree of regulation

6 The degree of regulation varies according to the class of body subject to audit. Some are subject to more extensive requirements than others.

(a) Government Departments are closely regulated by Statute and various administrative and financial requirements (e.g. the Government Accounting Manual and Departmental instructions).
(b) Non-Departmental Public Bodies are usually permitted an element of discretion in their activities, and are governed mainly by their constituting instrument. In addition administrative rules and financial requirements may be imposed.
(c) Local Authorities and Health Authorities are controlled to varying extents by specific mandatory or enabling legislation and Departmental circulars and internal regulations.
(d) Nationalised industries are normally governed by specific enabling legislation involving a minimum of control over general activities but restrictions on some specific aspects of their operations (e.g. accounts directions and powers of borrowing and investment).

7 The nature and extent of the external regulation and internal administrative arrangements of a body will affect the manner in which the audit should be conducted.

Scope and conduct of the audit

8 It is the responsibility of the management of the audited body to ensure compliance with all regulations applicable to that body, many of which will influence its day-to-day activities and operations. This responsibility should be discharged by the establishment, maintenance and control of systems designed to ensure that the body's activities are in accordance with the applicable regulations and by taking appropriate action whenever a breach of regulations occurs.

9 Although the auditor may not be required to examine or report on compliance with all the regulations affecting the body it will be necessary for him to ascertain the nature and extent of the particular regulated environment affecting the activities of the body and consider the impact of those regulations on the scope and conduct of the audit.

10 The auditor should consider in particular:

(a) the propriety of transactions in relation to regulations governing permitted activities of the body;

(b) compliance with other regulations which are fundamental to the activities and operations of the body;

(c) compliance with those regulations likely to have a direct effect on the form of financial statements and the amounts and the nature of disclosures therein.

He may also be given specific responsibility by statute or the terms of his engagement to report on compliance with particular regulations, for example in connection with local authority grant claims.

Procedures

11 The guidance given below relates to those audit procedures necessary for ascertaining, and determining compliance with, regulations. All auditing standards and guidelines to which reference is made below should be read in the context of the Auditing Guideline 'Applicability to the public sector of auditing standards and guidelines'.

Terms of engagement

12 Guidance on the procedures for confirming the terms of an auditor's appointment is contained in the Auditing Guideline 'Engagement letters'. The auditor should ensure that reference to the scope of the audit includes any special responsibilities imposed on the auditor by the regulated environment, such as testing and reporting where necessary on compliance with specific regulatory requirements.

Planning

13 The Auditing Guideline 'Planning, controlling and recording' gives guidance on matters to be considered when planning an audit. In addition to the matters set out therein the auditor will need, at the preparatory stage of his audit, to take account of the impact of regulations on the operation of the organisation and on the conduct of his audit. He should consider the potential risks arising from non-compliance with regulations and the materiality of the effect on the organisation's activities and financial statements.

14 The auditor should acquaint himself with the regulatory framework sufficiently to enable him properly to perform his audit. Besides being conversant with regulations affecting the auditor, he should familiarise himself with those regulations which he considers are likely to have a direct and material effect on the organisation and its financial reporting. Such regulations would include those which:

(a) have an effect on the organisation which is fundamental to its activities or operations; or
(b) affect its viability as a going concern and its ability to meet future commitments; or
(c) materially affect the financial statements.

He should also consider the impact on the audit of other regulations which may affect materially the organisation's activities. The auditor should, in order to identify significant pertinent regulations, consider the main framework of regulations, general duties of the organisation, its major discretionary powers and any limitations to the scope of its activities.

15 Identification of significant, pertinent regulations can be achieved by a combination of:

(a) examination of documents such as the constituting legislation, Charter, Memorandum and Articles of Association, and correspondence between the audited organisation and any supervisory body;
(b) examination of specific audit guidance issued by the CCAB accountancy bodies and any audit supervisory bodies;
(c) discussions with the audited organisation and any sponsoring or supervisory body, together with examination of Departmental instructions issued to staff within the Department, instructions issued by Departments to bodies they sponsor and instructions issued by Departments to other external bodies (e.g. local and health authorities); and
(d) in the first year of audit, discussions with the previous auditor and, thereafter, cumulative audit knowledge and experience.

16 In the first year of an assignment, or in the event of a major change of structure or activities of the body, the auditor will normally need to conduct a detailed review (as in paragraph 14) of the regulations likely to affect the audited body. In subsequent years he should satisfy himself as to the impact of changes in and additions to relevant regulations.

Systems and controls

17 Paragraph 3 of the Auditing Standard 'The auditor's operational standard' states that: "The auditor should ascertain the enterprise's system of recording and processing transactions and assess its adequacy as a basis for the preparation of financial statements." In addition the auditor should ascertain those systems designed to ensure compliance with the material regulations identified at the planning stage. He should review and assess such systems to the extent that he considers necessary.

Audit evidence

18 Having identified the requirements of relevant regulations the auditor should design and carry out appropriate tests and procedures to provide him with audit evidence as to the completeness, accuracy and validity of transactions contained in the accounting records and financial statements. Part of the auditor's tests on the validity of the transactions will include examining compliance with regulations.

Reporting

19 Paragraph 3 of the Auditing Standard 'The audit report' requires the auditor to refer expressly in his report on the financial statements to any matters prescribed by relevant legislation or other requirements. In the context of this guideline such requirements may include:

(a) an extension in scope of the audit reporting requirements (e.g. to make separate reports in the public interest under s.15, Local Government Finance Act 1982);
(b) giving positive assurance on particular matters (e.g. separate reports under s.4 Exchequer and Audit Departments Act 1921, in relation to stock and store accounts of government departments).

20 Upon discovery of significant non-compliance with relevant regulations (or in rare cases where compliance has resulted in the financial statements being misstated or presenting a misleading view), the auditor should draw the matter to the attention of management at a sufficient level of authority, or if appropriate, to the governing board or council of the audited body, to enable appropriate remedial or other action to be taken. Such action by management may include:

(a) taking steps to rectify the non-compliance;
(b) voluntary disclosure by the audited body to a Sponsoring Department or audit supervisory body;
(c) adjustments to, or further disclosure in, financial statements;
(d) adjustments or disclosure in other documents such as grant claims or annual reports.

21 The auditor will also need to consider whether the non-compliance materially affects his reporting responsibilities either due to the amounts involved or because it involves a significant breach of primary or secondary legislation which may be important to users of public sector financial statements. Where the non-compliance has been rectified and the auditor is satisfied that appropriate disclosures or adjustments have been made, he may not need to take any further action. However:

(a) where the non-compliance cannot be rectified; or
(b) it can be rectified, but the audited body has failed to take such action; or
(c) in either event the audited body has failed to make such disclosures or adjustments as the auditor considers necessary;

the auditor should determine whether the non-compliance materially affects his opinion on the financial statements. Where he considers his opinion is affected, he should qualify his audit report on the financial statements in accordance with the Auditing Standard 'Qualifications in audit reports'.

22 Irrespective of any remedial measures that the audited body might take, the auditor should consider whether his knowledge of an act or omission imposes further responsibilities on him under the general law, by specific regulation or terms of the engagement. Examples of these responsibilities are a requirement to submit a report to the body or to a Sponsoring Department or audit supervisory body; or, in the case of local government, to institute proceedings for restitution. In circumstances where the auditor believes he may be under a duty to take any such action, he should consider whether he should obtain independent legal advice and the extent to which he should liaise with the audited body.

Materiality

23 An auditor must exercise professional judgement in determining the materiality of the effect of regulations and non-compliance therewith, as well as the necessity for qualifying his audit opinion on the financial statements and for taking such other action as outlined in paragraph 22, above.

Pension schemes in the United Kingdom

(Issued November 1988)

Preface

This auditing guideline gives guidance on the special factors to be considered in the application of Auditing Standards to the audit of pension schemes. It is supplementary to, and should be read in conjunction with, auditing standards and related auditing guidelines. The guideline does not include guidance on those audit requirements specific to investment business carried out by pension scheme trustees under the terms of the Financial Services Act 1986, since at the time of writing those requirements have not been finalised.

This guideline sets out a framework for the relationship between the actuary and the auditor of a scheme. The controls and procedures that will be found in a well organised scheme are also noted.

This guideline is based on the legal position in the United Kingdom as at December 1987, including* The Occupational Pension Schemes (Disclosure of Information) Regulations 1986 (S.I. 1986/1046), as amended by The Occupational Pension Schemes (Disclosure of Information) (Amendment) Regulations 1986 and 1987 (S.I. 1986/1717, S.I. 1987/1105). These regulations are made under the Social Security Act 1975 and under the Social Security Pensions Act 1975 as amended by the Social Security Act 1985, and are generally effective for all accounting periods starting on or after 1 November 1986.

There is no equivalent legislation in the Republic of Ireland, and therefore references to statutory or regulatory requirements will not apply in that country. Guidance will be issued for the Republic of Ireland in due course.

The guideline also refers to Statement of Recommended Practice No. 1 (SORP 1), 'Pension scheme accounts', published by the Accounting Standards Committee in May 1986 and The Occupational Pension Schemes (Auditors) Regulations 1987 (S.I. 1987/1102). A number of other regulations have been made dealing with detailed aspects of pension schemes, such as money purchase contracting out regulations (S.I. 1987/1101) and contribution regulations (S.I. 1987/1108).

The user of this guideline should ensure that he is familiar with all relevant legislation.

The meaning of some of the pensions terminology used in this guideline is given in Appendix 2 which includes extracts from 'Pensions Terminology — A Glossary for Pension Schemes' published jointly by the Pension Management Institute and the Pensions Research Accountants Group in 1984. The definitions are reproduced with kind permission of those bodies.

Terms which are explained in Appendix 2 are emboldened in the text of the guideline on the first occasion on which they are used.

*The equivalent legislation in Northern Ireland is contained in:

The Occupational Pension Schemes (Disclosure of Information) Regulations (Northern Ireland) 1986 (1986/225)

The Occupational Pension Schemes (Disclosure of Information) (Amendment) Regulations (Northern Ireland) 1986 (1986/319)

Social Security Pensions (Northern Ireland) Order 1975

Social Security (Northern Ireland) Order 1985

Introduction

Scope of the guideline

1 This auditing guideline has been written in the context of the audit and accounts requirements of:

The Occupational Pension Schemes (Disclosure of Information) Regulations 1986,
The Occupational Pension Schemes (Disclosure of Information) (Amendment) Regulations 1986 and 1987, and
The Occupational Pension Schemes (Auditors) Regulations 1987.

These regulations are collectively referred to in this guideline as "the Disclosure Regulations".

The guideline applies to all audits carried out under those requirements, which apply to all occupational pension schemes in the United Kingdom except:

— unfunded schemes,
— public service pension schemes
— schemes with fewer than two members, and
— death benefit only schemes

Parts of this guideline, in particular the description of the accounting requirements and guidance on audit reports, may not be applicable to those pension schemes outside the Disclosure Regulations. Nevertheless, the principles contained in this guideline are relevant to the audit of all pension schemes.

Scheme arrangements

2 In addition to state pension provisions, employers in the United Kingdom and Ireland commonly make pension arrangements for groups of employees to which the employees may themselves contribute. Such arrangements are known as **occupational pension schemes**. Where they involve contributions into a trustee-administered fund, the trustees are also a party to the arrangements.

3 There are many different types of pension scheme arrangement. The main areas of difference between them are:

(a) the basis for determining benefits (see paragraph 4);
(b) the method of **funding** adopted (see paragraphs 5 to 8);
(c) the nature of investments held by the fund (see paragraphs 9 and 10); and
(d) the manner in which investments are managed (see paragraph 11).

These matters may be included in the **trust deed** which governs the scheme and which is often supplemented by detailed **rules**.

Benefits

4 Schemes may be established in terms of **defined contributions** or **defined benefits**, or with an element of both.

Funding

5 Pension scheme liabilities may be financed in the following ways:

(a) **pay-as-you-go**;
(b) **terminal funding**;
(c) advance provision within the employer's own balance sheet; and
(d) funding via an external trust fund.

The first three methods are, for the purposes of regulation and of this guideline, considered to be **unfunded**. The fourth and most common method is considered to be funded.

6 There is a large variety of possible funding methods. A particular scheme's funding method and level of contributions will be determined by the employer and the trustees in accordance with the trust deed or other documentation and after consultation with the actuaries and other parties to the scheme (such as employees and unions).

7 Schemes must, subject to certain limitations, also allow employees to improve their accumulated pension and benefit rights by making **additional voluntary contributions** (AVCs), which may be invested in the general fund of the scheme or in a separate insurance policy, building society account or other designated account.

8 Defined benefit schemes may become **underfunded** or **overfunded**, that is have an actuarial **deficiency** or **surplus**. The employer is rarely contractually obliged to make good any underfunding so that promised benefits can be met, although many employers correct underfunding voluntarily. Conversely the trustees of an overfunded scheme may occasionally have to pay to the employer part of the surplus arising from an actuarial valuation, although other options may be available such as reduction in future contributions or use of the surplus to enhance benefits.

Fund investments

9 The funds of pension schemes will usually be comprised of one or more investments including, for example, ordinary shares, fixed interest securities and insurance policies. **Insured schemes** are schemes where the only long-term investments are insurance policies. Where the policies guarantee promised benefits at all times the scheme is described as **fully insured.**

10 Self-administered schemes may invest in a variety of United Kingdom and foreign assets, the trustees playing a major role in the determination of the scheme's investment policy. Schemes, particularly major schemes, may employ designated managers to administer their investments. Other schemes often invest in **managed funds**, which are either unitised (i.e. represented by units in a fund which are valued periodically to take account of reinvested income and capital growth) or **segregated funds**. Although an insurance company may manage such a fund, and the managed fund is technically an insurance contract, a scheme with managed fund investments is not considered to be an insured scheme for the purposes of this guideline.

Investment management

11 Trustees may appoint an agent to manage the scheme's investments. They may also delegate the custody of the assets to an investment manager, whether internal or external, or to a separate agent. Nevertheless the trustees will remain ultimately responsible under trust law for the management and custody of the assets (see also paragraph 14).

Multi-employer and unitised investment arrangements

12 A multi-employer investment arrangement, that is one with a number of sponsoring employers, may be an amalgamation of the investments of a number of smaller schemes with differing rules and differing contribution and benefit rates. Commonly the investments of the schemes are pooled under the common control of one (main or **commingled**) fund, which may be an investment holding company or a fund constituted under a trust deed. The main fund may be unitised. Sub-funds purchase or sell units, at current value, depending on whether benefits in a period exceed contributions. These arrangements are distinct from the situation where a pension scheme has several participating employers, such as the subsidiaries within a group of companies or companies within a particular industry.

Regulatory background

13 The environment in which a pension scheme operates is different from that of most commercial enterprises. The auditor should be familiar with the regulatory background to pension schemes and the accounting and taxation aspects of their operation before commencing his audit.

Trust law

14 Most funded pension schemes are constituted as trusts and are governed by trust law. A trust is usually established by a legal document, the trust deed, which places the responsibility for the stewardship and custody of the assets on one or more trustees. The general duties and powers, including investment powers, of trustees are derived from the Trustee Act 1925 and the Trustee Investments Act 1961* but such powers are frequently extended by the trust deed and any accompanying rules. Trustees may delegate their authority under the trust deed, but cannot delegate their responsibility. Trustees must act in accordance with the terms of the trust, unless these are overridden by legislation, to protect the interests of beneficiaries of the scheme as between the beneficiaries themselves, and to ensure that no one who is not entitled receives any trust property. Where a trustee is also a director or employee of the sponsoring employer, his actions as trustee must not be influenced by his dual capacity.

Social security legislation

15 Detailed regulations affecting occupational pension schemes in the United Kingdom are set out in social security legislation. The Social Security Pensions Act 1975 set up a state scheme which provides a pension comprising a **basic pension** and an additional earnings related pension under SERPS (State Earnings Related Pension Scheme). If an occupational pension scheme meets certain criteria and assumes certain obligations it may, having obtained the appropriate certificate, "**contract out**" of SERPS. As a result of contracting out, employees and employers pay lower national insurance contributions.

16 The **Occupational Pensions Board** (OPB) exercises limited financial and regulatory supervision over contracted-out schemes. It has the power to issue, vary or withdraw contracting-out certificates.

17 The trustees of contracted-out schemes must make certain annual returns to the OPB. For self-administered defined benefit schemes these include Form OP21 which must contain certain detailed financial confirmations. The form must be submitted annually to the OPB within 3 months of the end of the scheme's year. The statement includes:

(a) confirmation of the date of the latest accounts of the scheme which have been audited;

(b) details of any audit qualification;

(c) confirmation that payment of contributions at the appropriate rate for the last scheme year has been made;

(d) details of any self-investment or concentration of investment for the last scheme year; and

(e) confirmation that the appropriate actuary has been given the opportunity to consider any change which might affect the scheme's current actuarial certificate.

*The equivalent legislation in Northern Ireland is contained in the Trustee Act (Northern Ireland) 1958, and the Trustee Amendment Act (Northern Ireland) 1962.

The OPB allows trustees to request the auditor to sign Form OP21. This does not form part of the audit of the scheme accounts and may therefore involve additional work.

18 The Social Security Act 1985, which amended the Social Security Pensions Act 1975, has increased the degree of regulation of pension schemes. The Disclosure Regulations made under those Acts require trustees to make specified information about the scheme available to the members, including audited annual accounts.

Financial reporting

19 The trustees have a statutory duty, under **the Acts**, to produce an annual report of the scheme. It will principally comprise:

(a) a trustees' report — covering the general activity, history and development of the scheme;

(b) the audited accounts;

(c) the latest available actuarial statement (see paragraph 25(a) below) — covering the progress of the scheme towards meeting its potential liabilities and obligations to members and the security of the **accrued benefits** of members; and

(d) an investment report — covering the investment policy and performance of the investments.

Whilst the individual components of the annual report are separate, it will be necessary for the user to read the whole report to gain a full and proper appreciation of the scheme's financial position. (See paragraphs 72 and 73 on the extent of the auditor's responsibilities in relation to the annual report.)

Audited accounts

20 The Disclosure Regulations require the audited accounts to include:

(i) a revenue account which discloses the financial additions to and withdrawals from the fund during the accounting period;

(ii) a statement of net assets;

(iii) reconciliation of the movement in the total value of the fund, this reconciliation may be shown as a separate statement or may be incorporated into the revenue account or the statement of net assets;

(iv) additional information required by Schedule 3 to S.I. 1986/1046 and such information as is necessary to meet the statutory requirement to show a true and fair view of the financial transactions of the scheme during the scheme year and of the disposition, at the end of the scheme year, of the assets and liabilities; and

(v) a report by the auditor.

The Disclosure Regulations set out the information to be included in audited accounts. SORP 1 'Pension scheme accounts', published by the Accounting Standards Committee sets out recommended practices on accounting policies, content of accounts and disclosures. The Disclosure Regulations require accounts to include a note stating whether or not the accounts have been prepared in accordance with SORP 1, and if not, an indication of where there are any material departures from those guidelines although there is no requirement to justify non-compliance.

Audit

21 The Disclosure Regulations require trustees of occupational pension schemes to 'obtain' audited accounts. The auditor must be qualified to act as auditor of a company, or be approved by the Secretary of State for Social Services, and must comply with independence requirements set out in the Disclosure Regulations. He is required by

Regulation 7(5) of S.I. 1986/1046 to state whether or not in his opinion:

(i) the requirements of Regulation 7(4)(a) are satisfied, that is that the accounts:

(a) show a true and fair view of the financial transactions of the scheme during the scheme year and of the disposition, at the end of the scheme year, of the assets (not including insurance policies which are specifically allocated to the provision of benefits for, and which provide all the benefits payable under the scheme to, particular members or other persons in respect of particular members or both) and liabilities, other than liabilities to pay pensions and benefits after the end of the scheme year; and

(b) contain the information specified in Schedule 3;

and

(ii) contributions payable to the scheme during the scheme year have been paid in accordance with the scheme rules or contracts under which they were payable, and with the recommendation of the actuary, if appropriate.

If the auditor's opinion on any of the matters required to be covered is negative or qualified, his report should include a statement of the reasons.

22 The Social Security Pensions Act 1975 has been amended by Section 11 of the Social Security Act 1986 to give the Secretary of State for Social Services power to make regulations with regard to:

(a) the appointment, resignation and removal of auditors of occupational pension schemes;

(b) the duty of employers and auditors of employers to disclose information to the trustees or managers of occupational pension schemes and to the auditors of such schemes;

(c) the duty of trustees or managers of an occupational pension scheme to disclose information and to make available documents to the auditors of the scheme.

Details of the Regulations in this regard are set out in the Disclosure Regulations, specifically in The Occupational Pension Schemes (Auditors) Regulations 1987. The Disclosure Regulations require the statement by an outgoing auditor dealing with relevant circumstances connected with his resignation to be reproduced in the annual report.

Taxation

23 In order to enjoy the advantages of available statutory tax reliefs, a pension scheme must obtain the approval of the **Superannuation Funds Office** of the Inland Revenue (SFO). This approval is granted if the scheme complies with specific requirements and may be withdrawn if compliance does not continue. **Exempt approved schemes** are those pension schemes approved by the SFO which are exempt from United Kingdom taxation on investment income and capital gains arising out of their investments. Tax suffered at source on investment income can be reclaimed by such a pension scheme. Repayment may not be allowed by the Inland Revenue until the **definitive trust deed** and rules have been approved.

24 Taxation arises on pension arrangements, *inter alia*, as follows:

(a) Where SFO approval has not been granted, has been withdrawn or has been limited.

(b) Where a scheme has an 'excess surplus' under the Government Actuary's guidelines which has not been dealt with in accordance with the Finance Act 1986, and as a result part of the scheme's exemption has been lost.

(c) Where a scheme incurs VAT on expenditure it may not be able to reclaim that tax. Many schemes do not have any taxable outputs and therefore any input tax remains an expense of the scheme. This is a complex area and reference should be made to the VAT leaflet 'Funded Pension Schemes' No . 700/17/83 for further details.

(d) A scheme will be liable to stamp duty on investment transactions.

(e) Tax suffered at source on overseas investment income and gains may not be recoverable.

(f) Tax deductible from pension payments and refunds of contributions.

(g) Tax on certain commutation payments as explained in paragraph 19.28 of Inland Revenue booklet 12 'Occupational Pension Schemes: approval under FA 1970, as amended'.

Where a scheme's assets include shares in companies, those companies, even if wholly owned, do not enjoy the tax exemptions granted to the scheme.

A scheme's advisers and agents

25 A scheme will normally use the services of a number of advisers and agents. They may include:

(a) *The actuary:* The actuary may advise the trustees, the employer or both on the contributions required to meet the scheme's funding objectives. In some cases the actuary may be an employee of the sponsoring employer or, where the scheme is an insured scheme, of the insurance company. The actuary may himself be a trustee of the scheme. Under the Disclosure Regulations the trustees must obtain a full actuarial valuation of the fund at least once in every three and a half years, although a more frequent valuation may be required under the trust deed. Each actuarial valuation must be accompanied by an actuarial statement for inclusion in the annual report. The actuary may update the statement between full valuations. The actuary may also advise the trustees on other aspects of the scheme's operations such as the calculation of individual benefits and the production of statutory certificates, as referred to in paragraph 17 above. (An Audit Brief 'The work of a pension scheme actuary' has been published by the Auditing Practices Committee and this gives more details of an actuary's work for a pension scheme and the sponsoring employer.)

(b) *The investment manager:* An investment manager may be employed to advise the trustees on which investment policy to adopt or to implement the trustees' own investment policy. He may be an employee of the scheme or of an external financial services organisation. The extent of involvement of external investment managers differs between schemes. They may make investment decisions, prepare the detailed investment records for the scheme and hold title to the scheme investments through nominees. Investment management is an activity which requires authorisation under the Financial Services Act 1986. External investment managers will need to be authorised by one of the means available under the Act. In addition, an in-house manager who takes day-to-day investment decisions on the investments within an occupational scheme will also need to be authorised. Authorised persons have to observe rules for the conduct of their business. If all day-to-day investment decisions are delegated to an external investment manager, then other persons connected with the scheme, for example an in-house review committee to which the external managers report on an infrequent basis, would not need to be authorised.

(c) *The property adviser:* The property adviser will advise the trustees on suitable investments. He may manage property lettings and supervise the progress of property developments. However, the trustees will often employ other independent advisers for periodic independent valuations of the property portfolio (see Appendix 1 to SORP 1). Property investment, other than that included in collective investment schemes, is excluded from the provisions of the Financial Services Act 1986, but some forms of property-related investment, e.g. property unit trusts, are within the scope of the Act.

(d) *The insurance company:* There are various methods by which insurance companies provide services to pension schemes. Where the scheme is insured, including where it is fully insured, the scheme's investments are in the form of insurance policies. The insurance company that has issued the policies has responsibility for management of the underlying investments. The insurance company may also act as agent for the paying of benefits and arrange for one of its staff to act as actuary to the scheme. Where the scheme is self-administered and has insurance policy investments, the insurance company may be involved in valuing the policies for the purposes of inclusion in the accounts. Where a self-administered scheme invests in a managed fund which is administered by an insurance company, that company is acting as an investment manager rather than as an insurer, although the managed fund policy may technically constitute an insurance contract.

(e) *The custodian:* A custodian may be appointed to keep the documents of title to the scheme's investments. Sometimes referred to as a custodian trustee, he may hold the investments through a nominee company. Arrangements for communicating between the custodian, investment manager, stockbroker and trustee will vary between schemes.

(f) *The administrator:* An administrator may be appointed to carry out certain actions on behalf of the trustees, such as receipt of contributions, payment of benefits, purchase and sale of assets and maintenance of scheme records. The administrator might be the sponsoring employer or one of his employees, an insurance company or a pension consultant. The term 'administrator' is defined under the Finance Act 1970 and is used by the SFO to describe a person having specific duties under the Finance Acts.

(g) *The sponsoring employer:* In addition to being a party to the scheme in his own right, the sponsoring employer is responsible for deducting employees' contributions and paying all contributions to the trustees. He may also deal with the payment of pension benefits on behalf of the trustees, supply the scheme with other information about members and **pensioners** and employ the trustees' staff.

Auditing procedures

26 The following distinctive aspects of pension scheme arrangements will frequently require special consideration in identifying key audit areas:

(a) the existence and contents of the trust deed and rules regulating the scheme;

(b) the specific matters, particularly contributions receivable, upon which the auditor is required to report under the Acts and Disclosure Regulations;

(c) the possible close involvement of the employer, from whom significant cashflow in the form of the contributions is received, in the running of the scheme;

(d) the importance of maintaining accurate membership records over a long period of time, and the extent to which the trustees rely on the sponsoring employer or other third party for the maintenance of those records;

(e) the predominance of investments amongst the scheme's assets, and the extent to which the management and custody of and the cash accounting for those investments is delegated to a third party;

(f) the extent of the involvement of the employer or his employees in determining the deployment of the scheme's assets; and

(g) the extent to which benefits payable under, and transfers out of, the fund are calculated and settled by the administrators.

The key role played by the actuary in relation to the scheme will also impact on the planning of the auditor's work. The following procedures expand upon or are supplementary to those given in the Operational Auditing Guidelines.

Planning

Trust deed and scheme rules

27 The auditor should obtain a copy of the trust deed and scheme rules (and any supplemental deeds or other amendments), these set out the conditions which govern the operation of the scheme. The auditor should review trustees' minutes with particular regard to changes in the trust deed or rules and any other significant items. He should identify those matters which are relevant to his audit opinion, such as the types of investment authorised and the bases for calculating benefits payable and contributions receivable. Furthermore he should plan his audit so that he has a reasonable expectation of detecting material misstatements in the accounts resulting from breaches of the trust deed or scheme rules. A failure by the scheme to adhere to its rules is a breach of trust and may also result in the scheme's tax privileges being lost. The auditor should ensure that those breaches of trust revealed by the audit are brought to the attention of the trustees, and that, where appropriate, their effect is properly reflected in the annual report.

28 The auditor should plan his audit so that he has a reasonable expectation of detecting material misstatements in the accounts resulting from breaches of statute and irregularities and errors which are material and might adversely affect the true and fair view given by the scheme's accounts. In addition he will need to acquaint himself with the rules for calculating taxation deductions and payments to the Department of Health and Social Security on benefits and refunds such as **state scheme premiums**.

The status of the scheme

29 Once the scheme has obtained Inland Revenue and OPB approval, the approval will remain in force until or unless revoked. The auditor should be alert to the possibility that approval can be revoked and should be satisfied that approval is still valid. Where approval for a new scheme has not yet been granted or approval has been revoked, the auditor should consider whether, in the light of any indemnity given by the employer, the accounts adequately disclose the existence of a contingent liability to pay tax on income and capital gains should full approval not be received or renewed.

Liaison with other parties

30 As part of his audit, the auditor will need to communicate with some or all of the scheme's advisers and agents. The auditor should consult them at an early stage to ensure that his audit work is properly planned and that he gains a full understanding of each adviser's role in the scheme's operations. It is desirable that the right of direct access to advisers and agents be agreed with the trustees and recorded in the auditor's letter of engagement. Restrictions in the access afforded to the auditor may result in the scope of his work being limited and give rise to a qualified audit opinion.

31 Particular care will be necessary when the scheme has more than one employer. It will be necessary to liaise with the various employers, and perhaps with their auditors. Where the scheme is unitised the auditor must be aware of the rules for valuing units and apportioning income and capital gains or losses.

32 The degree of involvement of third parties connected with the scheme will differ and the auditor must consider whether information received directly from such third parties can be accepted as an independent confirmation (such as a bank letter) or should be regarded as more in the nature of a management representation. The auditor should inspect contracts or letters of engagement between the scheme and each adviser to decide on the nature of the scheme's relationship with that party and the nature of the appropriate audit evidence required. He should also consider whether the information received is consistent with over evidence available to him.

Engagement letter

33 In the letter of engagement to the appointing body setting out his responsibilities, the auditor should include, in addition to the items set out in the Auditing Guideline 'Engagement letters', the following matters:

(a) the extent of his right of access to information and explanations from advisers, agents, the sponsoring employer and their auditors (see paragraph 22 above concerning statutory rights to information);

(b) his statutory responsibility under the Disclosure Regulations to report on the contributions payable to the scheme;

(c) the fact that he will plan his audit so that he has a reasonable expectation of detecting material misstatements in the accounts resulting from breaches of trust or statute and will report to the trustees any breaches revealed by his audit whether or not resulting in material misstatement (the letter should make it clear that the audit should not be relied upon to disclose all breaches which may exist);

(d) his professional responsibility to review the other parts of the annual report to satisfy himself that they are consistent with and do not undermine the credibility of the audited accounts;

(e) that the auditor's responsibility in relation to reports by the scheme's actuary and insurer is limited to that of understanding the implications of those reports for the scheme's accounts;

(f) the extent of other work to be carried out by him for the pension scheme at the trustee's request such as verifying data supplied by the scheme to the actuary or signing Form OP21; and

(g) whether it is the employer or the trustees who will be responsible for the payment of the auditor's fees.

Accounting policies

34 The auditor should ascertain whether the policies adopted for the scheme's accounts are appropriate and are satisfactorily disclosed. The Disclosure Regulations require that assets generally be stated at market value. SORP 1 recommends policies which should be adopted in respect of the valuation of investments, associated and subsidiary companies, long term insurance policies and AVCs. If the policies adopted differ from those recommended then, in accordance with the Disclosure Regulations the departure from SORP 1 should be noted in the accounts.

The audit approach

35 The primary function of pension scheme accounts is to record the stewardship of the trustees. Accordingly a significant influence on the audit approach to be adopted will be the need to assess the way in which the trustees have discharged that stewardship responsibility. Whilst the items in a pension scheme's statement of net assets and revenue account are individually significant, because they record distinct aspects of the scheme, a more significant aspect for the auditor in deciding on his audit approach will be the nature, distribution and value of the assets of the scheme and the actuary's assessment of the relationships of those assets to the long-term liabilities. These factors will influence the planning of the audit in relation to:

(a) materiality and audit risk;

(b) the balance between the testing of transactions and the testing of assets and liabilities; and

(c) the degree of reliance that can be placed on analytical review.

36 When planning the nature and extent of his audit work, the auditor should have regard to the relationships that exist between separate items within the accounts, and between items in the accounts and non-accounting information given in the annual report or otherwise available (e.g. the relationships between investment holdings and investment income, and between the number of pensioners and benefit expenditure).

37 The relationships which will be of most significance to the pension scheme audit include:

(a) The individual items and amounts of investment income will be directly related to investment holdings and can be compared to published data (e.g. interest rates, dividend details and results from independent investment performance measurement comparisons).

(b) Changes in membership and members' pensionable remuneration during the financial year will directly affect the contribution income (e.g. company mergers, pay increases, redundancies).

(c) The level of benefits payable will be influenced by changes in the number or class of pensioners (e.g. early retirement schemes, deaths).

Accounting systems and internal control

38 The trustees have a duty under trust law to maintain adequate accounting records to enable them to carry out their duties including discharging their responsibilities for investment decisions and safeguarding the scheme's assets. Since these responsibilities cannot be delegated, the trustees will need to ensure that they themselves have adequate accounting systems and controls available to them to demonstrate proper stewardship of the scheme's assets even where certain administrative or investment activities are undertaken by agents.

39 The extent and nature of accounting systems, procedures and internal controls of a pension scheme will depend mainly upon the size of the scheme, the extent to which the trustees delegate the administration of the scheme and the types of investment involved. Consequently the systems of a large self-administered fund with in-house investment management will differ from those found in a small insured scheme. Segregation of duties, especially in the area of cash control, and other features of good internal control are as important to pension schemes as to other organisations. However formalised procedures and internal control for certain transactions may not exist because of the infrequency of particular types of transaction (e.g. benefits payable on the death in service of members).

40 In his review of a pension scheme's accounting system and internal controls the auditor will need to consider the extent of the trustees' control over their agents and advisers. The trustees will need to ensure that those to whom the day-to-day administration has been delegated are reputable and competent, that their responsibilities and lines of communication are clearly defined, that conflicts of interest are minimised, and that fees charged are reasonable. The controls over day-to-day administration, including management, organisation, segregation of duties, personnel and supervision, and detailed internal checks will be similar to those found in many types of organisations and are described in the Auditing Guideline 'Internal controls'. These may exist both within and between the trustees' staff and other agents and advisers.

41 Many smaller schemes are administered by one of the senior officers or employees of the sponsoring employer (for example, the company secretary). In such schemes the scope for developing internal controls may be limited, especially because of a lack of segregation of duties. Where this is so, or where control over administration does not exist, it is unlikely that the auditor will be able to place significant reliance on internal controls for the purposes of his audit. He will, therefore, base his audit approach on substantive testing procedures.

Procedures and controls

42 Paragraphs 43 to 52 below illustrate important administrative procedures and controls which the auditor would normally expect to find in a well organised pension scheme. Other types of controls that may exist are set out in the Auditing Guideline 'Internal controls'. The auditor will generally wish to structure his audit to identify and record important procedures and controls and to test them where appropriate as part of his overall audit approach.

Contributions receivable

43 Procedures and controls for contributions receivable include:

(a) checking that contributions are received on a timely basis from the employer, on behalf of both the employer and employees, in accordance with the scheme rules or at rates based on actuarial recommendations;

(b) prompt investment of contributions received; and

(c) identification of the element of contributions which are AVCs or relate to life assurance premiums.

Benefits payable

44 Procedures and controls for benefits payable include:

(a) checking calculations of benefits and taxation deducted (if any) for compliance with the scheme's rules, membership records, actuarial advice and relevant legislation;

(b) checking changes in pension payments (amount and payee) to supporting evidence; and

(c) periodic confirmation of the continued existence of pensioners and others in receipt of benefits.

The pension payroll system may actually form part of the employer's payroll system. In any case, pension payments are often made using normal payroll systems, and the controls applicable to payroll systems used by employers should also be applied to pension schemes.

Transfers in and out

45 Procedures and controls for transfers in and out include:

(a) checking amounts payable in respect of pension obligations transferred out of the scheme or of refunds with scheme rules, membership records, actuarial tables or advice and other supporting documentary evidence;

(b) checking amounts receivable on the transfer of members to the scheme with supporting documentary evidence, actuarial advice and the scheme rules;
(c) checking amounts of state scheme premiums (if any) due to the Department of Health and Social Security with documentary evidence; and
(d) checking that all payments from the trustees to the sponsoring employer have been reported to the Inland Revenue and the correct tax deducted and accounted for.

AVCs

46 Procedures and controls for AVCs include:

(a) procedures to ensure that AVC arrangements are within Inland Revenue rules;
(b) checks over contributions and benefits as for the main scheme; and
(c) procedures to ensure that AVCs are paid promptly to the trust for the benefit of the individual and are subject to the appropriate degree of segregation, if any, from general funds.

Administration expenses

47 Procedures and controls for administration expenses include an examination to ensure that administration expenditure and the costs of investment transactions are incurred only in accordance with the scheme's trust deed and rules. In general, the trustees will be entitled to recover from the trust fund expenses incurred in the carrying out of the trusts. However, the **trust documents** may provide that the employer will bear some or all of these expenses.

Investment transactions

48 Procedures and controls for investment transactions include:

(a) recording investment policy and approval by trustees of specific investments;
(b) periodic review by trustees of investment performance;
(c) reconciliation of investment transaction records to asset and cash records; and
(d) checks on the completeness of investment income, including tax refunds.

Where investment transactions are delegated to an investment manager, the trustees will need to ensure that they have adequate records to exercise proper control (e.g. by retaining transaction and valuation listings supplied by the investment manager).

Assets

49 Procedures and controls for assets include:

(a) agreement of asset records maintained by the trustees to those of custodians;
(b) holding of assets in safe custody under the control of persons other than those responsible for the keeping of records;
(c) holding of fidelity insurance against misdeeds of staff concerned with investment transactions and the holding of assets, whether employed by the trustee or another party, such as the investment manager;
(d) prompt banking of receipts to appropriate bank accounts; and
(e) adequate arrangements for control and communication of signatories to banks and investment institutions.

Membership records

50 The trustees of the pension scheme will need to ensure that reliable membership records are maintained which are adequate to enable them to fulfil their responsibilities to the scheme. In some cases the records may be kept by the employer or an administrator on behalf of the trustees.

51 Procedures and controls for membership records include periodic checks of the continued accuracy of membership records, and of the information used to update them, to appropriate authorities or directly with the members (e.g. by use of direct confirmation of the continuing existence of individual members). This applies to employees, pensioners and **deferred pensioners.**

52 Such checks are necessary because the membership records will be used by the actuary in determining the present and future liabilities of the scheme and thus the appropriate level of contributions, and by those responsible for administering the scheme in calculating the amount of benefit to be paid in the event of the member dying, leaving service or becoming entitled to other benefits. Inaccurate membership records may therefore lead to incorrect transactions in the future and to the scheme not discharging its responsibilities to deferred pensioners.

Audit evidence

Contributions, benefits and membership records

53 The Occupational Pension Schemes (Auditors) Regulations 1987 require employers and their auditors to disclose appropriate information to the auditors of occupational pension schemes (see paragraph 22).

54 As noted earlier in paragraph 21(ii) the auditor has a specific audit responsibility in respect of contributions because Regulation 7 of S.I. 1986/1046 requires him to state expressly in his audit report "whether or not in his opinion contributions payable to the scheme during the scheme year have been paid in accordance with the scheme rules or contracts under which they were payable, and with the recommendation of the actuary, if appropriate." His work in this area is essentially concerned with ensuring that contributions due to the scheme are paid on the basis described in the rules, that they have been properly calculated, and relate to the pensionable pay of identified members of the scheme.

55 In order to verify the accuracy of contributions received and benefits paid by the scheme, the auditor will wish to make use of information supplied by the sponsoring employer and the pension scheme's membership records. In addition the auditor may find it appropriate to discuss with the actuary aspects of his recommendations, particularly those relating to contributions. Details in the payroll and personnel records of the employer will normally be used to calculate the amount of contributions payable to the scheme, and will also be used either to update the membership records of the scheme or directly to calculate the amount of any particular benefit payable (e.g. by reference to salary history).

56 The auditor will need to obtain evidence to satisfy himself that the scheme's membership records are accurate to the extent that he uses them to verify contributions and benefits. His work should include checking the reconciliation of total number of members in terms of those joining and leaving the scheme and reviewing evidence of the existence of members and of their ages and salary details. Where he is also asked to verify the accuracy of data supplied to the scheme's actuary, he may have to carry out further examination of the membership records.

57 The scheme auditor will need to obtain independent evidence in relation to information supplied by the employer to the scheme. Where the auditor acts for both the scheme and the employer, his work on the audit of the employer's accounts and access to his records for any additional tests may enable him to obtain such evidence. Where the auditor does not also act for the employer, or where there are many employers, he should consider obtaining direct confirmation from the employer of the amounts paid as contributions, the information used in calculating those amounts and any other information supplied to the scheme. The scheme auditor may need to discuss with the trustees whether he or the employer's auditor should perform the audit work on the employer's payroll records, in order to enable the scheme auditor to give his opinion that contributions have been paid in accordance with the rules and recommendation of the actuary as required by the Disclosure Regulations. If the work is to be done by the employer's auditor, the form of any report to be given by the employer's auditor should be agreed in advance with the scheme auditor.

58 As well as supplying the scheme with the information referred to above, the employer is a party to the scheme and often also acts as agent for payment of pension benefits. The scheme auditor will therefore usually need to obtain an agreed form of report on that information from the employer's auditor. The nature and scope of the work appropriate to the scheme audit may well be different from that required by the employer's auditor in the latter's audit testing on the employer's accounts.

59 The scheme auditor should therefore agree the nature and scope of work to be carried out by the employer's auditor in relation to the payment of benefits. The extent to which the scheme auditor may rely on the employer's auditor will be governed by the general principles contained in the Auditing Guideline 'Group financial statements — reliance on the work of other auditors'.

Investment transactions and balances

60 Under the provisions of the Financial Services Act 1986 the trustees may manage the investments of the scheme through an 'authorised person' (i.e. a member of a self-regulating organisation (SRO) authorised by the Securities and Investment Board (SIB) or a person or firm authorised directly by SIB) and/or they may themselves be an authorised person. The investments covered by that Act include shares, debentures, government securities, options and futures. Property and deposits are not covered by that Act. Where the trustees are authorised and governed by the rules of a SRO, they will be required to comply with any record-keeping requirements; the audit considerations will be similar to those of other investment businesses.

61 Where the trustees use an authorised investment manager, the rules of the relevant SRO will require him to provide the trustees with contract notes for each transaction. A contract note must specify certain details including the date, time, description, size, unit price, consideration and fee for the transaction. It must be despatched to the trustees immediately on completion of the contract. Where the trustees purchase units in an insurance company managed fund, an allocation statement would be issued instead of a contract note.

62 An authorised investment manager is also required to provide a periodic statement of transactions he has made on behalf of the investor. This must include a valuation of the portfolio he manages and details of income received in the period. In most cases the statements will form a basis for the scheme's accounts.

63 Where the scheme employs external investment administrators they will each be in one of the following categories:

- — authorised investment businesses (as authorised under the Financial Services Act 1986);
- — insurers (as governed by the Insurance Companies Act 1982);
- — banks (as recognised by the Banking Act 1987);

— administrators of investments not regulated by any of the above statutes (e.g. property).

Insurers acting as managers of managed funds are classified as authorised investment businesses for the purpose of regulation.

64 Details which should be available from those managing the scheme's investments, and which will generally provide sufficient evidence, include:

Authorised investment businesses	— contract notes and statements (see paragraphs 61 - 62)
	— direct confirmation of investment holdings
Insurers	— periodic statements of cash premiums paid (where appropriate)
	— valuations
Bankers and deposit takers	— bank statements
	— direct confirmation of balances
Property managers etc.	— detailed statements of transactions made and assets held. (It will be necessary for the nature and frequency of these statements to be agreed between the trustees and the managers.)

65 The Auditing Guideline 'Audit evidence' requires evidence to be reliable as well as sufficient and relevant. The Auditing Guideline 'Reliance on other specialists' sets out the principles to be followed by the auditor when he wishes to place reliance on audit evidence provided by other specialists. The following may be relevant in assessing the reliability of independent information about investments other than listed securities:

(a) whether the contract between the investment manager and the trustees is at arms length;

(b) the extent to which returns made to regulatory authorities have been audited and the conclusions of such audits (e.g. the DTI returns of an Insurance Company);

(c) other forms of protection available under investor protection legislation (e.g. Financial Services Act 1986); and

(d) the published accounts of managed funds.

66 In the rare event that the auditor still lacks adequate evidence in this area of the scheme's accounts, he may request the trustees to make use of their right under the rules of SROs to inspect the investment manager's records.

Investment valuations

67 The valuations of domestic and foreign marketable securities and exchange rates may usually be verified by reference to published market prices and rates. SORP 1 recommends appropriate valuation methods to use.

68 The value placed on unlisted investments and property will be provided by the trustees, possibly on the basis of advice received from the fund's external advisers or in-house valuers. The matters referred to in paragraph 65 will be particularly relevant in relation to the valuation of unlisted securities by other specialists. Independent published evidence of market prices and income related to listed securities can be used to check the reliability of statements about listed securities. The value placed on an insurance policy investment will usually be provided by either the insurer or the scheme's actuary. Appendix 2 of SORP 1 gives guidance on the method for arriving at a valuation. The principles contained in the Auditing Guideline 'Reliance on other specialists' should be followed in such instances.

Insured schemes

69 An insured scheme is defined as one in which one or more insurance policies are the only long-term investment medium. The benefits will not necessarily be guaranteed by the insurance company. The insurance policies will be included at a valuation in the statement of net assets (unless they are specifically allocated to the provision of benefits for, and provide all the benefits payable under the scheme to, particular members or other persons in respect of particular members or both, see paragraph 70). The insurance company may carry out, *inter alia*:

(a) the receipt and investment of contributions;

(b) the valuation of the policy in an acceptable manner;

(c) the payment of benefits on behalf of the scheme; and

(d) the actuarial valuation and provision of the actuary's statement for inclusion in the annual report.

Where the actuary is independent of the insurance company, the auditor will also need to communicate with the actuary regarding items (b) and (d) above. Where the actuary is employed by the insurance company, such separate communication may not be necessary.

Fully insured schemes

70 A fully insured scheme is defined as one where the trustees have effected an insurance contract in respect of each member which guarantees benefits corresponding at all times to those promised under the rules. The policies are designated (or, where a member has left service, occasionally assigned) to the member and it is not appropriate that they be included in the net assets statement of the scheme pursuant to Regulation 7 (4)(a)(ii) of S.I. 1986/1046. The accounts of such schemes will be confined to a statement of the transactions of the scheme (i.e. contributions received and passed to the insurance company and, to the extent that they come within the trustees' responsibility, benefits paid by the insurance company to beneficiaries) and a net assets statement. Policies which have been specifically allocated to individual members will not be treated as assets: instead the cost of acquiring the policies should be treated as the cost of discharging the pension obligation at the time of allocation. Currently, fully insured schemes are usually defined contribution arrangements.

71 The auditor of a fully insured scheme will be primarily concerned with the transactions of the scheme and the continued existence of the policies which guarantee the payment of benefit. The scheme actuary will normally be an actuary employed by the insurance company. The auditor will need to consult the insurance company in order to ascertain that the conditions of the policies have not been breached to the detriment of any guaranteed benefits.

Review of the annual report

72 The audited accounts will be published as part of the annual report together with the trustee's report, the actuary's statement and the investment report. The auditor's opinion does not extend to these reports. Much of the information contained in them, however, will have been encountered by the auditor during the course of his work. Before completing his report on the accounts which will be included in the annual report, the auditor should satisfy himself that the other parts of the annual report are consistent with, and do not undermine the credibility of the audited accounts. Guidance about these matters is included in the Auditing Guideline: 'Financial information issued with audited financial statements'.

73 Where the auditor's opinion as to whether contributions payable to the scheme have been properly paid (see paragraph 21) is to be qualified, the Disclosure Regulations require the trustees to include in their report a statement giving an account of the reasons and a statement of how the discrepancy has been or is likely to be resolved. The auditor will be particularly concerned as to the content of that statement.

The actuary's statement

74 The actuary's statement forms one part of the annual report. The actuary's opinion is central to gaining an understanding of the state of affairs of a scheme. Although not expressing an opinion on the actuary's work, the auditor should review the statement so as to:

(a) understand more fully the scheme's operation;

(b) be aware of the implications of the actuary's opinion for the future operation of the scheme;

(c) ensure that there is no obvious inconsistency with the accounts; and

(d) establish whether in general the actuary has been provided with information (detailed membership data and known employer or scheme plans for future developments) which is consistent with that used in preparing the accounts as at the valuation date or the nearest accounting date to it. This should preferably be done before the actuary's statement is prepared.

75 The auditor's work in relation to the actuary's statement will often be carried out through discussion with the actuary or by correspondence. The auditor should obtain the consent of the trustees to approach the actuary and should be given freedom to discuss with the actuary any matters relating to the scheme which the auditor considers relevant to the actuary's work and vice versa.

76 The auditor should have an appreciation of the various matters considered by the actuary, the factors which may affect his valuation and the items included in a full valuation. The actuary may also wish to have an appreciation of the matters considered by the auditor (a discussion of these matters, together with suggested audit procedures, is set out in the Audit Brief 'The work of a pension scheme actuary').

Reporting

The audit report

77 The Disclosure Regulations require an auditor to report whether, in his opinion the accounts show a true and fair view of the financial transactions of the scheme and of the disposition of its assets and liabilities. These liabilities do not include liabilities to pay pensions and benefits after the end of the year.

78 The principles set out in the Auditing Standard 'The audit report' are applicable to the audit report on pension scheme accounts. The audit report should therefore identify those to whom it is addressed and the accounts to which it relates. The auditor should also state whether the accounts have been audited in accordance with approved Auditing Standards. The audit report should be addressed in accordance with the trust deed. Where the deed is silent, the report should be addressed to the trustees and members. The auditor should, however, be aware that trustees have a statutory duty to make the annual report available to members.

79 The scope paragraph of the audit report will encompass the note to the accounts which refers to the actuary's statement. The auditor does not express an opinion on the actuary's statement. He should therefore ensure that a note consistent with the following wording in paragraph 45 of SORP 1 is included but that it does not itself reproduce the actuary's opinion:

> "The accounts summarise the transactions and net assets of the scheme. They do not take account of liabilities to pay pensions and other benefits in the future. The actuarial position of the fund, which does take account of such liabilities, is dealt with in the statement by the actuary on pages 00 to 00 of the annual report and these accounts should be read in conjunction therewith."

Providing such a note is included, it is not necessary to refer to the excluded liabilities in the auditor's report. However, if that part of the note dealing with the excluded liabilities is omitted, a qualification of the auditor's report will be required. The Disclosure Regulations require the accounts to indicate any material departure from SORP 1, and as the omission of the part referred to above would be such a departure, it will be necessary that the accounts indicate the fact of departure. However, it is unlikely that the simple statement of the departure would be adequate to highlight the exclusion of future liabilities. Accordingly the qualification should be in the form of an 'except for' reservation to the true and fair view of the assets and liabilities.

80 If the assets intended to cover some or all of the liabilities of the scheme are in the form of insurance policies the benefits of which have been assigned to individual members, these assets will be correctly excluded from the scheme accounts and this exclusion should be referred to in the notes to the accounts. There is however no requirement, actual or implied, in the regulations for this note. Nevertheless the absence of such a note should be dealt with in a qualification of the auditor's report in a similar manner to that referred to in the previous paragraph.

81 Regulation 7(5)(b) of S.I. 1986/1046 also requires the auditor to include "a statement whether or not in his opinion contributions payable to the scheme during the scheme year have been paid in accordance with the scheme rules or contracts under which they were payable, and with the recommendation of the actuary, if appropriate". This opinion should be given in a separate paragraph below the opinion on the accounts. This opinion on contributions is separate from the opinion on the accounts and must not be presented so as to appear to be a qualification of that opinion or an emphasis of matter in relation to that opinion. However, a qualification on contributions will imply that the rules of the scheme will have been breached, and the principles of paragraphs 27 and 28 will apply.

82 The wording of the opinion on contributions is more specific than the opinion required on the accounts. It requires the auditor to consider the amounts of contributions payable to the scheme and, where the trust deed or rules are specific, the dates of payment. Where the trust deed or rules are not specific, the auditor should consider qualifying his report if in his opinion the contributions are not paid within a reasonable period. In judging what is reasonable, the auditor should have regard to the usual timetable of payments, the situation at the time of the last actuarial valuation and any advice from the actuary.

83 It may be necessary for the auditor to consider whether results of audit tests on contributions require a qualified opinion to be given on contributions paid. Criteria to be considered in this respect will include whether any discrepancies favour one particular member or group of members, and the extent to which the growth of the fund has suffered because of a failure to pay contributions to the scheme in a proper manner.

84 The auditor may, for example, in the case of a scheme having several participating employers, be unable to obtain sufficient evidence on contributions to give an unqualified opinion. The scope of his examination might be expressly stated as being limited to the transactions as recorded in the books of the scheme.

85 An example of an unqualified audit report is set out in Appendix 1.

Qualifications in audit reports

86 Where the auditor is not in a position to report affirmatively on the scheme accounts or on contributions payable to the scheme, he should qualify his report by referring to all material matters about which he has reservations. The following are examples of matters which may give rise to a qualified opinion in relation to pension scheme accounts:

(a) a limitation in the scope of the audit, for example if the auditor has not been allowed access to certain records held by others;

(b) a material misstatement resulting from a breach of the trust deed or scheme rules;

(c) the trustees have not complied with the Acts or Disclosure Regulations (this will include paragraph 9 of Schedule 3 to S.I. 1986/1046 which requires material departures from SORP 1 to be disclosed);

(d) the auditor has not inspected the statement by a previous auditor required under the Occupational Pension Schemes (Auditors) Regulations 1987, or that statement is not attached to the annual report; and

(e) the auditor is unable to confirm that contributions have been received from the employer in accordance with the scheme rules or actuary's advice.

87 Non-compliance with SORP 1 will not of itself lead to a qualification of the audit report. However, paragraph 9 of Schedule 3 to S.I. 1986/1046 does require that the accounts contain "a statement whether the accounts have been prepared in accordance with parts 2 to 4 of Statement of Recommended Practice 1 ... and if not, an indication of where there are any material departures from those guidelines". Accordingly, the auditor will need to qualify his opinion if:

(a) the accounts have been prepared in accordance with SORP 1 but do not contain a statement to that effect; or

(b) the accounts have not been prepared in accordance with SORP 1 and do not contain a statement to that effect together with an adequate indication of material departures.

The qualification will be on the grounds that the accounts do not contain the information specified in Regulation 7 of and Schedule 3 to S.I. 1986/1046.

Appendix 1

88 Example of an unqualified audit report

AUDITORS' REPORT TO THE TRUSTEES AND MEMBERS OF ...

We have audited the accounts on pages ... to ... in accordance with approved Auditing Standards.

In our opinion the accounts give a true and fair view of the financial transactions of the scheme during the year ended ... and of the disposition at that date of its assets and liabilities and contain the information specified in Regulation 7 of and Schedule 3 to the Occupational Pension Schemes (Disclosure of Information) Regulations 1986.*

In our opinion the contributions payable to the scheme during the year ended ... have been paid in accordance with the scheme rules and with the recommendation of the actuary.

Auditors

Date

* The above example is based on legislation in Great Britain. In the case of Northern Ireland the reference in the second paragraph would be to Regulation 7 of and Schedule 3 to the Occupational Pension Schemes (Disclosure of Information) Regulations (Northern Ireland) 1986.

Appendix 2

Glossary of terms

89 Accrued Benefits	The benefits for service up to a given point in time. They may be calculated in relation to current earnings or projected final earnings. A member is not necessarily entitled to receive accrued benefits should he leave the scheme prior to retirement. Another common meaning is the benefits which would be payable if all the members left service.
Active Member	A member of a pension scheme who is currently accruing benefits under that scheme, other than deferred pensioners.
The Acts	The Social Security Acts 1973, 1975, 1985 and 1986 and the Social Security Pensions Act 1975, as amended.
*Additional Voluntary Contributions (AVC)	Contributions over and above a members' normal contributions, if any, which a member elects to pay in order to secure additional benefits.
*Approved Scheme	An occupational pension scheme which is approved by the Inland Revenue, thus avoiding the tax penalty in Section 23 of the Finance Act 1970.
*Basic Pension	The flat rate state pension paid to all who meet the minimum contribution requirements while in employment.
*Commingled Fund	A term sometimes used to describe a common investment fund.
*Common Investment Fund	An arrangement whereby the assets of two or more pension schemes, usually operated by a single employer, are pooled for investment.
*Concentration of Investment	The investment of an unduly high proportion of the assets of a pension scheme in a single enterprise. The OPB requires contracted out schemes to report concentration of over 10 per cent. The Disclosure Regulations and SORP 1 require disclosure where there is a concentration of investment which exceeds 5 per cent.
*Contract Out	To use a statutory arrangement under which an occupational pension scheme meeting certain conditions provides its members with specified benefits to replace part of their earnings related state scheme benefits. Lower contributions are payable to the state scheme in respect of employees who are contracted out.
*Contributions Equivalent Premium	A type of state scheme premium which may be paid when a member leaves after a relatively short period of contracted out employment, in return for which the state scheme will take over the obligation to provide his guaranteed minimum pension.
*Deferred Pensioner	A person entitled to preserved benefits. Sometimes referred to as a deferred member.
*Deficiency	The excess of the actuarial value of liabilities over the actuarial value of assets, on the basis of the valuation method used.

*** Definition taken from 'Pensions Terminology — A Glossary for Pension Schemes' published by the Pensions Management Institute and the Pensions Research Accountants Group in 1984. Reproduced with kind permission.**

*Defined Benefit Scheme	A pension scheme in which the rules specify the benefits to be paid, and the scheme is financed accordingly.
*Defined Contribution Scheme	An alternative term for a money purchase scheme, normally one where the rate of contribution is specified in the rules.
Definitive Trust Deed	See 'Trust Document' below.
Disclosure Regulations	The Occupational Pension Schemes (Disclosure of Information Regulations 1986 (S.I. 1986/1046) as amended by The Occupational Pension Schemes (Disclosure of Information) (Amendment) Regulations 1986 and 1987 (S.I. 1986/1717, S.I. 1987/1105), The Occupational Pension Schemes (Auditors) Regulations 1987 (S.I. 1987/1102).
*Discontinuance Valuation	An actuarial valuation to establish the degree of solvency if a scheme were wound up. The liabilities are calculated as the cost of providing the existing benefits for current and deferred pensioners and accrued benefits, ignoring possible future earnings increases, for active members and their dependants. The assets are taken at market value.
*Exempt Approved Scheme	An approved scheme which is established under an irrevocable trust (or, exceptionally, subject to a formal direction under Section 21(1)(b) of the Finance Act 1970) thus giving rise to the tax reliefs specified in the Finance Acts.
*Fully Insured Scheme	A scheme where the trustees have effected an insurance contract in respect of each member which guarantees benefits corresponding at all times to those promised under the rules.
*Funding	The provision in advance for future liabilities by the accumulation of assets, normally external to the employers' business.
* Funding Rate	A term sometimes used to describe the rate of contributions.
Guaranteed Minimum Pension	The minimum pension which a pension scheme provides as one of the conditions of contracting out under the Acts. The state benefits payable in respect of a contracted out employee are reduced by the amount of the guaranteed minimum pension. The Social Security Act 1986 permits defined contribution schemes to contract out without guaranteeing this minimum pension.
*Insured Scheme	A pension scheme where the sole long-term investment medium is an insurance policy (other than a managed fund policy).
*Level of Funding	The propoi.ion at a given date of the actuarial value of liabilities for pensioners' and deferred pensioners' benefits and for members' accrued benefits which is covered by the actuarial value of assets excluding the actuarial value of future contributions. The term may also be used in relation to the results of a discontinuance valuation.
*Managed Fund	An investment contract by means of which an insurance company offers participation in one or more funds operated on similar lines to unit trusts.
*Member	An employee or former employee entitled to benefit from a pension scheme. Sometimes used to refer only to an active

	member. For some statutory purposes the term members may include employees who are prospective members.
*Money Purchase Scheme	A pension scheme in which the benefits are directly determined by the value of contributions paid in respect of each member.
*Occupational Pension Scheme	An arrangement, other than accident insurance, organised by an employer or on behalf of a group of employers, to provide pension and/or benefits for members on leaving service or retiring and, after a member's death, for his or her dependants.
Occupational Pensions Board (OPB)	A statutory body whose duties include the supervision of the statutory arrangements for contracting out. It also investigates and reports on pension topics referred to it from time-to-time by the Government.
*Overfunded Scheme	A scheme with an actuarial surplus.
*Pay-as-you-go	An arrangement under which benefits are paid out of revenue and no provision is made for future liabilities. The state scheme is pay-as-you-go.
*Pension Scheme	An arrangement, other than accident insurance, to provide pension and/or other benefits for members on leaving service or retiring and, after a member's death, for his or her dependants.
*Pensioner Trustee	An individual or body widely involved with pension schemes and accepted under SFO requirements as a trustee of a small self-administered scheme.
*Pensioner	A person who is currently entitled to a pension from a pension scheme.
*Preserved Benefits	Benefits arising on termination of employment or of pension scheme membership, payable later.
*Rules	The detailed provisions of a pension scheme, normally set out in a formal way and usually given authority by a trust document.
*Segregated Fund	An arrangement whereby the investments of a particular pension scheme are managed by an insurance company independently of other funds under its control.
*Self-Administered Scheme	A pension scheme where the assets are invested, other than wholly by payment of insurance premiums, by the trustees, an in-house manager or an external investment manager. Although on the face of it the term self-administered should refer to the method of administering contributions and benefits, in practice the term has become solely related to the way in which the investments are managed.
*Self-Investment	The investment of a scheme's assets in the business of the employer or that of an associated company, or loans made to the employer or associated company. The OPB requires contracted out schemes to report self investment of over 10 per cent. The Disclosure Regulations and SORP 1 require disclosure of particulars of any self-investment in excess of 5 per cent of the total value of net assets of the scheme.

SERPS	The State Earnings Related Pension Scheme.
*State Scheme Premium	A payment which may be made when either the pension scheme or a member of it ceases to be contracted out, in return for which the state scheme will provide the equivalent of the whole or a part of the guaranteed minimum pension. A state scheme premium may be an accrued rights premium, a contributions equivalent premium, a limited revaluation premium or a pensioner's rights premium.
*Superannuation Funds Office (SFO)	The branch of the Inland Revenue which deals with the approval of pension schemes under the relevant tax legislation.
*Surplus	The excess of the actuarial value of assets over the actuarial value of liabilities on the basis of the valuation method used.
*Terminal Funding	An arrangement whereby a payment to meet the capitalised value of a benefit is made only at or about the time when the benefit is due to commence. (Not common in the United Kingdom except in respect of discretionary pension increases.)
*Transfer Payment	A payment made by one pension scheme to another, for example when a member changes employment, to enable the receiving pension scheme to give additional benefits.
*Transfer Value	A term commonly used to mean transfer payment.
*Trust Deed	See 'Trust Document' (below).
*Trust Document	Any deed, board resolution or other document which establishes or alters a pension scheme and governs its management. An interim trust deed may be used to establish a pension scheme on broadly stated terms leaving the detailed provisions and the rules to be provided later by a definitive trust deed.
*Trustee	A person or body holding, alone or jointly, the title to property for the benefit of another. In a pension scheme the trust document often gives the trustees further responsibilities.
Underfunded Scheme	A scheme with an actuarial deficiency.
*Unfunded Scheme	A pension scheme which is based on pay-as-you-go or under which funds are set aside only at retirement.
Valuation Basis	The collection of assumptions used by an actuary in the valuation of a pension scheme.
*Valuation Method	The approach used by the actuary in an actuarial valuation. Two main categories of approach are defined under accrued benefits valuation method and prospective benefits valuation method. A variety of methods can be used but the method or methods used in a particular case should be made clear in the actuarial report. More detail of the methods is set out in the Audit Brief 'The work of a pension scheme actuary'.

Banks in the United Kingdom

(Issued March 1989)

Preface

This Auditing Guideline on bank audits contains guidance on the special factors to be considered in the application of Auditing Standards to banks and is intended to assist:

(a) the auditors of a bank to comply with Auditing Standards when carrying out their audit work and in preparing their report on the financial statements;

(b) the reporting accountants of a bank in reporting on matters specified by the Bank of England in accordance with the guidance issued by the Bank of England; and

(c) in outlining the contents of the reports referred to in paragraph 5(b) of the guideline.

The guideline is supplementary to, and should be read in conjunction with, the Auditor's Operational and Reporting Standards and related guidelines.

The Banking Act 1987 (the Act) introduced important new responsibilities for the auditors of authorised institutions.

The two main implications of the Act for auditors are:

(a) The Bank of England is empowered to obtain information from an institution and to require that this information be reported upon by a 'reporting accountant' (appointed by the institution and normally expected to be the auditor). The Bank of England has indicated that it will require reports on internal control systems and accounting and other records, and on banks' returns used for prudential purposes.

(b) Section 47 of the Act provides that no duty, for example that of confidentiality to his client, to which an auditor of an authorised institution or a person appointed under Sections 8(5) or 39(1)(b) of the Act (the reporting accountant) shall be subject will be contravened "by reason of his communicating in good faith to the Bank, whether or not in response to a request made by it, any information or opinion on a matter to which this section applies and which is relevant to any function of the Bank under this Act".

It is this section which makes it clear that auditors and reporting accountants are able to communicate to the Bank of England by way of a formal report, at a meeting or by any other means on any matters relating to the institution's affairs arising out of their appointment which are relevant to any function of the Bank of England under the Act.

One of the main aims of the guideline is to satisfy the requirements of Section 47(5) o the Act which allows HM Treasury to make regulations for auditors specifying circustances in which matters are to be communicated to the Bank of England if guidance is not issued by the profession.

The contents of this guideline have the approval of the Bank of England and the Treasury.

This guideline is based on the law as at 1 October 1987.

Introduction

1 Throughout this guideline, the term 'bank' refers to any institution which is authorised under the Banking Act 1987 to take deposits in the UK. Banks which are incorporated in Great Britain are subject to the audit provisions of the Companies Act 1985 and those incorporated in Northern Ireland to the provisions of the Companies (Northern Ireland) Order 1986. The scope of the statutory audit of a bank's financial statement is, therefore, no different from that of the generality of companies in Great Britain and Northern

Ireland. The Banking Act 1987 gives the Bank of England power to require information from a bank and may require that this information be reported upon by an accountant or other person with relevant professional skill (who may be the auditor). The auditors will therefore have additional responsibilities if acting as reporting accountants under the Banking Act 1987.

2 This guideline therefore distinguishes between the two types of assignment relating to banks:

(a) the audit of the financial statements and related reports in accordance with the Companies Act 1985 (see paragraphs 16 to 64); and

(b) reporting under Section 39 of the Banking Act 1987 (see paragraphs 65 to 191).

3 In the case of banks which are not subject to the provisions of the Companies Act 1985 (for example, UK branches of overseas banks), the terms of engagement are a matter of contract between the auditors and their clients.

4 The guideline refers to 'auditors' when discussing work carried out for the purposes of paragraph 2(a) above, and to 'reporting accountants' when considering other types of assignment under paragraph 2(b) above. It is important to note that the reporting accountants may be the auditors.

5 The auditors or reporting accountants of a bank are required to form an opinion and report as follows:

(a) The auditors are required to report to the members whether, in their opinion, the annual financial statements give a true and fair view and have been properly prepared in accordance with the Companies Act 1985. However, where a bank presents financial statements using the provisions of Part III of Schedule 9 to the Companies Act 1985 the auditors are only required to report on whether the accounts have been properly prepared. (It is nevertheless provided in the Companies Act 1985 that the financial statements shall not be deemed not to give a true and fair view simply because they have been prepared using the provisions of Part III of Schedule 9 to that Act.)

(b) The reporting accountants are required to report to the directors, or to the senior manager in the case of a branch, in accordance with specific instructions received by the bank from the Bank of England, on:

(i) the accounting and other records and the systems of internal control; and

(ii) Bank of England returns used for prudential purposes.

(c) Both auditors and reporting accountants are entitled to report to the Bank of England in exceptional circumstances in order to protect the interests of depositors ('*ad hoc* reports').

6 Auditors or reporting accountants may be asked by the Bank of England to perform other specific assignments. The reports generated by such assignments are outside the scope of this guideline.

7 It is particularly important that the auditors or reporting accountants of a bank undertake an engagement only after considering their own competence and the adequacy of their resources (including relevant experience) to carry out their duties. In assessing their competence and resources the auditors or reporting accountants should bear in mind the type and range of the bank's activities and nature of its systems. For example, highly specialised computer systems will require different skills from those necessary to evaluate manual systems. Similarly, different skills may be required for a large banking organisation offering a wide range of highly specialised services (such as corporate finance), to those required for a smaller organisation.

Legislation

The Banking Act 1987

8 The Banking Act 1987 has replaced the Banking Act 1979 as the statute relating to the regulation of banks. It regulates deposit-taking in order to protect depositors and to fulfil the UK's obligations under the EC First Credit Institutions Directive on the protection of shareholders and third parties, and provides for the establishment of a Board of Banking Supervision to give advice to the Bank of England on the exercise of its regulatory functions. The main provisions of the Act deal with:

(a) the creation of a single category of 'authorised institution' (referred to in this guideline as a 'bank') to replace the two tier system established by the 1979 Act;

(b) the laying down of specific criteria for authorisation, including the requirement that business be conducted in a 'prudent manner';

(c) the powers of the Bank of England to require information, to instigate investigation procedures, to refuse, restrict or revoke authorisation and to give directions to a bank during and after the revocation process;

(d) the restriction of the use of banking names and descriptions;

(e) the establishment of lines of communication between auditors and reporting accountants and the Bank of England, and the corresponding provision for disclosure of information by the Bank of England to the auditors or reporting accountants;

(f) the establishment of a statutory duty for authorised institutions to report large exposures to the Bank of England;

(g) the further development of the Deposit Protection Scheme set up by the 1979 Act;

(h) the establishment of restrictions on disclosure of information; and

(i) the imposition of requirements on overseas institutions with, or proposing to set up, representative offices in the UK.

Appendix 1 details the provisions of the Banking Act 1987 which are of most interest to auditors and reporting accountants.

9 Section 47 of the Act provides that, where auditors or reporting accountants communicate information to the Bank of England in good faith, on a matter of which they become aware in their capacity as auditors or reporting accountants and which is relevant to any function of the Bank of England under the Act, they shall not be regarded as having contravened any duty to which they may be subject. Guidance on the communication between bank auditors or reporting accountants and the Bank of England is given in this guideline in paragraphs 171 to 191.

10 Section 39(3) of the Act gives the Bank of England the power to obtain such information and documents from banks as it may reasonably require for the performance of its functions under the Act. Section 39(4) gives it like power to obtain documents which can be required from a bank under Section 39(3) from any other person who appears to be in possession of them. This may include the auditors or reporting accountants of a bank. Section 39(4) thus refers only to documents which could be required of the bank itself. As a bank would not normally have copies of the auditors' or reporting accountants' working papers, it follows that the Bank of England would not be able to obtain copies of such working papers under Section 39(4).

11 Section 41(5) of the Act imposes a duty on the auditors and reporting accountants of a bank to produce to investigators appointed by the Bank of England under Section 41(1) all documents relating to the bank concerned which are in their custody or power. This would appear to include the auditors' or reporting accountants' own working papers. If in doubt, legal advice should be sought.

The Financial Services Act 1986

12 The Financial Services Act 1986 is designed to provide a framework for protecting the customers of investment businesses and affects banks to the extent that they are involved in these businesses. Banks which are so involved will require prior authorisation and be subject to regulation by the Securities and Investments Board (SIB) or self-regulating organisations (SROs) in respect of such business. Auditors should be aware that this may give rise to additional responsibilities.

13 If a bank is listed by the Bank of England under Section 43 of the Financial Services Act 1986, it will have particular responsibilities for maintaining records and systems of control which are outlined in general terms in the Bank of England's paper "The Regulation of the Wholesale Markets in Sterling, Foreign Exchange, and Bullion" (April 1988). There may also be special features in the application of the requirements of the Banking Act 1987 to discount houses. This guideline does not provide specific guidance on these requirements and features; further guidance can be obtained from the Wholesale Markets Supervision Division of the Bank of England.

The Companies Act 1985

14 The form and content of the financial statements of banks is governed by the Companies Act 1985 and Statements of Standard Accounting Practice (SSAPs). In addition, from time to time, the Committee of London and Scottish Bankers (CLSB), the British Bankers' Association (BBA) and the accountancy bodies provide, in an advisory capacity, guidance and recommendations to their members on accounting issues.

15 A banking company is designated a 'specific category' company by Section 257 of the Companies Act 1985 and, as such, may prepare its final statements in accordance with Schedule 9 of the Act which does not prescribe standard formats for financial statements. Schedule 9 also provides for certain banks under authority of the Department of Trade and Industry to gain exemption from particular disclosure requirements.

Auditing under the Companies Act 1985

Background

Areas for consideration

16 This section of the guideline comments on matters either peculiar to or of particular importance in the audit of a bank under the Companies Act 1985.

Accounting records

17 In common with all companies incorporated under the Companies Act 1985, banks are subject to the requirements of Section 221 of that Act, which provides that accounting records must be kept in accordance with that section. Auditors of banks are subject to the duty imposed by Section 237(2) of the Companies Act 1985, that they should form an opinion as to whether proper accounting records have been kept.

18 In forming their opinion on the financial statements under the Companies Act 1985, the auditors should consider the implications and effects of any matters to which they, or other reporting accountants, draw attention in the report to the directors or senior manager on the accounting and other records and internal control systems.

19 The auditors should therefore have regard to such factors as:

(a) the guidance given by the Bank of England as to its interpretation of the statutory requirement for the maintenance of adequate accounting and other records for Banking Act purposes (BSD/1987/2);

(b) the size and structure of the bank and its organisation and management; and

(c) the nature, volume and complexity of the bank's transactions.

Internal control systems

20 A system of internal controls is defined in the Auditing Guideline 'Internal controls' as being:

"the whole system of controls, financial and otherwise, established by management in order to carry on the business of the enterprise in an orderly and efficient manner, ensure adherence to management policies, safeguard the assets and secure as far as possible the completeness and accuracy of the records."

21 The auditors of any company including a bank are required by Auditing Standards to assess the internal control systems only to the extent that they wish to place reliance on those systems in arriving at their opinion as to whether the financial statements give a true and fair view. As the special features of banking outlined in paragraph 22 below mean that the auditors will normally have to place significant reliance on the systems of control, a careful evaluation of these systems, including computer-based accounting and information systems, and their relationship with the risk of material misstatement in the financial statements will be essential. If the auditors conclude that they can rely on the system of controls, they may be able to limit the level of substantive tests required to form their opinion on the financial statements.

22 Systems of internal control in a bank are vital for management in ensuring orderly and prudent operations at the bank and are also important in assisting the directors in preparing financial statements which give a true and fair view, for example, because of the following special features of the business of banking:

(a) A bank deals in money or assets readily convertible into money. In the case of most commercial organisations, most movements of cash are the result of a related movement of goods and some audit assurance may, therefore, be obtained by reference to this relationship. This is not available, however, in the case of banks and similar financial organisations. Assurance must, therefore, be provided by adequate systems of control, particularly over the handling of cash and other negotiable assets. In most enterprises the transfer of funds from one party to another is effected through the medium of a cheque or other negotiable instrument. Although such instruments are used in banks, it is also common for payment to be effected electronically such as by telex, CHAPS or SWIFT. As the centralised communications departments which exist in larger institutions will often process very high volumes and a high value of transactions each day, the need for strong and effective controls over the whole area of funds transfer is particularly important. If, as a result of the widespread use of automated money and funds transfer systems, the auditors experience difficulty in identifying adequate audit trails, they will need to reconsider their audit approach.

(b) The substantial scale of transactions, both in terms of volume and relative value, makes it essential that control systems are in place to ensure that transactions are recorded promptly, accurately and completely and are checked and proved, and that records are reconciled at appropriate intervals in order to identify and investigate differences promptly. In the case of large banks, the volume of transactions can be so great that the auditors cannot express an opinion without obtaining considerable assurance from adequate systems of control. Accounting for the large volumes of similar transactions will frequently involve the use of computers. The auditors will need to have, or be able to call upon, the necessary expertise to satisfy themselves that they have a sufficient understanding of the systems relevant to their audit work, so that they can justify from their written record of the systems and their compliance tests, the reliance that they have placed on its internal controls.

(c) The geographical dispersal of some banks' operations means that, in order to maintain control over dispersed activities, banks need to ensure not only that there are sufficient controls at each location, but also that there are effective communication procedures between the various locations and the centre.

(d) Increasingly, the activities of banks result in the creation of assets and liabilities which do not appear on their balance sheets, perhaps as a result of forward foreign exchange dealing or specialised off balance sheet products such as swaps. The fact that the resultant cash flow may not take place for a considerable time creates the risk that wrongly recorded or unrecorded positions may exist and that these may not be detected for some time, thereby exposing the bank to risk of loss. Consequently, banks have developed important operational controls to mitigate such risks.

(e) The provisions of the Taxes Acts require banks to operate Composite Rate Tax, Mortgage Interest Relief at Source and to act as paying and collecting agents. In addition the VAT position of a bank can be particularly complex. These areas may give rise to a significant liability if not properly dealt with. Accordingly, an effective control system is essential to ensure that the record keeping requirements of the Taxes Acts and VAT law are satisfied, and that tax is accounted for promptly and accurately.

23 For the purpose of identifying relevant controls, the principal activities of banks may be classified as follows:

(a) loans, advances, trade finance and related income and expense;

(b) customer accounts, cash, transfer of funds, nostro accounts and related income and expense;

(c) market deposits and related income and expense;

(d) dealing in foreign exchange, futures, options, commodities, bullion and related income, expense, gains and losses;

(e) investments, dealing securities and related income, expense, gains and losses; and

(f) trustee and advisory activities (including portfolio management) and related income and expense.

Examples of detailed controls under each of these heads are given in Appendix 2.

24 The overall audit objective is to ensure that the financial statements give a true and fair view of the state of the bank's affairs at a given date and of the results for the year then ended, and comply with statutory and other relevant requirements.

25 Audit steps likely to be required to satisfy this overall objective, can be identified as follows:

(a) to determine the reliability of the bank's systems of internal control;

(b) to ensure that all material balances exist, are complete, and are fairly stated at the balance sheet date;

(c) to ensure that all income and expenditure, gains and losses are properly accounted for;

(d) to ascertain the recoverability and hence the realisability at the balance sheet date, of any loans, investments and other related credit exposures;

(e) in relation to trustee activities, to ascertain whether controls exist to give reasonable assurance that the bank has fulfilled its fiduciary duties; and

(f) to ensure that all material commitments and liabilities, contingent or otherwise, are identified, provided for, or adequately disclosed in the financial statements.

26 The delegation of management functions may form part of the bank's systems of control. The auditors will need to understand both the extent and nature of any delegation of management functions, and the systems of control employed by the directors over delegated functions.

27 In the context of banking operations, the system of internal controls should also be adequate to meet the relevant authorisation criteria, in particular to enable the bank's directors and management to conduct its business in a prudent manner on a day-to-day basis, and to ensure the complete, accurate and timely production of such information as the Bank of England, or other supervisory body, may require. As discussed in paragraphs 68-136, these controls will be reported on by the reporting accountants. Management must exercise judgement in determining the scope and nature of the controls adopted and should review, monitor and test the systems regularly to ensure that they remain effective. In exercising this judgement, management should give consideration to the detailed control objectives set down in the Bank of England Guidance Note 'Accounting and other Records and Internal Control Systems and the Reporting Accountants' Reports Thereon' issued in September 1987 (BSD/1987/2) and the need for financial statements to give a true and fair view. Auditors are not required to complete all the functions of reporting accountants in carrying out their work. However, they should be aware of the criteria for authorisation in assessing the results of their audit work, particularly when considering the question of going concern.

Automation

28 As a result of the large number of transactions undertaken and records held by banks and the need for swift and accurate information processing and retrieval, many banking functions are often highly automated, including: funds transfer systems, the accounting function, the processing and recording of retail customer transactions, the dealing room and the supply of dealing and management information.

29 The auditors should assess the extent, nature and impact of automation within the bank and plan and perform their work accordingly. The Auditing Guideline 'Auditing in a computer environment' will be especially relevant in the audit of banks. In particular:

(a) the required level of technical computer knowledge and skills is likely to be extensive and may require the auditor to obtain advice and assistance from staff with specialist skills;

(b) bank audits are particularly suitable for the use of audit software and other types of Computer Assisted Audit Techniques; and

(c) reliance on internal controls for audit purposes is likely to require the evaluation and testing of general controls relating to the environment within which computer based systems are developed, maintained and operated.

Branches

30 Many banks operate a network of branches. The auditors' approach to such branches will principally be determined by the degree of head office control over the business and accounting functions at each branch and by the scope and effectiveness of the bank's inspection and/or internal audit visits. The extent and impact of visits from regulators should also be considered. Where branches maintain separate accounting records, the extent of audit visits and work on each branch will also be dependent on the materiality of, and risks associated with, the operations of each branch and the extent to which controls over branches are exercised centrally. Where the branch accounting records are centralised, the auditors should obtain reasonable assurance that the systems of control over branches are operating satisfactorily either by visiting branches, or by ensuring that an adequate system of branch inspection by internal auditors exists. Particular attention should be paid both to the difficulties of exercising head office control and to the differences in nature and degree of risk that may arise in overseas branches. In the case of smaller branches, attention should be focused upon the exceptions to a bank's normal control procedures caused by staffing levels (e.g. the greater difficulty of ensuring adequate segregation of duties) and to the consequent need for an increased level of control from outside the branch.

Operational guidelines

Planning, controlling and recording

31 Paragraph 2 of 'The auditor's operational standard' states that "the auditor should adequately plan, control and record his work". When planning the audit of a bank, auditors should refer to the Auditing Guideline 'Planning, controlling and recording', and in particular should consider the following matters:

(a) the overall financial environment in which the bank operates and its types of business;

(b) the extent of computer systems and the reliance placed on these systems by the bank;

(c) the legal framework in which the bank operates;

(d) the audit risk involved. The assessment of this is crucial and should be undertaken very carefully, particularly where the circumstances and management of the bank indicate that the engagement is likely to be high risk;

(e) key audit areas, in particular individual areas where there is a high risk of material misstatement. These should be identified at an early stage of the audit to ensure that work is concentrated on these areas;

(f) the adequacy and scope of the internal audit or inspection function;

(g) the timing and nature of the audit work to be carried out;

(h) the use of staff with adequate training and experience.

32 The auditors should also consider the following additional matters when planning the audit:

(a) the requirements of any Guidance Notes issued by the Bank of England;

(b) any formal communications between the Bank of England and the bank, including all correspondence, minutes or notes of meetings relevant to the reporting accountants' examination of the accounting and other records, internal control systems and Bank of England returns used for prudential purposes. The Bank of England has stated that it will inform the auditors of any matter which it believes to be of such importance that the auditors' knowledge of it could significantly affect the way in which they carry out their audit (see also paragraph 56);

(c) the contents of the most recent reports prepared by the reporting accountants on accounting and other records, internal control systems and on Bank of England returns used for prudential purposes.

Copies of the Guidance Notes mentioned at (a) may be obtained from the Bank of England. Copies of the documents mentioned at (b) and (c) should be requested from the client.

33 Paragraph 6 of the Auditing Guideline 'Planning, controlling and recording' states: "In order to plan his work adequately the auditor needs to understand the nature of the business of the enterprise, its organisation, its method of operating and the industry in which it is involved, so that he is able to appreciate which events and transactions are likely to have a significant effect on the financial statements."

34 In gaining an understanding of the underlying operations of the bank and in assessing the nature of the exposures arising from the business, auditors will normally find it helpful to adopt a 'top down' approach by:

(a) gaining an understanding of the overall structure of the bank, the environment in which it operates and the financial statements as a whole;

(b) dividing the bank and its financial statements into manageable parts based for example on separate lines of business, financial statement components or phases of processing transactions. Often this division will follow the departmental splits used by the bank;

(c) determining the relationships of each part to the whole, the particular risks and related audit objectives for each part and the nature and degree of audit testing required.

35 The overall objective of this approach is to identify those aspects of the business which have a significant impact on the financial statements and those parts of the financial statements for which risk of material misstatement exists and to concentrate the audit work on these areas.

Analytical review procedures

36 The auditors should include appropriate overall and detailed analytical review procedures at all stages of their work. The Auditing Guideline 'Analytical review' outlines the contribution that can be made by analytical review as the planning stage, in obtaining evidence and in reviewing the financial statements. Analytical reviews are of particular significance to the audits of banks to highlight exceptions, large or unusual transactions and variations from the norm, as a basis for directing the auditors to further detailed investigation into changes in the business or particular problem areas. As a result of the nature of banking risks, banks must possess management information systems which are both reliable and appropriate to the business undertaken. The auditors may use such information, having regard to the adequacy of the overall controls over its production.

Banking risks

37 Fundamental to the auditors' approach is an understanding of the multi-dimensional nature and extent of the risks and related exposures in a banking environment. These risks include:

(a) credit risk: the risk that a debtor or counterparty will be unable to meet his obligations;

(b) interest rate risk: the risk that arises from the mismatching of interest rates (e.g. funds borrowed at rates linked to LIBOR and employed at fixed rates), maturities or currencies;

(c) position risk: the risk that changes to the values of assets, liabilities and commitments will occur as a result of movements in relative prices (e.g. as a result of changes in the market price of tradeable assets/securities, in exchange rates or interest rates);

(d) liquidity risk: the risk that arises from the possibility of the bank having insufficient funds to meet the demands of depositors or other counterparties;

(e) settlement risk: the risk that one side of a transaction will be settled without value being received from the counterparty;

(f) systems failure risk: the risk that arises either from internal systems breakdowns or external payment and clearing systems breakdowns. These systems include both manual and computer procedures. Breakdowns include computer malfunctions ranging from temporary faults to prolonged failure.

38 Given the scale of banking operations, significant exposures can arise within short periods of time. A major feature of a bank's system of control is likely to be the existence of pre-established and approved exposure limits and subsequent monitoring of exposures against these limits. The effectiveness of the monitoring procedures will depend on the quality and timeliness of management information. The systems operated by the bank should ensure that:

(a) the nature of the exposures arising from the business of the bank are properly identified by management and that appropriately determined limits have been set and approved for permitted exposures;

(b) appropriate procedures exist for monitoring the level of exposures which involve an appropriate degree of aggregation of the exposures, not only within, but across the different activities of the bank or group, in particular covering interest rate, exchange rate and credit exposure;

(c) exposures exceeding limits are identified and reported promptly through the appropriate reporting channels and action results.

39 There are no special considerations in relation to the controlling and recording of the bank auditors' work.

Accounting systems

40 The auditors should follow the guidance given in the Auditing Guideline 'Accounting systems' together with the guidance given in paragraphs 17 to 19 above.

Audit evidence

41 Paragraph 4 of 'The auditor's operational standard' states that "the auditor should obtain relevant and reliable audit evidence sufficient to enable him to draw reasonable conclusions therefrom". The auditors of a bank will need to ensure that they have gathered sufficient evidence to support their opinion on the financial statements.

42 The auditors' judgement of what is sufficient evidence to enable them to form their opinion on whether the financial statements give a true and fair view will be influenced amongst other things, by their knowledge of the bank's business, the environment in which it operates and the risk of misstatement.

43 The auditors of a bank should be aware of the value of evidence obtained from independent sources and of consistent evidence obtained from different sources both inside and outside the bank.

44 The level of substantive testing will be determined by reference to the auditors' judgement of the audit evidence required to enable them to express an opinion on the financial statements. This judgement will be based on the evaluation of the system of control, the results of the compliance tests and the assessment of materiality in the particular audit areas concerned. Examples of compliance and substantive tests specific to banks are given in Appendix 2.

Internal controls

45 The auditors' objective in examining the bank's system of internal controls is to assess whether they can rely on these controls in determining the audit work necessary to form their opinion on the bank's financial statements.

46 Paragraph 5 of 'The auditor's operational standard' states that "if the auditor wishes to place reliance on any internal controls, he should ascertain and evaluate those controls and perform compliance tests on their operation".

47 The requirements of the Banking Act 1987 and the Bank of England should result in a strong system of internal control and auditors should be able to place considerable reliance on such internal controls. They should closely follow the Auditing Guideline 'Internal controls', in conjunction with the guidance given in paragraphs 20 to 27.

48 Attention is drawn to the sections in the Auditing Guideline 'Internal controls' on 'Management responsibility' and 'Limitations on the effectiveness of internal controls'. In particular, it should be noted that no system, however elaborate, can offer a guarantee against fraudulent collusion.

Reliance on internal auditors

49 Internal audit has a dual function in an internal control system:

(a) as one of the controls within the system;

(b) as a control operating to check whether the other controls are in place and effective.

50 The extent to which the auditors will be able to take account of the work of the internal auditors will depend upon their assessment of the effectiveness of both these functions of internal audit. In making this assessment the auditors should have regard to the matters set out in the Auditing Guideline 'Reliance on internal audit'.

51 The nature of a bank's business and the particular opportunities that exist in a bank for fraud and misappropriation through collusion, mean that an important part of the auditors' work will be to assess the scope and quality of the work of the internal auditors and the action taken by management as a result of their reports, where reliance is intended to be placed on this work in determining the nature and level of their audit tests. The auditors should consider participating with the internal auditors in parts of their work such as branch visits, so as to see their work at first hand.

Review of financial statements

52 Paragraph 6 of the Auditing Standard 'The auditor's operational standard' states that: "The auditor should carry out such a review of the financial statements as is sufficient in conjunction with the conclusion drawn from the other audit evidence obtained, to give him a reasonable basis for his opinion on the financial statements."

53 When reviewing the financial statements of a bank, the auditors should pay close attention to transactions shortly before and after the year end. Such a review should include:

(a) large deposits or loan repayments received shortly before the year end which are repaid or re-advanced shortly afterwards. This will require a good deal of judgement to identify any window-dressing transactions;

(b) transfers between the trading security and investment security portfolios which take advantage of different valuation policies;

(c) the reclassification of hedging and trading transaction/positions to take advantage of different timing of profit and loss recognition;

(d) the reclassification of assets within liquidity profiles or under balance sheet headings.

54 The auditors should consider whether the accounts comply with all relevant statutory requirements, and whether the accounting policies adopted are such as will enable them to express an unqualified opinion on the financial statements.

55 SSAP 2 requires the disclosure of accounting policies. There are important areas of bank accounting, which the auditors should consider carefully for each bank audit engagement, where either: (i) different accounting policies are adopted by other banks; or (ii) the accounting treatment of a transaction is highly judgemental. The appropriate treatment is likely to be dependent upon the nature of the item, however, any treatment adopted should be in accordance with the fundamental accounting concepts set out in SSAP 2. A number of these areas are discussed in (a)-(g) below:

(a) provisions for bad and doubtful debts
— provisions for bad and doubtful debts are determined by management based on its assessment of their recoverability. Such determination should involve the consistent application of clearly established accounting policies and should be carried out on a prudent basis. Differing accounting treatments are used, for example, in respect of unpaid interest receivable and the timing of write-offs of bad debts against provisions;

(b) valuation of securities
— dated securities held as long-term assets (perhaps until maturity) are generally accounted for at cost plus or minus the amortisation of any discount or premium, or at cost less provision for permanent diminution. Dealing securities are usually valued individually, at the lower of cost and market value, or at market value. These alternative accounting treatments may lead to similar securities being given different values in financial statements depending on the purpose for which they were purchased and/or held;

(c) off-balance-sheet transactions
— the volume of transactions which fall to be treated by banks as off balance sheet has increased significantly in recent years. The off-balance-sheet business of banks can be divided into four main categories: (i) guarantees and contingents (further subdivided into direct credit substitutes, trading contingents and indemnities); (ii) commitments (revocable and irrevocable); (iii) interest rate and foreign exchange rate related transactions; and (iv) securitisation and sub-participations. The auditors should consider whether it is appropriate that such transactions remain off balance sheet, and consider the disclosure requirements which might be appropriate in respect of such transactions;

(d) treasury instruments
— in recent years there has been a variety of new instruments coming onto the market such as financial futures, interest rate and currency swaps, forward (or future) rate agreements and options. Banks undertake such transactions as principal to create a dealing position or for hedging purposes, or as intermediary or broker. It is generally accepted that the accounting treatment of such transactions should reflect their purpose. Where a trading transaction has been

undertaken, the instrument may be revalued or 'marked to market' and the resulting profit or loss taken to revenue immediately. If the instrument is used to match another transaction or to hedge an existing position then the accounting treatment adopted mirrors the accounting treatment of the matched transaction or hedged position. Criteria should be established by a bank to define when a match or hedge is undertaken and to ensure the appropriate accounting symmetry. This method of accounting gives rise to the need to establish at the time of the transaction the purpose for which an instrument is transacted and whether the bank's intentions in relation to that transaction may change over time;

(e) foreign exchange

— foreign currency transactions are usually of greater significance for banks than for the generality of companies. Profits and losses from foreign currency activities arise and are recognised as a result of:

(i) revaluation of spot positions;

(ii) revaluation of forward contracts or positions.

For foreign currency trading, profits and losses on uncompleted forward transactions are usually recognised in the accounts. In certain circumstances spot and forward contracts are matched and the profit or loss arising therefrom is transferred to the profit and loss account over the life of the related contracts. The results of foreign currency dealing activities can vary from bank to bank depending on the policy adopted for recognising matched contracts and the basis of revaluing forward contracts;

(f) fees and commissions

— banks account for such income either: (i) on a receipts basis; or (ii) be recognising immediately a portion of income which is intended to offset the initial costs of performing the transaction and crediting the remainder over the period of the related facility; or (iii) on some other accruals basis appropriate to the nature of the transaction;

(g) taxation

— there are also important areas of bank taxation which the auditors should consider carefully for each bank audit engagement. Whilst the profits of a bank are taxed in a manner broadly similar to the profits of any other trading company, a number of differences arise from the special nature of a banking trade and the transactions which a bank undertakes:

(i) such differences may arise from the application of tax principles to a bank trade, e.g. the taxation of the profits on disposal of 'banking investments' as part of trading income on a realisation basis and the inclusion of interest payable and receivable generally on an accruals basis. In addition, where a practice has not been agreed, judgement may need to be exercised as to whether certain transactions (e.g. foreign currency transactions, fees and transactions in treasury instruments) will be taxed on an accruals basis or whether a strict realisation basis may be required;

(ii) as a result of the nature of a banking trade certain distinctions such as that between capital and revenue may become blurred. Given the multi-currency nature of banking, the appropriate tax treatment of exchange gains and losses may be a significant factor which should be considered;

(iii) the geographical dispersal of many banks' operations also means that both UK and overseas taxation must be considered. Relationships between UK and overseas branches and subsidiaries should be reviewed in order to determine whether additional tax liabilities might arise through additional attribution of profits into particular territories including the UK.

Reporting under the Companies Act 1985

Reporting to members on the financial statements

56 The Bank of England has confirmed that it will take the initiative in reporting to the auditors any matter it believes to be of such importance that the auditors' knowledge of it could significantly affect the form of their report or the way in which they carry out their audit. In the absence of any notification, the auditors are therefore entitled to assume that the Bank of England has considered the need to take such an initiative and has concluded that it has no matters to report.

57 The auditors' report on the financial statements of banks incorporated under the Companies Act 1985 which do not take advantage of the permitted disclosure exemptions available under Paragraph 27 of Schedule 9 to that Act, is expressed in true and fair view terms. If the financial statements do not give a true and fair view, the auditors' report should be qualified in accordance with the Auditing Standard 'Qualifications in audit reports'.

58 Where a bank has taken advantage of the exemptions permitted by Schedule 9 of the Companies Act 1985, the auditors are not required to report whether in their opinion the financial statements of the bank give a true and fair view. As a result, the auditors should normally only report whether the financial statements are properly prepared in accordance with the Companies Act 1985. The following is an appropriate form of report:

AUDITORS' REPORT TO THE MEMBERS OF..

We have audited the financial statements on pages ... to ... in accordance with approved Auditing Standards.

In our opinion, the financial statements have been properly prepared in accordance with the provisions of the Companies Act 1985 applicable to banking companies.

Auditor

Date

59 If the auditors are unable to given an unqualified audit opinion on whether the financial statements have been properly prepared in accordance with the Companies Act 1985, they should state the reasons for their qualification. An example of an appropriate form of report may be:

AUDITORS REPORT TO THE MEMBERS OF..

We have audited the financial statements on pages ... to ... in accordance with approved Auditing Standards.

The information concerning ... has not been disclosed in accordance with ... of the Companies Act 1985.

Except for the omission of the disclosure referred to above, in our opinion, the financial statements have been properly prepared in accordance with the provisions of the Companies Act 1985 applicable to banking companies.

Auditors

Date

60 It should be noted that the Bank of England requires delivery of a bank's audited financial statements to it within six months of the end of the accounting reference period (Bank of England Policy Notice, BSD/1983/1).

Reporting to management

61 The Auditing Guideline 'Internal controls' stresses the importance of notifying management of any significant control weaknesses which the auditors have noted during the course of their work. The auditors should therefore report, as soon as possible, significant weaknesses in internal controls which come to their attention during the course of their audit to an appropriately senior level of management of the bank.

62 The usual means of communicating weaknesses will be the management letter and the auditors should follow the guidance laid down in the Auditing Guideline 'Reports to management'. A management letter is additional to, and is not a substitute for either the auditors' report under the Companies Act 1985 or the reporting accountants' reports under the Banking Act 1987.

Co-operation with reporting accountants

63 If the auditors are not also acting as reporting accountants, they should be prepared to co-operate with the reporting accountants and, after obtaining their client's permission to do so, make available such information as the reporting accountants may reasonably require in order to discharge their duties. The auditors should also carefully consider whether there are any particular matters relating to the audit which in their opinion should be drawn to the attention of the reporting accountants.

Discussions with the Bank of England after completion of the report under the Companies Act 1985

64 A trilateral discussion with the bank and the Bank of England will be held after the auditors have issued their report on the bank's statutory accounts. The trilateral discussion will cover:

(a) the audit, presentation and content of the bank's accounts;

(b) matters related by the Bank of England, or those which the bank or its auditors have drawn to its attention during the year, either at routine prudential meetings or at *ad hoc* meetings, including how such matters have been resolved to the satisfaction of the auditors or have been reflected or treated in the accounts; and

(c) matters brought to the Bank of England's attention in a written notice in accordance with Section 46 of the Banking Act 1987, or the bank's or its auditors' intention to give such written notice (see paragraph 65).

Reporting under the Banking Act 1987

Auditors' notices to the Bank of England

65 Auditors have a statutory duty to give written notice to the Bank of England in the following circumstances:

(a) If they decide to include in their report any qualifications as to a matter mentioned in Section 236 of the Companies Act 1985, or any statement about accounting records pursuant to Section 237 of that Act (Banking Act 1987, s. 46(2)(c)).

The decision to give written notice will only be taken after extensive discussions with management, and when a problem is either irremediable or when the circumstances indicate that the auditors intend to qualify.

(b) If they resign before the expiration of their term of office or intend not to seek reappointment (Banking Act 1987, s. 46(2)(a) and (b)). Similarly, a bank is required to notify the Bank of England if it proposes to terminate the appointment of its auditors or not to reappoint them (Banking Act 1987, s. 46(1)).

Reporting accountants' reports for the Bank of England

66 As stated in paragraph 5 the reporting accountants will be required to report to the directors of the bank or to the senior manager in the case of a branch, on the following matters, for onward transmission to the Bank of England:

(a) accounting and other records and internal control systems;

(b) Bank of England returns used for prudential purposes.

67 The reporting accountants may also need to report to the Bank of England either via the bank or, in exceptional circumstances, directly. Guidance on such reporting is given in paragraphs 171 to 191.

Accounting and other records and internal control systems

The requirements

68 The Banking Act 1987 explicitly places a requirement on banks to maintain accounting and other records, and internal control systems, "such as to enable the business of the institution to be prudently managed and the institution to comply with the duties imposed on it by or under this Act" (Banking Act 1987, Schedule 3, paragraph 4(7) and (8)).

69 It is the responsibility of a bank's directors and management to ensure that adequate records and systems are maintained and the responsibility of the Bank of England to judge whether a bank has maintained adequate records and systems as part of its overall judgement as to whether all the criteria for authorisation are being met.

70 As supervisor, the Bank of England is concerned with obtaining evidence to enable it to form a view as to whether the Banking Act's requirements on accounting and other records and internal control systems are met. It will do this *inter alia* by considering any evidence provided by the reporting accountants.

71 The Bank of England has interpreted the requirements of the Act in its Guidance Note 'Accounting and other Records and Internal Control Systems and the Reporting Accountants' Reports Thereon' (BSD/1987/2). Reporting accountants should be familiar with the contents of this Guidance Note.

72 The Bank of England will require banks to appoint reporting accountants to report to the directors of UK incorporated banks and to the senior manager of UK branches of overseas incorporated banks whether, in the reporting accountants' opinion, accounting and other records and internal control systems have been maintained by management throughout the period examined in accordance with the Bank of England's interpretation of the requirements of the Act. In forming their opinion, the reporting accountants should have regard *inter alia* to the nature and scale of the business of the bank.

73 It may be necessary for the reporting accountants to carry out a full review of the records and systems each year. The Bank of England will determine, in consultation with the bank and its reporting accountants, whether a rolling programme of examinations may be carried out over a number of years. In such cases, the Bank of England has said that, at a trilateral planning meeting each year, it will discuss and agree the areas on which the reporting accountants are to report and will then write to the bank requesting that the agreed work be done. The letter of instruction or letter of engagement should detail the agreed areas of work (see paragraphs 94 and 95).

74 It is expected that normally the auditors will be appointed as reporting accountants in making these reports. The reporting accountants should aim to combine audit work with work for Banking Act purposes, if at all feasible.

75 Work carried out by the reporting accountants to identify weaknesses in the record keeping system will overlap with, and influence the work carried out on, the systems of internal control and on information in the Bank of England returns used for prudential purposes (see paragraphs 137 to 161 below). If the reporting accountants are also the auditors, it may also influence the work carried out for the purposes of reporting under Sections 236 and 237 of the Companies Act 1985.

76 The Bank of England does not expect, however, that reporting accountants will be able to given an unqualified opinion on the records and systems in every bank, but that they may need to draw the Bank of England's attention in their report to a number of matters which have come to their attention in the course of their work. The circumstances which might give rise to such an opinion qualified by exceptions may include those detailed in paragraph 133 below.

77 An engagement to express an opinion on a bank's records and systems of control for Banking Act purposes differs in purpose and in scope from a study and evaluation of the records and systems made as part of an examination of financial statements in order to express an opinion on whether those statements give a true and fair view.

78 Given these differences, which are discussed in paragraphs 80 to 88 below, the reporting accountants are unlikely to be able to rely solely on work carried out for audit purposes and therefore they should adopt additional procedures as necessary.

The differences between a review of accounting records and internal control systems for audit and for Banking Act purposes

Accounting and other records

79 The Auditing Guideline 'Accounting systems' draws the attention of auditors of enterprises subject to legislation other than the Companies Act 1985 to the "need to consider their specific duties relating to accounting records".

80 When planning the work which they may need to undertake as a result of the reporting requirements, the reporting accountants will need to consider any timing factors, particularly as, if they are also acting as auditors, any qualifications made in their report on accounting and other records should be considered when making their report on the financial statements under the Companies Act 1985 (see also paragraph 18). However, it may be possible to give an unqualified opinion on the accounting records for Companies Act purposes, and a qualified opinion on the records for Banking Act purposes over the same period.

81 The Companies Act requirement is that records must exist, sufficient to disclose with reasonable accuracy, the financial position of a company at any one point in time. It is possible that a breakdown in the record keeping system may not always result in the expression of a qualified opinion on the financial statements by the auditors. In a Banking Act context, however, the Bank of England has provided guidance on the accounting and other records which banks should keep. Reporting accountants should therefore consider, in the light of that guidance, drawing the attention of the Bank of England to breakdowns in the maintenance of records by giving an opinion qualified by exceptions (see paragraphs 132 to 133).

82 As reporting accountants are required to report on the operation of accounting and other records throughout the period under review, their evaluation and detailed testing will be spread over this period (see paragraphs 89 to 98 below).

Internal control systems

83 The Auditing Guideline 'Internal controls' states that it is the responsibility of the directors and management of an organisation to establish and maintain the systems of internal control which they consider most appropriate in the particular circumstances of their organisation (see also paragraph 69).

84 In an evaluation of internal controls made as part of an audit, the auditors' conclusion is an intermediate step in forming an opinion on the financial statements as a whole. They may decide not to rely on internal control procedures either because: (a) the procedures are not satisfactory for their purpose; or (b) the audit effort required to permit reliance on the system would not be cost effective. Accordingly, the testing of controls in an audit will generally be more limited than that undertaken for a report for Bank of England purposes, where an opinion is expressed on those internal controls alone.

85 The scope of the study and evaluation of internal control systems in an engagement to express an opinion on the system of controls, or certain elements of that system as required by the Bank of England, generally differs from the scope of an internal controls review within an audit. For the report required by the Bank of England, the reporting accountants may be required to examine additional control areas and may be required to examine all control areas in more detail although the procedures employed may be similar in nature. For example, if the reporting accountants are also the auditors, the evaluation and testing of internal control systems carried out for Bank of England purposes may serve as a basis for reliance on such controls in determining the nature, timing and extent of audit testing. Similarly, if the reporting accountants are also the auditors, the work required of them may be an extension of the work undertaken for audit purposes. Furthermore, the auditors need not apply procedures in an audit which duplicate procedures that have been applied for the purpose of an expression of an opinion on the specified elements of a bank's system of internal control (e.g. those areas of internal control on which a report is commissioned by the Bank of England possibly as part of a rolling programme of work).

86 Where they are relevant to areas of the bank which fall within the scope of the report on accounting and other records and systems of internal control, the reporting accountants should normally consider both manual and programmed applications controls as well as the general controls over the computer environment. The applications controls typically to be considered would include those outlined in Appendix 3.

87 Where a rolling programme of work is commissioned and certain areas specified for report each year, the reporting accountants will need to consider how wide ranging their examination of the specified areas should be. Certain internal controls may affect a number of different areas and the reporting accountants should discuss the extent to which these should be included in the scope of their review, with the Bank of England at the planning meeting (see paragraph 91). Examples of internal controls which may affect a number of areas are given in Appendix 4.

88 As reporting accountants are required to report on the operation of internal controls throughout the period under review, their evaluation and detailed testing of the control system will be spread over this period (see paragraphs 89 to 98 below).

The reporting accountants' work

Study and evaluation

89 The reporting accountants should follow recognised procedures by:

(a) planning the scope of their work;

(b) reviewing and documenting the accounting and other records and systems in operation;

(c) testing compliance with the system; and
(d) evaluating the results of these tests.

Planning

90 The reporting accountants should follow the guidance laid down in the Auditing Guideline 'Planning, controlling and recording' when planning the scope of their work.

91 A trilateral planning meeting will be held between the Bank of England, the reporting accountants and the bank to define and agree the scope of the reporting accountants' examination of records and systems. Such meetings will provide an opportunity for:

(a) reporting accountants to obtain confirmation of the records and systems to be examined and to discuss any practical problems anticipated in carrying out their work, including those posed by any computer system in operation;
(b) reporting accountants to ask the Bank of England for clarification on any aspect of its Guidance Notes on records and systems, and on any other matter relevant to their examinations and to their reports;
(c) the Bank of England to inform the reporting accountants and the bank of matters which it considers relevant to the work to be carried out by the reporting accountants;
(d) the bank to inform its reporting accountants and the Bank of England of any matters relevant to the examinations and to the reports; and
(e) the bank, by virtue of its size and the complexity of its operations, to obtain the Bank of England's agreement to a rolling programme of examinations of records and systems spread over a number of years and to the scope of the examinations for the current year.

92 If the bank is listed by the Bank of England under Section 43 of the Financial Services Act 1986 (see paragraph 13), the Wholesale Markets Supervision Division of the Bank of England may require the reporting accountants to carry out additional work and the scope of any such work should be agreed beforehand. A separate meeting may be called for this purpose.

93 Under Section 83 of the Banking Act 1987 the Bank of England is empowered to disclose information as follows:

(a) for the purpose of enabling or assisting it to discharge its functions under the Act;
(b) to an auditor if it enables or assists the Bank of England to discharge its functions under the Act, or is otherwise in the interests of depositors;
(c) if seeking advice from a qualified person on any matter of law, accountancy, valuation or any other matter requiring the exercise of professional skill, to ensure that the person is properly informed with respect to the matters on which his advice is sought.

94 As noted in paragraph 91 above, the planning meeting provides an opportunity for the Bank of England to inform the reporting accountants of any matters of which it is aware which might affect the way in which the reporting accountants go about their work, or to which they should pay particular attention in their examination, or to confirm that it is not aware of any such matters. It will then issue a letter of instruction to the bank indicating any such matters.

95 The reporting accountants should then obtain a letter of instruction from the bank based on the results of the discussions at the planning meeting and on the letter of instruction which it has received from the Bank of England, or should issue a letter of engagement, and ensure that this is acknowledged in writing by their client.

96 The reporting accountants should obtain copies of the following documents when planning their work:

(a) if they are not also the auditors, the latest financial statements of the bank and the audit report on them, together with a copy of the latest management letter issued by the auditors. They should also seek their client's permission to discuss any matters relevant to their examination with the auditors (for co-operation between auditors and reporting accountants see paragraph 63);

(b) all correspondence and all minutes or notes of meetings that the bank has held with the Bank of England which are relevant to the reporting accountants' examination of the accounting and other records and internal control systems.

97 The reporting accountants should also enquire of their client whether any other reports have been commissioned from other specialists relating to the establishment and maintenance of accounting and other records and internal control systems during the period under examination. If any such reports exist they should request a copy.

98 Reporting accountants should also ensure that they are aware of any other relationships between their firm and the bank which could materially affect their work as reporting accountants (see paragraph 117).

Review

99 It will be necessary for the reporting accountants to familiarise themselves with the overall system of organisational and management control (i.e. how the bank satisfies itself that the internal controls are adequate and are maintained) and, in particular, to consider the accounting systems, including management information systems, in order to facilitate their evaluation of the controls in operation.

100 The Bank of England indicates in its Guidance Note that, subject to size considerations, a bank should maintain certain organisational, administrative and other records and controls, including a manual containing a full description of day to day operational procedures and controls, both computer-based and manual, and documentation on accounting and control systems, including a record of changes made to the systems and the date of and authority for their implementation. The reporting accountants should review any such documentation for accuracy and completeness in those areas on which they have been instructed to report.

101 The reporting accountants' review should include checking the documentation of the system, which management will have recorded by means of narrative notes, flowcharts, checklists or a combination of these methods. The reporting accountants will thereby obtain an understanding of:

(a) the flow of transactions through the accounting system;

(b) the specific control objectives that relate to points in the flow of transactions and handling of assets and liabilities where errors or irregularities could occur;

(c) the specific control procedures or techniques that the bank has established to achieve specific control objectives; and

(d) the overall system of organisational and management control.

102 The reporting accountants should review the accounting and order records to ensure that these are adequate to meet the requirements of the Bank of England Guidance Note. The scope and nature of the accounting and other records which are required for the business to be conducted in a prudent manner should be commensurate with a bank's needs and particular circumstances and should have regard to the manner in which the business is structured, organised and managed, to its size and to the nature, volume and complexity of its transactions and commitments.

103 While it is the responsibility of directors and management to decide what management information is required and who should receive it, the reporting accountants should also satisfy themselves that, having regard to the nature and scale of the business, the management information systems are adequate and, in particular, that they address all significant aspects of the business and provide senior management with regular information on the significant risks which the bank faces. In the case of larger more complex banks or in important potentially high risk areas, the reporting accountants may require to seek the assistance of experts in the relevant fields.

104 The accounting and other records should be located where they will best assist management to conduct the business of the bank in a prudent manner on a day-to-day basis. If the accounting and other records of a UK branch of an overseas incorporated bank are kept outside the United Kingdom, there should be arrangements which allow local management to have immediate access to them.

Testing

105 The reporting accountants should review the internal control systems with management to confirm that there is reason to suppose that, *prima facie*, the accounting system operates in the manner recorded.

106 Generally, audit tests can be classified as either substantive or compliance, based upon the auditors' objective in using the procedure. The objective of a substantive test is to gather evidence as to the completeness, accuracy and validity of the information contained in the financial statements. The objective of a compliance test is to gather evidence relating to the existence and effectiveness of specific internal controls. Therefore, a particular test may be either compliance or substantive, depending on what the auditors are attempting to determine.

107 The reporting accountants are not required to express an opinion on financial statements but to form an opinion on whether the bank's accounting and other records and internal control systems have been maintained throughout the period examined in accordance with the requirements of the Bank of England's Guidance Note BSD/ 1987/ 2. In that guidance note, the Bank of England emphasises that it is seeking information about significant or pervasive weaknesses. This is discussed in more detail in paragraphs 132 to 133.

108 The type of testing to be carried out will be compliance, as the objective is to test the effective functioning of internal controls and the maintenance of accounting and other records. Testing should, therefore, ordinarily include tests to determine whether the control procedure is being performed and tests of the correctness of the information subject to the internal control being tested. The tests may involve re-performance by the reporting accountants. For example, if the control being tested was the check on the arithmetical accuracy of an interest accrual or revaluation by an accounts clerk, the compliance test of control should include:

- examination of the accounts clerk's initial on the appropriate document, indicating by whom and when the document had been prepared;
- examination of a supervisor's initial, indicating by whom and when the check had been performed; and
- re-performance of the calculation of the accrual or revaluation to check its arithmetical accuracy.

Compliance tests include tests of detail (requiring inspection of documents) and tests using observation and enquiry techniques. The type of test selected will depend on the control identified and the objective of the test.

109 The accounting and other records and systems of internal control to be examined and reported on will be those in operation throughout the period under review and not those in existence at a specified date. Accordingly, the testing of records and controls will have to be spread over the period of the review, to provide adequate evidence to support the opinions given.

110 Management may change the form of accounting and other records and systems of internal control during the period under review. The extent to which the reporting accountants should consider superseded records and controls should be agreed with the Bank of England prior to the commencement of the examination and any agreed limitation in the scope of the work should be referred to in the letter of instruction or engagement (see paragraphs 94 and 95).

111 Most banks operate computer-based systems and the reporting accountants should have regard to the Auditing Guideline on 'Auditing in a computer environment' and in particular should consider using Computer Assisted Audit Techniques (see paragraph 29).

112 It is unlikely that detailed compliance testing will be required of all elements of a system of control. The reporting accountants should consider the use of observation and enquiry techniques in appropriate circumstances and the use of the work of internal auditors. They should also consider the impact of any rolling programme of examination determined by the Bank of England. A system of rotating emphasis on key areas and locations may be acceptable and practicable, particularly in larger banks.

Evaluation

113 In evaluating a system of internal control for the purpose of expressing an opinion, the reporting accountants should consider the results of their review of the design of the system and of their tests of compliance. For this purpose, they should identify weaknesses in the system and evaluate whether they are material to achievement of the control objectives set down by the Bank of England, either individually or in combination.

The role of internal audit

114 The Bank of England considers that internal audit should be an integral part of any internal control system established and maintained by management. The existence, scope and objectives of an internal audit department are, however, dependent upon the judgement of management as to its own needs and duties, the size and structure of the bank and the risks inherent in its business.

115 Although there is no statutory requirement that a bank must establish an internal audit department, this will be an effective way for management to ensure that the systems of internal control operate as prescribed. Where a bank is unable to set up such a function, whether for reasons of size, economy or otherwise, it may set up alternative arrangements perhaps involving the use of independent accountants or other external suitably qualified persons.

116 The nature and degree of technical skills required for a person to be 'competent' to carry out internal audit functions will depend on the nature of the business and the complexity of the systems on which he is required to report. For example, a person engaged by a bank to carry out an internal audit of the controls built into a bank's computer systems will require specialist knowledge of computer security and control. The reporting accountants will need to be satisfied that the bank overcomes any disadvantages inherent in the alternatives mentioned in paragraph 115 above.

117 The reporting accountants should consider the adequacy of the internal audit procedures on the basis set out in the paragraphs on internal audit in the Auditing Guideline 'Internal controls'. The reporting accountants must remember that they are required to report on whether or not the systems have been maintained in accordance with the Bank of England guidance. Key questions that they should consider regarding the systems of internal audit include:

(a) Is the system structured so that it can perform an independent appraisal function?
(b) Is the organisation and staffing adequate?
(c) Is the work adequately planned and controlled?
(d) Does the programme ensure comprehensive coverage of the whole system within an adequate period of time?
(e) Are the techniques used satisfactory?
(f) Are adequate procedures employed for reporting?
(g) Is there adequate follow-up of reports?

118 Particular consideration must be given to internal audit reporting procedures, especially where there is a senior official able to influence the operation of control overall or in particular parts of the bank's operations. In such a case, reporting should be direct to the board and not just to that official. There should be arrangements in place whereby the board can be satisfied that the systems of control, internal audit and report are regularly reviewed for adequacy and that internal audit reports are reviewed. The board may set up a committee with responsibilities, *inter alia*, for this area of its functions and for ensuring adequate follow-up of reports received. The reporting accountants should review these board procedures as part of their review of internal audit, in particular, taking into account the technical qualifications and experience available.

119 In forming their opinion on the adequacy of the systems, the reporting accountants must have regard to the need for evidence to support their conclusions, and the Auditing Guideline 'Audit evidence' should be followed. For example, evidence of the establishment of systems is much greater if the directors approve new procedures which materially affect the control systems, and if the directors minute any regular review of procedures. Evidence of the maintenance of internal audit systems should be provided by proper documentation of internal audit programmes, work carried out, conclusions reached and reports made.

120 Where the internal audit department is well established, the reporting accountants may seek to limit the extent of their detailed testing by relying on the work of internal auditors or by other direct assistance. In doing so they should consider the matters outlined in the Auditing Guideline 'Reliance on internal audit'.

Branches

121 If control systems and accounting records which exist over or at an overseas branch of a UK incorporated bank are to be included in their reports, the reporting accountants should ensure that this is defined in the scope of work agreed both with the Bank of England and with the bank.

122 The reporting accountants may need to place reliance on the internal audit function, as outlined in paragraphs 114 to 120. It may also be necessary for the reporting accountants to arrange for work to be carried out by local accountants. Any work undertaken by such accountants will be the ultimate responsibility of the primary reporting accountants who should ensure that procedures have been correctly carried out.

123 Reporting accountants will be appointed to report on UK branches of institutions incorporated overseas. Controls and records of such branches may well be operated and maintained overseas. If control of part of a bank's operations is exercised outside the United Kingdom, the scope of the reporting accountants' work will probably be restricted to considering the adequacy of the information reported to the overseas entity and compliance with delegated authority. This restriction of scope should be agreed with the Bank of England and the bank at the time of the trilateral planning meeting and incorporated in the letter of instruction or engagement (see paragraphs 94 and 95).

124 In the case of UK branches of institutions incorporated overseas, reporting accountants should consider the internal audit arrangements established locally or at head office (insofar as they cover the activities of the branch). In such circumstances reporting accountants will have to consider the extent to which they can rely on the work of the internal audit function having regard to the independence of such a function (particularly where established locally) and the difficulties in evaluating fully an internal audit department based at the head office. Similar considerations may apply to banks which are subsidiaries of overseas institutions and to situations where a home country supervisory authority itself carries out an examination.

Representations by management

125 The reporting accountants should follow the guidance given in the Auditing Guideline "Representations by management" and may wish to obtain a letter of representation from management covering, *inter alia*, the following areas:

(a) acknowledging management's responsibility for establishing and maintaining accounting and other records and the system of internal control;

(b) stating that management has disclosed to the reporting accountants all material weaknesses in the records and systems of which it is aware and also those areas for which management believes the cost of corrective action may exceed the benefits;

(c) describing any irregularities involving management or employees who have significant roles in the system of internal control;

(d) stating whether there were any changes made subsequent to the reporting date which would significantly affect the systems of internal control, including any corrective action taken by management with regard to material weaknesses; and

(e) confirming that management has made available to the reporting accountants all correspondence and all minutes or notes of meetings that the bank has held with the Bank of England which are relevant to the reporting accountants' examination of the accounting and other records and internal control systems.

Confirmation from the Bank of England

126 The Bank of England has confirmed that it will take the initiative in reporting to the reporting accountants any matter it believes to be of such importance that the reporting accountants' knowledge of it could significantly affect the form of their report or the way in which they carry out their work. In the absence of any notification, the reporting accountants are therefore entitled to assume that the Bank of England has considered the need to take such an initiative and has concluded that it has no matters to report. In the case of a UK branch of a bank incorporated overseas, reporting accountants are also entitled to assume that the Bank of England would be aware of, and would inform them of, any material concerns of the home country supervisor.

The report

127 The report will be used by the Bank of England to assist it in making a judgement as to whether the overall criteria for authorisation have been met and in particular, whether the criteria for maintaining adequate records and systems have been met. The report should therefore be prepared with the Bank of England's responsibility in mind.

128 The reporting accountants should ensure that their report includes:

(a) a description of the scope of the engagement or reference to an accompanying letter of instruction or engagement;

(b) the date on which the report was signed and the period to which the opinion relates;

(c) a statement that the establishment and maintenance of the accounting and other records and the systems of internal control are the responsibility of management;

(d) a brief explanation of the broad objectives and inherent limitations of the system of internal control;

(e) their opinion on whether, having regard to the nature and scale of the bank's business, the records and systems examined by them were established and were maintained during the period examined, in accordance with the Bank of England's Guidance Note;

(f) any other matters or explanations relevant to their opinion.

129 Further to paragraph 128(d) above, there are inherent limitations that should be recognised in considering the potential effectiveness of any system of internal control. Particularly significant for the purpose of reports on internal control is that any projection of a current evaluation of an internal control system to future periods is subject to the risks that the procedures may become inadequate because of changes in conditions and that the degree of compliance with prescribed procedures may deteriorate. The reporting accountants would normally refer to such matters in their reports.

130 An example of the form of report required by the Bank of England is as follows:

THE DIRECTORS, XYZ BANK LIMITED THE SENIOR MANAGER, ABC BRANCH

Dear Sir(s)

In accordance with your letter of instruction dated [ ], a copy of which is attached, we have examined the accounting and other records and internal control systems of XYZ Bank Limited (ABC Branch) which were in existence during the year ended [ ].

Our examination has been carried out having regard to the Bank of England's Guidance Note BSD/1987/2 dated September 1987 and in accordance with the Auditing Guideline 'Banks in the United Kingdom'.

As directors (senior manager) of XYZ Bank Limited (ABC Branch) you are responsible for establishing and maintaining adequate accounting and other records and internal control systems. In fulfilling that responsibility you must assess the expected benefits and related costs of management information and of control procedures. The objective is to provide reasonable, but not absolute, assurance that assets are safeguarded against loss from unauthorised use or disposition, that banking risks are properly monitored and evaluated, that transactions are executed in accordance with established procedures and are recorded properly, and to enable you therefore to conduct the business in a prudent manner.

Because of inherent limitations in any accounting and internal control system, errors or irregularities may nevertheless occur and not be detected. Also, projection of any evaluation of the systems to future periods is subject to the risk that management information and control procedures may become inadequate because of changes in conditions or that the degree of compliance with those procedures may deteriorate.

In our opinion, having regard to the nature and scale of its business, during the year ended [ ],

either the accounting and other records and internal control systems examined by us were established and maintained in accordance with the requirements of the Guidance Note (with the exception of the matters set out in the appendix attached to this report),

or the accounting and other records and internal control systems examined by us were not established and maintained in accordance with the requirements of the Guidance Note for the reasons set out in the appendix attached to this report.

Yours faithfully

A Reporting Accountant

131 The above examples includes three alternative forms of specimen wording which cater for the following situations:

(a) The exceptional situation, where the reporting accountants have no reservations about the bank's accounting and other records and/or systems of internal control; in this situation, the penultimate paragraph of the report should be inserted without the words in parenthesis (an unqualified opinion).

(b) The typical situation, where the reporting accountants have some reservation(s) about the bank's accounting and other records and/or systems of internal control but have formed the view, on the basis of the evidence which they have seen, that the weakness is not pervasive; in this situation, the penultimate paragraph of the report should be inserted in its entirety (an opinion qualified by exceptions).

(c) The situation where the reporting accountants have severe reservations about the bank's accounting and other records and/or systems of internal control, and have formed the view, on the basis of the evidence which they have seen that the weakness is pervasive; in this situation, the final paragraph of the report should be inserted (an adverse opinion).

132 As noted in paragraphs 76 and 81, the reporting accountants may have to draw attention in their report to a number of matters which have come to their notice during the course of their work. Although it will not be unusual for a report to draw attention to a number of matters, reporting accountants are not required to report all omissions, weaknesses and failures in the existence, nature, scope and effectiveness of records and systems, however minor. They are, however, required to report those which individually or collectively are, in their opinion, significant and result in there not being reasonable assurance that the requirements set out in the Bank of England's Guidance Note have been met. Reportable matters should include all significant weaknesses which the reporting accountants have noted during the course of their work and which they have reported or intend to report to management.

133 The Bank of England has indicated that the circumstances giving rise to an opinion qualified by exceptions would include those where:

(a) certain records and systems do not exist and the reporting accountants consider that they should exist in order to assist management to conduct the business of the bank in a prudent manner on a day-to-day basis;

(b) there is, or has been, a significant weakness in, or failure of, significant systems during the period examined; or

(c) the reporting accountants are unable to form an opinion on a particular aspect of the records and systems and therefore wish to bring details of the matter to the attention of the Bank of England to place it in a better position to judge whether the criteria for authorisation are satisfied.

134 The Bank of England does not expect reporting accountants to examine, assess or report on management's banking judgements and decisions. The assessment of the quality of management and of its banking decisions is a supervisory judgement for the Bank of England to make.

135 If, after discussing the matter with their client, the reporting accountants conclude that they will give an adverse opinion (as set out in paragraph 131 (c)), or that the issue of a report will be delayed, they must immediately inform the Bank of England in writing giving their reasons. They should also send the bank a copy of their letter.
The decision to give written notice will only be taken after extensive discussions with management and when a problem is either irremediable or when the circumstances indicate that the reporting accountants intend to give an adverse opinion.

136 The report must be completed, dated and submitted to the directors of a UK incorporated bank, or the managers of a UK branch of an overseas incorporated bank within three months of the end of the period examined. The bank must then pass the report, together with any comments management sees fit to make, to the Bank of England within one month of the date of the report.

Bank of England returns used for prudential purposes
The requirements

137 The management of banks are required by the Bank of England to submit to it a number and variety of returns, mainly on a quarterly basis within the integrated banking statistics system.

138 Preparation and submission of the returns is the responsibility of the bank's management who should be aware of Section 94 of the Banking Act relating to the knowing or reckless provision of false or misleading information. In particular, Section 94(3) states that:

> "An authorised institution or former authorised institution shall be guilty of an offence if it fails to provide the Bank with any information in its possession knowing or having reasonable cause to believe —
>
> (a) that the information is relevant to the exercise by the Bank of its functions under this Act in relation to the institution; and
>
> (b) that the withholding of the information is likely to result in the Bank being misled as to any matter which is relevant to and of material significance for the exercise of those functions in relation to the institution."

139 The Bank of England has emphasised the importance which it attaches to the returns submitted by banks and intends to exercise the powers derived from Section 39(1) of the Banking Act to require institutions to appoint reporting accountants to examine and report upon the returns submitted to the Bank of England and any other returns which are used for prudential purposes to enable or assist the Bank of England to exercise its duties and functions under the Act. On occasion, the Bank of England may agree with a particular bank, that it will accept prudential information in addition to, or instead of, the information contained in standard returns. Such information could also fall to be reported upon by reporting accountants.

140 These proposed new reporting arrangements are intended to reassure the Bank of England about the reliability of the information it receives from a bank. The Bank of England will review the returns and any reports obtained thereon to assess whether the interests of depositors are not at risk because of adverse changes in the bank's financial position or in its management resources. It will be for the Bank of England to judge, in the light of all the information available to it, whether the requirements of the Act are satisfied.

141 The Bank of England has said that after consultation with each institution and after submission of the relevant returns, it will select the particular return or range of returns which it wishes to have examined and reported on from those submitted by the bank's management, and will inform the bank in writing of its decision. It intends to ensure that all relevant returns are examined over a period of time judged appropriate for each institution.

142 The information provided on returns is based upon information drawn from accounting and other records presented in an alternative format. The reporting accountants are required to form an opinion and report upon whether in their opinion the information contained in the returns examined is, in all material respects:

(a) complete in so far as all the relevant information contained in the accounting and other records at the reporting date has been extracted therefrom and recorded in the returns;

(b) accurate in so far as it reflects correctly information contained in, and extracted from, the accounting and other records at the reporting date;

(c) prepared in accordance with the Bank of England's current reporting instructions (including notes and definitions) and any further written rulings that apply specifically to the particular bank; and

(d) prepared, in the case of a UK incorporated bank, using the same accounting policies as those applied in its most recent statutory accounts.

The reporting accountants' work

Reporting instructions and other documentation from the Bank of England

143 The Bank of England has issued a Guidance Note on 'Reporting Accountants' Reports on Bank of England Returns used for Prudential Purposes' (BSD/1987/3) which gives guidance on the scope of the reporting accountants' examinations of returns and specifies the form of their report.

144 The Bank of England's Guidance Note states that reporting accountants are expected to have a proper understanding and working knowledge of:

(a) the returns submitted by a bank as well as the Bank of England's current reporting instructions (including notes and definitions) and any further rulings that have been agreed in writing between the Bank of England and an individual bank to reflect its particular circumstances;

(b) the policy notices published by the Bank of England which relate to the returns; for example, those on subordinated loan capital, and on the measurement of capital;

(c) the Bank of England's Guidance Note on 'Accounting and other Records and Internal Control Systems and The Reporting Accountants' Reports Thereon' (BSD/1987/2) issued in September 1987; and

(d) the Bank of England's Guidance Note on 'The Bank of England's Relationship with Auditors and Reporting Accountants' (BSD/1987/4) issued in December 1987.

145 In pursuance of this, the Bank of England will make available copies of the documents referred to in paragraph 144, to reporting accountants on their appointment and will ensure that reporting accountants are informed of any alterations to the documents and recent replacements or superseding documentation as and when they are issued. Before commencing an assignment, reporting accountants should request from the Bank of England a list of all the current documentation available which they need to undertake their work.

146 The reporting accountants should obtain from the bank copies of all correspondence, minutes or notes of meetings held between the bank and the Bank of England relevant to the reporting accountants' examination of the Bank of England returns used for prudential purposes.

147 The Bank of England has emphasised that if reporting accountants feel that its reporting instructions do not fully and unambiguously cater for the circumstances and nature of a particular material transaction or series of transactions, they should ask the bank to seek clarification of these matters from the Bank of England and include details of the treatment of this transaction or transactions in their report, or in an appendix thereto. This information should be given regardless of the nature of the opinion expressed in the report.

Relationship with reports on accounting and other records and internal control systems

148 The accounting and other records and internal controls systems of a bank are subject to separate reporting requirements as outlined in paragraphs 68 to 78. In making their report on the returns used for prudential purposes, the reporting accountants are thus not expected to form an opinion on the accuracy of the information contained in the accounting and other records *per se*, but simply to report on the extraction of information from those records for inclusion on the returns, taking account of any journal or other adjustments. They are also not required to report on the effectiveness of the systems of control which a bank has set up, firstly to provide and ensure the quality of the information in the records and secondly to ensure the correct transfer of information from records to returns.

149 Accountants reporting on prudential returns should, however, be aware of the requirement for institutions to maintain adequate accounting and other records and internal control systems, and, if they are not acting as reporting accounts for the report on records and systems, should obtain a copy of the most recent report from the bank. They should consider whether it is necessary to mention a qualification in the report on records and systems in their report on a return, although such a reference need not constitute a qualified opinion on the information contained in that return.

150 The reporting accountants should also enquire of their client whether any other reports have been commissioned from other specialists relating to the establishment and maintenance of accounting and other records, internal control systems or prudential returns, during the period under examination. If any such reports exist they should request a copy.

Materiality

151 When specifying to the bank the particular return or range of returns which it wishes to have examined (see paragraph 141 above), the Bank of England will also specify the level of materiality which the reporting accountants should take into account in reporting.

This level will vary from bank to bank and from one return to another but the level will be set to ensure that the Bank of England will be informed of all matters which are likely to affect its supervisory judgement. The returns specified and the materiality level required should then be notified to the reporting accountants by way of a letter of instruction from the bank. Alternatively, the reporting accountants should send a letter of engagement to the bank and ensure that this is acknowledged in writing by their clients.

Testing

152 The extent of testing required will vary from bank to bank as this will be dependent on the underlying accounting and other records.

153 In testing for completeness and accuracy, reporting accountants should trace on a sample basis the extraction of information contained in the accounting and other records to the relevant returns and vice versa. Any material adjustments made to the accounting and other records in compiling the returns should be reviewed for reasonableness. Reporting accountants should also review the information being submitted in the returns to ensure that it is consistent in all material aspects with the Bank of England's current reporting instructions (including notes and definitions) and any further written rulings that apply specifically to the particular bank. Reporting accountants should confirm with the management of a UK incorporated bank that the returns have been prepared using the same accounting policies as those applied in its most recent statutory accounts and should test the application of these policies.

Groups

154 Certain returns may contain information prepared on a consolidated basis and reporting accountants should discuss with the Bank of England the extent to which they should extend their examination to the records of any group company from which information has been extracted for consolidation in the return. In the case of group companies which are also banks and, therefore, subject to examination of their records and internal control systems by a reporting accountant, the guidance given in this guideline should be followed. If however, a group company is not a bank, its records and internal control systems will not have been examined by reporting accountants unless the Bank of England has used the provisions of Section 39 of the Banking Act 1987 to require the group company to provide information and to commission reporting accountants. To the extent that information in a return has been extracted from accounting and other records and subject to internal control systems which have not been subject to review, the reporting accountants may consider it appropriate to refer to this in their report on the return.

155 Where a group includes overseas subsidiaries, difficulties may be experienced in forming an opinion on the matters laid down in paragraph 143. In these circumstances, the reporting accountants should ensure that the precise scope of their engagement is set out in the letter of instruction received from or letter of engagement issued to the bank. If subsidiaries are not to be included in the engagement, that fact should be clearly stated.

Branches

156 Where information contained in the accounting and other records of an overseas branch of a UK incorporated bank is required for the completion of a return, either the reporting instructions for that particular return will make this clear or the Bank of England will issue a further ruling, specific to the bank. Reporting accountants should satisfy themselves that the requirements of paragraph 142 above have been met in respect of the information extracted from the accounting and other records of the overseas branch.

Ad hoc reports

157 In the course of their work examining a return, the reporting accountants may discover that it contains material errors or omissions which have not been reported to the Bank of England. In such circumstances, they should follow the guidance laid down in paragraphs 181 to 191 as regards the procedures to be followed when making an *ad hoc* report under Section 47 of the Banking Act 1987.

The report

158 Paragraph 142 above gives details of the opinion required of reporting accountants. An example of the report required by the Bank of England is as follows:

THE DIRECTORS, XYZ BANK LIMITED

THE SENIOR MANAGER, ABC BRANCH

Dear Sir(s)

In accordance with your letter of instruction dated [ ], a copy of which is attached, we have examined those returns referred to which you have submitted to the Bank of England. We attach a copy of the returns which we have initialled for the purpose of identification. Our examination has been carried out having regard to the Bank of England's Guidance Note BSD/1987/3 dated October 1987 and in accordance with the Auditing Guideline 'Banks in the United Kingdom'.

In our opinion, in all material respects, the information contained in the returns examined by us:

either has been completely and accurately extracted from the accounting and other records and has been prepared and presented in accordance with the current reporting instructions (and specific written rulings) issued by the Bank of England [and using the same accounting policies as those applied in the most recent statutory accounts] (with the exception of the matters set out in the appendix attached to this report),

or has not been completely and accurately extracted from the accounting and other records and has not been prepared and presented in accordance with the current reporting instructions (and specific written rulings) issued by the Bank of England [and has not used the same accounting policies as those applied in the most recent statutory accounts] for the reasons set out in the appendix attached to this report.

Yours faithfully

A Reporting Accountant

This report may require adaptation to meet the individual circumstances of each bank.

159 In the case of the requirement contained in paragraph 142(d), reporting accountants are required to report to the Bank of England that the accounting policies used are the same as those applied in a UK bank's most recent statutory accounts. Where this is not so, the reporting accountants should report the circumstances and provide a quantification of the effect of the different policies, if practicable. The Bank of England has said that it will not consider a report to be 'qualified' merely because it contains a statement of the application of different accounting policies.

160 If, after discussing the matter with their client, the reporting accountants conclude that they will give an adverse opinion on a particular return, they should inform the Bank of England in writing without delay. Guidance on when the decision to give written notice is taken is given in paragraph 135. The letter should contain their reasons for the adverse opinion and a copy should be sent to their client.

161 The reporting accountants' report should be addressed to the directors in the case of a UK incorporated bank, and to their senior manager in the case of a UK branch of an overseas institution. The report should be completed, dated and submitted to the institution not more than three months after the date of the Bank of England's letter of instruction to the bank. The bank must then submit the report to the Bank of England, together with such comments as management sees fit to make, not more than one month after the date of the report.

Trilateral meetings with reporting accountants

Introduction

162 The Bank of England's system of supervision has always been based on regular meetings with banks at which the discussions have focused on returns used for prudential purposes and other financial information.

163 Meetings between the Bank of England and a bank's auditors to discuss a bank's affairs have hitherto been exceptional. However, with the introduction of a system of regular reporting on accounting and other records, and internal control systems and on returns used for prudential purposes, the Bank of England believes it should have the opportunity to meet the reporting accountants preparing these reports annually and, when necessary, on other occasions ('*ad hoc* meetings' with reporting accountants). Similarly, the Bank of England believes that it should have the opportunity to meet a bank's auditors each year and, when necessary, on other occasions ('*ad hoc* meetings' with auditors). These meetings will usually be conducted on a trilateral basis, involving the Bank of England, the bank and the auditors or reporting accountants.

The role of auditors and reporting accountants in the supervisory process

164 In the first year of appointment an initial planning meeting involving the bank, the Bank of England and the reporting accountants will be held to discuss and agree the scope of their work (see paragraphs 91 to 94). This initial meeting may be particularly helpful if, for example, the bank or its reporting accountants need to raise important questions about the Bank of England's Guidance Notes, or where, by virtue of its size and the complexity of its operations, the bank wishes to obtain the Bank of England's agreement to a rolling programme of examinations spread over a number of years. A later meeting will be held after the reports have been submitted which will provide an opportunity to discuss the work carried out, the reports on accounting and other records and internal control systems and the reports on returns made to the Bank of England for prudential purposes. In future years, it is expected that planning and review matters will be dealt with at the same meeting. At that meeting, if the auditors are also the reporting accountants, it is also expected that the Bank of England will wish to discuss the statutory accounts and the auditors' report (see paragraph 64).

165 The Bank of England will only need to hold separate meetings with auditors and with reporting accountants when:

(a) the timing of receipt of both the auditors' report and of the reporting accountants' reports differs; and

(b) different firms are appointed as auditors and as reporting accountants.

166 The agenda for a trilateral meeting will be prepared by the Bank of England and circulated in advance. Auditors and reporting accountants are expected to participate fully in trilateral meetings. Accordingly, they will be expected to contribute to the discussion of matters arising from the statutory audit and from their work under the Banking Act 1987. Thus, they will be expected to discuss with the Bank the affairs of the bank including, if necessary, information obtained about its customers obtained in the course of that work. However, the Bank recognises that it would not be appropriate for auditors or reporting accountants to report to the Bank information about the bank or its customers which they have obtained through their professional relationship with another client which is not the bank's associated body as defined in Section 47(4) of the Banking Act 1987. Normally it is expected that they will discuss with their client any report or matter which they wish to raise at a meeting with the Bank of England before the report is issued or the meeting held.

167 As stated in paragraph 164 above, trilateral discussions between the Bank of England, a bank and its reporting accountants will be held after the reports on records and systems and on returns used for prudential purposes have been forwarded to the Bank of England by the bank's management.

168 These discussions will assist the Bank of England in forming its judgement about whether the criteria for authorisation relating to records and systems are met. In particular they will cover:

(a) matters which arise from the reporting accountants' examinations and those to which their reports refer;
(b) management's comments on the reports;
(c) reporting accountants' explanations of a change in a previously reported intention to qualify a report or for the reason for and nature of a qualified report;
(d) any other matter which the Bank of England considers relevant to its judgement;
(e) any step or course of action which may be necessary in the light of the reports; for example, the commissioning of a more detailed report on a particular aspect of the bank's records and systems; and
(f) an agreement as to the scope, or a change to the previously agreed scope, of the next period's examination of records and systems thereby avoiding the need for a separate planning meeting (see paragraphs 91 and 94).

169 Any party may seek to call a trilateral meeting at any other time if important matters affecting the bank come to their attention. Normally, auditors or reporting accountants should raise their concerns with the bank first and if the problem cannot be resolved to their satisfaction, suggest that the bank asks the Bank of England to convene the meeting. However, if the bank refuses to do so or fails to do so within a period of time specified by the auditors or reporting accountants, the auditors or reporting accountants should contact the Bank of England direct and request that a meeting is held.

170 In exceptional circumstances, for example, those outlined in paragraphs 184 and 185, the auditors or reporting accountants may consider it necessary to draw the attention of the Bank of England to information about the bank without its knowledge. Before doing so, however, they should consider whether a representative of the bank at appropriate senior level should be informed and invited to attend the meeting with the Bank of England (see also paragraph 187(c)).

Ad hoc reports

Statutory provisions

171 The following paragraphs of this guideline have been prepared to assist auditors and reporting accountants in understanding the circumstances in which they should take the initiative in bringing important matters to the attention of the Bank of England.

Auditors and reporting accountants

172 Section 47 of the Act provides that no duty to which an auditor of an authorised institution, or a person appointed under Sections 8(5) or 39(1)(b) of the Act (the reporting accountant), shall be subject will be contravened "by reason of his communicating in good faith to the Bank, whether or not in response to a request made by it, any information or opinion on a matter to which this section applies and which is relevant to any function of the Bank under the Act". It is this section which makes it clear that auditors and reporting accountants are able to communicate with the Bank of England by way of a formal report, at a meeting or by any other means on any matters relating to the bank's affairs arising out of their appointment and which are relevant to any function of the Bank of England under the Act. These matters include those which are relevant to the reports made by reporting accountants, to the regular discussions with the Bank of England and to those exceptional circumstances which are referred to in paragraphs 184 and 185. The Bank believes that auditors or reporting accountants may communicate a matter to the Bank with the protection of Section 47 regardless of the source of that information, provided they become aware of the matter in their capacity as auditors or reporting accountants of that client bank.

173 Confidentiality is an implied term of auditors' and reporting accountants' contracts with their clients, but in Section 47 circumstances it does not prevail since they are entitled to communicate information or opinions relating to the business or affairs of the bank or any associated body of the bank without contravening the duty of confidence owed to the bank and its associated bodies. The Bank recognises that it would not be appropriate for auditors or reporting accountants to report to the Bank information obtained through their professional relationship with another client which is not the bank's associated body.

174 References in the following paragraphs of the guideline to 'reporting under Section 47' refer to reporting with the protection of Section 47 of the Banking Act 1987.

175 It is important to stress that the Bank of England expects that the management of the bank will continue to be its primary source of information and that the normal reporting procedures, including the reports on records, systems and returns, the prudential meetings and annual trilateral meetings will normally provide it with all the information it needs to carry out its responsibilities under the Act.

176 Auditors and reporting accountants cannot, however, be expected to be aware of all circumstances which, had they known of them, would have led them to exercise their right to report under Section 47. That section does not require auditors to change the scope of their audit work, nor the frequency or timing of their audit visits, nor does it require the reporting accountants to vary the scope and timing of their examination.
Neither auditors nor reporting accountants have an obligation to seek out grounds for making a report under Section 47; the section does not place an obligation on auditors or reporting accountants to conduct their work in such a way that there is reasonable certainty that they will discover an occurrence of the kind described in paragraph 181. It is only when auditors become aware in the ordinary course of their audit work, or reporting accountants become aware during their examination, of such an occurrence that they should make detailed enquiries with Section 47 specifically in mind.

177 Auditors and reporting accountants should, however, ensure that they are made aware of any other relationships which exist between any department of their firm and the client bank which could affect their work. As noted in paragraph 178, the Banking Act 1987 does not give protection to auditors and reporting accountants if a matter is not reported to the Bank of England. The Bank of England expects that auditors and reporting accountants will ensure that they are informed of all potentially 'reportable' matters by all the other departments within their firm which have a relationship with their client bank.

It would, therefore, be prudent for such firms to establish adequate systems of interdepartmental communication to ensure any maters which may give rise to a report under Section 47 are brought to the attention of the appropriate auditors or reporting accountants. However, the Bank of England expects banks to advise their auditors or reporting accountants when they appoint a third party (including another department of the same firm) to review, investigate or report on any aspect of their records and systems and to provide them with copies or reports by such a third party promptly after their receipt.

178 Auditors and reporting accountants should realise that there are circumstances in which Section 47 will not provide protection, for example, where they could be held to have acted maliciously or in bad faith. The Act does not, therefore, provide complete immunity from all types of legal action by all parties affected, or subsequently affected, by the auditors' action in reporting to the Bank. Auditors and reporting accountants may, therefore, wish to consider taking legal or other professional advice before making the decision whether or in what manner to report and in order, for example, to ensure that the form and content of their report are such as to secure the protection of Section 47 and that it only includes relevant material. However, auditors should recognise that speed of reporting may well be important in order to protect the interests of depositors. There is no protection given by the Act if the auditors or reporting accountants fail to report to the Bank of England.

The Bank of England

179 Information which is confidential and has been obtained by the Bank of England under, or for the purposes of, the Act can only be disclosed in given circumstances. However, under Section 83(2) of the Act, the Bank of England is not precluded from disclosing information "to the auditor of an authorised institution or former authorised institution if it appears to the Bank that disclosing the information would enable or assist the Bank [to discharge its functions under the Act] ... or would otherwise be in the interests of depositors". Similarly Section 83(1) allows the Bank of England to disclose information to reporting accountants. It should be noted that disclosure by the Bank of England of confidential information to auditors or to reporting accountants is to them only; they are not generally free to pass that information to others, such as their client bank.

180 The Bank of England has confirmed that it will take the initiative in bringing a matter to the attention of a bank and its auditors or reporting accountants:

(a) when it believes that it is of such importance that the auditors' or reporting accountants' knowledge of it could significantly affect the form of their audit or other report or the way in which they carry out their reporting responsibilities (see also paragraphs 56 and 126); and

(b) when the disclosure is for the purpose of enabling or assisting the Bank of England to discharge its functions under the Act or will otherwise be in the interests of depositors.

The Bank of England will indicate whether management of the bank have been informed of the matter and if so, who has been advised.

Taking the initiative

181 The profession has developed a criterion for use by auditors or reporting accountants in deciding whether to take the initiative in making an *ad hoc* report in addition to their regular reporting responsibilities. The criterion is that the auditors or reporting accountants should take the initiative when they consider it expedient to do so in order to protect the interests of depositors because there has been a material loss or there exists a significant risk of material loss. This criterion can be more fully explained as follows:

(a) there must be an adverse occurrence, or a change in the auditors' or the reporting accountants' perception of an existing situation, which may include an adverse change in the circumstances of the bank; and

(b) the position described in (a) above has given rise to a material loss or indicates that a reasonable probability exists that a material loss may arise; and

(c) the position is such that the interests of depositors might be better safeguarded if the Bank of England were aware of it.

182 As stated in paragraph 176, the auditors or reporting accountants are not required to seek out grounds for making a report. It is only where they become aware during the ordinary course of their work that the criterion might be satisfied that they should take the matter further.

Reporting via the bank

183 It is important for auditors or reporting accountants to act in a manner that will preserve their professional relationship with their client. Normally, therefore, they should ask the bank to draw matters about which they are concerned to the attention of the Bank of England. Examples of circumstances encountered in which the criterion set out in paragraph 181 may be met and the matter reported via the bank, are:

(a) where it has come to the attention of the auditors or reporting accountants that there is an extreme situation, such as evidence of imminent financial collapse, where it it obvious that the Bank of England must be informed;

(b) where the auditors or reporting accountants have evidence of an occurrence which has led or is likely to lead to a material diminution of the bank's net assets;

(c) when the auditors or reporting accountants form the opinion that there has been a significant failure of or that there is a significant weakness in, the accounting and other records or the internal control systems;

(d) when the auditors or reporting accountants form the opinion that management has reported financial information to the supervisor which is misleading in a material particular (or become aware that management has failed or does not intend to report something and the failure to report is, or would be, materially misleading).

Reporting direct to the Bank of England[1]

184 In exceptional circumstances, where it is in the interests of protecting depositors that the management of the bank should not be informed in advance, the auditors or reporting accountants should report direct to the Bank of England. Examples of these circumstances are:

(a) where there has been an occurrence which causes the auditors or reporting accountants no longer to have confidence in the integrity of the directors or senior management, e.g. where they believe that a fraud or other misappropriation has been committed by the directors or senior management of the bank, or they have evidence of the intention of directors or senior management to commit such fraud or misappropriation;

(b) where there has been an occurrence which causes the auditors or reporting accountants no longer to have confidence in the competence of the directors or

[1]There are other circumstances in which the auditors must give written notice to the Bank of England (see paragraph 65).

senior management to conduct the business of the bank in a prudent manner so as to protect the interests of depositors, e.g. where they have discovered that the directors or senior management are acting in an irresponsible or reckless manner with respect to the bank's affairs, or they have evidence of an intention so to act.

185 Additionally, as outlined in paragraph 187(b), a direct report should be made where the bank will not itself inform the Bank of England of a matter, having been advised to do so by the auditors or reporting accountants or where it has not done so within the period of time specified, or where there is not adequate evidence that the bank has properly reported the matter in question.

Reporting procedures

186 In forming a view as to whether it is expedient to report a matter to the Bank of England, the auditors or reporting accountants should follow the procedures in making enquiries and obtaining and assessing relevant evidence which are a normal part of forming a professional judgement in relation to an audit or investigation.

187 Where the auditors or reporting accountants become aware of a matter which in their professional judgement they consider ought to be reported to the Bank of England, they should consider adopting the following procedures, bearing in mind that speed may be of the essence.

(a) The auditors or reporting accountants should consider the facts and unless inappropriate in the circumstances, discuss the matter with the management of the bank.

(b) In normal circumstances, they should establish whether the matter has already been reported by the bank through the usual channels, and if so, obtain from the bank a copy of the Bank of England's written acknowledgement sufficient to establish that the matter has been properly reported

If the matter has not already been reported by management, the auditors or reporting accountants should write to the bank setting out their views and requesting the directors or management to inform the Bank of England of the matter, within a specified period of time. They should then obtain from the bank, evidence of prompt acknowledgement from the Bank of England, sufficient to establish that the matter has been properly reported.

In the absence of such evidence, it may be appropriate for the auditors or reporting accountants to report the matter direct to the Bank of England, and to inform the management of the bank of the contents of their report.

If the directors or management have not informed the Bank of England, and continue to refuse to inform the Bank of England within the specified period of time, the auditors or reporting accountants should report direct to the Bank of England.

(c) If the situation is sensitive, for example in the circumstances outlined in paragraph 184(a) and (b), it may be inappropriate to discuss the matter with the normal levels of management. The auditors or reporting accountants should, therefore, consider reporting to the appropriate senior level within the bank with a view to the Bank of England being informed of the situation by a senior representative of the bank. The auditors or reporting accountants should then obtain evidence from the bank of prompt acknowledgement by the Bank of England sufficient to establish that the matter has been properly reported. In the absence of such evidence, it will then be appropriate for the auditors or reporting accountants to report direct to the Bank of England.

In exceptional circumstances where the auditors or reporting accountants feel that in the interests of speed and/or, because of the nature of the matter, it is not appropriate or practical to inform or discuss the matter with anyone connected with the bank, the auditors or reporting accountants should make an appropriate written or other report direct to the Bank of England.

188 Auditors or reporting accountants should satisfy themselves that their decision will stand up to examination at a future date on the basis of the following considerations:

- — what they knew at the time;
- — what they should have known in the course of their audit or investigatory work;
- — what they should have concluded; and
- — what they should have done.

189 Speed of reporting will often be important to the protection of the interests of depositors. A report should be made as soon as the auditors or reporting accountants reasonably can after forming the view that it is expedient to do so in order to protect the interests of depositors. For auditors this may well mean ensuring that an *ad hoc* report is made to the Bank of England in advance of making their report under the Companies Act 1985, and for reporting accountants in advance of making the normal reports required by the Bank of England.

190 Auditors and reporting accountants should note that in the situations outlined in paragraphs 184 and 185 above, making an *ad hoc* report alone may not discharge all their responsibilities. An example of this would be reporting accountants who are also auditors considering the implications of the *ad hoc* report for their opinion on the financial statements.

191 To ensure that the Bank of England is informed promptly of matters which meet the criterion, a firm acting as auditors or reporting accountants should ensure:

(a) that all staff responsible for banking assignments are aware of the provisions of the appropriate legislation and the contents of this guideline, and are able to identify situations in which Section 47 might operate; and

(b) that satisfactory procedures exist to ensure that any information, which may be the subject of an *ad hoc* report, obtained by staff in the course of their work, is passed on to the partner responsible without unnecessary delay.

192 Appendix 1 — Banking Act 1987: important provisions for auditors and reporting accountants

Section	
	Applications for authorisation
8(5)	Power to require an accountant's report on information provided to the Bank in connection with an application for authorisation.
	Power to obtain information and require production of documents
39(1)(b)	Power to require an authorised institution to provide the Bank with a report by an accountant on information which the Bank has or may reasonably require for the performance of its functions under the Act.
39(6)	Section 39(1)(b) powers exercisable in relation to group and other connected companies of an authorised institution.
39(7)	Section 39(1)(b) powers exercisable in relation to certain persons connected with an authorised institution which is a partnership.

39(8)	Section 39(1)(b) powers exercisable in relation to a former authorised institution (and certain persons connected with it).
39(10)	Section 39(1)(b) powers exercisable in relation to significant shareholders.
	Investigations
41(1)	Power to appoint competent persons to investigate authorised and former authorised institutions (and certain group and other connected persons).
41(5)	Duty of auditor (and reporting accountant) to provide information etc. to competent persons.
	Audited accounts to be open to inspection
45	Requirement for an authorised institution to keep most recent audited accounts at UK offices where it holds itself out as accepting deposits.
	Notification in respect of auditors
46(1)	Requirement for an authorised institution incorporated in the UK to notify the Bank with respect to proposed or actual changes of auditor.
46(2)	Requirement for an auditor of an authorised institution appointed under Section 384 of the Companies Act 1985 to notify the Bank if he resigns, decides not to seek reappointment or decides to qualify accounts.
46(3)	Requirement in Section 46(2) also applied to an auditor of a former authorised institution.
	Communication by auditor etc. with the Bank
47	Ability of auditor and reporting accountant to communicate to the Bank certain information or opinion notwithstanding duties to client (whether an authorised or a former authorised institution).
	Disclosure of transactions by authorised institutions with chief executives and managers
90	Amendment of provisions in Companies Act 1985 (and Northern Ireland equivalent) relating to disclosure in accounts by authorised institutions of transactions with chief executives and managers.
	False or misleading information
94(1)	Criminal offence for any person knowingly or recklessly to provide the Bank with materially false information if the information is provided in purported compliance with requirement imposed by or under the Act or in circumstances when provider knew, or reasonably ought to have known, that the information would be used by the Bank for exercising its functions under the Act.
94(2)	Criminal offence knowingly or recklessly to provide materially false or misleading information in connection with application for authorisation under the Act
94(3)	Criminal offence for authorised (or former authorised) institution to fail to disclose to the Bank information relevant to its supervisor when it knew, or reasonably ought to have known, that it was so relevant and that the withholding of the information was of material significance to the exercise of the Bank's functions in relation to the institution.
	Other
105	Meaning of 'director', 'controller', 'manager' and 'associate'.

106 Interpretation.

Schedule

Schedule 3 Minimum criteria for authorisation.

Schedule 7 Amendments of Companies Act 1985 (Section 331(5) and 744; and paragraphs 14(a) and 17(a) of Schedule 6 to that Act).

193 Appendix 2 — Examples of controls and audit tests

This appendix details for each area of activity identified in paragraph 23:

(i) examples of controls which may be compliance tested; and

(ii) examples of substantive tests.

It should be noted that, although the majority of the controls listed will be present in each bank, this list is by no means prescriptive.

(A) Loans, advances and trade finance

(i) ***Controls which may be compliance tested***

Segregation of duties

(a) adequate segregation of duties between those who transact business, control receipt and custody of security, transfer and receive funds and maintain accounting records;

(b) dual control maintained for negotiable security;

(c) adequate control procecedures in relation to staff holidays.

Physical

(a) adequate physical control maintained over security held and negotiable instruments including dual control;

(b) segregation of funds held pending remittance from bank's own funds;

Authorisation and approval

(a) formal policies and authority limits established for the operation as a whole;

(b) overall monitoring of total facility limits;

(c) adequate authorisation of facilities for new customers;

(d) maintenance of complete loan files;

(e) credit investigations and evaluations performed on all applications prior to extending facilities;

(f) up-to-date list of counterparties with whom the bank is prepared to act together with appropriate limits;

(g) formal approval of loans, applications and all related commitments by appropriate officers or committees prior to disbursements;

(h) prior formal approval of renewal of facilities and any excesses over previously agreed limits;

(i) controls to ensure all required documentation in place prior to commitments under facilities;

(j) comparison to policy guidelines as to margin of security, quality of borrower, type of business;

(k) proper authorisation for provisions and write-offs;

(l) clearly defined procedure and policy for timing of write-offs;

(m) regular independent inspection of security and loan agreement to records;

(n) regular independent valuation of security and comparison to commitments;

(o) proper authorisation of release of security only against release of commitment;

(p) insurance of assets held as security;

(q) all letters of credit issued to be authorised by two signatories;

(r) all payaways to be authorised by two signatories;

(s) all limit excesses approved by senior official;

(t) appropriate checklist of all documentation for completeness, authorisation, validity and compliance with local regulations;

(u) standard application form for issue of letter of credit;

(v) checking to ensure funds received from collecting bank/drawee prior to remitting of proceeds to customer/remitting bank.

Arithmetical and accounting

Loans and advances

(a) comparison between listings of new loans and facilities with underlying documentation as a check on processing;

(b) properly approved reconciliations between general and subsidiary ledgers with prompt follow-up of reconciling items;

(c) adequate procedures to ensure that all related income is properly accounted for and received;

(d) adequate procedures to control cut-off;

(e) proper accounting and reporting for all foreign exchange denominated transactions;

(f) proper records maintained for potential recoveries of amounts written off;

(g) consistent basis adopted for establishment of any general provision;

(h) procedures for taking into account all interest receivable, fees, contingent liabilities and other related facilities when establishing provisions.

Trade finance

(a) immediate recording of all letters of credit, collections and bills purchased/discounted in register using sequential numbering;

(b) use of memorandum ledger accounts for contingent liabilities arising under letters of credit issued and bills.

(c) maintenance of general ledger accounts to record bills purchased/discounted;

(d) regular reconciliation between registers, memorandum ledger accounts and general ledger accounts with prompt follow-up of reconciling items;

(e) proper accounting for income and commission;

(f) standard form for all letters of credit with allocation of unique sequential number;

(g) procedures to identify bills which are due for payment.

Supervision

Loans and advances

(a) policies and authority limits established for facilities, subject to regular review at an appropriate level;

(b) regular review of any system of classification by quality of borrower;

(c) particular monitoring of specially identified classified accounts;

(d) reporting of concentrations by connected borrowers, industry and country;

(e) reporting of accounts with overdue interest or principal repayments, limit excesses or other out-of-order characteristics;

(f) controls to trace, segregate and monitor entries over dormant balances;

(g) periodic reviews for identification and establishment of provisions against bad and doubtful loans

Trade finance

(a) formal policies and authority limits established and subject to regular review at an appropriate level;

(b) maintenance of maturity diary;

(c) noting of bills not paid on due date and the chasing of overdue bills.

(ii) ***Substantive tests***

(a) agreement of facilities and drawdowns to source documents;

(b) testing calculation of interest and accruals;

(c) review of provisioning procedures and assessment of the adequacy of provisioning;

(d) review of loan files;

(e) testing of masterfile amendments;

(f) testing/checking of security;

(g) review of exceeded facilities;

(h) review of suspense accounts;

(i) performance of circularisation of balances or transactions;

(j) inspection of collateral or circularisation of holders of collateral;

(k) analytical review of balances and income compared with prior periods or budgets.

(B) Customer accounts, cash, transfer of funds and nostro accounts

(i) ***Controls which may be compliance tested***

Segregation of duties

Customer accounts and cash

(a) adequate segregation of duties between those who control receipt and custody of cash, transfer and receive funds and maintain accounting records;

(b) dual control over signature plates for cheque signing machines;

(c) signature controls on bankers payments, cheques and bankers drafts and effective review of underlying documentation;

(d) dual control over receipt of mail;

(e) adequate control procedures in relation to staff holidays.

Transfer of funds (telex, SWIFT, CHAPS)

(a) adequate segregation of duties between those responsible for initiation, coding, authentication, transmittal, settlement and reconciliation functions;

(b) dual control over composition of test keys;

(c) adequate control procedures in relation to staff holidays.

Physical

Customer accounts and cash

(a) teller area has adequate physical protection;

(b) physical control over till contents;

(c) control over spare keys to tills;

(d) surprise counts of till cash, and vault funds according to a systematic plan;

(e) relief tellers have separate floats or transfers of floats between tellers properly documented;

(f) reserve cash kept in vault under adequate security control;

(g) controls over stocks of unused cheques, bankers drafts, bankers payments, travellers cheques and other blank documentation;

(h) access to contents of ATMs properly secured.

Transfer of funds (telex, SWIFT, CHAPS)

(a) physical segregation of both testing and transmission areas;

(b) restricted access to communications areas;

(c) physical or software locks to prevent unauthorised access;

(d) restricted access to issued and unissued test keys;

(e) encryption of communication lines.

Authorisation and approval

Customer accounts and cash

(a) formal policies established;

(b) authorisation procedures for drawing from reserve cash;

(c) control procedures relating to issue of travellers' cheques;

(d) authorisation controls on non-EFT payments;

(e) properly authorised reconciliation of branch and head office clearings accounts to control accounts, review and follow up procedures for all old and unusual items and exception reporting system for overdue response/clearance items and unusually high balances;

(f) evidence of identity for withdrawals, e.g. signature, cheque guarantee card and checking of identity prior to cheque clearance;

(g) balance enquiry to support evidence of sufficient funds/undrawn facility for withdrawals;

(h) limits on tellers' funds and vault cash to reduce exposure;

(i) cash cards issued only to properly authorised customers;

(j) control and dormant accounts.

Nostro accounts

(a) formal policies established;

(b) formal authorisation for opening and closing of nostro accounts;

(c) regular issue and update of list of authorised signatures.

Transfer of funds (telex, SWIFT, CHAPS)

(a) formal transfer policies established;

(b) all payment instructions over a certain amount require two appropriate signatures;

(c) limits on amount of transfers by signatories;

(d) independent verification of authorising signatures;

(e) messages/transactions released into systems only on approval by duly authorised individuals;

(f) appropriate limits set for each operating unit;

(g) password control to automated test key systems;

(h) maintenance and review of log of all transfers;

(i) all transfers of funds require test keys;

(j) independent evidenced comparison of transfer messages with source documents;
(k) individuals entering and approving messages/transactions are identifiable for each message/transaction;
(l) adequate control over issue and maintenance of passwords and passwords changed on a regular basis;
(m) all amendments to messages/telex forms properly authorised;
(n) input validation controls over primary processing documents;
(o) all incoming messages properly authenticated and processed.

Arithmetical and accounting
Customer accounts and cash
(a) immediate recording in books;
(b) cheques restrictively endorsed upon receipt;
(c) daily balancing of tills and investigation of variances;
(d) regular reconciliation of control accounts;
(e) control over opening accounts;
(f) sequence control over bankers payments, cheques and bankers drafts;
(g) detailed analysis of branch and head office clearings accounts readily available;
(h) proper reconciliation procedures governing related control and suspense accounts relating to ATMs;
(i) control over standing data amendments.

Nostro accounts
(a) regular preparation of reconciliations between nostro and third party confirmations and outstanding items promptly followed up.

Supervision
(a) policies established subject to regular review at an appropriate level;
(b) independent review and approval of nostro account reconciliations and prompt follow-up of outstanding items.

(ii) ***Substantive tests***
(a) checking of cash records, including cash counts;
(b) checking of daily clearing reconciliation: in-debits and credits, out-debits and credits and other payments and receipts, such as direct debit and CHAPs;
(c) agreement of entries to source documents;
(d) testing of interest calculation and recording;
(e) testing of amendments to masterfiles;
(f) testing of SWIFT/telex control logs, including sequence and continuation testing to ensure no unregistered transfers;
(g) circularisation of all nostro banks;
(h) circularisation of customer accounts;
(i) testing of suspense accounts;
(j) testing of interest accruals;
(k) testing of cut-off;
(l) testing of nostro reconciliations.

(C) Market deposits

(i) ***Controls which may be compliance tested***

Segregation of duties

(a) adequate segregation of duties amongst those who initiate deals, effect settlement, post ledgers, and have custodial responsibility for negotiable instruments;

(b) independent check of calculations on deal slips;

(c) independent checking to deal slip of deal manifold set produced as by-product of processing, if appropriate;

(d) adequate control procedures in relation to staff holidays.

Physical

(a) use of security printing device for Certificates of Deposit (CDs);

(b) maintenance of register of negotiable instruments issued independently of custodian of unissued paper;

(c) negotiable instruments and collateral stored on premises kept in locked, fireproof safe or vault;

(d) dual control over negotiable instruments and unissued CDs;

(e) reconciliation of depositories' statements to detail records of money market instruments;

(f) comprehensive insurance cover for all negotiable instruments on premises;

(g) regular and surprise counts of negotiable instruments by independent staff.

Authorisation and approval

(a) formal trading policies and dealing limits established;

(b) placings only made with approved counterparties;

(c) appropriate and prior approval clearly documented for deals in excess of pre-set limits;

(d) counterparty receives authorised confirmation for all deals despatched by staff independent of dealers;

(e) all alterations to deal slips authorised by dealers;

(f) controls over input of interest rate amendments;

(g) controls over input of market values for revaluation of money market instruments.

Arithmetical and accounting

(a) input validation controls over primary processing documents;

(b) maturity listings reconciled to manual records kept by position keepers or dealers;

(c) reconciliations of subsidiary and general ledgers, subject to supervisory review;

(d) sequence control over deal slips and control over spoilt deal slips.

Supervision

(a) policies subject to regular review at an appropriate level;

(b) independent review and follow up of outstanding items on nostro reconciliation;

(c) review and authorisation of valuations of negotiable instruments by senior management;

(d) deal listings checked by staff independent of the dealers to incoming counterparty confirmations and overdue confirmations followed up;

(e) analysis of deals by broker to ensure no undue concentration of business with any one broker;
(f) review and authorisation of brokers payments;
(g) independent review of interest rates on deals (possibly in course of review of interest matching of loans/deposits);
(h) assets periodically reviewed for recoverability and sufficiency of collateral.

(ii) ***Substantive tests***

(a) testing of completeness of recording deals;
(b) agreement of deal ticket details to accounting records;
(c) testing of accruals and revaluations;
(d) testing of amendments to masterfiles;
(e) agreement of limits used to supporting documents;
(f) testing of amortisation of profits/losses on arbitrage transactions;
(g) testing of brokerage charges to supporting documents;
(h) circularisation of counterparties to deals;
(i) circularisation of nostro accounts;
(j) circularisation of brokers used;
(k) checking of collectability of funds;
(l) testing of cut-off;
(m) testing balances to authorised limit list.

(D) Foreign exchange, futures, options and commodities dealing

(i) ***Controls which may be compliance tested***

Segregation of duties

(a) segregation of duties amongst those who initiate deals, effect settlement, post ledger and prepare revaluations;
(b) deal listings reconciled to the accounting records and checked by staff independent of the dealers to incoming counterparty confirmations and overdue confirmations followed up;
(c) adequate control procedures in relation to staff holidays.

Physical

(a) comprehensive security procedures over vault and movements of commodities (e.g. bullion) in/out;
(b) reconciliation of custodian statements to detailed internal commodity records;
(c) comprehensive insurance cover for all commodities on premises;
(d) regular and surprise counts of commodity stocks held on premises by independent staff.

Authorisation and approval

(a) formal trading procedures and dealing limits established, e.g. counterparty settlement and currency exposure;
(b) procedures for approval of counterparties established;
(c) deals only made with approved counterparties;
(d) appropriate approval clearly documented for deals in excess of pre-set limits;
(e) counterparty receives authorised confirmation for all deals, despatched by staff

independent of dealers;

(f) all alterations to deal slips authorised by dealers;

(g) review of all arbitrage deals to ensure valid.

Arithmetical and accounting

(a) independent check of calculations of deal slips;

(b) independent checking to deal slip of deal manifold set produced as by-product of processing of deal slip if appropriate;

(c) input validation controls over primary processing documents;

(d) regular independent agreement of accounting records of outstanding contracts with contingency accounts and position keepers' records or dealers' records;

(e) independent review and reconciliation of revaluation and other suspense accounts;

(f) independent review and follow up of outstanding items on nostro reconciliations;

(g) analysis of deals by broker to ensure no undue concentration of business with any one broker;

(h) controls over input of market prices and exchange rates for revaluation purposes;

(i) sequence controls over deal slips and control over spoilt deal slips.

Supervision

(a) trading policies and dealing limits subject to regular review;

(b) independent review and approval of prices/exchange rates on deals;

(c) review and authorisation of revaluations by senior management.

(ii) ***Substantive tests***

(a) checking of daily clearing reconciliation: in-debits and credits, out-debits and credits and other payments and receipts, such as direct debit and CHAPs;

(b) agreement of entries to source documents;

(c) testing of interest calculation and recording;

(d) testing of amendments to masterfiles;

(e) testing of SWIFT/telex control logs, including sequence and continuation testing;

(f) circularisation of all nostro banks;

(g) circularisation of customer accounts;

(h) testing of suspense accounts;

(i) testing of interest accruals;

(j) testing of cut-off;

(k) testing year-end revaluations;

(l) testing the reconciliation of dealer records to accounting records;

(m) checking within the bank's internal limits.

(E) Investments and dealing securities

(i) ***Controls which may be compliance tested***

Segregation of duties

(a) segregation of duties amongst those who initiate deals or underwriting and other commitments, effect settlement and post ledgers, prepare revaluations and have custodial responsibility for securities;

(b) deal listings checked by staff independent of the dealers to incoming counterparty confirmations and overdue confirmations followed up;
(c) dual control over access to negotiable securities;
(d) adequate control procedures in relation to staff holidays.

Physical

(a) negotiable securities stored on the premises kept in locked fireproof safe or vault;
(b) reconciliation of depositories' statements to detailed records of securities;
(c) comprehensive insurance cover for all negotiable securities on the premises;
(d) regular and surprise securities counts by independent staff.

Authorisation and approval

(a) formal policies for dealing and approval of counterparties established;
(b) deals only made with approved counterparties;
(c) appropriate approval clearly documented for deals in excess of pre-set limits;
(d) counterparty receives authorised confirmation for all deals (other than those through stockbrokers) despatched by staff independent of dealers;
(e) all alterations to deal slips authorised by dealers;
(f) authorisation of managing, underwriting and selling group commitments.

Arithmetical and accounting

(a) input validation controls over primary processing documents;
(b) independent checking of deal manifold set produced as by-product of processing of deal slip if appropriate;
(c) agreement of dealers' position records to accounting records and review of same;
(d) reconciliations of subsidiary and general ledgers, subject to supervisory review;
(e) sequence control over deal slips;
(f) independent review and follow up of outstanding items on nostro reconciliations;
(g) independent check of calculations of all fees and commissions and allocation of underwriting expenses;
(h) security revaluation prices obtained from independent recognised market makers;
(i) controls over input of valuation prices;
(j) all interest and dividend income due is diarised and overdue amounts followed up;
(k) independent check of calculation on deal slip;
(l) reconciliation to brokers' statements;
(m) authorisation of payments to brokers;
(n) instruction reports regularly issued;
(o) unsettled transaction reports regularly issued.

Supervision

(a) trading policies and dealing limits, subject to regular review;
(b) analysis of deals to ensure no undue concentration of business with any one broker;
(c) independent review of yields/market prices on deals;
(d) periodic revaluations of all securities and review and authorisation of revaluations by senior management.

(ii) ***Substantive tests***

(a) testing of limits to source documents;
(b) agreement of deal tickets to counterparty contract notes;
(c) agreement of accounting records to deal tickets;
(d) testing of the computer system with test data;
(e) testing of valuations;
(f) agreement of income to source documents;
(g) testing of calculation of income and capital profits;
(h) agreement of deals to customers' instructions;
(i) circularisation of custodians;
(j) checking of security position reconciliation;
(k) testing of unmatched instruction reports and unsettled transaction reports;
(l) circularisation of counterparty accounts;
(m) testing of completeness of recording and cut-off;
(n) testing of agency accounts.

(F) Trustee and advisory activities (including portfolio management)

(i) ***Controls which may be compliance tested***

Segregation of duties

(a) adequate segregation of duties between initiation, recording, authorisation and cash and securities handling;
(b) adequate control procedures in relation to staff holidays.

Physical

(a) dual control over safekeeping and adequate physical security;
(b) storage of negotiable securites in locked, fireproof safe/vault;
(c) control over receipt and despatch of all share certificates and other title documents;
(d) maintenance of register of items held and regular agreement both to physical holdings and customer records by independent personnel;
(e) comprehensive insurance cover for any assets and securities on the premises.

Authorisation and approval

(a) formal policies established;
(b) authorised agreement with customers for all new fiduciary/advisory accounts;
(c) adequate controls to acknowledge, record and suitably invest any assets received on a timely basis;
(d) purchases/sales approved either by customer where non-discretionary or by responsible official if discretionary;
(e) controls over confirmations, as for investments;
(f) controls over brokers, as for investments.

Arithmetical and accounting

(a) regular reporting to customer of current holdings, values and transactions;
(b) checking of income received to recording of expected receipts and follow-up of differences;
(c) recording and control of bonus and rights issues;

(d) control over income received direct by customer, trustee or other individual to ensure proper accountability and recording;
(e) adequate segregation between capital and income receipts;
(f) correct accounting for related taxation;
(g) segregation between trustee and own account transactions;
(h) prompt recording of purchase and sales including procedures to allocate stock transactions to respective customers;
(i) matching of transaction records to contract notes;
(j) maturities diary for redemptions, projects and collection of income;
(k) reconciliation between total securities holding and individual customer portfolio records.

Supension

(a) policies subject to regular review at an appropriate level;
(b) approved list of brokers and other counterparties;
(c) monitoring, approval and regular charging of fees on agreed bases;
(d) insurance cover adequate and regularly monitored in relation to assets held;
(e) formal rules on conflict of interest and dealing;
(f) implementation and monitoring of special requests from customers;
(g) review/monitoring of fees charged to customers.

(ii) ***Substantive test***

(a) agreement of deal tickets to confirmations and supporting documentation;
(b) testing of deals to management agreement with customer to ensure that they are within the bank's dealing authority;
(c) agreement of entries in customer account to deal tickets and customer instructions;
(d) agreement of payment in customer account to deal ticket and customer instructions;
(e) testing execution of customers' instructions by agreeing to deal ticket and fund transfer;
(f) testing the calculation of management fees;
(g) checking aggregation of total securities positions to individual customers' portfolios;
(h) circularisation of custodians ensuring that replies relate to client or customer account only;
(i) circularisation of time deposits and money at call;
(j) circularisation of customers.

194 Appendix 3 — Application and general controls over the computer environment

Application controls to be considered will typically include those relating to:

(a) the organisation of the relevant bank departments;
(b) the management review of activities;
(c) pre-computer processing of transactions;

(d) input and processing of transactions by computer;

(e) maintenance of computer files of transactions and balances;

(f) post-processing actions on the output from computer systems;

(g) reconciliation of computerised records with related assets.

The general controls to be considered will be those controls relating to the development, maintenance and operation of computer systems that are designed to control the following risks:

(a) risks arising in the development and enhancement of new computer systems (Development);

(b) risks of errors during data processing, development and amendment to programs (Errors);

(c) risks of loss, including being unable to continue operation or recover from a breakdown or disaster, caused by an accident or otherwise (Business Interruption);

(d) risks relating to unauthorised access to the computer system, its application and data files (Fraud and unauthorised access to confidential information).

195 Appendix 4 — Examples of controls which affect a number of areas

(a) Controls over the authorisation and correct recording of:

 (i) nostro transactions; and

 (ii) transactions using funds transfer systems.

(b) Controls over financial planning and budgeting.

(c) Controls governing the provision of adequate management accounting information.

(d) Controls over the documentation and communication of:

 (i) accounting policies; and

 (ii) operational procedures and controls.

(e) Controls over effective personnel selection routines.

(f) Controls over establishing, monitoring and reporting risk.

(g) Controls over management review of systems, e.g. internal audit.

(h) Controls over communication with the Bank of England and other regulatory authorities.

(i) Computer controls.

Guidance for internal auditors

(Issued June 1990)

Preface

This guideline provides advice to internal auditors about the main issues and procedures which they need to consider as part of their work. It should also be of benefit to organisations considering establishing an internal audit function.

The guideline is written in the context of internal audit work in both the commercial and public sectors. It should be read in conjunction with the Explanatory Foreword to Auditing Standards and Guidelines and the Auditing Guidelines 'Reliance on internal audit' and 'The auditor's responsibility in relation to fraud, other irregularities and errors'. Internal auditors may also find it helpful to refer to the Audit Brief 'Value for money audit' issued by the Auditing Practices Committee of CCAB Limited (June 1990).

Internal auditors should also have regard to the ethical statements issued by the accountancy bodies and also to any requirements regarding internal audit set out in relevant statutes or regulations.

A glossary of terms used in the guideline is given in the appendix.

Objectives and scope of internal audit

1 Internal audit is an independent appraisal function established by the management of an organisation for the review of the internal control system as a service to the organisation. It objectively examines, evaluates and reports on the adequacy of internal control as a contribution to the proper, economic, efficient and effective use of resources.

2 The essentials for effective internal auditing are:

(a) *independence*

The internal auditor should have the independence in terms of organisational status and personal objectivity which permits the proper performance of his duties (paragraphs 11 to 14).

(b) *staffing and training*

The internal audit unit should be appropriately staffed in terms of numbers, grades, qualifications and experience, having regard to its responsibilities and objectives. The internal auditor should be properly trained to fulfil all his responsibilities (paragraphs 15 to 26).

(c) *relationships*

The internal auditor should seek to foster constructive working relationships and mutual understanding with management, with external auditors, with any other review agencies and, where one exists, with the audit committee (paragraphs 27 to 37).

(d) *due care*

The internal auditor should exercise due care in fulfilling his responsibilities (paragraphs 38 to 44).

(e) *planning, controlling and recording*

The internal auditor should adequately plan, control and record his work (paragraphs 45 to 58).

(f) *evaluation of the internal control system*

The internal auditor should identify and evaluate the organisation's internal control system as a basis for reporting upon its adequacy and effectiveness (paragraphs 59 to 62).

(g) *evidence*
The internal auditor should obtain sufficient, relevant and reliable evidence on which to base reasonable conclusions and recommendations (paragraphs 63 to 69).

(h) *reporting and follow-up*
The internal auditor should ensure that findings, conclusions and recommendations arising from each internal audit assignment are communicated promptly to the appropriate level of management and he should actively seek a response. He should ensure that arrangements are made to follow up audit recommendations to monitor what action has been taken on them (paragraphs 70 to 78).

3 The terms of reference for the internal audit function should be formally confirmed by the organisation and should have proper regard to the contents of this guideline; demonstrable independence of the function is crucial to its effectiveness.

4 For certain public sector organisations the need for an internal auditing function is prescribed by statute and this provides a basis for defining specific standards and guidance for the practice of internal auditing in those organisations. The Government Internal Audit Manual and the National Health Service Internal Audit Manual are examples of internal auditing standards and guidance prescribed for specific organisations.

5 To achieve full effectiveness the scope of the internal audit function should provide an unrestricted range of coverage of the organisation's operations, and their internal auditor should have sufficient authority to allow him access to such records, assets and personnel as are necessary for proper fulfilment of his responsibilities.

6 It is a management responsibility to determine the extent of internal control in the organisation's systems which should not depend on internal audit as a substitute for effective controls. Internal audit, as a service to the organisation, contributes to internal control by examining, evaluating and reporting to management on its adequacy and effectiveness. Internal audit activity may lead to the strengthening of internal control as a result of management response.

7 One of the objectives of internal auditing is to assist management in the pursuit of value for money. It is achieved through economic, efficient and effective use of resources.

8 It is a management responsibility to maintain the internal control system and to ensure that the organisation's resources are properly applied in the manner and on the activities intended. This includes responsibility for the prevention and detection of fraud and other illegal acts.

9 The internal auditor should have regard to the possibility of such malpractice and should seek to identify serious defects in internal control which might permit the occurrence of such an event.

10 An internal auditor who discovers evidence of, or suspects, malpractice should report firm evidence, or reasonable suspicions, to the appropriate level of management. It is a management responsibility to determine what further action to take.

Independence

11 Independence is achieved through the organisational status of internal audit and the objectivity of internal auditors.

Organisational status

12 The status of internal audit should enable it to function effectively. The support of management is essential. Internal audit should be involved in the determination of its own priorities, in consultation with management. Accordingly the head of internal audit should have direct access to, and freedom to report to, all senior management including the chief executive, board of directors and, where one exists, the audit committee.

Objectivity of the internal auditor

13 Each internal auditor should have an objective attitude of mind and be in a sufficiently independent position to be able to exercise judgement, express opinions and present recommendations with impartiality.

(a) The internal auditor, notwithstanding his employment by the organisation, should be free from any conflict of interest arising either from professional or personal relationships or from pecuniary or other interests in an organisation or activity which is subject to audit.

(b) The internal auditor should be free from undue influences which either restrict or modify the scope or conduct of his work or over-rule or significantly affect judgement as to the content of the internal audit report.

(c) The internal auditor should not allow his objectivity to be impaired when auditing an activity for which he has had authority or responsibility.

(d) An internal auditor should be consulted about significant proposed changes in the internal control system and the implementation of new systems and make recommendations on the standards of control to be applied. This need not prejudice that auditor's objectivity in reviewing those systems subsequently.

(e) An internal auditor should not normally undertake non-audit duties but where he does so, exceptionally, he should ensure that management understands that he is not then functioning as an internal auditor.

14 Where any of the situations referred to in paragraphs 13(a) to (c) arise, this should be clearly declared by the internal auditor so that consideration can be given to the need for alternative arrangements for the audit assignment.

Staffing and training

15 The effectiveness of internal audit depends substantially on the quality, training and experience of its staff. The aim should be to appoint staff with the appropriate background, personal qualities and potential. Thereafter, steps should be taken to provide the necessary experience, training and continuing professional education.

Staffing

16 The internal audit unit should be managed by a head of internal audit who should be suitably qualified and should possess wide experience of internal audit and of its management. He should plan, direct, control and motivate the resources available to ensure that the responsibilities of the internal audit unit are met.

17 The full range of duties may require internal audit staff to be drawn from a variety of disciplines. The effectiveness of internal audit may be enhanced by the use of specialist staff, particularly in the internal audit of activities of a technical nature.

18 The internal audit unit should employ staff with varying types and levels of skills, qualifications and experience in order to satisfy the requirements of each internal audit task.

19 The head of internal audit should participate in the recruitment and selection of his staff. New entrants to internal audit work should have time to familiarise themselves with the activities of the internal audit unit and the organisation, and to demonstrate their suitability for audit work.

Training

20 The organisation has a responsibility to ensure that the internal auditor receives the training necessary for the performance of the full range of duties.

21 Training should be tailored to the needs of the individual. It should include both the theoretical knowledge and its practical application under the supervision of suitably competent and experienced internal auditors. Account should be taken of:

(a) internal audit objectives and priorities;

(b) the type of internal audit work;

(c) previous training, experience and qualifications; and

(d) personal development in the light of the needs of the organisation and the internal audit unit.

22 Training should be a planned and continuing process at all levels and should cover:

(a) basic training — providing the knowledge of basic auditing principles and practices which all internal auditors should possess;

(b) development training — in general audit skills and techniques and inter-personal skills, to improve the effectiveness of those currently employed in internal audit; and

(c) specialised training — for those responsible for the internal audit of activities which require special skills or knowledge.

23 Other forms of staff development should be considered according to particular needs. These may include periods of attachment to other parts of the organisation or secondment to other organisations.

24 The internal auditor should keep abreast of current developments, improvements, new techniques and practices in auditing.

25 The internal auditor should maintain technical competence through professional development which may include:

(a) private reading and study; and

(b) participation in professional activities such as attending meetings, courses and conferences, lecturing, writing articles and papers and contribution to research groups.

26 The head of internal audit should co-ordinate and keep under review, the training requirements of internal auditors. He should be responsible for preparing training profiles which identify the training requirements for different grades of internal auditor, and should maintain personal training records for each individual. In large organisations this may be performed by a designated training officer.

Relationships

27 In order that the internal auditor may properly perform all his tasks it is necessary for all those with whom he has contact to have confidence in him. Constructive working relationships make it more likely that internal audit work will be accepted and acted upon, but the internal auditor should not allow his objectivity to be impaired.

Organisational relationships

28 The head of internal audit should prepare the internal audit plan in consultation with senior management. The internal auditor should arrange the timing of internal audit assignments in consultation with the management concerned, except on those rare occasions where an unannounced visit is a necessary part of the audit approach. Consultation can lead to the identification of areas of concern or of other interest to management.

29 Matters which arise in the course of the audit are confidential and discussion should be restricted to management directly responsible for the area being audited unless they have given express agreement to broaden the discussion.

30 Discussions with management are necessary when preparing the audit report. This is an essential feature of the good relationship between the auditor and the management.

Relationships with external audit

31 The relationship between internal and external audit needs to take account of their differing roles and responsibilities. Internal audit is an independent appraisal function within the organisation and internal auditors are direct employees. The external auditor usually has a statutory responsibility to express an independent opinion on the financial statements and stewardship of the organisation.

32 The aim should be to achieve mutual recognition and respect, leading to a joint improvement in performance and the avoidance of unnecessary overlapping of work. It should be possible for the external and internal auditors to rely on each other's work, subject to limits determined by their different responsibilities, respective strengths and special abilities. Consultations should be held and consideration given to whether any work of either auditor is adequate for the purpose of the other. The internal auditor does not automatically have a right of access to the records of the external auditor. However, the relationship between the internal and external auditor will usually be such that the external auditor will be able to allow access to the necessary records.

33 Since internal audit evaluates an organisation's internal control system the external auditor may need to be satisfied that the internal audit function is being planned and performed effectively. This review needs to be seen by both parties as a necessary part of the working relationship (see the Auditing Guideline 'Reliance on internal audit').

34 Regular meetings should be held between internal and external auditors at which joint audit planning, priorities, scope and audit findings are discussed and information exchanged. The benefits of joint training programmes and joint audit work should also be considered.

Review agencies and specialists

35 Certain information obtained during an internal audit assignment may assist a review agency, such as management services or consultants, which is seeking to secure improvements in the organisation's performance. Management's formal approval should be obtained before releasing any audit report or other information to a review agency.

36 The internal auditor should establish a regular dialogue with review agencies and obtain their reports for information, for review and for comment where proposals may affect internal control arrangements.

37 Where it is necessary for the internal auditor to have contact with other specialists the same basic principles about information apply as in the case of review agencies.

Due care

38 The internal auditor cannot be expected to give total assurance that control weaknesses or irregularities do not exist.

39 In order to demonstrate that due care has been exercised the internal auditor should be able to show that his work has been performed in a way which is consistent with this guideline.

40 The internal auditor should possess a thorough knowledge of the aims of the organisation and the internal control system. He should also be aware of the relevant law and the requirements of relevant professional and regulatory bodies.

Ethical standards

41 The ethical statements issued by the accountancy bodies are relevant to the work of internal auditors.

42 The internal auditor must be impartial in discharging all responsibilities; bias, prejudice or undue influence must not be allowed to limit or over-ride objectivity. At all times, the integrity and conduct of each internal auditor must be above reproach. He should not place himself in a position where responsibilities and private interests conflict and any personal interest should be declared. Gifts or other rewards should not be accepted.

43 The internal auditor should not improperly disclose any information obtained during the course of his work.

Quality of internal audit performance

44 The head of internal audit should promote and maintain adequate quality standards in the internal audit unit. He should establish methods of evaluating the work of his staff to ensure that the internal audit unit fulfils its responsibilities and has proper regard to this guideline.

Planning, controlling and recording

45 Internal audit work should be planned, controlled and recorded in order to determine priorities, establish and achieve objectives, and ensure the effective and efficient use of audit resources.

Planning

46 The main purposes of internal audit planning are:

(a) to determine priorities and to establish the most cost-effective means of achieving audit objectives;

(b) to assist in the direction and control of audit work;

(c) to help ensure that attention is devoted to critical aspects of audit work; and

(d) to help ensure that work is completed in accordance with pre-determined targets.

47 The stages of internal audit planning are:

(a) to identify the objectives of the organisation;

(b) to define internal audit objectives;

(c) to take account of relevant changes in legislation and other external factors;

(d) to obtain a comprehensive understanding of the organisation's systems, structure, and operations;

(e) to identify, evaluate and rank risks to which the organisation is exposed;

(f) to take account of changes in structures or major systems in the organisation;

(g) to take account of known strengths and weaknesses in the internal control system;

(h) to take account of management concerns and expectations;

(i) to identify audit areas by service, functions and major systems;

(j) to determine the type of audit: e.g. systems, verification or value for money;

(k) to take account of the plans of external audit and other review agencies; and

(l) to assess staff resources required, and match with resources available.

48 The internal auditor should prepare strategic, periodic and operational work plans.

49 The strategic plan should usually cover a period of between two to five years during which all major systems and areas of activity will be audited. It should set out the audit objectives, audit areas, type of activity and frequency of audit and an assessment of resources to be applied.

50 The periodic plan, typically for a financial or calendar year, translates the strategic plan into a schedule of audit assignments to be carried out in the ensuing period. It should define the purpose and duration of each audit assignment and allocate staff and other resources accordingly and should be formally approved by management.

51 Operational work plans should be prepared for each audit assignment as it is arranged covering:

(a) objectives and scope of the audit;

(b) time budget and staff allocation; and

(c) methods, procedures and reporting arrangements, including supervision and allocation of responsibilities.

52 All internal audit plans should be sufficiently flexible to respond to changing priorities.

Controlling

53 Control of the internal audit unit and of individual assignments is needed to ensure that internal audit objectives are achieved and work is performed effectively. The most important elements of control are the direction and supervision of the internal audit staff and review of their work. This will be assisted by an established audit approach and standard documentation. The degree of control and supervision required depends on the complexity of assignments and the experience and proficiency of the internal audit staff.

54 The head of internal audit should establish arrangements:

(a) to allocate internal audit assignments according to the level of and proficiency of internal audit staff;

(b) to ensure that internal auditors clearly understand the responsibilities and internal audit objectives;

(c) to communicate the scope of work to be performed and agree the programme of work with each internal auditor;

(d) to provide and document evidence of adequate supervision, review and guidance during the internal audit assignment;

(e) to ensure that adequate working papers are being prepared to support internal audit findings and conclusions; and

(f) to ensure that internal audit's performance is in accordance with the internal audit plan or that any significant variations have been explained.

55 The head of internal audit should establish arrangements to evaluate the performance of the internal audit unit. He may also prepare an annual report to management on the activities of the internal audit unit in which he gives an assessment of how effectively the objectives of the function have been met.

Recording

56 Internal audit work should be properly recorded because:

(a) the head of internal audit needs to be able to ensure that work delegated to staff has been properly performed. He can generally do this only by reference to detailed working papers prepared by the internal audit staff who perform the work;

(b) working papers provide, for future reference, evidence of work performed, details of problems encountered and conclusions drawn; and

(c) the preparation of working papers encourages each internal auditor to adopt a methodical approach to his work.

57 The head of internal audit should specify the required standard of internal audit documentation and working papers and ensure that those standards are maintained.

58 Internal audit working papers should always be sufficiently complete and detailed to enable an experienced internal auditor with no previous connection with the internal audit assignment subsequently to ascertain from them what work was performed and to support the conclusions reached. Working papers should be prepared as the internal audit assignment proceeds so that critical details are not omitted and problems not overlooked. These should be reviewed by internal audit management.

Evaluation of the internal control system

59 Controls ensure that processes act to meet the system's objectives.

60 The main objectives of the internal control system are:

(a) to ensure adherence to management policies and directives in order to achieve the organisation's objectives;

(b) to safeguard assets;

(c) to secure the relevance, reliability and integrity of information, so ensuring as far as possible the completeness and accuracy of records; and

(d) to ensure compliance with statutory requirements.

61 When evaluating internal control systems the internal auditor should consider the effect which all the controls have on each other and on related systems.

62 As part of the planning process the internal auditor should identify the whole range of systems within the organisation. For those systems to be examined, the internal auditor should establish appropriate criteria to determine whether the controls are adequate and assist in achieving the objectives of the system. The stages of a system's audit would normally be:

(a) to identify the system parameters;

(b) to determine the control objectives;

(c) to identify expected controls to meet control objectives;

(d) to review the system against expected controls;

(e) to appraise the controls designed into the system against control objectives;

(f) to test the actual controls for effectiveness against control objectives;

(g) to test the operation of controls in practice; and

(h) to give an opinion based on audit objectives as to whether the system provides an adequate basis for effective control and whether it is properly operated in practice.

Evidence

63 Internal audit evidence is information obtained by an internal auditor which enables conclusions to be formed on which recommendations can be based.

64 The internal auditor should determine what evidence will be necessary by exercising judgement in the light of the objectives of the internal audit assignment. This judgement will be influenced by the scope of the assignment, the significance of the matters under review, the relevance and the reliability of available evidence and the cost and time involved in obtaining it.

65 The collection and assessment of internal audit evidence should be recorded and reviewed to provide reasonable assurance that conclusions are soundly based and internal audit objectives achieved.

Sufficiency

66 An internal auditor should obtain the evidence considered necessary for the achievement of the internal audit assignment objectives. This is influenced by, for instance:

(a) the level of assurance required;

(b) the objectives and scope of the internal audit assignment;

(c) the scale of activity under review and the degree of risk involved;

(d) the cost and time involved in obtaining evidence; and

(e) the reliability of the evidence.

Relevance

67 The relevance of the internal audit evidence should be considered in relation to the objectives of the internal audit assignment.

Reliability

68 Reliable evidence can be achieved through the use of the appropriate internal audit techniques which should normally be selected in advance, but which may be expanded or altered as necessary during the internal audit assignment.

69 In order to place reliance on evidence an internal auditor should be satisfied with its nature, extent, adequacy, consistency and relevance to the internal audit assignment and with the methods governing its collection.

Reporting and follow-up

70 The primary purposes of internal audit reports are to provide management with an opinion on the adequacy of the internal control system, and to inform management of significant audit findings, conclusions and recommendations. The aim of every internal audit report should be:

(a) to prompt management action to implement recommendations for change leading to improvement in performance and control; and

(b) to provide a formal record of points arising from the internal audit assignment and, where appropriate, of agreements reached with management.

71 Reporting arrangements, including the format and distribution of internal audit reports, should be agreed with management. The head of internal audit should ensure that reports are sent to managers who have a direct responsibility for the unit or function being audited and who have the authority to take action on the internal audit recommendations. Internal audit reports are confidential documents and their distribution should be restricted to those managers who need to know, to the audit committee and to the external auditor.

72 While the internal auditor may clear minor matters which do not indicate a consistent or systematic weakness with members of staff directly involved, matters of consequence should be reported formally in writing to management.

73 The internal auditor should produce clear, constructive and concise written reports based on sufficient, relevant and reliable evidence, which should:

(a) state the scope, purpose, extent and conclusions of the internal audit assignment;

(b) make recommendations which are appropriate and relevant, and which flow from the conclusions; and

(c) acknowledge the action taken, or proposed, by management.

74 The internal auditor should make an interim report, orally or in writing, where it is necessary to alert management to the need to take immediate action to correct a serious weakness in performance or control, or where there are reasonable grounds for suspicion of malpractice. Consideration should also be given to interim reporting where there is a significant change in the scope of the internal audit assignment or where it is desirable to inform management of progress. Interim reporting does not diminish or eliminate the need for final reporting.

75 The internal auditor should normally meet with management to discuss the audit findings at the completion of fieldwork for each internal audit assignment and the formal written report should be presented to management as soon as possible thereafter.

76 Before issuing the final report, the internal auditor should normally discuss the contents with the appropriate levels of management, and may submit a draft report to them, for confirmation of factual accuracy.

77 If the internal auditor and management disagree about the relevance of the factual content of the draft audit report, the internal auditor should consider whether reference should be made to this in the final report.

78 It is management's responsibility to ensure that proper consideration is given to internal audit reports. The internal auditor should ensure that appropriate arrangements are made to determine whether action has been taken on internal audit recommendations or that management has understood and assumed the risk of not taking action.

Appendix — Glossary of terms used in the guideline

Organisation:	The body for which the internal auditor is providing an internal audit service.
Audit committee:	A committee of directors, usually without executive responsibility, or top-ranking managers, which considers both the external and internal audit plans and activity with a specific brief to review internal control arrangements.
Management:	A comprehensive term including all persons who have responsibility at various levels for activities which may be the subject of internal audit.
Internal auditor:	An individual who takes responsibility for carrying out internal audit work within an organisation whether as an employee or as an external agency.
System:	A series of inter-related procedures, composed of processes and controls designed to operate together to achieve a planned objective.
Internal control:	The regulation of activities in an organisation through systems designed and implemented to facilitate the achievement of management objectives.
Internal control system:	The whole system of controls, financial and otherwise, established by the management in order to carry on the business of an organisation in an orderly and efficient manner, ensure adherence to management policies, safeguard assets and secure as far as possible the completeness and accuracy of records.
Controls:	The individual components of an internal control system are known as 'controls' or 'internal controls'. These ensure that processes work to meet the system's objectives.

Communications between auditors and Regulators under Sections 109 and 180(1)(q) of the Financial Services Act 1986

(Issued July 1990)

Preface

This guideline refers to auditors, audits and to reports on the annual financial statements. Firms authorised by recognised professional bodies (RPBs) may not have auditors as such nor be required by their RPB to submit audited financial statements. They may, however, be required to submit reports on specific matters, such as client money, which have to be reported on by an independent reporting accountant.

Although Sections 109 and 180(1)(q) of the Financial Services Act 1986 refer only to the auditors of authorised persons, the rules of the RPBs generally make provisions having a similar effect. The provisions may be set out in the terms of appointment of the independent reporting accountant or elsewhere.

This guideline is applicable to the independent reporting accountants of firms authorised by RPBs even though the guideline refers only to auditors, audits and reports on annual financial statements.

Introduction

1 The Financial Services Act 1986 (the Act) was introduced to protect investors and, therefore, is concerned with ensuring that investment business in the United Kingdom is conducted in accordance with the relevant regulations and rules by persons who are fit and proper and are authorised to conduct such business.

2 The regulatory powers of the Act are vested in the Secretary of State for Trade and Industry, but Section 114 enables him to transfer most of his functions under the Act to a designated agency. Most of the relevant functions have been transferred to the Securities and Investments Board (SIB), which has exercised its powers to recognise self-regulating organisations (SROs), recognised professional bodies (RPBs) and certain other bodies. This guidance is concerned only with investment businesses which are regulated by SIB, an SRO or an RPB.

3 Investment businesses must be regulated by either SIB, an SRO or an RPB, depending on what they are and what investment business activities they do. For example, a unit trust management company might be authorised by IMRO, one of the SROs, whereas a firm of accountants might be authorised by its institute, an RPB. For convenience, this guideline uses the term 'Regulator' to refer to the relevant regulatory body. However, certain functions under the Act remain the responsibility of the Secretary of State, regardless of which Regulator authorises the investment business.

4 Who may conduct investment business, and the manner in which he must conduct it, is governed by detailed rulebooks issued by the appropriate Regulator. Compliance with the rulebooks is monitored in four principal ways:

- through internal monitoring by the authorised business of compliance with the financial and other regulations and by the authorised business informing its Regulator when it becomes aware that it has breached certain of the rules;
- through the requirement that management of an authorised business submits regular

financial returns to its Regulator;

- through powers given to the Regulators to monitor and inspect the businesses being regulated; and
- by requiring the auditors to make certain reports.

5 The rules require the auditor to confirm to the Regulator that he has obtained such information and explanations and carried out such work as is necessary to enable him to report annually to the Regulator on the authorised business's compliance with certain financial rules and regulations. The precise reporting requirements vary from Regulator to Regulator, and more restricted or extensive reports may be required. In general terms, however, these reports cover:

- the authorised business's annual financial statements and accounting records;
- the authorised business's statement of financial resources; and
- the adequacy of the authorised business's system of control over its clients' money and other property throughout the period under review and compliance with the respective rules at a point in time (normally the balance sheet date).

6 In the course of performing the work necessary to discharge these routine reporting responsibilities or in carrying out his other auditing functions, the auditor may become aware of matters which he considers need to be brought to the Regulator's attention, other than through the medium of the routine formal report (an '*ad hoc* report').

7 This guideline is concerned only with *ad hoc* communications between auditors and Regulators:

- by auditors to Regulators under Section 109; and
- by Regulators to auditors under Section 180(1)(q), or the corresponding regulations in the SROs' or RPBs' rulebooks.

It does not cover the auditor's approach to the audit of an authorised business or his routine reporting responsibilities.

8 The auditor should bear in mind that certain expressions used in the Act and in a Regulator's rules may be matters for legal interpretation. There may, therefore, be circumstances in which, notwithstanding the guidance given in this Auditing Guideline, an auditor will wish to take legal advice.

Communications by the auditor

9 Section 109(1) of the Act provides that:

> "No duty to which an auditor of an authorised person may be subject shall be regarded as contravened by reason of his communicating in good faith to the Secretary of State, whether or not in response to a request from him, any information or opinion on a matter of which the auditor has become aware in his capacity as auditor of that person and which is relevant to any functions of the Secretary of State under this Act."

SIB is the designated agency of the Secretary of State for most purposes of the Act and the auditor would communicate with SIB or the Secretary of State under this section. However, the auditor would normally communicate with an SRO or RPB under Section 109(5) as described below.

10 Section 109 (5) of the Act provides that Section 109 applies to:

"(a) the communication by an auditor to a recognised self-regulating organisation or recognised professional body of matters relevant to its function of determining whether a person is a fit and proper person to carry on investment business; and

(b) the communication to such an organisation or body or any other authority or person of matters relevant to its or his function of determining whether a person is complying with the rules applicable to his conduct of investment business."

Under this sub-section, the auditor can communicate with the relevant SRO or RPB on the matters specified in Section 109(5).

11 Section 109 does not lay down any rules nor does it specify the circumstances in which the auditor is to communicate any matter to the Regulator. Rather, it provides for these matters to be governed by professional bodies, with a reserve power vested in the Secretary of State to make relevant rules which he may exercise if he considers that the auditor of an authorised business is not subject to satisfactory rules or guidance on Section 109 issued by the auditor's professional body.

12 This guideline contains guidance on the circumstances in which matters should be brought to the attention of the Regulator. In interpreting this guidance, the auditor should bear in mind the fundamental objectives of the legislation, to which reference is made in Section 109(5). These are to ensure that the Regulator is able to fulfil his function of determining whether a person carrying out investment business is a 'fit and proper person' to do so, and that he is complying with the rules applicable to his conduct of investment business.

13 Confidentiality is an implied term of an auditor's contract with his client, but in certain circumstances such as under Section 109 it does not prevail, since he is entitled to communicate information or opinions on a matter relating to the business or affairs of the authorised business relevant to the Regulator's functions under the Act without the duty of confidentiality owed to the client being regarded as having been contravened.

14 The matters which may be communicated under Section 109 depend on the functions of the individual Regulator under the Act. Any matters relevant to any of its functions under the Act may be communicated to SIB. The information which may be communicated to an SRO or RPB is restricted by Section 109(5) to that which relates to whether the authorised business is 'fit and proper' and whether the regulated business is complying with the SRO's or RPB's rules applicable to the conduct of investment business.

15 In most cases information will be communicated to the authorised business's own Regulator but there may be occasions where the auditor will need to pass information to another Regulator. This may be because the information is relevant to SIB's or the Secretary of State's functions under the Act (which are wider than the SROs' and RPBs' functions) and is passed to SIB or the Secretary of State under Section 109(1). It may also be because the information does not relate to the authorised business being audited and is being communicated under the provision of Section 109(3) to SIB, the Secretary of State, one of the SROs or RPBs as appropriate (see paragraph 21).

16 Matters which may be reported are not restricted to problems of solvency, or other financial requirements, but include evidence of dishonesty or serious incompetence (which would preclude the authorised person from satisfying the 'fit and proper' test), and material failure to observe the rules or regulations applicable to conduct of investment business.

17 Clearly the potential scope of matters which may be reported is very wide, but as explained in paragraph 22 this does not, of itself, require the auditor to extend the scope of his work in order to discover matters that may be reportable.

18 The auditor is able to communicate with the Regulator by way of:

- a formal report;
- a meeting; or

- by any other means,

on any matters of which he becomes aware in his capacity as the authorised business's auditor and which are relevant to the Regulator's function under the Act. Full notes or minutes of any conversations or meetings with the Regulator on the subject should be made.

19 This communication can be made either on the auditor's initiative or in response to a request from the Regulator for information. The auditor should co-operate with the Regulator and respond to any requests from the Regulator for information, provided he has no reason to doubt that the request is relevant to the Regulator's function under the Act. The auditor may communicate a matter to the Regulator with the protection of Section 109 regardless of the source of that information, provided he became aware of the matter in his capacity as auditor of the authorised business and he does so in good faith.

20 Matters of which the auditor becomes aware 'in his capacity as auditor' may not be restricted to those matters identified during the course of the audit work by the auditor and the audit staff. A matter which is relevant to the functions of the Regulator and which is identified during the course of work for the authorised business by another partner (or member of staff) such as a management consultant or tax partner may be deemed to be known to the auditor (see also paragraph 23). However, any matters identified during work performed for another client which is *not* an authorised business cannot be communicated to the Regulator with the protection of Section 109, even though the matters identified may relate to an authorised business.

21 Section 109(3) provides:

> "The matters to be communicated ... include matters relating to persons other than the authorised person".

Thus, the right to communicate matters to a Regulator is not restricted to information obtained by the auditor about his client, the authorised business, but could include, for example, information obtained in his capacity as auditor of the authorised business concerning another person who is (say) a customer of the authorised business. The other person need not be an authorised business. This right is always subject to the overriding requirement that the information has come to the auditor's attention in his capacity as the auditor of the authorised business and that it is relevant to the functions of the Regulator under the Act as provided in Sections 109(1) or 109(5).

22 The auditor cannot be expected to be aware of all circumstances which, had he known of them, would have led him to exercise his right to report under Section 109. That section does not require the auditor to change the scope of his audit or other work for the authorised business, nor the frequency or timing of his visits. The auditor has no obligation to seek out grounds for making a report under Section 109; the section does not place an obligation on the auditor to conduct his work in such a way that there is reasonable certainty that he will discover a notifiable matter. It is only when the auditor does become aware in the ordinary course of this work of such a matter, or of circumstances which suggest the existence of such a matter, that he should make detailed enquiries with Section 109 specifically in mind.

23 The auditor should ensure that he is made aware of any other engagement which may exist between any department of his firm and the authorised business and of any information which another department of his firm has obtained pursuant to that engagement, if these matters are relevant to his work as an auditor. It would therefore be prudent for the audit firm to establish adequate systems of inter-departmental and inter-office communication to ensure any matters which are relevant to the audit work and may give rise to a report under Section 109 are brought to the attention of the auditor. For example, if the management consultancy arm of a firm is employed to advise on accounting systems because there has been a material breakdown, this may give rise to a report under Section 109.

24 The auditor should also ensure that:

(a) all staff responsible for authorised business engagements are aware of the provisions of Section 109 and the contents of this guideline, and are able to identify situations in which they might apply; and

(b) satisfactory procedures exist to ensure that any information, which may be the subject of an *ad hoc* report, obtained by staff in the course of their work, is passed on to the partner responsible without delay.

25 Although SIB and the SROs expect an authorised business to advise its auditor when it appoints a third party (including another department of the same firm) to review, investigate or report on any aspects of its records and systems and to provide the auditor with copies of reports by such a third party promptly after their receipt, the auditor should still ensure that his own procedures address this point (see paragraph 23).

26 The auditor should realise that Section 109 will not provide protection where he could be held to have acted maliciously or in bad faith or if the information reported is outside the scope of the section. The Act does not, therefore, provide complete immunity from all types of legal action by all parties affected, or subsequently affected, by his action in reporting to the Regulator.

27 An auditor is protected, however, even if the information which he communicates falls short of proof, or the opinion which he communicates cannot be verified. An auditor who can demonstrate that he has acted reasonably and in good faith in informing the Regulators of a reportable matter which he thinks has occurred would not be held in breach of duty to his client even if, after an investigation, it were found there was not a matter which needed to be reported. These are areas where the auditor may wish to consider taking legal advice before making a report.

28 Whilst no breach of statutory duty might arise, it should be appreciated that there is no protection given by the Act if the auditor, after becoming aware of an occurrence, fails to report, promptly, or at all, to the Regulator. Furthermore, auditors should recognise that speed of reporting is likely to be important in order to protect the interests of investors.

Ad hoc reports

29 Investments in financial markets carry inherent risks. It is not the purpose of the Act, nor the duty of the auditor, to protect the investor from the normal risks of investments which are appropriate for him. The auditor should, however, take the initiative and ensure that an *ad hoc* report under Section 109 is made to the Regulator by either the authorised business or himself if he considers investors have incurred, or are at significant risk of incurring, a material loss as a result of persons regulated under the Act carrying on business in a manner that is not fit and proper or that is in breach of the regulations.

30 This can be more fully explained as follows:

(a) there must be a significant adverse occurrence or a change in the auditor's perception of an existing situation, that may include an adverse change in the circumstances of the business; and

(b) the situation described in (a) above has:

(i) given rise to or has indicated that a reasonable probability exists that it may give rise to:

- a material financial loss to the business; or
- loss of control over the assets or records; or

(ii) indicated that there is evidence of:

- dishonesty or serious incompetence; or
- serious failure to observe rules or regulations for the conduct of the regulated business; and

(c) the position is such that because of a significant risk which is material to the collective interests of investors, the investors' interests would be better safeguarded if the Regulator were aware of the position, even if only to organise protective action.

One measure by which materiality of a loss or potential loss may be judged is by reference to the relevant financial resource rules. The authorised business's ability to continue trading will depend on its ability to make good any losses which might have been incurred and still meet the financial resources requirement.

31 The auditor should bear in mind that his decision may have to stand up to examination at a future date on the basis of the following considerations:

- what he knew at the time;
- what he should have known in the course of his audit;
- what he should have concluded; and
- what he should have done.

Reporting via the authorised business

32 Where the auditor becomes aware of a matter which, in his professional judgement, he considers ought to be reported to the Regulator, he should consider the facts and, unless inappropriate in the circumstances (described in paragraph 35), discuss the matter with the management of the authorised business.

33 It is important for the auditor to act in a manner that will respect his professional relationship with his client. Normally, therefore, the auditor should ask the authorised business to draw matters about which he is concerned to the attention of the Regulator. Examples of the circumstances encountered in which the situation set out in paragraphs 29 and 30 may be met are:

(a) the auditor discovers a failure by the authorised business to comply with the relevant rules laid down by the Regulators which may have material consequences (e.g. accounting records not kept in accordance with the clients' money rules);

(b) it has come to the attention of the auditor that the procedures, records or systems fail significantly to comply with, or to demonstrate compliance with, conduct of business requirements to which the authorised business is subject;

(c) the auditor forms the opinion that there has been breakdown or a failure of the accounting or the internal control systems which may have material consequences;

(d) the auditor forms the opinion that management has reported financial information to the Regulator which is misleading in a material respect, or becomes aware that management has failed or does not intend to report something (e.g. as required by the Financial Notification Regulations) and the failure to report is, or would be, materially misleading;

(e) there is an extreme situation, such as evidence of imminent financial collapse, and it is obvious that the Regulator must be informed.

34 Where the authorised business will not itself inform the Regulator of a matter, having been advised to do so by the auditor, or where it has not been done within the period of time specified, or where there is not adequate evidence that the client has properly reported the matter in question, the auditor should make such a report direct to the Regulator.

Reporting direct to the Regulator

35 In exceptional circumstances, where the auditor doubts whether management are fit and proper persons to carry on investment business and it would be in the interest of protecting investors that the management of the authorised business should not be informed in advance, the auditor should report direct to the Regulator. Examples of these circumstances are:

(a) where there has been an occurrence which causes the auditor no longer to have confidence in the integrity of the directors or senior management, e.g. where he believes that a fraud or other irregularity has been committed by the directors or senior management of the authorised business, or he has evidence of the intention of directors or senior management to commit such a fraud or other irregularity;

(b) where there has been an occurrence which causes the auditor no longer to have confidence that the directors or senior management will conduct the business of the authorised business in a prudent manner so as to protect the interests of investors, e.g. where he has discovered that the directors or senior management are acting in an irresponsible or reckless manner with respect to the affairs of the business or its clients, or he has evidence of their inclination so to act.

36 The auditor should also report direct to the Regulator when speed is of the essence and there may not be time to follow the reporting procedures outlined in paragraph 37 below. For example, when he becomes aware that the authorised business may be about to cease being authorised, whether as a result of its own action or that of its Regulator or otherwise, the auditor should consider the need to disclose to the appropriate Regulator any information in his possession relevant to the functions of the Regulator without delay. The fact of such impending cessation of authorisation may bring forward the desirability of disclosing matters to the Regulator, in order that he may take appropriate action while the business is still subject to the rules of the Regulator, particularly where such matters bear on the security of third party interests. It is also in the auditor's own interest to act before authorisation ceases whilst he has the benefit of the protection given by Section 109.

Reporting procedures

37 In normal circumstances, where an auditor concludes that an *ad hoc* report to the Regulator is necessary, he should adopt the following procedures, bearing in mind that speed may be of the essence:

(a) He should establish whether the matter has already been reported by the authorised business through the usual channels, and, if so, obtain from the authorised business a copy of the notification to the Regulator and a copy of the Regulator's written acknowledgement sufficient to establish that the matter has been properly reported.

(b) If the matter has not been reported to the Regulator, the auditor should consider whether it may be possible and sufficient to submit or accelerate his routine report.

(c) If the auditor decides that an *ad hoc* report is necessary, he should immediately discuss the matter with the directors or management and request them to inform the Regulator. He should follow this with a written request setting out his views and requesting the directors or management to inform the Regulator of the matter within a specified period of time sufficient for the authorised business to obtain advice but short enough to ensure that the risk of damage is limited. The auditor should then seek from the authorised business evidence of prompt notification to and acknowledgement from the Regulator sufficient to establish that the matter has been properly reported.

(d) If the directors or management of the authorised business have not informed the Regulator, and continue to refuse to inform the Regulator within the specified period of time, the auditor should discuss the matter with any non-executive directors or the audit committee. Alternatively, the auditor could inform the non-executive directors or audit committee in writing when he brings the matter to the attention of the executive directors. If the directors or management do not take necessary action, the auditor should report direct to the Regulator.

38 In exceptional circumstances, such as those outlined in paragraphs 35 and 36, it is not appropriate or practical for the auditor to inform, or discuss the matter with anyone connected with the authorised business, including non-executive directors or the audit committee. In these circumstances, the auditor should make an appropriate written or other report direct to the Regulator.

39 The auditor should note that making an *ad hoc* report alone may not discharge all his responsibilities. For example he should consider the implications of the matter giving rise to the *ad hoc* report for his opinion on the financial statements.

Communications by the Regulator

40 The Act also deals with communications by Regulators to auditors of authorised persons. Section 180(1)(q) permits the communication of information which is otherwise restricted under Section 179, to auditors of authorised persons for the purpose of enabling them to discharge their functions under the Act without the consent of the person from whom it is received or to whom it relates. Restricted information is defined in Section 179 as information obtained by a primary recipient (SIB or the Secretary of State in this case) for the purpose of discharging its functions under the Act. The SROs and RPBs are not listed as primary recipients, but there are corresponding regulations in their rulebooks. If SIB were to pass restricted information to one of them, the SRO or RPB would be bound by the provisions of Section 179 and would, therefore, need to use the provisions of Section 180(1)(q) to enable it to pass information to the auditor.

41 The Regulators have indicated that they will take the initiative in bringing a matter to the attention of an auditor of an authorised business, whether under the provisions of Section 180(1)(q) or corresponding provisions in the rulebooks, where they believe that it is of such importance that the auditor's knowledge of it could significantly affect the form of his audit report or the way in which he carries out his reporting responsibilities. The Regulators have also indicated that they will inform the auditor whether the authorised business's management has been informed of the matter and, if so, who has been advised.

42 If the auditor is not informed by the Regulator of any matter he is entitled to assume that the Regulator has no such information. Accordingly there is no need for the auditor to request the Regulator to confirm this. SIB and the SROs have stated that they will normally not respond to general enquiries from auditors seeking confirmation that there is no relevant information in connection with annual audits.

General business insurers in the United Kingdom

(Issued March 1991)

Preface

This guideline gives guidance on the special factors to be considered in the application of Auditing Standards to general business insurers in the United Kingdom. It is supplementary to, and should be read in conjunction with, Auditing Standards and related Auditing Guidelines.

The contents of this guideline have the approval of the Department of Trade and Industry. This guideline is based on the law in effect at 30 September 1990.

Introduction

1 Throughout this guideline, the term "insurer" refers to any company subject to the Companies Act 1985 ("the Companies Act") and authorised under the Insurance Companies Act 1982 ("the Insurance Act") to write general insurance or **reinsurance** business (i.e. basically non-life insurance) in the United Kingdom. This guideline does not attempt to deal with specific legislative features affecting insurance undertakings governed by other legislation such as friendly societies, or with Lloyd's syndicates. Technical insurance terms, printed in bold type where they first appear in the guideline, are defined in the Appendix.

2 Auditors of insurers have the following duties:

- to report to members on the financial statements in accordance with the requirements of Section 235 of and paragraph 28A of Schedule 9 to the Companies Act;
- to report on the returns to be deposited by the insurer with the Secretary of State for Trade and Industry in accordance with the requirements of Section 21 of the Insurance Act ("the DTI Return"); and
- to communicate with the Secretary of State for Trade and Industry in certain circumstances ("*ad hoc* reports") in accordance with Section 21A of the Insurance Act.

3 It is particularly important that auditors undertake audit engagements for insurers only after considering their own competence and the adequacy of their resources to carry out their duties (including relevant experience). In assessing their competence and resources, auditors should bear in mind the type and range of the insurer's activities and the nature of its systems. Auditors will, in particular, need to have a proper understanding of:

- the nature of insurance business, the characteristics of various classses of business, the structure of the insurance market and the various types of organisation within the market;
- the regulatory environment and in particular the accounting methods peculiar to insurance business, the accounting and audit requirements of the Companies Act applicable to insurers and the reporting and audit requirements of the Insurance Act; and

- the audit approach to key areas of general insurance business, in particular **claims provisions**, where the auditor may neeed to form an opinion on matters often involving substantial uncertainty.

4 These matters are addressed in this guideline. The guideline is not intended to be comprehensive but rather to give an indication of those areas peculiar to insurance business of which auditors need to be aware; it does not cover other areas, such as investments, except where these are peculiar to insurance, although they may be an important aspect of an insurer's operations. This guideline will not by itself be sufficient to provide all the detailed knowledge required of auditors of a general business insurer in all circumstances which might arise.

Background

General

5 Insurance takes a wide variety of forms but, in essence, transfers risk for a consideration.

Utmost good faith

6 In insurance contracts there is a far higher degree of obligation imposed on the parties than in most contracts, as the contract is based on mutual trust and utmost good faith (*uberrima fides*). This means that both parties, the insurer and the insured, have an obligation to disclose fully all relevant facts relating to the contract. In practice this means that both parties and, where appropriate, any intermediary but in particular the prospective insured (who alone will know all of the information relating to the risk which is necessary for the insurer to determine a fair premium) must disclose all relevant material information before the contract is agreed. The duty to disclose is onerous and may result in litigation. In the event of non-disclosure or misrepresentation of any material facts by one of the parties, the contract is voidable *ab initio* by the other party. If the breach was fraudulent, there may in addition be grounds for an action for damages.

Indemnity

7 The principle of indemnity applies to most general business insurance contracts. It requires that, as far as possible, the insurance should restore the insured to the same financial position as immediately before the loss. There are a number of exceptions (for example, new for old home contents policies). In addition, if the full value insured is inadequate and a partial loss occurs, the **claim** may be subject to "averaging". This means that the insurer will only meet a proportion of the claim equal to the ratio of the sum insured to the full value of the item insured.

Subrogation

8 If indemnity applies to a policy and the insured is able to make other recoveries (such as the salvage value) to reduce his loss, the insurer is entitled to the benefit of those recoveries; this principle is known as **"subrogation"**.

Industry structure

9 The principal types of organisation writing general business insurance in the United Kingdom, in certain cases as "composites" also writing life and other long-term insurance business, are:

- Proprietary companies
  Proprietary insurers are usually companies limited by shares where the members are investors (rather than policyholders).

- Mutuals
  A mutual insurer is usually a company limited by guarantee, its members being the policyholders.
- Branches of insurers incorporated overseas
- Lloyd's syndicates
  Lloyd's is an insurance market comprising individual underwriting members ("Names") grouped into syndicates.

Sources of business

10 The two basic sources of business are:

- Direct selling
  The insurer is in direct contact with the insured as a result of advertising, or direct mail, or a branch network, or a sales force employed by the insurer.
- Intermediaries
  Insurance intermediaries advise and assist the insured in arranging insurance. In addition to arranging insurance coverage, they frequently deal with claims and other matters in the administration of the insurance contracts which they place.

Other sources of business include participation in pools and reinsurance accepted

11 A pool, which is usually managed by a third party, is an administrative arrangement for the acceptance of risks on behalf of the members of the pool. The risks are shared in predetermined proportions between the insurers in the pool. A pool arrangement is often used either where the risks are individually too large to be borne by a single insurer, or in circumstances where the risks are complex and require a considerable, costly investment in expertise by an insurer before the risks can be assessed and an appropriate premium calculated.

Reinsurance

12 Insurers may transfer (or **"cede"**) a part of the risks assumed to another insurer; in this case, the direct insurer is referred to as the cedant and the accepting insurer as the reinsurer. The reinsurer may, in turn, transfer (or **"retrocede"**) a part of the risks assumed; in this case, the insurer retroceding the business is known as the "retrocessionaire". A reinsurance contract does not absolve the **ceding company** of any liability to the insured; reinsurance is a separate contract to which the original insured is not a party.

13 The purpose of reinsurance is to manage and spread risk; it is used in particular:

- to protect the capital base from a **catastrophe** or to prevent over-concentration of risks of a particular type or in a particular area;
- to reduce the risk of loss on any one contract, and so give flexibility to the underwriter to write risks which would otherwise be unacceptably large;
- to increase the volume of business written without increasing the capital base to an equivalent extent;
- to reduce the likelihood of wide variations in the overall underwriting result, comparing one year with another; and
- to obtain a wider spread of risk by way of reciprocal arrangements with other insurers.

14 There are two basic forms of reinsurance: proportional and non-proportional. In the case of a proportional reinsurance **treaty**, the premiums and claims are divided in agreed proportions between the ceding company and the reinsurer. Proportional reinsurance can take the form of quota share (which states the proportion of each risk that is to be reinsured) or surplus (which allows the ceding company more flexibility to retain within specified limits a part of the risk). In a non-proportional reinsurance arrangement, the premiums and claims are not shared in the same proportions by the reinsurer. There is a variety of forms of non-proportional reinsurance of which "excess-of-loss" (including **"stop-loss"**) is the most common. Under an **excess-of-loss** treaty the reinsurer, in consideration for a premium, undertakes to pay all claims in excess of a specified amount (called a **"retention"**), usually up to a maximum amount.

15 There are two methods of reinsurance: **facultative** and **treaty**. With the facultative method of reinsurance, each risk to be reinsured is offered to the reinsurer who accepts or rejects it individually. Under the treaty method of reinsurance, an agreement is entered into between the ceding company and the reinsurer whereby all risks written by the ceding company that fall within the terms and limits of the treaty will be reinsured with the reinsurer automatically. The limits and terms of the treaty can be, for example, monetary, geographic or class of business.

Legislation

Insurance Companies Act 1982

16 The principal legislation governing the conduct of insurance business is the Insurance Act and the related regulations, in particular the Insurance Companies Regulations 1981 and the Insurance Companies (Accounts and Statements) Regulations 1983. The Insurance Act gives wide-ranging supervisory powers to the Department of Trade and Industry ("DTI") in respect of:

- authorisation;
- monitoring; and
- intervention.

No person may carry on any insurance business in the United Kingdom unless authorised to do so under Section 3 or 4 of the Insurance Act (except where the insurance business is carried on by a member of Lloyd's, by a registered friendly society or by a trade union or employers' association providing provident benefits or strike benefits only). Authorisation may be obtained only after submitting satisfactory information as to the manner in which business is proposed to be carried on and such other particulars required by regulation. Authorisation is given for specified classes of business.

17 In order to assist the DTI in monitoring insurers, the Insurance Act requires that every insurer shall prepare and submit to the DTI a return for each financial year. The form and content of this return is specified by regulation and, in respect of general business, must include:

- a statement of assets;
- a statement of liabilities;
- a calculation of the required minimum margin of solvency;
- a statement of solvency showing the excess or deficiency of net assets over the required minimum margin of solvency;
- revenue accounts and certain additional information;
- a statement of other income and expenditure; and
- a summary of reinsurance business accepted and ceded, and information on major cedants and reinsurers.

18 The regulations contain requirements concerning *inter alia*:

- the matching of assets and liabilities;
- the localisation of assets;
- the admissibility of assets;
- the basis of valuation of assets; and
- the calculation of the minimum margin of solvency.

The basis of admissibility and valuation of assets for the purposes of the returns is conservative; the regulations seek to put the assets on to a realisation basis (but there is no attempt to put the net assets on to a full liquidation basis which would involve provision for all costs of winding up the business).

19 Where no detailed regulations concerning liabilities have been issued, the amounts at which liabilities are to be stated are in accordance with regulation 52 of the Insurance Companies Regulations 1981, namely "in accordance with generally accepted accounting concepts, bases and policies or other generally accepted methods appropriate for insurance companies".

20 The DTI Return must be accompanied by a directors' certificate and an auditor's report in prescribed form; this is set out in Part I of Schedule 6 to the Insurance Companies (Accounts and Statements) Regulations 1983. The directors' certificate must, if such is the case, include statements that:

- for the purpose of preparing the DTI Return, proper accounts and records have been maintained and adequate information obtained by the insurer, and that an appropriate system of control has been established and maintained over transactions and records;
- the insurer is in compliance with the requirements for matching and localisation of assets specified by regulation;
- assets and liabilities have been valued in accordance with the relevant regulations; and
- if the insurer accounts for any of its business over a period longer than one year, that:
  - premiums and considerations have been retained in the fund subject only to discharging liabilities of that business and transfer of any profits after closing of the account at the end of the appropriate period; and
  - any shortfall in the fund has been made good.

The auditor's report on the DTI Return is required to state whether it is reasonable for the directors to have made these statements.

21 The DTI has considerable powers of intervention, including:

- control of the nature, location and custody of assets;
- restricting the volume of business to be written;
- requiring the submission of more frequent returns or specified information;
- withdrawal of authorisation; and
- the right to petition the Court to wind up the insurer.

Companies Act 1985

22 The statutory requirements relating to financial statements prepared for submission to members are set out in the Companies Act. Insurance companies are exempted from Schedule 4 and Schedule 4A to the Companies Act. Insurers are permitted (but not required) to prepare financial statements in accordance with the requirements of Schedule

9 (i.e. broadly in accordance with the previous requirements originally contained in the Companies Acts 1948 and 1967). However, if insurers do not draw up statements in accordance with Schedule 9, their financial statements must comply with the requirements of Schedule 4 and 4A.

23 Paragraph 28(1) of Schedule 9 to the Companies Act exempts insurers from certain disclosure requirements of the Schedule. The most important exemptions relate to disclosure of the amounts of, and movements in, provisions and reserves. Where insurers use the exemptions available to them, the statement of accounting policies would normally indicate that fact. Any heading in the financial statements which contains, or is affected by movements in, reserves must indicate that fact (but the amounts do not need to be quantified).

21 Whilst Section 255 of the Companies Act requires that the balance sheet and profit and loss account of an insurer give a true and fair view, paragraph 28(2) of Schedule 9 states that, for the purposes of the Companies Act, an insurer's financial statements shall not be deemed not to give a true and fair view by reason only of the fact that disclosure exemptions have been used.

25 Schedule 9 does not specify formats for financial statements; it does, however, require the financial statements to disclose specific information. In addition, many of the disclosure requirements imposed by other parts of the Companies Act that apply to the generality of companies also apply to insurers; for example, Schedule 5 (Miscellaneous matters to be dealt with in the notes), Schedule 6 (Details of loans and other transactions favouring directors and officers) and Schedule 7 (Matters to be dealt with in the Directors' Report).

26 The European Commission has proposed a directive on the financial statements of insurance undertakings. If this directive is adopted it will, in due course, be implemented by legislation in the United Kingdom and will replace existing provisions of the Companies Act applicable to the financial statements of insurers.

Accounting

27 An insurer's financial statements will usually include one or more underwriting revenue accounts which show the underwriting results for various classes of business; the items dealt with in revenue accounts are usually referred to as **"technical items"**. Historically, investment income and certain expenses have not been shown in the revenue account, but a number of insurers now allocate some of the investment return to revenue accounts; the total of the underwriting result and the allocated investment return is sometimes referred to as the "insurance result".

28 The underwriting revenue accounts may be drawn up on one of three accounting bases:

- the annual basis;
- the deferred annual basis; or
- the fund basis.

29 Under the annual basis of accounting, the incurred cost of claims and expenses is charged against the earned proportion of premiums written. The incurred cost of claims comprises paid claims adjusted by the net movement in provisions, including:

- paid claims to the extent not provided in prior years;
- the net change in provisions for outstanding claims including claims incurred but not reported (**"IBNR"**);

- related claims settlement expenses, and
- the net movement in provisions for unexpired risks and premium deficiencies (where appropriate).

Expenses are stated net of movements in **deferred acquisition costs**. Premiums written are adjusted by the net movement in **unearned premiums**. Income, claims and expenses for the accounting period are stated on an accruals basis. The underwriting result will therefore represent primarily that for the current **accident year** together with adjustments to premiums and claims provisions for previous accident years.

30 The deferred annual basis of accounting is of limited application, being principally restricted to proportional treaty reinsurance business assumed. The basic principle is that the determination of the underwriting results is deferred by one year, the most recent year being referred to as the **"open year"** and previous years as "closed years", by which time periodic accounts together with notification of the reinsurer's share of outstanding claims should have been received. At the balance sheet date, provisions will include:

- for the closed year, outstanding claims and unearned premiums (frequently computed as a fixed percentage of **written premiums**) for all treaties in force; and
- for the open year, the balance of premiums less paid claims and expenses for the open year to the extent to which this data has been notified.

Total provisions will need to be assessed to check that they are likely to be adequate to cover estimated outstanding liabilities and, if net losses are foreseen for the open treaty year, this should be recognised by increasing the balance carried forward.

31 Under the fund basis, notified premiums and claims are analysed by **underwriting year**. The result of each underwriting year is not determined until "closure", usually at the end of the third **development year** but, in the case of some insurers, the recognition of profit may be deferred until the fourth development year. The question of computing earned and unearned premiums does not arise under the fund basis. At the balance sheet date, the balance of the fund represents:

- the amount estimated to be required to meet all net outstanding liabilities for all closed underwriting years; and
- the balance of notified premiums less paid claims and expenses for the open underwriting years.

This balance may need to be increased if ultimate net losses are predicted for any of the open years. The underwriting result for the accounting period will therefore represent that attributable to the underwriting year being closed together with adjustments in reassessing previously closed years and for the recognition of any foreseeable losses for one or more open underwriting years.

32 Provisions under the deferred annual basis and the fund basis are often described in financial statements as "insurance funds".

33 Statements of Standard Accounting Practice ("SSAPs") apply to the financial statements of insurers except in so far as the requirements of SSAPs are overridden by the exemptions in Schedule 9 to the Companies Act. Insurers are therefore expected to comply with SSAPs except where disclosure exemptions have been utilised in their published financial statements.

34 The differences between insurance and other business activities, and the differences between particular classes of insurance, have resulted in a range of accounting policies and bases. In May 1990 the Association of British Insurers issued a Statement of

Recommended Practice (the "ABI Statement"), "franked" by the Accounting Standards Committee, in order to narrow the difference and variety in the accounting treatments. The purpose of the ABI Statement was to set out recommneded practice in four areas:

- premiums;
- claims;
- unexpired risks; and
- expenses (with special reterences to **acquisition costs**).

Auditing

Planning the audit

Introduction

35 The Auditing Standard "The auditor's operational standard" requires that "the auditor should adequately plan, control and record his work" and general guidance on these matters is given in the Auditing Guideline "Planning, controlling and recording". Given the importance of computer processing within many insurers, the guidance in the Auditing Guideline "Auditing in a computer environment" is likely to be of particular relevance to the auditor. Reference should also be made to the sections in the Auditing Guideline "Internal controls" on management responsibility and limitations on the effectiveness of internal controls. The following paragraphs deal only with particular aspects of general insurance business that are likely to need consideration by the auditor.

36 The auditor should bear in mind throughout the planning and conduct of the audit of the financial statements that the information contained in the DTI Return is also subject to audit. Accordingly the auditor should plan to integrate his work for the purpose of reporting on the financial statements in accordance with the Companies Act with that for the purpose of reporting on the DTI Return.

Understanding the business

37 In order to identify the critical audit areas and plan the audit work adequately, the auditor needs to understand the particular features and characteristics of the insurer's business and the environment in which the insurer operates. The relevant background may include, *inter alia*:

- the classes of insurance written, the nature of the risks and the policy terms;
- the market in which the insurer operates and the methods by which business is transacted;
- the nature of, and changes in, the legal environment in which the risk resides;
- the reinsurance arrangements, including the terms on which reinsurance has been ceded and the overall effect of the reinsurance programme;
- changes from previous periods in underwriting practices, agency arrangements, reinsurance arrangements and claims settlement procedures; and
- the composition of the investment portfolio and its suitability having regard to the nature of the business in force.

38 Conditions affecting the market generally will also need to be considered, for example:

- changes in market capacity and any consequential effect on premium rates;
- matters likely to affect claims **experience** in the classes or business written; and
- investment conditions.

Organisational structure and accounting information

39 Procedures of accounting significance may be carried out at several locations, such as:

- acceptance of risk;
- recording of policy details; and
- investigation, evaluation and payment of claims.

In such circumstances the auditor will need to consider the extent to which common systems and controls are in operation.

40 An insurer may delegate underwriting authority to an agent who will accept business on its behalf and submit accounts or statements periodically. Considerations affecting the audit approach to this situation are set out in paragraphs 54 and 55 below.

Systems and internal controls

41 The administration of insurance business depends on the accurate collation, processing and storing of large volumes of data for the purposes of:

- policy records;
- claims records;
- underwriting statistics; and
- accounting.

42 The directors of an insurer are required to give a certificate on the DTI Return that, for the purpose of preparing the return, an appropriate system of control has been established and maintained by the company over its transactions and records. Furthermore, as indicated in paragraph 20, the auditor is required to report whether, in his opinion, it was reasonable for the directors to make such a statement. The audit work will therefore need to be planned not only to assess the reliance to be placed on controls in determining the work necessary to express an opinion on the financial statements but also to enable the auditor to form an opinion on the system of control for the purposes of forming an opinion on the matters contained in the directors' certificate on the DTI Return. In order to do this, a preliminary assessment of the control environment should be made at the planning stage.

43 Most insurers place considerable reliance on computerised systems and the insurance industry is making increasing use of on-line and distributed systems; data may be directly input or amended through remote terminals by the insurer's own staff or, in some cases, by intermediaries. Computer systems may not provide a visible audit trail, particularly for detailed analyses. The audit of the controls over the computer system and the use of computer assisted audit techniques may be the only practicable means of checking the aggregation of data or calculations performed by computer (such as the provision for unearned premiums). The use of such software will need to be planned before the audit commences to give sufficient time for program development or amendment.

44 The auditor will be concerned not only with the accurate derivation of amounts shown in the financial statements but also with the accuracy and consistency of:

- detailed analyses of premiums and claims by classes of business, risk groups and currency for the purposes of the DTI Return; and
- statistics used in the evaluation of provisions for outstanding claims.

Technical provisions

45 For most insurers, the estimation of provisions for outstanding claims and other

technical provisions is crtitical, not only because it is likely to have a material effect upon results and net assets, but also because it is an area of considerable uncertainty and frequently involves a high degree of judgement. A small change in the aggregrate amount of provisions is likely to have a sugnificant effect on the results and net assets of an insurer. Considerations affecting the audit approach in this area are set out in paragraphs 73 to 77 below.

46 In planning the audit approach to outstanding claims provisions, the auditor should consider whether a statistician or an actuary should be involved in the audit, and may wish to refer to the Auditing Guideline "Reliance on other specialists".

Reinsurance security

47 Where business is reinsured, the financial stability of the reinsurers and their ability to meet current and prosective liabilities may be of significance to the financial statements of the cedant, in that, in particular, provisions are frequently calculated after taking credit for anticipated reinsurance recoveries. This is therefore a vitally important aspect of the financial statements of insurers where there is significant reinsurance of risks assumed. Considerations affecting the audit approach to reinsurance ceded are set out in paragraph 64 and in relation to reinsurance recoveries in paragraphs 84 and 85.

Analytical review

48 Audit planning should include an analytical review of available financial information in order to assist in assessment of overall risk and identification of critical audit areas. This should include:

- a review of interim of management accounts; and
- comparisons of various operating and other ratios with like periods in previous years.

A considerable number of ratios and performance indicators are commonly used in the insurance industry and the following will generally be useful in reviewing the financial statements of an insurer:

- the ratio of claims incurred to **earned premiums** (the claims ratio) which, subject to an allowance for expenses, is an indicator of actual experience compared with that anticipated at the time of underwriting;
- the ratio of expenses (including commissions) to written premiums (the **expense ratio**) which is an indicator of expense levels in relation to the volume of business;
- the sum of these two ratios (the **combined ratio**) is an approximate indicator of underwriting profitability before taking account of the investment return;
- the ratio of unearned premiums to written premiums, which should be reasonably stable if the level of business is stable;
- commissions incurred to written premiums which may highlight changes in the commission structure or business mix;
- claims outstanding to claims paid where a change in the ratio may indicate changing settlement patterns or a change in business mix;
- claims outstanding to shareholders' funds which indicates reserves available to cover adverse deviations on claims provisions;
- the **solvency ratio**, the ratio of net assets to annual written premiums, is an indicator of the margin available to meet various contingencies, in particular adverse movements in investment values and unexpectedly severe claims experience; and
- investment yield — a significant change in income from invested funds may indicate,

for example, a shift in investment philosophy towards higher risk investment.

The premium cycle

49 The premium cycle includes the following phases:

- underwriting;
- policy issue;
- premium billing and collection;
- commissions; and
- reinsurance.

Audit objectives

50 The audit objectives for the premium cycle may be summarised as being to check that:

- appropriate controls exist over undewriting and issue of policies;
- the insurer accounts for all premiums to which it is entitled and for all return premiums for which it is liable;
- all commissions payable and receivable are properly recorded;
- all risks over specified retention limits are reinsured with approved reinsurers; and
- reinsurance premiums payable are properly recorded and reported to reinsurers.

51 The audit objectives for premium recognition and reporting may be summarised as being to check that:

- premium revenue is recognised only to the extent that the period of risk has expired (see paragraph 90);
- commissions and other acquisition expenses are deferred only to the extent that they can be fully recovered against future earnings from the business acquired (see paragraph 97); and
- disclosures relating to premiums are properly made in the financial statements.

Underwriting

52 The insurer should have documented procedures to ensure that all risks are underwritten at the appropriate level of authority. These procedures, which the auditor should review, should embrace:

- particulars of all risks which may be underwritten;
- the maximum cover (before and after reinsurance);
- risks and extent of cover which can be delegated (e.g. by way of binding authorities);
- concentrations of risk and aggregate exposures;
- the risks and extent of cover which may be ceded and details of approved reinsurers;
- the checking and approval of rate books and amendments thereto by the underwriters;
- the controls to ensure that correct rates have been applied to the risks underwritten including, where appropriate, controls over any computerised rate book;
- the controls over the checking of the proposal form, cover notes and other documents and the issue of policy documents and all amendments thereto;
- the controls which ensure that no policy is sent out until the risk has been underwritten;
- procedures governing the issue of renewal notices;
- the controls to ensure that reinsurance cover is obtained in accordance with the

insurer's guidelines; and

- the controls exercised by senior management to ensure that underwriting guidelines are being followed.

53 Insurers may delegate authority for underwriting and for claims settlement by:

- issuing specific authority to an underwriting agent or to an intermediary; or
- participation in a pool.

This delegation reduces the insurer's control not only over the transactions themselves but also over the recording of them. The auditor will therefore need to review the arrangements for the delegation of authority for underwriting and/or claims settlement to ascertain the controls which the insurer exercises over the delegated activities and the reporting procedures for them. The auditor will need to consider, in particular, the extent to which reliance can be placed upon:

- third party confirmations; and
- the work of other auditors.

Intermediaries

54 Business should be accepted only from intermediaries approved in accordance with the specified guidelines of the insurer. The insurer should have procedures to ensure that its requirements have been met before business is accepted from an intermediary.

55 Audit tests in relation to facilities granted to intermediaries should, in general, cover a review of:

- authorisation of delegated authority including the use of cover notes;
- the insurer's risk monitoring procedures;
- accounting for contracts written and control over the receipt of premiums; and
- accounting for claims and control of the payment of claims.

Document control

56 Documents which provide evidence of insurance cover should be pre-numbered and the insurer should maintain numerical records of the documents issued and details of the recipient. It is important that forms should only be available to authorised employees of the insurer or to authorised intermediaries. In either case, the insurer should have proper procedures over the control and use of such forms, and the auditor should test these procedures.

Recording of premiums

57 The auditor should test the insurer's procedures for ensuring that new business has been accurately recorded and should test that individual agents' accounts are reconciled to the control account.

58 For certain types of business, notably **London Market** business, there may be a considerable delay between signing the **slip** (or otherwise underwriting the risk) and being notified of the premiums due. In these circumstances, it is important that the insurer should have procedures for estimating premiums in respect of business written, and the auditor will need to consider the degree of certainty attaching to the insurer's estimates of premiums and the extent to which the premiums should be recognised prior to receipt.

59 The auditor needs to be satisfied that premium income is not significantly overstated as a result of the inclusion of **pre-debited** income (i.e. premiums charged in anticipation that the policyholder will renew the policy). The auditor should consider in particular:

- the nature and extent of pre-debiting, and
- recent lapse rates and the effect which they are likely to have on premium income.

60 It is often not possible at the inception of a policy to determine the premium exactly. In these cases, a **deposit premium** (often an estimate of the expected premium or related to the premium for the previous year) will be charged with any balance due being charged retrospectively.

61 The auditor should consider the extent to which policies are subject to reprospective premium adjustment. It may be appropriate to recognise the additional premium where sufficient evidence exists to support the amount due.

62 Reliable statistical data on historical premium and claims notification and settlement are essential for the establishment of appropriate unrecorded premium and claims provisions and for the purposes of the DTI Return. These statistics are organised into the groupings best suited to the nature of the insurer's portfolio of risks and may include groupings by class of business and currency. The auditor will need to check the analysis of the coding of these items since reliance will be placed on the aggregated statistical data for the calculation of claims provisions and for the purposes of the DTI Return.

Reinsurance assumed

63 Inwards reinsurance is derived either from treaty or facultative business. The insurer should maintain a record of all treaties and should ensure that it receives regular (typically quarterly) statements (or **"bordereaux"**) from the ceding company of premiums, commissions, claims, expenses and retentions. These are often received six or nine months in arrears, and consequently proportional inwards treaties are usually accounted for on a deferred annual basis. The auditor should be concerned particularly with the following in respect of inwards treaty business:

- treaties are underwritten at an appropriate level of authority and in accordance with the insurer's guidelines;
- controls exist to ensure that statements are received on a regular basis;
- statements are reviewed and checked before being entered into the accounting records; and
- treaty results are reviewed by senior management on a regular basis.

For facultative business, similar controls should exist except that each individual risk must be approved at an appropriate level of authority.

Reinsurance ceded

64 The auditor should, in particular, consider the following areas in respect of reinsurance ceded:

- the insurer has procedures for identifying, approving and monitoring reinsurers;
- the insurer has ceded business only to approved reinsurers;
- the insurer maintains an up-to-date record of all in-force policies by underwriting year;
- the risks and covers ceded are in accordance with the insurer's guidelines and the terms of the reinsurance contract;
- premiums, retentions, commissions and expenses are accounted for in accordance with the terms of each reinsurance contract;
- treaties have been authorised at an appropriate level of authority;
- statements are sent out in accordance with the requirements of the reinsurance

contract;

- details on the statements are in agreement with the insurer's records;
- the insurer has notified the reinsurer promptly where the contract requires such notification; and
- the insurer monitors the status of all treaties which are in the course of being negotiated.

Commissions

65 The auditor should consider the many, and sometimes complex, types of commission that the insurer will bear or receive. Normally these commissions are related to the amounts of the premiums and should be tested together with premiums. Additionally, the auditor should test those commissions that are based on aggregate premium volumes or on profits of certain business.

The claims cycle

66 The claims cycle includes the following phases:

- initial intimation of loss;
- recording of claim;
- estimation of the amount of claim settlement;
- admission and settlement of claim; and
- recovery in respect of salvage, subrogation and reinsurance.

Audit objectives

67 The audit objectives for the claims cycle may be summarised as being to check that:

- all claims are recorded as soon as they are notified;
- a preliminary estimate is made for the likely cost of every claim;
- claims data are accurately recorded;
- claims provisions are regularly reviewed;
- admission and settlement of claims is performed at the appropriate level of authority;
- claims provided in the period arise only from risks insured under policies validly issued by the insurer;
- claims provisions and settlements are supported by appropriate documentation;
- claims disbursements are strictly controlled; and
- all recoveries in respect of salvage and subrogation or from reinsurers are properly recorded and collected.

68 The audit objectives for claims recognition and reporting may be summarised as being to check that:

- claims provisions, including IBNR, are adequate (see paragraph 100);
- credit is taken only for reinsurance which is recoverable in respect of claim provisions including IBNR (see paragraph 100); and
- disclosures relating to claims are properly made in the financial statements.

Initial intimation of loss

69 The auditor should check that the insurer has procedures for ensuring that all claims or known losses are captured immediately by its systems, even where the amount of information available initially may be limited.

Recording of claims

70 Once intimation of a loss has been received, an initial assessment of the claim should be made and entered into the accounting records. The auditor should check that the insurer has procedures to ensure that:

- a valid policy was in force at the date of occurrence of the event;
- premiums have been paid on the policy; and
- *prima facie* the policy covered the event which resulted in the claim being made.

71 Audit procedures for the recording of claims should cover:

- the accuracy of claims data; and
- identification of all claims where an estimate of the loss is not available.

72 In order to produce statistical data, each claim is assigned a statistical code which identifies the class of business, the underwriting year and the accident year. The auditor will need to check the allocation of these codes since reliance will be placed on the aggregated statistical data for the calculation of claims provisions and the analyses for the purposes of the DTI Return.

Claims estimates

73 Claims estimates form the basis of the provision in the financial statements for known outstanding losses. It is often possible to make a reasonable initial estimate of the amount of a claim for certain types of business; however, for some classes of business, it may be difficult to provide an initial estimate of the amount of the claim, particularly for certain **long-tail** classes of business. These estimates may involve a high degree of judgement. Every claim should be supported by a file which includes all relevant correspondence, notes of meetings and, in the more complex cases, loss **adjusters'** reports, medical reports, legal opinions, etc. The insurer should have a procedure for ensuring that claims estimates are made at an appropriate level of authority. Because the estimation of claims provisions is often a matter of judgement, the auditor should compare past provisions with subsequent settlements to provide an indication of the accuracy of past estimates.

74 The auditor should check that procedures exist to ensure that outstanding claims are reviewed on a regular basis, and that claims provisions are updated when new information is received on a claim.

75 It is important for the auditor to test that claims cover the risks of all notified but unsettled claims and that all settled or invalid claims are excluded. Common problems are the failure to clear records when claims are settled and the failure to reduce or eliminate estimates when information is received which indicates a reduced liability or no liability.

76 The provisions should be based on the anticipated ultimate cost of settlemnt of claims and the claims provisions should make allowance for direct settlement costs (such as the fees of loss adjusters, lawyers and doctors), and may also make provision for indirect expenses.

77 Certain insurers discount their claims provisions to reflect the time value of money in relation to the funds available for investment pending the settlement of claims. Whether or not claims are discounted, the need to establish adequate gross provisions is the same; discounting is a separate issue. However, discounting of claims provisions requires careful consideration by an auditor, as there are no generally accepted accounting principles in the United Kingdom in this area (although the ABI Statement makes certain recommendations as regards discounting). It is clearly important therefore that financial statements should make clear any accounting policies adopted by insurers in relation to the discounting of claims provisions.

78 Audit procedures in respect of estimates for known outstanding claims should include a review of the following:

- the adequacy of the statistics maintained by the insurer for each class of business;
- the insurer's past record of establishing adequate claims provisions;
- the insurer's procedures for ensuring that claims are reviewed at an appropriate level of authority;
- the insurer's procedures for ensuring that claims provisions are reviewed on a regular basis;
- the reasonableness of claims provisions in the light of information contained in the claims files;
- the effect of inflation, currency fluctuation and other economic factors on claims costs;
- comparison of settlements and related provisions;
- correspondence and other documentation related to London Market business and reinsurance assumed;
- the level of reliance on particular reinsurers and the extent of exposure in the event of their failure;
- correct calculation of reinsurance recoveries; and
- the procedures for ensuring that there is full inclusion of claims.

Admission and settlement of claims

79 The admission and settlement of claims should be carefully controlled and the insurer should have various levels of authority relating to the size and nature of the claim. It may also be necessary to obtain the approval of reinsurers before a claim is either admitted or settled in accordance with any requirements of the particular reinsurance contracts.

80 Settlements are often paid directly to third parties rather than to the insured. It is particularly important, therefore, for the auditor to check that there is strong control over cash disbursements. It is also important to check that the claims provision is reduced or eliminated immediately a payment is made.

81 Audit procedures for claims payments should cover a review of procedures in respect of the following:

- the admission of the claim;
- ensuring that a valid policy is in force when the event occurs giving rise to the claim;
- the authorisation of settlements and controls over disbursements;
- obtaining reports from professional advisers or loss adjusters where appropriate;
- the release of claims provisions;
- the investigation of significant differences between claims payments and provisions; and
- controls over the accumulation of claims.

82 The auditor should consider the principal sources of business (e.g. direct business, intermediaries, participation in pools and reinsurance accepted) and the extent to which producers of business have authority for settling claims.

Salvage and subrogation

83 It is important that an insurer sets up claims provisions taking account of salvage and subrogation, and controls the subsequent collection of these funds when a claim is settled. The auditor will need to be satisfied that the amount recognised by the insurer in respect of salvage and subrogation recoveries is supported by appropriate documentation.

Reinsurance recoveries

84 The auditor will need to satisfy himself that reinsurance balances reflect recoveries in respect of settled claims in accordance with the terms of the reinsurance contracts. The audit approach to reinsurance ceded is set out in paragraph 64 and proper controls by the insurer should ensure that the amounts recoverable are properly calculated. However, the auditor will also need to be reasonably satisfied that the reinsurers are, and will be when amounts are due to be paid, in a position to discharge their obligations. The auditor should not seek to carry out his own review of reinsurers that is management's responsibility but rather he should check that the insurer itself has appropriate systems and procedures for this. Such procedures should include a regular review of all reinsurers (not merely those to whom business is currently ceded) and, in particular, obtaining and reviewing current information on the reinsurer on a regular basis. The auditor should review selected reinsurers for the purposes of assessing the nature and quality of the information obtained and the reasonableness of the review procedures and conclusions. The auditor should also review the spread of risk among reinsurers to identify any excessive reliance on or exposure to specific reinsurers.

85 The auditor should check that the insurer has controls over the accumulation of claims arising from particular events or during particular periods for excess-of-loss cover. The controls exercised by an insurer may include management review of exception reports of large claims and claims occurring on a given date or at the same location. The auditor will therefore need to test these controls.

Technical provisions

86 The relevance of the audit procedures described in this section will vary according to the type of business written, the basis of accounting which is adopted and the resulting provisions and funds, which generally comprise:

- unearned premiums;
- unexpired risks;
- claims outstanding;
  - notified;
  - incurred but not reported ("IBNR"); and
- funds:
  - open years;
  - closed years.

The following table illustrates some of the wide variety of business written, types of claim and likely bases of accounting which may be encountered:

Nature of business written	*Reported outstanding claims*	*Incurred but not reported claims (IBNR)*	*Likely accounting basis*
Direct **short-tail**	Case estimates/formula basis	Generally straightforward to evaluate on a formula or statistical basis	Annual
Proportional reinsurance	Dependent on notification from cedant for treaty as a whole. Often delayed	Estimates required in the absence of outstanding claim advices from cedants for each treaty in force	Deferred annual or fund basis
	No individual claim notification	Exposure to IBNRs may depend upon treaty wording. Statistical projections by underwriting/treaty year	
Non-proportional reinsurance	Long reporting delays; estimates may escalate. Statistical projections by underwriting year	Difficult to assess. Statistical projection	Fund basis

There are many other types of business, but claims on longer-tail business , including most forms of reinsurance, are generally more difficult to evaluate than other types of claims.

Risk factors

87 In planning the audit of technical provisions, the auditor should consider areas of special risk, including:

- any rapid growth in premium income, new lines of business and reliance upon new underwriters or new sources of business;
- the possibility of unrecorded premiums for classes where underwriting losses are expected;
- the degree and appropriateness of reliance upon reinsurers or retrocessionnaires, especially where high percentages of business written are ceded or retroceded and also any material changes in reinsurance protection (e.g. increased retentions);
- small populations or concentrations of risks written where claims frequency and severity are more likely to fluctuate;
- high exposure to lines of business which may be unprofitable and where claims experience has deteriorated, or is likely to do so;
- the degree of inherent uncertainty and difficulty in assessing the ultimate cost of claims, particularly where there is a significant IBNR element, because claims are not settled for many years and the assessment of liability is largely based upon statistical

projections where the range of possible outcomes is wide;

- the effect of domestic and overseas inflation and currency fluctuations; and
- business written in jurisdictions where jury awards, punitive damages, interest penalties or contingency fees are common.

Audit approach

88 The nature, extent and timing of audit procedures on technical provisions will be affected by:

- the degree of reliance which can be placed on the insurer's controls over claims processing (including controls over the receipt of post, claims advices, claims files, procedures for recording, investigating and evaluating report claims), the processing of premiums, the determination of reinsurance recoveries due and the maintenance of accurate statistical records (see paragraph 72 above);
- the nature of, and changes in:
  - business in force, and the mix of treaty and facultative, proportional and non-proportional (including excess-of-loss) reinsurance assumed, short and long-tailed business;
  - outwards reinsurance arrangements;
  - claims and premium processing procedures, computer systems, statistical reports and methods used for quantifying and assessing technical provisions (both gross and net of reinsurance); and
  - authorities given to third parties for settling claims;
- the adequacy of technical provisions at previous balance sheet dates;
- the nature and composition of technical provisions and the relative materiality of each class of business; and
- the extent to which the insurer's classification of business in force for management and financial reporting purposes is consistent with the accounting classes specified in the DTI Return.

89 The audit approach will comprise analytical review, overall evaluations and checks for reasonableness, statistical appraisals, reperformance of calculations and validation of estimates and substantive tests by reference to individual claims files and advices received from cedants, observations and enquiry. The emphasis of the work will tend to vary according to the particular circumstances and may be identified at the planning stage of the audit by means of an analytical review on the basis of interim financial information (e.g. substantive tests on case estimates for reported claims on direct business and statistically based projections for long-tail business, including reinsurance assumed).

Unearned premiums

90 The provision for unearned premiums is usually calculated by reference to the unexpired period of risk of the policies concerned, and premiums are therefore recognised as revenue evenly over the term of policies. However, in some instances this basis is not appropriate, for example policies where the cover provided declines on a predetermined basis over the term of the policy or where risks are seasonal in nature.

91 The auditor should ascertain the method used by the insurer to calculate unearned premiums and, in the light of his knowledge of the insurer's business, consider whether the method is appropriate. Unearned premiums are often calculated by computer, and the most efficient audit approach may be to test the controls over the computer program or to use audit software to check the calculations.

92 Analytical review may be useful in assessing the provision for unearned premiums; tests may include:

- reviewing unearned premiums in total and by class for unusual fluctuations from normal or expected levels; and
- reviewing the ratio of unearned premiums to written premiums.

93 Substantive tests should normally include tests:

- to check that unearned premiums are derived from a record of all premiums written and in force at the year end, and that inception dates and terms of policies are accurately recorded;
- of individual calculations of unearned premiums; and
- to check that proper account is taken of outwards reinsurance agreements.

94 Where the insurer assumes business through treaties or participation in pools or associations, the auditor should be satisfied that the reliability and timeliness of reports from ceding insurers or intermediaries is taken into account in the calculations.

Unexpired risks

95 The auditor should check that additional provision is made if there is evidence that the provision for unearned premiums may not be sufficient to cover acquisition costs, policy maintenance expenses, claims and claims settlement expenses attributable to the unexpired term of insurance policies. Such a provision is normally described as a provision for unexpired risks but sometimes as a provision for premium deficiencies.

96 The auditor should check that any provision for unexpired risks has been assessed separately for all significant classes of business written by an insurer.

Deferred acquisition costs

97 Policy acquisition costs are those costs which are primarily related to the acquisition of insurance business and which vary either directly (e.g. commissions) or indirectly (e.g. underwriting salaries) with such business. Where an insurer uses the annual basis of accounting, it is normally appropriate that such costs should be written off on the same basis as the related premium revenue is recognised. Where the annual basis of accounting is not used the acquisition costs incurred but which relate to future periods and which are recoverable may be carried forward. The auditor should ascertain the method used by the insurer to calculate deferred acquisition costs and, in the light of knowledge of the insurer's business, consider whether the method is acceptable and consistent with previous years and with the calculation of provisions for unearned premiums.

98 Analytical review may include reviewing:

- deferred acquisition costs in total and by line of business for unusual fluctuations from normal or expected levels;
- the ratio of deferred acquisition costs to unearned premiums and written premiums; and
- the ratio of commissions deferred to commissions incurred.

99 Substantive tests should normally include reviews to check that:

- only properly deferrable acquisition costs are included;
- expenses which are not directly related to the acquisition of business are excluded;
- commissions received on reinsurance outwards are offset against deferred acquisition

costs to the extent to which they relate to the recovery of acquisition costs;

- adequate provision has been made for unexpired risks where anticipated claims, claims settlement expenses and acquisition costs are expected to exceed the related premium income; and
- the detailed calculation of deferred acquisition costs is checked.

Outstanding claims (including IBNR)

100 The auditor should carry out an analytical review of the provisions for outstanding claims. In particular, the auditor should, where appropriate:

- confirm that statistical reports, claims development or run-off statements (e.g. by major class of business, underwriting/accident year, gross and net of reinsurance) for the periods reconcile with amounts processed in the financial records;
- review and test the basis for dealing with transactions in foreign currencies;
- obtain and review whatever relevant statistical information is available, and ascertain what steps management take with regard to this information. Obtain and review copies of any management assessments or reports (e.g. on adequacy of prior year provisions, projections of provisions needed, estimates of fully developed premium income and ultimate claims ratios of underwriting/accident year, statistical or actuarial reports);
- note the adequacy of outstanding claims and IBNR provisions made at previous year-ends in the light of subsequent development of such claims. Obtain explanations for any unsatisfactory trends in the development of such provisions and ascertain whether any corrective action has been taken. Examine also data on prior year claims development as published in the insurer's own DTI Returns;
- ascertain the extent to which savings/deficits on prior year provisions for reported claims are attributable in the aggregate to paid claims and revised estimates on remaining outstanding claims;
- consider overall reasonableness of the provision for IBNR claims having regard to:
  - — seasonal factors;
  - — the nature of, and changes in, the mix of business in force, outwards reinsurance arrangements, claims processing procedures and claims department organisation; and
  - — the average cost of incurred or paid claims when compared with the average cost per IBNR claim, as provided at the balance sheet date.
- review the relationship (both gross and net of reinsurance) of the following individual provisions, where relevant, as a percentage of written premiums in the light of corresponding percentages in previous years, subsequent claims development and changes in premium levels, rating and exposure:
  - — reported outstanding claims;
  - — IBNRs;
  - — total outstanding claims (i.e. aggregate of above);
  - — unearned premiums (gross or net of deferred acquisition costs);
  - — unexpired risks/premium deficiencies;
  - — total technical provisions (i.e. total of above); and
  - — total insurance funds (open and closed years).

- for business where individual claims are accounted, compare current and previous trends having regard to the following and obtain explanations for any unusual movements (e.g. by major class of business, by development year for each accident year, gross and net of reinsurance):
  - — the number and frequency of claims (including IBNR);
  - — the average cost of paid, outstanding and incurred claims;
  - — the number of claims settled at no cost; and
  - — reopened claims.
- for major lines of business and by minor currencies the auditor should review the pattern of development in subsequent financial years for each accident or underwriting year, noting percentage growth factors from year to year, of:
  - — paid claims (gross and net of reinsurance);
  - — paid and reported outstanding claims (gross and net of reinsurance);
  - — booked premiums (gross and net of reinsurance) which in some cases may be recorded net of commissions;
  - — paid claims ratios (i.e. paid claims as a percentage of earned (accident year) or fully developed (underwriting year) premiums; and
  - — projected ultimate claims ratios.
- obtain explanations for any unusual trends;
- consider whether provisions for estimated reinsurance recoveries may be overstated due to reinsurance protections not existing to the extent that they are taken into account;
- consider the provision made for outstanding liabilities (analysed appropriately by underwriting/accident year) in the light of past developments and form a judgement as to whether the provision is likely to be adequate in the light of past developments, and current and expected circumstances. The auditor should consider the respective merits of projections based upon paid claims and known incurred claims;
- review the following ratios and obtain explanations for any unusual trends:
  - — paid claims as a percentage of outstanding claims;
  - — paid claims as a percentage of incurred claims; and
  - — outstanding claims as a percentage of incurred claims.
- consider the following in relation to previous years and obtain explanations for unusual movements (e.g. of major class of business, by year):
  - — numbers of policies/treaties in force;
  - — average premium per policy;
  - — claims frequency per policy; and
  - — average incurred claim cost per policy.
- consider whether the results of the above reviews are reasonable by major reporting class and overall:
  - — when compared with similar information for previous years;
  - — in the light of known industry trends; and
  - — taking into account changes in the circumstances of the business, including:

    (i) changes in the rate of economic and social inflation, including trends in litigation awards, which may differ substantially from the rate of economic inflation (both may vary geographically and over time);

(ii) emergence of previously unrecognised claims that are not reflected in the statistics; and

(iii) statistics in a currency other than the currency of settlement which may be distorted by currency fluctuations; and

- examine and test, as appropriate, any separately computed provision for reopened claims and review the historical trend for reopened claims.

Claims settlement costs

101 Provisions should be made within outstanding claims and IBNR provisions for direct claims settlement costs, such as loss adjusters' fees, survey fees and legal costs. Such expenses are normally allocated to the related individual claims and would therefore be included in the cost of paid and incurred claims and in the statistics used to project IBNR requirements.

102 Additional provision should be made for direct claims settlement costs which cannot be readily attributed to individual claims, such as claims department overheads.

103 Substantive tests might include:

- confirming that the method of providing for indirect claims settlement expenses relating to reported outstanding and IBNR claims is appropriate and consistent with previous years;
- if provision is made on a formula basis (e.g. based on the ratio of actual paid indirect **claims expenses** to paid claims), reviewing the basis of the formula and checking the calculation of the provision; and
- checking that account has been taken of the fact that some of the indirect expenses will already have been incurred in respect of outstanding claims (e.g. claims department overheads) in setting provisions; a lower factor may therefore be applicable to reported outstanding claims than to IBNR claims.

Insurance funds

104 Classes of business which are long-tail or subject to considerable delays in notification of premiums and claims may be accounted for on a funded basis (but direct liability business, although it is long-tail business, has traditionally been accounted for on an annual basis).

105 Premiums, claims, commissions and related expenses are allocated to insurance funds for each class of business and underwriting year and no profit is taken until the year is closed, normally at the end of the third year of development. No separate provisions are made specifically for unearned premiums, outstanding claims, IBNR, deferred acquisition costs or unexpired risks. Instead, an assessment is made at the end of each open year as to whether the fund for that year is likely to be adequate to meet anticipated losses on the basis of available information; the method for doing so is similar to that adopted in assessing IBNR requirements and audit procedures will be similar. When the year is closed, a detailed assessment is made of the amount of the various outstanding items which is transferred to the next year.

106 The fund assessment may include a separate projection of the development of premium income relating to the relevant underwriting years. This should be reviewed using the same principles which apply to claims projections.

107 Insurance funds should be reviewed to identify any "cross-funding" that may have occurred whereby profits anticipated on one class of business or underwriting year are notionally applied to cover losses on other classes or other years of the same class elsewhere. The appropriateness of any cross-funding will require careful consideration by the auditor.

Insurance debtors and creditors

108 Insurance balances receivable from or payable to policyholders, intermediaries and other insurers are fundamentally no different from the debtors and creditors of any other business. Accordingly, the audit techniques that should be applied are in principle broadly similar. However, there are a number of accounting practices adopted by the insurance industry in respect of balances with intermediaries and agents which are dissimilar to those of other concerns. The following matters may require particular attention in auditing insurance balances:

(a) In many cases, particularly with London Market business, accounting by intermediaries to insurers is net and the brokers ledger is both a debtors and creditors ledger with both debit and cash entries. Reconciliation problems are therefore more likely to be encountered.

(b) In certain lines of business, where the amount of risk and hence the premium payable may depend on, for example, a declaration in relation to numbers of employees, stock levels etc., an insurance company may issue a provisional premium note in advance of receiving the declaration in an attempt to accelerate its cash flow. Intermediaries frequently do not recognise provisional premiums.

(c) The insurance contract may allow the policyholders extended credit (for example, the payment of an annual motor premium by monthly instalments). The insurer will treat the whole premium as written premium but only the amount due as a current receivable with the deferred premium being debited to another account.

(d) Under proportional reinsurance treaties, the ceding company is often allowed to retain temporarily a proportion of the cash due to the reinsurer in respect of his shares of the premiums and to set up premium reserves. The treaty normally stipulates when the ceding company has to release these retentions. Premium retentions represent a deferred receivable to the reinsurer whose accounting systems should be capable of changing them to a current receivable at the time stipulated under the treaty.

(e) Where an insurance company has given a delegated underwriting authority to an intermediary it is dependent on the intermediary for information about the risks written in its name and the related premiums and claims. This information is often not received on a timely basis.

(f) The London Market reinsures risks from all over the world. Between the original direct insurer of the risk and the London Market reinsurer there will often be a chain of other insurance companies and intermediaries. As a result information, and particularly cash, can take a considerable time to pass through this chain and reach London Market companies.

(g) Reinsurance intermediaries in the London Market account and settle on a "net" basis to reinsurers.

Reconciliation of accounts

109 In view of the problems and differences that may exist between the intermediary's account with the insurer and the insurer's account with the intermediary, it is imporant that the account should be regularly reconciled and that the insurer should follow up unreconciled items with the intermediary. The reconciliation may be difficult for a number of reasons including the following:

- the insurer may be unable to match the cash received from the intermediary against the open items on its own ledger. Such "unallocated cash" can reach significant amounts;
- closings received from the intermediary may have been queried by the insurer's technical department;
- some intermediaries only show on their statements items due for payment. Most insurance companies debit the intermediary at the inception of a policy even though the intermediary may be allowed several months' credit; and
- many intermediaries have separate regional subsidiaries or separate subsidiaries for specialist types of business, such as reinsurance of aviation. Unless the insurance company's accounting system recognises these distinctions, reconciliation will be very difficult to achieve.

110 Apart from checking that the amounts included in agents and intermediaries accounts are valid, a way of substantiating these balances is to perform a positive circularisation of a representative sample. In certain circumstances, individual transactions rather than the whole account may need to be confirmed.

111 If the response is poor alternative procedures will need to be performed. These are likely to include reviewing the following:

- age analysis;
- unmatched items and suspense accounts; and
- the agent/intermediary's past performance.

Amounts due from reinsurers

112 The auditor should ascertain whether the reinsurer agrees the balances and, if it agrees, consider whether it has the ability to pay the amount due. The auditor should review the insurer's files of reinsurers to ascertain whether bordereaux or notification of claims have been sent and whether individual claims or balances are disputed by the reinsurer. The auditor should also check that a valid policy was in force at the time of the occurrence of an event giving rise to the claim.

113 Credit reviews of reinsurers should be performed by management (see paragraph 84).

114 The traditional approach to the substantive testing of trading balances, particularly receivable balances, is to seek direct confirmation of those balances from the third parties. However, such confirmation of reinsurance balances may not be effective. The value of premium or claim ceded to a reinsurer is determined by the reinsured. Accordingly the reinsurer can confirm only that the account is unsettled at the confirmation date, not that it is the true amount receivable or payable. It may be necessary, therefore, to perform other substantive tests on items included in the balance by reference to the original insurance transactions, and the reinsurance arrangements relating to those transactions.

Reporting

Companies Act 1985

115 The auditor's responsibilities in relation to the financial statements of insurers under the Companies Act are the same as those for the generality of companies. However, where an insurer takes advantage of the disclosure exemptions, the auditor should report, in accordance with the requirements of paragraph 28A of Schedule 9, along the following lines:

AUDITORS' REPORT TO THE MEMBERS OF XYZ LIMITED

We have audited the financial statements on page 000 to 000 in accordance with Auditing Standards.

In our opinion, the financial statements have been properly prepared in accordance with the provisions of the Companies Act 1985 applicable to insurance companies.

Auditors

Date

Insurance Companies Act 1982

116 The auditor has the following responsibilities under Section 21 of the Insurance Act in relation to returns submitted to the DTI:

- to state whether, in his opinion, the parts of the return required to be audited have been properly prepared in accordance with the regulations; and
- to state whether, in his opinion and according to the information and explanations he has received:
  - — the directors' certificate has been properly prepared in accordance with the regulations; and
  - — it was reasonable for the persons giving the certificate to have made the statements therein.

As indicated in paragraph 20, the directors' certificate, on which the auditor is required to express a view, is required to state *inter alia* that, for the purposes of the DTI Return, "an appropriate system of control had been established and maintained by the company over its transactions and records"; the auditor is therefore required in effect to express a view on this statement

117 The auditor is also required by Section 21 to state, if such is the case, that:

- for the purposes of preparing the DTI Return, proper accounting records have not been maintained or proper returns have not been received from branches; and
- he has not obtained all the information and explanations necessary for the purposes of his report.

118 The form and content of the auditor's report is specified in Part III of Schedule 6 to The Insurance Companies (Accounts and Statements) Regulations 1983. The following form of report would usually be appropriate for an insurer which carries on only general insurance business:

AUDITORS' REPORT TO THE SECRETARY OF STATE FOR TRADE AND INDUSTRY PURSUANT TO REGULATION 27 OF THE INSURANCE COMPANIES (ACCOUNTS AND STATEMENTS) REGULATIONS 1983

We have examined forms [insert numbers of relevant forms actually included in the DTI Return] together with the information furnished pursuant to Regulations 17 and 19 of the Insurance Companies (Accounts and Statements) Regulations 1983 and the related notes on page 000.

In our opinion these forms together with the information furnished pursuant to Regulations 17 and 19 and the related notes have been properly prepared in accordance with the provisions of the Insurance Companies (Accounts and Statements) Regulations 1983. [See note]

In our opinion and according to the information and explanations we have received:

(i) the certificate on pages 000 and 000 annexed in accordance with Regulation 26(a) has been properly prepared in accordance with the Regulations; and

(ii) it was reasonable for the persons giving the certificate to have made the statements therein, but, in relation to the statements required by paragraph 2 of Part I of Schedule 6 to the Insurance Companies (Accounts and Statements) Regulations 1983 this opinion is given only to the extent that it applies to information required by Regulations 17 and 19.

Auditors

Date

Note: Where the requirements to furnish information have been modified by an Order issued by the Secretary of State, the words "as modified by an Order date [ ] issued by the Secretary of State" should be inserted at the end of this sentence. Such orders relate, for example, to dispensation from giving information which is commercially sensitive.

Qualifications

119 If the audit report on the financial statements is qualified, the auditor will need to consider the extent to which the report on the DTI Return can be issued, or how the Return should reflect this.

120 If a report has been issued to the DTI in the circumstances set out in paragraphs 121 to 139, the auditor will need to consider its effect upon the audit report on the financial statements and the report on the DTI Return.

Ad hoc reports under the Insurance Companies Act 1982

General considerations

121 Section 135 of the Financial Services Act 1986 inserted a new section, Section 21 A, into the Insurance Act which states that:

> "No duty to which an auditor of an insurance company to which this Part of this Act applies may be subject shall be regarded as contravened by reason of his communicating in good faith to the Secretary of State, whether or not in response to a request from him, any information or opinion on a matter of which the auditor has become aware in his capacity as auditor of that company and which is relevant to any functions of the Secretary of State under this Act".

It is this section which makes it clear that the auditor is able to communicate with the DTI by way of a formal report, at a meeting or by any other means on any matters relating to the insurer's affairs arising out of his appointment and which are relevant to any functions of the DTI under the Insurance Act.

122 The auditor of an insurer which is also an authorised investment business will, by virtue of Section 109 of the Financial Services Act, be able to disclose to the relevant supervisor matters relating to supervisory functions under the Financial Services Act as well as disclosing to the DTI matters relevant to its supervisory functions under the Insurance Act.

123 It is important to stress that the DTI expects that the management of the insurer will continue to be its primary source of information for regulatory purposes and that the normal reporting procedures will usually provide it with all the information it needs to carry out its responsibility under the Insurance Act.

Responsibility of the auditor

124 The ability to communicate matters to the DTI is not restricted to information obtained by the auditor about the insurer itself. Under Section 21A, an auditor may communicate any relevant matter about anything which has come to his attention in his capacity as the auditor of an authorised insurer and which is relevant to any functions of the Secretary of State under the Insurance Act. Thus, in his communications with the DTI, the auditor may address not only the affairs of the insurer but also, for example, information about ceding companies obtained in the course of his audit of the insurer. The Insurance Act does not give protection in relation to disclosure of information by the auditor otherwise than in his capacity as auditor of the insurer.

125 The auditor cannot be expected to be aware of all circumstances which would, had he known of them, have led him to exercise his right to report under Section 21A. That section does not require the auditor to change the scope of his audit work, nor the frequency or timing of his audit visits beyond that required to enable a report to be made on the return to the DTI under the Insurance Act and on the financial statements of the insurer under the Companies Act 1985. The auditor does not have an obligation to seek out grounds for making a report under Section 21A (i.e. the section does not place an obligation on the auditor to conduct his work in such a way that there is reasonable certainty that he will discover an occurrence of the kind described in paragraph 128). It is only when the auditor becomes aware in the ordinary course of his audit work of such an occurrence, that he should make detailed enquiries with Section 21A specifically in mind.

126 The auditor should, however, ensure that he is made aware of any other relationships which exist between any department of his firm and the insurer which could affect his work. As noted in paragraph 127, the Insurance Act does not give protection to the auditor if a matter is not reported to the DTI. The DTI expects that the auditor will ensure that he is informed of all potentially "reportable" matters by all other departments within his firm which have a relationship with the client insurer. It would, therefore, be prudent for such firms to establish adequate systems of inter-departmental communication to ensure all matters which may give rise to a report under Section 21A are brought to the attention of the appropriate auditor. However the DTI expects insurers to advise their auditor when they appoint a third party (including another department of the same firm) to review, investigate or report on any aspect of their records and systems and to provide him with copies of reports by such a third party promptly after their receipt.

127 The auditor should realise that there are circumstances in which Section 21A will not provide protection, for example, where he could be held to have acted maliciously or in bad faith. Section 21A does not, therefore, provide complete immunity from all types of legal action by all parties affected, or subsequently affected, by his action in reporting. The auditor may, therefore, wish to consider taking legal or other professional advice from an appropriately qualified source before making the decision whether, or in what manner, to report. However, it should be borne in mind that speed of reporting may well be important in order to protect the interests of existing and prospective policyholders. There is no protection given by Section 21A if the auditor fails to report to the DTI.

Taking the initiative

128 The profession has developed a criterion for use by the auditor in deciding whether to take the initiative in making an *ad hoc* report in addition to his regular reporting responsibilities. The criterion is that the auditor should take the initiative when he considers it expedient to do so in order to protect the interests of policyholders. This criterion can be more fully explained as follows:

- there must be an adverse occurrence, or a change in the auditor's perception of an existing situation, which may include an adverse change in the circumstances of the insurer; and
- the position described above has given rise to a material loss or indicates that a reasonable probability exists that a material loss may arise; and
- the position is such that the interests of existing and prospective policyholders might be better safeguarded if the DTI were aware of it.

129 As stated in paragraph 125, the auditor is not required to seek out grounds for making a report. It is only where he becomes aware during the ordinary course of his work that the criterion might be satisfied that he should take the matter further.

Reporting via the insurer

130 It is important for the auditor to act in a manner that will preserve his professional relationship with the insurer. Normally, therefore, he should ask the insurer to draw matters about which he is concerned to the attention of the DTI. Examples of circumstances encountered in which the criterion may be met, and the matter reported via the insurer, are:

- when, in the auditor's opinion, the insurer does not or may not, at present, have the required margin of solvency;
- where it has come to the attention of the auditor that there is an extreme situation. such as evidence of imminent financial collapse, where it is obvious that the DTI must be informed;
- where the auditor has evidence of an occurrence which has led or is likely to lead to a material diminution of the insurer's net assets;
- where the auditor forms the opinion that there has been a significant failure of, or that there is a significant weakness in, the accounting and other records or the internal control systems;
- the discovery of an insurer's failure to comply with the Insurance Act and related regulations; and
- when the auditor forms the opinion that the management has reported financial information to the DTI which is misleading in a material particular (or become aware that management has failed, or does not intend, to report something and the failure to report is, or would be, materially misleading).

Reporting direct to the DTI

131 In exceptional circumstances, where it is in the interests of protecting policyholders that the management of the insurer should not be informed in advance, the auditor should report direct to the DTI. Examples of such circumstances are:

- where there has been an occurrence which causes the auditor no longer to have confidence in the integrity of the directors or senior management, e.g. where he believes that a fraud or other misappropriation has been committed by the directors or senior management of the insurer, or he has evidence of the intention of directors or senior management to commit such fraud or misappropriation; and
- where there has been an occurrence which causes the auditor no longer to have confidence in the competence of the directors or senior management to conduct the business of the insurer in a prudent manner so as to protect the interests of existing

and prospective policyholders, e.g. where he has discovered that the directors or senior management are acting in an irresponsible or reckless manner with respect to the insurer's affairs, or he has evidence of an intention so to act.

132 Additionally, as outlined in paragraph 134, a direct report should be made where the insurer will not himself inform the DTI of a matter, having been advised to do so by the auditor, or where the insurer has not done so within the period of time specified, or where there is not adequate evidence that the insurer has properly reported the matter in question.

Reporting procedures

133 In forming a view as to whether it is expedient to report a matter to the DTI, the auditor should follow the procedures in making enquiries and obtaining and assessing relevant evidence which are a normal part of forming a professional judgement in relation to an audit.

134 Where the auditor becomes aware of a matter which in his professional judgement he considers ought to be reported to the DTI, he should consider adopting the following procedures, bearing in mind that speed may be of the essence:

(a) The auditor should consider the facts and, unless inappropriate in the circumstances, discuss the matter with the management of the insurer.

(b) In normal circumstances, he should establish whether the matter has already been reported by the insurer and if so, obtain from the insurer a copy of the DTI's written acknowledgement sufficient to establish that the matter has been properly reported. If the matter has not already been reported by management, the auditor should write to the insurer setting out his views and requesting that the DTI be informed of the matter, within a specified period of time. He should then obtain from the insurer evidence of prompt acknowledgement from the DTI, sufficient to establish that the matter has been properly reported. In the absence of such evidence, it may be appropriate for the auditor to report the matter direct to the DTI, and to inform the management of the insurer of the contents of his report. If the directors or management have not informed the DTI, and continue to refuse to inform them within the specified period of time, the auditor should report direct to the DTI.

(c) If the situation is sensitive, for example in the circumstances outlined in paragraph 131, it may be inappropriate to discuss the matter with the normal levels of management with whom the auditor normally deals. The auditor should therefore consider reporting to the appropriate senior level within the insurer with a view to the DTI being informed of the situation by a senior representative of the insurer. The auditor should then obtain evidence from the insurer of prompt acknowledgement by the DTI sufficient to establish that the matter has been promptly reported. In the absence of such evidence, it will then be appropriate for the auditor to report direct to the DTI. In exceptional circumstances where the auditor feels that in the interests of speed and/or, because of the nature of the matter, it is not appropriate or practical to inform or discuss the matter with anyone connected with the insurer, the auditor should make an appropriate written or other report direct to the DTI.

135 The auditor should bear in mind that his decision may have to stand up to examination at a future date on the basis of the following considerations:

- what he knew at the time;
- what he should have known in the course of his audit;
- what he should have concluded; and

- what he should have done.

136 Speed of reporting will often be important to the protection of the interests of existing and prospective policyholders. A report should be made as soon as the auditor reasonably can after forming the view that it is expedient to do so in order to protect the interests of existing and prospective policyholders. For the auditor this may well mean ensuring that an *ad hoc* report is made to the DTI in advance of making his report on the financial statements of the insurer or on the DTI Return.

137 The auditor should note that in the situations outlined in paragraphs 130 and 131 above, making an *ad hoc* report alone may not discharge all his responsibilities. An example of this would be the need for the auditor to consider the implications of the *ad hoc* report for his opinion on the financial statements.

138 To ensure that the DTI is informed promptly of matters which meet the criterion, the auditor should ensure that:

- all staff responsible for insurance assignments are aware of the provisions of Section 21A and the contents of this guidance and are able to identify situations in which they might operate; and
- satisfactory procedures exist to ensure that any information, which may be the subject of an *ad hoc* report, obtained by staff in the course of their work, is passed on to the partner responsible without unnecessary delay.

Communications by the DTI

139 The DTI is mindful of the role of auditors and the supervisory benefits of closer cooperation. The DTI has confirmed that it will consider, in appropriate cases, informing auditors of factors which may be relevant to their functions.

Appendix — Glossary of terms

140 This glossary is not intended to be comprehensive; it deals only with certain technical insurance terms used in the guideline.

Accident year. The calendar year in which the accident or claim occurs.

Acquisition costs. Costs incurred in the acquisition of new and renewal insurance contracts. Acquisition costs include those costs that vary with, and are primarily related to, the acquisition of insurance contracts (e.g. commissions, certain underwriting and policy issue costs and inspection fees).

Adjuster. A person who investigates a claim and negotiates settlement with the claimant on behalf of the insurer. The adjuster may be independent or may be an employee of the insurer.

Bordereaux. Detailed listings of premiums and/or claim transactions usually prepared monthly and rendered to interested parties. These listings are frequently rendered by ceding companies to reinsurers and by large general agents to companies.

Catastrophe. Fire, earthquake, storm, explosion and other similar events that result in substantial claims. Catastrophic claims (the whole of the claims of an insurance company arising out of a single catastrophic event) are usually protected by excess-of-loss treaties in order to limit any one such series of claims to a specific amount.

Cede. To transfer liability in connection with a risk, or a portion of it, from the original insurer to the reinsurer.

Ceding company. The original or primary insurer who reinsures with another company, which is called the reinsurer.

Claim. A notification by or on behalf of the insured of an event within the terms of an insurance contract giving rise to a liability of the insurer.

Claims expenses. The expenses incurred in the investigation, adjustment, and settlement of claims. There are two types of claims expenses: allocated and unallocated; however, there are no generally accepted definitions of these two terms. Allocated claim expenses are frequently considered to include direct expenses incurred in settling claims that can be attributed to specific cases including such items as court costs and legal fees. The remainder are considered to be unallocated claims expenses.

Claims provision. An amount set aside for payment of claims incurred but not yet paid.

Claims ratios. The expression in terms of ratios of the relationship of claims to premiums. Two ratios in common usage are (1) the paid claims ratio (paid claims divided by written premiums or earned premiums) and (2) the incurred claims ratio (incurred claims divided by earned premiums).

Closing. An advice from a broker or bureau notifying a premium receipt, a payment due, a claim payment or a recovery due.

Combined ratio. The aggregate of the expense and claims ratios. (See **"expense ratio"** and **"claims ratio"**.)

Cover note. Confirmation of insurance or reinsurance cover.

Deferred acquisition costs. (See also **"Acquisition costs"**.) Acquisition costs which are carried forward from one accounting period to the next.

Deposit premium. A premium or part-premium paid at the inception of an insurance or reinsurance contract.

Development year. A year subsequent to the accident year during which claims experience develops.

Direct business. Business where policies are issued to provide the primary insurance on a given hazard.

Earned premium. The *pro rata* portion of the premium applicable to the expired period of the policy.

Excess-of-loss treaty. A type of reinsurance treaty used extensively, which provides that the reinsurer pays all or a specified percentage of claims arising from a particular occurrence or event (frequently of a more or less catastrophic nature) in excess of a fixed amount and up to a stipulated limit. Such treaties do not usually apply to specific policies but apply to aggregate claims incurred under all policies subject to the particular hazards reinsured. The premium is usually a percentage of net premiums written by the insurer for the hazards subject to such reinsurance.

Expense ratio. The percentage of underwriting expenses including commission incurred to premiums written.

Experience. This refers to the claim ratio status of a particular risk, a particular coverage, or a particular carrier, etc.

Exposure. The criterion used in measuring the extent of a hazard assumed by the carrier. From the statistical standpoint of ratemaking for property and liability insurance, exposure is the product of the amount of insurance at risk and the policy period expressed in years. Also, exposure is the state of being in danger of a claim occurring from a particular hazard.

Facultative reinsurance. Reinsurance arrangements under which each risk to be reinsured is offered to and is either accepted or rejected by the reinsurer. So-called facultative reinsurance arrangements are, therefore, only permissive and do not obligate the ceding company to cede or the reinsurer to accept.

IBNR (claims incurred but not reported). Claims resulting from accidents or occurrences that have taken place but on which the insurer has not yet received notices or reports of a claim.

In-force. A policy which is in effect and has not expired or been cancelled.

Localisation of assets. The maintenance of assets in such places and in such currencies as are suitable to meet the related liabilities.

London Market. The London Market consists of Lloyd's syndicates and other insurers with underwriting offices located in the City of London. The Market specialises in dealing with large international and complex insurances such as marine, aviation and transit risks, long-tail liability risks and reinsurances.

Long-tail. Business where there is a significant period of time between the occurrence of an event giving rise to a claim and settlement of the claim.

Open year. An insurance or reinsurance year of account that is not closed or finalised. Adopted in fund accounting by Lloyd's syndicates and by some insurers in respect of certain classes of business.

Pre-debited income. The debiting of a renewal premium at a rate of premium where the cover is not yet agreed by the agent or the insured on the due date for policy renewal.

Reinsurance. (1) A procedure whereby the original insurer relieves itself of part or all of an insurance risk by passing it on (reinsuring it) to another insurance company. (2) A contract in which the reinsurer (the first party) in consideration of a premium agrees to indemnify the reinsured (the second party) against a risk insured by the reinsured under a policy in favour of the insured (third party). The reinsured may be referred to as the original or primary insurer or the ceding company.

Retrocede. To reinsure reinsurance assumed. For example: A accepts reinsurance from B and then in turn reinsures with C a whole or part of the reinsurance assumed from B. The reinsurance ceded to C by A is called a retrocession.

Retention. The amount of any risk which an insurer keeps for its own account, being net of any part of the risk which is reinsured.

Short-tail. Business where there is only a short period of time between the occurrence of an event giving rise to a claim, and settlement of the claim.

Slip. A piece of paper used in the London Market to record the acceptance of risk by an underwriter.

Solvency ratio. The ratio of net assets to premiums written.

Stop-loss insurance. A stop-loss agreement is designed to prevent the ceding company's loss from exceeding a specific predetermined limit. For example, if under an agreement indemnifying a company against claims in excess of a 70 per cent claims ratio the ceding company's claims ratio exceeds 70 per cent, then recovery will be made from the reinsurer for the amount needed to reduce the claims ratio to 70 per cent.

Subrogation. In contracts of indemnity, the right of an insurer to stand in the place of the insured and exercise all the rights or remedies available to the insured, whether already enforced or not.

Technical items. Items relating to accounting for underwriting activity.

Technical provisions. Amounts set aside in respect of commitments arising from insurance contracts.

Treaty. A term historically applied to reinsurance contracts as distinct from facultative reinsurance arrangements.

Underwriting year. The year to which business is allocated; for non-treaty business it is normally determined by closing date, and for treaty business, by inception date.

Unearned premium. The amount of premium on a policy representing the unexpired period of the policy.

Written premiums. Premiums receivable for policies commencing in a period.

Life insurers in the United Kingdom

(Issued October 1991)

Preface

This guideline gives guidance on the special factors to be considered in the application of Auditing Standards to life insurers in the United Kingdom. It is supplementary to, and should be read in conjunction with, Auditing Standards and related Auditing Guidelines.

Insurers are permitted to draw up accounts under Schedule 9 to the Companies Act 1985, rather than under Schedule 4 which is applicable to the generality of companies. Accordingly, life insurers may take advantage of the disclosure exemptions available under Schedule 9, the most important of which relates to the disclosure of the amounts of, and movements in, provisions and reserves. As a result of the use of disclosure exemptions, the audit objective, as regards the balance on a life fund which contains undisclosed reserves, is to be satisfied that it is at least sufficient to meet liabilities to the policyholders whereas, if disclosure exemptions were not utilised, the audit objective would be to be satisfied that not only was it sufficient but also that it was not demonstrably excessive. The European Commission has put forward proposals for an insurance accounts directive which, when enacted in the United Kingdom, is likely to result in the withdrawal of the exemptions currently available to insurers.

The contents of this guideline have the approval of the Department of Trade and Industry. This guideline is based on the law in effect at 31 December 1990.

Introduction

1 Throughout this guideline, the term insurer refers to any company subject to the Companies Act 1985 ('the Companies Act') and which is authorised under the Insurance Companies Act 1982 ('the Insurance Act') to write long-term insurance or **reinsurance** business in the United Kingdom (abbreviated for convenience in this guideline to 'life insurance'). This guideline does not attempt to deal with specific legislative features affecting insurance undertakings governed by other legislation, such as friendly societies. Technical insurance terms, printed in bold type where they first appear in the guideline, are defined in the Appendix.

2 Auditors of insurers have the following duties:

- to report to members on the financial statements in accordance with the requirements of Section 235 of, and paragraph 28A of Schedule 9 to, the Companies Act;
- to report on the returns to be deposited by the insurer with the Secretary of State for Trade and Industry in accordance with the requirements of Section 21 of the Insurance Act ('the DTI Return'); and
- to communicate with the Secretary of State for Trade and Industry in certain circumstances ('*ad hoc* reports') under Section 21A of the Insurance Act.

3 It is particularly important that auditors undertake audit engagements for insurers only after considering their own competence and the adequacy of their resources to carry out their duties (including relevant experience). In assessing their competence and resources, auditors should bear in mind the type and range of the insurer's products and the nature of its systems. Auditors will, in particular, need to have a proper understanding of:

- the nature of life insurance, the characteristics of various products, the structure of the life insurance market its taxation and the various types of organisation within the market;

- the regulatory environment and in particular the accounting methods peculiar to life insurance business, the accounting and audit requirements of the Companies Act applicable to insurers and the reporting and audit requirements of the Insurance Act; and
- the audit approach to key areas of life insurance business, particularly the valuation of long-term liabilities.

4 The matters above are addressed in this guideline. The guideline is not intended to be comprehensive but rather to give an indication of those areas peculiar to life insurance business of which auditors need to be aware; it does not cover other areas, such as investments, except where these are peculiar to insurance, although they may be an important aspect of an insurer's operations. This guideline will not by itself be sufficient to provide all the detailed knowledge required of auditors of an insurer in all circumstances which might arise.

Background

General

5 The basic purpose of life insurance is to provide cover in relation to an insured life for a specified period or until death of the insured, for a consideration. However, life insurance policies fulfil a wide variety of purposes including 'investment' contracts and annuities. 'Life insurance' comprises, for the purposes of this guideline, those classes of long-term business set out in Schedule 1 the Insurance Act as follows:

- life and annuity;
- marriage and birth;
- **linked long term**;
- **permanent health**;
- **tontines**;
- capital redemption; and
- pension fund management.

6 Life insurance may be categorised as either industrial business or ordinary business. Industrial business is a specialised area of life insurance subject to a different legislative framework. The most important distinguishing features of industrial business are the relatively low average unit premium levels and sums assured and the method of collection of premiums. Premiums are collected in cash by visiting the policyholder at regular weekly or monthly intervals. Business other than industrial business is known as 'ordinary business'.

Industry structure

7 The principal types of organisation writing life insurance in the United Kingdom, in certain cases as composites writing general and other insurance business are:

- Proprietary companies
  Proprietary insurers are usually companies limited by shares where the members are investors (rather than policyholders).
- Mutuals
  A mutual insurer is usually a company limited by guarantee, its members being the policyholders.

- Branches of insurers incorporated overseas.

In addition certain Lloyds' syndicates underwrite life business.

Sources of business

8 The two basic sources of business are:

- Direct selling
  The insurer is in direct contact with the insured as a result of advertising or direct mail, or a branch network, or a sales force employed by the insurer.
- Intermediaries
  Insurance intermediaries advise and assist the insured in arranging insurance following the 'polarisation' requirements of the Financial Services Act 1986 ('FSA'); life insurance intermediaries are divided between **independent financial advisers** and **appointed representatives**.

Another source of business is reinsurance accepted.

Life insurance contracts

9 Life insurance products are designed to meet one or more of the following purposes:

- provision of a lump sum on death (risk contracts);
- accumulation of funds (**investment contracts**) including the accumulation of funds for the provision of pensions (pension business);
- provision of payments over a period in return for a capital sum including the payment of pensions and the purchase of the right to future payments (**annuities** and pension annuities); and
- provision of payments in the event of ill health or incapacity (permanent health).

Contracts may be entered into by or on behalf of individual policyholders or by employers on behalf of a specified group of person. Life insurance contracts are generally not cancellable by the insurer.

10 In order to qualify as a life insurance contract for the purposes of the Insurance Act, a contract must fall within one of the specified classes set out in paragraph 5 above.

11 Certain policies ('qualifying policies') benefit from specific tax advantages set out in Part XIII, Chapter II of the Income and Corporation Taxes Act 1988.

12 Life insurance contracts can be divided into three generic types:

- link contracts — where the benefit is determined by reference to the market value of a segregated group of assets (or indices) to which the policy is linked, or, in some cases, to a stated minimum guaranteed sum assured, whichever is the higher. Units are notionally allocated to each policy on the payment of each premium, on the basis specified in the policy, being units in either an internal investment fund of the insurer (an **internal linked fund**) or in an external authorised unit trust;
- **with-profit** contracts — where the policyholder participates in the **surplus** (or 'profits') of the insurer and the benefit is expressed as a guaranteed minimum sum at the end of the term or earlier death together with bonuses declared during the term of the policy and/or on the termination of the policy; and
- without-profit contracts — where the policyholder does not participate in the surpluses of the insurer and the benefit is expressed as a fixed sum at the end of the term or at earlier death, or as a fixed annuity payable immediately or from the occurrence of a future event.

Risk contracts

13 Risk contracts are designed to give rise to a claim only in the event of death and can be divided into two generic types:

- whole life; and
- term.

A **whole life contract** provides for payment of a sum on death whenever death occurs. Term contracts by contrast provide for payment only if death occurs during the contract term. Variations of such contracts include mortgage protection policies where the sum assured declines as the loan is repaid, and 'family income policies' where the benefit is expressed as a sum paid regularly for the balance of the term remaining at the time of death.

Investment contracts and pension business

14 Investment contracts may provide for either regular premiums for a specified period (or earlier death) or a single premium. Examples of investment contracts are income bonds where a regular income is provided to the policyholder and endowment policies where the benefits are payable at the end of a term or on earlier death. Pensions business comprises contracts where the accumulated benefit is payable at or after minimum retirement age and must be applied by the policyholder at least in part in the provision of an annuity.

Annuities

15 Annuities may be for a fixed or variable amount; typically variable annuities rise by a fixed annual percentage or by reference to a UK index of inflation and for fixed terms or for life. Annuities may be written by reference to more than one life, for example to pay a regular sum while two assureds survive and following the first death to pay a lower sum to the survivor for the rest of their life. The most common form of life insurance annuity contract is a pension annuity but insurers also write immediate and deferred annuity business.

Permanent health insurance

16 These contracts, which have terms of five or more years, pay an 'annuity' related to a period of illness or incapacity rather than a period of survival (although payments would cease on the earlier of death or on reaching normal retirement age).

Reinsurance

17 Insurers may transfer (or **cede**) a part of the risks assumed to another insurer; in this case the direct insurer is referred to as the cedant and the accepting insurer as the reinsurer (or reassurer). The reinsurer may, in turn, transfer (or **retrocede**) a part of the risks assumed: in this case, the insurer retroceding the business is known as the 'retrocessionaire'. A reinsurance contract does not absolve the **ceding company** of any liability to the insured; reinsurance is a separate contract to which the original insured is not a party.

18 The purpose of reinsurance is to manage and spread risk; it is used for example:

- to protect the capital base from a **catastrophe** or to prevent over-concentration of **mortality risks** or **morbidity risks**;
- to reduce the risk of loss on any one contract including **substandard lives** and so to eliminate wide variations in underwriting results; and
- to enable an increase in the volume of business written without increasing the capital base to an equivalent extent.

19 Life reinsurance may take the form of proportional contract whereby premiums and claims are divided in agreed proportions between the ceding company and the reinsurer. Certain reinsurance contracts may only result in the cession of the mortality risk element, with the insurer retaining the investment risk. Certain treaties often referred to as financing treaties provide a method of supporting the expansion of an insurer's long-term business by relieving the effect of new business strain on solvency margins.

20 There are two methods of reinsurance: **treaty** and **facultative**. Under the treaty method of reinsurance an agreement is entered into between the ceding company and the reinsurer whereby all risks written by the ceding company that fall within the terms and limit of the treaty will be reinsured with the reinsurer automatically. With the facultative method of reinsurance each risk to be reinsured is offered to the reinsurer who accepts or rejects it individually. The majority of risks are placed by **surplus treaty** reinsurance. A small number of large risks are placed facultatively. The limits and terms of treaties can be, for example, monetary, geographic or class of business.

Legislation

Insurance Companies Act 1982

21 The principal legislation governing the conduct of insurance businsess is the Insurance Act and the related regulations, in particular the Insurance Companies Regulations 1981 ('the 1981 Regulations') and the Insurance Companies (Accounts and Statements) Regulations 1983 ('the 1983 Regulations'). The Insurance Act gives wide ranging supervisory powers to the Department of Trade and Industry ('DTI') in respect of:

- authorisation;
- monitoring; and
- intervention.

22 No person may carry on any insurance business in the United Kingdom unless authorised to do so under Section 3 or 4 of the Insurance Act (except where the insurance business is carried on by a member of Lloyd's, by a registered friendly society or by a trade union or employers' association providing provident benefits or strike benefits only). Authorisation may be obtained only after submitting satisfactory information as to the manner in which business is proposed to be carried on and such other particulars required by regulation. Authorisation is given for specified classes of business.

23 In order to assist the DTI in monitoring insurers, the Insurance Act requires that every insurer shall prepare and submit to the DTI a return for each financial year. The form and content of this return is specified by the 1983 Regulations and, in respect of long-term business, must include:

- a statement of assets;
- a statement of liabilities;
- a calculation of the required minimum **margin of solvency**;
- a statement of solvency showing the excess or deficiency of net assets over the required minimum margin of solvency;
- revenue accounts;
- an analysis of premiums, claims and expenses;
- a summary of changes in business and an analysis of new business;
- expected income from **admissible** non-linked **assets** and an analysis of admissible

non-linked fixed interest securities;

- an analysis of holdings in authorised unit trusts and other assets directly matching liabilities in respect of linked benefits;
- an analysis of units in internal linked funds and a balance sheet and revenue account for internal linked funds;
- a statement of other income and expenditure;
- a valuation summary (Schedule IV); and
- a summary of business in force (Schedule V) which need only be submitted every five years.

24 An insurer is required by Section 28 of the Insurance Act to identify by means of separate funds:

- assets attributable:
  - — to long-term business; and
  - — to other business; and
- liabilities attributable:
  - — to ordinary long-term business;
  - — to industrial long-term business; and
  - — to other business.

Separate forms (Form 13 — analyses of admissible assets) are required in the DTI Return for long-term business and for other business. Section 136 of the FSA inserts a new section, Section 31A, into the Insurance Act which requires insurers to secure that adequate arrangements are in force to ensure that transactions affecting the assets of the insurer do not operate unfairly between different funds. This applies not only to those required by Section 28 to be separately identified but also to any other funds separately identified in the accounting or other records of the insurer.

25 The 1981 Regulations contain requirements concerning *inter alia*:

- the matching of assets and liabilities;
- the **localisation of assets**;
- the admissibility of assets;
- the permitted links for linked business;
- the basis of valuation of assets; and
- the calculation of the minimum margin of solvency.

The basis of valuation and admissibility of assets for the purposes of the returns applies only to assets not included in internal linked funds; the regulations seek to put the assets on to a realisation basis (but there is no attempt to put the net assets on to a full liquidation basis which would involve provision for all costs of winding up the business).

26 The 1981 Regulations also cover the valuation (or 'determination') of long-term insurance liabilities, and require them to be computed on actuarial principles making proper provision for all liabilities on prudent assumptions.

27 Under Section 18 of the Insurance Act, the insurer is required to cause an investigation to be made into the financial condition of its long-term business:

- once in every period of 12 months; and
- at any other time when there is to be a distribution of surplus.

Such an investigation is conducted by an actuary ('the Actuary'), appointed as actuary to the insurer for the purposes of the Insurance Act, who is required:

- to value the liabilities of the insurer attributable to long-term business; and
- to determine any excess over those liabilities of the assets representing the long-term business fund.

For this purpose, the valuation of assets and the determination of liabilities have to be made in accordance with any applicable regulations, namely those contained in Parts V and VI of the1981 Regulations. The Actuary is also subject to guidance issued by the Institute of Actuaries and the Faculty of Actuaries. This guidance, contained principally in Guidance Note GN1, amplifies the professional responsibilities and duties of the Actuary and, in effect, extends the requirements of the Insurance Act and the related regulations in a number of areas. The following responsibilities of the Actuary are of relevance in the context of the audit:

- although the Actuary is appointed and remunerated by the insurer (and may be a director or employee of the insurer), the Actuary has responsibilities and obligations to the DTI which arise from its supervisory functions aimed at the protection of policyholders;
- the Actuary should take all reasonable steps to ensure that he is satisfied at all times that if he were to carry out an investigation into the financial condition of the insurer the position would be satisfactory; and
- the Actuary should advise the directors of the insurer on the extent to which it would be appropriate to distribute any surplus to policyholders or to transfer it to shareholders and make recommendations for its specific allocation.

28 The Actuary is required as part of his statutory duties to report to the DTI in a prescribed form on investigations carried out under Section 18 of the Insurance Act. The form and content of this report and of any statement of long-term business are prescribed by Regulation 24 of the 1983 Regulations, detailed requirements being specified in Schedules 4 and 5 respectively. It is also the professional duty of the Actuary to report first in writing to the directors of the insurer on the results and implications of any such investigation, whether or not an allocation of surplus is involved. When making recommendations in respect of proposed allocation of surplus, the Actuary must include sufficient information and commentary as may be necessary to enable the directors to consider the appropriateness of the allocation and to understand its implications for the future conduct of the insurer's long-term business.

29 Regulation 26(b) and Part II of Schedule 6 of the 1983 Regulations require the Actuary to provide a certificate each year as part of the DTI Return which:

'(a) shall state if such be the case,

(i) that in his opinion proper records have been kept by the company adequate for the purpose of the valuation of the liabilities of its long-term business;

(ii) that the mathematical reserve as shown in Form 14, together, if the case so require with an amount specified in the certificate (being part of the excess of the value of the admissible assets representing the long-term business funds over the amount of those funds shown in Form 14) constitute proper provision at the end of the financial year for the liabilities (other than liabilities which had fallen due before the end of the financial year) arising under or in connection with contracts for long-term business including any increase in those liabilities arising from a distribution of surplus as a result of an investigation as at that date into the financial condition of the long-term business; and

(iii) that for the purposes of subparagraph (ii) above the liabilities have been assessed in accordance with Part VI of the Insurance Companies Regulations [1981] in the context of assets valued in accordance with Part V of those Regulations, as shown in Form 13; and

(b) shall state the amount of the required minimum margin, required Community minimum margin or required United Kingdom minimum margin as the case may be applicable to the company's long-term business immediately following the end of the financial year (including any amounts resulting from any increase in liabilities arising from a distribution of surplus as a result of the investigation into the financial condition of the long-term business)'.

The 1983 Regulations provide that, if he considers it necessary, the Actuary shall add to the certificate such qualification, amplification or explanation as may be appropriate.

30 The DTI Return must be accompanied by a directors' certificate in prescribed form; this is set out in Part I of Schedule 6 to the 1983 Regulations. The directors' certificate must, if such is the case, include statements that:

- for the purpose of preparing the DTI Return, proper accounts and records have been maintained and adequate information obtained by the insurer, and that an appropriate system of control has been established and maintained over transactions and records;
- the insurer is in compliance with the requirements for matching and localisation of assets specified by regulation;
- assets and liabilities have been valued in accordance with the relevant regulations;
- the requirements of Sections 28 to 31 of the Insurance Act have been complied with (except in the case of an insurer which has no shareholders and carries on no business other than long-term business);
- any transactions of the fund with a connected party have been no less than fair to the fund;
- any guarantees given by the fund on behalf of a related party are disclosed;
- in the case of a United Kingdom company **pure reinsurer**, United Kingdom deposit company or external company which has financial commercial or administrative links with any other entity carrying on insurance business that the returns in respect of long-term business are not distorted by agreements between the entities concerned or by any arrangements which could affect the apportionment of expenses and income; and
- that the insurer has complied with Section 31A of the Insurance Act during the period covered by the return.

The auditor's report on the DTI Return is required to state whether it is reasonable for the directors to have made these statements.

31 The DTI has considerable powers of intervention including:

- control of the nature location and custody of assets;
- restricting the volume of business to be written;
- requiring the performance of a valuation of liabilities;
- requiring the submission of more frequent returns or specified information;
- withdrawal of authorisation; and

- the right to petition the Court to wind up the insurer.

Financial Services Act 1986

32 Insurers are also governed by certain of the provisions of the FSA which was enacted for the purposes of controlling the conduct of investment business. Under the FSA only authorised or exempted persons may carry on investment business.

Social Security Act 1975

33 Certain provisions of the Social Security Act 1975 are of significance to insurers writing pension business. In particular restrictions are placed on the uses to which accumulated approved pension scheme funds may be put and insurers, when disbursing such funds, are required to ensure that the disbursements are not in breach of the restrictions.

Companies Act 1985

34 The statutory requirements relating to financial statements prepared for submission to members are set out in the Companies Act. Insurers are exempted from Schedule 4 and Schedule 4A to the Companies Act. Insurers are permitted to prepare financial statements in accordance with the requirements of Schedule 9 (i.e. broadly in accordance with the previous requirements originally contained in the Companies Acts 1948 and 1967). However, if insurers do not draw up statements in accordance with Schedule 9, their financial statements must comply with the requirements of Schedule 4 and Schedule 4A.

35 Paragraph 28(1) of Schedule 9 to the Companies Act exempts insurers from certain disclosure requirements of the Schedule. The most important exemptions relate to disclosures of the amounts of, and movements in, provisons and reserves. Where insurers use the exemptions available to them, the statement of accounting policies would normally indicate that fact. Any heading in the financial statements which contains, or is affected by movements in, reserves must indicate that fact (but the amounts do not need to be quantified).

36 Whilst Section 255 of the Companies Act requires that the balance sheet and profit and loss account of an insurer give a true and fair view, paragraph 28(2) of Schedule 9 states that, for the purposes of the Companies Act, an insurer's financial statements shall not be deemed not to give a true and fair view by reason only of the fact that disclosure exemptions have been used.

37 Schedule 9 does not specify formats for financial statements; it does, however, require the financial statements to disclose specific information. In addition, many of the disclosure requirements imposed by other parts of the Companies Act that apply to the generality of companies also apply to insurers; for example, Schedule 5 (Miscellaneous matters to be dealt with in the notes), Schedule 6 (Details of loans and other transactions favouring directors and officers) and Schedule 7 (Matters to be dealt with in the Directors' Report).

38 The European Commission has proposed a directive on the annual financial statements of insurance undertakings. If this directive is adopted, it will, in due course, be implemented by legislation in the United Kingdom and will replace existing provisions of the Companies Act applicable to the financial statements of insurers.

Accounting

39 An insurer's financial statements will usually disclose the assets attributed (a) to the long-term business, and (b) to other insurance business and, except in the case of mutual insurers, to shareholders' funds.

40 Transactions attributable to long-term insurance business are accounted for on a fund basis in a revenue account. The balance of funds is maintained at a level which is at least sufficient to cover liabilities to the policyholders. Historically, insurers writing exclusively long-term business have tended to include all investment income and expenses in the revenue account, but a number of insurers allocate certain items not attributable to long-term business to the profit and loss account. The profit and loss account is mainly comprised of income and expenditure relating to shareholders' other business and the transfer to or from the long-term business fund, transfers from the fund being governed by the requirements of the Insurance Act. The taxation relating to the transfer to or from the long-term business fund may be shown wholly or partly in either the revenue account or in the profit and loss account.

41 Although there is no specified format for the revenue account for the purposes of the financial statements, it will normally be made up of the following items:

- premium income;
- investment income;
- appreciation/depreciation in the value of investments;
- transfer from/to investment reserve;
- claims;
- commissions;
- management expenses;
- taxation;
- transfer to/from profit and loss account;
- net increase in **long-term fund**;
- long-term fund brought forward; and
- long-term fund carried forward.

42 Any surplus of the balance on the long-term fund over the valuation of long-term liabilities will be dealt with in one or more of the following ways:

- allocated as bonuses to with-profits policyholders in accordance with the memorandum and articles of the insurer subject to Section 30 of the Insurance Act;
- allocated to shareholders (i.e. transferred to the profit and loss account); or
- carried forward unappropriated within the long-term fund.

The amount of the unappropriated surplus is not required to be disclosed in the financial statements.

43 Statements of Standard Accounting Practice ('SSAPs') apply to the accounts of insurers except in so far as the requirements of SSAPs are overridden by the exemptions in Schedule 9 to the Companies Act. Insurers are therefore expected to comply with SSAPs, except where disclosure exemptions have been utilised in their published financial statements.

44 The differences between insurance and other business activities, and the differences between particular classes of insurance, have resulted in a range of accounting policies and bases. In May 1990, the Association of British Insurers issued a Statement of Recommended Practice (the 'ABI Statement'), franked by the Accounting Standards Committee, in order to narrow the areas of difference and variety in the accounting treatments used. The ABI Statement sets out recommended practice in the following areas:

- premiums;
- claims; and
- expenses (with special reference to **acquisition costs**).

Auditing

Planning the audit

Introduction

45 The Auditing Standard 'The auditor's operational standard' requires that 'the auditor should adequately plan, control and record his work' and general guidance on these matters is given in the Auditing Guideline 'Planning, controlling and recording'. Having regard in particular, to the role of the Actuary referred to in paragraph 27 in connection with the determination or long-term liabilities, the auditor may also wish to refer to the Auditing Guideline 'Reliance on other specialists'. Given the importance of computer processing within many insurers, the guidance given in the Auditing Guideline 'Auditing in a computer environment' is likely to be of particular relevance to the auditor. Reference should also be made to the sections in the Auditing Guideline 'Internal controls' on management responsibility and limitations on the effectiveness of internal controls. The following paragraphs deal only with particular aspects of life insurance business that are likely to need consideration by the auditor.

46 The auditor should bear in mind throughout the planning and conduct of the audit of the financial statements that the information contained in the DTI Return is also subject to audit. Accordingly, the auditor should plan to integrate his work for the purpose of reporting on the financial statements in accordance with the Companies Act with that for the purpose of reporting on the DTI Return.

Understanding the business

47 In order to identify the critical audit areas and plan the audit work adequately, the auditor needs to understand the particular features and characteristics of the insurer's business, and the environment in which the insurer operates. The relevant background may include, *inter alia*:

- the classes of business written, and the nature of the risks policy terms and benefits;
- the major distribution channels used by the insurer to market products;
- the nature of, and changes in, the legislative, regulatory and fiscal environments;
- significant changes from prior years in levels of new business by major class;
- new products;
- composition of the investment portfolio and its suitability having regard to the nature, period and currency of the liabilities;
- the basis of valuation of long-term liabilities;
- the treatment of provisions and reserves; and
- changes in **bonus rates** and bonus philosophy.

The single most important aspect in relation to the audit of the financial statements will be the valuation of long-term liabilities and the effect which this has on the emergence of surplus.

48 Conditions affecting the market generally will also need to be considered, for example:

- changes in investment conditions;
- changes in taxation; and
- the effects of new factors such as AIDS;

and the impact these may have on bonus policy or solvency.

Organisational structure and accounting information

49 Procedures of accounting significance may be carried out at several different locations. These procedures may include:

- underwriting and acceptance of risk;
- premium collection;
- policy and valuation records;
- payment of policy claims and maturities; and
- investment accounting.

In such circumstances the auditor will need to consider the extent to which common systems and controls are in operation.

50 The records of business in force ('the master file') are the records maintained by an insurer in respect of policyholders. It is the single most important record of activity and is used to generate information for the financial statements. In particular, the master file:

- constitutes an important accounting record for originating the collection of future premiums and the payment of recurring benefits; and
- constitutes the base data used for the valuation of long-term liabilities, including details of units allocated to policyholders in respect of unit linked business.

It is also used extensively for:

- recording clients' personal information;
- monitoring premium balances;
- calculating benefits due to policyholders;
- measuring the amount of new business written, the **lapse rate** and other performance indicators; and
- estimating future profits and bonus rates.

Systems and internal controls

51 The administration of insurance business depends on the accurate collation, processing and storage of large volumes of data. Amongst the data that will be held is information relating to:

- policyholder details;
- insured life details;
- policy records;
- valuation of liabilities;
- bonus declaration
- maturities, surrenders and claims; and
- accounting.

Much of the information stored by insurers must be retained for many years. For example, the date of inception of a policy, or the annual premium or the basic sum assured may be used in the determination of the amount of a claim or surrender or maturity value. Consequently, special attention must be paid to controls over the security of the data, and to ensure that appropriate access controls exist to prevent unauthorised changes to data.

52 The directors of an insurer are required to give a certificate in the DTI Return that, for the purpose of preparing the DTI Return, an appropriate system of control has been established and maintained by the insurer over its transactions and records, including a statement that they have complied with Section 31A of the Insurance Act as described in paragraph 24 above. As indicated in paragraph 30, the auditor is required to report whether, in his opinion, it was reasonable for the directors to make the statements set out in these two certificates. The audit work will therefore need to be planned not only to assess the reliance to be placed on controls in determining the work necessary to express an opinion on the financial statements and the DTI Return, but also to form an opinion on the system of control for the purposes of forming an opinion on the matters contained in the directors' certificate in the DTI Return and that the transactions of the insurer have not operated unfairly between the insurer's funds. In order to do this, a preliminary assessment of the control environment should be made at the planning stage.

53 Most insurers place considerable reliance on computerised systems and the insurance industry is making increasing use of on-line and distributed systems; data may be directly input or amended through remote terminals by the insurer's own staff or, in some cases, by intermediaries. Computer systems may not provide a visible audit trail, particularly for detailed analyses. The audit of the controls over the computer system and the use of computer assisted audit techniques may be the only practicable means of checking the aggregation of data or calculations performed by computer (such as those involved in the processing of master file data). The use of such software will need to be planned before the audit commences to give sufficient time for program development or amendment.

54 The auditor will be concerned not only with the accurate derivation of amounts shown in the financial statements but also with the completeness, accuracy, validity and consistency of:

- detailed analyses of premiums and claims for the purposes of the DTI Return; and
- master file data used in the valuation of long-term liabilities.

Reinsurance security

55 Where business is reinsured, the circumstances surrounding the reinsurance treaties and the ability of reinsurers to meet current and prospective obligations may be of significance to the financial statements of the insurer. This is therefore a vitally important aspect of the financial statements of insurers where there is significant reinsurance of risks assumed and accordingly, the insurer's reinsurance strategy and programme should be considered at the planning stage.

Analytical review

56 Audit planning should include an analytical review of available financial information in order to assist in assessment of overall risk and identification of critical audit areas. This should include:

- a review of interim or management accounts; and
- comparison of various operating and other ratios with prior year data.

A considerable number of ratios and performance indicators are commonly used in the insurance industry and the following will generally be useful in reviewing the financial statements of an insurer:

- new business premium income to budget and prior year figures, separately for single premium and recurring business — this review should indicate any shift in the pattern of business accepted;
- lapse ratio — a comparison of this ratio with prior years may indicate changes in the persistency of business in force and in the quality of new business production;
- initial commission to new business premium income — this may indicate a change in commission rates or in the mix of business;
- claims, surrenders and annuities as compared with prior year experience — this may indicate features requiring further investigation;
- **free assets** (as shown by the DTI Return) to liabilities — this is an indicator of the margin available to the insurer to withstand adverse conditions or to sustain a major expansion of the business; and
- investment income yield — a significant change in income from invested funds may indicate, for example, a shift in investment philosophy.

The premium cycle

57 The premium cycle includes the following phases:

- acceptance of business;
- policy issue;
- premium billing and collection;
- commissions; and
- reinsurance.

58 The audit objectives for the premiums cycle may be summarised as being to check that:

- appropriate controls exist over the acceptance of business and issue of policy documents;
- the insurer accounts for all premiums to which it is entitled;
- all commissions payable and receivable are properly recorded;
- reinsurance premiums payable are properly recorded; and
- premium income recording systems are capable of producing the appropriate analysis of information for use in:
  - — the calculation of long-term liabilities; and
  - — updating the master file including, in the case of unit linked business, the creation and allocation of units to the relevant policies at correctly calculated prices.

59 The audit objectives for premium recognition and reporting may be summarised as being to check that:

- revenue is recognised only to the extent that it is due in respect of in force business;
- commissions and other acquisition costs are properly identified and accounted for; and
- disclosures relating to premiums are properly made in the financial statements.

60 The insurer should have documented procedures to ensure that all risks are underwritten at the appropriate level of authority within the insurer following an appropriate review of the relevant data. These procedures will be based on the completion of an application or proposal form by the prospective policyholder which will give information required by the underwriter to determine:

- whether or not the prospective risk should be accepted;
- the premiums which should be charged; and
- the extent of risk which the company can accept (and accordingly determine the risk to be ceded to a reinsurer).

The auditor should establish that these procedures operate effectively because the assumptions underlying provisions for long-term liabilities will depend upon new business applications having been properly processed in accordance with predetermined criteria.

61 The auditor should assess the controls operating over completeness of recording of all documentation supporting the premium cycle, in particular:

- applications for new business should be processed promptly to ensure that:
  - — a basis is established for recording and controlling cash received with applications in settlement of the first premium;
  - — bank mandates for direct debits are put into effect in time to collect premiums when due; and
- renewal premium notices and premium variation notices should be effectively controlled to ensure that premiums are collected promptly including those collected by intermediaries.

62 The auditor should establish that an insurer's systems and controls are adequate to record completely and accurately all premiums and other significant data promptly. Data which will be of significance because of their relevance in particular to the valuation of long-term liabilities include:

- particulars of policyholder;
- details of the insured (date of birth, sex, occupation etc);
- special terms;
- premium;
- sum insured;
- unit linked information (including the number or units allocated to the policyholder and the internal linked funds or other assets to which the policy is linked);
- maturity date; and
- reinsurance.

The auditor will need to be satisfied that significant data are processed properly from new business applications and premium systems to the master file and that the cut off for the accounting records and the master file is consisent. Demands for premiums and direct debits to collect premiums, including policies where premiums increase each year, will often be generated automatically by computerised premium systems and from the master file. In these circumstances, the auditor will need to evaluate and test systems and controls in order to form an opinion as to the reliability of the data generated.

63 The insurer should have appropriate procedures in relation to reinsurance assumed to ensure that:

- it is subject to appropriate underwriting controls and is only accepted after proper consideration of the risks involved;
- if the business is treaty business, any business accepted is within the terms of the

treaty; and

- regular reports are received from ceding insurers.

The auditor should test these controls so as to be reasonably satisfied that the insurer is able:

- to identify all risks which it has reinsured to a sufficient extent to make proper provision for those risks; and
- to calculate and check reinsurance premiums receivable or commissions payable.

64 There should be appropriate controls to ensure that account is taken of all reinsurance cover purchased and that:

- provision is made for reinsurance premiums payable;
- credit is taken for commission receivable;
- allowance is made for reinsurance recoverable when providing for liabilities (including assessing the security of the reinsurer); and
- the insurer's procedures are adequate to ensure that the reinsurer is properly notified of all claims and any other information required under the reinsurance arrangements.

65 Commission is normally payable as follows:

- initial commission — a substantial commission payable on sale of the policy (which may be recoverable from intermediaries at least to some extent if the policy lapses within a specified period); and
- renewal commission — payable annually at a much lower rate.

Reinsurance commissions may also be borne or received whenever business is accepted or ceded. The auditor needs to be satisfied that the insurer has procedures to ensure that apropriate provision is made for commissions and that account is taken of policy lapses.

66 Insurers will sometimes assist in the funding of intermediaries' operations by advancing sums to the intermediaries before commissions are earned. The sums advanced will be repayable by the intermediary if commission is not earned equivalent to the amount advanced and intermediaries may be required to pay interest at a commercial rate on the sums advanced. The auditor needs to understand the terms on which these advances are made so as to establish whether the accounting treatment properly reflects the arrangements with the intermediaries.

The claims cycle

67 The claims cycle includes the following phases:

- initial intimation of the claim;
- recording of claim;
- admission and settlement of claim; and
- recovery in respect of reinsurance.

Audit objectives

68 The audit objectives for the claims cycle may be summarised as being to check that:

- all claims are recorded as soon as they are notified;
- claims data are accurately recorded;
- admission and settlement of claims is performed at the appropriate level of authority;
- claims settlements are supported by appropriate documentation;

- claims disbursements are strictly controlled;
- recoveries from reinsurers are properly recorded and collected;
- the claims recording system is capable of producing information analysed for updating business in force files, and, in the case of unit linked business, cancelling the units allocated to the policy at correctly calculated prices; and
- there is a proper cut off between the recording of claims payable and the provision for long-term liabilities.

69 The audit objectives for claims recognition and reporting may be summarised as being to check that:

- claims provisions are adequate;
- only reinsurance which is recoverable in respect of claims provisions is taken into account; and
- disclosures relating to claims are properly made in the financial statements.

70 The auditor should establish that the insurer's systems and controls are adequate to record completely and accurately claims and other significant data promptly. The auditor will need to be satisfied that significant data are processed properly from claims recording systems to the master file and that the accounting records and the master file are consistent.

71 The insurer should have systems which are adequate to record claims immediately on notification and to ensure that:

- claims are subject to appropriate checking of the contractual liability and verification before payment; and
- all claims notified to the insurer are processed and settled as soon as is practicable.

The insurer's procedures for verifying claims should be clearly documented and should state what documentary evidence is required for payment of claims. Systems should identify policies maturing and generate information to enable payment to be made promptly. The insurer should also have a procedure for verifying the continued existence of **annuitants**.

72 The insurer's systems must ensure that, if a claim is notified which should give rise to a recovery from reinsurers, procedures are instituted to notify the reinsurer. The auditor should satisfy himself that the insurer has appropriate procedures to ensure that:

- all reinsurance recoveries have been identified;
- reinsurance recoverable has been properly accounted for; and
- reinsurers have been notified of claims.

Valuation for long-term liabilities

The valuation approach

73 The determination of the amount of the long-term insurance liabilities for the purposes of the Insurance Act is the responsibility of the Actuary (see paragraph 27 to 29); there is no corresponding responsibility in relation to financial statements prepared in accordance with the requirements of the Companies Act.

74 Whenever, as part of an investigation of the financial condition of the long-term business, a detailed valuation of liabilities is carried out in accordance with the requirements of the Insurance Act it will have regard to:

- the principles contained in the guidance given by the Institute of Actuaries and the

Faculty of Actuaries (see paragraph 27);

- the provisions of the 1981 Regulations;
- the general nature of the assets and liabilities; and
- the need, where applicable, to release surplus in a manner consistent with the equitable declaration of bonuses to with-profit policyholders.

75 The principles or the assumptions may have to be varied from time to time to ensure that an adequate standard of providing for liabilities can be maintained in changing conditions and that surpluses can be released equitably as between shareholders and the different classes and generations of policyholders. In any event, the determination of the amount of long-term liabilities for the purposes of the Insurance Act will have to satisfy the minimum standards laid down in the 1981 Regulations in 'making proper provision for all liabilities on prudent assumptions in regard to the relevant factors'.

76 In determining the amount of the long-term liabilities for the purposes of the Insurance Act (or 'mathematical reserves' as they are referred to in the 1981 Regulations) the following matters would *inter alia* be taken into account:

- the nature and term of the assets held to match the liabilities making provision for any possible future adverse changes;
- the need for liabilities to be covered by revenue arising solely from the related assets and future premium income;
- the need for future premiums to be taken into account to no greater extent than the discounted value of expected future premiums utilising a net premium method of valuation; the net premium method can make due allowance for a **zillmerisation** adjustment to spread the acquisition costs of new business (up to 3½% of the capital sum at risk restricted to the actual costs if lower);
- the need for interest rates for discounting not to exceed 92½% of the weighted average (using assets valued in accordance with the 1981 Regulations) of the gross redemption yields of any fixed interest securities held and the running yields of other assets held. In the case of future investment returns for new money more than three years in the future the maximum rate of interest is 7⅕% gross of tax;
- relevant published tables for mortality and morbidity together with the insurer's own claims experience if significantly different;
- provision for future expenses (including an allowance for inflation) in respect of existing contracts;
- provision for the exercise of any policyholder options in existence; and
- taxation.

No policy may be treated as an asset and no credit may be taken for future voluntary discontinuances unless this results in higher provisions being required.

77 Apart from the minimum bases specified above, specific provisions are established for the purposes of the valuation of liabilities under the Insurance Act. These are recommended as minimum levels and are covered either by guidance notes issued jointly by the Institute of Actuaries and the Faculty of Actuaries or by notes issued specifically by the Government Actuary's Department ('GAD'). The notes cover *inter alia*:

- specific minimum methods for testing for mismatches between assets and liabilities;
- specific provisions for tax on future capital gains;
- methods for testing maturity guarantees on unit linked policies; and

- specific 'reserves' to be established.

78 For the purposes of the DTI Return the responsibility for expressing an opinion on the adequacy of the 'mathematical reserves' is that of the Actuary; the auditor may therefore, for the purposes of the DTI Return, rely upon the certificate given by the Actuary. However, for the purposes of expressing an opinion on the financial statements in accordance with the Companies Act the auditor takes full responsibility for expressing an opinion on the financial statements including the amount of the long-term fund.

79 The auditor's objectives in relation to the amount of the long-term liabilities and any distribution of surplus will be:

- to obtain reasonable assurance that the assets of the long-term fund are not less than the related liabilities;
- to establish whether, if a surplus in any fund has been ascertained, either its amount or the proportion distributed to shareholders has been materially affected by a change in the valuation approach or assumptions or by exceptional circumstances that may require disclosure in the financial statements having particular regard to the provisions of paragraph 28(1) of Schedule 9 to the Companies Act; and
- to satisfy himself that, in the case of a proprietary insurer, any distribution of surplus made by the insurer complies with Sections 29 and 30 of the Insurance Act, and with the articles of association.

80 The auditor should consider any relevant reports made to the directors by the Actuary and discuss with him matters relevant to the valuation of long-term liabilities. The audit approach should be sufficient to ascertain from this and from other tests and procedures:

- that systems, procedures and controls exist and are operating satisfactorily to establish the reliability of information contained in the valuation database;
- the consistency of the accounting records and the valuation database;
- that the assets used for the purposes of the valuation are those recorded in the accounting records;
- that adequate procedures and controls exist and are operating satisfactorily to coordinate and process the valuation data for the purpose of the valuation, reports and certificates provided by the Actuary;
- the validity of any transfer of surplus from the long-term fund;
- the implications of any formal reports by the Actuary to the directors of the insurer or of any correspondence between the insurer and the Actuary or between either of them and the DTI, the GAD or any other regulatory body;
- the implications of any matters relating to record keeping, systems or controls brought to the attention of the management of the insurer by the auditor;
- that the Actuary is prepared to give the certificate set out in paragraph 29 above and would give similar comfort, if required, with regard to the financial statements for the purposes of the Companies Act;
- that the extent of disclosures in the financial statements is consistent with a true and fair view;
- the quantum of **free reserves**.

Assumptions

81 The determination of the amount of long-term liabilities for the purpose of the

Insurance Act involved the making of appropriate assumptions concerning the following, each of which is dealt with in more detail below;

- mortality and morbidity;
- expenses;
- interest; and
- taxation.

In addition in determining the amount of long-term liabilities for purposes other than the Insurance Act the insurer should make assumptions regarding the likelihood of in force regular premium business lapsing or becoming paid up as a result of the cessation of premiums.

Mortality and morbidity

82 The Institute of Actuaries and the Faculty of Actuaries periodically issue Mortality Tables relevant to different groups of people, and a valuation should make reference to the Mortality Tables used. Adjustments may be made to reflect the experience of a particular insurer where this differs from the standard tables and the specific guidance issued from time to time by the Institute of Actuaries and the Faculty of Actuaries or by the GAD. For permanent health contracts, morbidity consideratons may have as much significance as mortality. Morbidity is dealt with in a manner similar to that for mortality using standard tables as a base.

Expenses

83 Insurers normally account for expenses by charging them to revenue as incurred. 'The ratio of expenses to premiums receivable in a period will vary depending on a number of factors. The costs of writing new business are normally much higher than for processing renewal premiums in view, in particular, of the market practice of paying a high proportion of Commisions in the first year. Additionally, an insurer normally has substantial fixed costs and signficant changes in business volumes will therefore affect the expense ratio. Therefore expenses should be analysed in sufficient detail to allow expense levels to be projected with acquisition and renewal expenses separately identified. Allowances will also need to be made for inflation. An aspect which will require particular consideration for a new or rapidly expanding insurer is any **expense overrun**. This should be analysed and the impact on the assumptions assessed to determine whether any change to those assumptions is appropriate.

84 The high cost of writing new business has an adverse effect on the net assets of the insurer. This 'new business strain' arises because the initial provisions which will need to be set up in respect of a new policy cannot be financed by the first premium since that will have been largely (or even entirely) offset by expenses and commission. Zillmerisation (or derivatives of that technique) may be used to modify the valuation or a long-term policy by increasing the part of the future premiums for which credit is taken so as to allow for initial expenses.

Interest

85 An assumption for future interest rates is required in a valuation of long-term liabilities so as to discount future cash flows to present value. Adoption of a prudent rate also provides a buffer against unforeseen interest rates changes or other adverse fluctuations. The rate of interest used may be adjusted for tax in valuing non-pension business.

Linked liabilities

86 The valuation of linked liabilities must be based on the value of the assets notionally allocated to policyholders. Consistency between asset valuations and liability valuations is therefore more exacting than for 'conventional' business although the same general principles apply. In particular it will be necessary, for the purpose of reporting on Forms 47, 48, and 49 of the DTI Return, for the auditor to check the separate identification of assets matching linked liabilities and, for the purpose of reporting on Forms 50 and 51 of the DTI Return, for the auditor to check the units in force in and movement in the value of each internal linked fund. This will include checks on the calculation of unit prices and reviews or the value of units created and cancelled and the amounts deducted on account of management charges and taxation from each internal linked fund.

Deferred taxation

87 Insurers have to consider equity between policyholders arising from, in particular, the possibility of a reduction in the number of policyholders and the size of the fund at some future date. For unit linked business, this may be achieved by recognising projected tax liabilities on a discounted basis for the purposes of the valuation. An alternative approach for non-linked business is to establish a specific deferred tax provision separately in the financial statements. The auditor must obtain a proper understanding of the basis of the valuation of long-term liabilities so as, in particular, to ensure that deferred taxation is appropriately recognised on a consistent basis.

Determination of surplus

88 Simplistically, the valuation of assets and liabilities at a given date will provide a measure of the surplus or deficit, as the surplus is derived from margins in the premium rates, experience in claims or expenses and investment performance. However, as has already been indicated, interest and other assumptions for the purposes of the valuation under the Insurance Act will be conservative and are often set so as to allow a surplus to emerge in an orderly manner over a period of time. The valuation process will frequently include an analysis of the surplus for the financial period to establish how it has emerged. This will enable the divergence of actual experience from that assumed to be evaluated. Apart from the restrictions of surplus which result from conservative assumptions, the valuation may reflect contingency provisions in relation to any uncertainties. Provisions may also be established outside the long-term business fund to allow for mismatches and other contingencies or to reflect depreciation in investment values.

89 The auditor should satisfy himself that any distributions of surplus made by the directors of a proprietary company comply with Sections 29 and 30 of the Insurance Act. The auditor should therefore establish from the reports to the directors by the Actuary, augmented as appropriate by consultation with the Actuary, whether:

- the distributions have been made out of the **established surplus**;
- any participating policyholders have received not less than their minimum entitlement under the insurer's statutes; and
- the transfers to profit and loss account from surplus in which participating policyholders are eligible to participate are not such as to require the company to give notice to the Secretary of State under Section 30 of the Insurance Act.

Under Section 268 of the Companies Act, surplus transferred to the profit and loss account constitutes realised profits for the purpose of determining whether a distribution may be made in accordance with the Companies Act (notwithstanding that there may be significant unrealised investment appreciation within the long-term fund). No dividend may be declared if long-term liabilities exceed long-term assets unless this is made good by a transfer from shareholders' funds.

Insurance debtors and creditors

90 Insurance balances receivable from or payable to intermediaries and other insurers are fundamentally no different from the debtors and creditors of any other business. Accordingly, the audit techniques that should be applied are in principle broadly similar.

Unpaid premiums

91 In general, audit tests for unpaid premiums should be carried out in accordance with normal audit procedures in relation to debtors to verify recoverability, existence and validity of the debt. However, for life insurance policies involving an investment element, the amount of the unpaid premium will often be recoverable from the 'reserve value' of the policy, or be deductible from the policy proceeds in the event of claim surrender or maturity. The period over which premiums are outstanding should be comparatively short, and long-outstanding premiums should be investigated, recognising any special terms which may be available to the policyholder. For many life assurance policies, where there are unpaid premiums, the policy lapses or becomes paid up after a prescribed period of grace (the period of which varies between different insurers and classes of business); other insurers allow automatic premium loans whereby the reserve value of the policy is utilised to pay outstanding premiums.

Outstanding claims

92 The treatment of liabilities is based on a clear distinction between claims which have been notified and those which have not. A specific provision is normally made in the financial statements for claims which have been notified but have not been settled by the end of the accounting period whilst the liability for claims notified after the end of the accounting period should, unless otherwise provided, be covered by the valuation of long-term liabilities. Where a claim is payable and the policy or contract remains in force, as arises under a continuous disability policy or in the settlement of an annuity contract, the amounts when due for payment are usually treated as claims payable. Audit tests should be carried out in relation to cut off procedures with a view to ensuring that liabilities to policyholders are neither duplicated nor omitted entirely either from outstanding claims or from the valuation of liabilities. The amount provided for settling all claims arising from events which have occurred and been notified before the end of the accounting period is usually based on the estimated ultimate cost at which the claims are expected to be settled, including interest, if applicable, under the insurer's stated practice, less amounts already paid in respect of these claims. As the amount of the claim is predetermined, it will not be necessary to take account of the effect of inflation unless there is a specific policy condition to that effect. The accounting liability for claims outstanding relating to unit linked business is usually provided at the time at which the policy or contract ceases under the terms of the policy to participate in the fund. Audit tests should be designed to confirm that proper cut off procedures are in place.

93 Usually it will not be necessary to set up a separate provision for claims incurred but not reported as, until recorded as a claim, the liability will be included in the valuation of long-term liabilities. Where a claim has been incurred on a policy which has been reinsured **claims recoveries**, estimated where appropriate, should be accounted for in the same accounting period as the cost of the related claim. Audit tests should be directed to ensure that cut off procedures are adequate and that reinsurance recoverables have not been omitted.

Reinsurers' balances

94 The auditor should ascertain whether the reinsurer agrees the balances and, if it agrees, consider whether it has the ability to pay the amount due. The auditor should review the insurer's files relating to reinsurers to ascertain whether individual claims or balances are disputed by the reinsurer. Clearly reconciliations should be up-to-date and there should be no long-outstanding or disputed items. Particular care should be taken to ensure that reinsurance recoveries have been raised on all notified claims for which payment or provision has been made. Amounts due from or to reinsurers will normally be covered by direct confirmation.

Agents' balances and advance commission

95 There are certain accounting practices adopted by the insurance industry in respect of balances with independent intermediaries and appointed representatives, which may require particular attention:

- proper cut off procedures should be in force for the recognition of premium income, commission and claims paid;
- reconciliations of balances with agents should be carried out by the insurer at regular intervals; long-outstanding or unreconciled items should be carefully reviewed; and
- accounting for commissions to intermediaries on indemnity terms (see paragraph 66).

Reporting

Companies Act 1985

96 The auditor's responsibilities in relation to the financial statements of insurers under the Companies Act are the same as those for the generality of companies. However, where an insurer takes advantage of the disclosure exemptions, the auditor should report, in accordance with the requirements of paragraph 28 to Schedule 9, along the following lines:

> AUDITORS' REPORT TO THE MEMBERS OF XYZ LIMITED
>
> We have audited the financial statements on pages ... to ... in accordance with Auditing Standards.
>
> In our opinion, the financial statements have been properly prepared in accordance with the provisions of the Companies Act 1985 applicable to insurance companies.
>
> Auditors
>
> Date

Insurance Companies Act 1982

97 The auditor has the following responsibilities under Section 21 of the Insurance Act in relation to the returns submitted to the DTI:

- to state whether, in his opinion, the parts of the return required to be audited have been properly prepared in accordance with the regulations; and
- to state whether, in his opinion and according to the information and explanations he has received:
  - — the directors' certificate has been properly prepared in accordance with the regulations; and
  - — it was reasonable for the persons giving the certificate to have made the statements therein.

As indicated in paragraph 30, the directors' certificate on which the auditor is required to express a view is required to state *inter alia* that, for the purposes of preparing the DTI Return, 'an appropriate system of control had been established and maintained by the company over its transactions and records'; the auditor is therefore required in effect to express a view on this statement. Furthemore, the auditor is required to express an opinion on the directors' certificate that they have complied with Section 31A of the Insurance Act.

98 The auditor is also required to state, if such is the case, that:

- for the purposes of preparing the DTI Return, proper accounting records have not been maintained or proper returns have not been received from branches;
- the DTI Return is not in agreement with the accounting records and returns received from branches; and
- he has not obtained all the information and explanations necessary for the purposes of his report.

99 The form and content of the auditor's report is specified in Part III of Schedule 6 to the 1983 Regulations. The following form of report would usually be appropriate for an insurer which carries on only ordinary long-term insurance business:

AUDITORS' REPORT TO THE SECRETARY OF STATE FOR TRADE AND INDUSTRY PURSUANT TO REGULATION 27 OF THE INSURANCE COMPANIES (ACCOUNTS AND STATEMENTS) REGULATIONS 1983

We have examined forms [insert numbers of relevant forms actually included in the DTI Return] and the related notes on page ...

In our opinion these forms together with the related notes have been properly prepared in accordance with the provisions of the Insurance Companies (Accounts and Statements) Regulations 1983.

In our opinion and according to the information and explanations we have received:

(i) the certificate on pages ... and ... annexed in accordance with Regulation 26 (a) (other than so much of it as relates to the statement required by Regulation 29) has been properly prepared in accordance with the Regulations; and

(ii) it was reasonable for the persons giving the certificate to have made the statements therein.

In giving this opinion, we have relied on:

(i) the certificate of the Actuary on page ... with respect to the mathematical reserves and required minimum margin of the company; and

(ii) on the identity and value of any **implicit items** as they have been admitted in accordance with Regulation 10(4) of the Insurance Companies Regulations 1981.

Auditors

Date

Qualifications

100 If the audit report on the financial statements is qualified, the auditor will need to consider the extent to which the report on the DTI Return can be issued, or how the Return should reflect this.

101 If a report has been issued to the DTI in the circumstances set out in paragraphs 102 to 120, the auditor will need to consider its effect upon the audit report on the financial statements and the report on the DTI Return.

Ad hoc reports under the Insurance Companies Act 1982

General considerations

102 Section 135 of the FSA inserts a new section, Section 21A, into the Insurance Act which states that:

> 'No duty to which an auditor of an insurance company to which this Part of this Act applies may be subject shall be regarded as contravened by reason of his communicating in good faith to the Secretary of State, whether or not in response to a request from him, any information or opinion on a matter of which the auditor has become aware in his capacity as auditor and which is relevant to any functions of the Secretary of State under this Act.'

It is this section which makes it clear that the auditor is able to communicate with the DTI by way of a formal report, at a meeting or by any other means on any matters relating to the insurer's affairs arising out of his appointment and which are relevant to any function of the DTI under the Insurance Act.

103 The auditor of an insurer which is also an authorised investment business will, by virtue of Section 109 of the FSA, be able to disclose to the relevant supervisor matters relating to supervisory functions under the FSA as well as disclosing to the DTI matters relevant to its supervisory functions under the Insurance Act.

104 It is important to stress that the DTI expects that the management of the insurer and, where appropriate, the Actuary will continue to be its primary sources of information for regulatory purposes and that the normal reporting procedures will usually provide it with all the information it needs to carry out its responsibilities under the Insurance Act.

Responsibility of the auditor

105 The ability to communicate matters to the DTI is not restricted to information obtained by the auditor about the insurer itself. Under Section 21A, an auditor may communicate any relevant matter about anything which has come to his attention in his capacity as the auditor of an authorised insurer and which is relevant to any functions of the Secretary of State under the Insurance Act. Thus, in his communications with the DTI, the auditor may address not only the affairs of the insurer but also the information about other insurers obtained in the course of his audit of the insurer. The Insurance Act does not give protection in relation to disclosure of information obtained by the auditor otherwise than in his capacity as auditor of the insurer.

106 The auditor cannot be expected to be aware of all circumstances which would, had he known of them, have led him to exercise his right to report under Section 21A. That section does not require the auditor to change the scope of his audit work, nor the frequency or timing of his audit visits beyond that required to enable a report to be made on the return to the DTI under the Insurance Act and on the financial statements of the insurer under the Companies Act. The auditor does not have an obligation to seek out grounds for making a report under Section 21A (i.e. the section does not place an obligation on the auditor to conduct his work in such a way that there is reasonable certainty that he will discover an occurrence of the kind described in paragraph 109). It is only when the auditor becomes aware in the ordinary course of his work of such an occurrence that he should make detailed enquiries with Section 21A specifically in mind.

107 The auditor should, however, ensure he is made aware of any other relationships which exist between any department of his firm and the insurer which could affect his work. As noted in paragraph 108, the Insurance Act does not give protection to the auditor if a matter is not reported to the DTI. The DTI expects that the auditor will ensure that he is informed of all potentially 'reportable' matters by all other departments within his firm which have a relationship with the client insurer. It would, therefore, be prudent for such firms to establish adequate systems of inter-departmental communication to ensure any matters which may give rise to a report under Section 21A are brought to the attention of the appropriate auditor. However, the DTI expects insurers to advise their auditor when they appoint a third party (including another department of the same firm) to review, investigate or report on any aspect of their records and systems and to provide them with copies of reports by such a third party promptly after their receipt.

108 The auditor should realise that there are circumstances in which Section 21A will not provide protection, for example, where he could be held to have acted maliciously or in bad faith. Section 21A does not, therefore, provide complete immunity from all types of legal action by all parties affected, or subsequently affected, by his action in reporting. The auditor may, therefore, wish to consider taking legal or other professional advice from an appropriately qualified source before making the decision whether, or in what manner, to report. However, it should be borne in mind that speed of reporting may well be important in order to protect the interests of existing and prospective policyholders. There is no protection given by Section 21A if the auditor fails to report to the DTI.

Taking the initiative

109 The profession has developed a criterion for use by the auditor in deciding whether to take the initiative in making an *ad hoc* report in addition to his regular reporting responsibilities. The criterion is that the auditor should take the initiative when he considers it expedient to do so in order to protect the interests of the policyholders. This criterion can be more fully explained as follows:

- there must be an adverse occurrence, or a change in the auditor's perception of an existing situation, which may include an adverse change in the circumstances of the insurer: and
- the position described above has given rise to a material loss or indicates that a reasonable probability exists that a material loss may arise; and
- the position is such that the interests of existing and prospective policyholders might be better safeguarded if the DTI were aware of it.

110 As stated in paragraph 106, the auditor is not required to seek out grounds for making a report. It is only where he becomes aware during the ordinary course of his work that the criterion might be satisfied that he should take the matter further.

Reporting via the insurer

111 It is important for the auditor to act in a manner that will preserve his professional relationship with the insurer (including that with the Actuary). Normally, he should ask the insurer to draw matters about which he is concerned to the attention of the DTI. Examples of circumstances encountered in which the criterion may be met, and the matter reported via the insurer, are:

- when, in the auditor's opinion, the insurer does not or may not at present, have the required minimum margin of solvency;
- where it has come to the attention of the auditor that there is an extreme situation, such as evidence of imminent financial collapse, where it is obvious that the DTI must be informed;

- where the auditor has evidence of an occurrence which has led or is likely to lead to a material diminution of the insurer's net assets;
- when the auditor forms the opinion that there has been a significant failure of, or that there is significant weakness in, the accounting and other records or the internal control systems;
- the discovery of an insurer's failure to comply with the Insurance Act and related regulations made thereunder; and
- when the auditor forms an opinion that management has reported financial information to the DTI which is misleading in a material particular (or become aware that management has failed or does not intend to report something and the failure to report is, or would be, materially misleading).

Reporting directly to the DTI

112 In exceptional circumstances, where it is in the interests of protecting existing and prospective policyholders that the management of the insurer should not be informed in advance, the auditor should report directly to the DTI. In the case of an insurer carrying on long-term business, it may still be appropriate to discuss the matter with the Actuary. Examples of such circumstances are:

- where there has been an occurrence which causes the auditor no longer to have confidence in the integrity of the directors or senior management e.g. where he believes that a fraud or other misappropriation has been committed by the directors or senior management of the insurer, or he has evidence of the intention of directors or senior management to commit such fraud or misappropriation; and
- where there has been an occurrence which causes the auditor no longer to have confidence in the competence of the directors or senior management to conduct the business of the insurer in a prudent manner so as to protect the interests of existing and prospective policyholders, e.g. where he has discovered that the directors or senior management are acting in an irresponsible or reckless manner with respect to the insurer's affairs, or they have evidence of an intention to so act.

113 Additionally, as outlined in paragraph 115, a direct report should be made where the insurer or, where appropriate, the Actuary will not themselves inform the DTI of a matter, having been advised to do so by the auditor or where they have not done so within the period of time specified, or where there is not adequate evidence that the insurer or the Actuary has properly reported the matter in question.

Reporting procedures

114 In forming a view as to whether it is expedient to report a matter to the DTI, the auditor should follow the procedures in making enquiries and obtaining and assessing relevant evidence which are a normal part of forming a professional judgement in relation to an audit.

115 Where the auditor becomes aware of a matter which in his professional judgement he considers ought to be reported to the DTI, he should consider adopting the following procedures, bearing in mind that speed may be of the essence.

(a) The auditor should consider the facts and, unless inappropriate in the circumstances, discuss the matter with the management of the insurer and with the Actuary.

(b) In normal circumstances, he should establish whether the matter has already been reported by the insurer or the Actuary and if so, obtain from the insurer or the Actuary a copy of the DTI's written acknowledgement sufficient to establish that the matter has been properly reported. If the matter has not already been reported by management or the Actuary, the auditor should write to the insurer setting out his views and requesting that the DTI be informed of the matter within a specified period of time. A copy of this letter should also be provided to the Actuary. He should then obtain from the insurer or the Actuary evidence of prompt acknowledgement from the DTI, sufficient to establish that the matter has been properly reported. In the absence of such evidence, it may be appropriate for the auditor to report the matter directly to the DTI, and to inform the management of the insurer and the Actuary of the contents of his report. If the directors or management or the Actuary have not informed the DTI, and continue to refuse to inform them within the specified period of time, the auditor should report direct to the DTI.

(c) If the situation is sensitive, for example in the circumstances outlined in paragraph 112, it may be inappropriate to discuss the matters with the levels of management with whom the auditor normally deals. The auditor should therefore consider reporting to the appropriate senior level within the insurer with a view to the DTI being informed of the situation by a senior representative of the insurer. In the case of an insurer carrying on long-term business it will normally still be appropriate for the auditor also to discuss the matter with the Actuary. The auditor should then obtain evidence from the insurer or the Actuary of prompt acknowledgement by the DTI sufficient to establish that the matter has been properly reported. In the absence of such evidence, it will then be appropriate for the auditor to report direct to the DTI. In exceptional circumstances where the auditor feels that in the interests of speed and/or, because of the nature of the matter, it is not appropriate or practical to inform or discuss the matter with anyone connected with the insurer, the auditor should make an appropriate written or other report direct to the DTI.

116 The auditor should bear in mind that his decision may have to stand up to examination at a future date on the basis of the following considerations:

- what he knew at the time;
- what he should have known in the course of his audit;
- what he should have concluded; and
- what he should have done.

117 Speed of reporting will often be important to the protection of the interests of existing and prospective policyholders. A report should be made as soon as the auditor reasonably can after forming the view that it is expedient to do so in order to protect the interests of existing and prospective policyholders. For the auditor this may well mean ensuring that an *ad hoc* report is made to the DTI in advance of making his report on the financial statements of the insurer or on the DTI Return.

118 The auditor should note that in the situations outlined in paragraphs 111 and 112 above, making an *ad hoc* report alone may not discharge all his responsibilities. An example of this would be the need for the auditor to consider the implications of the *ad hoc* report for his opinion on the financial statements.

119 To ensure that the DTI is informed promptly of matters which meet the criterion, the auditor should ensure that:

- all staff responsible for insurance assignments are aware of the provisions of Section 21A and the contents of this guidance and are able to identify situations in which they might operate; and
- satisfactory procedures exist to ensure that any information, which may be the subject

of an *ad hoc* report, obtained by staff in the course of their work, is passed on to the partner responsible without unnecessary delay.

Communications by the DTI

120 The DTI is mindful of the role of auditors and the supervisory benefits of closer cooperation. The DTI has confirmed that it will consider, in appropriate cases, informing auditors of factors which may be relevant to their function.

Appendix — Glossary of terms

This glossary is not intended to be comprehensive; it deals only with certain technical terms used in this guideline.

Acquisition costs. Costs incurred in the acquisition of new and renewal insurance contracts. Acquisition costs include those costs that vary with, and are primarily related to, the acquisition of insurance contracts (e.g. commissions, certain underwriting and policy issue costs and inspection fees).

Admissable assets. Assets available to meet the liabilities and margin of solvency of an insurer after valuation in accordance with Part V of the 1981 Regulations.

Annuitants. Persons in receipt of an annuity.

Annuity. A periodic payment (strictly, an annual payment) made from a stated or contingent date and continued for a fixed period, or for as long as the annuitant or annuitants live. In practice, annuity payments are most frequently made on a monthly basis; however, they may be made at any other interval that is agreed upon.

Appointed representatives. Term established by the FSA to denote those who distribute investment products from only one insurer. They must, however, give best advice.

Bonus rates. The amount of the bonus payments allocated to with-profits policyholders by way of distribution of established surplus in a particular year.

Catastrophe. Total claims of an insurer arising out of a single catastrophic event (e.g. conflagration, earthquake, storm, explosion or similar event).

Cede. To transfer liability in connection with a risk, or a portion of it, from the original insurer to the reinsurer.

Ceding company. The original or primary insurer who reinsures with another company, which is called the reinsurer.

Established surplus. The excess of admissible assets representing the whole or part of a long-term fund over liabilities, as determined by an investigation by the Actuary, attributable to the related business.

Expense overrun. The excess of expenses incurred over that expected and allowed for in the establishment of premium rates.

Facultative reinsurance. Reinsurance arrangements under which each risk to be reinsured is offered to and is accepted or rejected by the reinsurer. So-called facultative reinsurance arrangements are, therefore, only permissive and do not obligate the ceding company to cede or the reinsurer to accept.

Free assets. Assets over and above those required to meet long-term liabilities and the margin of solvency.

Free reserves. The excess of the long-term business fund over the 'mathematical reserves' and other specific provisions included in the determination of liabilities and the margin of solvency in accordance with the 1981 Regulations.

Implicit item. Items which may be included in the determination of liabilities for the purposes of the DTI Return. These include hidden reserves, future profits and zillmerisation. The consent of the DTI is required.

Independent financial advisers. Term established by the FSA to denote those who distribute a range of investment products, including life insurance, from more than one insurer, and who are required to give best advice.

Internal linked funds. Specified assets by reference to which the value of policyholder benefits is determined.

Investment contracts. Long-term contracts the main purpose of which is the accumulation of capital for the policyholder.

Lapse rate. The rate at which insurance policies terminate through failure of the insured to continue making premium payments. It is usually expressed as a ratio of the number of policies on which the insured failed to make premium payments during a given period, to the total number of policies at the beginning of the period from which thoses lapses occurred.

Localisation of assets. The maintenance of assets in such places and in such currencies as are suitable to meet the related liabilities.

Long-term fund. A pool of assets owned by a life company out of which it meets claims under life insurance policies as and when they arise.

Margin of solvency. The difference between the assets and liabilities of an insurance company. A minimum margin of solvency is required to be maintained in accordance with Part II of the 1981 Regulations.

Mathematical reserves. The amount, calculated in accordance with the requirements of the Insurance Act, which is required to be provided to cover liabilities arising under contracts for long-term business.

Morbidity risk. The risk of an insured becoming ill or disabled.

Mortality risk. The risk of an insured life ending through death of the insured.

Permanent health. The provision of insurance providing specified benefits against the risk of incapacity through accident, sickness or infirmity for a period of at least five years or until normal retirement age where the insurance is not cancellable by the insurer or is so only in special specified circumstances.

Pure reinsurer. An insurer for which authorisation to carry on business in the United Kingdom is restricted to reinsurance.

Reinsurance. (1) A procedure whereby the original insurer relieves itself of part or all of an insurance risk by passing it on (reinsuring it) to another insurance company. (2) A contract in which the reinsurer (the first party) in consideration of a premium agrees to idemnify the reinsured (the second party) against the risk insured by the reinsured under a policy in favour of the insured (third party). The reinsured may be referred to as original or primary insurer or the ceding company.

Retrocede. To reinsure reinsurance assumed. For example: A accepts reinsurance from B and then in turn reinsures with C a whole or part of the reinsurance assumed from B. The reinsurance ceded to C by A is called a retrocession.

Substandard lives. Insurance of persons who do not meet the standards set for insurance at regular rates. Substandard insurance may be issued for physical, moral or mental reasons, or because of occupation, residence etc.

Surplus. The amount by which the total value of assets of the long-term fund exceeds the liabilities to policyholders.

Surplus treaty. Reinsurance by a ceding company of that part of a risk that exceeds the retention established by the ceding company.

Tontines. Life insurance policy providing for dividends payable after a period of years to the surviving persisting members of an initial group. A pure tontine policy also provides that no surrender values are payable upon lapse; thus, all profits from lapse are divided among the survivors.

Treaty. A term historically applied to reinsurance contracts as distinct from facultative reinsurance arrangements.

Whole life contract. Insurance that may be kept in force for a person's entire life by paying one or more premiums. It is paid for in one of three different ways: (1) ordinary life insurance (premiums are payable as long as the insured lives), (2) limited payment life insurance (premiums are payable over a specified number of years), and (3) single-premiums life insurance (a lump-sum amount paid at the inception of the insurance contract). The insurance contract pays a benefit (contractual amount adjusted for items such as policy loans and dividends, if any) at the death of the insured. Whole life insurance contracts also build up non-forfeiture benefits.

With-profit. Term used to describe policies where the policyholders are eligible to participate in established surplus. Also a term used to describe the separate funds established in respect of such business.

Zillmerisation. An adjustment to the valuation of long-term business reserves to recognise the heavy initial expenses of writing such business.

Bank reports for audit purposes

(Issued 30 June 1982)

Introduction

1 Paragraph 4 of the auditor's operational standard states that the auditor should obtain relevant and reliable audit evidence. This guideline is designed to assist auditors in complying with this standard with respect to amounts due to and from banks, and assets held by them.

2 The practice of obtaining independent certificates or reports from banks is an important feature in the proper discharge of auditors' responsibilities. Bank reports assist auditors to ascertain the existence and the amount of liabilities and the existence amount, ownership and proper custody of assets; they also provide other information relevant to the audit of financial statements.

3 The standard audit request letter in the appendix to this guideline has been prepared following discussions with the Committee of London Clearing Bankers, and the Committee of Scottish Clearing Bankers. The standard letter has been prepared primarily for the purpose of obtaining information from the clearing banks. Many companies, however, also have dealings with other banks or licensed deposit-taking institutions, and auditors will normally need reports from them. The British Bankers' Association had indicated that the standard letter may not always be appropriate for requests to such organisations, particularly where specialised or limited services are offered, and that consequently no undertaking can be given by their members to answer every question on every occasion. Separate guidance relating to Ireland will be issued in due course. The standard request letter set out in the guideline should be used for all requests to banks after 1 October 1982.

Background

4 The information which auditors regularly need from banks is substantially the same for most audits, and can be obtained in a standard letter of request. The use of such a letter, designed to cover all normal banking activity and to facilitate the extraction of information from banking records, should smooth the processing of these audit requests. The answers received should assist in highlighting areas which require particular audit attention.

5 As the clearing banks keep their customer records in a more or less similar manner, the use of a standard letter should facilitate the efficient preparation of their replies. The banks accept the need for their assistance in these matters, and a standard letter gives them a clearer understanding of auditors' requirements.

6 Auditors should therefore request information from banks in the form of the standard letter set out in the appendix and in accordance with the procedures in paragraphs 11 - 13 below. It is intended that this standard letter should be primarily for audit purposes, but if it is used when members are only concerned with the preparation of accounts and not with the audit of, for instance, sole traders, partnerships or other non-statutory organisations, then any reference in it to an audit should be deleted. For certain purposes other than verification at the year-end (for example for work of an accounting nature, interim audits and accountants' reports on solicitors' accounts), it may be necessary to seek confirmation only of selected items from the standard request. In such cases the letter should not be headed 'standard request for bank report'.

7 The attached standard letter is a revision of the one set out in the Statement issued in

1976, following experience gained in the use of that earlier version. It now includes enough space for the banks to enter their replies on a copy of the letter, which should be sent at the same time as the main audit request.

8 As indicated in paragraph 3 above, in the case of institutions other than clearing banks it may often be more appropriate for the auditor to make a specific request for the information he requires rather than to use the standard letter. If he is unable to obtain any of the information he requires, he must consider the effect of this on his audit opinion.

Authority to disclose

9 Banks will require the explicit authority of their customers to disclose the requested information. They will always require such authority in writing, and this may be obtained either on each occasion a bank report is requested, or as an authority which continues until further notice. In the former case it is recommended that the authority should be evidenced by the customer's counter-signature to the letter of request; in the latter case the letter of request should refer to the customer's written authority given on a specified earlier date. In the case of a joint account, the authority should be given by all parties to the account.

Disclaimer

10 The introduction to the letter states that there is no contractual relationship between banker and auditor. In addition, the banks may add a disclaimer at the end of their reply, the text of which may be as follows:

> "This reply is given solely for the purpose of your audit without any responsibility to you on the part of the bank, its employees or agents, but it is not to relieve you from any other enquiry or from the performance of any other duty."

Counsel has given the opinion that the inclusion of the introductory statement and of a disclaimer of this nature does not significantly impair the value of the information given as audit evidence. The information given by a reputable bank should not be regarded as inaccurate or likely to be inaccurate simply because the giving of it is not actionable. Accordingly, an auditor can reasonably rely upon information given by a banker, provided it is not clearly wrong, suspicious or inconsistent in itself, ambiguous or in conflict with other evidence gathered in the course of an audit.

Procedures

11 Auditors should, where appropriate, adopt the following procedures in connection with requests to banks for audit purposes:

(a) The standard letter set out in the appendix to this guideline should be sent in duplicate on each occasion by the auditor on his own note paper to each bank branch with which it is known that the client holds an account or has had dealings since the end of the previous accounting reference period.

(b) Auditors should ensure that the bank receives the client's authority to permit disclosure. This authority must be evidenced by:

(i) the client's counter-signature to the standard letter; or

(ii) a specific authority contained in an accompanying letter; or

(iii) a reference in the standard letter to the client's specific written authority, given on a specified earlier date, which remains in force.

(c) The letter should reach the branch at least two weeks in advance of the date of the client's financial year-end. This should enable the banks to provide the information within a reasonable time after the year-end. It should be borne in mind, however, that many requests arise at the same time and at a period of peak activity for the banks. Special arrangements should therefore be made with the banks in those cases where, because of time constraints on the audit, a reply is required within a few days of the company's year-end.

(d) The dates to be entered on the standard letter are normally the closing dates of:
   (i) the client's accounting reference period for which the report is requested; and
   (ii) the client's previous accounting reference period for which a full bank report was compiled. If, exceptionally, audited accounts are produced other than for an accounting reference period, alternative dates should be substituted.

(e) In reviewing the bank's reply, it is important for auditors to check that the bank has answered all questions in full.

(f) Auditors will need to check the authenticity of any letters not received directly from the bank branch concerned. If an auditor receives a bank report without having made a previous request, he should check with the branch concerned that the report has been prepared in compliance with the terms of the standard letter.

12 The standard letter should be used in its complete form for all audit requests in respect of year-end financial statements and should not normally be altered or extended. In certain circumstances supplementary requests for additional information may be required for audit purposes. For administrative reasons the letter containing these supplementary requests should be submitted where possible at the same time as the standard letter. Where supplementary information is requested the banks will, as indicated above, require authority to disclose this. If the wording of the authority is not sufficiently comprehensive, additional authority may be required. For some information, such as security lodged by a third party, authority from someone other than the customer may be required.

13 The banks may choose not to reply on the copy standard letter itself, but instead on their own note paper. If this is the case, the auditor should check that the list of replies corresponds with the questions on the standard letter and that there have been no omissions.

Appendix

Standard letter of request for bank report for audit purposes

(i) *The form of the letter should not be amended by the auditor.*

(ii) *Sufficient space should be left for the bank's replies (two-thirds of each page is recommended).*

The Manager,

....(Bank)

....(Branch)

Dear Sir,

....(Name of Customer)

STANDARD REQUEST FOR BANK REPORT
FOR AUDIT PURPOSES
FOR THE YEAR ENDED ....

In accordance with your above-named customer's instructions given

(1) hereon
(2) in the attached authority
(3) in the authority dated ... already held by you

Delete as appropriate

please send to us, as auditors of your customer for the purpose of our business, without entering into any contractual relationship with us, the following information relating to their affairs at your branch as at the close of business on .... and, in the case of items 2, 4 and 10 during the period since.. For each item, please state any factors which may limit the completeness of your reply; if there is nothing to report, state 'none'.

We enclose an additional copy of this letter, and it would be particularly helpful if your reply could be given on the copy letter in the space provided (supported by an additional schedule stamped and signed by the bank where space is insufficient). If you find it necessary to provide the information in another form, please return the copy letter with your reply.

It is understood that any replies given are in strict confidence.

Information requested *Reply*

Bank accounts

1 Please give full titles of all accounts whether in sterling or in any other currency together with the account numbers and balances thereon, including NIL balances:

(a) where your customer's name is the sole name in the title;
(b) where your customer's name is joined with that of other parties;
(c) where the account is in a trade name.

NOTES

(i) Where the account is subject to any restriction (e.g. a garnishee order or arrestment), this information should be stated.
(ii) Where the authority upon which you are providing this information does not cover any accounts held jointly with other parties, please refer to your customer in order to obtain the requisite authority of the other parties. If this authority is not forthcoming please indicate.

2 Full titles and dates of closure of all accounts closed during the period.

3 The separate amounts accrued but not charged or credited at the above date, of:

(a) provisional charges (including commitment fees); and
(b) interest.

4 The amount of interest charged during the period if not specified separately in the bank statement.

Information requested	*Reply*

5 Particulars (i.e. date, type of document and accounts covered) of any written acknowledgement of set-off, either by specific letter of set-off, or incorporated in some other document or security.

6 Details of:

(a) overdrafts and loans repayable on demand, specifying dates of review and agreed facilities;

(b) other loans specifying dates of review and repayments;

(c) other facilities.

Customer's assets held as security

7 Please give details of any such assets whether or not formally charged to the bank.

If formally charged, give details of the security including the date and type of charge. If a security is limited in amount or to a specific borrowing, or if there is to your knowledge a prior, equal or subordinate charge, please indicate.

If formally charged, indicate nature of security interest therein claimed by the bank.

Whether or not a formal charge has been taken, give particulars of any undertaking given to the bank relating to any assets.

Customer's other assets held

8 Please give full details of the customer's other assets held, including share certificates, documents of title, deed boxes and any other items listed in your registers maintained for the purpose of recording assets held.

Contingent liabilities

9 All contingent liabilities, viz:

(a) total of bills discounted for your customer, with recourse;

(b) date, name of beneficiary, amount and brief description of any guarantees, bonds or indemnities given to you by the customer for the benefit of third parties;

(c) date, name of beneficiary, amount and brief description of any guarantees, bonds or indemnities given by you, on your customer' be-

Information requested	*Reply*
half, stating where there is recourse to your customer and/or to its parent or any other company within the group;	
(d) total of acceptances;	
(e) total sterling equivalent of outstanding forward foreign exchange contracts;	
(f) total of outstanding liabilities under documentary credits;	
(g) others — please give details.	

Other information

10 A list of other banks, or branches of your bank, or associated companies where you are aware that a relationship has been established during the period.

Yours faithfully

Disclosure authorised for and on behalf of

....

....

(Name of customer)

....

....

(Signed in accordance with the mandate for the conduct of the customer's bank account.)

....

(Official stamp of bank)

....

(Authorised signatory)

....

(Position)

....

(Date)

Notes to the standard letter

(References are to item numbers in the standard letter)

1 Bank accounts: The phrase 'all accounts' includes details of all current, deposit, loan and foreign currency accounts and other advances or facilities, money held on deposit receipt. The reply should indicate whether the balance is in favour of the bank or customer, and account numbers. Where a number of deposits have been made or uplifted during the year, it is not necessary to give details of each separate deposit transaction as would be required in the case of the opening and closing of accounts.

3 Accrued charges: These can be quoted only on a provisional basis; the rate for national allowances will not be fixed until near the end of the charging period.

4 Analysis of charges: For the purposes of profit and loss disclosure requirements it is only necessary to ask for details of interest charged. (But see note 6 (b) below in respect of balance sheet disclosure requirements). The details of the rate of interest applicable to any interest-bearing accounts, or the appropriate formula by which interest is calculated, should only be required exceptionally.

5 **Set-off:** Auditors will need to have an understanding of the principles governing set-off, but it should not normally be necessary to make enquiries beyond the question as put in the standard letter. Details should be available from the relevant documents. A right of set-off may exist even when there are no written arrangements.

6 **Loans and other facilities:** The following details are not normally required;

(a) the date term loans were granted if new or renewed during the period;

(b) rate of interest charged or similar form of compensation (which information is only required by the Companies Acts to be disclosed for facilities which are wholly or partly repayable in more than five years' time);

(c) the purpose of the facility;

(d) loan repayment arrangements, where these are included in a written agreement which is available for inspection by the auditor.

7 and **8 Customer's assets:**

(a) *Security* includes details of charge, mortgage or other claims or security registered (e.g. debenture, memorandum of deposit); assets charged and, where appropriate, cross reference to facility specifically secured.

(b) *Assets* include bonds, stock and share certificates, investments, bearer or other securities; title deeds relating to freehold, leasehold or other property; certificates of tax deposit, bills of exchange or other negotiable instruments receivable (other than cheques); shipping and other commercial documents, deposit receipts (as distinct from any account represented by the deposit receipt);
the names of persons who are able to obtain release of the assets should be ascertained from the customer and are usually covered by the bank mandate.

(c) *Lien:* auditors should be aware that any assets held by the bank for safe custody may be subject to some form of banker's lien, although this may only operate under particular conditions. It should be necessary to enquire only in exceptional circumstances.

(d) *Bearer securities:* detailed enquiries on bearer securities should be made of the bank only when evidence cannot be obtained from the customer or his banking records.

9 **Contingent liabilities:** The liabilities under indemnities given in respect of missing bills of lading do not have an expiry date. From time to time the banks take a view on old liabilities and remove some of them from their records. Certain of these old liabilities may not therefore be shown in the figure quoted by the bank, but it cannot be guaranteed that no claim will be incurred subsequently.

10 Other information: Banks are often asked for introductions to other branches or banks for the purpose of establishing new sources of finance. The provision of any available information relating to introductions or new accounts will assist auditors to satisfy themselves that they have information about all their client's banking relationships.

Notes on matters excluded from the standard letter

Supplementary requests

The standard letter contains all items found to be regularly required for audit purposes.

In cases of doubt, or specific requirements, auditors may wish to make supplementary requests regarding other items which are not regularly required. These may include the following:

(a) copies of bank statements;
(b) copies of paying-in slips for specified lodgement of specified dates;
(c) details showing make-up of those lodgements;
(d) any list of securities or other documents of title which have been lodged by a bank with its customer as security for deposit with that bank. (This particular matter would probably apply only between banking organisations);
(e) interest on any account paid to or by third parties, and the names of those third parties;
(f) receipts for fire and other insurances, and similar documents in the bank's possession;
(g) returned paid cheques;
(h) stopped cheques — these are normally presented through the banking system within the audit period, and therefore there should be no need to seek specific details;
(i) details of third party security, including directors' guarantees; if this information is required, the request must be accompanied by a specific authority from the appropriate third parties;
(j) details of outstanding forward foreign exchange contracts, including the particulars of each contract, the dates of maturity and the currencies concerned.

Notes

(i) The cost of providing audit information falls on the customer and supplementary requests should be kept to a reasonable minimum.
(ii) Depending on the terms of the authority which has been given, it may be necessary to seek specific authorisation for the disclosure of supplementary information.

Bank mandates

Auditors may require supplementary information about bank mandates as independent verification that board resolutions concerning a company's banking affairs have been duly communicated to the bank so that they may ensure that only authorised persons are acting on behalf of the company. Auditors should ensure that they receive copies of all such resolutions from their clients.

Attendance at stocktaking

(Issued October 1983)

Preface

Paragraph 4 of the Auditing Standard, 'The auditor's operational standard' states that: "The auditor should obtain relevant and reliable audit evidence sufficient to enable him to draw reasonable conclusions therefrom".
This auditing guideline gives guidance on how that paragraph may be applied in relation to attendance at stocktaking. It is supplementary to and should be read in conjunction with the auditor's operational and reporting standards and related guidelines.

Introduction

1 The value of stock and work in progress ('stocks') in the financial statements of a trading enterprise will often be material to the profit and loss account and to the balance sheet and, as such, is of great importance to the financial statements. There are three main elements in the audit of stocks: existence, ownership and valuation. This guideline is primarily concerned with the first of these elements.

Responsibilities

2 It is the responsibility of the management of an enterprise to ensure that the amount at which stocks are shown in the financial statements represents stocks physically in existence and includes all stocks owned by the enterprise. Management satisfies this responsibility by carrying out appropriate procedures which will normally involve ensuring that all stocks are subject to a count at least once in every financial year. Further, where the auditor attends any physical count of stocks in order to obtain audit evidence, this responsibility will not be reduced.

3 In the case of a company incorporated under the Companies Acts, management also has responsibilities to maintain proper accounting records and to include all statements of stocktakings in those records.

4 It is the responsibility of the auditor to obtain audit evidence in order to enable him to draw conclusions about the validity of the quantities upon which are based the amount of stocks shown in the financial statements. The principal source of this evidence are stock records, stock control systems, the results of any stocktaking and test-counts made by the auditor himself. By reviewing the enterprise's stock records attendance at stocktaking to obtain the necessary audit evidence.

Attendance as a means of providing evidence

5 Where stocks are material in the enterprise's financial statements, and the auditor is placing reliance upon management's stocktake in order to provide evidence of existence, then the auditor should attend the stocktaking. This is because attendance at stocktaking is normally the best way of providing evidence of the proper functioning of management's stocktaking procedures, and hence of the existence of stocks and their condition.

6 Evidence of the existence of work in progress will frequently be obtained by a stocktake. However, the nature of the work in progress may be such that it is impracticable to determine its existence by a count. Management may place substantial reliance on internal controls designed to ensure the completeness and accuracy of records of work in progress. In such circumstances there may not be a stocktake which could be attended by the auditor. Nevertheless, inspection of the work in progress will assist the auditor to plan his audit procedures, and it may also help on such matters as the determination of the stage of completion of construction or engineering work in progress.

Types of stocktaking

7 Physical verification of stocks may be by means of a full count (or measurement in the case of bulk stocks) of all the stocks at the year end or at a selected date before or shortly after the year end, or by means of a count of part of the stocks in which case it may be possible to extrapolate the total statistically. Alternatively, verification may be by means of the counting or measurement of stocks during the course of the year using continuous stock-checking methods. Some business enterprises use continuous stock-checking methods for certain stocks and carry out a full count of other stocks at a selected date.

8 Paragraphs 9 and 10 set out some special considerations in circumstances where the count is carried out at a date which is not the same as that of the financial statements or where it takes place throughout the year. The principal procedures which the auditor would normally carry out in relation to his attendance at any count of stocks are set out in paragraphs 11 - 21 of this guideline.

9 The evidence of the existence of stocks provided by the stocktake results is most effective when the stocktaking is carried out at the end of the financial year. Stocktaking carried out before or after the year end may also be acceptable for audit purposes provided records of stock movements in the intervening period are such that the movements can be examined and substantiated. The auditor should bear in mind that the greater the interval between the stocktaking and the year end the greater will be his difficulties in substantiating the amount of stocks at the balance sheet date. Such difficulties will, however, be lessened by the existence of a well developed system of internal control and satisfactory stock records.

10 Where continuous stock-checking methods are being used, the auditor should perform tests designed to confirm that management:

- (a) maintains adequate stock records that are kept up to date;
- (b) has satisfactory procedures for stocktaking and test-counting, so that in normal circumstances the programme of counts will cover all stocks at least once during the year; and
- (c) investigates and corrects all material differences between the book stock records and the physical counts.

The auditor needs to do this to gain assurance that the stock-checking system as a whole is effective in maintaining accurate stock records from which the amount of stocks in the financial statements can be derived. It is unlikely that he will be able to obtain such assurance if the three matters above are not confirmed satisfactorily, in which circumstances a full count at the year end may be necessary.

Procedures

11 The following paragraphs set out the principal procedures which may be carried out by an auditor when attending a stocktake, but are not intended to provide a comprehensive list of the audit procedures which the auditor may find it necessary to perform during his attendance.

Before the stocktaking: planning

12 The auditor should plan his audit coverage of a stocktake by:

- (a) reviewing his working papers for the previous year, where applicable, and discussing with management any significant changes in stocks over the year;

(b) discussing stocktaking arrangements and instructions with management;
(c) familiarising himself with the nature and volume of the stocks, the identification of high value items and the method of accounting for stocks;
(d) considering the location of the stock and assessing the implications of this for stock control and recording;
(e) reviewing the systems of internal control and accounting relating to stocks, so as to identify potential areas of difficulty (for example cut-off);
(f) considering any internal audit involvement, with a view of deciding the reliance which can be placed on it;
(g) ensuring that a representative selection of locations, stocks and procedures are covered, and particular attention is given to high value items where these form a significant proportion of the total stock value;
(h) arranging to obtain from third parties confirmation of stocks held by them, but if the auditor considers that such stocks are a material part of the enterprise's total stock, or the third party is not considered to be independent or reliable, then arranging where appropriate either for him or for the third party's auditor to attend a stocktake at the third party's premises; and
(i) establishing whether expert help needs to be obtained to substantiate quantities, or to identify the nature and condition of the stocks, where they are very specialised.

13 The auditor should examine the way the stocktaking is organised and should evaluate the adequacy of the client's stocktaking instructions. Such instructions should preferably be in writing, cover all phases of the stocktaking procedures, be issued in good time and be discussed with those responsible for carrying out the stocktaking to ensure the procedures are understood and that potential difficulties are anticipated. If the instructions are found to be inadequate, the auditor should seek improvements to them.

During the stocktaking

14 During the stocktaking, the auditor should ascertain whether the client's staff are carrying out their instructions properly so as to provide reasonable assurance that the stocktaking will be accurate. He should make test counts to satisfy himself that procedures and internal controls relating to the stocktaking are working properly. If the manner of carrying out the stocktaking or the results of the test-counts are not satisfactory, the auditor should immediately draw the matter to the attention of the management supervising the stocktaking and he may have to request a recount of part, or all of the stocks.

15 When carrying out test-counts, the auditor should select items both from count records and from the physical stocks and should check one to the other to gain assurance as to the completeness and accuracy of the count records. In this context, he should give particular consideration to those stocks which he believes, for example from the stock records or from his prior year working papers, to have a high value either individually or as a category of stock. The auditor should include in his working papers items for subsequent testing, such as photocopies of (or extracts from) rough stocksheets and details of the sequence of stocksheets.

16 The auditor should determine whether the procedures for identifying damaged, obsolete and slow moving stock operate properly. He should obtain (from his observations and by discussion e.g. with storekeepers) information about the stock's condition, age, usage and, in the case of work in progress, its stage of completion. Further, he should ascertain that stock held on behalf of third parties is separately identified and accounted for.

17 The auditor should consider whether management has instituted adequate cut-off procedures i.e. procedures intended to ensure that movements into, within and out of stocks are properly identified and reflected in the accounting records. The auditor's procedures during the stocktaking will depend on the manner in which the year end stock value is to be determined. For example, where stocks are determined by a full count and evaluation at the year end, the auditor should test the arrangements made to segregate stocks owned by third parties and he should identify goods movement documents for reconciliation with financial records of purchases and sales. Alternatively, where the full count and evaluation is at an interim date and year end stocks are determined by updating such valuation by the cost of purchases and sales, the auditor should perform those procedures during his attendance at the stocktaking and in addition should test the financial cut-off (involving the matching of costs with revenues) at the year end.

18 In addition, the auditor should:

(a) conclude whether the stocktaking has been properly carried out and is sufficiently reliable as a basis for determining the existence of stocks;

(b) consider whether any amendment is necessary to his subsequent audit procedures; and

(c) try to gain from his observations an overall impression of the levels and values of stocks held so that he may, in due course, judge whether the figure for stocks appearing in the financial statements is reasonable.

19 The auditor's working papers should include details of his observations and tests, the manner in which points that are relevant and material to the stocks being counted or measured have been dealt with by the client, instances where the client's procedures have not been satisfactorily carried out and the auditor's conclusions.

After the stocktaking

20 After the stocktaking, the matters recorded in the auditor's working papers at the time of the count or measurement should be followed up. For example, details of the last serial numbers of goods inwards and outwards notes and of movements during the stocktaking should be used in order to check cut-off. Further, photocopies of (or extracts from) rough stocksheets and details of test-counts, and of the sequence of rough stocksheets, may be used to check that the final stocksheets are accurate and complete.

21 The auditor should ensure that continuous stock records have been adjusted to the amounts physically counted or measured and that differences have been investigated. Where appropriate, he should ensure also that management has instituted proper procedures to deal with transactions between stocktaking and the year end, and also test those procedures. In addition, he should check replies from third parties about stocks held by or for them, follow up all queries and notify senior management of serious problems encountered during the stocktaking.

Auditing in a computer environment

(Issued June 1984)

Preface

This guideline describes how the principles of an external audit should apply in a computer environment, including that relating to smaller computers.

Auditors unaccustomed to auditing in a computer environment are advised to obtain detailed practical guidance on the particular processing situations which they might meet and on the techniques which they might have to employ. Such auditors are also advised to use the detailed guidance available through their accountancy body and to attend appropriate training courses.

Introduction

1 Auditing standards prescribe the basic principles and practices to be followed in the conduct of an audit. 'The auditor's operational standard' and the guidelines on planning, controlling and recording, accounting systems, audit evidence, internal controls and review of financial statements apply irrespective of the system of recording and processing transactions. However, computer systems do record and process transactions in a manner which is significantly different from manual systems, giving rise to such possibilities as a lack of visible evidence and systematic errors. As a result, when auditing in a computer environment, the auditor will need to take into account additional considerations relating to the techniques available to him, the timing of his work, the form in which the accounting records are maintained, the internal controls which exist, the availability of the data and the length of time it is retained in readily useable form, as further described below.

2 Computers have a wide range of capabilities and changes continue to be made as a result of new technology. With the introduction of smaller computers, there is a greater likelihood of weak internal controls. This will normally lead to greater emphasis being placed on substantive testing of transactions and balances, and on other procedures such as analytical review, rather than on compliance testing. Furthermore, where smaller volumes of transactions are processed, substantive testing may in the circumstances be the more efficient method of obtaining audit evidence.

Background

3 Audits are performed in a computer environment wherever computer-based accounting systems, large or small, are operated by an enterprise, or by a third party on behalf of the enterprise, for the purpose of processing information supporting the amounts included in the financial statements.

4 The nature of computer-based accounting systems is such that the auditor is afforded opportunities to use either the enterprise's or another computer to assist him in the performance of his audit work. Techniques performed with computers in this way are known as computer-assisted audit techniques ('CAATs') of which the following are the major categories:

(a) use of 'audit software' — computer programs used for audit purposes to examine the contents of the enterprise's computer files;

(b) use of 'test data' — data used by the auditor for computer processing to test the operation of the enterprise's computer programs.

5 Where there is a computer-based accounting system, many of the auditor's procedures may still be carried out manually. For instance, the ascertainment of the accounting system and assessment of its adequacy will normally be performed manually, and in appropriate circumstances the auditor may also decide to select manual audit techniques.

Knowledge and skills

6 When auditing in a computer environment, the auditor should obtain a basic understanding of the fundamentals of data processing and a level of technical computer knowledge and skills which depending on the circumstances may need to be extensive. This is because the auditor's knowledge and skills need to be appropriate to the environment in which he is auditing, and because ethical statements indicate that he should not undertake or continue professional work which he is not himself competent to perform unless he obtains such advice and assistance as will enable him competently to carry out his task.

Planning, controlling and recording

7 Paragraph 2 of 'The auditor's operational standard' states that "the auditor should adequately plan, control and record his work". The principles relating to planning, controlling and recording are the same in a computer environment as in other circumstances, but there are additional considerations that need to be taken into account.

Planning

8 In order to plan and carry out an audit in a computer environment, the auditor will need an appropriate level of technical knowledge and skill. As part of his additional planning considerations, he should decide at an early stage what effect the system itself, and the way it is operated, will have on the timing of and the manner in which he will need to perform and record his work. In this respect, he may have had the opportunity to consider these matters during the development and implementation of the system.

9 The auditor should also consider the use of CAATs, as this may have a significant effect on the nature, extent and timing of his audit tests. As indicated in paragraph 10 below, in certain circumstances the auditor will need to use CAATs in order to obtain the evidence he requires, whereas in other circumstances he may use CAATs to improve the efficiency or effectiveness of his audit. For example, the availability of audit software may mean that substantive tests can be performed more economically or quickly than substantive tests performed manually, which may persuade him to place less reliance on internal controls and to reduce his compliance testing accordingly.

10 In choosing the appropriate combination of CAATs and manual procedures, the auditor will need *inter alia* to take the following into account:

(a) Computer programs often perform functions of which no visible evidence is available. In these circumstances it will frequently not be practicable for the auditor to perform tests manually.

(b) In many audit situations the auditor will have the choice of performing a test either manually or with the assistance of a CAAT. In making this choice, he will be influenced by the respective efficiency of the alternatives, taking into account:
   (i) the extent of compliance or substantive testing achieved by both alternatives;
   (ii) the pattern of cost associated with the CAAT;
   (iii) the ability to incorporate within the use of the CAAT a number of different audit tests.

(c) In some cases, the auditor will need to report within a comparatively short timescale. In such cases it may be more efficient to use CAATs because they are quicker to apply, even though manual methods are practicable and may cost less.

(d) There is a need before using a CAAT to ensure that the required computer facilities, computer files and programs are available. Furthermore, given that enterprises do not retain copies of computer files and programs for an indefinite period, the auditor should plan the use of any CAAT in good time so that these copies are retained for his use.

(e) The operation of some CAAT's requires frequent attendance or access by the auditor. The auditor may be able to reduce the level of his tests by taking account of CAAT's performed by the internal auditors, but the extent to which he can do this in any given situation will depend, amongst other things, on his assessment of the effectiveness and relevance of the internal audit function.

(f) Where the enterprise's accounting records include computer data, the auditor will need to have access to that data. Further, where the auditor wishes to perform a CAAT, it is often necessary for the enterprise to make computer facilities available to the auditor to enable him to discharge his responsibilities.

Controlling

11 Whether or not the audit is being carried out in a computer environment, audit procedures should always be controlled to ensure that the work has been performed in a competent manner. Where CAAT's are used, however, particular attention should be paid to:

(a) the need to co-ordinate the work of staff with specialist computer skills with the work of others engaged on the audit;

(b) the approval and review of the technical work by someone with the necessary computer expertise.

12 It is acceptable for an auditor to use a CAAT on copies of computer records or programs, provided he has taken steps to gain reasonable assurance that the copies are identical to the originals.

Recording

13 The standard of the audit working papers relating to computer-based accounting systems, and the retention procedures in respect of them should be the same as those adopted in relation to other aspects of the audit. Where the technical papers differ materially from the other working papers, for instance where they consist of computer output or magnetic media, it may be convenient to keep these separate from the other working papers.

14 Where a CAAT is used, it is appropriate that the working papers indicate the work performed by the CAAT, the results of the CAAT, the auditor's conclusions, the manner in which any technical problems were resolved and may include any recommendations about the modification of the CAAT for future audits.

Accounting systems

15 Paragraph 3 of 'The auditor's operational standard' states that "the auditor should ascertain the enterprise's system of recording and processing transactions and assess its adequacy as a basis for the preparation of financial statements". The principles relating to this are the same in a computer environment, but it should be borne in mind that many computer-based accounting systems are specified in far greater detail than non-computer-based accounting systems. In assessing the adequacy of the accounting system as a basis for the preparation of financial statements, the auditor is likely to receive a more detailed record of the enterprise's system than would otherwise be the case.

Audit evidence

16 Paragraph 4 of 'The auditor's operational standard' states that "the auditor should obtain relevant and reliable audit evidence sufficient to enable him to draw reasonable conclusions therefrom". The principles relating to the obtaining of audit evidence do not change because the audit is being carried out in a computer environment.

17 However, the availability of computer facilities results in opportunities for auditors to use computers. CAATs may be used at various stages of an audit to obtain audit evidence. For instance where the auditor chooses to place reliance on internal controls, he may use a CAAT to assist in the performance of compliance tests. Furthermore, he may also use CAATs to perform substantive tests, including analytical review procedures.

Internal controls

18 Paragraph 5 of 'The auditor's operational standard' states that "if the auditor wishes to place reliance on any internal controls, he should ascertain and evaluate those controls and perform compliance tests on their operation". The principles relating to internal controls are the same in a computer environment as in any other environment, but there are additional considerations which are discussed in paragraphs 19-24 below.

19 Internal controls over computer-based accounting systems may conveniently be considered under the following two main headings:

(a) Application controls. These relate to the transactions and standing data appertaining to each computer-based accounting system and are therefore specific to each such application. The objectives of application controls, which may be manual or programmed, are to ensure the completeness and accuracy of the accounting records and the validity of the entries made therein resulting from both manual and programmed processing.

(b) General controls. Controls, other than application controls, which relate to the environment within which computer-based accounting systems are developed, maintained and operated, and which are therefore applicable to all the applications. The objectives of general controls are to ensure the proper development and implementation of applications, and the integrity of program and data files, and of computer operations. Like application controls, general controls may be either manual or programmed.

20 Application controls and general controls are inter-related. Strong general controls contribute to the assurance which may be obtained by an auditor in relation to application controls. On the other hand, unsatisfactory general controls may undermine strong application controls or exacerbate unsatisfactory application controls.

21 As with controls in other circumstances, the evaluation of application controls and general controls will be assisted by the use of documentation designed to help identify the controls on which the auditor may wish to place reliance. Such documentation can take a variety of forms but might consist of questions asking whether there are controls in a system which meet specified overall control objectives, or which prevent or detect the occurrence of specified errors or omissions. For application controls, an integrated set of internal control questions may be used covering controls over both the manual part and the programmed part of the application, and the impact of relevant general controls.

22 Where preliminary evaluation of the application controls and general controls discloses the absence of, or uncompensated weaknesses in, controls, and therefore the auditor cannot rely on the controls, he should move directly to substantive tests which may be assisted by the use of CAATs.

23 However, where preliminary evaluation reveals application controls or general controls which may meet the auditor's objectives, he should design and carry out compliance tests if he wishes to rely on those controls. In determining whether he wishes to place reliance on application controls or general controls, the auditor will be influenced by the cost effectiveness and ease of testing and by the following matters:

(a) Where application controls are entirely manual the auditor may decide to perform compliance tests in respect of the application controls only, rather than to place any reliance on general controls. However, before he can place reliance on application controls which involve computer programs, the auditor needs to obtain reasonable assurance that the programs have operated properly, by evaluating and testing the effect of relevant general controls or by other tests on specific parts of the programs.

(b) Sometimes a programmed accounting procedure may not be subject to effective application controls. In such circumstances, in order to put himself in a position to limit the extent of his substantive testing, the auditor may choose to perform his compliance tests by testing the relevant general controls either manually or by using CAATs, to gain assurance of the continued and proper operation of the programmed accounting procedure. Where as a result of his compliance tests the auditor decides he cannot place reliance on the controls, he should move directly to substantive tests.

(c) As indicated in paragraph 1, there is in a computer environment the possibility of systematic errors. This may take place because of program faults or hardware malfunction in computer operations. However, many such potential recurrent errors should be prevented or detected by general controls over the development and implementation of applications, the integrity of the program and data files, and of computer operations. As a result, the controls which the auditor may evaluate and test may include general controls.

(d) On the other hand, the extent to which the auditor can rely on general controls may be limited because many of these controls might not be evidenced, or because they could have been performed inconsistently. In such circumstances, which are particularly common where small computers are involved, if he wishes to limit his substantive tests, the auditor may obtain assurance from compliance tests on manual application controls or by tests on specific parts of the programs.

24 In performing compliance tests on application or general controls, the auditor should obtain evidence which is relevant to the control being tested. Procedures the auditor may consider include observing the control in operation, examining documentary evidence of its operation, or performing it again himself. In the case of programmed application controls, the auditor may test specific parts of the programs, or re-perform them, by taking advantage of CAATs. He may also obtain evidence by testing relevant general controls.

Review of financial statements

25 Paragraph 6 of 'The auditor's operational standard' states "the auditor should carry out such a review of the financial statements as is sufficient, in conjunction with the conclusions drawn from the other audit evidence obtained, to give him a reasonable basis for his opinion on the financial statements". CAATs (particularly audit software) may be of assistance to auditors in carrying out certain aspects of this work.

Third party service organisations

26 Where enterprises use a third party service organisation such as a computer service bureau or a software house for the purpose of maintaining part or all of their accounting records and procedures, the auditor still has a responsibility to follow 'The auditor's operational standard'. However, the auditor may encounter practical obstacles, as the enterprise may be placing some reliance on the proper operation of internal controls exercised by the third party. Consequently, where the auditor finds it impracticable to obtain all the information and explanations that he requires from the enterprise itself (because the enterprise may not be maintaining sufficient controls to minimise that reliance) he should perform other procedures. These may include taking the steps he considers necessary to enable him to rely on the work performed by other auditors or carrying out procedures at the premises of the third party.

Prospectuses and the reporting accountant

(Issued February 1986)

Preface

A reporting accountant's responsibilities, and the procedures he will apply in carrying out his work, are not identical with those of an auditor although there are a number of similarities.

In particular, when an accountant's report is to be included in listing particulars, the Yellow Book requires him to express an opinion as to whether the financial information contained in his report gives a true and fair view. It is generally agreed to be best practice to extend this Yellow Book requirement to all prospectuses and circulars. A 'true and fair view' opinion is therefore usually included in all accountants' reports.

A further similarity is the reliance which third parties may place on the accountants' report, and the expectations of such third parties concerning the professional standards of skill and care which the reporting accountant will employ.

This guideline gives procedural and reporting guidance in respect of accountants' reports prepared for inclusion in prospectuses, listing particulars, circulars and similar documents. It also provides guidance on the comfort letters which the reporting accountant is frequently required to prepare.

Definitions of the terms used in the guideline are given in Appendix 1.

This guideline should be read in conjunction with the Auditing Standards and the related Auditing Guidelines.

Introduction

1 A prospectus is an invitation to the public to subscribe for, or to purchase, shares or debentures in a company. There are a variety of circumstances in which prospectuses may be issued including, for example, when a company is applying for admission to the Stock Exchange's Official List or its Unlisted Securities Market, when a company is being launched onto one of the over-the-counter markets, or when shares are being issued under the Business Expansion Scheme. The form and content of prospectuses vary according to the circumstances in which they are issued. When issued in connection with an application for admission to the Official List, the document is known as the 'listing particulars'.

2 When a listed or USM company proposes certain types of transaction it may be required by the Stock Exchange to issue a circular to its shareholders, to inform them of the proposal and, in some cases, to obtain their approval. This may be necessary, for example, when a substantial acquisition or disposal of assets is being made (for a listed company, a 'Class 1' circular). An accountant's report may be required to be included in the circular. The principles contained in this guideline with reference to prospectuses also apply to the preparation of accountant's reports for inclusion in circulars.

3 The table below identifies the regulations which prescribe the minimum contents of prospectuses and circulars issued in different circumstances. This guideline does not attempt to reproduce or summarise these regulations, and it should therefore be read in conjunction with them.

Circumstances	**Regulations concerning minimum contents of prospectuses and circulars**
Application for admission to the Official List	Section 3 of the Yellow Book*
Application for admission to the Unlisted Securities Market	Section C of the Green Book and, when new securities are being issued, Schedule 3 Companies Act 1985**
All other prospectuses involving the marketing of new securities	Schedule 3 Companies Act 1985**
Circulars	Section 6 of the Yellow Book or Section D of the Green Book

4 The reporting accountant will need to be familiar with the regulations governing the minimum contents of the particular type of document of which his report will form a part.*** However, in some circumstances the contents will extend beyond the minimum required by the regulations. For example, when a company is being introduced to the Unlisted Securities Market and no marketing of new shares is to take place, even though there is no requirement in the regulations for an accountant's report to be presented, such a report is often still required by the sponsor to the introduction.

5 Where securities are to be listed, or traded in the USM, the directors of the company issuing the shares or debentures to the public are required to state that they accept full responsibility for the completeness and accuracy of the information contained in the prospectus. The prospectus will include information on the company's financial affairs and may also include reports by 'experts', one of whom is likely to be the reporting accountant. The sponsor to the issue will coordinate the preparation of the prospectus and any reports which it will contain.

6 The sponsor may require the reporting accountant to prepare a detailed report covering various aspects of the company's business, including its management, profit record, assets and liabilities, and prospects. This type of report, known as the 'long-form' report, is often the basis of the accountant's report to be included in the prospectus (the 'short-form' report). It is, however, outside the scope of this guideline.

7 A prospectus need not include a profit forecast. However, if a profit forecast is included, the Stock Exchange requires the reporting accountant to examine and prepare a separate report on the accounting policies and calculations for the forecast. Guidance on this subject is given in the statement entitled 'Accountants' reports on profit forecasts' issued in 1978 by the accountancy bodies, and is not dealt with in this guideline.

* The Stock Exchange (Listing) Regulations 1984 (SI 1984 No 716) bring into effect in the United Kingdom the Listing Particulars directive (EEC Council Directive No 80/390/EEC) which sets out the requirements for information to be disclosed in listing particulars. These requirements, together with the additional requirements of the Stock Exchange itself, are set out in the Yellow Book. Where application has been made to the Council of the Stock Exchange for admission of securities to listing, and the Council has approved the applicable listing particulars, the provisions of the Companies Act 1985 relating to prospectuses do not apply.

** Equivalent Irish legislation Northern Ireland: Schedule 3 Companies Act (Northern Ireland) 1960 Republic of Ireland: Schedule 3 Companies Act 1963.

*** The reporting accountant should also be aware of the requirements of Part III of the Companies Act 1985 and of the Prevention of Fraud (Investments) Act 1958, especially in so far as they relate to statutory liabilities for documents issued in connection with the issue of shares or debentures to the public.

The accountant's report

8 The accountant's report gives an independent statement, supported by an opinion, of financial information for the company concerned or, if it has subsidiaries, for the group, which together with the other information in the prospectus may assist potential investors in making the decision whether or not to invest.

9 The contents of the accountant's report will usually include:

(a) profit and loss accounts, dividends and earnings per share of the company or, if it has subsidiaries, of the group in respect of each of the five immediately preceding completed accounting periods;

(b) balance sheet information:

  (i) for listed companies — balance sheets of the company or, if it has subsidiaries, of the group at the end of each of the five immediately preceding completed accounting periods;

  (ii) for other companies — balance sheets of the company and, if it has subsidiaries, of the group at the end of the last completed accounting period;

(c) source and application of funds statements of the company or, if it has subsidiaries, of the group in respect of each period reported on;

(d) notes to the profit and loss accounts, balance sheets, and source and application of funds statements;

(e) accounting policies on which the financial information has been prepared;

(f) any other matters which the reporting accountant considers relevant for the purposes of his report; and

(g) the reporting accountant's opinion as to whether the financial information gives a true and fair view.

The above list illustrates only the principal items which may appear in the accountant's report, and it is not intended to be exhaustive. According to the circumstances of the prospectus or circular additional information may be necessary. The minimum information to be included in the accountant's report is set out in the Section 4 of the Yellow Book, in the case of listing particulars and circulars for listed companies, and in Schedule 3 Companies Act 1985 for other types of prospectus. The reporting accountant should refer to the appropriate regulations to determine the detailed requirements.

10 The financial information contained in an accountant's report, together with any financial information contained elsewhere in the prospectus, does not constitute full accounts as defined by Section 254 Companies Act 1985. Accordingly, elsewhere in the prospectus, a statement should be made, as required by Section 255 Companies Act 1985, that the financial information does not constitute full accounts and that (if it be the case) full accounts have been delivered to the Registrar of Companies and that such accounts have been reported on by the auditor with or without qualification.

The reporting accountant

11 For the purposes of prospectuses other than listing particulars, the reporting accountant must be the company's auditor, who may be appointed either to act alone, or jointly with another accountant. For listing particulars there is no such requirement, although the Yellow Book does require the reporting accountant to be independent of the company to the same extent as an auditor.

12 Where the auditor is appointed as reporting accountant, the audit partner should wherever possible involve another partner who is not connected with the audit engagement, so as to provide a fresh view of the matters reported on. To minimise duplication of effort, this second partner need only assist at important stages of the work. For example, he should participate in agreeing the principal terms of the engagement letter, planning the work to be carried out, reviewing the draft prospectus, and agreeing the treatment of any contentious matters.

13 When the company's auditor is not appointed either as sole or joint reporting accountant, he should be aware that the reporting accountant will need access to information contained in his audit files. In principle, therefore, the auditor should be prepared to co-operate with the reporting accountant and to make available to him such information as he may require for the purpose of his report.

Procedures

14 The principles set out in 'The auditor's operational standard' are appropriate to the conduct of the reporting accountant's work. The following procedures amplify those given in the operational guidelines which support 'The auditor's operational standard', and which are applicable to this type of engagement.

Planning, controlling and recording

15 The reporting accountant should agree the terms of his engagement with the company, and also with the sponsor. This should be done even where the reporting accountant has an existing audit engagement with the company. The principles contained in the Auditing Guideline 'Engagement letters' should be applied, with appropriate modifications. An engagement letter should be prepared, dealing with, *inter alia*:

(a) the preparation of any long-form report;
(b) the audit of any interim accounts which may be necessary;
(c) the preparation of a short-form report for inclusion in the prospectus or circular;
(d) the nature of any comfort letters required in relation to the directors' statements concerning borrowings, the adequacy of working capital, or other financial information;
(e) the review of any profit forecasts and the preparation of an accountant's report thereon to be included in the prospectus with the forecasts;
(f) the reporting accountant's need to have the opportunity to attend meetings at which the prospectus will be drafted, to receive draft copies of the prospectus, and generally to be satisfied with the form and context of his report in the final version before giving his consent to the issue of the prospectus;
(g) the timescale for preparation and publication of the prospectus, and the deadlines which are to be met; and
(h) the reporting accountant's need to be able to communicate with the company's auditors and other professional advisors.

The reporting accountant should request that the engagement letter is acknowledged and confirmed in writing.

16 When joint reporting accountants are appointed the detailed work involved in preparing the accountants' report may, for practical reasons, be divided between them. This should be agreed between the joint reporting accountants, and may form part of the engagement letter. However, irrespective of any such arrangement, the joint reporting accountants are jointly and severally responsible for the entire accountants' report. Accordingly, the firms of accountants should liaise with each other on a regular basis, having particular regard to any problems which are identified. Procedures by which such consultations are to take place should be agreed at the planning stage.

17 In planning the detailed procedures to be carried out, the reporting accountant should conduct a preliminary review of the affairs of the company, and of the financial information which will form the basis of his report. As well as assisting the planning of his work, this review may also indicate whether there may be factors likely to restrict the scope of his work, or give rise to a qualification of his report, or are such that the company or its sponsor might decide not to proceed, or the purpose of the prospectus might fail to be achieved. If any such factors are identified they should be reported immediately to the company and the sponsor. In practice this preliminary review may often be carried out before the engagement has been formally accepted.

18 The extent of the work which the reporting accountant will need to carry out in relation to his report will be influenced by whether all the financial statements to be reported upon have previously been subjected to audit, and whether the reporting accountant himself audited the financial statements on which the report is to be based.

19 Where the latest completed accounting period reported on by the company's auditors ended more than six months before the date of publication of the listing particulars for a new listing, The Stock Exchange's normal requirement regarding the age of the figures reported on will not be satisfied. The equivalent maximum period for the Unlisted Securities Market is nine months. In these circumstances an audit of financial statements drawn up to an interim date will normally be required.

20 Where other material financial information has not been audited it will be necessary to carry out audit work before it can be included in the accountant's report, in order to ensure that it can provide a satisfactory basis for his opinion. Audit work will also be required where financial information has been a constituent part of audited financial statements, without having been the specific subject of an audit opinion, e.g. the results of a single division or branch of a large company. Even if he does not carry out the detailed additional audit work himself, the reporting accountant should be closely involved in its planning, control and review.

21 The reporting accountant should apply the procedures described in the Auditing Guideline 'Events after the balance sheet date' to ensure that any significant events between the dates of the latest audited financial statements and publication of the prospectus are identified and correctly reflected in the financial information reported on.

22 The reporting accountant should control and record his work. This will involve the direction and supervision of his staff and the review of their work, and the preparation of working papers to record the procedures carried out. A large part of the work performed will often take the form of reviewing files and documents, and discussions with the company's management, staff and professional advisors. Particular care should be taken to ensure that the working papers adequately reflect the nature of these procedures, the evidence examined and the conclusions reached.

Evidence

23 The reporting accountant should obtain relevant and reliable evidence sufficient to enable him to prepare the financial information to be included in his report and to form an opinion on that information.

24 To assist the reporting accountant in presenting his report and forming an opinion as to whether the financial information it contains gives a true and fair view, he should review and discuss with management the features and trends of the results during the relevant period.

25 The reporting accountant should review the audit working papers relating to the periods to be covered by his report. Where the reporting accountant was not himself the auditor for these periods, he will need to liaise with the auditor in order to make use of his working papers, and to obtain the information and explanations necessary to answer any questions resulting from this review. The reporting accountant may also seek further clarification from the auditor of any important issues arising from his discussions with management.

26 The object of this review of the audit working papers is to enable the reporting accountant to determine the extent to which he is able to rely on the audit work already performed, and to ascertain whether any further procedures are necessary. Careful consideration should be given to any problems which arose during the audit of the financial statements for the relevant periods, and to the manner in which they were resolved. It must be emphasised that the fact that an audit has been previously carried out does not reduce the responsibility of the reporting accountant for his report and the opinion it contains.

27 As part of his review of the audit working papers, the reporting accountant should undertake a general assessment of the company's accounting systems and records during the period covered by his report, in order to determine their reliability as sources of evidence.

28 The reporting accountant should pay particular attention to any difficult or contentious points which come to light during his discussions with the company's management or auditors, and to matters critical to the ascertainment of profit or the presentation of results.

29 If the reporting accountant cannot satisfy himself in all material aspects by the procedures outlined above, he may need to undertake further detailed audit procedures. Where it is impracticable for him to carry out auditing procedures relating to earlier years, his reservations should be stated in his report. However, if additional assurance is required by the reporting accountant only in respect of the latest period under review, then it may still be possible to arrange for supplementary audit procedures in the relevant areas to be carried out.

Review of financial statements

30 The reporting accountant will need to review the relevant financial statements at several stages of his work, for example:

(a) as part of his planning and preliminary review procedures (see paragraph 17);

(b) during his review of the audit working papers (see paragraphs 25 to 28); and

(c) in order to determine whether any adjustments are required to the figures for the purposes of his report (see paragraphs 34 to 44).

31 In carrying out a review of the financial statements, the reporting accountant should give special attention to any matters which have resulted in qualified audit reports. He will need to consider carefully the significance of any such qualifications for his own report. In some cases uncertainties which gave rise to a qualified audit report may have been resolved, and in other cases it may be possible to make adjustments to the reported results in order to avoid any need to qualify the opinion in the accountant's report. Where the reporting accountant concludes that he need not, for the purposes of his report, repeat a previously qualified audit opinion, he should indicate in his report how the matter was resolved — for example as a result of adjustments made or additional procedures carried out.

32 The reporting accountant will need to review the appropriateness of all the accounting policies, as well as their compliance with Statements of Standard Accounting Practice and the consistency of their application. Wherever practicable all the financial information included in the accountant's report should be set out on the basis of the current accounting policies, i.e. the policies to be adopted for the current accounting period.

33 The use of analytical review procedures as part of the review of the financial statements will enable the reporting accountant to form a better understanding of the nature of the business and of the principal factors influencing its development during the relevant period. Any unusual features or unexpected fluctuations need to be adequately explained if the reporting accountant is to obtain the assurance he needs for his report.

Adjustments to reported figures

Background to adjustments

34 The financial information included in the accountant's report should be based on the audited financial statements for the periods reported on. However, in order to ensure that the financial information is presented on a consistent and comparable basis the reporting accountant may need to make adjustments to the figures previously reported in the financial statements. The Yellow Book requires the reporting accountant to make any adjustments necessary for the purpose of his report.

35 The number of adjustments should be kept to the minimum considered necessary by the reporting accountant. Adjustments need only be made if the amounts involved are material.

36 The reporting accountant should state in his report that all the adjustments he considers necessary have been made, or that no adjustments were necessary.

37 In addition to any adjustments, the reporting accountant should also make such changes to the presentation of information contained in the financial statements as he considers necessary, so that matters of particular importance in the context of the prospectus are given due prominence.

The nature of adjustments

38 Adjustments to previously reported figures should only be made:

(a) to ensure that the financial information for all the years reported on is stated on a consistent basis (see paragraph 39);
or

(b) to ensure that the financial information is in all other respects properly comparable, for example, by correcting any fundamental accounting errors in the financial statements of the periods reported on.

39 To enable the financial information to be stated on a consistent basis two different types of adjustment may be required;

(a) Adjustments should be made to ensure that, wherever practicable, all the financial information in the report is stated on the basis of the current accounting policies.

(b) If there has been a change in the group structure in the period reported on (for example, the acquisition or disposal of a subsidiary company or business, or a reorganisation of the group) it may sometimes be appropriate to make adjustments so that the effects of the change on the results of the group and its state of affairs do not distort the financial information. (Some examples of this type of adjustment are given in Appendix 2.)

40 If the audit report on the financial statements of one of the periods reported on was qualified, the reporting accountant may be able to make adjustments so that the financial information in his report gives a true and fair view, and thus avoid the need to qualify his opinion on the financial information. For example, if the qualification was due to the uncertainty surrounding a material accounting estimate, the reporting accountant may, with the benefit of hindsight, have sufficient information to correct the estimate if it was subsequently shown to be materially incorrect.

41 However, although adjustments may be made in respect of accounting policies, adjustments should not normally be made to the company's accounting estimates, provided there were no fundamental errors. The effect of correcting an estimate in a later period should normally be reflected in the result of that period. The reporting accountant should consider whether separate disclosure in the profit and loss tabulations as an exceptional item is necessary. Consideration should also be given to any additional disclosure which may be necessary by way of notes.

The statement of adjustments

42 Where adjustments have been made, the reporting accountant is required to prepare a 'statement of adjustments', showing how the audited financial statements have been adjusted to arrive at the figures in his report. Although no particular format is required for the statement, it must be sufficiently detailed to reconcile the figures in the audited financial statements with those in the accountant's report.

43 For clarity, material reclassifications of balance sheet items should be included in the statement of adjustments, even where they do not affect the results of any of the periods reported on.

44 The Stock Exchange requires the statement of adjustments to be made available for public inspection. The statement of adjustments may also be made available for public inspection in other cases. In addition, a draft version of the statement of adjustments for a listed company must be submitted to the Quotations Department of the Stock Exchange at least 14 days before publication of the listing particulars. For all companies other than listed companies the statement of adjustments must also be filed with the Registrar of Companies.

Reporting

45 The reporting accountant should address his report jointly to the directors of the company and to the sponsor.

46 The accountant's report should be dated. The date used by the reporting accountant should be that on which the directors authorise the issue of the prospectus.

47 The reporting requirements regarding the financial information are contained in the regulations relevant to the type of prospectus being prepared. Paragraphs 48 to 53 below are concerned with the general principles to be followed by the reporting accountant in expressing his opinion on the financial information.

The reporting accountant's opinion

48 The opinion is usually situated near the beginning of the report, together with a number of other matters, which collectively form an introduction to the statement of financial information.

49 This introduction should also identify:

(a) the entity being reported on (see paragraph 50);

(b) the auditors of the financial statements throughout the period; and

(c) whether any financial statements have been prepared for submission to the members for accounting periods later than the last period covered by the report.

50 In order that the entity being reported on may be clearly defined, it may be necessary to give details of the group structure, significant changes during the period, and any reorganisation which has taken place since the date of the last audited financial statements. Where there has been a change in company name during the period, this also should be explained. If this information is complex and results in a paragraph which is disproportionately long in the context of the introduction section as a whole, it may be appropriate to include it as a separate paragraph in a prominent position elsewhere in the accountant's report.

51 The reporting accountant's opinion should draw attention to the following matters:

(a) that the financial information is based on the audited financial statements of the company and its subsidiary companies;

(b) that all adjustments considered necessary by the reporting accountant for the purpose of his report have been made (or that no adjustments were considered necessary);

(c) that the reporting accountant has carried out his work in accordance with this guideline; and

(d) whether or not the financial information gives a true and fair view.

52 The following form of wording may be appropriate for the introductory and opinion section of the report, and includes an example of an unqualified opinion: "We have examined the audited financial statements of ... ('the Company') and its subsidiaries for the five years ended .... The Company and its subsidiaries are referred to as 'the Group'. XYZ & Co/We have acted as auditors of the Group throughout the period covered by this report. No financial statements have been prepared for the Group in respect of any period subsequent to .... The financial information set out in paragraphs ... to ... below is based on the audited financial statements of the Group after making such adjustments as we consider necessary. Our work has been carried out in accordance with the Auditing Guideline: Prospectuses and the reporting accountant.

In our opinion, the financial information, (which has been prepared in accordance with the historical cost convention, as modified by the revaluation of land and buildings), gives a true and fair view of the profits and losses, and source and application of funds of the Group for each of the five years ended on ..., and of the state of affairs of the Group at the end of each of those years."

53 If the reporting accountant has reservations on any material matters, then his report must be qualified. All reasons for the qualification must be stated, together with the amounts involved if this is relevant and practicable. The Auditing Standard 'Qualifications in audit reports' should be followed. The reporting accountant should be aware that in practice a qualification which casts doubt on the reported profits or the balance sheet figures may cause the prospectus not to be issued. Therefore, if any matter comes to his attention which could give rise to a qualification of his report, he should assess its likely effect and advise the directors and the sponsor at the earliest opportunity.

Letters of consent

54 If a prospectus contains any statement purporting to be made by an expert, the expert must have given and not withdrawn his consent to the issue of the prospectus with the statement in the form and context in which it is included. A statement to the effect that he has given and not withdrawn his consent must be made in the prospectus. The reporting accountant is one of the experts coming within the scope of this requirement.

55 Financial and other information is contained throughout a prospectus and not only in the accountant's report. Whilst the reporting responsibility of the reporting accountant does not extend beyond his own report, he should consider the document as a whole. He should be satisfied that nothing contained within the prospectus as a whole is inconsistent with the information in his report, and that all relevant matters which have come to his attention have been properly reflected. In particular he should take steps to make himself aware of all the principal issues arising during the drafting of the prospectus. He should give consent to the publication of the prospectus containing his report only if he is satisfied with the form and context in which his report appears in the published document.

56 An appropriate form of letter of consent to the directors of the company and the sponsor may be as follows:

"We hereby consent to the issue of the prospectus/circular dated ..., issued in connection with ..., with the inclusion therein of our report dated ... and the references thereto, and the references to our name, in the form and context in which they appear. We attach a copy/final proof of the document initialled by us for the purpose of identification."

57 The reporting accountant's letter of consent should be dated with the same date as the prospectus.

58 The Stock Exchange requires the letter of consent to be available for public inspection at the time of publication of the prospectus. The letter of consent may also be made available for public inspection in other cases. For all companies other than listed companies the letter of consent must be filed with the Registrar of Companies.

59 If, at any time before allotment takes place under the prospectus, the reporting accountant becomes aware that the prospectus contains an untrue statement purporting to be made by him, he should withdraw his consent in writing, and give reasonable public notice of the withdrawal and the reasons for it.

Comfort letters

60 In addition to preparing an accountant's report as prescribed by the relevant regulations, the reporting accountant may be required by the directors of the company or by the sponsor to prepare reports on a number of other matters. These reports are not intended for publication, and are not required by statute or by any other regulations. The scope of such reports is entirely at the discretion of the directors of the company and the sponsor, and should normally be agreed in the engagement letter.

61 The purpose of these additional reports is to provide independent assurance regarding financial information included in the prospectus other than as part of the accountant's report. For this reason they are known as 'comfort letters'.

62 Comfort letters are usually required in relation to the directors' statement included in the prospectus concerning:

(a) the adequacy of working capital; and

(b) the aggregate of borrowings at the latest practicable date.

These are considered in more detail in the following paragraphs. Other matters which may be the subject of comfort letters include:

(i) any pro-forma financial statements shown in the prospectus to indicate the effect of a major acquisition or reorganisation of the group;

(ii) taxation clearances and indemnities; and

(iii) any other financial information, wherever it is situated in the prospectus.

The reporting accountant's responsibility in respect of profit forecasts included in the prospectus is mentioned in paragraph 7.

Reports on working capital requirements

63 The Stock Exchange requires that the directors of the company state that in their opinion the company's working capital is sufficient for the requirements of the business or, if not, how it is proposed to provide the additional working capital thought by the directors to be necessary. The directors are solely responsible for this statement. However it is customary for the directors and the sponsor to ask the reporting accountant to review and report to them on the cash flow forecast prepared for this purpose, and this may include a request for a commentary on the assumptions on which it is based.

64 The approach to such an assignment involves obtaining and reviewing the forecasts prepared by the management of the company and comparing the cash flow shown by these forecasts with the facilities and resources available, or to become available, to the company. The extent of the facilities and resources available should normally be confirmed directly to the reporting accountant by the appropriate third party.

65 The forecasts should normally cover at least one year from the date of the prospectus and should include forecasts of profit, cash flow and financial position at the end of the period together with detailed assumptions used in their preparation. In addition to checking the arithmetical accuracy of the forecasts and that they are properly derived from the stated assumptions, the reporting accountant will also need to review the assumptions. If any assumption appears to be unrealistic, or if any important assumption has not been stated, he should consider drawing attention to it in his comfort letter. The degree of review required will in part depend on whether forecasts made in the past have proved reliable, and on the extent of the surplus of resources over the estimated cash flow requirements.

66 As the directors have sole responsibility for their statement regarding the adequacy of working capital, the reporting accountant should satisfy himself that they have considered all the relevant information with due care. He should ensure that the directors' approval of the working capital forecasts and the underlying assumptions is recorded in the board minutes.

67 The report should clearly identify the information on which it is based. The form of the report will usually be that in the opinion of the reporting accountant the directors' statement has been made with due care and the forecast is properly compiled on the basis of the underlying assumptions.

Reports on borrowings

68 The Stock Exchange requires disclosure of details of any loan capital, borrowings, mortgages or charges and indebtedness and contingent liabilities, as at the most recent practicable date. In this context borrowings include bank overdrafts, liabilities under acceptances (other than normal trade bills), acceptance credits, hire purchase commitments, and other guarantees. Significant finance lease commitments should also be stated.

69 In determining the amount of bank indebtedness, either the figure in the cash book or the figure on the bank statement may be used. However, the two figures should be reconciled where practicable, and the reporting accountant should investigate any unusual or large uncleared items and consider referring to them in his comfort letter.

70 The date at which borrowings and bank indebtedness are stated will not usually be the end of an accounting period. Therefore audited financial statements are unlikely to be available, and the reporting accountant will have less evidence on which to base his opinion concerning the figure for borrowings than he would at the end of an accounting period. In these circumstances he will have to place substantial reliance on management as to the identification of those parties from whom there are outstanding borrowings. These should be substantiated by direct confirmation from the lenders of the amounts outstanding at the relevant date. In view of the reliance placed on these representations, the reporting accountant should ensure that they are formally confirmed by the directors and recorded in the board minutes.

71 The report should clearly identify the information on which it is based, and should refer to the following:

(a) without carrying out an audit, the reporting accountant's procedures cannot necessarily be expected to reveal all significant matters concerning borrowings;

(b) reliance has been placed on the representations of management as to the completeness of the amounts shown in the statement of borrowings; and

(c) nothing has come to the reporting accountant's attention to indicate that any adjustments should be made.

Appendix 1

72 Definition of terms

The Stock Exchange	The Stock Exchange of the United Kingdom and the Republic of Ireland.
The Official List	the Official List of the Stock Exchange.
USM	the Unlisted Securities Market of the Stock Exchange.
Prospectus	any prospectus, notice, circular, advertisement or other invitation, offering to the public for subscription or purchase any shares in or debentures of a company.
Listing particulars	a document of the type required to be published as a condition of admission of securities to the Official List.
Circular	a circular issued by a listed or USM company to its shareholders as required by the Stock Exchange, and which does not constitute listing particulars or a prospectus.
The Yellow Book	The Stock Exchange's publication 'Admission of Securities to Listing'.
The Green Book	The Stock Exchange's publication 'The Stock Exchange — Unlisted Securities Market'.
Reporting accountant	an independent accountant engaged in preparing a report for inclusion in a prospectus, listing particulars or circular.
Sponsor	a merchant bank, issuing house or stockbroker appointed by a company to assist in preparing a prospectus, listing particulars or circular.

Appendix 2

73 Examples of adjustments following changes in group structure

The purpose of this appendix is to illustrate some of the types of adjustments which may be made to previously reported figures for the purpose of the accountant's report, arising as a result of changes in the group structure. The examples given are not an exhaustive list, and the treatments described are not definitive. In any particular case the reporting accountant will need to consider carefully the suitability of adjustments in the light of the specific circumstances.

74 *Results and balance sheets*
It may be appropriate to prepare the financial information on the following basis:

(a) Acquisition by issue of share capital during the period reported upon.	Include the results of the acquired entity for the whole period.

(There may be difficulties in presenting the balance sheets and statements of sources and applications of funds whether merger or acquisition accounting principles have been applied. This may be due to differences in year-ends or the inability to attribute fair values to periods prior to acquisition. Adjustment may not, therefore, be appropriate. The notes in the accountant's report should, however, provide a reconciliation of movements on reserves and the table of results. Additional information may also be necessary to ensure that the balance sheets give a true and fair view of the financial position.)

(b) Acquisition subsequent to the period reported upon.	Present the financial information on the acquired entity as a separate section in the accountant's report.

(It should also be noted that the Companies Act requires an accountant's report to be prepared for any business to be acquired out of the proceeds of a share issue to the public, but in the case of listing particulars only the provisions of the Yellow Book will apply.)

(c) Acquisition for cash during the period reported upon.	Include the results of the acquired entity from the date of acquisition.

(Where acquisition accounting has been used, consideration should also be given to disclosing separately the results of the acquired business for the periods prior to acquisition.)

(d) Acquisition for a combination of cash and shares during the period reported upon.	Include the results of the acquired entity for the whole period.

(Consideration should be given to an adjustment for notional interest on the cash element of the purchase price for the period prior to the acquisition date.)

(e) Disposals of a subsidiary or discontinuation of a material section of the business.	Show separately the results of that section of the business in the profit and loss table.
(f) Reorganisations prior to issue of shares to the public.	Where, for example, companies under common control but legally unconnected are formed into a legal group prior to issue or flotation, the accountant's report should be prepared on a combined basis and should explain fully the basis of preparation in the introductory paragraphs of the report.

75 *Earnings per share*
Consequential adjustments may arise in calculating earnings per share for each period covered by the accountant's report. The principles in Statement of Standard Accounting Practice No. 3 should be followed as far as practicable. If an acquisition has been made for shares, the number of shares used in the calculation would normally be increased throughout the period covered by the accountant's report even if acquisition accounting

was applied in the statutory financial statements. This would correspond to the increase in reported earnings reflecting the results of the acquired business.

Difficulties may result where there has been a capital reconstruction since the date of the last audited financial statements. When calculating earnings per share it may be appropriate to employ the number of shares in issue immediately prior to the issue to the public.

76 *Accounting policies*

Where a report is being prepared on an entity which is being acquired by another, consideration should be given to applying the accounting policies to be adopted as a result of the change in ownership. Adjustments should be made to earlier years' figures, if necessary, to show the results for all periods on the same basis. If it is not practicable to make the adjustments, the policies adopted in the earlier and later years, and the effect in the year of change, should be stated.

Reports to management

(Issued December 1986)

Preface

Paragraphs 21 and 22 of the Auditing Guideline 'Internal Controls' state:

> "It is important that the auditor should report, as soon as practicable, significant weaknesses in internal controls which come to his attention during the course of an audit to an appropriately senior level of management of the enterprise. Any such report should indicate that the weaknesses notified are only those which have come to the attention of the auditor during the course of his normal audit work and are not necessarily, therefore, all the weaknesses which may exist.

The fact that the auditor reports weaknesses in internal controls to management does not absolve:

(a) management from its responsibility for the maintenance of an adequate internal control system; or

(b) the auditor from the need to consider the effect of such weaknesses on the extent of his audit work and on his audit opinion."

A report to management arising out of an audit assignment is also a suitable medium for providing constructive advice on improvements to the financial and accounting efficiency of the client's business.

Reports to management should not be confused with specific responsibilities which may be imposed on the auditor in some sectors (by statute, regulation, or agreement) to report to a third party on the adequacy of a client's internal control arrangements.

The purpose of this guideline is to provide guidance on the procedures involved in making a report to management on matters arising out of an audit assignment.

Introduction and purpose

1 Reports to management are known by various names, for example management letters, post audit letters and letters of weaknesses. The report should preferably be communicated in writing to the client, but may take the form of a record of a discussion held with management, to be included in the auditor's working papers. In smaller companies, for example, it may be more cost effective to discuss with management the various matters to be reported and after such a meeting to provide a note of the observations and action which the client intends to take. The principles outlined in this guideline should be followed whatever method is used to report to management on matters which have arisen during the audit.

2 The auditor's statutory duty is to express an opinion on the financial statements and this responsibility is not reduced by any report made to management. A report to management is additional to, and is not a substitute for, the exercise of the auditor's statutory duties.

3 Principal purposes of a report to management are:

(a) to enable the auditor to give the comments he wishes on the accounting records, systems and controls that he has examined during the course of his audit. Areas of weakness in systems and controls that have come to his attention and might lead to material errors should be highlighted and brought to management's attention, together with any advice for their improvement;

(b) to provide management with other constructive advice. The auditor might, for example, be able to suggest areas where economies could be made or where resources could be used more efficiently;

(c) to communicate matters that have come to the auditor's attention during the audit that might have an impact on future audits.

4 The auditor would not normally make a report to management where there are no significant matters to bring to management's attention. In such a case the auditor may wish, solely as a matter of courtesy, to inform management that no report will be forthcoming.

Planning

5 A report to management will normally be a natural by-product of the audit, and the auditor should incorporate the need to report in the planning of the audit.

6 In addition to advising the client in an engagement letter that the auditor will report to the client's management any weaknesses in the client's systems which he thinks should be brought to its attention, the auditor should add that he may also comment on other matters.

7 The auditor should also refer in the engagement letter to any arrangements agreed with the client for submitting to, or requesting from, other group companies, any reports to management which might arise (see further at paragraph 25 *et seq*).

8 To be effective, a report to management should be made as soon as possible after completion of the audit procedures giving rise to comment. Where the audit work is performed on more than one visit, it will often be appropriate to report to management after interim audit work has been completed as well as after the final visit. If there are procedures that need to be improved before the financial year end the auditor should raise them in a letter or in discussion at an interim stage. As soon as an accounting breakdown is identified or serious weaknesses are apparent, senior management should be informed without delay.

Contents

9 Generally, where the following matters arise out of the audit, they should be included in a report to management:

(a) weaknesses in the structure of accounting systems and internal controls;

(b) deficiencies in the operation of accounting systems and internal controls;

(c) inappropriate accounting policies and practices; and

(d) non-compliance with legislation, accounting standards, or other regulations.

An auditor may have specific reporting duties imposed on him by statute or regulation. For example, the auditor of a company incorporated under the Companies Act has a specific duty to report where, in his opinion, proper accounting records have not been kept. Where a qualified audit report is required to discharge such a duty, a report to management cannot be regarded as a substitute.

10 The auditor may also wish to include in the report comments on potential economies, improvements in efficiency, or other constructive advice which might be of assistance to the client organisation.

11 Reports to management should explain clearly the implications of any matters raised. The use of specific examples identified during the audit to illustrate these matters helps readers to understand the nature of the problems which require action.

12 It is normally helpful for the auditor to make recommendations for improvements on the matters raised. This should not however delay the issuing of any report to management. It should be borne in mind that determination of appropriate improvements in systems and the assessment of the cost-effectiveness of additional controls may be complex issues that in any event are management's responsibility.

13 Points made in previous years' reports should be reviewed. Where they have not been dealt with effectively the auditor should enquire why appropriate action has not been taken. If the auditor considers the points still to be significant, they should be included again in his current report, otherwise there is a risk that the auditor may give an impression that he is satisfied that the weakness has been corrected.

14 Where the work of internal audit reveals weaknesses in internal controls, the external auditor should consider whether it is enough to draw management's attention to a report of internal audit or whether he should also report to management himself, particularly where he considers management response to internal audit reports is inadequate or where the weaknesses are significant.

Format and presentation

15 The report should be clear, constructive and concise. Careful presentation will help the recipient to understand the significance of the comments and devise corrective actions.

16 It is important that matters of concern should be discussed and recorded as they arise to ensure that the auditor has properly understood the situation. These discussions should take place with appropriate members of the client's staff at an operating level and should not necessarily be limited to executives concerned solely with finance and accounting. When the points in the report are drafted they should be cleared for factual accuracy with the client's staff concerned.

17 The auditor should explain that his report to management only includes those matters which have come to his attention as a result of the audit procedures, and that it should not be regarded as a comprehensive statement of all weaknesses that exist or of all improvements that might be made.

18 The report may contain matters of varying levels of significance and the inclusion of detail may make it difficult for senior management to identify points of significance. The auditor can deal with this by giving the report a 'tiered' structure so that senior management can consider any major points, and other points can be brought to the attention of less senior personnel. Alternatively, by agreement with the client, this objective might best be achieved by preparing separate reports for different levels of management, and reporting that this has been done.

19 Where different members of management are responsible for different regions, branches or functions, the report may have separate sections relating to the various areas of responsibility.

20 When submitting his report the auditor should use his best endeavours to ensure that its contents reach those members of management who have the power to act on the findings. It is usually appropriate to address the report, or that part of the report containing the major points, to the Board of Directors or equivalent body even if the receipt of a report of less important points is delegated by the Board. The auditor may agree with the client to address his report to the client's audit committee.

21 The auditor should preferably communicate his report in writing to the client, but the volume or nature of his comments may be such that a written report is unnecessary inappropriate or not cost-effective. In these circumstances the report should consist of a record of a discussion with management which should be minuted or otherwise recorded in writing. Management should be provided with a copy of this note to ensure the discussion has been fairly reflected. The written record of any such discussions should preferably form part of the audit working papers.

Management response

22 The auditor should request a reply to all the points raised, indicating what action management intends to take as a result of the comments made in the report. It should be made clear in the report that the auditor expects at least an acknowledgement of its receipt or, where he considers it appropriate, the directors' discussion of the report to be recorded in the board minutes.

23 Where matters have been discussed with client staff as and when they arise, the auditor should consider whether to incorporate responses made by staff in the final form of a report. This will be particularly useful where, say, senior management receive the report and need to be informed of the action taken by their staff.

24 Where the report to management takes the form of a record of the auditor's discussions with management, this record should preferably include management's response and any intended action.

Groups of companies

25 The management of a holding company may wish to be informed of significant points arising in the reports to the managements of its subsidiaries. Where the auditor is responsible for the audit of all the companies in the group, the management of the holding company may request that an additional report be addressed to the holding company summarising points of significance to the group that were made in the individual reports to the managements of the subsidiaries. The auditor may agree to this request. However, as a report to management is a confidential matter between the auditor and the management of the company concerned, he should first obtain permission from the managements of the subsidiary companies to disclose the contents to the holding company.

26 Where other auditors are involved, the auditor of the holding company will usually request that he should receive copies of reports sent to the managements of subsidiary companies, so that he is aware of any significant internal control weaknesses or accounting weaknesses in those companies. The request should normally be made through the holding company to the management of the subsidiary companies concerned. Should such a request be received by the auditor of a subsidiary company he should obtain permission from the management of the subsidiary before complying.

27 If the auditor of a holding company wishes to report to the management of the holding company on matters contained in the reports to the managements of subsidiaries, whether or not their financial statements are audited by him, he should first ensure that the managements of the subsidiary companies concerned and their auditors both agree to this procedure, and that no breach of confidence takes place.

28 All these arrangements for groups should be established at the planning stage, and should be recorded in the engagement letters.

Third parties interested in reports to management

29 Any report made to management should be regarded as a confidential communication. The auditor should therefore not reveal the contents of the report to any third party without the prior consent of the management of the organisation.

30 In practice the auditor has little control over what happens to the report once it has been despatched. Occasionally management may provide third parties with copies of the report, for example, their banks or certain regulatory authorities. Therefore care should be taken to protect the auditor's position from exposure to liability in negligence to any third parties who may seek to rely on the report.

31 As a general rule a liability in negligence could arise where an auditor carries out work for a client in circumstances where the auditor knows or ought to foresee that:

(a) his work is liable to be relied upon by a third party; and

(b) the third party may suffer financial loss as a result.

An express disclaimer of liability will normally provide a high degree of protection against unforeseen liability to third parties who may choose to rely on the report to management. To achieve this the auditor should state clearly in his report that:

(i) the report has been prepared for the private use of his client;

(ii) it must not be disclosed to a third party without the written consent of the auditor; and

(iii) no responsibility is assumed by the auditor to any other person.

Use of disclaimer paragraphs may not however give full protection from liability where the auditor knows or ought reasonably to know that a report to management may be passed on to a third party who would rely upon it. Thus the auditor should recognise that, for example, his client's bankers may occasionally request a copy of the report to management and may make use of it on the assumption that the auditor has performed his duties to the client to an acceptable standard. The auditor should therefore clarify with the client whether his report to management is likely to be submitted by the client to any regulatory body or other interested parties.

The auditor should ensure that his comments are factually accurate, his opinions reasonably held and stated, and that remarks of a personal nature are carefully considered. This is particularly necessary when this report contains comments which are critical of members of the client's management or other staff and could lay the auditor open to a charge of defamation.

The auditors' statement on the summary financial statement

(Issued May 1991)

Preface

1 The purpose of this guideline is to clarify the auditors' responsibilities in connection with summary financial statements issued by listed companies under Section 251[1] of the Companies Act 1985 and to describe how the principles of the Auditing Standard 'The audit report' should be applied to the auditors' statement on the summary financial statement.

2 All references are to the Companies Act 1985 ('the Act') as amended by the Companies Act 1989.

Background

3 Under Section 238(1) of the Act a company is required to send to every member of the company copies of:

- the company's annual accounts;
- the directors' report for the financial year; and
- the auditors' report on those accounts.

4 However, Section 251(1) states that:

"A public company whose shares, or any class of whose shares, are listed need not, in such cases as may be specified by regulations made by the Secretary of State, ... send copies of the documents referred to in Section 238(1) to members of the company, but may instead send them a summary financial statement".

For this purpose 'listed' means admitted to the Official List of The International Stock Exchange of the United Kingdom and the Republic of Ireland Limited.

5 The summary financial statement must be derived from the annual accounts and directors' report, and must explicitly follow the detailed requirements concerning its form and content which are set out in the Companies (Summary Financial Statement) Regulations 1990 (SI 1990/514)[2], referred to in this guideline as 'the Regulations' (Section 251(3)).

6 Section 251(4) specifies that the summary financial statement shall:

" (a) state that it is only a summary of information in the company's annual accounts and the directors' report;

(b) contain a statement by the company's auditors of their opinion as to whether the summary financial statement is consistent with those accounts and that report and complies with the requirements of this section and regulations made under it;

[1]The equivalent legislation in Northern Ireland is contained in Article 259 of the Companies (Northern Ireland) Order 1986. There is no equivalent legislation in the Republic of Ireland.

[2]The equivalent regulations in Northern Ireland are contained in The Companies (Summary Financial Statement) Regulations Northern Ireland 1990 (SR 378 of 1990).

(c) state whether the auditors' report on the annual accounts was unqualified or qualified, and if it was qualified set out the report in full together with any further material needed to understand the qualification;

(d) state whether the auditors' report on the annual accounts contained a statement under:

(i) Section 237(2) (accounting records or returns inadequate or accounts not agreeing with the records and returns); or

(ii) Section 237(3) (failure to obtain necessary information and explanations), and if so, set out the statement in full".

The auditors' procedures

7 The summary financial statement must contain a statement of the auditors' opinion on the matters specified in Section 251(4)(b) (see paragraph 6 above). Therefore, when planning the audit of the annual accounts of a listed company, the auditors should ascertain whether a summary financial statement will be prepared. Where applicable, the auditors' engagement letter should refer to their responsibilities in relation to the summary financial statement (see the Auditing Guideline 'Engagement letters'). It will usually be desirable for the auditors to carry out their work on the summary financial statement at the same time as, rather than after, completing the audit, so that their statement under Section 251(4)(b) and their audit report can be issued at the same time. The auditors should therefore encourage the directors to take this into account when they are planning the timetable for the preparation of the annual accounts.

8 The auditors' procedures in relation to the summary financial statement will be directed towards consideration of the matters on which they are required, by Section 251(4)(b), to express an opinion, namely:

- whether it is consistent with the annual accounts and the directors' report; and
- whether it complies with the requirements of Section 251 and of the Regulations.

It should be noted, however, that these opinions are not independent of each other; it is a requirement of the Regulations that the summary financial statement includes not only the detailed information specifically prescribed by the Regulations but also any other information necessary to ensure that it is consistent with the annual accounts and directors' report (see paragraph 1(2) of Schedules 1 and 2 to the Regulations).

Consistency

9 The auditors are required to state whether in their opinion the summary financial statement is consistent with the annual accounts and the directors' report. The auditors are not required to form an opinion on whether the summary financial statement gives a true and fair view.

10 It is in any event most unlikely that the summary financial statement could give a true and fair view in any practical situation, as much of the detailed information from which it has been extracted is not presented. The summary financial statement is required (by Section 251(4)(a)) to include a statement that it is only a summary and also (by the Regulations) to include in a prominent position a statement that it does not contain sufficient information to allow for a full understanding of the company's results and its state of affairs.

11 In order to be satisfied that the summary financial statement is consistent with the annual accounts and directors' report, the auditors will not merely be concerned with whether the detailed information required by the Regulations has been properly extracted and transferred to the summary financial statement. They should also consider whether the summary financial statement needs to contain any other information (i.e. in addition to that specifically prescribed) in order to ensure that it is consistent with the annual accounts and directors' report.

12 Matters which may give rise to an inconsistency include:

- information which has been inaccurately extracted from the annual accounts and directors' report (for example, incorrect classification of balance sheet items);
- information which, in the auditors' opinion, has been summarised in a manner which is not consistent with the annual accounts and directors' report (for example, unduly selective summarisation of the directors' report); and
- omission from the summary financial statement of information which is not specifically required by the Regulations but which, in the auditors' opinion, is necessary to ensure consistency with the annual accounts and directors' report (for example, omission of information relating to an exceptional item or a non-adjusting post balance sheet event which the auditors consider fundamental to a shareholder's understanding of the company's results or financial position).

13 When the auditors identify what they believe may be an inconsistency they should discuss the matter with the directors or senior management, as appropriate, so that they may eliminate the inconsistency, for example by including additional information in the summary financial statement or by making appropriate amendments to the annual accounts or directors' report.

14 If discussion with the directors or senior management does not result in the elimination of the inconsistency, the auditors should qualify their statement under Section 251(4)(b). The qualified statement should include a description of the inconsistency (see also paragraph 19 below).

Compliance with Section 251 and the Regulations

15 In order to give the statement of opinion required by Section 251(4)(b) the auditors will need to give consideration to the specific and detailed requirements of Section 251 and the Regulations.

16 Section 251(3) states that the summary financial statement shall be derived from the annual accounts and directors' report. The auditors will therefore need to consider whether the summary financial statement contains any material which, although it is not inconsistent with the annual accounts and directors' report, is nevertheless not properly derived from them in the manner specified by the Regulations.

17 If the auditors' report on the annual accounts was qualified, or if it included a statement under Section 237(2) or (3), the auditors will need to consider whether the qualified report or statement is accurately reproduced in the summary financial statement, as required by Section 251(4)(c) and (d). They should also consider whether a reader of the summary financial statement will be able to understand the circumstances giving rise to the qualified audit report or statement. Usually the requirement to reproduce in the summary financial statement the full text of the qualified report or statement will ensure this. But Section 251(4)(c) requires that any further material needed to understand the qualified report should also be set out. Therefore, where the qualification includes a reference to a note to the annual accounts but does not explicitly state all the relevant information contained in that note, such information should also be reproduced in the summary financial statement.

18 The auditors should satisfy themselves that the other items required by Section 251 and the Regulations (such as the statements referred to in paragraph 10 above) are also included in the summary financial statement.

19 An inconsistency between the summary financial statement and the annual accounts and directors' report will also mean that the summary financial statement is not properly derived from them and does not comply with the Regulations; it will therefore lead to a qualification of the auditors' statement on the grounds of non-compliance with Section 251 and the Regulations as well as on the grounds of the inconsistency.

Other considerations

20 The summary financial statement may be issued as part of some other form of communication to members of the company, such as a newsletter. Where this occurs, the summary financial statement should form a separate and clearly identified part of the larger document. The auditors' statement on the summary financial statement will refer only to the summary financial statement and not to any other material included in the same document. However, the auditors should ensure that they are not associated with any information which could be misleading. They should therefore urge the directors not to issue any document containing the summary financial statement until they have had an opportunity to read the other material which will be included with it. The auditors should make arrangements to see, prior to publication, any document in which the summary financial statement is to be included. If they disagree with any of this material they should discuss the matter with the directors. If the amendments the auditors consider necessary are not made, they should consider taking legal advice.

The auditors' statement

21 The auditors' statement on the summary financial statement will incorporate the following elements:

- Addressee — the Act does not specify that the auditors' statement should be addressed; in the absence of any other requirement it should be addressed to the members of the company.
- Scope of statement — the summary financial statement should be clearly identified.
- Opinion — the auditors should express their opinion as to whether the summary financial statement is consistent with the annual accounts and the directors' report and whether it complies with the requirements of Section 251 and the regulations made under it.
- Date — the auditors' statement should be dated on or as soon as possible after the date of their audit report on the annual accounts (see paragraph 7 above). In any event it cannot be dated before the date of that report or before the date on which the summary financial statement is approved by the board of directors.

An example of such a statement is given in the Appendix to this guideline. If the auditors cannot give the opinion indicated above, they should qualify their statement in accordance with the Auditing Standard 'The audit report'.

Appendix — Example of a statement on the summary financial statement

AUDITORS' STATEMENT TO THE MEMBERS OF XYZ PUBLIC LIMITED COMPANY

In our opinion the summary financial statement above/overleaf is consistent with the annual accounts and directors' report of XYZ Public Limited Company for the year ended 31 December 19.. and complies with the requirements of Section 251 of the Companies Act 1985 and the regulations made thereunder.

Auditors

Date

Section 8
Statements of Auditing Standards

Contents

The scope and authority of APB pronouncements

(Issued May 1993)

Reproduced with the permission of the Auditing Practices Board

The Auditing Practices Board

1 The Auditing Practices Board ('APB') was established in 1991 by the Consultative Committee of Accountancy Bodies ('CCAB') to advance standards of auditing and associated review activities in the United Kingdom and Republic of Ireland and to provide a framework of practice for the exercise of the auditors' role. The CCAB comprises six principal accountancy bodies in the United Kingdom and Republic of Ireland, namely:

- The Institute of Chartered Accountants in England and Wales
- The Institute of Chartered Accountants of Scotland
- The Institute of Chartered Accountants in Ireland
- The Chartered Association of Certified Accountants
- The Chartered Institute of Management Accountants; and
- The Chartered Institute of Public Finance and Accountancy.

2 In addition to practising auditors, members of the APB include persons from the business and academic worlds, the public sector and the legal profession. The members are appointed by a selection committee consisting of the Presidents of the members of the CCAB, the chairman of the APB and nominees of the Bank of England and the London Stock Exchange. This committee makes appointments from nominations made by the accountancy profession, the Bank of England, the London Stock Exchange, the National Audit Office, the Audit Commission, the Securities and Investments Board, the United Kingdom Department of Trade and Industry and the Republic of Ireland Department of Enterprise and Employment.

3 Under its constitution the APB has up to eighteen voting members and not more than five non-voting members. The Chairman and up to eight other voting members are required to be practising auditors.

Objectives of APB

4 The APB is committed to leading the development of auditing practice in the United Kingdom and the Republic of Ireland so as to:

- establish high standards of auditing;
- meet the developing needs of users of financial information; and
- ensure public confidence in the auditing process.

5 To achieve these objectives, the APB intends to:

- take an active role in the development of statutes, regulations and accounting standards which affect the audit profession;
- promote ways of increasing the value of audits and of ensuring their cost effectiveness;
- consult with the users of financial information to ensure that the APB provides an effective and timely response to their developing needs and to issues raised

by them;

- advance the wider public's understanding of the roles and responsibilities of auditors; and
- establish and publish statements of the principles and procedures with which auditors are required to comply in the conduct of audits, and other explanatory material to assist in their interpretation and application. Pronouncements will have due regard to international developments.

The scope and authority of APB pronouncements

Introduction

1 The pronouncements of the Auditing Practices Board ('APB') fall into three principal categories: Statements of Auditing Standards ('SASs'), Practice Notes and Bulletins. This paper explains the scope and authority of the three types of pronouncement and the distinctions between them. The APB also issues consultative documents and research studies to stimulate public debate and comment on auditing practice and related services, and other documents to inform readers of matters of general interest relating to the work of auditors or of the APB.

2 As well as financial statements, audit and related service engagements may involve other financial information, or non-financial information such as:

- the adequacy of internal control systems;
- compliance with statutory, regulatory or contractual requirements;
- economy, efficiency and effectiveness in the use of resources ('value-for-money' auditing); and
- environmental practices.

3 The APB recognises the fundamental importance of professional judgment being applied by auditors in all audit and related service engagements. The pronouncements of the APB are published with the objective of establishing a framework of prescriptive, persuasive and other guidance designed to support and assist auditors in this regard.

Scope of Statements of Auditing Standards

4 SASs contain basic principles and essential procedures ('Auditing Standards'), which are indicated by bold type[1] and with which auditors are required to comply, except where otherwise stated in the SAS concerned, in the conduct of any audit of financial statements. SASs are also published containing Auditing Standards which apply, as stated therein, to other audits and related services provided by auditors.

5 In addition to SASs of general application the APB issues SASs containing additional Auditing Standards applicable to the conduct of audits of certain types of entities, such as those within specialised industries.

6 SASs also include explanatory and other material which, rather than being prescriptive, is designed to assist auditors in interpreting and applying Auditing Standards.

7 Auditing Standards need not be applied to matters whose effect is in the auditors' judgment not material.

[1] For identification purposes, each Auditing Standard has a unique reference number (for example, SAS 600.1 identifies the first Auditing Standard in SAS 600 'Auditors' reports on financial statements').

8 Each SAS specifies the date from which it becomes effective.

Authority of Auditing Standards

9 The members of the CCAB (the accountancy bodies) have undertaken to adopt all SASs promulgated by the APB. Apparent failures by auditors to comply with the Auditing Standard contained within SASs are liable to be enquired into by the appropriate committee established under the authority of the relevant accountancy body, and disciplinary or regulatory action may result.

10 In order to be eligible for appointment in Great Britain as auditors of companies or of any of the other entities which require their auditors to be eligible for appointment as auditors under Section 25 of the Companies Act 1989, persons must be registered with a supervisory body recognised under the Companies Act 1989 (a recognised supervisory body or 'RSB') and must be eligible for appointment under the rules of that RSB. The Companies Act 1989 requires RSBs to have rules and practices as to the technical standards to be applied in company audit work and as to the manner in which these standards are to be applied in practice.[2] Each RSB adopts SASs in order to meet that requirement and each is required to have arrangements in place for the effective monitoring and enforcement of compliance with the Auditing Standards contained within SASs.

11 Auditors who do not comply with Auditing Standards when performing company or other audits in Great Britain make themselves liable to regulatory action by the RSB with whom they are registered which may include the withdrawal of registration and hence of eligibility to perform company audits.

12 In the Republic of Ireland legislative requirements concerning qualifications for appointment as auditor and recognition of bodies of accountants are contained in the Companies Act 1990. This Act requires bodies of accountants to have satisfactory rules and practices as to technical and other standards. The Act also empowers the Minister for Enterprise and Employment to revoke or suspend recognition or authorisation of a body of accountants or individual auditor.

13 All APB pronouncements and in particular Auditing Standards are likely to be taken into account when the adequacy of the work of auditors is being considered in a court of law or in other contested situations.

14 Guidance on the reporting implications where there are limitations on the scope of the work undertaken by auditors, or where auditors consider it necessary in exceptional circumstances to depart from auditing standards, is given in the SAS 'Auditors reports on financial statements'.

Development of SASs

15 The APB is committed to wide consultation in the preparation of SASs. Prior to issuing SASs, the APB issues exposure drafts for general public comment and may issue other consultative documents in relation to proposed SASs. The APB also seeks out those with a special expertise or interest in the topic under consideration for consultation where necessary. The approval of at least three quarters of the voting members of the APB is required before a SAS can be issued.

International Standards on Auditing

16 The APB supports the International Auditing Practices Committee of the Interna-

[2] In Northern Ireland, equivalent requirements are contained in Part III of the Companies (Northern Irelan) Order 1990.

tional Federation of Accountants ('IFAC') in its aim of improving the harmonisation of auditing practices throughout the world. SASs are formulated with due regard to international developments, in particular the International Standards on Auditing ('ISAs') issued by IFAC.

17 Each SAS explains its relationship to the ISA dealing with the same topic. In most cases, complying with the Auditing Standards within a SAS ensures compliance with the basic principles and essential procedures identified within the relevant ISA. Where the provisions of a SAS and an ISA differ, the Auditing Standards contained within the SAS should be complied with in respect of audits of entities reporting within the United Kingdom and the Republic of Ireland.

Practice Notes and Bulletins

18 The APB also issues

- Practice Notes, to assist auditors in applying Auditing Standards of general application to particular circumstances and industries, and
- Bulletins, to provide auditors with timely guidance on new or emerging issues.

Practice Notes and Bulletins are persuasive rather than prescriptive. However, they are indicative of good practice and have similar status to the explanatory material in SASs, even though they may be developed without the full process of consultation and exposure used for SASs.

19 As occasion arises, Bulletins are likely to be developed into, or to be include within, SASs or Practice Notes. Similarly, some Practice Notes will at a later date be developed into, or be include within SASs.

Pronouncements of predecessor body

20 The APB has adopted the Auditing Standards and Guidelines prepared by its predecessor body, the Auditing Practices Committee, and these remain in force until withdrawn or replaced by SASs or Practice Notes. The old Auditing Standards and the new Auditing Standards contained within SASs have the same status. Auditing Guidelines have the same status as Practice Notes.

Statement of Auditing Standards 100 — Objective and general principles governing an audit of financial statements

(Issued March 1995)

Reproduced with the permission of the Auditing Practices Board

Statements of Auditing Standards ('SASs') are to be read in the light of 'the scope and authority of APB pronouncements'. In particular, they contain basic principles and essential procedures ('Auditing Standards'), indicated by paragraphs in bold type, with which auditors are required to comply in the conduct of any audit. SASs also include explanatory and other material which is designed to assist auditors in interpreting and applying Auditing Standards. The definitions in the Glossary of terms are to be applied in the interpretation of SASs. 5

Introduction

1 The purpose of this SAS is to establish standards and provide guidance on the objective and principles governing an audit of financial statements. The objective of an audit of financial statements is to enable auditors to give an opinion on those financial statements taken as a whole and thereby to provide reasonable assurance that the financial statements give a true and fair view (where relevant) and have been prepared in accordance with relevant accounting or other requirements.

2 In undertaking an audit of financial statements auditors should:

(a) carry out procedures designed to obtain sufficient appropriate audit evidence, in accordance with Auditing Standards contained in SASs, to determine with reasonable confidence whether the financial statements are free of material misstatement;

(b) evaluate the overall presentation of the financial statements, in order to ascertain whether they have been prepared in accordance with relevant legislation and accounting standards; and

(c) issue a report containing a clear expression of their opinion on the financial statements. (SAS 100.1)

3 Financial statements are normally prepared and presented annually and are directed primarily toward the information needs of an entity's shareholders, proprietors or equivalent body of persons. Generally, financial statements are prepared with the objective that they present a true and fair view of the state of affairs of the entity at the period end and of the profit or loss for that period.

4 A degree of imprecision is inevitable in the preparation of all but the simplest of financial statements because of inherent uncertainties and the need to use judgment in making accounting estimates and selecting appropriate accounting policies. Accordingly, financial statements may be prepared in different ways and yet still present a true and fair view.

5 The auditors' opinion enhances the credibility of the financial statements by providing reasonable assurance from an independent source that they present a true and fair view. However, the user cannot assume that the auditors' opinion is a guarantee as to the future viability of the entity nor an assurance as to the efficiency or effectiveness with which management has conducted the affairs of the entity.

Responsibility for the financial statements

6 The responsibility for the preparation and presentation of the financial statements is that of the directors of the entity. Auditors are responsible for forming and expressing an opinion on the financial statements. The audit of the financial statements does not relieve the directors of any of their responsibilities.

Scope

7 The scope of the work required to conduct an audit in accordance with the Auditing Standards contained in SASs is determined by the auditors. Factors which influence auditors' judgment in this regard include the requirements of, and the guidance contained in, SASs, the requirements of relevant professional bodies, legislation and regulations and the terms of the audit engagement. Although the basic principles of auditing are the same in the public and the private sectors, auditors of public service bodies often have wider objectives and additional duties and statutory responsibilities, laid down in legislation, directives or codes of practice.

Reasonable assurance

8 An audit carried out in accordance with Auditing Standards is designed to provide reasonable assurance that the financial statements taken as a whole are free from material misstatement. The term 'reasonable assurance' is therefore central to an audit undertaken in accordance with Auditing Standards. The view given in financial statements is itself based on a combination of fact and judgment and, consequently, cannot be characterised as either 'absolute' or 'correct'. When reporting on financial statements auditors provide a level of assurance which is reasonable in that context but, equally, cannot be absolute.

9 The work undertaken by auditors to form an opinion is permeated by the exercise of judgment, in particular regarding:

(a) the gathering of evidence: for example, in deciding the nature, timing and extent of audit procedures; and

(b) the drawing of conclusions based on the evidence gathered: for example, assessing the reasonableness of the estimates made by the directors in preparing the financial statements.

10 The extent to which audit risk (that auditors may give an inappropriate opinion on financial statements) can be reduced is restricted due to the inherent limitations of any audit. Such limitations include those resulting from:

- the impracticality of examining all items within an account balance or class of transactions;
- the inherent limitations of any accounting and control system;
- the possibility of collusion or misrepresentation for fraudulent purposes; and
- most audit evidence being persuasive rather than conclusive.

11 Auditors recognise the possibility that material misstatement may exist and plan and perform the audit with that possibility in mind. This involves examining critically and with professional scepticism the information and explanations provided and not assuming that they are necessarily correct.

12 In addition to audit risk, auditors are also exposed to loss or injury to their professional practice from litigation, adverse publicity, or other events arising in connection with financial statements that they have audited and reported on. This exposure is present even though they have performed their audit in accordance with Auditing Standards and have reported appropriately on those financial statements. Even if auditors assess this exposure as low, they do not perform less extensive procedures than would otherwise be appropriate under Auditing Standards.

Ethical principles

13 In the conduct of any audit of financial statements auditors should comply with the ethical guidance issued by their relevant professional bodies. (SAS 100.2)

14 The ethical principles which govern auditors' professional responsibilities include:

- integrity;
- objectivity
- independence;
- professional competence and due care;
- professional behaviour; and
- confidentiality.

Compliance with International Standards on Auditing

15 With the exception that paragraphs 1 (an objective rather than an Auditing Standard) and 11 (covered by other Auditing Standards) are considered to be more appropriately expressed as guidance rather than as basic principles or essential procedures, compliance with this SAS ensures compliance in all material respects with International Standard on Auditing 200 'Objective and General Principles Governing an Audit of Financial Statements'.

Effective date

16 Auditors are required to comply with the Auditing Standards contained in this SAS in respect of audits of financial statements for periods ending on or after 23 December 1995.

Statement of Auditing Standards

110 — Fraud and error

(Issued March 1995)

Reproduced with the permission of the Auditing Practices Board

*Statements of Auditing Standards ('SASs') are to be read in the light of 'The scope and authority of APB pronouncements'. In particular, they contain basic principles and essential procedures ('Auditing Standards'), indicated by paragraphs in bold type, with which auditors are required to comply in the conduct of any audit. SASs also include explanatory and other material which is designed to assist auditors in interpreting and applying Auditing Standards. The definitions in the Glossary of terms are to be applied in the interpretation of SASs.**

Introduction

1 The purpose of this SAS is to establish standards and provide guidance on the auditors' responsibility to consider fraud and error in an audit of financial statements. This SAS refers to error as well as fraud because, having identified a matter which could cause a misstatement in the financial statements, auditors will be concerned to establish the circumstances giving rise to that matter and whether such misstatement was an error or occasioned by fraudulent conduct.

2 Auditors should plan and perform their audit procedures and evaluate and report the results thereof, recognising that fraud or error may materially affect the financial statements. (SAS 110.1)

3 No precise legal definition of fraud exists. It is for the court to determine in a particular instance whether fraud has occurred. Auditors need to be alert to conduct which may be dishonest before considering whether it may be fraudulent. In particular circumstances, conduct may be dishonest in some respect but not fraudulent: for example, conduct which breaches an undertaking to follow a specified course of conduct required by a regulator. Where specific breaches of laws or regulations are concerned, auditors follow the principles and essential procedures set out in SAS 120 'Consideration of laws and regulations'.

4 For the purpose of this SAS 'fraud' comprises both the use of deception to obtain an unjust or illegal financial advantage and intentional misrepresentations affecting the financial statements by one or more individuals among management, employees or third parties. Fraud may involve:

- falsification or alteration of accounting records or other documents;
- misappropriation of assets or theft;
- suppression or omission of the effects of transactions from records or documents;
- recording of transactions without substance;
- intentional misapplication of accounting policies; or
- wilful misrepresentations of transactions or of the entity's state of affairs.

The implications of such matters and the extent to which it is reasonable to expect auditors

* Revised March 1995

to detect fraudulent conduct are considered in paragraphs 18 to 22 below. Appendix 2 contains commentary on the interpretation of relevant aspects of the Theft Act 1968, which is one of the most common statutes to which reference may be appropriate.

5 Auditors may encounter circumstances in which it is unclear whether possible misstatement arises from intent to mislead, from accidental oversight, from aggressive business practices or from unethical conduct. Where this is the case, they need to consider the nature of the circumstances in which the misstatement arose and any explanation received in order to determine whether error or fraud is involved. Auditors carry out this assessment in the context of assessing whether the financial statements give a true and fair view.

6 For the purpose of this SAS, 'error' refers to unintentional mistakes in financial statements, such as:

- mathematical or clerical mistakes in the underlying records and accounting data;
- oversight or misinterpretation of facts; or
- unintentional misapplication of accounting policies.

7 'Directors' means the directors (or shadow directors) of a company or other entity, the partners, proprietors, committee of management or trustees of other forms of entity, or equivalent persons responsible for the reporting entity's affairs, including the preparation of its financial statements.

8 In the context of this SAS, 'management' means those persons, who may include directors, who have executive responsibility for the conduct of the entity's operations and the preparation of its financial statements.

9 Guidance on the auditors' responsibility for the detection and reporting of material misstatements resulting from non-compliance with law or regulations when carrying out an audit of financial statements is provided in SAS 120 'Consideration of law and regulations'. Guidance on the auditors' responsibility to report direct to regulators in the financial sector is provided in SAS 620 'The auditors' right and duty to report to regulators in the financial sector'.

Responsibilities of the directors

10 It is the responsibility of the directors to take such steps as are reasonably open to them to prevent and detect fraud. This includes:

- taking steps to provide reasonable assurance that the activities of the entity are conducted honestly and that its assets are safeguarded;
- establishing arrangements designed to deter fraudulent or other dishonest conduct and to detect any that occurs; and
- ensuring that, to the best of their knowledge and belief, financial information, whether used in the entity or for financial reporting, is reliable.

They are also responsible for preparing financial statements that give a true and fair view of the state of affairs of a company or group and of its profit or loss for the financial year. Neither the assignment of particular responsibilities to management nor the audit process relieves the directors of these fundamental responsibilities.

11 In addition, directors and officers of companies have responsibility to provide information required by the auditors, to which they have a legal right of access under Section 389A of the Companies Act 1985. That section also provides that it is a criminal offence to give to the auditors information or explanations which are misleading, false or deceptive.

12 The following steps, among others, may assist the directors in discharging their responsibilities for the prevention and detection of fraud and error:

- the practices contemplated in the document 'Internal control and financial reporting' giving guidance for directors of listed companies developed in response to the recommendation of the Cadbury Committee;
- the steps taken to develop within the entity an appropriate control environment, which is itself dependent upon the attitude, awareness and actions of directors;
- the development of a Code of Conduct, ensuring employees are properly trained in and understand its provisions, monitoring compliance and taking appropriate disciplinary action in cases of non-compliance;
- the institution and operation of appropriate systems of internal control including monitoring their effectiveness and taking corrective action where necessary.

13 In order to assist them in achieving the objectives in paragraph 10, directors of larger entities will often assign particular responsibilities to:

- an internal audit function
- a legal department
- a compliance function, and/or
- an audit committee.

14 In planning and conducting their work, auditors seek to obtain reasonable assurance that financial statements are free from material misstatement, whether caused by error or by fraud. Doing so involves the auditors considering whether they may place reliance upon aspects of the internal control system (such as where there is an effective independent internal audit department) and, specifically, assessing the risk of material misstatement arising from fraud or error. However, an audit conducted in order to express an opinion on the view given by financial statements cannot be regarded as providing any further assurance on the adequacy of an entity's systems or on the actual incidence of fraud. Directors may therefore wish to commission more detailed investigations in particular instances of concern.

15 In certain sectors or activities (for example financial services), there are detailed laws and regulations that specifically require directors to have systems to safeguard the entity's assets and to ensure the reliability of its financial reporting.

16 Given the responsibility of directors to prepare financial statements that give a true and fair view of the state of affairs of a company and of its profit or loss for the financial year, it is necessary, where material error or fraud has occurred, for them to correct the accounting records and ensure that the matter is appropriately reflected and/or disclosed in the financial statements.

Responsibility of the auditors

Prevention

17 It is not the auditors' function to prevent fraud and error. The fact that an audit is carried out may, however, act as a deterrent.

The extent to which the detection of fraud or error may reasonably be expected

18 Auditors plan, perform and evaluate their audit work in order to have a reasonable expectation of detecting material misstatements in the financial statements arising from error or fraud. However, an audit cannot be expected to detect all errors or instances of fraudulent or dishonest conduct. The likelihood of detecting errors is higher than that of detecting fraud, since fraud is usually accompanied by acts specifically designed to conceal its existence, such as management introducing transactions without substance, collusion between employees or falsification of records. Consequently, 'reasonable expectation' in the context of fraud must be construed having regard to the nature of the fraud and, in particular, the degree of collusion, the seniority of those involved and the level of deception concerned.

19 An audit is subject to the unavoidable risk that some material misstatements of the financial statements will not be detected, even though the audit is properly planned and performed in accordance with Auditing Standards. This risk is higher with regard to misstatements resulting from dishonest or fraudulent conduct. The reasons for this include the following:

- the effectiveness of audit procedures is affected by the inherent limitations of the accounting and internal control systems and by the use of selective testing rather than the examination of all transactions;
- much of the evidence obtained by the auditors is persuasive rather than conclusive in nature;
- dishonest or fraudulent conduct may take place over a number of years but may only be discovered in a later year (for example because a fictitious asset becomes material to the financial statements); and
- dishonest or fraudulent conduct may involve conduct designed to conceal it, such as collusion, forgery, override of controls or intentional misrepresentations being made to the auditors.

20 The subsequent discovery of material misstatement of the financial statements resulting from fraud or error existing during the period covered by the auditors' report does not, in itself, indicate that the auditors have failed to adhere to the basic principles and essential procedures of an audit or have been otherwise at fault.

21 While the existence of effective accounting and internal control systems may reduce the probability of misstatement of financial statements resulting from fraud and error, there is always some risk of internal controls failing to operate as designed. Furthermore, any accounting and internal control systems may be ineffective against fraud committed by management, particularly if it involves collusion, internally or with third parties.

22 The detection of fraud committed by management poses particular difficulties for the auditor because management can be in a strong position to commit a fraud and conceal it from others within the entity and from the auditors. Actions that management may take to commit and conceal fraud include:

- introducing complexity into the corporate structure, commercial arrangements with third parties, transactions or internal systems;
- collusive acts with employees or third parties, whether related parties or otherwise;
- the override of internal controls set up to prevent or detect fraud;
- influencing accounting policies, financial statement presentation and accounting estimates affecting financial information used within the business or for external reporting;
- manipulating evidence available to, or responses to evidence requested by, the

auditors, delaying the provision of evidence or making representations and responses to audit enquiries that lack integrity or are deliberately untruthful.

Auditors in the public sector

23 The responsibilities of auditors of entities in the public sector as regards fraud and error are similar to those of auditors of limited companies and other entities in the private sector. The basic principles and essential procedures set out in this SAS therefore apply equally to auditors in both the private and public sector. However, in some ways the responsibilities of auditors of entities in the public sector go beyond those in the private sector by virtue of statutory or other prescribed duties and obligations.

The approach to be adopted by auditors

24 When planning the audit the auditors should assess the risk that fraud or error may cause the financial statements to contain material misstatement. (SAS 110.2)

Conditions or events which increase the risk of fraud and error include:

- previous experience or incidents which call into question the integrity or competence of management or other staff;
- particular financial or reporting pressures within an entity;
- weakness in the design and operation of the accounting and internal control systems;
- unusual transactions;
- problems in obtaining sufficient appropriate audit evidence; and
- inadequate control over data in an information systems environment.

Examples of these conditions or events are set out in Appendix 1.

25 Based on their risk assessment, the auditors should design audit procedures so as to have a reasonable expectation of detecting misstatements arising from fraud or error which are material to the financial statements. (SAS 110.3)

26 In order to have a reasonable expectation of detecting error or fraud, auditors:

(a) include in the engagement team personnel competent to plan and conduct the audit having regard to the size and complexity of the entity concerned and to the industry in which the entity operates;

(b) make a preliminary assessment of the control environment and of conditions and characteristics of the business that might indicate increased risk of fraud or error.

(c) obtain an understanding of the business, its organisational and commercial arrangements and the nature of its transactions, focusing on the substance of the arrangements and transactions, not just the form;

(d) if proposing to rely on the operation of controls to reduce the extent of their substantive procedures, evaluate the strengths and weaknesses of the internal control system, including any internal audit department. This will include an assessment of the potential for management override and the checks and balances that exist in order to guard against this. Attention should be paid to any areas of special weaknesses in the systems and to the adequacy of internal control procedures over those aspects of the business where there is specific risk of increased fraud or error;

(e) obtain from management an understanding of any events of which they are aware during the period involving dishonest or fraudulent conduct and any material weaknesses or breakdowns in the accounting records or controls and, where appropriate, obtain written representations.

(f) are alert throughout the conduct of the audit to audit evidence indicating unusual events or actions, such as:

- control overrides;
- unusual transactions;
- insubstantial responses to audit enquiries, delays or vague representations;
- unusual accounting judgements.

(g) obtain sufficient reliable audit evidence that puts appropriate emphasis on external evidence or evidence created by the auditors. Particular attention is paid to the quality of audit evidence generated by the company or by third parties with whom the company has a relationship.

27 Unless the audit reveals evidence to the contrary, the auditors accept representations as truthful and records and documents as genuine.[1] However, auditors plan and perform the audit with an attitude of professional scepticism, recognising that conditions or events may be found that indicate fraud or error may exist.

28 When conducting an audit where the risk assessment or the audit evidence obtained suggests that there may be fraudulent or dishonest conduct by directors or senior management, the level of professional scepticism and the degree to which evidence independent of the entity is sought is increased. In such circumstances, auditors place less emphasis on management representations and documents generated or provided by the entity.

Procedures when there is an indication that fraud or error may exist

29 When auditors become aware of information which indicates that fraud or error may exist, they should obtain an understanding of the nature of the event and the circumstances in which it has occurred, and sufficient other information to evaluate the possible effect on the financial statements. If the auditors believe that the indicated fraud or error could have a material effect on the financial statements, they should perform appropriate modified or additional procedures. (SAS 110.4)

30 The extent of such modified or additional procedures depends on the auditors' judgement as to:

(a) the types of fraud or error indicated;

(b) the identity of the persons involved;

(c) the likelihood of the occurrence of fraud or error;

(d) the likelihood that a particular type of fraud or error could have a materiai effect on the financial statements, possibly including those of prior years; and

(e) the extent to which it is realistic to expect that further procedures are likely to clarify the position.

Unless circumstances clearly indicate otherwise, the auditors cannot assume that an instance of fraud or error is an isolated occurrence. If necessary, the auditors adjust the nature, timing and extent of their substantive procedures.

31 When evaluating the possible effect of dishonest or fraudulent conduct on the financial statements, the auditors consider its potential materiality. This includes an evaluation of:

1 See SAS 440 — Management representations

- the potential financial consequences, such as fines, penalties, damages, threat of expropriation of assets, enforced discontinuance of operations and litigation;
- whether the potential financial consequences require disclosure, and if so, the adequacy of any disclosure;
- whether breaches of laws and regulations may be involved; or
- whether the potential financial consequences are so serious as to call into question the view given by the financial statements.

Such an evaluation may require the assistance of the entity's directors, legal advisers bankers or other advisers.

32 As the assessment of the effect of dishonest or fraudulent conduct may involve consideration of matters which do not lie within the competence and experience of individuals trained in the audit of financial information, it may be necessary for auditors to obtain appropriate expert advice (whether through the entity or independently) in order to make their assessment of the possible effect on the entity's financial statements. Where this is the case, auditors are required to meet the standards set out in SAS 520 'Using the work of an expert'.

33 When the auditors become aware of, or suspect that there may be, instances of error or fraudulent conduct, they should document their findings and, subject to any requirement to report them direct to a third party, discuss them with the appropriate level of management. (SAS 110.5)

34 Depending on the circumstances, the methods which auditors may decide to adopt to document their findings include taking copies of records and documents and making minutes of conversations. When discussing with management findings which indicate the possibility of fraud, they ensure so far as possible that there is no communication with any person who may be implicated in the events which they are investigating.

35 If the directors do not provide sufficient information to satisfy the auditors' concerns in relation to the suspected or actual error or fraudulent conduct, the auditors may consider it prudent to obtain legal advice about the application of law or regulations to the particular circumstances (including, for example, Section 389A of the Companies Act 1985 — see paragraph 11 above) and the possible effects on the financial statements.

36 The auditors may need, with the entity's permission, to consult the entity's lawyer as to the possible legal consequences of any fraudulent conduct. However, where it is not possible to consult the entity's own lawyer, or it is not appropriate to rely on the entity's lawyer's opinion, or where the auditors so wish, or it is not clear what further action, if any, the auditors ought to take, they may obtain their own legal advice.

37 When adequate information about the suspected or actual error or fraud cannot be obtained, the auditors ensure that the board of directors is aware of the position, and consider the implications of the lack of audit evidence for their report on the financial statements (as required by SAS 110.9) and whether any obligation arises to report to third parties (see SAS 110.10, 110.11 and 110.12 below).

38 The auditors should consider the implications of suspected or actual error or fraudulent conduct in relation to other aspects of the audit, particularly the reliability of management representations. (SAS 110.6)

39 If the auditors consider that error or fraudulent conduct may have or has occurred, they re-evaluate their assessments of audit risk, reconsider whether their other audit procedures have been performed with an appropriate degree of professional scepticism and consider the validity of management representations. Factors affecting the auditors' risk assessment on discovering a possible instance of fraudulent conduct include:

- any apparent failure of specific control procedures;
- the level of management or employees involved; and
- the concealment, if any, of the act.

For example, a series of suspected or actual instances of error or fraudulent conduct which are financially immaterial may be symptomatic of management's probity and hence may throw doubt on the integrity of the financial statements and perhaps even the future prospects of the entity.

Reporting fraud or error

40 The action taken by auditors to report an event varies in relation to its nature and the gravity of its consequences. For example, if the suspected or actual error or fraud is likely to have a substantial effect on the financial statements but there is little firm evidence yet available, auditors nevertheless need to consider whether the matter requires inclusion in their report in accordance with the requirements of SAS 600 concerning either fundamental uncertainties or circumstances in which a qualified opinion is to be expressed. If the matter is fully documented but the effect is not material, then unless the auditors conclude that an apparently isolated incident is part of a wider pattern calling into question the probity of the entity's management no reference need be made in the financial statements or in their report.

Reporting to management

41 The auditors should as soon as practicable communicate their findings to the appropriate level of management, the board of directors or the audit committee if:

(a) they suspect or discover fraud, even if the potential effect on the financial statements is immaterial (save where SAS 110.12 applies); or

(b) material error is actually found to exist. (SAS 110.7)

42 In determining an appropriate representative of the entity to whom to report occurrences of apparent fraud or material error, the auditors need to consider all the circumstances. With respect to apparent fraud, the auditors report the matter to the appropriate higher level of authority within the entity which they do not suspect of involvement in the fraud. If the auditors suspect that members of senior management, including members of the board of directors, are involved, it may be appropriate to report the matter to the audit committee. Where no higher authority exists, or the auditors are precluded by the entity from obtaining sufficient appropriate audit evidence to evaluate whether fraud or error which is material to the financial statements has, or is likely to have, occurred, or if the auditors believe that the report may not be acted upon or are unsure as to the person to whom to report, they may wish to obtain legal advice.

43 Where the auditors determine that the matter involves error rather than suspected fraud, they will request the directors to make appropriate amendments to the financial statements. If such amendments are not made, the auditors need to consider whether their opinion on the financial statements ought to be qualified, as required by SAS 600.

Reporting to addressees of the auditors' report on the financial statements

44 Where the auditors conclude that the view given by the financial statements could be affected by a level of uncertainty concerning the consequences of a suspected or

actual error or fraud which, in their opinion, is fundamental, they should include an explanatory paragraph referring to the matter in their report. (SAS 110.8)

45 Where the auditors conclude that a suspected or actual instance of fraud or error has a material effect on the financial statements and they disagree with the accounting treatment or with the extent, or the lack, of disclosure in the financial statements of the instance or of its consequences they should issue an adverse or qualified opinion. If the auditors are unable to determine whether fraud or error has occurred because of limitation in the scope of their work, they should issue a disclaimer or a qualified opinion. (SAS 110.9)

46 In determining whether disclosures concerning the matter are adequate, or whether an explanatory paragraph needs to be included in their report, auditors base their decision primarily on the adequacy of the overall view given by the financial statements. Steps taken to regularise the position, or the possible consequences of qualification, are not, on their own, grounds on which the auditors may refrain from qualifying their opinion or from including an explanatory paragraph reflecting a fundamental uncertainty.

47 When determining whether the directors have appropriately treated a possible or actual instance of dishonesty or fraud that may require disclosure in the financial statements, auditors have regard to whether the financial statements are free of material misstatements, whether shareholders require the information to enable them to assess the performance of the company and any potential implications for its future operations or standing. Corrections to the financial statements need to be made in respect of errors identified. Where a suspected or actual instance of dishonest or fraudulent conduct needs to be reflected in the financial statements, a true and fair view will require that sufficient particulars are provided to enable users of the financial statements to appreciate the significance of the information disclosed. This would usually require the full potential consequences to be disclosed and, in some cases, it may be necessary for this purpose that the financial statements indicate that dishonest or fraudulent conduct is or may be involved.

48 When considering whether the financial statements reflect the possible consequences of any suspected or actual dishonest or fraudulent conduct, auditors have regard to the requirements of SSAP 18 'Accounting for contingencies'. Suspected or actual dishonest or fraudulent conduct may require disclosure in the financial statements because, although the immediate financial effect on the entity may not be material, there could be future material consequences such as fines or litigation.

Reporting to third parties

49 Paragraphs 53 to 60 below give guidance to auditors on the circumstances in which to report to third parties who have a proper interest in receiving such information. In addition, auditors of financial institutions subject to statutory regulation, who are required to report certain information direct to the relevant regulator, have separate responsibilities.

Guidance on these responsibilities is given in SAS 620 'The auditors' right and duty to regulators to report in the financial sector', and the associated Practice Notes.

50 Where the auditors become aware of a suspected or actual instance of fraud they should:

(a) consider whether the matter may be one that ought to be reported to a proper authority in the public interest; and where this is the case;

(b) except in the circumstances covered in SAS 110.12, discuss the matter with the board of directors, including any audit committee. (SAS 110.10)

51 Where, having considered any views expressed on behalf of the entity and in the light of any legal advice obtained, the auditors conclude that the matter ought to be reported to an appropriate authority in the public interest, they should notify the directors in writing of their view and, if the entity does not voluntarily do so itself or is unable to provide evidence that the matter has been reported, they should report it themselves. (SAS 110.11)

52 When a suspected or actual instance of fraud casts doubt on the integrity of the directors, auditors should make a report direct to a proper authority in the public interest without delay and without informing the directors in advance. (SAS 110.12)

53 Confidentiality is an implied term of the auditors'contract. The duty of confidentiality, however, is not absolute. In certain exceptional circumstances auditors are not bound by the duty of confidentiality and have the right or duty to report matters to a proper authority in the public interest. Auditors need to weigh the public interest in maintaining confidential client relationships against the public interest in disclosure to a proper authority. Determination of where the balance of public interest lies requires careful consideration. Auditors whose suspicions have been aroused need to use their professional judgement to determine whether their misgivings justify them in carrying the matter further or are too insubstantial to deserve reporting.

54 Examples of circumstances which may cause the auditors no longer to have confidence in the integrity of the directors include situations:

- where they suspect or have evidence of the involvement or intended involvement of the directors in possible fraud which could have a material effect on the financial statements; or
- where they suspect or have evidence that the directors are aware of such fraud and, contrary to regulatory requirements or the public interest, have not reported it to a proper authority within a reasonable period.

55 Auditors are protected from the risk of liability for breach of confidence or defamation provided that:

- in the case of breach of confidence;
  - — disclosure is made in the public interest, and
  - — such disclosure is made to an appropriate body or person, and
  - — there is no malice motivating the disclosure, and
- in the case of defamation;
  - — disclosure is made in their capacity as auditors of the entity concerned, and
  - — there is no malice motivating the disclosure.

In addition, auditors are protected from such risks where they are expressly permitted or required by legislation to disclose information (see paragraph below).

56 'Public interest' is a concept that is not capable of general definition. Each situation must be considered individually. Matters to be taken into account when considering whether disclosure is justified in the public interest may include:

- the extent to which the suspected or actual fraud is likely to affect members of the public;
- whether the directors have rectified the matter or are taking, or are likely to take, effective corrective action;
- the extent to which non-disclosure is likely to enable the suspected or actual fraud to recur with impunity;

- the gravity of the matter; and
- the weight of evidence and the degree of the auditors' suspicion that there has been an instance of fraud.

57 When reporting to proper authorities in the public interest it is important that auditors only report to one which has a proper interest to receive the information.[2] Which body or person is the proper authority in a particular instance depends on the nature of the suspected or actual fraud. Proper authorities could include, in the United Kingdom, the Serious Fraud Office, the Crown Prosecution Service, police forces, the Securities and Investments Board and the Self Regulating Organisations it has recognised, the Recognised Professional Bodies recognised by the SIB under the Financial Services Act 1986, the International Stock Exchange, the Panel on Takeovers and Mergers, the Society of Lloyd's, the Bank of England, local authorities, the Charity Commission for England and Wales, the Scottish Office for Scottish Charities, the Inland Revenue, HM Customs and Excise and the Department of Trade and Industry. Comparable bodies in the Republic of Ireland could include the Garda Fraud Squad, the Revenue Commissioners, the Irish Stock Exchange and the Department of Enterprise and Employment. In cases of doubt as to the appropriate authority, auditors are advised to consult with their professional body. Auditors in the United Kingdom may wish to refer the facts to the Investigations Division of the Department of Trade and Industry with a view to investigation by that Division.

58 Auditors receive the same protection even if they only have a reasonable suspicion that fraud has occurred. Auditors who can demonstrate that they have acted reasonably and in good faith in informing an authority of an instance of fraud which they think has been committed would not be held by the court to be in breach of duty to the client even if, an investigation or prosecution having occurred, it were found that there had been no offence.

59 Auditors may need to take legal advice before making a decision on whether the matter should be reported to a proper authority in the public interest.

60 Auditors need to remember that their decision as to whether to report, and if so to whom, may be called into question at a future date, for example on the basis of:

- what they knew at the time;
- what they ought to have known in the course of their audit;
- what they ought to have concluded; and
- what they ought to have done.

Auditors may also wish to consider the possible consequences if financial loss is occasioned as a result of fraud which they suspect (or ought to suspect) has occurred but decide not to report.

61 In addition to the duty of auditors of businesses in the financial sector to report direct to regulators in certain circumstances (see paragraph 49 above), auditors and others have a statutory duty to take the initiative to report to the appropriate authorities suspected money-laundering related to drug trafficking and terrorism.[3] A failure to report in these to circumstances is itself a criminal offence.

3 See Criminal Justice Act 1993.

2 (See Initial Services v. Putterill (1967) All England Law Reports 3, page 145 and Lion Laboratories Ltd v. Evans (1984) All England Law Reports 2, page 417)

Withdrawal from the engagement

62 The auditors may conclude that withdrawal from the engagement is necessary in certain circumstances, for example if they consider that the shareholders have not been given the information they require and see no opportunity for reporting such information to the shareholders whilst continuing as auditors. Factors that may affect the auditors' conclusion include the implications if the highest authority within the entity is suspected of involvement with the suspected or actual fraud, which may affect the reliability of management representations, and the effects on the auditors of continuing association with the entity. In reaching such conclusion, the auditors may need to seek legal advice.

63 Resignation by auditors is a step of last resort. It is normally preferable for the auditors to remain in place to fulfil their statutory duties, particularly where minority interests are involved. However, there are circumstances where there may be no alternative to resignation, for example where the directors of a company refuse to issue its financial statements or the auditors wish to inform the shareholders or creditors of the company of their concerns and there is no immediate occasion to do so.

64 Guidance for auditors on the circumstances of withdrawing from engagements is provided in ethical guidance issued by the accountancy bodies.[4]

Overseas activities

65 Where any of the activities of a company or group are carried on outside the United Kingdom or the Republic of Ireland, the auditors should take steps to ensure that the audit work in relation to the detection and reporting of any fraud and error is planned and carried out in accordance with the requirements of this SAS. (SAS 110.13)

66 The requirements of this SAS apply irrespective of whether the overseas activities are carried on by a subsidiary of a United Kingdom or Irish parent, a division of the company based overseas or employees operating from the United Kingdom or the Republic of Ireland.

Compliance with International Standards on Auditing

67 Compliance with this SAS and with relevant ethical guidance ensures compliance in all material respects with International Standard on Auditing 240 'Fraud and Error'.*

Effective date

68 Auditors are required to comply with the Auditing Standards contained in this SAS in respect of audits of financial statements for periods ending on or after 30 June 1995. Adoption of the requirements when reporting on financial statements for financial periods ending before that date is encouraged.

4 Reference should be made to the appropriate section of the relevant guidance to members. For auditors of limited companies in Great Britain who cease to hold of office, the requirements of Section 394 of the Companies Act 1935 apply.

* Revised March 1995.

Appendix 1

Examples of conditions or events which may increase the risk of fraud or error occurring

Included below are examples of conditions or events which may increase the risk of either fraud or error, or in some cases both. It is not an exhaustive checklist of such conditions or events.

1 Previous experience or incidents which call into question the integrity or competence of management

- Management dominated by one person (or a small group) and no effective oversight board or committee.
- Complex corporate structure where complexity does not seem to be warranted.
- High turnover rate of key accounting and financial personnel.
- Personnel (key or otherwise) not taking holidays.
- Significant and prolonged under-staffing of the accounting department.
- Frequent changes of legal advisors or auditors.

2 Particular financial reporting pressures within an entity

- Industry volatility.
- Inadequate working capital due to declining profits or too rapid expansion.
- Deteriorating quality of earnings, for example increased risk taking with respect to credit sales, changes in business practice or selection of accounting policy alternatives that improve income.
- The entity needs a rising profit trend to support the market price of its shares due to a contemplated public offering, a takeover or other reason.
- Significant investment in an industry or product line noted for rapid change.
- Pressure on accounting personnel to complete financial statements in an unreasonably short period of time.
- Dominant owner-management.
- Performance-based remuneration.

3 Weaknesses in the design and operation of the accounting and internal controls system

- A weak control environment within the entity.
- Systems that, in their design, are inadequate to give reasonable assurance of preventing or detecting error or fraud.
- Inadequate segregation of responsibilities in relation to functions involving the handling, recording or controlling of the entity's assets.
- Indications that internal financial information is unreliable.
- Evidence that internal controls have been overridden by management.
- Ineffective monitoring of the operation of system which allows control overrides, breakdown or weakness to continue without proper corrective action.
- Continuing failure to correct major weakness in internal control where such correc-

tions are practicable and cost effective.

4 Unusual transactions

- Unusual transactions, especially near the year end, that have a significant effect on earnings.
- Complex transactions or accounting treatments.
- Unusual transactions with related parties.
- Payments for services (for example to lawyers, consultants or agents) that appear excessive in relation to the services provided.

5 Problems in obtaining sufficient appropriate audit evidence

- Inadequate records, for example incomplete files, excessive adjustments to accounting records, transactions not recorded in accordance with normal procedures and out-of-balance control accounts.
- Inadequate documentation of transactions, such as lack of proper authorisation, supporting documents not available and alteration to documents (any of these documentation problems assume greater significance when they relate to large or unusual transactions).
- An excessive number of differences between accounting records and third party confirmations, conflicting audit evidence and unexplainable changes in operating ratios.
- Evasive, delayed or unreasonable responses by management to audit inquiries.
- Inappropriate attitude of management to the conduct of the audit — e.g. time pressure, scope limitation and other constraints.

6 Some factors unique to an information systems environment which relate to the conditions and events described above

- Inability to extract information from computer files due to lack of, or non-current, documentation of record contents or programs.
- Large numbers of program changes that are not documented, approved and tested.
- Inadequate overall balancing of computer transactions and data bases to the financial accounts.

Appendix 2

Examples of offences under the Theft Act 1968[1]

The Theft Act 1968 (the Act) only applies to England and Wales. In Scotland, such matters are dealt with, if at all, under common law. In the Republic of Ireland, there is no such equivalent legislation. In Northern Ireland, the equivalent legislation is the Theft Act (Northern Ireland) 1969.

Definitions within the Act

1 The basic definition of theft is to be found in the Act. Section 1 of the Act provides that:

1 References to the Theft Act 1968 also include references to the Theft Act (Northern Ireland) 1969.

(a) a person is guilty of theft if he dishonestly appropriates property belonging to another with the intention of permanently depriving the other of it; and 'thief' and 'steal' shall be construed accordingly; and

(b) it is immaterial whether the appropriation is made with a view to gain, or is made for the thief's own benefit.

Theft is an arrestable offence, and punishable on conviction on indictment by imprisonment for a term not exceeding ten years.

2 The Act does not define dishonesty, that being a question of fact to be decided on the circumstances of each case. The Act does, however, provide for certain circumstances in which the appropriation of property belonging to another is not to be treated as dishonest. These include cases in which a person appropriating property does so in the belief that he has in law the right to deprive the other of it, or in the belief that he would have had the other's consent if the other had known of the appropriation and the circumstances of it.

Obtaining property, or pecuniary advantage, by deception

3 Under Section 15 of the Act, a person who by any deception dishonestly obtains property belonging to another with the intention of permanently depriving the other of it commits an arrestable offence. Obtaining property covers obtaining ownership, possession or control of it. 'Obtain' includes obtaining for another, or enabling another to obtain or retain. 'Deception' means any deception, deliberate or reckless, by words or conduct as to fact or law, including a deception as to the present intention of the person using the deception or any other person.

4 Under Section 16 of the Act, a person who by any deception (defined as above) dishonestly obtains for himself or another any pecuniary advantage commits an arrestable offence. A pecuniary advantage within the meaning of Section 16 is obtained for a person where:

(a) he is allowed to borrow by way of overdraft, or to take out any policy of insurance or annuity contract, or obtains an improvement of the terms on which he is allowed to do so; or

(b) he is given the opportunity to earn remuneration or greater remuneration in an office or employment, or to win money by betting.

5 The Theft Act 1978 creates a range of offences and replaces Section 16(2)(a) of the Act. The offences created are:

(a) dishonestly obtaining services from another by deception;

(b) evading liability by deception. The offence is committed where a person by deception dishonestly secures the remission of a liability to make payment, or, with intent to make permanent default, dishonestly induces a creditor or person claiming payment on his behalf to wait for or forgo payment, or dishonestly obtains exemption from or abatement of liability to make payment; and

(c) dishonestly making off without payment, where it is known that payment on the spot is required or expected, and with intent to avoid payment.

False accounting

6 Under Section 17 of the Act, it is an arrestable offence:

(a) dishonestly to destroy, deface, conceal or falsify any account or record or document made or required for any accounting purpose; or

(b) in furnishing information for any purpose dishonestly to produce or make use of any account or any record or document as aforesaid which, to the knowledge of the person producing or making use of it, is or may be misleading, false or deceptive in a material particular, with a view to gain for oneself or another or with intent to cause loss to another.

For this purpose, a person who makes or concurs in making an entry which is or may be misleading, false or deceptive in a material particular, or who omits or concurs in omitting a material particular, is treated as falsifying the account or document.

7 Under Section 34(2) of the Act, 'gain' and 'loss' are to be construed for the purposes of the Act as extending not only to gain or loss in money or other property, but also to any such gain or loss whether temporary or permanent; and 'gain' includes a gain by keeping what one has, as well as a gain by getting what one has not, and 'loss' includes a loss by not getting what one might get, as well as a loss by parting with what one has.

Liability of company officers for certain offences by company

8 Under Section 18[2] of the Act, where the offences of obtaining property by deception, obtaining pecuniary advantage by deception or false accounting are command by a body corporate and are proved to have been command with the consent or connivance of any director, manager, secretary or other similar officer of the body corporate, or any person who was purporting to act in any such capacity, that person as well as the body corporate is guilty of the offence and is liable to be proceeded against and punished accordingly.

False statements by directors, etc

9 Under Section 19 of the Act, where an officer of a body corporate or an unincorporated association (or person purporting to act as such), with intent to deceive members or creditors about its affairs, publishes or concurs in publishing a written statement or account which to that person's knowledge is or may be misleading, false or deceptive in a material particular, that person commits an arrestable offence.

Suppression, etc, of documents

10 Under Section 20 of the Act, a person who dishonestly, with a view to gain whether personal or for another or with intent to cause loss to another, destroys, defaces or conceals any valuable security, any will or other testamentary document or any original document of, or belonging to, or filed or deposited in, any court of justice or any government department, commits an arrestable offence. Similarly, a person who dishonestly procures execution of a valuable security commits an arrestable offence. This applies in relation to the making, acceptance, endorsement, alteration, cancellation, or destruction in whole or in part of a valuable security, and in relation to the signing or sealing of any paper or other material in order that it may be made or converted into, or used or dealt with as a valuable security, as if that were the execution of a valuable security.

11 A valuable security means any document creating, transferring, surrendering or releasing any right to, in or over property, or authorising the payment of money or delivery of any property, or evidencing the creation, transfer, surrender or release of any such right, or the payment of money or delivery of any property, or the satisfaction of any obligation.

2 There is no equivalent section in Northern Ireland legislation

Statement of Auditing Standards 120 — Consideration of law and regulations

(Issued March 1995)

*Statements of Auditing Standards ('SASs') are to be read in the light of 'The scope and authority of APB pronouncements'. In particular, they contain basic principles and essential procedures ('Auditing Standards'), indicated by paragraphs in bold type, with which auditors are required to comply in the conduct of any audit. SASs also include explanatory and other material which is designed to assist auditors in interpreting and applying Auditing Standards. The definitions in the Glossary of terms are to be applied in the interpretation of SASs.**

Introduction

1 The purpose of this SAS is to establish standards and provide guidance on the auditors' responsibility to consider law and regulations in an audit of financial statements.

2 Auditors should plan and perform their audit procedures, and evaluate and report on the results thereof, recognising that non-compliance by the entity with law or regulations may materially affect the financial statements. (SAS 120.1)

3 'Non-compliance with law or regulations' in this SAS refers to acts of omission or commission by the entity being audited, either intentional or unintentional, which are contrary to law (comprising common law and statute) or regulations. Such acts include transactions entered into by, or in the name of, the entity or on its behalf by its directors or employees. For the purpose of this SAS, non-compliance with law or regulations does not include personal misconduct (unrelated to the business activities of the entity) by the entity's directors or employees. Nor does it include civil wrongs, for example breaches of duties in contract or tort.

4 'Directors' means the directors (including shadow directors) of a company or other entity, the partners, proprietors, committee of management or trustees of other forms of entity or equivalent persons responsible for directing the entity's operations and preparing its financial statements.

5 In the context of this SAS, 'management' means those persons, who may include directors, who have executive responsibility for the conduct of the entity's operations and the preparation of its financial statements.

6 Whether an act constitutes non-compliance with law or regulations is a legal determination that is ordinarily beyond the auditors' professional competence. However, auditors' training, experience and understanding of the entity and its industry may enable them to recognise that some acts coming to their attention may constitute non-compliance with law or regulations. The determination as to whether a particular act constitutes or is likely to constitute non-compliance with law or regulations is generally based on the advice of an informed expert qualified to practise law, but ultimately can be determined only by a court of law.

* Revised March 1995

7 Laws and regulations vary considerably in their relation to the financial statements. Some laws and regulations relate directly to the preparation of, or the inclusion or disclosure of specific items in, the financial statements. Examples of such laws and regulations are given in paragraph 23 below. Other laws and regulations provide a legal framework within which the entity conducts its business.Thus some entities operate in heavily regulated industries (such as banks and chemical companies); others are subject only to the many laws and regulations that generally relate to the operating aspects of the business (such as those relating to occupational safety and health and equal opportunities). Therefore determining the type of procedures necessary in a particular instance needs to take account of the particular entity concerned and the complexity of the regulations with which it is required to comply. In general, a small company which does not operate in a regulated area will require few specific procedures compared with a large multinational corporation carrying on complex, regulated business.

8 Non-compliance with law or regulations may result in financial consequences for the entity, such as fines or litigation. Generally, the further removed possible non-compliance with law or regulations is from the events and transactions normally reflected in financial statements or the less material the possible financial consequences, the less likely the auditors are to become aware of or recognise it in the course of their audit.

9 This SAS applies to audits of financial statements and does not apply to other engagements in which the auditors are specifically engaged to test and report separately on compliance with specific laws or regulations.

10 Guidance on the auditors' responsibility for the detection and reporting of material misstatements resulting from fraud or error when carrying out an audit of financial statements is provided in SAS 110 'Fraud and error'. Guidance on the auditors' responsibility to report direct to regulators in the financial sector is provided in SAS 620 'The auditors' right and duty to report to regulators in the financial sector'.

Responsibilities of the directors

11 It is the responsibility of the directors:

- to take appropriate steps to provide reasonable assurance that the entity complies with law and regulations applicable to its activities;
- to establish arrangements for preventing any non-compliance with law or regulations and detecting any that occurs; and
- to prepare financial statements that give a true and fair view of the state of affairs of a company or group and of its profit or loss for the financial year.

Neither the assignment of particular responsibilities to management nor the audit process relieves the directors of these fundamental responsibilities.

12 In addition, directors and officers of companies have responsibility to provide information required by the auditors, to which they have a legal right of access under Section 389A of the Companies Act 1985. That section also provides that it is a criminal offence to give to the auditors information or explanations which are misleading, false or deceptive.

13 The following steps, among others, may assist the directors in discharging their responsibilities for the prevention and detection of non-compliance with law or regulations:

- maintaining an up-to-date register of significant laws and regulations with which the entity has to comply within its particular industry;

- monitoring legal requirements and any changes therein and ensuring that operating procedures are designed to meet these requirements;
- instituting and operating appropriate systems of internal control;
- developing a Code of Conduct, ensuring employees are properly trained in and understand its provisions, monitoring compliance and taking appropriate disciplinary action in cases of non-compliance;
- engaging legal advisers to assist in monitoring legal requirements; and
- maintaining a record of complaints.

In larger entities, these policies and procedures may be supplemented by assigning appropriate responsibilities to:

- an internal audit function;
- a legal department;
- a compliance function; and/or
- an audit committee.

14 In certain sectors or activities (for example financial services), there are detailed laws and regulations that specifically require directors to have systems to ensure compliance. These laws and regulations could, if breached, have a material effect on the financial statements. In addition, the directors are required to report certain instances of non-compliance to the proper authorities on a timely basis.

15 Given the responsibility of the directors to prepare financial statements that give a true and fair view of the state of affairs of a company and of its profit or loss for the financial year, it is necessary, where possible non-compliance with law or regulations has occurred which may result in a material misstatement in the financial statements, for them to ensure that the matter is appropriately reflected and/or disclosed in the financial statements.

Responsibilities of the auditors

Prevention

16 It is not the auditors' function to prevent non-compliance with law or regulations.The fact that an audit is carried out may, however, act as a deterrent.

Detection

17 Auditors plan, perform and evaluate their audit work in order to have a reasonable expectation of detecting material misstatements in the financial statements. When doing so, they recognise that material misstatements may arise from non-compliance with law or regulations. However, an audit cannot be expected to detect all possible non-compliance with law and regulations.

18 An audit is subject to the unavoidable risk that some material misstatements of the financial statements will not be detected, even though the audit is properly planned and performed in accordance with Auditing Standards. This risk is higher with regard to misstatements resulting from non-compliance with law or regulations due to such factors as the following:

- there are many laws and regulations, relating principally to the operating aspects of the entity, that typically do not have a material effect on the financial statements and where the consequences of any non-compliance are not captured by the accounting and internal financial control systems;
- the effectiveness of audit procedures is affected by the inherent limitations of the

accounting and internal control systems and by the use of selective testing rather than the examination of all transactions;

- much of the evidence obtained by the auditors is persuasive rather than conclusive in nature; and
- non-compliance with law or regulations may involve conduct designed to conceal it, such as collusion, forgery, override of controls or intentional misrepresentations being made to the auditors.

Money laundering

19 When, in the course of their work, auditors become aware of evidence which, in their view, leads them to suspect the laundering of money which either derives from drug trafficking or is related to terrorist offences, they are required by the Criminal Justice Act 1993 to report their suspicions to the appropriate authority. Under the terms of the Act, it is a criminal offence to disclose the reporting of such suspicions to any other party where this may prejudice a criminal investigation. Auditors therefore need to be aware that they are under a statutory obligation not to disclose the matter to the directors if the latter may be implicated in the laundering.

Auditors in the public sector

20 The responsibilities of auditors of entities in the public sector as regards law and regulations are similar to those of auditors of limited companies and other entities in the private sector. The basic principles and essential procedures set out in this SAS therefore apply equally to auditors in both the private and public sector. However, in some ways the responsibilities of auditors of entities in the public sector go beyond those in the private sector by virtue of statutory or other prescribed duties and obligations.

The auditors' consideration of compliance with law and regulations

21 The auditors plan and perform the audit with an attitude of professional scepticism. They recognise that the audit may reveal conditions or events that could lead to questioning whether an entity is complying with law and regulations. For audit purposes laws and regulations relevant to the audit can be regarded as falling into two main categories:

(a) those which relate directly to the preparation of, or the inclusion or disclosure of specific items in, the financial statements of the entity; and

(b) those which provide a legal framework within which the entity conducts its business and which are central to the entity's ability to conduct its business and where noncompliance may reasonably be expected to result in the entity ceasing operations, or call into question its continuance as a going concern.

22 The auditors should obtain sufficient appropriate audit evidence about compliance with those laws and regulations which relate directly to the preparation of, or the inclusion or disclosure of specific items in, the financial statements. (SAS 120.2)

23 Those laws and regulations which relate directly to the preparation of, or the inclusion or disclosure of specific items in, the financial statements include:

- those which specify the form and content of financial statements, such as Schedule 4 to the Companies Act 1985;
- those which determine the circumstances under which a company is prohibited from making a distribution except out of profits available for the purpose, such as Section 263 of the Companies Act 1985;

- those laws which require auditors expressly to report non-compliance, such as the requirements of the Companies Act 1985 relating to the maintenance of proper accounting records or the disclosure of particulars of directors' remuneration in a company's financial statements; financial reporting requirements for particular industries.

24 Where statutory requirements exist which require the auditors to report, as part of the audit of the financial statements, whether the entity complies with certain provisions of laws or regulations, the auditors need:

(a) to have a sufficient understanding of such laws and regulations in order to consider them when auditing the assertions related to the determination of the amounts to be recorded and the disclosures to be made; and

(b) to test for compliance with such provisions.

Compliance with the Taxes Acts

25 The auditors' responsibility to express an opinion on an entity's financial statements does not extend to determining whether the entity has complied in every respect with applicable tax legislation. Auditors need to obtain sufficient appropriate evidence to give reasonable assurance that the amounts included in the financial statements in respect of taxation are not materially misstated. This will usually include making appropriate enquiries of those advising the entity on taxation matters (whether within the audit firm or elsewhere).

26 Where the firm appointed as auditors is not responsible for computing and agreeing the entity's tax liabilities, those responsible for conducting the audit will, in their capacity as auditors, seek to obtain assurance that the amounts included in the financial statements in respect of tax liabilities are not materially misstated. At the time the auditors express their opinion on the financial statements, those amounts are often estimates yet to be agreed with the Inland Revenue. If the auditors become aware that the entity has failed to comply with the requirements of tax legislation, they will need to follow the procedures for reporting set out later in this SAS.

27 However, accounting firms appointed as auditors to report on an entity's financial statements frequently act as its tax advisors and in this capacity are responsible for computing the entity's tax liabilities and agreeing them with the tax authority on the entity's behalf. This additional service is often carried out by partners and staff other than those involved in the audit. Ethical standards of the accountancy bodies prescribe the action to be taken by tax advisors who become aware of a client's non-compliance with tax legislation.[1] Where the same firm acts as both auditors and tax advisors, therefore, any apparent non-compliance with the Taxes Acts of which those responsible for the audit become aware in the course of their work needs to made known to the partner responsible for tax matters, so that appropriate action should be taken. The auditors also need to assess the effect of the matter on their opinion on the financial statements, as set out in SAS 120.10 and 120.11. However, where appropriate action is taken by those responsible for taxation services to the entity, it will not normally be necessary for the auditors to follow the other reporting requirements of this SAS (those contained in paragraphs 56 to 70).

28 The auditors should perform procedures to help identify possible or actual instances of non-compliance with those laws and regulations which provide a legal

1 Professional requirements are set out in relevant sections of guidance issued to members of each accountancy body.

framework within which the entity conducts its business and which are central to the entity's ability to conduct its business and hence to its financial statements, by:

(a) obtaining a general understanding of the legal and regulatory framework applicable to the entity and the industry, and of the procedures followed to ensure compliance with that framework;

(b) inspecting correspondence with relevant licensing or regulatory authorities;

(c) enquiring of the directors as to whether they are on notice of any such possible instances of non-compliance with law or regulations; and

(d) obtaining written confirmation from the directors that they have disclosed to the auditors all those events of which they are aware which involve possible non-compliance, together with the actual or contingent consequences which may arise therefrom. (SAS 120.3)

29 Laws and regulations are central to an entity's ability to carry out its business when either:

- compliance is a pre-requisite of obtaining a licence to operate in the business concerned (for example, compliance with regulations for financial resources in the case of an entity authorised under the Financial Services Act 1986); or
- non-compliance may reasonably be expected to result in the entity ceasing operations, or otherwise call into question the entity's continuance as a going concern (for example where the non-compliance accounts for a substantial proportion of profits, or through the level of fines or damages which could result).

30 The auditors need to obtain a general understanding of those laws and regulations which provide a legal framework within which the entity conducts its business. This includes a general understanding of those laws and regulations which are specific to an industry, such as:

- in a company in which a major activity is the development of a single property, the planning regulations or consents;
- in a waste disposal company, the terms of licences held by the company under which it is allowed to dispose of hazardous waste; and
- those laws and regulations in relation to which the company is required to provide financial information to regulatory or other authorities and where non-compliance may affect the company's ability to continue trading.

31 To obtain this general understanding, the auditors:

- enquire of management as to the laws or regulations (and any changes therein) that may be central to the entity's ability to conduct its business;
- enquire of management concerning the entity's policies and procedures regarding compliance with laws and regulations, in particular those which may be central to its ability to conduct its business;
- discuss with management the policies or procedures adopted for identifying, evaluating and accounting for litigation, claims and assessments;
- use their existing knowledge of the entity's industry and business and of its regulatory environment; and
- discuss the legal and regulatory framework with auditors of subsidiaries in other countries (for example, if the subsidiary is required to adhere to the securities regulations of the parent company).

32 Other than as set out in SAS 120.2 and 120.3 (paragraphs 22 and 28), the auditors are not required to plan and perform other procedures to identify possible instances of non-compliance with law or regulations, because to do so is outside the scope of an audit of financial statements.

33 When carrying out their procedures for the purpose of forming an opinion on the financial statements, the auditors should in addition be alert for instances of possible or actual non-compliance with law or regulations which might affect the financial statements. (SAS 120.4)

34 There may be a wide range of laws and regulations falling into this category, many of which fall outside the expertise of individuals trained in financial auditing. There can therefore be no assurance that auditors appointed to report on an entity's financial statements will detect all material breaches of such laws and regulations. However, when auditors suspect the existence of breaches which could be material, they need to consider whether and how the matter ought to be reported, as set out later in this SAS.

35 Procedures that may bring such non-compliance to the auditors' attention include:

- reading minutes of board and management meetings
- enquiring of the entity's directors and legal counsel concerning litigation, claims and assessments; and
- performing substantive tests of details of transactions or balances.

Procedures when possible non-compliance with law or regulations is discovered

36 The Appendix to this SAS sets out examples of the types of information that may come to the auditors' attention and which may indicate non-compliance with law or regulations.

37 When the auditors become aware of information which indicates that non-compliance with law or regulations may exist, they should obtain an understanding of the nature of the act and the circumstances in which it has occurred and sufficient other information to evaluate the possible effect on the financial statements. (SAS 120.5)

38 When evaluating the possible effect on the financial statements, the auditors consider:

- the potential financial consequences, such as fines, penalties, damages, threat of expropriation of assets, enforced discontinuance of operations and litigation;
- whether the potential financial consequences require disclosure; and if so, the
- adequacy of any disclosure; and
- whether the potential financial consequences are so serious as to call into question the view given by the financial statements.

39 As the assessment of compliance with laws and regulations may involve consideration of matters which do not lie within the competence and experience of individuals trained in the audit of financial information, it may be necessary for auditors to obtain appropriate expert advice (whether through the entity or independently) in order to make their assessment of the possible effect on the entity's financial statements. Where this is the case, auditors are required to meet the standards set out in SAS 520 'Using the work of an expert'.

40 When the auditors become aware of or suspect that there may be non-compliance with law or regulations, they should document their findings and, subject to any requirement to report them direct to a third party, discuss them with the appropriate

level of management. (SAS 120.6)

41 Depending on the circumstances, the methods which auditors may decide to adopt to document their findings include taking copies of records and documents ar' making minutes of conversations.

42 If the directors do not provide sufficient information to satisfy the auditors' concerns in relation to the suspected non-compliance to show that the entity is in fact in compliance, the auditors may consider it prudent to obtain legal advice about the application of law or regulations to the particular circumstances (including, for example, Section 389A of the Companies Act 1985 — see paragraph 12 above) and the possible effects on the financial statements.

43 The auditors normally, with the entity's permission, consult the entity's lawyer as to whether non-compliance with a law or regulation is involved and the possible legal consequences. However, where it is not possible to consult the entity's own lawyer, or it is not appropriate to rely on the entity's lawyer's opinion, or where the auditors so wish, or it is not clear what further action, if any, the auditors ought to take, they may obtain their own legal advice.

44 When adequate information about the suspected non-compliance with law or regulations cannot be obtained, or where the entity has no procedures to ensure compliance with laws and regulations, the auditors ensure that the board of directors is aware of the position, consider the implications of the lack of audit evidence for their report on the financial statements (as required by SAS 120.11) and whether any obligation arises to report to third parties (see SAS 120.12 and SAS 120.13 to 120.15 below).

45 The auditors should consider the implications of suspected or actual non-compliance with law or regulations in relation to other aspects of the audit, particularly the reliability of management representations. (SAS 120.7)

46 If the auditors consider that non-compliance with law or regulations may have or has occurred, they reconsider their assessments of audit risk and the validity of management representations. Factors affecting the auditors' risk assessment on discovering a possible instance of non-compliance with law or regulations include:

- any apparent failure of specific control procedures;
- the level of management or employees involved; and
- the concealment, if any, of the act.

For example, a series of suspected or actual instances of non-compliance with law or regulations which are financially immaterial may be symptomatic of management's general disregard for the law and hence may throw doubt on the integrity of the financial statements and perhaps even the future prospects of the entity.

Reporting non-compliance with law or regulations

47 The action taken by auditors to report a suspected or actual non-compliance with law or regulations varies in relation to its nature and the gravity of its consequences. For example, if the non-compliance is likely to have a substantial effect on the financial statements but there is little firm evidence yet available, auditors nevertheless need to consider whether the matter requires inclusion in their report in accordance with the requirements of SAS 600 concerning either fundamental uncertainties or circumstances in which a qualified opinion is to be expressed. If the matter is fully documented but the effect is not material, then unless the auditors conclude that an apparently isolated incident is part of a wider pattern aimed at circumventing a major element of the laws and regulations which apply to the entity concerned, no reference need be made in the financial statements or their report.

Reporting to management

48 The auditors should, as soon as practicable (save where SAS 120.15 applies), either:

(a) communicate with management, the board of directors or the audit committee; or

(b) obtain evidence that they are appropriately informed,

regarding any suspected or actual non-compliance with law or regulations that comes to the auditors' attention. (SAS 120.8)

49 If, in the auditors' judgement, the suspected or actual non-compliance with law or regulations is material or is believed to be intentional, the auditors should communicate the finding without delay. (SAS 120.9)

50 If the auditors suspect that there has been an instance of possible non-compliance with law or regulations, the auditors report the matter to the appropriate higher level of authority within the entity which they do not suspect of involvement in the non-compliance. If the auditors suspect that members of senior management, including members of the board of directors, are involved, it may be appropriate to report the matter to the audit committee or, in the case of suspected money laundering, direct to the appropriate authority. Where no higher authority exists, or if the auditors believe that the report may not be acted upon or are unsure as to the person to whom to report, they may wish to obtain legal advice.

Reporting to addressees of the auditors' report on the financial statements

51 Where the auditors conclude that the view given by the financial statements could be affected by a level of uncertainty concerning the consequences of a suspected or actual non-compliance which, in their opinion, is fundamental, they should include an explanatory paragraph referring to the matter in their report. (SAS 120.10)

52 Where the auditors conclude that a suspected or actual instance of non-compliance with law or regulation has a material effect on the financial statements and they disagree with the accounting treatment or with the extent, or the lack of any disclosure in the financial statements of the instance or of its consequences they should issue an adverse or qualified opinion. If the auditors are unable to determine whether non-compliance with law or regulations has occurred because of limitation in the scope of their work, they should issue a disclaimer or a qualified opinion. (SAS 120.11)

53 In determining whether disclosures concerning the matter are adequate, or whether an explanatory paragraph needs to be included in their report, auditors base their decision primarily on the adequacy of the overall view given by the financial statements. Steps taken to regularise the position (for example, where there has been an unauthorised material transaction for which authority has subsequently been obtained), or the possible consequences of qualification, are not, on their own, grounds on which the auditors may refrain from qualifying their opinion or from including an explanatory paragraph reflecting a fundamental uncertainty.

54 When determining whether a suspected or actual instance of non-compliance with law or regulations requires disclosure in the financial statements, auditors have regard to whether shareholders require the information to enable them to assess the performance of that company and any potential implications for its future operations or standing. Where a suspected or actual instance of non-compliance needs to be reflected in the financial statements, a true and fair view will require that sufficient particulars are provided to enable users of the financial statements to appreciate the significance of the information disclosed.This would usually require the full potential consequences to be disclosed and, in some cases, it may be necessary for this purpose that the financial statements indicate that non-compliance with law or regulations is or may be involved.

55 When considering whether the financial statements reflect the possible consequences of any suspected or actual non-compliance, auditors have regard to the requirements of SSAP 18 'Accounting for contingencies'. Suspected or actual non-compliance with law or regulations may require disclosure in the financial statements because, although the immediate financial effect on the entity may not be material, there could be future material consequences such as fines or litigation. For example, an illegal payment may not itself be material but may result in criminal proceedings against the entity or loss of business which could have a material effect on the true and fair view given by the financial statements.

Reporting to third parties

56 When the auditors become aware of a suspected or actual non-compliance with law and regulations which gives rise to a statutory duty to report, they should make a report to the appropriate authority without undue delay. (SAS 120.12)

57 Paragraphs 62 to 70 below give guidance to auditors on the circumstances in which to report in the public interest to third parties who have a proper interest in receiving such inhrmation. In addition, auditors of financial institutions subject to statutory regulation, who are required to report certain information direct to the relevant regulator, have separate responsibilities. Guidance on these responsibilities is given in SAS 620 'The auditors' right and duty to report to regulators in the financial sector' and the associated Practice Notes.

58 The procedures and guidance in SAS 620 can be adapted to circumstances in which auditors of other types of entity become aware of a suspected instance of non-compliance with law or regulations which they are under a statutory duty to report.

59 Where the auditors become aware of a suspected or actual instance of non-compliance with law or regulations which does not give rise to a statutory duty to report to an appropriate authority they should:

(a) consider whether the matter may be one that ought to be reported to a proper authority in the public interest; and where this is the case

(b) except in the circumstances covered in SAS 120.15, discuss the matter with the board of directors, including any audit committee. (SAS 120.13)

60 Where, having considered any views expressed on behalf of the entity and in the light of any legal advice obtained, the auditors conclude that the maner ought to be reported to an appropriate authority in the public interest, they should notify the directors in writing of their view and, if the entity does not voluntarily do so itself or is unable to provide evidence that the matter has been reported, they should report it themselves. (SAS 120.14)

61 Auditors should report a matter direct to a proper authority in the public interest and without discussing the matter with the entity if they conclude that the suspected or actual instance of non-compliance has caused them no longer to have confidence

in the integrity of the directors. (SAS 120.15)

62 Confidentiality is an implied term of the auditors' contract. The duty of confidentiality, however, is not absolute. In certain exceptional circumstances auditors are not bound by the duty of confidentiality and have the right or duty to report matters to a proper authority in the public interest. Auditors need to weigh the public interest in maintaining confidential client relationships against the public interest in disclosure to a proper authority. Determination of where the balance of public interest lies requires careful consideration. Auditors whose suspicions have been aroused need to use their professional judgement to determine whether their misgivings justify them in carrying the matter further or are too insubstantial to deserve reporting.

63 Examples of circumstances which may cause the auditors no longer to have confidence in the integrity of the directors include situations:

- where they suspect or have evidence of the involvement or intended involvement of the directors in possible non-compliance with law or regulations which could have a material effect on the financial statements; or
- where they are aware that the directors are aware of such non-compliance and, contrary to regulatory requirements or the public interest, have not reported it to a proper authority within a reasonable period.

64 Auditors are protected from the risk of liability for breach of confidence or defamation provided that:

- in the case of breach of confidence:
  - – disclosure is made in the public interest, and
  - – such disclosure is made to an appropriate body or person, and
  - – there is no malice motivating the disclosure, and
- in the case of defamation:
  - – disclosure is made in their capacity as auditors of the entity concerned, and
  - – there is no malice motivating the disclosure.

In addition, auditors are protected from such risks where they are expressly permitted or required by legislation to disclose information (see paragraph 70 below).

65 'Public interest' is a concept that is not capable of general definition. Each situation must be considered individually. Matters to be taken into account when considering whether disclosure is justified in the public interest may include:

- the extent to which the suspected or actual non-compliance with law or regulations is likely to affect members of the public;
- whether the directors have rectified the matter or are taking, or are likely to take, effective corrective action;
- the extent to which non-disclosure is likely to enable the suspected or actual non-compliance with law or regulations to recur with impunity;
- the gravity of the matter;
- whether there is a general management ethos within the entity of disregarding law or regulations; and
- the weight of evidence and the degree of the auditors' suspicion that there has been an instance of non-compliance with law or regulations.

66 When reporting to proper authorities in the public interest it is important that, in order to suspect retain the protection of qualified privilege, auditors report only to one who has a proper interest to receive the information.[2] Which body or person is the proper authority in a particular instance depends on the nature of the suspected or actual non-compliance. Proper authorities could include, in the United Kingdom, the Serious Fraud Office, the Crown Prosecution Service, police forces, the Securities and Investments Board and the Self Regulating Organisations it has recognised, the Recognised Professional Bodies recognised by the SIB under the Financial Services Act 1986, the International Stock Exchange, the Panel on Takeovers and Mergers, the Society of Lloyd's, the Bank of England, local authorities, the Charity Commissioners for England and Wales, the Scottish Office For Scottish Charities, the Inland Revenue, HM Customs and Excise, the Department of Trade and Industry and the Health and Safety Executive. Comparable bodies in the Republic of Ireland could include the Garda Fraud Squad, the Revenue Commissioners, the Irish Stock Exchange and the Department of Enterprise and Employment. In case of doubt as to the proper authority to approach, auditors are advised to consult with their professional body. Auditors in the United Kingdom may wish to refer the facts to the Investigations Division of the Department of Trade and Industry with a view to investigation by that Division.

67 Auditors receive the same protection even if they have only a reasonable suspicion that non-compliance with law or regulations has occurred. Auditors who can demonstrate that they have acted reasonably and in good faith in informing an authority of a breach of law or regulations which they think has been committed would not be held by the court to be in breach of duty to the client even if, an investigation or prosecution having occurred, it were found that there had been no offence.

68 Auditors may need to take legal advice before making a decision on whether the matter should be reported to a proper authority in the public interest.

69 Auditors need to remember that their decision as to whether to report, and if so to whom, may be called into question at a future date, for example on the basis of:

- what they knew at the time;
- what they ought to have known in the course of their audit;
- what they ought to have concluded; and
- what they ought to have done.

Auditors may also wish to consider the possible consequences if financial loss is occasioned by non-compliance with law or regulations which they suspect (or ought to suspect) has occurred but decide not to report.

70 In Addition to the duty of auditors of businesses in the financial sector to report direct to regulators in certain circumstances (see paragraph 57 above), auditors and others have a statutory duty to take the initiative to report to the appropriate authorities suspected non-compliance with law or regulations related to drug trafficking, money laundering and terrorism. A failure to report in these circumstances is itself a criminal offence.

Withdrawal from the engagement

71 The auditors may conclude that withdrawal from the engagement is necessary in certain circumstances, for example if they consider that the shareholders have not been given information they require and see no opportunity for reporting such information to the

2 See Initial Services v. Putterill (1967) All England Law Reports 3, page 145 and Lion Laboratories Ltd v. Evans (1984) All England Law Reports 2, page 417.

shareholders whilst continuing as auditors. Factors that may affect the auditors' conclusion include the implications if the highest authority within the entity is suspected of involvement with the suspected or actual non-compliance, which may affect the reliability of management representations, and the effects on the auditors of continuing association with the entity. In reaching such conclusions, the auditors may need to seek legal advice.

72 Resignation by auditors is a step of last resort. It is normally preferable for the auditors to remain in office to fulfil their statutory duties, particularly where minority interests are involved. However, there are circumstances where there may be no alternative to resignation, for example where the directors of a company refuse to issue its financial statements or the auditors wish to inform the shareholders or creditors of the company of their concerns and there is no immediate occasion to do so.

73 Guidance for auditors on the circumstances of withdrawing from engagement is provided in ethical guidance issued by the accountancy bodies.[3]

Overseas activities

74 Where any of the activities of a company or group are carried on outside the United Kingdom or the Republic of Ireland, the auditors should take steps to ensure that the audit work in relation to the detection and reporting of any non-compliance with local law and regulations is planned and carried out in accordance with the requirements of this SAS. (SAS 120.16)

75 The requirements of this SAS apply irrespective of whether the overseas activities are carried on by a subsidiary of a United Kingdom or Irish parent company, a division of the company based overseas or employees operating from the United Kingdom or the Republic of Ireland.

Compliance with International Standards on Auditing

76 Compliance with this SAS and with relevant ethical guidance ensures compliance in all material respects with International Standard on Auditing 250 'Consideration of Laws and Regulations in an Audit of Financial Statements'.*

Effective date

77 Auditors are required to comply with the Auditing Standards contained in this SAS in respect of audits of financial statements for financial periods ending on or after 30 June 1995. Adoption of the requirements when reporting on financial statements for financial periods ending before that date is encouraged.

Appendix

Indications that non-compliance may have occurred

Examples of the type of information that may come to the auditors' attention and may indicate that non compliance with law or regulations has occurred are listed below:

3 Reference should be made to the appropriate section of the relevant guidance to members. For auditors of limited companies in Great Britain who cease to hold office, the requirements of section 394 of the Companies Act 1985 apply.

* Revised March 1995.

- Investigation by government department or payment of fines or penalties;
- Payments for unspecified services or loans to consultants, related parties, employees or government employees;
- Sales commissions or agents' fees that appear excessive in relation to those normally paid by the entity or in its industry or to the services actually received;
- Purchasing at prices significantly above or below market price;
- Unusual payments in cash, purchases in the form of cashiers'cheques payable to bearer or transfers to numbered bank accounts;
- Unusual transactions with companies registered in tax havens;
- Payments for goods or services made other than to the country from which the goods or services originated;
- Existence of an accounting system that fails, whether by design or by accident, to provide adequate audit trail or sufficient evidence;
- Unauthorised transactions or improperly recorded transactions;
- Media comment.

Statement of Auditing Standards 130 — The going concern basis in Financial Statements

Reproduced with the permission of the Auditing Standards Board

Statements of Auditing Standards ('SASs') contain basic principles and essential procedures ('Auditing Standards'), indicated by paragraphs in bold type, with which auditors are required to comply in the conduct of any audit. SASs also include explanatory and other material which is designed to assist auditors in interpreting and applying Auditing Standards. The definitions in the Glossary of terms are to be applied in the interpretation of SASs.

Introduction

1 The purpose of this SAS is to establish standards and provide guidance for auditors in respect of their consideration of the going concern basis in financial statements prepared by directors.

2 When forming an opinion as to whether financial statements give a true and fair view, the auditors should consider the entity's ability to continue as a going concern, and any relevant disclosures in the financial statements. (SAS 130.1)

The applicability and scope of this SAS

3 This SAS contains standards and guidance for auditors in relation to the going concern basis that is generally presumed in financial statements which are required to be properly prepared in accordance with the Act, and to give a true and fair view. In the absence of specific legal or other provisions to the contrary, the principles and procedures embodied in the SAS apply also to the audit of the financial statements of other entities, including those within the public sector.

4 This SAS does not establish standards nor provide guidance about going concern in any other context, such as that of an engagement to report on an entity's future viability. In particular, Bulletin 1994/1 'Disclosures relating to corporate governance (Revised)' gives advice to auditors in connection with any statement regarding going concern made by the directors in compliance with the Code of Best Practice published by the Committee on The Financial Aspects of Corporate Governance ('the Cadbury Report'). Guidance for directors in relation to such a statement is contained in 'Going Concern and Financial Reporting: Guidance for directors of listed companies'.

Going concern as an accounting concept

5 Appendix 1 to this SAS summarises, in relation to going concern, the legal and professional accounting requirements with which directors comply in preparing financial statements. Under these accounting requirements (and consequently for the purposes of this SAS) the going concern basis is considered as an accounting concept in accordance with which financial statements are generally prepared on a presumption that 'the entity will continue in operational existence for the foreseeable future'. Accordingly, in financial statements:

(a) assets are recognised and measured on the basis that the entity expects to recover (through use or realisation) the recorded amounts in the normal course of business; and

(b) liabilities are recognised and measured on the basis that they will be discharged in the normal course of business.

Where the directors are unable to accept the going concern presumption on the basis of their own information and judgments, the entity may not be able to recover (through use or realisation) the amounts recorded in the financial statements in respect of its assets. There may also be changes in the amounts and dates of maturities of liabilities. In these circumstances, the amounts and classification of assets and liabilities in the financial statements would need to be adjusted by the directors if the effects were material.

6 An important consequence of the legal and professional accounting requirements is that, when preparing financial statements, the directors should satisfy themselves as to whether the going concern basis is appropriate. Even if it is appropriate, it may still be necessary for the financial statements to contain additional disclosures, for instance relating to the adoption of that basis, in order to give a true and fair view.

7 Accordingly, the auditors' procedures in complying with this SAS are intended to provide them with assurance that:

(a) the going concern basis used in the preparation of the financial statements as a whole is appropriate; and

(b) there are adequate disclosures regarding that basis in the financial statements in order that they give a true and fair view.

8 The auditors' procedures necessarily involve a consideration of the entity's ability to continue in operational existence for the foreseeable future. In turn, that necessitates consideration both of the current and the possible future circumstances of the business and the environment in which it operates.

Foreseeable future: guidance and inherent limitations in application

9 In defining the going concern accounting concept, Statement of Standard Accounting Practice Number 2 ('SSAP 2') uses the term 'foreseeable future' without further elaboration. Neither the Act nor accounting standards expand on that term in the context of going concern.

10 Any consideration involving the foreseeable future involves making a judgment, at a particular point in time, about future events which are inherently uncertain. The following factors are relevant.

(a) In general terms, the degree of uncertainty increases significantly the further into the future the consideration is taken. The manner in which the uncertainty increases with time depends on the circumstances of each particular entity.

(b) Any judgment about the future is based on information available at the time at which it is made. Subsequent events can overturn a judgment which was reasonable at the time it was made.

11 Accordingly, the foreseeable future depends on the specific circumstances at a point in time, including the nature of the entity's business, its associated risks and external influences.

12 As a consequence, it is not possible to give any certainty in relation to going concern. Any judgment made, whether by directors or auditors, although reasonable at the time, can be valid only at that time and can be overturned by subsequent events.

Consideration of going concern by the directors and auditors

13 In assessing going concern, directors take account of all relevant information of which they are aware at the time. The nature of the exercise entails that the directors look forward, and there will be some future period to which they will pay particular attention in assessing going concern. It is not possible to specify a minimum length for this period: it is recognised in any case that any such period would be artificial and arbitrary since in reality there is no 'cut off point' after which there should be a sudden change in the approach adopted by the directors. The length of the period is likely to depend upon such factors as:

- the entity's reporting and budgeting systems; and
- the nature of the entity, including its size or complexity.

Where the period considered by the directors has been limited, for example, to a period of less than one year from the date of approval of the financial statements, the directors will have determined whether, in their opinion, the financial statements require any additional disclosure to explain adequately the assumptions that underlie the adoption of the going concern basis.

14 The basis for the auditors' procedures is the information upon which the directors have based their assessment and the directors' reasoning. The auditors assess whether this constitutes sufficient appropriate audit evidence for their purpose and whether they concur with the directors' judgment about the need for additional disclosures.

15 The following factors in particular may affect the information available to auditors, and whether the auditors consider this information constitutes sufficient audit evidence for the purposes of their audit.

(a) *The nature of the entity (its size and the complexity of its circumstances, for instance).* This SAS applies to the audits of the financial statements of all sizes of entity. The larger or more complex the entity the more sophisticated is likely to be the information available and needed to support the assessment of whether it is appropriate to adopt the going concern basis.

(b) *Whether the information relates to future events, and if so how far into the future those events lie.* The information relating to the period falling after one year from the balance sheet date is often prepared in far less detail and subject to a greater degree of estimation than the information relating to periods ending on or before one year from the balance sheet date.

16 Appendix 2 illustrates how the auditors might decide to apply the SAS in certain circumstances. Example 1 within that Appendix is of particular relevance to entities with 'uncomplicated circumstances', which includes many smaller companies.

Definitions

17 The following definitions apply for the purposes of interpreting the requirements and the guidance in this SAS.

18 *The going concern basis:* Financial statements prepared under the presumption that the entity is carrying on business as a going concern are described in this SAS as being prepared on the going concern basis.

19 *The Act:* for Great Britain, 'the Act' refers to the Companies Act 1985. For Northern Ireland, the equivalent legislation is provided by the Companies (Northern Ireland) Order 1986 and for the Republic of Ireland by the Companies Acts 1963 to 1990.

20 *Directors:* the directors of a company or other body, the partners, proprietors, committee of management or trustees of other forms of entity, or equivalent persons responsible for directing the entity's operations and preparing its financial statements.

Audit evidence

21 The auditors should assess the adequacy of the means by which the directors have satisfied themselves that:

(a) it is appropriate for them to adopt the going concern basis in preparing the financial statements; and

(b) the financial statements include such disclosures, if any, relating to going concern as are necessary for them to give a true and fair view.

For this purpose:

(i) the auditors should make enquiries of the directors and examine appropriate available financial information; and

(ii) having regard to the future period to which the directors have paid particular attention in assessing going concern, the auditors should plan and perform procedures specifically designed to identify any material matters which could indicate concern about the entity's ability to continue as a going concern. (SAS 130.2)

22 The examples in Appendix 2 illustrate the importance of planning the audit approach regarding going concern. The auditors' approach includes a preliminary assessment (at the stage at which they are developing an overall audit plan) of the risk that the entity may be unable to continue as a going concern.

23 The auditors may need to consider some or all of the following matters:

- whether the period to which the directors have paid particular attention in assessing going concern is reasonable in the entity's circumstances and in the light of the need for the directors to consider the ability of the entity to continue in operational existence for the foreseeable future;
- the systems, or other means (formal or informal), for timely identification of warnings of future risks and uncertainties the entity might face;
- budget and/or forecast information (cash flow information in particular) produced by the entity, and the quality of the systems (or other means, formal or informal) in place for producing this information and keeping it up to date:
- whether the key assumptions underlying the budgets and/or forecasts appear appropriate in the circumstances;
- the sensitivity of budgets and/or forecasts to variable factors both within the control of the directors and outside their control;
- any obligations, undertakings or guarantees arranged with other entities (in particular, lenders, suppliers and group companies) for the giving or receiving of support;
- the existence, adequacy and terms of borrowing facilities, and supplier credit; and
- the directors' plans for resolving any matters giving rise to the concern (if any) about the appropriateness of the going concern basis. In particular, the auditors may need to consider whether the plans are realistic, whether there is a reasonable expectation that the plans are likely to resolve any problems foreseen and whether the directors are likely to put the plans into practice effectively.

24 In many entities the headroom between the financial resources required in the foreseeable future and the facilities available is large. In others, it will often be marginal. The nature and scope of the auditors' procedures depends on the circumstances. The extent of the procedures is influenced primarily by the excess of the financial resources available to the entity over the financial resources that it requires. The entity's procedures (and the auditors' procedures) need not always be elaborate in order to provide sufficient appropriate audit evidence. For example, auditors may not always need to examine budgets and forecasts for this purpose. This is particularly likely to be the case in respect of entities with uncomplicated circumstances. Many smaller companies fall into this category. Thus for example:

- regarding the systems or other means for timely identification of warnings of future risks and uncertainties, the directors might consider that it is appropriate simply to keep abreast of developments within their individual business and their business sector. In the circumstances, the auditors might concur with the directors; or
- the directors might not, as a matter of course, prepare periodic cash flow and other budgets, forecasts or other management accounts information apart from the accounting records required by law and outline plans for the future. In the directors' view, this might be acceptable where the business is stable. In the circumstances the auditors might concur with the directors. Hence the auditors' procedures regarding budgets, forecasts and related issues might comprise discussion of the directors' outline plans in the light of other information available to the auditors.

The auditors' examination of borrowing facilities

25 In examining borrowing facilities the auditors could decide, for example, that it is necessary:

(a) to obtain confirmations of the existence and terms of bank facilities; and

(b) to make their own assessment of the intentions of the bankers relating thereto.

The latter assessment could involve the auditors examining written evidence or making notes of meetings which they would hold with the directors and, occasionally, with the directors and the entity's bankers. In making their assessment of the bankers' intentions the auditors ascertain, normally through enquiries of the directors, whether the bankers are aware of the matters that are causing the auditors to decide that such an assessment is necessary. It is also important that the relationships between the auditors, the directors and the bankers are clarified and understood.

26 The auditors might be more likely to decide that it is necessary to obtain confirmations of the existence and terms of bank facilities, and to make their own assessment of the intentions of the bankers relating thereto, in cases where, for example:

- there is a low margin of financial resources available to the entity;
- the entity is dependent on borrowing facilities shortly due for renewal;
- correspondence between the bankers and the entity reveals that the last renewal of facilities was agreed with difficulty, or that, since the last review of facilities, the bankers have imposed additional conditions as a prerequisite for continued lending;
- a significant deterioration in cash flow is projected;
- the value of assets granted as security for the borrowings is declining; or

- the entity has breached the terms of borrowing covenants, or there are indications of potential breaches.

27 In accordance with SAS 600 'Auditors' report on financial statements' the auditors consider whether any inability to satisfy themselves regarding the existence and terms of borrowing facilities and the intentions of the lender relating thereto, and/or the factors giving rise to this inability, need to be:

- disclosed in the financial statements in order that they give a true and fair view; and/ or
- referred to (by way of an explanatory paragraph or a qualified opinion) in the auditors' report.

28 The British Bankers' Association has assisted in drafting the guidance above and in Appendix 2, regarding the auditors' examination of the entity's banking facilities. The guidance aims to improve communications between directors, auditors and bankers, whilst stressing the importance of each party's clear understanding of their relationships to each other. The guidance does not alter existing practice regarding confirmation letters from bankers about their intentions concerning facilities.

Determining and documenting the auditors' concerns

29 The auditors should determine and document the extent of their concern (if any) about the entity's ability to continue as a going concern. In determining the extent of their concern, the auditors should take account of all relevant information of which they have become aware during their audit (SAS 130.3)

30 In addition to information obtained having regard to the future period to which the directors have paid particular attention, the information of which the auditors are aware includes:

(a) any information of which they have become aware relating to the period thereafter; and

(b) their other audit evidence (such as their knowledge of the entity, its industry and possible developments therein).

31 The auditors might be more likely to conclude that there is a significant level of concern about the entity's ability to continue as a going concern if, for example, indications such as the following are present:

Financial

- an excess of liabilities over assets;
- net current liabilities;
- necessary borrowing facilities have not been agreed;
- default on terms of loan agreements, and potential breaches of covenant;
- significant liquidity or cash flow problems;
- major losses or cash flow problems which have arisen since the balance sheet date and which threaten the entity's continued existence;
- substantial sales of fixed assets not intended to be replaced;
- major restructuring of debt;
- denial of (or reduction in) normal terms of trade credit by suppliers;
- major debt repayment falling due where refinancing is necessary to the entity's

continued existence;

- inability to pay debts as they fall due;

Operational

- fundamental changes in the market or technology to which the entity is unable to adapt adequately;
- externally forced reductions in operations (for example, as a result of legislation or regulatory action);
- loss of key management or staff, labour difficulties or excessive dependence on a few product lines where the market is depressed;
- loss of key suppliers or customers or technical developments which render a key product obsolete;

Other

- major litigation in which an adverse judgment would imperil the entity's continued existence; and
- issues which involve a range of possible outcomes so wide that an unfavourable result could affect the appropriateness of the going concern basis.

However, in situations such as these the auditors may have obtained sufficient appropriate evidence causing them to conclude that there is not a significant level of concern about the entity's ability to continue as a going concern. Appendix 2, Example 1 contains such a situation.

32 The auditors could consider that there is a significant level of concern about the entity's ability to continue as a going concern, or they could disagree with the preparation of the financial statements on the going concern basis. In such cases (whether or not this is because of potential insolvency) the auditors might decide to write to the directors drawing their attention to the need to consider taking suitable advice. In particular, the directors of an entity may need to obtain advice from specialist accountants or lawyers on the appropriateness and implications of continuing to trade while they know, or ought to know, that the entity is insolvent.

Written confirmations of representations from the directors

33 The auditors should consider the need to obtain written confirmations of representations from the directors regarding:

(a) the directors' assessment that the company is a going concern; and

(b) any relevant disclosures in the financial statements. (SAS 130.4)

34 Such written confirmations are necessary in respect of matters material to the financial statements when those representations are critical to obtaining sufficient appropriate audit evidence In view of their importance, it is appropriate for such confirmations to be provided by the directors, rather than other levels of the entity's management.

35 If they are unable to obtain such written confirmations of representations as they consider necessary from the directors, the auditors consider whether:

- in the light of SAS 600 'Auditors' report on financial statements', there is a limitation on the scope of their work which requires a qualified opinion in 'except for' or 'disclaimer' terms; or
- the failure of the directors to provide the written confirmations could indicate that there is concern.

Assessing disclosures in the financial statements

36 The auditors should consider whether the financial statements are required to include disclosures relating to going concern in order to give a true and fair view. (SAS 130.5)

37 If the going concern basis is inappropriate at the balance sheet date or significantly uncertain in the foreseeable future, this affects the manner in which the other fundamental accounting concepts are applied in the financial statements. It is thus important, where there is concern as to the entity's ability to continue as a going concern, that readers of the financial statements have a proper understanding of the context in which the directors have satisfied themselves that the financial statements prepared on the going concern basis show a true and fair view. Therefore, in such cases, if the financial statements do not include disclosures relating to the entity's ability to continue as a going concern, the auditors consider:

- whether the financial statements give a true and fair view; and hence
- whether they need to qualify their audit opinion in respect of disagreement with the disclosure of this matter in the financial statements.

38 In particular, if the future period to which the directors have paid particular attention is, as described in paragraph 13, not very long, the directors will have determined whether, in their opinion, the financial statements require any additional disclosures to explain adequately the assumptions that underlie the adoption of the going concern basis. The auditors assess whether they concur with the directors' judgments regarding the need for additional disclosures and their adequacy. Disclosure, however, does not eliminate the need to make appropriate judgments about the suitability of the future period as an adequate basis for assessing the position.

39 To avoid repetition, the text in the financial statements might refer readers to specific disclosures located elsewhere in the annual report (for instance in the Operating and Financial Review). The auditors take account of such specified disclosures in considering the adequacy of disclosures in the financial statements.

Reporting on the financial statements

40 In relation to going concern Appendix 4 summarises, in flowchart form, how auditors formulate their opinion as to whether the financial statements give a true and fair view.

41 When auditors of regulated financial entities consider that they might need to either qualify their audit opinion or add an explanatory paragraph to their report, they may have a duty to inform the appropriate regulator at an early stage in the audit. In such cases the regulator might, if it has not already done so, specify corrective action to be taken by the entity. At the time at which they formulate their report, the auditors take account of matters such as:

- any views expressed by the regulator;
- any legal advice obtained by the directors; and
- the actual and planned corrective action.

42 Where the auditors consider that there is a significant level of concern about the entity's ability to continue as a going concern, but do not disagree with the preparation of the financial statements on the going concern basis, they should include an explanatory paragraph when setting out the basis of their opinion. They should not qualify their opinion on these grounds alone, provided the disclosures in the financial statements of the matters giving rise to the concern are adequate for the

financial statements to give a true and fair view. (SAS 130.6)

43 This requirement is consistent with SAS 600, 'Auditors' report on financial statements'. The explanatory paragraph describes clearly the nature of the matters giving rise to the auditors' concern and refers to the relevant disclosures in the financial statements. The auditors use their judgment to decide the extent to which it is necessary for the description in their report to repeat information taken from the notes to the financial statements. The extent of the auditors' concern is one factor affecting the nature and extent of the description in the auditors' report. The prime consideration is clarity of communication. The description is normally identified within the auditors' report through the use of the subheading 'Going concern'.

44 The auditors might have concluded that there is a significant level of concern about the entity's ability to continue as a going concern. In these cases the auditors do not normally regard the disclosures as adequate unless (in addition to any disclosures otherwise required, for example by accounting standards) the following matters are included in the financial statements:

- a statement that the financial statements have been prepared on the going concern basis;
- a statement of the pertinent facts;
- the nature of the concern;
- a statement of the assumptions adopted by the directors, which should be clearly distinguishable from the pertinent facts;
- (where appropriate and practicable) a statement regarding the directors' plans for resolving the matters giving rise to the concern; and
- details of any relevant actions by the directors.

Neither the guidance above, nor the illustrative examples in Appendix 2, regarding disclosures in the financial statements constitute accounting standards.

45 If the period to which the directors have paid particular attention in assessing going concern is less than one year from the date of approval of the financial statements, and the directors have not disclosed that fact, the auditors should do so within the section of their report setting out the basis of their opinion, unless the fact is clear from any other references in their report. They should not qualify their opinion on the financial statements on these grounds alone. (SAS 130.7)

46 Where, in forming their opinion, the auditors have based their assessment of going concern on a period to which the directors have paid particular attention which is less than one year from the date of approval of the financial statements, it is appropriate for the auditors to disclose that fact within the basis of their opinion, unless it is disclosed in the financial statements or accompanying information (for example, the Operating and Financial Review). In deciding whether to disclose the fact, the auditors assess whether the evidence supplied to them by the directors is sufficient to demonstrate that the directors have, in assessing going concern, paid particular attention to a period of one year from the date of approval of the financial statements.

47 A determination of the sufficiency of the evidence supplied to the auditors by the directors will depend on the particular circumstances. However, to be sufficient the evidence may not require formal cash flow forecasts and budgets to have been prepared for the period ending one year from the date of approval of the financial statements. Although such forecasts and budgets are likely to provide the most persuasive evidence alternative sources of evidence may also be acceptable. Often, the auditors through discussion with the directors of their plans and expectations for that period may be able to satisfy themselves that the directors have in fact paid particular attention to a period of one year from the date of approval of the financial statements. Appendix 3 illustrates circumstances where formal budgets and forecasts have, with justification, not been provided for the entire twelve month period yet the auditors are able to conclude that the directors have paid particular attention to the period ending one year from the date of approval of the financial statements.

48 The auditors qualify their opinion if they consider that the directors have not taken adequate steps to satisfy themselves that it is appropriate for them to adopt the going concern basis. This might arise, for example, when the auditors do not consider that the future period to which the directors have paid particular attention in assessing going concern is reasonable in the entity's circumstances. This is a limitation on the scope of the auditor's work, as they are unable to obtain all the information and explanations which they consider necessary for the purpose of their audit.

49 Where the auditors disagree with the preparation of the financial statements on the going concern basis, they should issue an adverse audit opinion. (SAS 130.8)

50 Where the going concern presumption is inappropriate:

- even disclosure in the financial statements of the matters giving rise to this conclusion is not sufficient for them to give a true and fair view; and
- the effect on financial statements prepared on that basis is so material or pervasive that the financial statements are seriously misleading. Accordingly, an adverse opinion is appropriate in such cases.

Application to groups

51 The principles and procedures set out in this SAS apply also to the audit of consolidated financial statements.

52 It may be appropriate, on the grounds of materiality, for the group financial statements to be prepared on the going concern basis even though it is inappropriate for the individual financial statements of one or more members of the group to be prepared on the going concern basis.

Preliminary announcements

53 The London Stock Exchange does not explicitly require a preliminary announcement to refer to the company's ability to continue as a going concern. However, the auditors would be unlikely to agree a preliminary announcement if they have concluded that there is a significant level of concern about that matter which is not appropriately disclosed in the announcement.

Financial statements not prepared on the going concern basis

54 In rare circumstances, in order to give a true and fair view, the directors may have prepared financial statements on a basis other than that of a going concern. If the auditors consider this other basis to be appropriate in the specific circumstances, and if the financial statements contain the necessary disclosures, the auditors should not qualify their audit opinion in this respect. (SAS 130.9)

55 Some enterprises are formed for a specific purpose, such as a joint venture to undertake a construction project, and are wound up or dissolved when the purpose is achieved. Under these circumstances the financial statements may be prepared on a basis that reflects the fact that assets may need to be realised other than in the ordinary course of operations. In these circumstances the auditors may wish, without qualifying their opinion, to refer in their report to the basis on which the financial statements are prepared; the auditors may do this in the introductory paragraph of their report.

Compliance with International Standards on Auditing

56 Compliance with the auditing standards contained in this SAS ensures compliance in all material respects with the basic principles and essential procedures in International Standard on Auditing 570 'Going Concern'.*

Effective date

57 Auditors are required to comply with the requirements of this SAS in respect of audits of financial statements for financial periods ending on or after 30 June 1995. Adoption of the requirements when reporting on financial statements for financial periods ending before that date is encouraged.

Withdrawal of material in other guidance

58 This SAS supersedes guidance given to auditors in the Auditing Guideline 'The auditors' consideration in respect of going concern'.

Appendix 1
Preparation of the Financial Statements: Note on legal and professional requirements

Company law and accounting standards

1 The Act specifies certain accounting principles which should normally be adopted in preparing the financial statements of a company. One of these principles is that:

> 'the company shall be presumed to be carrying on business as a going concern' (paragraph 10 of Schedule 4 to the Act).

However such a presumption is not conclusive and may be disregarded if the facts of the particular situation so require. The term 'going concern' is not defined in the Act but, as discussed below, is defined in SSAP 2.

2 Paragraph 15 of Schedule 4 to the Act states that departures from the Act's accounting principles *may* be made if it appears to the directors that there are 'special reasons' for doing so. The financial statements must disclose any such departure, the reasons for it and its effect. 'Special reasons' would include circumstances where the directors conclude, on the basis of the facts as they appear to them, that it is appropriate to depart from the going concern presumption.

3 Furthermore, in addition to that particular provision of the Act, Section 226 of the Act contains an overriding requirement for directors to prepare financial statements which give a true and fair view of the state of affairs of the company as at the end of the financial year and of its profit or loss for the financial year.

4 If compliance with the provisions of the Act would not be *sufficient* to give a true and fair view, the Act requires the directors to give the necessary additional information in the financial statements. If, in 'special circumstances', compliance with the provisions of the Act is *inconsistent* with the requirement to give a true and fair view, the Act requires the

*Revised March 1995.

directors to depart from the particular provision to the extent necessary to give a true and fair view. The financial statements must disclose the particulars of any such departure, the reasons for it and its effect.

5 Accordingly, directors cannot assume that preparing the financial statements on the going concern basis and in accordance with the other provisions of the Act will necessarily result in the financial statements giving a true and fair view. Whilst, in general, compliance with accounting standards is also necessary to meet the requirement to prepare financial statements giving a true and fair view, such compliance is not of itself sufficient to ensure that a true and fair view is given in all cases.

Accounting standards and the definition of 'going concern'

6 SSAP 2 identifies going concern as one of the fundamental accounting concepts and defines going concern thus:

> 'the enterprise will continue in operational existence for the foreseeable future. This means in particular that the profit and loss account and balance sheet assume no intention or necessity to liquidate or curtail significantly the scale of operation'.

7 SSAP 2 also provides that if financial statements are prepared on the basis of assumptions which differ materially from those concepts the facts should be explained in the financial statements. This is similar to the statutory requirement to disclose departures from accounting principles. However, there are currently no more detailed accounting standards or guidance dealing specifically with going concern as an accounting principle.

Appendix 2

Illustrative examples of audit procedures and auditors' reports

The appendix is illustrative only and does not form part of the Auditing Standards. The purpose of the appendix is to illustrate the application of the Auditing Standards to assist in clarifying their meaning in a number of commercial situations. The examples focus on particular aspects of the situations illustrated and are not intended to be a comprehensive discussion of all the relevant factors that might influence either the directors' or auditors' assessments of the appropriateness of the going concern basis. As auditors would need to exercise judgment in the circumstances described it is possible that different auditors may arrive at different conclusions. This does not, however, detract from the examples which demonstrate thought process and the implications for an audit report once certain conclusions have been reached by the auditors. These examples neither modify nor override the Auditing Standards.

Example 1 — A company with uncomplicated circumstances and a significant bank overdraft

Situation 1

- Auditors consider that the possibility of the overdraft facility not being renewed is remote.
- Unqualified auditors' report without an added explanatory paragraph.

Situation 2

- The possibility of the overdraft facility not being renewed is not remote, but auditors do not consider there is a significant level of concern about the ability of the company to continue as a going concern.
- Relevant disclosures in the financial statements.
- Unqualified auditors' report without an added explanatory paragraph.

Situation 3

- As above except that the nature of the business is such that there can be considerable variation in the timing of cash inflows, and the auditors consider there is a significant level of concern about the ability of the company to continue as a going concern.
- Relevant disclosures in the financial statements.
- Unqualified auditors' report with an added explanatory paragraph.

Example 2 — A large processing company

Situation 1

- Directors have plans mitigating exposure to price fluctuations.
- Unqualified auditors' report without an added explanatory paragraph.

Situation 2

- Large contract tender may not be accepted.
- Unqualified auditors' report with an added explanatory paragraph.

Example 3 — Auditors disagree that disclosures are adequate

Example 1 — A Company with uncomplicated circumstances and a considerable bank overdraft

Situation 1

1 In this case, in their capacity as accountants and financial advisors, the auditors also act as agents for the directors in that they:

- prepare the financial statements to be audited;
- extract the extended trial balance upon which the financial statements are based;
- prepare other financial information, such as the outline plans referred to below; and
- assist the directors in financial matters generally, based on information supplied to them by the directors. The directors take responsibility for the financial information and decisions, and the auditors ensure that they remain, and are seen to remain, independent. In these circumstances the auditors consider that the financial information can act as audit evidence.

2 When planning the audit, the auditors become aware of the following matters.

- The company does not prepare periodic cash flow and other budgets, forecasts or other management accounts information apart from the accounting records required by law. In view of the size, lack of complexity and stability of the business, the auditors might concur with the directors' view that such information is not required for the purposes of the directors' assessment of going concern in the context of the preparation of the financial statements.
- From their knowledge of the company's circumstances based on previous experience (including previous audits) and their discussions with the directors about the financial year (including discussions prompted by a review of the year end extended trial balance), the company still appears to operate under relatively stable conditions, for example regarding customers, suppliers and competitors. The trial balance shows a net asset position and that the company continues to be profitable.
- Based on discussions, the directors' outline plans for the future do not appear to be inconsistent with the other information available to the auditors at this stage

of the audit. The outline plans consist of considering the company's performance during the financial year, and adjusting for key circumstances, both those under the directors' control (such as 'one-off' capital expenditure) and those which the directors estimate will be different (such as planned sales, and price rises for materials).

- As in prior years the company has a significant bank overdraft. The bankers have in the past always renewed an adequate overdraft facility and the company has to date been able to operate well within it. The date on which the bankers are due to consider renewal of overdraft facilities is after the likely date of approval of the financial statements.

It is emphasised that views reached by the auditors at this stage are preliminary only, and may be confirmed or otherwise by subsequent audit work.

3 The auditors' initial assessment might be that there is not a significant level of concern about the ability of the company to continue as a going concern. They plan:

- to perform their other audit work with an awareness that there may be nevertheless situations which cause them to consider that there is a significant level of concern about the ability of the company to continue as a going concern; and
- to obtain evidence as to whether the company has, to the date of their report, operated well within its overdraft facility.

The auditors consider that this will be sufficient in these circumstances to satisfy the SAS's requirements on audit evidence.

4 Having completed their audit, the auditors consider that:

- the results of their procedures confirm their preliminary assessments, in particular the preliminary decision not to seek a letter from the bankers regarding maintenance and renewal of the overdraft facility;
- the information in the financial statements, and that received during their preparation and audit, does not suggest that there is a significant level of concern about the ability of the company to continue as a going concern;
- having reconsidered the directors' outline plans for the future, the plans do not appear to be inconsistent with the other information of which the auditors are aware; and
- there is no reason to disagree with the directors' view, based on their discussions with the bankers, that it is likely that the bankers will renew an overdraft facility which meets the anticipated needs of the company by a reasonable margin.

5 The directors consider that no special disclosures are required in the financial statements. The auditors agree, and accordingly, the auditors do not consider it necessary to qualify their audit opinion or to add an explanatory paragraph to their audit report.

Situation 2

1 The circumstances and audit work are as in Situation 1 except as follows.

2 The auditors' past experience and preliminary planning procedures reveal that the company has, on several occasions in the past few years, exceeded its agreed bank facility. In the past the bankers have not withdrawn the facility, but the auditors are aware that the company's relationship with the bankers is worsening. In these circumstances the bankers have for some time requested and received each quarter management accounts covering the year to date. (As a result, recent financial information is available. Had the bankers not adopted this practice the auditors would have decided whether it was appropriate to base their work on other available sources of information about financial performance and position after the balance sheet date. For instance, the auditors might have decided to base their work on a recently updated trial balance.)

3 Towards the end of the audit, the auditors examine the most recent management accounts. In particular, they consider whether the management accounts and any assumptions underlying their preparation are inconsistent with other information of which they are aware. The directors have started to implement a cost reduction exercise, and this appears to be reasonable and proceeding according to plan. The management accounts show that the company is so far managing to remain within its current overdraft facility, and the directors' outline plans (which take account of the cost reduction exercise) indicate that the company should be able to continue to do so.

4 The auditors scrutinise the company's correspondence and notes of conversations between the directors and the bankers, who examine the draft financial statements and the most recent management accounts. The auditors also examine a letter which they have requested the directors to obtain from the bankers regarding maintenance and renewal of overdraft facilities. The letter (addressed to the directors with a copy sent by the bankers directly to the auditors) contains a number of normal banking caveats. From the comments made in the letter it is evident that:

- the bankers have not made a decision about the continuance of the facilities:
- the bankers will continue to monitor the facilities in the light of information which becomes available to them; and
- (subject to the foregoing) the bankers will consider renewal of the facility on the agreed review date, which falls after the date on which the directors plan to approve the financial statements.

5 On this basis the auditors decide that:

- in the absence of indications that the facility may be exceeded in the 12 month period to the anniversary of the date of approval of the financial statements which they are auditing; and
- together with the results of other audit work;

they consider that there is concern about the ability of the company to continue as a going concern, but not of such significance as to require to be highlighted in the audit report.

6 In this particular case, the possibility that adequate overdraft facilities will not be renewed is not remote. The financial statements thus contain disclosures such as those shown below.

Extract from notes to the financial statements

Note 12 Creditors: amounts falling due within one year	*19x1*	*19x0*
	£	£
Current instalments due on debenture loans	xx	xx
Bank overdrafts	xx	xx
Obligations under finance leases	xx	xx

The company meets its day to day working capital requirements through an overdraft facility which is repayable on demand. The company expects to operate within the facility currently agreed and within that expected to be agreed on (date), when the company's bankers are due to consider its renewal for a further year. These views are based on the company's plans and on the successful outcome of discussions with the company's bankers.

7 If the note to the financial statements illustrated above omitted the narrative paragraph, the auditors might decide that the disclosures in the financial statements were insufficient to give a true and fair view of the state of the company's affairs. If so, they would qualify their audit opinion, for example as follows.

Extract from the auditors' report

Qualified opinion arising from disagreement as to the adequacy of a disclosure in the financial statements

In our opinion, the financial statements should disclose the following matters. The company meets its day to day working capital requirements through an overdraft facility which, in common with all such facilities, is repayable on demand. We understand from the directors that they expect that the company will continue to operate within the facility currently agreed and within that which they expect will be agreed on (date), when the company's bankers are due to consider renewing the facility for a further year. The directors inform us that their views are based on their plans and on discussions with the company's bankers but that, inherently, there can be no certainty in relation to those views.

Except for the absence of the disclosure referred to in the paragraph above, in our opinion the financial statements give a true and fair view of the company's state of affairs as at 31 December 19.. and have been properly prepared in accordance with the Companies Act 1985. In our opinion the financial statements give a true and fair view of the company's profit for the year ended 31 December 19.. .

Registered auditors
Address
Date

Situation 3

1 The circumstances and audit work are as in Situation 2, except that the nature of the business is such that there can be considerable unpredictable variation in the timing of cash inflows. Because of this the company's bankers have frequently requested and received a rolling cash flow forecast (supported by a sensitivity analysis) covering the year ahead.

2 Since the last balance sheet date, the company has operated within its overdraft facility, and towards the end of the audit, the auditors examine the latest available cash flow forecast. This covers the year ending 9 months from the date on which the directors plan to approve the financial statements. The cash flow sensitivity analysis prepared by the directors takes into account the cost reduction exercise and reveals the following.

- The 'best case' shows the company can remain within the current overdraft facility.
- The 'worst case' shows that the company would exceed its current overdraft facility throughout the period covered.
- The 'most likely' case shows the company would remain within the current overdraft facility, but would be close to it on several occasions during the period covered.

3 The auditors scrutinise correspondence and notes of conversations between the directors and the bankers, who examine the draft financial statements, the cash flow information and forecast and the sensitivity analysis. The auditors also examine a letter from the bankers regarding renewal of overdraft facilities. The letter is similar to that mentioned in Situation 2, and is addressed to the directors with a copy sent by the bankers directly to the auditors. The renewal is scheduled to be considered by the bankers at a date which falls after the date on which the directors plan to approve the financial statements. The auditors consider that the frequent requests by the bankers for cash flow forecasts indicates considerable concern on the part of the bankers. Taking into account all the information available to them, the auditors might decide to request the directors to arrange a tripartite meeting between the auditors, the directors and the bankers. Following any such meeting the auditors would make appropriate notes in their working papers.

4 The auditors update their audit work on the cash flow forecast and sensitivity analysis to cover the period falling after that covered by these documents. They do this principally through discussion with the directors of the outline plans for this period.

5 The financial statements contain disclosures such as those shown below.

Extract from notes to the financial statements

Note 1 Basis of preparing the financial statements

The company meets its day to day working capital requirements through an overdraft facility which is repayable on demand.

The nature of the company's business is such that there can be considerable unpredictable variation in the timing of cash inflows. The directors have prepared projected cash flow information for the period ending 9 months from the date of their approval of these financial statements. On the basis of this cash flow information and discussions with the company's bankers, the directors consider that the company will continue to operate within the facility currently agreed and within that which they expect will be agreed on (date), when the company's bankers are due to consider renewing the facility for a further year. However, the margin of facilities over requirements is not large and, inherently there can be no certainty in relation to these matters. On this basis, the directors consider it appropriate to prepare the financial statements on the going concern basis. The financial statements do not include any adjustments that would result from a withdrawal of the overdraft facility by the company's bankers.

6 In these circumstances the auditors consider that they are able to form an audit opinion, but that they have a significant level of concern about the ability of the company to continue as a going concern. Hence, whilst they do not qualify their audit opinion, they include a suitable explanatory paragraph when setting out the basis of their opinion, as set out below.

7 The guidance in paragraph 61 of SAS 600 'Auditors' report on financial statements' states that the explanatory paragraph describes:

> '... the matter giving rise to the fundamental uncertainty and its possible effects on the financial statements, including (where practicable) quantification.'

Extreme circumstances are necessary to support adjustment of financial statements onto a basis of accounting other than the going concern basis. In this example, the auditors do not disagree with the preparation of the financial statements on the going concern basis. The Board considers that it may be misleading for the auditors' report to refer to the possible effects on the financial statements of the matter giving rise to the fundamental uncertainty. The example below, therefore, omits such references.

Extract from the 'Basis of opinion' section of the auditors' report

Going concern

In forming our opinion, we have considered the adequacy of the disclosures made in note 1 of the financial statements concerning the uncertainty as to the continuation and renewal of the company's bank overdraft facility. In view of the significance of this uncertainty we consider that it should be drawn to your attention but our opinion is not qualified in this respect.

Example 2 — A Large processing company

Situation 1

1 The company is a large producer of basic foodstuffs. Key features of its business are:

- turnover comprises a high volume of sales with relatively low individual unit prices;
- there is a strong relationship (in terms of quantities) between inputs to and outputs from the processes;
- there are relatively few suppliers (mainly foreign) for the key raw materials; and
- the use of an integrated standard costing system with sophisticated stock controls.

2 These features require and permit the company to operate a sophisticated management information system (with rolling budgets and forecasts prepared 12 months ahead) in order to monitor and control stock levels and raw material prices in particular.

3 In these circumstances a wealth of detailed records and forecasts is available to the auditors, and so, regarding going concern, they are careful to focus on the records and forecasts relevant to identifying material matters which may cause them to have a significant level of concern about the company's ability to continue as a going concern.

4 From their knowledge of the company's circumstances based on previous experience, the auditors are aware that the company's cash flow and results are very sensitive to raw materials prices, including the effects of foreign exchange differences. This initial assessment is confirmed when the auditors finish planning their audit, when they also become aware that the company's gearing ratio is increasing. The auditors' response is to plan to examine the rolling cash flow forecasts for the period ending one year from the date of approval of the financial statements in conjunction with evidence of appropriate forward contracts and options which will be in place during that period. However, these forward contracts and options are unlikely to cover the whole of that period and so in addition the auditors plan to assess how effective the directors have been during the year under audit in mitigating these exposures to fluctuating prices and exchange rate changes. This, together with the auditors' experience from previous audits of the directors' effectiveness in mitigating exposure, will enable the auditors to establish the directors' 'track record' in this area. The auditors consider that the combined evidence they obtain from these and their other audit procedures will be sufficient in these circumstances to satisfy the SAS's requirements on audit evidence.

5 The auditors' initial assessment, at the planning stage of the audit, is that there is not a significant level of concern about the ability of the company to continue as a going concern. Subsequent work confirms this. Accordingly, the auditors consider it appropriate neither to qualify their audit opinion, nor to add an explanatory paragraph to their report.

6 The financial statements contain disclosures such as those shown below.

Extract from notes to the financial statements

Note 20 Financial commitments

In the ordinary course of business the company enters into forward contracts and options. The aim is to hedge the company's exposure to the potentially adverse effects of fluctuating prices for raw materials and foreign exchange rate changes.

Situation 2

1 The circumstances, disclosures in the financial statements and the audit work are as in Situation 1, except as follows. The auditors have completed their audit work and consider that the financial statements, which contain the following disclosures, give a true and fair view.

Extract from notes to the financial statements

Note 2 Going concern

The company has placed a tender with a current major customer for a two year contract. The customer's decision is awaited, but if awarded to the company, the contract would comprise a significant proportion of the company's forecasted turnover over the contract period. Until reaching a decision regarding the tender, the customer is making a monthly decision whether or not to extend the most recently agreed contract for a further month.

The directors have a number of alternative plans for utilising the company's resources and generating income should it not be awarded the contract. However the company has yet to submit tenders for several of these alternative contracts.

The directors consider that in preparing the financial statements they have taken into account all information that could reasonably be expected to be available. On this basis, they consider that it is appropriate to prepare the financial statements on the going concern basis. This assumes that either the contract is awarded to the company or that the directors' alternative plans are successful. The financial statements do not include any adjustments that would result if the contract were not awarded to the company and the directors' alternative plans were not successful.

2 The auditors consider that they have obtained all the evidence which may reasonably be expected to be available, but that there is a significant level of concern about the ability of the company to continue as a going concern. This is reflected in the wording they decide to use in the explanatory paragraph they include when setting out the basis of their opinion describing the matters giving rise to their concern in their unqualified auditors' report on the financial statements.

Extract from the 'Basis of opinion' section of the auditors' report

Going concern

In forming our opinion, we have considered the adequacy of the disclosures made in note 2 of the financial statements concerning the uncertainty over the possible outcome of a tender for a two-year contract placed by the company with a current major customer. In view of the significance of this uncertainty we consider that it should be drawn to your attention, but our opinion is not qualified in this respect.

Example 3 — auditors disagree that disclosures are adequate

1 The auditors consider that there is a significant level of concern about the ability of the company to continue as a going concern. The financial statements do not disclose the fact that borrowing covenants have been breached and the related borrowings have not been reclassified as amounts falling due within one year. The auditors are not aware of any agreement from the lenders to waive the breach. The auditors thus do not consider that the disclosures in the financial statements of the matters giving rise to this concern are adequate to give a true and fair view of the state of affairs of the company and of the group as at the balance sheet date. The true and fair view given by the profit and loss account is not affected because the only material result of the breach is that the related borrowings become repayable on demand. Set out below is an extract from the financial statements.

Extract from notes to the financial statements

Note 1 Basis of preparing the financial statements

The directors are currently negotiating with lenders to the group for new terms for amounts borrowed totalling £A. In addition, the directors' plans for raising funds of approximately £B from a share issue by the company are at an advanced stage. Both matters have already been announced publicly.

The financial statements have been prepared on the going concern basis which assumes that the company and its subsidiaries will continue in operational existence for the foreseeable future.

The validity of this assumption depends on the successful conclusion of the negotiations with the group's lenders and the raising of additional funds by a share issue. Certain of these arrangements will require the approval of shareholders in a general meeting. The financial statements do not include any adjustments that would result if negotiations were not concluded successfully.

Whilst the directors are presently uncertain as to the outcome of both the matters mentioned above, they believe that it is appropriate for the financial statements to be prepared on the going concern basis.

2 The following is an extract from the auditors' report.

Extract from the 'Basis of opinion' section of the auditor's report

Going concern

In forming our opinion, we have considered the adequacy of the disclosures made in note 1 of the financial statements concerning the directors' efforts to renegotiate loans and raise further capital. In view of the significance of the fact that the preparation of the financial statements on the going concern basis assumes the successful conclusion of both these matters, we consider that these disclosures should be brought to your attention. Our opinion is not qualified in this respect, but certain aspects of the disclosures give rise to a qualification as described below.

Qualified opinion arising from disagreement about an accounting treatment and the adequacy of a disclosure in the financial statements

In our opinion the financial statements should disclose the fact that the company and certain of its subsidiaries have not complied with covenants relating to certain of their borrowings included in the financial statements. Under the terms of these covenants, the publication of these financial statements gives rise to defaults relating to certain of the group's borrowings as a consequence of which the related borrowings become repayable on demand. These related borrowings should have been reclassified as amounts falling due within one year, which would have reduced the figures recorded in the financial statements for 'net current assets' and 'creditors: amounts falling due after more than one year' by £C.

Except for the absence of the disclosures, and the failure to reclassify the relevant borrowings, referred to in the paragraph above, in our opinion the financial statements give a true and fair view of the state of affairs of the company and the group as at 31 December 19.. and have been properly prepared in accordance with the Companies Act 1985. In our opinion the financial statements give a true and fair view of the profit of the group for the year ended 31 December 19.. .

Appendix 3
Illustrative examples of the auditors' assessment of whether evidence provided to them by the directors, concerning the attention they have paid to the period one year from the date of approval of the financial statements, is sufficient

The appendix is illustrative only and does not form part of the Auditing Standards. The purpose of the appendix is to illustrate the application of the Auditing Standards to assist in clarifying their meaning in a number of commercial situations. The examples focus on particular aspects of the situations illustrated and are not intended to be a comprehensive discussion of all the relevant factors that might influence either the directors' or auditors' assessment of the appropriateness of the going concern basis. As auditors would need to exercise judgment in the circumstances described it is possible that different auditors may arrive at different conclusions. This does not, however, detract from the examples which demonstrate thought process and the implications for an audit report once certain conclusions have been reached by the auditors. These examples neither modify nor override the Auditing Standards.

Example 1 — A small company producing specialised computer application software

Extract from auditors' risk assessment

This owner managed company employs a few highly trained and highly paid computer system designers to design application software for use by transportation enterprises, such as airlines and bus companies, in preparing their timetables and fare structures. Few companies are engaged in this field and the supply of suitably trained staff is limited. The system designers, who met at University, have been with the company since its formation. They all have an equity interest in the company.

Although the company has only been in existence for five years it has established a reputation for excellence in its field. Its reputation derives from the skill and expertise of its individual employees rather than from anything attaching to the company itself.

A significant amount of time is spent by the designers in pure research activities developing new products. In addition the time needed to develop individual systems relating to an established product can be considerable. In addition to design of new systems the company maintains those systems it has installed on a contractual basis and undertakes training courses in the use of the systems for the employees of its customers.

The company is thinly capitalised and relies primarily on advances from its customers supplemented by short term bank borrowings for its day to day cash requirements.

The company employs a part time bookkeeper to prepare the financial statements, cash flow forecasts and maintain the books of account.

The company has usually been in a position to choose which contracts it accepts and has not had difficulty in recovering its costs. The company is not economically dependent on any one transportation enterprise.

The company updates each month a rolling cash flow projection with a six month time horizon. The company does not prepare projections for a longer period as it perceives its management need is to be able to manage effectively its short term cash flow. The company has negotiated a line of credit with its bankers which it would be able to utilise to overcome short term cash shortages.

Assessment by auditors of whether there is sufficient evidence that the directors have paid particular attention to a period of twelve months

When the auditors assess whether the directors have, in assessing going concern, paid particular attention to a period of one year from the expected date of approval of the financial statements they:

(a) review the cash flow forecasts for the six month period from the expected date of approval of the financial statements; and

(b) then enquire of the directors the steps they have taken to assess the appropriateness of the going concern basis for the subsequent six month period.

The directors inform the auditors that they do not consider there is any need for cash flow forecasts to be prepared beyond six months because:

- the cash flow forecasts show a net cash inflow for the period;
- they have reviewed in detail the assumptions implicit in the forecast with the bookkeeper and concur with them;
- the company has a significant backlog of orders which will occupy half of the designers for at least the next year;
- the company is actively tendering for both systems design and maintenance contracts in the United Kingdom and Europe and is considering expanding into the Americas;
- the company has recently renewed its arrangements with its bankers for a further year;
- the design employees seem to be settled and stimulated and there is no reason to believe that they will leave the company in the foreseeable future; and
- in the unlikely event that the company did not win many of the tenders it could modify its existing expansion plans which have been necessitated by an increase in maintenance contracts. Rather than employ new staff to undertake this work existing staff could be reassigned to it.

The auditors conclude that the directors have paid particular attention to the period ending one year after their approval of the financial statements.

Example 2 — an enterprise in the fashion industry

Extract from auditors' risk assessment

This company employing 1,000 people designs and manufactures ladies fashion-wear. Its business is seasonal and it presents two major collections per year one in the spring and one in the autumn.

The company has attracted established designers and they are regarded as one of the leading manufacturers.

Almost all of the company's sales orders are received from the major retailers when they show their collections. Although some of the garments are manufactured prior to the showing of the collection the majority of them will be manufactured in the four months immediately following the showing.

The company's finance director is a qualified accountant with a staff of 6. Because of the seasonal nature of the business the company prepares its detailed budgets and cash flow forecasts until the end of the next season. The company's year end is 30 June and the directors expect to approve the financial statements during October. Detailed cash flow forecasts are only available to the end of February in the following year a period of only four months from the approval of the financial statements.

The company which has been marginally profitable over the last few years has a small line of credit with its bank but is financed primarily through the factoring of its debtors.

Assessment by auditors of whether there is sufficient evidence that the directors have paid particular attention to a period of twelve months

When the auditors assess whether the directors have, in assessing going concern, paid particular attention to a period of one year from the expected date of approval of the financial statements they would;

(a) review the cash flow forecasts for the four month period from the expected date of approval of the financial statements; and

(b) then enquire of the directors the steps they have taken to assess the appropriateness of the going concern basis for the subsequent eight month period.

The directors inform the auditors that they do not consider there is any need for additional cash flow forecasts to be prepared beyond the end of February in the following year because:

- the cash flow forecasts show a net cash inflow for the period and the present cash position is strong because of a recent sale of debtors from the present collection;
- the directors have reviewed in detail the assumptions implicit in the forecast and concur with them;
- the designers are working on the next collection and they believe, based on discussions with some of the retailers, that they have some good general ideas which will appeal to their customers if translated into imaginative detailed designs;
- discussions with the major retailers indicate that they expect demand to be high next season;
- the company's relationship with its factor is good and they do not expect any difficulties in selling their debtors in the future;
- the company anticipates no major capital expenditures in the next twelve months. Most of the machinery is less than five years old and in any event is financed by lease arrangements rather than by purchase; and
- the company has recently renewed its arrangements with its bankers for a further year.

The auditors conclude that the directors have paid particular attention to the period ending one year after their approval of the financial statements.

Auditors' options when they conclude that the directors have not paid particular attention to the period ending one year after the approval of the financial statements

The two examples above illustrate that the auditors may conclude that the directors have paid particular attention, to the period ending one year after the approval of the financial statements, even though they have not prepared cash flow forecasts for that period.

The auditors may conclude in slightly different situations that the directors have not paid particular attention to the period ending one year after the approval of the financial statements. If this is the case the auditors need to consider the impact on their audit report which may be either:

(a) they may conclude that there is a significant level of concern about the entity's ability to continue as a going concern (but they do not disagree with the use of the going concern basis). In which case the directors include a note to the financial statements and the auditors include an explanatory paragraph when setting out the basis of their opinion (in accordance with paragraph 42 of the SAS); or, less probably;

(b) they may conclude that the directors have not paid particular attention to the period ending one year from the date of approval of the financial statements but there is no significant level of concern. Then if the directors:

    (i) refer to the period paid particular attention to, in the annual report, the auditors need not refer to the period in their basis of opinion (in accordance with paragraph 46 of the SAS); however

    (ii) if the directors do not refer to the period paid particular attention to, the auditors would do so in the section of their report setting out their basis of opinion (in accordance with paragraph 45 of the SAS); or

(c) they may conclude that the directors have not taken adequate steps to satisfy themselves that it is appropriate to adopt the going concern basis. Accordingly, there is a limitation of scope which gives rise to a qualified audit report (in accordance with paragraph 48 of the SAS).

Appendix 4

Going concern and reporting on the financial statements

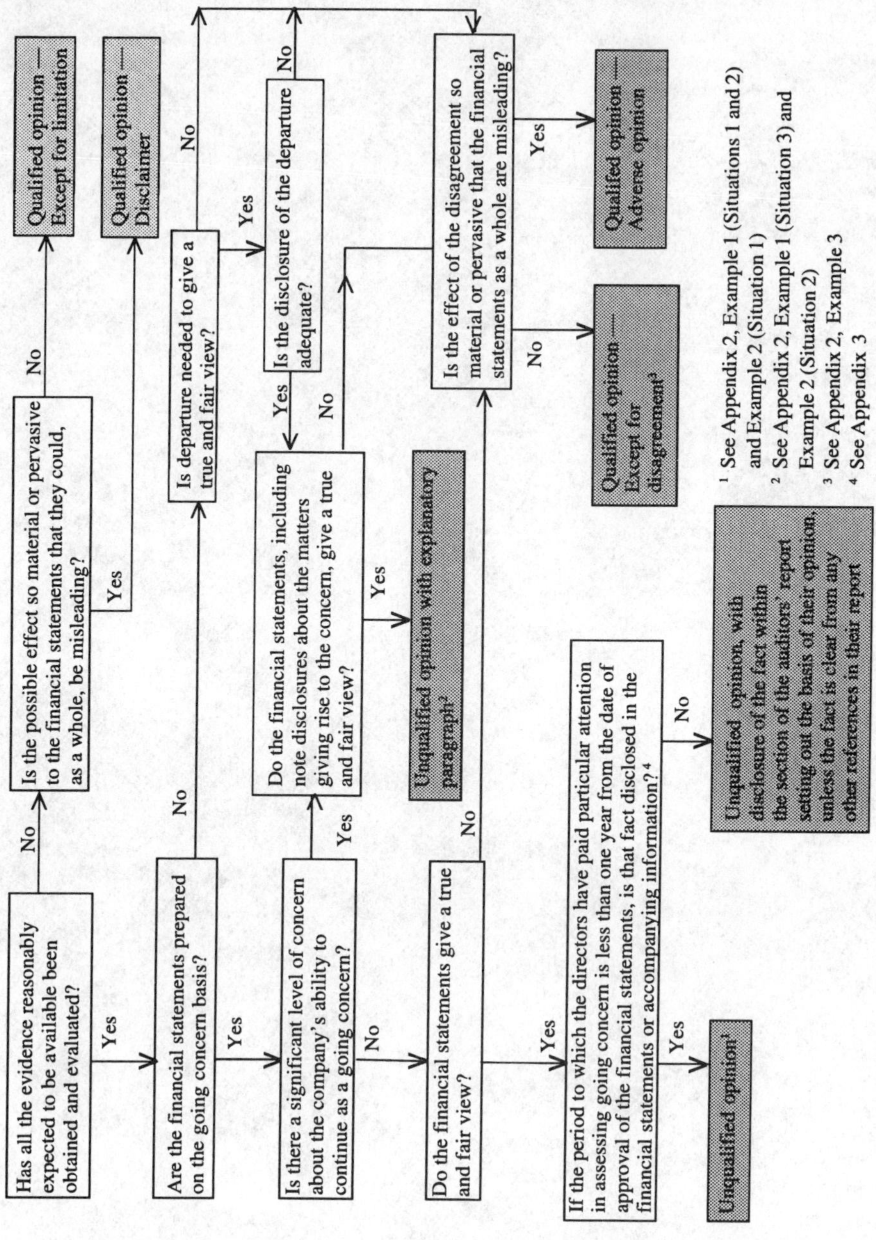

[1] See Appendix 2, Example 1 (Situations 1 and 2) and Example 2 (Situation 1)
[2] See Appendix 2, Example 1 (Situation 3) and Example 2 (Situation 2)
[3] See Appendix 2, Example 3
[4] See Appendix 3

Statement of Auditing Standards

140 — Engagement Letters

(Issued March 1995)

Reproduced with the permission of the Auditing Practices Board

Statements of Auditing Standards ('SASs') are to be read in the light of 'The scope and authority of APB pronouncements'. In particular, they contain basic principles and essential procedures ('Auditing Standards'), indicated by paragraphs in bold type, with which auditors are required to comply in the conduct of any audit. SASs also include explanatory and other material which is designed to assist auditors in interpreting and applying Auditing Standards. The definitions in the Glossary of terms are to be applied in the interpretation of SASs.

Introduction

1 The purpose of this SAS is to establish standards and provide guidance to auditors on:

(a) agreeing with clients the terms of engagements by means of audit engagement letters; and

(b) the contents of audit engagement letters.

2 The auditors and the client should agree on the terms of the engagement, which should be recorded in writing. (SAS 140.1)

3 For the purpose of this SAS 'client' means the addressees of the auditors' report, or, when as will often be the case it is not practical to agree such terms with this body, the entity itself through the board of directors or the audit committee.

4 The terms of the engagement are normally recorded in an engagement letter and their acceptance by the client evidenced by signature by a person at an appropriate level within the entity, for example the finance director or equivalent, although other forms of contract may be used. In the public sector due account is to be taken of the relevant legislative requirements on the appointment of auditors and the arrangements under which an engagement is defined.

5 This SAS is intended to assist auditors in the preparabtion of engagement letters relating to audits of financial statements. While the principles of the guidance may also be helpful in relation to other audit-related services, such as reporting on interim statements or Cad- bury Code compliance statements, it is not intended to cover matters that may be relevant to such engagements. When these and other services such as tax, accounting, or management advisory services are to be provided, auditors often prepare separate engagement letters so as to distinguish clearly the statutory audit from other services. In particular, the provision of investment business advice as defined by the Financial Services Act 1986 usually requires the preparation of a separate engagement letter. The distinction between the statutory audit and other services is particularly important because auditors are not able to limit their liability in respect of the statutory audit.

Procedures

6 Auditors should agree the terms of their engagement wlth new clients in writing.

Thereafter auditors should regularly review the terms of engagement and if appropriate agree any updating in writing. (SAS 140.2)

7 The agreement of an engagement letter is in the interests of both auditors and client. It is therefore desirable that the contents be agreed prior to the audit appointment (and the letter sent soon after) and, in any event, before the commencement of the first audit assignment. Subsequently, the regular review of the engagement letter helps the auditors and the client avoid misunderstandings with respect to the engagement.

Recurring audits

8 As part of the annual planning process, auditors consider whether a new engagement letter is required. The following factors may make the agreement of a new letter appropriate:

- any indication that the client misunderstands the objective and scope of the audit;
- a recent change of management, board of directors or audit comminee;
- a significant change in ownership, such as a new holding company;
- a significant change in the nature or size of the client's business; and
- any relevant change in legal or professional requirements.

It may be appropriate to remind the client of the original letter when the auditors decide a new engagement letter is unnecessary for any period.

Audit of components

9 When the auditors of a parent entity are also auditors of its subsidiary undertaking, branch or division (component), a separate engagement letter may, in many cases, be unnecessary. The factors which influence the decision whether or not to agree a separate engagement letter with the component include:

- who appoints the auditors of the component;
- whether a separate report is to be issued on the component;
- whether the terms for each component are the same;
- legal and regulatory requirements;
- the extent of any work performed by other auditors; and
- the degree of ownership by the parent.

If the auditors send one letter relating to the group as a whole, it identifies the components for which they are appointed as auditors. The directors of the parent entity are requested to forward the letter to the boards of directors of the components concerned. Each board is requested to confirm that the terms of the engagement letter are accepted.

Changes in nature of engagement

10 Auditors who, before the completion ot the audit, are requested to change the engagement to one which provides a different level of assurance, should consider the appropriateness of so doing. If auditors consider that it is appropriate to change the terms of engagement, they should obtain written agreement to the revised terms. (SAS 140.3)

11 A request by the client for the auditors to change the terms of engagement prior to completion may result from:

- a change in circumstances affecting the need for the service;

- a misunderstanding as to the nature of an audit or of the related service originally requested; or
- a restriction on the scope of the engagement, whether imposed by management or caused by circumstances.

Any such request, and the reason given for it, require careful consideration by the auditors, particularly of the implications of a restriction on the scope of the engagement.

12 If auditors consider that it is not appropriate to change the terms of engagement, they consider their position and may need to take legal advice, or, if appropriate, consult a regulatory body. If auditors are unable to agree to a change of engagement and are not permitted to continue the original engagement, they withdraw and consider whether there is any obligation, contractual or otherwise, to report to other parties, such as the board of directors or shareholders, the circumstances necessitating the withdrawal.

13 Auditors of limited companies in Great Britain who cease to hold office as auditors are required to comply with the requirements of Section 394 of the Companies Act 1985 regarding the statement to be made by them in relation to their ceasing to hold office. Equivalent requirements for Northern Ireland are contained in Article 401A of the Companies (Northern Ireland) Order 1986 and, for the Republic of Ireland, are contained in Section 185 of the Companies Act 1990.

Principal contents

14 Auditors should ensure that the engagement letter documents and confirms their acceptance of the appointment, and includes a summary of the responsibilities of the directors and of the auditors, the scope of the engagement and the form of any reports. (SAS 140.4)

15 Matters normally dealt with relating to the principal relevant responsibilities of the directors and of the auditors and to the scope of the audit are illustrated in the example of an audit engagement letter in the Appendix, which is drafted in a form to apply to limited company clients. In the case of other entities, the matters relating to the responsibilities of directors and auditors are modified in accordance with the requirements of relevant legislation or, in the case of non-statutory audits, the terms agreed with the client.

Form of reports

16 The engagement letter normally refers to the form of reports or other communication of results of the engagement to be issued by the auditors in addition to the statutory reports to the members, such as a report to the directors or management on any identified material weaknesses in, or observations on, the accounting and internal control system. The letter might also refer to matters such as the intended confidentiality of such reports and, where appropriate, to the conditions, if any, on which permission may be given to the directors to make those reports available to others.

Other matters

17 Other matters which may be dealt with in the engagement letter include:

- fees and billing arrangements;
- procedures where the client has a complaint about the service;
- where appropriate, arrangements concerning the involvement of:
  - — other auditors and experts in some aspect of the audit;
  - — internal auditors and other staff of the entity:

- arrangements, if any, to be made with the predecessor auditors, in the case of an initial audit;
- any restriction of the auditors' liabilities to the client (when such possibility exists);
- where appropriate, the country by whose laws the engagement is to be governed;
- a reference to any further agreements between the auditors and the client; and
- a proposed timetable for the engagement.

Compliance with International Standards on Auditing

18 Compliance with this SAS ensures compliance in all material respects with International Standard on Auditing 210 'Terms of Audit Engagements'.

Effective date

19 Auditors are required to comply with the Auditing Standards contained in this SAS in respect of audits of financial statements for periods ending on or after 23 December 1995.

Appendix

Example of an Audit Engagement Letter

This form of letter has been drafted to apply to limited company clients. It is not necessarily comprehensive or appropriate to be used in relation to every company, and it must be tailored to specific circumstances — for example, to the special reporting requirements of regulated entities, or of small companies to which certain exemptions are given.

To the directors of ....

The purpose of this letter is to set out the basis on which we (are to) act as auditors of the company (and its subsidiary undertakings) and the respective areas of responsibility of the directors and of ourselves.

Responsibilities of directors and auditors

1.1 As directors of the above company, you are responsible for ensuring that the company maintains proper accounting records and for preparing financial statements which give a true and fair view and have been prepared in accordance with the Companies Act 1985 *(or other relevant legislation — note 1).* You are also responsible for making available to us, as and when required, all the company's accounting records and all other relevant records and related information, including minutes of all management and shareholders' meetings.

1.2 We have a statutory responsibility to report to the members whether in our opinion the financial statements give a true and fair view and whether they have been properly prepared in accordance with the Companies Act 1985 *(or other relevant legislation).* In arriving at our opinion, we are required to consider the following matters, and to report on any in respect of which we are not satisfied *(note 2)*:

(a) whether proper accounting records have been kept by the company *(note 3)* and proper returns adequate for our audit have been received from branches not visited by us;

(b) whether the company's *(note 3)* balance sheet and profit and loss account are in agreement with the accounting records and returns;

(c) whether we have obtained all the information and explanations which we consider necessary for the purposes of our audit; and

(d) whether the information given in the directors' report is consistent with the financial statements.

In addition, there are certain other matters which, according to the circumstances, may need to be dealt with in our report. For example, where the financial statements do not give details of directors' remuneration or of their transactions with the company, the Companies Act 1985 requires us to disclose such matters in our report.

1.3 We have a professional responsibility to report if the financial statements do not comply in any material respect with applicable accounting standards, unless in our opinion the non-compliance is justified in the circumstances. In determining whether or not the departure is justified we consider:

(a) whether the departure is required in order for the financial statements to give a true and fair view; and

(b) whether adequate disclosure has been made concerning the departure.

1.4 Our professional responsibilities also include:

- including in our report a description of the directors' responsibilities for the financial statements where the financial statements or accompanying information do not include such a description; and
- considering whether other information in documents containing audited financial statements is consistent with those financial statements.

Scope of audit

2.1 Our audit will be conducted in accordance with the Auditing Standards issued by the Auditing Practices Board, and will include such tests of transactions and of the existence, ownership and valuation of assets and liabilities as we consider necessary. We shall obtain an understanding of the accounting and internal control systems in order to assess their adequacy as a basis for the preparation of the financial statements and to establish whether proper accounting records have been maintained by the company. We shall expect to obtain such appropriate evidence as we consider sufficient to enable us to draw reasonable conclusions therefrom.

2.2 The nature and extent of our procedures will vary according to our assessment of the company's accounting system and, where we wish to place reliance on it, the internal control system, and may cover any aspect of the business's operations that we consider appropriate. Our audit is not designed to identify all significant weaknesses in the company's systems but, if such weaknesses come to our notice during the course of our audit which we think should be brought to your attention, we shall report them to you. Any such report may not be provided to third parties without our prior written consent. Such consent will be granted only on the basis that such reports are not prepared with the interests of anyone other than the company in mind and that we accept no duty or responsibility to any other party as concerns the reports.

2.3 As part of our normal audit procedures, we may request you to provide written confirmation of certain oral representations which we have received from you during the course of the audit on matters having a material effect on the financial statements. In connection with representations and the supply of information to us generally, we draw your attention to Section 389A of the Companies Act 1985 *(note 4)* under which it is an offence for an officer of the company to mislead the auditors.

2.4 In order to assist us with the examination of your financial statements, we shall request sight of all documents or statements, including the chairman's statement, operating and financial review and the directors' report, which are due to be issued with the financial statements. We are also entitled to attend all general meetings of the company and to receive notice of all such meetings.

2.5 The responsibility for safeguarding the assets of the company and for the prevention and detection of fraud, error and non-compliance with law or regulations rests with yourselves. However, we shall endeavour to plan our audit so that we have a reasonable expectation of detecting material misstatements in the financial statements or accounting records (including those resulting from fraud, error or non-compliance with law or regulations), but our examination should not be relied upon to disclose all such material misstatements or frauds, errors or instances of non-compliance as may exist.

2.6 *(Where appropriate — note 5)* We shall not be treated as having notice, for the purposes of our audit responsibilities, of information provided to members of our firm other than those engaged on the audit (for example information provided in connection with accounting, taxation and other services).

2.7 Once we have issued our report we have no further direct responsibility in relation to the financial statements for that financial year. However, we expect that you will inform us of any material event occurring between the date of our report and that of the Annual General Meeting which may affect the financial statements.

Other services

3 You have requested that we provide other services in respect of ...... The terms under which we provide these other services are dealt with in a separate letter. We will also agree in a separate letter of engagement the provision of any services relating to investment business advice as defined by the Financial Services Act 1986.

Fees

4 Our fees are computed on the basis of the time spent on your affairs by the partners and our staff and on the levels of skill and responsibility involved. Unless otherwise agreed, our fees will be billed at appropriate intervals during the course of the year and will be due on presentation.

Applicable law

5 This [engagement letter] shall be governed by, and construed in accordance with, [English] law. The Courts of [England] shall have exclusive jurisdiction in relation to any claim, dispute or difference concerning the [engagement letter] and any matter arising from it. Each party irrevocably waives any right it may have to object to an action being brought in those Courts, to claim that the action has been brought in an inconvenient forum, or to claim that those Courts do not have jurisdiction.

Agreement of terms

6 Once it has been agreed, this letter will remain effective, from one adudit appointment to another, until it is replaced. We shall be grateful if you could confirm in writing your agreement to these terms by signing and returning the enclosed copy of this letter, or let us know if they are not in accordance with your understanding of our terms of engagement.

Yours faithfully

We agree to the terms of this letter

....

Signed for and on behalf of (company)

Notes

1 Relevant legislation for the Republic of Ireland is the Companies Acts 1963 to 1990 and for Northern Ireland is the Companies (Northern Ireland) Order 1986.

2 In the Republic of Ireland, auditors are required to report additionally on matters (a) to (d) as identified in section 1.2 of the example engagement letter, and on whether there existed at the balance sheet date a financial situation which, under Section 40(1) of the Companies (Amendment) Act 1983, would require the convening of an extraordinary general meeting of the company. Hence this sentence would read: ' . . we are required to consider the following matters and to report on:'

3 The reference to 'company' does not need to be altered in the case of groups as Section 237 of the Companies Act 1985 refers only to the company being audited and not to any parent company or subsidiary or associated undertaking.

4 Relevant references for the Republic of Ireland are Sections 193(3), 196 and 197 of the Companies Act 1990. The relevant reference for Northern Ireland is Article 397A of the Companies (Northern Ireland) Order 1986.

5 When accounting, taxation or other services are undertaken on behalf of an audit client, information may be provided to members of the audit firm other than those engaged on the audit. In such cases, it may be appropriate for the audit engagement letter to include this or a similar paragraph to indicate that the auditors are not to be treated as having notice, for the purposes of their audit responsibilities, of such information, to make it clear that a company would not be absolved from informing the auditors directly of a material matter.

6 ***Additional paragraph — Complaints procedures***

Certain professional bodies require members to notify clients of their own complaints procedures and of the clients' right to make complaints to those professional bodies. This might appropriately be included in the engagement letter in a form such as the following:

> ' We aim to provide you with a fully satisfactory service and [name] as engagement partner will seek to ensure that this is so. If, however, you are unable to deal with any difficulty through [him][her] and [his][her] team please contact [name]. We undertake to look into any complaints promptly and to do what we can to resolve the position. If you are still not satisfied you may of course take up the matter with [professional body] by whom we are regulated for audit purposes.'

Statement of Auditing Standards 150 — Subsequent events

(Issued March 1995)

Reproduced with the permission of the Auditing Practices Board

Statements of Auditing Standards ('SASs') are to be read in the light of 'The scope and authority of APB pronouncements'. In particular, they contain basic principles and essential procedures ('Auditing Standards'), indicated by paragraphs in bold type, with which auditors are required to comply in the conduct of any audit. SASs also contain explanatory and other material which is designed to assist auditors in interpreting and applying Auditing Standards. The definitions in the Glossary of terms are to be applied in the interpretation of the SASs.

Introduction

1 The purpose of this SAS is to establish standards and provide guidance on auditors' responsibility regarding 'subsequent events' occurring:

(a) between the period end and the date of the auditors report;

(b) between the date of the auditors report and the issue of the financial statement; and

(c) after the financial statements have been issued, but before they are laid before the members, or equivalent.

These three stages — and auditors' responsibilities in relation to them — leading to the laying of financial statements before members apply to all entities. However, in practice, one or more of the stages may be so short as not to require separate consideration by auditors, for example where the meeting at which the directors of a small owner-managed entity approved the financial statements, and the auditors report is signed, is immediately followed by the entity's annual general meeting.

2 Auditors should consider the effects of subsequent events on the financial statements and on their report. (SAS 150.1)

3 'Subsequent events' means both those relevant events (favourable or unfavourable) which occur and those facts which are discovered between the period and the laying of the financial statements before the members, or equivalent. 'Relevant events' are those which:

- provide additional evidence relating to conditions existing at the balance sheet date; or
- concern conditions which did not exist at the balance sheet date, but which may be of such materiality that their disclosure is required to ensure that the financial statements are not misleading.

Discovery of facts is relevant in this context if the discovery reveals material misstatements in the financial statements.

4 This SAS does not provide guidance on facts discovered after the laying of the financial statements before the members. Such facts may result in the directors issuing revised accounts as defined by relevant legislation.

Subsequent events between the period end and the date of the auditors' report

5 Auditors should perform procedures designed to obtained sufficient appropriate audit evidence that all material subsequent events up to the date of their report which require adjustment of, or disclosure in, the financial statements have been identified and properly reflected therein. (SAS150.2)

6 Auditors focus these procedures on any matters they may have become aware of during the course of the audit which may be susceptible to change after the period end. Such procedures are in addition to those which may be applied to specific transactions occurring after period end to obtain audit evidence as to account balances as at the period end, for example the testing of cut-offs of sales and stocks and payments to creditors.

7 The procedures to identify subsequent events which may require adjustment of, or disclosure in, the financial statements are performed as near as practicable to the date of the auditors' report and generally include some or all of the following:

- enquiring into, and considering the effectiveness of, the procedures management has established to ensure that subsequent events are identified;
- reading minutes of the meeting of members, the board of directors and audit and executive committees held after period end and enquiring about matters discussed at meetings for which minutes are not yet available;
- reviewing relevant accounting records and reading the entity's latest available financial information, such as interim financial statements, budgets, cash flow forecasts and other related management reports; and
- making enquiries of management as to whether any subsequent events have occurred which might affect the financial statements.

The extent to which the results of these procedures require reviewing and updating immediately before the date of the auditors' report depends on the length of time which has elapsed between when these procedures were initially performed and the date of their report and the susceptibility of items to change over time.

8 Examples of specific enquiries which may be made of management are:

- the current status of items involving subjective judgement or which were accounted for on the basis of preliminary data, for example, litigation in progress;
- whether new commitments, borrowings, or guarantees have been entered into;
- whether sales of assets have occurred or are planned;
- whether the issue of new shares or debentures, or an agreement to merge or to liquidate, has been made or is planned;
- whether any assets have been destroyed, for example by fire or flood;
- whether there have been any developments regarding risk areas and contingencies;
- whether any unusual accounting adjustments have been made or are contemplated; and
- whether any events have occurred or are likely to occur which might bring into question the appropriateness of accounting policies used in the financial statements as would be the case, for example, if such events might call into question the validity of the going concern basis.

9 When placing reliance on other auditors, for example those of a division, branch or subsidiary undertaking, principal auditors satisfy themselves that the other auditors have performed appropriate procedures relating to the subsequent events in the period up to the date of the principle auditors' report.

Subsequent events discovered after the date of the auditors' report but before the financial statements are issued

10 The directors have the responsibility to issue financial statements which give a true and fair view and are not otherwise misleading. They may therefore reasonably be expected to inform the auditors of any material subsequent events which may affect the financial statements occurring or discovered during the period from the date of the auditors' report to the date the financial statements are issued (for example to members). However, auditors do not have any obligation to perform procedures or make enquiries regarding the financial statements after the date of their report.

11 When, after the date of their report but before the financial statements are issued, auditors become aware of subsequent events which may materially affect the financial statements, they should establish whether the financial statements need amendment, should discuss the matter with the directors and should consider the implications for their report, taking additional action as appropriate. (SAS 150.3)

12 When the directors amend the financial statements, the appropriate action is for the auditors to carry out the audit procedures necessary in the circumstances, to extend the procedures referred to in paragraphs 6 to 9 above to the date of their new report and to provide the directors with a new report on the amended financial statements, dated the day on which this new report is signed.

13 When the directors do not amend the financial statements before issuing them, in circumstances where the auditors believe they need to be amended, paragraph 19 below applies.

Subsequent events discovered after the financial statements have been issued but before their laying before the members, or equivalent

14 After the financial statements have been issued, auditors have no obligation to perform procedures or make enquiries regarding such financial statements.

15 When, after the Financial statements have been issued, but before they have been laid before the members or equivalent, auditors become aware of subsequent events which, had they occurred and been known of at the day of their report, might have caused them to issue a different report, they should consider whether the financial statements need amendment, should discuss the matter with the directors, and should consider the implications for their report, taking additional action as appropriate. (SAS 150.4)

16 Two cases may be distinguished:

(a) an event which occurred before the date of the auditors' report, but which the auditors became aware of thereafter; and

(b) an event which occurred after the date of the auditors' report.

In the former case, the auditors considered with the directors whether the financial statements should be revised (for example, under the statutory provisions relating to the revision of company annual financial statements and directors' reports as set out in Sections 245 to 245C of the Companies Act 1985 and in Articles 253 to 253C of the

Companies (Northern Ireland) Order 1986). There are no statutory provisions for revising financial statement in the latter case, although the auditors may wish to take advice on whether it might be possible to withdraw their report. In both cases, other possible courses of action include the making of a statement by the directors or auditors at the annual general meeting. In any event legal advice may be helpful.

17 When the directors revise the financial statements, the appropriate action for the auditors to take includes:

- carrying out the audit procedures necessary in the circumstances;
- considering, where appropriate, whether Sock Exchange regulations require the revision to be publicised;
- considering whether there is any requirement, in the case of businesses authorised under the Financial Services Act 1986 or other regulated businesses, to communicate with the appropriate regulator;
- reviewing the steps taken by the directors to ensure that anyone in receipt of the previously issued financial statements together with the auditors report thereon is informed of the situation; and
- issuing a new report on the revised financial statements.

18 When auditors issue a new report, they:

(a) refer in their report to the note to the financial statements which more extensively discusses the reason for the revision of the previously issued financial statements, or set out such reason in their report;

(b) refer to the earlier report issued by them on the financial statements;

(c) date their new report not earlier than the date the revised financial statements are approved; and

(d) have regard to the guidance relating to reports on revised annual financial statements and directors' reports as set out in APB's Practice Note 8 'Reports by auditors under company legislation in the United Kingdom'.

19 If the directors do not revise the financial statements which the auditors believe need to be revised and these statements are issued but have not yet been laid before the members or equivalent, or if the directors do not intend to make an appropriate statement at the annual general meeting, then the auditors consider steps to take on a timely basis to prevent reliance on their report. For example, they may consider making an appropriate statement at the annual general meeting. They may also consider taking legal advice on their position. Auditors do not have a statutory right to communicate directly in writing with the members although, if they resign or are removed or are not re-appointed, they have, for example, various duties and rights under company law.

Compliance with International Standards on Auditing

20 With the exception that paragraphs 18(a) and (b) are considered to be more appropriately expressed as guidance rather than as basic principles or essential procedures, compliance with this SAS ensures compliance in all material respects with the guidance in International Standard Auditing 560 'Subsequent Events' which relates to audit work. The guidance given therein which relates to the offering of securities to the public has not been reflected in the SAS.

Effective date

21 Auditors are required to comply with the Auditing Standards contained in this SAS in respect of audits of financial statements for periods ending on or after 23 December 1995.

Statement of Auditing Standards 160—Other information in documents containing audited financial statements

(Issued March 1995)

Reproduced with the permission of the Auditing Practices Board

Statements of Auditing Standards ('SASs') are to be read in the light of 'The scope and authority of APB pronouncements'. In particular, they contain basic principles and essential procedures ('Auditing Standards'), indicated by paragraphs in bold type, with which auditors are required to comply in the conduct of any audit. SASs also include explanatory and other material which is designed to assist auditors in interpreting and applying Auditing Standards. The definitions in the Glossary of terms are to be applied in the interpretation of SASs.

Introduction

1 The purpose of this SAS is to establish standards and provide guidance on auditors' consideration of other information in documents containing audited financial statements. Nothing in this SAS refers to other information which is released in conjunction with financial statements without the auditors' knowledge and consent.

2 An entity usually issues on an annual basis a document which includes its audited financial statements together with the auditors' report thereon. This document is frequently referred to as the 'annual report'. In issuing such a document, an entity may also include, either by statute or custom, other financial and non-financial information. For the purpose of this SAS, such other financial information and non-financial information is called 'other information'.

3 Examples of other information include a directors' report required by statute, a chairman's statement, an operating and financial review, financial summaries, employment data, planned capital expenditures, financial ratios and selected quarterly data.

4 An audit of financial statements is directed towards the expression of an opinion by the auditors as to whether the financial statements give a true and fair view. Accordingly, auditors have no responsibility to report that the other information is properly stated. They may, however, be asked as a separate engagement, or be required by specific legislation, to review elements of it (for example, the auditors' review of the directors' statement of compliance with the Cadbury Code).

5 Auditors should read the other information. If as a result they become aware of any apparent misstatements therein, or identify any material inconsistencies with the audited financial statements, they should seek to resolve them. (SAS 160.1)

6 The principles of this SAS apply to audits of the financial statements of all types of entity as, irrespective of any statutory responsibilities regarding the other information, auditors give consideration to all the other information when issuing a report on the financial statements. This is because the credibility of the financial statements and the related auditors' report may be undermined by inconsistencies between the financial statements and the other information, or by misstatements within the other information. For certain types of entity, there may be specific legal requirements to follow, for example those relating to information in the directors' report of a limited company.

Auditors' consideration of other information

7 If auditors identify an inconsistency between the financial statements and the other information, or a misstatement within the other information, they should consider whether an amendment is required to the financial statements or to the other information and should seek to resolve the matter through discussion with the directors. (SAS 160.2)

8 A misstatement within the other information exists when the other information is stated incorrectly or presented in a misleading manner.

9 An inconsistency exists when the other information contradicts, or appears to contradict, information contained in the financial statements. An inconsistency may raise doubt about the audit conclusions drawn from audit evidence previously obtained and, possibly, about the basis for the auditors' opinion on the financial statements.

Unresolved misstatements and inconsistencies

10 If, after discussion with the directors, the auditors conclude that the financial statements require amendment and no such amendment is made, they should consider the implications for their report. If, after discussion with the directors, the auditors conclude that the other information requires amendment and no such amendment is made, they should consider appropriate action. (SAS 160.3)

11 In some circumstances, for example when auditing the financial statements of limited companies in the United Kingdom and Republic of Ireland, auditors have a statutory responsibility to consider whether the information given in the directors' report is consistent with the financial statements with which it is issued. If they are of the opinion that it is not, they are required to make reference to the inconsistencies in their report. The relevant provisions of the statutory framework in the United Kingdom and Republic of Ireland relating to limited companies are detailed in Appendix 2.

12 Matters which may require resolution or reference in an explanatory paragraph within the auditors' report include:

- an inconsistency between amounts or narrative appearing in the financial statements and the directors' report;
- an inconsistency between the bases of preparation of related items appearing in the financial statements and the directors' report, where the figures themselves are not directly comparable and the different bases are not disclosed; and
- an inconsistency between figures contained in the financial statements and a narrative interpretation of the effect of those figures in the directors' report.

An example of an auditors' report on an inconsistency between the directors' report and the financial statements in circumstances where it is the directors' report that requires amendment is set out in Appendix 3.

13 If auditors conclude that the other information contains any misstatements or inconsistencies with the financial statements, in circumstances other than those in which paragraph 11 applies, and they are unable to resolve them through discussion with the directors, they may need to seek legal advice on appropriate action, which may involve including in their report an explanatory paragraph describing the matter. In particular, they may need legal advice on whether they would be protected by qualified privilege from a defamation claim if they were to refer to the matters in their report or subsequently.

14 Auditors of a limited company may use their right under Section 390 of the Companies Act 1985[1] to be heard at any general meeting of the members 'on any part of the business of the meeting which concerns them as auditors'.

15 Auditors may also consider resigning from the audit engagement. In the case of auditors of limited companies, the requirements of Section 394 of the Companies Act 1985 for auditors to make a statement on their ceasing to hold office as auditors apply.[2]

16 A flow chart to assist in determining a course of action regarding material misstatements in other information and inconsistencies between the financial statements and the other information is included as Appendix 1.

Timing considerations

17 In order that auditors can consider the other information included in the annual report, they make appropriate arrangements with the entity to obtain timely access to such information prior to the date of their report. SAS 600 'Auditors' reports on financial statements' requires all other information to be approved by the entity, and auditors to consider all necessary evidence, before the audit opinion is expressed.

Compliance with International Standards on Auditing

18 International Standard on Auditing 720 'Other Information in Documents Containing Audited Financial Statements' includes the following requirements which are not reflected in Auditing Standards in this SAS:

(a) 'If an amendment is necessary in the other information and the entity refuses to make the amendment, the auditor should consider including in the audit report an emphasis of matter paragraph describing the material inconsistency or taking other actions.'

As explained in paragraph 13, it is considered inappropriate for auditors to refer to such matters in their report without seeking legal advice. Accordingly, guidance in this regard is included as an explanation of the requirement of the Auditing Standard requiring auditors in these circumstances to 'consider appropriate action'.

(b) 'When the auditor still considers there is an apparent misstatement of fact, the auditor should request management to consult with a qualified third party, such as the entity's legal counsel and should consider the advice received.'

This has not been included as an Auditing Standard as it represents one of the many possible solutions after auditors find themselves in disagreement with management. Such disagreements need to be resolved in the most appropriate way in the circumstances, which may not always be through third party advice.

19 Compliance with this SAS therefore ensures compliance in all material respects with International Standard on Auditing 720 'Other Information in Documents Containing Audited Financial Statements'.

1 The relevant reference for the Republic of Ireland is Section 193(5) of the Companies Act 1990 and for Northern Ireland is Article 395 of the Companies (Northern Ireland) Order 1986.

2 The relevant reference for the Republic of Ireland is Section 185 of the Companies Act 1990 and for Northern Ireland is Article 398 of the Companies (Northern Ireland) Order 1986.

Effective date

20 Auditors are required to comply with the Auditing Standards contained in this SAS in respect of audits of financial statements for periods ending on or after 23 December 1995.

Appendix 1
Determining a course of action regarding material misstatements and inconsistencies

The process described below is to be followed in respect of each individual material inconsistency between the financial statements and the other information, and each material misstatement within the other information.

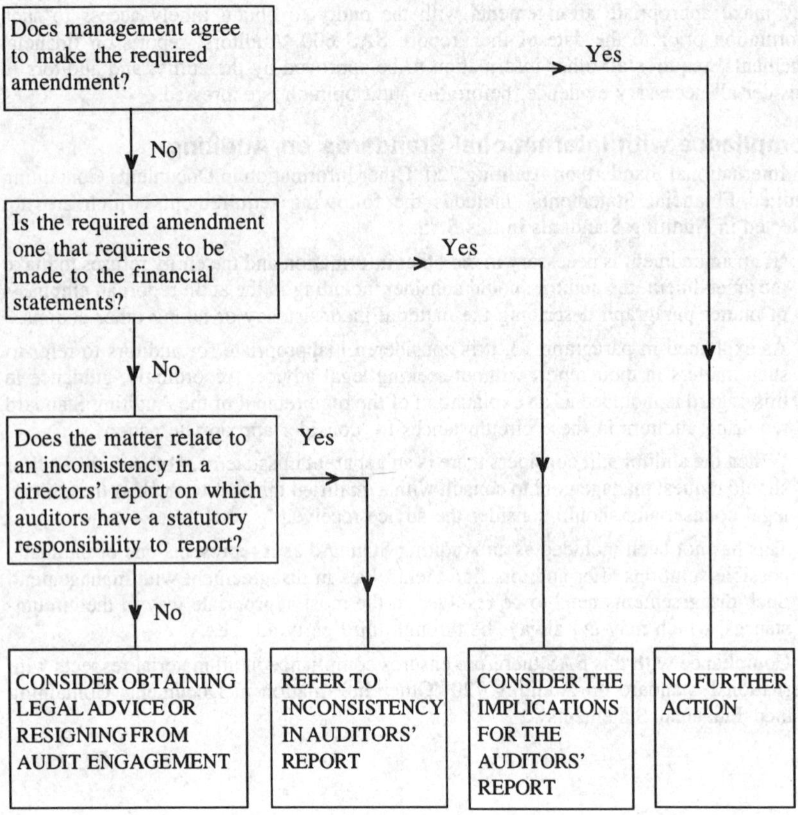

Appendix 2

Statutory framework

Great Britain and Northern Ireland

Section 235(3) of the Companies Act 1985 sets out one of the statutory responsibilities of auditors as follows:

> 'The auditors shall consider whether the information given in the directors' report for the financial year for which the annual accounts are prepared is consistent with those accounts; and if they are of the opinion that it is not they shall state that fact in their report.'

The equivalent legislation in Northern Ireland is Article 243(3) of the Companies (Northern Ireland) Order 1986.

Republic of Ireland

Section 15 of the Companies (Amendment) Act 1986 sets out the following statutory responsibility of auditors:

> 'It shall be the duty of the auditors of a company, in preparing the report in relation to the company required by Section 163 of the Principal Act, to consider whether the information given in the report of the directors of the company relating to the financial year concerned is consistent with the accounts prepared by the company for that year and they shall state in the report whether, in their opinion, such information is consistent with those accounts.'

Appendix 3

Auditors' report arising from Section 235(3) of the Companies Act 1985 — inconsistency between the financial statements and the directors' report

AUDITORS' REPORT TO THE SHAREHOLDERS OF XYZ LTD — EXTRACTS

Opinion

In our opinion the financial statements give a true and fair view of the state of the company's affairs as at 31 December 19.. and of its profit [loss] for the year then ended and have been properly prepared in accordance with the Companies Act 1985.

Inconsistency between the financial statements and the directors' report

In our opinion, the information given in paragraph 7 of the directors' report is not consistent with these financial statements. That paragraph states without amplification that the company's trading resulted in a profit before tax of £X. The profit and loss account, however, states that the company incurred an operating loss for the year of £Y and a profit from the sale of land of £Z.

Note: *This form of report is not a qualified report for the purposes of Sections 240(3)(d) or 271(4) of the Companies Act 1985, as the opinion on the financial statements is unaffected.*

Statement of Auditing Standards 200 — Planning

(Issued March 1995)

Statements of Auditing Standards ('SASs') are to be read in the light of 'The scope and authority of APB pronouncements'. In particular, they contain basic principles and essential procedures ('Auditing Standards'), indicated by paragraphs in bold type, with which auditors are required to comply in the conduct of any audit. SASs also include explanatory and other material which is designed to assist auditors in interpreting and applying Auditing Standards. The definitions in the Glossary of terms are to be applied in the interpretation of SASs.

Introduction

1 The purpose of this SAS is to establish standards and to provide guidance on planning an audit of financial statements. This SAS is framed in the context of recurring audits. In a first audit, auditors are likely to need to extend the planning process beyond the matters discussed herein.

2 Auditors should plan the audit work so as to perform the audit in an effective manner. (SAS 200.1)

3 Planning entails developing a general strategy and a detailed approach for the expected nature, timing and extent of the audit.

4 Auditors formulate the general audit strategy in an overall audit plan, which sets the direction for the audit and provides guidance for the development of the audit programme. The audit programme sets out the detailed procedures required to implement the strategy. Where, because of the size or nature of the entity, the details of the overall audit plan can be adequately documented in the audit programme, or vice versa, separate documentation of each may not be necessary.

Planning the work

5 Planning is necessary for audits of entities of all sizes. The objectives of planning the audit work, which takes place before the detailed audit work begins, include:

- ensuring that appropriate attention is devoted to the different areas of the audit;
- ensuring that potential problems are identified; and
- facilitating review.

Planning also assists in the proper assignment of work to members of the audit team and their briefing, and in the co-ordination of work done by other auditors and experts, so that the audit may be performed in an efficient and timely manner.

6 An understanding of the entity's affairs and, as far as practicable, of the nature and of the scope of the work they are to carry out is necessary for all members of the audit team before the audit field work starts.

7 Obtaining knowledge of the entity's business is required as an important part of planning the work. The auditors' experience with the entity and knowledge of its business assists in the identification of events, transactions and practices which may have a

material affect on the financial statements.

8 Planning varies according to the size of the entity and the complexity of the audit. For example, on some small audits planning may be carried out at a meeting with the directors or management of the entity or when the entity's records become available to the auditors for audit. When the auditors assist in the preparation of the financial statements, sufficient flexibility is required in the overall audit plan to take account of any areas of audit risk identified, and evidence obtained, during that exercise.

9 Auditors may need to discuss elements of the overall audit plan and certain audit procedures with the entity's management and staff, and with any audit committee, to improve the effectiveness of the audit and to co-ordinate audit procedures with work of the entity's personnel, including internal auditors. The overall audit plan and the detailed audit procedures to be performed, however, remain the auditors' responsibility. When such discussions occur, care is required not to compromise the independence and validity of the audit.

The overall audit plan

10 Auditors should develop and document an overall audit plan describing the expected scope and conduct of the audit. (SAS 200.2)

11 The amount of detail in the record of the overall audit plan is to be sufficient to guide the development of the detailed audit procedures to be performed. However, the precise form and content of the overall audit plan, and the formality with which it considers matters affecting the scope of the audit and the audit work to be undertaken, vary depending on the size of the entity, the complexity of the audit, the need for members of the audit team to be briefed and the specific methodology and technology the auditors use.

12 Matters for auditors to consider in developing the overall audit plan may include:

Knowledge of the entity's business

- general economic factors and industry conditions affecting the entity's business;
- important characteristics of the entity, its business, principal business strategies, its financial performance and its reporting requirements, including changes since the previous audit;
- the operating style and control consciousness of directors and management; and
- the auditors' cumulative knowledge of the accounting and internal control systems and any expected changes in the period.

Further guidance on these matters is given in SAS 210 'Knowledge of the business'.

Risk and materiality

- the setting of materiality for audit planning purposes;
- the expected assessments of risks of error and the identification of significant audit areas;
- any indication, including the experience of past years, that misstatements that could have a material affect on the financial statements might arise because of fraud or for any other reason; and
- the identification of complex accounting areas including those involving accounting estimates.

Nature, timing and extent of procedures

- the relative emphasis expected to be placed on tests of control and substantive procedures;

- the effect on the audit of the use of information technology by the entity or the auditors;
- the work of any internal audit function and its expected effect on external audit procedures;
- procedures which need to be carried out at or before the year end; and
- the timing of significant phases of the preparation of the financial statements.

Co-ordination, direction, supervision and review

- the involvement of other auditors, including other offices of the same firm, in the audit of components, for example subsidiary undertakings, branches and divisions;
- the involvement of, and communications with, experts, other third parties and internal auditors;
- the number of locations; and
- staffing requirements.

Other matters

- any regulatory requirements arising from the decision to retain the engagement;
- the possibility that the going concern basis may be inappropriate;
- the terms of the engagement and any statutory responsibilities; and
- the nature and timing of reports or other communications with the entity that are expected under the engagement.

The audit programme

13 Auditors should develop and document the nature, timing and extent of planned audit procedures required to implement the overall audit plan. (SAS 200.3)

14 In developing the detailed audit procedures to be performed, auditors consider the assessments of risks of error and the amount of audit evidence that the procedures are planned to provide. They also consider the co-ordination of audit work with any work on preparing the financial statements, the timing of tests of controls and substantive procedures, the co-ordination of any assistance expected from the entity, the composition of the audit team and the involvement of other auditors or experts. The other matters noted in paragraph 12 above may also need to be considered further during the development of the record of planned audit procedures.

15 The documentation may take the form of an audit programme which sets out the audit procedures the auditors intend to adopt and includes reference to other matters such as the audit objectives, timing, sample size and basis of selection for each area. It serves as a set of instructions to the audit team and as a means to control and record the proper execution of the work. The level of detail in the audit programme depends on the complexity of the audit, the extent of other documentation and the experience of the members of the audit team.

Changes to the audit work planned

16 The audit work planned should be reviewed and, if necessary, revised during the course of the audit. (SAS 200.4)

17 Changes in conditions, or unexpected results of audit procedures, may require changes to the overall audit plan or the planned audit procedures. Changes to the planned audit procedures are documented so that there is an accurate record of the nature, timing and extent of the audit procedures performed. A record of changes to the overall audit plan may be necessary to explain the general strategy finally adopted for the audit.

Compliance with International Standards on Auditing

18 Compliance with this SAS ensures compliance in all material respects with International Standard on Auditing 300 'Planning'.

Effective date

19 Auditors are required to comply with the Auditing Standards contained in this SAS in respect of audits of financial statements for periods ending on or after 23 December 1995.

Statement of Auditing Standards

210 — Knowledge of the business

(Issued March 1995)

Reproduced with the permission of the Auditing Practices Board

Statements of Auditing Standards ('SASs') are to be read in the light of 'The scope and authority of APB pronouncements'. In particular, they contain basic principles and essential procedures ('Auditing Standards'), indicated by paragraphs in bold type, with which auditors are required to comply in the conduct of any audit. SASs also include explanatory and other material which is designed to assist auditors in interpreting and applying Auditing Standards. The definitions in the Glossary of terms are to be applied in the interpretation of SASs.

Introduction

1 The purpose of this SAS is to establish standards and provide guidance to auditors on obtaining knowledge of the business of the entity to be audited and how to use that knowledge.

2 Auditors should have or obtain a knowledge of the business of the entity to be audited which is sufficient to enable them to identify and understand the events, transactions and practices that may have a significant effect on the financial statements or the audit thereof. (SAS 210.1)

3 Knowledge of the business is used by auditors in, for example, assessing risks of error, in determining the nature, timing and extent of audit procedures and in considering the consistency and reliability of the financial statements as a whole when completing the audit.

4 The auditors' level of knowledge for an engagement normally includes a general knowledge of the economy and the industry within which the entity operates, and a more particular knowledge of how the entity operates. The level of knowledge required by auditors is less than that possessed by the directors. An illustrative list of matters to consider in a specific engagement is set out in the Appendix.

5 The extent to which auditors need formally to document their knowledge of the business depends upon its complexity and the number of persons who will be engaged on the audit, as well as the need to cover possible departure, illness or incapacity of key members of the audit team. Auditors prepare such documentation to a level sufficient to facilitate proper planning of the audit.

Obtaining the knowledge

Prior to acceptance of an engagement

6 Prior to acceptance of an engagement, auditors obtain a preliminary knowledge of the industry and of the ownership, directors, management and operations of the entity to be audited, sufficient to enable them to consider their ability to undertake the audit.

7 Knowledge obtained prior to acceptance of an engagement generally includes:

- knowledge from previous relevant experience;
- knowledge from enquiries of predecessor auditors;

- specific rules or regulations pertaining to the industry;
- accounting standards applicable to the industry;
- an initial perception of the viability of the business; and
- the perceived integrity of the directors and management.

Auditors also required sufficient knowledge to enable them to assess whether there is a requirement for staff with specialist audit expertise (for example computer audit specialists) or other experts.

Following acceptance of an engagement

8 Following acceptance of an engagement, auditors obtain further and more detailed knowledge and information sufficient to enable them to plan the audit and develop an effective audit approach.

9 To the extent practicable, auditors obtain the required knowledge at the start of the engagement. However, obtaining the required knowledge of the business is a continuous and cumulative process of gathering and assessing the information and relating the resulting knowledge to audit evidence and information at all stages of the audit. Further information obtained as the audit progresses enables auditors to update and augment that knowledge, and may require them to re-assess it.

Updating knowledge for succeeding periods

10 In succeeding periods, auditors consider the information gathered previously and perform procedures designed to identify significant changes that have taken place since the last audit.

Sources of knowledge

11 Auditors can obtain a knowledge of the industry and the entity from a number of sources, for example:

- previous experience with the entity and its industry;
- visits to the entity's premises and plant facilities;
- discussion with people within the entity (for example directors, internal auditors, computer personnel and senior operating personnel);
- discussion with other auditors and with legal and other advisors who have provided services to the entity or within the industry;
- discussion with knowledgeable people outside the entity (for example economists, industry regulators);
- publications related to the industry (for example government statistics, surveys, texts, trade journals, reports prepared by banks and securities dealers, financial newspapers);
- legislation and regulations that significantly affect the entity;
- documents produced by the entity (for example minutes of meetings, material sent to shareholders or filed with regulatory authorities, promotional literature, prior years' annual and financial reports, budgets, internal management reports, interim financial reports, management policy manuals, manuals of accounting and internal control systems, charts of accounts, job descriptions, marketing and sales plans); and
- professional literature giving industry-specific guidance.

Using the knowledge

12 Understanding the business and using this information appropriately assists auditors in:

- assessing risks and identifying problems;
- planning and performing the audit effectively and efficiently; and
- evaluating audit evidence.

13 Auditors make judgements about many matters throughout the course of the audit where knowledge of the business is important, for example:

- considering risks pertaining to the entity's business activities and the directors' response thereto;
- identifying areas where special audit considerations and skills may be necessary;
- developing the overall audit plan and the audit programme;
- considering the complexity of the entity's information systems and any effect on the audit approach;
- determining a materiality level and assessing whether the materiality level chosen remains appropriate;
- assessing inherent risk and control risk;
- assessing audit evidence to establish its appropriateness and the validity of the related financial statement assertions;
- evaluating accounting estimates and representations by the directors or management;
- recognising conflicting information (for example contradictory representations);
- recognising unusual circumstances (for example undisclosed related party transactions, possible fraud or non-compliance with law or regulations, or unexpected relationships of statistical operating data with reported financial results);
- making informed enquiries and assessing the reasonableness of answers; and
- considering the appropriateness of accounting policies and financial statement disclosures.

14 The audit engagement partner should ensure that the audit team obtains such knowledge of the business of the entity being audited as may be reasonably be expected to be sufficient to enable it to carry out the audit work effectively. (SAS 210.2)

15 Such knowledge may be transmitted initially by means of the overall audit plan or an audit briefing meeting and subsequently during the course of the audit.

16 The audit engagement partner also ensures that the audit team understands that need to be alert for and to share additional information.

Compliance with International Standards on Auditing

17 Compliance with this SAS, in conjunction with SAS 470 'Overall review of financial statements', ensures compliance in all material respects with International Standards on Auditing 310 'Knowledge of the business'.

Effective date

18 Auditors are required to comply with the Auditing Standards contained in this SAS in respect of audits of financial statements for periods ending on or after 23 December 1995.

Appendix
Matters to consider in relation to knowledge of the business

This list is provided for illustrative purposes only. It is not exhaustive, nor is it intended that all matters listed willl be relevant to every engagement.

General economic factors

- General level of economic activity (for example recession, growth).
- Interest rates and availability of financing.
- Inflation.
- Government policies:
  - — monetary;
  - — fiscal;
  - — taxation — corporate and other;
  - — financial incentives (for example government aid programmes);
  - — tariffs, trade restriction.
- Foreign currency rates and controls.

The industry — conditions affecting the client's business

- The market and competition.
- Cyclical or seasonal activity.
- Changes in product technology.
- Business risk (for example high technology, high fashion, ease of entry for competition).
- Declining or expanding operations.
- Adverse conditions (for example declining demand, excess capacity, serious price competition).
- Key ratios and operating statistics.
- Specific accounting practices and problems.
- Environmental requirements and problems.
- Regulatory framework.
- Specific or unique practices (for example relating to labour contracts, financing methods, accounting methods).

The entity

Directors, management and ownership

- Corporate structure — private, public, government (including any recent or planned changes).
- Beneficial owners, important stakeholders and related parties (local, foreign, business reputation and experience) and any impact on the entity's transactions.

- The relationships between owners, directors and management.
- Attitudes and policies of owners.
- Capital structure (including any recent or planned changes).
- Organisational structure.
- Group structure.
- Subsidiaries' audit arrangements.
- Directors' objectives, philosophy, strategic plans.
- Acquisitions, mergers or disposals of business activities (planned or recently executed).
- Sources and methods of financing (current, historical).
- Board of directors:
  - composition;
  - business reputation and experience of individuals;
  - independence from and control over operating management;
  - frequency of meetings;
  - existence and membership of audit committee and scope of its activities;
  - existence of policy on corporate conduct;
  - changes in professional advisors (for example lawyers).
- Operating management:
  - experience and reputation;
  - turnover;
  - key financial personnel and their status in the organisation;
  - staffing of accounting department;
  - incentive or bonus plans as part of remuneration (for example based on profit);
  - use of forecasts and budgets;
  - pressures on management (for example over-extended, dominance by one individual, support for share price, unreasonable deadlines for announcing results);
  - management information systems;
- Internal audit function (existence, quality).
- Attitude to internal control environment.

The entity's business — products, markets, suppliers, expenses, operations

- Nature of business(es) (for example manufacturer, wholesaler, financial services, import/export).
- Location of production facilities, warehouses, offices.
- Employment (for example by location, supply, wage levels, union contracts, pension commitments, government regulation).
- Products or services and markets (for example major customers and contracts,

terms of payment, profit margins, market share, competitors, exports, pricing policies, reputation of products, warranties, order book, trends, marketing strategy and objectives, manufacturing processes).

- Important suppliers of goods and services (for example long-term contracts, stability of supply, terms of payment, imports, methods of delivery such as 'just-in-time').
- Stocks (for example locations, quantities).
- Franchises, licences, patents.
- Important expense categories.
- Research and development.
- Foreign currency assets, liabilities and transactions by currency, hedging.
- Legislation and regulations that significantly affect the entity.
- Information systems — current, plans to change.
- Debt structure, including coveneants and restrictions.

Financial performance — factors concerning the entity's financial condition and profitability

- Accounting policies
- Earnings and cash flow trends and forecasts.
- Leasing and other financial commitments.
- Availability of lines of credit.
- Off balance sheet finance issues.
- Foreign exchange and interest rate exposures.
- Comparison with industry trends.

Reporting environment — external influences which affect the directors in the preparation of the financial statements

- Legislation.
- Regulatory environment and requirements.
- Taxation.
- Accounting requirements.
- Measurement and disclosure issues peculiar to the business.
- Audit reporting requirements.
- Users of the financial statements.

Statement of Auditing Standards

220 — Materiality and the audit

(Issued March 1995)

Reproduced with the permission of the Auditing Practices Board

Statements of Auditing Standards ('SASs') are to be read in the light of 'The scope and authority of APB pronouncements'. In particular, they contain basic principles and essential procedures ('Auditing Standards'), indicated by paragraphs in bold type, with which auditors are required to comply in the conduct of any audit. SASs also include explanatory and other material which is designed to assist auditors in interpreting and applying Auditing Standards. The definitions in the Glossary of terms are to be applied in the interpretation of SASs.

Introduction

1 The purpose of this SAS is to set standards and provide guidance in auditors' consideration of materiality and its relationship with the risk that they might give an inappropriate opinion on the financial statements (audit risk).

2 Auditors should consider materiality and its relationship with audit risk when conducting an audit. (SAS 220.1)

3 'Materiality' is an expression of the relative significance or importance of a particular matter in the context of financial statements as a whole. A matter is material if its omission would reasonably influence the decisions of an addressee of the auditors' report; likewise a misstatement is material if it would have a similar influence. Materiality may also be considered in the context of any individual primary statement within the financial statements or of individual items included in them. Materiality is not capable of general mathematical definition as it has both qualitative and quantitative aspects.

Consideration of materiality

4 Auditors plan and perform the audit to be able to provide reasonable assurance that the financial statements are free of material misstatement and give a true and fair view. The assessment of what is material is a matter of professional judgement and includes consideration of both the amount (quantity) and nature (quality) of misstatements.

5 Auditors consider the possibility of misstatements of relatively small amounts that cumulatively, could have a material effect on the financial statements. For example, a relatively small error in a month-end procedure could be an indication of a potential material misstatement if that error is repeated each month.

6 Auditors are also alert to the nature of misstatements relating to qualitative aspects of a matter. Examples of qualitative misstatements are the inadequate or inaccurate description of an accounting policy when it is likely that a user of the financial statements could be misled by the description.

7 Materiality is considered at both the overall financial statement level and in relation to individual account balances, classes of transactions and disclosures. Materiality may be influenced by considerations such as legal and regulatory requirements and considerations relating to individual financial statement account balances and relationships. This process may result in different materiality considerations being applied depending on the aspect of the financial statements being considered. For example, the expected degree of accuracy of certain statutory disclosures, such as directors' emoluments, may make normal materiality considerations irrelevant.

Materiality and audit work

8 Auditors should consider materiality when determining the nature, timing and extent of audit procedures. (SAS 220.2)

9 The assessment of materiality during audit planning, based on the latest available reliable financial information, assists in the determination of an efficient and effective audit approach. In determining an audit approach to the different areas within the financial statements, this preliminary materiality assessment helps auditors decide such questions as what items to examine and whether to use sampling techniques. This enables them to select audit procedures that, in combination, reduce audit risk to an acceptably low level.

10 The assessment of materiality during audit planning may differ from that at the time of evaluating the results of audit procedures. This may be because of a change in circumstances or in a change in the auditors' knowledge as a result of the audit, for example, if the actual results of operations and financial position are different from those they expected when the audit was planned.

11 If auditors identify factors which result in the revision of their preliminary materiality assessment, they consider the implications for their audit approach and may modify the nature, timing and extent of planned audit procedures. For example, if, after planning for specific audit procedures, they determine that the acceptable materiality level is lower than was previously assessed, the risk of failing to detect a material misstatement necessarily increases. They compensate for this by carrying out more audit work.

Evaluating the effect of misstatements

12 In evaluating whether the financial statements give a true and fair view, auditors should assess the materiality of the aggregate of uncorrected misstatements. (SAS 220.3)

13 The aggregate of uncorrected misstatements comprises:

(a) specific misstatements identified by the auditors, including uncorrected misstatements identified during the audit of the previous period if they affect the current period's financial statements; and

(b) their best estimate of other misstatements which cannot be quantified specifically.

14 Auditors consider whether the aggregate of uncorrected misstatements is material. If they conclude that the misstatements may be material they consider reducing audit risk by extending audit procedures or requesting the directors to adjust the financial statements. In any event the directors may want to adjust the financial statements for the misstatements identified. If the directors refuse to adjust the financial statements and the results of extended audit procedures do not enable the auditors to conclude that the aggregate of uncorrected misstatements is not material, they consider the implications for their report.

Compliance with International Standards on Auditing

15 With the exception that the first sentence of paragraph 4 and the final sentence of paragraph 14, which are reflected in Auditing Standards in other SASs, are considered to be more appropriately expressed in this SAS as guidance rather than as basic principles or essential procedures, compliance with this SAS ensures compliance in all material respects with International Standard on Auditing 320 'Audit Materiality'.

Effective date

16 Auditors are required to comply with the Auditing Standards contained in this SAS in respect of audits of financial statements for periods ending on or after 23 December 1995.

Statement of Auditing Standards 230 — Working papers

(Issued March 1995)

Reproduced with the permission of the Auditing Practices Board

Statements of Auditing Standards ('SASs') are to be read in the light of 'The scope and authority of APB pronouncements'. In particular, they contain basic principles and essential procedures ('Auditing Standards'), indicated by paragraphs in bold type, with which auditors are required to comply in the conduct of any audit. SASs also include explanatory and other material which is designed to assist auditors in interpreting and applying Auditing Standards. The definitions in the Glossary of terms are to be applied in the interpretation of SASs.

Introduction

1 The purpose of this SAS is to establish standards and provide guidance regarding working papers in the context of the audit of financial statements.

2 Auditors should document in their working papers matters which are important in supporting their report. (SAS 230.1)

3 Working papers are the material that auditors prepare or obtain, and retain in connection with the performance of the audit. Working papers may be in the form of data stored on paper, film, electronic media or other media. Working papers support, amongst other things, the statement in the auditors' report as to the auditors' compliance or otherwise with Auditing Standards, and thus record compliance with Auditing Standards to the extent that this is important in supporting their report.

4 Working papers are the record of:

(a) the planning and performance of the audit;

(b) the supervision and review of the audit work; and

(c) the audit evidence resulting from the audit work performed which the auditors consider necessary and on which they have relied to support their report.

Form and content of working papers

5 Working papers should record the auditors' planning, the nature, timing and extent of the audit procedures performed, and the conclusions drawn from the audit evidence obtained. (SAS 230.2)

6 Auditors should record in their working papers their reasoning on all significant matters which require the exercise of judgement, and their conclusions thereon. (SAS 230.3)

7 The extent of working papers is a matter of professional judgement since it is neither necessary or practical to document every matter auditors consider. Auditors base their judgement as to the extent of working papers upon what would be necessary to provide an experienced auditor, with no previous connection with the audit, with an understanding of the work performed and the basis of the decisions taken. However, even then, that experienced auditor may only be able to obtain a comprehensive understanding of all

aspects of the audit by discussing them with the auditors who prepared them.

8 It is in those areas of the audit that involve difficult questions of principle or judgement that auditors' judgement may be questioned subsequently, particularly by a third party who has the benefit of hindsight. In such circumstances it is important to be able to demonstrate the relevant facts that were known at the time the auditors reached their conclusion.

9 Auditors draw conclusions relating to specific financial statement assertions. However, all such conclusions are arrived at within the context of their report. That report relates to the financial statements taken as a whole, and not to the individual assertions embodied in the financial statements.

10 The form and content of working papers are affected by matters such as:

- the nature of the engagement;
- the form of the auditors' report;
- the nature and complexity of the entity's business;
- the nature and condition of the entity's accounting and internal control systems;
- the needs in the particular circumstances for direction, supervision and review of the work of members of the audit team; and
- the specific methodology and technology the auditors use.

11 Working papers are designed and organised to meet the circumstances and the auditors' needs for each individual audit. The use of standardised working papers (for example checklists, specimen letters, standard organisation of working papers) may improve the efficiency with which such working papers are prepared and reviewed. While they facilitate the delegation of work and provide a means to control its quality, it is never appropriate to follow mechanically a standard approach to the conduct and documentation of the audit without regard to the need to exercise professional judgement.

12 To improve audit efficiency, auditors may utilise schedules, analyses and other documentation prepared by the entity. In such circumstances, auditors require evidence that such information is properly prepared.

13 Working papers include where relevant:

- information concerning the legal and organisational structure of the entity;
- extracts or copies of important legal documents, agreements and minutes;
- information concerning the industry, economic environment and legislative environment within which the entity operates;
- evidence of the planning process and any changes thererto;
- evidence of the auditors' understanding of the accounting and internal control systems;
- evidence of inherent and control risk assessments and any revisions thereof;
- evidence of the auditors' consideration of the work of internal audit and their conclusions thereon;
- analysis of transactions and balances;
- analysis of significant ratios and trends;
- a record of the nature, timing and extent of auditing procedures undertaken and the results of such procedures;
- details of procedures regarding components whose financial statements are audited by other auditors;

- copies of communications with other auditors, experts and other third parties;
- copies of correspondence with the entity, reports to directors or management and notes of discussions with the entity's directors or management concerning audit matters;
- letters of representation from the entity's directors or management;
- a summary of the significant aspects of the audit including details of the information available, the amounts involved, management's views, the conclusions reached and how these matters are resolved or treated; and
- copies of the approved financial statements and auditors' reports.

14 Working papers typically record when and by whom audit procedures are undertaken and when and by whom they are reviewed. A written record of points raised during the review of working papers need not be retained providing the working papers demonstrate evidence of the extent of the review process and are updated to record the resolution of any significant matters noted.

15 In the case of recurring audits, some working paper files may be classified as 'permanent' audit files which are updated with new information of continuing importance, as distinct from 'current' audit files which contain information relating primarily to the audit of a single period.

Confidentiality, safe custody and ownership of working papers

16 Auditors should adopt appropriate procedures for maintaining the confidentiality and safe custody of their working papers. (SAS 230.4)

17 There are no specific statutory requirements regarding the period of retention of audit working papers. Auditors exercise judgement to determine the appropriate period of retention bearing in mind the possible needs of their client, for example that audited information may need to be included in a prospectus at some future date, and their own needs, including any regulatory requirements. Prior to their destruction, auditors consider whether there is likely to be a need to refer to them again.

18 Working papers are the property of the auditors. They are not a substitute for, nor part of, the entity's accounting records.

19 Auditors comply with ethical guidance as to the confidentiality of working papers. Portions of, or extracts from, the working papers may be made available to the entity at the discretion of the auditors, provided such disclosure does not undermine the independence or the validity of the audit process. Information is generally not made available to other third parties (including parent companies or subsidiary undertakings or their auditors) without the permission of the entity.

Compliance with International Standards on Auditing

20 Compliance with this SAS ensures compliance in all material respects with International Standard on Auditing 230 'Documentation'.

Effective date

21 Auditors are required to comply with the Auditing Standards contained in this SAS in respect of audits of financial statements for periods ending on or after 23 December 1995.

Statement of Auditing Standards 240 — Quality control for audit work

(Issued March 1995)

Reproduced with the permission of the Auditing Practices Board

Statements of Auditing Standards ('SASs') are to be read in the light of 'The scope and authority of APB pronouncements'. In particular, they contain basic principles and essential procedures ('Auditing Standards'), indicated by paragraphs in bold type, with which auditors are required to comply in the conduct of any audit. SASs also include explanatory and other material which is designed to assist auditors in interpreting and applying Auditing Standards. The definitions in the Glossary of terms are to be applied in the interpretation of SASs.

Introduction

1 The purpose of this SAS is to establish standards and provide guidance on quality control over:

(a) policies and procedures of auditors regarding audit work generally; and

(b) procedures regarding the work delegated to assistants on an individual audit.

2 Quality control policies and procedures should be implemented both at the level of the audit firm and on individual audits. (SAS 240.1)

3 In this SAS the following terms have the meaning attributed below:

(a) 'audit engagement partner' means the person who assumes ultimate responsibility for the conduct of the audit and for issuing an opinion on the financial statements;

(b) 'auditors' or 'audit firm' mean the partners of a firm or a sole practitioner or a company or organisation providing audit services, as appropriate;

(c) 'personnel' means all partners and professional staff engaged in the audit firm's audit practice; and

(d) 'assistants' means personnel involved in an individual audit, including experts employed by the auditors (see SAS 520 'Using the work of an expert') other than the audit engagement partner.

Audit firm

4 Audit firms should establish and monitor quality control policies and procedures designed to ensure that all audits are conducted in accordance with the Auditing Standards contained in SASs and should communicate those policies and procedures to their personnel in a manner designed to provide reasonable assurance that the policies and procedures are understood and implemented. (SAS 240.2)

5 The nature, timing and extent of auditors' quality control policies and procedures depend on a number of factors such as the size and nature of the practice, geographic dispersion, organisation and appropriate cost/benefit considerations. Accordingly, the policies and procedures adopted by different auditors vary as does the extent of their documentation.

1 Auditors may find it helpful to refer to the ethical guidance or Audit Regulations or other regulations dealing with these matters.

6 The quality control policies to be adopted by auditors usually incorporate the following[1]:

(a) professional requirements — personnel adhere to the principles of independence, integrity, objectivity, confidentiality and professional behaviour;

(b) skills and competence — personnel have attained and maintained the technical standards and professional competence required to enable them to fulfil their responsibilities with due care;

(c) acceptance and retention of clients — prospective clients are evaluated and existing clients are reviewed on an ongoing basis. In making a decision to accept or retain a client, the auditors' independence and ability to serve the client properly and the integrity of the client's management are considered;

(d) assignment — audit work is assigned to personnel who have the degree of technical training and proficiency required in the circumstances;

(e) delegation (direction supervision and review) — sufficient direction, supervision and review of work at all levels is carried out in order to provide confidence that the work performed meets appropriate standards of quality;

(f) consultation — consultation, whenever necessary, within, or outside the audit firm occurs with those who have appropriate expertise; and

(g) monitoring — the continued adequacy and operational effectiveness of quality control policies and procedures are monitored.

Individual audits

7 For each audit, the audit engagement partner should apply quality control procedures appropriate to the particular audit which ensure compliance with Auditing Standards. (SAS 240.3)

8 Any work delegated to assistants should be directed, supervised and reviewed in a manner which provides reasonable assurance that such work is performed competently. (SAS 240.4)

9 The audit engagement partner and personnel with supervisory responsibilities consider the professional competence of assistants performing work delegated to them when deciding the extent of direction, supervision and review appropriate for each assistant.

Direction

10 Appropriate direction of assistants to whom work is delegated involves informing them of their responsibilities and the objectives of the procedures they are to perform. It also involves informing them of matters such as the nature of the entity's business and possible accounting or auditing problems which may affect the nature, timing and extent of audit procedures with which they are involved. Means of communicating audit directions, in addition to briefing meetings and informal oral communications, include audit manuals and checklists as well as the audit programme and the overall plan.

Supervision

11 Supervision is closely related to both direction and review and may involve elements of both.

12 Personnel with supervisory responsibilities perform the following functions during the audit:

(a) monitor the progress of the audit to consider whether:

(i) assistants have the necessary skills and competence to carry out their assigned tasks;

(ii) assistants understand the audit directions; and

(iii) the work is being carried out in accordance with the overall audit plan and the audit programme;

(b) become informed of and address significant accounting and auditing questions raised during the audit, by assessing their significance and modifying the overall audit plan and the audit programme as appropriate; and

(c) resolve any differences of professional judgement between personnel and consider the level of consultation that is appropriate.

Review

13 Work performed by each assistant is reviewed by personnel of appropriate experience to consider whether:

(a) the work has been performed in accordance with the audit programme;

(b) the work performed and the results obtained have been adequately documented;

(c) any significant audit matters have been resolved or are reflected in audit conclusions;

(d) the objectives of the audit procedures have been achieved; and

(e) the conclusions expressed are consistent with the results of the work performed and support the audit opinion.

14 The following are reviewed on a timely basis:

(a) the overall audit plan and the audit programme;

(b) the assessments of inherent and control risks, including the results of tests of control and the modifications, if any, made to the overall audit plan and the audit programme as a result thereof;

(c) the documentation obtained from substantive procedures and the conclusions drawn therefrom, including the results of consultations; and

(d) the financial statements, proposed audit adjustments and the proposed auditors' report.

15 The process of reviewing an audit before issuing the auditors' report may include, particularly in the case of large complex audits, requesting personnel not otherwise involved in the audit to perform certain additional procedures, for example to read the annual report or to consider specific areas of audit judgement.

Compliance with International Standards on Auditing

16 Compliance with this SAS ensures compliance in all material respects with International Standard on Auditing 220 'Quality Control for Audit Work'.

Effective date

17 Auditors are required to comply with the Auditing Standards contained in this SAS in respect of audits of financial statements for periods ending on or after 23 December 1995.

Statement of Auditing Standards

300 - Accounting and Internal Control Systems and Audit Risk Assessments

(Issued March 1995)

Statements of Auditing Standards ('SASs') are to be read in the light of 'The scope and authority of APB pronouncements'. In particular, they contain basic principles and essential procedures ('Auditing Standards'), indicated by paragraphs in bold type, with which auditors are required to comply in the conduct of any audit. SASs also include explanatory and other material which is designed to assist auditors in interpreting and applying Auditing Standards. The definitions in the Glossary of terms are to be applied in the interpretation of SASs.

Introduction

1 The purpose of this SAS is to establish standards and provide guidance on audit risk and its components: inherent risk, control risk and detection risk, and also on the auditors' approach to obtaining an understanding of the accounting and internal control *systems*. In some circumstances specific legislation and regulations require auditors to undertake procedures additional to those set out in this SAS.

2 **Auditors should:**

(a) obtain an understanding of the accounting and internal control systems sufficient to plan the audit and develop an effective audit approach; and

(b) use professional judgement to assess the components of audit risk and to design audit procedures to ensure it is reduced to an acceptably low level. (SAS 300.1)

3 'Audit risk' means the risk that auditors may give an inappropriate audit opinion on financial statements. Audit risk has three components: inherent risk, control risk and detection risk.

4 'Inherent risk' is the susceptibility of an account balance or class of transactions to material misstatement, either individually or when aggregated with misstatements in other balances or classes, irrespective of related internal controls.

5 'Control risk' is the risk that a misstatement that could occur in an account balance or class of transactions and that could be material, either individually or when aggregated with misstatements in other balances or classes, would not be prevented, or detected and corrected on a timely basis, by the accounting and internal control systems.

6 'Detection risk' is the risk that auditors' substantive procedures (tests of details of transactions and balances or analytical procedures) do not detect a misstatement that exists in an account balance or class of transactions that could be material, either individually or when aggregated with misstatements in other balances or classes.

7 'Accounting system' means the series of tasks and records of an entity by which transactions are processed as a means of maintaining financial records. Such systems

identify, assemble, analyse, calculate, classify, record, summarise and report transactions and other events.

8 'Internal control system' comprises the control environment and control procedures. It includes all the policies and procedures (internal controls) adopted by the directors and management of an entity to assist in achieving their objective of ensuring, as far as practicable, the orderly and efficient conduct of its business, including adherence to internal policies, the safeguarding of assets, the prevention and detection of fraud and error, the accuracy and completeness of the accounting records, and the timely preparation of reliable financial information. Internal controls may be incorporated within computerised accounting systems. However, the internal control system extends beyond those matters which relate directly to the accounting system.

9 'Control environment' means the overall attitude, awareness and actions of directors and management regarding internal controls and their importance in the entity. The control environment encompasses the management style, and corporate culture and values shared by all employees. It provides the background against which the various other controls are operated. However, a strong control environment does not, by itself, ensure the effectiveness of the overall internal control system. Factors reflected in the control environment include:

- the philosophy and operating style of the directors and management;
- the entity's organisational structure and methods of assigning authority and responsibility (including segregation of duties and supervisory controls); and
- the directors' methods of imposing control, including the internal audit function, the functions of the board of directors and personnel policies and procedures.

10 'Control procedures' are those policies and procedures in addition to the control environment which are established to achieve the entities specific objectives. They include in particular procedures designed to prevent or to detect and correct errors. The latter may be a particular focus of high level controls in small or owner-managed entities. Specific control procedures include:

- approval and control of documents;
- controls over computerised applications and the information technology environment,
- checking the arithmetical accuracy of the records;
- maintaining and reviewing control accounts and trial balances;
- reconciliations;
- comparing the results of cash, security and stock counts with accounting records;
- comparing internal data with external sources of information; and
- limiting direct physical access to assets and records.

11 Auditors are only concerned with those policies and procedures within the accounting and internal control systems that are relevant to the financial statement assertions. The understanding of relevant aspects of the accounting and internal control systems, together with the inherent and control risk assessments, enables auditors to:

- assess the adequacy of the accounting system as a basis for preparing the financial statements;
- identify the types of potential misstatements that could occur in the financial statements;

- consider factors that affect the risk of misstatements; and
- design appropriate audit procedures.

12 When planning their audit, auditors consider the likelihood of error in the light of inherent risk and the system of intemal control (control risk) in order to determine the extent of work (and hence the level of detection risk) required to satisfy themselves that the risk of error in the financial statements is sufficiently low.

Inherent risk

13 In developing their audit approach and detailed procedures, auditors should assess inherent risk in relation to financial statement assertions about material account balances and classes of transactions, taking account of factors relevant both to the entity as a whole and to the specific assertions. (SAS 300.2)

14 In the absence of knowledge or information to enable auditors to make an assessment of inherent risk for a specific account balance or class of transactions they assume that inherent risk is high. However, when an assessment is made and inherent risk is not considered to be high, they document the reasons for their assessment and are able to reduce the work they would otherwise carry out.

15 To assess inherent risk, auditors use their professional judgement to evaluate numerous factors, having regard to their experience of the entity from previous audits, any controls established by management to compensate for a high level of inherent risk (as described in paragraph 32 below), and their knowledge of any significant changes which have taken place. Examples of relevant factors are:

At the entity level

- the integrity of directors and management;
- management experience and knowledge and changes in management during the period, for example inexperience may affect the preparation of the financial statements of the entity;
- unusual pressures on directors or management, such as tight reporting deadlines, market expectations or other circumstances that might predispose them to misstate the financial statements, for example the industry experiencing a large number of business failures or an entity that is close to breaching borrowing covenants;
- the nature of the entity's business, for example the potential for technological obsolescence of its products and services, the complexity of its capital structure, the significance of related parties and the number of locations and geographical spread of its production facilities; and
- factors affecting the industry in which the entity operates, for example economic and competitive conditions as indicated by financial trends and ratios, regulatory requirements and changes in technology, consumer demand and accounting practices common to the industry.

At the account balance and class of transactions level

- financial statement accounts likely to be susceptible to misstatement, for example accounts which required adjustment in the previous period or which involve a high degree of estimation;
- the complexity of underlying transactions and other events which might require the use of the work of an expert;
- the degree of judgement involved in determining account balances;

- susceptibility of assets to loss or misappropriation, for example assets which are highly desirable and movable such as cash;
- the quality of the accounting systems;
- the completion of unusual and complex transactions, particularly at or near periods end; and
- transactions not subjected to ordinary processing.

Accounting system and control environment

16 In planning the audit, auditors should obtain and document an understanding of the accounting system and control environment sufficient to determine their approach. (SAS 300.3)

17 Auditors obtain an understanding of the accounting system sufficient to enable them to identify and understand:

(a) major classes of transactions in the entity's operations;

(b) how such transactions are initiated;

(c) significant accounting records, supporting documents and accounts in the financial statements; and

(d) the accounting and financial reporting process, from the initiation of significant transactions and other events to their inclusion in the financial statements.

18 An understanding of the control environment enables auditors to assess the likely effectiveness of control procedures. A strong control environment, for example one with strong budgetary controls and an effective internal audit function, increases the effectiveness of control procedures. A small entity's control environment may be strengthened by the close involvement of the directors, including their review of financial information.

19 Based on their understanding of the accounting system and control environment, auditors can make a preliminary assessment of the adequacy of the system as a basis for the preparation of the financial statements, and of the likely mix of tests of control and substantive procedures.

20 As control procedures are often incorporated within accounting systems, gathering information to obtain the understanding of the accounting system is likely to result in some understanding of specific control procedures. In any event, as the accounting system, control environment and control procedures are closely related, auditors often seek to obtain information about all the relevant aspects of the accounting and internal control systems ('the systems') as one exercise. However, in order to design and select the appropriate audit tests it may be necessary for them to undertake additional work to obtain a more detailed understanding of specific control procedures.

21 When seeking an understanding of the accounting systems and control environment sufficient to plan the audit, auditors obtain a knowledge of the design and operation of the systems. This understanding also assists the auditors' assessment of inherent risk. In order to obtain this knowledge, they often perform 'walk-through tests', that is tracing one or more transactions through the accounting system and observing the application of relevant aspects of the internal control system.

22 The nature, timing and extent of the procedures performed by auditors to obtain an understanding of the systems vary with, among other things:

- materiality considerations;
- the size and complexity of the entity;

- their assessment of inherent risk;
- the complexity of the entity's computer systems;
- the type of internal controls involved; and
- the nature of the entity's documentation of specific internal controls.

23 Usually, the auditors' understanding of the systems is obtained through previous experience with the entity updated as necessary by:

(a) enquiries of appropriate supervisory and other personnel at various organisational levels within the entity, together with reference to documentation such as procedures manuals, job descriptions and systems descriptions;

(b) inspection of relevant documents and records produced by the systems; and

(c) observation of the entity's activities and operations, including the information technology function's organisation, personnel performing control procedures and the nature of transaction processing.

Internal controls and their inherent limitations

24 Internal controls established by the directors relating to the accounting system are concerned with achieving objectives such as:

- transactions are executed in accordance with proper general or specific authorisation;
- all transactions and other events are promptly recorded at the correct amount, in the appropriate accounts and in the proper accounting period so as to permit preparation of financial statements in accordance with the applicable reporting framework (e.g. relevant legislation and applicable accounting standards);
- access to assets is permmitted only in accordance with proper authorisation; and
- recorded assets are compared with the existing assets at reasonable intervals and appropriate action is taken with regard to any differences.

25 An internal control system can only provide the directors with reasonable confidence that their objectives are reached because of inherent limitations such as:

- the usual requirement that the cost of an internal control is not disproportionate to the potential loss which may result from its absence;
- most systematic internal controls tend to be directed at routine transactions rather than non-routine transactions;
- the potential for human error due to carelessness, distraction, mistakes of judgement and the misunderstanding of instructions;
- the possibility of circumvention of internal controls through collusion with parties outside or inside the entity;
- the possibility that a person responsible for exercising an internal control could abuse that responsibility, for example by overriding an internal control; and
- the possibility that procedures may become inadequate due to changes in conditions or that compliance with procedures may deteriorate over time.

These factors indicate why auditors cannot obtain all their evidence from tests of the system of internal control.

Control risk in the small business

26 Auditors obtain an appropriate level of audit evidence to support their audit opinion regardless of the size of the entity. However, many internal controls relevant to large entities are not practical in the small business; for example, in small businesses accounting procedures may be performed by few persons who may have both operating and custodial responsibilities and, consequently, segregation of duties may be severely limited. Inadequate segregation of duties may, in some cases, be offset by other control procedures and close involvement of an owner or manager in strong supervisory controls where they have direct personal knowledge of the entity and involvement in transactions — though this in itself may introduce other risks. In circumstances where segregation of duties is limited and evidence of supervisory controls is lacking, the audit evidence necessary to support the auditors' opinion on the financial statements may have to be obtained entirely through the performance of substantive procedures and any audit work carried out in the course of preparing the financial statements. What follows is to be read with this in mind.

Control risk

27 If auditors, after obtaining an understanding of the accounting system and control environment, expect to be able to rely on their assessment of control risk to reduce the extent of their substantive procedures, they should make a preliminary assessment of control risk for material financial statement assertions, and should plan and perform tests of control to support that assessment. (SAS 300.4)

28 If, as a result of their work on the accounting system and control environment, auditors decide it is likely to be inefficient or impossible to rely on any assessment of control risk to reduce their substantive procedures, no such assessment is necessary and control risk is assumed to be high.

Preliminary assessment of control risk

29 The preliminary assessment of control risk is the process of evaluating the likely effectiveness of an entity's accounting and internal control systems in preventing and correcting material misstatements. This entails consideration of the design of the accounting and internal control systems to assess their likely effectiveness. There is, however, always some control risk because of the inherent limitations of any internal control system.

30 The more effective the entity's accounting and internal control systems are assessed to be, the lower the auditors' assessment of control risk. Where auditors obtain satisfactory audit evidence from tests of control as to the effectiveness of the accounting and internal control systems, the extent of substantive procedures may be reduced.

31 Auditors may conclude that the accounting and internal control systems are not effective, or they may decide that it is likely to be inefficient to adopt an audit approach which relies on tests of control. In these circumstances they plan the audit approach on the basis that sufficient appropriate audit evidence needs to be obtained entirely from substantive procedures and from any audit work carried out in the preparation of the financial statements.

Relationship between the assessments of inherent and control risks

32 Management often react to situations where inherent risk is high by designing accounting and internal control systems to prevent and detect misstatements and therefore, in many cases, inherent risk and control risk are highly interrelated. In such situations, the effects of inherent and control risk may be more appropriately determined by making a combined assessment.

Documentation of understanding and assessment of control risk

33 When control risk is assessed at less than high, auditors document the basis for that conclusion.

34 Different techniques may be used to document information relating to accounting and internal control systems and the assessment of control risk. Selection of a particular technique is a matter for the auditors' judgement. Common techniques, used alone or in combination, are narrative descriptions, questionnaires, checklists and flow-charts. The form and extent of this documentation is influenced by the size and complexity of the entity and the nature of the entity's accounting and internal control systems. Generally, the more complex the entity's accounting and internal control systems and the more extensive the auditors' procedures, the more extensive the documentation needs to be.

Tests of control

35 Tests of control are performed to obtain audit evidence about the effective operation of the accounting and internal control systems — that is, that properly designed controls identified in the preliminary assessment exist in fact and have operated effectively throughout the relevant period. They include tests of elements of the control environment where strengths in the control environment are used by auditors to reduce control risk assessments.

36 Some of the procedures performed to obtain the understanding of the accounting and internal control systems may not have been specifically planned as tests of control but may provide audit evidence about the effectiveness of the operation of internal controls relevant to certain assertions and, consequently, serve as tests of control. For example, in obtaining the understanding of the accounting and internal control systems pertaining to cash, auditors may obtain audit evidence about the effectiveness of the bank reconciliation process through enquiry and observation.

37 In these circumstances, when auditors conclude that procedures performed to obtain the understanding of the accounting and internal control systems also provide audit evidence about the operating effectiveness of policies and procedures relevant to a particular financial statement assertion, they may use that evidence, on its own or (if not in itself sufficient) with other appropriate audit evidence, to support a control risk assessment at less than high.

38 Tests of control may include:

- corroborative enquiries about, and observation of, internal control functions;
- inspection of documents supporting controls or events to gain audit evidence that internal controls have operated properly, for example verifying that a transaction has been authorised or a reconciliation approved;
- examination of evidence of management reviews, for example minutes of management meetings at which financial results are reviewed and corrective action decided on;
- reperformance of control procedures, for example reconciliation of bank accounts, to ensure they were correctly performed by the entity; and
- testing of the internal controls operating on specific computerised applications or over the overall information technology function, for example access or program change controls.

39 When obtaining evidence about the effective operation of internal controls, relevant factors for auditors to consider are how they were applied, the consistency with which they were applied during the period and by whom they were applied. The concept of effective operation recognises that some deviations may have occurred. Deviations from prescribed controls may be caused by such factors as changes in key personnel, significant seasonal fluctuations in volume of transactions and human error. In particular, staff changes in key internal control functions may increase control risk. If there have been such changes in the period under review, auditors may need to modify their tests of control to confirm effective operation during and after the period of change.

40 If substantially different controls are used at different times during the period, auditors consider each separately. A breakdown in internal controls for a specific portion of the period requires separate consideration of the nature, timing and extent of the audit procedures to be applied to the transactions and other events of that period.

41 Auditors may find it necessary, or may prefer, to use computer-assisted audit techniques. The use of such techniques, for example file interrogation tools or audit test data, may be appropriate when the accounting and internal control systems provide no visible evidence documenting the performance of internal controls which are programmed into a computerised accounting system.

Quality and timeliness of audit evidence

42 As described in SAS 400 'Audit evidence', certain types of audit evidence obtained by auditors are more reliable than others. Usually, auditors' observations provide more reliable audit evidence than merely making enquiries, for example they might obtain audit evidence about the proper segregation of duties by observing the individual who applies a control procedure or by making enquiries of appropriate personnel. Audit evidence obtained by some tests of control, such as observation, pertains only to the point in time at which the procedure was applied. Auditors may decide, therefore, to supplement these procedures with other tests of control capable of providing audit evidence about other periods of time before or after that point.

43 If intending to rely on tests of control performed in advance of the period end, audltors should obtain sufficient appropriate audit evidence as to the nature and extent of any changes in design or operation of the entity's accounting and internal control systems within the accounting period since such procedures were performed. (SAS 300.5)

44 Auditors may decide to perform some tests of control at an interim audit visit in advance of the period end. However, they cannot rely on the results of such tests without considering the need to obtain further evidence relating to the remainder of the period. Factors to be considered include:

- the results of the interim tests;
- the length of the remaining period;
- whether any changes have occurred in the accounting and internal control systems during the remaining period;
- the nature and amount of the transactions and other events and the balances involved;
- the control environment; and
- the nature, timing and extent of the substantive procedures which they plan to undertake.

45 Likewise, in determining the appropriate audit evidence to support a conclusion about control risk, auditors may consider the audit evidence obtained in previous audits having regard to the guidance in paragraph 44 above. In a continuing engagement, auditors have knowledge of the accounting and internal control systems through work carried out previously but update this information and consider the need to obtain further audit evidence. The longer the time elapsed since part of the accounting and internal control system was subject to tests of control, the less persuasive are the results of that work in providing audit evidence to support an assessment of control risk that is less than high.

Final assessment of control risk

46 Having undertaken tests of control, auditors should evaluate whether the preliminary assessment of control risk is supported. (SAS 300.6)

47 Whenever deviations are detected, auditors make specific enquiries in order to consider their implications. It may be that, in the circumstances, they can obtain sufficient appropriate audit evidence to conclude that, despite those deviations, their preliminary assessment is supported. On the other hand, if they conclude that the deviation rate is such that the preliminary assessment is not supported, they amend their assessment of control risk unless audit evidence obtained from other tests of control supports that assessment.

48 If the evaluation of deviations results in auditors concluding that the assessed level of control risk needs to be revised, they modify the nature, timing and extent of their planned substantive procedures.

Detection risk

49 Auditors should consider the assessed levels of inherent and control risk in determining the nature, timing and extent of substantlve procedures required to reduce audit risk to an acceptable level. (SAS 300.7)

50 The level of detection risk relates to the auditors' substantive procedures (tests of details of transactions and balances and analytical procedures). It is primarily the consequence of the fact that auditors do not, and cannot, examine all available evidence: auditors seek reasonable confidence and so do not examine all items, nor all evidence concerning any item that is examined. Moreover, as audit evidence is generally persuasive rather than conclusive, some detection risk is usually present even if they examine all evidence available of an account balance or an entire class of transactions.

51 To form their audit opinion, auditors obtain sufficient appropriate audit evidence as to whether the financial statements are free of material misstatement. Internal controls, even if fairly simple and unsophisticated, may contribute to this evidence. The auditors' control risk assessment, together with the inherent risk assessment, influences the nature, timing and extent of substantive procedures to be performed to reduce detection risk, and therefore audit risk, to an acceptably low level.

52 While tests of control and substantive procedures are distinguishable as to their purpose, the results of either type of procedure may contribute to the purpose of the other. Misstatements discovered in conducting substantive procedures may cause auditors to modify the previous assessment of control risk.

53 Regardless of the assessed levels of inherent and control risks, auditors should perform some substantive procedures for financial statement assertions of material account balances and transaction classes. (SAS 300.8)

54 The assessed levels of inherent and control risks cannot be sufficiently low to eliminate the need for auditors to perform any substantive procedures for material account balances and transaction classes. However, these substantive procedures may comprise only analytical procedures where such procedures provide sufficient appropriate evidence.

55 The auditors' assessment of the components of audit risk may change during the course of an audit, for example information may come to their attention when performing substantive procedures that differs significantly from the information on which they originally assessed inherent and control risks. In such cases, they modify the planned substantive procedures based on a revision of the assessed levels of inherent and control risks for the relevant financial statement assertions.

56 When both inherent and control risks are assessed as high, auditors consider whether substantive procedures can provide sufficient appropriate audit evidence to reduce detection risk, and therefore audit risk, to an acceptably low level. For example, they may not be able to obtain sufficient evidence about the completeness of income in the absence of some internal controls. When auditors determine that detection risk regarding a material financial statement assertion cannot be reduced to an acceptably low level, they consider the implications for their report.

Communication of weaknesses

57 As a result of obtaining an understanding of the accounting and internal control systems and of performing audit procedures, auditors may become aware of weaknesses in the systems. Guidance on the communication of such weaknesses to directors or management is included in SAS 610 'Reports to directors or management'.

Compliance with International Standards on Auditing

58 International Standard on Auditing 400 'Risk Assessments and Internal Control' includes the following requirements which are not reflected in Auditing Standards in this SAS:

(a) 'The auditor should obtain an understanding of the accounting system sufficient to identify and understand:
  - (a) major classes of transactions in the entity's operations;
  - (b) how such transactions are initiated;
  - (c) significant accounting records, supporting documents and accounts in the financial statements; and
  - (d) the accounting and financial reporting process, from the initiation of significant transactions and other events to their inclusion in the financial statements.'

(b) 'The auditor should obtain an understanding of the control environment sufficient to assess directors' and management's attitudes, awareness and actions regarding internal controls and their importance in the entity.'

(c) 'The auditor should obtain an understanding of the control procedures sufficient to develop the audit plan.'

As the SAS contains an Auditing Standard requiring auditors to obtain and document an understanding of the accounting system and control environment sufficient to determine their audit approach, it is considered more appropriate to include the requirements in (a), (b) and (c) above as guidance rather than as Auditing Standards.

(d) 'The preliminary assessment of control risk for a financial statement assertion should be high unless the auditor:
  - (a) is able to identify internal controls relevant to the assertion which are likely to prevent or detect and correct a material misstatement; and
  - (b) plans to perform tests of control to support the assessment.'

This requirement is inherent in SAS 300.4 in paragraph 27 above. It is therefore considered sufficient for the corresponding idea to be included as guidance only in paragraph 31 above. This states that, when auditors conclude that they do not wish to rely on tests of control, they plan the audit approach on the basis that sufficient appropriate audit evidence needs to be obtained entirely from substantive procedures and from any audit work carried out in the preparation of the financial statements.

(e) 'The auditor should document in the audit working papers:

(a) the understanding obtained of the entity's accounting and internal control systems; and

(b) the assessment of control risk.'

This requirement is reflected generally in SAS 200 'Planning' and SAS 230 'Working papers'.

(f) 'The higher the assessment of inherent and control risk, the more evidence the auditor should obtain from the performance of substantive procedures.'

This requirement is reflected in SAS 400 'Audit evidence'.

(g) 'When the auditor determines that detection risk regarding a financial statement assertion for a material account balance or class of transactions cannot be reduced to an acceptably low level, the auditor should express a qualified opinion or disclaimer of opinion.'

This requirement is reflected in SAS 600 'Auditors' reports on financial statements'.

(h) 'The auditor should make management aware, on a timely basis and at an appropriate level of responsibility, of material weaknesses in the design or operation of the accounting and intemal control systems, which have come to the auditors' attention.'

This requirement is reflected generally in Auditing Standards in SAS 610 'Reports to directors or management'.

59 With the explanations noted in paragraph 58, compliance with this SAS ensures compliance in all material respects with International Standard on Auditing 400 'Risk Assessments and Internal Control'.

Effective date

60 Auditors are required to comply with the Auditing Standards contained in this SAS in respect of audits of financial statements for periods ending on or after 23 December 1995.

Statement of Auditing Standards 400 — Audit evidence

(Issued March 1995)

Reproduced with the permission of the Auditing Practices Board

Statements of Auditing Standards ('SASs') are to be read in the light of 'The scope and authority of APB pronouncements'. In particular, they contain basic principles and essential procedures ('Auditing Standards'), indicated by paragraphs in bold type, with which auditors are required to comply in the conduct of any audit. SASs also include explanatory and other material which is designed to assist auditors in interpreting and applying Auditing Standards. The definitions in the Glossary of terms are to be applied in the interpretation of SASs.

Introduction

1 The purpose of this SAS is to establish standards and provide guidance on the quantity and quality (or reliability) of evidence to be obtained by auditors, and the procedures for obtaining that evidence.

2 Auditors should obtain sufficient appropriate audit evidence to be able to draw reasonable conclusions on which to base the audit opinion. (SAS 400.1)

3 Audit evidence is obtained in a number of ways, including from an appropriate mix of tests of control and substantive procedures. In some circumstances, evidence may be obtained entirely from substantive procedures and enquiries made to ascertain the adequacy of the accounting system as a basis for the preparation of the financial statements.

Sufficient appropriate audit evidence

4 Sufficiency and appropriateness are interrelated and apply to audit evidence obtained from both tests of control and substantive procedures. Sufficiency is the measure of the quantity of audit evidence; appropriateness is the measure of the quality or reliability of audit evidence and its relevance to a particular assertion. Usually, audit evidence is persuasive rather than conclusive, and auditors therefore often seek audit evidence from different sources or of a different nature to support the same assertion.

5 Auditors seek to provide reasonable, not absolute, assurance that the financial statements are free from material misstatement. In forming their audit opinion, therefore, auditors do not normally examine all of the information available. Appropriate conclusions can be reached about a financial statement assertion using a variety of means of obtaining evidence, including sampling.

6 The auditors' judgement as to what is sufficient appropriate audit evidence is influenced by such factors as:

- the assessment of the nature and degree of risk of misstatement at both the financial statement level and the account balance or class of transactions level;
- the nature of the accounting and internal control systems, including the control environment;
- the materiality of the item being examined;
- the experience gained during previous audits and the auditors' knowledge of the

business and industry;

- the findings from audit procedures, and from any audit work carried out in the course of preparing financial statements, including indications of fraud or error; and
- the source and reliability of information available.

7 If unable to obtain sufficient appropriate audit evidence, auditors consider the implications for their report.

Tests of control

8 In seeking to obtain audit evidence from tests of control, auditors should consider the sufficiency and appropriateness of the audit evidence to support the assessed level of control risk. (SAS 400.2)

9 The aspects of the relevant parts of accounting and internal control systems about which auditors seek to obtain audit evidence are:

(a) design: the accounting and internal control systems are capable of preventing or detecting material misstatements; and

(b) operation: the systems exist and have operated effectively throughout the relevant period.

Substantive procedures

10 In seeking to obtain audit evidence from substantive procedures, auditors should consider the extent to which that evidence together with any evidence from tests of controls supports the relevant financial statement assertions. (SAS 400.3)

11 Financial statement assertions are the representations of the directors that are embodied in the financial statements. By approving the financial statements, the directors are making representations about the information therein. These representations or assertions may be described in general terms in a number of ways, one of which is as follows:

(a) existence: an asset or a liability exists at a given date;

(b) rights and obligations: an asset or a liability pertains to the entity at a given date;

(c) occurrence: a transaction or event took place which pertains to the entity during the relevant period;

(d) completeness: there are no unrecorded assets, liabilities, transactions or events, or undisclosed items;

(e) valuation: an asset or liability is recorded at an appropriate carrying value;

(f) measurement: a transaction or event is recorded at the proper amount and revenue or expense is allocated to the proper period; and

(g) presentation and disclosure: an item is disclosed, classified and described in accordance with the applicable reporting framework (for example relevant legislation and applicable accounting standards).

12 Audit evidence is usually obtained to support each financial statement assertion. Audit evidence regarding one assertion (for example, existence of stock) does not compensate for failure to obtain audit evidence regarding another (for example, its valuation). Tests may, however, provide audit evidence about more than one assertion (for example, testing subsequent receipts from debtors may provide some audit evidence regarding both their existence and valuation).

13 Programmes of detailed audit procedures are sometimes drawn up by auditors by reference to 'audit objectives'. Such objectives may provide a satisfactory way of enabling auditors to satisfy themselves that the planned work will result in appropriate evidence being obtained, provided that the objectives cover all the relevant financial statement assertions made by the directors.

14 The nature, timing and extent of substantive procedures depends, amongst other factors, on the auditors' assessments of the control environment and accounting systems generally and of the inherent and control risks relating to each assertion, as well as on any evidence obtained from audit work performed during the preparation of the financial statements. In particular, where tests of control provide satisfactory evidence as to the effectiveness of accounting and internal control systems, the extent of relevant substantive procedures may be reduced, but not entirely eliminated.

15 Substantive procedures may be incorporated within other procedures. For example, tests of control may be designed as dual purpose tests to provide evidence of a substantive nature, and such evidence may also be obtained as part of the work carried out to make preliminary assessments of risks of error.

16 The reliability of audit evidence is influenced by its source: internal or external, and by its nature: visual, documentary or oral. While the reliability of audit evidence is dependant on individual circumstance, the following generalisations may help in assessing that reliability:

- audit evidence from external sources (for example confirmation received from a third party) is more reliable than that obtained from the entity's records;
- audit evidence obtained from the entity's records is more reliable when the related accounting and internal control system operates effectively;
- evidence obtained directly by auditors is more reliable than that obtained by or from the entity;
- evidence in the form of documents and written representations is more reliable than oral representations; and
- original documents are more reliable than photocopies, telexes or facsimiles.

17 Audit evidence is more persuasive when items of evidence from different sources or of a different nature are consistent. When audit evidence from one source is inconsistent with that from another, auditors determine what additional procedures are necessary to resolve the inconsistency.

18 Auditors consider the relationship between the cost of obtaining audit evidence and the usefulness of the information obtained. However, the existence of difficulty or experience is not in itself a valid basis for omitting a necessary procedure.

Procedures for obtaining audit evidence

19 Auditors obtain audit evidence by one or more of the following procedures; inspection, observation, enquiry and confirmation, computation and analytical procedures. The choice of such procedures is dependent, in part, upon the periods of time during which the audit evidence sought is available and the form in which the accounting records are maintained.

Inspection

20 Inspection consists of examining records, documents or tangible assets. Inspection of records and documents provides audit evidence of varying degrees of reliability depending on their nature and source and the effectiveness of internal controls over their processing.

Three major categories of documentary audit evidence, listed in descending degree of reliability as audit evidence, are evidence:

(a) created and provided to auditors by third parties;

(b) created by third parties and held by the entity; and

(c) created and held by the entity.

Inspection of tangible assets provides reliable audit evidence about their existence but not necessarily as to their ownership or value.

Observation

21 Observation consists of looking at a process or procedure being performed by others, for example the observation by auditors of the counting of stock by the entity's staff or the performance of internal control procedures, in particular those that leave no audit trail.

Enquiry and confirmation

22 Enquiry consists of seeking information of knowledgeable persons inside or outside the entity. Enquiries may range from formal written enquiries addressed to third parties to informal oral enquiries addressed to persons inside the entity. Responses to enquiries may provide auditors with information not previously possessed or with corroborative audit evidence.

23 Confirmation consists of the response to an enquiry to corroborate information contained in the accounting records. For example, auditors may seek direct confirmation of debts by communication with debtors.

Computation

24 Computation consists of checking the arithmetical accuracy of source documents and accounting records or performing independent calculations.

Analytical procedures

25 Analytical procedures consist of the analysis of relationships between items of financial data, or between items of financial and non-financial data, deriving from the same period, or between comparable financial information deriving from different periods or different entities, to identify consistencies and predicted patterns or significant fluctuations and unexpected relationships, and the results of investigations thereof.

Compliance with International Standards on Auditing

26 Compliance with this SAS ensures compliance in all material respects with International Standard on Auditing 500 'Audit Evidence'.

Effective date

27 Auditors are required to comply with the Auditing Standards contained in this SAS in respect of audits of financial statements for periods ending on or after 23 December 1995.

Statement of Auditing Standards 410 — Analytical Procedures

(Issued March 1995)

Reproduced with the permission of the Auditing Practices Board

Statements of Auditing Standards ('SASs') are to be read in the light of 'The scope and authority of APB pronouncements'. In particular, they contain basic principles and essential procedures ('Auditing Standards'), indicated by paragraphs in bold type, with which auditors are required to comply in the conduct of any audit. SASs also include explanatory and other material which is designed to assist auditors in interpreting and applying Auditing Standards. The definitions in the Glossary of terms are to be applied in the interpretation of SASs.

Introduction

1 The purpose of this SAS is to establish standards and provide guidance on the applications of analytical procedures during and audit.

2 Auditors should apply analytical procedures at the planning and overall review stages of the audit. (SAS 410.1)

3 'Analytical procedures' means the analysis of relationships:

(a) between items of financial data, or between items of financial and non-financial data, deriving from the same period; or

(b) between comparable financial information deriving from different periods or different entities,

to identify consistencies and predicted patterns or significant fluctuations and unexpected relationships, and the results of investigations thereof.

4 The analytical procedures required by paragraph 2 above are designed primarily to assist in planning the audit and as part of the evaluation of the financial statements. Analytical procedures may also be performed as substantive procedures designed to obtain audit evidence directly.

Nature and purpose of analytical procedures

5 Analytical procedures include the consideration of comparisons of the entities financial information with, for example:

- comparable information for prior periods;
- anticipated results of the entity, from budgets or forecasts;
- predictive estimates prepared by the auditors, such as an estimation of the depreciation charge for the year; and
- similar industry information, such as a comparison of the entity's ratio of sales to trade debtors with industry averages, or with the ratios relating to other entities of comparable size in the same industry.

6 Analytical procedures also include consideration of relationships:

- between elements of financial information that are expected to conform to a predicted pattern based on the entity's experience, such as the relationship of gross profit to sales; and

- between financial information and relevant non-financial information, such as the relationship of payroll costs to number of employees.

7 Various methods may be used in performing the above procedures. These range from simple comparisons to complex analysis using advanced statistical techniques. Analytical procedures may be applied to consolidated financial statements, financial statements of components (such as subsidiary undertakings, divisions or branches) and individual element of financial information. The auditors choice of procedures, methods and level of application is a matter of professional judgement.

8 Analytical procedures are used by auditors:

(a) to assist in planning the nature, timing and extent of other audit procedures;

(b) as substantive procedures when their use can be more effective or efficient than other procedures in reducing detection risk for specific financial statement assertions; and

(c) as part of the overall review of the financial statements when completing the audit.

Analytical procedures in planning the audit

9 Auditors should apply analytical procedures at the planning stage to assist in understanding the entity's business, in identifying areas of potential audit risk and in planning the nature, timing and extent of other audit procedures. (SAS 410.2)

10 Analytical procedures at this stage are usually based on interim financial information, budgets and management accounts. However, for those entities with less formal means of controlling and monitoring performance, it may be possible to extract relevant financial information from the accounting system (perhaps when preparing the draft financial statements), VAT returns and bank statements. Discussions with management, focused on identifying significant changes in the business since the prior financial period, may also be useful.

11 Application of analytical procedures may indicate aspects of the entity's business of which the auditors were previously unaware and assist in determining the nature, timing and extent of other audit procedures.

Analytical procedures as substantive procedures

12 The decision about whether to use analytical procedures as substantive procedures and the nature, timing and extent of their use is based on the auditors judgement about the expected effectiveness and efficiency of the available procedures in reducing detection risk for specific financial statements assertions. Auditors usually enquire of management as to the availability and reliability of information needed to apply analytical procedures and the results of any such procedures performed by the entity. It may be efficient to use analytical data prepared by the entity, provided the auditors are satisfied that such data is properly prepared.

13 When intending to apply analytical procedures as substantive procedures, auditors consider a number of factors such as:

- the plausibility and predictability of the relationships identified for comparison and evaluation. For example, there is a strong relationship between certain selling expenses and turnover in businesses where the sales force is paid by commission;
- the objectives of the analytical procedures and the extent to which their results are reliable;

- the degree to which information can be disaggregated, for example analytical procedures may be more effective when applied to financial information on individual sections of an operation or to financial statements of components of a diversified entity, than when applied to financial information relating to the entity as a whole;
- the availability of information, both financial (such as budgets or forecasts) and non-financial (such as the number of units produced or sold);
- the relevance of the information available, for example whether budgets are established as results to be expected rather than as goals to be achieved;
- the comparability of the information available, for example broad industry data may need to be supplemented to be comparable with that of an entity that produces and sells specialized products; and
- the knowledge gained during previous audits, together with the auditors' understanding of the effectiveness of the accounting and internal control systems and the types of problems that in prior periods have given rise to accounting adjustments.

14 The reliability of the information used in analytical procedures is likely to be enhanced if it comes from sources independent of, rather than internal to, the entity. If the information is produced internally, its reliability is enhanced if it is produced independently of the accounting system or there are adequate controls over its preparation. The necessity for evidence on the reliability of such information depends on the results of other audit procedures and on the importance of the results of analytical procedures as a basis for the auditors' opinion.

15 The extent of reliance that auditors place on the results of analytical procedures when used as substantive procedures may also depend on the following factors:

(a) other audit procedures directed towards the same financial statement assertions. For example, other procedures auditors undertake in reviewing the collectability of debtors, such as the review of subsequent cash receipts, may confirm or dispel questions arising from the application of analytical procedures to an edged profile of customers' accounts;

(b) the accuracy with which the expected results of analytical procedures can be predicted. For example, auditors normally expect greater consistency in comparing the relationship of gross profit to sales from one period to another than in comparing discretionary expenses, such as research or advertising; and

(c) the frequency with which a relationship is observed, for example a pattern repeated monthly as opposed to annually.

16 The application of analytical procedures is based on the expectation that relationships between data exist and continue in the absence of known conditions to the contrary. The presence of these relationships provides audit evidence as to the financial statement assertions relating to the data produced by the accounting system. However, reliance on the results of analytical procedures depends on the auditors' assessment of the risk that the analytical procedures may identify relationships as expected whereas, in fact, a material misstatement exists.

Analytical procedures as part of the overall review when completing the audit

17 When completing the audit, auditors should apply analytical procedures in forming an overall conclusion as to whether the financial statements as a whole are

consistent with their knowledge of the entity's business. (SAS 410.3)

18 The conclusions drawn from the results of such procedures are intended to corroborate conclusions formed during the audit regarding individual components or elements of the financial statements and to assist in arriving at the overall conclusion as to whether the financial statements as a whole are consistent with the auditors' knowledge of the entity's business. However, they may also identify areas requiring further procedures.

Investigating significant fluctuations or unexpected relationships

19 When significant fluctuations or unexpected relationships are identified that are inconsistent with other relevant information or that deviate from predicted patterns, auditors should investigate and obtain adequate explanations and appropriate corroborative evidence. (SAS 410.4)

20 The investigation of significant fluctuations and unexpected relationships normally begins with enquiries of management, followed by corroboration of management's responses:

(a) by comparing them with the auditors knowledge of the entity's business and with other evidence obtained during the course of the audit; or

(b) if the analytical procedures are being carried out as substantive procedures, by undertaking additional audit procedures where appropriate to confirm the explanations received.

21 If management is unable to provide an explanation or if the explanation is not considered adequate, auditors determine the audit procedures to be undertaken to obtain an explanation for the fluctuation or relationship noted.

Compliance with International Standards on Auditing

22 Compliance with this SAS ensures compliance in all material respects with International Standard on Auditing 520 'Analytical Procedures'.

Effective date

23 Auditors are required to comply with the Auditing Standards contained in this SAS in respect of audits of financial statements for periods ending on or after 23 December 1995.

Statement of Auditing Standards 420 — Audit of Accounting Estimates

(Issued March 1995)

Reproduced with the permission of the Auditing Practices Board

Statements of Auditing Standards ('SASs') are to be read in the light of 'The scope and authority of APB pronouncements'. In particular, they contain basic principles and essential procedures ('Auditing Standards'), indicated by paragraphs in bold type, with which auditors are required to comply in the conduct of any audit. SASs also include explanatory and other material which is designed to assist auditors in interpreting and applying Auditing Standards. The definitions in the Glossary of terms are to be applied in the interpretation of SASs.

Introduction

1 The purpose of this SAS is to establish standards and provide guidance on the audit of accounting estimates contained in financial statements. This SAS is not intended to be applicable to the examination of prospective financial information, though many of the procedures outlined herein may be suitable for that purpose.

2 Auditors should obtain sufficient appropriate audit evidence regarding accounting estimates. (SAS 420.1)

3 'Accounting estimate' means an approximation of the amount of an item in the absence of a precise means of measurement. Examples are:

- allowances to reduce stocks and debtors to their estimated realisable value;
- depreciation provisions;
- accrued revenue;
- provision for deferred taxation;
- provision for a loss from a lawsuit;
- profits or losses on construction contracts in progress; and
- provision to meet warranty claims.

4 Directors and management are responsible for making accounting estimates included in financial statements. These estimates are often made in conditions of uncertainty regarding the outcome of events that have occurred or are likely to occur and involve the use of judgement. As a result, audit evidence obtained is generally less conclusive when accounting estimates are involved. Consequently, in assessing the sufficiency and appropriateness of audit evidence on which to base the audit opinion, auditors are more likely to need to exercise judgement in their consideration of accounting estimates than in other areas of the audit.

The nature of accounting estimates

5 The determination of a complex accounting estimate may involve a high degree of special knowledge and judgement. For example, estimating a provision for slow-moving or surplus stocks may involve considerable analyses of current data and a forecast of future sales.

6 Accounting estimates may be determined as part of the routine accounting system operating on a continuing basis, or may be non-routine, operating only at period end. In many cases, accounting estimates are made by using a formula based on experience, such as the use of standard rates for depreciating each category of fixed assets or a standard percentage of sales revenue for computing a warranty provision. In such cases, the formula is reviewed regularly by management or the directors, for example by reassessing the remaining useful lives of assets or by comparing actual results with the estimate and adjusting the formula when necessary.

7 If the uncertainty associated with an item, or the lack of objective data, makes it incapable of reasonable estimation, auditors consider the implications for their report.

Audit procedures

8 Auditors should obtain sufficient appropriate audit evidence as to whether an accounting estimate is reasonable in the circumstances and, when required, is appropriately disclosed. (SAS 420.2)

9 The evidence available to support an accounting estimate is often more difficult to obtain and less conclusive than evidence available to support other items in the financial statements.

10 An understanding of the procedures and methods, including the accounting and internal control systems, used by management and directors in making accounting estimates is often important in order for auditors to plan the nature, timing and extent of their procedures.

11 Auditors should adopt one or a combination of the following approaches in the audit of an accounting estimate:

(a) review and test the process used by management or the directors to develop the estimate;

(b) use an independent estimate for comparison with that prepared by management or the directors; or

(c) review subsequent events. (SAS 420.3)

Review and testing the process used by management or directors

12 The steps normally involved in the review and testing of the process used by management or the directors are:

(a) evaluation of the data and consideration of the assumptions on which the estimate is based;

(b) testing of the calculations involved in the estimate;

(c) comparison, where possible, of estimates made for prior periods with actual results of those periods; and

(d) consideration of management's or the directors' review and approval procedures.

Use of an independent estimate

13 Auditors may make or obtain an independent estimate and compare it with the accounting estimate prepared by management or the directors. When using an independent estimate auditors generally evaluate the data, consider the assumptions and test the calculation procedures used in its development. It may also be appropriate to compare independent estimates made for prior periods with actual results of those periods.

Review of subsequent events

14 Transactions and events which occur after period end may provide audit evidence regarding an accounting estimate made by management or the directors. The auditors' review of such transactions and events may reduce, or even remove, the need for them to review and test the process used to develop the accounting estimate or to use an independent estimate in assessing the reasonableness of the accounting estimate.

Evaluation of results of audit procedures

15 Auditors should make s final assessment of the reasonableness of the accounting estimate based on their knowledge of the business and whether the estimate is consistent with other audit evidence obtained during the audit. (SAS 420.4)

16 Auditors consider whether there are any significant subsequent transactions or events which affect the data and the assumptions used in determining the accounting estimate.

17 As a result of the uncertainties inherent in accounting estimates, evaluating differences can be more difficult than in other areas of the audit. When there is a difference between their estimate of the amount best supported by the available audit evidence and the estimated amount included in the financial statements, the auditors determine whether such a difference requires adjustment. If the difference is reasonable, for example because the amount in the financial statements falls within a range of acceptable results, it may not require adjustment.

18 Auditors consider whether individual differences which appear reasonable are biased in one direction so that, on a cumulative basis, they have a material effect on the financial statements. In such circumstances, they assess the reasonableness of the accounting estimates taken as a whole.

19 If auditors believe the difference is unreasonable, management or the directors are requested to revise the estimate. If they refuse to revise the estimate, the difference is considered a misstatement and is considered with all other misstatements in assessing whether the effect on the financial statements is material.

Compliance with International Standards on Auditing

20 Compliance with this SAS ensures compliance in all material respects with International Standard on Auditing 540 'Audit of Accounting Estimates'.

Effective date

21 Auditors are required to comply with the Auditing Standards contained in this SAS in respect of audits of financial statements for periods ending on or after 23 December 1995.

Statement of Auditing Standards 430 — Audit Sampling

(Issued March 1995)

Reproduced with the permission of the Auditing Practices Board

Statements of Auditing Standards ('SASs') are to be read in the light of 'The scope and authority of APB pronouncements'. In particular, they contain basic principles and essential procedures ('Auditing Standards'), indicated by paragraphs in bold type, with which auditors are required to comply in the conduct of any audit. SASs also include explanatory and other material which is designed to assist auditors in interpreting and applying Auditing Standards. The definitions in the Glossary of terms are to be applied in the interpretation of SASs.

Introduction

1 The purpose of this SAS is to set standards and provide guidance on the design and selection of an audit sample and the evaluation of the sample results. This SAS applies equally to both statistical and non-statistical sampling methods. It applies to any audit using sampling whether related to financial statements or not. Nothing contained in this statement is intended to preclude non-statistically based samples where there are reasonable grounds for believing that the results may be relied on for the purpose of the test.

2 When using either statistical or non-statistical sampling methods, auditors should design and select an audit sample, perform audit procedures thereon and evaluate sample results so as to obtain appropriate audlt evidence. (SAS 430.1)

3 In forming their audit opinion, auditors do not normally examine all of the information available. It is generally impractical to do so and valid conclusions can be reached using audit sampling.

4 'Audit sampling' means the application of audit procedures to less than 100% of the items within an account balance or class of transactions to enable auditors to obtain and evaluate audit evidence about some characteristic of the items selected in order to form or assist in forming a conclusion concerning the population which makes up the account balance or class of transactions.

5 It is important to recognise that certain testing procedures do not come within the definition of sampling. Tests performed on 100% of the items within a population do not involve sampling. Likewise applying audit procedures to all items within a population which have a particular characteristic (for example all items over a certain amount) does not qualify as audit sampling with respect to the portion of the population examined, nor with regard to the population as a whole, since the items were not selected from the total population on a basis that was expected to be representative.

6 Statistically based sampling involves the use of techniques from which mathematically constructed conclusions about the population can be drawn. Auditors draw a judgemental opinion about the population from non-statistical methods.

Design of the sample

7 When designing the size and structure of an audit sample, auditors should consider the specific audit objectives, the nature of the population from which they wish to sample, and the sampling and selection methods. (SAS 430.2)

Audit objectives

8 Auditors first consider the specific audit objectives to be achieved and the audit procedures which are most likely to achieve those objectives. In addition, when audit sampling is appropriate, consideration of the nature of the audit evidence sought and possible error conditions or other characteristics relating to that evidence assists auditors in defining what constitutes an error and what population to use for sampling. For example, when performing tests of control over an entity's purchasing procedures, auditors may be concerned with matters such as whether an invoice was clerically checked and properly approved. On the other hand, when performing substantive procedures on invoices processed during the period, auditors are concerned with matters such as the proper reflection of the amounts payable and of the monetary amounts of such invoices in the financial statements.

Population

9 The population is the entire set of data from which auditors wish to sample in order to reach a conclusion. Therefore the population from which the sample is drawn has to be appropriate and complete for the specific audit objective. For example, if the auditors' objective is to test for overstatement of debtors, the population may be defined as the debtors listing. On the other hand, when testing for understatement of creditors, the population is not the creditors listing but rather subsequent disbursements, unpaid invoices, suppliers' statements, unmatched goods received notes or other populations that can provide evidence of understatement of creditors.

10 The individual items that make up the population may be described as sampling units. The population can be divided into sampling units in a variety of ways. For example, if the auditors' objective is to test the validity of debtors, the sampling unit may be defined as customer balances or individual customer invoices. In monetary unit sampling each £1 of, for example, a debtors balance listing is the sampling unit. Auditors define the sampling unit in order to obtain an efficient and effective sample to achieve the particular audit objectives.

11 To assist in the efficient and effective design of the sample, stratification may be appropriate. Stratification is the process of dividing a population into sub-populations each of which is a group of sampling units, which have similar characteristics (often monetary value). The strata are explicitly defined so that each sampling unit can belong to only one stratum. This process can be used to reduce the variability of the items within each stratum. Stratification therefore enables auditors to direct audit effort towards the items which, for example, contain the greatest potential monetary error. For example, they may direct attention to larger value items for debtors to detect material overstatement errors.

Sample size

12 When determining sample sizes, auditors should consider sampling risk, the amount of error that would be acceptable and the extent to which they expect to find errors. (SAS 430.3)

13 Examples of some factors affecting sample size are contained in the Appendix.

Sampling risk

14 Sampling risk arises from the possibility that the auditors' conclusion based on a sample, may be different from the conclusion that would be reached if the entire population were subjected to the same audit procedure.[1]

15 Auditors are faced with sampling risk in both tests of control and substantive procedures as follows:

(a) tests of control

(i) the risk of placing a higher than necessary assessment on control risk, because the error in the sample is greater than the error in the total population; or

(ii) the risk of placing a lower than required assessment on control risk, because the error in the sample is less than the error in the population as a whole.

(b) substantive tests

(i) the risk of concluding that a recorded account balance or class of transactions is materially misstated when it is not, because the error in the sample is greater than the error in the population as a whole; or

(ii) the risk of concluding that a recorded account balance or class of transactions is acceptable when it is materially misstated, because the error in the sample is less than the error in the population as a whole.

16 Sample size is affected by the degree of sampling risk that auditors are willing to accept from the results of the sample, which depends upon the importance of the results of the audit procedure involving sampling to the auditors' conclusions. The greater their reliance on the results, the lower the sampling risk auditors are willing to accept and the larger the sample size needs to be. Auditors consider sample size in the context of the overall risk assessment (see SAS 300 'Accounting and internal control systems and audit risk assessments').

Tolerable error

17 Tolerable error is the maximum error in the population that auditors are willing to accept and still conclude that the audit objective has been achieved. Tolerable error is considered during the planning stage and, for substantive procedures, is related to the auditors' judgement about materiality. The smaller the tolerable error, the larger is the sample size as a proportion of the population.

18 In tests of control, the tolerable error is the maximum rate of deviation from a prescribed control procedure that auditors are willing to accept in the population and still conclude that the preliminary assessment of control risk is valid. In substantive procedures, the tolerable error is the maximum monetary error in an account balance or class of transactions that auditors are willing to accept so that, when the results of all audit procedures are considered, they are able to conclude, with reasonable assurance, that the financial statements are not materially misstated.

1 Sampling risk can be contrasted with non-sampling risk which arises when auditors use any audit procedures. Non-sampling risk arises because, for example, most audit evidence is persuasive rather than conclusive, or auditors might use inappropriate procedures or might misinterpret evidence and thus fail to recognise an error. Auditors attempt to reduce non-sampling risk to a negligible level by appropriate planning, direction, supervision and review.

Expected error

19 If auditors expect error to be present in the population, a larger sample than when no error is expected generally has to be examined to conclude that the actual error in the population is not greater than the planned tolerable error. The size and frequency of errors is important in assessing the sample size. Larger sample sizes arise, for the same overall error, if there are a few large errors compared to where there are many small ones. Smaller sample sizes result when the population is expected to be error free. If the expected error rate is high then sampling may not be appropriate. In determining the expected error in a population, auditors consider such matters as the size and frequency of errors identified in previous audits, changes in the entity's procedures and evidence available from other procedures.

Selection of the sample

20 Auditors should select sample items in such a way that the sample can expected to be representative of the population in respect of the characteristics being tested. (SAS430.4)

21 For a sample to be representative of the population, all items in the population are required to have an equal or known probability of being selected.

22 While there are a number of selection methods, three methods commonly used are:

- random selection, which ensures that all items in the population have an equal chance of selection, for example by use of random number tables;
- systematic selection, which involves selecting items using a constant interval between selections, the first interval having a random start. When using systematic selection, auditors ensure that the population is not structured in such a manner that the sampling interval corresponds with a particular pattern in the population; and
- haphazard selection, which may be an acceptable alternative to random selection provided auditors are satisfied that the sample is representative of the entire population. This method requires care to guard against making a selection which is biased, for example towards items which are easily located, as they may not be representative.

Evaluation of sample results

23 Having carried out, on each sample item, those audit procedures which are appropriate to the particular audit objective, auditors should:

(a) analyse any errors detected in the sample; and

(b) draw inferences for the population as a whole. (SAS 430.5)

Analysis of errors in the sample

24 In analysing the errors detected in the sample, auditors first determine that an item in question is in fact an error. In designing the sample, auditors define those conditions which constitute an error by reference to the audit objectives. For example, in a substantive procedure relating to the recording of debtors, a misposting between customer accounts does not affect the total debtors. Therefore, it may be inappropriate to consider this an error in evaluating the sample results of this particular procedure, even though it may have an effect on other areas of the audit such as the assessment of doubtful debts.

25 When the expected audit evidence regarding a specific sample item cannot be obtained, auditors may be able to obtain sufficient appropriate audit evidence through performing alternative procedures. For example, if a positive debtors confirmation has been requested but no reply received, auditors may be able to obtain sufficient appropriate audit evidence of the debt by reviewing subsequent payments from the customer. If they are able to perform satisfactory alternative procedures, the item is not treated as an error.

26 Auditors also consider the qualitative aspects of the errors. These include the nature andcause of the error and the possible effect of the error on other phases of the audit.

27 In analysing the errors discovered, auditors may observe that many have a common feature, for example type of transaction, location, product line or period of time. In such circumstances, they may decide to identify all items in the population which possess the common feature, thereby producing a sub-population, and extend audit procedures in this area. They may then perform a separate analysis based on the items examined for each sub-population, so that they have sufficient appropriate audit evidence for each sub-population.

Inferences to be drawn from the population as a whole

28 Auditors project the error results of the sample to the population from which the sample was selected, ensuring that the method of projection is consistent with the method used to select the sampling unit. The projection of the sample involves estimating the probable error in the population (by extrapolating the errors found in the sample), and estimating any further error that might not have been detected because of the imprecision of the technique. This is in addition to the consideration of the qualitative aspects of any errors found.

29 Auditors consider whether errors in the population might exceed the tolerable error. To accomplish this, they compare the projected population error to the tolerable error taking into account the results of other audit procedures relevant to the specific control or financial statement assertion. The projected population error used for this comparison in the case of substantive procedures is net of adjustments made by the entity. When the projected population error exceeds the tolerable error, they re-assess the sampling risk and, if that risk is unacceptable, consider extending the audit procedure or performing alternative audit procedures, either of which may result in them proposing an adjustment to the financial statements.

Compliance with International Standards on Auditing

30 Compliance with this SAS ensures compliance in all material respects with International Standard on Auditing 530 'Audit Sampling'.

Effective date

31 Auditors are required to comply with the Auditing Standards contianed in this SAS in respect of audits of financial statements for periods ending on or after 23 December 1995.

Appendix

Some factors influencing sample size

SAS 430.3 states that 'when determining sample sizes, auditors should consider sampling risk, the amount of error that would be acceptable and the extent to which they expect to find errors'. Factors affecting sample size are set out in the tables below.

The Auditing Standards and guidance included in SAS 220 'Audit materiality', SAS 300 'Accounting and internal control systems and audit risk assessments' and SAS 400'Audit evidence' are also relevant when using these tables.

Table 1 — Some factors influencing sample size for tests of controls

Factor	**Impact on sample size**
Sampling risk	• The greater the reliance on the results of a test of control using audit sampling, the lower the sampling risk auditors are willing to accept and, consequently, the larger the sample size. • The lower the assessment of control risk, the more likely auditors are to place reliance on audit evidence from tests of control. • A high control risk assessment may result in a decision not to perform tests of control.
Tolerable error rate	The higher the tolerable rate the lower the sample size and vice versa.
Expected error rate	• If errors are expected, a larger sample usually needs to be examined to confirm that the actual error rate is less than the tolerable error rate. • High expected error rates may result in a decision not to perform tests of control.
Number of items in population	Virtually no effect on a sample size unless population is small.

Table 2 — Some factors influencing sample size for substantive tests

Factor	Impact on sample size
Inherent risk[1]	• The higher the assessment of inherent risk, the more audit evidence is required to support the auditors' conclusion.
Control risk[2]	• The higher the assessment of control risk, the greater the reliance on audit evidence obtained from substantive procedures. • A high control risk assessment may result in the decision not to perform tests of control and reliance entirely on substantive procedures.
Detection risk[3]	• Sampling risk for substantive tests is one form of detection risk. The lower the sampling risk auditors are willing to accept, the larger the sample size. • Other substantive procedures may provide audit evidence regarding the same financial statement assertions and reduce detection risk. This may reduce the extent of the auditors' reliance on the results of a substantive procedure using audit sampling. • The lower the reliance on the results of a substantive procedure using audit sampling, the higher the sampling risk auditors are willing to accept and, consequently, the smaller the sample size.
Tolerable error rate	The higher the monetary value of the tolerable error the small the sample size and vice versa.
Expected error rate	If errors are expected, a larger sample usually needs to be examined to confirm that the actual error rate is less than the tolerable error rate.
Population value	The less material the monetary value of the population to the financial statements, the smaller the sample size that may be required.
Numbers of items in population	Virtually no effect on sample size unless population is small.
Stratification	If it is appropriate to stratify the population this may redirect the sample and lead to a smaller sample size.

1 Inherent risk is the susceptibility of an account balance or class of transactions to material misstatement, either individually or when aggregated with misstatements in other balances or classes, irrespective of related internal controls.

2 Control risk is the risk that a misstatement that could occur in an account balance or class of transactions and that could be material, either individually or when aggregated with misstatements in other balances or classes, would not be prevented, or detected and corrected on a timely basis, by the accounting and internal control systems.

3 Detection risk is the risk that auditors' substantive procedures do not detect a misstatement that exists in an account balance or class of transactions that could be material, either individually or when aggregated with misstatements in other balances or classes.

Statement of Auditing Standards 440 — Management representations

(Issued March 1995)

Reproduced with the permission of the Auditing Practices Board

Statements of Auditing Standards ('SASs') are to be read in the light of 'The scope and authority of APB pronouncements'. In particular, they contain basic principles and essential procedures ('Auditing Standards'), indicated by paragraphs in bold type, with which auditors are required to comply in the conduct of any audit. SASs also include explanatory and other material which is designed to assist auditors in interpreting and applying Auditing Standards. The definitions in the Glossary of terms are to be applied in the interpretation of SASs.

Introduction

1 The purpose of this SAS is to establish standards and provide guidance on the use of management representations as audit evidence, the procedures to be applied in evaluating and documenting management representations and the action to be taken if management refuses to provide confirmation of appropriate representations.

2 During an audit many representations are made to the auditors, either unsolicited or in response to specific enquiries. They may consider certain of these representations to be critical to obtaining sufficient appropriate audit evidence on which to base their audit opinion. The auditors may also require representations on general matters, for example that the directors have made all accounting records available to the auditors.

3 The possibility of misunderstandings between auditors and management is reduced when oral representations are confirmed in writing. Written confirmation of representations may take the form of:

(a) a representation letter from management; or

(b) a letter from the auditors outlining their understanding of management's representations, duly acknowledged and confirmed in writing by management; or

(c) minutes of meetings of the board of directors, or similar body, at which such representations are approved.

An example of representations from management in the form of a letter is set out in the appendix.

4 Auditors should obtain written confirmation of appropriate representations from management before their report is issued. (SAS 440.1)

5 In the context of management representations, 'management' includes directors, officers and others who perform senior managerial functions.

6 ' Directors' means the directors of a company or other body, the partners, proprietors, committee of management or trustees of other forms of entity, or equivalent persons responsible for directing the reporting entity's affairs and preparing its financial statements.

Acknowledgement by the directors of their responsibility for the financial statements

7 Auditors should obtain evidence that the directors acknowledge their collective responsibility for the preparation of the financial statements and have approved the financial statements. (SAS 440.2)

8 Auditors normally obtain evidence of the directors' acknowledgement of such collective responsibility and approval by receiving a signed copy of the financial statements which incorporate a statement of the directors' responsibility for the financial statements. They can also receive it from:

(a) relevant minutes of meetings of the board of directors or similar body, or by attending such a meeting; or

(b) a written representation from the directors.

9 When auditors have responsibility for reporting on the financial statements of a group of companies, acknowledgement by the directors of their responsibility for the Financial statements applies to both the group financial statements and the financial statements of the parent undertaking.

Representations by management as audit evidence

10 In addition to obtaining representations from the directors as to their responsibility for the financial statements, auditors often rely on representations by management as part of their audit evidence.

11 Auditors should obtain written confirmation of representations from management on matters material to the financial statements when those representations are critical to obtaining sufficient appropriate audit evidence. (SAS 440.3)

12 It is advisable for auditors to discuss such matters with those responsible for giving the written confirmation before they sign it to ensure that they understand what it is that they are being asked to confirm.

13 Written confirmation of representations is normally requested from an appropriate level of management and limited to matters that are considered material to the financial statements, either individually or collectively.

14 When representations to the auditors relate to matters which are material to the financial statements, they:

(a) seek corroborative audit evidence;

(b) evaluate whether the representations made by management appear reasonable and are consistent with other audit evidence obtained, including other representations; and

(c) consider whether the individuals making the representations can be expected to be well-informed on the particular matters.

15 Representations by management cannot be a substitute for other audit evidence that auditors expect to be available. If auditors are unable to obtain sufficient appropriate audit evidence regarding a matter which has, or may have, a material effect on the financial statements and such audit evidence is expected to be available, this constitutes a limitation on the scope of the audit, even if a representation from management has been received on the matter. In these circumstances it may be necessary for them to consider the implications for their report.

16 In certain instances, such as where knowledge of the facts is confined to management (for example, when the facts are a matter of management intentions), or when the matter is principally one of judgement or opinion (for example, on the trading position of a particular customer), management representations may be the only audit evidence available. In some exceptional cases, the matter may be of such significance that the auditors refer to the representations in their report as being relevant to a proper understanding of the basis of their opinion.

17 When auditors have responsibility for reporting on group financial statements, where appropriate they obtain written confirmation of representations relating to specific matters regarding both the group financial statements and the financial statements of the parent undertaking. The means by which they obtain these representations depends on the group's methods of delegation of management control and authority. They may be able to obtain the required representations regarding the group financial statements from the management of the parent undertaking because of the level of their involvement in the management of the group. Alternatively, they may obtain certain representations regarding matters material to the group financial statements directly from the management of the subsidiary undertakings, or by seeing relevant representations by management to the auditors of those subsidiary undertakings, in addition to those obtained from the management of the parent undertaking.

18 If a representation appears to be contradicted by other audit evidence, the auditors should investigate the circumstances to resolve the matter and consider whether it casts doubt on the reliability of other representations. (SAS 440.4)

19 The investigation of apparently contradictory audit evidence regarding a representation received usually begins with further enquiries of management, to ascertain whether the representation has been misunderstood or whether the other audit evidence has been misinterpreted, followed by corroboration of management's responses. If management is unable to provide an explanation or if the explanation is not considered adequate, further audit procedures may be required to resolve the matter.

Basic elements of a management representation letter

20 When requesting a management representation letter, auditors request that it be addressed to them, that it contain specified information and that it be appropriately dated and approved by those with specific knowledge of the relevant matters.

21 It is usually appropriate for the auditors to request that the management representation letter be discussed and agreed by the board of directors or similar body, and signed on their behalf by the chairman and secretary, before they approve the financial statements, to ensure that the board as a whole is aware of the representations on which the auditors intend to rely in expressing their opinion on those financial statements. The auditors may also wish to consider whether to take the opportunity to remind the directors that, under Section 389A of the Companies Act 1985, it is an offence to mislead the auditors.[1]

22 A management representation letter is normally dated on the day the financial statements are approved.

23 If there is any significant delay between the date of the management representation letter and the date of the auditors' report, the auditors may consider it necessary to obtain further representations regarding the intervening period.

1 Relevant legislative references for the Republic of Ireland are to Sections 193(3), 196 and 197 of the Companies Act 1990 and, for Northern Ireland, to Article 397A of the Companies (Northern Ireland) Order 1986.

Action if management refuses to provide written confirmation of representations

24 If management refuses to provide written confirmation of a representation that the auditors consider necessary, the auditors should consider the implications of this scope limitation for their report. (SAS 440.5)

25 In such circumstances, it may no longer be appropriate for the auditors to place reliance on other representations made by management during the course of the audit.

Compliance with International Standards on Auditing

26 Compliance with this SAS ensures compliance in all material respects with International Standard on Auditing 580 'Management Representations'.

Effective date

27 Auditors are required to comply with the Auditing Standards contained in this SAS in respect of audits of financial statements for periods ending on or after 23 December 1995.

Appendix

EXAMPLE OF A MANAGEMENT REPRESENTATION LETTER

The following example of management representations from a company to its auditors is in the form of a letter, but it is not intended to be a standard letter, nor to imply that management representations must necessarily be in the form of a letter. Representations by management vary from one entity to another and from one year to the next.

Although seeking representations from management on a variety of matters may serve to focus management's attention on those matters, and thus cause management specifically to address those matters in more detail than would otherwise be the case, auditors are cognisant of the limitations of management representations as audit evidence as set out in SAS 440.

(Company letterhead)

(To the auditors) (Date)

We confirm to the best of our knowledge and belief, and having made appropriate enquiries of other directors and officials of the company, the following representations given to you in connection with your audit of the financial statements for the period ended 31 December 19..

(1) We acknowledge as directors our responsibilities under the Companies Act 1985 for preparing financial statements which give a true and fair view and for making accurate representations to you. All the accounting records have been made available to you for the purpose of your audit and all the transactions undertaken by the company have been properly reflected and recorded in the accounting records. All other records and related information, including minutes of all management and shareholders' meetings, have been made available to you.

(2) The legal claim by ABC Limited has been settled out of court by a payment of £258,000. No further amounts are expected to be paid, and no similar claims have been received or are expected to be received.

(3) In connection with deferred tax not provided, the following assumptions reflect the intentions and expectations of the company:

(a) capital investment of £450,000 is planned over the next three years;

(b) there are no plans to sell revalued properties; and

(c) we are not aware of any indications that the situation is likely to change so as to necessitate the inclusion of a provision for tax payable in the financial statements.

(4) The company has not had, or entered into, at any time during the period any arrangement, transaction or agreement to provide credit facilities (including loans, quasi-loans or credit transactions) for directors or to guarantee or provide security for such matters.

(5) There have been no events since the balance sheet date which necessitate revision of the figures included in the financial statements or inclusion of a note thereto.

As minuted by the board of directors at its meeting on . . . . . .(date)

____________________ ____________________

Chairman Secretary

Other signatories may include those with specific knowledge of the relevant matters, for example the chief financial officer.

The paragraphs included in the example above relate to a specific set of circumstances. Set out below are examples of other issues which, depending on the particular circumstances, the materiality of the amounts concerned to the financial statements and the extent of the other audit evidence obtained regarding them, may be the subject of representations from management:

- *the extent of the purchase of goods on terms which include reservation of title by suppliers;*
- *the absence of knowledge of circumstances which could result in losses on long-term contracts;*
- *the reasons for concluding that an overdue debt from a related party is fully recoverable; and*
- *confirmation of the extent of guarantees, warranties or other financial commitments relating to subsidiary undertakings or related parties.*

Statement of Auditing Standards
450 — Opening balances and comparitives

(Issued March 1995)

Reproduced with the permission of the Auditing Practices Board

Statements of auditing Standards ('SASs') are to be read in the light of 'The scope and authority of APB pronouncements'. In particular, they contain basic principles and essential procedures ('Auditing Standards'), indicated by paragraphs in bold type, with which auditors are required to comply in the conduct of any audit. SASs also include explanatory and other material which is designed to assist auditors in interpreting and applying Auditing Standards. The definitions in the Glossary of terms are to be applied in the interpretation of SASs.

Introduction

1 The purpose of this SAS is to establish standards and provide guidance regarding auditors' consideration of opening balances taken from the preceding period's financial statements and their consideration of comparative figures in financial statements.

2 Auditors should obtain sufficient appropriate audit evidence that amounts derived from the preceding period's financial statements are free from material misstatements and are appropriately incorporated in the financial statements for the current period. (SAS 450.1)

3 'Opening Balances' means those account balances which exist at the beginning of the period. Opening balances are based upon the closing balances of the preceding period and reflect the effect of transactions of preceding periods and accounting policies applied in the preceding period.

4 'Comparatives' are the corresponding amounts and other related disclosures from the preceding period which are part of the current period's financial statements as required by relevant legislation and applicable accounting standards. Such comparatives are intended to be read in relation to the amounts and other disclosures relating to the current period. Except where there has been a prior year adjustment or change in accounting policy, the opening balanced are consistent with the balance sheet comparatives.

5 'Continuing Auditors' means the auditors who audited and reported on the preceding periods financial statements and continue as auditors for the current period.

6 'Incoming Auditors' means the auditors who are auditing and reporting on the current period's financial statements not having audited and reported on those for the preceding period which were either reported on by predecessor auditors or were unaudited.

7 'Predecessor auditors' means the auditors who previously audited and reported on the financial statements of an entity and who have been replaced by the incoming auditors.

Opening balances

8 Auditors should obtain sufficient appropriate audit evidence that:

(a) opening balances have been appropriately brought forward;

(b) opening balances do not contain errors or misstatements which materially

affect the current period's financial statements; and

(c) appropriate accounting policies are consistently applied or changes in accounting policies have been properly accounted for and adequately disclosed. (SAS 450.2)

9 In the event that auditors are unable to obtain sufficient appropriate audit evidence, they consider the implication for their report.

Continuing auditors

10 If continuing auditors issued an unqualified report on the preceding period's financial statements and the audit of the current period has nor revealed any matters which cast doubt on those financial statements, the procedures regarding opening balances need not extend beyond ensuring that opening balances have been appropriately brought forward and that current accounting policies have been consistently applied.

11 If a qualified report was issued on the preceding period's financial statements the auditors, in addition to carrying out the procedures in paragraph 10, consider whether the matter which gave rise to the qualification has been resolved and properly dealt with in the current period's financial statements.

Incoming auditors

12 The sufficiency and appropriateness of the audit evidence required by incoming auditors regarding opening balances depends on such matters as:

- the accounting policies followed by the entity;
- whether the preceding period's financial statements were audited and, if so, whether the auditors' report was qualified;
- the nature of the opening balances relative to the current period's financial statements.

13 Incoming auditors perform the procedures in paragraphs 10 and 11, recognising that audit work on the current period normally provides evidence regarding opening balances. Other procedures which incoming auditors might perform include the following:

- consultations with management and review of records, working papers and accounting and control procedures for the preceding period; and
- substantive testing of any balances in respect of which the results of other procedures are considered unsatisfactory. Particular emphasis may need to be given to such testing where the previous financial ststements were unaudited, for example if a company has taken advantage in the previous year of the exemptions from audit conferred under Sections 249A to 249E of the Companies Act 1985. If in these circumstances it is not possible for auditors to obtain sufficient appropriate audit evidence, they consider the implications for their report.

An example of extracts from an auditors' report where the auditors were unable to obtain sufficient evidence about opening balances is set out in Appendix 1.

14 The above procedures normally enable incoming auditors to obtain suffcient appropriate audit evidence about the opening balances, and consultations with predecessor auditors are not normally necessary. Except in the case of certain public sector appointments predecessor auditors have no legal or ethical obligation to provide information and do not normally allow access to their working papers. However, they are expected to co-operate with incoming auditors to provide clarification of, or information on, specific accounting matters where this is necessary to resolve particular difficulties.

Comparatives

15 Auditors should obtain sufficient appropriate audit evidence that:

(a) the accounting policies used for the comparatives are consistent with those of the current period and appropriate adjustments and disclosures have been made where this is not the case;

(b) the comparatives agree with the amounts and other disclosures presented in the preceding period and are free from errors in the context of the financial statements of the current period; and

(c) where comparatives have been adjusted as required by the relevant legislation and accounting standards, appropriate disclosures have been made. (SAS 450.3)

16 The comparatives form part of the financial statements on which the auditors express an opinion, although they are not required to express an opinion on the comparatives as such. Their responsibilty is to establish whether the comparatives are the amounts which appeared in the preceding period's financial statements or, where appropriate, have been reinstated either to achieve consistency and comparability with the current period's amounts or to reflect a change of accounting policy or the correction of a fundamental error.

17 In the event that auditors are unable to obtain sufficient appropriate audit evidence, they consider the implications for their report as discussed below.

Continuing and incoming auditors

18 As auditors do not express an opinion on comparatives as such, the extent of audit procedures performed with respect to comparatives is significantly less than for the audit of the current period's financial statements and is normally limited to ensuring that the comparatives have been correctly brought forward and are appropriately classified. Since comparatives are presented in the context of the current period's financial statements, the materiality of any misstatements is judged in terms of their relationship to the current period.

19 When the auditors' report on the preceding period was qualified, and the matter which gave rise to the qualification is unresolved and:

- is material in the context of the current period's opening balances as well as comparatives, the report on the current period's financial statements is qualified regarding opening balances and comparatives (an example of extracts from an appropriate auditors' report where comparatives are required by law is given in Appendix 2); or

- does not affect opening balances but is material in the context of the current period's financial statements, the report on the current period's financial statements refers to the comparatives. If comparatives are required by law or regulation, the reference is in the form of a qualification on the grounds of non-compliance with that requirement. If comparatives are presented solely as good practice, the reference is in the form of a explanatory paragraph. An example of extracts from an appropriate auditors' report is given in Appendix 3.

20 If the auditors' report on the preceding period was qualified but the matter which gave rise to the qualification has been resolved and properly dealt with in the financial statements, the current report does not normally refer to the previous qualification. However, if the point is material to the current period, the current report explains how the matter resulting in the qualification has been dealt with and may include a qualification on the current period's financial statements (for example, if a provision which the auditors considered should have been made in the previous period is made in the current period).

21 In certain unusual circumstances auditors may become aware of a material misstatement which affects the preceding period's financial statements on which the auditor's report was without qualification. In such circumstances:

(a) if the preceding period's financial statements have not been revised and reissued with a new auditors' report, the auditors ensure that the comparatives agree with the revised financial statements;

(b) if the preceding period's financial statements have not been revised and reissued but the comparatives have been properly restated, the auditors do not qualify their report providing adequate disclosure has been given; and

(c) if the preceding period's financial statements have not been revised and reissued, and the comparatives have not been properly restated, the auditors consider the implications for their report.

Incoming auditors — audited comparatives

22 When the financial statements of the preceding period were audited by other auditors, incoming auditors assume audit responsibility for the comparatives only in the context of the financial statements as a whole. The incoming auditors read the preceding period's financial statements and, using the knowledge gained during the current audit, consider whether they have been properly reflected as comparatives in the current period's financial statements.

23 Although incoming auditors are not required to re-audit the financial statements of the preceding period, if they become aware of a possible material misstatement of comparatives, the procedures in paragraph 21 apply.

Incoming auditors — unaudited comparatives

24 When the financial statements of the preceding period were unaudited, for example if a company has taken advantage in the previous year of the exemption from audit conferred by Sections 249A to 249E of the Companies Act 1985, the incoming auditors consider whether there is clear disclosure in the financial statements that the comparatives are unaudited. They are not relieved of carrying out, as far as is appropriate, procedures regarding comparatives as identified in paragraphs 22 and 23. In the event that they are unable to obtain sufficient appropriate audit evidence, or if there is not adequate disclosure, they consider the implications for their report.

Compliance with International Standards on Auditing

25 Compliance with this SAS (together with SAS 600 'Auditors' reports on financial statements') ensures compliance in all material respects with International Standard on Auditing 510 'Initial Engagements — Opening Balances'. As at the date of publication of this SAS, there is no equivalent International Standard on Auditing dealing with compartives.

Effective date

26 Auditors are required to comply with the Auditing Standards contained in this SAS in respect of audits of financial statements for periods ending on or after 23 December 1995.

Appendix 1

Auditors' Report if unable to obtain evidence regarding opening balances

Auditors' Report to the Shareholders of XYZ Ltd — Extracts

Basis of opinion

We planned our audit so as to obtain all the information and explanations which we considered necessary in order to provide us with sufficient evidence to give reasonable assurance that the financial statements are free from material misstatement, whether caused by fraud or other irregularity or error. However, the evidence available to us was limited because we were not appointed auditors of the company until 30 June 19X5 and in consequence it was not possible for us to perform the auditing procedures necessary to obtain sufficient appropriate audit evidence as regards [*specify and evaluate the balances involved*] included in the preceding year's financial statements at £ . . . Any adjustment to [*these figures*] would have a consequential effect on the profit for the year ended 31 December 19X5. . .

Qualified opinion arising from limitation in audit scope

In our opinion, the financial statements give a true and fair view of the state of the company's affairs as at 31 December 19X5 and, exept for any adjustments that might have been found to be necessary had we been able to obtain sufficient evidence concerning [*specify the balances involved*] as at 1 January 19X5, of its profit [loss] for the year then ended and have been properly prepared in accordance with the Companies Act 1985.

In respect alone of the limitation on our work relating to [*specify the opening balances involved*]:

- we have not obtained all the information and explanations that we considered necessary for the purpose of our audit; and
- we were unable to determine whether proper accounting records had been maintained.

Appendix 2

Auditors' Report if the report on the preceding period was qualified and the matter has not been resolved

Auditors' Report to the Shareholders of XYZ Ltd — Extracts

Qualified opinion arising from disagreement about accounting treatment

Included in the debtors shown on the balance sheet of 31 December 19X4 and 31 December 19X5 is an amount of £Y which is the subject of litigation and against which no provision has been made. In our opinion, full provision of £Y should have been made in the year ended 31 December 19X4 reducing profit before tax for the year ended 31 December 19x4 and net assets at 31 December 19X4 and 31 December 19X5 by that amount.

Except for the absence of this provision, in our opinion the financial statements give a true and fair view of the state of the company's affairs as at 31 December 19X5 and of its profit [loss] for the year then ended and have been properly prepared in accordance with the Companies Act 1985.

Appendix 3

Auditors' Report if the report on the preceding period was qualified, the matter has not been resolved but does not affect opening balances

Auditors' Report to the Shareholders of XYZ Ltd — Extracts

Basis of opinion
We conducted our audit in accordance with Auditing Standards issued by the Auditing Practices Board, except that the scope of our work was limited as explained below . . .

We planned and performed our audit so as to obtain all the information and explanations which we considered necessary in order to provide us with sufficient evidence to give reasonable assurance that the financial statements are free from material misstatement, whether caused by fraud or other irregularity or error. In forming our opinion we also evaluated the overall adequacy of the presentation of information in the financial statements. However, the evidence available to us was limited in relation to the comparatives in the current year's financial statements which are derived from the financial statements for the year ended 31 December 19X4. In our report on those financial statements we stated that, because we were appointed auditors on 30 June 19X4, it was not possible for us to perform the auditing procedures necessary to obtain sufficient appropriate audit evidence concerning the quantities and condition of certain stock and work in progress included in the balance sheet at 31 December 19X3 at £ . . . Any adjustment to this figure would have a consequential effect on the profit for the year ended 31 December 19X4 and, consequently, our opinion on the financial statements for the year ended 31 December 19X4 was qualified because of this limitation in audit scope. Accordingly the amounts shown as cost of sales and profit for the year ended 31 December 19X4 may not be comparable with the figures for the current period.

Qualified opinion arising from limitation in audit evidence about comparatives
In our opinion the financial statements give a true and fair view of the state of the company's affairs at 31 December 19X5 and of its profit [loss] for the year then ended and, except for any adjustments to the comparatives which might have been found to be necessary had we been able to obtain sufficient evidence concerning certain stock and work in progress at 31 December 19X3, have been properly prepared in accordance with the Companies Act 1985.

Statement of Auditing Standards 470 — Overall review of financial statements

(Issued in March 1995)

Reproduced with the permission of the Auditing Practices Board

Statements of Auditing Standards ('SASs') are to be read in the light of 'The scope and authority of APB pronouncements'. In particular, they contain basic principles and essential procedures ('Auditing Standards'), indicated by paragraphs in bold type, with which auditors are required to comply in the conduct of any audit. SASs also include explanatory and other material which is designed to assist auditors in interpreting and applying Auditing Standards. The definitions in the Glossary of terms are to be applied in the interpretation of SASs.

Introduction

1 The purpose of this SAS is to establish standards and provide guidance on auditors' overall review of financial statements prior to the expression of an audit opinion.

2 Auditors should carry out such a review of the financial statements as is sufficient, in conjunction with the conclusions drawn from the other audit evidence obtained, to give them a reasonable basis for their opinion on the financial statements. (SAS 470.1)

3 An overall review of the financial statements is performed by auditors at the completion phase of the audit, after having accumulated audit evidence about individual items or groups of items. The performance of such a review requires appropriate levels of experience and skill.

Compliance with accounting regulations

4 Auditors should consider whether the information presented in the financial statements is in accordance with statutory requirements and that the accounting policies employed are in accordance with accounting standards, properly disclosed, consistently applied and appropriate to the entity. (SAS 470.2)

5 When considering whether the accounting policies adopted by management are appropriate, auditors have regard to:

- policies commonly adopted in particular industries;
- policies for which there is substantial authoritative support;
- whether any departures from applicable accounting standards are necessary for the financial statements to give a true and fair view; and
- whether the financial statements reflect the substance of the underlying transactions and not merely their form.

6 In reviewing the financial statements to ensure compliance with statutory requirements, accounting standards and other applicable regulations, auditors may find it helpful to use a checklist or other aide memoire.

Review for consistency and reasonableness

7 Auditors should consider whether the financlal statements as a whole and the assertions contained therein are consistent wlth their knowledge of the entity's business and with the results of other audit procedures, and the manner of disclosure is fair. (SAS 470.3)

8 The principal considerations when carrying out such a review are:

(a) whether the financial statements adequately reflect the information and explanations previously obtained and conclusions previously reached during the course of the audit;

(b) whether it reveals any new factors which may affect the presentation of, or disclosures in, the financial statements;

(c) whether analytical procedures applied when completing the audit, such as comparing the information in the financial statements with other pertinent data, produce results which assist in arriving at the overall conclusion as to whether the financial statements as a whole are consistent with their knowledge of the entity's business;

(d) whether the presentation adopted in the financial statements may have been unduly influenced by the directors' desire to present matters in a favourable or unfavourable light; and

(e) the potential impact on the financial statements of the aggregate of uncorrected misstatements (including those arising from bias in making accounting estimates) identified during the course of the audit and the preceding period's audit, if any.

Compliance with International Standards on Auditing

9 No International Standard on Auditing has been issued on auditors' overall review of financial statements prior to the expression of an audit opinion.

Effective date

10 Auditors are required to comply with the Auditing Standards contained in this SAS in respect of audits of financial statements for periods ending on or after 23 December 1995.

Statement of Auditing Standards 500 — Considering the work of internal audit

(Issued March 1994)

Reproduced with the permission of the Auditing Practices Board

Statements of Auditing Standards ('SASs') are to be read in the light of 'The scope and authority of APB pronouncements'. In particular, they contain basic principles and essential procedures ('Auditing Standards'), indicated by paragraphs in bold type, with which auditors are required to comply in the conduct of any audit. SASs also include explanatory and other material which is designed to assist auditors in interpreting and applying Auditing Standards. The definitions in the Glossary of terms are to be applied in the interpretation of SASs.

Introduction

1 The purpose of this SAS is to establish standards and provide guidance to external auditors in considering the work of internal audit. This SAS applies when an entity employs its own internal audit staff and also when an entity's internal audit function is undertaken by a third party or the external auditors. This SAS does not deal with instances when internal audit personnel assist the external auditors in carrrying out external audit procedures. The procedures noted in this SAS apply only to internal audit activities which are relevant to the audit of the financial statements.

2 **External auditors should consider the activies of internal audit and their effect, if any, on external audit procedures. (SAS 500.1)**

3 'Internal audit' means an appraisal or monitoring activity established by management and the directors for the review of the accounting and internal control systems as a service to the entity. It functions by, amongst other things, examining, evaluating and reporting to management and the directors on the adequacy and effectiveness of components of the accounting and internal control systems.

4 The external auditors have sole responsibility for the audit opinion expressed and for determining the nature, timing and extent of external audit procedures. All judgements relating to the audit of the financial statements are those of the external auditors. That responsibility is not reduced by any use made of internal audit work. However, internal audit work may serve to provide external auditors with audit evidence.

Scope and objectives of internal audit

5 The scope and objectives of internal audit vary widely and depend on the size and structure of the entity and the requirements of its management and directors. Generally, internal audit activities include one or more of the following:

- review of the accounting and internal control systems: the establishment of adequate accounting and internal control systems is a responsibility of management and the directors which demands proper attention on a continuous basis. Often, internal audit is assigned specific responsibility for reviewing the design of the systems, monitoring their operation and recommending improvements thereto;

- examination of financial and operating information: this may include review of the means used to identify, measure, classify and report such information and specific enquiry into individual items including detailed testing of transactions, balances and procedures;
- review of the economy, efficiency and effectiveness of operations including non-financial controls of an organisation;
- review of compliance with laws, regulations and other external requirements and with internal policies and directives and other requirements including appropriate authorisation of transactions; and
- special investigations into particular areas, for example suspected fraud.

Relationship between internal and external auditors

6 The role of internal audit is determined by management and the directors and its objectives differ from those of the external auditors who are engaged to report independently on the financial statements. The external auditors' primary concern is whether the financial statements are free of material misstatement. The internal audit function's objectives vary according to the requirements of management and the directors and, generally, less emphasis is placed on materiality considerations.

7 Nevertheless some of the means of achieving their respective objectives are often similar and thus certain of the work of internal auditors may be useful in determining the nature, timing and extent of external audit procedures. If an entity has an audit committee, monitoring the activities of the internal audit function and the relationship between the entity's internal and external auditors is often one of that committee's responsibilities.

8 Even when the internal audit function is undertaken by a third party or the external auditors, it is part of the entity's activities. Irrespective of the degree of internal audit's autonomy and objectivity it cannot achieve the same degree of independence as required of external auditors when expressing an opinion on the financial statements.

Understanding and assessment of the role and scope of internal audit

9 The external auditors should obtain a sufficient understanding of internal audit activies to assist in planning the audit and developing an effective audit approach. (SAS 500.2)

10 An effective internal audit function often allows a modification in the nature and timing, and a reduction in the extent, of procedures performed by the external auditors but cannot eliminate them entirely. However, in some cases, having considered the activities of internal audit, the external auditors may decide that internal audit work will have no effect on external audit procedures. Nevertheless, external auditors normally find it helpful to be aware of conclusions drawn by internal audit.

11 The effectiveness of the internal audit function may be an important factor in the external auditors' assessment of the control environment, and their related assessment of audit risk.

12 During the course of their planning the external auditors should perform assessment of the internal audit function if they consider that it may be possible and desirable to rely on certain internal audit work in specific audit areas for the purpose of the external audit of the financial statements. (SAS 500.3)

13 The external auditors' assessment of the internal audit function for planning purposes can often be based largely on knowledge obtained from past reviews of internal audit work. This assessment influences their judgement about the use which may be made of the work of internal audit in modifying the nature, timing and extent of external audit procedures.

14 When obtaining an understanding and performing an assessment of the internal audit function, the important criteria are:

(a) *organisational status*: internal audit's specific status in the organisation and the effect this has on its ability to be objective. In the ideal situation, the internal audit function reports to the highest level of management, but also has a direct line of communication to the entity's main board or audit committee, and is free of any other operating responsibility. External auditors consider any constraints or restrictions placed on internal audit. In particular, the internal auditors need to be free to communicate fully with the external auditors;

(b) *scope of function*: the nature and extent of the assignments which internal audit performs. External auditors also consider whether management and the directors act on internal audit recommendations and how this is evidenced;

(c) *technical competence*: whether internal audit work is performed by persons having adequate technical training and proficiency as internal auditors. External auditors may for example, review the policies for hiring and training the internal audit staff and their experience and professional qualifications; and

(d) *due professional care*: whether internal audit work is properly planned, supervised, reviewed and documented. The existence of adequate audit manuals, work programmes and working papers may be considered.

Timing of liaison and co-ordination

15 When planning to use internal audit work, the external auditors consider internal audit's plan for the period and discuss it at as early a stage as possible. Where internal audit work is to be a factor in determining the nature, timing and extent of the external auditors' procedures, it is desirable to agree in advance the timing of such work, the extent of audit coverage, test levels and proposed methods of sample selection, documentation of the work performed and review and reporting procedures.

16 Liaison with internal audit is more effective when meetings are held at appropriate intervals during the period. The external auditors need to be advised of, and have access to, relevant internal audit reports and need to be kept informed of any significant matter that comes to the attention of the internal auditors which may affect the work of the external auditors. Similarly, the external auditors generally inform internal audit of any significant matters which may affect internal audit work. The external auditors inform management or the directors, including the head of the internal audit function, of any significant factors noted which may result in improved economy, efficiency or effectiveness in their future use of the work of internal audit.

Evaluating specific internal audit work

17 When the external auditors use specific internal audit work to reduce the extent of their audit procedures, they should evaluate that work to confirm its adequacy for their purposes. (SAS 500.4)

18 The evaluation of specific internal audit work involves consideration of the adequacy of the scope of work and related audit programmes and whether the assessment of the key internal audit function remains appropriate. This evaluation may include consideration of whether:

- the work is performed by persons having adequate technical training and proficiency as internal auditors;
- the work of assistants is properly supervised, reviewed and documented;
- sufficient appropriate audit evidence is obtained to afford a reasonable basis for the conclusions reached;
- the conclusions reached are appropriate in the circumstances;
- any reports prepared by internal audit are consistent with the results of the work performed;
- any exceptions or unusual matters disclosed by internal audit are properly resolved;
- amendments to the external audit programme are required as a result of matters identified by internal audit work; and
- there is a need to test the work of internal audit to confirm its adequacy.

19 The nature, timing and extent of the testing, if any, of the specific internal audit work which the external auditors consider necessary depends on their judgement as to the risk and materiality of the area concerned, the assessment of the internal audit function and the results of the other evaluation procedures set out in paragraph 18 above. Such tests may include examination of items already examined by internal audit, examination of other similar items and observation of internal audit procedures.

20 In the event that the external auditors conclude that the internal audit work is not adequate for their purposes, they extend their procedures beyond those originally planned to ensure that sufficient appropriate audit evidence is obtained to support the conclusions reached.

Compliance with International Standards on Auditing

21 With the exception that SAS 500.4 in paragraph 17 does not include a requirement to test the work of internal audit to confirm its adequacy, as the adequacy of such work can often be assessed using some of the other procedures outlined in paragraph 18 and the criteria for determining whether to test the work of internal audit are set out in paragraph 19, compliance with this SAS ensures compliance in all material respects with International Standard on Auditing 610 'Considering the Work of Internal Auditing'.

Effective date

22 Auditors are required to comply with the Auditing Standards contained in this SAS in respect of audits of financial statements for periods ending on or after 23 December 1995.

Statement of Auditing Standards

510 — The relationship between principal auditors and other auditors

(Issued March 1995)

Reproduced with the permission of the Auditing Practices Board

Statements of Auditing Standards ('SASs') are to be read in the light of 'The scope and authority of APB pronouncements'. In particular, they contain basic principles and essential procedures ('Auditing Standards'), indicated by paragraphs in bold type, with which auditors are required to comply in the conduct of any audit. SASs also include explanatory and other material which is designed to assist auditors in interpreting and applying Auditing Standards. The definitions in the Glossary of terms are to be applied in the interpretation of SASs.

Introduction

1 The purpose of this SAS is to establish standards and provide guidance to both principal auditors and other auditors regarding the use by principal auditors, reporting on the financial statements of an entity, of other auditors' work on the financial information of one or more components included in the financial statements of the entity. The statutory requirements relating to companies incorporated in the United Kingdom and the Republic of Ireland for other auditors to co-operate with principal auditors are explained in more detail in paragraphs 16-21 below and in the attached Appendix. In certain parts of the public sector where the responsibilities of principal and other auditors are governed by statutory provisions, these override the provisions of this SAS. This SAS does not deal with those instances where two or more auditors are appointed as joint auditors nor does it deal with the auditors' relationship with predecessor auditors.

2 When using the work of other auditors, principal auditors should determine how that work will affect their audit. (SAS 510.1)

3 'Principal auditors' means auditors with responsibility for reporting on the audit of financial statements of an entity when those financial statements include financial information of one or more components audited by other auditors.

4 'Other auditors' means auditors, other than the principal auditors, with responsibility for reporting on the financial information of a component which is included in the financial statements audited by the principal auditors. Other auditors include affiliated firms, whether using the same name or not, and correspondent firms, as well as unrelated auditors.

5 'Component' means a division, branch, subsidiary undertaking, joint venture, associated undertaking or other entity whose financial information is included in financial statements audited by the principal auditors

Acceptance as principal auditors

6 Auditors should consider whether their own participation is sufficient to enable them to act as principal auditors. (SAS 510.2)

7 For this purpose principal auditors consider:

- the materiality of the portion of the financial statements which they do not audit;
- the degree of their knowledge regarding the business of the components;
- the nature of their relationship with the firms acting as other auditors;
- their ability where necessary to perform additional procedures to enable them to act as principal auditors; and
- the risk of material misstatements in the financial statements of the components audited by other auditors.

Principal auditors' procedures

8 When planning to use the work of other auditors, principal auditors should consider the professional qualifications, experience and resources of the other auditors in the context of the specific assignment. (SAS 510.3)

9 Some of the factors to be considered are membership of a relevant professional organisation or the standing of any firm with which the other auditors are affiliated. These factors can be supplemented when appropriate by enquiries of third parties, reference to the other auditors' professional organisation and by discussions with the other auditors. The principal auditors' assessment may be influenced by the review of previous audit work of the other auditors.

10 Principal auditors should obtain sufficient appropriate audit evidence that the work of the other auditors is adequate for the principal auditors' purposes. (SAS 510.4)

11 In order to obtain this evidence, the principal auditors advise the other auditors of the use that is to be made of their work and make the necessary arrangements for the co-ordination of their efforts at the initial planning stage of the audit. This involves informing the other auditors about matters such as areas requiring special consideration, procedures for the identification of inter-entity transactions that may require disclosure and the timetable for completion of the audit. In addition, the principal auditors advise the other auditors of, and obtain representations from them as to compliance with:

(a) the independence requirements regarding both the entity and the component; and

(b) the relevant accounting, auditing and reporting requirements.

12 The principal auditors may also discuss with the other auditors the audit procedures applied, may review a written summary of the other auditors' procedures (which may be in the form of a questionnaire or checklist) or may review working papers of the other auditors. They may wish to perform these procedures during a visit to the other auditors. The nature, timing and extent of the principal auditors' procedures depend on the circumstances of the engagement and their assessment of the professional qualifications, experience and resources of the other auditors.

13 The principal auditors may conclude that it is not necessary to apply procedures such as those described in paragraph 12 because of evidence previously obtained that acceptable quality control policies and procedures are complied with in the conduct of the other auditors' practice. For example, when they are affiliated firms, their continuing formal relationship may provide for procedures that give that comfort, such as periodic inter-firm review, tests of operating policies and procedures and review of working papers of selected audits.

14 The principal auditors should consider the significant findings of the other auditors. (SAS 510.5)

15 The principal auditors may consider it appropriate to discuss with the other auditors, and the directors or management of the component, the audit findings or other matters affecting the financial statements of the component and to request copies of reports to directors or management issued by the other auditors. They may also decide that supplementary tests of the records or the financial statements of the component are necessary. Such tests may, depending on the circumstances, be performed by the principal auditors or the other auditors.

Co-operation between auditors

16 Other auditors, knowing the context in which the principal auditors intend to use their work, should co-operate with and assist the principal auditors. (SAS 510.6)

17 Other auditors carry out their work in the knowledge that the financial information on which they report is to be included within the financial statements which are reported on by the principal auditors. In many circumstances when the component is a subsidiary undertaking, there is a statutory obligation on the other auditors, and the component which they audit, to give the principal auditors such information and explanations as they may reasonably require for the purpose of their audit. Where there is no statutory obligation on the other auditors and the principal auditors advise that they intend to use the other auditors' work, the other auditors may require permission from the component to communicate with the principal auditors on matters pertaining to the component's audit. If the component refuses such permission, the other auditors bring this to the attention of the principal auditors so that the principal auditors can discuss and agree an appropriate course of action with the directors of the entity which they audit.

18 If in undertaking their audit procedures the other auditors identify any matter which they consider likely to be relevant to the principal auditors' work, they bring it to the attention of the principal auditors as may be most appropriate in the circumstances. For example, they may communicate directly with the principal auditors, providing consent is granted by the component or there exists a statutory obligation, or it may require reference to be made within their auditors' report. In any event, whenever they cannot carry out any aspect of their work as requested, the other auditors inform the principal auditors.

19 The other auditors have sole responsibility for their audit opinion on the financial statements of the component which they audit. Accordingly, they plan and execute their audit in a manner which enables them to report on the component without placing reliance on the principal auditors necessarily informing them of matters which have come to their attention and which may have an important bearing on the financial statements of the component. This may involve the other auditors seeking representations directly from the directors or management of the entity audited by the principal auditors.

20 There is no obligation, statutory or otherwise, on principal auditors to provide information to other auditors. However, in undertaking their work principal auditors may identify matters which they assess to be relevant to the other auditors' work. In these circumstances, principal auditors discuss and agree an appropriate course of action with the directors of the entity which they audit.

21 The course of action agreed with the directors may involve principal auditors communicating directly with the other auditors, or the directors informing the component or the other auditors. However, there may be circumstances where sensitive commercial considerations dictate that information cannot be passed on to the component or the other auditors. In this event, principal auditors are not required to take further action as to do so would be in breach of the principle of client confidentiality.

Reporting considerations

22 When the principal auditors are satisfied that the work of the other auditors is adequate for the purposes of their audit, no reference to the other auditors is made in the principal auditors' report.

23 The principal auditors have sole responsibility for their audit opinion and a reference to the other auditors in the principal auditors' report may be misunderstood and interpreted as a qualification of their opinion or a division of responsibility, neither of which is appropriate.

24 When the principal auditors conclude that adequate evidence about the work of the other auditors cannot be obtained and they have not been able to perform sufficient additional procedures with respect to the financial statements of the component audited by the other auditors, they consider the implications for their report.

25 Any report of the other auditors containing a qualified opinion or an explanatory paragraph referring to a fundamental uncertainty requires the principal auditors to consider whether the subject of the qualification or the fundamental uncertainty is of such a nature and significance, in relation to the financial statements of the entity on which they are reporting, that it needs to be reflected in their report.

Compliance with International Standards on Auditing

26 The requirement for auditors to consider the implications for their report is included as a basic principle and essential procedure in SAS 600 'Auditors' reports on financial statements' and therefore paragraph 24 is considered to be more appropriately expressed as guidance rather than as a basic principle or essential procedure. In conjunction with SAS 600, compliance with this SAS ensures compliance in all material respects with International Standard on Auditing 600 'Using the Work of Another Auditor'.

Effective date

27 Auditors are required to comply with the Auditing Standards contained in this SAS in respect of audits of financial statements for periods ending on or after 23 December 1995.

Appendix
Statutory framework

1 If a parent company and its subsidiary undertaking are companies incorporated in Great Britain, Section 389A(3) of the Companies Act 1985 imposes a duty on the subsidiary undertaking and its auditors to 'give to the auditors of any parent company of the undertaking such information and explanations as they may reasonably require for the purposes of their duties as auditors of that company'. Similar obligations regarding companies incorporated in Northern Ireland and the Republic of Ireland are set out in Article 397A(3) of the Companies (Northern Ireland) Order 1986 and Section 196(1) of the Companies Act 1990 respectively.

2 Where a parent company is incorporated in Great Britain but its subsidiary undertaking is not, Section 389A(4) of the Companies Act 1985 imposes a duty on the parent company, if required by its auditors to do so, to 'take all such steps as are reasonably open to it to obtain from the subsidiary undertaking such information and explanations as they may reasonably require for the purposes of their duties as auditors of that company'. Similar obligations on parent companies incorporated in Northern Ireland and the Republic of Ireland are set out in Article 397A(4) of the Companies (Northern Ireland) Order 1986 and Section 196(2) of the Companies Act 1990 respectively.

Statement of Auditing Standards 520 — Using the work of an expert

(Issued March 1995)

Reproduced with the permission of the Auditing Practices Board

Statements of Auditing Standards ('SASs') are to be read in the light of 'The scope and authority of APB pronouncements'. In particular, they contain basic principles and essential procedures ('Auditing Standards'), indicated by paragraphs in bold type, with which auditors are required to comply in the conduct of any audit. SASs also include explanatory and other material which is designed to assist auditors in interpreting and applying Auditing Standards. The definitions in the Glossary of terms are to be applied the interpretation of SASs.

Introduction

1 The purpose of this SAS is to establish standards and provide guidance on using the work of an expert to obtain audit evidence. Auditors have sole responsibility for their opinion, but may use the work of an expert. Such an expert may be engaged by an entity to provide specialist advice on a particular matter which affects the financial statements or by auditors in order to obtain sufficient appropriate audit evidence regarding certain financial statement assertions.

2 **When using the work performed by an expert, auditors should obtain such appropriate audit evidence that such work is adequate for the purpose of the audit. (SAS 520.1)**

3 'Expert' means a person or firm possessing special skill, knowledge and experience in a particular field other than auditing.

4 The auditors' education and experience enables them to be knowledgeable about business maners in general, but they are not expected to have the expertise of a person trained for, or qualified to engage in, the practice of another profession or occupation.

5 An expert may be engaged by the entity or the auditors. The expert may also be employed by the entity or the auditors.

6 When auditors use the work of an expert employed by them or by an associated firm, that work is used in the employee's capacity as an assistant on the audit as contemplated in SAS 240 'Quality control for audit work'. Accordingly, in such circumstances the requirements of SAS 240 apply as well as those of this SAS.

Determining the need to use the work of an expert

7 During the audit the auditors may obtain, in conjunction with the entity or independently, audit evidence in the form of reports, opinions, valuations or statements of an expert. Examples are:

- valuations of certain types of assets, for example land and buildings, plant and machinery, works of art, precious stones, unquoted investments and intangible assets;
- determination of quantities or physical condition of assets, for example minerals stored in stockpiles, underground mineral and petroleum reserves and the remaining useful life of plant and machinery;

- determination of amounts using specialised techniques or methods, for example pensions accounting and actuarial valuations;
- the measurement of work completed and to be completed on contracts in progress; and
- legal opinions concerning interpretations of agreements, statutes and regulations, or on the outcome of litigation or disputes.

8 When determining whether to use the work of an expert, the auditors review:

(a) the importance of the matter being considered in the context of the financial statements;

(b) the risk of misstatement based on the nature and complexity of the matter being considered; and

(c) the quantity and quality of other available relevant audit evidence.

9 If the auditors determine that it is appropriate to seek to use the work of an expert, the approach is discussed and may be agreed with management or the directors. If management or the directors are unable or unwilling to engage an expert, the auditors may consider engaging an expert or whether sufficient appropriate audit evidence can be obtained from other sources. If unable to obtain sufficient appropriate audit evidence, they consider the implications for their report.

Competence and objectivity of the expert

10 When planning to use the work of an expert the auditors should assess the objectivity and professional qualifications, experience and resources of the expert. (SAS 520.2)

11 Normally, this involves considering the expert's:

(a) professional certification, or licensing by, or membership of, an appropriate professional body; and

(b) experience and reputation in the field in which the auditors are seeking audit evidence.

12 The risk that an expert's objectivity is impaired increases when the expert is:

(a) employed by the entity; or

(b) related in some other manner to the entity, for example by being financially dependent upon, or having an investment in, the entity.

13 If the auditors are concerned about the competence or objectivity of the expert they may discuss their reservations with management or the directors and consider whether sufficient appropriate audit evidence can be obtained. They may undertake additional audit procedures or seek evidence from another expert. If unable to obtain sufficient appropriate audit evidence, they consider the implications for their report.

The expert's scope of work

14 The auditors should obtain sufficient appropriate audit evidence that the expert's scope of work is adequate for the purposes of their audit. (SAS 520.3)

15 Audit evidence may be obtained through a review of the terms of reference, which are often set out in written instructions from the entity to the expert. Such instructions to the expert may cover such matters as:

- the objectives and scope of the expert's work;
- a general outline as to the specific matters the expert's report is to cover;

- the intended use of the expert's work, including the possible communication to third parties of the expert's identity and extent of involvement;
- the extent of the expert's access to appropriate records and files; and
- information regarding the assumptions and methods intended to be used by the expert and their consistency with those used in prior periods.

In the event that these matters are not clearly set out in written instructions to the expert, the auditors may seek to communicate with the expert directly to obtain audit evidence in this regard.

Assessing the work of the expert

16 The auditors should assess the appropriateness of the expert's work as audit evidence regarding the financial statement assertions being considered. (SAS 520.4)

17 This involves assessment of whether the substance of the expert's findings is properly reflected in the financial statements or supports the financial statement assertions, and consideration of:

- source data used;
- assumptions and methods used;
- when the expert carried out the work;
- the reasons for any changes in assumptions and methods compared with those used in the prior period; and
- results of the expert's work in the light of the auditors' overall knowledge of the business and the results of other audit procedures.

18 When considering whether the expert has used source data which is appropriate in the circumstances, the auditors may consider the following procedures:

(a) making enquiries regarding any procedures undertaken by the expert to establish whether the source data is sufficient, relevant and reliable; and

(b) reviewing or testing the data used by the expert.

19 The appropriateness and reasonableness of assumptions and methods used and their application are the responsibility of the expert. The auditors do not have the same expertise and, therefore, cannot necessarily challenge the expert's assumptions and methods. However, they seek to obtain an understanding of the assumptions and methods used and to consider whether they are reasonable, based on their knowledge of the business and the results of other audit procedures, and compatible with those used for the preparation of the financial statements.

20 If the results of the expert's work are not consistent with other audit evidence, the auditors attempt to resolve the inconsistency by discussions with the entity and the expert. Applying additional procedures, including possibly engaging another expert, may also assist in resolving the inconsistency.

21 If the auditors are not satisfied that the work of an expert provides sufficient appropriate audit evidence and there is no satisfactory alternative source of such evidence, they consider the implications for their report.

22 When the auditors are satisfied that the work of an expert provides appropriate audit evidence, reference is not made to the work of the expert in their report. Such a reference may be misunderstood and interpreted as a qualification of the auditors' opinion or a division of responsibility, neither of which is appropriate.

Compliance with International Standards on Auditing

23 Compliance with this SAS ensures compliance in all material respects with International Standard on Auditing 620 'Using the Work of an Expert'.

Effective date

24 Auditors are required to comply with the Auditing Standards contained in this SAS in respect of audits of financial statements for periods ending on or after 23 December 1995.

Statement of Auditing Standards

600 — Auditors' Reports on Financial Statements

(Issued May 1993)

Reproduced with the permission of the Auditing Practices Board

Statements of Auditing Standards ('SASs') contain basic principles and essential procedures, ('Auditing Standards'), indicated by paragraphs in bold type, with which auditors are required to comply in the conduct of any audit. SASs also include explanatory and other material which is designed to assist auditors in interpreting and applying Auditing Standards.

Introduction

1 The purpose of this Statement of Auditing Standards is to establish standards and provide guidance on the form and content of auditors' reports issued as a result of an audit of the financial statements of an entity ('the reporting entity'). Much of the guidance provided can be adapted to auditors' reports on financial information other than financial statements.

2 **Auditors' reports on financial statements should contain a clear expression of opinion, based on review and assessment of the conclusions drawn from evidence obtained in the course of the audit. (SAS 600.1).**

3 An appreciation of the inter-relationship between the responsibilities of those who prepare financial statements and those who audit them is also necessary to achieve an understanding of the nature and context of the opinion expressed by the auditors. Readers need to be aware that it is the directors (or equivalent persons) of the reporting entity and not the auditors who determine the accounting policies followed. Auditors' reports therefore also set out the respective responsibilities of directors and auditors.

4 It will aid communication with the reader if the auditors' report is placed before the financial statements and, where the directors set out their responsibilities themselves, if this description is immediately before the auditors' report.

5 The requirements of the SAS are intended to achieve informative reporting by auditors within the reporting obligations current at its date of issue. Further developments may in the future alter the matters on which auditors are required to report or the manner in which they are required to report: such changes will be reflected in amendments to the requirements in this SAS when appropriate.

Nature of assurance provided

6 The view given in financial statements is derived from a combination of fact and judgment, and consequently cannot be characterised as either 'absolute' or 'correct'. When reporting on financial statements, therefore, auditors provide a level of assurance which is reasonable in that context but, equally, cannot be absolute. Consequently it is important that the reader of financial statements is made aware of the context in which the auditors' report is given.

Applicability

7 This SAS applies to all reports issued by auditors which express an opinion in terms

of whether financial statements give a true and fair view, or where statutory or other specific requirements prescribe the use of a term such as 'presents fairly' or 'properly prepared in accordance with'.

Definitions

8 The following definitions apply in interpreting the requirements of this SAS.

9 *Financial statements:* the balance sheet, profit and loss account (or other form of income statement), statements of cash flows and total recognised gains and losses, notes and other statements and explanatory material, all of which are identified in the auditors' report as being the financial statements.

10 *Directors:* the directors of a company, the partners, proprietors or trustees of other forms of enterprise or equivalent persons responsible for the reporting entity's affairs, including the preparation of its financial statements.

11 *Material:* a matter is material if its omission or misstatement would reasonably influence the decisions of a user of the financial statements.

Materiality may be considered in the context of the financial statements as a whole, any individual primary statement within the financial statements or individual items included in them.

12 *Inherent uncertainty:* an uncertainty whose resolution is dependent upon uncertain future events outside the control of the reporting entity's directors at the date the financial statements are approved.

13 *Fundamental uncertainty:* an inherent uncertainty is fundamental when the magnitude of its potential impact is so great that, without clear disclosure of the nature and implications of the uncertainty, the view given by the financial statements would be seriously misleading.

The magnitude of an inherent uncertainty's potential impact is judged by reference to:

- the risk that the estimate included in the financial statements may be subject to change;
- the range of possible outcomes; and
- the consequences of those outcomes on the view shown in the financial statements.

Basic elements of the auditors' report

14 Auditors' reports on financial statements should include the following matters:

(a) a title identifying the person or persons to whom the report is addressed;

(b) an introductory paragraph identifying the financial statements audited;

(c) separate sections, appropriately headed, dealing with:

(i) respective responsibilities of directors (or equivalent persons) and auditors;

(ii) the basis of the auditors' opinion;

(iii) the auditors' opinion on the financial statements;

(d) the manuscript or printed signature of the auditors; and

(e) the date of the auditors' report. (SAS 600.2).

15 The use of a standard format for auditors' reports on financial statements assists the reader to follow the report's contents. The section headings indicate to the reader the nature of the matters contained in the section concerned: for example, where a qualified opinion is expressed, the heading 'Qualified opinion' may be used.

16 Auditors draft each section of their report on financial statements to reflect the requirements which apply to the particular audit engagement. However, the use of common language in auditors' reports assists the reader's understanding. Accordingly, Appendix 2 includes examples of auditors' reports on financial statements to illustrate wording which meets the Auditing Standards contained in this SAS.

Title and addressee

17 An appropriate title is used to distinguish clearly the auditors' report from other information relating to the reporting entity with which it may be published.

18 The auditors' report on the financial statements of a company is addressed to its members (normally the shareholders) because the audit is undertaken on their behalf. The auditors' report on financial statements of other types of reporting entity is addressed to the appropriate person or persons, as defined by statute or by the terms of the individual engagement.

Identification of financial statements

19 The purpose of the introductory section of the auditors' report, identifying the financial statements that have been audited, is to ensure that there is no ambiguity regarding the information to which the auditors' opinion relates. The introductory section may refer to the accounting convention and accounting policies which have been followed in preparing the financial statements.

Statements of responsibility and basis of opinion

20 (a) Auditors should distinguish between their responsibilities and those of the directors by including in their report:

(i) a statement that the financial statements are the responsibility of the reporting entity's directors;

(ii) a reference to a description of those responsibilities when set out elsewhere in the financial statements or accompanying information; and

(iii) a statement that the auditors' responsibility is to express an opinion on the financial statements.

(b) Where the financial statements or accompanying information (for example the directors' report) do not include an adequate description of directors' relevant responsibilities, the auditors' report should include a description of those responsibilities. (SAS 600.3).

21 The matters to be included in the description of the directors' responsibilities reflects the specific requirements applicable to the reporting entity. A description of the responsibilities of a company's directors is normally considered adequate when it includes the following points:

(a) company law requires directors to prepare financial statements for each financial year which give a true and fair view of the company's (or group's) state of affairs at the end of the year and profit or loss for the year then ended;

(b) in preparing those financial statements, the directors are required to:

- select suitable accounting policies and then apply them on a consistent basis, making judgments and estimates that are prudent and reasonable;

- *(large companies only*[1]*)* state whether applicable accounting standards have been followed, subject to any material departures disclosed and explained in the financial statements;
- *(where no separate statement on going concern is made by the directors)* prepare the financial statements on the going concern basis unless it is not appropriate to presume that the company will continue in business.

(c) the directors are responsible for keeping proper accounting records, for safeguarding the assets of the company (or group) and for taking reasonable steps for the prevention and detection of fraud and other irregularities.

These points may be adapted for different requirements applicable to different categories of reporting entity, for example to reflect special legal requirements relating to small companies, insurance companies or banks, or specific requirements applicable to a non-corporate entity.

22 In the case of reporting entities other than companies, auditors assess the adequacy of the description by reference to statutory or any other specific requirements with which the reporting entity's directors are required to comply.

23 Illustrative wording of a description of the directors' responsibilities, which may be included in auditors' reports on company financial statements where the directors' statement is inadequate, is shown in Appendix 3. Auditors' reports on the financial statements of other reporting entities provide equivalent details, reflecting appropriate legal and regulatory requirements when necessary to do so.

24 Auditors should explain the basis of their opinion by including in their report:

(a) a statement as to their compliance or otherwise with Auditing Standards, together with the reasons for any departure therefrom;

(b) a statement that the audit process includes:

(i) examining, on a test basis, evidence relevant to the amounts and disclosures in the financial statements;

(ii) assessing the significant estimates and judgments made by the reporting entity's directors in preparing the financial statements;

(iii) considering whether the accounting policies are appropriate to the reporting entity's circumstances, consistently applied and adequately disclosed;

(c) a statement that they planned and performed the audit so as to obtain reasonable assurance that the financial statements are free from material misstatement, whether caused by fraud or other irregularity or error, and that they have evaluated the overall presentation of the financial statements. (SAS 600.4).

25 A reference to compliance with Auditing Standards is necessary in order to provide assurance that the audit has been carried out in accordance with established standards.

26 In some exceptional circumstances, a departure from Auditing Standards may be appropriate to fulfil the objectives of a specific audit more effectively. If this is the case, the auditors explain the reasons for that departure in their report. Other than in such exceptional and justifiable circumstances, a departure from an Auditing Standard is a

[1]'Large' in this context means those companies which fall outside the categories of small and medium-sized companies as defined in the Companies Act 1985.

limitation on the scope of work undertaken by the auditors. In such circumstances the auditors assess whether a qualified opinion or disclaimer of opinion is required, as set out in SAS 600.7.

27 In certain circumstances, auditors are required by statute to follow other comparable standards, such as the Code of Audit Practice for Local Authorities and the National Health Service in England and Wales or the requirements of the Scottish Accounts Commission. Where this is the case, auditors refer to these standards.

28 In some circumstances, auditors may be required to report whether the financial statements have been properly prepared in accordance with regulations or other requirements, but are not required to report on whether they give a true and fair view. Where the special circumstances of the reporting entity require or permit the adoption of policies or accounting bases which would not normally permit a true and fair view to be given, auditors would refer to those circumstances in the paragraphs dealing with the respective responsibilities of directors and auditors (unless the matter is included in a separate statement given by the directors) and may draw attention to them in the basis of opinion section of the report.

29 Auditors may wish to include additional comment in this part of their report to highlight matters which they regard as relevant to a proper understanding of the basis of their opinion.

Expression of opinion

30 An auditors' report should contain a clear expression of opinion on the financial statements and on any further matters required by statute or other requirements applicable to the particular engagement. (SAS 600.5).

31 An auditors' report may include an unqualified opinion or qualified opinion. The circumstances giving rise to each type of opinion are set out below and example reports illustrating each form of opinion are contained in Appendix 2.

Unqualified opinions

32 An unqualified opinion on financial statements is expressed when in the auditors' judgement they give a true and fair view (where relevant) and have been prepared in accordance with relevant accounting or other requirements. This judgement entails concluding whether *inter alia*:

- the financial statements have been prepared using appropriate accounting policies, which have been consistently applied;
- the financial statements have been prepared in accordance with relevant legislation, regulations or applicable accounting standards (and that any departures are justified and adequately explained in the financial statements); and
- there is adequate disclosure of all information relevant to the proper understanding of the financial statements.

Qualified opinions

33 A qualified opinion is issued when either of the following circumstances exist:

(a) there is a limitation on the scope of the auditors' examination (see SAS 600.7); or

(b) the auditors disagree with the treatment or disclosure of a matter in the financial statements (see SAS 600.8);

and, in the auditors' judgment, the effect of the matter is or may be material to the financial statements and therefore those statements may not or do not give a true and fair view of the matters on which the auditors are required to report or do not comply with relevant accounting or other requirements.

Adverse opinions

34 An adverse opinion is issued when the effect of a disagreement is so material or pervasive that the auditors conclude that the financial statements are seriously misleading (see SAS 600.8). An adverse opinion is expressed by stating that the financial statements do not give a true and fair view.

35 When the auditors conclude that the effect of a disagreement is not so significant as to require an adverse opinion, they express an opinion that is qualified by stating that the financial statements give a true and fair view except for the effects of the matter giving rise to the disagreement.

Disclaimers of opinion

36 A disclaimer of opinion is expressed when the possible effect of a limitation on scope is so material or pervasive that the auditors have not been able to obtain sufficient evidence to support, and accordingly are unable to express, an opinion on the financial statements (see SAS 600.7).

37 Where the auditors conclude that the possible effect of the limitation is not so significant as to require a disclaimer, they issue an opinion that is qualified by stating that the financial statements give a true and fair view except for the effects of any adjustments that might have been found necessary had the limitation not affected the evidence available to them.

Compliance with relevant accounting requirements

38 The auditors' opinion is expressed in the context of the particular accounting requirements applicable to the financial statements concerned and normally includes, in addition to an opinion on the view given by the financial statements, an opinion on whether or not those requirements have been followed. For example, an auditors' report on the financial statements of a company incorporated in Great Britain includes the words '. . . and have been properly prepared in accordance with the Companies Act 1985'.

39 Save in exceptional circumstances, compliance with accounting standards is necessary to give a true and fair view.

40 Financial statements are normally required to contain particulars of any material departure from an accounting standard which applies to the reporting entity, together with the financial effects of the departure unless this would be impracticable or misleading in the context of giving a true and fair view.

Requirements of company law

41 In the context of financial reporting by companies, directors are required by law to prepare annual accounts which consist of a balance sheet and profit and loss account together with accompanying notes and which give a true and fair view of the state of affairs of the company (or group) at the end of the financial year and of the profit or loss of the company (or group) for that year. Company law requires the auditors to state whether in their opinion the company's annual accounts give such a view.

42 There is no specific legal requirement that companies should comply with accounting standards. However, legislation in the UK gives specific recognition to accounting standards and requires large companies to state in their financial statements whether those statements have been prepared in accordance with such standards and to give particulars of any material departure and the reasons for it — paragraph 36A of Schedule 4 to the

Companies Act 1985.

43 It is likely that a Court would infer from this requirement, taken together with other changes introduced into UK company law by the Companies Act 1989, that financial statements which meet the Act's requirements will follow rather than depart from accounting standards, and that any departure would be regarded as sufficiently abnormal to require justification. Therefore, in general, compliance with accounting standards is necessary to meet the requirement of company law that the directors prepare annual accounts which give a true and fair view of a company's (or group's) state of affairs and profit or loss.

Primary statements

44 Accounting standards contained in Financial Reporting Standards require, in certain circumstances, further 'primary statements' in addition to the balance sheet and profit and loss account. It follows from the principle stated in the last paragraph that, where required by an accounting standard, these further primary statements are normally necessary in order that the annual accounts give a true and fair view, as required in the United Kingdom by the Companies Act 1985 or the Companies (Northern Ireland) Order 1986 and, in the Republic of Ireland, the Companies Acts 1963 to 1990. The annual accounts, including the additional primary statements required by accounting standards, are referred to by the term 'financial statements'.

45 Accordingly, reference in an auditors' opinion on a company's financial statements to the primary statements required by accounting standards is unnecessary. It may also be misleading to the reader of the auditors' report, in that it may appear to detract from the role of the additional primary statements in supporting the information contained in the company's balance sheet and profit or loss account so as to give a true and fair view as required by the law.

46 Auditors may be requested to report separately on one or more primary statements. When making such a separate report, they need to ensure that in doing so no impression is given that the primary statement(s) referred to is other than integral to the financial statements as a whole and that it is clear to a reader that the primary statement is necessary to give a true and fair view of the state of affairs and profit or loss for statutory purposes.

Non-compliance with accounting standards

47 When the auditors conclude that the financial statements of a company do not comply with accounting standards, they assess:

(a) whether there are sound reasons for the departure;

(b) whether adequate disclosure has been made concerning the departure from accounting standards;

(c) whether the departure is such that the financial statements do not give a true and fair view of the state of affairs and profit or loss.

In normal cases, a departure from accounting standards will result in the issue of a qualified or adverse opinion on the view given by the financial statements.

48 Where no explanation is given for a departure from accounting standards, its absence may of itself impair the ability of the financial statements to give a true and fair view of the company's state of affairs and profit or loss. When auditors conclude that this is so, a qualified or adverse opinion on the view given by the financial statements is appropriate, in addition to a reference (where appropriate) to the non-compliance with the specific requirement of company law referred to in paragraph 42 above.

Small companies — Great Britain and Northern Ireland

49 Directors of companies which fall within the category of small companies as defined by company legislation in the UK may draw up financial statements taking advantage of a number of exemptions from the full requirements of company law.[2] Financial statements prepared using these exemptions are nevertheless required to give a true and fair view, and the legislation further specifically provides that they shall not be deemed not to do so by reason only of the fact that advantage has been taken of the exemptions.

50 Auditors reporting on the financial statements of a small company prepared using these exemptions are permitted (but not required) to report in terms which omit reference to whether a true and fair view is given, referring only to the proper preparation of those statements in accordance with the requirements of company law applicable to small companies. However, their legal obligation to consider whether the financial statements give a true and fair view as required by company law remains unchanged. The requirement for a clear expression of opinion (contained in SAS 600.5) is therefore best met by referring to the true and fair view, except for particular circumstances in which the auditors consider it impossible to do so.

51 Illustrative wording for an auditors' report on financial statements of a small company taking advantage of the exemptions is given in Example 5 of Appendix 2.

Further matters required by statute or other regulations

52 Further opinions or information to be included in the auditors' report may be determined by specific statutory requirements applicable to the reporting entity, or, in some circumstances, by the terms of the auditors' engagement. Such matters may be required to be dealt with by a positive statement in the auditors' report or only by exception. For example, in the Republic of Ireland auditors are required to state whether, in their opinion, proper books of account have been kept, whereas company legislation in the United Kingdom requires auditors to report only when a company has not maintained proper accounting records.

53 Where further opinions are required by statute or other regulation, matters which result in qualification of such an opinion may also result in a qualification of the auditors' opinion on the financial statements: for example, if proper accounting records have not been maintained and as a result it proves impracticable for the auditors to obtain sufficient evidence concerning material matters in the financial statements, their report indicates that the scope of their examination was limited and includes a qualified opinion or disclaimer of opinion on the financial statements arising from that limitation, as required by SAS 600.7.

Fundamental uncertainty

54 (a) **In forming their opinion on financial statements, auditors should consider whether the view given by the financial statements could be affected by inherent uncertainties which, in their opinion, are fundamental.**

(b) **When an inherent uncertainty exists which:**

(i) in the auditors' opinion is fundamental; and

(ii) is adequately accounted for and disclosed in the financial statements;

the auditors should include an explanatory paragraph referring to the fundamental uncertainty in the section of their report setting out the basis of their opinion.

[2] Set out in Schedule 8 to the Companies Act 1985, as inserted by SI 1992 No. 2452.

(c) **When adding an explanatory paragraph, auditors should use words which clearly indicate that their opinion on the financial statements is not qualified in respect of its contents. (SAS 600.6).**

Inherent uncertainties

55 Inherent uncertainties about the outcome of future events frequently affect, to some degree, a wide range of components of the financial statements at the date they are approved. It is not possible for the directors to remove the uncertainties by obtaining more information at the date they approve the financial statements: the statements can reflect only the working assumptions of directors as to their financial outcome and, where material, describe the circumstances giving rise to the uncertainties and their potential financial effect.

56 In forming an opinion, auditors take into account the adequacy of the accounting treatment, estimates and disclosures of inherent uncertainties in the light of evidence available at the date they express that opinion.

57 Auditors recognise that, in preparing financial statements, directors are required to analyse relevant existing conditions, including uncertainties about future events and their effect on financial statements. An audit includes assessment of whether there is sufficient evidence to support the directors' analysis and resulting estimates and disclosures given in the financial statements. Usually auditors are able to obtain sufficient evidence concerning the directors' assessment of the outcome of inherent uncertainties by considering various types of evidence, including the historical experience of the reporting entity.

58 Forming an opinion on the adequacy of the accounting treatment of inherent uncertainties involves consideration of:

- the appropriateness of accounting policies dealing with uncertain matters;
- the reasonableness of the estimates included in the financial statements in respect of inherent uncertainties; and
- the adequacy of disclosure.

59 Auditors distinguish between circumstances in which an unqualified opinion is appropriate and those in which a qualification or disclaimer of opinion is required due to a limitation on the scope of their work. An inherent uncertainty can be expected to be resolved at a future date, at which time sufficient evidence concerning its outcome would be expected to become available. When evidence does or did exist (or reasonably could be expected to exist) but that evidence is not available to the auditors, the scope or their work is limited and a qualification or disclaimer of opinion is appropriate.

60 Where auditors conclude that the accounting policies followed lead to material misstatements in the financial statements, or that the estimates included in the financial statements are materially misstated, or that disclosures relating to uncertainty are inadequate, a qualified or adverse opinion is required by SAS 600.8.

Fundamental uncertainties

61 In some circumstances, the degree of uncertainty about the outcome of a future event and its potential impact on the view given by the financial statements may be very great. Where resolution of an inherent uncertainty could affect the view given by the financial statements to the degree that the auditors conclude that it is to be regarded as fundamental, they include an explanatory paragraph when setting out the basis of their opinion describing the matter giving rise to the fundamental uncertainty and its possible effects on the financial statements, including (where practicable) quantification. Where it is not possible to quantify the potential effects of the resolution of the uncertainty, the auditors include a statement to that effect. Reference may be made to notes in the financial statements but such a reference is not a substitute for sufficient description of the fundamental uncertainty so that a reader can appreciate the principal points at issue and their implications.

62 Communication with the reader is enhanced by the use of an appropriate sub-heading differentiating the explanatory paragraph from other matters included in the section describing the basis of the auditors' opinion.

63 In determining whether an inherent uncertainty is fundamental, auditors consider;

(a) the risk that the estimate included in the financial statements may be subject to change;

(b) the range of possible outcomes; and

(c) the consequences of those outcomes on the view shown in the financial statements.

64 Inherent uncertainties are regarded as fundamental when they involve a significant level of concern about the validity of the going concern basis or other matters whose potential effect on the financial statements is unusually great. A common example of a fundamental uncertainty is the outcome of major litigation.

Opinions expressed

65 An unqualified opinion indicates that the auditors consider that appropriate estimates and disclosures relating to fundamental uncertainties are made in the financial statements. It remains unqualified notwithstanding the inclusion of an explanatory paragraph describing a fundamental uncertainty. The explanatory paragraph is included as part of the basis for the auditors' opinion so as to make clear that it describes a matter which the auditors have taken into account in forming their opinion, but that it does not qualify that opinion.

66 When the auditors conclude that the estimate of the outcome of a fundamental uncertainty is materially misstated or that the disclosure relating to it inadequate, they issue a qualified opinion.

67 A disclaimer of opinion is issued by auditors as a result of an inherent uncertainty which in their opinion is fundamental only when a limitation of the scope of their work directly affects their assessment of the adequacy of its accounting treatment and disclosure.

Limitation of audit scope

68 When there has been a limitation on the scope of the auditors' work that prevents them from obtaining sufficient evidence to express an unqualified opinion:

(a) the auditors' report should include a description of the factors leading to the limitation in the opinion section of their report;

(b) the auditors should issue a disclaimer of opinion when the possible effect of a limitation on scope is so material or pervasive that they are unable to express an opinion on the financial statements;

(c) a qualified opinion should be issued when the effect of the limitation is not so material or pervasive as to require a disclaimer, and the wording of the opinion should indicate that it is qualified as to the possible adjustments to

the financial statements that might have been determined to be necessary had the limitation not existed. (SAS 600.7).

69 In considering whether a limitation results in a lack of evidence necessary to form an opinion, auditors assess:

(a) the quantity and type of evidence which may reasonably be expected to be available to support the particular figure or disclosure in the financial statements; and

(b) the possible effect on the financial statements of the matter for which insufficient evidence is available. When the possible effect is, in the opinion of the auditors, material to the financial statements, there will be insufficient evidence to support an unqualified opinion.

70 Inherent uncertainties do not arise from, or give rise to, a limitation on the auditors' work and are considered under SAS 600.6.

71 A description of the factors leading to a limitation enables the reader to understand the reasons for the limitation and to distinguish between:

(a) limitations imposed on the auditors (for example, where not all the accounting records are made available to the auditors or where the directors prevent a particular procedure considered necessary by the auditors from being carried out); and

(b) limitations outside the control of the auditors or the directors (for example, when the timing of the auditors' appointment is such that attendance at the entity's stock-take is not possible and there is no alternative form of evidence regarding the existence of stock).

72 When the proposed terms of an audit engagement include a limitation on the scope of the auditors' work such that they believe the need to issue a disclaimer exists, they would normally not accept such a limited engagement as an audit engagement, unless required by statute to do so.

73 Where a scope limitation is imposed by circumstances, auditors would normally attempt to carry out reasonable alternative procedures to obtain sufficient audit evidence to support an unqualified opinion.

Disagreement on accounting treatment or disclosure

74 Where the auditors disagree with the accounting treatment or disclosure of a matter in the financial statements, and in the auditors' opinion the effect of that disagreement is material to the financial statements:

(a) the auditors should include in the opinion section of their report:

(i) a description of all substantive factors giving rise to the disagreement;

(ii) their implications for the financial statements;

(iii) whenever practicable, a quantification of the effect on the financial statements;

(b) when the auditors conclude that the effect of the matter giving rise to disagreement is so material or pervasive that the financial statements are seriously misleading, they should issue an adverse opinion;

(c) in the case of other material disagreements, the auditors should issue a qualified opinion indicating that it is expressed except for the effects of the matter giving rise to the disagreement. (SAS 600.8).

75 An auditors' report including a qualified opinion arising from disagreement includes a description of the reasons for qualification and the effects on the financial statements. Whilst reference may be made to relevant notes in the financial statements, such reference is not a substitute for sufficient description of the circumstances in the auditors' report so that a reader can appreciate the principal points at issue and their implications for an understanding of the financial statements.

Date and signature of the auditors' report

76 (a) Auditors should not express an opinion on financial statements until those statements and all other financial information contained in a report of which the audited financial statements form a part have been approved by the directors, and the auditors have considered all necessary available evidence.

(b) The date of an auditors' report on a reporting entity's financial statements is the date on which the auditors signed their report expressing an opinion on those statements. (SAS 600.9).

77 The report may be signed in the name of the auditors' firm, the personal name of the auditor, or both as appropriate. The signature is normally that of the firm because the firm as a whole assumes responsibility for the audit. To assist identification, the report normally includes the location of the auditors' office. Where appropriate, their status as registered auditors is also stated.

Date of the auditors' report

78 Dating the auditors' report informs the reader that the auditors have considered the effect on the financial statements of events or transactions of which they are aware which occurred up to that date.

79 The auditors are not in the position to form their opinion until the financial statements (and any other financial information contained in a report of which the audited financial statements form a part) have been approved by the directors and the auditors have completed their assessment of all the evidence they consider necessary for the opinion or opinions to be given in their report. This assessment includes events occurring up to the date the opinion is expressed. Auditors therefore plan the conduct of audits to take account of the need to ensure, before expressing an opinion on financial statements, that the directors have approved the financial statements and any accompanying financial information and that the auditors have completed a sufficient review of post balance sheet events.

80 The date of the auditors' report is, therefore, the date on which, following:

(a) receipt of the financial statements and accompanying documents in the form approved by the directors for release;

(b) review of all documents which they are required to consider in addition to the financial statements (for example the directors' report, chairman's statement or other review of an entity's affairs which will accompany the financial statements); and

(c) completion of all procedures necessary to form an opinion on the financial statements (and any other opinions required by law or regulation) including a review of post balance sheet events;

the auditors sign (in manuscript) their report expressing an opinion on the financial statements for distribution with those statements.

81 The form of the financial statements and other financial information approved by the directors, and considered by the auditors when signing a report expressing their opinion, may be in the form of final drafts from which printed documents will be prepared. Subsequent production of printed copies of the financial statements and auditors' report does not constitute the creation of a new document. Copies of the report produced for circulation to shareholders or others may therefore reproduce a printed version of the auditors' signature showing the date of actual signature.

82 Before signing a report expressing their opinion after consideration of final drafts of the financial statements and other accompanying documents, auditors will need to consider whether the form of draft documents is sufficiently clear for them to assess the overall financial statement presentation. When the auditors conclude that this is not the case, it will be necessary for them to defer signing their report until it is possible for them to do so.

83 If the date on which the auditors sign their report is later than that on which the directors approved the financial statements, the auditors take such steps as are appropriate:

(a) to obtain assurance that the directors would have approved the financial statements on that later date (for example, by obtaining confirmation from specified individual members of the board to whom authority has been delegated for this purpose); and

(b) to ensure that their procedures for reviewing subsequent events cover the period up to that date.

Registrar of companies

84 The copy of the auditors' report which is delivered to the registrar of companies is required to state the name of the auditors and be signed by them. Where the auditors sign their report in a form from which a final printed version is produced, they may sign copies for identification purposes in order to provide the registrar with appropriately signed copies. No further active procedures need to be followed at that later date.

Compliance with International Standards on Auditing

85 Compliance with the auditing standards contained in this SAS will ensure compliance in all material respects with the basic principles and essential procedures proposed in the exposure draft of International Standard on Auditing 'Auditors' report on financial statements'.

Effective date

86 Auditors are required to comply with the requirements of this SAS in respect of audits of financial statements for financial periods ending on or after 30 September 1993. Adoption of the requirements when reporting on financial statements for accounting periods ending before that date is encouraged.

Note on legal requirements applicable to companies

i Reference should be made to the legislation itself for an understanding of the relevant points of law. This section lists only the main sections of the relevant Acts containing provisions in relation to auditors' reports on financial statements.

Legal requirements in Great Britain

References are to the Companies Act 1985 as amended by the Companies Act 1989.

ii The main sections of the Companies Act containing provisions relating to auditors' reports on financial statements are as follows:

Section 235 auditors to report to the member of the company on any financial statements of the company laid before it in general meeting;

Section 236 signature of auditors' reports;

Section 237 auditors to report to members in certain circumstances;

Section 246 exemptions for small and medium-sized companies;

Section 251 summary financial statements.

Summary financial statements

iii In the UK, listed companies may send a summary financial statement to shareholders and debenture holders in place of the full report and accounts. Such summary financial statements are required to include a statement from the company's auditors confirming that the summary financial statement is consistent with the full financial statements, but need not include the auditors' report on the financial statements, unless this is qualified.

iv In order to ensure that recipients of a summary financial statement are aware that further information is contained in the full report, it is appropriate for auditors to extend the information given in their report on a summary financial statement so as to draw attention to the fact that the auditors' report includes information on the responsibilities of directors and auditors, on the basis of the auditors' opinion and, where considered appropriate, to draw attention to fundamental uncertainties.

v Guidance on the work to be undertaken before issuing such a statement is contained in the Auditing Guideline 'Auditors' reports on summary financial statements'. Illustrative wording for an auditors' statement on a summary financial statement is shown in Example 6 of Appendix 2 to this SAS. This example supersedes the example contained in the Auditing Guideline.

Significance of qualified opinions

vi The term 'qualified' in relation to auditors' reports has a particular meaning in company law. For example, the term is defined for the purposes of Part VII of the Companies Act 1985 (accounts and audit) in Section 262 of the Act as meaning:

> 'that the report does not state the auditors' unqualified opinion that the accounts have been properly prepared in accordance with this Act or, in the case of an undertaking not required to prepare accounts in accordance with this Act, under any corresponding legislation under which it is required to prepare accounts'.

vii The issue of a qualified report has significance for a number of other provisions in company law. The principal examples are:

- *re-registration of a private company as public — Section 43*

  Section 46 defines 'unqualified' for the purposes of Section 43 as 'stating without material qualification the auditors' opinion that the balance sheet has been properly prepared in accordance with this Act'. A qualification is material unless the auditors state in their report that the matter giving rise to the qualification is not material for the purpose of determining (by reference to the company's balance sheet) whether at the balance sheet date the amount of the company's net assets was not less than the aggregate of its called up share capital and undistributable reserves.

- *requirements for last annual accounts when these form the relevant accounts for determining the legality of a proposed distribution — Section 271*

  Section 271(3) provides that, in this circumstance, the auditors must have made their report on the annual accounts before the directors and shareholders determine whether a dividend may be paid.

  A company may not pay a dividend based on financial statements which receive a qualified report from its auditors unless the auditors make a further report stating whether or not the matter giving rise to the qualification is material to assessing the legality of the dividend. The auditors are not, however, required to 'approve' the dividend or comment on whether its payment is prudent.

viii A number of other uses, outside company law, are made of auditors' reports on financial statements. These include:

- the Banking Act 1987 (in the UK);
- the requirements of regulators of investments businesses; and
- the requirements to be met before a listing on the London Stock Exchange may be obtained.

Legal requirements in Northern Ireland

ix The legal requirements in Northern Ireland are contained in The Companies (Northern Ireland) Order 1986 (as amended) and are very similar to those in Great Britain. References in the Order which correspond to the legal references in paragraph ii above are as follows:

- Section 243;
- Section 244;
- Section 245;
- Section 256;
- Section 259.

Legal requirements in the Republic of Ireland

x The legal requirements in the Republic of Ireland are contained in the Companies Acts, 1963 to 1990.

xi The main sections of the Act that govern the duties of auditors are as follows:

Companies Act 1990

Section 193	auditors' report and right of access to books and of attendance and audience at general meetings;
Section 194	duty of auditors if proper books of account are not kept.

Companies (Amendment) Act 1986

Section 15 consideration by auditors of consistency of directors' report with company accounts;

Section 18 provision in relation to documents delivered to registrar of companies.

Significance of qualified opinions

xii Section 9(11) of the Companies (Amendment) Act 1983 equates to Section 46 of the Companies Act 1985 in Great Britain and Section 49(3) and (4) of the Companies (Amendment) Act 1983 correspond to Section 271 of the Companies Act 1985 in Great Britain.

Appendix 1

Forming an opinion on financial statements

1 This appendix sets out in the form of a flowchart the steps involved in forming an opinion as to whether a set of financial statements presents a true and fair view of the reporting entity's state of affairs and profit or loss. The flowchart is intended to provide guidance to readers in understanding the Statement of Auditing Standards. It does not form part of the Standards themselves.

2 The flowchart is drawn up on the basis that the directors make no further amendments to the financial statements following the audit. In practice, directors may make amendments in response to comments by the auditors: any amendment of the financial statements (for example, to provide additional disclosure in order to give a true and fair view) would require auditors to begin the sequence of questions afresh.

3 In applying the logic in the flowchart, auditors may find it necessary to address the questions for discrete sections of the financial statements as well as for the financial statements as a whole.

4 The principal matters which auditors consider in forming an opinion may be expressed in three questions:

(1) *Have they completed all procedures necessary to meet Auditing Standards and to obtain all the information and explanations necessary for their audit?* This question is considered in paragraphs 68 to 73 of the SAS.

(2) *Have the financial statements been prepared in accordance with the applicable accounting requirements?* This question is considered in paragraphs 38 to 51 of the SAS.

The flowchart refers to these requirements as GAAP (generally accepted accounting practice) as a convenient shorthand to indicate those accounting requirements which apply in the case of the particular financial statements concerned. In the case of a company subject to company legislation in Great Britain, this will normally mean that the financial statements have been prepared in accordance with Schedule 4 and (if appropriate) 4A to the Companies Act 1985 — Sections 226(3) and 227(4) — and with applicable accounting standards.

As a starting point, compliance with applicable accounting requirements is likely to result in financial statements giving a true and fair view. However, compliance alone may be insufficient in a particular instance. Section 226(4) and (5) and Section 227(5) and (6) therefore *require* directors of a company to provide additional information or even depart from the rules in order to give a true and fair view.

Similarly, a breach of the rules, whether by omission or substitution of an alternative accounting treatment, may mean that a true and fair view is not given, but departures from the rules are needed in some specific cases so that a true and fair view can be given.

Hence the third question:

(3) *Do the financial statements, as prepared by the directors, give a true and fair view?*

Forming an opinion on financial statements

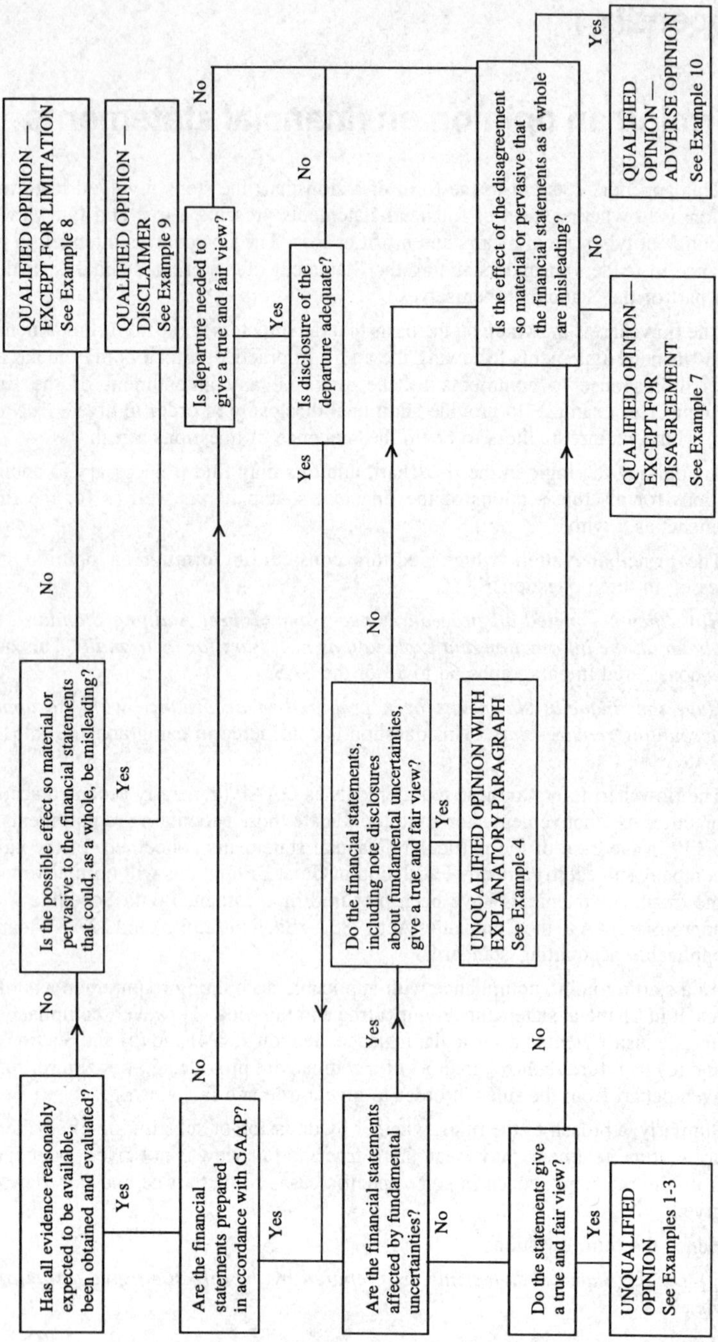

Questions concerning limitation and disagreement are presumed to involve matters considered to be material

Appendix 2

Examples of auditors' reports on financial statements

Unqualified opinions

1 Company incorporated in Great Britain.

2 Company incorporated in the Republic of Ireland.

3 Company incorporated in Northern Ireland.

4 Explanatory paragraph dealing with a fundamental uncertainty.

5 Company incorporated in Great Britain using exemptions available for small companies.

6 Opinion on a summary financial statement.

Qualified opinions

7 Disagreement.

8 Limitation on the auditors' work.

9 Disclaimer of opinion.

10 Adverse opinion.

11 Qualified opinion and explanatory paragraph dealing with a fundamental uncertainty.

12 Omission of primary statement.

Example 1 — unqualified opinion: company incorporated in Great Britain

Auditors' report to the shareholders of XYZ PLC

We have audited the financial statements on pages ... to ... which have been prepared under the historical cost convention[3] [as modified by the revaluation of certain fixed assets] and the accounting policies set out on page ... .

Respective responsibilities of directors and auditors

As described on page ... the company's directors are responsible for the preparation of financial statements. It is our responsibility to form an independent opinion, based on our audit, on those statements and to report our opinion to you.

Basis of opinion

We conducted our audit in accordance with Auditing Standards issued by the Auditing Practices Board. An audit includes examination, on a test basis, of evidence relevant to the amounts and disclosures in the financial statements. It also includes an assessment of the significant estimates and judgments made by the directors in the preparation of the financial statements, and of whether the accounting policies are appropriate to the company's circumstances, consistently applied and adequately disclosed.

We planned and performed our audit so as to obtain all the information and explanations which we considered necessary in order to provide us with sufficient evidence to give reasonable assurance that the financial statements are free from material misstatement, whether caused by fraud or other irregularity or error. In forming our opinion we also evaluated the overall adequacy of the presentation of information in the financial statements.

Opinion

In our opinion the financial statements give a true and fair view of the state of the company's affairs as at 31 December 19.. and of its profit [loss] for the year then ended and have been properly prepared in accordance with the Companies Act 1985.

Registered auditors *Address*

Date

[3] A reference to the convention draws attention to the fact that the values reflected in the financial statements are not current but historical and, where appropriate, to the fact that there is a mixture of past and recent values.

Example 2 — unqualified opinion: company incorporated in the Republic of Ireland

Auditors' report to the shareholders of XYZ PLC

We have audited the financial statements on pages ... to ... which have been prepared under the historical cost convention [as modified by the revaluation of certain fixed assets] and the accounting policies set out on page ... .

Respective responsibilities of directors and auditors

As described on page ... the company's directors are responsible for the preparation of financial statements. It is our responsibility to form an independent opinion, based on our audit, on those statements and to report our opinion to you.

Basis of opinion

We conducted our audit in accordance with Auditing Standards issued by the Auditing Practices Board. An audit includes examination, on a test basis, of evidence relevant to the amounts and disclosures in the financial statements. It also includes an assessment of the significant estimates and judgments made by the directors in the preparation of the financial statements, and of whether the accounting policies are appropriate to the company's circumstances, consistently applied and adequately disclosed.

We planned and performed our audit so as to obtain all the information and explanations which we considered necessary in order to provide us with sufficient evidence to give reasonable assurance that the financial statements are free from material misstatement, whether caused by fraud or other irregularity or error. In forming our opinion we also evaluated the overall adequacy of the presentation of information in the financial statements.

Opinion

In our opinion the financial statements give a true and fair view of the state of the company's affairs as at 31 December 19.. and of its profit [loss] for the year then ended and have been properly prepared in accordance with the Companies Acts 1963 to 1990.

We have obtained all the information and explanations we consider necessary for the purposes of our audit. In our opinion, proper books of account have been kept by the company. The financial statements are in agreement with the books of account.

In our opinion, the information given in the directors' report on pages ... to ... is consistent with the financial statements.

The net assets of the company, as stated in the balance sheet on page ..., are more than half of the amount of its called up share capital and, in our opinion, on that basis there did not exist at (date) a financial situation which, under Section 40(1) of the Companies (Amendment) Act 1983, would require the convening of an extraordinary general meeting of the company.

Registered auditors *Address*

Date

Example 3 — company incorporated in Northern Ireland

Auditors' report to the shareholders of XYZ PLC

We have audited the financial statements on pages ... to ... which have been prepared under the historical cost convention [as modified by the revaluation of certain fixed assets] and the accounting policies set out on page ... .

Respective responsibilities of directors and auditors

As described on page ... the company's directors are responsible for the preparation of financial statements. It is our responsibility to form an independent opinion, based on our audit, on those statements and to report our opinion to you.

Basis of opinion

We conducted our audit in accordance with Auditing Standards issued by the Auditing Practices Board. An audit includes examination, on a test basis, of evidence relevant to the amounts and disclosures in the financial statements. It also includes an assessment of the significant estimates and judgments made by the directors in the preparation of the financial statements, and of whether the accounting policies are appropriate to the company's circumstances, consistently applied and adequately disclosed.

We planned and performed our audit so as to obtain all the information and explanations which we considered necessary in order to provide us with sufficient evidence to give reasonable assurance that the financial statements are free from material misstatement, whether caused by fraud or other irregularity or error. In forming our opinion we also evaluated the overall adequacy of the presentation of information in the financial statements.

Opinion

In our opinion the financial statements give a true and fair view of the state of the company's affairs as at 31 December 19.. and of its profit [loss] for the year then ended and have been properly prepared in accordance with the Companies (Northern Ireland) Order 1986.

Registered auditors *Address*

Date

Example 4 — unqualified opinion with explanatory paragraph describing a fundamental uncertainty

Auditors' report to the shareholders of XYZ PLC

We have audited the financial statements on pages ... to ... which have been prepared under the historical cost convention [as modified by the revaluation of certain fixed assets] and the accounting policies set out on page ... .

Respective responsibilities of directors and auditors

As described on page ... the company's directors are responsible for the preparation of financial statements. It is our responsibility to form an independent opinion, based on our audit, on those statements and to report our opinion to you.

Basis of opinion

We conducted our audit in accordance with Auditing Standards issued by the Auditing Practices Board. An audit includes examination, on a test basis, of evidence relevant to the amounts and disclosures in the financial statements. It also includes an assessment of the significant estimates and judgments made by the directors in the preparation of the financial statements, and of whether the accounting policies are appropriate to the company's circumstances, consistently applied and adequately disclosed.

We planned and performed our audit so as to obtain all the information and explanations which we considered necessary in order to provide us with sufficient evidence to give reasonable assurance that the financial statements are free from material misstatement, whether caused by fraud or other irregularity or error. In forming our opinion we also evaluated the overall adequacy of the presentation of information in the financial statements.

Fundamental uncertainty

In forming our opinion, we have considered the adequacy of the disclosures made in the financial statements concerning the possible outcome to litigation against B Limited, a subsidiary undertaking of the company, for an alleged breach of environmental regulations. The future settlement of this litigation could result in additional liabilities and the closure of B Limited's business, whose net assets included in the consolidated balance sheet total £... and whose profit before tax for the year is £... . Details of the circumstances relating to this fundamental uncertainty are described in note ... . Our opinion is not qualified in this respect.

Opinion

In our opinion the financial statements give a true and fair view of the state of affairs of the company and of the group as at 31 December 19.. and of the group's profit [loss] for the year then ended and have been properly prepared in accordance with the Companies Act 1985.

Registered auditors *Address*

Date

Example 5 — company incorporated in Great Britain, using accounting exemptions available for small companies

Auditors' report to the shareholders of XYZ Ltd

We have audited the financial statements on pages ... to ... which have been prepared under the historical cost convention [as modified by the revaluation of certain fixed assets] and the accounting policies set out on page ... .

Respective responsibilities of directors and auditors

As described on page ... the company's directors are responsible for the preparation of financial statements. It is our responsibility to form an independent opinion, based on our audit, on those statements and to report our opinion to you.

Basis of opinion

We conducted our audit in accordance with Auditing Standards issued by the Auditing Practices Board. An audit includes examination, on a test basis, of evidence relevant to the amounts and disclosures in the financial statements. It also includes an assessment of the significant estimates and judgments made by the directors in the preparation of the financial statements, and of whether the accounting policies are appropriate to the company's circumstances, consistently applied and adequately disclosed.

We planned and performed our audit so as to obtain all the information and explanations which we considered necessary in order to provide us with sufficient evidence to give reasonable assurance that the financial statements are free from material misstatement, whether caused by fraud or other irregularity or error. In forming our opinion we also evaluated the overall adequacy of the presentation of information in the financial statements.

Opinion

In our opinion the financial statements give a true and fair view of the state of the company's affairs as at 31 December 19.. and of its profit [loss] for the year then ended[4] and have been properly prepared in accordance with the provisions of the Companies Act 1985 applicable to small companies.

Registered auditors *Address*

Date

[4] When reporting on the financial statements of a small company which takes advantage of the exemptions available under Schedule 8 to the Companies Act 1985 (as inserted by SI 1992 No 2452), auditors may consider that were it not for paragraph 14(1) of the schedule, a true and fair view is not given because of the use of some or all of these exemptions. In such circumstances, they may give the form of report allowed by paragraph 14(3) of Schedule 8, as follows:

'In our opinion, the financial statements have been properly prepared in accordance with the provisions of the Companies Act 1985 applicable to small companies'.

When the auditors consider that a true and fair view is not given for other reasons, they should qualify their opinion as required by the Auditing Standards contained in this SAS.

Example 6 — auditors' statement on a summary financial statement

Auditors' statement to the shareholders of XYZ PLC
We have audited the summary financial statement set out above/on page ... .

Respective responsibilities of directors and auditors
The summary financial statement is the responsibility of the directors. Our responsibility is to report to you our opinion as to whether the statement is consistent with the full financial statements and directors' report.

Basis of opinion
We conducted our audit in accordance with Auditing Standards issued by the Auditing Practices Board. The audit of a summary financial statement comprises an assessment of whether the statement contains all information necessary to ensure consistency with the full financial statements and directors' report and of whether the detailed information required by law has been properly extracted from those documents and included in the summary statement.

Our report on the company's full financial statements includes information on the responsibilities of directors and auditors relating to the preparation and audit of financial statements and on the basis of our opinion on the financial statements.

Opinion
In our opinion the summary financial statement above/on page ... is consistent with the full financial statements and directors' report of XYZ plc for the year ended ... and complies with the requirements of the Companies Act 1985, and regulations made thereunder, applicable to summary financial statements.

Registered auditors *Address*
Date

Example paragraphs for inclusion in the basis of opinion section where applicable

(1) *referring to a fundamental uncertainty:* Our report on the group's full financial statements included an explanatory paragraph concerning a fundamental uncertainty arising from the outcome of possible litigation against B Ltd, a subsidiary undertaking of the company, for an alleged breach of environmental regulations. Details of the circumstances relating to this fundamental uncertainty are described in note ... of the summary financial statement. Our opinion on the full financial statements is not qualified in this respect.

(2) *referring to a qualified opinion:* Our opinion on the company's full financial statements was qualified as a result of a disagreement with the accounting treatment of the company's leased assets. Details of the circumstances giving rise to that opinion are set out in note ... of the summary financial statement.

Example 7 — qualified opinion: disagreement

Auditors' report to the shareholders of XYZ PLC

We have audited the financial statements on pages ... to ... which have been prepared under the historical cost convention [as modified by the revaluation of certain fixed assets] and the accounting policies set out on page ... .

Respective responsibilities of directors and auditors

As described on page ... the company's directors are responsible for the preparation of financial statements. It is our responsibility to form an independent opinion, based on our audit, on those statements and to report our opinion to you.

Basis of opinion

We conducted our audit in accordance with Auditing Standards issued by the Auditing Practices Board. An audit includes examination, on a test basis, of evidence relevant to the amounts and disclosures in the financial statements. It also includes an assessment of the significant estimates and judgments made by the directors in the preparation of the financial statements, and of whether the accounting policies are appropriate to the company's circumstances, consistently applied and adequately disclosed.

We planned and performed our audit so as to obtain all the information and explanations which we considered necessary in order to provide us with sufficient evidence to give reasonable assurance as to whether the financial statements are free from material misstatement, whether caused by fraud or other irregularity or error. In forming our opinion we also evaluated the overall adequacy of the presentation of information in the financial statements.

Qualified opinion arising from disagreement about accounting treatment

Included in the debtors shown in the balance sheet is an amount £Y due from a company which has ceased trading. XYZ plc has no security for this debt. In our opinion the company is unlikely to receive any payment and full provision of £Y should have been made, reducing profit before tax and net assets by that amount.

Except for the absence of this provision, in our opinion the financial statements give a true and fair view of the state of the company's affairs as at 31 December 19.. and of its profit [loss] for the year then ended and have been properly prepared in accordance with the Companies Act 1985.

Registered auditors *Address*

Date

Example 8 — qualified opinion: limitation on the auditors' work

Auditors' report to the shareholders of XYZ PLC

We have audited the financial statements on pages ... to ... which have been prepared under the historical cost convention [as modified by the revaluation of certain fixed assets] and the accounting policies set out on page ... .

Respective responsibilities of directors and auditors

As described on page ... the company's directors are responsible for the preparation of financial statements. It is our responsibility to form an independent opinion, based on our audit, on those statements and to report our opinion to you.

Basis of opinion

We conducted our audit in accordance with Auditing Standards issued by the Auditing Practices Board, except that the scope of our work was limited as explained below.

An audit includes examination, on a test basis, of evidence relevant to the amounts and disclosures in the financial statements. It also includes an assessment of the significant estimates and judgments made by the directors in the preparation of the financial statements, and of whether the accounting policies are appropriate to the company's circumstances, consistently applied and adequately disclosed.

We planned our audit so as to obtain all the information and explanations which we considered necessary in order to provide us with sufficient evidence to give reasonable assurance that the financial statements are free from material misstatement, whether caused by fraud or other irregularity or error. However, the evidence available to us was limited because £... of the company's recorded turnover comprises cash sales, over which there was no system of control on which we could rely for the purpose of our audit. There were no other satisfactory audit procedures that we could adopt to confirm that cash sales were properly recorded.

In forming our opinion we also evaluated the overall adequacy of the presentation of information in the financial statements.

Qualified opinion arising from limitation in audit scope

Except for any adjustments that might have been found to be necessary had we been able to obtain sufficient evidence concerning cash sales, in our opinion the financial statements give a true and fair view of the state of the company's affairs as at 31 December 19.. and of its profit [loss] for the year then ended and have been properly prepared in accordance with the Companies Act 1985.

In respect alone of the limitation on our work relating to cash sales:

- we have not obtained all the information and explanations that we considered necessary for the purpose of our audit; and
- we were unable to determine whether proper accounting records had been maintained.

Registered auditors *Address*

Date

Example 9 — disclaimer of opinion

Auditors' report to the shareholders of XYZ PLC
We have audited the financial statements on pages ... to ... which have been prepared under the historical cost convention [as modified by the revaluation of certain fixed assets] and the accounting policies set out on page ... .

Respective responsibilities of directors and auditors
As described on page ... the company's directors are responsible for the preparation of financial statements. It is our responsibility to form an independent opinion, based on our audit, on those statements and to report our opinion to you.

Basis of opinion
We conducted our audit in accordance with Auditing Standards issued by the Auditing Practices Board, except that the scope of our work was limited as explained below.

An audit includes examination, on a test basis, of evidence relevant to the amounts and disclosures in the financial statements. It also includes an assessment of the significant estimates and judgments made by the directors in the preparation of the financial statements, and of whether the accounting policies are appropriate to the company's circumstances, consistently applied and adequately disclosed.

We planned our audit so as to obtain all the information and explanations which we considered necessary in order to provide us with sufficient evidence to give reasonable assurance that the financial statements are free from material misstatement, whether caused by fraud or other irregularity or error. However, the evidence available to us was limited because we were appointed auditors on (date) and in consequence we were unable to carry out auditing procedures necessary to obtain adequate assurance regarding the quantities and condition of stock and work-in-progress, appearing in the balance sheet as £ ... . Any adjustment to this figure would have a consequential significant effect on the profit for the year.

In forming our opinion we also evaluated the overall adequacy of the presentation of information in the financial statements.

Opinion: disclaimer on view given by financial statements
Because of the possible effect of the limitation in evidence available to us, we are unable to form an opinion as to whether the financial statements give a true and fair view of the state of the company's affairs as at 31 December 19.. or of its profit [loss] for the year then ended. In all other respects, in our opinion the financial statements have been properly prepared in accordance with the Companies Act 1985.

In respect alone of the limitation on our work relating to stock and work-in-progress:

- we have not obtained all the information and explanations that we considered necessary for the purpose of our audit; and
- we were unable to determine whether proper accounting records had been maintained.

Registered auditors *Address*

Date

Example 10 — adverse opinion

Auditors' report to the shareholders of XYZ PLC

We have audited the financial statements on pages ... to ... which have been prepared under the historical cost convention [as modified by the revaluation of certain fixed assets] and the accounting policies set out on page ... .

Respective responsibilities of directors and auditors

As described on page ... the company's directors are responsible for the preparation of financial statements. It is our responsibility to form an independent opinion, based on our audit, on those statements and to report our opinion to you.

Basis of opinion

We conducted our audit in accordance with Auditing Standards issued by the Auditing Practices Board. An audit includes examination, on a test basis, of evidence relevant to the amounts and disclosures in the financial statements. It also includes an assessment of the significant estimates and judgments made by the directors in the preparation of the financial statements, and of whether the accounting policies are appropriate to the company's circumstances, consistently applied and adequately disclosed.

We planned and performed our audit so as to obtain all the information and explanations which we considered necessary in order to provide us with sufficient evidence to give reasonable assurance as to whether the financial statements are free from material misstatement, whether caused by fraud or other irregularity or error. In forming our opinion we also evaluated the overall adequacy of the presentation of information in the financial statements.

Adverse opinion

As more fully explained in note ... no provision has been made for losses expected to arise on certain long-term contracts currently in progress, as the directors consider that such losses should be off-set against amounts recoverable on other long-term contracts. In our opinion, provision should be made for foreseeable losses on individual contracts as required by Statement of Standard Accounting Practice 9. If losses had been so recognised the effect would have been to reduce the profit before and after tax for the year and the contract work in progress at 31 December 19.. by £... .

In view of the effect of the failure to provide for the losses referred to above, in our opinion the financial statements do not give a true and fair view of the state of the company's affairs as at 31 December 19.. and of its profit [loss] for the year then ended. In all other respects, in our opinion the financial statements have been properly prepared in accordance with the Companies Act 1985.

Registered auditors *Address*

Date

Example 11 — qualified opinion and fundamental uncertainty

Auditors' report to the shareholders of XYZ PLC

We have audited the financial statements on pages ... to ... which have been prepared under the historical cost convention [as modified by the revaluation of certain fixed assets] and the accounting policies set out on page ... .

Respective responsibilities of directors and auditors

As described on page ... the company's directors are responsible for the preparation of financial statements. It is our responsibility to form an independent opinion, based on our audit, on those statements and to report our opinion to you.

Basis of opinion

We conducted our audit in accordance with Auditing Standards issued by the Auditing Practices Board. An audit includes examination, on a test basis, of evidence relevant to the amounts and disclosures in the financial statements It also includes an assessment of the significant estimates and judgments made by the directors in the preparation of the financial statements, and of whether the accounting policies are appropriate to the company's circumstances, consistently applied and adequately disclosed.

We planned and performed our audit so as to obtain all the information and explanations which we considered necessary in order to provide us with sufficient evidence to give reasonable assurance as to whether the financial statements are free from material misstatement, whether caused by fraud or other irregularity or error. In forming our opinion we also evaluated the overall adequacy of the presentation of information in the financial statements.

Fundamental uncertainty

In forming our opinion, we have considered the adequacy of the disclosures made in the financial statements concerning the possible outcome of negotiations for additional finance being made available to replace an existing loan of £... which is repayable on 30 April 19... The financial statements have been prepared on a going concern basis, the validity of which depends upon future funding being available. The financial statements do not include any adjustments that would result from a failure to obtain funding. Details of the circumstances relating to this fundamental uncertainty are described in note ... . Our opinion is not qualified in this respect.

Qualified opinion arising from disagreement about accounting treatment

The company leases plant and equipment which have been accounted for in the financial statements as operating leases. In our opinion, these leases should be accounted for as finance leases as required by Statement of Standard Accounting Practice 21. If this accounting treatment were followed, the finance leases would be reflected in the company's balance sheet at £X and the profit for the year would have been reduced by £Y. The financial statements do not include an explanation for this departure from an applicable accounting standard as required by the Companies Act 1985.

Except for the failure to account for the leases referred to above as required by SSAP 21, in our opinion the financial statements give a true and fair view of the state of the company's affairs as at 31 December 19.. and of its profit [loss] for the year then ended and have been properly prepared in accordance with the Companies Act 1985.

Registered auditors *Address*

Date

Example 12 — qualified opinion: Disagreement arising from omission of a primary statement required by Financial Reporting Standards

Auditors' report to the shareholders of XYZ PLC

We have audited the financial statements on pages ... to ... which have been prepared under the historical cost convention [as modified by the revaluation of certain fixed assets] and the accounting policies set out on page ... .

Respective responsibilities of directors and auditors

As described on page ... the company's directors are responsible for the preparation of financial statements. It is our responsibility to form an independent opinion, based on our audit, on those statements and to report our opinion to you.

Basis of opinion

We conducted our audit in accordance with Auditing Standards issued by the Auditing Practices Board. An audit includes examination, on a test basis, of evidence relevant to the amounts and disclosures in the financial statements. It also includes an assessment of the significant estimates and judgments made by the directors in the preparation of the financial statements, and of whether the accounting policies are appropriate to the company's circumstances, consistently applied and adequately disclosed.

We planned and performed our audit so as to obtain all the information and explanations which we considered necessary in order to provide us with sufficient evidence to give reasonable assurance as to whether the financial statements are free from material misstatement, whether caused by fraud or other irregularity or error. In forming our opinion we also evaluated the overall adequacy of the presentation of information in the financial statements.

Qualified opinion arising from omission of cash flow statement

As explained in note ... the financial statements do not contain a statement of cash flows as required by Financial Reporting Standard 1. Net cash flows for the year ended 19.. amounted to £... and in our opinion information about the company's cash flows is necessary for a proper understanding of the company's state of affairs and profit [loss].

Except for the failure to provide information about the company's cash flows, in our opinion the financial statements give a true and fair view of the state of the company's affairs as at 31 December 19.. and of its profit [loss] for the year then ended and have been properly prepared in accordance with the Companies Act 1985.[5]

Registered auditors *Address*

Date

[5] Omission of a primary statement normally results in the issue of an opinion qualified as to the effect on the view given by the financial statements and the compliance with the Companies Act's other specific requirements, because the Act requires additional information to be included in financial statements when necessary to give a true and fair view.

Appendix 3

Statement of directors' responsibilities

Example wording of a description of the directors' responsibilities for inclusion in a company's financial statements.

Company law requires the directors to prepare financial statements for each financial year which give a true and fair view of the state of affairs of the company and of the profit or loss of the company for that period. In preparing those financial statements, the directors are required to:

- select suitable accounting policies and then apply them consistently;
- make judgments and estimates that are reasonable and prudent;
- state whether applicable accounting standards have been followed, subject to any material departures disclosed and explained in the financial statements[6];
- prepare the financial statements on the going concern basis unless it is inappropriate to presume that the company will continue in business[7].

The directors are responsible for keeping proper accounting records which disclose with reasonable accuracy at any time the financial position of the company and to enable them to ensure that the financial statements comply with the Companies Act 1985. They are also responsible for safeguarding the assets of the company and hence for taking reasonable steps for the prevention and detection of fraud and other irregularities.

[6] Large companies only.

[7] If no separate statement on going concern is made by the directors.

Statement of Auditing Standards 610 — Reports to directors or management

(Issued March 1995)

Statements of Auditing Standards ('SASs') are to be read in the light of 'The scope and authority of APB pronouncements'. In particular, they contain basic principles and essential procedures ('Auditing Standards'), indicated by paragraphs in bold type, with which auditors are required to comply in the conduct of any audit. SASs also include explanatory and other material which is designed to assist auditors in interpreting and applying Auditing Standards. The definitions in the Glossary of terms are to be applied in the interpretation of SASs.

Introduction

1 The purpose of this SAS is to establish standards and provide guidance on auditors' reports to directors, including any audit committee, or to management, at an appropriate, level, of weaknesses in the accounting and intemal control systems and other matters including errors, identified during the audit. In some circumstances specific legislation and regulations require auditors to issue reports on the adequacy of an entity's internal control systems which require auditors to undertake procedures additional to those set out in this SAS.

2 Auditors should consider the matters which have come to their attention during the audit and whether they should be included in a report to directors or management. (SAS 610.1)

3 'Directors' means the directors of a company or other body, the partners, proprietors, committee of management or trustees of other forms of entity, or equivalent persons responsible for directing the entity's operations and preparing its financial statements.

4 'Management' means those persons who have executive responsibility for the conduct of the entity's operations and the preparation of its financial statements.

5 The principal purposes of reports to directors or management are for auditors to communicate points that have come to their attention during the audit:

- on the design and operation of the accounting and internal control systems and to make suggestions for their improvement;
- of other constructive advice, for example comments on potential economies or improvements in efficiency; and
- on other matters, for example comments on adjusted and unadjusted errors in the financial statements or on particular accounting policies and practices.

6 If auditors consider that SAS 600 'Auditors' reports on financial statements' requires the qualification of the auditors' report, or other reference to a matter in the report a report to directors or management cannot be regarded as a substitute. To avoid inconsistencies between reports to directors or management and auditors' reports, auditors preparing either report have regard to other such reports issued, or proposed, in respect of the same period.

Material weaknesses in the accounting and internal control systems

7 When material weaknesses in the accounting and internal control systems are identified during the audit, auditors should report them in writing to the directors, the audit committee or an appropriate level of management on a timely basis. (SAS 610.2)

8 A material weakness in the accounting and internal control systems is a condition which may result in a material misstatement in the financial statements. If the directors or management have detected a material weakness and, in the view of the auditors, have taken appropriate corrective action, the auditors do not need to report to directors or management on the matter. In these circumstances they normally document the considerations which resulted in their conclusion that no report to directors or management in respect of this matter is needed.

9 Usually, material weaknesses in the accounting and internal control system are communicated to directors or management in a written report issued by the auditors. In some circumstances it may be appropriate for the relevant matters to be raised orally with directors or management, followed by a file note circulated to those attending the meeting to provide a record of the auditors' observations and any responses of the directors or management.

10 When no material weaknesses in the accounting and internal control systems are identified during the audit, the auditors may choose not to issue a report to directors or management. When auditors do not intend to issue a report to directors or management they may consider it appropriate to inform them that no report is to be issued.

Other matters regarding reports to directors or management

11 In the course of the audit, the auditors may identify weaknesses in the accounting and internal control systems other than material weaknesses, or other matters which they consider appropriate to bring to the attention of directors or management. Usually these matters are included in a report to directors or management, together with details of any material weaknesses, although they may be issued in a separate report. The auditors may consider it appropriate to raise these matters orally with directors or management and in these circumstances they normally prepare a file note to provide a record of their observations.

12 In any report to directors or management, auditors explain that the report is not a comprehensive statement of all weaknesses which exist or of all improvements which may be made, but that it documents only those matters which have come to their attention as a result of the audit procedures performed. Auditors may wish to refer to their audit approach in the report to directors or management, particularly the work undertaken on the accounting and internal control systems, to help directors or management appreciate the nature, timing and extent of the audit procedures which have resulted in the identification of the matters included in the report.

13 To be effective, a report to directors or management is best made as soon as possible after completion of the audit procedures giving rise to comment. Where the audit work is performed on more than one visit, it is often appropriate to report to directors or management after the interim visit as well as after the final audit visit, but making clear that the overall audit work is only partially complete and further matters may still arise.

14 Normally, auditors ask for a reply to the points raised in a report to directors or management, indicating the actions that the directors or management intend to take as a result of the comments made in the report.

15 Where significant matters raised in previous reports to directors or management have not been dealt with effectively, the auditors enquire why appropriate action has not been taken. If they consider that a point is still significant, consideration is given to repeating the point in the current report, otherwise there is a risk that they may give an impression that they are satisfied that the weakness has been corrected or is no longer significant. Similarly, they may wish to reinforce a point previously raised by internal audit.

Addressees of report to directors or management

16 When submitting a report to directors or management, auditors consider which directors or members of management have the power and responsibility to act on their findings. Normally, it is appropriate to address the report to the board of directors, audit committee or similar body. The report may contain matters of varying levels of significance which may make it appropriate for a tiered report to be issued, so that the board can consider any major points and receipt of a report of less important matters can be delegated to management.

Groups of companies

17 The directors or management of the parent undertaking of a group of companies may wish to be informed of significant points arising in the reports to the directors or management of its subsidiary undertakings. In these circumstances, permission is needed from the directors or management of the subsidiary undertakings to disclose the contents of any reports to directors or management to the parent undertaking or the principal auditors. Normally, such arrangements for groups are established at the planning stage and are recorded in the instructions to the auditors of subsidiary undertakings and relevant engagement letters.

Third parties interested in reports to directors or management

18 Any report to directors or management is a confidential communication. Thus auditors require the prior consent of the directors or management if they are to provide a copy of a report to directors or management to a third party.

19 In practice auditors have little control over what happens to the report once it has been dispatched. Occasionally directors or management may provide third parties with copies of the report, for example their banks or certain regulatory authorities. It is appropriate, accordingly, to ensure that third parties who see the report understand that it was not prepared for their benefit. Accordingly care is required to protect auditors from exposure to liability to any third parties who may seek to rely on a report which was not intended for their use. Thus auditors normally state in their report to directors or management that:

(a) the report has been prepared for the sole use of the entity;

(b) it must not be disclosed to a third party, or quoted or referred to, without the written consent of the auditors; and

(c) no responsibility is assumed by the auditors to any other person.

20 As a general rule liability in negligence to a third party may only arise in circumstances where auditors carry out work for an entity knowing:

- that their work is to be relied upon by a third party;
- the purpose for which that third party intends to rely on it; and
- that the third party may suffer financial loss if the report is relied on having been negligently prepared.

An express disclaimer of liability normally provides protection against an unforeseen liability to a third party.

21 In the public or regulated sectors, auditors may have a duty to submit a management letter annually, and also to submit copies of management letters to relevant regulatory or funding bodies. In the public sector, there may also be a requirement or expectation that such letters will be made public and in such circumstances the reservations on their use in paragraphs 19 and 20 may not always be appropriate.

Compliance with International Standards on Auditing

22 No specific International Standard on Auditing has been issued on reports to directors or management. Compliance with this SAS ensures compliance with the section entitled 'Communication of Weaknesses' in International Standard on Auditing 400 'Risk Assessments and Internal Control'.

Effective date

23 Auditors are required to comply with the Auditing Standards contained in this SAS in respect of audits of financial statements for periods ending on or after 23 December 1995.

Statement of Auditing Standards 620 — The Auditors' right and duty to report to regulators in the financial sector

(Issued March 1994)

Statements of Auditing Standards ('SASs') contain basic principles and essential procedures, ('Auditing Standards'), indicated by paragraphs in bold type, with which auditors are required to comply in the conduct of any audit. SASs also include explanatory and other material which is designed to assist auditors in interpreting and applying Auditing Standards.

Introduction

1 The purpose of this SAS is to establish standards and provide guidance on the circumstances in which auditors of a financial institution subject to statutory regulation (a 'regulated entity') are required to report direct to a regulator information which comes to their attention in the course of the work undertaken in their capacity as auditor of the regulated entity. This may include work undertaken to express an opinion on the entity's financial statements, other financial information or on other matters specified by legislation or by a regulator.

2 Auditors of regulated entities should bring information of which they have become aware in the ordinary course of performing work undertaken to fulfil their audit responsibilities to the attention of the appropriate regulator without delay when:

(a) they conclude that it is relevant to the regulator's functions having regard to such matters as may be specified in statute or any related regulations; and

(b) in their opinion there is reasonable cause to believe it is or may be of material significance to the regulator (SAS 620.1).

3 Auditors of regulated entities generally have special reporting responsibilities in addition to their responsibility to report on financial statements. These special reporting responsibilities take two forms:

(a) *a responsibility to provide a report on matters specified in legislation or by a regulator.* This form of report is often made on an annual or other routine basis and does not derive from another set of reporting responsibilities. The auditors are required to carry out appropriate procedures sufficient to form an opinion on the matters concerned. These procedures may be in addition to those carried out to form an opinion on the financial statements;

(b) *a statutory duty to report certain information, relevant to the regulators' functions, that come to the auditors' attention in the course of their audit work.* The auditors have no responsibility to carry out procedures to search out the information relevant to the regulator. This form of report is derivative in nature, arising only in the context of another set of reporting responsibilities, and is initiated by the auditors on discovery of a reportable matter.

4 The statutory duty to report to a regulator applies to information which comes to the attention of auditors in their capacity as such. In determining whether information is obtained in that capacity, two criteria in particular need to be considered: first, whether the person who obtained the information also undertook the audit work; and if so, whether it was obtained in the course of or as a result of undertaking the audit work. Appendix 2 to this SAS sets out guidance on the application of these criteria.

5 Auditors may have a statutory right to bring information to the attention of the regulator in particular circumstances which lie outside those giving rise to a statutory duty to initiate a direct report. Where this is so, auditors may use that right to make a direct report relevant to the regulator on a specific matter which comes to their attention when they conclude that doing so is necessary to protect the interests of those for whose benefit the regulator is required to act.

6 This SAS deals with both forms of direct reports. Guidance on the auditors' responsibility to provide special reports on a routine basis on other matters specified in legislation or by a regulator is given in the Practice Note 'Investment businesses' and Auditing Guidelines dealing with the audits of other regulated entities.

7 The Standards and explanatory material in this SAS complement but do not replace the legal and regulatory requirements applicable to each regulated entity. Where the application of those requirements, taking into account any published interpretations, is insufficiently clear for the auditors to determine whether a particular circumstance results in a legal duty to make a report to a regulator, or a right to make such a report, it may be appropriate to take legal advice.

Definitions

8 *The Acts:* In the United Kingdom, these comprise the Banking Act 1987, Financial Services Act 1986, Building Societies Act 1986, Insurance Companies Act 1982 and the Friendly Societies Act 1992, and regulations made under those Acts, and any future legislation including provisions relating to the duties of auditors similar to those contained in those statutes.

9 In the Republic of Ireland, *the Acts* comprise the Central Bank Acts 1942 to 1989, the Building Societies Act 1989, the Trustees Savings Bank Act 1989, the Insurance Act 1989, the European Communities (Undertakings for Collective Investment in Transferable Securities) Regulations 1989, the Unit Trusts Act 1990, the ACC Bank Act (Section 4) Regulations 1992, the ICC Bank Act (Section 3) Regulations 1993 and, in the case of investment companies, the Companies Act 1990 and any future legislation including provisions relating to the duties of auditors similar to those contained in those Acts, together with other regulations made under them.

10 *Audit:* for the purpose of this SAS, the term *audit* refers both to an engagement to report on the financial statements of a regulated entity and to an engagement to provide a report on other matters specified by statute or by a regulator undertaken in the capacity of auditor.

11 *Auditors:* the term 'auditors' should be interpreted in accordance with the requirements of the Acts. Guidance on its interpretation is contained in Practice Notes relating to each area of the financial sector to which the duty applies.

12 *Control environment:* the overall attitude, awareness and actions of directors and management regarding internal controls and their importance in the entity. Factors

reflected in the control environment include:

- management's philosophy and operating style;
- the entity's organisational structure and methods of assigning authority and responsibility (including segregation of duties and management supervisory controls); and
- management's methods of imposing control including the internal audit function, the functions of the board of directors and personnel policies and procedures.

13 *Directors:* the directors of a company or other body, the partners, proprietors, committee of management or trustees of other forms of enterprise or equivalent persons, and members of senior management responsible for aspects of the conduct of a regulated entity's business.

14 *Material significance:* the term 'material significance' requires interpretation in the context of the specific legislation applicable to the regulated entity. A matter or group of matters is normally of material significance to a regulator's functions when, due either to its nature or its potential financial impact, it is likely of itself to require investigation by the regulator. Further guidance on the interpretation of the term in the context of specific legislation is contained in Practice Notes dealing with the rights and duties of auditors of regulated entities to report direct to regulators.

15 *Regulated entity:* an individual, company or other type of entity authorised to carry on business in the financial sector which is subject to statutory regulation.

16 *Regulator:* such persons as are empowered by the Acts to regulate business in the financial sector. The term comprises the Bank of England, the Securities and Investment Board, Self-Regulating Organisations and Recognised Professional Bodies, the Department of Trade and Industry, the Building Societies Commission, the Friendly Societies Commission, the Central Bank of Ireland and such other bodies as may be so empowered in future legislation.

Appointment as auditors and ceasing to hold office

17 Before accepting appointment, auditors follow the procedures identified in the ethical guidance and Audit Regulations issued by their relevant professional bodies.

18 In the case of regulated entities, auditors would in particular obtain an understanding of the appropriate statutory and regulatory requirements and a preliminary knowledge of the management and operations of the entity, so as to enable them to determine whether a level of knowledge of the business adequate to perform the audit can be obtained. The procedures carried out by auditors in seeking to obtain this preliminary understanding may include discussion with the previous auditors and, in some circumstances, with the regulator.

19 On ceasing to hold office, auditors may be required by statute or by regulation to make specific reports concerning the circumstances relating to that event, and would also follow the procedures identified in the ethical guidance issued by the relevant professional body.

20 In addition, auditors of regulated entities would assess whether it is appropriate to bring any matters of which they are then aware to the notice of the regulator. Under legislation in the UK, this may be done either before or after ceasing to hold office, as the auditors' statutory right to disclose to a regulator information obtained in the course of their appointment is not affected by their removal, resignation or otherwise ceasing to hold office.

Conduct of the audit

21 The duty to make a report direct to a regulator does not impose upon auditors a duty to carry out specific work: it arises solely in the context of work carried out to fulfil other reporting responsibilities. Accordingly, no auditing procedures in addition to those carried out in the normal course of auditing the financial statements, or for the purpose of making any other specified report, are necessary for the fulfilment of the auditors' responsibilities.

22 It will, however, be necessary for auditors to take additional time in carrying out a financial statement audit or other engagement to assess whether matters which come to their attention should be included in a direct report and, where appropriate, to prepare and submit the report. These additional planning and follow-up procedures do not constitute an extension of the scope of the financial statement audit or of other work undertaken to provide a specified report relating to a regulated entity. They are necessary solely in order to understand and clarify the reporting responsibility and, where appropriate, to make a report.

23 The circumstances in which auditors are required by statute to make a report direct to a regulator include matters which are not considered as part of the audit of financial statements or of work undertaken to discharge other routine responsibilities. For example, the duty to report would apply to information of which they become aware in the course of their work which is relevant to the regulator's criteria for fit and proper persons, although auditors are not otherwise required to express an opinion on such matters. However, the legislation imposing a duty to make reports direct to regulators does not require auditors to change the scope of their audit work, nor does it place on them an obligation to conduct their work in such a way that there is reasonable certainty that they will discover all matters which regulators might consider as being of material significance. Therefore, whilst auditors of regulated entities are required to be alert to matters which may require a report, they are not expected to be aware of all circumstances which, had they known of them, would have led them to make such a report. It is only when auditors become aware of such a matter during the conduct of their normal audit work that they have an obligation to determine whether a report to the regulator is required by statute or appropriate for other reasons.

24 Similarly, auditors are not responsible for reporting on a regulated entity's overall compliance with rules with which it is required to comply nor are they required to conduct their work in such a way that there is reasonable certainty that they will discover breaches. Nevertheless, breaches of rules with which a regulated entity is required to comply may have implications for the financial statements and, accordingly, auditors of regulated entities need to consider whether any actual or contingent liabilities may have arisen from breaches of regulatory requirements. Breaches of a regulator's requirements may also have consequences for other matters on which auditors of a regulated entity are required to express an opinion.

Planning

25 When gaining a knowledge of the business for the purpose of their audit, auditors of a regulated entity should obtain an understanding of its current activities, the scope of its authorisation and the effectiveness of its control environment. (SAS 620.2)

26 Auditing Standards require auditors to gain a sufficient understanding of the reporting entity's business to plan and perform their audit effectively and to assess the risk of material misstatements in the financial statements.

27 In the context of a regulated entity, the auditors' understanding of its business needs to extend to the applicable statutory provisions, the rules of the regulator concerned and any guidance issued by the regulator on the interpretation of those rules, together with other guidance issued by the APB.

28 Auditors are also required to assess the risk of misstatements in the financial statements, or of other errors in relation to other matters on which they are required to report. In making such an assessment they take into account the control environment, including the entity's higher level procedures for complying with the requirements of its regulator. Such a review gives an indication of the extent to which the general atmosphere and controls in the regulated entity are conducive to compliance, for example through consideration of *inter alia:*

- the adequacy of procedures and training to inform staff of the requirements of relevant legislation and the rules or other regulations of the regulator;
- the adequacy of procedures for authorisation of transactions;
- procedures for internal review of the entity's compliance with regulatory or other requirements;
- the authority of, and any resources available to, the compliance officer; and
- procedures to ensure that possible breaches of requirements are investigated by an appropriate person and are brought to the attention of senior management.

29 In some areas of the financial sector, conducting business outside the scope of the entity's authorisation is a serious regulatory breach, and therefore of material significance to the regulator. In addition, it may result in fines, suspension or loss of authorisation.

30 Where the auditors' review of the reporting entity's activities indicates that published guidance by the regulator may not be sufficiently precise to enable them to identify circumstances in which it is necessary to initiate a report, they would consider whether it is necessary to discuss the matters specified in legislation with the appropriate regulator with a view to reaching agreement on its interpretation.

31 Similarly, where a group includes two or more companies separately regulated by different regulators, there may be a need to clarify the regulators' requirements in any overlapping areas of activity. However, the statutory duty to make a report as presently defined arises only in respect of the legal entity subject to regulation. Therefore auditors of an unregulated company in a group that includes one or more other companies which are authorised by regulators would not have a duty to report matters to the regulators of those companies.

32 When a regulated entity is subject to provisions of two or more regulators, the auditors need to take account of their separate reporting requirements in planning and conducting their work. Arrangements may exist for one regulatory body to rely on financial monitoring being carried out by another body (the 'lead regulator') and where this is the case, routine reports by the regulated entity's auditors may be made to the lead regulator alone.

33 However, the auditors' statutory duty to report cannot be discharged by reliance on the lead regulator informing others. Therefore, where auditors conclude that a matter is of material significance to one regulator, they need to assess the need for separate reports informing each regulator of matters which the auditors conclude are or may be of material significance to it.

Supervision and control

34 Auditors should ensure that all staff involved in the audit of a regulated entity have an understanding of:

(a) the provisions of applicable legislation;

(b) the regulator's rules and any guidance issued by the regulator; and

(c) any specific requirements which apply to the particular regulated entity,

appropriate to their role in the audit and sufficient (in the context of that role) to enable them to identify situations which may give reasonable cause to believe that a matter should be reported to the regulator. (SAS 620.3)

35 Auditing Standards require auditors to exercise adequate control and supervision over staff conducting work on an audit. Consequently, in planning and conducting the audit of a regulated entity auditors need to ensure that staff are alert to the possibility that a report to its regulator may be required.

36 Auditing firms also need to establish adequate procedures to ensure that any matters which are discovered in the course of or as a result of audit work and may give rise to a duty to report are brought to the attention of the partner responsible for the audit on a timely basis.

37 The right and duty to report to a regulator applies to information of which auditors become aware in their capacity as such. They do not extend automatically to any information obtained by an accounting firm regardless of its source. Consequently partners and staff undertaking work in another capacity are not required to have detailed knowledge of the regulator's requirements (unless necessary for that other work) nor to bring information to the attention of the partner responsible for the audit on a routine basis.

38 However, as discussed further in Appendix 2, firms need to establish lines of communications, commensurate with their size and complexity, sufficient to ensure that non-audit work undertaken for a regulated entity which is likely to have an effect on the audit is brought to the attention of the partner responsible for the audit, who will need to determine whether the results of non-audit work undertaken for a regulated entity ought to be assessed as part of the audit process.

Identifying matters requiring a report direct to regulators

39 Where an apparent breach of statutory or regulatory requirements comes to the auditors' attention, they should:

(a) obtain such evidence as is available to assess its implications for their reporting responsibilities; and

(b) determine whether, in their opinion, there is reasonable cause to believe that the breach is of material significance to the regulator. (SAS 620.4)

40 The precise matters which give rise to a statutory duty on auditors to make a report to a regulator derive from the relevant Acts. Broadly, such matters fall into three general categories:

(a) the financial position of the regulated entity;

(b) its compliance with requirements for the management of its business; and

(c) the status of its directors as fit and proper persons.

Further detailed guidance on the interpretation of these matters in the context of specific legislation applicable to each type of regulated entity is contained in Practice Notes dealing with the rights and duties of auditors of regulated entities to report direct to regulators.

41 In assessing the effect of an apparent breach, auditors take into account the quantity and type of evidence concerning such a matter which may reasonably be expected to be available. If the auditors conclude that they have been prevented from obtaining all such evidence concerning a matter which may give rise to a duty to report, they would normally make a report direct to the regulator without delay.

42 An apparent breach of statutory or regulatory requirements may not of itself give rise to a statutory duty to make a report. There will normally be a need for some further investigation and discussion of the circumstances surrounding the apparent breach with the directors in order to obtain sufficient information to determine whether it points to a matter which is or may be of material significance to the regulator. For example, a minor breach which has been corrected by the regulated entity and reported (if appropriate) to the regulator, and which from the evidence available to the auditors appears to be an isolated occurrence, would not normally give the auditors reasonable cause to believe that it is or may be of material significance to the regulator.

43 When determining whether a breach of statutory or regulatory requirements gives rise to a statutory duty to make a report direct to a regulator, auditors consider factors such as:

- whether the breach, though minor, is indicative of a general lack of compliance with the regulator's requirements or otherwise casts doubt on the status of the directors as fit and proper persons;
- whether a breach which occurred before the auditors' visit to the regulated entity was reported by the entity itself and has since been corrected, such that, at the date of the auditors' discovery, no breach exists;
- whether the circumstances giving rise to a breach which occurred before the auditors' visit to the regulated entity continue to exist, or the entity's directors have not taken corrective action, or the breach has re-occurred; and
- whether the circumstances suggest that an immediate report to the regulator is necessary in order to protect the interests of depositors, investors, policyholders, clients of the entity or others in whose interests the regulator is required to act.

44 Auditors would normally seek evidence to assess the implications of a suspected breach before reporting a matter to the regulator. However, the auditors' responsibility to make a report does not require them to determine the full implications of a matter before reporting: they are required to exercise their professional judgment as to whether or not there is reasonable cause to believe that a matter is or may be of material significance to the regulator. In forming that judgment, auditors undertake appropriate investigations to determine the circumstances but do not require the degree of evidence which would be a normal part of forming an opinion on financial statements. Such investigations would normally include:

- enquiry of appropriate level of staff;
- review of correspondence and documents relating to the transaction or event concerned; and
- discussion with directors, or other senior management where appropriate.

In the case of a life company, it would also be appropriate to consult with the appointed actuary, who also has various statutory duties under insurance companies legislation.

45 The potential gravity of some apparent breaches may be such that an immediate report to the regulator is essential in order to enable the regulator to take appropriate action: in particular, prompt reporting of a loss of client assets may be necessary to avoid further loss to investors or others in whose interests the regulator is required to act. Auditors are therefore required to balance the need for further investigation of the matter with the need for prompt reporting.

46 On completion of their investigations, auditors need to ensure that the facts and the basis for their decision (whether to report or not) is adequately documented such that the reasons for that decision may be clearly demonstrated should the need to do so arise in future.

Reliance on other auditors

47 Auditors with responsibilities for reporting on financial statements including financial information of one or more components audited by other auditors are required to obtain sufficient appropriate audit evidence that the work of the other auditors is adequate for the purposes of their audit. The same principle applies to reliance on another auditor in a different type of engagement. Auditors of a regulated entity who rely on work undertaken by other auditors need to establish reporting arrangements such that the other auditors bring to their attention matters arising from their work which may give rise to a duty to report to a regulator.

48 The nature of the reporting arrangements will depend on the nature of the work under taken by the other auditors. For example, the statutory duty to make a report relates to the legal entity subject to regulation rather than to the entire group to which that entity may belong. Consequently, the auditors of a holding company authorised by one regulator would not be expected to have knowledge of all matters which come to the attention of a subsidiary's auditors. They would, however, have a duty to report, where appropriate, matters which arise from their audit of the regulated entity's own financial statements and of the consolidated group figures.

49 Where the audit of a regulated entity is undertaken by joint auditors, knowledge obtained by one auditing firm is likely to be deemed to be known by the other. Care will therefore be needed in agreeing and implementing arrangements to exchange information relating to matters which may give rise to a duty to report to a regulator.

Reporting

The auditors' statutory duty to report direct to regulators

50 When the auditors conclude, after appropriate discussion and Investigations, that a matter which has come to their attention gives rise to a statutory duty to make a report, they should bring the matter to the attention of the regulator without undue delay in a form and manner which will facilitate appropriate action by the regulator. When the initial report is made orally, the auditors should make a contemporaneous

written record of the oral report and should confirm the matter in writing to the regulator. (SAS 620.5)

51 Except in the circumstances referred to in paragraph 54 auditors seek to reach agreement with the directors on the circumstances giving rise to a report direct to the regulator. However, where a statutory duty to report arises, the auditors are required to make such a report regardless of:

(a) whether the matter has been referred to the regulator by other parties (including the company, whether by its directors or otherwise); and

(b) any duty owed to other parties, including the regulated entity's directors and its shareholders (or equivalent persons).

52 Except in the circumstances set out in paragraph 54, auditors send a copy of their written report to the directors and (where appropriate) audit committee of the regulated entity.

53 In normal circumstances, auditors would wish to communicate with the regulator with the knowledge and agreement of the regulated entity's directors. However, in some circumstances immediate notification of the discovery of a matter giving reasonable grounds to believe that a reportable matter exists will be necessary — for example, a phone call to alert the regulator followed by a meeting to discuss the circumstances.

54 When the matter giving rise to a statutory duty to make a report direct to a regulator casts doubt on the integrity of the directors or their competence to conduct the business of the regulated entity, the auditors should make their report to the regulator without delay and without informing the directors in advance. (SAS 620.6)

55 Speed of reporting is essential where the circumstances cause the auditors no longer to have confidence in the integrity of the directors. In such circumstances, there may be a serious and immediate threat to the interests of depositors or other persons for whose protection the regulator is required to act; for example where the auditors believe that a fraud or other irregularity may have been committed by, or with the knowledge of, the directors, or have evidence of the intention of the directors to commit or condone a suspected fraud or other irregularity.

56 In circumstances where the auditors no longer have confidence in the integrity of the directors, it is not appropriate to provide the directors with copies of their report. Since such circumstances will be exceptional and extreme, the auditors may wish to seek legal advice as to their responsibilities and the appropriate course of action.

Money laundering

57 When, in the course of their work, auditors become aware of evidence indicating the presence of laundering of money which either derives from drug trafficking or is related to terrorist offences, they are required by the Criminal Justice Act 1993 to report their suspicions to the appropriate authority. Under the terms of the Act, it is a criminal offence to disclose the reporting of such suspicions to any other party where this may prejudice a criminal investigation. Auditors therefore need to be aware that, whilst they may disclose such circumstances to the regulator, they are under a statutory obligation not to disclose the matter to the directors where the latter may be implicated in the laundering.

The auditors' right to report direct to regulators

58 When a matter comes to the auditors' attention which they conclude does not give

rise to a statutory duty to report but nevertheless may be relevant to the regulator's exercise of its functions, they should:

(a) consider whether the matter should be brought to the attention of the regulator under the terms of the appropriate legal provisions enabling auditors to report direct to the regulator; and, if so

(b) advise the directors that in their opinion the matter should be drawn to the regulators' attention.

Where the auditors are unable to obtain, within a reasonable period, adequate evidence that the directors have properly informed the regulator of the matter, they should make a report direct to the regulator without undue delay. (SAS 620.7)

59 Auditors may become aware of matters which they conclude are relevant to the exercise of the regulator's functions even though they fall outside the statutory definition of matters which must be reported to a regulator. In such circumstances, the Acts provide auditors with protection for making disclosure of the matter to the appropriate regulator.

60 Where the auditors consider that a matter which does not give rise to a statutory duty to report is nevertheless, in their professional judgment, such that it should be brought to the attention of the regulator, it is normally appropriate for them to request the directors of the regulated entity in writing to draw it to the attention of the regulator.

Contents of a report initiated by auditors

61 When making or confirming in writing a report direct to a regulator, the auditors should:

(a) state the name of the regulated entity concerned;

(b) state the statutory power under which the report is made;

(c) state that the report has been prepared in accordance with SAS 620 'The auditors' right and duty to report to regulators in the financial sector';

(d) describe the context in which the report is given;

(e) describe the matter giving rise to the report;

(f) request the regulator to confirm that the report has been received;

(g) state the name of the auditors, the date of the written report and, where appropriate, the date on which an oral report was made to the regulator and the name and title of the individual to whom the oral report was made. (SAS 620.8)

62 Such a report is a by-product of other work undertaken by the auditors. As a result it is not possible for them or the regulator to conclude that all matters relevant to the regulator were encountered in the course of their work. The auditors' report therefore sets out the context in which the information reported was identified and indicates the extent to which the matter has been investigated and discussed with the directors.

Context of a report

63 Matters to which the auditors may wish to refer when describing the context in which a report is made direct to a regulator include:

- the nature of the appointment from which the report derives. For example, it may be appropriate to distinguish between a report made in the course of an audit of financial statements and one which arises in the course of a more limited engagement, such as an appointment under Section 39 of the Banking Act 1987;

- the applicable legislative requirements and interpretations of those requirements which have informed the auditors' judgment;
- the extent to which the auditors have investigated the circumstances giving rise to the matter reported;
- whether the matter reported has been discussed with the directors;
- whether steps to rectify the matter have been taken.

Communication of information by the regulator

64 The Acts provide that, in certain exceptional circumstances, regulators may pass confidential information to another party. The precise circumstances in which regulators may disclose information varies, but in general they may do so if considered necessary to fulfil their own obligations under the appropriate Act, or, in some cases, to enable the auditors to fulfil their duties either to the regulated entity or, in other cases, to the regulator. Confidential information remains confidential in the hands of the recipient.

65 Insofar as the law permits, regulators have confirmed that they will consider taking the initiative in bringing a matter to the attention of the auditors of a regulated entity in circumstances where:

(a) they believe the matter is of such importance that the auditors' knowledge of it could significantly affect the form of their report on the entity's financial statements or other matters on which they are required to report, or the way in which they discharge their reporting responsibilities; and

(b) the disclosure is for the purpose of enabling or assisting the regulator to discharge its functions under the Acts.

66 Auditors need to be aware that there may be circumstances in which the regulators are unable to disclose such information. Where the auditors of a regulated entity are not informed by the regulator of any matter, therefore, they cannot assume that there are no matters known to the regulator which could affect their judgment as to whether information is of material significance. However, in the absence of disclosure by the regulator, auditors can only form their judgment in the light of evidence to which they have access.

Relationship with other reporting responsibilities

67 When issuing a report expressing an opinion on a regulated entity's financial statements or on other matters specified by legislation or a regulator, auditors:

(a) should consider whether there are consequently reporting issues affecting their opinion which arise from any report previously made direct to the regulator in the course of their appointment; and

(b) should assess whether any matters encountered in the course of their audit indicate a need for a further direct report. (SAS 620.9)

68 The circumstances which give rise to a report direct to a regulator may involve an uncertainty or other matter which requires disclosure in the financial statements. Auditors will therefore need to consider whether the disclosures made in the financial statements are adequate for the purposes of giving a true and fair view of the regulated entity's state of affairs and profit or loss. Where they conclude that an uncertainty which has resulted in such a report is fundamental, the auditors are required by SAS 600 'Auditors' reports on financial statements' to include an explanatory paragraph drawing attention to the matter in their report.

69 Similarly, circumstances giving rise to a report direct to a regulator may also require reflection in auditors' reports on other matters required by legislation or another regulator.

70 In fulfilling their responsibility to report direct to a regulator, it is important that auditors not only assess the significance of individual transactions or events but also consider whether a combination of such items over the course of the work undertaken for their primary reporting responsibilities may give the auditors reasonable ground to believe that they constitute a matter of material significance to the regulator, and so give rise to a statutory duty to make a report.

71 As there is no requirement for auditors to extend the scope of their work to search for matters which may give rise to a statutory duty to report, such an assessment of the cumulative effect of evidence obtained in the course of an audit would be made when reviewing the evidence in support of the opinions to be expressed in the reports the auditors have been appointed to make. Where such a review leads to the conclusion that the cumulative effect of matters noted in the course of the audit is of material significance to the regulator, it will be appropriate for a report to be made as set out in SAS 620.8. However, reports indicating a 'nil return' are not appropriate.

Compliance with International Standards on Auditing

72 No International Standard on Auditing has been issued on the auditors' legal responsibility to make a report to regulators.

Effective date

73 The statutory duty to report to regulators is in force in the Republic of Ireland and in the United Kingdom comes into effect on 1 May 1994 in the case of banks, building societies, investment businesses and friendly societies. The duty applies to auditors of insurance companies in the UK from 1 July 1994. Auditors in the UK are required to comply with this SAS from those dates.

74 The duty on auditors to report to regulators does not have retrospective effect. However, auditors in the United Kingdom may identify matters before the duty comes into force which they conclude would give rise to a statutory duty to report to a regulator after that date. In such circumstances, auditors are encouraged to consider using their right to initiate a report under the existing provisions of the Acts.

Withdrawal of material in other guidance

75 The SAS supersedes guidance given to auditors on reports made direct to regulators contained in:

(a) Section 2 of Practice Note 1 'Investment businesses';

(b) paragraphs 166 to 177 of the Auditing Guideline 'Building Societies in the United Kingdom';

(c) paragraphs 171-191 of the Auditing Guideline 'Banks in the United Kingdom';

(d) paragraphs 121-139 of the Auditing Guideline 'General business insurers in the United Kingdom';

(e) paragraphs 112-120 of the Auditing Guideline 'Life insurers in the United Kingdom'.

Note on legal requirements

i Reference should be made to the legislation itself for an understanding of the relevant points of law. In interpreting the legal requirements it is also appropriate to refer to guidance published by the regulators and that contained in Practice Notes issued by the Auditing Practices Board.

Legal requirements in the United Kingdom

ii The auditors' right to report to a regulator is contained in:

(a) Building Societies Act 1986, Section 82;

(b) Banking Act 1987, Section 47;

(c) Insurance Companies Act 1982, Section 21A;

(d) Financial Services Act 1986, Section 109;

(e) Friendly Societies Act 1992, Section 79.

iii The auditors' duty to report to a regulator is set out in the following Statutory Instruments:

(a) The Building Societies (Auditors) Order 1994;

(b) The Accountants (Banking Act 1987) Regulations 1994;

(c) The Auditors (Insurance Companies Act 1992) Regulations 1994;

(d) The Auditors (Financial Services Act 1986) Rules 1994;

(e) The Friendly Societies (Auditors) Order 1994.

Legal requirements in the Republic of Ireland

iv The auditors' duty to report to a regulator is set out in:

(a) the Building Societies Act 1989, Section 89(i);

(b) the Central Bank Act 1989, Section 47;

(c) the Trustee Savings Bank Act 1989, Section 38(i);

(d) the Insurance Act 1989, Section 35(i);

(e) the European Communities (Undertakings for Collective Investment in Transferable Securities) Regulations 1989, Sections 83(2) to (7);

(f) the Unit Trusts Act 1990, Section 15;

(g) the ACC Bank Act, 1992 (Section 4) Regulations 1992;

(h) the ICC Bank Act, 1992 (Section 3) Regulations 1993; and

(i) the Companies Act 1990, Section 258.

Appendix 1

The regulatory framework

1 In both the United Kingdom and the Republic of Ireland, legislation exists in the principal areas of financial services to protect the interests of investors, depositors in banks and other users of financial services. Regulated entities operating in the financial sector are required to comply with legal and regulatory requirements concerning the way their business is conducted. Compliance with those rules is monitored in four principal ways:

- internal monitoring by the directors of the regulated entity;
- submission of regular returns by the regulated entity to the regulator;
- monitoring and, in some cases, inspection of the entity by the regulator;
- reports by the reporting entity's auditors on its financial statements and other specified matters required by legislation or by the regulator.

Responsibility for ensuring compliance

2 Ensuring compliance with the requirements with which a regulated entity is required to comply in carrying out its business is the responsibility of the directors of a regulated entity. It requires adequate organisation and systems of controls. The regulatory framework provides that adequate procedures for compliance must be established and maintained. The directors of a regulated entity are also normally required to undertake regular reviews of compliance and to inform the regulator of any breach of the rules and regulations applicable to its regulated business. In addition, regulators may undertake compliance visits.

3 Auditors of regulated entities normally have responsibilities for reporting on particular aspects of its compliance with the regulator's requirements. However, they have no direct responsibility for expressing an opinion on an entity's overall compliance with the requirements for the conduct of its business, nor does an audit provide any assurance that breaches of requirements which are not the subject of regular auditors' reports will be detected.

The role of auditors

4 Directors of regulated entities have primary responsibility for ensuring that all appropriate information is made available to regulators. Normal reporting procedures (including auditors' reports on records, systems and returns, and regular meetings with directors and/or senior management and auditors) supplemented by any inspection visits considered necessary by the regulators should provide the regulators with all the information they need to carry out their responsibilities under the relevant Act.

Routine reporting by auditors

5 Regulators' requirements for reports by auditors vary. In general terms, however, such reports may include opinions on:

- the regulated entity's annual financial statements;
- the regulated entity's compliance with requirements for financial resources; and
- the adequacy of the regulated entity's system of controls over its transactions and in particular over its clients' money and other property.

6 As a result of performing the work necessary to discharge their routine reporting responsibilities, or those arising from an appointment to provide a special report required by the regulator, the auditors of a regulated entity may become aware of matters which they consider need to be brought to the regulator's attention sooner than would be achieved by routine reports by the entity or its auditors.

7 Auditors of regulated entities normally have a right to communicate in good faith information they consider is relevant to the regulator's functions.

The auditors' statutory duty to report to the regulator

8 In addition, auditors are required by law to report direct to a regulator when they conclude that there is reasonable cause to believe that a matter is or may be of material significance to the regulator. The precise matters which result in a statutory duty to make such a report vary, depending upon the specific requirements of relevant legislation and the regulator's rules. In general, however, a duty to report to a regulator arises when the auditors become aware that:

- the regulated entity is in serious breach of
  — requirements to maintain adequate financial resources, or
  — of requirements for its directors to conduct its business in a sound and prudent manner (including the maintenance of systems of control over transactions and over any clients' assets held by the business); or
- there are circumstances which give reason to doubt the status of its directors or senior management as fit and proper persons.

Confidentiality

9 Confidentiality is an implied term of auditors' contracts with their client entities. However in the circumstances leading to a right or duty to report, auditors are entitled to communicate to regulators in good faith information or opinions relating to the business or affairs of the entity or any associated body without contravening the duty of confidence owed to the entity and, in the case of a bank, building society and friendly society, its associated bodies.

10 The statutory provisions permitting auditors to communicate information to regulators relate to information obtained in their capacity as auditors of the regulated entity concerned. Auditors and regulators therefore should be aware that confidential information obtained in other capacities may not normally be disclosed to another party.

Appendix 2

The application of the statutory duty to report to regulators

Introduction

1 The statutory duty to report to a regulator applies to information which comes to the attention of auditors in their capacity as such. However, neither the term 'auditor' nor the phrase 'in the capacity of auditor' are defined in the legislation, nor has the court determined how these expressions should be construed.

2 As a result, it is not always clearly apparent when an accounting firm should regard itself as having a duty to report to a regulator. For example, information about a regulated entity may be obtained when partners or staff of the firm which is appointed as its auditor carry out work for another client entity; or when the firm undertakes other work for the regulated entity. Auditors, regulated entities and regulators need to be clear as to when the normal duty of confidentiality will be overridden by the auditors' statutory duty to report to the regulator.

3 In order to clarify whether or not an accounting firm should regard itself as bound by the duty, the APB has developed, in conjunction with HM Treasury and the regulators, guidance on the interpretation of the key conditions for the existence of that duty, namely that the firm is to be regarded as auditor of a regulated entity and that information is obtained in the capacity of auditor.[1]

4 Guidance on the interpretation of the term 'auditor' in the context of each Act is contained in the separate Practice Notes dealing with each area affected by the legislation.

5 This appendix sets out guidance on the interpretation of the phrase 'in the capacity of auditor'. The Board nevertheless continues to hold the view, expressed in the exposure draft of this SAS, that the meaning of the phrase should be clarified in legislation in the longer term.

In the capacity of auditor

6 In determining whether information is obtained in the capacity of auditor, two criteria in particular should be considered:

(a) whether the person who obtained the information also undertook the audit work; and if so,

(b) whether it was obtained in the course of or as a result of undertaking the audit work.

7 It is then necessary to apply these criteria to information about a regulated entity which may become known from a number of sources, and by a number of different individuals within an accounting firm. Within a large firm, for example, information may come to the attention of the partner responsible for the audit of a regulated entity, a partner in another office who undertakes a different type of work, or members of the firm's staff at any level. In the case of a sole practitioner who is the auditor of a regulated entity, information about a regulated entity may also be obtained by the practitioner in the course of work other than its audit.

[1] See debate in the House of Commons, Hansard 15 February 1994, cols 853 to 856.

Non-audit work carried out in relation to a regulated entity

8 Where partners or staff involved in the audit of a regulated entity carry out work other than its audit (non-audit work) information about the regulated entity will be known to them as individuals. In circumstances which suggest that a matter would otherwise give rise to a statutory duty to report if obtained in the capacity of auditor, it will be prudent for them to make enquiries in the course of their audit work in order to establish whether this is the case from information obtained in that capacity.

9 However where non-audit work is carried out by other partners or staff, neither of the criteria set out in paragraph 6 is met in respect of information which becomes known to them. Nevertheless the firm should take proper account of such information when it could affect the audit so that it is treated in a responsible manner, particularly since in partnership law the knowledge obtained by one partner in the course of the partnership business may be imputed to the entire partnership. In doing so, two types of work may be distinguished: first, work which could affect the firms' work as auditors and, secondly, work which is undertaken purely in an advisory capacity.

10 A firm appointed as auditor of a regulated entity needs to have in place appropriate procedures to ensure that the partner responsible for the audit function is made aware of any other relationship which exists between any department of the firm and the regulated entity when that relationship could affect the firm's work as auditors. Common examples of such work include accounting work, particularly for smaller entities, and provision of tax services to the regulated entity.

11 *Prima facie*, information obtained in the course of non-audit work is not covered by either the right or the duty to report to a regulator. However, the firm appointed as auditor needs to consider whether the results of other work undertaken for a regulated entity need to be assessed as part of the audit process. In principle, this is no different to seeking to review a report prepared by outside consultants on, say, the entity's accounting systems so as to ensure that the auditor makes a proper assessment of the risks of mis-statement in the financial statements and of the work needed to form an opinion. Consequently, the partner responsible for the audit needs to make appropriate enquiries in the process of planning and completing the audit (see SAS 620.2, SAS 620.9). Such enquiries would be directed to those aspects of the non-audit work which might reasonably be expected to be relevant to the audit. When, as a result of such enquiries, those involved in the audit become aware of issues which may be of material significance to a regulator such issues should be considered, and if appropriate reported, following the Auditing Standards set out in this SAS.

12 Work which is undertaken in an advisory capacity, for example to assist the directors of a regulated entity to determine effective and efficient methods of discharging their duties, would not normally affect the work undertaken for the audit. Nevertheless, in rare instances, the partner responsible for such advisory work may conclude that steps considered necessary in order to comply with the regulator's requirements have not been taken by the directors or that the directors intend in some respect not to comply with the regulator's requirements. Such circumstances would require consideration in the course of work undertaken for the audit, both to consider the effect on the auditors' routine reports and to determine whether the possible non-compliance is or is likely to be of material significance to the regulator.

Work relating to a separate entity

13 Information obtained in the course of work relating to another entity audited by the same firm (or the same practitioner) is confidential to that other entity. Auditors are not required, and have no right, to report to a regulator confidential information which arises from work undertaken by the same auditing firm for another client. However, as a matter of sound practice, individuals involved in the audit of a regulated entity who become aware (in a capacity other than that of auditors of a regulated entity) of a matter which could otherwise give rise to a statutory duty to report would normally make enquiries in the course of their audit of the regulated entity to establish whether the information concerned is substantiated.

14 In carrying out their work, auditors are required to have due regard to whether disclosure of non-compliance with laws and regulations to a proper authority is appropriate in the public interest. Standards and guidance on this general professional obligation are set out in [draft] SAS 120 'Compliance with laws and regulations'.

Conclusion

15 The phrase 'in his capacity as auditor' limits information subject to the duty to report to matters of which auditors become aware in their capacity as such. Consequently, it is unlikely that a partnership can be said to be acting in its capacity as auditor of a particular regulated entity whenever any apparently unrelated material comes to the attention of a partner or member of staff not engaged in that audit, particularly if that material is confidential to another client.

16 The statutory duty to report to a regulator therefore does not extend automatically to any information obtained by an accounting firm regardless of its source. Accounting firms undertaking audits of regulated entities need, however, to establish lines of communication, commensurate with their size and organisational structure, sufficient to ensure that non-audit work undertaken for a regulated entity which is likely to have an effect on the audit is brought to the attention of the partner responsible for the audit and to establish procedures for the partner responsible for the audit to make appropriate enquiries of those conducting such other work as part of the process of planning and completing the audit.

Appendix 3

Action by the auditors on discovery of a breach of a regulator's requirements

1 This appendix sets out in the form of a flowchart the steps involved in assessing whether a report to a regulator is required when a breach of the regulator's requirements comes to the attention of the auditors.

2 The flowchart is intended to provide guidance to readers in understanding the Statement of Auditing Standards. It does not form part of the Auditing Standards contained in the SAS.

Action by the auditors on discovery of a breach of a regulator's requirements

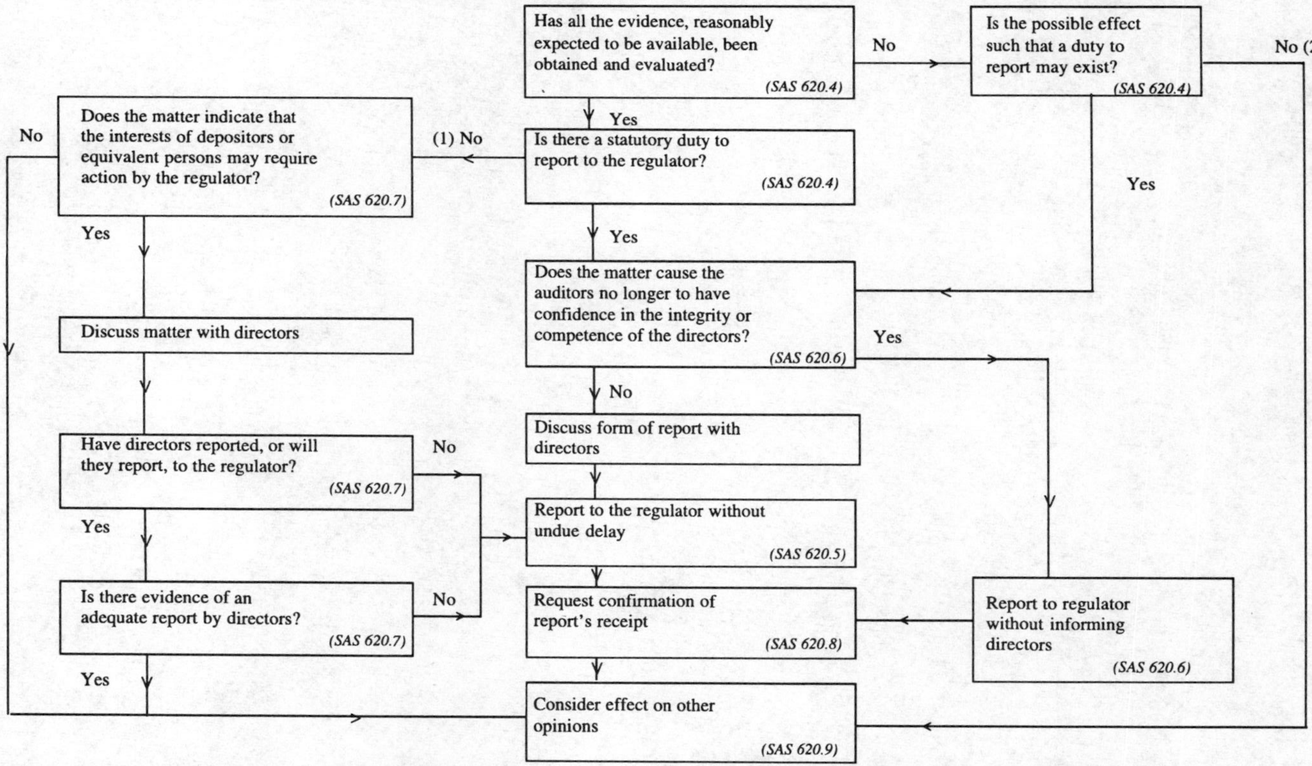

(1) This route would be followed only when a distinct right to report to the regulator exists. Otherwise, where no duty to report exists, auditors would next consider effect on other opinions.

(2) Where the auditors consider that a distinct right to report to the regulator exists, they would next consider the question marked (1).